DICTIONARY
OF
LABOUR BIOGRAPHY

DICTIONARY
OF
LABOUR BIOGRAPHY

Edited by
GREG ROSEN

First published in Great Britain 2001
by Politico's Publishing
8 Artillery Row, London, SW1P 1RZ, England

Tel.: 020 7931 0090
Email: publishing@politicos.co.uk
Website: http://www.politicos.co.uk/publishing

A catalogue record for this book is available from the British Library.

ISBN 1 902301 18 8

Printed and bound in Great Britain by St Edmundsbury Press
Typeset in Bembo by Duncan Brack.

Picture acknowledgements:
Sir Ken Jackson (p. xiii): Andrew Wiard
Thanks to *Tribune* for assistance with cover photographs

CONTENTS

FOREWORD
by
Rt Hon. the Lord Callaghan of Cardiff KG

This unique one-volume *Dictionary of Labour Biography* brings to life the politics of the Labour Party, past and present, through the personalities who shaped it. It recalls the courage and conviction of those who fought to build and renew the party they loved over the past century and the trauma of the fraternal battles that weakened it.

Here you will find Keir Hardie, the name revered above all the pioneers, Arthur Henderson, J R Clynes, Jimmy Maxton, the Webbs, Ramsay MacDonald (before he lost his way) – who all brought vision, ideas, and organisational vitality to the fledgling party. There are the recruits from liberalism: Haldane, Hobson and Christopher Addison. There are the 'Big Five' of the 1940s: Attlee, Bevin, Cripps, Dalton and Morrison, who combined practicality and idealism in building a new post-war Britain. There is Nye Bevan, the father of the NHS, and Ellen Wilkinson and George Tomlinson, who brought schools for all. There is Hugh Gaitskell, who we lost at the height of his powers, and my old friends and Cabinet colleagues Douglas Houghton and Merlyn Rees, who did so much for the Labour Movement over so many years.

It ranges widely from thinkers and polemicists – Tawney, Orwell, Shaw, Harold Laski and John P Mackintosh – by way of Fenner Brockway and Michael Foot, the great voices of radical dissent, all the way through to the giants who built and sustained the bedrock of the trade union movement – Walter Citrine, Sam Watson, Jack Cooper, Les Cannon, Frank Cousins and Bill Carron.

But it also includes the unsung organisers, like Jim Middleton, Morgan Phillips, Reg Underhill and Jim Cattermole. One omission that I would like to see remedied in future editions of this *Dictionary* is more of an account of some of the women organisers like Dr Marion Phillips and Sara Barker who formed the party's powerful Women's Sections, which gave political voice to the exploited women of the workforce. Their graft and dedication behind the scenes were instrumental in turning Labour from a party of protest into a party that could achieve the power to change Britain for the better.

To call up these names from the past is to remind ourselves that Labour was more than a political party. Moral force and faith in the face of hostility and contempt gave strength to its leaders and to the rank and file. Labour grew out of the hardships and injustices suffered by our people, and it was deep conviction and organisation which enabled them to triumph over their struggles and trials and win social justice. It is their legacy on which Tony Blair builds today in a very different society.

James Callaghan

FOREWORD
by
Sir Ken Jackson

It gave me great pleasure to be asked to write a foreword to this *Dictionary of Labour Biography*.

As Britain's oldest trade union, celebrating our 150th anniversary this year, we understand how important it is to celebrate our past. It is the past in which we take pride that forged us into Britain's most forward-thinking trade union and most long-standing advocate of industrial partnership. Just as we champion industrial partnership in the workplace, so we champion partnership with the Labour Party; we are proud of our historic Labour link.

Our strength as a union is the strength of the Labour Movement as a whole – our members, the men and women whose hard work built its success. That is why I welcome the fact that this volume brings to life the stories of so many of them. The famous – the infamous, even – but also the less-than-famous, those without whom so little of what the Labour Party has achieved could have been built, but whose names, if ever added to the foundation stones, have been rubbed away by the dust of time. I welcome too, the range of contributors to this book, nearly one hundred and fifty in all, who have been united in tribute to the Labour Party.

It was to build a brighter future for working people that the Labour Party was formed. It has been a long journey since then. Sometimes it has been a difficult one. But on that journey, the people who built and have since sustained the Labour Party have achieved a great deal for working people: achievements that deserve celebration. The better we understand our past, the more we will have to celebrate in the future.

Sir Ken Jackson
General Secretary, Amalgamated Engineering and Electrical Union

GUIDE AND ACKNOWLEDGEMENTS

The Labour Party is about values and it is about people, labouring people: that is what makes it the Labour Party. To understand the contemporary Labour Party, to understand why the party came to be where and what it is now, we must understand both the philosophical topography over which it has driven but also the perspective, personality and outlook of the successive drivers. Driving the Labour Party being a collective operation, that means understanding not just the drivers but the co-drivers, map-readers, map-designers, mechanics and, of course, the back-seat drivers too.

It is our past that underpins and defines our present. It also helps us to put our current Labour government, its challenges, trials, tribulations, personalities and achievements, in a broader context. That past, the formative experiences of those who built and sustained Labour for much of the last century and the interplay of their personalities, is not a history that is easily, or affordably, accessible. Diaries and memoirs are predominantly those of a few big players, and some are opaque, to say the least. Likewise, biographies tend to concentrate on the prominent few. In reality, the many, far from being but a passive canvas upon which Labour's historians can paint, themselves helped to make history and through it our present.

That is why a host of writers agreed to illuminate what, for a black-and-white era, is a history steeped in colour – by contributing to this one-volume *Dictionary of Labour Biography*. Authors include trade-union leaders, current and former MPs and ministers, historians, peers and journalists. Some have been Labour activists all their lives. Others have not. But all are united in recognising the importance of those people who built and have sustained the Labour Party. Without their efforts and generosity, this book could not have been written. I would like to take this opportunity to thank them, each and every one.

The pen-portraits in this volume include every single Labour Cabinet Minister to date. In addition, there are biographies of other key parliamentarians, thinkers and polemicists, trade-union leaders, Labour and TUC general secretaries, Labour's backroom fixers and organisers, and prominent mavericks. Some are more expansive – Bernard Donoughue on Wilson, Denis MacShane on Bevin and Phillip Whitehead on Benn, Thomas and others stand out – and others focus more narrowly. Each entry nevertheless includes basic biographical information and in addition aims to assess the significance of their subject in the Labour Party and the mark they made in and on the party in government and opposition. Entries are listed alphabetically according to the name by which the individual has been most commonly known. Individuals ennobled part-way during their political career are given both their name and their title in the contents and the entry's heading and are positioned according to the name by which they are more commonly known (thus Lord Glenamara appears under 'S' as Ted Short; Lord Merlyn-Rees under 'R' as Merlyn Rees; but William Warrender Mackenzie under 'A' as Lord Amulree). Constraints of space and time have meant inevitably that I have not been able to include entries on all whom I had originally intended. I hope to remedy that in a second edition!

It is worth noting several points about the way the Labour Party structure has evolved over the years. The Shadow Cabinet was known until 1951 as the Executive Committee of the Parliamentary Labour Party, when its name was changed to avoid confusion with the National Executive Committee (NEC) of the party. First elected in 1923, it consisted of 12 elected Commons members until it was expanded to 15 in 1981 and 18 in 1988. The exception to this was during the 1931–35 parliament, when the reduced circumstances of the Labour Party meant that there were only seven elected Commons members. There are in addition six ex-officio members – Leader, Deputy Leader, Commons Chief Whip, Lords Leader, Lords Chief Whip and elected Labour peers' representative. It was only in 1955 that the practice of appointing departmentally specific Shadow Ministers was begun – up until then, the operation of the Shadow Cabinet was far less structured. Also, although the Parliamentary Labour Party has always had a separate chair than the Party Leader when Labour has been in government, it was only in 1970 that the practice began of electing a separate PLP chair in opposition. From 1951–64, for example, it had been successively Clement Attlee, Hugh Gaitskell and Harold Wilson. Until 1922, there was no party leader as such, only the Chairman. In 1922, Ramsay MacDonald became the first Chairman also to be Parliamentary Party Leader, the Vice-Chairman post being simultaneously renamed that of Deputy Leader. Until 1978, when Callaghan became Leader of the Labour Party, the post was literally that of Leader of the Parliamentary Party only, although it was not until 1981 that the system of leadership election by MPs alone was replaced by an electoral college with 40% of the votes allocated to the trade unions, 30% to the Parliamentary Party and 30% to constituency parties. In 1994, Tony Blair became the first Labour leader to be elected by one member, one vote following the rule changes agreed by party conference during John Smith's leadership in 1993.

In addition to the contributors, I owe an overwhelming debt of gratitude to all those whose patient support for and encouragement of my historical endeavours made this book possible. I would like to pay tribute to the team at Politico's: to Iain Dale, whose commitment to this project from the start has been unstinting; to John Berry, who has been endlessly helpful, supportive and accommodating; to Duncan Brack, who gave generous advice from his own editorial experience and whose considerable typesetting and formatting abilities fortuitously complemented the editor's strengths in other areas; and to Sean Magee for his expert guidance. I would also like to thank Mark Seddon and Barckley Sumner at *Tribune* for their encouragement and for their generosity in letting me plunder the wonders of the *Tribune* photo library.

I am especially grateful to Sir Ken Jackson for the generous support and encouragement he has given me in my undertaking of this *Dictionary* and indebted to him and to Lord Callaghan for their kindness in agreeing to contribute forewords. D-J Collins, friend and colleague, has been a valued advisor on this book as on so much else. John Lloyd, whose passion for Labour history is an inspiration to all who know him, John Gibbins and John Spellar, have all endured my preoccupation with the past with admirable stoicism and been generous with their knowledge and insights. I must also thank for their encouragement and suggestions Simon Baugh, Chris Bishton, Michael Dugher, Richard Fulham, Ian Geary, Ann Marshall, Joe McGowan, John Park, Julian Richards, Mark Tami, Tom Watson, and Sarah Welfare, and for their ebullient good cheer the staff of the AEEU canteen, who have a deserved reputation for brewing the best tea in Bromley. At BiE, Jessica Bawden and Alastair Graham were supportive throughout, alongside Jim Cattermole, whose decades of service to the Labour Movement are recognised in this volume. Rex Osborn, a stalwart comrade-in-arms through many battles, Jayant Chavda and Dickson Mabon have been prodigiously helpful, giving invaluable encouragement and advice. To Merlyn Rees, Paul Richards and Tam Dalyell I am indebted for wise counsel at crucial junctures, and to Eleanor Jupp for her faith and enthusiasm, particularly during the travails of proofing. I am supremely grateful to a number of contributors who stepped into the breach on a number of entries as deadlines loomed and without whom this volume would be not nearly so complete as it is, namely: Jackie Ashley, Lewis Baston, Ted Graham, Nigel Griffiths, Joe Haines, Helen Liddell, Calum MacDonald, Peter Metcalfe, Austin Mitchell, Robert Pearce, Stephen Pollard, Paul Routledge, Robert Taylor and Damien Welfare.

I would also like to thank for their advice, assistance and encouragement Andrew Adonis, Peter Archer, Matt Carter, Dick Clements, Richard Elsen, Rory Fisher,

Geoffrey Foote, George Foulkes, Mark Glover, Roy Grantham, Arthur Greenan, Laura Higgs, Kevin Jefferys, Gavin Kelly, Phil Kelly, Fraser Kemp, Peter Kilfoyle, Phil Larkin, Roger Liddle, Bronwen Maddox, Kevin Maguire, Seema Malhotra, Kenneth O Morgan, Gina Page, Matthew Seward, David Seymour, Maeve Sherlock and Phillip Whitehead. In addition I owe a great deal to John Brown, who remains the great unsung hero of Edinburgh University's history department and a guiding light to his students past and present, to Bernard Crick, to Una and Deirdre Mackintosh, and to Lorna Davidson, Mark Dolan, James Longworth, Ed Pybus and Will Sergeant for all their encouragement in this and other projects. I have also benefited from the insights and comradeship of many Labour activists with whom I have campaigned over the years, including Beth Egan, a beacon of Fabian fortitude, the inimitable Adam Bowen, Jeannie Boyle, Colin Dingwall, Alex Foulkes, Nick Small, Catherine Stihler, Liz Wilson, Philippa Wood, Judy Bax and Nicky Gavron.

Greg Rosen
August 2001

For Fred, Maria and Alex,
who made it all possible

LABOUR
BIOGRAPHIES

Diane Abbott   (1953–)

Diane Abbott is politically the diametrical opposite of Tony Blair's ideal Labour MP. Born on 27 September 1953 in Paddington, the daughter of Reginald, a welder, and Julie, a psychiatric nurse, she was from 1987 to 1997 Labour's only black woman MP, before being joined by Oona King who ironically had fought against her in Hackney North's selection for the 1997 election. She was educated at Harrow County Girls Grammar School, where she was a contemporary in the drama society of Michael Portillo, then at Newnham College, Cambridge, where she studied History.

Abbott was elected as MP for Hackney North and Stoke Newington in 1987 and has held the seat ever since. The constituency comprises extensive poverty-stricken local authority estates combined with the trendy *Guardian*-reading enclave of Stoke Newington. Appropriately for a seat represented by a black MP it is one of the most ethnically diverse constituencies in the UK, with large West African, Caribbean, Turkish, Kurdish and Asian communities and the Hassidic Jewish community in Stamford Hill.

A Labour Party member from 1971, Abbott was a civil servant, local government press officer and TV journalist before going into politics. Part of the multi-cause Bennite left (she was active in CND and the Campaign for Labour Party Democracy) that swept through the London Labour Party in the late 1970s and early '80s, she was elected as a Labour councillor in Westminster in 1982, the hard left's *annus mirabilis* in local government. She served just four years in opposition, but is fond of lecturing Hackney councillors on the basis of her local government experience.

Having built a network of contacts in the hard left she was put on their NEC slate from 1984 onwards. She missed getting selected as PPC for Brent East (being beaten by Ken Livingstone) and Westminster North, but in 1985 deselected Ernie Roberts MP to win the selection in Hackney North & Stoke Newington by just seven votes. Ironically she was opposed by Livingstone's supporters and *Labour Left Briefing*.

Abbott's power base in the local Labour Party since then has been the natural loyalty of ethnic minority members, combined since they came to terms with her selection with the backing of *Briefing*, a number of whose leading lights live in the seat. She suffered a major blow in 1996 when the faction of Hackney Labour councillors who were most identified with supporting her effectively expelled themselves from Labour by forming a separate group on the council after an internal split. They have since mainly joined the Lib Dems and Tories and Abbott has had to adapt to the more vigorous electoral battle that this has created in previously safe Labour Hackney.

Abbott has tried to build alliances locally with community groups outside the Labour Party, appealing for personal support by disassociating herself from the local Labour councillors and Tony Blair's government. Internally, she is not afraid to pick a fight, calling local councillors to their faces 'the most unrepresentative Labour group since universal suffrage', describing her opponents on the constituency general committee to the author with a throw-away 'All you white boys in suits look the same to me' and in 1992 refusing to allow her long-serving and highly organised constituency party secretary to be her election agent, a move activists speculated was because she thought it was important to have a black agent. She is at daggers drawn with her parliamentary neighbour Brian Sedgemore MP over local council issues and her backing for Ken Livingstone in the Labour Party's London mayoral selection.

In Parliament she missed over 30 three-line whips in a year in the most recent figures issued to her CLP. It may or may not have been coincidental that very many of these votes were on issues where she was known to publicly disagree with the government's position. She is a member of the Campaign Group in the PLP, and assiduously courts the left in the constituencies, helping her to get elected to the NEC from 1994 until MPs were barred from the CLP section.

She is a respected campaigner and a principled rebel on race, asylum and immigration issues, and on the social security issues that also impact hugely in Hackney. However, the frequency of her rebellions has tended to reduce the impact of her critique of New Labour so that the instances where she does have a good point are taken less seriously, as does the impression that her attacks on New Labour figures are as much personal as political.

Condemned to a perennial back-bench role, she has refused to tread the path towards ministerial office and loyalty followed by more career-minded former left-wingers like Dawn Primarolo and Michael Meacher. She has been an active member of the Foreign Affairs Select Committee since 1997, if appearing to let the side down when a newspaper diary columnist implied that she had been caught snoozing after lunch in the midst of a committee cross-examination of the Foreign Secretary. Following Ken Livingstone's election as Mayor of London, Abbott was appointed to his cabinet with responsibility for women and equality. She is at pains to point out that this is an advisory rather than an executive role.

Abbott was married to David Thompson in 1991 but the two separated in 1993. Despite her working-class black origins she can come across as extremely patronising and aloof. She combines a role as one of the half-dozen most hard left Labour MPs with a long-term friendship with disgraced Tory Jonathan Aitken, who was her parliamentary pair and is godfather to her son.

Luke Akehurst

Brian Abel-Smith (1926–96)

Within the Labour Party Brian Abel-Smith was an influential figure behind the scenes from the 1950s until the end of the 1970s. As an advisor to Richard Crossman when the party was in opposition, and between 1968 and 1970 when Crossman was Secretary of State for Health and Social Security, Abel-Smith helped to form the pensions plans, which were summarised during the 1964 election by the slogan, 'Retirement on half pay for all'. These provided the basis for a Bill before Parliament in 1970 that was lost when the Conservatives unexpectedly won the election. But between 1974 and 1978 Abel-Smith resumed the role of special advisor within the department at Barbara Castle's invitation when she became Secretary of State; and this time earlier planning reached fruition with the 1975 Act's introduction of state earnings-related pensions.

Throughout these years superannuation policy was part of a wider attempt to revise post-war health and welfare reforms, both to make them more effective in limiting poverty and to adapt them to changing social circumstances. Within the party there was a major intellectual shift which involved a loss of faith in the Beveridge Plan as implemented after the War. By the time of the 1975 Act, however, the optimistic belief that the Welfare State could be successfully reconstructed was beginning to wane. Central to it had been a redefinition of poverty, in relative terms, of the sort which Abel-Smith and Peter Townsend had made in their pamphlet, *The Poor and the Poorest*, published in 1965. However, by 1978, when Abel-Smith ceased to be a government advisor, increasing poverty was weakening confidence that poverty could be contained and diminished. After 1979 he had no direct involvement either in the formation of policy or in party divisions during the long years of opposition and the struggle to come to terms with the success of Thatcherism.

Brian Abel-Smith was born on 6 November 1926 into an upper-class family, remotely related to royalty. Throughout his life he had 'adequate means, though not rich' (in the words of his *Times* obituary). After school at Haileybury and national service, he graduated from Cambridge with a second in Economics and began research, first becoming widely known as a result of the memorandum which he and Richard Titmuss contributed to the Guillebaud Committee's Report in 1956. The committee had been appointed by the Conservatives on their return to power in the hope that it would recommend cuts in National Health Service spending. Titmuss and Abel-Smith showed that in fact the cost of the NHS had fallen as a share of GDP since its introduction; in real terms it had risen only slightly, and per head of population it had remained steady.

The history and organisation of health services in Britain and elsewhere remained one of Abel-Smith's main interests, along with pensions policy. He also wrote on the reform of the legal system, which he believed failed if judged as a social service. He had a distinguished academic career, becoming a lecturer at the LSE in 1955, a reader in 1961, and succeeding Titmuss as Professor of Social Administration in 1965. He also produced a long list of publications, written alone or in collaboration with others, and enjoyed membership of various official inquiries and periods as an advisor to WHO and to the ILO. He intentionally avoided a political career. Although he was one of the bright young men Dalton picked out to encourage into parliament, and others in the 1950s tried to persuade him in this direction, he turned down the chance of safe seats, such as Bishop Auckland at the time of the 1959 election, because he was frightened that his homosexuality might be exposed in the public glare of politics. Even after homosexuality had been decriminalised, he guarded his privacy.

Whether he would have been more influential if he had become an MP and a cabinet minister is doubtful. He was one of the contributors to *Conviction*, a collection of essays published in 1958, which attracted considerable attention as a statement of belief by a new generation of socialist intellectuals. Their later careers diverged, some ending up on the political right, and only one of them, Peter Shore, made it into a Labour cabinet. Abel-Smith, it might be argued, was at least as influential as an advisor as Shore ever was as a minister.

Abel-Smith died in April 1996. There is no biography. Peter Townsend's notice in the *Independent*, 9 April, is the most enlightening of the obituaries. Abel-Smith's entry in *Who's Who* lists his extensive publications on health, the NHS and social services.

Dr John Brown

3

Sir Richard Acland Bt. (1906–90)

Herbert Asquith once said that mankind was divided into three species – 'Men, women and Aclands'. The utopian idealist Dick Acland kept up the tradition of a long line of independent-minded personalities involved in British politics, and his own brand of Christian Socialism played an important footnote in the unusual political circumstances of the 1930s and '40s.

Acland was born on 26 November 1906 in Broadclyst, Devon, the son of Sir Francis Acland, the fourteenth baronet, who was at that time Liberal MP for Richmond in York-shire, and was later a minister under Lloyd George. The Acland family had a rich historical lineage. The baronetcy was created in 1644 when the Aclands' garrison was the only one in Devon that stayed loyal to King Charles I. Other members of the family included one who went to fight for Britain in the American War of Independence only to swap sides when he got there; another was the only Tory MP to vote for the Great Reform Act, and Acland's grandfather was Education Minister in Gladstone's last government.

Educated at Rugby School and Balliol College, Oxford, Acland qualified as a barrister, practising until 1934. In the family tradition, he unsuccessfully contested as a Liberal the local seats of Torquay in 1929 and Barnstaple in 1931. He was elected for Barnstaple in 1935, a seat he held for the next ten years.

But he did not remain a Liberal. In the 1930s he moved to support the fight against fascism and appeasement, getting involved with the Left Book Club and moves for a Popular Front. As a result, he found himself associating frequently with diverse figures such as Harold Laski and the Communist Harry Pollitt, joining forces with Stafford Cripps and Nye Bevan to achieve the famous 1938 Bridgewater by-election victory for an Independent Progressive. These political stances led to Acland's shift to supporting the economic solutions offered by the left, and combined with his non-conformist tradition he developed his own distinctive brand of Christian Socialism. In 1936 he married Anne Alford, and they went on to have three sons. He succeeded to his father's baronetcy in 1939.

His views were exemplified in his best-selling 1940 Penguin paperback *Unser Kampf*, which called for extensive common ownership of land and industry, and emphasised the moral dimension to the war. He published a series of pamphlets including *What It Will Be Like* and *How It Can Be Done*, and set up a radical group based on one entitled *Forward March*. In 1942 this combined with the 1941 Committee, a group concerned with more mechanistic aspects of the war effort and inspired by the radical wartime broadcasts of J B Priestley and whose chief patron was *Picture Post* owner Edward Hulton; together the two formed the Common Wealth Party. The Party advocated Acland's common ownership principles, arguing for mass nationalisation, immediate independence for India and aid for the Third World.

The most significant role played by Common Wealth was its breaking of the wartime by-election truce whereby the main parties had agreed not to contest each other's vacant seats. Common Wealth dived in and put up candidates against what it saw as 'reactionary' candidates, and scored three dramatic successes, with Acland being joined in the Commons by Common Wealth MPs for Eddisbury, Skipton and Chelmsford.

For a time, Common Wealth tapped in to the aspirations of voters for the future once the war was over. With the wide-ranging reforms suggested by the 1942 Beveridge Report backing it up, the Christian-based idealism of Acland filled a gap. Acland was an effective campaigner, but even his efforts were overwhelmed by Labour's 1945 landslide. In that election all but one of the Common Wealth candidates (including Acland himself in Putney) were defeated. Acland promptly joined Labour, and Common Wealth rapidly disappeared – its only MP joined Labour straight after the election. Common Wealth had served two purposes as far as the Labour Party's future was concerned – it laid the ground (and in some ways, heralded victory) for the radical reforming agenda of the Attlee government and helped to instil the belief that such reforms, including Beveridge, were both necessary and desirable in the post-war reconstruction. On a more mundane level, the party acted as a conduit through which people like Desmond Donnelly, George Wigg and of course Acland himself found their way into the Labour Party.

Following his switch to the Labour Party, Acland was chosen as the 'clean' Labour candidate in the 1947 Gravesend by-election to replace the sleaze-tainted Gerry Allighan, who had been expelled from the Commons for a breach of parliamentary privilege. It is suggested that Herbert Morrison personally picked Acland to be the candidate. The by-election was eventful; *The Times* recalled Kent miners parading through the streets of Gravesend by the light of their lamps, and on Acland's victory Morrison sang 'Oh What A Beautiful Morning' to the assembled press.

Back in the Commons, Acland served as Second Church Estates Commissioner from 1950 to 1951. He soon fell in with the Keep Left crowd, which opposed Ernest Bevin's Cold War policies, and it was defence which led to Acland's final change of allegiance. When the British development of a hydrogen bomb was announced in 1955 and wasnot opposed by Labour, Acland resigned his seat in protest. He sought to stand as an independent against a Labour candidate in the ensuing by-election, but the Conservative government called the 1955 general election soon after. In the resulting contest, Acland split the vote and denied Labour candidate Victor Mishcon the seat, handing it to the Tory Peter Kirk.

After this defeat and a brief spell teaching at Wandsworth Grammar School, Acland retreated to the family's spiritual home of Exmoor, and became a lecturer at St Luke's College of Education in Exeter until 1974. He kept up his campaigning for peace and equality, and into the 1980s was speaking out on the plight on the Third World. Acland continued publishing pamphlets and books on a variety of subjects throughout his life, including *Forward Speaking, Nothing Left To Believe?, Why So Angry?, We Teach Them Wrong, Sexual Morality, Curriculum or Life, The Next Step* (1974) and *Hungry Sheep* (1988). He died on 23 November 1990, at a time when British politics was dominated by the Conservative leadership contest.

Two other small legacies have flowed from Acland. In 1943, in keeping with his principles of common ownership, he donated the ancestral estate of Killerton to the National Trust. The house was subsequently rented back from the trust as a hall of residence for St Luke's College, with Acland as Warden. After his death, debate over whether stag hunting should be banned on the land (contrary to Acland's wishes) was a great controversy at Trust AGMs. And in Gravesend, Acland donated the classic bellwether seat to psephologists – since the Tories won in 1955, Gravesend and its successor Gravesham has been the only parliamentary seat that has always gone the way of the overall winning party.

Acland was an idiosyncratic figure, forged in the unusual politics of his time. But he appears to be universally remembered as a decent, principled idealist in the Liberal aristocratic tradition.

The abiding impression is one of a political life dominated by politics as a moral crusade; in Acland's own words, 'Do not ask "Is it expedient?" Simply ask "Is it right?"'

Matthew Seward

Willie Adamson (1863–1936)

Heavily built and retaining a bristling chestnut moustache until his later years, Willie Adamson was, despite not being a particularly heavy hitter, Scottish Secretary in both of Ramsay MacDonald's governments and, briefly, Labour's leader.

Following the resignation of Arthur Henderson from the Lloyd George Coalition Cabinet and from the Chairmanship of the Parliamentary Labour Party (PLP), William Adamson was in October 1917 elected unopposed as PLP Chairman and Commons Labour leader in his stead, joining the Privy Council in 1918. He was not, however, a success and his absence from Parliament through illness for much of 1919 and 1920 contributed to his being replaced as PLP Chair by J R Clynes. Solid, industrious and widely trusted, he was nonetheless a poor debater. Manny Shinwell depicted him in *The Labour Story* as 'a dour and phlegmatic Scottish miners' leader very much out of his depth in the Commons'.

There were some who did not take him particularly seriously. Hugh Dalton confided to his diary on 23 March 1919: 'Much mockery of Adamson coming and announcing that, to become His Majesty's Opposition, all the Labour Party needed was two additional clerks, a typist and a messenger. The Speaker refused to recognise the Labour Party as unqualified opposition, because of the Sinn Fein and the possibility of this and Liberal Sections reuniting.' As a minister he developed a certain reputation. One particular story was regaled in the memoirs of several colleagues including those of future Scottish Secretary, Tom Johnston: 'To most supplementary questions in the House of Commons [Adamson] had a stock answer: it was that he would give the answer "due consideration." And once when some of his interrogators became annoyed, and one of them, Mr Pringle, asked whether after he had given the due consideration to the due consideration he had previously promised, he would give due consideration to the advisability of giving an answer to the question, Willie imperturbably replied amid roars of laughter that he would give the point raised by honourable members due consideration!'

He was not, however, entirely inactive as a minister. He was a supporter of the Scottish Home Rule Association and as Scottish Secretary he came out strongly for devolution. In May 1924 he backed the Private Member's Bill by Clydeside Labour MP George Buchanan, subsequently talked out by the Conservatives at second reading, for a single-chamber Scottish Assembly for dealing with Scottish legislation within the UK framework.

He was also a staunch free-trader and on 24 April 1930 wrote to MacDonald attacking the proposal to compel millers to purchase a certain quota of their wheat from English farmers as forcing Scottish consumers to pay higher prices 'solely to ensure an increased return to English farmers.'

By 1929, according to Tom Johnston's *Memoirs*, Macdonald was amongst those who regarded Adamson's time as a player as over. Despite Adamson having been consistently re-elected to the shadow cabinet every year since 1923, MacDonald initially suggested to Adamson that he should go to the Lords as titular Scottish Secretary, 'and do the ceremonial stuff,' whilst Johnston himself took charge in the Commons as Under-Secretary of State. Both were happy to agree to this and were duly sworn to secrecy whereupon Adamson asked, 'Can I no' tell my wife about the Lords?' To this MacDonald assented, whereupon Adamson asked, 'And my son?' 'Your what!' shouted the PM. 'I didn't know you had a son. That arrangement is off. I am against appointing peers who have heirs to inherit their titles!' He therefore became Scottish Secretary with first Johnston and later Joe Westwood as his deputy. In 1931, Adamson was amongst the nine members of MacDonald's Cabinet who rebelled against the proposal to cut the dole.

Born in Halbeath, near Dunfermline, on 2 April 1863, he attended a school run by the local mining engineer's wife. Family poverty led him down the mines as an eleven-year-old pit-boy, where he remained until the age of 38. His mother Flora had worked in the pits until the Act of 1842 and his father, James Adamson, a coalminer, died before the young William left school. He had four children by his wife, Christine Marshall, whom he married in 1887.

Attempts by mine-owners to drive down wages and maintain long hours and appalling conditions produced a climate of industrial militancy in the Scottish mines. Adamson's activism in his local miners' association during the 1890s was sufficient to propel him by 1902 to the assistant secretaryship and in 1908 to the general secretaryship of the Fife and Kinross Miners Association. A devout Baptist, he also co-founded the Dunfermline Temperance Council and a local mutual society. Politically, his early allegiance to the Liberal Party shifted to support for Labour in advance of the Lib-Lab Miners Federation of Great Britain. In 1905 he was elected a Labour Councillor in Dunfermline and in 1910 he fought West Fife for Labour at both General Elections. Defeated by a Liberal in January 1910, he became in December the first Scottish miner to become an MP.

As an MP he urged the nationalisation of the mines and, despite the death in action of his eldest son, he vigorously opposed the enemy, Prussian militarism, during the Great War. He continued his trade-union involvement through the 1920s, preoccupied increasingly with the growing communist-inspired militancy in the Scottish mining associations, in particular in Fife and Lanarkshire. A staunch democrat, he favoured conciliation and arbitration as the means by which the trade unions could secure better conditions for working people. As Tom Johnston recollected in his *Memoirs*, 'With caution personified with a capital P, he carried on for years a relentless warfare with the communists in his county, and his motto in that warfare as I once told him was the motto on the Covenanters banner at Tippermuir, "Jesus and No Quarter."' In the summer of 1928 the battle came to a head, following his suspension from local union office by the Communists who had by now gained control of the Fife union, Adamson, backed by the National Union of Scottish Mineworkers' executive, founded a rival Fife, Clackmannanshire and Kinross Miners Association.

Losing his seat in the 1931 General Election disaster, he failed narrowly to regain it in 1935, beaten by the Communist Willie Gallagher. His wife died that year and on 23 February 1936 he died of pneumonia in a Dunfermline nursing home.

Greg Rosen

Dr Christopher Addison (1st Viscount Addison)   (1869–1951)

In his first conference speech as Prime Minister, Tony Blair contrasted his hopes that the twenty-first century would be one of the progressives with the domination of the twentieth by the Conservatives. This continuing theme of his premiership highlights what he sees as the split of the progressives in the early part of the century into the Liberal and Labour Parties.

Christopher Addison, one of the most low-profile and under-rated British political figures of the first half of the twentieth century, was in many ways a personification of this split. The only minister to serve in both post-war governments, he began his political career under Lloyd George's wing and finished it as Attlee's mentor, thus marking a place alongside the leaders of the two most radical reforming governments seen until 1997.

Addison was born on 19 June 1869 in Hogsthorpe, Lincolnshire, to a farming family. His initial upbringing in farming life taught him lessons he retained throughout his life and which came to be especially useful when a minister in the responsible ministry. Educated at Trinity College in Harrogate he got into Sheffield Medical School and later St Bartholomew's Hospital. Once qualified, he carved out a notable career as an anatomist – he was Professor of Anatomy at Sheffield and lecturer in the subject at Charing Cross and St Bartholomew's hospitals. Secretary of the Anatomical Society, he prepared the twelfth edition of *Ellis's Demonstrations of Anatomy*. He is probably the only cabinet member to have ever given his name to a part of the human body (Addison's plane) and is one of only three post-war Cabinet ministers to hold a medical degree (along with the 'Radio Doctor' Charles Hill and David Owen).

It was his experiences as a doctor that led him directly into politics. Seeing the appalling problems of social deprivation and dearth of basic public health motivated him into involvement with Liberal politics, and he entered parliament in the first general election of 1910 for Hoxton. He was brought close to Lloyd George early on, when Addison's expertise in the field came to the fore during the passage of the National Health Insurance Bill. He joined the government as Parliamentary Secretary to the Board of Education at the outbreak of war in August 1914, and in May 1915 transferred to the Ministry of Munitions under Lloyd George. At this department, new methods of what was essentially 'war socialism' were instituted, massively increasing production through state control of private industries. Huge savings to the taxpayer were achieved, and Addison took over as Minister on Lloyd George's accession to the Premiership in December 1916, hasving been created a Privy Counsellor that June. Addison had further opportunity to work on social reform as the Minister for Reconstruction from July 1917.

One of the most crucial roles he ever performed, however, was as the very first Minister of Health, from June 1919 until April 1921. Originally appointed as President of the Local Government Board, he changed the law to create the new ministry, which was also responsible for housing and thereby fulfilling the (misquoted) notion of creating 'homes fit for heroes to live in'.

There was a housing shortage due to the interruption of the war, and Addison's solution was an ambitious programme of state-assisted housing. What came to be known as the Addison Act of 1919 provided for councils to build almost unlimited housing with low, controlled rents, and the government making up the shortfall in huge subsidies. The cost of such a programme to the taxpayer led to a public outcry, and in April 1921 Addison was moved by Lloyd George – he spent a few months as Minister Without Portfolio before resigning in July.

Addison had felt increasingly frustrated both in government and with Lloyd George and elements of the Liberal Party, and after losing his Shoreditch seat in 1922 he joined the Labour Party, which he saw as the principal vehicle by which the social reforms he desired might come about. He unsuccessfully contested Hammersmith South in 1924, and then wrote a series of books outlining his view on the housing debate and other issues, in *The Betrayal of the Slums* (1922), *Politics from Within* (two volumes, 1924) and *Practical Socialism* (two volumes, 1926). He followed these publications up in the 1930s with *Four and a Half Years* (two volumes, 1934) and *A Policy for British Agriculture* (1939).

In the 1929 election he won Swindon for Labour, and was immediately appointed to the government as Parliamentary Secretary to the Ministry of Agriculture, where he was able to use his farming background to its full in approaching policy questions. He served as the Minister for Agriculture from 1930–1, taking through the first Agricultural Marketing Acts. He opposed Ramsey MacDonald and Philip Snowden over unemployment benefit cuts in 1931 and in the election of that year lost his seat.

He regained his seat in a 1934 by-election but lost it in the following year's general election. At the behest of Clement Attlee he was created Baron Addison in 1937, and also married for the second time, this time to Dorothy Low. His first wife Isobel had died three years earlier.

After spending time writing, in 1940 Attlee appointed him Labour leader in the House of Lords, a position he held throughout the war and eventually until 1951. On Labour's 1945 landslide victory, he became Leader of the House of Lords and Secretary of State for the Dominions, and was raised to a Viscountcy and made a Knight of the Garter. He was the only Lords leader this century never to actually lead from the Lords chamber, which was the home of the Commons from 1941 (when the Commons chamber was bombed) until 1952 – the House of Lords sat in the Robing Room.

It was in his task as Lords leader that he performed a crucial role in the success of the Labour government. For whilst Labour had a huge majority in the Commons, in the Lords they were faced with an overwhelming majority of Tory hereditary peers. Addison however gained widespread respect from all sides of the House, which facilitated the passage of Labour's manifesto commitments through the upper House. Essential to his success was the relationship he developed with the Conservative leader in the Lords, the Marquess of Salisbury. The Salisbury-Addison convention that the Lords should not oppose at second reading measures promised in a party's manifesto was devised, and has stood the test of time over the rest of this century as one of the most important parliamentary conventions.

Addison served as Dominions Secretary until 1947 and as the first Secretary of State for Commonwealth Relations for a few months in 1947, participating in a number of important overseas conferences in that capacity. But his advancing age (by 1951 he was 82 – the oldest person to hold ministerial office this century) meant that he gave up his other ministerial roles to concentrate on seeing through the government's programme in the Lords. But he continued to perform an important role as one of Attlee's key confidants and advisers in the Cabinet, and as the only minister in the government with experience of the previous postwar reconstruction.

Addison served out the entirety of the Attlee government, and died at Radnage in Buckinghamshire on 11 December 1951, soon after Labour's election defeat that year.

In many ways, Christopher Addison was one of the most influential but historically under-sung figures of British politics in the first half of this century. Referring to Addison's work after the Great War, Peter Hennessy has described him as 'the father of the council house', and to this extent, Addison's influence lasted until the early 1980s when the Thatcher government's introduction of the right to buy fundamentally altered the local government housing scene. The memorable achievements of the Attlee government would be much less had it not been for Addison's skilful approach to the House of Lords and his success in seeing through the passage of legislation. All subsequent Labour governments also have him to thank for the negotiation of the Salisbury-Addison convention, without which the Lords could have wrecked many a manifesto commitment.

Key biographies of Addison are R J Minney's *Viscount Addison: Leader of the Lords* (1958) and *Portrait of a Progressive: the Political Career of Christopher, Viscount Addison* (1980) by Kenneth and Jane Morgan.

Matthew Seward

A V Alexander (1ˢᵗ Viscount/1ˢᵗ Earl Alexander of Hillsborough) (1885–1965)

Albert Victor Alexander was a significant figure in Labour and Co-operative politics from the 1920s to the 1940s, and is one of the few Labourites to have been awarded an earldom. He remains the leading Co-operator in Labour Party history, and his work in defence ministries between 1929 and 1950 was particularly notable.

Alexander was born on 1 May 1885 at Weston-super-Mare, Somerset. His father, a blacksmith and artisan engineer, died in 1886, and Alexander and his sisters were brought up in Bristol by their mother. In 1898 Alexander left school, and then worked as a clerk for the Bristol School Board (to 1903) and then for Somerset County Council; by 1919 he was chief clerk of Somerset's higher education department. He was also active in the National Association of Local Government Officers, eventually becoming secretary of the Somerset County Council branch. In 1908 he married Esther Ellen Chapple, a teacher: under her influence he joined the Baptist Church, soon becoming a lay preacher. (In 1956 he was to become President of the Council of Protestant Churches.) They had a son, who died in infancy, and a daughter.

Alexander served in the Army throughout the First World War, leaving in 1919 with the rank of captain. In 1920 he was appointed secretary to the parliamentary committee of the Co-operative Congress, and in 1921 played a leading part in the successful resistance to the government's plans to tax the profits of Co-operative Societies. This successful campaign raised his profile in Co-operative politics, and in 1922 he was adopted as Labour and Co-operative candidate for Sheffield Hillsborough, which he won at that year's general election and held in subsequent elections in 1923, 1924 and 1929.

In Ramsay MacDonald's first minority Labour government of 1924 Alexander was appointed Parliamentary Secretary to the Board of Trade. Between the fall of that government in late 1924 and Labour's re-election in 1929 he did not secure election to the shadow cabinet; it was thus a surprise to many when he was appointed to the 1929 cabinet as First Lord of the

Admiralty. Alexander was one of the few ministers to enhance his reputation between 1929 and 1931. Among other things he was partly responsible for the 1930 London Naval Treaty. In August 1931 he was one of nine ministers who refused to accept a cut in unemployment benefit as a way of balancing the budget. On the fall of the government, and its replacement by a National administration under MacDonald, he was elected to the Shadow Cabinet; but at the 1931 general election, he lost Hillsborough by a convincing majority.

Between 1931 and 1935 Alexander returned to work for the Co-operative Congress, and at the 1935 election he won back Hillsborough for Labour. In the 1935 Parliament he emerged as one of the PLP's leading figures, being elected to the Shadow Cabinet every year between 1935 and the outbreak of war, and topping the poll in 1939: at various times he was even mentioned as a possible replacement for Attlee, although few took this likelihood too seriously. In this period his main achievement was to work with Hugh Dalton and others to change the PLP's line from voting against the Service Estimates to abstaining, an important symbolic switch in Labour's increasing recognition of the likelihood of war with Nazi Germany.

On the outbreak of war in 1939, Alexander was appointed to liaise with the new First Lord, Winston Churchill, on Admiralty matters. When the latter formed his Coalition government in May 1940, Alexander was the obvious choice to take over as First Lord. He held the position until 1945. Once again, he proved a strong proponent of the Navy's case, and was frequently seen in full uniform attending launches and so on; indeed, his habit of referring to 'my navy' tended to support the view of those, like Dalton, who saw him as a rather pompous and even in some ways ridiculous figure. However, with Churchill acting as Minister of Defence, Alexander's scope for independent action was inevitably limited.

On the break-up of the Coalition, Alexander returned to opposition. At the 1945 general election, he held Hillsborough by a majority of over 10,000, and in the new Labour government Attlee appointed him First Lord once again. He also served on the cabinet mission to India in 1946. With the reorganisation of the defence ministries under the umbrella of the Ministry of Defence that took place towards the end of that year, Alexander was removed from the Admiralty in October, to become Minister without Portfolio, before in December taking over as Minister of Defence. Alexander remained there until February 1950, but he was not seen as being particularly successful. He had great difficulties with the service chiefs, was embarrassed by having to make two U-turns on the length of time conscripted servicemen should serve, was seen as too favourable towards the Admiralty, and was not very effective in prioritising between the different services. He was created Viscount Alexander of Hillsborough in the 1950 New Years Honours List, and after Labour's majority was slashed at the February 1950 general election, he was shifted from Defence to become Chancellor of the Duchy of Lancaster. He remained in the latter post until Labour left office in October 1951.

At this point Alexander became deputy Labour leader in the House of Lords, and in 1955 he succeeded Earl Jowitt as leader. He was created 1st Earl Alexander of Hillsborough in 1963. He remained leader (and thus, ex-officio, a member of the shadow cabinet) until the 1964 general election, when he was finally replaced by Lord Longford. Alexander died in London on 11 January 1965, and his title became extinct.

A. V. Alexander was a staunch centre-right Labourite. He was generally regarded, at least until late in his ministerial career, as a safe pair of hands, if rather uninspiring and at times pompous. All in all, Alexander deserves to be remembered as a figure of some importance within the Labour party, and not least as one who, more effectively than most, combined Labour and Co-operative concerns effectively.

Alexander wrote no memoirs, and his published works were little more than pamphlets: see, for example, *Parliament and the Consumer* (1929) and *The World Court: The Way to Peace* (1935). There is only one, short, biography: J. Tilley, *Churchill's Favourite Socialist: A Life of A. V. Alexander* (1995).

Andrew Thorpe

Wendy Alexander (1963–)

The Labour Party was built on the development of visionary ideas, and their achievement by practical means. Wendy Alexander is perhaps the best contemporary example of a politician who has combined idealism with the efficient delivery of real progress.

Wendy Alexander was born in Glasgow on 27 June 1963. Her family moved to Bishopton, Renfrewshire, in 1970, when her father became the Church of Scotland minister there. Her mother worked as a doctor, and both her parents remain committed Labour Party activists. She attended Park Mains High School, Erskine, before winning a place at Pearson College in Vancouver. She graduated from Glasgow University in 1986, with a degree in Modern and Economic History, then in Industrial Relations from Warwick University in 1987.

Having joined the Labour Party aged 15, Alexander became fully involved in student politics during her time at Glasgow University. As Convenor of the Democratic Left, an anti-Tory, anti-Trotskyite, broad coalition of all those on the Left, she was instrumental in ensuring that the Trotskyites never gained control of Scottish Labour Students. Following graduation from Warwick, Wendy Alexander worked briefly as researcher for the MPs George Galloway and Sam Galbraith, and then edited a publication for the Local Economic Development Information Service. In 1988 she became Research Officer for the Scottish Labour Party, a post she filled until late 1992, following which, she worked for the Socialist Group in the European Parliament.

At this point, Alexander made a move away from politics. In 1994 she completed an MBA at INSEAD, the French international business school and went to work as a management consultant for Booz, Allen and Hamilton. But the link was never truly severed. In 1997, Donald Dewar, then Scottish Secretary, appointed Alexander as his Special Adviser. She worked, not only on a broad range of policy areas, but also on the drafting of the Scotland Act, the bill which secured the formation of the Scottish Parliament.

In May 1999 she was elected as MSP for Paisley North, and was appointed Minister for Communities. This portfolio gave her responsibility for social inclusion, housing, equalities and Local Government. She soon produced plans to transfer Glasgow's housing stock into community ownership, making it possible not only to lift the burden of debt from the housing stock, and gain access to increased levels of investment, but also to give tenants democratic control over their own communities. These plans are to be put to a ballot of tenants in the autumn of 2001, and if accepted will lead to a huge improvement in Glasgow's housing stock.

With her responsibility for local government came the opportunity to repeal Section 2(a) of the Local Government Act, better known as Section 28, prohibiting 'the promotion of homosexuality and other pretended family relationships'. The move should have surprised no-one, as the legislation had always been bitterly opposed by the Left; what was surprising was the unprecedented vitriol of the anti-repeal campaign, *Keep the Clause*. Despite the increasingly vicious attacks on the Executive, and on Alexander personally, the legislation stayed, in essence, on track, and the clause was duly repealed. There are those who claim that Alexander's unbending stance on Section 28 has caused her personal political damage; however, few on the Left would dispute that it was simply the right thing to do, and this, for Alexander, was the most important point. Following the death of Donald Dewar in October 2000, the new First Minister, Henry McLeish, appointed Alexander Minister for Enterprise and Lifelong Learning. This move delighted her, giving her the opportunity to bring her experience of industry to bear on the fight for social justice.

In a reflection of her original intended career as a doctor, Alexander's first publications dealt with the world of medicine: *First Ladies of Medicine* (1987) and a contribution to *The World is Ill Divided: Women's Work in Scotland* (1990). She followed this with several contributions to works on devolution: *The State and the Nations* (1996) and *The Ethnicity Reader* (1997). Since her election to the Scottish Parliament, her contributions to publications have focused on the work of the Parliament; *A Different Future – A Moderniser's Guide to Scotland* (1999) and *New Gender Agenda* (2000).

Alexander has been described as an arch-moderniser, but this does not reflect her deeply held convictions and continued commitment to changing the world single-handed, a commitment which few politicians are able to maintain, let alone act on. Alexander has been a constant supporter of devolution, but she has no truck with Nationalism; delivering remains the priority, devolution the vehicle to make it possible. Wendy Alexander is on a mission to deliver social justice to the Scottish people, a mission which she sees as inextricably intertwined with the achievement of economic prosperity and industrial modernisation. Alexander has stuck by the ideals that she was raised with, and now she has the opportunity to put them into practice. With her levels of determination and enthusiasm it seems likely that she will succeed.

Judith Begg

Frank Allaun (1913–)

Frank Allaun represented the East division of Salford in the Commons for some 28 years. In that time, despite never achieving ministerial office (the nearest he came was as PPS to the Secretary of State for the Colonies) Allaun nevertheless distinguished himself as a fierce campaigner for causes he passionately believed in; unilateral nuclear disarmament, a free press and good housing. His election to the Labour Party's National Executive Committee in 1967 (a body he remained on for the following 16 years) allowed him to promote such causes but it also gave him a platform to push a cause he was equally passionate about – Labour party democracy. In so doing Allaun was placed in the thick of much debate and division in the Labour Party.

Frank Allaun was born in Manchester on 27 February 1913 to Harry and Hannah Allaun.

His parents sent Allaun to a prestigious local school, Manchester Grammar. Before joining the Labour Party, Allaun channelled the political energies that stem from the idealism of youth into the Communist Party eventually becoming the North West's Regional Organiser of the Young Communist League. It was also at this time that Allaun discovered his passion for writing and thus embarked on a long career as a campaigning journalist as a regular contributor to the ILP's *Labour's Northern Voice*. Following Manchester Grammar Allaun trained as an accountant at night school but accountancy was never for him. Instead his passion for journalism eventually led Allaun to the post of Town Hall Correspondent on the *Manchester Guardian* after the war.

The war of course had a massive impact on Allaun's outlook, as it did for so many politicians of his generation. Despite not seeing frontline combat himself (Allaun worked at Metro Vickers as an engineer instead), the destruction and inhumane brutality of the war forged a lasting influence on Allaun. It was also the war which, arguably, convinced Allaun of the need to follow the road of parliamentary democracy in pursuit of socialism, leading him to join the Labour Party. It was not long before the campaigning journalist (who by now had been promoted to industrial correspondent) started to make a name for himself on the political scene. In 1951 he stood for the Manchester seat of Moss Side. Moss Side then was a safe Conservative seat and the incumbent, Florence Horsbrugh, won a comfortable majority of almost 11,000. Although a setback for Allaun, this campaign was pretty much of a 'dry run' and allowed Allaun to impress the Labour Party enough for him to win selection to fight the safe Labour seat of Salford East four years later in 1955.

Throughout the 1950s and 1960s, Allaun was involved in the anti-nuclear movement and played a full part in the protests. He was an early activist in the Direct Action Committee which organised the first Aldermaston march (which was later taken over by CND). To this day Allaun is still involved in the peace movements and remains President of Labour Action for Peace (an organisation of which he was Chair for many years up until his retirement from the Commons in 1983). A Labour Action for Peace model resolution for the 1989 Labour Party Conference read, 'We reaffirm our continued commitment to the unconditional removal of all nuclear weapons and nuclear bases from British soil and waters within the first Parliament of the next Labour Government.' Such words could easily have been penned by Allaun himself. Today, Allaun is as committed as ever to such views with the passion with which those in the Labour movement have become accustomed and it is no wonder that today he is campaigning hard in newspapers against America's proposed national missile defence program.

In 1964 Allaun was appointed as PPS to the Secretary of State for the Colonies, Anthony Greenwood. But his rise up the greasy pole of government was to be remarkably short-lived. Less then six months later, in March 1965, Allaun resigned and would never see any glimmer of ministerial office again. Instead he stood in the annual beauty contest of the Labour party's NEC elections, winning a place in 1967. That year the left made decisive gains in the constituency section, and Allaun was elected alongside Tony Benn (still on his personal ideological journey), Barbara Castle, Tom Driberg, Anthony Greenwood, Joan Lestor and Ian Mikardo. Allaun had stood the previous year but had missed out by one place.

Over the following years the Labour party NEC was to assume more importance as the centre ground of many of the battles with the left that paralysed the Labour Party in the late

1970s and early 1980s. Throughout that time Allaun, who always carried the support of many activists, became at times something of an apologist for but in the main a fellow traveller of the left. In the 1980s, for example, he supported motions backing mandatory reselection of MPs and refused to endorse the expulsion of Militant Tendency supporters; they were 'good socialists' as far as he was concerned. Such a complement, however, did not extend to those Labour Party members who eventually joined the SDP. At an NEC meeting on 8 September 1980 the minutes record that Allaun proposed that a letter be written to the Labour supporters of the Social-Democratic Alliance (a grass-roots grouping of the traditional Labour right that included prominent London local government figures like John O'Grady, Douglas Eden, Stephen Haseler, Roger Fox and Jim Daly, and counted as its president Lord George-Brown) that they should undertake to give a commitment not to stand as candidates against the Labour Party or otherwise face expulsion.

As an NEC member Allaun was an outspoken opponent of the Falklands war, leading the *Daily Star* to brand him along with other leftwingers such as Benn and Stuart Holland as members of the loony left who were 'no friends of their country, of freedom, or their own party' (*Daily Star*, 15 April 1982). In later years Allaun was to be an equally strident opponent of the Gulf War.

But Allaun was by no means an unreconstructed Bennite. Allaun always had and to this day still has a deep attachment to Michael Foot, stretching back to the days when they campaigned together against the nuclear deterrent. Allaun would often declare himself a 'Foot man' although he did not always agree with him. Allaun, for example, could not wholeheartedly support Benn in his challenge for the Deputy Leadership against Denis Healey. Benn records in his diaries that Allaun first said he would think about supporting him, then decided to support him but finally made an about turn and withdrew his support (*Benn Diaries 1980–1990*, 20 March 1981). Similarly Allaun always supported the notion of a broad left slate for Shadow Cabinet elections combining the best of those on the soft and hard left from both the Tribunites and the Campaign Group.

Proposed boundary changes in the early 1980s meant that there would be only one Salford seat after the 1983 general election and thus Allaun decided to retire. He now lives in Prestwich, Greater Manchester, and is active in Bury South Labour Party while still writing regular columns for the *Morning Star, Tribune* and the *Socialist Campaign Group News*. For those on the left Allaun will be remembered as a passionate campaigner for peace and an opponent of nuclear arms. For those on the right he will be viewed as a fellow traveller of the hard left who despite seeing himself as a 'Foot man' supported Benn and Heffer at every opportunity on the NEC and did nothing to help stop the rot in the 1980s Labour Party.

His first wife Lilian died in 1986, he married Millie in 1989. He has one son and one daughter. His publications include: *Stop the H Bomb Race (1959); Heartbreak Housing (1966); Your Trade Union and You (1970); No Place Like Home (1972); The Wasted 30 Billions (1975); Question and Answers on Nuclear Weapons (1981); Spreading the News: a Guide to Media Reform (1989);* and *The Struggle for Peace (1992).*

Jonathan Ashworth

Lord Amulree (William Warrender Mackenzie)   (1860–1942)

Although Lord Amulree served in the cabinet of the second Labour government, his links to the party were only ever tenuous, and were abruptly severed in August 1931 when he chose to follow Ramsay MacDonald into the National government. It is therefore not surprising that he is now a forgotten figure in the party's history.

William Warrender Mackenzie was born at Scone, Perthshire, on 19 August 1860. The son of a prosperous farmer, he was educated at Perth Academy and Edinburgh University, graduating in 1885. In 1886 he was called to the Bar, and began a successful legal career, which included acing as a joint editor of Halsbury's *Laws of England*. In 1914 he became a King's Counsel. During the First World War, he was called upon to arbitrate a number of industrial disputes, particularly over wages, and most of his time for the next decade was to be concerned with this type of work, serving as the first president of the Industrial Court between 1919 and 1926. His efforts were broadly appreciated by many trade unionists, and he came to be seen as, in broad terms, a friendly figure by the Labour leadership.

There is no evidence that he was a member of the Labour party before 1929, but in June of that year he was ennobled, as 1st Baron Amulree, by MacDonald's second Labour government, which was desperate to strengthen Labour's extremely weak position in the House of Lords. Amulree was given no post within the government, but that changed in October 1930, when the Secretary of State for Air, Lord Thomson, was killed in the R101 disaster. MacDonald was, by this time, in considerable difficulties with his cabinet. Since it was increasingly faction-ridden, he did not want to favour one side over another. A number of junior ministers were pressing for promotion, but MacDonald had a low opinion of them all. In addition, Labour's front bench in the Lords was so weak that a replacement would almost certainly have to be found who was already in the Upper House. Accordingly, MacDonald asked Amulree – who had hitherto had no discernible interest in aviation – to take over. This was essentially an appointment of a non-party figure, loyal only to MacDonald, at a time when dealing with the party had become almost too much for MacDonald to bear. In that sense, it was symbolic of the increasing difficulties between the premier and many of his colleagues. There was little to distinguish Amulree's period as Secretary of State for Air. The R101 disaster had been a bitter blow to the Ministry. Even more seriously, in a context of severe restrictions on expenditure and planning for the 1932 World Disarmament Conference, and with more experienced cabinet colleagues fighting for resources for the Army and Navy against the still youthful RAF, there was little scope for Amulree to make much impact.

In the August 1931 crisis that led to the fall of the government, Amulree, predictably, supported MacDonald, and voted in favour of the proposal to cut unemployment benefit as a means of resolving the financial crisis. On the fall of the government, his offer to remain at the Air Ministry was accepted, although he was excluded from the ten-member emergency cabinet. However, he was too lightweight a figure to survive after the October 1931 general election, since the Conservatives – by far the largest group within the government – were very much underrepresented in the ministry, and on 5 November he was replaced by the Marquess of Londonderry. Amulree remained associated with MacDonald's 'National Labour' organisation for some years after 1931, and was serving on its executive committee until at least 1936. He died on 5 May 1942, and his son succeeded to the peerage.

In many ways, Amulree was similar to the non-Labour ministers appointed in 1924. That he could become a cabinet minister in a Labour government said a great deal about MacDonald's inability to bring on talent within the party and his failure to manage the ambitions of his colleagues and subordinates, but little more than that.

There is no biography. Among his works is *Industrial Arbitration in Great Britain* (1929).

Andrew Thorpe

Peter Archer (Lord Archer of Sandwell) (1926–)

Peter Kingsley Archer rose from an unprivileged background to achieve distinction in both the law and politics. He was probably the only Law Officer of the Crown to have been even temporarily a mineworker. Like so many Labour politicians of his generation, he was held back by the Tory hegemony of 1979–1997, although his gentle nature and tendency to view fellow human beings in a kindly light might anyway have prevented him from reaching the highest offices.

Born 20 November 1926, he attended Wednesbury High School for Boys, leaving at the age of 16 after taking Higher School Certificate (the equivalent of A levels). His parents were apolitical, but young Peter was influenced by reading Ramsay MacDonald's *Problems of a Socialist Government* in the public library: he did not know that MacDonald had subsequently betrayed socialism. A local Methodist minister, the Rev. Percy Jackson, active in the Social Credit movement, succeeded in talking Peter out of joining the Young Communists in the sixth form.

He obtained temporary employment for a year with the District Audit service in Birmingham. The District Auditor, E R Southgate, a former postman, impressed on the young man the need to study for a degree in order to get on in life. Peter therefore embarked on an external degree in law by correspondence from University College, London. He wanted to do his war service in the Army, as his father had done in the First World War, but instead, by the luck of the ballot, was sent to work in the mines as one of 'Bevin's Boys'. For four years he studied in his spare time, obtaining an LLB in 1946 and an Intermediate BA in Philosophy in 1947. He must have been an unusual miner. On demobilisation in 1948 he went to the London School of Economics to study full time for an LLM, awarded in 1950. So he never returned to the District Audit. Yet another degree followed, in Philosophy at UCL in 1952, financed by a scholarship from the enlightened benchers of Gray's Inn. He had certainly taken Southgate's advice to heart. He was called to the Bar in 1952.

In the meantime he had joined the Labour Party in 1948, being elected (as often happens) ward secretary within three weeks. In 1954 he married Margaret Smith ('Miff'), a local deputy head teacher. They had one son, John.

He stood for the Conservative seat of Hendon South in 1959. He had already become the PPC there when a by-election occurred in Wednesbury in 1958. Despite his strong Black Country connections he felt he could not try for Wednesbury, and had to watch John Stonehouse secure the safe seat which the latter held until his imprisonment. Archer had to wait another eight years before entering Parliament. He gradually developed a common law practice at the Bar including personal injury and divorce cases, and the then unusual speciality of employment and trade union disputes.

He had come to the attention of two experienced talent scouts, the West Midlands Regional Agent, Reg Underhill, and his deputy, Bert Williams. In 1964 he fought the marginal seat of Brierly Hill, but the Conservative held on. Just before the March 1966 election Arthur Henderson QC stood down from his safe seat of Rowley Regis and Tipton. When a long-serving MP retires selectors usually pick a contrasting successor, but the CLP was content to select one Methodist barrister to follow another, and Archer defeated Betty Boothroyd, Bryan Stanley and Guy Barnett for the nomination. He held the seat, with boundary changes later renamed Warley West, for over 30 years.

From 1967 to 1970 Archer served as PPS to the Attorney General, acquiring experience which he was to put into practice in the following Labour government. In 1969 he was sent for three months to represent his country on the United Nations' 'Third Committee' on human rights. He retained a keen interest in international human rights, being active in Amnesty International and the Anti-Slavery Society. When Labour lost office in 1970 he pursued his practice at the Bar, becoming Queen's Counsel in 1971. There was a shortage of 'silks' doing criminal work in the early 1970s, so he tried his hand in the criminal courts. It was useful experience for a future Law Officer.

In February 1974 Labour took office again. Wilson chose Archer to be the new Solicitor-General. Along with Sam Silkin, the Attorney-General, he broke with precedent by refusing the knighthood which had until that time automatically gone with the job. Silkin took the high-profile decisions, for example on prosecuting journalist Duncan Campbell and others under the Official Secrets Act. Archer's duties included representing the Government in the courts, domestic and occasionally European. Being ex-officio a law officer for Northern Ireland, he also had to authorise prosecutions there.

When James Callaghan became Prime Minister Archer retained his position. As the Party drifted towards internecine struggle Archer was naturally both a loyalist and a conciliator: along with colleagues he founded the group 'Labour First'.

In Opposition he remained on the front bench and was elected to the Shadow Cabinet from 1981 to 1987; after covering Legal Affairs (1979–82) and Trade, Prices and Consumer Protection (1982–83), he was Shadow Northern Ireland Secretary from 1983 to 1987. The absence of partisan rhetoric suited his style. He was Chair of the Fabian Society in 1980 and became its President in 1993. He also served as Chair of the Council on Tribunals and President of the World Disarmament Campaign.

In 1992 he stood down from the Commons and was created Lord Archer of Sandwell. He has been popular and effective in the Lords, serving as an Opposition Foreign Affairs Spokesman (1992–97). He scored a notable, symbolic victory when he successfully proposed an amendment which abolished the death penalty for treason and piracy, thus removing it altogether from the statute book. He has been a firm defender of civil liberties generally and trial by jury in particular. His values have remained constant throughout a long career. His publications include *The Queen's Courts; Communism and the Law; The International Protection of Human Rights;* and *Purpose in Socialism.*

David Bean QC

Hilary Armstrong (1945–)

Hilary Armstrong's 2001 promotion to Chief Whip saw her join the Cabinet, albeit with observer status, after more than twelve years on the Labour front bench. Born on 30 November 1945, Armstrong was educated at Sunderland's Monkwearmouth comprehensive, West Ham Technology College, and then the University of Birmingham. After an early career as a social worker and lecturer, she inherited the North West Durham seat from her own father at the 1987 general election, although with significant boundary changes. Her father, the Rt Hon. Ernest Armstrong, a former schoolmaster and Sunderland councillor, had held the seat since 1964 and had served as a whip under Harold Wilson and as an Under-Secretary of State at Education (1974–75) and Environment (1975–79) before becoming a Deputy Speaker.

After a brief spell on the education select committee, Neil Kinnock quickly promoted her into a junior education spokesperson's job in 1988, a role with which she continued until the 1992 election defeat. John Smith then took her on to be his PPS, before returning her to her tasks as a spokesperson in 1994, as a junior member of Gordon Brown's Treasury team. Blair moved her on at his first reshuffle to the Local Government spokesperson's job that she retained in various forms into and throughout the first term of the Labour government.

She formed her political views during her early career in community-based social work, further flavoured by a stint with VSO in Kenya. Coupled with her Methodism, this emphasis on working with socially excluded groups has led to a communitarian-style political outlook based on a desire to move away from statist delivery to locally organised policy.

Elected to the Labour NEC during her stint as John Smith's PPS, she emerged as the crucial figure in the decision by the MSF union not to oppose OMOV at the 1993 conference – as it turned out, the decisive turning point in John Smith's reform attempt. A gut Labour politician, she was also effective working behind the scenes on the NEC Women and Local Government committees, and has been described as one of the key lieutenants of Sally Morgan, the former political secretary to Prime Minister Blair.

A constitutional moderniser, she worked well with the Liberal Democrat front bench on reform of local government. As Chief Whip, she lines up alongside the similarly pro-reform Robin Cook and his deputy Stephen Twigg, prompting hopes that some of the more arcane practices in the Commons might finally be due for reform

Peter Metcalfe

Clement Attlee (Earl Attlee) (1883–1967)

Clement Richard Attlee was born on 3 January 1883, to the Putney family of a wealthy city solicitor, Henry Attlee. He was educated at home until he was nine, and showed early on his remarkable latent for absorbing information like a sponge and retaining it. He learned Italian so thoroughly that, six decades later, he amazed his political colleagues by addressing the socialist international conference in Milan in fluent Italian.

At nine he was sent to Northaw Place, a boarding preparatory school at Potters Bar in Hertfordshire. The two clergymen who ran it were interested in cricket and in the Bible, in that order, and in very little else, so they gave him the detailed knowledge of, and fascination for, cricket statistics which made him, as one political colleague put it, a 'walking Wisden'.

Haileybury in Hertfordshire was chosen as his public school, and he went there in 1896. In 1901, the year of Queen Victoria's death, Attlee entered University College, Oxford. Then he trained for the bar, but without much enthusiasm, as he told his first biographer, Roy Jenkins: 'I rather thought of some profession in which a living could be made while in my leisure time I could continue my reading in literature and history and learn more of art and antiquities'. His other ambition, though he did not talk about it until he retired, was to be a poet.

He passed his bar examinations in 1905. But his life changed one night when he visited the East End of London, with the vague idea of doing some charitable work among the poor. Attlee, straight from work in his silk hat and tail coat, walked gingerly through Stepney's disgusting, uncleaned streets to Haileybury House, set up by his old school as a club for poor East End children. He quickly became deeply involved, and started to manage the club in 1907.

Deciding that charity was not enough to end poverty, and political action was required, he joined the Independent Labour Party, and conquered his shyness sufficiently to start addressing open-air ILP meetings in 1908. In 1912 he took a job teaching at the London School of Economics, but two years later, when war was declared in August 1914, he chose to enlist in the army straight away – even though the ILP had always said that if war came, socialists should refuse to fight.

He had what was known as 'a good war' – he was wounded, admired for his efficiency and bravery, and promoted to Major. Back in Stepney in 1919, he threw himself into East End Labour politics, and bought a lease on a big, dilapidated old house in Limehouse called Norway House. He converted the first floor into a flat for himself. The ground floor he gave to the Limehouse Labour Party for its headquarters, complete with canteen, card tables and a three-quarter-size billiard table, and in 1920 he was Stepney's mayor.

While mayor he wrote *The Social Worker*, which contains probably the clearest statement of the principles which underlay his political philosophy, and the philosophy of the government he led a quarter of a century later. In particular, it attacks the idea that looking after the poor can be left to voluntary action. Charity, he says, is a cold, grey, loveless thing. If a rich man wants to help the poor, he should pay his taxes gladly, not dole out money at whim.

Charity, he says, 'is only possible without loss of dignity between equals. A right established by law, such as that to an old age pension, is less galling than an allowance made by a rich man to a poor one, dependent on his view of the recipient's character, and terminable at his caprice ...'

On 10 January 1922 he married Violet Millar, and in November of the same year was elected Labour MP for Limehouse, soon becoming Labour leader Ramsay MacDonald's PPS. When MacDonald formed the first Labour government two years later, Attlee, who had by then earned himself a reputation as a solid and reliable parliamentarian, became Under-Secretary of State for War.

In the late 1920s he left the ILP, which had been his political home ever since he became a socialist. The ILP, he wrote in his autobiography, 'became more and more irresponsible under the leadership of Jimmy Maxton. With many others I found it necessary to part company with this organisation. This was a matter of very great regret, for I had spent my political life in its ranks.'

He was disappointed not to get a job in MacDonald's second government in 1929, but became Chancellor of the Duchy of Lancaster as a result of the resignation of Sir Oswald Mosley in May 1930. A further reshuffle in March 1931 made him Postmaster General, still outside Cabinet. But in the election later that year, Labour was decimated by the National Government, led by the man who until a few weeks previously had led the Labour government, Ramsay MacDonald.

The Labour leader, Arthur Henderson, lost his seat, and so did all remaining members of the MacDonald cabinet. Only three of Labour's 46 MPs had any front bench experience: Attlee, George Lansbury, and Sir Stafford Cripps, who had been Solicitor General for a year, but was very new to the Party and had only been in the House for a year. There was only one conceivable leader, Lansbury, and only one conceivable deputy leader, Attlee.

When Lansbury retired in 1935, the real battle for the succession was between Attlee and Herbert Morrison, who had lost his seat in 1931 but was now back in parliament. Morrison believed all his life that had he been an MP in 1931, he would have won the leadership in 1935, but this seems unlikely. The truth is that, after they had been betrayed by the showy and snobbish MacDonald, Attlee's modest suburban ways appealed to the Party.

The characteristics which became the stuff of affectionate anecdote later were already present, like his terseness, his addiction to *The Times* crossword puzzle, his fascination with cricket, and his strange and rather exaggerated devotion to Haileybury, to University College Oxford, and even to his prep school, Northaw House. People say that he never had an image. But the truth was that these things were his image. He turned suburban mannerisms and staccato, pronounless sentences into precious political assets.

In a growingly dangerous international situation, he knew that he needed to get his party, despite its pacifist traditions, to think seriously about defence. So, as he wrote in his autobiography, 'As soon as the 1935 parliament met, I determined to take steps to create a better understanding of defence problems in the Party ... I ... formed a Defence Committee which met regularly and discussed defence problems ... The result was seen in the far more informed contribution which Labour men were able to make in Service debates.'

In 1940 Attlee played a key part in the formation of a coalition government under Winston Churchill, making it clear that Labour would not serve under Neville Chamberlain. Two days after Germany invaded Holland and Belgium, on Friday May 10, Attlee and the new Prime Minister, Winston Churchill, agreed on the composition of a new government. Attlee was determined not to hold things up by bargaining over offices, for he remembered how vital decisions were delayed during the Dardanelles campaign while Conservatives and Liberals bargained for places in Asquith's coalition of 1915. Attlee himself became Lord Privy Seal, and a member of the war cabinet.

He was a much more powerful figure during the war than his low public profile suggested. Behind the scenes his voice was often crucial, and never more so than just before the fall of France. French Prime Minister Paul Reynaud wanted Britain to try to negotiate a general peace with Hitler. Attlee was the first to speak in the war cabinet, and it was his contribution that effectively destroyed Reynaud's idea.

Only Attlee and Churchill were in the war cabinet from start to finish, and Attlee did most of the nuts and bolts work. There was a sense of almost audible relief around Whitehall when it was known that Attlee, not Churchill, would be in the chair at cabinet, for the meeting would be far more efficiently conducted and would last half the time. He was sharp with any minister who spoke too long or was not properly briefed, and he kept debates as short as possible. In February 1942 Churchill gave him the title of Deputy Prime Minister, and he also became Dominions Secretary until September 1943, when he became Lord President of the Council.

At the 1945 election, Labour was returned with 393 seats and an overall majority for the first time ever, and Attlee became Prime Minister. Until December 1946 he followed Churchill's example in serving as his own Minister of Defence. He held up the adoption of a thoroughgoing Cold War policy until January 1947. Right up until then – unlike his Foreign Secretary, Ernest Bevin – he believed that the United Nations would be given the power to create a new world order, and that Britain could negotiate with the Russians.

He acted decisively over India, appointing Louis Mounbatten as Viceroy and giving him full powers to reach an agreement. He and Mountbatten enabled Britain, against all the odds, to withdraw in good order from a large slice of Empire. Mountbatten wrote to Attlee: 'Without your original guidance and your unwavering support nothing could have been accomplished out here.'

But the central job of the 1945 government, as Attlee saw it, was the creation of the welfare state, whose design was to be found in the wartime Beveridge report. On 5 July 1948 the National Health Service came into existence after a titanic struggle between Health Minister Aneurin Bevan and the doctors. In addition, on the same day, Attlee was able to announce 'the most comprehensive system of social security ever introduced into any country.'

Four Acts came into force that day: the National Insurance Act, the Industrial Injuries Act, the National Assistance Act, and the NHS Act. They were all based on a new principle: that 'we must combine together to meet contingencies with which we cannot cope as individual citizens.'

In the same year the government nationalised inland transport – railways, canals and road haulage – and the great utilities, electricity and gas. The Bank of England had been nationalised in 1945. Iron and steel followed in 1949. Altogether, the Attlee government brought about a fifth of the economy into public ownership.

Attlee drove these measures through against a background of dire warnings that the war-shattered economy could not afford them. He gave his reply to Parliament in 1946, and it remains a standing rebuke to Labour ministers who say that we must have a better deal for the poorest – but now is never the right time to do it.

'The question is asked – can we afford it? Supposing the answer is "No," what does that mean? It really means that the sum total of the goods produced and the services rendered by the people of this country is not sufficient to provide for all our people at all times, in sickness, in health, in youth and in age, the very modest standard of life that is represented by the sums of money set out in the Second Schedule to this [National Insurance] Bill. I cannot believe that our national productivity is so slow, that our willingness to work is so feeble or that we can submit to the world that the masses of our people must be condemned to penury.'

At the February 1950 election, Labour polled the highest popular vote any party had ever polled, even more than in 1945, nearly three per cent more than the Conservatives. The swing to the Conservatives was only 3.3%. But Labour's overall majority was down to five, because many of its votes went to build up massive majorities in safe Labour seats. The redistribution of seats which had taken place during the Parliament had transferred huge blocks of Labour votes from marginal to safe seats and probably lost Labour about 30 MPs. Redistribution meant also that Attlee himself now sat as MP for Walthamstow West.

Attlee was forced to go to the country again in October 1951, this time against the background of a bitter cabinet division between Hugh Gaitskell and Aneurin Bevan over charging for teeth and spectacles on the NHS. Yet still he came near to winning the election – and did win it, in the sense that Labour polled more votes than the Conservatives. But it got fewer seats; Churchill's Conservatives had an overall majority of 17.

Attlee led Labour through the General Election of May 1955. Retiring as leader and as an MP in December 1955, he was created Earl Attlee and Viscount Prestwood and became in 1956 a Knight of the Garter. He had been made a Companion of Honour in 1945 and was awarded an Order of Merit in 1951. His beloved Vi died in 1964 at the age of 68, and Attlee moved into a flat at 1 Kings Bench Walk in the Temple. He died in his sleep on 8 October 1967.

Attlee published his memoirs, *As it Happened*, in 1954. His other publications include: *The Social Worker* (1920); *The Town Councillor* (1925); *The Will and the Way to Socialism* (1935); *The Labour Party in Perspective* (1937); *Collective Security Under the United Nations* (1958); and *Empire into Commonwealth* (1961). Francis Williams' *A Prime Minister Remembers*, based on interviews with Attlee, appeared in 1961. Attlee papers are held at the Bodleian Library, Oxford, and Churchill College, Cambridge. Biographies include Roy Jenkins, *Mr Attlee* (1948); Kenneth Harris, *Attlee* (1982); Trevor Burridge, *Clement Attlee: A Political Biography*, (1985); and Francis Beckett, *Clem Attlee* (1997).

Francis Beckett

Alice Bacon (Baroness Bacon of Leeds and Normanton) (1909–93)

Alice Bacon was born into a Yorkshire mining family and into the Labour movement on 10 September 1909. Her father, Benjamin, was a miner and a West Riding county councillor. She went first to elementary schools in Normanton and then to Normanton Girls' Grammar School. During this time she was a leading light of the Labour League of Youth, which introduced her to national politics at a young age.

Bacon trained as a schoolteacher at Stockwell training college and as an external student at London University, and then worked as a secondary school teacher. During her political career she was often described as having the manner of a schoolmistress, with a didactic, commonsensical approach to speaking, which could be effective and persuasive but rankled with Labour intellectuals such as Richard Crossman, who could not abide her flat Yorkshire vowels. Denis Healey described her as 'a bonny Yorkshire lass of immense common sense and strong character, she had more than a touch of Jane Eyre about her. No Rochester ever entered her life, but she had a personal devotion to Hugh Gaitskell which went beyond politics.' Education was always one of her main political interests, at a time when it was regarded as a political backwater, and she was an early advocate of comprehensive schools.

Her contribution to Labour history was mostly through her long service on the National Executive Committee; she first won a place in 1941 and served continuously until she stepped down from parliament in 1970. She was chair of the Labour Party in 1950–51. Alice Bacon was elected MP for Leeds North East in July 1945, overturning a large Conservative majority, and following boundary changes which added suburban Tory territory to North East she moved in 1955 to Leeds South East, where she remained until 1970.

Alice Bacon was one of Gaitskell's staunchest supporters on the NEC and not unwilling to get involved in his 'dirty work', including the attempted expulsion of Bevan in 1955; she was also a notably disciplinarian chair of the Organisation Subcommittee. She and the National Agent, Sara Barker, would suspend and reorganise constituency parties suspected of Trotskyite infiltration with a fervour that would make New Labour's efforts at enforcing its will on local parties seem timid. She seriously proposed that the right and the Bevanites should use different lifts at Transport House when turning up for NEC meetings. As well as being a fierce battler in the bitter internal Labour politics of the 1950s, Bacon was also involved in policy development, fraternal visits and Labour's general election campaign committees in 1959–66.

Bacon was appointed Minister of State, second in command at the Home Office, in October 1964, having been a Shadow Home Office Minister since 1959. For the first year the department was under the benign but ineffective regime of Frank Soskice, and Bacon made much of the running on the biggest Home Office issue, immigration control. She oversaw the introduction of the 1965 Immigration Act and persuaded the 1965 Labour conference to endorse this moderately restrictive (but nowhere near as illiberal as the 1968 Act) measure. She then served under Roy Jenkins, her remit including drugs policy. She expressed her strong personal disapproval of cannabis, but established the liberalising Wootton committee to investigate the drug laws. She joined the Privy Council in 1966.

On 29 August 1967 Alice Bacon moved to Minister of State at the Department of Education and Science, under Patrick Gordon Walker and Ted Short, where she helped administer Labour's policies of comprehensive schooling and expanding higher education. She was not a Wilson loyalist on the NEC; she participated in the plots against him in 1968 and 1969 over the new General Secretary and *In Place of Strife*. Her decision to stand down from parliament in 1970 was in order to take care of her aunt, who had previously cared for Bacon's own parents in their old age. She went straight to the Lords as Baroness Bacon of Leeds and Normanton and contributed actively to the Labour cause in the 1970s and early 1980s, particularly on Home Office matters, education and local government. She died on 24 March 1993. Alice Bacon's was a notably unselfish life, devoting her energies to the Labour Party, Hugh Gaitskell and the improvement of educational and social conditions.

Lewis Baston

Oliver Baldwin (1st Viscount Corvedale and 2nd Earl Baldwin of Bewdley)   (1899–1958)

Baldwin is not a name one immediately associates with the Labour Party. Rather it conjures up images of the Conservative Prime Minister Stanley Baldwin, who engineered much of interwar Britain's era of Conservative dominance. However, Oliver Ridsdale Baldwin's career does more than justify his own place in twentieth-century political history, for he successfully emerged from his fathers shadow with a completely different political outlook and ethos.

His career is perhaps more extraordinary, given that his upbringing and education should have led him in the political footsteps of his famous father, rather than creating the self-proclaimed socialist and Labour MP. Moreover, Baldwin was not only a politician, but also an author, soldier, journalist, playwright and colonial governor. Each achievement was the result of Baldwin's adaptability and a reflection of his diverse character.

Baldwin was born on 1 March 1899, the elder son of Stanley and Lucy Baldwin, of Astley Hall, Worcestershire. At this time his father was the owner of a great iron and steel business, entering Parliament in 1908. Oliver was educated privately at St. Aubyn's School, Rottingdean. This was followed by four years at Eton, up until July 1915, which he described in his autobiography, *The Questing Beast* (1932), as 'the most useless and unhappy years of my life up until then.' Many have attributed this dislike for education to his nonconformist roots, which he inherited from both sides of his family.

Having joined the cadets in May 1916, Baldwin had the opportunity to demonstrate his physical courage, for in 1917 he was commissioned in the Irish Guards and in May 1918 saw action in France. He spent the early months of 1920 in Algeria and Morocco and wrote about this time of his life in the publication, *Six Prisons and Two Revolutions*. In Armenia, Baldwin witnessed the invasion of the Bolshevik army and was briefly imprisoned, demonstrating an early rebellious streak that was to emerge consistently throughout his life. These foreign experiences further isolated him from Conservative politics, partly owing to his disillusionment with Lord Curzon's foreign policy and his increasing association with the Armenian radicals. Nonetheless, soldiering would remain one of his great loves, and during the Second World War he became a Major in the Intelligence Corps, serving in Egypt, Palestine, Syria, Eritrea and Algeria from 1940 to 1943.

However, it was in the early 1920s that Baldwin began to articulate his own set of political beliefs. At the time this was attributed partly to his having met in 1922 John Boyle, Baldwin's lifelong partner with whom he set up home in London. Others simply pointed to Baldwin's contentious streak, as immediately after his father became PM in 1923 he declared himself a socialist and promptly left the family home. This contrast between the Conservative father and socialist son aided rumours that their relationship was often strained and formal. However, such differences did not affect the natural affection they held for each other, exhibited in their correspondence in Cambridge.

Joining the SDF in 1922 Baldwin thence progressed to Labour politics. He stood unsuccessfully for parliament at Dudley in 1924 before winning the seat in 1929. However, moving to Chatham in 1931 and Paisley in 1935, he was twice defeated. It was not until 1945 that he returned to the Commons, as Labour MP for Paisley, carrying the courtesy title Viscount Corvedale. Never a minister, he was, however, briefly a PPS: to Jack Lawson in 1946 and to Fred Bellenger in 1947, successively Attlee's Secretaries of State for War.

It was Oliver Baldwin's association with Oswald Mosley and his New Party that caused the most political controversy. His relationship with Mosley was close and in February 1931 Baldwin resigned the Labour whip, joined the New Party and even contributed to the drafting of the party manifestos, though he resigned from the New Party the following day and rejoined the Labour Party. Thus he never endorsed or associated himself with any of Mosley's fascist tendencies. However, this episode reflects not only Baldwin's wilfulness, but also his haphazard political judgement. Baldwin himself often felt his political career was something of a failure, feeling that his theoretical principles and high ideals were not reflected in the reality of Labour politics. On the death of his father in December 1947, Oliver automatically succeeded to the earldom and was forced to resign his Commons seat and adjust to life in the Lords. Despite all this, his brief career in the Commons forged many of Baldwin's closest friendships, including those with Labour stalwarts such as James Maxton, Ben Tillet, Seymour Cocks and Arthur Greenwood.

In 1948 the Labour Government appointed the new 2nd Earl Baldwin as Governor of the Leeward Islands. His open hostility to the actions of the British Government in sending out missions of inquiry and inspection attracted criticism. His outspoken views and eccentric behaviour nearly cost him his position, and on being recalled by the Colonial Secretary, Arthur Creech-Jones, for 'consultation' Baldwin talked openly to the press of his expectations of a 'carpeting'. He was, however, a popular governor and V C Bird, one of the main local Labour leaders, publicly backed Baldwin's continuation as Governor. Hence, after apologising and retracting some of his previous statements, Baldwin was returned to the island, continuing in post until 1950. This incident gave the Conservatives a degree of political capital, but Baldwin was genuinely concerned about the condition of the island, one of the poorest in the West Indies.

This concern for those less fortunate than himself was demonstrated throughout his various careers. As a politician, soldier, playwright, journalist and author he displayed generosity, loyalty and a belief in the principles that had guided him as a young man. His propensity for causing controversy was legendary, but he was not a deliberate troublemaker. Rather, he simply said what he thought, and this was often the cause of some discussion amongst more reserved politicians.

Earl Baldwin of Bewdley died in a London hospital on 10 August 1958; he was 59. Very little has been written on any part of the career of this fascinating man and principled politician. He was somewhat of a black sheep, isolated in equal measure by society's view of homosexuality and by his own ability to shock and amuse. However, his diverse and colourful life, and his sortie into Labour politics, are testament to a man who did not always accept the status quo and broke away from the conservative future that had seemed his destiny.

Jennifer Gerber

Ed Balls   (1967–)

It is a sign of the respect he commands that Ed Balls, the Oxford (Keble) and Harvard (Kennedy Scholar) educated Chief Economic Adviser to the Chancellor has been tipped to enter Number Eleven in his own right ever since he began work for Gordon Brown as a 27-year-old back in 1994. Indeed, by the time he started with Brown he had already clocked up an impressive CV, as a teaching fellow at Harvard and then as the economics leader writer of the *Financial Times*.

Yet despite featuring in a conference speech of Michael Heseltine (and despite his 'new Labour society wedding' of 1998 to MP and junior minister Yvette Cooper) his profile remained relatively overshadowed by Charlie Whelan until in 1999 he was elevated above the ranks of mere special advisers to become Chief Economic Adviser. This ostensibly political appointment to an official position caused some protests from the Tories, but the issue soon died down since it was, after all, merely the formal confirmation of what had been known to be true ever since May 1997.

Born on 25 February 1967, Ed Balls was brought up by his parents, Michael and Carolyn, in Norwich until they moved to Nottingham when he was aged eight. There he attended the independent Nottingham High School. Ed's father Michael, an academic, had secured a grammar school scholarship and read Zoology at Keble College, Oxford, despite being brought up by just one parent following the premature death of his father, a gas company truck driver.

Ed Balls allegedly came to the attention of Gordon Brown after writing a 1992 Fabian Society pamphlet calling for Bank of England independence in the wake of the British ejection from ERM. With Charlie Whelan and Gordon Brown, he formed the triumvirate that transformed Labour's economic policy and credibility before, during and after the 1997 election defeat.

If Brown provided the vision and Whelan the PR, it was Balls who drove the detailed ideas. It was his Fabian plan for granting independence to the Bank of England that the Chancellor handed to officials upon entering the Treasury in 1997. And it was Balls who drove the so-called 'Americanisation' of Labour economic policy in opposition that drew heavily on the thinking of New Democrat intellectuals Larry Summers and Larry Katz. He has suffered minor setbacks: he was lampooned for writing 'neo-classical endogenous growth theory' into a Brown speech, and a fly-on-the-wall documentary of life inside the Treasury revealed his influence and caused inevitable jealousy amongst rivals.

Balls has partly managed the rivalries of colleagues by claiming to have no political ambition in his own right. It is true, indeed, that he shows little desire or aptitude for the mechanical business of low politics and schmoozing in the Strangers' Bar. But the fig leaf cannot last forever – why else might a man universally acknowledged as amongst the most powerful in Britain want to give that all up for the obscurity of the backbenches, unless he hopes to emerge on to the front bench and take political power in his own right?

Melissa Robinson

Thomas Balogh (Lord Balogh)　　　　　　　　(1905–85)

Despite a relatively brief and junior ministerial post, Thomas Balogh's influence in the postwar Labour Party was considerable. He was an economist of note and an important influence on the thinking of many significant Labour figures, not least Harold Wilson.

Balogh was born in Budapest on 2 November 1905 into a professional, middle-class family. He was educated at the city's Minta Gymnasium. The school, nicknamed the Winchester of Hungary, produced a long line of Hungarian intellectuals including Nicholas Kaldor. Kaldor, another Hungarian émigré economist influential in Labour circles, and Balogh were very much linked in the public mind and were variously nicknamed 'the Hungarian Mafia' and 'Buda and Pest' amongst other (mostly unflattering) things. Balogh went on to study law and economics at the Universities of Budapest and then Berlin before spending two years doing postgraduate research at Harvard. He went on to work as an economic researcher at the Banque de France, the Reichsbank in Germany and the Federal Reserve in America.

His first academic article was published in the *Economic Journal* and made a sufficiently favourable impression on its editor, John Maynard Keynes, for him to help Balogh secure a job with the banking firm O.T. Falk and Sons in 1932. He moved into academia in 1934 when he joined the Economics faculty at University College, London. Balogh remained at UCL until 1939 when he moved to Balliol College, Oxford, where his students included Roy Jenkins. He maintained his links with Balliol until he died.

Balogh's significance within the Labour Party emerged in the late 1940s. He was the informal economic advisor to the Keep Left group of MPs including Dick Crossman, Michael Foot and Ian Mikardo. Crossman, Foot and Mikardo wrote the pamphlet *Keep Left* in 1947 which, under the influence of Balogh, called for a state-engineered export drive domestically coupled with a revised position in the emergent Cold War between the superpowers. Instead of siding with either the USA or the Soviet bloc, Britain should seek to cooperate with Europe in developing a socialist third bloc, independent of the superpowers, which could play a mediating role in world politics and provide an alternative model of development for the Third World. Balogh developed the themes of *Keep Left* in his book *The Dollar Crisis: Causes & Cures* (Blackwell, 1949) where he proposed moves towards a planned European economy as a solution to the USA's enormous economic dominance. European goods were to be given preferential status within Europe. This would give a boost to European economies, enabling them to maintain full employment and achieve a more equitable distribution of income; the policy was to be supplemented with greater state control of the domestic economy. This state regulation and planning of the economy proves a consistent theme throughout Balogh's political career, though he, like most of the Keep Left group, were later opponents of Britain's membership of the Common Market.

The Keep Left group were a small, inexperienced and not particularly influential group of MPs within the Labour Party. But in the wake of the resignations from the government of Aneurin Bevan, John Freeman and Harold Wilson in 1951 over the imposition of charges for false teeth and spectacles, Keep Left emerged as the forum for left-wing opposition to the conduct of government policy. Keep Left evolved into the Bevanite faction in the wake of Labour's 1951 election defeat and Balogh continued his association with it.

In the 1950s Balogh developed the technocratic approach of *The Dollar Crisis*. He was sceptical of the reliance of Hugh Gaitskell's followers on Keynesian economic management, instead inextricably linking the pursuit of equality with technocratic economic controls – economic planning, greater public ownership and controls over investment were prerequisites of sustainable moves towards greater equality. He was convinced of the greater economic efficiency of the planned economy and that the competitive threat would come from the Soviet bloc rather than the USA or Europe. His technocratic agenda brought him into closer alliance with Harold Wilson. Despite being regarded with suspicion by much of the Left, Wilson remained a high-profile Bevanite, and his thinking on economic matters was developing along the same lines as Balogh's, emphasising strategic control of the economy. This emphasis on planning soon came to override the concern with public ownership and marked a division between Balogh, Wilson and Crossman and their former Bevanite allies such as Mikardo, who continued to emphasise the need for nationalisation.

One of Balogh's recommendations was for a diminishing of the role of the Treasury across all areas of policy-making. In a chapter on the civil service that he contributed to Hugh Thomas' book on *The Establishment* (Blond, 1959), Balogh claimed that the responsibility for Britain's relative economic underperformance lay with the Treasury and their conservatism and lack of technical expertise. Because of this he advocated the establishment of a new economic ministry that would take on some of the Treasury's functions. Wilson's closeness to Balogh on this issue is clear. Within weeks of being elected party leader in 1963 Wilson had charged Balogh with drawing up plans for a new economics department. The department was to oversee the implementation of a broad-ranging national plan which was to be drawn up and administered by highly skilled economic technicians. These plans were the basis for the Department for Economic Affairs, which was established after Labour's election victory in 1964.

Balogh was appointed as economic advisor to Wilson after the election. He was firmly established as one of Wilson's 'kitchen cabinet' and enjoyed being close to the centre of power. He also had a reputation for spectacular rudeness and rarely disguised his impatience with the civil service. However, despite his closeness to Wilson, his influence in office was more limited than he might have hoped. Despite the institutional changes he advocated such as the DEA or the Industrial Reconstruction Corporation, designed to promote productivity through encouraging industrial mergers, he must have been disappointed at the conduct of policy in a number of areas. The DEA and economic planning, in particular the planning of incomes via a rigorous incomes policy (a subject he returned to in 1970 in his Fabian pamphlet *Labour & Inflation*), failed to achieve the significance he had wanted. Michael Shanks, an economist who worked with Balogh, said that the impression was that planning 'took place on an essentially *ad hoc* basis as a reaction to crisis' (in Michael Hatfield's *The House the Left Built* (Gollancz, 1978), p.28).

Balogh had been elevated to the House of Lords in 1968 and from Labour's return to office in 1974 until December 1975, he was Minister of State for Energy. He had maintained an interest in North Sea oil since the first discoveries were made in the 1960s. Typically he thought that a stricter regime of controls on the oil industry was necessary to maximise the benefits of the oil fields to the British economy. He played a key role in setting up the British National Oil Corporation to give the state a direct state in North Sea oil and became its deputy director in 1976, becoming its economic advisor in 1978.

After Labour's election defeat in 1979 he used his position in the House of Lords to attack the Conservative government of Margaret Thatcher, in particular on matters relating to oil and to economic policy. Throughout his involvement in politics he retained a high profile as an academic economist and had acted as an advisor to numerous governments in the developing world. He married psychotherapist Pen Gatty in 1945, leaving her for Catherine Storr in 1970. He died on 21 January 1985.

There is no biography of Balogh yet, but his fellow Labour Party economist Andrew Graham wrote an article, 'Thomas Balogh (1905–1985)' in *Contemporary Record* (Vol.6, No.1, summer 1992) reviewing his life's work. His role in the development of North Sea oil policy is covered by his former student June Morris in 'Thomas Balogh and the Fight for North Sea Revenue' *Contemporary Record* (Vol. 12, No.2, summer 1998).

Dr Philip Larkin

George Barnes   (1859–1940)

A leader of both the Parliamentary Labour Party and the Amalgamated Society of Engineers (ASE) – now part of the Amalgamated Engineering and Electrical Union) – George Nicoll Barnes also served as a member of Lloyd George's coalition government.

Born at Lochee, Dundee on 2 January 1859, Barnes was the second of five sons of James Barnes, a Yorkshire-born journeyman machine-maker, and Catherine Adam Langlands, from Kirriemuir, Angus. He was educated at a church school until the age of 11, when he became a clerk in a jute mill, earning seven shillings a week. His apprenticeship as an engineer started at the age of 13 and led him from Lambeth to Dundee and back to London, where he worked for eight years with a firm in Fulham and for a short period at Woolwich Arsenal.

When he joined the ASE Barnes became allied with John Burns and Tom Mann, both of whom considered it their duty to shake up the 'respectable and deadly dull' engineers by promoting socialist political action. When Tom Mann challenged the Liberal John Anderson for the General Secretaryship in 1891 and only narrowly lost, Barnes was working as the secretary of the organising committee in London, where Mann had his greatest strength. In 1889 Barnes was elected to the executive of the ASE and in 1892 became assistant secretary. He was one of four ASE men to stand as Independent Labour Party candidates in the 1895 election, in his case at Rochdale, but was unsuccessful.

In 1896 Barnes was elected General Secretary of the ASE on a platform pushing for the 8–hour week, with a majority over Anderson of over 8,000. Sidney and Beatrice Webb recommended him because of his 'vigorous energy… great official experience, proved integrity and the strictest regularity of habits.' He remained in office until 1908. In his first year of office he faced the challenge of the great engineering lockout of 1897–98. Barnes's stubborn determination contributed to the symbolic importance of the conflict, and his election as General Secretary was widely seen as a major step in the growth of socialism within the trade union movement.

After forming part of the ASE delegation to the Labour Representation Committee (LRC) founding conference in 1900, Barnes went on to be elected as the LRC candidate for Glasgow Blackfriars in 1906, defeating Andrew Bonar Law, later a Tory Prime Minister. He held the seat until 1918 when it was redefined as Glasgow Gorbals, which he represented until his retirement in 1922.

After serving as Party Vice-Chairman in the Commons from 1908 to 1910, Barnes rose briefly to succeed Arthur Henderson as chairman (essentially leader) of the 29 members of the Parliamentary Labour Party from 1910 to 1911, an important period covering two general elections.

Barnes was active in promoting social and employment issues in Parliament such as pensions, unemployment maintenance and labour exchanges. His experience as chair of the National Committee of Organised Labour for Pensions earlier in the century paid off when he became the first-ever Minister of Pensions in Lloyd George's coalition government in December 1916, joining the War Cabinet in May 1917.

In August 1917 Barnes again succeeded Henderson on his resignation from the War Cabinet, as Minister without Portfolio. When Labour Party support for the coalition government was withdrawn prior to the 1918 general election, Barnes decided to remain in the cabinet. He became the effective leader of the National Democratic Party (NDP) of pro-coalition Labour MPs and was re-elected on this basis at the 1918 general election, along with fellow minister John Hodge and thirteen other NDP candidates. He remained a member of the Lloyd George Coalition Cabinet until January 1920, retiring from Parliament at the 1922 election, at which only one NDP candidate secured election. The NDP dissolved in 1923.

As an attendee of the Peace Conference in Paris he played a central part in the establishment of the International Labour Organisation (ILO) as an important component of the League of Nations, and represented Great Britain at the first ILO conference in 1919.

After a period of pursuing his interests in travel and peace in retirement, George Barnes died on 21 April 1940. As a key trade union leader he had seen the ASE through an intense transitional period of political and technological change. In his study of the unions and the ILP David Howell writes, 'How much was Barnes the aggressive socialist militant, as his opponents loved to portray him ?' His transition from militant trade unionist to patriotic coalitionist indicates the complexity of political choices for working-class politicians in the early part of the century.

His autobiography, *From Workshop to War Cabinet,* was published in 1924. Barnes also published *The History of the Amalgamated Society of Engineers* (1901), *Industrial Conflict: The Way Out* (1924), *The History of the International Labour Office* (1926) and numerous pamphlets. Useful information on his career is contained in David Howell, *British Workers and the Independent Labour Party 1888–1906* (Manchester: Manchester University Press, 1983) ; Paul Adelman, *The Rise of the Labour Party 1880 to 1945* (London: Longman, 1996); D James, T. Jowitt and K. Laybourn (eds.), *The Centennial History of the Independent Labour Party* (Halifax: Ryburn Academic Publishers, 1992); and Henry Pelling, *The Origins of the Labour Party 1880–1900* (1954).

Sarah Welfare

Joel Barnett (Lord Barnett of Heywood and Royton)   (1923–)

Joel Barnett was born on 14 October 1923 in North Manchester where he still lives, and after elementary school attended Manchester Central High School. After his war service, spent in Germany, he trained as an accountant. In 1949 he married Lilian Goldstone. They have one daughter. He later had his own accountancy practice in central Manchester.

For many years he was the treasurer of the Manchester Fabian Society where his report at their annual general meeting was a particular feature. Treating it with mock earnestness he ended his report with the words 'It's only money'. Only someone professionally engaged with finance and with a due regard for its importance could illustrate so clearly its limitations in certain circumstances.

In 1956 he became the only Labour councillor in Prestwich and with a subsequent victory he became the leader of a two-member Labour group. Subsequently, in 1959, he fought the Runcorn constituency and a Conservative majority of 12,000. In 1961 he was selected for Heywood and Royton, a Conservative marginal seat with no centre, forming a horseshoe around Rochdale, and in 1964 he won it with a majority of 816. As Joel put it, he surrounded the 27-stone MP, Cyril Smith.

Joel and I entered the House of Commons together with Edmund Dell, a close friend of ours. The three of us played an active part in the long and complex 1965 Finance Bill debates where Joel's professional expertise was particularly useful. These were the debates which established his role. In 1967 he followed me as Chairman of the Parliamentary Labour Party back-bench Treasury Committee.

In 1965 Joel and I decided to spend one month each year looking at the economies of different countries. In the years 1965–71 we studied the economies of the six Common Market countries three times as well as the USA, China, Japan, Indonesia, Hong Kong, and Singapore. We made a particular study of inflation in South America in 1969. In opposition after 1970 we both became front-bench spokesmen on the Treasury.

Following the 1974 General Election Joel became Treasury Chief Secretary, becoming a Privy Counsellor in 1975. His main achievement was the introduction of cash limits on expenditure. At a time of high and variable inflation the control of spending plans in real terms, that is by inflation-proofing, was no longer possible and cash limits were an essential way of controlling spending plans. Following the importance attached to the tight control of public expenditure, he joined the Cabinet in 1977. The other important innovation he introduced was what became known as the Barnett formula. Rather than have extensive annual discussions on expenditure allocations in Scotland and Wales, a formula was devised as a percentage of total expenditure for each of the countries. Intended as an interim measure it has lasted over 25 years. Joel himself says it should now be replaced with Barnett Mark 2.

His skills were particularly valuable in Finance Bill legislation. The Conservative opposition in Committee, first led by Margaret Thatcher before she became Prime Minister, was carefully selected. Nearly all of its members became senior Ministers and the majority subsequently became Cabinet Ministers. The debates were lengthy, with many sittings lasting through the night. It was frequently acknowledged that they were responded to with courtesy and skilled argument.

Following the defeat of the Labour Government in 1979 Joel became Chairman of the Public Accounts Committee. It was his decision which led to the Chevaline updating of our nuclear weapons being made public and accountable. Hitherto, it was not known even to members of the Cabinet.

In 1983 the Boundaries Commission brought to an end the constituency of Heywood and Royton. It was absorbed into three existing ones, each with sitting Labour members. Joel found himself without a seat and was made a peer as Lord Barnett of Heywood and Royton in 1983, serving as an Opposition front-bench Treasury Spokesman (1983–86). Margaret Thatcher, then Prime Minister, wanted him to become a European Commissioner, which Joel declined. This was a repeat of the invitation four years earlier which, as a Member of Parliament he had declined. He was made deputy Chairman of the BBC in June 1986 and, following the death of Stuart Young in August, he became Acting Chairman, reverting to Deputy Chairman on the appointment of Duke Hussey as Chairman of the Governors.

From the outset of his appointment he was left in no doubt of the hostility to the BBC of Margaret Thatcher who repeatedly called the licence fee a 'compulsory levy with criminal sanctions'. It was Joel's outstanding contribution – supported by Duke Hussey – that he succeeded in playing it long and saved the BBC as we know it. I called it his Scheherezade role.

He became Chairman of British Screen Finance in 1985; a Trustee of the V&A; a Trustee of the Hallé Orchestra (1982–93); and Chairman of the Hansard Society for Parliamentary Government (1985– 90). He was made an Hon. LLD at Strathclyde University in 1983. He has been Chairman of the Economic Committee in the House of Lords and his contributions to debates, particularly on economic matters, are influential. His commentary on public life and his humour tinged with a degree of irreverence are widely appreciated. He has appeared on the boards of a number of companies and his business advice is much respected. In 1984 he wrote *Inside the Treasury*, a record of his experience over five years.

Rt Hon. Lord Sheldon

David Basnett (Lord Basnett) (1924–89)

David Basnett was at the centre of Labour's history during some of its most controversial years, and as General Secretary from 1973 to 1986 of the General and Municipal Workers Union (GMWU) – known as the General, Municipal, Boilermakers and Allied Trade Unions after he successfully engineered a merger with the boilermakers in 1982 – he played a pivotal role in delivering support to the election of a Labour Government.

Elected as General Secretary of what was then the GMWU in 1973, his early years saw the most ambitious efforts at co-operation between government and the trade union movement. The social contract delivered pay restraint, but it also gave unions an important role in discussions on pensions and social security reform, employment law and economic management. David Basnett was at the heart of these discussions as one of the TUC's Neddy six, though his contribution was always overshadowed by the personalities of Jack Jones of the TGWU and the AUEW's Hugh Scanlon. This was not just a matter of personal charisma; it also reflected the fact that the drama of industrial relations had until then been in the industrial sector rather than in public services.

Basnett's more low-key approach only came to the fore in the later stages of the government, with the retirement of these two big voices and growing tensions over public sector pay. In what proved to be a decisive turning point for the Labour Party, he presided over the 1978 TUC Congress, the last under the Labour Government. Prime Minister Jim Callaghan addressed the delegates and was widely expected to use the Congress to launch an autumn election. Instead he broke into song and, under the impression that he was leading them into an election battle, delegates gave him a massive ovation. When the Prime Minister announced only a few days later that there would be no autumn election there was anger amongst trades unionists, who thought they had been deliberately misled.

But underlying the political events there was also a deeper turning point in relations between unions and government. The social contract itself had come to an end a year earlier, when the TUC had withdrawn its agreement, though the government had stumbled on with a unilateral pay norm. By the 1978 pay round, the dams were ready to burst. Claims by the Ford unions and then lorry drivers broke the psychological 10 per cent barrier. Then in January local authority unions, including Basnett's own members, went on strike in support of a claim for up to 40 per cent, presaging the Winter of Discontent that sealed the government's fate.

Basnett's own role during these conflicts was always to be as supportive as he could be to the Government. But with more decentralised bargaining structures he could not contain all the pressures from within his own union, and the growing disparities between private and public sectors were undeniable. Looking back on this period, Basnett still saw the cooperation on pay during 1974–79 as a positive experience. In a Fabian pamphlet in 1982, he rejected so-called free collective bargaining and advocated a broad framework of cooperation between unions and Government on pay, economic management and the social wage. This was not, in fact, far removed from the initial ambitions of the social contract.

After the election defeat, his attentions turned to reconciling the internal problems of the Labour Party and it was during these years that his political role became most overt. Together, Basnett and the left-wing Clive Jenkins were the power brokers in the struggle over the future structure of the party and the choice of the next leader. Despite his centre-right politics, the experience of pay restraint led Basnett to oppose Denis Healey and he sought a deal that would ensure that Callaghan would remain as leader until a new system of electing his successor was in place.

Basnett's own proposal for the new electoral college arrangement would in fact have given more votes to Labour MPs than the three-way split that subsequently emerged. In the event, Callaghan decided to resign early, leaving the votes in the hands of MPs alone, who delivered an unexpected victory to Michael Foot. The electoral college was not in fact tested until the Deputy Leadership contest in 1981, and by then Basnett had overcome his misgivings about Healey in the face of greater concerns about the left's campaign for Tony Benn.

When Foot resigned after the 1983 defeat Basnett quickly emerged as a kingmaker, urging the party to skip a generation in favour of Neil Kinnock. In itself, his call did not change the outcome, since Kinnock won comfortable majorities in all three sections. But the trade unions did have a crucial impact in a way that has been largely ignored, and which was not welcomed by the Kinnock camp at the time. For the first time, unions realigned their voting for NEC candidates on political rather than industrial lines, delivering a right-wing majority that was to prove decisive for Kinnock as his reforms progressed. Basnett and the GMB were central to negotiating the deals with the other unions that made this possible.

David Basnett's trade-union loyalties and support for Labour were borne both of his personal experience as a trade union officer and of a long family tradition. He was born in Liverpool on 9 February 1924 into a family of trade unionists – his father Andrew was the Liverpool regional secretary of the GMWU – and served as a wartime RAF pilot flying Sunderland flying boats over the Atlantic before himself becoming a GMWU Liverpool regional officer in 1948. He went on to become the union's first national education officer in 1955 and a national officer for the chemical and glass industries from 1960, playing a leading role in the seven-week Pilkington's dispute in the 1970s, which shaped much of his thinking about the limits of existing collective bargaining structures.

A serious and thoughtful man, nicknamed the Bishop by industrial correspondents, David Basnett seemed to epitomise an older style of trades unionism. But this image does not do justice either to the changes in collective bargaining and in the Labour Party that he sought to promote, nor to the difficult circumstances in which both unions and the Government were operating during the 1970s.

Created Lord Basnett in 1987, he was an active Labour peer but also spent considerable time with his wife Kathleen Molyneaux, whom he had married in 1956, and son Paul, dealing with the consequences of the serious rugby injuries sustained by his other son Ian in 1984. He died of cancer at home in Leatherhead on 25 January 1989.

Chris Savage

Margaret Beckett   (1943–)

Margaret Beckett (née Jackson) was born in Ashton-under-Lyne on 15 January 1943, the youngest of three daughters. The long illness and early death of her father (1955) and the resulting hardship dominated her childhood. After her father died, the family moved to Norwich and she began to excel academically, eventually studying Metallurgy and becoming one of only 20 women amongst 24,000 apprentices linked to Manchester University. She followed her scientific career until she was 27, but began to show an interest in politics as soon as she arrived in Manchester, joining first the Labour Club until, at the age of 20, she was shocked by the Sharpville Massacre into joining the Labour Party proper. She stood in municipal elections (unsuccessfully) before joining the Labour Party staff as a researcher from 1970 to 1974.

From there, her political career accelerated. She met her future husband, Leo, at the 1972 Party Conference. As chairman of the local party in Lincoln, he was seeking a candidate to take on Dick Taverne, who had just defected from Labour to sit as Democratic Labour, a proto-SDP. Margaret fitted the bill, and won the seat in the October 1974 election, immediately becoming PPS to Overseas Development Minister Judith Hart, whose Political Advisor she had been since the formation of the Labour government in February of that year. In January 1975 she became an assistant Whip, and then from March 1976 until Labour lost power, a Parliamentary Under-Secretary of State for Education. Despite the setback of losing her seat in 1979, she returned to Parliament in 1983 as MP for Derby. After serving as an Opposition Front-Bench Spokesman on Health and Social Security (1984–89), election to the Shadow Cabinet in 1989 resulted in her appointment as Shadow Chief Secretary to the Treasury, a post she held until after the 1992 election defeat, when she became Deputy Leader and Shadow Leader of the House of Commons. She became a Privy Counsellor in 1993.

But the rapid rise through Labour's ranks came to an end with the death of John Smith. As well as standing to retain the leadership she had inherited from him (she was leader from May–July 1994), she also opened up the deputy leadership for contest – and lost both. Blair made her Shadow Secretary of State for Health in 1994 and then in 1995 for Trade and Industry, a portfolio she retained into ministerial office. She became Leader of the House of Commons in 1998.

But her route up the career ladder does little to illuminate the central questions of her career. The most important debate is over where on the spectrum of Labour Party ideology she should be placed. Some would argue she is firmly of the Left, citing ample evidence: she opposed joining the EEC; backed Arthur Scargill in the miners' strike; opposed expelling the Militant Tendency and the ditching of unilateralism; and as late as 1995 abstained on the decision to deselect hard-Left Liz Davies from the Leeds North East candidacy. Most telling of all, she was considered lukewarm (to the point of disloyalty to John Smith) over the plans to adopt

One Member One Vote, the memory of which episode contributed greatly to John Prescott's later victory over her for the deputy leadership.

But others argue that Beckett is no more left-wing than many of her current cabinet colleagues on whom the New Labour colours have settled more easily. Indeed, there is evidence that she should be bracketed in the same category as the many Labour ex-researchers who have become so commonplace in the House, with ambition her driving force. She has twice taken the front-bench jobs of colleagues who had resigned over principles she might have been expected to share (on the first occasion, in March 1976, she was accused of treachery by the Left after taking Joan Lestor's education job despite an alleged pact with other Labour women not to do so). She angrily severed her links with the left-wing Campaign Group in 1988 when they backed a challenge by Tony Benn against Neil Kinnock's leadership. She was labelled 'class traitor of the month' by *Labour Left Briefing*. As Shadow Chief Secretary, it was she who pioneered the tight approach to spending commitments ('Beckett's Law') for which Labour became famous. As Shadow Trade and Industry Secretary she helped reconcile business to a Labour victory to such an extent that policies such as the minimum wage barely surfaced in the election campaign. Moreover, few can dispute that her public loyalty to Blair has been unstinting.

The second question about Margaret Beckett is why she chose to resign the Deputy Leadership in 1994. Perhaps she felt that, having been Leader through a successful European election campaign, she did not want to return to the Deputy's position. Perhaps she sensed a Blair victory and was not sure she could work with him unless her own mandate was reconfirmed. But the official suggestion that she was motivated by administrative convenience to allow both jobs to be contested together can surely not be the whole truth.

Fortunately, the third question – to assess her Cabinet career – is easier to answer, for her record must be viewed as a success. Prior to the 1997 election, she was widely tipped in the media to be on the list for an early sacking from government, and every year at Shadow Cabinet elections rumours circulated that Blair wanted her out. But despite a serious policy wobble over coal-mine closures at the DTI and being blamed for presiding over a lacklustre 1999 European election campaign, her record has been extremely steady and her stock has risen. As her friends point out, a cursory review of the problems surrounding the 2000 mayoral elections demonstrates that her responsibility for the failures of the 1999 Euro-election campaign must be limited to say the least. At the DTI her successors in the post have had their problems too, and she will have been proud to have introduced the minimum wage and the legislation to reinstate the right to trade union recognition, for example. Indeed, her record stands in contrast to those of some younger and more accident-prone cabinet colleagues who the media thought would soon be promoted above her.

A respected and successful Leader of the House, she was regularly deployed as a spokesperson in defence of general government policy, indicating the confidence held in her ability to communicate clearly and not make mistakes in even the most pressured media interviews. Her performance was rewarded after the election of June 2001 with promotion to run the new Department of the Environment, Food and Rural Affairs.

She once said of herself 'I am a terrible pessimist. I always expect the worst, on the basis that hopefully at least I won't be disappointed.' Despite the setbacks on policy and to her personal ambition, she has surely now reached a position that allows her to look back and consider that, in her own case, her caution has proved to be unnecessary.

Peter Metcalfe

Tony Benn (2nd Viscount Stansgate) (1925–)

Tony Benn was a child of the House of Commons. He grew up in its shadow. His father and both grandfathers had sat there before him, and in his last parliament he was able to listen to his own son Hilary's maiden speech. Yet this consummate parliamentarian frequently challenged and sometimes enraged the political establishment – and that was just in the Labour Party! Few politicians have been born and bred in such a well-connected household (on the site of the present Millbank Tower); fewer have spent so much of their adult life in a process of constant self-radicalisation, excoriating privilege from the Crown downwards.

Anthony Neil Wedgwood Benn was born on 3 April 1925, the second son of William Wedgwood Benn, then a Liberal MP, and his much younger wife Margaret. Through Westminster School and Oxford he seemed to be progressing to a relaxed political career. An MP at 25, replacing Stafford Cripps; a key aide to Hugh Gaitskell at the time of the Labour leader's response to Eden's broadcast justifying his Suez policy; a member of the NEC by 1959: his new roles gave him access and influence. 'I really felt that at that house at that moment I was at the centre of the world' he wrote of the furious clashes between Gaitskell and the BBC in 1956. In the 1959 election the youthful Wedgwood Benn produced (and starred in) new-style election broadcasts. He subsequently became, at Gaitskell's invitation, the youngest member of the Shadow Cabinet.

He was very much his father's son. He had inherited the older man's relish for argument, and sympathy for minorities, at home and abroad. 'Dare to be a Daniel, dare to stand alone,' his father said. The son could be a Daniel too, even when the lions were intent upon fighting each other. In 1960 young Wedgie made a confused attempt to mediate between the embattled Gaitskell and his challenger Harold Wilson, and a muddled resignation from the NEC, to which he was not re-elected that year. Days later he inherited from his father the one thing he had never wanted – the Stansgate viscountcy. Benn's elder brother had been killed in the war. He had been happy for his father to enter the Lords; Tony was not. For years he had collected support for a change in the law to permit disavowal of a peerage, from Churchill downwards. Many Tories had been, or were, in his position. His father's death, he argued, had taken two people out of Parliament. He had been elected by the voters of Bristol.

The campaign to change the law was a very British fossil hunt. The Earl Marshal, Garter King at Arms and other luminaries argued that an hereditary peerage could never be disclaimed. The party leaderships were lukewarm, Macmillan because many of his ministers feared the return of Lords Home and Hailsham to the Commons, Gaitskell because he was out of sorts with the reluctant viscount.

The campaign took more than two and a half years. Benn was tenacious. He fought and won a by-election, and was formally disbarred. He became a household name, in his internal exile. In all this episode he was supported by his wife Caroline, with whom he had replicated the close and energetic family home in which he grew up. The former Caroline DeCamp of Cincinnati had married Tony Benn after meeting him at Oxford. It was a union that mattered profoundly to both for the rest of their lives, until her death following a long battle with cancer in 2001. Her American eye for the absurdities of English inequality helped to radicalise Benn in the Sixties, as the couple's children were to do in the Seventies. The ability to ask awkward questions, but not always to stay upon an answer, grew on him, although as his biographer puts it, 'He was an Establishment politician from his short haircut to his polished shoes' in the days of flower power and protest.

In the Wilson governments of the 1960s, however, he was initially seen as the exemplar of the technological revolution, symbolically opening the Post Office Tower as Postmaster-General, and on his knees before the Queen showing her beautiful new stamps – on which her head no longer appeared. He was promoted to the new technology ministry after the 1966 election, where his refusal to be shocked by the new made him happy with 'Mintech's' mission. To this he added responsibility for the state-owned utilities and much of manufacturing industry after 1969. Some key projects, like Concorde, will always be associated with Benn's advocacy, but most of his causes did not prosper as Labour's hopes soured. Industry was insufficiently modernised, both in the boardroom and the shop floor, where the White Paper *In Place of Strife* became a misnomer, not a practice. Benn's own frustration showed through, as he moved away from his brief to argue for more popular access to broadcasting, or for a tougher resistance to the emergent radicalism that followed Enoch Powell's 'rivers of blood' speech in Wolverhampton. Each time the carefully signalled vehemence left his leader Harold Wilson (a premature 'feelgood' prime minister) squirming.

The 1970 election defeat was not expected by Wilson, and it shattered him. For Benn it was a liberation. For the next decade, although he never held the great offices of state, he was in many ways the most formative influence in the Labour Party. Before 1970 his colleagues had underrated, even patronised him. Tony Crosland, who had known him since his undergraduate days, told his wife 'there's nothing wrong with Jimmy ('James' was the Benn family's own pet name for him) except that he's a bit cracked.' Now they took him seriously, and circumstances helped him on his way. The Wilson government had applied for membership of the Common Market, and had been rebuffed by De Gaulle. There were fervent pro-Europeans in its ranks, but much of the Cabinet, including Benn, looked at the economic record of the six founder members and hoped that the same medicine would cure the British sickness.

When the incoming Heath government re-applied, and secured terms similar to those Wilson's negotiators believe he would have accepted, the issue split the Labour Party wide open. Factions swirled around the pragmatic Wilson; pro-marketeers led by the new Deputy Leader, Roy Jenkins, rejectionists spurred on by Michael Foot and Peter Shore.

Benn argued a third way; put the issue to a referendum of the whole people. Initially his colleagues scoffed at the idea, but after two years of party strife over Europe the shadow cabinet voted in favour of the referendum option. The vote goaded Jenkins to resign the deputy leadership, which in turn further weakened the pro-Europeans, some already at odds with their constituencies – after they had supported the principle of entry in October 1971, against an ill-advised three-line whip. Benn had already challenged for the deputy leadership once, and he now had a new position of power. At a critical moment he succeeded to the chair of the Labour Party itself. He used this vigorously to radicalise it from the left, and made key changes in the organisation at Transport House. The left's candidate for the general secretaryship, Ron Haywood, secured it on Benn's casting vote as chairman.

'Participation 72' saw the chairman nurturing a plenitude of sub-committees. He was, observers recall, 'exciting, inspirational, sometimes dangerous.' The Public Sector Group was the brightest blossom of all. Benn's support for its proposal to nationalise twenty-five leading companies, which carried the NEC but was fudged by the leadership, doubled press attacks on 'Chairman Benn'. He was derisively portrayed as wild-eyed, a little mad.

These attacks on Benn and his family led him to drastic if symbolic action. His entries in reference books were pruned or removed altogether. He became, and remained for the duration, plain Tony Benn. Some saw this as a charade, along with the mugs of tea and trade union banners with which his life and offices were adorned. But the fact is that he was enthused by what working-class politics could achieve, in the days of the Upper Clyde sit-in and the two NUM strikes which ultimately brought Heath's government down. His belief that the shop floor worker and the 'liftman at Broadcasting House' should have a say in the shaping of their world never left him. It made his five years as a cabinet minister from 1974 to 1979 more difficult, because of the negative response his enthusiasms invoked.

Initially he was Secretary of State for Industry, abuzz with ideas for industrial re-organisation, worker co-operatives and the National Enterprise Board. Benn's proposed NEB was seen as the wrong solution to a real problem by his cabinet colleagues. 'A naïve dream ... that (he) can persuade the hundred thousand different entrepreneurial components of private industry into one harmonious equivalent of the Russian Gosplan' said one. Harold Wilson wanted the plans toned down. Benn wanted to tone them up. The word went round Whitehall that he did not have the Prime Minister's full confidence. It was duly noted, not least by Sir Anthony Part, the Permanent Secretary. His nonco-operation reinforced Benn's view that there would always be an establishment conspiracy against radical change, which only the mass of the people could frustrate. Yet it was the mass of the people, for better or worse, who frustrated him in 1975. The referendum on continued Common Market membership, for which he had so long campaigned, was duly held in 1975. Enoch Powell on the right, and most of the Labour left, were prominent No campaigners. In the Cabinet the dissenting minority (Foot, Castle, Shore and Benn) were free to campaign. By common consent Benn had the highest profile, and the most vituperative press. (Newspapers were overwhelmingly for a Yes vote). He woke on 6 June 1975 to find a 2–1 vote in favour of the Common Market, through the constitutional procedure he himself had devised.

He was swiftly removed from Industry, but not from the Government. Wilson, the saying went, had been too shrewd to take Benn off the chessboard, he had castled him with Eric Varley instead. Neither then nor later, during the agonies of the IMF loan debate, did Benn resign. He was one of the six leadership contestants when Wilson resigned, coming fourth with 37 votes, and adopted the novel tactic in the IMF argument of circulating the minutes of the 1931 cabinet crisis, in which his father had participated. Those who came to see him at the Department of Energy found this most energetic of ministers less demonic than they had expected: courteous, thoughtful, offering them over lunch not cracked mugs of tea but the wine he never drank himself.

Bringing North Sea oil onshore, dealing with the imbalance in favour of the nuclear lobby: these were competently done, without any deeper sense of how the great energy utilities might change. The Secretary of State's thoughts and hopes were elsewhere. He registered the alarm and disillusion of the Labour rank-and-file. He detested the Lib-Lab pact into which Wilson's successor James Callaghan was soon forced for want of a parliamentary majority. His own power base was the NEC. He was to be top of the annual poll for ten consecutive years. He was chair of the Home Policy Sub-Committee, and the most popular fringe speaker at Conference. Two grassroots pressure groups, the Labour Co-ordinating Committee set up specifically for 'people disillusioned with the progress of the Wilson/Callaghan government', and the Campaign for Labour Party Democracy, fanned out across the country. Policies were the target for the former, people for the latter. Benn's supporters were common in both. Out beyond them, exploiting disillusion for a different end, were an assortment of Trotskyite sects whose interest in the Labour party was principally parasitic. The industrial strife of 1978–79 and the final fall of the Callaghan government, were promising ground for the diverse hopes of all these groups.

Freed from office and collective responsibility for a Labour government's actions, Benn seemed to have found his historic moment. He did not stand for the shadow cabinet. His book *Arguments for Socialism* was seen as his own personal manifesto. Some reviews dubbed it 'Arguments for me'. He endorsed proposals for the compulsory re-selection of MPs, and argued that the NEC should have a final say over the election manifesto. The 1979 conference carried both motions, and the activists almost won on proposals for an electoral college to choose the party leader. The principle of such a college was accepted by an NEC commission dominated by the trades union leaders. The Labour right began to talk of secession in line with the siren calls of Roy Jenkins. The scene was set for the 1980 conference at Blackpool.

Whether Benn was the sorcerer or the sorcerer's apprentice is beside the point. The furniture began to fall about, and the convulsion continued. In a remarkable oration he let slip all the frustrations of the years of government. There must be a new Industry Act extending public ownership 'within a matter of days', withdrawal from the Common Market 'within a couple of weeks', made possible by the instant 'creation of a thousand peers'. Later in the week he was back at the rostrum condemning cabinet ministers who he claimed had tamely colluded in the destruction of party policy. To the onlooker he must have seemed on the very threshold of personal success. The future apostates of the SDP were packing their bags before he had finished. But old associates were appalled. Michael Foot and Peter Shore listened aghast. Shore said later, 'He was in these Labour governments which he so savagely attacked longer than anyone else except Denis Healey'. Why was Benn so plausible? 'He's an insider, he was there, he knew. Secondly he has a tremendous gift for communication, and thirdly because he has this capacity for self-deception which is absolutely essential if you are going to persuade others that you are right.' Benn himself maintained that it was necessary to prove 'that we were a serious left, and we weren't playing games.' In this he succeeded.

When Callaghan stood down as leader, the veteran Foot was helped over his own misgivings to run as the left's candidate against Denis Healey. He won, aided by the secret votes of some of those now waiting to join the SDP. Foot and Healey now had to bridge their own differences to keep the party together. To the consternation of many of his supporters Tony Benn was eager for a new joust. Though never previously a joiner of factions (the eclectic Fabians apart) Benn had recently added himself to the parliamentary Tribune Group. Its members thought that the new recruit would consult his peers. Robin Cook and others scoured the Palace of Westminster, but Benn was not to be found. By the morning light his press release was discovered; he meant to stand for the deputy leadership. He wanted to test the new machinery of the Electoral College. In vain Michael Foot argued that if that was his purpose he should challenge the leader. The myriad factions who lived on the alphabet soup of the Labour left urged him on. The mass rallies which Labour had called against unemployment were 'wrecked by a sectarian mob … screaming applause for Tony Benn and execrations on Denis Healey,' in Foot's embittered recollection.

The Bennites had always been a shifting group. On this issue many on the 'soft left' were unnerved that Benn might actually win. More than a dozen Labour MPs had defected to the breakaway SDP. Unions' delegate conferences and constituency activists were targeted by the shock troops. It would be close. At this time Benn was struck down by a disease of the nervous system, Guillain-Barré syndrome, which temporarily incapacitated him. It did not abate the sustained press attacks on him. Nor did the time of reflection persuade him to counsel moderation to some of his own supporters. Just before the election Benn was charged by Neil Kinnock, in a *Tribune* article, with fostering antagonism in the party. Kinnock was already seen by Foot (and himself) as a potential heir. His advice to the left was simple: when the choice came down to Benn or Healey, abstain. Thirty seven MPs did so. The electoral college divided 50.426% for Healey, 49.574% for Benn. The high tide would ebb thereafter. Had the college been divided differently, for example one third for each section, the result would have been reversed. But in that event the split in the Labour Party would have been far greater. Benn argued after the 1983 electoral debacle that at least those who voted Labour (the smallest proportion since 1918) had clearly voted for genuine socialism. This purifying reduction would have been taken even further under a Benn leadership.

1983 marked a personal defeat for Tony Benn. Redistribution rubbed out his historic constituency. He was forced into a run-off with his neighbour Michael Cocks, Labour's Chief Whip. He lost, fought an adjoining marginal seat, and lost again. He was out of the Commons when the PLP elected its new leader – inevitably, Neil Kinnock. Benn was thus temporarily crippled both physically and politically. Within a few months he was back, selected with NUM help for the Derbyshire industrial seat of Chesterfield. In a neat juxtaposition he replaced Eric Varley, the minister with whom he had been 'castled' in 1975. He brought to the selection all the cool appraisal and skill which make him such a formidable competitor. Observers in the selection conference noted that when a delegate had a sudden epileptic fit during his speech the candidate instantly clicked his stop-watch to keep a check on stoppage time while the man received help. He was returned by the electors of Chesterfield after a skilful, low-key campaign.

Within a few weeks the miners were on strike, following Arthur Scargill in his challenge to the Thatcher government. If Benn had doubts about the NUM's refusal to call a strike ballot, and the reliance on mass picketing against working miners and obdurate police, he kept them to himself. He was still there when his constituents marched back behind their bands and banners in March 1985.

The Labour leadership had been embarrassed by the violence of the strike and the failure to ballot. It was even less happy about the infiltration of the party by the Militant Tendency. There was a clamour for action. As long as the left held a majority on the NEC enquiries into Militant were muted. The Tendency was entrenched in Liverpool, but it had sympathisers around the country. At the 1985 Labour conference Kinnock launched a furious attack on the Militants in local government. Benn and his parliamentary allies protested the purge, but it went on. Erstwhile allies who, a few years before, had told the world that they wanted him as their leader, or as their companion on a desert island, began to back away. He became confined on a political desert island of his own, with the hard left Campaign Group as his principal allies.

In 1987, Labour was moving back towards the middle ground, in line with Neil Kinnock himself. Unilateral disarmament and the commitment to leave the EEC were disavowed. The election campaign, which began with a personalised broadcast in which Kinnock's conference attack on Militant featured prominently, at least halted Labour's precipitate electoral decline. The Tories remained solidly in power, however, and Benn decided to test his belief that a less revisionist Labour policy would have offered a real alternative. He made a last, forlorn, challenge for the Labour leadership in tandem with Eric Heffer. The result was a rebuff from all sections of the College he had striven so hard to create, giving him only 11.3% of the total vote against 88.6% for Neil Kinnock.

This defeat marked the beginning of a process that marginalized Benn's influence in the counsels of the Labour Party under three successive leaders in the 1990s. He never returned to the shadow cabinet, and had few reliable allies on the NEC while he remained there. His voice remained clear, however, in opposition to the poll tax, to the war against Saddam Hussein, and to violations of civil liberties in Britain. A series of conferences at Chesterfield and elsewhere brought the extra-parliamentary left together as an alternative voice.

Harold Wilson had once famously jeered that 'Tony Benn has immatured with age.' After his sixtieth year a different process occurred. His opinions settled. He became a lucid critic of many of the absurdities of the British state, and for younger MPs he spoke in an historic, republican tradition that went back to the Levellers and the Chartists. With each succeeding parliament until he retired in 2001 his voice became more cherished for its maturity. The inconsistencies of former days, and his opacity about one member/one vote in the Labour Party, mattered less. The publication of five volumes of his diaries, and the retention of the vast archive he had collected, will keep historians busy for a generation. With those of Crossman and Castle, Benn's diaries (which became a best-selling BBC tape) provide a multi-dimensional view of how cabinet government worked.

Through all these later years the Benn family remained especially close. As a campaigner for comprehensive education and a political biographer, Caroline Benn made her own distinct contribution. When she died, after a long battle with cancer, the Benn children paid their tribute at St Margaret's, Westminster, in words and music of their own creation.

Tony Benn was serene in their affection. He had changed the course of British politics, often in precisely the opposite direction to what he intended. He was an authentic alternative voice. On that day, only a few weeks away from his own retirement, it mattered not only that he had dared to be a Daniel, but that he had been a very fine dad as well.

Phillip Whitehead MEP

William Wedgewood Benn (1ˢᵗ Viscount Stansgate)   (1877–1960)

William Wedgwood Benn had a political career that spanned the first half of the twentieth century, and mirrored many of the changes in society and politics over the period. He began as a radical Liberal, serving the Liberal administrations of 1906 and 1910, and ended his career as a minister in the Labour Government of Clement Attlee. William Wedgwood Benn was also a decorated soldier and airman, and founded a veritable political dynasty as father of Tony Benn MP and grandfather of Hilary Benn, MP for Leeds Central since June 1999.

William Wedgwood Benn was himself the son of a Member of Parliament. His father, John Benn, was Liberal Member of Parliament for Wapping from 1892 to 1895, and was re-elected at Devonport at a by-election in 1904. William Wedgwood Benn was born on 10 May 1877 in London, and from an early age was involved in campaigning in London's East End with his father. He was educated at the Lycée Condorcet, Paris, and University College London, where he graduated in 1898 with first class honours in French, and became a Fellow. He was President of the Union Debating Society, and during a debate in which Benn was opposing the Boer War he was thrown from a window by 'patriotic' students.

At the 1906 General Election Benn was elected Liberal Member of Parliament for St George's, Tower Hamlets, his father's old seat, and at 28 was the youngest MP in the House. The *Evening News* described him as 'slim, boyish-looking and clean-shaven … and eyes sparkling with enthusiasm. Although young in years, Mr Benn is by no means young politically, for, as the son of William Benn MP, he has been born and brought up amid parliamentary surroundings. From the cradle he has been able to devote himself entirely to one hobby – politics.' He became PPS to Reginald McKenna, First Lord of the Admiralty and subsequently Asquith's Chancellor.

After the January 1910 General Election Benn joined Asquith's government as a Whip, serving until the formation of the wartime coalition in May 1915. Benn became increasingly disillusioned with David Lloyd George, then Chancellor of the Exchequer, after the Marconi scandal in 1912. Despite his Government position, Benn supported the trade union movement, and raised funds for the 1912 London dockers strike.

After the outbreak of the First World War, Benn resigned his seat to join the Army. He was commissioned into the Middlesex Yeomanry and served in Egypt and Gallipoli in 1915. Between May and December 1916 he transferred into the Royal Navy Air Service and flew as a navigator in 41 missions, winning the DSO. He went on to win the DFC, the French Croix de Guerre, and the Italian Military Cross. He published his war memoir in 1919, entitled *In the Side Shows*.

In 1918 Benn was elected Liberal Member of Parliament for Leith, the only non-coalition Liberal gain of the election, and became a leading light of the small group of Asquith supporters who refused to support Lloyd George and his Liberal-Conservative coalition, dubbed the 'Wee Frees'. In 1920 Benn married Margaret Holmes. During 1924 he urged a supportive attitude to the first Labour government. He remained a 'radical Liberal' in Parliament until February 1927, 'small of stature, vigorous in debate and swift in repartee,' as Lord Beaverbrook described him in *The Decline and Fall of Lloyd George*. Following the appointment of Lloyd George, whose convictions he did not trust, as leader of the re-merged Liberal Party in October 1926, he resigned and joined the Labour Party.

Unlike most party defectors, Benn resigned his seat. He was elected to Parliament again in a by-election in 1927 in Aberdeen North. After the Labour victory in 1929, Ramsay MacDonald appointed Benn Secretary of State for India. Benn broke with MacDonald after being asked to support the introduction of tariffs, and in 1931 lost his seat to a National Government candidate. He stood in 1935 for Dudley, but was defeated. In 1937, he was returned at a by-election for Manchester Gorton. In November 1937 he stood for the Labour Party Parliamentary Committee (Shadow Cabinet) and was elected in seventh place. He was re-elected in 1938 and 1939.

When the Second World War started, Benn, by now 63, enlisted as a Pilot Officer in the RAF, and flew several operations. He became an Air Commodore, and worked as Director of Public Relations for the Air Ministry. In 1940, Attlee asked Benn to become a Labour Peer. All peerages were hereditary, and so the title would pass to Benn's eldest son Michael, who agreed to take on the role. William Wedgwood Benn became the first Viscount Stansgate in 1941.

Both Benn's sons, Michael and Anthony, joined the Royal Air Force during the Second World War. Tony served in South Africa and Rhodesia. Michael was killed in 1944 when his aircraft crashed at Chichester, making Tony Benn heir to the title Viscount Stansgate.

William Wedgwood Benn served in the 1945 Attlee cabinet as Secretary of State for Air until October 1946, when Attlee rearranged the service ministries under a single minister in cabinet. He continued to support Labour from the backbenches, and became President of the Inter-Parliamentary Union in 1947, and in 1957 Honorary President. William Wedgwood Benn died in London, aged 83, on 17 November 1960.

His obituary in the *Times* said, 'By his death British public life is deprived of one of its most vivid personalities and the House of Lords loses one of its most endearing, irrepressible, provocative and witty debaters. "Wedgie Benn" was a fighter to the end of his days.'

At the one hundredth anniversary of his birth, his son Tony Benn said of his father: 'He was a lifelong radical. The simple radical and democratic and human values which he consistently upheld are very important because our political and religious liberties are founded upon them. I am therefore profoundly grateful to have started my life, and learned my politics from, such a teacher, such a father, and such a friend.'

Paul Richards

Annie Besant (née Wood) (1847–1933)

To include in a dictionary of Labour biography a woman who left England for India seven years before the founding of the Labour Party may seem somewhat peculiar. However Annie Besant's early life and works were consumed with many of the causes which were to become signature issues for the party once it was founded in 1900. The prescience of her wide body of writing and her many campaigns, in addition to her relationships with key radicals and reformers, ensured that her ideas influenced the early Labour movement long after she had moved on to her new passions of theosophy and Indian independence.

Born in London in 1847 to Irish parents who left their homeland after the 1845 famine, Annie's lineage provided no hint of her future role campaigning for social justice. Indeed her sole political relative, great-uncle Sir Matthew Wood, member for the City 1817–1843, was noted chiefly for his friendship with and devout loyalty to Queen Caroline.

Annie's peaceful childhood ended aged 5 with her father's sudden death. Subsequent financial troubles saw the family move to Harrow, where her mother took in boys from the school until an elderly philanthropic woman, Miss Ellen Maryatt, temporarily adopted 8-year-old Annie. The next seven years were spent undertaking a privileged and unconventional education on Miss Maryatt's Dorset estate, where the emphasis was on developing free thinking and composition skills rather than the rote learning predominant in contemporary schools.

The fervently evangelical beliefs of her teacher influenced Annie, whose scriptural knowledge and oratorical skills were developed on Sundays when Bible study was the only permitted activity. A European trip in her mid-teens reinforced Annie's religious commitment as she witnessed the grandeur and pomp of European churches. After confirmation in Paris she renounced theatres and balls as representatives of the devil on earth. She later dismissed such behaviour ('little prig that I was') but her unworldliness combined with a desire to serve God through tending the poor and sick, meant that at the age of 18 she stumbled into marriage to an older clergymen, Frank Besant, a rigid, charmless man. Their unhappy union, during which Annie increasingly doubted the veracity of core Christian tenets, produced a son and a daughter (Digby, born 1869, and Mabel, born 1871) before they separated eight years later. After a protracted and unpleasant court battle, Frank gained custody of their children in 1879.

The year after her separation Annie began her acquaintance with Charles Bradlaugh, an encounter which was to shape her activity and passions over the next two decades. Recognising the intellect which had been latent during her years fulfilling the role of a clergyman's wife, Bradlaugh encouraged her to write for the *National Reformer*. Annie thrived as an author; her output included pieces on spiritualism, secular education, atheism, science, economics, literature and agricultural reform. The variety of interests explored in this post was an early indicator of the scope of issues she was later to champion.

Annie finally renounced the conventional religiosity of her Victorian upbringing when she became Vice President of the National Secular Society in 1874, but there was always something religious in the passion with which she approached her various causes and she eventually dedicated her last years to leading the new world-wide religion of theosophy. By the late 1870s she was established as a leading thinker in radical circles and attracted popular attention in 1877 as a defendant in the Knowlton trial, prosecuted for her role in publishing a book explicitly promoting birth-control methods.

1880 saw one of her lesser-known but self-professed greatest triumphs as she helped her partner Bradlaugh resist the demand to take the oath upon taking his seat in the House of Commons as the newly elected member for Northampton. Annie believed that this was an essential battle to affirm that the House belonged to the people before the monarchy, aristocracy or church.

By 1885 Annie had joined the Fabian Society after attending a debate between Bradlaugh and H M Hyndman on, 'Will socialism benefit the English people?'. She decided that 'the case for Socialism was intellectually complete and ethically beautiful'. She fast established herself as a favourite author and debater within this elite circle, contributing to *Fabian Essays* (1885) and developing a close relationship with G B Shaw who claimed to have based the character Raina in *Arms and the Man* on Annie.

When the depression of 1886 caused the already inadequate living standards of the poor to degenerate further, Annie's concern for social justice moved on from expression in the written word and debating chamber to action. She noted that 'Society must deal with the unemployed or the unemployed will deal with society'. Unlike Fabian colleagues who preferred the gradualist road to socialism, Annie attended public meetings, urging the workers to demonstrate and protest their need for jobs and food. The subsequent Trafalgar Square riots saw Annie participating and fighting with police.

Annie's concern then turned to the conditions of the working poor. Her investigations in this area included interviews with employees of Bryant & May which led to her article, 'White Slavery in London', in an 1888 edition of the *Pall Mall Gazette*. This article inspired the matchgirls' strike later that year. Annie's leading role in organising this campaign, which successfully raised wages and living conditions, was to ensure her place in socialist history.

Increasingly frustrated with the Fabians' apparent concern for better drainage systems rather than immediate societal reform, Annie moved further to the left and, as a member of the Social Democratic group, was elected to the London School Board in the autumn of 1888. Although elected politics was to be a short-lived career, she sucessfully argued for free school meals and medical treatment in elementary schools, before deciding not to stand for re-election.

At the peak of her political fame and abilities, Annie's spiritual interest was reawakened by a meeting in 1889 with Madame Blavatsky, the founder of a new religion called theosophy. Annie gradually resigned her political affiliations to immerse herself more fully in her new passion. In 1893 Annie left England to pursue her religious life in India where she became president of the Theosophical Society from 1907 until her death in 1933.

Annie's concern for justice was not entirely eclipsed by the religious duties which occupied the latter part of her life; she established schools in India and became a major figure in the Indian Independence Movement. However, the seeds which Annie had sown in England from 1874 to 1889 during her time as a leading light in almost every campaign associated with intellectual, social and political freedom continued to grow strongly long after she had moved on to pastures and passions new.

Key texts on Annie Besant include her own *Annie Besant: An Autobiography* (1893); T. Besterman, *Mrs Annie Besant* (1934); R. Dinnage, *Annie Besant* (1986); A. Taylor, *Annie Besant: A Biography* (1992); and G. West, *Mrs Annie Besant* (1947).

Beth Egan

Aneurin Bevan (1897–1960)

If there is one personification of the radical, romantic, rebellious left of the Labour Party, then it is Nye Bevan. The image of the reckless rebel, always arguing for the most extreme position and kicking against the constraints of political leadership and discipline, is a compelling one, but it is also amounts to much less than the reality of Bevan's contribution to the history of the

Labour Party. In the end, Bevan was more frustrated by his inability to lead and shape the Labour Party than he was satisfied by the role of romantic rebel leader; and in the end it was the example of Bevan the practical politician that established the benchmark against with all other Labour ministers and their achievement continue to be measured, not least by the ministers themselves.

Bevan was the son of David Bevan, a miner from Tredegar, Monmouthshire, and was born on 15 November 1897: he was born into the Labour movement. The household gods of the young Bevan's home were nonconformity in spiritual matters, and Robert Blatchford and the *Clarion* in matters temporal. Hating the discipline of school, Bevan educated himself: he was an avid consumer of the works held in the local library. His intellectual arrogance was born of this self-education. At 13 he was working in the Tytryst Colliery and working his way through the shelves of the Tredegar Workmen's Institute Library, reading a mix of ripping yarns, Rider Haggard and Jack London, and socialist literature, most importantly, H.G Wells. By 19 Bevan was active in the ILP and chair of the Tredegar lodge of the South Wales Miners' Federation. In 1919 he went to London, to the Central Labour College, and spent two years studying economics, politics and history at the college. He was influenced strongly by Marx and Engels, but much more by the *Communist Manifesto* than *Das Kapital*: though he retained a stubborn and life-long faith in central planning. He wrote of the *Manifesto* in *Plebs* magazine in 1921: 'The *Communist Manifesto* stands in a class by itself in Socialist literature. No indictment of the social order ever written can rival it. The largeness of its conception, its profound philosophy and its sure grasp of history, its aphorisms and its satire, all these make it a classic of literature, while the note of passionate revolt which pulses through it, no less than its critical appraisement of the forces of revolt, make it for all rebels an inspiration and a weapon'. Back in South Wales there followed unemployment, until, in 1926, he became a full-time union official and launched himself on his political career.

His wages of £5 a week were paid by the members of the local Miners' Lodge. On 15 April 1926, the Tredegar Iron and Coal Company, like all colliery companies, posted at the pit-head lock-out notices. When the General Strike started on 3 May 1926, Bevan soon emerged as one of the leaders of the South Wales miners. After the TUC leaders called off the strike, the miners remained locked out for six months. Bevan was largely responsible for the distribution of strike pay in Tredegar and for the formation of the Council of Action, an organisation that helped to raise money and provide food for the miners. In his work as a union official and in his central organisational role during the strike, Bevan displayed qualities of maturity and resourcefulness both well above his years and in marked contrast to the picture that his opponents often painted of him. He showed clearly in this period the executive ability that made him a fine minister and the rash radicalism that prevented him from being in a political position from which he could compete for power.

Following a short local council career (Tredegar District Council, 1922–28; County Council, 1928–29), during which it gave him pleasure to expand the holdings of the local library considerably, Bevan was elected for Ebbw Vale in 1929. His sharp tongue, brilliant speaking technique and fast wit allowed him quickly to make a mark in the House of Commons. His success at Westminster built on his radical reputation at home to earn him the lasting enmity of the *Western Mail*. 'Every mannerism that he (Aneurin Bevan) cultivates, every speech he delivers, even the expression he wears in the most familiar photographs, bear witness to a profound consciousness of his own superiority. Socialists may believe in the equality of other folk, but Mr. Bevan always conveys the impression of living at a greater intellectual altitude than the rest of the miners' leaders.' This was a frequent form of attack on Bevan. It was born of his natural aristocracy of intellect and bearing. People from his class, for critics like the *Western Mail,* were not supposed to be the aristocrats of politics. But Bevan felt himself and his class to be the equal of, if not to say superior too, any other class in society.

Bevan's disdain was directed in turn at the three outstanding political personalities of the era. First, at Ramsay MacDonald and the National Government's plan for the means test: the 'purpose of the means test,' he wrote, 'is not to discover a handful of people receiving public money when they have means to supply themselves. The purpose is to compel a large number of working-class people to keep other working-class people, to balance the Budget by taking £8 to £10 millions from the unemployed.' At Neville Chamberlain in just about every respect: 'Listening to a speech by Chamberlain is like paying a visit to Woolworth's: everything in it place and nothing above sixpence'. And finally, and throughout the war, at Churchill: 'He is a man suffering from petrified adolescence'.

In each of the great causes of the interwar period, Bevan was on the left of the party, on occasion even flirting with other parties and finally expelled by Labour for a time. He walked up to the promise of Oswald Mosley but saw, before middle-class intellectuals like John Stratchey, that there was nothing to Mosley but vanity. What appealed to him about the New Party was the promise of action and not the antics or charisma of Mosley, whom he never trusted.

In 1934 Bevan married Jennie Lee, a match which grew into a formidable political and personal partnership The fight against fascism and the fight against mass unemployment were the governing obsessions of Bevan's life as war approached. His consistency of outlook took him towards the Popular Front and he was expelled, along with Cripps in 1938, for refusing to accept the policy of non-intervention in the Spanish Civil War.

When war came, Bevan's stature had grown to the extent that he was often cited as the most effective opponent of the Chamberlain government. He firmly supported the parliamentary coup which brought in Churchill as war leader, and then became the focus of parliamentary opposition to the heavy censorship imposed on radio and newspapers and to wartime Regulation 18B, which gave the Home Secretary the powers to lock up citizens without trial. Though often attacking Churchill, he reserved especial venom for members of his own party in the coalition. For example in March 1942 he roasted Herbert Morrision, already an enemy, over the threat to ban the *Mirror* because of a Zac cartoon: 'I do not like the *Daily Mirror* and I have never liked it. I do not see it very often. I do not like that form of journalism. I do not like the strip-tease artists. If the *Daily Mirror* depended upon my purchasing it, it would never be sold. But the *Daily Mirror* has not been warned because people do not like that kind of journalism. It is not because the Home Secretary is aesthetically repelled by it that he warns it. I have heard a number of honourable members say that it is a hateful paper, a tabloid paper, a hysterical paper, a sensational paper, and that they do not like it. I am sure the Home Secretary does not take that view. He likes the paper. He is taking its money (waves cuttings of articles written by Morrison for the *Daily Mirror*).' Bevan led the calls for the nationalisation of the coal industry and the full implementation of the Beveridge Report, and advocated the opening of a Second Front in Western Europe to aid Russia. He was elected to the constituency section of Labour's NEC in 1944, on which he served until 1954, returning later as Party Treasurer from 1956 to 1960.

At the beginning of the 1945 General Election campaign Bevan made plain the depth of his tribal instincts in the political battle against the Tories: 'We have been the dreamers, we have been the sufferers, now we are the builders. We enter this campaign at this general election, not merely to get rid of the Tory majority. We want the complete political extinction of the Tory Party.' He was not opposed to coalitions to win wars, but he was an early and firm advocate of the ending of the political truce: there was nothing coalition-minded about his approach. His narrow sectarianism occasionally tilted him towards insulting the Tories rather too fulsomely for the taste of the leadership, as in the famous 'lower than vermin' speech, but on policy he was actually more broad-minded than his rhetoric often suggested.

Clement Attlee, in perhaps his most inspired appointment, brought Bevan into Cabinet as Minister of Health in 1945. In 1946 Parliament passed the revolutionary National Insurance Act. It instituted a comprehensive state health service, effective from 5 July 1948. The Act provided for compulsory contributions for unemployment, sickness, maternity and widows' benefits and old age pensions from employers and employees, with the government funding the balance. The National Insurance Act created the structure of the Welfare State and after the passing of the National Health Service Act in 1948, people in Britain were provided with free diagnosis and treatment of illness, at home or in hospital, as well as dental and ophthalmic services. As Minister of Health, Aneurin Bevan was now in charge of 2,688 hospitals in England and Wales. It was the decision to nationalise the hospitals that made the profound difference in the structural changes brought about by the creation of the NHS. This decision was Bevan's and its implementation was down to his skill, patience and application as a Minister. It is the most significant and lasting reform in the history of the Labour Party and it was achieved by the force of personality of one man. The survival of the NHS is a testament to Bevan's ability and vision as a minister; that it was his only lasting concrete political achievement is equally a testament to the political failure of the five years after the fall of the Labour government – a fall he helped precipitate through resignation, having already been moved within Cabinet from Health to be Minister of Labour in January 1951

Bevan's resignation as Minister of Labour over teeth and spectacles in April 1951 was more of a power struggle than a clash of principles. Gaitskell played the crisis for political advantage as much as for the principle of the expenditure on rearmament he needed. Bevan was outplayed on principle – he had already conceded the imposition of charges – and he was outgunned in the politics of the crisis because it was impossible for Attlee to accept the resignation of his Chancellor a week before Budget day. His political position never recovered. The money raised by charges was utterly irrelevant to the rearmament package: dishing Bevan was the point.

Ministerial office had changed Bevan from a sectarian to a national and international statesman, but he now found himself as the figurehead of an oppositional faction: the misnamed Bevanites. He was not a factional leader and he did want to accept the discipline of the group. His central preoccupation was how to defeat the consolidators. The Morrisonian wing of the party had essentially won the argument that the creation of a mixed-economy welfare state was the destination of the Labour Party. For Bevan and others, it was the beginning, not of ever more nationalisation but of a truly developmental state, a growing and nurturing welfare state and a new kind of society. Bevan tried to work out these ideas in his deeply disappointing work of political theory, *In Place of Fear*. 'This is an entirely new situation, bringing about new adaptations and new values. So long as parliaments divest themselves of economic power then democratic institutions were bound to be always the whipping-boys for private enterprise. This happens no matter how experienced the individuals are, no matter how knowledgeable they are. That is the reason why no democracy in the modern world is safe unless it becomes a socialist democracy. There is no halfway house here at all. It may be that we are moving towards an eclectic society; we are not going to have a monolithic society; we are not going to have a society in which every barber's shop is nationalized. But we must have a society in which the democratic institutions and the elected representatives of the people have their hands on the levers of economic power.'

In Place of Fear was published in 1952, perhaps the high point of Bevan's fame and the high tide of Bevanism as a political force. Thereafter the left was ruthlessly defeated by a combination of big trades union bosses and the political right and centre. In turn the political ideas of Bevanism were taken over by the revisionist ideology of Tony Crosland and his *The Future of Socialism*. By the time Gaitskell defeated Bevan and Morrison for the leadership (he got 70 votes to Gaitskell's 157 and Morrison's 40), the fate of Labour's left was sealed. The oppositional tone of Bevanism became increasingly linked to unilateral nuclear disarmament, a policy which Bevan, Shadow Foreign Secretary from November 1956 until his death in 1960, did not agree with. When he turned on his supporters, he was not supporting the possession of nuclear weapons, nor agreeing with the NATOists and the advocates of the Atlantic alliance. Rather he was trying, in much of that famous speech, to spell out a third way between the two. However those are not the passages that get quoted, and this is:' I knew this morning that I was going to make a speech that would offend and even hurt many of my friends. I know that you are deeply convinced that the action you suggest is the most effective way of influencing international affairs. I am deeply convinced that you are wrong. It is therefore not a question of who is in favour of the hydrogen bomb, but a question of what is the most effective way of getting the damn thing destroyed. It is the most difficult of all problems facing mankind. But if you carry this resolution and follow out all its implications and do not run away from it you will send a Foreign Secretary, whoever he may be, naked into the conference chamber.' Following on from that speech he formed a working relationship with Gaitskell, who had already promoted him from shadowing Labour to become Shadow Colonial Secretary in February 1956 and Shadow Foreign Secretary in November of that year. Bevan was elected Deputy Leader unopposed in November 1959 but died of cancer in Asheridge on 6 July 1960.

In all of these tumultuous political events Bevan was imaginative, creative and inspirational in all he said but he was frustrated at every turn in the scope he could enjoy for effective political action. His faith in a meritocracy that would reward his natural ability with high office was evidence of both the rather unscheming nature of his ambition and his innate naivety. The ambition was real enough but it was always the slave of the rhetoric: over and again in the 1930s and even more in the 1950s, Bevan lost out to those with less natural brilliance but better discipline and sounder tactics. His champions, most notable Michael Foot, would argue that was his greatness. This is true up to a point. The virtuous foundation of his ambition remained unsullied and the big offices of state, and ultimately the leadership of the Labour Party itself, went elsewhere. Purity was purchased at the price of achieving real change. Biographies of Bevan include: Michael Foot, *Aneurin Bevan* (two volumes, London, 1962, 1973); John Campbell, *Nye Bevan, A Biography* (London, 1987, 1994); Vincent Brome, *Aneurin Bevan*, (London, 1953); and Mark Krug, *Aneurin Bevan, Cautious Rebel* (London, 1963).

Professor Brian Brivati

Ernest Bevin   (1889–1951)

Foreign Secretaries fall into four categories – the decorative (who make pretty speeches – David Owen is a good example), the institutional (who faithfully read out a line defined by FCO officials – Lord Carrington was one), the reactive (who wait for No 10 or other countries to make policy and then respond to it – Sir Malcolm Rifkind is one such) and the weather-makers – the political foreign secretaries who define and shape British foreign policy and take it into new directions. Run-of-the-mill Prime Ministers prefer to appoint one of the first three categories. Great Prime Ministers look for weather-making Foreign Secretaries. Clement Attlee, Britain's greatest peace-time Prime Minister in the twentieth century, had no hesitation in allowing the giant figure of Ernest Bevin to occupy the Foreign Secretary post for nearly all of the reforming Labour government of 1945 to 1951.

The new direction Bevin gave foreign policy – breaking free of the Conservative isolationism associated with Joseph and Neville Chamberlain, shaping the global institutions (UN, NATO, GATT, OECD) that have stood the test of time, burying British imperialism, developing a nuclear deterrent, bringing America under the Atlantic Alliance into a permanent relationship with Europe and arguing down those who thought Stalinist tyranny should be appeased – constitute a period of foreign policy creativity without parallel in British history.

Ernest Bevin, one of the giants of twentieth-century international politics, was very much a weather-making Foreign Secretary. He came to the office after decades of hard political experience. He had built one of the greatest trade unions in the world out of disparate worker organizations. He had been involved in a lifelong international ideological struggle with communism and with its national-imperial expression – the Soviet Union and its satellite organizations. He reshaped the Labour Party in the 1930s, reinforcing its labourist traditions and focusing its policy-making away from constitutional or radical creativity in the direction of bread-and-butter welfarism and tangible improvements in the lives of the poor and the unskilled working class he incarnated and represented so brilliantly.

It is impossible to understand Ernest Bevin the Foreign Secretary without understanding his trade union life – including a wide international experience – or his lifetime as a political leader involved intimately in the policy debates of the inter-war years.

Ernest Bevin was born in a Somserset village on 9 March 1881, a seventh child. He did not know and never knew who his father was. His mother died when he was eight years old. At 13 he was working as a labourer in a bakery. He died in 1951 having served as Foreign Secretary in a Labour Government and having built Britain's greatest trade union of workers, the Transport and

General Workers. Either achievement would have made its mark in history. Bevin's TGWU had huge influence in the Labour Party during his time as its General Secretary in the 1920s and 1930s and when he was a Minister between 1940 and 1951. The union continued to wield massive influence within the Labour Party for the rest of the twentieth century. Bevin's vision of what a trade union should be and do and his insistence that Labour was a party which, in his own visceral metaphor, 'grew out of the bowels of the trade unions' shaped British politics until the reforms associated with Tony Blair in the 1990s. Even now Labour is the last remaining democratic left party in Europe where trade unions still have an institutional presence within the party – holding seats in the Executive, having union votes in the selection of the Leader and Prime Minister, and using their block votes to shape party policy.

Bevin's heritage remains more than fifty years after his death. The same is true of the broad outline of foreign policy as shaped by Bevin during his period as Foreign Secretary. The great institutions of the post-1945 world like the United Nations, NATO, GATT (now the World Trade Organisation), the OECD and the IMF were all brought into being with Bevin's active engagement and support. Bevin did not come to the Foreign Office without international experience. In 1917, he was chosen to be the TUC delegate at the convention of the American Federation of Labor. It was at the height of the U-boat campaign against Atlantic shipping and other more senior TUC leaders found reasons to contribute to the war effort at home rather than risk a sea voyage to America. The young Bevin had no such cares and began a lifelong love affair with America. The AFL offered the British fraternal delegate one of those big-jewelled rings Americans wear to show allegiance to a college, regiment or union. Bevin's fingers were so big the ring had to be taken away to be enlarged.

When Bevin came to build his union's headquarters, Transport House, located at the heart of political and administrative power in Westminster, he modelled it on the AFL (now AFL-CIO) office which overlooks the White House in Washington. In the 1920s and 1930s Bevin went abroad regularly for international trade union conferences and took a leading role in shaping the International Labour Organisation. There he dealt with the differing ideological and national passions and conflicts that disfigured inter-war Europe and later gave rise to the Cold War. He also witnessed the rise of anti-colonialism as a new cause and while in Geneva during the long summer sessions of the ILO he observed the failure of the League of Nations to function effectively.

Therefore, far from his being a novice in international affairs when he was made Foreign Secretary in 1945, no other senior Labour politician had travelled so widely, so regularly and with such consistent dealing with representatives of other countries. Hugh Dalton was widely seen as Labour's Foreign Secretary in waiting. Dalton was an old Etonian academic who spoke European languages, but in terms of consistent involvement with policy issues abroad Bevin's active trade union internationalism in the 1920s and 1930s gave the union leader more experience and understanding of 'abroad' than the cultured intellectual Dalton.

It is Bevin the trade unionist who commands most attention in the Labour pantheon. He moved quickly through the ranks of the smaller transport workers unions in the first two decades of the century. The British economy is par excellence a trading economy. Trade within the UK and trade between the Britain and the rest of the world defines what Napoleon admiringly called *'une nation des commerçants'* – a nation of traders, not shopkeepers as the remark is sometimes falsely translated. The early twentieth-century transport revolution brought about by the invention of the combustion engine helped to proletarise hundreds of thousands of workers who found their employment organised along strict Taylorist lines. Bevin seized upon this large group of disparate workers and wielded them into one union, and then used the union as a huge power bloc within political life. Bus drivers, lorry drivers, delivery workers, even taxi drivers turned to Bevin's TGWU for help.

Another key group of workers Bevin sought to organise were dockers. He was National Organiser of the Docker's Union from 1910 to 1921, folding it into the Transport and General Workers Union, the large amalgamated conglomerate union which he led as General Secretary from 1921 to 1940. He became known as the 'Dockers KC' after producing a meagre plate of food in front of a government commission in order to show what the British docker was expected to feed to his family on the basis of the pay cuts being sought by employers.

A fierce advocate of the working class that Victorian and Edwardian capitalism had left impoverished, badly housed, and with minimal welfare rights, Bevin saw in trade union organisation the mechanism that would deliver social justice for his members. The TGWU became a catch-all general trade union that recruited any and all categories of workers not organised by the craft and sectoral unions. In the automobile industry, for example, the skilled workers belonged to the AEU and to other specialist metal industry unions, but the general assembly line worker was left unorganised. This opened the way for TWGU recruiters, notably the Coventry-based union organiser Jack Jones, to win a huge place for the TGWU amongst manufacturing workers.

As a result, British industry after 1945 faced a multiplicity of unions inside each workplace, leading to endless demarcation disputes and industrial relations difficulties arising from inter-union rivalry and positioning. Unlike the United States, where a single automobile workers' union was created, or the united industrial unions of Germany or the Nordic countries, Bevin's TGWU was present everywhere in British workplaces but without the unity of organizational strength to allow one single channel of worker representation.

But to ask Bevin to re-organise the institutional framework of British trade unionism is to indulge in retrospective fantasy politics. Bevin was unable to escape from the limitation of British labourism. In contrast to the European social democratic tradition, where the party as a mass movement came first and trade unions as the worker expression of social democracy came second, the organization of, first, craft unions – the AEU dating back to 1851 – and then the new unions of the 1890s led to the Labour Party being founded as an expression of trade unionist politics rather than trade unions being shaped to conform to social democratic thinking.

Thus Bevin saw the Labour Party as a union-based political organization. He insisted in the 1930s that Labour should resist radical or overly ideological left politics. He denounced the pacfcist Labour leader, George Lansbury, for 'hawking his conscience from conference to conference, asking what he should do with it.' It was the brutal, offensive language of a trade union bully. Although there is a great deal of Bevin hagiography, it was clear that he was an extremely authoritarian leader who brooked little debate or different opinions in his own union and found opposing political views from Labour politicians hard to accept.

At a time when social democracy in Sweden was reaching out to forms of historic compromise with employers (the no-strike, no lock-out Saltsbjoden agreement of 1938 opened the way to decades of social partnership in Sweden) or the New Deal on offer from Roosevelt in the United States was proposing forms of reformism based on a compromise between class and capital, Bevin maintained support for nationalisation plus welfare rights sustained by adversarial 'them and us' trade union politics.

The British establishment began co-operating with Bevin at an early stage. He sat on the Macmillan Committee on banking whose analysis was rejected by Ramsay MacDonald and Philip Snowden. This led to the collapse of the 1931 Labour government and paved the way for the long anti-union years of Conservative-controlled National Government policies of the 1930s.

Despite his opposition to the Tory politics of the 1930s, Bevin never indulged in leftism. On the contrary he fashioned an anti-communist politics *avant la lettre*. Bevin paid lip service to the creation of the Soviet Union. Like many socialist trade unionists he held out great hopes for the Bolshevik revolution in 1917 and supported a dockers' boycott of arms shipments to the counter-revolutionary armies sent by Lloyd George to destroy the revolution. But this early sympathy faded. Lenin's insistence that trade unions should be smashed and split unless they accepted unconditional control by local communist parties and submitted themselves to Moscow was not acceptable to the proud and patriotic working-class leader, Bevin. During the General Strike of 1926 he was confronted with the ultimate dilemma of socialist transformation. To be sure, trade unions could bring the state to a standstill, but were they prepared to take it over? Baldwin posed the question to Bevin and other TUC leaders and they decided that their purpose was not revolution but reform, amelioration and a transformation of the condition of working people and the economy they lived under within the boundaries set by electoral democracy. Thus militant shop stewards who challenged Bevin's authority were as much an enemy as the employers who refused his claims.

For Bevin, the Communist Party in Britain and the Soviet Union was an undemocratic enemy. The communist trade unionists Bevin grappled with on the international stage were, he believed, stooges of a vile dictatorship. Historians have sought to portray an era of post-1945 labour movement history as representing a trade union cold war, initiated by Bevin and put into effect by anti-communist underlings working secretly in the Foreign Office. Yet Bevin was anti-communist long before 1945. Like Michael Foot, from the left, or Denis Healey from the right, Bevin had no illusions about the absolute fight to the finish needed between communism and democratic socialism. His support for activity to counter the well-financed communist attempts to control trade unions and political movements after 1945 was not Cold War specific. It was a continuation by other means of an anti-communist politics rooted in rejection of Lenin and Trotsky's contempt for democracy and for working-class organisations they did not control. Stalin continued this Leninist-Trotskyist politics while Bevin stood in the social-democratic European tradition of hostility towards Soviet communism.

This down-to-earth right-wing Labourism strengthened rather than weakened his role as one of the dominant figures in inter-war Labour politics. He was active in the Labour Party, seeking to control and influence its line in the 1930s. As pacifism – the equivalent in the 1930s of the unilateral nuclear disarmament movements a generation or two later – took off and the Labour Party refused to support rearmament programmes, Bevin gave a lead in calling for Britain to get ready to fight the Nazis. But it was a Britain-first policy. Bevin equally supported the policy of non-intervention in Spain – mainly on the grounds that the anti-Franco fight would, if successful, benefit communism. In the event the Republic's defeat encouraged Hitlerism. If Bevin was right to resist pacificism in Britain he was wrong to oppose the sending of arms to help the Republican cause win in Spain.

Within his own union and within the Labour Party, Bevin was a conservative authoritarian. He broke apart opposing groups and was content to see Labour leftists like Stafford Cripps and Aneurin Bevan threatened with expulsion from the party. Today's generation can barely tell the difference between Bevan and Bevin, yet their fight – the unions versus the intellectuals, the incrementalists versus the radical reformers, the man of organisation versus the man of oratory – shaped the Labour Party for decades. Bevin's successors as TGWU leaders distrusted the left and intellectual politicians and always placed a premium on the institutional prerogatives of the trade union over the possibilities of extending the Labour Party's reach to the non-industrial middle classes.

However to back-project the failings of later twentieth-century Labourism on to Bevin is hindsight historiography. As war broke out in 1939, it was clear that, first, it would be an industrial war of matériel as much as of men; second, it would require the mobilisation of every man and woman whether into the armed services or the home front; third, that in contrast to the First World War it could not be fought by the Establishment or ruling class alone. 'A bayonet is a weapon with a worker attached to each end' was one reproach that lingered. In May 1940 the war began in earnest and the isolationist Conservative premier, Neville Chamberlain, with his vulgar proto-Majorite disdain for trade unions, was removed from Downing Street. It was obvious that to harness all the nation's vigour not just a coalition government was needed but that the embodiment of working-class identity and self-organisation, Ernest Bevin, would have to be at the centre of the War Cabinet.

A Commons seat was found for him in Wandsworth, and Bevin started organising the flow of labour into factories in order to deliver the necessary output to fight the war. He took quasi-dictatorial powers to direct labour, conscripting men to go down the mines – the 'Bevin Boys' as they were called. At the same time he insisted on workers' canteens being established so that a hot meal was served to men who had known the dole and the means test only a few years previously. Trade union officials were brought into the war effort. For the first time, the British state began to appreciate the contribution that trade unionists could bring to the organisation of efficient production. The full-employment economy that resulted began to lead to higher wages.

Bevin became popular, and on visits to factories with Churchill received as many if not more cheers than the Prime Minister. When the two leaders went to meet troops preparing for the invasion of France the soldiers reminded them about what happened after 1918. They anxiously asked Bevin: 'There will be jobs for us when we get home, won't there, Ernie?' Thus Bevin's presence in the wartime cabinet ensured that the Beveridge report and other wartime preparations for what became the welfare state were given priority and profile.

There was another aspect of Bevins' wartime government role that has not properly been understood. Bevin, and other Labour ministers, began fully to understand that government could be made to work for national and for labour interests. The planning and controls needed for war, as well as the rationing and health advice that led to better health outputs for most citizens, showed that Conservative laissez-faire administration was not the last word. More important, citizens saw Labour ministers in a coalition government and doing a better job than their Conservative *confrères*. Having made 'No coalition politics' the watchword of Labour politics after the disaster of 1931, it was a training period in the grand coalition government of 1940–45 that paved the way for the great reforming Attlee government of 1945. The world in which British citizens today live is still framed by decisions taken by Attlee, Bevin et al in a way that none of the successor Labour government of the 1960s or 1970s matched.

Bevin lay at its heart not just as Foreign Secretary but as a great domestic political figure whose speeches and other interventions dominated post-war Labour Party politics. Although he stopped being TGWU General Secretary in 1940 he remained close to the trade unions. After 1945 he remained in close touch with the political and organisational direction of the unions. When he travelled to the United States he spent an evening seeing old trade union chums, and he took an active interest in the politics of the World Federation of Trade Unions, the unified international labour body, which split in 1947 over the old question of whether communists and Moscow should control trade unions around the world.

This suspicion of communist motives meant that from the start of his period of office as Foreign Secretary, Bevin was never likely to fall in with the policy agenda of the Soviet Union and Stalin. The key economic problem facing Britain was rebuilding the shattered domestic economy without the huge reserves and foreign remittances which the war had consumed. The United States offered the only lifeline. Bevin spotted the implications of Secretary of State George Marshall's Harvard speech in May 1947 and realised that it could be converted into a plan that would bring Britain and the rest of Europe the credit lines needed for economic growth to take off again.

Side-lining the Treasury, which might have expected to have some say in transatlantic economic policy, Bevin moved quickly to create the institutional framework that became known as the Marshall Plan. He did so while maintaining the turn to collectivist welfare social policy that was implemented across Europe by the great reforming governments after 1945. It little mattered whether these governments were headed by Labour in Britain, de Gaulle in France or social democrats in Nordic countries. The same mix of state control of key industries, allied with compulsory insurance and cradle-to-grave welfare rights, plus a strong role for trade emerged as the European norm. But the basic fundamentals of the market economy were not challenged. Britain remained dependent on trade and overseas capital flows. The City still existed. Class hierarchies were not challenged. Bevin enjoyed the Old Etonians who worked for him at the Foreign Office. When he challenged his private secretary by asking if anyone from a similar background – illegitimate, with only elementary education – had been in charge of foreign affairs ever before the reply was imperturbable: 'Well, Secretary of State, I think you'll find there are remarkable similarities between you and Cardinal Wolsey.' The Oxbridge-trained diplomats had Bevin eating out of their hands thereafter.

The turn to America was heightened by the Berlin crisis and the announcement of the Truman doctrine, which saw the United States picking up part of Britain's unsustainable burden to control access to oil fields across the Near East region. The out-and-out declaration of the Cold War by Stalin led to NATO and the permanent linkage with the United States which, after two centuries of suspicious jockeying between the two Anglo-Saxon powers, became a given in the second half of the twentieth century.

Bevin was no yes-man for Washington. He opposed the creation of a Jewish state in Palestine and was accused of latent anti-semitism. He promoted the creation of a British nuclear weapon not to support the United States but to have some claim to status and influence. 'I don't care how we do it, but it must have a Union Jack on it,' he said, using a metaphor that de Gaulle or other leaders thereafter who insisted that national status demanded nuclear weaponry would echo.

He oversaw the retreat from the Indian empire, but Britain shipped out settlers to East Africa and sought to strengthen possessions elsewhere in Asia. British troops put down colonial rebellions, and while Britain avoided the imbroglios of other ex-imperial powers such as France in Vietnam and North Africa or the Dutch in Indonesia, Bevin still saw the red-coloured map as the natural order of things.

He failed utterly to see the future importance of Europe. He called his opposite number in France, the distinguished resistance leader Georges Bidault, 'Biddle' and said of the Germans 'I can't 'elp it but I 'ates them'. All good John Bull stuff, but despite a strong pro-European awareness amongst Labour MPs and some of his junior ministers, Bevin refused to join the Schumann Plan, the forerunner of the European Community, and started Britain down the long road of semi-isolation and suspicious semi-detachment from Europe which has been the hallmark of British European policy during most of the succeeding half-century. In this Bevin was guided by the young Labour intellectual, Denis Healey. A deeply cultured European Healey was suspicious of what he saw as the Catholic and capitalist roots of European Christian democracy, and failed to understand the deeper social and inclusive policies that were taking root in Europe. Nor did Bevin or Healey appreciate the extent to which state power in France, where far more of the economy had been taken out of private owernship than in Britain, or social democratic partnership politics in the German or Nordic industries, would lead to an economic revival on mainland Europe that would see Britain fall significantly behind her continental rivals in terms of growth and GDP per capita.

This is not the wisdom of hindsight. Politicians and commentators at the time urged Britain to become a full player in Europe, to share power in order to offer leadership. The then much weaker European nations looked to Britain for such leadership. It was not on offer. Bevin had been born at the height of imperial confidence and had risen with this class, never above it, to occupy the commanding heights of the British state. His politics was as marked by what he opposed – communism, foreigners telling Brits what to do, reformist ideas, criticism of trade unions – as by the causes and ideas he advanced.

As a result Bevin lay at the heart of some of the worst divisions that plagued the politics of the Attlee government. On issue after issue – Palestine, the Soviet Union, colonial problems – the Labour Party split in parliament, at its conference, and in its activist core. Bevin was a giant beast in the post-war political jungle but he trampled his opponents ruthlessly and rarely sought to conciliate when the alternative of a crushing retort or the threat of an expulsion was available. The greatness of Bevin's foreign policy achievements have stood the test of time. His quarrels have faded. At the time, however, they contributed to a loss of morale in the Government. Attlee's team had solved many of the pre-war economic and social problems but by 1950 these Edwardian socialists were worn out and seemed to offer only more of the same to a post-war generation looking to a brighter, gayer, more varied life.

Bevin himself became exhausted in office. Non-stop work, an indifference to exercise and a healthy appetite for drink had been part of his being for decades. After the election victory in 1950, Attlee decided to move Bevin and replace him with his disliked rival, Herbert Morrison. As a farewell, every official, from Permanent Under-Secretary to door-keeper, in the Foreign Office donated sixpence to buy him a memento. It was a demotic moment of egalitarianism in an institution where place and protocol rule. Bevin had shown that great political genius when applied to the affairs of state could produce foreign policy which shaped the world and left an enduring mark on his country. That, together with his work as the greatest builder of British trade unionism, gives Bevin a place in history which few politicians of any party have matched before, then or since. He died on 14 April 1951, as Labour MP for East Woolwich.

When Robin Cook, a successor Labour Foreign Secretary, took office in 1997, he placed a bust of Ernie Bevin, in the handsome room overlooking Horse Guards Parade which the Foreign Secretary occupies. There Cook and his team would plan a new era of foreign affairs under Labour. But they built on the foundations left by Bevin. The classic three–volume biography *Ernest Bevin* by Alan Bullock is the standard work.

Denis MacShane MP

Rodney Bickerstaffe (1945–)

Rodney Bickerstaffe was born in Doncaster on 6 April 1945. Bickerstaffe's roots are important to him. He recently declared 'I came from the working class. I'm proud of that class and I'm proud to work for it'. Working for that class is exactly what Bickerstaffe has done so superbly in his thirty-five years in the trade union movement.

Bickerstaffe's first experience of the trade union movement was when his mother, a member of the National Union of Public Employees (NUPE), took him to a union meeting when he was just eight years old. Bickerstaffe became a NUPE official in 1966 as an Area Officer in Yorkshire. In 1974 he became Deputy Divisional Officer for the North-East, whilst in 1975 he was appointed Divisional Officer of the newly-created Northern Division which encompassed Tyneside, County Durham, Cleveland, Cumbria and Northumberland. Two years later Bickerstaffe was promoted to NUPE Head Office, with responsibility for NUPE members employed in universities, local government and the water industry. In July 1981 Bickerstaffe was appointed General Secretary of NUPE. He worked in partnership with the late Alan Fisher, before assuming full responsibility in June 1982. At the merger, in July 1993, of COHSE, NALGO and NUPE to form UNISON, Britain's largest trade union (currently representing 1.3 million members), Bickerstaffe became Associate General Secretary.

In addition to being a past President of the TUC, Bickerstaffe has also been elected as President of the European Public Services Committee, representing seven million workers in Europe, and Vice-President of Public Services International which represents twenty million workers worldwide.

In his final speech as General Secretary of UNISON at UNISON National Conference

2000 Bickerstaffe stressed that 'The true basis for any caring society must be public services provided from the public purse, staffed by men and women properly trained and decently paid. There's no place at all for profit out of the elderly and dying or the young'. It is the vigorous and skilful pursuit of these socialist ideals which has characterised Bickerstaffe's career.

Within the Labour movement Bickerstaffe is most closely associated with the policy many see as the greatest single achievement of the Labour Government of 1997–2001: the national minimum wage. By the time of its introduction on 1 April 1999, Bickerstaffe had been campaigning for a statutory national minimum wage for over thirty years. Whilst describing the introduction of the minimum wage as a 'historic victory for the low paid', he has consistently campaigned for a minimum wage of well over £4 an hour unhampered by restrictions regarding age and duration of employment.

More recently Bickerstaffe hit the headlines for his role in the defeat of the Labour Party leadership over the issue of pensions at the centennial Labour Party Annual Conference in September 2000. Bickerstaffe spoke with passion and conviction in support of a motion calling for the restoration of the link between earnings and pensions, the UNISON pensions policy. 60 per cent of delegates voted to support the motion whilst 39 per cent voted, with the party leadership, not to restore the link. It was the first time the Labour Party leadership had been defeated on a motion at party conference for six years. In April 2001 Bickerstaffe succeeded Jack Jones as President of the National Pensioners' Convention.

As for other issues, Bickerstaffe is a vocal campaigner against the current Labour Government's PFI initiatives, whilst he joined the Labour Government in opposing the fuel protests of September 2000, arguing that it was a 'bosses' blockade'.

Characteristic of the humility of the man who has earned such widespread affection in the Labour movement is the fact that at Labour Party Annual Conference, as delegates approaching the main hall 'run the gauntlet' of leaflet-proffering activists endeavouring to entice them to numerous fringe meetings, it is not unheard of to be handed leaflets by Bickerstaffe himself. Many delegates will recall Bickerstaffe handing them an invitation to a fringe meeting on travellers' rights, another issue highly important to him.

A measure of the high regard in which Bickerstaffe is held within the trade union movement is the TUC press release regarding his retirement as General Secretary of UNISON, dated 12 July 1999: 'Rodney Bickerstaffe has been a tower of strength to the TUC and the conscience of the movement. He represents the best in our movement and tradition'. Labour NEC member Tony Robinson described Bickerstaffe as 'the most effective trade union leader of the nineties' and as part of the Labour Party's Centenary commemoration in Doncaster Bickerstaffe was the second speaker on the bill, behind his close friend Deputy Prime Minister John Prescott.

Richard Burgon

Tessa Blackstone (Baroness Blackstone of Stoke Newington) (1942–)

Tessa Ann Vosper Blackstone (Baroness Blackstone of Stoke Newington) could be regarded as one of the most important women in the Labour Party of her time, not just for her deep experience in education and the arts and her wider policy interests, but also in her key role as co-founder and Chairman of IPPR in the decade prior to Labour's return to power. She has shared strong relationships and support with leading Party figures since she came to prominence as an advisor to the Central Policy Review Staff, Cabinet Office (1975–78). She was the author of a controversial report on the Foreign Office, and she proved herself bright, able to challenge, extremely headstrong and fiercely determined.

These attributes have been consistent throughout Blackstone's career from life as a student, through her teaching years, her difficult job at ILEA in the early 1980s, and then at Birkbeck College. Her role at the college, known mainly for its part-time degrees for mature students, was to turn around an institution in major financial and organisational difficulties. She succeeded in doing so, fighting for funding and presiding over major organizational changes.

She inevitably upset people on the way – people at the receiving end of her leadership have seen her as authoritarian and difficult to work with. But the mission of the college (named after its founder, George Birkbeck) to provide for people to study by night and have a second chance as adults was something she instinctively identified with.

Tessa was born on 27 September 1942, daughter of the late Geoffrey Blackstone CBE, GM and Joanna Vosper. She was educated at Ware Grammar School, Hertfordshire, and went on to study Sociology at the London School of Economics, from where she later gained a PhD. Through the 1960s and 1970s she taught at Enfield College, the LSE and the Institute of Education. Her parents were a significant influence in her life – they were well off but had a strong social conscience and pushed her hard to achieve. But her interest in politics was ignited by childhood experiences when she encountered the poverty and squalor in which others lived. The events shocked and moved her deeply and led to her profound sense of social injustice.

At the London School of Economics she became actively involved in the Socialist Society (Soc Soc). She fell in love with Tom Evans, then president of the LSE, whom she married when aged 20. She joined the Labour Party in 1964. Tom and Tessa had two children together – Benedict and Liesel. Benedict was born just weeks before Tessa started her first teaching job, leading to tough years combining work and a young family. Her marriage to Tom ended in 1975 though they remained good friends, and she spent much time with her children nursing their father through his last year until his death from cancer in 1985. She now has three grandchildren.

Her contributions to the Labour Party in opposition and in government have been considerable. She twice sought the Labour nomination for a general election, firstly in Hackney North and Stoke Newington in 1979, and secondly in 1981 in Hertford and Stevenage, where she lost the selection by one vote, after an initial tie-break. She was precluded from public office during her time as Deputy Education Office (Resources) at ILEA (1983–86), but was awarded a life peerage in 1987.

During the 1970s and 80s she was member of the NEC Sub-Committee on Education and Science. In the period 1988–1997 she held posts including Opposition spokesperson on Education and Science (1988–96), Treasury (1990–92), Trade and Industry (1992–96) and Foreign Affairs (1992–97).

This experience prepared her for jobs in Government. She has held the posts of Minister of State at the Department for Education and Employment (DfEE) (1997–2001) under David

Blunkett – a significant job in Labour's first term with the priorities for government being 'education, education, education' – and in June 2001 was appointed Minister for the Arts. Both were posts for which she was welcomed as someone with experience on the inside and knowledge of how the system worked – a 'critical friend' as well as a champion. Her arts experience has included being Member of the Board, Royal Opera House (1991–1997), Chairman of the Ballet Board (since 1997), Member of the Board of Trustees, The Natural History Museum, and Chairman of the Advisory Council of the BBC (1987–91).

Yet there are mixed views on the legacy from her time at the DfEE – the Further Education (FE) sector perhaps benefiting more than Higher Education (HE) from DfEE policy. In her time at the DfEE, HE policy concentrated on issues of access to HE for those from deprived areas, Foundation degrees (degrees for those who might not otherwise achieve one) and equal opportunities for HE staff. There was also an increase in quality assurance reviews, which added to HE costs and, some would argue, did not produce much benefit, except in terms of increased accountability.

The focus on access to HE/FE for those who might not have had the same opportunity previously can in large part be attributed to Blackstone. There has been more support for part-time students, single parents and the disabled as well as maintenance allowances for 16–19 year olds. But the targeting of funding is related to the introduction of tuition fees. There are mixed views on the effect this has had on applications to universities.

Those in favour of tuition fees, even if on a pragmatic rather than ideological basis, argue that those who can afford to should make a contribution, thereby allowing more resources to be targeted at those who previously missed out. Blackstone certainly furthered the view that sustainable funding for higher education has to be sourced through a partnership between taxpayers, parents and students, and an often overlooked fact is that more rigorous means testing has led to approximately 50 per cent of students being exempt.

There is no doubt that the policy was deeply unpopular with students and the decision was overruled in Scotland, where moves are being made so that students no longer pay up-front fees. The policy is also criticised for having deterred mature students and those from poorer families and ethnic minorities, though this remains unclear and the subject of much disagreement amongst academics – for example, in times of economic boom applications for study may well go down. But the choices of the Labour government in student funding and in targeted support are very close to Blackstone's own philosophy – which is essentially a sense of egalitarianism tempered by pragmatism. But she is serious about government continuing to play its part. There was a serious attempt by the Treasury to reduce HE funding per student by 3 per cent, which she saw off.

In summary, her work has led to an increasingly successful emphasis on getting more people from poor backgrounds to apply to university and on the use of devices such as summer schools to assist, but some say this is offset by the funding issues and the deterrence of poor students by fees and loans. Gender balance is not much changed, but universities are beginning slowly to adopt policies which should help in due course.

Blackstone has been at the centre of debate on the reform of A levels. She has been crucial in her support for different strands of Labour education policy, arguing that they are compatible – you can widen access and introduce reform as well as maintaining standards. There have been sceptics, and if Labour succeeds in winning the argument Blackstone will have played a major role in moving it forward.

But she has seen her role also as genuinely changing attitudes to learning more widely. She believes one of her biggest challenges has been to try to change perceptions to create a genuinely learning society. She has wanted to make further education available in communities opening up chances for young people and older people, and make learning more flexible.

Whether her work has helped set the foundations for radical change in education in Britain remains to be seen. But other areas which have affected her popularity are the abolition of maintenance grants for poorer students, which many saw as a step too far, and also in not beginning to tackle the issue of academic funding and morale much earlier.

There is also a question as to whether universities gained more from the DTI or DfEE policy. The starting-to-be-successful emphasis on reaching out to business and the community, and the more effective exploitation of universities as hubs for clusters, sources of skills transfer and more entrepreneurial students and academics is largely the result of policies pursued by the DTI, which has also generated large increases in resources available for university research.

Blackstone has been committed to the principles of the Labour Party since her student days and gained distinguished sponsors including Sir Klaus Moser, who taught her as a student and remained a lifelong friend. She has been consistent in her views throughout her life, believing passionately that the market cannot be left without intervention, and that the state has a responsibility to provide a wide range of public services available on an equitable basis. Overall, respect for her has been marked by the conferral of seven honorary doctorates, and it is likely that she will continue to be a prominent figure for some time to come.

Seema Malhotra

Tony Blair   (1953–)

In the opening years of the twenty-first century, it was clear that Tony Blair was the most successful politician Labour had seen since at least Harold Wilson. But in the great sweep of things, how important a leader for Britain is he? That is still harder to say. His stunning 1997 general election victory over John Major's Conservatives, exhausted by office and divided by Europe, ended an 18–year period during which it had often seemed that Labour would never rule again, and might not survive as a political force. Repeating that success in June 2001 made him the first Labour leader to win a full second term – and he did it with a majority that gave the party every hope of a third term too.

After years when centre-left politics appeared to be permanently exiled and degenerating into futile exhibitionism, Tony Blair gave Labour, or 'New Labour', something as close to absolute power as parliamentary democracies inside the EU in the modern world can offer. He was able to reshape his administration, shifting the Foreign Secretary Robin Cook to lead the Commons, and declaring a crusade for better-funded and radically reformed public services. He had the kind of unfettered authority no Labour Prime Minister before him had enjoyed.

But what did he wish to do with this power? Was this really the rebirth of progressive politics, finding new ways to redistribute from the powerful and established to the excluded, or those who were simply underpaid, undereducated and schooled to have few ambitions? Was it a recasting of Britain's democracy and her place in the world, as advocated by the constitutional reformers who had been embraced by his predecessor John Smith and by the Europhiles? Was it European Britain or not? Mr Blair's default-mechanism, unideological and somewhat bland answer was that he stood for 'modernisation'. New Labour would produce a New Britain, a young country, 'Cool Britannia' (though that was not one of his phrases).

Early on, he did indeed move with lightning speed. Referendums were fought and won to establish a Scottish Parliament, a Welsh National Assembly and a new government for London, headed by an elected mayor. Gordon Brown's plans to give independence on monetary affairs to the Bank of England were revealed and implemented, surprising the country. The minimum wage arrived, a long Labour ambition, set at such a low level that it killed virtually no jobs. After his second victory, he reshaped Whitehall to give himself more personal authority and held out the prospect of changes that would transform traditional ways of running schools and the health service. Standing in Downing Street, he gave a broad hint of wanting to press ahead with a referendum on the euro – hours before appointing a Eurosceptic, Jack Straw, as Foreign Secretary. A little more grizzled and lined, with a rather larger family, this was nevertheless a familiar Tony Blair, the smiling 40–something Sphinx. He was neither left nor right but simply progressive. What mattered was what worked.

Yet, in the way of things, much did not work. Economic disasters like the foot and mouth outbreak; real ones, on the rail system; symbolic ones, like the Millennium Dome; and a feeling that the Government was over-haughty, too close to big business and becoming mired in low-level sleaze took the gloss off the Blair project. In his 2001 election campaign, he faced furious voters who felt the Health Service had failed them, or who resented student fees, or who thought teachers were being shabbily treated. These encounters appeared to shock him and the need for 'delivery' was central to his second government's idea of itself. There was no triumphalism. The scale of the election victory was somewhat undercut by the lowest turnout in a general election since 1918; fewer than one in four voters had actually chosen New Labour. Looking ahead, the agonisingly difficult choice about a euro referendum included a steep mountain of public hostility. The Blair revolution could not be safe yet with so few ardent followers.

Tony Blair is sometimes accused of being an actor. His paternal grandparents really were, but they put his father, Leo Blair, up for adoption with a family of Clydeside socialists, from whom the Prime Minister's surname comes. Leo Blair was, in his youth, a leading Young Communist but he became a successful barrister, law lecturer and local TV star, moving to the right to such an extent that he was looking for a seat as a Conservative candidate when he was struck dumb by a stroke at the age of 40. That last ill-fortune apart, there are obvious and irresistible echoes here. Leo's son was also a youthful rebel who became more conformist, even conservative in later life, and was also a barrister and an early success on TV. Born on 6 May 1953, Tony Blair was, like his father, never part of the Labour Party's natural family but was adopted by it. Probably, the Prime Minister's complicated relationship with authority, the mix of rebellion and the desire to be accepted, derived from his wish to measure up to his highly political, driven and media-savvy father, and then from a private education, first at prep school in Durham, and then at Fettes College, the grandly gothic public school in Edinburgh.

At Fettes he was initially unhappy – not surprisingly, in the disciplinarian, conformist atmosphere of a Scottish public school of the time – and even tried to run away. Later he became something of a counter-culture star, the long-haired, smoking and drinking, infuriatingly clever rebel and talented actor remembered by former teachers.

At St John's College, Oxford, where he read History from 1972 to 1975, Tony Blair's life took on a double meaning. He was known as a sexy, trendy rock singer and all-round good-time boy by most friends but also became a committed, socially-conscious Christian and discovered the Scottish philosopher John Macmurray as an intellectual influence. In the highly political atmosphere of the time he joined occasional protest marches but avoided membership of any party or the numerous Marxist groups then fashionable. Nevertheless, by the time he arrived to study for the Bar in London, aged 22, he was interested enough in politics to join the Labour Party. That same year, by accident of alphabet, he found himself sitting next to an intellectually outstanding rival for a scholarship place, Cherie Booth. They met again when both were taken on as pupils by Derry Irvine, the abrasive and brilliant lawyer and close friend of John Smith. Within three years, the two ambitious and moderate-left lawyers had married, with Irvine, later made Lord Chancellor by Blair, playing what he described as the role of 'Cupid, QC.'

Tony Blair later implied that he had joined the Labour Party to change it, 'out of growing concern at the unrest that sectarian elements from the ultra-left were causing'. Others said it was a sharp career move at a time when it was easier to get nominated for Labour seats than Tory ones, though others again defend him on the grounds that joining Labour at all in those days hardly looked like a career move. Certainly, his early voting and speaking record in the Hackney South party suggested that he was on the then relatively unpopular centre-right of the party. He never toyed with defecting to the SDP and was strongly hostile to the Bennite 'hard left', then in its heyday. His first real political blooding came in the 1982 Beaconsfield by-election, fought during the crisis weeks of the Falklands War. He suffered a smashing defeat in a strong Conservative constituency, but impressed a string of senior Labour figures, including Neil Kinnock and Michael Foot, when they came to support his campaign. Foot later gave him a warm personal letter of endorsement ('a most entertaining, attractive and obviously first-rate candidate') which later helped swing the safe Labour Sedgefield constituency party to choose him as their one. He was energetically opposed to the Trotskyist Militant Tendency but stressed his deep involvement in labour law, working for the trade unions and on civil liberties cases, and at this stage was a member of CND. Having struggled to find a seat, and with a deal with Cherie that whoever got first into parliament would support the other's political ambitions, he won the Sedgefield nomination at the last minute against left-wing opposition and with considerable luck.

He entered the Commons, then, in May 1983 at the age of 30, after one of Labour's most shattering national defeats ever. Much of Blair's later politics should be seen against the background of this debut, arriving to sit for a party which seemed to be destroying itself through extremism, division and poor organisation. It would have been much easier, surely, for an ambitious, middle-class man to seek a political career with the then triumphant Tories.

But the luck which had landed him in Derry Irvine's chambers and then helped to get him Sedgefield continued. As one of only 32 new Labour MPs, he had more of a chance of shining than many newcomers in an ordinary new Parliament and won his first frontbench job, as a Treasury spokesman, after only 18 months. He is often criticised now for caring too little for backbenchers' rights; certainly he has had very little experience of life as a backbencher. During this 1983–87 parliament, he opposed British membership of the European Monetary System (earlier he had publicly backed the party line of leaving the EEC); he supported the legal position of the striking miners; and he made a name for himself with sharp, well-presented and concise speeches.

His most important political activity, however, took place well away from the chamber or the public. This was his friendship and mutual conversation with Gordon Brown, another bright and frustrated rising Labour star, though a man who knew far more about the Labour movement. The Scottish MP became a close personal friend, sharing an office and increasingly Blair's analysis of Labour's future and desperate need to modernise. At this stage, Brown was clearly the senior of the two, a far more confident parliamentary performer and much more media-savvy too. Blair argued and soaked up a lot.

In public, however, Blair's speeches in that and in the 1987–92 parliament sounded pretty conventional for a moderate socialist politician of the period – attacking the greed of the City traders, opposing privatisation of the electricity and gas industries, hammering the Tory government over insider trading and warning against the rule of 'market forces' in takeover cases. He was under the wing of Roy Hattersley, the leading centre-right figure in the party at the time, but was now attracting the attention of Neil Kinnock himself. He was offered a series of key promotions, first as Energy spokesman in 1988, after his first election to the shadow cabinet, then Employment in 1989. In this job he reversed Labour's support for the traditional pre-entry closed shop, a bold stroke which raised his profile hugely. Indeed, it was around this time that he was first talked about as a possible successor by Neil Kinnock. Throughout the period, he was pushing the need for Labour to reach out far more vigorously to the middle ground and was a staunch, though rarely leading, supporter of Kinnock's long battle to make the party electable. The need for modernisation was only underlined by Kinnock's inability to push Labour far enough, fast enough, and by his resignation following another general election defeat in 1992.

Both Blair and Brown agreed not to stand as deputy to the new leader John Smith, allowing him to balance the party with a left-leaning number two, Margaret Beckett. But this period was intensely frustrating for Tony Blair, perhaps the worst time of his adult life. Despite his own Scottish private education, Blair had little sympathy for or understanding of the distinctively Scottish-presbyterian moralism of Smith, with its emphasis on relatively high taxes, redistribution and social equality. To the modernisers, Smith was a trade union-influenced throwback who could not reach out to Middle England. From 1992 to 1994, Blair used his time as Shadow Home Secretary to map out a tougher, more traditionalist line on law and order, family values and community, summed up by the famous soundbite (which Brown authored, and then gave him gratis) 'tough on crime, tough on the causes of crime'. He and Brown both learned some ruthless electoral lessons from the 'New Democrats' and the successful, if entirely unsocialist, campaign for the White House fought by Bill Clinton in 1992. Finally, he and the other modernisers constantly pushed for internal Labour reforms, culminating in Smith's dramatic confrontation at the 1993 party conference over 'one member, one vote', which the Labour leader narrowly won but which was an experience he did not wish to repeat. At this stage in his career, Blair was pessimistic about his own and Labour's future, frustrated at being out of the inner circle. In fact, his high profile on law and order and impatience at the rate of change had marked him out, for Smith, as his likeliest successor. In the words of John Rentoul, Blair's biographer, 'If Neil Kinnock had left one legacy to the party, it was to make desperation respectable. There was now a large body of opinion at grass roots and activist level that wanted to win at almost any cost.'

When John Smith died suddenly of a heart attack on 12 May 1994, Tony Blair quickly decided that he had become the senior partner in the Blair-Brown practice and, notwithstanding any vague earlier understandings, stood for the leadership himself. This horrified Gordon Brown, but Blair's urgent connection with Middle England and the 'desperation' identified by Rentoul persuaded enough movers and shakers that it had to be Blair. After a famous dinner at Islington's Granita restaurant, Brown did the decent thing and declined to split the modernising vote. Blair took 57 per cent of the electoral college votes, easily beating John Prescott and Margaret Beckett, and became the leader of a party he quickly took to calling New Labour. From then until the 1997 general election, his energies were spent on reshaping the party message, ditching the old Clause 4, part IV commitment to common ownership of the means of production, distribution and exchange, and agreeing tight limits on future spending and taxing – a juggernaut of change that electrified spectators and stunned many traditional Labour people.

Internally, he produced a tightly controlled, almost Leninist party machine, driven by close friends such as Peter Mandelson, with a ruthless commitment to victory over John Major's by now utterly exhausted and divided Conservatives. All this paid off with a general election victory so complete that Blair himself wondered whether it was not too big: it rendered any formal co-operation with the Liberal Democrats, which he had favoured in the interests of a new progressive alliance, redundant.

In office, the first phase of New Labour reform continued the breathtaking speed of internal changes before the election. These included: legislation for a referendum on Scottish and Welsh devolution, then the setting up of an Edinburgh Parliament and a Welsh Assembly; Gordon Brown's introduction of Bank of England independence over monetary policy and major changes to the tax and benefit system to benefit low-income families and job-seekers; Britain's first national minimum wage; the removal of most hereditary peers from the House of Lords; a huge repayment of national indebtedness, made possible by tight spending constraints and a buoyant economy inherited from the Tories; the cutting of many primary class sizes; and dramatic progress in the interminable Northern Ireland peace process. Blair's over-adroit wooing of different sections of the national press with different agendas, offering them contrasting stories and punishing hostile journalism, made 'spin' a major media story and eventually brought a severe punishment; but in the early years it helped give him, and New Labour, unimaginably strong opinion-poll ratings.

But there was always another side to the picture. Perhaps inevitably, the sheer scale of the Commons majority produced a certain swank, even arrogance, in his government: flash parties in Downing Street, the endorsement of gushing media and sports stars and a too-clever-by-half publicity machine left an unpleasant taste in many mouths. Peter Mandelson, then Trade Secretary and a hugely controversial figure in the party, was forced to resign over an undeclared loan to pay for an expensive house. There were rows over fund-raising, which sat unhappily with a party which had tormented Major's Conservatives over 'sleaze' just a few years earlier.

A series of' personal errors, notably Blair's attempts to fix the Labour leadership of the Welsh Assembly and to prevent Ken Livingstone from becoming the first elected Mayor of London, then the unpopularity of the Dome and rising satire about the power of his Press Secretary Alastair Campbell, took the shine off 'Teflon Tony'. The Conservative leader William Hague, dismissed as a joke early on, began hitting Blair hard and painfully in their weekly Commons confrontations.

Blair's worst period since becoming leader six years earlier ran from the early summer of 2000 to the following spring. He was slow-handclapped and booed by the Women's Institute, saw his party's poll ratings slide significantly and made an ill-judged attempt to be tougher than ever on crime by allowing the police to exact summary fines on hooligans, only to find the police rejecting the notion and Lord Tebbit attacking him for being authoritarian. To cap it all, his 16–year-old son Euan was found collapsed, drunk, in Leicester Square, arrested by police and cautioned. After that came the real crisis of the fuel protests, when parts of Britain were brought to a halt by truckers and farmers livid with the effect of fuel duty and rising petrol costs. More worryingly for Mr Blair and his Chancellor, they had the public on their side. The Government won through, but looked rattled. Again, the 1999/2000 rise of only 75p in the basic state pension produced a pensioners' protest that won centre-stage at the party's Brighton conference and forced a rare open acknowledgement of misjudgement and an apology. Some observers wondered whether the birth of an unexpected fourth baby, Leo, had exhausted the Prime Minister.

There is an angry anti-Blair view in the country, ranging from fuel protestors and supporters of foxhunting, and now spread strongly among farmers and other countryside people, who found his government's handling of the 2001 foot-and-mouth epidemic slow and ineffectual. His great good luck has been that this disaffection did not translate into support for William Hague's Conservatives at the polls; he was fighting a party regarded by voters as being untrustworthy on public services and still addicted to the tax-cutting politics of the Eighties. But on the question of the euro above all, he will be faced with making a stand which will infuriate and harden opposition . On that, at least, there is no easy third way, no national consensus to be had.

Mr Blair, however, is a tough man who has brushed aside many obstacles on his road to the top. He has a wily sense of political strategy constantly missed by his opponents, sustained by a strong Christian faith, and has a restless social conscience too easily dismissed by Labour critics who call him 'Tory Blair'. By British political standards he is still a relatively young man, and with his fresh personal mandate and his sense that time is always short, it is far too early to judge his real place in British history.

Key books on Tony Blair include: *Tony Blair* by John Rentoul (1995); *Tony Blair* by Jon Sopel (1995); *Blair's 100 Days* by Derek Draper (1997); and *The Unfinished Revolution* by Philip Gould (1998).

Andrew Marr

Robert Blatchford (1851–1943)

Robert Blatchford was the son of an actor and was born in Maidstone in 1851. His father died when he was only two years old, and by the age of fourteen he was an apprentice brushmaker. However, he disliked this work and ran away to join the army. Before leaving the service in 1878 he had reached the rank of sergeant major. After trying various jobs he became a freelance journalist. He worked for several different newspapers before becoming the leader writer for the *Chronicle* in Manchester and it was these journalistic experiences that turned Blatchford into a socialist.

In 1890 Blatchford founded the Manchester Fabian Society and the following year Blatchford along with four other members launched a socialist newspaper called *The Clarion*. Blatchford was the editor and he decided that the paper would follow a 'policy of humanity; a policy not of party, sect or creed; but of justice, of reason'. The first edition sold 40,000 copies but after a few months settled down to about 30,000 copies a week.

In 1893 Blatchford's compiled some of his articles about socialism and published them in a single volume entitled *Merrie England*. This book was an immediate success, its cheaper edition alone selling over 2,000,000 copies. Influenced by the ideas of William Morris and others, Blatchford in his book emphasised the importance of the arts and the values of the countryside. This publication was so popular that it was translated into several different languages. Former Labour leader J R Clynes wrote in *The British Labour Party* (1948) that 'The spirit which a book like *Merrie England* cultivated and expressed went further in making a socialist than even the renowned Nine Chapters of Karl Marx. To build was the task of a man who could produce a book to make the plan of Socialism plain to workmen who would not require a dictionary for the meaning of any word.'

Unfortunately by the turn of the century, Blatchford was upsetting many of his socialist supporters by his nationalistic views on foreign policy. He spoke out vehemently for the Boer War and warned against what he saw as the German menace. 'I'm not a jingo, I'm opposed to the war. But I cannot go with other socialists that support the enemy. My heart is with the British soldier.' Blatchford also changed his views on equal rights and strongly opposed polices of the NUWSS and the WSPU.

This drastic change in views led Blatchford to move away from the left completely after the First World War and become a passionate advocate of the British Empire. During the 1924 General Election he openly supported the Conservative Party and declared his loyalty to Stanley Baldwin. Robert Blatchford died on 17 December 1943.

Maria Bell

David Blunkett (1947–)

Whatever else he goes on to achieve following his promotion to Home Secretary in the wake of Labour's June 2001 election victory, David Blunkett will be remembered as the first Education Secretary since Rab Butler who left state schools in a better state than he found them in. If you can judge a man by his enemies, Blunkett is surely a paragon. From the left – especially the teaching unions – he was assailed for treating with private schools and business, and for introducing heretical notions such as rewarding good teachers. The right found it more difficult to attack him, since his insistence on the importance of standards, and his palpable success in improving them, offered little ammunition. Blunkett's reformist zeal confused many people, who took too literally his history as a crusading 1980s local authority leader with a left-wing Labour power base. But Blunkett is a far more complex and interesting character than that, and the fact that his career has not travelled along well-trodden lines is, on further analysis, hardly surprising.

In some ways Blunkett was indeed the identikit Old Labour figure – leader of a radical Sheffield council, committed to the idea that government alone can achieve certain goals, and an economic Keynesian. As leader of Sheffield Council between 1980 and his election to Parliament for Sheffield Brightside in 1987 (the seat he has continued to represent), he established local industrial plans, with an employment department in his town hall. He led the fight against rate capping and refused to set a rate. He was, from 1983 onwards, repeatedly – and uniquely – elected to Labour's National Executive Committee from the constituency section, usually topping the poll, and the only non-MP to be elected in the CLP section; his success was due almost entirely to his status as a leader of the left (or the 'soft left', in the language of the time). But as a friend of both Tony Blair and David Blunkett once put it to me, explaining their political journeys: 'As Blair has gone from sensible to very sensible, Blunkett has moved from insane to sensible.' Even on the NEC, however, in the 1980s he showed that he was a far subtler politician than that. His backing for Neil Kinnock's drive to expel Militant in the mid 1980s was critical. Most of his left-wing colleagues either voted against or abstained on the expulsions as they came before the NEC. Blunkett saw Militant in its true colours, and his support for Kinnock helped carry the day across the party at a time when success was touch and go.

Once in the Commons, his rise was inexorable. In November 1989 he became deputy local government spokesman under Bryan Gould, and was elected to the Shadow Cabinet in 1992, serving first as Health spokesman and taking the Education brief in 1994 (which was combined with Employment in 1995). The story of Blunkett's life is powerful. He was born on 6 June 1947 in Sheffield, into a poor family, blind as a result of a rare genetic mismatch between his parents. It is impossible to read his 1995 autobiography, *On A Clear Day* (a rare example of a political autobiography genuinely written by the subject and moving from first page to last) without admiring the man. He refuses to wallow in self-pity but instead relates matter-of-factly the terrible agonies of his childhood. At the age of four he was sent away to the Manchester Road School for the Blind. He was allowed only one visit a month from his parents. As he puts it in his book: 'Obviously this has a profound effect on an infant, who feels totally abandoned and terrified, particularly when he cannot see who or what is around him. It was one of the worst experiences of my life…I desperately missed the hugging and affection of home.' He later graduated from Sheffield University.

He has never traded on his blindness. Those who underestimate him or feel pity for him soon come to regret it, as his political and intellectual skills need no outside compensation. His father died of an horrific work injury, falling into a giant vat of boiling water, leaving his mother in true poverty: 'I do not use the term lightly. Those who have never experienced real poverty are all too often sentimental about it and about poor people in general. I have to smile at this and think if only you knew what it was like, you would know all about aspirations and expectations and why it was that, in the community in which I grew up, escaping the poverty trap and achieving success were the key aims.' It hardly requires psychoanalysis to see that these early experiences explain almost all of Blunkett's political views. This is the crux of the man. Education, for Blunkett, is about escape – from poverty, from low expectations and from limited horizons. As a fellow Cabinet Minister put it about him: 'This is where he differs from Blair. On policy, there's almost nothing between them. Blunkett's motivation is class based. He hates the idea that working-class children should be denied a proper education. Blair's outlook is much more New Labour, and is based on ideas of "the knowledge society" and "skills shortages."' The received wisdom at the beginning of his term as Education Secretary was that he was the stooge for Blair's agenda. This was quite wrong. Far from being forced to dance to his tune, many of the boldest initiatives emerged from Blunkett himself. He is the perfect salesman because he believes in the product to his very core.

He is also in many ways deeply conservative. As he has said, 'recent research has shown that children's lack of numeracy can be put down to the fact that calculators have taken over from the use of their brains. Yes, I am a fundamentalist when it comes to education; I believe in discipline, solid mental arithmetic, learning to read and write accurately, plenty of homework, increasing expectations and developing potential'. No Conservative could have put it better. But Blunkett, quite rightly, could never see why the devil should always have the best tunes. There is nothing socialist about illiteracy.

Blunkett's outlook was perfectly illustrated when, in March 1998, the British Council sponsored an overseas tour of the play *Shopping and Fucking*. Blunkett said that 'I don't know how much they are spending. But if they are spending a penny on it, it's a penny too much.' The play was 'full of foul language. Shakespeare didn't need that, did he?'

It is that combination of outrage at the injustice that denies poor children the same opportunities as the better off, and a traditional respect for the basics, which makes Blunkett the powerful force he is. His own experience taught him the importance of a basic grounding and confirmed his contempt for 'progressive' attitudes, especially in the classroom. The principal of his last school, for instance, typified the problem: 'His view was that exams were unnecessary, that they narrowed academic and intellectual development and that it was therefore a waste of time for pupils to study for them. Such an attitude angers me to this day because he had a PhD. I wonder how he thought he could become head of a college without qualifications'.

Unlike many senior Labour politicians, Blunkett still has his own power base. He is no one's creature. He has the protection and strength which flow from his hero-like position in the party, and a rare ability to communicate and engage with the public. It is anyone's guess how high that combination will see him fly.

Stephen Pollard

Margaret Bondfield (1873–1953)

Margaret Grace Bondfield was a woman who devoted much of her life to the advancement of the trade-union movement, and whilst her Parliamentary career was brief, she made her mark on history as the first-ever female member of the Cabinet.

Margaret Bondfield was born near Chard in Somerset on 17 March 1873. She was the tenth of eleven children of a lace worker, William Bondfield, a nonconformist with radical sympathies. Margaret left elementary school at 13, and was for the next two years a supply teacher in the local boys school. Aged 15, she became a drapers' assistant in Brighton, where she became interested in the Women's Movement and expanded her knowledge by reading widely under the influence of a female Liberal friend. For the next 11 years, Bondfield worked in shops both in London and the provinces, working long hours for low wages.

In 1894, now living and working in London, Bondfield joined the Shop Assistants Union, and became in 1896 the first woman delegate to its conference. She served as its Assistant Secretary from 1898 until she stepped down to concentrate her activities on the wider Labour movement in 1908. In 1899 she published a paper on 'The Conditions of Employment in Shops' in the *Economic Journal*. In 1899 she became also the first female delegate to the Trades Union Congress (TUC), delivering a speech in support of the historic resolution which led to the formation of the Labour Party. Her involvement with the TUC was extensive. In 1917 she was the first woman to be elected to its Parliamentary Committee, the forerunner of the General Council, of which she became the first woman Chair in 1923–24.

In 1902 she met Mary Macarthur, who became a close personal friend as well as a colleague. Her biographer of 1924, M A Hamilton, wrote that, 'In the years between 1903 and 1921, the romance of her life – and a very real romance – was her association with Mary Macarthur.' Macarthur founded the National Federation of Women Workers in 1906, the first general union for women, and Bondfield became extensively involved.

During this period the teetotal Bondfield was a member of the Ideal Club, a debating and social group based in Tottenham Court Road, where she met George Bernard Shaw and the Webbs. She was first attracted to the Social Democratic Foundation, but subsequently moved to the ILP and the Fabian Society. From 1908 to 1913 she served on the ILP Executive and lectured widely on their behalf. Following the death of Mrs Ramsay MacDonald she became organising secretary of the Women's Labour League, which subsequently became the women's section of the Labour Party.

She opposed the First World War, later opposing conscription, advocating a negotiated peace and becoming involved with the Union for Democratic Control. However, she also held positions on the Central Committee on Women's Employment and the War Emergency Women's National Committee.

After the War, Bondfield became Vice-President of the International Federation of Working Women, and from 1921 to 1938 the Chief Women's Officer of the General and Municipal Workers Union following its absorption of her National Federation of Women Workers. A devout anti-Communist, particularly after taking part in a joint TUC-Labour Party delegation to the Soviet Union, she opposed the Communist Party's application to affiliate to the Labour Party in 1920. Though involved in the TUC's decision to call the General Strike of 1926, she supported the decision to end it and was in general a political ally of JH Thomas of the NUR.

She contested Woolwich in the LCC election of 1910, the first at which women were allowed to stand, and in 1913, and unsuccessfully fought the Northampton by-election of April 1920 against a Coalition Liberal. Undeterred by defeat she re-fought Northampton at the General Election of 1922 before finally becoming Northampton's MP at the general election of 1923, only to lose the seat in the election that marked the defeat of MacDonald's first government at the end of 1924. Returning to Parliament at the Wallsend by-election of 1926, she was defeated in the electoral disaster of 1931 and, after failing to regain Wallsend at the general election of 1935, she announced her intention not to return to Parliament.

Despite this brief parliamentary career, Bondfield not only managed to become the first woman to hold ministerial rank, as Parliamentary Secretary at the Ministry of Labour in 1924, but was also the first female member of the Cabinet, serving as Minister of Labour from 1929 to 1931. She was made a Privy Counsellor in 1929 and a Companion of Honour in 1948.

As Minister of Labour, despite boosting the rates of unemployment benefit and removing the 'genuinely seeking work' condition for claimants, Bondfield nevertheless became unpopular with the left of the Party. When MacDonald sought to secure economies in public expenditure in 1931 she backed him, though she remained with Labour when he formed the National Government. The Unemployment Insurance Anomalies Bill of July 1931, designed to tackle benefit fraud, caused further unpopularity by removing certain categories of benefit.

In 1938, Bondfield travelled in Mexico, studying labour conditions there. She also published an autobiography, *A Life's Work* (1949) and served as Chair of the Women's Group on Public Welfare from 1939 to 1949. She died on 16 June 1953 in a Surrey nursing home.

Margaret Bondfield contributed symbolically to the advancement of women by becoming the first female Cabinet Minister. However, perhaps more substantially, by pressing forward the case for union representation in traditionally female industries, she played a large part in ensuring that women became part of the labour movement and had access to the protection and collective action afforded to men.

Judith Begg

Albert Booth (1928–)

Albert Booth brought to public life a passion for detail that brought him success and a highly-principled nature, which proved his undoing. From relatively humble origins as an engineering draughtsman, he rose to become a member of the Cabinet in Jim Callaghan's government, as Secretary of State for Employment, a position he filled with quiet competence rather than distinction. He lost his seat at Westminster in the Tory landslide of 1983, proving even more unpopular with his constituents than his political mentor, Michael Foot, because of his dogged support for CND in a shipbuilding town dominated by Vickers, makers of the Polaris submarines.

Albert Edward Booth was born on 28 May 1928 and educated at St. Thomas's School, Winchester, South Shields Marine School and Rutherford College of Technology. Politically active from his teens, he was a member of the National Consultative Committee of the Labour League of Youth and an election agent in 1951. By the age of 24, he was secretary of his constituency party and a member of Tynemouth Borough Council from 1962 to 1965. A keen union man, he also chaired the local Trades Council.

In 1964 he contested the safe Conservative seat of Tynemouth and did sufficiently well to secure nomination at Barrow-in-Furness in 1966, when he almost doubled Labour's majority to eight thousand. His future seemed assured. An assiduous member of the Tribune Group (more left-wing in the 1970s than it became later), he attracted the attention of Tony Benn, Foot and other leading figures on the Parliamentary left, often attending their dinner parties with his wife Joan. His draughtsman's eye for detail made him a natural choice for the Commons Select Committee on Statutory Instruments, which he chaired from 1970 to 1974. He was also an Opposition spokesman on trade and industry.

After Labour's victory in the 'who rules' election rashly called by Edward Heath in February 1974, Booth followed his champion Foot to Employment as Minister of State. When Harold Wilson resigned in April 1976 and Foot moved to become Leader of the House, Benn lobbied for the Employment portfolio, arguing that Booth should take his place at Energy. But Foot had already promised the job to his protégé, Albert, and Callaghan confirmed the move, which brought with it Privy Council status. In Cabinet, Booth loyally supported Callaghan's Social Contract incomes policy with the TUC, despite being sponsored at Westminster by his hard-left union the AUEW (TASS), which was intransigently opposed. He also refused to resign over cuts in public spending.

In Opposition after 1979, Booth was elected to the Shadow Cabinet, becoming Shadow Transport Secretary 1979–83, but is also remembered as the Labour politician who first hired Peter Mandelson as a researcher following his unhappy departure from the staff of Congress House. Booth's political career was cut short at the age of 55, when the voters of Barrow-in-Furness rejected him and Michael Foot's Labour Party in the general election of 1983, in greater part over the policy of unilateral nuclear disarmament. Booth had supported unilateralism to the extent of leading a CND march through his constituency, prompting dismay and admiration in equal measure among friends.

Following the defeat, he moved into industry, as executive director of the South Yorkshire Passenger Transport Executive, but did not give up politics or the hope of re-entering Parliament. In 1984 he was Treasurer of the Labour Party and in 1987 he contested Warrington South, losing to a former political aide in Thatcher's Number Ten. A courteous, unassuming man, Albert Booth belonged to a different age to the one that spawned Tony Blair. In retirement, he lived quietly in Beckenham and, although entitled to an ex-MP's Westminster pass, was rarely seen there.

Paul Routledge.

Cherie Booth (1954–)

Cherie Booth is a prominent Queen's Counsel (QC) who is highly regarded for her expertise in public and employment law. Her importance in Labour history rests on the way she has personified the modern Labour woman's dilemma when faced with conflicting professional and personal aspirations. To her and Labour's credit, she is quite unlike any of her predecessors. She is the first wife of a prime minister to be politically active in her own right, have a successful professional career, turn her public profile to the advantage of a string of good causes, raise three children, give birth to a fourth child while resident in Downing Street, and support a committed and active husband, in full view of an intrusive media.

Cherie Booth was born in Bury, Lancashire, on 23 September 1954, and is the daughter of the accomplished actor, Anthony Booth. Brought up in Waterloo, Liverpool, as a Roman

Catholic by her mother, Gale Booth, she joined the Labour Party as a teenager in 1970 and has been a member ever since. She was educated at Seafield Grammar School, Crosby, and studied law at the London School of Economics (LSE) where she obtained first class honours (LLB). She also became an Honorary Fellow of the LSE in 1999. She was called to the Bar at Lincoln's Inn in 1976 where she came top of her class in her Bar exams and became a barrister. Cherie Booth and Tony Blair met as trainee barristers and married in 1980. They have four children (Euan 1984; Nicky 1985; Kathryn 1988, and Leo 2000, the first birth to a Prime Minister's wife since 1848). In the first half of the 1980s, before the demands of her children and legal career took over, Cherie was an active executive member of the Labour Co-ordinating Committee, the influential ginger group from Labour's mainstream left which played a decisive role in re-newing the antiquated structures and politics of the Labour Party. Cherie contested the safe Conservative seat of Thanet North for Labour in the general election of 1983. That year her husband became an MP and went on to become Prime Minister.

Cherie Booth's legal career has paced her husband's political career. She became one of the youngest-ever woman QCs in 1995; an Assistant Recorder (a part time junior judge) in 1996, and a Recorder (a part-time judge) in June 1999. She has not shied away from controversial or high profile court cases. She has represented a solicitor against the Law Society; the TUC against the Government over parental leave; a gay rights case against South West Trains; and an injured child against the Criminal Injuries Compensation Board following a well-known ma-chete attack on a nursery in 1996. She has contributed chapters to publications, covering her specialism of public and employment law, including the 1998 edition of *Jordan's Employment Law Service*. She has also publicly supported family-friendly employment policies, job shares, stronger protection against gender harassment and the Human Rights Act, incorporating the European Convention on Human Rights into British law. She has lectured publicly on sub-jects such as the case for a more equal employment environment and became a Fellow of the Institute of Advanced Legal Studies in 1998.

A reluctant celebrity, Cherie Booth has used, to the benefit of others, the media interest in her activities. She has found time to play a role on behalf of the cancer charities Sargent Can-cer Care for Children and Breast Cancer Care. She has assisted education projects through in-volvement with the LSE, John Moores University Liverpool, the Open University, the Kids Club Network and even the Islington Music Centre. She has also made time for Refuge and the Citizenship Foundation.

In Cherie Booth, Labour has provided Britain with a remarkable example of what a deter-mined and talented woman can achieve. She has already set a standard for prime ministerial spouses in the 21st century that will be hard to equal.

Rex Osborn

Betty Boothroyd (Baroness Boothroyd) (1929–)

Betty Boothroyd, or 'Madam Speaker' as she became known to the public in her final Commons incarnation, was with Mo Mowlam arguably the most popular and prominent woman politician in the Parliaments of 1992–2001. Her style and flair made her, the first woman Speaker and only the third Labour MP to be elected to an office held continuously by the Conservatives 1928–65, the first Speaker in history to be a household name. In July 1992, within three months of becoming Speaker, she had been acclaimed 'Parliamentarian of the Year' by the *Spectator* – hardly a natural political soulmate. In May 1997 she was re-elected Speaker unopposed on the nomination of her friend and parliamentary colleague Gwyneth Dunwoody.

Her achievement in even becoming Speaker was considerable – beating former Tory Cabinet Minister Peter Brooke by 372 to 238 votes in the first contested election in over forty years. Seventy-four Conservative MPs led by former Thatcher Cabinet Minister John Biffen and ranging from 'wets' like Robert Adley, Edwina Curry, Jim Lester and Emma Nicholson to the more right-wing Sir Rhodes Boyson and Sir Nicholas Fairbairn backed her, despite pressure from the Tory Whips. She had not even always seemed the likely Labour candidate: former engineering toolmaker Sir Harold Walker, a former Employment Minister under Jim Callaghan and the AEEU-sponsored MP for Doncaster, had been the senior Deputy Speaker since 1983, whilst Boothroyd had been Third Deputy Speaker only since 1987.

Perhaps ironically for a Speaker who would rise so effortlessly above Parliamentary squabbles, Boothroyd's political hinterland was in the backroom battles for the soul of the Labour Party. One of the leading women members of the Manifesto Group of social-democratic loyalist Labour backbenchers, she was on the Manifesto/Campaign for Labour Victory slate for Labour's NEC Women's Section from 1977, securing election in February 1981 to the vacancy created by Shirley Williams's defection to the SDP. In his *Senate of Lilliput* of January 1983, the then *Daily Telegraph* sketchwriter Edward Pearce characterised Boothroyd as the new, improved Shirley Williams: 'crisper than Mrs Williams and has, literally professional command of TV. How often does either party get the allegiance of a Tiller Girl with brains... She is an asset and will be used as one.' From 1981 until her decision not to re-stand in September 1987 on becoming Third Deputy Speaker, she was a key NEC loyalist, working closely with John Golding, Gwyneth Dunwoody and Shirley Summerskill against Militant, Bennery and unilateralism.

As Paul Routledge phrased it in his superlative Boothroyd biography, *Madam Speaker* (1995), it was 'difficult to put a credit card' between her political views and those of the Labour MPs who joined the SDP. A staunch and longstanding pro-European, she had resigned her only government post (Assistant Whip for the West Midlands, the first woman to be a Labour government Whip) in November 1975, having been appointed only in October 1974, to concentrate fully on her role as a nominated (pre-direct elections) MEP from 1975 to 1977. Her mentors Sir Geoffrey de Freitas and Lord Walston were two of the leading pro-European Jenkinsites of the era. Indeed the nucleus of the SDP has often been seen in the so-called 'Walston Group' that met at Walston's Albany apartment in the early 1970s to plot a Jenkinsite future for Labour. Lord Walston, a former junior Foreign Office and Trade minister 1964–67 had been as Harry Walston a Liberal and Labour parliamentary candidate before being created one of the first Labour Life Peers in 1961. Boothroyd was his secretary from 1962 until she entered Parliament at the West Bromwich by-election of May 1973 (it was renamed West Bromwich West following boundary changes in February 1974). A farmer and substantial landowner, he became a close friend as well as her employer, giving her use of a fourteenth-century cottage on his Cambridgeshire estate where she has lived for many years. Cambridge blue Squadron-Leader Sir Geoffrey de Freitas (whose secretary she was 1952–60 when he was a leading Gaitskellite front-bencher) had been PPS to fellow Old Haileyburyan Clement Attlee and a junior minister 1946–51. Walston became SDP spokesman on agriculture and foreign affairs and de Freitas would almost certainly have joined the SDP but for his illness and untimely death early in 1981. Boothroyd, like most of her fellow GMB-sponsored MPs, did not.

Born on 8 October 1929 in Dewsbury, Yorkshire, the only child of textile workers, Archibald and Mary Boothroyd, she herself confessed 'I came out of the womb into the Labour movement': her parents were Labour Party and Textile Workers' Union members and activists whilst her uncle was a Labour Councillor. She attended Eastborough Board School with Sir Marcus Fox, also a contemporary at the Vivienne School of Dancing before becoming a Conservative MP and Chairman of the 1922 Committee. Leaving Eastborough aged 12 she attended Park Mansion School before winning a scholarship aged thirteen to Dewsbury Technical College. It was then that she famously became, aged seventeen, a Tiller Girl, having toured during the latter war years as a singer and dancer with the Swing Stars Band. Meanwhile she was becoming a keen Labour activist, joining the Labour League of Youth aged sixteen, and by the time of the fall of the Attlee government in 1951 had risen to the National Consultative Committee.

In 1952, having been an unsuccessful Labour candidate in the Dewsbury Council elections, she left her Dewsbury secretarial job at the Road Haulage Association for a similar post at Labour Party HQ at Transport House, soon moving to the Commons to become secretary to both de Freitas and the Bevanite Barbara Castle, for whom she also worked until 1958. Though it was de Freitas who became a close friend and political mentor as well as an employer, her friendships with members of the Keep Left/Bevanite circle, including her Hornsey flatmate Jo Richardson who was then secretary to both Ian Mikardo and the Keep Left Group, perhaps help explain why Boothroyd was less inclined than those who joined the SDP to despair completely of the Labour Party in 1981. She enjoyed the social side of Hornsey Constituency Labour Party, frequently joining her flatmate Jo Richardson, the Castles, Terry Lancaster and other young Bevanites for a bitter in the Flask pub in Highgate, despite her firm Gaitskellite Atlanticist views. She was also firmly involved in the trade union movement: an APEX member, she was chair of the Parliamentary Staffs trade union 1955–60. Before winning West Bromwich West she unsuccessfully fought the Leicester South-East by-election in November 1957, Peterborough at the 1959 general election, Nelson and Colne at the by-election of June 1968, and Rossendale at the 1970 general election. Before winning West Bromwich West the only election she had won was to Hammersmith Borough Council in May 1965, on which she served until 1968. When the SDP was formed she still had the energy and the will to stand and fight the militant left within Labour: 'loyal to Dewsbury rather than Albany', as Routledge put it. On her retirement as Speaker in 2000 she was created Baroness Boothroyd.

Greg Rosen

Arthur Bottomley (Lord Bottomley of Middlesborough) (1907–95)

The two peaks of Arthur Bottomley's lifetime of service to the Labour movement came at the beginning and towards the end of his political career. At the age of 32 on the outbreak of war he became ARP controller for his native Walthamstow, and later Deputy Regional Commissioner for the whole of South-East England. He gave outstanding leadership in this role during the years of the London air raids and earned an early OBE. At the age of 57, following the General Election of October 16 1964, he joined the new Labour Cabinet as Secretary of State for Commonwealth Affairs. He was immediately plunged into the crisis in Central Africa with the threatened rebellion in Southern Rhodesia. Within days he was in Northern Rhodesia, about to become Zambia, for the Independence celebrations. But before the Union flag could come down at midnight on 22 October, he had to negotiate successfully a 59th minute settlement with Dr Kenneth Kaunda. The rest of his period of office was preoccupied in dealing with the impending Rhodesian Unilateral Declaration of Independence. It involved chairing difficult meetings of Commonwealth Ministers, who demanded direct British military intervention, and even more difficult meetings with a defiant and devious Ian Smith during two visits to Salisbury.

Inevitably, as the Rhodesian rebellion occupied the stage for the United Kingdom, Arthur Bottomley's role was overshadowed by that of the Prime Minister, Harold Wilson. Together they paid a memorable visit to Salisbury in October 1965 on the eve of UDI. It included a bizarre dinner party at which an innocent Essex cricket story from Arthur provoked, from Ian Smith's Cabinet colleagues, behaviour of such prurience that it shocked their more puritan visitors from London.

After UDI the drama entered a new phase, and by the time the next meeting took place at sea, on HMS *Tiger*, Arthur Bottomley had moved, as part of a major Cabinet reshuffle in August 1966, to the less contentious post of Minister of Overseas Development, a post he held until his retirement from Cabinet in August 1967. Bottomley brought to both these ministerial tasks an experience of international negotiations from his posts in the first post-war Labour Government as Parliamentary Under-Secretary of State for Dominions (1946–47) and as Secretary for Overseas Trade at the Board of Trade (1947–51), where he had succeeded the young Harold Wilson. He became a Privy Counsellor in 1951. Equally important was the fact that, during the long years in Opposition (1951–64), he built up a fund of goodwill and personal understanding with the leaders of the newly independent Commonwealth countries by his leading role in the Commonwealth Parliamentary Association. He led the Labour delegations to CPA conferences in Malaysia, Malawi, Mauritius, Canada and Australia. He was Chairman of the Commonwealth and Colonies Group of the Parliamentary Labour Party in 1963 in the run-up to the General Election.

Arthur Bottomley was born in East London on 7 February 1907. He was educated at the Gamuel Road Secondary School. supplemented by extension classes at Toynbee Hall where Clem Attlee had worked after returning from the First World War. He became a Labour member of the Walthamstow Borough Council at the age of 22. In 1935, he was appointed the London Organiser of the National Union of Public Employees. He remained with both organisations until his election to Parliament for the Chatham division of Rochester in 1945. Boundary changes made it the marginal Rochester & Chatham constituency in 1950, but he continued to hold it until 1959, having become since November 1957 an elected member of the shadow cabinet and Shadow Commonwealth Secretary.

He returned to NUPE for a couple of years until he won a by-election in 1962 in Middlesbrough East (later in 1974 Teeside, Middlesbrough) which he held until 1983. In 1984, he went to the Lords as Baron Bottomley of Middlesbrough, where he continued to be active as Chairman of the Attlee Foundation, President of the British & India Forum and of the Britain and Burma Society (a country to which he had led a special Parliamentary Labour Party mission in 1962).

Arthur's wife, Dame Bessie Bottomley, whom he married in 1936, gave great service to the Labour Party in Walthamstow in education, in hospital management and as a JP. They were a strong partnership – the Sydney and Beatrice Webb of Walthamstow. They had no children, but throughout their lives went out of their way to encourage young people in Parliament and elsewhere in the Labour movement. Arthur died on 3 November 1995. Arthur Bottomley's publications were: *Why Britain should Join the Common Market* (1959); *Two Roads to Colonialism* (1960); *The Use and Abuse of Trade Unions* (1961); and *Commonwealth Comrades and Friends* (1986).

Rt. Hon. Lord Thomson of Monifieth

Herbert Bowden (Lord Aylestone) (1905–94)

Herbert William Bowden was born on 20 January 1905 and after wartime service in the RAF (1941–45) and a spell on Leicester City Council (1938–45) was elected Labour MP for Leicester South from 1945–50 and for Leicester South-West until 1967, when he entered the House of Lords as Lord Aylestone. He was PPS to Postmaster-General Wilfred Paling, 1947–49, and in the Whips Office 1949–51. During the long years of opposition he served as Opposition Deputy Chief Whip under Attlee from 1951 to 1955 and was then appointed Opposition Chief Whip by Hugh Gaitskell – with whom he had a close working relationship. As early as December 1954 fellow Labour MP Fred Bellenger had lunched Gaitskell and Bowden together, telling them that one day Herbert would be Chief Whip and Gaitskell Leader, so they had better get along.

They did. Their first conversation was about withdrawing the whip from the Bevanites. This set the tone for what the historian of party discipline Eric Shaw has called the years of 'democratic centralism'. Bowden was a disciplinarian party loyalist, who supported the attempt to expel Nye Bevan in 1955 and campaigned with Gaitskell against the adoption of unilateralist candidates in winnable seats in the run-up to the 1964 election, working closely and in secret with the Campaign for Democratic Socialism. He was awarded a CBE in 1953 and joined the Privy Council in 1962.

After Gaitskell's death he remained Opposition Chief Whip until Wilson recognised Bowden's ultimate loyalty to the party and appointed him Lord President and Leader of the House of Commons on Labour's return to government in 1964. As Lord President he advised a reluctant Tony Benn that he had better take the oath of allegiance to the Queen.

After the 1966 election, when Wilson's power was more firmly consolidated, Bowden was first moved to become Secretary of State for Commonwealth Affairs, in August 1966, where he battled with the Rhodesian problem, and then in August 1967 sent to head the Independent Broadcasting Authority, after which he left the Commons. He was given a life peerage as Lord Aylestone that same year, though, as Richard Crossman put it, he always remained 'a Chief Whip at heart.'

In 1969 he was considered as chair for a committee of enquiry into secrecy. Wilson suggested Aylestone but his Principal Private Secretary, Michael Halls, opposed this on the grounds that his association with television would have made him 'too liberally minded' and he might produce a report 'almost Swedish' in tone. In fact Bowden was, and remained, deeply old Labour in his instincts and politics, but with personal loyalties that tied him to the Gaitskellite-Jenkinsite wing of the party. He was generally considered a success at the IBA and retained the post until 1975, when on his retirement he became a Companion of Honour.

He enjoyed a distinguished Indian summer in the House of Lords, joining the SDP in 1981 (joining its steering committee and becoming its first leader in the Lords) from friendship and disillusion with the party he had been loyal to rather than through any deep conviction. He was not, for example, an early pro-European. Nevertheless, he joined the Liberal Democrats in 1992. He died on 5 May 1994. He married Louisa Brown in 1928, with whom he had a daughter.

Professor Brian Brivati

Bessie and Jack Braddock   (1899–1970 and 1890–1963)

Depending on one's point of view, the partnership of John (Jack) and Elizabeth Margaret (Bessie) Braddock was forged either in heaven or in hell. Bessie was a local Liverpool girl, educated at local elementary schools, born on 24 September 1899 to socialist Hugh Bamber and his wife 'Ma' Bamber, an activist icon in her own time. Whilst her background was comfortable compared to her neighbours, Bessie soon showed that Bamber blood flowed freely through her veins. Whether assisting down-and-outs, or agitating for improved working conditions as a clerk for the Warehouse Workers Union, there was a restless determination about Bessie.

Indeed it was entirely appropriate that she met Jack in the ILP rooms in Upper Parliament Street, Liverpool. Of her relationship, she was to say: 'You don't get time for courting. We just realised that sooner or later we would marry.' They did, on 9 February 1922.

Her lifelong partner Jack was more than a match for the fearsome Bessie. A former boxer, he had been born in Hanley, Staffordshire, in 1890 and was en route to Canada via Liverpool when he was sucked into Liverpool politics. He never made that intended trip across the ocean. He was a colourful character, immediately noticeable by his habitual stetson hat. He began his working life in Liverpool as a wagon builder and ended up as an insurance agent. Jack was to be a local anchor while Bessie sailed off to the national stage at Westminster.

However, the seven years between their first meeting and their wedding were to reflect a youthful political romanticism consonant with the revolutionary zeitgeist of the times. Undergoing repeated arrests, they were in the habit of hiding visiting revolutionaries from the police, like Count Malatesta, or the Russian Zuzenko. The latter was hidden in Garston, South Liverpool, from where Jack and Bessie took him on surreptitious cinema visits.

With the formation of the Communist Party, the Braddocks were natural recruits. Indeed, Jack became its local leader for five years, whilst Bessie became the treasurer. Disillusionment soon set in, and they both left the Communist Party in 1924, throwing themselves into Labour Party activity. Jack was to become a councillor within five years, remaining on the council from 1929 until his death in 1963, and was Labour leader for the final fifteen years, from 1948.

Whilst Bessie followed Jack onto the council in 1930, her ambitions took a different turn when she was adopted as prospective parliamentary candidate for Liverpool Exchange in 1936. She remained on the council until 1961, despite having finally won her parliamentary seat from the Tories in 1945.

Jack's considerable energies were devoted to moulding an effective Labour machine in Liverpool, particularly as leader of the Labour Group. He attacked Labour's left wing with all the fervour of a convert, once describing his internal rivals as 'flat-faced Muscovites from Garston.' He and Bessie, however, were always ready to take on the right wing also. Their belief in direct action led them to pollute the beer supply at a newly established fascist club.

In his virulently anti-left rhetoric, he was joined by Bessie, who was eventually to hone it, at the instigation of Herbert Morrison, into a bitter anti-Bevan crusade. She was a leading opponent of the left on Labour's NEC from 1947 to 1948 and from 1958 to 1969. Over time, this political fundamentalism was to have Bessie suspended from the City Council Labour group, excluded from the House of Commons and facing a split constituency party.

Nevertheless, Bessie remained a difficult opponent. For example, she was a firm supporter locally of birth control clinics, to the fury of both local Catholics and Protestants in those sectarian times. Yet she opposed family allowances, as they would 'allow employers to cut men's wages and undermine the trade union concept of a living wage.'

Wartime ambulance driver Bessie took no hostages as she and Jack grew increasingly litigious. They took on, amongst others, the local Protestant political leader, Alderman Longbottom; Labour councillor Reg Bevins (later a Tory Minister); and Express Newspapers. Their longstanding combativeness had metamorphosed into a more sophisticated form than setting about opponents.

Jack's death on 12 November 1963 was to signal an abrupt end to all that. Bessie remained an implacable foe of the left in all of its guises. However, the spark had gone and her retirement in 1970, followed by her death in November of that year, marked the close of a unique era in a city renowned for the singularity of its political life.

Peter Kilfoyle MP

Tom Bradley (1926–)

Tom Bradley was an influential member of the Parliamentary Labour Party, respected particularly for the authority and perception with which he spoke on transport issues, and also as a committed European during a period when holding such a view was frequently not in fashion in the Labour Party. He was also President of the Transport Salaried Staffs' Association, the senior lay position in the union, at a time of considerable change, and sometimes turmoil, in the railway industry as traffic levels continued to fall and the quest for reductions in costs intensified.

Thomas George Bradley was born on 13 April 1926 in Kettering, and was educated at Kettering Central School. In 1953 he married Joy (née Starmer). They had two sons. When he left school Tom Bradley became a clerk on the railways, joining the then Railway Clerks' Association in 1942. He was a member of the Kettering Branch and served as a branch officer from 1946 to 1958. He also held office as President of Kettering Trades Council.

In 1958 he was elected to the Association's Executive Committee representing the Midlands East Division. Three years later he was elected as the Association's National Treasurer, the second most senior lay position. He served as Treasurer for three years before being elected National President in 1965 following Ray Gunter's resignation from that position on his appointment as a cabinet minister in the newly elected Labour Government.

Bradley was TSSA President until 1977 when he resigned from the post in order to become Acting General Secretary following the early retirement of David Mackenzie. He served as Acting General Secretary from January to May 1977, when he ceased to hold any office in the TSSA following his defeat by the Assistant General Secretary in the election for a new General Secretary.

Bradley was a member of Kettering Constituency Labour Party. He was elected to Northamptonshire County Council in 1952, becoming an Alderman in 1961 and served on Kettering Borough Council from 1957 to 1961. He was the youngest candidate to contest the 1950 General Election when he stood in Rutland and Stamford. He stood again in Rutland and Stamford in the 1951 and 1955 General Elections and in the 1959 General Election he was the Labour candidate in Preston South. In a by-election in 1962 he was elected as Member of Parliament for Leicester North-East. He remained MP for the constituency, which subsequently became Leicester East in 1974, until his defeat at the general election in 1983.

His maiden speech in Parliament was on the Offices, Shops and Railway Premises Bill that introduced minimum standards of working conditions and accommodation – legislation that the Association had sought for the railway industry since 1912. As a former railway clerk, he was able to describe in detail the poor working conditions which he and his colleagues had inherited from the private railway companies and which still remained a fact of life for many.

With the return of a Labour Government in 1964, Tom Bradley became Parliamentary Private Secretary to Roy Jenkins as the Minister of Aviation from 1964 to 1965, as the Home Secretary from 1965 to 1967 and as the Chancellor of the Exchequer from 1967 to 1970. Following the Labour Party's election defeat in 1970 Bradley became an opposition spokesman on Transport from 1970 to 1974, but did not take up a ministerial post in either of the 1974 Labour Governments. Following the Party's election defeat in 1979 he became Chairman of the Select Committee on Transport, holding that post until 1983.

He was a trade union representative on the National Executive Committee of the Labour Party from 1966 to 1981 and was Vice Chairman of the Party in 1974–1975 and Chairman of the Party in 1975–76. He resigned from the Labour Party in 1981 on his defection to the newly formed Social Democratic Party. One of the leaders of the new SDP was Roy Jenkins, for whom Tom Bradley had been Parliamentary Private Secretary from 1964 to 1970 and whose views and outlook he shared, particularly on Europe and on the leftward lurch of the Labour

Party at that time. It was as the Social Democratic Party candidate that Bradley lost his Leicester East seat at the 1983 General Election. A committed European, he was Director, British Section, European League for Economic Co-operation from 1979 to 1991, and also served for a period as Chairman of the Trade Union Committee for Europe.

Tom Bradley had a hard act to follow as the successor to Ray Gunter as President of the TSSA. He proved, though, to be a popular and well respected President who made sure his Parliamentary responsibilities did not impinge on his union commitments. It may well have been his desire to maintain his close identification with the Association and its members that led to his not becoming a junior minister in either of the 1974 Labour Governments, which would almost certainly have necessitated his resignation as President of the TSSA. Despite his departure from the Labour Party, he was an intensely loyal person to causes, to organisations and to people in which and in whom he believed, as his commitment to Europe, to the TSSA and to Roy Jenkins showed. The feeling must be that that loyalty may have led to him not achieving the levels of attainment in the political field that his ability and integrity deserved.

Richard Rosser

H N Brailsford (1873–1958)

Maynard Keynes famously asserted that the world is ruled by ideas and little else. If Labour historians were to accept this maxim then Henry Noel Brailsford, internationalist, prolific author and influential journalist, would command a more prominent place among the giants of the Labour movement.

Born in Mirfield, a Yorkshire colliery town, on 25 December 1873, Brailsford was educated in Scotland. His father was a Wesleyan Methodist preacher who worked mainly in Glasgow, where Brailsford junior attended university on a scholarship from 1890 and achieved a first class honours degree. In 1897 he left a putative academic career in Glasgow for a position with the *Scots Pictorial*. Journalism was to dominate the next fifty years of Brailsford's life, though not before he enjoyed a youthful spell in the Philhellenic Legion, a volunteer force fighting for the Greeks in their struggle with Turkey. Initially, Brailsford worked as a foreign correspondent for the *Manchester Guardian* in the Balkans, France and Egypt. In 1899 he moved to London, contributing to the *Morning Leader*, the *Star* and the *Nation* as well as becoming leader writer for the *Daily News*.

By virtue of his travels, Brailsford was now seen as something of an expert on the Balkans. He was selected to head the British relief mission to Macedonia in 1903, an experience which inspired a cultural and historical survey of the region, published in 1906.

In 1907, Brailsford joined the Independent Labour Party. He was to remain active within the ILP for a quarter of a century as a leading exponent of public ownership, the minimum wage and international federation. This growing enthusiasm for politics induced a prolific period of literary output, including *War of Steel and Gold* (1914), *Origins of the Great War* (1914) and *Belgium and the Scrap of Paper* (1915). The War government, unimpressed with Brailsford's outspoken criticism, gave him the rare distinction of demanding his books be impounded.

1917 saw the publication of his most influential work to date: the strikingly-named *A League of Nations*, which called for the establishment of an international organisation responsible for trade, foreign investment and the distribution of raw materials. Despite the fact that Woodrow Wilson borrowed heavily from his precepts in creating the League, Brailsford was wary of the limitations inherent in the US President's post-war settlement. He criticised the Versailles Treaty, predicting it would inflame German militarism, while also maintaining that a League of Nations dominated by imperialist powers would not address the roots of international conflict. After the rise of Fascism and collapse of the League, Brailsford finally concluded that only a federal world-order of socialist countries could secure peace through joint economic planning and disarmament.

After the Great War, Brailsford returned to Central and Eastern Europe. *Across the Blockade* (1919) and *After the Peace* (1920) recounted for a British audience the terrible privation suffered by people in the defeated Powers. Travelling further East, he became one of the first wave of Western socialists to bring home lessons from the Soviet experiment. Like many of his contemporaries, Brailsford was inspired by evidence that planning could produce rapid economic growth but repulsed by the concomitant suppression of freedoms. He always remained a democratic socialist, believing in constitutional means for the realisation of socialism through radical reform of parliament and the common ownership of property.

In 1922, Brailsford was appointed editor of the revamped ILP newspaper, *New Leader*. With a new attention to presentation and young writers such as George Bernard Shaw, H G Wells and Bertrand Russell, it was one of the most successful radical newspapers ever published. After 1924, Ramsay MacDonald became a particular target for the *New Leader* as the radical ILP lost patience with the Labour Prime Minister's near-indiscernible gradualism. A bolder programme was offered by Brailsford himself and the economist John Hobson in 1926. *The Living Wage* set out ambitious plans for a minimum wage, family allowances, price controls, the nationalisation of the Bank of England and the introduction of planning in domestic and export industries. The clear intention of the fifty-page pamphlet was to spur their parliamentary leaders onto a more radical socialist course.

In that same year, Fenner Brockway ousted Brailsford as editor of the *New Leader* in circumstances which the new man later regretted – despite his proven ability, many on the left of the party had simply distrusted the Glasgow graduate for his middle-class background. Brailsford eventually left the ILP in 1932, turning his energies to working for *the New Statesman*, the Left Book Club and, after 1937, *Tribune* magazine. During the Second World War, Brailsford broadcast for the BBC Overseas Service and continued writing books including *Subject India* (1943) and *Our Settlement with Germany* (1944). After this time he retired from journalism and his output diminished. He died of a stroke on 23 March 1958.

Henry Noel Brailsford helped to popularise socialist ideas at a crucial time for the movement, as Labour was establishing itself as a party of power. His first-hand experience of poverty and degradation across the world made Brailsford a vocal opponent of imperialism and inspired the unstinting advocacy of federated world government that runs throughout his work.

Neill Harvey-Smith

Fenner Brockway (Lord Brockway)   (1888–1988)

Born on 1 November 1888 in Calcutta to the third of three generations of Christian missionaries, Fenner Brockway was educated at the School for the Sons of Missionaries in Blackheath. At school, his campaigning skills were in early evidence when he led a crusade against homosexuality and masturbation. Although his views were soon to become more liberal, he never lost the sense of politics as a moral and even spiritual quest.

In his teens, Brockway campaigned on behalf of the Liberal Party, but having been sent, in an early journalistic commission, to interview Keir Hardie, his outlook quickly changed. As Brockway himself wrote: 'I went to see him a young liberal. I left him a young socialist'. He joined the Independent Labour Party in 1907 and was to remain one of its key figures for the next four decades.

His journalistic skills led him to work for the ILP newspaper, the *Labour Leader*, and at the age of twenty-four he became its editor. His first major political challenge arrived in the shape of the Great War. An instinctive pacifist and anti-imperialist, he made the *Labour Leader* one of the chief voices against the conflict. He also founded the No-Conscription Fellowship with Clifford Allen and ultimately left his position on the *Labour Leader* to concentrate more on the Fellowship's support for conscientious objectors and its campaign for peace.

The decision had a high personal cost. As a newspaper editor Brockway was exempt from military service, but once he resigned his post, the full weight of the law was brought to bear and he spent the remaining years of the War doing hard labour in Wormwood Scrubs and Walton prison. Ironically, his irrepressible drive to write meant he was soon editing again, producing an underground prison newspaper, the *Walton Leader*, written on toilet paper.

Between the wars Brockway had a varied career. He became Organising Secretary of the ILP, worked for the Webbs' Prison System Enquiry Committee and edited *British Worker*, the newspaper of the labour movement during the General Strike. In May 1929, he was elected MP for East Leyton. However, this first phase of his parliamentary career was cut short when he lost his seat in the 1931 election following the debacle of MacDonald's National Government.

In the same year, Brockway made what he later described as 'a stupid and disastrous error' by throwing his considerable influence behind the ILP's decision to disaffiliate from the Labour Party. From that point on, he witnessed, with great sadness, the gradual decline of the organisation for which he had worked so hard.

However, during this period Brockway's own reputation grew, establishing him as a figure deeply involved in internationalism and struggles for rights and liberation overseas, most notably with regards to India. He also spent the 1920s and 1930s campaigning for pacifism inside the Labour Party, working within the Socialist International and becoming Chairman of the Central Board of Conscientious Objectors during the Second World War. The appointment was somewhat at odds with his rejection of pacifism in the face of the fascist threat but he continued to argue for the right to refuse military service on the grounds of personal liberty.

Following the Labour victory in 1945, Brockway was impressed by the Attlee Government and felt it was time to leave the withered ILP. In 1950, he began a parliamentary career that was to last until the end of his life. Elected as MP for Eton and Slough, the House of Commons offered a platform which allowed him to take on a truly international role. At a time when the British Empire was in rapid decline, he founded the Movement for Colonial Freedom in 1954 which aimed to mobilise British public support for liberation. He spoke regularly in the House of Commons on colonial matters, often being jokingly referred to as 'the Member for Africa'. And following the Suez Crisis, Brockway's long record as an anti-imperialist allowed him to play a key part in attempts to secure – not always successfully – a peaceful and fair transition to independence for numerous countries including Kenya, Tunisia, Madagascar, Ghana, Cyprus, Malta and British Guiana.

In this extraordinarily active period of his life, he also found time to organise early campaigns against apartheid in South Africa and nuclear weapons and to introduce regular Private Members Bills designed to outlaw racial discrimination.

He lost his seat in 1964 by eleven votes and after some soul-searching accepted a peerage and became Baron Brockway of Eton and Slough. Inside and outside the House of Lords, he continued campaigning on the issues for which he was now well-known. Despite heart problems and illnesses, often suffered during his many trips abroad, Fenner Brockway was writing and campaigning until his death on 28 April 1988, in Watford General Hospital, a few months short of his one hundredth birthday.

Brockway managed to combine five careers into one lifetime as journalist, leading party activist, social movement campaigner, parliamentarian, and unofficial diplomat and negotiator. Although he never held a government post, he skilfully employed all five roles to shape labour movement attitudes on race, internationalism and peace. However, he will certainly remain best-known as a man who became the prime domestic campaigner and a key international facilitator for the liberation of the British colonies.

Fenner Brockway wrote numerous books and pamphlets about the issues closest to his heart. Works of reminiscence and exposition of his core values include: *Inside the Left; Outside the Right; Towards Tomorrow;* and *98 Not Out*.

Adam Lent

George Brown (Lord George-Brown)   (1914–85)

George Brown was Deputy Leader of the Labour party 1960–70 and, as First Secretary of State and then Foreign Secretary in Harold Wilson's Government, Deputy Prime Minister from 1964 to 1968. He entered Parliament in 1945 for Belper, and quickly made his mark. He was Minister of Works and a Privy Counsellor in 1951 and rose steadily though the party during its thirteen years in Opposition. He challenged for the leadership on Hugh Gaitskell's death in 1963 but lost to Wilson by 144 votes to 103.

George Brown was in every sense a colourful character. He had a natural instinct for politics and a forceful personality. He had a first-class mind and could be passionate in debate. He was easily recognised by the public, which enjoyed his style and forgave him his shortcomings. Most of these resulted from a volatile temperament often fuelled by too much to drink. In the end he threw away his career. He was only 56 when he lost his seat but he made no significant contribution to politics thereafter. He sat in the House of Lords but left the Labour party in March 1976. He was an embarrassment rather than an asset to his old friends who founded the SDP when he chose to join them in 1981.

George Alfred Brown was born in Southwark on 2 September 1914, the son of a lorry driver. He left school at 16 and became a fur salesman. He then graduated into a full-time official of the Transport and General Union which sponsored him for Parliament. Already, at the Labour party conference of 1939, he had made a striking debut with a speech in favour of the expulsion of Sir Stafford Cripps. When, six years later, Hugh Dalton, then Chancellor of the Exchequer, held a Young Victors party for new Labour MPs, George Brown was amongst twelve of his most promising contemporaries, nine of whom were to become Ministers. Appointed PPS to Minister of Labour George Isaacs in 1945, and subsequently to Hugh Dalton in 1947, he served as Joint Parliamentary Under-Secretary at the Ministry of Agriculture from October 1947 until his appointment as Minister of Works in April 1951.

In the years of opposition after 1951, George Brown rose steadily in the party. He was elected to the shadow cabinet in 1955 and in November 1956 became its spokesman on Defence, after brief stints shadowing first Agriculture and then Labour. When the Soviet leader Nikita Khruschev came to London and was entertained by the National Executive Committee, George Brown had a noisy exchange with him that upset his colleagues but brought him into the public eye as a man of strong views, boldly expressed. In 1961 he became Shadow Home Secretary. He was a commanding speaker both in and out of Parliament and won praise for an impromptu civil liberties speech against the expulsion of African asylum seeker, Chief Enharo. Later, in 1962, he showed great skill in his robust advocacy of the case for Britain joining the Common Market at the end of a notable debate at the party conference.

George Brown was the obvious candidate of the right and centre of the party to succeed Hugh Gaitskell as leader. But he had already acquired a reputation of being unpredictable and sometimes 'overwrought'. A number of his natural supporters in the Parliamentary Labour Party preferred Jim Callaghan, or believed that Wilson, although the candidate of the left, was a safer all-round choice. In the event, Wilson's election was a blow to George Brown from which he never quite recovered. Wilson treated him fairly, recognising his qualities and his standing in the party and with the public. But Brown was suspicious and often imagined slights where there were none.

Initially, however, after a short pause to recover from the immediate shock of defeat, he knuckled down to widen his horizons, particularly on home affairs, and to prepare himself for government. When in October 1964 Wilson became Prime Minister, Brown, together with Jim Callaghan, made up the triumvirate upon which the Government was to depend.

Brown threw himself with immense energy into creating the Department of Economic Affairs, bringing together career civil servants and a very talented group of outsiders from business and academia. Within two months he had persuaded the CBI and the TUC to agree to a Declaration of Intent committing themselves to a voluntary incomes policy. Within a year there was a National Plan for sustained economic growth and Economic Planning Councils had been set up in almost every region. It was a huge personal achievement, the result of working immensely long hours, breaking every convention to get his own way and successively bullying and charming and ultimately exhausting those whose support he required.

But the parlous economic state of the country was an enemy of the DEA's work. Short-term problems defeated long-term strategies. The situation was aggravated by the

Government's failure to devalue the pound immediately after the election, a course which Brown advocated but Wilson and Callaghan opposed. The National Plan was out of date and hopelessly optimistic by the time it was published and a voluntary gave way to a statutory incomes policy in the summer of 1966. Regional Economic Planning Councils did some useful work but eventually lost their momentum. Within two years, the DEA was in decline and George Brown confessed to his friends that he personally was over the hill.

But when he was moved to the Foreign Office in August 1966 it was no humiliation. George Brown had long believed in Britain's membership of the European Economic Community and now was his chance to support the Labour Government's bid to enter. He was proud to follow in the footsteps of Ernest Bevin, a trade union leader who had become a great Labour Foreign Secretary. He soon acquired a reputation for being rough with officials and rude to their wives, and he did not much enjoy the confident ambience of the Foreign Office. But he gave his mind to difficult, detailed problems in the Middle East (including Britain's withdrawal from Aden) as well as the macro issues of the Cold War and Britain's relations with the United States at the time of Vietnam. He might have been an outstanding Foreign Secretary in a different era when heavy drinking and threats of resignation would have remained a private matter. But when in March 1968 he finally resigned, the event was no great surprise and, for some, a considerable relief.

In 1970, despite favourable opinion polls, Labour won its smallest share of the national vote for thirty-five years. In Belper there was a 5 per cent swing to the Conservatives, which was sufficient to push George Brown out. In his younger days he would have fought a by-election at the earliest opportunity and played a full part in rebuilding Labour in opposition. But he knew that he was well into the autumn of his political life and would never again command the same influence and status. He was created Lord George-Brown in 1970. He did some campaigning for friends in the elections of 1974, and the following year he supported a 'Yes' vote in the referendum on Britain's continued membership of the Common Market. But for the most part during the 1970s he earned a good living from newspaper articles and business ventures and his celebrity status. Finally, ill and in obvious decline, and having left his wife Sophie after over 40 years of marriage, he retired to a remote cottage in Cornwall and died in a Truro hospital on 2 June 1985.

The obituaries were a reminder of his larger-than-life career. 'Explosive and unpredictable but the nation loved him' was the *Daily Telegraph's* verdict. 'Hero-figure, fall guy, public entertainer' said the *Guardian*. In the *Financial Times* a former Cabinet Secretary described him as someone 'who always seemed to be at war with himself...finally betrayed by the defects of his personality'; and the *Times* honoured him with a leading article as 'The Nearly Man'.

George Brown was ultimately a tragic figure and his a wasted life. But for many years he brought his outstanding talents to the service of the Labour Movement, winning the admiration of his friends and the respect of many who differed from him. George Brown's autobiography was called *In my Way* (1972). See also *Tired and Emotional, the life of Lord George-Brown* by Peter Paterson (1993). Otherwise there are frequent references in the biographies and autobiographies of his contemporaries.

Rt Hon. Lord Rodgers of Quarry Bank

Gordon Brown   (1951–)

Slogans declaring 'schools and hospitals first' were plastered across billboards and on party battlebuses as Labour went in for the kill at the 2001 election. The contest with the Tories was fought for the first time on Labour territory, the future of public services, rather than tax cuts. Labour won a second consecutive clear victory at the polls for the first time in the party's history by successfully wresting the agenda from the Tories. Tony Blair as Labour leader and premier rightly took his bow, but those in the upper echelons of the Millbank Tower hierarchy were in little doubt that the strategy belonged to Gordon Brown.

The most successful Chancellor of the Exchequer the party has ever known had planned the campaign he chaired from before the 1997 triumph. In the enviable – if not unique – position for a Labour Treasury man of going into the contest boasting of his economic record, he could argue in the campaign that the party was opening the public purse rather than tightening its belt. Brown had teasingly introduced that slogan two months before when, winding up his final Budget before putting the government's fate in the hands of the electorate, he told MPs: 'We have made our choice: more investment, not less; stability the foundation; tax cuts we can afford; schools and hospitals first. I commend this Budget to the House.'

Defeating the Tories by offering what were record increases in public investment (genuine rises at that, unlike the triple-counted figures that backfired so spectacularly in 1998) when the Opposition was offering reductions to fund tax cuts worried some in No 10. A number of special advisers in the Blair court wanted the Prime Minister to force his Downing Street neighbour to offer 1p off the basic rate to reassure Middle Britain, and tried to bounce Brown with newspaper leaks of rows. But the Chancellor stood firm, proposing vaguer targeted cuts. He kept a repeat of the pledge four years earlier not to raise the basic or top income tax levels off the pledge card, though he agreed it should be in the manifesto. And when the Tories fanned fears during the campaign that Labour would abolish the ceiling on National Insurance contributions, Brown again resisted pressure from Blair to rule it out. A prudent Chancellor, even one who insists it is 'prudence with a purpose', never wants to close off a means of filling his coffers.

Brown is New Labour family but Old Labour friendly, a conviction politician who still believes in redistribution but does it by stealth and calls it fairness. He is Red Gordon, the democratic socialist committed to making Britain a fairer place by raising the incomes of the worst off and abolishing child poverty at home, while abroad he fights to relieve the debt burden crushing so many developing nations. Full employment has been restored as a central goal, an achievable goal at that, as those big rises in public spending promise to transform health and education. Anti-establishment and a closet republican, he is more at home hobnobbing with the leaders of the TUC than schmoozing with the bosses of the CBI and he could go to the Transport and General Workers Union conference in June 2001 to speak sincerely of 'our union' and 'our General Secretary' without delegates accusing him of hamming it up.

And he is also the Iron Chancellor, a chief architect of New Labour who believes Mrs Thatcher did not go far enough in encouraging enterprise and is convinced the private sector can deliver some public services more effectively than the state. Improved benefits are tied to work and during his first two years in Great George Street he stuck to expenditure targets inherited from the Conservatives that put hospitals and schools under an intolerable strain. Nigh on impossible to shift even if a decision is politically damaging, as in the case of the 75p peanuts for pensioners, he is sometimes accused of treating government colleagues with contempt.

Brown does not recognise the Red Gordon–Iron Chancellor split and argues that social justice and economic competence go hand in hand. Turning 50 in 2001, he was the dominant figure in the Government: chief executive to Tony Blair's chairman. He was the clear favourite to move from No 11 to No 10 should his colleague and friend step down as Prime Minister during the second term. Even jibes from his critics that he could never get the top job because voters would only back a 'happy family man' have dissolved. In August 2000 he married Sarah Macaulay, a PR consultant and fellow Raith Rovers fan. In July 2001 they announced she was pregnant, that vote-enhancing baby due in February 2002.

James Gordon Brown was born on 20 February 1951, the middle son of a Church of Scotland minister who imbued social justice and a deep sense of right and wrong in all three during their Fife upbringing. Prodigiously precocious, the Chancellor-to-be could, aged four, recite the Reverend Awdry's *Thomas the Tank Engine* when he was despatched to Kirkcaldy West primary school and skipped two grades in a couple of weeks. His father also took him to watch Raith Rovers, kindling a passion that has dogged him ever since. Brown, a keen sportsman, stopped playing contact games and sticks to tennis after a teenage rugby injury left him blind in his left eye. But unlike some of his New Labour colleagues, his passion for football is genuine and, marooned in London when Rovers made it to a Scottish cup final, he was forced to listen to the commentary on the phone while a friend in Edinburgh held the receiver next to a radio.

Brown was, unlike Blair, also consumed by politics from an early age and remembers listening while still only eight to reports of Hugh Gaitskell's defeat in 1959. Four years on and another Kirkcaldy old boy, Adam Smith, would have been proud of him when the interest in politics was fused with the first evidence of his economic flair when he produced, with his elder brother John, a newsletter sold for charity. Soon after his 15th birthday Brown had five straight As in his Highers and was writing fluently about politics, showing particular interest along with lifelong friend Murray Elder in Lloyd George and the historic 1909 Liberal budget.

At 16 he was at Edinburgh University where he was consumed by politics, eventually being elected Rector (1972–75) and publishing a labour of love on Red Clydesider James Maxton, even if his PhD was not completed until 1982. A part-time lectureship and work as a TV producer followed. Brown secured election to the Scottish Labour Party's executive in 1977 (serving until 1983–84, when he was Chair of the Scottish Labour Party) and contesting Edinburgh South at the 1979 election before he was elected to represent Dunfermline East in the House of Commons during Labour's catastrophic defeat of 1983. Still aged only 32, he was two years younger than Blair, who entered Parliament the same year.

His rise through the ranks of the PLP was rapid; from 1985 he was an opposition Trade and Industry spokesman, 1987–89 Shadow Chief Secretary to the Treasury, 1989–92 Shadow Trade and Industry Secretary, 1992 Shadow Chancellor and, from May 1997, Chancellor of the Exchequer. Early on he clearly had the edge on Blair, joining the shadow cabinet in 1987, ahead of him by two years, and making his name in 1988 by lacerating Tory Chancellor Nigel Lawson while standing in for John Smith (who had suffered his first heart attack) when the future Prime

Minister was still relatively unproven. Then Blair was to become Shadow Home Secretary after 1992 and used Brown's 'tough on crime, tough on the causes of crime' soundbite to dramatically enhance his reputation while the elder of the two redrew Labour's economic policies to ditch the tax-and-spend position that had been ruthlessly destroyed by John Major.

Smith's sudden death in 1994 stunned Brown, leaving him genuinely bereft. As he mourned, Mandelson and Alastair Campbell were already plotting Blair's leadership bid. Brown and Blair had a pact, the elder believing the younger would support him. But Blair emerged more ambitious and ruthless, manoeuvring his colleague and rival to back down. Those closest to Brown are adamant the pair made a fresh agreement. One part saw Blair conceding control of economic policy to his Shadow Chancellor; the other had Blair suggesting that he would step down during a second term and back Brown for the Labour leadership and, hopefully, the Premiership. That period in 1994 strained relations, but both men recognised they either succeeded or failed together, much of the infighting since having been the jousting between jealous rival followers rather than the two key figures in New Labour.

Brown never forgave Peter Mandelson, however, for privately backing Blair while suggesting to Brown that he was neutral. The result was an ongoing feud that spread beyond the two main protagonists and disrupted the party and government. Brown's supporters were blamed for the disclosure of Mandelson's secret £373,000 cut-price home loan at Christmas 1999 that forced the Chancellor's rival into his first resignation. Mandelson's second resignation after he lied about his role in the Hinduja passport affair could not be pinned on Brown, but he made little attempt to hide his contempt for his old foe. When the Hammond report was published after an internal inquiry and found no wrong-doing by Mandelson, Brown and John Prescott were heard joking during a joint trip to Yorkshire that he would never hold high office again anyway.

Brown is a workaholic and if he did not keep his pre-election promise to hit the ground running in 1997 it was only because he was out of the Treasury traps like a sprinter and kept up a pace more fitted to a machine than a man. Independence for the Bank of England was followed by reform of the City regulatory system. The minimum wage, working families tax credit and a host of initiatives followed. He could point to one million new jobs and significant increases in the living standards of the lowest paid among his achievements.

The £5bn windfall tax on the highly profitable privatised utilities was levied to fund the New Deal; tax credits scrapped on share deals by City institutions to raise a similar sum on an annual basis to ease borrowing. Brown punched Britain's weight on the world stage, playing a prominent role in IMF discussions to prevent a Far East recession spreading to the West and championing the case for Third World debt relief. Increasing Britain's aid spending in tandem with Clare Short was one of his greater if unsung achievements, reversing cuts imposed during a Tory era when charity stopped at the Channel Tunnel.

Cabinet colleagues complain that if the workaholic Chancellor would consult his colleagues more, he would be liked as well as respected. Brown creates enemies with his single-mindedness, occasionally exasperating Blair, while Stephen Byers and Alan Milburn head the queue of cabinet ministers complaining that he appears to wants to run their departments as well as the Treasury. Exclusive rather than inclusive, accused of ruling through a clique, he eased out Treasury Permanent Secretary Terry Burns and at one point was at daggers drawn with

Bank of England Governor Eddie George – the latter subsequently emerging as an ally in the debate over whether Labour should hold a euro referendum during its second term.

His thinking is heavily influenced by the US, hence his obsession with the value of the Private Finance Initiative and public-private partnerships which put his relations with those on the centre-left and in the public sector unions under genuine strain. Who provides a service, a public agency or private company, matters far less to him than the quality of the service delivered.

He is also de facto the keeper of the government's euro policy, whatever the concerns of No 10. Brown appears to have genuinely gone euro cautious after believing in opposition that Britain should join the single currency at the earliest possible opening. The crisis of October 1997, when his press secretary Charlie Whelan briefed the media from Whitehall's Red Lion public house that there would be no referendum in the first Parliament, was a personal disaster. But Brown turned it round, giving a sparkling performance in the Commons to announce five tests that were economic in content but political in purpose. Blair's own press secretary Alastair Campbell had suggested to Brown that the Prime Minister should make the statement after the Treasury had badly mishandled the first shift. Brown, not a man to mince his words, replied: 'Well, if that's the case, there's not much point in me being Chancellor.' The potentially explosive threat was instantly clear to Campbell, who immediately backed off.

When Blair described Brown as his Lloyd George, it was never fully clear whether he cast himself as H. H. Asquith. At the start of Labour's second term, Brown wanted speculation about the possibility of him succeeding Blair – as Lloyd George did Asquith – to end, because even a man still ambitious for the Premiership recognised that the speculation was destabilising. But there was no doubt he still had a burning desire to emulate Lloyd George, his hero from primary school all those years ago. Brown would not want to be remembered as the best Prime Minister Labour never had.

His publications include: *The Red Paper on Scotland* (ed. 1975, with Dr Henry Drucker); *The Politics of Nationalism and Devolution* (1980); *Scotland: the real divide* (ed. 1983); *Maxton* (1986); *Where there is Greed* (1989). Biographies of Brown include Paul Routledge, *Gordon Brown, the Biography* (1998); and Hugh Pym and Nick Kochan, *Gordon Brown – The First Year in Power* (1998).

Kevin Maguire

Nick Brown (1950–)

Nick Brown's part in the New Labour project is not easy to define. With a background in both the trade union movement (GMB Northern Region Legal Advisor, 1978–83), and as a councillor on Newcastle City Council (1980–83), he was first elected to Parliament in 1983, and currently holds the seat of Newcastle East and Wallsend with a large majority. Neither a New Labour clone, nor an Old Labour hack, Brown is an extremely likeable yet shrewd political operator. An intellectual heavyweight, Brown was born on 13 June 1950 and worked his way up via Swatenden Secondary Modern School, Tunbridge Wells Technical High School, and Manchester University. He realised early on that, if Labour were ever to become electable again, the party needed to overhaul its attitudes towards both employment and economic policy. Well respected by both Neil Kinnock and John Smith, he was appointed assistant spokesman on Legal Affairs only two years after entering Parliament. By 1987, he had joined the Shadow Treasury team and, with John Smith, played a crucial role in helping to weed out some of Labour's more eccentric economic policy commitments. It would be very wrong, however, to see him as an early architect of what became known as New Labour. Despite being Labour's deputy campaign co-ordinator and Shadow Deputy Leader of the House of Commons from 1992 to 1994, and in spite of a former career designing advertising campaigns for Proctor & Gamble, Brown always favoured the intellectual rigour of a well-argued policy over cheap, superficial gimmicks. Consequently, he is well respected across the political spectrum. Although he is, in crude terms, on the right of the party, he remains faithful to the ideals of the democratic socialist party which he joined as a teenager in the 1960s.

In the years leading up to the 1997 General Election, Brown's contribution was very important behind the scenes in keeping good discipline among Labour MPs. As Deputy Opposition Chief Whip, Brown had a reputation of being firm but fair. This was backed up by the fact that, when required, he could be extremely ruthless at ensuring that no maverick Labour MP stood in the way of the greater goal of expelling the Tories from power. After the election, he was rewarded with a promotion to the position of Chief Whip. The party management problems were now very different, with a large new intake of Labour MPs keen to make their mark. In such a situation, discipline was always going to be important, if the new Government was not to be seen as a large and inexperienced rabble. Insofar that they were not is credit to his management skills, and friends and foes alike admit that in his role as Chief Whip he was generally very effective.

For those more interested in personalities than in policies, the biggest mistake Nick Brown ever made was to back the wrong horse. Back in 1994, Brown had privately canvassed support for his long-standing friend, Gordon Brown, in the run-up to the Labour leadership election. This, in itself, although not a crime, did not endear him to the new leader, Tony Blair, who was keen to stamp his authority on the party. But worse was to come. Shortly after the general election, Brown was accused of providing material for an unofficial biography of the Chancellor, Gordon Brown, which highlighted the rivalry between the Brown and Blair camps. The Prime Minister was not amused, and it is widely believed that the sideways move of Nick Brown from the Chief Whip's office to the Ministry for Agriculture was Blair's way of getting revenge.

The rural hinterland was seen as a stepping stone for easing Brown out of the Cabinet altogether. However, Brown was not to be beaten so easily. Traditionally, agriculture is to Labour what unemployment is to the Tories: a no-win policy area. But given the fact that, when Brown took over, the agricultural industry was in complete meltdown, it would be fair to say that chalices rarely come more poisoned. Brown rose to the challenge. Although coming from an inner-city seat, and with little in the way of direct agricultural experience, Brown soon won the respect of farmers across the country with his honest, plain-speaking, and quick mastery of an unfamiliar and complex brief. And it is difficult to imagine who else could have crowbarred a quarter of a billion pounds out of the Treasury as a rescue package for an industry ravaged by BSE and a host of other disasters. Farmers may never be natural allies of the Labour movement, but because of Nick Brown, they have a lot to be thankful for.

However, his contribution whilst at the Ministry of Agriculture was not just to give new life to an industry that otherwise would have surely gone under. He must also take some credit for establishing the Food Standards Agency. Although a party manifesto commitment, Brown was responsible for getting it on the statute book. Having witnessed John Gummer's handling of the BSE crisis, Brown was keen to see that, in future, there should be no conflict of interest between the protection of the economic vitality of an industry and consumer safety. In particular, Brown passionately believed that the BSE crisis, created in part by Tory mismanagement, should never be allowed to happen again. Whilst campaigners will say that the provision is still not strong enough, it is nevertheless true that we all benefit from much greater food safety protection at the end of the first Labour term, thanks in part to Nick Brown's efforts whilst at the Ministry of Agriculture.

Despite all his best efforts, however, the handling of the foot-and-mouth outbreak in spring 2001 was not seen as MAFF's finest hour, and Blair took the opportunity of the 2001 post-election reshuffle to break up MAFF as a ministry. Though his detractors sought to scapegoat Nick Brown, his appointment as the new Minister for Work in June 2001 is a clear indication that his ministerial ability remains a valued asset to the government: along with John Spellar he is a non-Cabinet Minister who attends Cabinet, the traditional status of the Chief Whip's post he so enjoyed occupying.

Jake Turnbull

John Burns (1858–1943)

John Elliott Burns, a socialist hero of the 1880s and early 1890s, turned away from independent Labour representation and became a Liberal Cabinet minister, 1905–14. Although given to inflammatory rhetoric in the 1880s, Burns more characteristically exhibited the worthy features (anti-drink, anti-gambling) of the skilled worker. He had a high opinion of himself and exhibited hostility, even jealousy, towards Keir Hardie. To many in the Labour movement he was deemed to have 'sold out' to the Liberals in 1905.

Burns was born in Lambeth on 20 October 1858, the son of Alexander and Barbara Burns. His father was a Scottish engineer who had migrated to London in the 1850s. One of nine surviving children, Burns grew up in very modest circumstances, leaving school at ten or eleven. He attended night school and eagerly bought books. He saved sufficient to pay his way as an apprentice engineer. By 1878 he was active in radical politics. In 1881, after two years working for the United African Company, he returned to London a committed socialist.

Burns soon became probably the most effective working class orator in London. He was blessed with a very powerful voice and a strong presence. He was a star speaker for the Marxist Social Democratic Federation (SDF) and was elected to its executive committee in 1884. In 1885 he was the most successful of its parliamentary candidates, polling 598 votes in Nottingham West. He was prominent in the big London demonstrations of the period. He was arrested, tried but acquitted on a charge of riot over an SDF unemployed march to Trafalgar Square in 1886. The following year, after demonstrators tried to reach Trafalgar Square in disregard of a police ban, Burns received a six week prison sentence.

Burns had a powerful base of support in Battersea. After he had fallen out with the SDF leadership, the Battersea SDF branch became, in effect, his supporters' association. With its support, he topped the poll in early 1889 in the London County Council (LCC) election for Battersea. Later in the year, along with Tom Mann and Ben Tillett, he was a leader of the great London Dock strike. In that and the next few years Burns was at the height of his popularity and appeared the most important Labour figure. In October 1889 he was nominated to be the Socialist parliamentary candidate for Battersea. At the first socialist May Day in 1890 huge crowds marched to Hyde Park and the most popular of the many orators was Burns.

On the LCC Burns worked with the Progressives, who were Liberals and Radicals. He made a substantial impact in his early period (1889–94) but was less prominent later (1894–1907). Elected for Battersea in the 1892 general election, Burns got on badly with Keir Hardie, the other independent Labour MP, and increasingly preferred to work with Liberals and Radicals there too. Burns, backed by the Battersea Labour League, did not support the northern-based Independent Labour Party (ILP), when it was founded in 1893. Although Burns attended the foundation conference of the Labour Representation Committee in 1900, he did not align himself with it. He continued to act as a 'Lib-Lab' MP in Parliament and his politics, including his vigorous opposition to the Boer War and to tariffs, was similar to that of many Radicals. When Sir Henry Campbell-Bannerman formed a government in December 1905 he gave Burns the Cabinet post of President of the Local Government Board. It was said that Burns greeted this offer by congratulating Campbell-Bannerman for making such a popular move!

Burns, while President of the Local Government Board (1905–14), was notable for being an obstacle to radical change. Burns held many typical 'respectable' skilled worker attitudes, perhaps best summarised in his speech then pamphlet, *Brains Better than Bets or Beer: the Straight Tip to the Workers* (1902). He also shared many orthodox economic views concerning unemployment, and deplored many of the measures pressed successfully by Lloyd George and Churchill. After the 1909 Osborne Judgement, which undercut trade union funding of the Labour Party, Burns was among those in the Liberal Cabinet who did not wish to undo the law lords' verdict. In early 1914 Burns moved to be President of the Board of Trade. He resigned from the government in August 1914, in protest at British entry into the First World War. He did not stand again in the 1918 general election.

Burns married Martha Charlotte Gale in 1882. Their only child, a son, died in 1922. His wife died in 1936. Burns, who became something of a recluse, enjoying his library of books on the history of London and on politics, died on 24 January 1943. Biographies include: K D Brown, *John Burns*, (London, 1977); J Burgess, *John Burns: the Rise and Progress of a Rt. Honourable* (Glasgow, 1911); A P Grubb, *From Candle Factory to British Cabinet: the Life Story of the Rt Hon. John Burns* (London, 1908); W Kent, *John Burns: Labour's Lost Leader*, (London, 1950); and W Sanders, *Early Socialist Days* (London, 1927).

Professor Chris Wrigley

Noel Buxton (Lord Noel-Buxton of Aylsham)   (1869–1948)

Noel Buxton was one of a distinguished group of former Liberals who came into the Labour Party around the time of the First World War, frustrated by the compromised position of their former party, notably over foreign policy. He was born on 9 January 1869 in London, into a wealthy family; his father, Sir Thomas Fowell Buxton, was the director of a brewing company and his mother, Lady Victoria Noel, was the daughter of the Earl of Gainsborough. He came from a background which prized public service, and was particularly influenced by the example of his great grandfather, Sir Thomas Fowell Buxton, who was known as the 'Great Liberator' for his part in bringing about the abolition of slavery in the British empire: the condition of native peoples living under colonial rule was to be one of the many causes pursued by Noel Buxton during an active public life.

Noel Buxton spent most of his childhood on the family estate at Warlies in Essex. He was educated at Harrow, then studied at Trinity College, Cambridge, before going to work in the family brewery at Spitalfields. While living in the East End of London, he became involved in social work, and moved from this into local government, as a member of the Whitechapel Board of Guardians from 1897. With a group of radical liberals including CFG Masterman, he contributed to a study of social problems, *The Heart of Empire* (1901), writing on the issue of temperance. He fought his first Parliamentary contest in Ipswich in 1900 for the Liberal Party and was elected as Liberal MP for Whitby in 1905, though he lost the seat at the General Election of the following year. In January 1910 he became MP for North Norfolk. Whilst electioneering there he met his future wife, a Conservative, Lucy Pelham Burn, who was campaigning against him under the slogan 'No Noel for North Norfolk'. They married in 1914 and had six children. Although he had a long-standing commitment to social welfare, Buxton's main political interest by this time was in foreign affairs. He had travelled extensively and developed a passionate interest in the sufferings of minorities in the Balkans; with his brother Charles Roden Buxton, he helped found the Balkan Committee in 1902, which he headed until 1945. His writings on Eastern Europe included *Europe and the Turks* (1912) and *With the Bulgarian Staff* (1913).

He was involved in initiatives to promote peace between Britain and Germany and when war did break out in 1914 he and his brother Charles travelled to Bulgaria on a semi-official mission to secure Bulgarian neutrality. This set the scene for the most dramatic incident in his life, when the brothers were wounded in an attack by a Turkish would-be assassin in Bucharest. They became national heroes and a street in Sofia was named after them. During the war, Buxton continued to promote the possibility of a negotiated peace with the Germans. He found himself increasingly at odds with the Liberal Party's conduct of the war and was narrowly defeated in his constituency in 1918, standing as a 'Lib-Lab' candidate. He joined the Labour Party in 1919, and served as a member of its advisory committee on international questions. He became a close friend and travelling companion of the Labour leader, Ramsay MacDonald; there is an account of their motor tour of North Africa in his book *Travels and Reflections* (1929). Buxton regained North Norfolk in 1922, this time as a Labour MP. The Labour vote there seems to have been in large part a personal vote for Buxton, and his own politics remained heavily indebted to his Liberal background. He was never an ideological socialist, and argued that the Labour Party was merely carrying on what the Liberal Party should be doing, but no longer did.

In the first Labour Cabinet of 1924, Buxton was appointed Minister of Agriculture, though he had hoped for a role in the Foreign Office. As one of the Labour MPs representing an agricultural constituency, in one of the heartlands of the agricultural workers' union, he was perhaps an obvious choice. He proved a successful minister, and was responsible for piloting the Agricultural Wages Act of 1924 through parliament; this reinstituted minimum wage legislation for agricultural workers, and was one of the few constructive achievements of Ramsay MacDonald's first ministry. In 1929, when Labour returned to government, Buxton once more took on the agricultural portfolio, though he found his free trade principles difficult to reconcile with the demands of an industry sinking increasingly into depression and calling for protectionist measures. In June 1930, he retired from the Commons, on grounds of ill health, and accepted, with some reluctance, a place in the House of Lords as Lord Noel-Buxton of Aylsham: he was opposed on principle to hereditary political power. His wife Lucy took over as Labour candidate in North Norfolk, and narrowly managed to hang onto the seat at the 1930 by-election, though she lost it at the general election in the following year. With Noel Buxton as MP and Stephen Gee as agent, North Norfolk had been a success story for the Labour Party in rural England, but from 1930, Labour's strength there declined, and the seat was held by the Conservatives until 1945.

Noel-Buxton opposed MacDonald's decision to remain as Prime Minister in the National Government. During the 1930s, he devoted most of his energies towards charitable work, through his own family foundation, and as president (1930–48) of the Save the Children Fund. He had always been a vociferous critic of the Versailles settlement, and advocated the appeasement of Germany, endorsing its right to a colonial presence in Africa; he continued to argue for a negotiated peace after the outbreak of war in 1939. Germany appears in a poignant list amongst his papers, headed 'My Lost Causes'. He died on 12 September 1948 and was buried in the family churchyard in Upshire, Essex.

Although he served in two Labour governments, Noel Buxton's career of public service was defined throughout by a radical liberalism, which guided his approach to social welfare and foreign policy. A man of high principles, he was driven by an ethic of social responsibility, which found its outlet in philanthropic work as much as in political life. The key biography of Noel Buxton is the memoir by Mosa Anderson, *Noel Buxton. A Life* (London, 1952). Buxton drafted an autobiography, the typescript for which is in the archive at McGill University, Montreal, Canada. There is also useful material in his sister Victoria's biography of their brother Charles: Victoria De Bunsen, *Charles Roden Buxton: a Memoir* (1948).

Clare Griffiths

Stephen Byers (1953–)

Dubbed the 'fish man' by John Prescott, Stephen Byers is likely to remain infamous for advocating a weakening of Labour's links with the trade unions during a meal with journalists at the party's annual conference in 1996. One of New Labour's rising stars, Byers was quickly promoted after the 1997 general election, first as Education Minister, and then beat his long-standing rival Alan Milburn into the Cabinet when he was appointed Chief Secretary to the Treasury a year later.

He was made Trade and Industry Secretary following Peter Mandelson's first resignation from government in December 1998. During his tenure at the Department for Trade and Industry, Byers became one of the most outspoken and fervent supporters of Britain's entry into a European single currency in Tony Blair's administration. But, faced with job losses and a continuing crisis in the manufacturing industry, Byers' star began to wane by 2000 as critics claimed that he had failed to master his brief sufficiently competently to deserve further promotion in the Cabinet. In the post-election reshuffle of June 2001 he was moved to run the bulk of John Prescott's old empire as the new Secretary of State for Transport, Local Government and the Regions.

Byers was born 13 April 1953 in Wolverhampton, the son of Robert, an RAF radar technician, and Tryphena Mair. He attended Buxton County Primary and Chester City Grammar before he went on to study at Chester College of Further Education and gained a LLB at Liverpool Polytechnic. He joined the Labour Party in 1974 and, although he was a senior law lecturer at Newcastle Polytechnic until 1992, his political ambitions transpired quickly. He was elected to North Tyneside Metropolitan Borough Council in May 1980 and unsuccessfully fought Hexham in the 1983 general election.

He became Deputy Leader of North Tyneside Council in 1985 but failed to secure selections both for Blyth and Newcastle North. His quest for a parliamentary seat in the North East finally paid off in 1989 when he was selected for safe Wallsend after Ted Garrett announced he would not stand again after 25 years. Having previously had the disadvantage of being non-union sponsored, he secured UNISON backing after he reached the Commons. He retained Wallsend with a massive majority of 19,470 in the 1992 general election although the seat's boundaries were redrawn in 1995 and he is now the MP for Tyneside North.

He used his maiden speech to deplore the loss of shipbuilding jobs at Swan Hunter in his constituency. but his most long-standing interest has been in education. Not only was he chairman of education during years in local government, but he was also chairman of the National Employers Organisation for Teachers between 1990 and 1992 and served on the NEC's subcommittee on education. His various campaigns on the subject, once elected to Parliament, included protests against the 'fiasco surrounding the publication of the school examination results league tables' and the Assisted Places Scheme which, he alleged, had helped mostly middle-class parents. Even Tory-supporting newspapers admitted Byers deserved a 'gold star' for his work against the Education Bill enacting the opting out of schools.

He was quickly regarded as one of the new generation of bright, ambitious modernisers that formed part of Tony Blair's North East mafia and even complied with the stringent style rules laid down by Peter Mandelson when he shed his moustache in 1995. He was promoted to the position of Opposition Whip in 1994 and was appointed Assistant Spokesman on Education and Employment in David Blunkett's team in 1995. He became his deputy in the last pre-election reshuffle a year later.

His relationship with Labour's left hit turbulence after his briefing to journalists over the party's links with the union movement at its conference in Blackpool, and many observers suspected that he was being groomed by the leadership to fight a future New Labour government's battle to the death with the trade unions. But he was named Minister for school standards instead in May 1997, and moved quickly to introduce a White Paper on *Excellence in Schools* and introduced the second reading of the Education (Student Loans) Bill in July.

In his private life, Mr Byers briefly hit the headlines when he admitted in 1999 that he had fathered a love child when he was still a teenager but he now lives with his long-term partner Jan. He published *Rates and Unemployment* in 1992.

Sarah Schaefer

Jim Callaghan (Lord Callaghan of Cardiff) (1912–)

Leonard James Callaghan has been one of the major political figures in the United Kingdom of Great Britain and Northern Ireland in the last seventy years of the twentieth century. After 1945 and the election of the first Labour government with a majority in Parliament, he served as a junior minister at Transport (October 1947 – March 1950), the Admiralty (March 1950– October 1951) and, eventually, in the sixties, as Chancellor of the Exchequer and Home Secretary and, in the seventies, as Foreign Secretary and Prime Minister; the only figure in British politics to have achieved this feat. He has played a significant part m the political scene of the country as a whole and the Labour Party in particular. He represented Cardiff South for 42 years; he never neglected it.

James Callaghan typified the social background of the emerging Labour Party of the early twentieth century. Born on 27 March 1912, he was brought up in a one-parent family; his father, also James Callaghan, had died when he was a young boy. He was clever enough to pass the scholarship examination to Portsmouth Northern Secondary School, to achieve a good matriculation certificate when fifteen years of age and to pass the entrance examination for the civil service. But he had no university education, he often reflected ruefully, but then neither did most of those in his social class. He did read under the tutelage of the adult education bodies which flourished in the social scene of the time, supported by the ethos of the Fabian Society and the trade union movement. He married Audrey Elizabeth Moulton in 1938: they have a son and two daughters.

Later on he came under the influence of Harold Laski, as early on he had been under that of the Baptist Chapel. His basic socialism, however, did not come from books but from the reality of life. It was his strength, not weakness.

His union life was in a small organisation, the Inland Revenue Staffs Association, an early example of white-collar unionism. Passing the entrance exam for the position of tax officer was the relative equivalent of university entrance today. When he became a full-time union official he entered another field of endeavour. The place of the unions in the Party was important to Jim, they supported him when he was Treasurer of the Party 1967–76 (he served on Labour's NEC continuously throughout the period 1957–80). He entered battle on their side on a number of occasions, but they did not reciprocate on the economy in the seventies.

His Irish-born father had been a Chief Petty Officer in the Royal Navy – no mean feat and his father's memory was part of the wider influence in Jim's life in Portsmouth and Brixham. No wonder that with the advent of war young Callaghan became an officer in the Royal Navy. His service in the Far East provoked another influence on his beliefs – the need to aid colonial emancipation.

Thus it was that in the 1950s with election to the Shadow Cabinet every year from 1951 and on the NEC of the Labour Party, his main political interest was in colonial affairs. He met the emerging colonial leaders Tom Mboya, Kwame Nkrumah, Hastings Banda and Pandit Nehru and others. He appreciated their growing power and guided them often in the right tactical direction.

In all the political splits of the fifties Jim played for the middle ground, but always for the long-term aim of democratic socialism interlaced with the realisation that this development brings change in the realities themselves. It is not that problems end, but that problems themselves change. From 1951 to 1964 Labour was to be out of office, still supported by the old working class in the heavy industrial areas but spurned by the emerging social classes of white-collar suburbia. Governments win or lose elections but with all the troubles of a declining Churchill and the physical problems of Eden and Macmillan Labour only just won in 1964. The new triumvirate was Wilson, Brown and Callaghan. Bevan and Gaitskell had passed on.

Harold Wilson had become Prime Minister, George Brown the First Secretary of State at the Department of Economic Affairs and Jim Callaghan Chancellor of the Exchequer, having been Shadow Chancellor since 1961. With a small majority the government could not last long. It conducted itself well, however, and, above all, showed the new electorate that the Labour Party was not a bunch of undercover 'commies' and could govern. In March 1966 Wilson romped home with a large majority.

Basic issues, however, soon came home to roost. The value of sterling was suspect. The big three had agreed the new government could not devalue as in 1949. The pound was to be sacrosanct: one of the pillars of the Bretton Woods post-war settlement. It is very easy with hindsight to pontificate on the obvious need to have devalued. Free exchange rates were the result of the global economy, and the ending of the sterling balances were a consequence of our declining status.

Change in the Bank Rate was the stuff of politics. To devalue was failure. In my speech on the Queen's Speech of 1997 I quoted from Jim Callaghan's autobiography. On the first day he was Chancellor, he wrote: 'I was sitting at what had been Reggie Maudling's desk in the ground-floor study at 11 Downing Street. While I was reading the briefs which Treasury officials had prepared against the possibility of a Labour victory, he was in the upstairs flat with his wife, packing their belongings. On his way he put his head round the door, carrying a pile of suits over his arm. His comment was typical: "Sorry, old cock, to leave it in this shape. I suggested to Alec this morning that perhaps we should put up the bank rate but he thought that he ought to leave it all to you."'

The story of Jim's resignation over devaluation when it did become inevitable is part of Labour history, as was his subsequent transfer to the Home Office in November 1967. Immigration loomed there. The numbers had grown from year to year since the 1950s as cheap labour came in from the Caribbean, India and Pakistan. It forced change in immigration procedures and change in community-relations structures in the inner cities. Events, however, were to intervene when the nasty internal hatred in Kenya and Uganda, backed up by ill-thought-out 'citizenship' rules, forced out refugees. Callaghan as Home Secretary regulated the flow. Such a policy caused problems in the Labour Party itself even if it calmed the fears of the electorate. Enoch Powell caused fundamental problems for the Tory Party; he did the same for his political opponents as London dockers marched to his support. It all had an effect on the coming general election.

If immigration was negative in its effect on the Labour vote, despite a positive Race Relations Act and an urban aid programme, the response of Jim to the upsurge of violence in Northern Ireland showed the Labour Party in a good light. Jim in Belfast and Derry with the Army being welcomed by the Catholic population was the Home Secretary at his best.

Positive action was one thing but it did not cover up the splits in the party over the trade unions and Barbara Castle's white paper *In Place of Strife*. The basic divide on trade union law was there but it was exacerbated by Barbara Castle's response to the Donovan Report on the trade unions. Jim and the trade unions were against state regulation of the trade unions.

For whatever reason, despite public opinion polls giving more than a hope of a Labour Party victory, a Heath government came to power in 1970. In opposition again the old wounds reopened on Europe. The party was divided on the issue but with Jim as Shadow Foreign Secretary and his Council of Europe credentials a policy of 'renegotiation' headed off the immediate problem. By 1974 and the general election, with Labour as the biggest party and the pantomime talk of coalition between Heath and Thorpe, the reality of Labour's electoral weakness was plain. However, a minority Labour government came into power. The October 1974 General Election led to almost a repeat minority Labour Government; in fact it produced a majority of three.

There was no sign of a repeat of 1966 and certainly not of 1945. Politics was in the doldrums, with both main parties in Parliament divided on Europe and the electorate suspicious of them both. But there was a country to govern and there was work to be done.

Europe was still the main issue despite the Heath government's decision to enter. Renegotiation was the nub of the Foreign Secretary's policy. How to overcome the party split was the political question and an 'answer' was found in a referendum with members of the cabinet allowed to follow their own preferences. The 'Yes' vote won the day and Callaghan was one of its proponents without in any way weakening his pro-Atlantic principles.

He had learned as Chancellor that Britain was no longer a world power, and a further period in government had reinforced this view. So to keep us at the negotiating table needed the American alliance. On this basis Jim played an important part in Middle Eastern affairs and in Cyprus. He was a good and impressive Foreign Secretary, and this stood him in good stead when the political scene was transformed by Harold Wilson's resignation.

A few months earlier in 1975 Jim had taken me aside after the weekly Cabinet to tell me that Harold Wilson was to resign on his 60th birthday the following year; he had promised Mary. In retrospect these few prosaic words did not do justice to the surprise of the moment in the Foreign Secretary's room. Jim made it clear that he would be a candidate and asked me to be his campaign manager. In the meantime, no word to anybody.

The following year when the birthday arrived Harold announced his resignation to the world. A few weeks later after a series of votes by the Parliamentary Party Jim was elected leader and thus, after a visit to the Palace, he was Prime Minister.

On my way back to Northern Ireland I called in at his room to see him. He was to be the Prime Minister 'of the greatest country on earth' and emotional though that brief moment was it betokened his attitude to the new job which could not have been planned for but which arose out of events.

What do I recall about that period 1976–79 which ended with the disastrous election of 1979? One of the most significant events of his Premiership was the speech he made at Ruskin College, Oxford, in October 1976 initiating the Great Debate on Education which had an important effect on the world of education lasting to this day. He bothered about education at all levels, not only at the higher level. where he was the equivalent of Chancellor of the University of Wales at Swansea.

Another significant event in which I played a minor role was the Falklands conflict. In 1977 the Prime Minister called a meeting of the Defence and Overseas Policy Committee of the Cabinet. There were present David Owen, the lead minister because the subject being discussed was in the field of foreign affairs and defence. Fred Mulley, Secretary of State for Defence, was present, as also was the Chief of the Naval Staff. As Jim unfolded the story it became clear that the Argentinians were planning to invade the Falklands. To cut the story short, the Prime Minister wanted to authorise two frigates to be held off the Falklands, together with a hunter-killer submarine nearby. We all agreed, and he instructed that clear terms of engagement were to be prepared. How were the Argentinians to be alerted to the presence of the submarine and to face the consequences of any invasion they mounted? After the meeting Jim took the Head of SIS for a walk in the garden at Number 10 telling him what had been agreed and asking him to use his best endeavours to allow the Argentinians to 'find out' the situation. The Argentinians did find out and they changed their plans! As in Northern Ireland, Jim was at his best.

Overall the Labour Party was living from hand to mouth, with no majority in the Commons and dependent on the support of a few Liberal MPs operating the so-called Lib-Lab pact. Parliamentary life was difficult. The international economic situation was precarious, the home economy was bleak with high unemployment and inflation; the fall in the value of the pound illustrated the growing balance of payments deficit.

The story of the IMF negotiations alone and the interminable Cabinet meetings that occupied them, when we all had to face up to a situation not dissimilar in my view to 1931 and the co-operation with the Trade Unions fast disappearing, made for a crisis. It was of this period that Denis Healey bluntly said that without Jim Callaghan's political skill the government would never have survived the negotiations. The economic situation improved but the trade unions were not prepared then to provide further agreements on pay. The Cabinet agreed on a 5 per cent pay norm, realising that this meant more like 7 per cent because of wage drift, but the 5% figure was what was taken on board by the unions.

As a result there was an outbreak of strikes, not leadership led but leadership followed. 1979 opened with a series of strikes by lorry drivers, tanker drivers, health workers, dustmen, grave diggers and railway workers. It all shattered the government's economic strategy. The TUC/Labour agreement of February 1979 came too late.

The election was upon us and Jim had not been alone in the Cabinet in wishing to delay an autumn date but a minority government could not have won that election and when it came to May 1979, despite Jim Callaghan's personal popularity, which was higher than that of the Leader of the Opposition, the Labour Party was beaten.

The social structure of the electorate, as in industry, was changing. The spirit of equality in which Jim believed so much was over. The Thatcherite mood was in the ascendancy. After the election Jim Callaghan agreed to stay on as Leader of the Opposition for a short time to allow elections to take place for a successor. Michael Foot was his successor in 1980, but the long-term position required a Neil Kinnock to alter the structure of the Labour Party, then John Smith, to be followed by Tony Blair. Change required a new generation. Jim Callaghan had made a major contribution to the development of the Labour Party in particular and to British politics in general. He left the Commons in 1987 and continued to play his part in the House of Lords. It had been a long journey from Portsmouth to the Rt Hon. Lord Callaghan of Cardiff, KG. He published *A House Divided: the Dilemma of Northern Ireland*, in 1973, and his autobiography, *Time and Chance*, in 1987. His authorised biography, by Kenneth O Morgan, *Callaghan: A Life,* was published in 1997.

Rt Hon. Lord Merlyn-Rees

Alastair Campbell (1957–)

The Labour Party has had a long tradition of journalists turning their hands to the world of politics – among them Michael Foot, Tom Driberg and Gerald Kaufman – but none has succeeded in the way that Alastair Campbell has. He is arguably the most influential journalist that there has ever been in British politics and his achievements are remarkable by any standards. He has helped to redefine the communications culture of Whitehall; enabled the Labour Party to broaden its appeal with the electorate through the tabloid press; and played a major role in changing the nature of modern political discourse. He has succeeded through a combination of focus (concentrating only on his areas of expertise), discipline (no alcohol or long lunches) and dedication (working long hours in a highly pressured environment). His success has been underpinned by an instinctive grasp of the needs of political journalists and knowing exactly when and how to deliver what they want.

Alastair Campbell was born on 25 May 1957 in Keighley, Yorkshire. In the late sixties his family moved to Leicester and he spent his high school years at City of Leicester Boys' School before winning a place at Gonville and Caius College, Cambridge, to study Medieval and Modern Languages (French and German). Campbell's period at Cambridge was not the happiest period in his life as he has readily admitted: 'I could not hack it. I was too young and too chippy. I drank too much and stayed away – going to football matches to see Burnley.' However, his Cambridge experience was crucial in forming the anti-establishment outlook which would later guide his political philosophy as Tony Blair's Chief Press Secretary. Like many others in the Labour Party who studied at Oxbridge, he found the public school educated undergraduates to be risible both in terms of their privileged lifestyle and arrogance.

After a series of freelance writing jobs, and a brief spell as a croupier, Campbell joined the *Daily Mirror* on a traineeship and established himself as one of the paper's brightest reporters. He soon became political correspondent of the *Daily Mirror* and then political editor of the *Sunday Mirror*. During this period he formed two of his most important relationships. The first was with Fiona Millar, a fellow journalist, who would later become his partner and the mother of his children. The Millar family was part of the Labour establishment. Fiona's father, Bob, had written for *Tribune* and it was under his guidance that Campbell began to develop a closer interest in politics.

The second relationship was with Neil Kinnock, the then leader of the Labour Party. He got to know Kinnock whilst working in the lobby and almost immediately became his most loyal champion in Fleet Street as well as his speechwriter and political confidante. It was easy to see why the two men got on as they had much in common. Both possessed ebullient personalities, emotional temperaments and a fierce devotion to their friends. Many believe that had Labour won the 1992 general election, Campbell would have entered 10 Downing Street as Kinnock's press secretary. Instead Labour were defeated for the fourth time in a row, John Smith was elected leader and Campbell lost his influence with the party's establishment.

By this time Campbell was political editor of the *Daily Mirror*, a post he held until his move to *Today* in 1993, where he rejoined one of his former editors, Richard Stott. Campbell's career at *Today* was short-lived. In May 1994 John Smith died of a heart attack and in the immediate aftermath Campbell was one of the first journalists to predict that Tony Blair would become the next leader of the Labour Party. Four months later he was appointed Blair's chief press secretary. He brought tremendous journalistic flair to all Blair's speeches, articles and interviews – and ensured that Labour's communications had a sure populist touch. More significantly, he was instrumental in helping the new Labour leader reach parts of the electorate that had eluded his predecessors through carefully cultivating the tabloid press.

Since September 1994 Campbell has played a vital role in all the important events of Blair's leadership: the rewriting of Labour's Clause IV; the 1997 general election campaign; the Prime Minister's response to Princess Diana's death; the Good Friday Agreement; the 1999 war in Kosovo; the fuel protests of September 2000; and the foot-and-mouth crisis of spring 2001.

He has been a hugely controversial figure during this period, facing constant attacks in parliament and the press, and accusations that he is the real Deputy Prime Minister. The fact that he is powerful is not disputed, but it is important to remember that he is only powerful because of the immense power of the British media. Campbell learnt some harsh lessons during the eighties. He saw how a decent and civilised man – Neil Kinnock – was destroyed by the Tory press and never given the opportunity to connect with the electorate. He was determined that would not happen to Tony Blair. He has used his considerable skills with only one aim in mind – to ensure the election of a Labour Government. Unlike many in the upper echelons of modern politics he is not motivated by money or status: he has acquired his power for a purpose.

Alastair Campbell is a thoroughly modern political figure yet he possesses some thoroughly traditional Labour virtues: passion, loyalty and a visceral contempt for the Tories. The party has much to thank him for and there is no doubt that over time he will make an even greater contribution to British political life.

Jayant Chavda

Les Cannon (1920–70)

The mention of Les Cannon's name roused mid-twentieth-century trade union opinion more emphatically than any of his contemporaries. His intellectual power, organisational energy and unwillingness to tolerate fools were legendary. From 1945 to 1956 he was one of the Communist Party's most convincing voices. After 1956, until he died of cancer in December 1970, he exposed communist malfeasance in trade unions while restructuring the post-ballot-rigging Electrical Trade Union as an example to all of modern trade unionism.

Les Cannon was born in Wigan on 21 February 1920. He was the fourth of seven children. His father, Jim, was a miner and joined the Communist Party in 1920, although he was to leave it over the CP's aggressive attitude to the miners' leader, AJ Cook. Les' early life was dominated by his father's blacklisted unemployment and his bookishness. In 1936, he became an electrical apprentice with Wigan Corporation, studying himself to ONC level in electrical engineering. He joined the ETU in 1936 and the Communist Party in 1941. During the war, he worked in reserved occupations and by 1942 was the district secretary of the ETU in Wigan and elected to the union's executive council in 1945.

From 1945 to 1954, he was the union's leading spokesman on youth, automation, workstudy and other 'modern management techniques'. He battled to help the post-war production push and urged the merger of the Labour and Communist parties. However, as the Cold War deepened, Cannon was vocal in attacking late 1940s incomes restraint and the role of America in the world. His conviction style did not enamour him to everyone. An anonymous CP internal report prepared for Industrial Organiser Peter Kerrigan said of Les Cannon that 'a minor weakness is a certain tendency to dominate discussion and not listen sufficiently to what other comrades have to say. He tends to be a bit impatient in his attitude to people.' Syd Abbott, secretary of the Lancs and Cheshire Communist Party District Committee, said more directly on 29 October 1954 that Cannon was 'just a wireman with a head as big as a gasometer'. (It was probably the 'wireman' slur that got to Cannon.)

He was virtually full-time on union work all over the country. His reputation went beyond the union. He led the CP delegates at the World Youth Conference in 1947 (in preparing for which he first met Frank Chapple). Harry Pollit was a personal friend, and Willie Gallagher was best man at his wedding in Czechoslovakia to Olga later that year. By 1952 there were two sons, Oleg and Martin.

Cannon left the ETU executive council in 1954 to become Jon Vickers' assistant at the ETU's first trade union college at Esher. This was a vital role for the union in its unrivalled access to union activists and Cannon revelled in it. However, by 1956, his relationship with the Communist Party was becoming strained. He was often uncomfortable with the communists who ran the ETU. He resented the way they did nothing for him when he ran a strike at English Electric in 1950, was not pleased at the salary he was getting at Esher and could never get over the feeling that although Pollit and Co might see him as a natural successor to ETU President Frank Foulkes, the ETU communists did not appear so keen. In 1956, his friends in King St started to resent Cannon's dissatisfaction with the comparative failure of the British Road to Socialism to arrive anywhere. Cannon grew increasingly of the view, echoing his father's pre-war convictions, that British workers were too welded to their unions and the Labour Party to give a Leninist party any headway. He wrote papers for Pollit, culminating in his expressions of disillusion raised by Khruschev's 20th Congress speech, emphasised by the later events that year in Hungary. He left the CP, and the ETU communists got rid of him by shutting down Esher College completely. Cannon was back on the tools.

1957 saw the emergence within the ETU of different groups with a common loathing of the communist leadership. The issue that united them all was the growing conviction that since

1948 the union's leadership had only been able to remain in power because of systematic ballot rigging. Moderate Labour Party electricians were embarrassed at how their reputation stood in the movement. For all the official pride in what was called 'the fighting union', the moderates were irritated that the ETU always provided the CP with access to the TUC, CSEU and Labour Party conference agendas. Many of these opponents, particularly in Scotland, where they gathered round area official Jock Byrne, had their convictions reinforced by their Catholic faith. Small in number, but vocal, particularly in the building industry was a group of Trotskyists who thought the CP ETU leadership corrupt and venal personally. Alongside the ex-communists, this unlikely coalition looked to Cannon for leadership in overthrowing the communists at union headquarters at Hayes Court.

Cannon was at the centre of a reform group that issued unofficial circulars, wrote in labour magazines and were interviewed by Woodrow Wyatt and John Freeman on television. Frank Chapple, originally elected with CP support, kept harrying the executive and senior officials. Mark Young, another contracting electrician, was secretary of the Reform Group. The union made sure that Cannon was banned from holding office in the union, stopping him attending the 1958 TUC. They fiddled him out of his victory in 1957 for an EC seat. The intimidation was enormous, and Cannon must have thought more than once that it was not too late for him to pursue his interest in the law.

The 1959 general secretary election was fought in the most intense atmosphere. 106 branch votes were fraudulently ruled out by the leadership, handing apparent 'victory' to the Communist Frank Haxell. Les Cannon worked out how they did it. He, Frank Chapple and others knew some of the methods of routine fiddling from their communist past. Cannon identified the decisive method, where someone had gone from the union's head office to towns where the non-communist, Jock Byrne, had won, and posted a new replica envelope to head office. This envelope would now have an out-of-date Post Office stamp on it, and when the branch returns were put inside the 'late' envelope, they could be disallowed.

Byrne and Chapple took the case to the High Court. Gerald Gardiner was their barrister, Ben Hooberman their solicitor. Les Cannon had the key role, along with the plaintiffs, of assembling the evidence, which had to be identified and extracted from the ETU leadership under duress, with much destroyed before the hearing in the summer of 1961. Justice Winn decided Byrne had won the election and was the legitimate general secretary. When he took up his position, most senior officers and staff were communists or their sympathisers. Byrne needed Cannon at his old job at Esher again, where he could speak to the activists in explaining the implications of the trial.

The 1961 executive elections were independently supervised and turnouts in some areas rose over 100 per cent. The executive council was turned completely around politically. In 1963, Cannon won the union's presidency with 63 per cent of the vote in the highest turn-out the union had seen. In 1966, his closest ally Chapple won the general secretaryship after Byrne retired. With a new leadership and a supportive staff, Cannon embarked on a rich five years of trade union innovation.

Although the general secretary role in the ETU had always been the most dominant, Chapple was happy for Cannon to take centre stage on policy issues. Cannon revolutionised attitudes to pay. 'Fodder' based negotiations (where the only consideration was to keep up with the cost of living) were not sophisticated enough to gain the improvements that skilled men thought they were entitled to. Cannon was the first union leader to employ specialist work study experts to provide negotiators with the same level of management skills as the companies and industries the union negotiated with. Productivity improvement was the key to raising the pay and status of craftsmen. In electricity supply, basic wages were comparatively low and systematic overtime endemic. In electrical contracting, newly elected executive member Eric Hammond, Chapple and Cannon, based a new system on joint employer/union endorsement of electrician's skills, which raised wages substantially. With the touchstone contracting rate improved, it was easier to argue the case for electricians in manufacturing maintenance.

This success on behalf of the ordinary members' wages and conditions was the prime basis of Cannon's support in the union. It gave him the strength to take on the bitter left everywhere else. With Frank Chapple, he set about the reform of the union internally. First and foremost, his team took all elections out of the branches and more than doubled turnouts by introducing secret postal ballots. He expanded the policy conference, introduced conferences of shop stewards in each leading industry, introduced a full-time executive council and presided over the replacement of unrepresentative branch-based local committees with structures that represented the working shop stewards.

Outside the internal reform of the union Cannon spent his last six years in the public eye. He was comfortable in the media, and his evidence to the Donovan Commission on the future of the unions emphasised a social partnership approach that was ahead of its time. Walter Citrine wrote from retirement to say that he read the ETU's evidence to Donovan with 'care, enjoyment and pride'. His views on both *In place of Strife* and the Industrial Relations Bill in 1970 was to look at each proposal separately, rather than reject everything instinctively. He was appointed to the Industrial Re-Organisation Commission, and regained a place on the TUC general council, which was particularly sweet for Cannon remembering when he was banned from office by the CP leadership in 1958.

He was always fierce in his advocacy of payment for skill. He was convinced that the less well paid were best served by being uplifted by advances the employers made to skilled people. He famously denounced the Prices and Incomes Board for not understanding the power of feeling among underpaid craftsmen as well as the objective unhappiness felt by the unskilled poor. He was a visiting fellow at Nuffield College, reflecting how close in his wilderness years he had come to retraining in an academic discipline like law. He ran in tandem with Frank Chapple for only eight years before dying on 9 December 1970 at the age of 50. A biography, *The Road from Wigan Pier* by Olga Cannon and J R L Anderson, was published in 1973. Also worth reading is Keith Mason, *Front Seat*.

Dr John Lloyd

Edward Carpenter (1844–1929)

In modern-day politics Edward Carpenter is most often remembered for his advocacy of gay freedom but in his own time he was highly regarded by every aspect of the socialist and labour movements for his embodiment of a political vision that was just as much centred on the campaign against convention as on any fixed ideology. Born into a naval family in Brighton in 1844, he took a conventional route into ordination in the Church of England at the age of 25 through an academic career at Trinity Hall, Cambridge. He served as curate at St Edward's Church in Cambridge under Frederick Denison Maurice, the leading Victorian Christian Socialist, from whom he developed much of his social teaching.

But in 1874, spurred on by a growing appreciation of his own homosexuality and a deep frustration with academic life, he resigned his orders and became a teacher in the new University Extension Movement. For a few years he lived with a labourer in Sheffield whilst developing his belief in a form of communism based on genuine open human relationships. In 1883 he inherited a large amount of money from his father, and having met a working-class man George Merrill, he bought a farm in the small Derbyshire village of Millthorpe where he and Merrill lived openly as a couple. This took considerable courage, especially after the 1885 Criminal Law Amendment Act made all homosexual acts illegal and the 1895 Oscar Wilde trial showed how society could deal with offenders.

From the outset Carpenter was at the heart of the incipient labour and socialist movements. In 1883 he became a leading supporter of the Social Democratic Foundation, advancing Ramsay MacDonald £5 for its library. Two years later he joined William Morris and others in founding the Socialist League. Already his writings had acquired a strong socialist following and his song *England Arise* was to become a mainstay of the Labour Church Movement. In 1893 he was a founding member of the Independent Labour Party and he marched shoulder to shoulder with all the Movement's leading lights.

His major works, *Towards Democracy, England's Ideal* and *Civilisation, Its Cause and Cure,* all espoused a tolerant, libertarian brand of socialism that appealed to fundamental ethical principles rather than to scientific or ideological answers. And his passionate advocacy of male friendship and homosexuality, whilst not universally welcomed in the Labour movement, gained him a strong following amongst later writers, most notably E M Forster and Siegfried Sassoon. Forster wrote of him, 'Perhaps he never understood that for many people personal relationships are unimportant for the reason that their hearts are small. His own heart was great and made him a great man'.

Carpenter was also an ardent pacifist who opposed both the Boer and the First World Wars. He died in Guildford in 1929, less than a year after his long-term companion George.

Chris Bryant MP

Bill Carron (Lord Carron) (1902–69)

Bill Carron was born on 19 November 1902 in Kingston upon Hull, the younger of two sons of his Irish father John and his Yorkshire mother Frances. He attended St Mary's Roman Catholic Primary School, run by the Sisters of Mercy, and then Hull Technical College. He was forced to leave the technical college when his father died and became an apprentice at Rise, Downs and Thompson. His early working life was uneventful and he was not particularly active in the Union.

However, in 1931 he fell ill from eating strawberries and was confined to bed. Visited by one of the branch officials to pay him his sick benefit, he was persuaded, after argument, to become the branch secretary. In 1935 he moved to Reckitt & Coleman where he became a shop steward, union side chair of the Workers Committee and then Hull District President from 1940. It was a natural step to turn to full-time office as he was elected Divisional Organiser No 12 Division in 1945. When the post of Executive Council member for the East Midlands and East Anglia became vacant in 1950 he beat six rivals for that position. His election address attacked officials in the Communist Party who paid lip service to working-class unity but worked assiduously against Labour. His Catholicism and his anti-communism rather than his personal ambition drove his union career.

In 1956 he faced a huge dilemma. The post of President was vacant following the retirement of Bob Openshaw, yet his own Executive seat was also up for re-election. Under union rules he could not run for both. Most would have stuck to what they knew but Carron chose the tough option, defeating Reg Birch, the famous London communist, after trailing him on the first ballot. Carron's large majority was assisted by a *Panorama* programme made by Woodrow Wyatt drawing attention to the dangers of a communist victory. The publicity regularly transmitted in the *News of the World* continued to help the moderate cause for many years to come.

As President, he often prepared for the big events by meditation and retreat. His modest smiling demeanour and bland effrontery kept him one step ahead of his political opponents. He was happy to face both ways on policy and cast the Union's vote determinedly in support of the Labour leader Hugh Gaitskell and Wilson's Labour Government. He was accused of fashioning Carron's law.

His achievements were recognised both by the Government and by the Catholic Church. He was appointed Knight of the order of chivalry of St Gregory the Great in 1959, was knighted in 1963 and made a life peer in 1967, retiring as AEU President in November of that year. He was appointed a director of the Bank of England in 1963. Sadly his retirement was cut short by his sudden death on 3 December 1969. He was survived by his wife Mary, whom he had married in 1931, and daughters Hilary and Patricia.

John Gibbins

Barbara Castle (Baroness Castle of Blackburn) (1910–)

Barbara Castle's autobiography is most aptly entitled *Fighting All the Way*. For if there is one thing that stands out in Barbara's political career it is that she always fought like a tiger for what she believed to be right. She is still battling away today, at the age of 90, and, in the House of Lords as Baroness Castle of Blackburn, she has become the pensioners' champion.

Barbara was born in Chesterfield on 6 October 1910, the third child of Frank and Annie Betts. Frank Betts was an assistant surveyor of taxes with a voracious appetite for reading and politics. Sunday evening 'readings', where he would make sure his children read the books he thought they should, were a regular feature of family life. He went on to edit the ILP paper, the *Bradford Pioneer,* and it was through him that Barbara gained her interest in politics. She was educated at Bradford Girls Grammar School and St Hughs College, Oxford, with which, by her own admission, she had a 'love-hate' relationship.

In 1937 Barbara was elected to the St Pancras Borough Council. Her parliamentary career began with her selection as the Labour candidate for Blackburn in 1944, thanks to the party's Women's Section, who declared that if there were no women on the shortlist they would stop making tea and addressing envelopes, and to the man who was later to become her husband. Barbara has always said that one of the milestones of her career was her speech at Labour Conference in 1943 on Beveridge. It prompted the then night editor of the *Daily Mirror*, one Ted Castle (whom she married in 1944), to put her on the front page with the headline 'Jam yesterday, jam tomorrow, but never jam today'. It was this speech which brought her to the attention of that Blackburn selection committee.

On her arrival at the Commons, Barbara was invited by Stafford Cripps to be his Parliamentary Private Secretary (PPS) but she still managed to gain a reputation as a rebel, voting against the government in protest at the failure to uprate pensions immediately. This period too saw Barbara fighting hard for equal treatment for women, a cause which has always been dear to her heart. She moved an amendment to the National Insurance Bill which sought to make it compulsory for married women at work to join the insurance scheme, instead of relying on their husbands' insurance to earn them a reduced pension, payable only when their husbands retired. It was another thirty years before she achieved this goal as Secretary of State for Social Services.

It was Harold Wilson who gave Barbara her first Cabinet position in 1964, as Minister of Overseas Development, and made her a Privy Counsellor. It was a portfolio she relished. As a member of the Colonial sub-committee of the Labour Party's National Executive Committee (of which she was an elected member 1950–79), she had helped to develop party policy on small communities such as Cyprus and had, prior to Labour's victory in 1964, shadowed the subject from the front bench at Wilson's request. That policy called for just such a department, with Cabinet status, and Barbara was now in charge of it.

Her time at Overseas Development was, however, to be relatively short. In December of 1965, Harold Wilson invited her to become Minister of Transport with the words 'I want a tiger in my tank', recognising that there was a need for the government to develop an effective transport policy. Barbara was reluctant to take it, pleading that she could not drive. Wilson was determined. 'I think that is a good thing,' he replied; 'we cannot have Ministers of Transport knocking down people on pedestrian crossings.' It was a job she did not want, but was later to admit that she enjoyed it more than any of her ministerial posts. And, as the Minister who introduced seatbelts and the breathalyser, she did us all a great service indeed, though, at the time, she had to endure the most terrible abuse, particularly over the breathalyser. I recall her telling me many years later that it was virtually impossible for her to go into a pub. Her postbag was full of letters from angry drinkers. One of the worst said 'You've ballsed our darts matches up, so get out you wicked old B.' It was signed '3 regulars'. But Barbara had done what was necessary to change the culture of drinking and driving. It was a brave act by a politician who always had the courage of her convictions.

Barbara's next job was to be no less controversial. In April 1968, Harold Wilson moved her to the position of First Secretary of State and Secretary of State for Employment and Productivity. She wrote in her diary 'I am under no illusion that I may be committing political suicide … If I go down in disaster, as well I may, at least I shall have been an adult before I die.'

At the time, it may indeed have appeared to be a disaster. The government was plagued by a rash of unofficial strikes which were turning public opinion against the trade unions, and the Tories were clamouring for curbs on the unions. Barbara believed fervently in the concept, enshrined in the Donovan Report, that workers should have a right to organise themselves in trade unions and that the unions needed to be strengthened, not weakened. What she therefore wanted to do was to raise the status and the rights of trade unions, but to ask them in return to accept greater responsibilities in preventing the needless disruption of the country's economic life. And so *In Place of Strife* was born.

It was a White Paper far ahead, sadly, of its time. Its proposals included a 'conciliation pause' or a cooling-off period, a secret ballot before an official strike was declared, and the Industrial Relations Commission to have the final say on disputes about union recognition, without recourse to the courts. Its title *In Place of Strife* was an adaptation of Nye Bevan's *In Place of Fear*, where Nye Bevan himself had warned of the limitations of industrial action, particularly in a situation of economic crisis.

The rest, as they say, is history. *In Place of Strife* never happened and a serious attempt to modernise the trade union movement was lost for ever. One of its most vociferous opponents was Jim Callaghan who persuaded the Cabinet to his view. Had it been otherwise, we might never have seen the decimation of mining communities which resulted from the Tories' subsequent battle with the miners.

But Barbara did manage to get through the 1970 Equal Pay Act. As Barbara herself would admit, it was far from perfect but it did establish the principle that equal pay should apply to work of a similar nature, whether or not it was carried out by men or women. It is a fight we are still facing today, but without Barbara's Equal Pay Act, we would still be on the starting blocks.

Barbara's next ministerial job was as Secretary of State for Health and Social Services, with the re-election of a Labour government in 1974, having been switched in opposition from shadowing Employment to the DHSS in 1971. She achieved the best-ever pay rise for nurses, committed herself to the National Health Service by striving to phase out pay beds from the NHS, and founded the Child Benefit scheme which, for the first time, enabled payments to be made directly to mothers.

In 1976, when Jim Callaghan took over from Harold Wilson as Prime Minister, he decided to reap his revenge for *In Place of Strife*. Barbara was relieved of her Cabinet post and replaced by David Ennals. It was indeed a tragic loss to British politics.

It was then that Barbara decided to stand down as Member of Parliament for Blackburn, to be replaced in 1979 by Jack Straw, who had been one of her political advisers at the Department of Health. She went on to be an elected Member of the European Parliament (for Greater Manchester North 1979–84 and West 1984–89), and leader of the Labour Group in Europe (1979–85), where she continued to fight for the reform of the Common Agricultural Policy. She was created Baroness Castle of Blackburn in 1990.

It is impossible to pay tribute to the legacy Barbara Castle has left for British politics in such a short contribution, but I have tried. I had the privilege to work for Barbara as her constituency secretary for seven years, from 1974 to 1981. During that time she taught me a great many things, but one lesson above all. It is a lesson which all politicians should learn. It is 'Have the courage of your convictions and remember that nothing is impossible'. I should like that to be my epitaph. It certainly should be Barbara's. *The Castle Diaries 1974–76* were published in 1980 and *The Castle Diaries 1964–70* in 1984.

Janet Anderson MP

Jim Cattermole (1910–)

Jim Cattermole belongs to that illustrious group of Labour Party organisers who served the Party with distinction in the post-war years. After retirement he created a second career as Director of the Labour Movement in Europe, which at the age of 90 years he continued to work for into the new millennium.

Born James Cattermole in Coventry on 11 December 1910, his parents were active in the ILP and his father was a delegate to the TUC. After leaving King Edward's Grammar School, Camp Hill, Birmingham, in 1926, his father signed him up to the National Union for Distributive and Allied Workers (now USDAW) and he went to work at a Birmingham stockbrokers. From 1931 to 1945 he worked in the Birmingham office of the Sheffield Smelting Company, transferring his union membership to the precursor of APEX. He joined the Labour Party in 1929 and was active at county level, serving on the West Midlands Region Executive Committee and becoming Secretary of Tamworth CLP in 1937. As a delegate to the 1946 annual conference, chaired by Harold Laski, he moved a motion on pay for councillors. In 1945 he was appointed full-time Borough Party Secretary in Birmingham and led the organisation of the 1945 general election there, when the Party won ten out of the thirteen seats in the City. In 1948 he went to London as Assistant Regional Organiser and played an important part in the 1950 and 1951 General Elections. In 1953 he was appointed Regional Secretary for the East Midlands, where he remained until his retirement in 1972. When Harold Wilson called for an inquiry into the Party's 'penny-farthing' election organisation, Cattermole represented the Party's agents on it. They proposed that the Party nationally should pay the salaries of local agents. No action was taken until Tony Blair became Leader.

His work in organising by-elections resulted in Harold Nicholson, Kenneth Robinson, Roy Jenkins, Lena Jeger, Tom Bradley and Joe Ashton entering Parliament. During his service he was involved in eight general elections, in which five Labour governments were elected and twenty-two by-elections as well as local elections.

In addition to his work as an organiser, Cattermole was active in local government, serving on Solihull UDC 1945–46 and Nottinghamshire CC from 1975 to 1979 and on the Councils of the University of Nottingham and the Nottingham Polytechnic. Following Hugh Gaitskell's death in 1963 he was instrumental in establishing the Hugh Gaitskell Memorial Lecture at Nottingham University, where Gaitskell had had his first teaching post (as a tutor in the Department of Adult Education at what was then University College, Nottingham). He chaired the East Midlands Regional Council for Sport and Recreation and the Holme Pierrepoint water-sports centre when it staged Britain's first world rowing championship, and was associated with the creation of the River Trent slalom course, one of the two longest and fastest in the world.

He married Phylis Taylor in 1935. They were divorced in 1952. He settled in Nottingham and married Joan Mitchell, Professor of Political Economy at the university. He had three boys and a girl in his marriages.

He took early retirement in 1972. He had been asked to become Director of the Labour Committee for Europe under the urbane leadership of George Thomson MP. Initially his work involved organising visits by Labour and trade-union members to the organs of the then Community. Three years later came the referendum, the first major challenge. A Labour Campaign for Britain in Europe was launched. Cattermole was responsible for its organisation and arranged over 200 speaking engagements and debates at constituency meetings to carry the message to members. He worked closely with the Trade Union Alliance for Europe, presided over by Vic Feather, former General Secretary of the TUC, and David Warburton of the GMWU, which distributed 1.3 million leaflets.

In 1982 the Labour Committee for Europe faced its greatest crisis following the defection of leading members to the SDP. Cattermole set about restoring leadership and credibility. As an active member of his union APEX, he secured the support of its President, Denis Howell MP and the General-Secretary, Roy Grantham, as Chair and Treasurer respectively. The work of re-organisation was tackled vigorously. The next year, the Red Rose organisation, led by Arthur Palmer MP and the former editor of *Socialist Commentary*, Peter Stephenson, joined to form a new Labour Movement for Europe.

In 1985 *A Socialist Policy for Europe* by Geoffrey Harris and Richard Corbett was published. In 1990, *Europe Left* was first published, admirably edited by Anne Symonds. In 1995, *Despite the Opt-out*, setting out European achievements in spite of the lukewarm attitude of the Major government, was written by Pat Leighton and launched in the House. Four research groups were established on education, the environment, EMU and enlargement. Seminars were held and the final documents were circulated to all Constituency Labour Parties in 1996. The following year *Monetary Union,* written by Lynden Harrison MEP, was published and widely circulated in time for the 1997 general election.

Cattermole was an organiser par excellence. Through him a number of significant politicians had their entry to Parliament made easier. Because of him the Labour Movement for Europe survived to become a respected element in the Party.

Roy Grantham

Frank Chapple (Lord Chapple of Hoxton) (1921–)

Frank Chapple is among the most publicly recognisable of twentieth century trade union leaders. He was one of the most prominent ex-communists whose struggle against CP ballot-rigging and political support for discredited post-war East European regimes guaranteed that the British trade union movement remained broadly social democratic in political tone. His political strength was dependent on his capacity to appeal over the heads of unrepresentative activists to the broad sympathies of the members he represented. His willingness to speak out in support of this fundamental perception – that he was in politics to save his members from others in politics – enraged the left and gave courage to the ordinary shop stewards and branch officers of the electricians union.

Francis Joseph Chapple was born in Hoxton in East London on 8 August 1921. (He was later to take this part of London as his title when he was made a member of the House of Lords in 1985 following his retiral in 1984) His father was an illiterate shoe-repairer, and his mother worked on the family greengrocer's stall in Hoxton market. Chapple became an unindentured electrician when he left school, and was drawn to politics as the East End became the pre-war cockpit of dispute between fascists and anti-fascists. The Spanish Civil War also drew Chapple towards the Communist Party, and he joined the Electrical Trade Union in 1937 and the CP in 1939. (In joining the Shoreditch branch of the Young Communist League with playwright Ted Willis, he was able to boast later of the only YCL branch to produce two members of the House of Lords.)

Chapple developed his skills as an electrician while working across London in the contracting (construction) industry. As war approached, he worked at Royal Ordnance factories and the shiprepair yards on the Thames, often alongside the CP activists who were gaining control of the ETU at the same time. In 1943, he joined up with REME, and was in Normandy on D-Day plus twenty. By the end of the war he had witnessed the liberation of the prison camps and the unwilling repatriation of East Europeans who were supposed to be returning to a communist Elysium that Chapple was convinced existed. In 1947, he returned to England, although he was quickly sent to the World Youth Conference in Prague, where he first met Les Cannon and extended his CP networks. He worked in contracting again on his return to London, and became part of the local and national parallel organisation of Communist Party 'advisory committees'. These committees selected and organised support for CP candidates in the union, and Chapple knew how they worked – first-hand experience that was to prove vital in the organisational overthrow of the communists within the union in later years.

By 1956, his close proximity to the CP leaders of the ETU, particularly President Frank Foulkes and General Secretary Frank Haxell, was creating a sense of disillusion within his political faith. Foulkes was friendly and approachable, but Chapple did not like Foulkes' enjoyment of the good life. Haxell was different. He was a bully, and chose to surround himself with CP hacks in preference to competent communists. Chapple saw the ETU leadership get rid of Les Cannon from the union's college at Esher at just the time he personally felt their disapproval for seeking reform within the CP post-Hungary by gathering around the magazine organised by E P Thompson, *The Reasoner*. (Chapple has always been a voracious reader, lover of classical music and expert breeder and racer of pigeons.)

These post-Hungary issues were not resolved by a trip to Moscow in 1957, and the combined effects of the persecution of Les Cannon and his disappointment with the socialist homeland led him to leave the CP – but not before he had outmanoeuvred the Party leadership in winning a fairly easy ride onto the ETU's executive council in late 1957. With Cannon struggling against bans from holding office, Chapple used his executive seat with great courage and skill to keep up a persistent barrage of awkward questions of the leadership. As the 1959 General Secretary election approached, he persuaded all concerned to seek reform of the union through supporting the Catholic anti-communist Scottish area official Jock Byrne. When this election was clearly fiddled (through extra ballots appearing by post at CP branches and the ballots from 109 branches fraudulently being disallowed), Frank Chapple joined Jock Byrne in the High Court to win redress.

The ballot-rigging trial proved comprehensively how extensive the CP fraud was. Jock Byrne was declared the General Secretary, and went to the union's head office on 4 July 1961 – by this time ill and worn out. The executive was still CP dominated, and Byrne could only appoint apparently clerical grades of staff. But with Les Cannon back with the shop stewards at Esher College, Byrne appointed Frank Chapple as effectively his PA to overturn the CP machine. By 1962, the CP executive majority was overturned, and Chapple won his first national election in 1963 using the reformed secret postal ballot in a 26 per cent turnout that was more than twice the level of pre-1961 national elections. Frank Chapple was joined at the top of the union by new President Les Cannon the same year, and an epoch-making reform process started that designed a new union whose structure and policy reforms influenced unions beyond the ETU.

The introduction of secret postal ballots for union elections allowed Chapple always to appeal to a wider constituency than branch activists, whose motivation was so often political and not membership/industry led. The administration of the union needed clean lists of members to run these elections, and ex-ETU man Lord Citrine turned on the union's computer in 1967. The union organised staff workers in a distinctive section, recruitment was to become a specialist officers' skill, the union merged with the plumbers to form the EETPU in 1968, and management skills were turned to saving the union's finances through professional money management. This central theme of 'Trust the members' gave Chapple the support he needed to reform the position of electricians as craftsmen within the industrial community. Elected General Secretary in 1966 and re-elected every five years afterwards, he confronted the Wild West nature of construction. He designed a Joint Industry Board with local and national councils of equal union and employers. The JIB had an independent Chairman, and it set pay standards that rocketed electricians up the earnings scale as a reward for upskilling themselves and proving their skill through assessment. The same approach – of productivity-based negotiations in manufacturing and the public services maintenance teams – always gave Frank Chapple practical membership wage improvements to throw in the face of the left, who waxed sentimental about how great it had been when the ETU was a 'fighting union'.

After Les Cannon died prematurely in 1970, Chapple fought off a challenge to his leadership from ex-Reform Group colleague Mark Young, who was appointed General Secretary of the airline pilots union. Chapple then balloted the members to abolish the Presidency and form one focus of leadership. He spent 1966–70 on the National Executive Committee of the Labour Party, and in later years was on the TUC General Council, chairing Congress as President in 1983. He felt the drift to the left keenly, but he would not support every Labour Government initiative if it imperilled his belief in improving the standard of living for the union's members based on productivity. He did not like the 'overlordship' of the Commission on Industrial Relations. He hated the Prices and Incomes Board interference in the JIB productivity deals. He wrote in January 1967 that the union's loyalty to Labour must not be taken for granted. 'The hand and word of a friend and partner has been mistaken for the fealty of the vassal and the plea of a suppliant. The credit and goodwill afforded the Labour administration is not limitless and cannot extend to involving the union in self-destructive attitudes and actions.'

Throughout the first Thatcher government, Chapple despaired of the Labour Party's self de-struction. At the TUC, he opposed 'days of action' that attracted little support, but made the pub-lic think trade unions were willing to use industrial power for political ends. Chapple signed the Limehouse Declaration in 1981 and grew close to SDP MP John Grant. However, he knew that the union was never going to leave the Labour Party, and Chapple allocated political fund re-sources to strengthening the union's representation on Labour's local management committees, paralleling his understanding that the ballot-riggers had only been excluded from the union through building a mass campaign. The EETPU was the first union to advocate a union with-drawal from bloc vote democracy to one member one vote.

Chapple always said that skilled workers were not to be taken for granted politically, and that they left Labour in droves at the end of the 1970s. He did everything he could to keep skilled workers out of the Tory camp by finding a style and content for trade unionism that would sustain their interests. Just before he retired in 1984, he said in his 1983 TUC Presiden-tial address, 'Accepting that we ourselves have to make necessary reforms will not only give us a fighting chance of regaining the trust we have allowed to wilt; it would … have to be in touch with the times in which we live….we will have to stop wishing the world was like it once was, and face up to what it is. We have to broaden our base and not narrow it. We will have to improve further our internal democracy….positively encourage mass participation. Sometimes we appear to act as though we were the mouthpiece of a few. We must never treat our members with contempt or distrust their judgement.' Many were upset by the rough and keen ways in which he expressed himself. Few could ever say he did not represent millions in the content of what he said.

He published his autobiography, *Sparks Fly!*, in 1984, which he wrote with his friend, former Labour Employment Minister and SDP MP John Grant. *Strike Free* by Philip Basset (1986) and *Front Seat* by Keith Mason also have some insights. This author's *Light and Liberty* (1990) also covers much of his period of office in the EETPU.

Dr John Lloyd

1st Viscount Chelmsford (Frederic John Napier Thesiger) (1868–1933)

There can be few less likely inclusions in a pantheon of Labour heroes than the first Viscount Chelmsford, whose involvement with the Labour Party spanned just a few months in 1924. Described in the Lords by Curzon as 'an orthodox pillar of Conservatism' on 12 February 1924 and for a time chairman of Dorsetshire Conservative Association, Chelmsford was one of sev-eral non-socialist peers asked to join Ramsay MacDonald's first Labour Cabinet.

Frederic John Napier Thesiger was born at 7 Eaton Square, London, on 12 August 1868, the eldest of the five sons of Frederic Augustus Thesiger, second Baron Chelmsford, and Adria Fanny Heath, daughter of an officer in the Bombay army. His family originated in Saxony but had been pillars of the British establishment for generations. A distant uncle had served along-side Nelson at the Battle of Copenhagen; his grandfather, the first Baron Chelmsford, had been a Conservative MP, law officer and twice Lord Chancellor; and his father had been ADC to

Queen Victoria and had seen action in some of the most notable British military excursions of the second half of the nineteenth century. Educated at Winchester and Magdalen College, Oxford, and elected a fellow of All Souls College, Chelmsford followed in his grandfather's footsteps in being called to the bar by the Inner Temple in 1893. The next year he married Frances Charlotte Guest, daughter of the first Lord Wimborne, whose family were prominent Dorset Liberals. They had six children.

It was for public service, rather than his legal work, that Chelmsford became prominent. He served as a member of the London School Board from 1900 to 1904 before being elected to the London County Council (LCC). Some clue as to his future political career could be gleaned from Sidney Webb's recollection that Chelmsford, although a Moderate (as the Conservatives on the council were known), was 'genuinely progressive in sympathy'. In 1905, Chelmsford was elevated to the peerage on the death of his father from a heart attack during a game of billiards and began an eighteen-year period in Australia, as Governor of first Queensland and then, in 1909, of New South Wales. Chelmsford's *Dictionary of National Biography* entry states that 'tall, well built, good-looking, dignified, sociable and easy-mannered, he was admirably qualified for the personal and ceremonial duties of the King's representative in one of the overseas Dominions'. Significantly, he played an important role in helping New South Wales' first Labour government take power in 1912.

On returning to the UK in 1913 he was appointed an alderman of the LCC, but sailed for India as a captain of the 4th Dorset Regiment on the outbreak of war. He saw no action before his surprise appointment as Viceroy of India, in 1916, which was greeted 'with pessimism' by the Indian press (*Dictionary of National Biography*). Chelmsford quickly grasped the need for some move towards self-government, although he was more cautious than the Secretary of State for India, Edwin Montagu, who defined the goal of Indian policy in August 1917 as 'the progressive realisation of responsible government'. Chelmsford signed up to the Montagu-Chelmsford report of 1918 which led to the Government of India Act of the following year, but his vice-royalty was also remembered for the 1919 Amritsar massacre, for which, his *Dictionary of National Biography* entry concluded, 'Chelmsford and his colleagues must bear their share of the blame'.

Back in London in 1921, Chelmsford was created a Viscount and took on the chairmanship of the University College (London) Committee and, in 1923, was appointed to draft revised statutes for Oxford University. He was not a particularly active member of the House of Lords, speaking on nine occasions from 1921 to 1923, mostly on Indian or university questions. This was to change when, after the 1923 general election, Chelmsford was asked to join MacDonald's government as First Lord of the Admiralty, apparently on Haldane's recommendation. In a debate on 12 February 1924, Chelmsford, and other non-Labour colleagues such as Haldane and Parmoor, were attacked for their action by the Tories Curzon and Birkenhead, the latter saying of Chelmsford, 'He had not given the slightest indication of it until the very day on which we read that he had joined the Socialist Government' (*House of Lords Official Report*, 12 Feb 24, c113). Chelmsford replied that:

> It was bound to be the case, if the Labour Party of itself could not find representatives to look after their business in this House, that they would be obliged to look to those detached from politics, and to ask them whether they would come in on certain conditions.

When I was approached by the Prime Minister, it was made perfectly clear on what conditions I came in. I came in not as one who took the Labour label. I made that perfectly clear. I came in not as one who had taken the Labour label, but as one detached from politics, who was prepared, as a colleague, to help to carry on the King's Government on a disclosed programme … It was distinctly understood between ourselves that, if occasion arose where I was unable to follow the politics of the present Government, it would be regarded as fair on both sides that I should give in my resignation.

Perhaps mindful of his New South Wales experience, Chelmsford sought to help with the formation of the Labour government, particularly given its lack of spokesmen in the Lords. Furthermore, as Maurice Cowling argued of Chelmsford in *The Impact of Labour*, 'as an ex-Viceroy, he would be strong enough to stop Admiralty opinion in unsettling the Government in Parliament.' The appointment of several former Conservative and Liberal politicians in his government helped MacDonald build Labour's reputation as a responsible party of government.

Chelmsford made little mark on history as a Minister. Colin Cross has described him as 'a virtual non-entity' in his 1966 biography of Philip Snowden and Cowling judged that 'he gave MacDonald no satisfaction'. Chelmsford's major policy announcement concerned the cancellation of plans to develop the Singapore naval base and there was also a reduction in the number of cruisers to be purchased for the Navy, but these policies were Treasury-led. The First Sea Lord, Earl Beatty, was a more prominent advocate of the Admiralty than Chelmsford, who rarely spoke on naval matters after Labour lost the 1924 election.

After 1924, Chelmsford resumed his work for University College, London, continuing to speak in the Lords two or three times per year, until he again became a fellow of All Souls in 1929, and Warden of the college in 1932. He died of a heart attack in Wantage on 1 April 1933.

Robert Ingham

Walter Citrine (Lord Citrine) (1887–1983)

Citrine was the founder of the modern Trades Union Congress. As its General Secretary from shortly after the end of the General Strike of 1926 for the next twenty years, he worked to transform the TUC into an Estate of the Realm, the sole representative body of organised labour that would lobby and influence governments in the interests of trade unions and working people.

Under Citrine the TUC became a respected and respectable national institution with an influential voice in public life. He was a formidable figure – a brilliant administrator, a perceptive philosopher of modern industrial relations, a principled pragmatist who ensured the TUC was listened to and heeded by governments in peacetime as well as during the Second World War. It was Citrine – more than any other trade union leader of his generation except for Ernest Bevin, leader of the Transport and General Workers Union – who helped to shape the Labour movement in the mid-twentieth century.

Born on 22 August 1887 on Merseyside, the son of Alfred Citrine, he was trained as an electrician. In October 1914 he was elected as full-time district secretary of the Electrical Trades Union in his local area and four years later he became the union's Assistant General

Secretary. In that key job he saved the union from financial crisis and earned a rapid reputation for being an administrator. It was that skill which ensured his appointment in 1924 to become assistant to TUC General Secretary Fred Bramley. Less than two years later Citrine found himself in the top post after Bramley's sudden death.

His reputation was that of being a tidy-minded and methodical bureaucrat, who made the TUC a more professional and efficient organisation. But from the moment he was elected its General Secretary at the comparatively young age of 39, Citrine was determined to ensure the TUC became a more authoritative and coherent body, capable of speaking with clarity and decisiveness on behalf of its disparate affiliate trade union members. Although he was unable to equip the TUC with centralised powers which would subordinate the interests of individual unions to the greater good of the common labour interest, Citrine in alliance with Bevin went a long way to strengthen the organisation as a vital partner in the development of a limited corporatism in relations with the British state. He was keen in particular to ensure the TUC developed a distinctive and independent life of its own while retaining a close alliance with the Labour Party. Citrine was above all a realist, more than an ideologue. As he said on one occasion: 'The primary function of the trade union movement is to get better conditions here and now. Trade unionism should concentrate more upon trying to secure changes within capitalism which will elevate working-class standards.'

Citrine was keen to ensure the TUC practised responsibility, abandoning gesture politics for a measured role in the management of the political economy. But this did not mean he was a timid and grey administrator, anxious to display a studied moderation at all costs. Citrine was sensitive to the class character of British society but he was determined to ensure organised labour gained an effective voice in the making of public policy.

His attempts to develop a friendlier relationship with employers in a practical programme of common interest failed in the late 1920s, mainly because employers were unwilling to accept that trade unions should play a necessary role in their business affairs. But during the Second World War Citrine was able to ensure the TUC participated fully in the defeat of fascism. Under his leadership the organisation was turned into an indispensable body in the mobilisation of the workforce. A complex network of committees and forums was established that brought the TUC and employer associations together with the government to deal with and implement the wartime agenda. Citrine succeeded – despite the limited resources of the TUC – in liaison with Bevin as Minister of Labour and National Service in ensuring the voluntary character of industrial relations was preserved while accepting the state must be given the powers necessary to sustain war production. His commitment to what he described as a watchful though cordial collaboration between the TUC and the government ensured organised labour gained a legitimacy in the political economy it had never had before.

Citrine was also an effective figure in the development of international trade unionism. As president of the International Federation of Trade Unions during the 1930s, he witnessed the rise of Nazism at first hand. Although an opponent of the First World War, Citrine recognised that Hitler and his allies would only be stopped by the threat and the use of force. He rejected the pacifist sentiments of many in the Labour Party and accepted that collective security through the League of Nations would require a readiness by Britain and other democracies to take up arms to defer aggression. Citrine was also keen to encourage the development of free trade unionism

inside the British Empire and he established a close alliance with the American labour movement. A passionate anti-communist from the 1920s, he never suffered any illusions about the ty-
rannical nature of Stalin's Soviet Union. But during the Second World War he forged a close link
between the TUC and the Soviet labour movement in the struggle against Nazism.

Citrine was knighted in 1935 and became a Labour peer in 1946 when he moved from the
TUC to the recently formed National Coal Board. In his last years in public life, from 1947 to
1957, he became chairman of the Central Electricity Authority. He retired to south Devon and
died on 22 January 1983, his wife Doris, whom he had married in 1913, having predeceased
him in 1973.

Robert Taylor

David Clark (Lord Clark)   (1939–)

Dr. David George Clark was a model Labour MP. After he was first elected to Parliament in
1970, having joined the Party in 1959 (and the Co-operative Party in 1961), he served in the
Shadow Cabinet during the dark years of opposition in the 1980s and was eventually rewarded with a position in Cabinet on the Party's election in 1997. Yet, even when his time
in Cabinet came to an end he remained a faithful and loyal back-bencher fighting for the
modernisation of Parliament, finally retiring from the Commons at the election of 2001 and
accepting a peerage.

Clark was born into a working-class family on 19 October 1939 in Castle Douglas, Scotland,
to George Clark, a gardener, and Janet (Smith). He left school at 16, after attending Bowness Elementary and Windermere Grammar, and went to work as a forester (1956–57) before moving
on to a textile mill in Lancaster where he became a laboratory assistant (1957–59). Unable to
contemplate a lifetime in this occupation, Clark made a sudden decision to hand in his notice.
After a suggestion from one of the other residents in his lodgings, Clark decided to become a student teacher. He moved to Salford, Manchester, and the appalling social conditions made an immediate impact, leading him to join the Labour Party. Teaching during the day and attending
Manchester College of Commerce in the evenings to gain A levels, Clark made a conscious effort to improve his education. This, in turn, led him to go to Manchester University to get a degree (BA Econ) and he was elected President of the Student Union. Clark found a course at
UMIST that would enable him to undertake research and continue as President. In the second
year of the course he taught at Morecambe College of Further Education whilst continuing the
research – he eventually received an MSc.

On completion of his studies he began lecturing in Government and Administration at
Salford University (1965–70) and was also a tutor at the University of Manchester (1967–70).
As a result of his activity in the Party and having been the first Labour Student Union president at Manchester, he was asked to stand for election to Parliament in the constituency of
High Peak. He narrowly failed to gain the nomination (being defeated in a run-off after having been tied in first place) but succeeded in being selected for Manchester Withington. He
was defeated in the general election of 1966 but did help to decimate the Liberal Party vote in
the area. This appealed to those running the party in Liberal-held Colne Valley, and they asked

him to stand for nomination. Clark did so and went on to win the seat in 1970 only to lose it to the former Liberal MP in the February 1974 election. He failed to regain it in the October election of the same year.

After deciding that his future lay away from the constituency, because of boundary and demographic changes, Clark found it difficult to gain employment as his plan remained to re-enter Parliament. He eventually came to an agreement with Huddersfield University to head up a politics course on which they required assistance, and he worked as a senior lecturer from 1974 to 1979. He had already been selected to fight South Shields in the following election (1979) but could not be too involved in its affairs for fear of unsettling the sitting Labour MP who was due to retire. He contented himself by researching a PhD at Sheffield University, which was both a personal achievement and also acted as an 'insurance policy' in case of further periods of employment difficulty.

Although not planning or expecting to serve in the Shadow Cabinet, Clark served in many positions including Opposition Spokesperson on Agriculture and Food (1973–74); Defence (1980–81), when he resigned as his multilateral views did not coincide with those of the Labour Party; the Environment (1981–86); Environmental Protection and Development (1986–87); Food, Agriculture and Rural Affairs (1987–92); and Defence, Disarmament and Arms Control (1992–97). He was an elected member of the Shadow Cabinet from 1986. Given the successful extended period Clark spent at Defence, it was assumed that he would be given the same position in Cabinet on Labour entering Government. This was not to be the case as Clark himself realised. It was known that Donald Dewar would replace George Robertson as Secretary of State for Scotland, and Clark believed that Robertson would be allowed to fulfil his life's ambition and become Defence Secretary, leaving Clark himself with Agriculture.

As it was, Clark was made Chancellor of the Duchy of Lancaster. Here he was responsible for open government and drafting the promised Freedom of Information Bill. He believed that the proposals should be radical, opening up the British state to a degree of scrutiny never before seen. Unfortunately, this placed him in opposition to Lord Irvine (Lord Chancellor) and Jack Straw MP (Home Secretary) who both favoured a more closely guarded state. This conflict meant that Prime Minister Blair felt able to move him out of the Cabinet in 1998. He continued to live in the North East during his time in Cabinet, with his wife Christine (Kirby), who he married in 1970 and by whom he has one daughter, Catherine. He partly blames his decision to remain in the North East for his move to the back-benches. Clark's fate was widely anticipated in the press, for around 18 months before it actually happened, and it has been suggested that senior party figures sought to undermine his ideas and him personally. Clark, however, believes and accepts that it was part of a movement of power to Blair's generation of politicians.

In October 2000 he stood to become the new Speaker of the House of Commons, after receiving numerous representations, along with eleven other candidates. In keeping with his belief in 'modernisation', Clark wanted to discard the eighteenth-century costumes including the wig, silk stockings and buckle shoes for all but ceremonial duties. He backed a family-friendly House of Commons, complete with childcare facilities, and also believed that MPs should be allowed to take their laptop computers into committees. He was 'comprehensively defeated' (Sky News, 23 October 2000) but was one of those who came closest to defeating the eventual winner, Michael Martin MP. Clark was even said to be one of those considered for a position as Martin's deputy. Clark, though, remained unwilling to relinquish his position of influence on the back-benches.

Clark has a strong interest and concern in the environment and his Parliamentary activity in achieving amendments to the Wildlife and Countryside Act provided him with green credentials enabling him to amass votes in the Shadow Cabinet election in 1986. This forced Neil Kinnock (as leader of the Party), against his wishes, to make Clark opposition spokesperson on Environmental Protection and Development. Clark has long been associated with environmental causes and has held a number of positions – President of the Open Spaces Society (1979–88), President of the Northern Ramblers (1979–), Chairman of the Forestry Group (1979–) and Chairman of the All-Party National Parks Group. He even won a Green Ribbon Award for Lifetime Services to the Environment in 1998. Clark holds his putting of green issues onto the mainstream political agenda as one of his finest achievements.

Clark has also written a series of political publications – *We Do Not Want The Earth* (1992), *Victor Grayson, Labour's Lost Leader* (1985), *Colne Valley, Radicalism to Socialism* (1981) and *The Industrial Manager* (1966) – and has contributed various articles on management as well as Labour history. His interest in history has also led to him becoming a Trustee of the History of Parliament Trust. In addition, Clark is an advisor and non-executive director of the Homeowners Friendly Society, an organisation he helped to establish as a modern friendly society using contemporary methods of communication to assist people.

A very keen football supporter, Clark has inherited his father's love of Carlisle United, a joy which he shares with his daughter, and both try to see matches as often as possible. Clark is also a shareholder in the club. In addition, he is an avid hill walker, climber and mountaineer, especially in the Lake District.

After having been elected to Labour's shadow cabinet in the 1980s and 1990s, serving in a variety of positions, Clark was only briefly in Cabinet. However, far from becoming a disillusioned back-bench critic of the Party leadership he has continued to champion his favoured causes. Now, as one of Labour's senior Parliamentarians, he commands respect and is pleased with his contributions to the environmental agenda, in helping to set up the Food Standards Agency and in being the architect of the Freedom of Information legislation, even though this cost him his position in Cabinet.

Dr. Stuart Thomson

Charles Clarke (1950–)

Charles Clarke MP is an able Labour minister who has received rapid promotion since entering parliament at the 1997 election. Such promotion is not remarkable in the light of his previous political experience. Indeed, most of Charles Clarke's adult life has prepared him for a ministerial career. This promotion is also a recognition of the role Charles played in reviving Labour's fortunes after the 1983 general election. Charles was the political technician employed by Neil Kinnock to begin the process which eventually led to Labour victory in 1997. Neil Kinnock saw the need for modernisation and created the political context for it – but

Charles Clarke identified what was required in order to achieve it and defined the necessary objectives.

Charles Clarke was born in London on 21 September 1950, the son of a high-ranking civil servant, the late Sir Richard Clarke KCB. He was educated at Highgate School and King's College, Cambridge, where he became President of the Cambridge Students Union in 1972 and gained a degree in Maths and Economics (BA) in 1973. His experiences as a radical student led him to seek and win election to the executive of the National Union of Students (NUS) in 1973 and he joined the Labour Party in 1974. He was President of the NUS 1975–77.

In the period 1977–81 Charles Clarke took on a variety of roles and had several very different full-time and part-time jobs. He helped organise a World Youth Festival in Cuba (1977–78) and worked as Organiser for Hackney People in Partnership (1979–80). He was elected to Hackney Borough Council in a by-election in 1980, re-elected in 1982 and remained on the council until 1986. His years as Vice-Chair of Economic Development (1981–2) and as Chair of Housing for Hackney (1982–4) were educative and formative ones for Charles. In May 1980 Charles became the part-time researcher to Neil Kinnock MP. His other part-time employment at this time was as Organiser of the Community Challenge Conference for the Gulbenkian Foundation (1981–82) and as an adult education maths lecturer at the City Literary Institute (1981–3). In October 1984 Charles married Carol Pearson and they have two sons.

Following the election of Neil Kinnock to the Party leadership in 1983, Charles Clarke became the leader's full-time Political Secretary, and after the 1987 election he succeeded Dick Clements as Chief of Staff in the leader's office. From the day that Kinnock became party leader his team began the task of reforming the obsolescent Labour Party philosophy, image and machine. The long process took more time than Kinnock had and completion of the task was handed on to others. But it was in this period that the foundations were laid upon which New Labour and election victory were built. Charles was central to the project and for the nine years of Neil Kinnock's leadership (1983–92), he marshalled all elements of the strategy which moved the Party forward. Aside from the party leader, no individual shouldered the Party's weightiest burdens more than Charles Clarke did.

The Kinnock leadership team dispersed after Labour's defeat in the 1992 election. To try his hand in the private sector for a few years, Charles Clarke set up and ran his own company, Quality Public Affairs (1992–97). But he remained active and he became the Labour candidate for Norwich South, for which seat he was elected to Parliament in 1997. Since entering the Commons he has been a member of the Select Committee on Treasury Affairs (1997–98); Parliamentary Under-Secretary of State at the DfEE (July 1998); and Minister of State, the Home Office (July 1999). Along with Patricia Hewitt (with whom he served in Kinnock's office) he was the first of the May 1997 intake to get a ministerial post. In each role he has acquitted himself well in his ministerial work and in his handling of the media. He was appointed Chair of the Labour Party, joining the cabinet, after the 2001 election. Labour can be expected to rely on Clarke's combination of talents for some time to come.

Rex Osborn

Dick Clements (1928–)

Richard, or Dick, Clements, is a retired journalist and author who played a central part in the history and development of Labour's left. His writing skills and understanding for left politics combined to make him an influential figure on the Labour left throughout the 1960s, 70s and 80s.

Dick was born in London on 11 October 1928. His education at King Alfred's School, Hampstead, was cut short when, in 1940, he was evacuated from wartime London, first to Canada and then to the United States. His education continued at Gordon Junior High School, Washington DC. He returned to London in 1944 and enrolled at the Regent Street Polytechnic (1944–47). Dick joined the Labour Party while still a student in 1945 and, already ambitious to write, had joined the National Union of Journalists soon after he matriculated in 1947. It was this conjunction of a commitment to Labour and a desire to write which was to shape his career.

Dick served in the Merchant Navy (1947–49) before embarking on his long career in journalism by joining the writing staff of the *Middlesex Independent* (1949–51) and then the *Illustrated Leicester Chronicle* (1951–53). In 1952, having begun this promising journalistic career, Dick married Bridget MacDonald (granddaughter of Labour's first Premier, Ramsey MacDonald). Dick and Bridget have two sons.

In 1953, this promising journalistic career took a decidedly leftward turn. With a pen still his weapon of choice, Dick joined the Labour Party Headquarters staff, in Transport House, as editor of *Socialist Advance,* the monthly paper of the Labour League of Youth. In 1954 Dick went on to join the industrial staff of the *Daily Herald* and in 1956 the staff of *Tribune.* Here Dick found his journalistic home and here Dick wrote a number of publications, including *Glory Without Power: a Study of Trade Unions* (1959). After five years on the paper's staff, Dick became editor of *Tribune,* a post he held for over 20 years (1961–82). From this vantage point Dick Clements inspired and supported mainstream left thinking in the Labour Party. *Tribune* was an ideas forum for the parliamentary left (who were organised in a Tribune Group, known as Tribunite MPs and led by former *Tribune* editor, Michael Foot) but it also served the Labour Party as a whole. The arrangement was a model of how to make constructive left criticism from the inside, without destabilising the party or undermining its electability. In succeeding years, there were too many who failed to see the importance of such a model.

When Michael Foot became leader of the Labour Party in 1980, it was to Dick Clements he turned for guidance, appointing him his full time Political Adviser in 1982. Dick's measured advice was like a supportive arm to Michael Foot throughout the terrible days of internal party strife and the disastrous 1983 election campaign. When Neil Kinnock succeeded Foot as Labour leader in 1983 he determined to rebuild and reform the Labour Party using the Office of the Leader of the Opposition as a base. It was Dick Clements he employed as Executive Officer (a kind of Chief of Staff) to run that office (1983–87). Dick Clements oversaw the first steps toward party modernisation.

After the 1987 election Dick felt the need to get his pen back in action. For two years he worked as a freelance. Later he opted for a more settled existence, first with Considar International, a metal trading company developing trade links with the former Soviet Union (1989–93), then as Director of the Citizen's Income Trust until he retired in 1996.

As a writer and a political thinker Dick gave a guiding hand, with a gentle touch, to numerous Labour MPs and two who led the party with great courage through some of its most difficult times. It was a little easier to muster courage in such times with the calm and intelligent support of Dick Clements.

Rex Osborn

John Robert Clynes (1869–1949)

J R Clynes is among the least known of the Labour Party's leaders. Leader for only one year, 1921–2, he had been active as Vice-Chairman of the Parliamentary Labour Party (1918–21) under his predecessor William Adamson. He resumed the deputy leader role under Ramsay MacDonald (1922–31). Like Arthur Henderson, he was a major trade union figure in the Parliamentary Labour Party. Unlike Arthur Henderson he had a pre-1914 socialist background. However, he was very much a moderate, a voice of reasonableness and conciliation, in the Labour Party. He was at its fore 1908–31.

Born in Oldham on 27 March 1869, Clynes was the elder boy in Patrick and Bridget Clynes' family of seven. His father was a labourer who had migrated to Lancashire from Ireland in 1851. At the age of ten, J R Clynes became a 'little piecer' (a repairer of broken cotton threads), working six hours at Dowry Cotton Mills each morning and attending school in the afternoon. From the age of twelve he was a full-time piecer. He eagerly educated himself, buying books and reading in the Oldham Equitable Co-operative Society's library.

Clynes first displayed an interest in politics when attending meetings of the Irish National League. He first made an impact through writing a series of letters to the press about factory conditions, using the pseudonym 'Piecer'. He went on to be a founder member of a short-lived Piecers' Union. Although a frail and pale figure, Clynes was an effective speaker. While secretary of the Oldham branch of the National Union of Gasworkers and General Labourers, he impressed Will Thorne, the union's leader, and was appointed Lancashire District Organiser of the union in 1891 and five years later also became that area's secretary. A major trade union figure in Oldham, he became president of Oldham Trades Council, 1892–4, and its secretary 1894–1912. Clynes was President of his union from 1912.

Clynes was present at the foundation conference of the Independent Labour Party in 1893. He was a delegate at the Second International conference in Zurich later that year and at several other international conferences. He was also present at the foundation meeting of the Labour Representation Committee in February 1900. He served on its National Executive Committee, representing the trades councils (1904–8) and the trade unions (1909–39). He chaired the annual conference held at Portsmouth, January 1909.

Clynes stood unsuccessfully for Oldham council in 1901, 1902 and 1903. However, in the 1906 general election he was elected for Manchester North-East (later known as Manchester, Platting). He held the seat until 1931, even being returned unopposed in 1918. He won the seat back in the 1935 general election and remained an MP until he retired at the 1945 general election.

After Britain had entered the European war in 1914, Clynes was the leading ILP member in the Parliamentary Labour Party to support the war effort. In this he was in line with the preponderant view of trade union leaders. From early 1915 he served on the Munition Workers' Health Committee. At the time of the formation of the first wartime coalition government, May 1915, Clynes was opposed to the Labour Party participating. At the time of the formation of the second coalition government under Lloyd George, Clynes was in favour of Labour participation in view of what he judged to be a grave military and political situation.

In 1917–18 Clynes became the leading Labour figure in charge of food regulation. After the May 1917 engineering strikes he was appointed to the commission enquiring into the causes of industrial unrest. When Lloyd George appointed Lord Rhondda to be Food Controller (May 1917) he appointed Clynes to be Parliamentary Secretary to the Ministry of Food. When Rhondda died in July 1918, Clynes succeeded him as Food Controller. Thus he followed Arthur Henderson in being one of Labour's post-war leaders who had ministerial experience. His role at the Ministry of Food enhanced his reputation. At the end of the war Clynes was in favour of Labour remaining in Lloyd George's coalition, but when the Party decided otherwise, Clynes resigned from the government.

After the 1918 general election Clynes was elected Vice-Chairman of the Parliamentary Labour Party, in effect deputy leader. Clynes, along with Adamson, J H Thomas and (after a by-election) Arthur Henderson, opposed the Lloyd George coalition government and also made clear his commitment to democratic socialism, denouncing communism in Russia and at home. In February 1921 Clynes became Chairman of the Parliamentary Labour Party, with J H Thomas and Stephen Walsh as his Vice-Chairmen. He led the Labour Party into the 1922 general election, in which it gained 67 seats, raising its total to 142. However, in the post-election leadership election, Clynes was defeated by Ramsay MacDonald by 61 votes to 56. He served again as Vice-Chairman, 1922–31.

In January 1924 Clynes moved the vote of censure in the House of Commons which defeated Baldwin and led to the formation of the first Labour government. Clynes became Lord Privy Seal and Deputy Leader of the House of Commons. Clynes' main work was acting in the Commons for MacDonald, who was often away in his second role of Foreign Secretary. He occupied No 11 Downing Street. In the second Labour government (1929–31), Clynes was Home Secretary. Clynes' decisions included refusing Trotsky asylum in Britain. He also took much interest in prison reform, improving factory conditions and health and safety matters.

On his return to Parliament in 1935 Clynes was pressed to stand again as leader but declined. He remained a loyal and reliable elder statesman of the Labour Movement until he retired. His later years were clouded by the injuries his wife sustained from enemy action in the Second World War, which left her an invalid. He and Mary Elizabeth Harper, a textile worker, had married in 1893. He died on 23 October 1949 and she soon afterwards.

He published his two-volume *Memoirs* in 1937. Biographies include: Edward George, *From Mill-Boy To Minister: The Life of the Rt. Hon J R Clynes MP* (1918); 'A Parliamentary Colleague', 'Rt. Hon J R Clynes: Deputy Leader of the Labour Party' in Herbert Tracey (ed), *The Book of The Labour Party*, Vol 3 (London, Caxton Publishing Co, late 1920s) and J S Middleton, 'Clynes, John Robertson', *DNB*, 1950.

Professor Chris Wrigley

Ken Coates   (1930–)

Ken Coates had an enormous influence on the Labour Party of the 1970s through his leading role in the Institute for Workers Control (IWC), an organisation which brought together radical socialist advocates of the Yugoslav model of industrial democracy with leading trade unionists.

Kenneth Sidney Coates was born on 16 September 1930 and left school to work in the Nottinghamshire coalfields as a miner in 1948. After obtaining a State Scholarship to study at Nottingham University, he lectured there as an adult education tutor from 1960 to 1980. After a period of sectarian squabbling in Trotskyist groups, he was elected to the presidency of Nottingham City Labour Party, where he worked through the International Marxist Group (IMG) to criticise the Labour Government's support of the Vietnam War. The virulence with which he attacked Wilson led to his expulsion from the party in 1965, and he fought a five-year campaign, ultimately successful, to be reinstated. As editor of *The Week*, he worked through the Bertrand Russell Peace Foundation and, after breaking with the Trotskyists over his opposition to an unofficial dock strike in 1967, he helped to establish Spokesman Books as a vehicle for his own brand of radical politics. Thereafter, he stood out against attempts to set up a new Marxist party independently of Labour, calling instead for the left to fight for democracy within the Labour Party rather than be lost in a sectarian wilderness.

However, it was his leading role in the IWC which established his major contribution to Labour. The IWC had been set up in 1964 under the auspices of the Labour journal *Voice of the Unions*, and benefited from the rising industrial militancy of the decade. Coates emerged, with Tony Topham, as the principal ideologist of workers' control, arguing tirelessly against the old Labour model of the public corporation as a bureaucratic and remote body insensitive to consumers and despotic to its workers. The corporatist model of nationalisation, still espoused by Labour radicals such as Michael Foot, was challenged by the demand for a libertarian and decentralised polity, where companies were sensitive to the working-class community because they were democratically controlled by the workers themselves. Workers' participation was rejected as merely a ruse to preserve wage-slavery; it was workers' management which lay at the heart of the IWC vision of socialism. In pamphlets and books such as *Industrial Democracy in Great Britain* (1967) and *Can the Workers Run Industry?* (1968), Coates sought to recapture the syndicalist and guild socialist traditions of Labour, presenting himself as a witness in the tradition of radical Dissent.

The IWC's support of the shop stewards' movement as the embodiment of grass-roots democracy attracted trade unionists like Jack Jones (leader of the giant Transport and General Workers Union from 1969) and Hugh Scanlon (leader of the Engineers' Union from 1967). Both had their roots in shop-floor militancy and both expressed an interest in the more radical doctrines of industrial democracy. Most importantly, they controlled the votes of the two biggest unions in the Labour Party, and were able to push Labour decisively to the left after its election defeat in 1970. The effect of this was seen in 1973, when the Labour conference adopted a programme which stressed the need to shift power as well as wealth to working people through industrial democracy as well as public ownership.

Coates was elected a Labour MEP for Nottingham in 1989, but never lost his radical socialist roots – he fought passionately against the ending of Clause 4 of the party constitution in 1995, and (with Hugh Kerr) was expelled from the Labour Party in 1998 for openly opposing the centralisation of selection procedures for Labour's European Parliament candidates. He stood for the Alternative Labour List in the 1999 elections but was swamped by Labour at the polls, a victim at last of the machine against which he had fought through his life.

Geoffrey Foote

Michael Cocks (Lord Cocks of Hartcliffe) (1929–2001)

Michael Cocks was one of the four men who saved the Callaghan Government from defeat time and time again during the period 1976 to 1979. He was appointed Government Chief Whip in April 1976 when Wilson resigned and Callaghan became Prime Minister. By then he had been in the Government Whips' Office for two years, but that Government never had the luxury of any majority worth talking about. Jim Callaghan made three key appointments which helped his Government to survive until the ravages of the 'winter of discontent' in 1978–79 brought it to the verge of collapse, to be snuffed out – by one vote – in March 1979. These appointments were Michael Foot as Leader of the Commons, Michael Cocks as his Chief Whip and Walter Harrison as Cocks' deputy. It was Walter Harrison's job – each day – to scour the corridors of the Commons in order to secure a majority for the Government on any given day. One was enough, and often that was all they had.

Michael Cocks had to rule the Whip's Office with a rod of iron and as a result gained a reputation as a hard man. He had succeeded Bob Mellish as Chief Whip who was also bereft of numbers. Early in Cocks' reign there came the famous incidence of Michael Heseltine swinging the Mace, and earning his nickname of Tarzan. It also resulted in Margaret Thatcher breaking off 'the usual channels' for some time.

During the period from 1974 to 1979 government supporters in the Commons had the most arduous of tasks, for they had not only to sustain their Government and avoid defeat, but also to deliver the Manifesto programme. Trimming and tacking throughout that period was the order of the day, and it is largely to the credit of Michael Cocks and his Whips that there was only one major piece of legislation – the Nationalisation of Ship Repairing Bill – that had to be jettisoned. It was during that period that a significant number of Labour MPs died, substantially from, amongst other causes, the daily and nightly burden of being at Westminster and trudging through the Lobbies, Tony Crosland, Maurice Edelman and Hugh Delargy being amongst them. It was also a period when hitherto 'safe' Labour seats were lost in by-elections, huge Labour majorities in places like Workington and Ashfield being lost, only to be regained later. It was also a far from easy time both within the Party in the country and within the trade unions. It may appear that these matters did not directly affect the fortunes or otherwise within the Parliamentary Labour Party but that is not so. Labour MPs are subject to constituency pressures, and that in turn is reflected within Parliament. It was also a time when the Lib-Lab Pact was fashioned, devolution was an issue and the Scot Nats were rampant. Michael Cocks saw them all off.

Michael Francis Lovell Cocks was the son of Dr H F Lovell Cocks and was educated at Bristol University. He was first married to Janet MacFarlane in 1954 and they had two sons and two daughters. He married for a second time in 1979 to Valerie Davis. During his service as the Government Chief Whip – from 1976 to 1979 and on into opposition until 1985, Michael Cocks had to contend with running battles within his constituency party. He was, as his position demanded, tied to his duties at Westminster and, as would be his duty and inclination, to both advocate and defend the record of his Government – which of course was that of his constituency party. This was at a time when the procedure for mandatory reselection became the vogue, and despite leaving his post as Chief Whip in order to fight the reselection battle, he failed to be reselected and left the Commons in 1987. He entered the Lords as Lord Cocks of Hartcliffe and had the unusual but wholly acceptable situation of having as his two Supporters – those who introduce the new Peer to his fellow peers – both the then Opposition Chief Whip, Lord Ponsonby, and the then Government Chief Whip, Lord Bertie Denham. After the frenetic nature of his later period in the Commons, he took to the Lords like a duck to water.

When he entered the Commons in 1970 it was after he had been employed in various education posts since 1954 and was a lecturer at Bristol Polytechnic. He had already fought three parliamentary seats which would be viewed as unwinnable: at Bristol West in 1959 and at South Gloucester in 1964 and 1966. He served in the Government Whips Office before becoming Chief Whip in 1976 on Jim Callaghan becoming Prime Minister. Any majority soon went and the Lib-Lab Pact saw the Government through until that winter of discontent in 1978/79. It was Michael Cocks who announced to a stunned House of Commons in March 1979 that Airey Neave, Margaret Thatcher's Northern Ireland spokesman, had been blown to pieces within the precincts of the Palace of Westminster.

On going to the Lords in 1987 he quickly established his authority as a person who understood Parliamentary procedure and became a Deputy Chairman of the House, thus sitting upon the Woolsack, presiding over often contentious Committee Stages of bills, often long into the night. He was especially interested in the administration of the House and gained a reputation for asking searching and penetrating questions. In 1988 he became the Deputy Chairman of the London Docklands Development Corporation and in 1993 served as the Deputy Chairman of the Governors of the BBC. In the Lords he was always articulate on matters affecting the Middle East and the Arab–Israeli issues. He carried over into his service in the Lords a playing interest in the parliamentary cricket team, turning out for it many, many times. Michael Cocks maintained to the end the unspoken and unwritten code of Chief Whips, keeping close to his chest the many matters to which he became privy in his role as Government Chief Whip. From his official office at No 12 Downing Street, with its internal access through to No 11 (Chancellor) to No 10 (Prime Minister) and then to the Cabinet Office he was at the very heart of government for years. His is a story of knowing where the bodies lie. He never divulged these secrets, and tragically died at the height of his considerable parliamentary prowess of a heart attack on 26 March 2001.

Rt. Hon Lord Graham of Edmonton

G D H Cole (1899–1959)

George Douglas Howard Cole was one of the most influential socialist intellectuals to influence the Labour Party for much of the 20th century, shaping the party's thinking through various stages of its evolution. While he is not regarded as highly as in earlier years, his thought can be still be seen in much of Labour's commitment to a pluralist and decentralised society and nation.

Cole was born on 25 September 1889 at Cambridge, the son of a pawnbroker who shortly afterwards became a successful estate agent in Ealing. Educated at St Paul's School and Balliol College, Oxford, he took a Prize Fellowship at Magdalen in 1912. Cole became a socialist after reading the romances of William Morris at school, and the influence of Morris's paeans to medievalism and rejection of the utilitarian values of capitalism were to remain with him throughout his life. To this romantic outlook he added the intellectual influence of Rousseau's conception of the small republic. As a result, despite joining the Fabians at Oxford, he developed a profound dislike of the Webbs and their collectivist elitism.

Instead, influenced by the anarcho-syndicalist militancy then in the ascendant in France and combining it with the pluralism of J N Figgis, the republican politics of Rousseau and the medievalist romanticism of Morris, Cole took the guild socialist ideas then developing through the periodical *The New Age* and applied them to an industrial society. In his enormously influential *The World of Labour* (1913), which first brought Cole to the notice of the socialist left and the unions, and then in books such as *Self-Government in Industry* (1917) and *Guild Socialism Restated* (1920), Cole became the foremost advocate of the new doctrine. While accepting the class-war rhetoric common to the Left at that time, the essence of his guild ideas lay in his opposition to the slavery of the wage system, which destroyed individuality and creativity in the worker, reducing men to the status of a commodity. Cole saw the labour unrest of pre-war Britain as a natural reaction to such indignities, but he rejected the state socialist remedies proposed by the Fabians as merely substituting one tyrant – the private employer – for another, the 'servile state' (as it was described by Hilaire Belloc). Where the state socialists wished to use a centralised state to redistribute wealth, ignoring the relations of production which lay at the heart of the maldistribution of power in society, Cole saw slavery rather than poverty as the fundamental evil in society.

To remedy this evil, Cole looked to the self-government of small communities, grounded in the shop-floor democracy which he saw as embodied in a modern workers' committee, or guild. These guilds were to be the new trade unions, free of the union bureaucracy which had grown during the 19th century, concerned with the self-government of industry rather than the collective bargaining between employer and wage-labourer characteristic of capitalism and state socialism. The guild allowed the worker to be a positive and active citizen within the local community. While society was a plurality in which the citizen would function in a number of guises – consumer as well as producer, social and political as well as economic – and although regional and national federations of guilds would regulate and co-ordinate local guilds, it was the small unit of the workshop and the factory which were the fundamental units of democracy in an industrial society. It was the workers' management of industry which would serve as a form of genuine democracy, as opposed to the 'bare ballot-box democracy' which functioned to create a formal charade of popular rule in modern society. The guild democracy would be a functional democracy, representing social groups, rather than the formal political democracy which represented geographical constituencies which bore no relation to the social realities of class and status in the community.

There would still be a territorial state, as the nation was a legitimate political unit for Cole (he refused to accept the syndicalist demand for a general strike against war, correctly foreseeing that patriotism would swamp class consciousness), but in the event of a conflict of interests between the state and the guild, Cole took a libertarian approach. Where the state was sovereign in matters of defence and international affairs, it had no right to interfere in matters of industry or religion.

His frustration with the Webbs led him to resign from the Fabian Society in 1915 when, with friends such as William Mellor, the cartoonist Will Dyson and Conrad Noel (the Red Vicar of Thaxted in Essex), he founded the National Guilds League in April 1915. Through his work in the National Industrial Conference and the National Building Guild, Cole and the NGL sought to make guild socialism a reality, seeing it as the British form taken by the idea of soviet democracy sweeping Europe in the aftermath of the Russian Revolution. Ironically, just as the ILP adopted guild socialism as its aim at its 1922 conference, the economic depression destroyed the National Building Guild and severely weakened the trade unions which Cole saw as the vehicles of social change.

Isolated and politically impotent, Cole withdrew from the abstract heights of socialist theory in the 1920s to engage in a chronicling of the co-operative and trade union movement and of the Labour Party. Despite an attitude to woman as a low type of being and a growing disgust with all aspects of sex, he married Margaret Postgate in August 1918. They lived together in Chelsea and Oxford, where he became Robert Mynors Reader in Economics and a Fellow of University College in 1925. It was perhaps through his role as an academic mentor, first established in the 1920s through the 'Cole Group' (including Hugh Gaitskell), that he contributed most to the Labour movement, albeit intangibly.

Alert as ever to intellectual developments in Europe and in particular to the new corporatist ideas of a functional polity in which social and economic groups outside the formal political sphere of Parliament should have their say in government, Cole wrote *The Next Ten Years* (1929) as Labour's answer to the Lloyd George Liberal programme of overcoming the Depression. Taking on board the under-consumptionist economics of Hobson (to the end of his life he described himself as a Hobsonian in economics, not a Keynesian), Cole proceeded to outline a structure of economic planning in which the different interest groups would have some participation in decision-making. While he never lost his faith in local self-government, he now placed his stress on the active state as a transition to an ideal which was relegated to a distant future. However, his earlier libertarian functionalism had now become almost subsumed in a centralised polity in which the representatives of capital and labour planned the economy in alliance with the State.

A MacDonald loyalist in 1929, Cole was adopted as Labour candidate for the King's Norton division of Birmingham in 1930, but resigned before the election as a result of illness. His disillusionment with the 1929–31 Labour Government led him to lead the 'loyal grousers' of the Society for Socialist Inquiry and Propaganda and the New Fabian Research Bureau. Ernest Bevin of the Transport Workers Union was a prize ally, but Bevin broke with Cole when the latter negotiated with ILP dissidents to form the Socialist League in 1932. Thereafter, Cole espoused the Popular Front of Liberals, Socialists and Communists to defeat Fascism, but his direct political activities (he stood unsuccessfully as Labour candidate for Oxford University in 1945) were never as important as his intellectual influence.

Cole finally settled in Oxford in the autumn of 1940 to escape the Blitz (a diabetic, his nerves had already been badly affected by the insulin treatment), and became Chichele Professor of Political Thought at All Souls College in 1944. He had been closely associated with Nuffield College from its inception in 1937, and it was there that he helped to organise the wartime Nuffield Reconstruction Survey into the present conditions of industry and the population. Cole's own innovation was to hold a series of Private Conferences, mainly in Balliol College, which brought together progressive employers, trade unionists and socialist theorists in an attempt to develop a consensus on a mixed economy and socialist planning – the importance of these conferences in helping to form the post-war settlement of the mixed economy, welfare and planning is only now beginning to be recognised.

In his last years (he died on 14 January 1959), his interest in the republican ideas of direct democracy at the local level re-emerged in the 1950s in a series of articles and introductions to books such as Pribicevic's *The Shop Stewards Movement and Workers Control 1910–22* (1959). He saw the new shop stewards movement of the 1950s as a vehicle for social change and grassroots democracy, and the discussions in his Holywell flat strongly influenced socialists such as Stuart Hall and Charles Taylor to develop the ideas of the New Left which were to enjoy such influence in the 1970s through the Institute for Workers Control and the Bennite Left.

The key works on Cole are Margaret Cole's *The Life of G D H Cole* (1971) and A.W. Wright, *G D H Cole and Socialist Democracy* (1979).

Geoffrey Foote

A J Cook   (1883–1931)

A J Cook was an impassioned orator who had a great following among the British coal miners and who came, in the 1920s, to symbolise the miners' determined but ineffective struggle against the mineowners' insistence on lower wages and longer hours. As E P Harries wrote of him in *The British Labour Party* (1948), he attempted the impossible.'He was the successful firebrand on the platform at weekends. He tried to be the conciliatory negotiator during midweek. But his language was so extreme on the platform that he was not able to overcome the prejudices in the minds of those he met across the table.'

Arthur James Cook was born on 22 November 1883, the son of Selina and Tom Cook in Wookey, Somerset. Beginning his working life as a farm labourer he was undoubtedly influenced by his mother's religious convictions, becoming a Baptist lay-preacher, a training ground not unique for developing trade union leaders and labour figures of his generation.

At the tender age of 17 in 1901, out of financial necessity more than youthful adventure, Cook sought work in the booming South Wales coal-field, settling on the Trefor Colliery in Porth in the Rhondda. In 1906 he married Annie Edwards, the daughter of his landlord. An atavistic attendee at the Porth Baptist Chapel, he decided to join the South Wales Miners Federation and the ILP, becoming increasingly politicised to the extent that he and his wife were forced to leave their local chapel.

In 1911 Cook won a scholarship to the Central Labour College, London, and the following year he helped to write *The Miners' Next Step*, a report of the reform committee of the South Wales Miners' Federation. During World War One he was an outspoken pacifist. In 1917 he led attempts to resist the Government's plans to draft 20,000 miners from the pits into the army. For Cook, 'As a worker I have more regard for the interests of my class than any nation. The interests of my class are not benefited by this war, hence my opposition.' In 1919 Cook was elected to the Rhondda District Council, where he added colour to the dreary debates and worked hard on social matters, and was elected as Miners Agent on the Rhondda No.1 district of the South Wales Miners Federation. Working as he was at this point extremely closely with the communists, in 1918 and again in 1921, having had his house windows smashed and the house raided by the police, he was jailed for his leadership of striking miners. Elected to the Executive of the Miners' Federation of Great Britain in 1921, he became its Secretary in 1924. Now Secretary of the most potent and numerically strong union – boasting 800,000 members – Cook told the *Daily Herald*: 'I will not be satisfied until private enterprise in the mining industry is abolished'.

The stormclouds of depression were gathering over the British coal industry, however, and the next few years saw a period of shadow boxing between mine owners and the MFGB over wages and conditions. The government appointed a Royal Commission under Herbert Samuel in September 1925 to find a way forward for the coal industry which reported on 10 March 1926. It accepted a number of the Miners Union recommendations including the seven-hour day and national wage agreements but stated that wage reductions would be a preferable option to avoid colliery closures. Cook had declared in advance that the miners would not accept wage reductions or longer hours whatever the circumstances – 'Not a minute on the day, not a penny off the pay' – and was now boxed in. As E P Harries wrote, 'Cook roused the whirlwind. But instead of riding it, it carried him, until the miners were back at the end of six months stoppage, much more thoroughly beaten than they need have been in different circumstances.' The strike began on 1 May 1926 with a one million miner lock-out and became a general strike within days. When the Trades Union Congress abandoned the General Strike, Cook urged the miners to return to work, but, after their initial refusal, he directed their strike until they capitulated.

The following period was grim, particularly for those who had been steadfast and true throughout the 'lock-out'. Cook was defiant in the face of abject failure but became the target for those who sought a scapegoat for the tragic failure of 1926: Ramsay Macdonald dismissed Cook as 'incompetent'. Cook concluded that the best hope for the miners was the election of a Labour government, a position which drew criticism from the communists.

The government's draft Coal Bill of 1929 proposed a reduction in hours and a national levy to subsidise exports, but it omitted the points at issue between the mine-owners and the MFGB – namely national agreements on and the level of wage rates. When it became law in August 1930 it was substantially amended but little improved. Increasingly frustrated by the failures of the MacDonald government, Cook joined seventeen Labour MPs in signing the Mosley manifesto of December 1930 calling for protectionism, industrial rationalisation, public works and slum clearance. He did not, however, swallow the later Mosley agenda.

He failed properly to look after a leg injury sustained during a scuffle at a 1926 public meeting, and in January 1931 he had to have his right leg amputated (above the knee) to save his life. Cook kept to himself his contraction of cancer and died on 2 November 1931, aged only 46.

Ian Geary

Robin Cook   (1946–)

Robin Cook is one the finest parliamentary performers of his generation. His ruthless but witty demolitions of hapless Tory ministers in House of Commons debates were one of the bright spots of Labour's long spell in opposition. A leading member of the party's 'soft left', Cook has often seemed ill at ease with the rightward drift of New Labour and with the superficial nature of modern politics. His transition to government was bruising, but he proved to be an effective Foreign Secretary in age of economic interdependence and supranational politics. Following the post-election reshuffle of June 2001, it is likely that he will prove an equally effective Leader of the House of Commons.

Robin Cook was born in Bellshill, Lanarkshire, on 28 February 1946. Moving to Aberdeen at the age of four, his family moved to Edinburgh when he was fourteen. From a young age, he became interested in politics and learnt to spar with adversaries at Edinburgh Royal High School's debating society. At Edinburgh University, where he studied English Literature from 1964 to 1968, Cook was a leading member of the debating society and chairman of the Labour Club. In 1967–68 he was Chairman of the Scottish Association of Labour Students' Organisations.

After a brief career in teaching, Cook turned his full attention to politics. In the 1970 general election, he fought and lost Edinburgh North and became Secretary of Edinburgh City Labour Party, a post he held until 1972. From 1971 to 1974 Cook was elected to the Edinburgh Corporation, where he focused on housing. In the 1974 general election, on his twenty-eighth birthday, he won the seat of Edinburgh Central, increasing his majority when Harold Wilson went back to the country eight months later.

When he reached Westminster, Cook immediately fell in with the left wing of the Parliamentary Labour Party, frequently opposing decisions of the Wilson and Callaghan governments. He was in favour of a massive redistribution of wealth, state control of the economy, unilateral nuclear disarmament, cuts in defence spending, and was against British membership of the Common Market. Cook also opposed devolution, believing that any expression of nationalism was a betrayal of the working class.

Cook was finally appointed to Labour's front bench in December 1980 as an Opposition Treasury Spokesman (which he remained until 1983). When boundary changes turned his Edinburgh Central constituency into a marginal seat, Cook moved to and won the newly created seat of Livingston in the 1983 election, having fought off Tony Benn to win the nomination. He has been Livingston's MP ever since.

In November 1983 Cook was elected to the shadow cabinet for the first time and was named Labour's European spokesman, even though Cook was still unconvinced of the merits of European Community membership. Two years later Cook became the party's campaigns co-ordinator. He recognised the need to upgrade the party's campaign apparatus and to modernise local party structures. He played an early but key role in equipping Labour with modern campaigning techniques. He was spokesman on the City whilst briefly out of the shadow cabinet 1986–87.

As Shadow Social Services Secretary (July 1987–November 1989) and Health (to July 1992) Cook earned his spurs harrying the Tories for cutting social security benefits while reducing taxes for the wealthy, and for introducing market-oriented reforms to the NHS. One newspaper called him a 'one-man opposition' for his attacks on the Conservatives NHS reforms, which did much to boost Labour's popularity.

As Shadow Trade and Industry Secretary (July 1992 to October 1994) he harangued the government for its programme of coal mine closures. And as Shadow Foreign Secretary (from October 1994) Cook ridiculed the Tory divisions on Europe, further destabilising John Major's shaky administration.

His sharp-tongued wit and forensic grasp of detail were most brilliantly deployed against the Tory government in the arms-to-Iraq affair. Ministers and officials had several days to prepare their responses to the exhaustive and convoluted report drawn up by Sir Richard Scott in February 1996. Cook was given only two hours. Nevertheless, having sieved out the key findings, Cook trounced his opponent, Ian Lang, in the Commons debate, ridiculing the government's attempts to cover up the affair and avoid all responsibility. The government narrowly survived a subsequent Labour motion, but further serious damage to its credibility had been inflicted, and in some considerable style. Shortly after the debate, Tony Blair sent Cook a note congratulating him for one of the finest parliamentary performances of recent times.

Cook's stock had reached an all-time high. It was not to last. Although he was one of Labour's 'big four' senior figures during the last few years before the 1997 election and chairman of the National Policy Forum, he was clearly not in the vanguard of New Labour and his influence declined as that of the Blair-Brown-Mandelson troika grew. Rather than confronting the leadership over the course of policy, he chose instead to send the occasional warning shot. If anything, this only confirmed to his detractors within the party that Cook was 'unreliable'. Cook's standing was not helped by his testy relationship with Gordon Brown.

Cook's first few months as Foreign Secretary were turbulent. The most serious blow was the break-up in August 1997 of his marriage to Margaret, a consultant haematologist, whom he had met at Edinburgh University and married in 1969. Cook was waiting with Margaret at Heathrow airport for a flight to the US when he was told that the *News of the World* was planning to reveal his affair with Gaynor Regan, his secretary.

Cook decided there and then on a divorce (and later married Gaynor). Many commentators interpreted his decisiveness as a ruthless exercise in news management. Ironically for a man who had always kept his political and private lives separate, Cook's political authority was undermined. He had long accepted that his image counted against him. At this stage of his career, his private life did too.

A more substantive political test was his attempt to show that a Labour foreign policy could be different from a Conservative one. Shortly after becoming foreign secretary Cook announced that Labour's foreign policy would have an 'ethical dimension', with greater emphasis on human rights and regulation of the arms trade. However much the phrase has since been misinterpreted, it offered an infinitely flexible yardstick against which critics could judge the government's every measure. Thus when the government decided it was 'not practical' to revoke existing contracts for the sale of Hawk fighter jets to Indonesia, Cook's ethical intentions were ridiculed by left- and rightwing critics alike.

Despite such criticism, Cook has shown that a Labour foreign policy can amount to more than naked self-interest. His achievements include helping to push through an EU code of conduct on arms sales, a ban on the British use of anti-personnel landmines, and helping to establish an international criminal court. The government's robust support for military intervention in Kosovo points to the emergence of a new principle in British foreign policy, the doctrine of humanitarian intervention.

The biggest shift in Labour's foreign policy has, however, been on Britain's relations with Europe. The shift in Cook's attitudes to European integration matches that of his party. Like many left-wingers in the 1970s and early 1980s, Cook opposed British membership of the Common Market on the grounds that it was inimical to socialism and a dilution of economic sovereignty. Attitudes began to change in the mid-1980s, not least when the European Community appeared to offer some constraints on otherwise unbridled Thatcherism.

But even as Shadow Foreign Secretary, Cook was considered to be the Labour leadership's leading Eurosceptic. In fact, by the mid-1990s Cook's scepticism was aimed primarily at economic and monetary union which many on the left considered to be a 'bankers' plot'. With the euro-zone encompassing several countries led by centre-left governments, it became clear that the euro was indeed compatible with social democracy. By the end of Tony Blair's first government, Cook had become the most vociferous supporter of British membership of the single currency in the Cabinet.

Unusually for a politician, Cook has rarely tried to advance through the ranks of the party by making friends and destroying enemies. His reluctance to dedicate time to building broad alliances and his 'non-clubbable' nature has made it harder for him to prosper in New Labour. He has chosen instead to progress through hard work. His few distractions are riding, horse racing and amateur punditry.

But as Foreign Secretary, Cook succeeded in making personal relations work in his favour. On several occasions he courted controversy with his outspoken style of diplomacy. He also struck up close working relationships, with Madeleine Albright, the US secretary of state in particular, but also with other EU foreign ministers. It was a sign of his standing on the European stage that he was elected to the Presidency of the Party of European Socialists in May 2001.

Beyond foreign policy, Cook also played a key role in developing Labour's ideas on reshaping the constitution and headed the Labour-Liberal Democrat joint committee on constitutional reform. He is also a leading proponent of introducing a fairer voting system for Westminster elections. Although Cook's power inside Tony Blair's first government has waned, he is likely to play a critical role in any decision on the euro and on electoral reform, the two issues that will determine the fate of the second Labour government and the very nature of British politics. John Kampfner's biography, *Robin Cook*, was published in 1998.

Ben Hall

Jack Cooper (Lord Cooper) (1908–88)

Jack Cooper, General Secretary/Treasurer of the National Union of General and Municipal Workers (NUGMW) from 1962 to 1973 was a moderate trade union leader in the mould of his predecessor Tom Williamson and Arthur Deakin, the General Secretary of the Transport and General Workers' Union from 1945 to 1955. He was a firm believer in the authority of the union executive and full-time officials, especially its General Secretary; he was a strong supporter of good relations with employers; and he was fiercely loyal to the Labour leadership. At the same time, he was remarkably open to ideas. He was an early promoter of a broad range of new trade union services; he argued that British trade unions could learn much from Swedish methods of collective bargaining, including a wages policy; and long before it was fashionable, he was committed to the European idea.

Born at Stockton Heath on 7 June 1908, he was educated at Stockton Heath Council School and briefly at Lymn Grammar School before leaving school at sixteen to work at Crosfields Soap Works, Warrington. Fortunately for him, his uncle, Charles Dukes, who was by then Lancashire District Secretary before becoming General Secretary in 1934, appointed him a legal officer at the Manchester office of the union. In 1933, at the age of 25, he became a Lancashire District official; a National Industrial Officer in 1942; and Southern District Secretary in 1944.

In the longstanding tradition of the General and Municipal Workers, Cooper was also actively involved in Labour politics. He was a Manchester City Councillor from 1936 to 1942 and in 1949 he was elected to the London County Council. In 1950, he was returned as Labour MP for Deptford and was almost immediately appointed as PPS to Patrick Gordon Walker, the Secretary of State for Commonwealth Relations. However, the union executive understandably forced him to choose between a promising parliamentary future and his full-time post as Southern District Secretary. Jack Cooper opted to put his union career first and in 1952 was elected as Chairman of the NUGMW, an influential though unpaid position which he held with distinction for nine years. He served on the Labour party NEC 1952–57. When Tom Williamson retired in 1961, there were only two serious candidates, Jack Cooper and Fred Hayday, National Industrial Officer for the gas industry and son of Arthur Hayday, the former Midland District Secretary. Cooper won by 305,647 votes to 206,654 and took up his post at the beginning of 1962.

Immediately, Cooper set about modernising the union. First he built up its financial resources. At the 1963 Congress, he successfully argued for a big increase in members contributions and in 1964 he sold off the newly-built prestige central London headquarters and bought an older building near Esher. He significantly expanded the union's education, research and financial services. He also surrounded himself with talented people from a younger generation, including David Basnett, who succeeded him as General Secretary, Derek Gladwin, who later became Southern District Secretary (both of whom became Labour Peers) and John Edmonds, who followed Basnett as General Secretary in 1986.

Under Cooper's leadership, the union continued to support the Labour leadership. When Harold Wilson won the 1964 election, the union gave strong backing to the government's attempts to introduce a successful incomes policy, which Cooper believed would help his low-paid workers. While moving the address on the Queen's Speech in the Lords (he had been made a Life Peer in 1966 as Lord Cooper of Stockton Heath), he also argued for reform of industrial relations, including compulsory arbitration. Almost alone amongst the trade union leaders, he supported Barbara Castle's legislative proposals contained in *In Place of Strife* and, as TUC Chairman in 1970–1971, he found himself in the awkward position of supporting trade union registration under the Conservative Industrial Relations Act, while the trade unions were campaigning against the legislation. He seemed out of kilter with the times and the early

1970s found Jack Jones'TGWU and Hugh Scanlon's AUEW outpacing his union in the fierce competition for new members.

His outside appointments included being a member of the National Economic Development Council, Governor of the London Business School and also of Ruskin College and a Visiting Fellow of Nuffield College, Oxford. He married Nellie Spencer in 1934 and had three daughters. The marriage was dissolved in 1969, and he subsequently married Mrs Joan Rodgers. He died on 2 September 1988.

Rt Hon. Lord Radice

Frank Cousins (1904–86)

Frank Cousins, the General Secretary of the Transport and General Workers Union from 1956 to 1969, was the most forceful of all trade union leaders to emerge in the post-war years of Britain's Labour Movement. He, more than any other single union leader, played a crucial role in moving the Labour party and the trade union movement to the left and turned the TGWU, which was then the largest trade union in the country and a pillar of the Labour right-wing Establishment, into a driving force for radical left-wing reform and nuclear disarmament.

The reasons behind this quite remarkable success go beyond his own forceful and commanding personality. He emerged on the trade union and political scene at a moment of social, economic and even psychological change in the post-war development of organised labour in Britain. By the mid '50s a good deal of disillusion had set in to dampen the idealism of the immediate post-war years and the achievements of the Attlee Governments of 1945–51.

The battle between the right and left wings of the Labour Party, the growing turbulence across most of British industry, the seemingly perpetual economic crises besetting the country, together led to much of that disenchantment. And the split between right and left inside the Labour Party became sharper and more bitter than ever. This became focused on the fight for ideological supremacy, chiefly between the Gaitskellites on the right and the Bevanites on the left. Before Cousins emerged as general secretary of the TGWU the union was a bedrock of Gaitskellite support. Cousins' election in 1956 transformed that scene if not overnight then very quickly afterwards. Indeed, after the death of both Hugh Gaitskell and Aneurin Bevan within less than two years of each other, it was Cousins who played a vital role in helping Harold Wilson to become leader of the Labour Party and eventually Prime Minister. That, in turn, was to lead to Cousins joining the Wilson Cabinet as Britain's first Minister of Technology, after the General Election of 1964.

Frank Cousins was born on 8 September 1904 at 28, Minerva Street, Bulwell, Nottinghamshire, the eldest son in a family of ten [five sons, five daughters] of Charles Fox Cousins, a coal miner and his wife Hannah Smith, the daughter of a miner from Bulwell. He was educated at Beckett Road School in Wheatley, Doncaster, and King Edward Elementary School, Doncaster, which he left at the age of fourteen in 1918 shortly before the end of World War I. He immediately started work alongside his father at Brodsworth colliery in Doncaster. He worked underground, first as a trainee then at the coalface, joining the Yorkshire Miners' Association in his first week at work. The YMA was part of the Miners' Federation of Great Britain, forerunner of the National Union of Mineworkers. After working in the colliery for more than five years Cousins was injured and left to become a truck driver, first delivering coal locally and then, in 1931, as a long-distance lorry driver – by which time he had joined the Transport & General Workers Union led by Ernest Bevin, its founder.

Cousins' job was to ferry meat between Scotland and London and it was during his experiences as a truck driver in the early 1930s witnessing the widespread poverty and unemployment across the land, that, by his own admission, he became a convinced and dedicated socialist. In July 1938 he was appointed a full-time official of the TGWU as an organiser in the Doncaster district. It should be remembered that becoming a full-time trade union activist at that time was a calling quite the equal of working for a political party. They were bitter days for organised labour and being a member of a trade union implied a constant fight for justice and even recognition rights among employers. Cousins' role of recruiting and then retaining truck drivers and trying to negotiate terms with employers who were largely anti-union was a huge task and a considerable challenge to the courage of any young union official.

It was at that time he first met Ernest Bevin – probably a turning point in his career. Bevin noted the ability of this fearless, enterprising young ex-miner. Cousins' development as a full-time official moved fast from that point – but he still had to go through the ranks. He became a district organiser for South Yorkshire during the war years, based in Sheffield and in 1944 moved to London for his first national post as the national officer for the road haulage section of the TGWU. Four years later he was appointed national secretary for the group. Cousins already had a reputation as a radical and an 'awkward character'. His political views were in conflict with those of the TGWU general secretary, the redoubtable Arthur Deakin who was a rock of the Labour Establishment. Had Deakin remained in charge it is unlikely Cousins would have gone further up the union ladder. But a remarkable series of events thrust the rebel to national prominence.

Deakin died in 1955 before he could secure his preferred successor. The job of TGWU General Secretary, arguably the most important power-broking role in the British Labour Movement at that time, went to Deakin's number two, Arthur 'Jock' Tiffin – who would *not* have been Deakin's choice. And to everyone's amazement Cousins was appointed Tiffin's deputy largely by a union executive 'liberated' from Deakin's authority. Then came the final element in an extraordinary series of chance events – Tiffin died suddenly after a mere five months in office and on 2 January 1956 Cousins was appointed 'acting' general secretary. This was confirmed on 1 May 1956 after a union ballot of record proportions – Cousins won by 503,560 votes to 77,916, which was the largest ballot return in the history of any British trade union. That was a time when the TGWU ran membership ballots only for its general secretary.

From that moment the entire political balance of the Labour Movement shifted to the Left. It was, one might say, the 'Cousins Revolution'. Cousins' impact was immediate- especially on the industrial scene. The motor industry in particular was in turmoil as the first phase of automation began to bite into industrial relations and nearly 6,000 car workers in the Birmingham and Oxford plants of the old Austin-Morris group [later British Leyland] were sacked overnight. Cousins called a strike. Then came another major industrial conflict in defiance of the Macmillan Government's pay policy – Cousins called out his London busmen in a strike that lasted nearly two months and which he came near to losing, but in the end did not. At the same time the new TGWU leader was causing problems for his more conventional colleagues on the TUC General Council as well as in the Labour Party hierarchy. All this culminated in Cousins personally associating himself – along with his wife, Nance, and his family – with the Campaign for Nuclear Disarmament as well as with Cousins and family joining the Aldermaston Marchers. Then in 1960 at the Labour Party conference at Scarborough Frank Cousins led the campaign to 'Ban the Bomb' against Hugh Gaitskell's policy [to retain the bomb] and won the vote which precipitated Gaitskell's famous 'Fight, fight and fight again' speech. Cousins and the TGWU were forced to retreat from that position in the following year though he never, personally, retreated from his opposition to nuclear weapons – not even when he became a member of the Wilson Cabinet in 1964. Indeed that was to lead to increasing friction with the Prime Minister and other Cabinet colleagues, especially over Britain's relations with the United States and during the Vietnam War. Cousins remained a rebel within the Cabinet and in July 1966 resigned to return to the TGWU in his old post as General Secretary. However his resignation issue was not on defence policy but on the Government's decision to establish a statutory pay policy which he had always opposed. He also resigned his parliamentary seat at Nuneaton – a seat 'organised' for him after Wilson's election victory in 1964.

Back at the TGWU Frank Cousins continued to oppose statutory pay policy and remained a thorn in Government flesh right up to his retirement in 1969. Indeed it can be argued that he guaranteed a continuing problem for the Government, and subsequent Governments, since it was Cousins who ensured that his successor as TGWU leader would be Jack Jones with whom he had worked closely for many years. Cousins' final role was as founding father of the Community Relations Commission, set up in 1968 by the Wilson government as the first statutory authority charged with improving race relations. This was always an issue close to his heart. Indeed he decided to remain as Chairman of the CRC even after the defeat of the Wilson government in June 1970.

The incoming Conservative government of Edward Heath [now Sir Edward] persuaded Cousins to remain in the job and he agreed to do so for a brief spell in order to ensure a firm basis for the Commission. He then went into retirement, refusing numerous invitations to enter the House of Lords, to take a Governorship in one of the British colonies, or to assume some other major public role. He wanted to remain plain Mr Frank Cousins, socialist.

As Minister of Technology he was not a parliamentary success. He never came to terms with the House of Commons or Whitehall practice. Yet he laid the foundations in his brief tenure at Technology for much that has happened since in government-inspired technological development. Indeed if he had had his way much more would have been done, and perhaps achieved, in the British computer, aircraft, and machine tool industries.

Frank Cousins married in 1930 to Annie Elizabeth [always known as 'Nance'], daughter of Percy Judd, a railway clerk in Doncaster who later became Labour Mayor of the town. They had two sons, John and Michael, and a daughter, Brenda. Frank and Nance also adopted Frances, a child of Brenda, as their own daughter. Frank Cousins died on 11 June 1986 in Chesterfield, Derbyshire.

Biographies include: *The Awkward Warrior; Life and Times of Frank Cousins* by Geoffrey Goodman (Davis Poynter, 1979; republished by Spokesman Books, 1984); *Brother Frank* by Geoffrey Goodman (1969) and *Frank Cousins* by Margaret Stewart (1968).

Geoffrey Goodman

Bernard Crick   (1929–)

Professor Bernard Crick was born on 16 December 1929. He was educated at Whitgift School and University College London and was a graduate student in the Government Department at the LSE (1950–52). After spells at Harvard, McGill and Berkeley Universities, he became a lecturer in politics at the LSE in 1957 before becoming Professor of Political Theory and Institutions at Sheffield University (1965–71) and Professor of Politics at Birkbeck College London (1971–84). He edited the influential journal *Political Quarterly* from 1966 to 1980.

Bernard Crick has made very significant contributions to both political theory and practice. His book, *In Defence of Politics* (1962; revised edition, 2001) is a very elegant and rigorous defence of the autonomy of politics. Politics cannot be reduced to administration or politicians as managers. Equally, politics cannot be reduced to a by-product of general historical processes. Rather politics arises wherever there are conflicts of interest and where, unlike for example in a tribal order, they cannot be settled authoritatively. As the fundamental way of dealing with conflicts which arise out of the free actions of individuals, politics is essential to a free society. This conception of politics is defined very subtly in the book against the claims of ideology, nationalism, etc.

It is not at all fanciful to see the views represented in this very important book as providing the backdrop to his work on citizenship and its teaching in schools. At the invitation of David Blunkett, then Secretary of State for Education, Bernard Crick chaired the Committee on Teaching Citizenship in Schools (1997–98). This report led directly to citizenship becoming an important component in the national curriculum. If as *In Defence of Politics* argues, politics and political engagement are central to a free society, then learning about both political institutions and political values is central to both politics and citizenship. Crick has thus been in the rare position of being able to facilitate a practical embodiment of his basic political values. His recent book *Essays on Citizenship* brings together these theories.

The same set of values were also crucial to his work on the reform of Parliament which led to the publication of *The Reform of Parliament* in 1964. He argued that Parliament had two central functions: to make government more efficient by making opposition and scrutiny more effective and vigorous; and to communicate political issues to the public in vivid and exciting ways. He advocated the extension and strengthening of the committee system in the House of Commons and the provision of assistance to MPs. These concerns have stayed with him as his essay *To Make the Scottish Parliament a Model for Democracy* shows. One point about reform being in part to serve the transmission of political values and issues in a vivid way via the Parliamentary process clearly links this work with the position set out in *In Defence of Politics*.

After the election defeat of the Labour Party in 1983 Bernard Crick gave a spell-binding lecture at the Fabian Society on the need for Labour to create what he called a public doctrine – that is to say a set of linked principles and ideas which would underpin policy. A public doctrine would be less elaborate than an ideology or a fully-worked-out philosophical theory but it would equally rescue policy-making from a kind of mindless pragmatism which could not adopt a strategic approach. Largely as the result of Crick's lecture the Fabian Society funded the Socialist Philosophy Group which met for many years and out of whose meetings a significant number of books and pamphlets emerged. In March 1984, as a contribution to the formation of such a public doctrine, Crick published a very substantial Fabian Tract on *Socialist Values and Time*.

It is also important to recall that Crick published a much acclaimed biography of George Orwell in 1980. This is a first-rate biographical study of someone with a very uneasy and angular relationship to the British left. It reflects through Orwell's life issues about colonialism, anti-fascism, the likes of the working class and their political interests, and the implications of the development of totalitarian states and technology.

Professor the Lord Plant of Highfield

Stafford Cripps (1889–1952)

Although born a Victorian, Stafford Cripps was in every regard a model Edwardian gentleman, devoted to family, conspicuously honourable, independent of mind and modern of thought. Logic, science, intellectual rigour, personal integrity, faith – these were his political tools and he sought to apply them with a consistency and determination that brought him many supporters in the general public, though many of his colleagues found him unbending and arrogant. His somewhat tumultuous political career – which saw him expelled from the Labour Party, posted to Russia as Ambassador, promoted to Churchill's War Cabinet and readmitted to Labour in time to become President of the Board of Trade and Chancellor – was fashioned in the cauldron of two world wars. Few politicians have achieved so much in such a short life.

Richard Stafford Cripps was born the youngest of five children in London on 24 April 1889. It was a family of mixed political allegiance. His mother, Theresa, who died when he was only four years old, was one of the nine illustrious Potter sisters, who included Beatrice, the wife and Fabian colleague of Sidney Webb; Margaret, the equally resilient wife of the Liberal lawyer and politician Henry Hobhouse; and Kate, the Christian philanthropist wife of the economist Leonard Courtney. By contrast throughout Stafford's early years his father, Sir (Charles) Alfred Cripps, was a Conservative MP. Alfred had followed his own father's example in becoming a successful barrister and taking over the family home in Buckinghamshire, Parmoor, where the young Stafford was brought up following his mother's death by Alfred with help from Theresa's sister Mary Playne.

Like his father and two older brothers Stafford studied at Winchester, but instead of following the usual Wykehamist route to Oxford and despite winning a scholarship to New College, he accepted a place at the better-equipped University College London to read Chemistry under the celebrated Sir Arthur Ramsay. Although temperamentally and intellectually suited to the scientific life, Stafford was never to finish the course as during his father's 1910 General Election campaign in South Buckinghamshire he met and fell in love with the young daughter of another local Conservative businessman (and heiress to the Eno's Salts fortune), Isobel Swithinbank. A year later they were married and Stafford had resolved to follow his father and brother Seddon in pursuing a more lucrative legal career at his father's Inn of Court, the Middle Temple. In 1913, already the father of John and Diana, he was called to the bar.

The First World War marked Stafford for life. Unlike his brothers, he was declared unfit and saw no active service. Nevertheless he briefly drove a Red Cross van in France before being summoned, like many Ramsay students, to use his chemical expertise at the national explosives factory in Queensferry. Here, thanks to an excessive workload, his health deteriorated dramatically. Suffering from a nervous breakdown and severe colitis, he was forced into medical retirement for the rest of the war. Thereafter he had to take strict control of his diet, becoming teetotal and vegetarian.

When his health slowly recuperated after the war Stafford returned to the Bar and by dint of determined hard work and often brilliant forensic aptitude he forged an extremely successful career in the new field of patent and compensation law, becoming in 1927 Britain's youngest KC. His arguments are still cited in legal training.

Three things brought Stafford into Labour politics: the war, Christianity and his father. For during the war Alfred had aligned himself with the pacific forces on the left of British politics, becoming a Liberal peer in 1914 and eventually Lord President of the Council in the first Labour Cabinet in 1924. Alfred was also an extremely active member of the Church of England, instrumental in the founding of the new General Synod. Here too Stafford followed his father, his devout faith bolstered by the experience of debilitating illness. Throughout the 1920s Stafford, and (until his death in 1925) his former headmaster at Winchester, Bishop Burge, were the driving force behind the British Council of the World Alliance, an ecumenical Christian body that saw itself as a spiritual ally of the League of Nations.

Several legal cases brought Stafford into direct contact with the Labour Party, including the 1929 election tribunal in which Stafford defended the Labour MP for Plymouth Drake, J J Moses. But it was Herbert Morrison who first sought to get Stafford to join Labour, persuading him in 1930 to become the candidate for West Woolwich. Later that year, though, when Ramsay MacDonald was looking for a new Solicitor-General, he persuaded Stafford to abandon Woolwich in favour of Bristol East and in January 1931 in the dying moments of the second Labour Government Stafford became a Labour MP, a Knight of the Realm and a member of the front bench. When a few months later Stafford rejected MacDonald's offer to remain in post in the new National Government, he did so on political, not personal grounds. The Labour Government had been too meek.

The devastation that was wreaked on the Labour ranks in the 1931 election left many of its senior figures twiddling their thumbs in Transport House whilst the close but imperfect triumvirate of George Lansbury, Clement Attlee and Stafford Cripps ran the parliamentary show. Cripps rapidly became an ardent apostle for a Labour Party that would present a more radical alternative. He joined and soon led the Socialist League, he founded (and funded) the radical newspaper *Tribune,* and when the elderly Lansbury was ill, instead of accepting Attlee's suggestion that he should lead the parliamentary party, Cripps funded Attlee's salary as temporary Leader. The trade-union-led moderates like Dalton, Morrison and Arthur Henderson, ever mindful of electoral considerations, were incensed at both what Cripps said and how he said it and the 1930s saw regular internal Party battles over his call for the nationalisation of the banks, his initial opposition to 'capitalist rearmament' and his comments on the Royal Family. Nevertheless in 1934 he was elected to the NEC, the leading proponent of the left.

With the rise of fascism in Spain, Germany and Italy, Cripps' position changed. Hoping for a worldwide alliance of socialist states to combat fascism, he first sought to bind together the British left, including the Communist and Independent Labour Parties. This had the effect of both further antagonising Labour Party colleagues and turning the Socialist League into a virtual party within a party. When the Popular Front faltered he became one of the most defiant and assertive opponents of appeasement, advocating that Labour join with disaffected Tories, Liberals and others in order to oust Chamberlain and that Britain align itself with Russia to see off the fascist threat. The NEC finally expelled him at the end of January 1939 for circulating a memorandum calling for such a popular front and following his 'Petition Campaign' the Southport Labour Party conference confirmed the expulsion, along with those of G R Strauss and Aneurin Bevan. Bevan and Strauss' immediate instincts were to seek to return to the Labour fold. Cripps by contrast chose to travel, visiting Russia and China in the immediate run-up to the war.

When Chamberlain gave way to Churchill in May 1940, Cripps was a partyless MP in search of a job, and he was fortunate that Halifax, Attlee, Churchill and (reluctantly) Dalton all agreed to his being sent to Moscow as a special envoy and (subsequently) Ambassador, unique in both holding a parliamentary seat and a diplomatic post. Both the Germans and the Russians attributed the eventual German assault on Russia and Russia's joining the Alliance to Cripps' interventions, but he played a far more influential role in the subsequent battle for Allied support for Russia and as a counter-balance to Churchill's blind distrust of Stalin and Communist Russia.

When Cripps returned to London in 1942 amidst widespread coverage of the heroic Russian battle against the invading Germans, Churchill's and British military fortunes were at a low ebb and Cripps was feted as a potential replacement PM. Churchill appointed him to the War Cabinet as Lord Privy Seal in February 1942 but succeeded in keeping him at bay by giving him next to no power or real responsibility other than looking after the House of Commons – the one job a partyless MP was singularly ill-equipped to perform. In addition he sent him to India to try and negotiate a settlement.

Cripps' sojourn in the War Cabinet was brief, and having over-played his hand with threats of resignation, he was removed to the relative backwater of the Department of Aircraft Production in November 1942. Here he excelled, bringing his considerable management ability, his genuine fascination for engineering and his passionate belief in the cause to play in the concerted drive to make the planes Britain needed to win the war.

By the end of the war Cripps had begun to make his peace with his former Labour colleagues and just as he had refused MacDonald's request to stay on in the National Government in 1931, so when Labour left the Coalition in May 1945 he turned down Churchill's offer of a place in the Caretaker Government. It came as little surprise, therefore, when Attlee made Cripps President of the Board of Trade in the landslide Cabinet. It was a role that was well-suited both to his expertise and to his personal style. He relished the drive to improve productivity so as to save the country from post-war bankruptcy, and his own personal asceticism (only marred by his chain smoking) inspired confidence in a government that had to maintain ration-book austerity. In 1946 Cripps led the government team to try and resolve independence for India.

The ravages of post-war economics took an extreme toll on the Labour Government's economic strategy and during 1947 it became increasingly clear that a coherent economic strategy was essential, incorporating both trade and fiscal issues. Meanwhile Cripps was keen to see a change of Prime Minister, and when he alone of all the plotters went to confront Attlee he succeeded not in persuading the PM to stand down but of the need for greater economic harmonisation under Cripps' own leadership. On 29 September he added Minister for Economic Affairs to his responsibilities.

When Hugh Dalton resigned as Chancellor of the Exchequer only weeks later, Cripps was his natural successor. Still the force of his personality remained his strongest suit and despite the evident economic problems facing the country he achieved through 1948 and '49 a remarkable voluntary restraint in wages and dividends. By the summer of 1949, like several of his colleagues, Cripps was far from well, and he had to take hospital treatment in Switzerland whilst the Cabinet was considering devaluing the pound. Although initially opposed, and despite several public denials that he had any intention to do so, in September 1949 after a visit to the USA with Bevin, he devalued from $4.10 to $2.80. He felt deeply wounded by Churchill's assault on his integrity from the Opposition benches.

Despite ill health Cripps laboured on to the 1950 General Election and continued as Chancellor until he finally retired in October 1950. Most of his final months were spent in a clinic in Switzerland, where, accompanied by his wife Isobel, he died on 21 April 1952.

Cripps has been poorly served by history. Keeping only an intermittent diary and saving few papers, his reputation has suffered from being hidden from view. A couple of hagiographies appeared during his life (most notably Eric Estorik's in 1949), but the lengthy delay in his official biography has left him ignored by much of Labour history (though there are two recent biographies, by Simon Burgess and by me). Yet his achievements as a lawyer and politician are significant. Although it was Hitler's invasion of Russia that eventually made Stalin's mind up in favour of joining the Allies in the war, Cripps' assiduous long-term advocacy of such an alliance made its success possible. Although he did not frame the eventual settlement he was at the heart of every negotiation for Indian independence from the 1930s on. He played a significant role in establishing the Christian consensus in favour of what Archbishop William Temple termed 'the Welfare State' and without Cripps the Labour Government's economic strategy would undoubtedly have foundered sooner and more dramatically.

Cripps was no saint, however. He was a frequent conspirator who on several occasions sought to mount challenges to Attlee – all of which faltered and failed. And he could appear stubborn, arrogant and sanctimonious. As Churchill put it; 'There, but for the grace of God, goes God.'

Chris Bryant MP

Tony Crosland (1918–77)

At the age of twenty-two, Charles Anthony Raven Crosland confidently predicted he would achieve for the Labour Party what Edward Bernstein had done for the German SPD. By the end of his life, he arguably deserved this title, having written the most important revisionist book of the century, *The Future of Socialism*, and by setting out a new vision for socialism, economic growth and equality of opportunity which provided the backdrop for successive post-war Labour Governments. His intellectual legacy even stretches to the Blair Government that came to office twenty years after his death. Crosland also achieved a significant status as a formidable Labour politician. A close friend of Labour leader Hugh Gaitskell he build a reputation as a leading reformer, particularly as Secretary of State for Education and for Environment, and as Foreign Secretary in Callaghan's Government, he was widely tipped as a possible future Prime Minister.

Yet Crosland's life remains fascinating as much for its failures as for its successes. As perhaps the leading intellectual of his generation, Crosland never achieved the office of Chancellor of the Exchequer that undoubtedly would have provided the greatest test of his skills. Whilst an inspirational figure, his peers on the revisionist wing of the party looked more to his rival Roy Jenkins for leadership than to him. Ultimately, even Crosland's revisionist agenda was brought into doubt. By 1977, the Labour Government of which he was a leading member had been forced to abandon the key elements of the post-war economic consensus which Crosland had cherished. The debate about the merits of revisionism was one which was to continue long after its key exponent had departed.

Charles Anthony Raven Crosland was born on 29 August 1918 at St Leonards-on-Sea. His father Joseph Crosland was an important civil servant in the War Office and his mother Jessie was a college lecturer. Anthony lived with his two sisters at the family home in Golders Green and then Highgate, and enjoyed the relative luxury of a middle-class upbringing.

The most distinctive feature of Crosland's childhood was the family's religious beliefs, which deeply affected his life. The family had for many generations belonged to the Plymouth Brethren, a nonconformist sect with distinctive views about acceptable lifestyles. Taboos included smoking, the theatre and even voting in elections. Crosland certainly drew much from his parents' religious fervour, including a fundamental belief in equality which was to underpin his whole life, but he also developed a passion for attacking shibboleths and puritanical views within the Labour movement which were also derived from this strict upbringing.

He was educated at a private school in Highgate and, on winning a scholarship, at Trinity College, Oxford, which he entered in 1937. Pre-war Oxford provided an atmosphere in which Crosland's political beliefs flourished. The Labour Club, whose large membership included the Marxist sympathiser Denis Healey and Roy Jenkins, was the focal point for his political development, until disagreements over Russia's role in the Second World War led Crosland to form a breakaway 'democratic socialist' club in 1941. In future years, this organisation was to provide a useful forum in which Crosland could meet the Labour Party's leading politicians, many of whom, like Hugh Dalton, were to prove invaluable allies.

After the conclusion of the war, in which Crosland saw active service as a member of the Royal Welsh Parachute Regiment, he returned to Oxford to finish his studies, gaining a first in PPE in 1946. He was soon appointed a Fellow of Trinity College where he taught economics to undergraduates, but Crosland's focus had already turned to Westminster.

His parliamentary career was not without its highs and lows. With the assistance of Dalton, Crosland was elected as MP for South Gloucestershire in 1950, winning a 6,000 majority and retaining the seat a year later, despite the defeat of the Labour Government. But with the boundaries redrawn before the 1955 election, Crosland unwisely moved constituencies and was defeated in Southampton Test. It was not until 1959 that Crosland was returned to Parliament, this time for Grimsby and, after a recount, only by 101 votes. Crosland went on to strengthen Labour's hold on Grimsby and he successfully defended the seat on five successive occasions.

His time out of Parliament in the 1950s was not wasted, however. Indeed, during this period Crosland brought together the many articles and essays he had written over the preceeding years into one work of distinctive and original political analysis. *The Future of Socialism*, published in 1956, was a forceful account of the reasons why Labour must change its political and economic approach. Traditional capitalism had changed, he argued, and therefore the levers of traditional socialism, primarily nationalisation, were no longer necessary. Instead Crosland focused on the remaining pillars of socialism, which he argued were equality of opportunity and the abolition of class divisions. Crosland argued that the increase in public spending necessary to deliver the measures of equality of opportunity was to be paid, not through increased taxation, but through continued economic growth which, writing during the 'long boom' of the 1950s, he was confident would be easy to achieve.

The Future of Socialism was Crosland's greatest work and it helped to shift the political argument within Labour's ranks. Following the achievements of Labour's 1945–51 Governments, the Party appeared to split into the traditional left, who wanted a 'shopping list' of nationalisations, and the old right, who believed socialism was 'what a Labour Government does'. Both groups represented, in the words of Crosland's 1962 book, *A Conservative Enemy* within the Labour Party. In contrast, Crosland offered a revisionist approach which set out a radical course for Labour in a new age. His socialism was still about equality, but the means to deliver equality was now education and improved social and cultural life, not public ownership.

His revisionist works helped to increase his reputation as a formidable intellectual with the Labour Party. However his brash, often arrogant, personality and the small amount of time he spent in Westminster meant that Crosland appeared distant to many Parliamentary colleagues. In addition, while he was a loyal supporter of Gaitskell, he made little effort to provide a lead for the revisionist wing of the centre left – notwithstanding his role in the creation of the Campaign for Democratic Socialism in 1960. Both points were to prove extremely significant when Crosland's key supporter, the Labour leader Hugh Gaitskell, died suddenly in 1963 and was replaced by Harold Wilson.

Following the Labour victory in 1964, Crosland gained ministerial office, first at the Department of Economic Affairs and then in 1965 as Secretary of State for Education. It was in this post that Crosland most clearly displayed his clear thinking and forceful leadership within government, notably developing a comprehensive education system which ended the iniquitous 11–plus for thousands of children. It was Crosland's Woolwich speech of April 1965 that enshrined the 'binary principle', whereby technical colleges would not become universities but would be expanded under local authority control into a planned 30 Polytechnics. He was moved to the Board of Trade in August 1967, then again to the Department of Local Government and Regional Planning in 1969, a department that, renamed Environment, he continued to shadow in Opposition (1970–74), returning to government as Secretary of State for the Environment (1974–76).

But throughout this time, Crosland never won real favour with Wilson, particularly as he refused to stop mentioning 'the unmentionable' question of devaluation within Cabinet. The post of Chancellor, which he saw as his immediate objective, remained frustratingly elusive. In addition, Crosland also lost ground with Wilson's enemies, with the mantle of revisionist leader passing to Roy Jenkins. This was reinforced in the early 1970s, as the issue of Europe became more critical within Labour's ranks. Crosland's view was a pragmatic one, based on a need for Party loyalty, and he failed to support the pro-Europeans in the Tory lobby on the debate on the Common Market in 1971, a matter they were not to forget. This was evident first when he stood for the Deputy Leadership in 1972, coming third behind Ted Short and Michael Foot. Jenkins' supporters had still not forgiven him in 1976 when Wilson resigned and Crosland stood unsuccessfully for the leadership, winning only 17 votes.

With his old friend Jim Callaghan winning the leadership, Crosland was rewarded with the post of Foreign Secretary. This meant that he was a leading member of the Labour Cabinet that was forced to agree huge cuts in public expenditure to meet the terms of the IMF loan nego-tiated in 1976. For Crosland this struck at the heart of his whole analysis. The consensus about economics, the welfare state and the nature of capitalism established in the aftermath of the Second World War was disintegrating. Although when he said 'the party's over' to local author-ity leaders in 1975 he meant it in a different context, these words were understood as the de-mise of Crosland's own agenda. David Marquand, a close friend of Crosland, has argued that it is no co-incidence that within weeks of the Cabinet decision, Crosland suffered a massive stroke. He died in Oxford on 19 February 1977.

Crosland's legacy is much debated. Certainly his optimism in the 1950s in the rate of economic growth being sufficient to deliver real measures of equality of opportunity was overstated. This led some critics to abandon his whole approach and to return to public ownership as a solution. But it is significant that key members of the 1997 Labour Govern-ment, most notably Chancellor Gordon Brown, have sought to show how Crosland's ap-proach remains enduring. Moreover Crosland offered more than a political programme: he also offered a new way of understanding socialism. His radical agenda was a synthesis of left and right, and helped to inspire a generation to look beyond the achievements of the Attlee Governments. And for those today who still believe socialism has a future, Crosland's work remains an essential signpost for the way ahead.

Crosland was married twice, first to Hilary Sarson in 1952, which lasted less than a year be-fore they separated, and then to Susan Catling, a journalist, in 1964. His personal life reflected his dearly held libertarian views: he once argued that under socialism many people – includ-ing him – would be perfectly happy with 'sex, gin and Bogart'. This passion for freedoms also reflected a rejection both of the Brethren that he had grown up with and the puritanical Fabi-anism which valued a 'good filing system' above pleasure and enjoyment.

His main writings are: *Britain's Economic Problem* (1953); *The Future of Socialism* (1956); *The Conservative Enemy* (1962); *Socialism Now* (1974). Biographies include the wonderful personal story *Tony Crosland* (1982) by his wife, Susan Crosland, and Kevin Jefferys' admirable political biography *Anthony Crosland* (1999). There have also been published a number of essays on Crosland's work, including Lipsey and Leonard (ed) *The Socialist Agenda* (1981), and Leonard (ed) *Crosland and New Labour* (1999).

Matt Carter

Dick Crossman   (1907–74)

Richard Howard Stafford Crossman was born on 15 December 1907 in Bayswater, the third of the six children of the chancery lawyer Mr Justice Stafford Crossman and his wife Helen Elizabeth Howard, a first cousin of the Chichele Professor of the History of War at Oxford and a Fellow of All Souls. At the age of 12 he won a scholarship to Winchester, becoming Prefect of Hall and winning a scholarship to New College Oxford. It did not help his career in later life that he was senior to and far more academically gifted than another Wykhamist, Hugh Todd Naylor Gaitskell! Taking a brilliant First in Mods 1928 and Greats, 1930, he was offered a Fellowship by the Warden, H A L Fisher, Lloyd George's Education Minister and author of *The History of Europe*. Fisher told him to go to Germany for a year. Politics became his passion, sparked by the problems of the rise of Hitler.

And in 1931 he married Erika Simm (nee Landsberg), Jewish and communist. That she danced scantily attired on the high table at New College was described to me by Crossman's successor as Philosophy Tutor as 'de trop.' Divorce followed quickly and five years later Crossman married the divorced wife Zita Baker (née Davis), of one of his own colleagues as a Fellow of New College.

From 1932, he had lectured to huge undergraduate audiences and gained a reputation as a quite outstanding tutor for the cleverest of undergraduates. Weaker brethren were not encouraged to go to Crossman. In 1934 he was elected to the Oxford City Council on the slogan that he would get the refuse bins in North Oxford emptied three times a week, not twice a week. From 1936 to 1940 he led the Labour Group and played a prominent role for the non-appeasing side in the famous by-election. He had become a champion of rearmament in the Labour Party. In 1937 he fought and lost a by-election in West Birmingham, but as an enormously forceful candidate, appealed to George Hodgekinson and the influential men of the Coventry Labour Party, who adopted him in 1938, albeit his entry to the House of Commons was delayed until July 1945. He held the seat until 1974.

Crossman became Assistant Editor to Kingsley Martin at the *New Statesman*. More importantly, perhaps, he eked out a living by lecturing for the Workers' Educational Association, particularly in Staffordshire. This ill-remunerated activity brought him a contact with the roots of the party which he would not otherwise have had and gave him the appetite to work towards becoming an elected member of the National Executive Committee of the party in the constituency section.

In 1940 he was drafted into the Ministry of Economic Warfare, where his knowledge of German, combined with skills of the pen, made him most effective – irritating though he often was to his superiors, by not being a team player. In 1944 he was given the job, working to the American General Bedell Smith, of Assistant Chief of the Psychological Warfare Division at the Supreme Headquarters of the Allied Expeditionary Force. He had to be flown back from Algiers, life-threateningly ill with a jaundice-complicated appendicitis. Had it not been for the skill of Sir John Richardson, with whom in 1968–70 he was to negotiate as Secretary of State for Health and Social Security, meeting Richardson speaking on behalf of the Royal College of Surgeons, he would not have survived. 'It's a bit embarrassing turning down a man who has saved your life!' Part of the explanation for Crossman's recklessness as a journalist and a politician is that he thought that from day to day he was living on borrowed time.

In 1946, he was appointed by Ernie Bevin to the Anglo-American Palestine Commission. As Crossman was a gentile, Bevin did not expect or welcome Crossman's pro-Jewish stance, nor his deep friendship for Chaim Weitzman. (At 9 Vincent Square, Crossman kept in his basement study photographs of four people – his beloved and adored third wife Anne MacDougall, their children Patrick and Virginia and Chaim Weitzman).

Crossman persuaded his commission colleagues to allow an extra 100,000 European refugees into Palestine. Bevin was furious and blamed him for a 'stab in the back.' For 19 years he was to remain on the backbenches (though in 1959–60 and 1963–64 he was briefly spokesman for Pensions and Science respectively), but getting elected at the Morecambe Labour Conference in 1952 to the Labour NEC – on which he was to remain until 1967, choosing not to run of his own accord, on the grounds that it was healthy for the Pary that the NEC should be at arm's length from the Government.

He was one of the dynamic forces behind Aneurin Bevan, but was not altogether trusted by many left-wingers, since he defended the right of Harold Wilson to take Nye's place in the shadow cabinet when he resigned in 1954. However, this cemented his relationship with Wilson.

Of Crossman's period in office, it is impossible to truncate the activity of an issue-Secretary of State. The three volumes of Crossman Diaries stand comparison with those of Pepys and John Evelyn in the 17th Century and those of Hugh Dalton nearer our own time. During his period as Minister of Housing and Local Government (October 1964–August 1966), his fraught relationship with his Permanent Secretary, the formidable Dame Evelyn Sharpe, is covered in Volume One. As his PPS, I believe he had solid achievements in relation to the Rent Acts, combating the Rachmanism of the times, and in the planning field. Albiet he could bully civil servants, not one who worked with him would rather have gone through their careers without the experience. It was a period in their service which they remembered with awe and retrospective excitement.

As Lord President of the Council (August 1966–October 1968), his monument must be the setting up of Select Committees. He was a skilful and unexpectedly emollient negotiator and Leader of the House of Commons (August 1966–April 1968). When visitors arrived in the Lord President's Office, the most beautiful room in Whitehall, he was wont to point to a portrait on the wall and say, 'That's my political ancestor – Halifax, the Trimmer.' He came to grief over House of Lords' reform, having failed to 'square' Michael Foot, Iain MacLeod and Enoch Powell, and reconcile them with the agreement he had devised with Lord Carrington and Lord Jellicoe, whom he had supposed were negotaiting with the full authority of the Tories.

As Secretary of State for Health and Social Services (November 1968–June 1970), an elephantine Ministry based at the Elephant and Castle, he was effective in using the cases of Ely Hospital, Cardiff, Friern Barnett and South Ockenden to champion the cause of a different level of resources for mental health. However, the electoral cycle overtook his earnings-related pension scheme, to the details of which he had devoted so much of his frenetic, eclectic energy since the 1950s.

The Crossman Diaries are not daily diaries. They are weekly diaries, dictated on Sunday mornings at Prescot Manor into a machine. He is always wiser about the Monday or Tuesday than about Thursday or Friday since he knew what happened over 72 hours.

My abiding memory of Crossman is of his characteristically courageous behaviour on the night he had learned from the doctors that he had terminal cancer. He returned to Vincent Square, where I was his lodger, asked for a cup of tea, told me the gruesome news and then got up and said: 'Well, I'm going down to the study to check the Diaries. There's little time to lose!' He died at home in Prescot on Friday 5 April 1974.

Crossman was Editor of the *New Statesman* 1970–72. In addition to the *Diaries of a Cabinet Minister*, Crossman's *Backbench Diaries* (1951–63) were published in 1980. Crossman's other publications include *Plato Today* (1937); *Socrates* (1938); *Government and the Governed* (1939); *How We are Governed* (1939); *The Charm of Politics* (1958); *A Nation Reborn* (1960); *Planning for Freedom* (1965), and *Inside View* (1972). He edited *New Fabian Essays* (1952) and *The God that Failed (1950)*, a rejection of communism. Biographies include *Dick Crossman – a Portrait* by Tam Dalyell (1989) and *Crossman: The Pursuit of Power* by Anthony Howard (1990).

Tam Dalyell MP

Jack Cunningham   (1939–)

Jack Cunningham's service to the Labour movement, from teenage activist in 1955 to Minister for the Cabinet Office in 1999, has been characterised by skillful handling of tough challenges and unflinching loyalty. A powerful fire-fighter for a succession of party leaders, this PhD with a network of academic and industrial contacts and a taste for smart suits was a moderniser before it became fashionable.

Born John Cunningham in Newcastle-on-Tyne on 4 August 1939, he continues to live in the North East and support Newcastle United. His father, Andrew Cunningham, was Northern Secretary of the GMWU. Jack married Maureen Appleby in 1964; they have two daughters and a son.

Educated at Jarrow Grammar School and Bede College, Durham University, he earned an honours degree (1962) and a PhD (1966) in Chemistry. After two years as a research fellow at Durham, he became a regional officer for the GMWU, and won a seat on Chester-le-Street District Council. In 1969 he was about to take up a research post in Florida, but allowed his name to go forward for the Parliamentary nomination for Whitehaven, and he was elected for that west Cumbrian constituency in 1970.

Whitehaven constituency, renamed Copeland in 1983, stretches from Scafell Pike in the Lake District to industrial Whitehaven and Sellafield on the Irish Sea coast. The rivers and mountains contributed to Jack's enthusiasm for fishing and fell walking, while the nuclear industry at Sellafield has demanded the special political skills of a committed constituency MP.

It was not easy to defend a Labour majority of 1,894 with a 1987 manifesto commitment to phase out the constituency's main industry. His career has been built on the mutual loyalty between a high-flying politician and a remote rural constituency with unique local problems. He has struck the difficult balance between support for nuclear reprocessing and commitment to the environment, and he has not hesitated to criticise BNFL when necessary.

His father's conviction following the Poulson scandal in 1973 was a painful blow, but the young MP's career was boosted when Jim Callaghan, then Foreign Secretary, made Jack his

Parliamentary Private Secretary in 1974. He helped lead Jim Callaghan's leadership campaign in 1976, setting up the new Prime Minister's Downing Street political office before starting his ministerial career in Tony Benn's Energy Department.

As the Party lurched to the left in opposition in the 1980s, he was one of the prominent moderates who held the line against both the Militant Tendency and the breakaway SDP. He became Industry spokesman under Michael Foot, and he secured the only significant success of his leadership by organising the Darlington by-election victory in March 1983.

He backed Roy Hattersley in the leadership election, but went on to take a pivotal job as Neil Kinnock's Shadow Environment Secretary, 1983–89. That portfolio covered local government, so Jack Cunningham had to fight on two fronts, to defend local councils against attacks from the Thatcher government, and to restrain Militant-led Labour councillors who were provoking mayhem in Liverpool. He confronted the Trotskyite Militant Tendency, paving the way for Kinnock's famous 'grotesque chaos' Conference speech in Bournemouth in 1984, and he also led the opposition to the poll tax in the Commons, driving the Tory majority to a record low of 23.

As Labour's campaign co-ordinator from 1989 (doubling up as Shadow Leader of the House of Commons), he achieved a string of by-election victories and ran an effective general election campaign in 1992. He supported his friend John Smith for the leadership, and was appointed Shadow Foreign Secretary and a Privy Councillor. A long-standing Atlanticist as well as a committed European, he urged more proactive intervention in Yugoslavia and vigilance over Iraq. He worked closely with his deputy, George Robertson, on the Maastricht Treaty – insisting that Labour would vote against the opt-out from the Social Charter.

After supporting Tony Blair for the leadership in 1994, he moved first to shadow Trade and Industry, and then to the National Heritage portfolio, where he flagged up concerns about the profits of the National Lottery operator. He took a robust line with Michael Heseltine, refusing to commit a Labour government to underwrite the Millennium Dome project.

Returning to government in 1997, Cunningham was Blair's surprise choice for the crisis-ridden Ministry of Agriculture. He took a grip on the BSE crisis, with decisive initiatives to establish the independent Food Standards Agency; to set up the Phillips Enquiry into the causes of BSE; and to restore good relations with EU partners before the high-profile British Presidency. Dealings with MAFF civil servants and the NFU were difficult. Both were suspicious of his emphasis on consumer interests and the need to develop rural policies to reduce farmers' dependence on subsidies. Such suspicions may have inspired hostile briefings about the action taken on scientific advice to ban beef on the bone to prevent infection with new variant CJD.

In 1998 he was promoted to Minister for the Cabinet Office and Chancellor of the Duchy of Lancaster, with responsibility for co-ordinating and presenting government policy – 'the Cabinet Enforcer'- and also for the anti-drugs strategy. All his experience of political organisation and communication came to the fore in this task, and regular media appearances earned him the description of 'Minister for the Today Programme'. In 1999 he stepped down to enable the Prime Minister to shuffle Mo Mowlam from the Northern Ireland Office at a difficult stage in the peace process.

The range of responsibilities that Jack Cunningham has held in government and opposition demonstrates the scope of his talents. An academic scientist who became an MP, his campaigning and organisational skills have been of immense value to the Party. And he is one of the prominent mainstream Labour MPs who kept their nerve in the 1980s to prepare the ground for electoral success and government in the 1990s. A hard worker with a reputation as a hard man, he keeps things in perspective with a wide range of friends in industry as well as politics, an enthusiasm for fishing, music and Newcastle United, and a deep loyalty to his party, his constituency and, above all, his family.

John Home Robertson MSP

Hugh Dalton (Lord Dalton of Forest and Frith)   (1887–1962)

Edward Hugh John Neale Dalton was born in Neath, Glamorganshire, on 26 August 1887, the eldest son of the Reverend J N Dalton, KCVO, CMG who later became Canon Dalton at St. George's Chapel, Windsor, a formidable old-style cleric who, it is said, even Queen Victoria stood in awe of. Dalton went to Eton and King's College Cambridge, while his father tutored the future King George V. Arriving at Cambridge a Tory, at the beginning of his second term, in early 1907, he 'exchanged Joseph Chamberlain for James Keir Hardie and Sidney Webb' and joined the Cambridge University Fabian Society, where he became a leading light. From Cambridge he went to the LSE as a research student. Serving in the Royal Garrison Artillery in World War One he developed a life-long hatred of Germans. After the war he lectured at the LSE and fought Cambridge in the March 1922 by-election for the Labour Party. He fought and lost Maidstone in the general election of November 1922, Cardiff East in December 1923 and Holland-with-Boston at the by-election of July 1924. In October 1924 he finally won Peckham and in 1929 he switched to Bishop Auckland.

Already well-known as a political economist, he was elected to the shadow cabinet from December 1925 and served as Under-Secretary of State at the Foreign Office (Arthur Henderson's deputy) in the second Labour government of 1929–31. Re-elected to the shadow cabinet in September 1931, he lost his seat in Parliament at the general election the following month. He came back in 1935, speaking primarily on foreign affairs and became a leading figure within the Labour Party in pressing for a tough line against Hitler and support for increased military expenditure. He remained in the Commons until 1959, being re-elected to the shadow cabinet every year during Labour's years in opposition until in June 1955 he stood down, calling in a letter to Attlee, which he insisted on publishing in the *Daily Mirror,* on his fellow veterans to follow his example and make way for younger men, much to the fury of those of his colleagues with no such inclination. He served on Labour's NEC 1926–27 and from 1928 until his defeat at the hands of the Bevanites in 1952.

This simple biography of Dalton's life gives many clues to the complex personality and driven quality of his political career. The personal and the political were intertwined in Dalton's psyche to an extraordinary extent. First, his father gave him the regime, intellectual and social, against which to rebel, forming his deeply repressive sexuality as well as his burning ambition to succeed, preferably in ways that his father would despise and even better in ways which would destroy the world to which his father belonged. This sense of rebellion and personal confusion was compounded by the awkwardness of his physical appearance amid the beauty, elegance and charm of the set he attached himself to at Cambridge. His great passions for men like Rupert Brooke were possible because of his brilliance and his ability to perform, rather than his physical attractiveness. When many of his friends were killed in the war, he became and remained fixated on the guilt of the Germans. This trait, amongst others, would have made him a disaster as the post-war Foreign Secretary but made him absolutely perfect to run SOE.

When Labour entered the Churchill coalition in May 1940, Dalton became first Minister for Economic Warfare and then President of the Board of Trade in February 1942. His brief from Churchill at the first post was simple: set Europe ablaze. He was the ministerial head of the covert operations organisation called the Special Operations Executive and responsible for the attempt at blockade and other forms of economic warfare. As the tide of the war shifted, so he moved onto the Board of Trade and became increasingly political in his actions and planning. In both jobs the unconventionality of war, in which results mattered more than manners and procedures, suited Dalton perfectly. What could be achieved by will power, persuasion, nervous energy and ingenuity, was achieved. In the long run the apparatus of secret and economic war was largely irrelevant beside the effort of the Soviet army and the economic power of the USA, but wars are about more than logistics, and SOE provided the myth that the individual mattered. In purely morale terms, that it existed and that a figure like Dalton was running it was vital to the war effort and vital to the shift in allegiance that occurred through the 1940s and resulted in the 1945 Labour landslide.

Rebelling against family, emotionally crippled first by war and then by the death of his only child, Dalton became a driven politician. This drive produced a series of important works of political economy. The most important of his pre-war ideas was the capital levy. This was meant to be a once and for all progressive tax on private wealth.

The idea originated, in a modern form, in the aftermath of the First World War. A C Pigou and J M Keynes, with whom Dalton initially studied at Cambridge, both advocated the introduction of such a tax to pay for the cost of the war, and it was widely supported across the political spectrum for a short time. Dalton translated the idea of a capital levy from theoretical economics to practical politics in his 1923 polemic, *The Capital Levy Explained,* and it became Labour Party policy. The minority Labour governments (1924 and 1929–31) played down the significance of the commitment and it was never implemented.

The inter-war idea that private fortunes would be taxed for specific purposes, such as the repayment of war debt, declined in influence after the Second World War. However, the underlying principle became linked to the use of direct taxation for the redistribution of wealth to promote equality. In turn the capital levy influenced Labour's post-war tax policies, most notably in the form of the capital gains tax, which applied the tax on wealth in a progressive form, and the related increases in death duties.

This points to the wider legacy of Dalton as Chancellor of the Exchequer in the post-war Labour government. As the historian of Labour's tax policy, Richard Whiting, puts it, power was fused with radicalism. The tax burden was increased to pay for reconstruction and the construction of the welfare state at the same time as the economy grew and British industry recovered. The Bank of England was nationalised and the public sector expanded across the whole range of industries to which Labour were committed at the time of the general election in

1945. Dalton would have been a major architect of the government and might have been a countervailing force to the consolidators of the second half of the Parliament had he not made an appallingly stupid error. On the way to present his fourth Budget in November 1947 he briefed a lobby correspondent, John Carvel, on the contents of the emergency measures: 'No more on tobacco, a penny on beer; something on dogs and pools but not on horses; increased Petroleum Tax … Profits Tax doubled.' Carvel phoned it in to his paper, *The Star,* which had it on the streets before the speech. Attlee was glad to see the back of Dalton: 'Perfect ass' was the Prime Minister's later judgement.

Dalton was broken by the experience of government and the crisis which engulfed Labour during the winter of 1947. For the rest of his life he remained a presence but not a force in the Labour movement. From May 1948 until February 1950 he returned to Cabinet as Chancellor of the Duchy of Lancaster, leading the British delegation to the Council of Europe and playing a key part in shaping post-war European institutions. Appointed Minister of Town and Country Planning following the February 1950 election, he inherited responsibility for implementing the acts creating the new towns and National Parks, and for streamlining planning procedures. He became a champion of the countryside, announcing the first three National Parks – the Peak District, the Lake District and Snowdonia – and the creation of the Pennine Way. In February 1951 his ministry was expanded to include housing and local government, becoming the Ministry of Local Government and Planning, but he had little time to develop new policy initiatives before the fall of the Attlee government later that year. His key contribution was to champion and bring on talented young politicians, whom he both fell in love with and nurtured. Tony Crosland, Hugh Gaitskell (whose leadership ambitions he energetically championed over Morrison and Bevan), Roy Jenkins, and many others owed something to Dalton's constant scheming and intriguing on their behalf. But measured against his own sense of self-worth as an economist and the hopes with which he greeted Labour's triumph in 1945, the period from 1947 to 1962 has a tragically anti-climatic feel. His great rival Keynes would be the economic voice that defined an age, while Dalton, until rescued by the quality of his biographer, Ben Pimlott, quickly appeared quintessentially an interwar man. Created Lord Dalton of Forest and Frith in 1960, his final public appearance was in the chair at a rally of the anti-unilateralist Campaign for Democratic Socialism in February 1961. He died on 13 February 1962, at St Pancras Hospital, London. He was survived by his wife since 1914, Ruth, daughter of Thomas Hamilton Fox, a fellow socialist and former member of the London County Council who had for a few brief months in 1929 served as MP for Bishop Auckland after the death of the sitting MP to keep the seat warm for her husband who had not yet vacated Peckham, which he had opted to leave at the next election following a clash with the agent. Their only daughter had died in 1922 aged four and half.

His publications included: *With British Guns in Italy* (1919); *Principles of Public Finance* (1923); *Towards the Peace of Nations* (1928); *Practical Socialism for Britain* (1935); *Call Back Yesterday: Memoirs 1887–1931* (1953); *The Fateful Years: Memoirs 1931–45* (1957); *High Tide and After: Memoirs 1945–60* (1962). Ben Pimlott's masterly biography, *Hugh Dalton,* appeared in 1985 and Pimlott subsequently published edited editions of *The Hugh Dalton Diary* and *The Wartime Diary of Hugh Dalton.*

Professor Brian Brivati

Tam Dalyell (1932–)

At an early stage in his political career Tam Dalyell expressed the hope:'I am more concerned with doing something than being somebody.' Dalyell was that rare creature, a driven 'issue' politician. In the course of an unusually long parliamentary career his sense of purpose surprised and angered many people, including some senior figures on his own side.

Heir to the Baronetcy of The Binns, a Scottish title dating back centuries, Tam Dalyell was born in Edinburgh on 9 August 1932. He attended a number of schools in quick succession before settling at Harecroft Hall, an exclusive preparatory school 'for the sons of gentlefolk' in Cumbria, prior to Eton.

When national service beckoned, his chances of obtaining a commission in the Royal Scots Greys looked a formality. A portrait of his notorious ancestor, General 'Black Tam' Dalyell, founder of the regiment in 1678, hung in every mess. Failure at OCTU confined Dalyell to the ranks as a member of a tank crew stationed in Germany.

At university he was elected President of the Cambridge University Conservative Association. His contemporaries included future Tory luminaries Geoffrey Howe, Douglas Hurd, Patrick Jenkin and John Biffen. They were astonished when Dalyell embraced the Labour Party with sincere enthusiasm.

A teacher training course at Moray House was followed by service in schools in Edinburgh and Bo'ness. This experience convinced Dalyell an increase in the school leaving age hindered rather than helped many youngsters. His answer to the problem was typically imaginative: the introduction of ship schools. Between 1961 and 1982 more than a million children took part in the scheme, visiting ports throughout Europe and parts of north Africa. Dalyell, who was engaged as the first deputy Director of Studies, later observed:'I'm prouder of the role I played in the ship school scheme than anything else I've ever done.'

He first ran for parliament in 1959, contesting an unwinnable rural seat, Roxburgh, Selkirk & Peebles. Dalyell wasn't so much the candidate of choice as the only applicant interested enough to attend the final selection conference. His reward was the highest-ever Labour return in the constituency, an early sign that Border folk were beginning to tire of the Tories, and moving leftwards, at least as far as the Liberals.

Contesting the Borders convinced Dalyell he wanted to be an MP. His ambition was achieved with unexpected speed. Halfway through the 1959 parliament John Taylor, Deputy Chief Whip in the Labour opposition, and MP for West Lothian for more than a decade, died suddenly. Many people were surprised when a packed selection conference, attended by 133 delegates, many of them miners, favoured 'the young man from the big house, with the top-drawer accent and the Etonian education'.

He was not long an MP when Harold Wilson, then Shadow Chancellor, invited him to join the powerful Public Accounts Committee. The following year he played an important role at the heart of the campaign which committed Labour to redefining and restating socialism 'in terms of the scientific revolution'. Appointed PPS to Richard Crossman in 1964, his chances of promotion were further enhanced when he became a member of the first Select Committee on Science and Technology.

Significantly, however, his reputation as a well-informed, inquiring parliamentarian was also growing. His opposition to his own government's East of Suez policy infuriated ministerial colleagues. One well-orchestrated campaign forced the Ministry of Defence to abandon plans for a staging post on Aldabra, an uninhabited coral atoll in the Indian Ocean, which, as home to an almost extinct species of giant tortoise as well as many rare birds, was an ecological treasure. The same ministry also reacted badly when Dalyell admitted handing an unpublished parliamentary report on the germ warfare centre at Porton Down to a journalist. This indiscretion was judged a breach of privilege and a gross contempt of the House of Commons.

Dalyell's formal punishment was a reprimand from the Speaker, wearing a black cap, in accordance with an ancient rite since abandoned. The effect on his career did not end there, however: within a few months he was dropped from the Select Committee on Science and Technology.

Endeavouring to explain his failure to obtain a place on Labour's front bench, except for a brief period when he was science spokesman under Michael Foot, colleagues suggest he was 'never a team player'. His front-bench career ended because of his sustained opposition to the Falklands War: Michael Foot insisted all spokesman supported the main opposition line. Dalyell, who wanted to remain, later admitted: 'I knew in my bones I would never get back'. In fact, his reputation as a leading member of the 'awkward squad' conceals a passionate belief in the right of MPs to question the executive. On five separate occasions he was ordered to leave the chamber of the House of Commons for calling one Prime Minister a liar. Borneo, Porton Down, the Falklands, Lockerbie, Gulf War syndrome, Kosovo — Tam Dalyell is entitled to display the medals of many a hard fight in search of the truth.

His by-election victory in 1962 was the first of seven successful campaigns Dalyell waged in West Lothian. Boundary changes in 1983 caused the name to disappear from the parliamentary register. Dalyell continued in parliament as MP for Linlithgow, winning the seat four times before the century turned, and again in 2001 to succeed the retiring Sir Edward Heath as Father of the House.

An unrepentant supporter of 'Old' Labour he never subscribed to the idea that the party's 1997 success was due to the appeal of 'New' Labour. A passionate opponent of Scottish devolution, he was equally robust when arguing the case for Europe, voting against the Whips in favour of Britain joining the European Economic Community, and serving as a member of the European parliament between 1975 and 1979. His experience then convinced Dalyell that Europe would be better served with a nominated parliament, recruited from 'elected people' in each of the member states.

Tam Dalyell and Kathleen Wheatley married on 26 December 1963. They have one son and one daughter. He is the author of several books, including *The Case for Ship Schools* (1960), *Devolution: the End of Britain?* (1977) and *One Man's Falklands* (1982). He was also the subject of a biography, *Inside Outside,* by Russell Galbraith (2000).

Russell Galbraith

Alastair Darling (1953–)

A quiet revolutionary, highly competent and 'chillingly numerate', as Andrew Rawnsley put it, are some of the ways Alistair Darling has been described. He is also described as a man 'willing to talk openly about his transition from municipal left-winger to impeccable modernizer.' (Lord Hattersley, *Gaurdian*). But this does not do justice to a man who through his political journey has in many ways become the embodiment of New Labour, with a deep sense of commitment to democratic socialist beliefs and the passion to see lasting change in Britain. He has been key to Labour's reform of the welfare state, financial regulations and, in the early days, the foundations for constitutional reform, and was a key player in the discussions that changed the party between 1992 and 1997.

Alistair Darling was born on 28 November 1953 in London. His family moved to Scotland when he was aged 12, and settled in Edinburgh. He was educated at Loretto School, Lothian, a boarding school he did not enjoy, and went on to study Law at Aberdeen University. He married Maggie Vaughan, a journalist, in 1986 and has two children, Calum (b. 1988) and Anna (b. 1990).

Darling joined the Labour Party in 1977 when it was going through one of its most difficult times (an indication of its difficulties is evident from the fact that he might have joined a year earlier, had he received a reply to his letter). Politics was not new to his family, but the Labour Party was. His great uncle had been a Tory MP and his paternal grandfather a Liberal candidate in 1945. His late father had been a Conservative voter, though his mother voted Labour for the first time in 1997. He was elected MP for Edinburgh Central in 1987 – part of an intake of Scottish MPs who did not expect to be elected, but were rewarded with seats by the Scottish middle classes who were turning against Thatcherism.

His biggest political inspiration was Clement Attlee, whose achievements in the post-war period 1945–51 he has described as being of great significance in shaping Britain for 30 to 40 years. Attlee was a steady politician, preferring to solve problems through economics rather than political argument. Darling has also been seen as a bridge between different camps in the Party, described in the *Times* as 'the least partisan [of the Brown camp] with … one foot firmly in the Blair camp'. Attlee's legacy includes the development of the welfare state – the modernisation of which for the next 30 to 40 years is the cornerstone of Darling's work.

Post-1982 most of Darling's jobs were political. He was elected Lothian Regional Councillor (Haymarket-Tollcross area) in 1982, where he served until 1987. Between 1982 and 1986 he was on the Lothian and Borders Police Board, and from 1982 to 87 was Governor of Napier College, Edinburgh. In those years he served as Chair of the Regional Council's Transport Committee(1986–87), spoke out against the poll tax and complained to the Scottish Office that the Scottish Development Department had not given Edinburgh District Council the legal powers to supervise private landlords. This was to avoid the exploitation of the young single homeless. He was also Lothian Region Labour Party Secretary 1980–82.

His roles in opposition covered several of the big posts. In 1988 he was appointed Assistant Spokesman on Home Affairs, under Roy Hattersley, whom he persuaded to withdraw his opposition to a Bill of Rights. During 1988–92 he is credited with progressing Labour's constitutional change agenda. He co-authored Labour's Review Group proposals to democratise the legal system, made a start on the European Convention of Human Rights, spoke at a Fabian Society conference in favour of replacing the House of Lords with an elected second chamber and is credited with early work done on the Scottish Assembly and its electoral system. He was a member of the Plant Commission on Electoral Systems from 1990 to 1993.

In 1992 he became Opposition Frontbench Spokesman on Treasury, Economic Affairs and the City, beginning a close working relationship with Gordon Brown that saw him through to his key role in Cabinet as Chief Secretary to the Treasury in 1997–98, presiding with Brown over the first Comprehensive Spending Review. During the 1990s he was also a driving force behind the changes to financial regulations, spoke and wrote on stakeholding, and was part of the frontbench team that toured City boardrooms, said to have helped alleviate the City's concerns with a Labour government. He also served as a member of the party's Economic Commission in the mid-nineties.

In his own words, he is a 'reformer, not a radical', and his views have underpinned his approach to welfare reform – perhaps his greatest challenge so far and one in which he has courted controversy. He describes himself as of a generation that was brought up with the belief that the State had a large role to play – but what he believes had been lost sight of was that the state was an enabler rather than an end in itself. The state has a clear role to play in helping the individual get on, but there is also a need for individual responsibility.

His vision for welfare is that people out of work have a right to expect financial and educational support to help them back to work, but the role of the government and the individual needs to change. The state is not an end in itself but a device to help people help themselves – an approach embodied in the phrase 'Welfare to Work'.

The DSS as a ministry has been largely dismantled, and the department reformed as the Department of Work and Pensions, something Darling has fought for. It is a symbol of the active welfare state described in the 2001 manifesto, to promote work for those who can, rewards for those who save, volunteer, learn or train, and have pensioners share in the rising prosperity of the nation. Cash welfare is being divided into three categories: pensions, benefits for those who can't work, and a single approach for those who can work and who are of working age, with the point of welfare being to get people into work – or support people as they come off benefits.

Means testing has widened, and working closely with the Treasury, including rejecting calls to restore the earnings link, the approach has been to target the worse off and raise the income of the poorest. Pensions reform has been key, with the launch of the State second pension from April 2002 incentivising people to save, benefiting those on lower incomes, giving pension rights to carers and more to the disabled and those with broken work records. The introduction of the Stakeholder Pension is designed to create a system for those on low-to-moderate earnings to save at low cost, and help head off an impending crisis in the funding of pensions by the next generation of workers.

Change has not been easy, nor can the success of the approach yet be measured. Darling has had to preside over the disastrous 75p rise in the basic state pension, albeit on a long agreed formula for determining the rise, and also over continued cuts in benefits after taking over as Secretary of State for Social Security from Harriet Harman. This caused a backbench revolt over cuts in disability benefit, with more than 60 Labour MPs signing an amendment to his legislation, though some say the revolt could have been avoided had he consulted better; the reform of disability benefit was widely agreed to be necessary. This is perhaps his Achilles heel – he is not a 'clubbable' person and despite all his achievements and controversy, is not yet a household name.

Darling is solidly New Labour, believing in reform rather than revolution, full employment, strong public services, a better education system, wider opportunity for all, eradication of child poverty and a pragmatic use of the public and private sectors. Under Thatcher, he says, generations were written off, something no society can tolerate. However, he believes very strongly, as typified by his political journey, that it is no good just to have good intentions. A party has to be able to move from its vision to actually delivering it. He should be seen as someone who has contributed in a major way to the change the Labour Party had to make, despite his seeming anonymity (though he is well remembered at least for good looks, white hair and jet black eyebrows). He is a man who is in politics to make a difference, and as soon as he feels his time is over will return to full-time family life, the hardest compromise he has had to make in his public career.

Seema Malhotra

Ron Davies (1946–)

Until 26 October 1998, the Secretary of State for Wales was, to the English, a relatively unknown member of the Blair cabinet. However, after his 'moment of madness' with a man on Clapham Common, Ron Davies ensured that he became for a time (and for all the wrong reasons) a political figure whom everybody knew. Some ironically observed that at least the English media had finally noticed that the Cabinet had a Secretary of State for Wales. But the 'popular' press didn't really care, because now they could gleefully claim their first cabinet scalp of the new Labour Government.

All of this, sadly, misses the fact that Ron Davies had, in the five years leading up to the 1997 election, expertly brought the party's policy on devolution to fruition. He was successful in bringing both the Nationalists and the Liberals under the same roof as Labour in campaigning for a 'yes' vote, and ultimately deserves credit for securing the vote in favour of devolution which led to the establishment of the Welsh Assembly. Certainly, the mandate was secured by the smallest of majorities, but those Westminster-based critics of Davies who were keen to make political capital out of his downfall need to question whether Davies' successor, Alun Michael, would have been as successful in ensuring that a key manifesto commitment was supported by a majority of the Welsh people. Davies earned respect for his political beliefs from the main opposition parties, and there was a general consensus that he handled the lead-up to devolution extremely smoothly. It is perhaps a little ironic, therefore, that Davies had, before becoming an MP, been a staunch opponent of devolution in the late 1970s and early 1980s.

Born on 6 August 1946, in Machen, Gwent, Davies attended Bassaleg Grammar School, followed by Portsmouth Polytechnic, University College Wales and London University. He has been married twice, and has one daughter from his second marriage.

Prior to being elected to Caerphilly in 1983, Davies spent 15 years as a local councillor for both Rhymney Valley and Bedwas and Machen UDC. A former teacher and public sector employee, Davies had originally sought selection for Caerphilly in 1978, but only succeeded after the Labour incumbent, former Conway MP and Welsh Tourist Board Chair Ednyfed Hudson Davies, defected to the SDP. Once in Parliament, his promotion was relatively rapid, and he entered the Whips' office only two years after the 1983 General Election. He held this position for two years. In 1987, he was sacked by the then Chief Whip, Derek Foster, over a dispute as to whether Labour MPs had the right to elect their own Pairing Whip. This dispute did little to halt his rise through the party, and the same year Davies was promoted to become deputy spokesman for Agriculture.

Throughout the 1980s and early '90s, Welsh nationalism and separatism became increasingly popular. Separatism was in part fuelled by English holiday home purchases, Tory manufacturing policy and a hapless Tory minister who famously did not know the words to the Welsh national anthem. By the time Davies became Shadow Secretary of State for Wales in 1992 his constituents had also seen their fair share of pit and steelworks closures. It might have been very easy for the Welsh Nationalists to make political capital out of a neutered Welsh Labour Party suffering its fourth general election defeat. However, Davies ensured that Plaid Cymru did not make great inroads into the Labour heartlands of South Wales and the valleys. Indeed, his political acumen and leadership meant that, come 1997, Labour's position in Wales was still strong enough to declare Wales a 'Tory Free Zone'. Even by the standards of 1997, this was a great symbolic achievement for a man whose nation had suffered so much under Tory control from Westminster.

Davies himself was not a native Welsh speaker. However, unlike John Redwood, he made strenuous efforts to learn the language, and, by the time he became Secretary of State for Wales in 1997, he was fluent enough to take part in regular interviews and debates on Welsh language TV and radio. Whilst this may seem an insignificant achievement in political terms, nevertheless it was symptomatic of a man who cared greatly for his country's cultural history, and it certainly helped to win him respect among Welsh nationalists.

Davies had a reputation, both in opposition and in Government, of being a tough negotiator. Although he was seen as a 'consolidator', when first given the post of Shadow Secretary of State, in a bid to overcome divisions in the Welsh Labour Party, he was not afraid of speaking his mind. Opponents in the Party accused him of being abrasive and a bully, and his 'macho' reputation was enhanced by reports that he had come to blows with a journalist in a Westminster bar. A fellow Labour MP, Llew Smith, also accused Davies of threatening behaviour towards him, after he voiced his opposition to Labour's devolution programme. Despite all of this, friends who knew Davies were quick to point to his great sense of humour and generosity of spirit, both in and outside of the political arena.

After being forced to step down as Secretary of State for Wales, Davies was disappointed at being left out of Alun Michael's cabinet. Davies did briefly chair the Welsh Assembly's economic development committee, before further tabloid revelations about his personal life led him to resign. In 2000, he announced he would not stand again for Westminster, preferring to concentrate on the Welsh Assembly, of which he is still a member. However, in recent months he has been very critical of the 'talking shop' mentality of the Welsh Assembly. In particular, he believes the Assembly has been undermined by its obsession with posturing and procedural matters. Wayne David, the former chair of the EPLP, succeeded as MP for Davies' old Westminster seat in 2001.

It is sad that the man who did so much for Wales, from securing devolution and increased European funding to securing financial redress for the families of the Aberfan disaster, will nevertheless for many, only be remembered for a night on Clapham Common.

Jake Turnbull

Arthur Deakin (1890–1955)

Arthur Deakin's career was forged by the union for which he worked and by the man who created that union. Born in Sutton Coldfield on 11 November 1890, the union, which he joined in his teens when he began work for the steel works in Dowlais in South Wales, was initially the National Union of Gas Workers. His father, a cobbler, had died when he was a child and his mother's remarriage had taken the family to Merthyr Tydfil. As the amalgamation that was to form the largest trade union in the world was forced through by the power of Ernest Bevin's personality, so Arthur Deakin switched to the General Workers and then the Transport and General Workers.

Bevin was a leader who delegated to men he trusted and Deakin was one of a handful of the most trusted amongst the leadership of the TGWU. A full-time union official based in Shotton, Flintshire, since 1919, he moved to London in 1932 to become national secretary of the General Workers group within the TGWU. Whilst in Flintshire he was also, for a time, a Labour member, alderman and chairman of Flintshire County Council. In 1935 Bevin made Deakin TGWU Assistant General Secretary, and it is from this time, and not as often portrayed only after 1946 or even only after Bevin was dead, that Deakin developed a role and a power base of his own. Throughout the 1930s Bevin played multiple roles within the Labour movement and it was Deakin who often looked after the home patch and did much of the day-to-day running of the union. After 1940, Deakin's role was central. In contrast to Bevin and his difficult relations with the first two Labour governments, Deakin gave the postwar Labour government unconditional support. He therefore maintained much of the Bevin legacy of centralised leadership of the union and he also ensured that the TGWU block vote was securely behind the platform. The cost was direct threats from militant elements in the union to the survival of the amalgamation and, more importantly, the stifling of criticism from the union of Labour's industrial strategy. Ironically it is hard to imagine the Ernest Bevin of the 1930s being as cautious on domestic and industrial policy as Deakin was.

However, this loyalty was vital to the leadership after the defeat of 1951. Deakin was a dedicated anti-communist and rather unreflectingly transferred this opposition to the Bevanites and other non-communist members of the left of the party. Personally comfortable with the Conservative Party of the 1950s, he was able to maintain his union's position and defend free collective bargaining while leading the battle against communists and fellow travellers. He spearheaded, in support of Gaitskell, the lunacy of trying to expel Nye Bevan from the party in the run-up to the 1955 general election. His natural autocracy in the running of the union allowed him to use his influence on sponsored MPs and his block votes at party conferences to secure the Treasurership of the Labour Party for Hugh Gaitskell in 1954 and then the leadership in 1955. Though the trade union section did not then have a direct vote, it sponsored MPs who carried a much wider influence. Deakin organised the leaders of the other big unions behind Gaitskell's candidature.

Deakin managed the transition of the TGWU into the post-war world with skill and ensured that it maintained its dominant position. A flamboyant dresser and a cigar smoker, he appeared to fulfil many of the clichés associated with trade union barons. In fact he lived quietly, refused personal honours and was a member of the Primitive Methodist Church. His legacy, however, was not all positive from the perspective of the leadership. The autocracy with which the union was run and the difference in political outlook between much of the rank and file and the leadership was exposed sharply after Deakin's death, and no mechanism was in place for ensuring that the position of the union as loyal to leadership was maintained. The left asserted their position and under the leadership of Frank Cousins the influence of the TGWU swung behind the left. On all industrial and trade union matters Deakin's legacy to his union most approached that of Ernest Bevin. Though not the architect of the TGWU, Deakin deserves to be remembered as a key builder. In political terms his tenure most be seen as being a largely negative and restrictive one, which contributed to the bloody political conflicts of the 1950s which did so much to keep Labour out of power. He was made a Companion of Honour in 1949 and a Privy Counsellor in 1954. He died in Leicester on 1 May 1955. He had married Annie, the daughter of Robert George, in 1914.

Professor Brian Brivati

Edmund Dell (1921–99)

Edmund Dell was one of the most notable of the 1964 intake of Labour Members of Parliament. Born in London on 15 August 1921, he was the youngest of the three gifted children of Reuben and Frances Dell. He went to Owen's School, London, and then to Queen's College Oxford, where his studies were interrupted by his war service. He had been the London Boys Chess Champion. When we both came into the House there was a chess room. We played. I had determined to go for a draw. I nearly succeeded in this limited ambition.

When he went before the army commissioning board his studies in history were commented on. He was asked who he thought was the greatest English general. He knew that the expected answer was Wellington or Marlborough, but he replied: 'Cromwell'. Surprised by this answer he was asked for his explanation. 'Cromwell', he said, 'had to create his Model Army. He did not inherit one. And from nothing he created an army which beat the King.' He received his commission.

After his war service in the Royal Artillery he returned to Oxford and a first class honours degree in 1947, following his elder brother's similar distinction. The University offered and he accepted the position of Lecturer in Modern History. Two years later he was asked to join ICI and so began his industrial career. Throughout all this period his interest in politics remained. He served on the Manchester City Council from 1953 to 1960 and was Secretary of the Labour Group. In 1955 he was the unsuccessful Labour candidate in Middleton and Prestwich. In 1958 he was elected President of the Manchester and Salford Trades Council, an indication of his appeal to all parts of the Labour movement. One of his favourite quotations is in his book on the English Revolution, *The Good Old Cause*. This, which endeared him to his Council, was from Richard Rumboldt, a Leveller from the English Civil War: 'I am sure there was no man born with a saddle on his back nor any booted and spurred to ride him.'

Following a visit to South America for ICI, he was in 1963 faced with the opportunity of becoming a senior figure in the company if he were to abandon his political career. His friends insisted that he would be missing an important opportunity to play a prominent role in Parliament and Government, and this advice played a part in his decision not to accept the tempting offer put forward by ICI. He was offered and accepted a one-year Simon Research Fellowship at Manchester University and published articles and a Fabian pamphlet on *Brazil: the Dilemma of Reform*. Before the 1964 general election he was successful in becoming the Parliamentary candidate for Birkenhead following the retirement of Percy Collick. 1963 was also an important year for him when he married Susie Gottschalk, whom he knew from his Oxford days and for whom he had continued a long and eventually successful courtship.

In October 1964 he retained the seat of Birkenhead for Labour and on arriving at the House of Commons he became Parliamentary Private Secretary to Jack Diamond, then Chief Secretary to the Treasury and a previous MP for Blackley, Manchester. Soon realising that this position, while giving him an insight into the working of Government and the Treasury meant that he could not take part in economic or financial debates, he resigned. At a time of acute interest in all matters concerning the new government, his talent for avoiding publicity was well demonstrated. No-one noticed his resignation.

He had realised that a new Finance Bill would provide an opportunity to intervene with useful effect. Together with Joel Barnett and myself he made speeches which used his background of industrial and commercial experience. This was noted, and the general election of April 1966 brought about his appointment to Parliamentary Secretary at the Ministry of Technology and, in August 1967, to the Department of Economic Affairs. In April 1968 he became Minister of State at the Board of Trade and then in October 1969 at the Department of Employment and Productivity, becoming a Privy Counsellor in 1970.

In 1968 Robert Maxwell, then Labour MP for Buckingham and desperate for recognition, began a campaign 'I'm backing Britain'. This was an attempt by him to persuade everyone to buy or support British products and ideas. The means he used were populist and extravagant. Harold Wilson decided to provide public support for this campaign. He chose Edmund Dell to offer support from the Department of Trade. Edmund's participation in this overblown campaign was supremely successful. At a time when the campaign was littering the front pages he used his special talents to ensure that no-one realised that he was in any way involved.

After the General Election of 1970 he became an Opposition spokesman on Trade and Industry. Following the illness of Harold Lever in 1972 he became Chairman of the Public Accounts Committee. He realised that the benefits the country was getting from the taxation of North Sea oil were quite inadequate. The Report of the Committee led to the Revenue Petroleum Tax which he introduced when he became Paymaster General in the March 1974 Labour Government. As a Treasury Minister I assisted in this. This ensured that Britain received a proper contribution from the oil companies for the North Sea exploitation.

In April 1976 he became Secretary of State for Trade and played an important part in supporting Denis Healey's negotiations with the IMF. Increasingly he was tipped as a future Chancellor of the Exchequer. However, in the Autumn of 1978 he was offered the position of Chairman and Chief Executive of the Guinness Peat merchant bank, and in November 1978 he left Parliament. His presidency of the London Chamber of Commerce as well as his work in various working parties and committees on finance confirmed his reputation in this area. In 1980 he was named as the founder Chairman of Channel 4 and in that position he established the television channel as an important and innovative addition to the medium which, even after all these years, still bears some of the impressions from his founding years.

He was involved in prison reform, where he was much influenced by the work and the publications of his wife, Susi. He was one of the 'Three Wise Men' appointed in 1979 by the European Council to review the procedures of the European Community. This extended his already considerable interest in the development of the European Community, on which he was to write with insight and authority. He loved opera and was chairman of the finance committee of the English National Opera. A longstanding pro-European who had been one of the 69 Labour MPs to vote for EEC entry in 1971, he was a signatory of the Limehouse Declaration of 1981 and became a Trustee of the SDP. He was ambivalent, however, about the SDP-Liberal merger and although he joined the Liberal Democrats and served initially as a Trustee, he ceased involvement in the early 1990s. He died on 28 October 1999, shortly before the publication of his last book.

His publications included *The Good Old Cause* (with Christopher Hill, 1949); *The Politics of Economic Interdependence* (1987), *A Hard Pounding: Politics and Economic Crisis 1974–76* (1991); *The Chancellors: A History of the Chancellors of the Exchequer, 1945–90* (1996); and *Socialism* (2000).

Edmund had in the words of Peter Hennessy the combined qualities of character and mind. For me they were without equal. It was my unexpected privilege to meet such a man and to know him as a friend.

Rt Hon. Lord Sheldon

Donald Dewar (1937–2000)

Tributes come in different ways. Donald Dewar, Scotland's first First Minister, received a huge, emotional send-off at Glasgow Cathedral in October 2000. Following the shock of his death from a brain haemorrhage on 11 October, the cathedral was packed with politicians from all parties, including the Prime Minister and Leader of the Opposition, with members of the Royal Family, local Labour workers and many other friends and journalists. But what would have meant far more to Mr Dewar, who was neither religious nor much impressed by 'fuss' was the spontaneous applause in the streets of Glasgow as his cortege passed by. Few politicians in this cynical age would get such an instinctive popular tribute as the ripple of clapping and tears that followed his body through the city centre. He would have been both touched and delighted.

Mr Dewar's great personal popularity was partly the result of his unique position in political life – the author and first leader of Scotland's first Parliament since 1706 and her first democratic one ever. No-one else will have the (albeit journalistic) title 'father of the nation' which was showered on him by the same newspapers which, shortly before his death, had savaged him day after day. A passionately committed devolver almost all his political life, Mr Dewar helped ensure the commitment remained in the Labour manifesto after the death of his great friend the Labour leader John Smith. He later took the relevant legislation through the Commons and then oversaw the referendum approving the Edinburgh parliament. On 6 May 1999, he became an MSP for Anniesland in Glasgow, the same area he represented in the UK Parliament. With the Scottish Labour Party's success in that month, he formed the first administration, in coalition with Liberal Democrats, when the parliament was formally opened on 1 July 1999.

It was his proudest moment and it was a remarkable personal achievement. The 15 months that followed were, perhaps inevitably, something of a let-down. The new Scottish administration became embroiled in a bitter and at times vicious battle about its determination to repeal legislation banning the promotion of homosexuality in schools. Mr Dewar privately despaired at his country's Calvinist instincts. His ministerial team was raw and untested and made mistakes. Two special advisers were forced to resign after press allegations against them. A dreadful mess over the marking of Scottish examination results wore him down in the months before he died. The Scottish press, having got the parliament so many of the country's journalists had hankered after, then proved their independence from it with a constant stream of derisive attacks. And, to cap it all, an ambitious new parliamentary building at Holyrood, regarded as Mr Dewar's special 'baby', proved far slower to build and far more expensive than anyone had dreamed possible.

If, at times, Mr Dewar appeared tired and depressed in the months before his death, he had many sound reasons for that. Yet the affection he was held in was not simply about his one-off contribution to history, nor was it much undermined by the early disappointments of the new Scottish executive. It was personal. As a man Mr Dewar was about as far as it is possible to be from the slick, insincere and self-promoting characters modern politicians are popularly supposed to be. Gloomy, rude, intensely funny, ferociously hard-working, relentlessly unfashionable and darkly pessimistic, he was loved for himself by Scots who saw reflected in his gangling figure many national traits. A passionate Glaswegian – he did not have a passport for many years and liked to suggest that 'travel narrows the mind' – he was better read than many professors and had a deep love of Scottish art and literature. His conversation was provocative. His socialism was of the moderate, post-war Labour variety. He found the metropolitan glitz of New Labour both mildly amusing and mildly distasteful.

Donald Dewar was born on 21 August 1937, the single son of a Glasgow doctor and his wife, and was brought up in relative comfort in the city's West End. He attended Glasgow Academy and then Glasgow University, where he was president of the Union and debated with, among others, John Smith. A great admirer of Hugh Gaitskell, he joined the Labour Party at the age of 19 and was adopted as a candidate for Aberdeen South by 25. Though he failed to win it at his first try two years later, in 1964, he married and qualified as a solicitor that year. Then he won the seat in 1966. An energetic young MP in the Wilson years, he became Parliamentary Private Secretary to Tony Crosland and campaigned on issues from hanging to abortion from a strongly liberal perspective. His political career hit the buffers, however, when he lost his seat in the 1970 election. He returned to the law. During his time in the political wilderness, when he sometimes despaired of returning to the Commons, his marriage to Alison NcNair, broke up. She then married another lawyer, Derry Irvine, who later became Lord Chancellor in the 1997 Blair government and therefore a Cabinet colleague of Mr Dewar. The two men were never fully reconciled and Mr Dewar did not remarry, though he was close to his two children Ian and Marion. While other lawyers of his generation devoted themselves to private work, Mr Dewar spent five of his years outside the Commons as a social work reporter in Lanarkshire.

His crucial break came in 1978, when he won the Glasgow Garscadden by-election against a strong challenge from the SNP. He was delighted to be back in full-time politics. During the bitter years of opposition and infighting that followed Labour's 1979 defeat at the hands of Margaret Thatcher, he was a stalwart of the centre-right (Manifesto Group) faction in the party, opposing the various strands of leftism and Marxism that threatened to make Labour permanently unelectable, while solidly arguing the case for Scottish devolution. He became Labour's Scottish spokesman in 1983 and during the subsequent two parliaments, his dry wit, steadiness and forensic parliamentary skill won him enormous respect. One Conservative minister who faced him often across the despatch box wryly commented that Mr Dewar had 'the capacity to exhaust time and encroach upon eternity.' Under Mr Smith's leadership he became social security spokesman and one of the key members of the shadow cabinet; he was devastated by his old friend's sudden death. The final phase of Mr Dewar's career as the architect of devolution in the New Labour party of Tony Blair and Gordon Brown (another close friend) saw him rise to a position of national fame he never got used to and never quite liked. He seemed happiest when campaigning and working with his Glasgow constituents. One brief example of his unorthodox approach must suffice.

Shortly before he died, he entered a department store in the city and bore down on four women clustered round a hat stall. 'Well, good day,' he announced, 'I have to say that I don't think I ever seen four uglier women in my life.' After a brief shocked pause, they realised it was 'Big Donald' and shrieked with delighted laughter. Few other politicians could have risked that trick. But he knew his people and, right up to the end, they knew him.

Andrew Marr

Jack Diamond (Lord Diamond)   (1907–)

John Diamond – known as 'Jack' to most of his friends – became Lord Diamond in 1970 having served as Chief Secretary to the Treasury for six years, inside Harold Wilson's Cabinet for two of them. The son of the Reverend Solomon Diamond, he was born in Leeds on 30 April 1907 and educated there at Leeds Grammar School. He was very much a product of his time and background. Becoming a chartered accountant and moving to London in 1931, he was persuaded to join the Labour Party by Austen Albu (who himself later became a Labour MP and a Minister). Thereafter he brought his financial and administrative skills to the service of the Party whenever asked to do so.

Jack Diamond showed little interest in policy-making but had firm, mainstream convictions about the Labour Party being a party of conscience and reform, moderate, tolerant and fairminded. He seemed puzzled rather than angered by those, usually on the left of the party, who appeared to depart from the simple criteria which he believed defined a democratic socialist. He was loyal to those he served, especially Hugh Gaitskell when leader of the party and Jim Callaghan, his boss at the Treasury as Chancellor of the Exchequer. In 1981 he joined the SDP, together with Roy Jenkins, Dick Taverne and Bill Rodgers (thus making up the whole Treasury Ministerial team of 1969–70), and became the new party's leader in the House of Lords after 1982. But he was impatient with the inefficiency and indiscipline of the Liberals and did not support merger in 1988. After a short time in David Owen's rump party, he moved to the cross benches. In 1995 he rejoined the Labour Party, believing that it had now become, allowing for the passage of time, close to the kind of party that Hugh Gaitskell had sought to create.

As he passed his 90th birthday, he ceased to be active in debate but turned up unfailingly when summoned by a three-line whip. His mind was alert as ever. He learnt Greek so that he could read the classics and Arabic to read the Koran, seeing such disciplines as a way of keeping his brain alive. Otherwise he gave much time to his garden.

Jack Diamond was on the Labour Party headquarters list of prospective candidates when he presented himself in Manchester to the Blackley Labour party prior to the 1945 election. To his surprise he was selected because, so he explained, Catholics would not vote for a Protestant and Protestants would not vote for a Catholic but both were happy to choose a Jew. Apart from a short time as PPS to the Minister of Works in 1946, his main contribution during the 1945–50 Parliament was as a chairman of committees, a role for which his clear mind and persuasive manner strongly recommended him. He presided over the committee stage of the Gas Bill, the longest in that Parliament, although his own attitude to nationalisation was pragmatic rather than ideological.

In 1951 he lost his Blackley seat and did not return to Parliament until a by-election at Gloucester in 1957. But despite an active business life, he began to play an increasing behind-the-scenes role culminating in a close association with Hugh Gaitskell, after the latter's election as Leader in 1955. From 1950 to 1964 he was Treasurer of the Fabian Society and when the Campaign for Democratic Socialism was launched in 1960 in support of Gaitskell, he effectively became its mentor on money matters. Meanwhile, his training as an accountant made him an obvious member of the Shadow Treasury team and his skills were invaluable in dealing with the Finance Bill. In turn, this earned him the good opinion of Jim Callaghan and he was a natural appointment as Chief Secretary in Harold Wilson's Government of 1964. It was a measure of the trust in which he was widely held that his continued association with George Brown, to whom he was a wise counsellor, did nothing to lose the personal confidence of Wilson or Callaghan, although Brown was a thorn in both their sides.

Jack Diamond served as Chief Secretary for six years, declining the offer of a department of his own as Minister of Power because Callaghan asked him to stay at the Treasury. He was a steadying influence during that turbulent time and established the key role of the Chief Secretary in the control of public expenditure without alienating the Ministers whose plans he was often obliged to restrain. After losing Gloucester in 1970 and going to the Lords, he played a full part in its work and for five years was also Chairman of the Royal Commission on the Distribution of Income and Wealth. He published *Public Expenditure in Practice* in 1975 and, as co-author, *Socialism the British Way*, in 1948.

Jack Diamond has never courted publicity and is little known to the party outside Parliament. But his is a model of loyalty and service more common to the middle years of the 20th century than recent times.

Rt Hon. Lord Rodgers of Quarry Bank

Frank Dobson (1940–)

Frank Dobson will probably be unfairly remembered as the man who gave up the cabinet job he loved to go down to an ignominious third-place defeat at the hands of Ken Livingstone, innocent victim of Labour's mishandling of the London Mayor contest.

Dobson was born on 15 March 1940 near York, son of James, a railwayman, and Irene. He wears his family background in the railways as a badge of pride, and was sponsored by the NUR, later the RMT, rail union. He was educated at Archbishop Holgate's Grammar School, York and at the LSE where he studied economics. He joined the Labour Party in 1958, and whilst a student at the LSE he became heavily involved in the Holborn & St Pancras South Labour Party. He also met his future wife Janet at the LSE. They married in 1967 and went on to have three children – their daughter Sally has built a political career in her own right as a Millbank official.

Dobson's rise through the local Labour Party machine was given a kick-start by his good luck in moving in to a neighbouring flat to George and Irene Wagner, key figures in the group of friends who ran the Bloomsbury Labour Party and through it the CLP. The network of activists in the wards south of Euston Road is one that has supported and sustained him throughout his political career – he was fortuitous in getting involved in a local Labour Party that has traditionally been highly organised, with a permanent HQ and staff, one of the largest local memberships in the party and so near to central London that it has always been 'inside the loop' of national Labour Party affairs.

Dobson continues to live in Bloomsbury to this day, in a flat overlooking the British Museum. He is a familiar local figure to residents, seen walking out shopping in the community he represents. After holding a number of posts in the CLP, including editing its newsletter, Dobson was elected to Camden Council in 1971, becoming Leader within two years. He concentrated on housing issues, always a controversial area in crowded central London, and the provision of small parks and play areas to brighten up the lives of local residents. He is still involved in supporting the Coram's Fields park. His ward on Camden was Holborn, further cementing his power base in the south of the borough. Having previously worked for the CEGB and the Electricity Council, Dobson resigned as a councillor in 1975 to become Assistant Secretary to the Local Government Ombudsman.

He was selected as Labour candidate for Holborn & St Pancras South in 1978 in succession to Lena Jeger (who had herself succeeded her late husband) and became the local MP as Mrs Thatcher won power in 1979. Dobson was unfortunate in entering Parliament just in time to endure 18 years in opposition, but his talent for mastering a brief and taking on the Tories in a bluff, no-nonsense style led to a succession of high profile front bench roles: Deputy Spokesperson on Education (1981–83) and Health (1983–85), Spokesperson on Health (1985–87), Shadow Leader of the Commons (1987–89), Spokesperson on Energy (1989–92), Employment (1992–93), Transport (1993–94), and Environment and London (1993–97). Popular with fellow MPs and not associated with any faction within the party, with an image that has concentrated on loyalty to Labour per se rather than any particular ideological current within it, Dobson was from June 1987 consistently re-elected to the shadow cabinet.

In 1982 boundary changes amalgamated his constituency with part of Jock Stallard's St Pancras North. The two fought it out for the new selection and Dobson triumphed thanks to support from a number of key figures in the new parts of the seat added to his base in the southern wards.

As well as policy, Dobson excelled in campaigning and was a key player in a number of election campaigns. He took particular pride in leading the campaign to oust the fascist BNP's Derek Beacon from his Millwall seat on Tower Hamlets Council.

After the long years in opposition Dobson was one of the older members of Labour's shadow cabinet in the run-up to its 1997 triumph. Although valued by the party for his campaigning skills, his image as a hearty, bearded Yorkshireman with a penchant for (very) dirty jokes did not really fit in that easily with New Labour's champagne socialist image. 'Dobbo' himself projected himself as an 'Old Labour stalwart' and 'un-spun', though this could be seen as a clever bit of spin from someone keen to stay popular with the party's grassroots. Dobson's Old Labour credentials were certainly cultural rather than political – a leadership loyalist he has little time for the oppositionalists on the hard left. He likes, however, to recount the story that according to a newspaper league table of the Labour hierarchy he is 'to New Labour what Norway is to the European song contest – nul points'. Norway of course, he failed to add, has since won Eurovision.

Much to Dobson's surprise and to that of virtually every media pundit, he was rewarded for his years of hard slog with a seat in Cabinet in a job he loved, Health Secretary. Praised by NHS professionals for his handling of a difficult brief, he confounded the sneering predictions of the New Labour 'ultras'. His most difficult task was to begin the delivery of one of New Labour's five key pledges – cutting waiting lists by 100,000. Privately, he must have known that the pledge was something of a red herring, as length of time spent waiting might have been a better indicator, and the costs of delivering it were cutting into other NHS priorities. Dobson succeeded however in presiding over one of the largest hospital building programmes in British history and in squeezing greatly increased NHS funding out of a reluctant Gordon Brown.

Meanwhile Tony Blair had set about creating Britain's first directly elected mayor as part of the new arrangements for governing London. Unfortunately he neglected to think through who would be the Labour candidate and assumed that the obvious challenger, and Blair's last choice for the job, Ken Livingstone, would somehow fade away. It is not clear when Dobson privately decided to run, but throughout the summer of 1999 he protested that he had no interest in the job and fought to stay on at Health through a tricky summer reshuffle.

As late as Labour Party Conference that year Nick Raynsford thought he had a clear run and launched his campaign. Within days Dobson had suddenly announced he was a candidate and launched his own campaign. Raynsford bowed out, and Dobson also successfully co-opted as his deputy another candidate, Trevor Phillips. He did not however secure the withdrawal of his Camden neighbour, Hampstead MP Glenda Jackson. The two have never exactly been soulmates and their two CLPs fight like the Montagues and Capulets. Glenda's mishandling by Millbank ensured she did not stand aside for Frank.

Unfortunately, the campaign was hit by disaster before it ever got off the ground. None of this was of Dobson's making, for procedural decisions made either by Millbank or Downing Street made sure that a relentless media attack focused on the application of the party rulebook to the contest rather than Dobson's policies. Livingstone was put through a controversial panel vetting which succeeded in giving the impression that Blair wanted to block his candidature but did not even have the asset of achieving this as the panel backed down at the last moment. In retrospect Livingstone's subsequent willingness to stand against the Party suggests he was not fit to run as a Labour candidate and should have been barred.

Next, Labour imposed a flawed version of the electoral college instead of a straight

OMOV selection. Dobson and his team found out after the decision had been taken and were horrified. Not only did the decision make it look as though Ken was being picked on and increase the sympathy vote amongst instinctively democratic party members, but it also showed an appalling lack of knowledge of London Labour politics. Dobson himself was well aware that unlike at a national level, virtually every union affiliated to the London Party except the AEEU was controlled at a regional level by the left. A legally indisputable decision to bar left unions that had not paid their party dues looked to the uninitiated even shadier. Finally, again for sound legal reasons, Millbank refused to issue membership lists to the candidates and the Dobson campaign's legitimate possession of one was portrayed as a fix. Subsequent verdicts from the Data Protection Registrar confirmed after the campaign that Dobson's team had done nothing wrong.

In the end Dobson won a Pyrrhic victory over Livingstone by about 3 per cent of the electoral college. A heroic last-ditch drive to turn out Dobson's vote in the CLPs, particularly from the black and Asian communities, actually gave him his margin of victory, despite all the brouhaha about block votes. The election itself was something of an anti-climax. Livingstone never had to look over his shoulder whilst Labour voters and activists, disgusted by the selection process, just switched off. In the end Dobson seemed to be viewed almost with sympathy by a media which had relentlessly harried his campaign. An exhausted but dignified Dobson was lucky to avoid fourth place and had to settle for a humiliating third behind Livingstone and Tory Steve Norris.

Perhaps he was not too unhappy. Those close to him speak of him as a man who despite his long march through Labour politics has a highly developed hinterland and a contempt or perhaps pity for those with a single-minded obsession with politics. Dobson has a happy family life and a supportive wife and children and young grandchildren. Despite the wise-cracking image, he is a thoughtful character with a variety of cultural interests, particularly in history. He is not someone for whom politics is the be-all and end-all. The run-up to the general election campaign saw the old, relaxed, jovial Dobbo of pre-London Mayor days make a surprising come-back as head of Labour's attack campaign on the Tories and William Hague, a role he was ideally suited to.

Luke Akehurst

Desmond Donnelly (1920–74)

Desmond Donnelly was born on 16 October 1920 at Gohaingaon in the Sibsagar district of Assam where his father was a tea planter. Educated at Bembridge School on the Isle of Wight, Donnelly became a maverick Labour MP, once described by Richard Crossman as a 'very dubious and suspect' character, and then navigated a course from the extreme left to the extreme right of the Labour Party and ended in obscure circumstances in 1974, by which time he had become a Conservative. He contested, unsuccessfully, Evesham as a Common Wealth candidate in 1945. Common Wealth was one of four political parties Donnelly was to join in his ambitious search for fame and power over the remaining years of his life.

He won the safe Labour seat of Pembrokeshire in February 1950 and kept it as a Labour candidate until 1968. Even as a Bevanite in the late 1940s and early 1950s, he attempted to play both sides, carefully informing Hugh Dalton of full details of the Bevanites activities and attempting to carve out a position for himself as an expert on foreign and defence matters. He moved further and further to the right while Gaitskell was leader of the party. Gaitskell once commented that being the majority party in the period 1945–51 had attracted unsuitable types like Donnelly to the party in the search for power over principle. For Donnelly, Gaitskell's death in 1963 was an immense setback. Having deserted the Bevanites for the Gaitskellites, even Donnelly's political dexterity was not up to becoming a Wilsonian.

His moment of fame came when, with the Labour government elected in 1964 seeing its majority reduced by the loss of the Leyton by-election, he and fellow maverick Woodrow Wyatt held the balance of power in the vote on steel renationalisation. They argued that the government should drop full nationalisation in favour of state control. Wilson tried everything to win them over but they were determined to have their moment in the limelight. From opposing steel nationalisation Donnelly set about defending the myth of Britain's frontiers extending to the Himalayas and opposed the withdrawal of British troops from East of Suez. The cause was hopeless and Donnelly resigned the Labour whip in early 1968.

He followed his resignation with a series of personal attacks on the leadership, especially Wilson, and he was expelled from the party by the NEC. In response he founded the Democratic Party, which ran seven candidates in the 1970 election. One of these, Major Sir George FitzGerald, ran his campaign from a caravan with posters carrying slogans 'England for Sir George'. He lost his deposit to Jeffrey Archer. Six of the seven candidates also forfeited their deposits and though Donnelly kept his, he was defeated. He left the House a bitter and increasingly unbalanced man and, increasingly lonely and depressed, he committed suicide in a hotel room in West Drayton on 4 April 1974. He was often said to have had a strong sexual drive though no scandal was attached to his name in his lifetime. In 1947 he married Rosemary Taggart and they had twin sons and a daughter.

Ironically, one repercussion of his expulsion from the Labour Party was a judicial enquiry into the NEC's actions against the Constituency Labour Party in Pembrokeshire. This enquiry resulted in a new liberalisation of relations between the central party and CLPs which in turn gave the extreme left much greater scope for entryism. The young Bevanite Donnelly would no doubt have been delighted. His *Gadarene '68 – The Crimes, Follies and Misfortunes of the Wilson Government* was published in 1968.

Professor Brian Brivati

Bernard Donoughue (Lord Donoughue) (1934–)

Dr Bernard Donoughue was the first head of the 10 Downing Street Policy Unit, an innovation of Harold Wilson's after the first general election of 1974 but whose success owed everything to Donoughue's ability to turn a broad aspiration into an effective reality, aided by a staff of the highest quality. The Unit was, rightly, seen by the permanent civil service as offering the Prime Minister alternative advice – especially as Donoughue was given the title of Senior Policy Adviser – something which was traditionally anathema to them. Nevertheless, his friendly approach, easy charm and willingness to work with the civil service melted the initial opposition. He remained in the post when James Callaghan succeeded Wilson and stayed until Labour's election defeat in 1979. It was a tribute to the Unit's effectiveness that later Prime Ministers adopted and expanded it.

Donoughue was born on 8 September 1934 in Northamptonshire, the son of working-class parents who separated when he was 11. He grew up, first in a slum house and then on a council estate, coincidentally in the next village to the future Lady Falkender, with whom he was to clash frequently and dramatically during Wilson's second premiership.

After Northampton Grammar School and winning a scholarship to Lincoln College Oxford, where he took his doctorate, he had a varied career, working on the editorial staff of the *Economist* and the *Sunday Telegraph* before becoming a senior lecturer at the LSE in 1963, a post he held until seconded to Wilson in 1974. He married Carol Goodman in 1959, with whom he had four children. After leaving Downing Street he became Development Director of the Economist Intelligence Unit until 1981 when he joined his old friend Harold Evans, editor of the *Times*, as assistant editor. He left when Evans was dismissed by Rupert Murdoch in 1982 and took up senior posts with the City stockbrokers, Grieveson Grant and Kleinwort Benson. His private passions were music – he was Chairman of the Executive of the London Symphony Orchestra – and watching and playing football; he was a member of the Sports Council 1965–71 and a member of the Commission of Inquiry into Association Football 1966–68. In 1982 he returned to the LSE as a member of the Court of Governors, a position he had held before joining Wilson's staff. He was also a Fellow of Harvard and of the Roosevelt Centre for Policy Studies, Washington DC.

His highly successful career in politics, teaching and journalism had only one blemish. With some misgivings, he agreed in the late 1980s to join Robert Maxwell as vice-chairman of a new company which Maxwell had created. They did not get on. Donoughue found Maxwell impossible to work with and after Maxwell 'borrowed' £50m from a trust managed by the company he increasingly suspected Maxwell's probity and resigned early in 1990. Unfortunately for his reputation, he stayed until he was able to ensure that the 'borrowed' money had been replaced. When, shortly afterwards, Maxwell died and his frauds were exposed, it was inevitable that many of those who worked closely with Maxwell, Donoughue included, were unfairly tarnished.

Donoughue was a natural Gaitskellite, an early moderniser. After returning in 1961 from a year at Harvard – during which time he canvassed with the junior Senator from Boston, John F. Kennedy – he became active in the Campaign for Democratic Socialism, which was originally founded to oppose CND, but then widened its aims to defeat 'old' labour and propose reform. After Bill Rodgers, Secretary of CDS, resigned on becoming an MP, Donoughue, still not 30, succeeded him. His closeness to politicians like Rodgers, Roy Jenkins and Tony Crosland made him an object of suspicion among those in Wilson's circle, but a mutual friend of both men, Harry Kissin, a prominent financier, recommended him to Wilson, who first recruited him to work in his office during the first 1974 election and then asked him to form the Policy Unit. The intellectual power of the Unit – its original membership included Gavyn Davies, Andrew Graham, David Piachaud and Kay Carmichael – quickly made the Unit invaluable. The Prime Minister never went into a cabinet meeting without the Unit's comments on the brief supplied to him by the Cabinet Secretary. However, difficulties, political and personal, grew during his two years with Wilson. The early, almost gushing, reception from Marcia Williams, Wilson's political and personal secretary, rapidly turned to enmity as the Prime Minister looked to him and to me for advice. She demanded his sacking after only six months, or, at least, his removal from No 10. This failed when we made it clear that if one went both would go, a damaging departure which Wilson was not prepared to risk. Donoughue and I strenuously opposed Wilson's decision to defend in the Commons his secretary's involvement in a land deal near Wigan and his subsequent defiance of press criticism by making her a baroness, actions which only deepened the rift. Nevertheless, a great deal of work was done by the Unit, including the development of a plan to sell council houses, which, had it succeeded, might have changed the result of the 1979 election. Unfortunately, die-hard opposition, led, surprisingly, by Tony Crosland, ensured the proposal failed.

Donoughue was able to work more constructively and peacefully with Callaghan, particularly on education policy, where he was involved in the famous Ruskin speech of October 1976 which initiated the Great Debate on education standards. The problems of inflation, wage restraint and economic weakness inherited from previous governments, however, gradually grew to proportions which led to the Winter of Discontent and then defeat at the polls.

He was created Lord Donoughue of Ashton in 1985. When Tony Blair formed his government in 1997 he appointed Donoughue, who had shadowed Energy and Treasury Affairs 1991–92 and National Heritage 1992–97, to be a junior minister at Agriculture. It was a waste of Donoughue's abilities and he resigned the post after two years.

His books include *Trade Unions in a Changing Society* (1963); *British Politics and the American Revolution* (1964); co-authorship of *The People into Parliament* (1966); co-authorship of the acclaimed *Herbert Morrison, Portrait of a Politician* (1973) and *Prime Minister, The Conduct of Policy under Harold Wilson and James Callaghan* (1987).

Joe Haines

Tom Driberg (Baron Bradwell) (1905–76)

Thomas Edward Neil Driberg never held ministerial office, blaming 'deeply prejudiced puritans' such as Attlee and Wilson for barring him because of his homosexuality. He was however a leading figure of the Labour left in the 1940s and '50s, he held the chairmanship of the party in 1957–58 and prior to entering parliament was a well-known journalist for the *Daily Express*.

He also has the reputation of being one of the more colourful and outrageous Labour MPs, mainly due to his frank autobiography *Ruling Passions*, which was published posthumously in 1977. In it he described the three main passions of his life: promiscuous homosexual sex, left-wing politics and religion (he was a High Churchman and liturgist).

Born in Crowborough, Sussex on 22 May 1905 to elderly parents, he was the youngest of three brothers, though being the youngest by 15 years, he was very much a solitary child. His father, John James Steet Driberg, a retired Indian civil servant, was already sixty-five when he was born and his mother, Amy Mary Irving Bell, later told him he was meant to be a girl to keep her company in old age.

He was educated at the Grange School in Crowborough and then Lancing, where his contemporaries included author Evelyn Waugh and John Trevalyan, later the chairman of the British Board of Film Censors. Whilst at school his ruling passions began to emerge. Whilst the interest in religion and left-wing politics caused amusement and embarrassment to friends and family, his sexual desires resulted in his expulsion from Lancing during his final term, after making advances to younger boys.

Thanks to private tuition he was awarded a scholarship to Christchurch College, Oxford, where he led a decadent lifestyle, living way beyond the means of his monthly allowance. He made the most of his time at Oxford, making contacts and establishing friendships which would stand him in good stead later on in life. He mixed with people as diverse as Aleister Crowley, the Sitwells, Gertrude Stein and W H Auden.

He left university without a degree in 1927 and spent time living rough in London, earning money as a street artist before finding work in an all-night café in Soho. In spite of this lowlife existence, he later cited this period as one of the happiest times of his life. He maintained contacts with his Oxford friends, and one of them, Edith Sitwell, who was an admirer of his poetry, was horrified at his predicament. She stepped in to rescue him from the Soho low life by arranging a job for him on the *Daily Express*.

This was to be a major break in Driberg's life. After an initial trial period, he became a permanent reporter on the staff of the paper and remained on the *Express* for the next 15 years, by which time his national reputation as author of the *William Hickey* column helped him to be elected to Parliament.

His widely read column, entitled 'These Names Make News' focussed on gossip from London society; however it also enabled him to cover great events like the coronation of Pope Pius XII in 1939 and the Spanish Civil War.

In spite of his contacts with the Establishment, he was unable to prevent prosecution for indecency in 1935, following an incident in his 'not quite double' bed with two unemployed Scottish miners. He was able however to keep the case out of the newspapers with the assistance of *Express* proprietor Lord Beaverbrook. He attributed his acquittal to one of his character witnesses, Lord Sysonby, whose address at St James Palace had a considerable effect on the minds of the jury. One of the policemen investigating the charges came up to Driberg shortly before the trial and said 'why didn't you tell us who you were?' Driberg would not make the same mistake again.

He was first elected to Parliament as the independent member for Maldon in a by-election in 1942. He retained the seat as a Labour member in 1945, 1950 and 1951. In 1959 he was elected MP for Barking, a seat he held until he retired from Parliament in February 1974. In Parliament, Driberg was a prominent MP on the left and a close ally of Nye Bevan in the Labour Party's internecine warfare of the 1950s. He was first elected to Labours NEC in 1948 and remained a member until 1972.

His interests in Parliament were typically left-wing Labour, though he had strong connections to the anti-colonial movement and played a prominent role in the campaign for Burmese independence. To the surprise of many, including himself, he never held ministerial office. Whether this was due to his sexual exploits, his extreme left-wing politics or alleged spying for the KGB is uncertain. The Establishment protected Driberg, but they did not trust him.

He remained a prolific writer and journalist throughout his life, writing a weekly column for *Reynolds News*, later the *Sunday Citizen*, until 1967. He wrote biographies of Lord

Beaverbrook, art critic Hannan Swaffer and spy Guy Burgess, as well as an in-depth study of the moral rearmament movement. His failure to attain ministerial office excludes him from the ranks of the great Labour politicians of the twentieth century, but as an author and personality and as a prominent left-wing backbencher, he has a place in any history of the Labour Party. Created Lord Bradwell in January 1976, he died of heart failure in a London cab near Bayswater on 12 August 1976. He had married Mrs Ena Binfield in 1951, a Fabian friend of John Freeman and George Strauss who already had a son by another man, but even on their honeymoon (to a Brighton hotel) Driberg had sought to ensure they slept in separate rooms. 'She broke her marriage vows! She tried to sleep with me!' he complained to friends. They had lived apart since 1971 and she died in 1977.

Driberg's own autobiography *Ruling Passions* (1977) and Francis Wheen's biography *Tom Driberg: His Life and Indiscretions* (1990) are the key works on his life and both provide excellent anecdotes for dinner parties. He was also the subject of a play *Tom and Clem*, which ran at the Aldwych Theatre between April and July 1997. His own works include *Guy Burgess: A Portrait* (1960), *Swaff: The life and times of Hannan Swaffer* (1963) and *Beaverbrook: A study of Frustration and Power* (1956).

Colin Dingwall

Terry Duffy (1922–85)

Terry Duffy was born on 23 May 1922 in a Wolverhampton back-to-back, the second child of a family of eleven with a strong Catholic background. He was educated at St Joseph's Roman Catholic School, leaving at fourteen, and then worked in the Standard Motor Works as a sheet metal worker. His main interest then was boxing and he had professional offers before joining up at eighteen.

Typically he volunteered as soon as he could, for all three services on the same day it was said, and was claimed by the army, joining the Leicestershire Regiment. He achieved the rank of Regimental Sergeant Major, serving in Greece, Burma, North Africa and Italy, returning like many NCOs to become a shop steward, initially at the Norton Motorcycle factory but later at H M Hobson and Lucas Aerospace. As a Catholic he had strong anti-communist views and whilst convenor at H M Hobson he was persuaded to run for full-time office, aged 46, on the retirement of the post holder, Assistant Divisional Organiser No 16, a position he was re-elected to in 1973.

Both of these victories came under the system of branch balloting, which for years had been broadly neutral but which, following the retirement of Bill Carron in 1968, had suddenly started to favour the left. It was clear that, without change, the union would be taken over. John, later Sir John Boyd, General Secretary of the AEU, championed the cause of secret postal ballots to entrap the voice of the silent majority of moderate members, and the swing to the left was halted.

Terry Duffy was an early beneficiary, and his rise from then on was meteoric. He ran for the position of full-time Executive Council member in 1976, after taking legal action to stop a change in boundaries. He won, narrowly, and two years later succeeded Hugh Scanlon as the President of the AEU. He had swept from shop floor to the highest office in the union in just nine years.

This was an unprecedented achievement produced in part by his courage, guile and stamina and, in part, by his opponents continually underestimating him. He had no pretensions and generally undersold himself. When chairing the Unions National Committee he regularly got out of a tight spot with a joke or a tie-twiddling imitation of Oliver Hardy. Employers, supporters and opponents were taken in alike. Many saw him purely as a man of action, more interested in golf than anything else, and a political pushover. Most came to re-evaluate him.

Duffy was in the thick of all the big events in engineering: the shorter working week campaign of 1979, the Isle of Grain dispute in 1980, British Leyland on a number of occasions, the fight for the Labour Party against the left and the SDP.

As he neared retirement his health deteriorated. He suffered from emphysema, which gradually sapped his vitality but never his humour. As he lay dying the union fell out with the TUC over acceptance of money for postal ballots from government. Typically he sought to influence events from his sickbed. He died, aged 63, the following month during the Labour Party Conference, on 1 October 1985, the day of Neil Kinnock's famous speech attacking Militant. He would have cheered it to the rafters. His widow Joyce survived him. His brother Dennis was also an AEU full-time official, serving as divisional organiser in Wolverhampton.

John Gibbins

Gwyneth Dunwoody (1930–)

Though now popularly perceived as a maverick backbench battleaxe, Gwyneth Dunwoody was, during her years on Labour's NEC (1981–88), one of the key leadership loyalists who enabled Kinnock and Hattersley to take on Tony Benn, defeat Militant and reform the Party. It was Dunwoody who as Chair of the NEC Press and Publicity Sub-committee in September 1986 secured NEC backing for the Mandelson/Kinnock red rose logo for the Labour Party. Following the defeat of Shirley Williams at the 1979 general election, Dunwoody became, from November 1981 until October 1985, the only woman in Labour's Shadow Cabinet. In October 1983 Dunwoody became only the second woman to stand for Labour's Deputy Leadership, the first having been Shirley Williams in 1976. Like her running-mate Peter Shore, who stood for leader, she stood on a pro-import controls and anti-EEC but non-unilateralist and pro-NATO platform. Like Shore she came a poor fourth before suffering a sharp decline in the fortunes of her front-bench career. In July 1988, it was Dunwoody who as its Chair announced the dissolution of the Peter Shore/ Roy Hattersley-led Solidarity group of Labour MPs following the decline in its membership from some 40 five years previously to barely 25.

Gwyneth Patricia Dunwoody was born in Fulham on 12 December 1930, long before the area became a fashionable one, and was educated at Fulham County Secondary School. Her family was highly political. Her father, Morgan Phillips, was a General Secretary of the Labour Party, both her grandmothers were suffragettes, and her mother served as a minister in the House of Lords before being made the Lord Lieutenant of London.

She joined the Labour Party at sixteen in 1947 and in 1954 married Dr John Elliott Orr Dunwoody, a London doctor who was to serve as Labour MP for Falmouth and Camborne 1966–70. They had two sons and a daughter. In 1955 her husband became Senior House

Physician at Newton Abbott hospital in Devon, moving in 1956 to Totnes, where he remained until entering Parliament in 1966. Gwyneth meanwhile served on Totnes Borough Council 1963–66, and stood unsuccessfully for Parliament in Exeter in 1964. She won the seat in 1966, becoming alongside her husband, and the young David Owen in Plymouth, one of only three Labour MPs south-west of Bristol. Like her husband, but unlike Owen, she was defeated in 1970. Swiftly promoted, she was Parliamentary Secretary at the Board of Trade from 1967–70. It is rare for any husband and wife to serve as ministers in the same government at the same time but from 1969–70 the Dunwoodys managed it, when her husband served as Under-Secretary of State at the Department of Health and Social Security. Once she lost Exeter she became the Director of the Film Production Association of Great Britain for four years. Their marriage was dissolved in 1975. She won her current seat, NUR-sponsored Crewe (now Crewe and Nantwich), in February 1974, and it was from here that her political career was truly launched. She continued her commitments to the film industry as Director of the Association of Independent Cinemas from 1970 to 1976.

An active opponent of both devolution and the EEC, Gwyneth nevertheless served as a pre-direct election Member of the European Parliament from 1975 to 1979. Indeed, though a steadfast opponent of the hard left, her anti-EEC stance meant she was never close to those who joined the SDP. As deputy Foreign Affairs spokesperson (1979–80), she urged import controls on Japanese cars coming into the UK and was sceptical of the value of Japanese investment in Britain. On her election to the shadow cabinet she became Shadow Health Secretary (1981–83), spokesman on Parliamentary Campaigning and Information (1983–84), and on Transport (1984–85). As a close friend of Betty Boothroyd, she sponsored Boothroyd's bid to become Speaker, and was herself the only woman to declare herself in the race to succeed the first woman Speaker in the summer of 2000. She was a favourite of the backbenchers to take the role and serves as a Deputy Speaker in Westminster Hall as well as being a member of the Speaker's Panel of Chairmen.

Chair of the Transport Select Committee since 1997, she has earned a reputation for subjecting ministers to ferocious cross-examination. She has consistently campaigned against the privatisation of the transport system, in particular, the railway system, the London Underground and air-traffic control. From her position as Chair she has recently led three select committee investigations into the Labour Government's proposed plans to part-privatise air-traffic control, concluding that the committee had a number of concerns about the proposals and bringing her to clash with senior ministers. She was one of the main leaders of the Labour backbench rebellion over the legislation in May and November 2000. She went so far as to accuse the current Labour Cabinet of 'breathtaking arrogance' towards select committees, complaining that their attitude was 'dangerous for democracy.' Dubbed a 'self-confessed member of the awkward squad,' she would nevertheless rather call herself a 'pussycat.'

Having increasingly become an advocate of backbencher power, she does however retain traditionalist instincts in some areas. Whilst supporting the modernisation of Parliamentary procedure, she also fell foul of women MPs when she rejected the idea of breast-feeding in select and standing committee meetings, asserting that they would not be conducive either for the mother or baby. Many women MPs probably remembered her opposition through the 1980s to all-women Parliamentary shortlists. Still EEC-sceptic, she opposed the

Maastricht Treaty and the closed list system used in the 1999 European Elections. She rebelled against the Government over so-called 'cuts' to lone parent and disabled benefits, was opposed to sending troops into Kosovo and recently voted against a ban on fox-hunting.

She is Life President of the Labour Friends of Israel and Vice President of Socialist International Women. On a more irreverent note, she has a large collection of teddy bears, and sought in January 1998 to secure the return of Winnie the Pooh and his fellow characters from the New York Public Library to Great Britain when Tony Blair went to meet President Clinton soon after the Monica Lewinsky scandal broke out.

Jessica Asato

Evan Durbin (1906–48)

Evan Frank Mottram Durbin was one of the intellectual founders of revisionism and a key figure in Labour Party politics whose early death was held to have cut short a brilliant political career. Born in Bideford, Devon, on 1st March 1906, the son of a Baptist minister, he was educated at Taunton School before achieving a scholarship to New College, Oxford, in 1924. After an initial study of Zoology, he specialised in Economics, becoming a lecturer at the London School of Economics in 1930.

In the wake of the disastrous Labour election defeat in 1931, Durbin took a leading role in rethinking the meaning of socialist economic planning for the party. As a member of the Cole group, he worked in the New Fabian Research Bureau and the Society for Socialist Inquiry and Propaganda, though he refused to remain once they merged with ILP dissidents to form the Socialist League in 1932. Instead, together with his close friends Hugh Gaitskell and Douglas Jay, he joined the XYZ Club in 1934. This was a group of Labour sympathisers in the City formed by Nicholas Davenport in order to counter the Labour prejudice that finance was a necessarily hostile force. Durbin found the club an ideal forum for developing a Keynesian analysis which was to serve as a cornerstone of the corporate socialist programme which was emerging in the 1930s as a practical policy for a Labour government.

In books such as *Purchasing Power and Trade Depressions* (1933), in which Gaitskell collaborated, and *The Problem of Credit Policy* (1935), Durbin developed an economic theory which countered the dominant under-consumptionist economics of J A Hobson. He denied that low consumption was a cause of economic crisis, pointing to the success of capitalism in the 19th century as an example of how a restricted consumption could release the high investment of capital which was so essential to economic growth and national prosperity. He agreed with the underconsumptionists that the saving which resulted from a failure to spend money could result in a check on industrial expansion, but only if it was turned into a hoard. The problem could be resolved if that saving were turned into investment, enabling costs to be reduced and increasing consumption in its wake.

To Durbin, as to Keynes, the planless anarchy of traditional capitalism allowed savings to be turned into a hoard, leading to the Depression of the 1930s because it restricted investment as much as consumption and employment. Unlike Keynes, Durbin believed that only a state-directed economy – where government, banking, industrial and trade union action was centrally co-ordinated – could overcome the trade cycle of boom and slump which was so characteristic of private capitalism. In the interim period before the eventual establishment of such an economy, he rejected the panacea of breakneck credit expansion advocated by Mosley as causing a destructive inflation, advocating instead a moderately expansionary monetary policy through a policy of low interest rates and discriminatory taxation to encourage private investment of capital.

It was this interim period which was crucial to Durbin's politics. Rejecting the crisis politics of the Socialist League and the Popular Front strategy of alliance with the communists (whose support of the Moscow trials appalled him), Durbin elaborated a politics of moderation in his book, *The Politics of Democratic Socialism* (1940), which was to serve as a bible of revisionist socialism. Arguing that the totalitarian politics of communism and fascism were alien to the pragmatic British mind, he looked to parliamentary democracy as a necessary cushion against any social change which was so rapid that it would unsettle and possibly destroy the equilibrium and moderation of the British polity. He defined democratic government in terms of a method of resolving severe class differences. The freedom of the people to choose and oppose governments without being persecuted was a result of this method, which was based on a mutual understanding between the leading parties in Parliament to tolerate one another's political differences. Any radical challenge to the existing order, or conversely any radical challenge to the forces of change, would alarm the opposition into rash moves which could destroy any possibilities of a peaceful transition to socialism. It followed that parliamentary democracy to Durbin was already an integral part of a socialist society, binding the classes and parties into an organic nation whose quiet patriotism underlined an emotional unity.

It was his analysis of the changing nature of capitalist society which established Durbin in a line of thinkers who sought to escape from a Marxist analysis of their country (both the revisionists of the 1950s and the New Labour thinkers of the 1990s were to follow in his footsteps, often repeating his arguments). Durbin argued that the old divisions between a rich few and a propertyless many were being replaced as a result of the managerial revolution by the growth of a prosperous and stable middle class. This was manifested in a growing army of technicians, white-collar workers and suburban householders, but also in the increasing numbers of working-class people taking out small property holdings in the form of savings and mortgages which gave them a genuine stake in their society. Durbin argued that Labour must move out from its old trade union base to win over this middle class if it were to survive a an effective political force.

He had already stood for Parliament unsuccessfully as Labour candidate for East Grinstead in 1931 and Gillingham in 1935, and in 1940 he entered the Economic Section of the War Cabinet secretariat before becoming a personal assistant to Clement Attlee, the Labour leader, in 1942. The war brought out Durbin's British nationalism to the point of near-xenophobia, as can be seen in his comments on the French in *What Have we to Defend?* (1942). On his election as Labour MP for Edmonton in 1945, he served as a Parliamentary Secretary at the Ministry of Works from 1947 until his tragic death by drowning, saving his daughter and her friend on a Cornish beach on 3 September 1948. His death stunned Gaitskell, and his ideas were to be an inspiration to the revisionists in the Labour Party.

The key work is Elizabeth Durbin, *New Jerusalems: The Labour Party and the Economics of Democratic Socialism* (1985). Geoffrey Foote offers a different approach, bringing out the political aspects of Durbin's economic thought *in The Labour Party's Political Thought: A History* (1997 ed.).

Geoffrey Foote

Chuter Ede (Baron Chuter-Ede)   (1882–1965)

James Chuter Ede served as Home Secretary in the Labour Governments of 1945–51. He was born on 11 September 1882 in Epsom, Surrey, the son of James Ede, a grocer, and his wife, Agnes Mary Chuter. Both were staunch Noncomformists and Liberals, whose influence on their son was evident very early. He was educated at Epsom National School and Dorking National School. He won a scholarship to study at Christ's College, Cambridge, but was forced by lack of money to leave without completing his degree. From 1905, Ede tought in elementary schools in Surrey and became active in the Surrey County Teachers' Association and the local Liberal Association. In 1908, he was elected to the Epsom Urban Council and, six years later, to the Surrey County Council. With the outbreak of war in 1914, Ede enlisted in the Fifth East Surrey Regiment as a private and later served as a sergeant with the Royal Engineers.

During the war, Ede abandoned the Liberals for the Labour Party. He had always been a 'New Liberal' but Ede now perceived Labour as the more effective vehicle for achieving social reform and promoting trade union rights. Further, he saw himself as 'a person of a Liberal turn of mind but a Socialist in economics,' in part because of the experience of war. In 1918, Ede fought Epsom for the Labour Party. Five years later, he was elected MP for Mitcham but was defeated later the same year. In 1929, he became MP for South Shields and was again defeated in 1931. He won the seat back in 1935 and remained in the Commons until 1964. Ede also stayed active in local government, serving on the Epsom Urban Council (1908–27 and 1933–37) and as chairman of the Surrey County Council (1933–37). In 1927, he became a member of the London and Home Counties Joint Electricity Authority and was chairman from 1934 to 1940.

Ede's ministerial career began in 1940 when he became Parliamentary Secretary to the Ministry of Education in Winston Churchill's coalition Government. Working closely but quietly with the education minister, R. A. Butler, he played a major role in securing bipartisan agreement for the landmark Education Act of 1944, which introduced compulsory secondary schooling for all children in the state sector and divided secondary education between grammar schools, secondary moderns and technical schools.

In August 1945, Ede was appointed Home Secretary in the new Government of Clement Attlee. This was something of a surprise, not least to Ede himself, who had expected the Education post. But Attlee wanted to use his proven skills as an administrator, his experience in local government and his capacity for hard work for one of the most demanding departments.

During Ede's six-year tenure at the Home Office, the longest of the twentieth century, he took charge of a massive programme of legislation. In 1948 alone, there was the Criminal

Justice Act, which introduced major changes in the treatment of offenders and the criminal law; the British Nationality Act, which set the pattern of British nationality and naturalisation for over thirty years; the Children Act, which made provision for deprived children; the Representation of the People Act, which abolished the business and university graduate votes; and a new Civil Defence Act. In other parliamentary sessions, he piloted through the Fire Services Act, which gave responsibility for the service back to local authorities, honouring a promise by Herbert Morrison; a reorganisation of the police; changes to the magistrates courts; and major consolidations of the licensing and electoral laws.

Despite the size and scope of this programme, Ede is not remembered as one of the heroes of the Attlee Government. In part, this is because his achievements were largely tangential to the Government's central objectives. Most of the bills were initiated by the Home Office in order to update wartime regulations or to effect long-delayed changes. Indeed, the cautious approach taken in much of Ede's legislation failed to meet the aspirations of reformers. The Police Act of 1946, for example, did not effect radical change in the force, after pressure from the Police Federation.

His stance on the death penalty was a particular disappointment. During the debate on the criminal justice bill, the Labour MP Sydney Silverman put down an amendment in favour of abolition. On behalf of the government, Ede urged the Commons to reject it. He argued that public opinion did not favour change and that tough measures were needed to stem the rise in violent crime. When Silverman's amendment was passed by the Commons but rejected by the Lords, Ede then tabled a compromise clause limiting capital punishment to specified offences. The Lords rejected this too and he let the compromise clause lapse for fear of losing the entire bill. When the issue returned to the Commons in the mid-1950s, long after he had left office, Ede strongly supported abolition. A major reason for this change was the execution of Timothy John Evans, to whom he had denied a reprieve and whom Ede subsequently believed was innocent. He eventually secured the adoption of his compromise clause, which led, in time, to the complete abolition of the death penalty.

The indifference towards Ede may also be explained by his rectitude in completing a major overhaul of the electoral boundaries. The Labour Party paid a heavy price. The review gave suburban and middle-class areas more seats at the expense of the inner cities and may have reduced the party's margin over the Conservatives by as many as sixty seats. It won the 1950 General Election by five seats and was beaten the following year.

Ede, who also served as Leader of the House of Commons for the final six months of the Attlee Government, and in the Shadow Cabinet 1951–55, became PC (1944), CH (1953), DL (Surrey) and received honorary doctorates from Bristol (1956), Durham (1954) and Sheffield (1960). He was created Baron Chuter-Ede of Epsom in 1964 and changed his name by deed poll to Chuter-Ede. Viewed by contemporaries as earnest, deliberate in manner and somewhat austere, he was a teetotaler and non-smoker, whose hobbies included boating, horse-racing and photography. In 1917, Ede married Lilian Mary Stephens (died 1948) and they had no children. He died on 11 November 1965 in a Ewell nursing home.

Neil Stockley

John Edmonds   (1944–)

John Walter Edmonds is one of the new style of trade union leaders. Whereas in the past some trade union leaders left themselves open to accusations of being concerned with their own personal fiefdoms, Edmonds and others such as John Monks (General Secretary of the TUC, 1993–) are part of the moves towards 'new unionism'. This took into account the declining membership of the trade unions and their increasing irrelevance in industrial decision-making procedures. The emphasis has been placed upon modernisation – for the trade unions this meant recruitment and partnership (with each other, businesses and all political parties).

Edmonds has been leader of the GMB (formerly the General, Municipal, Boilermakers and Allied Trade Union) since 1986 and has extended his influence over the trade union movement since then, going on to be a member of the TUC General Council and its Executive Committee, becoming its President in 1998.

Edmonds was born on 28 January 1944 and raised in south London in a union-dominated family. His father, Walter Edmonds, was a shop steward for the TGWU (Transport and General Workers Union), his mother, Rose Edmonds, worked for a local paper company and his grandfather and uncle were both active in the print unions, being FOCs ('Father of the Chapel', the leader of a local union branch). Trade unionism was a fact of life. He recognised the south London in which he was raised to be differentiated. The affluent workers worked 'in the print' and took holidays. The less well-off worked in the docks and 'went hopping' in the hop fields of Kent as their break during the summer months.

After winning a London County Council scholarship whilst at primary school (Brunswick Park Primary) he went on to attend Christ's Hospital School. The school had an atmosphere of snobbery which affected the young Edmonds, as did its ethos of being a minor public school. The school did not allow the young man to develop his personality; instead the home environment allowed him to 'be himself'. A further scholarship meant that he was able to pursue his passion for history at Oriel College, Oxford. Not tempted by the more usual political route of studying PPE (Politics, Philosophy and Economics), although taking the economics options available in his course where possible, he took Modern History.

During his latter years at school, Edmonds became determined to become a trade union official and consolidated these ideas at Oxford. After a short time spent with a food company, the only job he could get in the GMWU (as the GMB was called at this time) was as a research assistant in the Research Department, preparing briefs and wage claims. He immediately tried to become a field officer (organiser) and managed it after only a couple of years, which placed him in the role of representing a variety of members in the union's Southern Region. This was a time of particular fulfilment and he loved the job as much as he had always hoped. His success and enthusiasm did not go unrecognised and he was promoted to become the union's youngest National Industrial Officer in 1972. He represented industries such as gas, electricity, nuclear energy, food companies such as Tate and Lyle, timber and packaging, the NHS and he also led on negotiations for local government workers. He also campaigned actively on behalf of disabled workers when he represented members at Remploy.

Since taking over as General Secretary Edmonds' greatest strength is seen to be his strategic thinking. His forward planning and ideas for his own union, as well as the movement more generally, have contributed significantly to a growing membership and level of influence. He saw developing an effective amalgamation policy during the unions' 'dark days' of the late 1980s and early 1990s, as essential in sustaining the core membership. This meant shifting the structure of the union to give a greater level of importance to the industrial, as opposed to the regional, identity. Edmonds was also one of the first union leaders to recognise the growing importance of women in the workplace and seek to provide them with greater opportunities within the GMB. This meant ensuring that women make up the same proportion of the governing body that they do in the membership as a whole. An active recruitment policy, still ongoing, looks to recruit more women, as well as from the service sector. Essentially the union began to push for rights at work and workers' rights as opposed to trade union immunities.

Edmonds describes relations with the Labour Party as a 'candid forum' and the relationship has not always been harmonious. The unions recognised that they had to reduce the size of their vote within the Party as it limited their freedom of movement as well as being electorally unhelpful for the Party. Yet this did not prevent the then leader of the Labour Party, John Smith (who Edmonds had championed for the position very shortly after Neil Kinnock resigned), from nearly losing a vote on OMOV at the hands of the unions; Edmonds, despite his support for OMOV, was wary of the form of the proposals on offer. Part of the 'new unionism' agenda means that whereas total support for the Party was correct during the years of Conservative Party rule in the 1980s and 1990s, following the Labour Party's election in 1997 they feel more able to speak out on behalf of their members and disagree publicly if necessary.

Edmonds is aware of the challenges that still remain for the GMB. The need for better communication techniques and organisation structures which deliver effective support and advice to members in an increasingly fragmented labour force are top of the agenda. Yet leaders such as Edmonds also maintain a very close eye at the European level on the need to influence policy there. The GMB is the only British union to have an office in Brussels, Edmonds helped to launch Trade Unionists for Europe to campaign for early entry into the single European currency, and he is also a member of the European TUC Executive. His prediction of the growth of the 'super-union', one which the GMB has done much to forward by being the successful merger partner for other unions, may well adopt a similar European dimension.

In addition to his trade union duties, Edmonds is a director of the Unity Trust Bank (1986–), a trade union member of the Forestry Commission (1995–), a Trustee of the NSPCC (1995–), a Trustee of the Institute of Public Policy Research (1988–) and is president of the Full Employment Forum. He has been a council member of ACAS (the Arbitration and Conciliation Service), member of the Consumers' Association council (1991–96), Director of the National Building Agency (1979–82) and a member of the Royal Commission on Environmental Pollution (1979–89). Edmonds was awarded an honorary Doctor of Law degree by Sussex University in 1994 and was a Visiting Fellow at Nuffield College, Oxford (1986–94). Away from work he is a keen cricketer, playing for a local club, and also enjoys carpentry.

Edmonds still lives, with his wife Linden (Callaby) by whom he has two daughters, in South London, an area which did so much to shape his outlook and politics.

Dr Stuart Thomson

Murray Elder (Lord Elder)   (1950–)

Murray Elder is a product of a famous Scottish education experiment which accelerated the progress through school of Fife's brightest youngsters. Born on 19 May 1950, he skipped the last year in primary school and went with 36 contemporaries straight into a special 'E' class at Kirkcaldy High School, along with his pre-school friend Gordon Brown. They later shared a flat in Edinburgh and Murray switched from a maths degree to economic history in a department with some inspirational lecturers like TC Smout.

His degree from Edinburgh University took him to London to work for the Bank of England in 1972. After four years in Exchange Controls he moved to the Economics Intelligence Unit in the Monetary Policy division. In spite of his banking career, Murray's politics had been shaped early by his left-wing father, a head teacher.

In 1980, on Gordon Brown's recommendation, John Smith interviewed him for a research job in the House of Commons. His co-employer was the outgoing Chancellor Denis Healey. Healey asked Murray why on earth he continued to wear a beard when these were unfashionable. 'It's none of your business,' came the reply, and Healey immediately offered him the job. His skills ranged far beyond research as a policy wonk of the old school – lots of reading, discussion and thought, though in 1989 he nevertheless experimented with the first focus groups in Scotland.

Murray's brief expanded to key policy issues at a time when Tony Benn was trying to take the party to the left. Indeed Healey had to beat Benn to become the party's Deputy Leader. These were the party's famine years – an election low of 1983 saw Labour reduced to 209 seats. Murray took part in this campaign for the first and last time as a Labour candidate – in the Ross, Cromarty & Skye seat, which Charles Kennedy took from the Tories. At least Murray saved his deposit. Michael Foot resigned. Neil Kinnock and Roy Hattersley took the helm with John Smith as the emerging force. But 1987 created a backlash in Scotland, when Labour picked up Tory strongholds but seemed no nearer to power. During this time Murray had become the party's Scottish Research Officer, then Scottish General Secretary. He worked with Donald Dewar ensuring that Labour played a leading role in the Scottish Constitutional Convention. Skilfully outflanking the Tories who refused to join and outmanoeuvring the Nationalists who ended up boycotting the Convention, Murray left the ground clear for a Labour re-grouping round the cause of Scottish devolution. He was a member of the Plant Commission on electoral reform, in part to ensure that the Scottish party was given enough room for manoeuvre in their discussions with the Liberals on the Constitutional Convention. That same year he almost lost his life when he was hit by heart failure, the consequence of rheumatic fever as a child. He was only saved by a then-rare heart transplant.

After the 1992 election defeat Neil Kinnock resigned and John Smith brought Murray south again as his Chief of Staff. John Smith and Murray were two peas from the same pod, laconic men combining sharp brains, direct talking and serious sobriety in public, while enjoying witty jokes and anecdotes and good malt whisky off duty. They also shared a love of the Scottish mountains. Politically, this was the time of OMOV – 'One member, one vote' – the first act of modernising the party. More than anyone, Murray worked behind the scenes to ensure John Smith could achieve it. Initially thought to be impossible, it was narrowly delivered at the Brighton conference in 1993.

In 1996 he rejoined Donald Dewar to prepare for the 1997 election. This work continued when Dewar became Secretary of State for Scotland. The work Murray had put into the Convention bore fruit when a coalition became necessary after the 1999 Scottish Parliament election resulted in a hung Parliament. In 1999, he was created Lord Elder, and is a member of the Lords Economic Affairs Committee.

Nigel Griffiths MP

David Ennals (Lord Ennals of Norwich) (1922–95)

An internationalist and tireless campaigner against injustice, David Hedley Ennals' political passions had their roots in his early upbringing. Born in Walsall on 12 August 1922, second of three sons of Arthur and Jessie Ennals, he was brought up in a practising Baptist family of international vision. A missionary uncle in the Congo and the strong support of their parents for the League of Nations led to all three brothers being active in the field of radical international politics: John as Secretary General of the World Federation of United Nations Associations and of the UK Immigrant Advisory Service, and Martin as General Secretary of the National Council for Civil Liberties, of Amnesty International and as founder of International Alert.

Educated at Queen Mary's Grammar School, Walsall, and briefly at the Loomis Institute, Connecticut, David began his working life early as a journalist in Walsall. From 1941 to 1946 he served in the Royal Armoured Corps, rising to the rank of Captain. Shortly before the D-Day landings he was sent into Normandy to inform the allies on German troop and gun positions. Two weeks later he was shot. His wounds were to cause him constant pain, necessitated numerous operations, and eventually led to the circulatory problem which would so badly affect his health.

Following demobilisation, he began to work for the cause of peace: from 1946 to 1947 as UNA's Regional Officer in Manchester, then as Secretary to the Council for Education in World Citizenship (1947–52), Secretary of UNA (1952–57), and Secretary to International Department of the Labour Party (1957–64). David had also by then become more actively engaged in frontline politics. A member of the Labour Party from his youth, he briefly transferred to the Liberals in 1949, fighting the constituency of Richmond for them in 1950 and 1951. In 1952 he rejoined the Labour Party. In 1962 he was selected as Labour candidate for the Conservative-held constituency of Dover, entering Parliament following the 1964 election at the age of 42. He was to hold this seat in 1966 but lose it in 1970 when Harold Wilson made him a Privy Counsellor in his resignation honours list.

The loss of Dover and the experience of sudden unemployment in his late forties, at a time when the mental illness of one of his children meant that he had continuing financial obligations, affected him deeply. His appointment later that year as Campaign Director of Mind happily developed his interest in mental health. Politics was in his blood, however, and, selected as Labour candidate for the marginal seat of Norwich North, he re-entered Parliament in 1974, holding the seat in 1979 but losing it in 1983. He entered the Lords later that year as Baron Ennals of Norwich.

His hard work, energy (Tam Dalyell described him as 'demonically energetic') and love of argument meant that David enjoyed speedy promotion. On entering the Commons in 1964 he quickly became PPS to Barbara Castle at the Ministry of Overseas Development, moving with her to the Department of Transport in 1965. In 1966 came his first Ministerial appointment, as Parliamentary Under Secretary of State for Defence for the Army. The following year he took a sideways move to the Home Office, where he had to handle the Commonwealth Immigration Act of 1968 – an act which caused his brother Martin to resign as public relations officer to the National Committee for Commonwealth Immigrants – and certainly caused David himself a great deal of anguish. 1968 saw him promoted as Minister of State at the Department of Health and Social Security under Dick Crossman.

When Harold Wilson's government returned to power in 1974 David was appointed Minister of State at the Foreign and Commonwealth Office under Jim Callaghan. In 1976 on Harold's resignation, he worked for Jim's election as leader and was rewarded with a seat in the Cabinet as Secretary of State for Health and Social Security. His previous experience there, his work with Mind, his strong interest in mental health, and his passionate belief in the NHS seemed to betoken a happy partnership and his Parliamentary Secretary welcomed him as 'a notably caring minister'. It was, however, to prove a poisoned chalice.

The Department presented a complex and unwieldy challenge which Barbara Castle, whom he succeeded, had contained by force of her personality and political flair. There were growing economic problems and the Treasury refused to meet the increasingly militant wage demands of the many low-paid public service workers or to provide the additional three billion pounds which David requested in 1978. This difficult situation was compounded by the Secretary of State's increasing ill health. A major thrombosis developed in his left leg during 1978, necessitating a number of operations in Westminster Hospital (as an NHS patient) and, since he insisted on remaining in control, key departmental meetings of ministers and officials had from time to time to be held in a side ward of the hospital. It also made it nigh impossible for the Secretary of State to stay on top of the complex difficulties which developed over the Winter of Discontent.

With the defeat of the by then minority Callaghan Government in 1979 David decided, with 'a sense of liberation' to retire to the back benches where he could devote his time to raising the profile of the many causes he supported. He continued this role in the Lords after 1983, in addition to being a frontbench spokesman there on Health, and despite his increasing suffering from ankylosing spondilitis. He died peacefully in his sleep at home in north London on 17 June 1995. He was 72.

David was twice married. His first marriage, to Eleanor Caddick in 1950, produced four children – Richard, Susie, Paul and Simon – to whom he remained devoted despite the drift in his marriage which ended in divorce in 1977. His second marriage, to Gene Tranoy, came later that year. They had one adopted son, Phuoc Ky, a refugee from Vietnam. Phuoc's death in May 1993 in a shooting incident (he was a rifleman with the Royal Greenjackets) was a cause of deep sadness, as were the deaths of his brothers, John in 1988 and Martin in 1991.

Generally seen as a radical, David brought ceaseless commitment and passion to the many causes he espoused. On the international front these included the UN, peacekeeping, arms control and opposition to all forms of injustice. He was an active Chair of the Anti-Apartheid Movement from 1960 to 1964 and, in 1966, travelled to Southern Rhodesia. during the days of

UDI on a fact-finding mission. He raised the cases of many refugees brought to his attention by Amnesty International, made visits to the Bihari community in Bangladesh and to perse-cuted tribes in Kenya, and visited the boat people being returned to Vietnam. He spoke out on the tragedies of Tibet and gave long-standing support, including time as Chairman, to the Ockenden Venture's work for refugee children.

Nearer home his concerns centred primarily on health and poverty. He remained devoted to the NHS. He was always commited to the problems of mental health, served as President of Mind, and, following a personal experience with Valium, raised the issue of addiction through prescription and promoted self-help groups for addicts. He chaired the Campaign for the Homeless and Rootless, was President of the College of Occupational Therapy, worked for the Children's Medical Charity and became a patron of the Alzheimer's Disease Society and of the National Society of Non-Smokers.

His speeches from the back benches reflect all of these interests and more. Publications came earlier and centre mostly on his international preoccupations of the time. *Strengthening the United Nations* (1957), was followed by *Middle East Issues* (1958), *United Nations Peace Force* (1960), *The United Nations on Trial* (1962) and *Out of Mind*, a book on mental health, (1973). It was only to be expected that his funeral would include readings from the Preamble to the UN Charter and from the UN Declaration of Human Rights. David was always a political animal; he was also ambitious. He got on well with his civil servants and was acknowledged both by them and by the ministers he served as a competent, committed and caring minister. However, his handling of the huge problems of the health and community services in which he so pas-sionately believed has been criticised by some of his colleagues, who felt that his deteriorating health meant that he was not always master of his undoubtedly difficult brief.

David was perhaps, first and foremost, an indefatigable and courageous campaigner against injustice. Much of his contribution to the Labour Party lay in his tireless raising and debating of these issues, not only in Parliament but up and down the land. He was unfailingly cheerful throughout pain and adversity. Courage, service and positive engagement characterised his at-titude to life. His vision was of an inclusive, belonging and international society where broth-erhood was a living practice. The Labour Party of his day became richer for this vision.

Lord Judd and Lady Chris Judd

Moss Evans   (1925–)

Moss Evans led Britain's biggest trade union during one of the most difficult periods the La-bour movement has ever faced. His opposition to government-imposed pay norms and his willingness to support his members in industrial action was a key element in the industrial un-rest of 1978–79 which helped to seal the fate of the Callaghan government. After the 1979 election defeat, he played a prominent part in the debates over the Labour Party's constitution and leadership.

Arthur Mostyn Evans was born in Cefn Coed, near Merthyr Tydfil, South Wales on 13 July 1925. When he was 12, his family moved to Birmingham after his father had lost his job as a miner during the Depression, moving back to Cefn Coed in 1940 when they were bombed out.

As the war drew to a close, Evans was posted to Ernest Bevin's 'special repair service', building Mulberry harbours and repairing bomb-damaged houses. It was while working in Berkshire in the summer of 1945 that he met his wife Laura. They remain married, with three daughters and two sons. Another son died in 1978.

After the war, Evans moved back to Birmingham, working at the Bakelite plant in Tyseley where he joined the TGWU. He became a shop steward, then chairman of the joint shop stewards committee and convenor, and took a six-month unpaid day release course at Birmingham University and a correspondence course at Ruskin College, Oxford.

By now, Evans was set for a career in the TGWU. In 1956, he became a full-time official district officer and in 1960 regional officer for the Midlands, moving to London in 1966 to take national responsibility for the engineering and chemical industries. In 1970, Evans was promoted to the position of National Organiser, one of the most influential positions in the TGWU. His reputation within the TGWU was cemented in 1970 and 1971, when he was charged with persuading a reluctant Ford workforce at Swansea, Daventry and Liverpool to accept a pay deal.

When Jack Jones announced his decision to step down, Evans, who was Jones's preferred candidate, quickly became the favourite to win the race to succeed him. Like all the other main candidates, Evans made his opposition to the Government's pay norms clear in the election campaign, and in 1977 he won the ballot decisively, by 349,548 votes to 119,241 for his nearest challenger, John Cousins, son of Jack Jones's predecessor Frank Cousins.

A vignette from September 1978 illustrates how close government and the trade unions then were. Mindful of the immense industrial strength of the TGWU at the time, James Callaghan telephoned Evans to suggest that he come to Transport House to meet the union's Finance and General Purposes Committee, to discuss pay policy. Evans knew that if anyone spotted the Prime Minister coming to Transport House to parley, they would smell trouble, so he suggested that the PM instead invite the committee to Downing Street. Yet, despite these top-level contacts, and the cordial personal relationship between Evans and leading members of the government, Callaghan included, the crisis which both men wished to avoid soon came about.

In September 1978, Ford car workers began an official dispute in support of a pay claim, which had been withdrawn because it breached the government's 5 per cent pay norm. Evans supported the strike, saying 'If the consequences are such that the government is going to suffer, so be it'. This was a signal that where there was a clash between his industrial role and his political role, it was the industrial which would take precedence. The strike succeeded, triggering further wage demands across the economy and dealing a heavy blow to the credibility of the government's pay policy.

During October 1978, Evans was involved in an episode which saw a chance for compromise over pay lost due to a series of mishaps. At a time when a document drawn up by the 'Neddy Six' union leaders was being put to the TUC General Council, Evans was absent on holiday in Malta. Though it had been booked for a long time, Evans insisted that he must stay in Britain, but relented when he was assured by TGWU colleagues that this was not necessary, confident that his support for the document would be given effect at the meeting. In the event, the two TGWU delegates on the General Council split their votes, the vote was tied, and the chance for compromise was lost. Evans returned to Britain to a torrent of criticism, including a newspaper article by the Chancellor Denis Healey, which criticised him personally. Evans admitted that the episode left the union looking foolish, reflecting wistfully that even though he had argued with TGWU colleagues that he should stay in Britain, 'it was always Evans who got the blame'.

Some observers, not least senior members of the Callaghan administration and their biographers, have said that Evans, a pleasant and affable man who professed his desire to remain 'one of the lads' upon his accession to the top job, lacked Jack Jones's force of personality and political judgement. They allege that he was neither willing nor able to maintain the political alliance with the Government, and that his support for striking workers led to a collapse in the Labour Government's authority, ushering in a period of Conservative hegemony.

However, it should be remembered that unlike his predecessor, Evans was faced with a disintegrating Labour administration whose pay policies were opposed by many ordinary trade unionists. Furthermore, Evans can claim the mantle of consistency. During his campaign for the General Secretaryship, Evans never made any secret of his support for a return to free collective bargaining in an orderly way. If there was a lack of judgement in this period, it may have been on the part of those who expected such a committed and experienced trade unionist to abandon the long-held beliefs on which he was elected, in order to support a government which had exhausted its natural well of support among working people.

Following the 1979 election defeat, Evans also emerged as a key player in the constitutional debates which racked the Labour Party. In much the same way as he had declared himself to be a supporter of greater involvement of lay activists and shop stewards in the TGWU, Evans supported 'democratising' the Party by widening the number of Party members involved in policy making and the election of the leader. He was a member of the Commission of Enquiry appointed by the National Executive Committee to investigate ways of reforming the Party's constitution, and at the meeting in Bishop's Stortford in June 1980, he provided the key vote which ensured that the Commission would support mandatory reselection of MPs.

At the Wembley special conference of January 1981, called to determine the method of selecting the Party Leader, Evans was mandated by his conference to support an Electoral College, but not one in which a single section had more than 50 per cent of the votes. Evans initially supported an equal three-way split for the Electoral College for the selection of leader but when this was rejected at the special conference, amid some confusion, he supported the formula which gave the trade unions 40 per cent. This triumphed over the formula giving the Parliamentary Party 50 per cent, with Evans's 1,250,000 block vote providing much of the eventual 1.5 million-vote margin.

Alas, his assessment in his speech to the Wembley conference that 'In a few years time, we will all be asking what the Dickens all the fuss was about', proved to be wide of the mark. The decision prompted the founders of the SDP to break with the Labour Party, while the Electoral College provided the Party's opponents with the opportunity to attack the Party for years after.

In the two elections for the Party leadership which took place during his tenure, he was an early and enthusiastic supporter of his fellow Welsh left-wingers Michael Foot and Neil Kinnock. Evans was one of the key influences behind Michael Foot's decision to stand for leader in 1980 as a full-time leader, and not just a caretaker figure, and he remained a staunch supporter during Foot's troubled tenure, rallying support for him after the disastrous Bermondsey by-election defeat in February 1983.

Though he would have placed himself firmly on the left of the Labour spectrum throughout his period as general secretary, he opposed Benn's 1981 deputy leadership challenge, calling it a distraction. Yet he was powerless to prevent the TGWU executive deciding to support Tony Benn, even though a hastily conducted branch ballot produced a majority for Denis Healey. His capacity for decisive action during much of 1981 was limited when he was forced to take four months off work, following surgery for stomach cancer.

After the 1983 election defeat, Evans swiftly moved to support Neil Kinnock's candidature, along with his fellow Welsh left-wing trade union leader, Clive Jenkins. He supported Kinnock on many occasions including Kinnock's attempt to prevent Conference endorsing cuts in defence spending and his one-member, one-vote reforms at the 1984 Party conference.

Evans retired as General Secretary on his sixtieth birthday, in July 1985, having announced his intention to do so in October 1983, in part due to ill-health. He then shepherded the union through a difficult period after complaints over the fairness of the ballot to elect his successor.

On his retirement, he professed his intention to spend time with his family and retired to Kings Lynn. Yet in 1991, he returned to the political fray, albeit on a smaller stage, as a Labour councillor for the Heacham ward on Kings Lynn and West Norfolk Borough Council. Evans was an active councillor, serving as leader of the Labour Group in opposition, as council leader and as Mayor in 1996. On his retirement he was appointed an Honorary Alderman of the Borough.

Moss Evans lives with his wife in Kings Lynn, enjoying the visits of his children and ten grandchildren and his hobbies of music, petanque, and horse racing. He is an active supporter of charity and community ventures – he is President of Heacham and District Age Concern, a member of Heacham Youth and Community Centre, and is a trustee of the 3R Centre, a charity he helped to set up which cares for abandoned racehorses.

David Mills

Charlie Falconer (Lord Falconer) (1951–)

People who work with Charlie Falconer tend to like him. Best known for his stewardship of the ill-fated Dome project and for being a former flatmate of Tony Blair, Lord Falconer is not the stereotype of a modern politician. Infectiously optimistic, genuine, thoughtful and unflappable, he brings to British politics formidable rigour in his thinking, coupled with a real desire to get things done. With talents like these, his future in the heart of government is assured.

His personal friendship with Tony Blair is only of passing interest when exploring his background and journey into politics. Like the Prime Minister, Charles Leslie Falconer chose the Labour Party rather than being born into it. But he was born into the law, on 19 November 1951. His great-grandfather had been a Church of Scotland minister; but his father, like his father before him, was an Edinburgh solicitor whose party loyalties had tended to shift. Grandfather Falconer had been an independent councillor who became Lord Provost of Edinburgh.

Charles' father had been a Liberal in his youth, and in the 1950s and '60swas a Conservative. But after Margaret Thatcher's accession to the Tory leadership in 1975 he drifted away from the party. John Falconer was closely involved in local hospital boards – an active citizen rather than a political one.

There was politics and politicians in the background however. The late John Smith lived close by in Edinburgh and the Falconers knew the Smiths well, both professionally and socially. A visit to Westminster to meet the newly-elected Smith in the early 1970s left a forcible impression on young Charles. Although interested in politics while studying History and Law at Queens College Cambridge, where he he went after Glenalmond, open allegiance and membership of a particular party 'wasn't the done thing'. He eventually joined the Labour Party in the late seventies. At about the same time Tony Blair moved in to the house Falconer had bought in Wandsworth, and together they were actively involved in local Labour Party life. Looking back on that time, Falconer recalls not just a profound disillusionment with the Callaghan government but also a deep frustration that the Labour Party did not have a coherent story to tell. In conversation, it was this lack of a persuasive argument, a clear and rigorous approach and the consequent inability to make a difference that exercised Falconer the most. His disenchantment with past policy and approach gives, perhaps, the best insight into his commitment and enthusiasm for Labour in government since 1997. The mantras of 'What matters is what works' and 'Pragmatism for a purpose' clearly match Falconer's own style of thinking and personal political motivation.

Through the 1980s Charlie Falconer built a formidable reputation, first as an employment and then as a more broadly commercial lawyer, becoming a QC in 1991. While his friend Tony Blair had increasingly focused on a political career, Falconer had largely subordinated politics to the Bar – though he did undertake extracurricular work for the party from time to time. Even before becoming leader, Blair had made it clear that he wanted to see successful people from other walks of life play a fuller role in parliament. After becoming leader, Blair recognised that he would need at least one new talented government law officer. It was therefore natural that he should encourage Falconer to become an MP. Sure enough, Falconer applied to stand in the safe seat of Dudley West shortly before the general election in 1997, but was unsuccessful. A series of exchanges at the NEC short-listing meeting regarding his children's private education proved his undoing. In his characteristically honest style, Falconer had told the panellists that he could not guarantee that he would reconsider his choice of education even if an incoming Labour Government were to demonstrably improve the quality of the state education sector. He would do what was in the best interests of his children.

Falconer clearly regrets his failure to become an elected Member of Parliament. His commitment to the process of democratic politics – making the case, winning an argument, gaining a mandate, delivering real change and then being accountable – is clear and absolute. But this has not negated an active role for him in government, first undertaking the job of Solicitor General in 1997 before moving to the Cabinet Office as Minister of State in July 1998, inheriting Peter Mandelson's membership of most key cabinet committees. He had a pretty shrewd idea that the Dome could be trouble for him – telling a meeting of Labour Party activists wryly that on the day he took over responsibility for the venture, the one-word caption on the picture of him behind the BBC newsreader changed with each bulletin. During the lunchtime news it said 'Dome'. At 6pm it read 'Supremo'. At 9pm it read, ominously, 'Crony'. But in an almost unnerving display of political determination he steered the project to completion, calmly and rationally facing the difficulties that emerged along the way, and balancing the undoubted (and in many ways disastrous) political fallout and the utterly damning National Audit Office report with the pragmatic calculation that it was sounder economically and in the wider interests of the communities of South-East London to see the thing through.

The Dome debacle has of course overshadowed much of his other work at the Cabinet Office. This is a shame, because far more telling of his own priorities and commitment to 'new politics' has been his work with the 'Active Communities Unit'. Here, alongside Paul Boateng at the Home Office, he has had responsibility for promoting and encouraging the giving of time to community involvement. Symbolic of the government's commitment to progressive policy, this practical and innovative approach seeks to enhance the well-being of communities through the supported work of voluntary organisations and individuals' own contribution of time and expertise. Redefining the relationship between state and individual is an underlying theme of New Labour philosophy and policy, not in a crude and dogmatic Thatcherite sense, but in an open, problem-solving manner. It is fitting that Charlie Falconer is clearly associated with this strand of work.

It is all too easy to portray Lord Falconer as the arch-Blair crony set up to act as the un-elected public whipping boy for unpopular government policies. Indeed, John O'Farrell predicted that he could look forward to a rosy future after the 2001 election as 'Minister for Very High Petrol Prices'. The truth of course is different. Having proved his tenacity as the public face for the Dome, he has now been appointed Minister for Housing and Planning – a challenging brief that will benefit from Falconer's rigour and commitment. Future elevation to the cabinet remains a distinct possibility.

Chris Naylor

Vic Feather (Lord Feather) (1908–76)

Vic Feather's period of office as General Secretary of the Trades Union Congress was brief but dramatic: its impact was far-reaching. Victor Feather was elected to the most senior post in the British trade union movement at the relatively late age of 61 after 30 years working for the TUC. Under the organisation's rules the General Secretary must retire at the age of 65. In the four years from 1969 to 1973 the TUC and Victor Feather were never far from the headlines, whether in negotiations with Harold Wilson and his employment secretary Barbara Castle or out on the streets in opposition to the draconian industrial relations policies of Edward Heath and Robert Carr. The image of those days was etched deep in the public and trade union memory and exerted a strong influence on both Conservative and Labour Governments for the rest of the twentieth century.

Victor Grayson Hardie Feather was born into a socialist household in a working-class area of Bradford on 10 April 1908: his Christian names were a tribute to two pioneers of parliamentary socialism – Victor Grayson and Keir Hardie. His father was a French polisher, while his mother struggled to bring up a family on his meagre earnings. The young Vic took up the family cause, attending socialist Sunday school, and by the age of 15 was addressing public meetings. His mentor was Frank Betts, whose daughter Barbara would later, as Barbara Castle, encounter Vic many years later in very different circumstances.

On leaving Hanson Secondary School, Vic Feather's family connections helped him obtain work with the local co-op, and it was through a Co-operative Union summer school that he met his wife Alice. They were married on 26 December 1930 and had two children – one daughter, Pat, and a son, Sandy, who followed the family trade as an official with the Iron and Steel Trades Confederation.

Vic Feather soon acquired a reputation as an activist in the shopworkers' union and, following unsuccessful attempts to be selected as a Labour parliamentary candidate, his talents were recognised by the TUC when he applied for a job in the Organisation Department. At the age of 29 he and his young family moved to London. His principal job was to liaise with the local trades union councils – a job which involved frequent conflicts with the communists who were then seeking to increase their influence within the trade unions. His contribution to the TUC's considerable work during the war years included accompanying a delegation to the Soviet Union. After the war he played an important role in helping trade union re-organisation first in Greece and later in Germany. He even played a part in helping resolve a dispute on Japanese railways. He continued his interest in international trade unionism after becoming General Secretary, playing a prominent part in the International Confederation of Free Trade Unions and helping found the European TUC.

In 1946, following the retirement of Walter Citrine, Feather was appointed Assistant Secretary – the number three job at the TUC with responsibility for arranging the annual Congress. Again he devoted much of his time to combating communist influence within the trades councils movement, but did so in a way that avoided both the McCarthy-inspired purges which plagued the United States or the splits between rival unions based on ideological grounds which were common in many other countries. The biggest test for the TUC came with allegations of ballot rigging by communists within the Electricians Union. Here Feather took a risk in going beyond the traditionally neutrality of TUC staff, giving covert assistance to those seeking to expose and publicise wrongdoing within the union.

In 1960, following Vincent Tewson's retirement, Feather became Assistant General Secretary. He and the General Secretary, George Woodcock, were as chalk and cheese. Woodcock was known for his formidable intellect, leading unions in far-reaching reviews of their structures and purpose in a changing world. Feather was left to deal with the difficult but essential business of sorting out inter-union relations and dealing with the nitty-gritty of union mergers. During this period he took on other wide-ranging responsibilities including involvement in Outward Bound and the Civic Trust and the Treasurership of the London Labour Party, which prior to his intervention was in considerable financial difficulties. He first came to the attention of the wider public when Woodcock was taken ill shortly before the 1966 Congress and Feather had to make the keynote speech on incomes policy. Three years later he was thrust into the limelight again, this time permanently, when Woodcock became chairman of the Commission on Industrial Relations on 1 March 1969. During the six months before the annual Congress confirmed his election as General Secretary, Feather was at the centre of the intense negotiations with Employment Secretary Barbara Castle over the government's far-reaching proposals set out in the white paper *In Place of Strife*.

This was the first attempt by a government in modern times to intervene in industrial relations matters which, according to the widely accepted doctrine of the time, were best sorted out by voluntary agreement between employers and unions. *In Place of Strife* could have destroyed the Wilson Government so bitter were the divisions within the Cabinet. It was thanks largely to Feather's negotiating skills that faces were saved all round with the so-called 'solemn and binding' undertaking by the TUC, which led to the withdrawal of the government threat to legislate.

The Conservative victory at the 1970 election came as a surprise to many. Its implications were enormous. Whilst Edward Heath was by no means as antagonistic to trade unions as his successor Margaret Thatcher, his government's proposals, in the shape of the Industrial Relations Bill, provoked enormous hostility from the unions. Whilst Feather, by nature, preferred negotiation to confrontation, this was a period in which the immovable object of trade union principle met the irresistible force of the law. In the end it was the law which gave way, and by the time Feather retired in 1973 the Industrial Relations Act had become more or less inoperative. However its shadow hung over the industrial relations policy of both the succeeding Wilson–Callaghan Government and the Thatcher Government whose 'step by step' approach to industrial relations law was clearly a conscious effort to avoid the set-piece confrontation faced by Heath in the early seventies.

In retirement Feather was made a Labour life peer and undertook a range of other public duties, including Governorship of the BBC. But within three years of leaving Congress House, on 28 July 1976, he died. Remarkably his memorial service, held at St Martin in the Fields, was attended by his three predecessors and former colleagues – Citrine, Woodcock and Tewson, as well as Len Murray, Norman Willis and myself – constituting, with Feather, a continuous line of General Secretaries from 1926 to the present day.

The key biography is *Victor Feather TUC,* a biography by Eric Silver (Gollancz, 1973). There are also extensive references in *The TUC from the General Strike to New Unionism* by Robert Taylor (Palgrave, 2000).

John Monks

Frank Field (1942–)

Frank Field was New Labour before Tony Blair thought of it. Frank Field is a radical reforming thinker, held in the highest esteem on all sides of the House, in tune with Labour voters rather than the party, who, for this reason, had spent most of his political life on the outside of the mainstream of the Labour Party until Tony Blair became leader in 1994. Under Blair the Party moved to Field, not vice versa. His abiding legacy to the Labour movement, undoubtedly, will be to have overturned the post-war consensus on the Left created by Richard Titmuss, the sociologist-social policy academic, that welfare payments do not affect people's behaviour – that is to say, that people do not alter their behaviour to ensure that they get the maximum amount of benefit possible. Field argues that they do.

From years of research, writing and, perhaps most important of all, listening to his Birkenhead constituents, Field developed the view that benefits have a large influence on behaviour and stressed the importance of work in shaping people's character. He concluded that human nature drives people to alter their behaviour to ensure that they receive the maximum amount of money on offer, as this is a rational economic reaction. Field has won the argument. His rallying cry was that the Left must understand this fundamental and clear human characteristic which is driven by the desire for self-improvement. It could only be at this point, that the Left could reform the welfare state, working with the grain of human nature, and thereby make it as popular as the NHS. This would allow the welfare state to become fair and be seen to be fair, as well as stopping the cost of the welfare state spiralling out of control. The post-1997 Labour Government reflects this new consensus, as do policies like the New Deal, where benefits are dependent on working.

As Labour's first and only Minister for Welfare Reform – a kind of super Minister of State responsible for overseeing reform across the whole department – Frank Field was famously brought into government to 'think the unthinkable' by Prime Minister Blair on Saturday 3 May 1997 (the same day that Harriet Harman was announced as Secretary of State for Social Security and before much of the Cabinet had been announced). As Minister for Welfare Reform, Field fundamentally clashed with Gordon Brown on the direction of welfare reform. This was largely because Brown wanted to target help to those most in need through means testing and salami-slice benefit cuts, in order to keep the £100 billion benefit budget from getting out of control and destabilising the rest of government spending.

Field powerfully argued that means tests are the 'cancer within the welfare state', penalising savings, encouraging dishonesty and discouraging work. Field wanted a return to universalism and compulsory savings in private vehicles owned by the individual to prevent the Treasury getting its 'sticky fingers on it'. He called this vision the Stakeholder Pension.

Field's successors in Government have distorted this original vision. Stakeholder pensions have become a non-compulsory second funded pension with a 1% charging structure for those with an income of between £11,000 and £20,000. Field's legacy also includes the concept of 'stakeholders', a phrase he first coined in the late 1980s – although Will Hutton lays a claim to have invented it too.

In the 'dark days' of the Thatcher governments, Field supported Thatcher's policy of allowing council tenants to buy their own council houses. He argued that Labour should support the aspirations of its core supporters to own their homes, and such policies should be Labour ones and not the reserve of the Tories. Thus he was arguing for New Labour aspirationalism, fighting the Tories in the centre ground, long before Blair.

Throughout his time in Parliament Field has been one of those rare MPs who is respected on all sides of the House. He is one of the few MPs whose Commons speeches are often listened to in silence – largely because he always has something interesting to say (he has been called a 'one man think-tank'), and because his views are always independently arrived at, free from the constraints of tribal loyalties, thought through with the utmost care and backed up with careful, original research. Indeed, his popularity with all sides of the House has, in some ways, served to increase the suspicion in which the left hold him and to increase the sense of him being an outsider. He is, as Matthew Parris described him in his BBC Radio 4 series, one of 'the awkward squad', that is someone who does not fit into one of the cosy tribes at Westminster and speaks his mind.

Frank Field was born in Enfield in North London on 16 July 1942. His mother, Annie Lague, had been moved to Enfield, away from the family's home in Chiswick, West London, as it was further way from the areas of London targeted by the Luftwaffe. Field was educated at Hogarth Junior School, St Clement Danes Grammar School and Hull University (BSc Economics). He also holds honorary degrees in social policy from Warwick University and Southampton University.

Field held a seat as a Labour councillor on Hounslow Borough Council in May 1964. He was Parliamentary candidate for Buckinghamshire South in 1966. He has represented the Merseyside constituency of Birkenhead since 1979. This should by rights be a safe Labour seat in that it is industrial in nature with poor housing and high unemployment. However it was heavily infiltrated by the Militant Tendency in the late 1980s, culminating in the Birkenhead Labour Party deselecting Field in favour of TGWU activist and Trotskyist Paul Davies in December 1989. Field immediately submitted a 150–page dossier detailing Militant infiltration in the local party to Labour Leader Neil Kinnock. He threatened to resign and cause a by-election, in which he would stand as an independent candidate, if the deselection stood. In January 1991 the NEC ruled that his reselection must be rerun. Field went onto win the rerun reselection vote with 53 per cent of the vote in June 1991.

Birkenhead is closely linked to Liverpool across the Mersey river, and is home to the Cammell Laird shipyard, an important shipbuilding and ship repair yard in the heyday of British ship building from the early part of the century until the 1980s. It built the famous *Ark Royal* aircraft carrier in the 1950s. Since the 1980s it has switched to ship repair work only but is now attempting to re-enter the new-build market.

Frank Field chaired the Social Security Select Committee from 1991 to 1997. He was also Shadow Church of England Commissioner from 1983 to 1997. He served on the Liaison Select Committee from 1983 to 1997 and the Parliamentary Ecclesiastical Committee from 1983 to 1997. He was a Shadow Health and Social Security Minister from 1983 to 1984, in Neil Kinnock's first year as Labour leader. Prior to that he was a Shadow Education and Science Minister from 1980 to 1981 under Michael Foot.

Field also took part in the Labour-instigated Borrie Commission on social security reform in 1993 and the Liberal Democrat-instigated Dahrendorf Commission on social security reform in 1994–95. His chairmanship of the Social Security Select Committee was regarded as a model for all other Select Committee chairs by the Whips of all parties in the House. Arguably a further legacy of Field's is to have provided the blueprint to enable select committees to be more powerful tools to hold the executive to account.

Certainly Field greatly impressed the Labour leadership with his handling of the committee, particularly in its grilling of the Maxwell brothers in the wake of the Maxwell pensions scandal, and he was duly promoted after the 1997 general election. He is rightly regarded as an expert in the field of welfare reform and has written on the subject since 1971.

As Minister for Welfare Reform, press reports soon revealed rifts between Field and Harman, the two apparently advocating fundamentally different approaches to welfare. Harman was backed by Brown, and Field sought to use Blair to give him the leverage he needed over Harman to drive his ideas through. In the end Field came to the conclusion that the only way he had a chance of driving his ideas through against the opposition of Brown and

Harman was to be the Secretary of State for Social Security – the position he had argued he needed when No 10 telephoned him on Saturday 3 May 1997.

In 1998 Harriet Harman was dismissed from the Cabinet and Field was not offered her position, although he was offered the role of Fraud Tsar – a Minister to drive out fraud across all Government departments. He made it clear to Blair that he only wanted to be Secretary of State for Social Security to drive through his vision and, when still not offered the post, resigned. Since returning to the back benches, he has remained loyal to the Labour leadership, although in the summer of 2000 he did criticise the government for being more 'spin than substance'. The media interest generated by his comments illustrates his ongoing influence in politics.

Before entering Parliament Frank Field was a lecturer at Southwark College for Further Education (1964–68) and at the Hammersmith College for Further Education (1968–69). Director of the Child Poverty Action Group (1969–79), he was the founding Director of the Low Pay Unit from 1974 to 1979.

In Parliament he was an unpaid consultant to the Civil and Public Services Association from 1982 to 1997. He also wrote regular or occasional columns for several national publications including *The Guardian, The Independent, The Times, The Daily Telegraph, The Sunday People* and *The Catholic Herald*. Frank Field is unmarried and has a flat in London and Birkenhead. He has two brothers.

Field is the author of the following publications: (ed jntly) *Twentieth-Century State Education*, 1971; (ed jntly) *Black Britons*, 1971; (ed) *Low Pay*, 1973; *Unequal Britain*, 1974; (ed) *Are Low Wages Inevitable?* 1976; (ed) *Education and the Urban Crisis*, 1976; (ed) *The Conscript Army: A Study of Britain's Unemployed*, 1976; (jntly) *To Him Who Hath: A Study of Poverty and Taxation*, 1976; (with Ruth Lister) *Wasted Labour*, 1978 (Social Concern Book Award); (ed) *The Wealth Report*, 1979; *Inequality in Britain: Freedom, Welfare and the State*, 1981; *Poverty and Politics*, 1982; *The Wealth Report II*, 1983; *Policies Against Low Pay*, 1984; *The Minimum Wage: Its Potential and Dangers*, 1984; *What Price A Child?* 1985; *Freedom and Wealth in a Socialist Future*, 1987; *The Politics of Paradise*, 1987; *Losing Out: The Emergence of Britain's Underclass*, 1989; (jntly with Matthew Owen) *Private Pensions For All*, 1993; *An Agenda for Britain*, 1993; (jntly with Matthew Owen) *National Pensions Savings Plan*, 1994; (jntly with Matthew Owen and Liam Halligan) *Europe Isn't Working*, 1994; (jntly with Paul Gregg) *Who Gets What, How and For How Long?* 1994; (jntly with Matthew Owen) *Beyond Punishment: Hard Choices on the Road to Full Employability*, 1994; *Making Welfare Work*, 1995; *How To Pay For The Future: Building A Stakeholder's Welfare*, 1996; *Stakeholder Welfare*, 1997; *Reforming Welfare*, 1997; *Reflections on Welfare Reform*, 1998; and numerous important newspaper articles and essays in other collections of essays including: 'Moore gives the Trade Unions the chance to steal the ball', *The Sunday Times* 16 October 1988; *Employment Audits in the Full Employment Seminar*, 1995, and *The State of Dependency*, 2000.

Christopher Kelsey

Barbara Follett (1942–)

Barbara Follett is Labour MP for Stevenage. Like many of her parliamentary colleagues, she has overcome difficulties in life to become a Labour MP. But she is unusual in the way she has drawn on her misfortune and experience to strengthen the Labour Party. She is also one of the few MPs who have played a major part in transforming the image of Labour, primarily through practical steps to increase the number of women MPs in the Parliamentary Labour Party.

Barbara Follett was born in Kingston, Jamaica, on Christmas Day 1942. Her father, Vernon Hubbard, was from Manchester and went to the Caribbean to set up the local branches of a British insurance company. In 1946 he returned to Britain with Barbara, her mother and her sister. After a year in Jersey, where Barbara's brother was born, they settled in Billericay, Essex. In 1952 the family moved again, to Ethiopia, where Vernon Hubbard set up the country's first insurance company in partnership with Emperor Haile Selassie.

Travel and the Ethiopian setting made Barbara an unconventional teenager. But travel and the Ethiopian setting also, in part, led to her father's alcoholism. In 1957, at a banquet given by the Emperor for Yugoslavia's President Tito, Mr Hubbard fell into a drinks trolley during the loyal toast. This was deemed an insult to the emperor and Hubbard was asked to leave the country. The family went to Cape Town, where Barbara finished her schooling and began a university degree in art. But by 1962 drinking cost her father his job, so Barbara went to work for Barclays Bank to supplement the money her mother earned as a shop assistant. The degree had to be put off for 30 years.

In 1963 Barbara married Richard Turner. They went to Paris where he did a doctorate, she taught at the Berlitz School of Languages (1963–64) and their daughter Jann was born (1964). They returned to South Africa in 1966 to run his mother's fruit farm in Stellenbosch. A second daughter, Kim, was born in 1968. The same year Barbara's broken father died at the age of 56.

The unconventional teenager had become a conventional white South African farmer's wife, but there was an unconventional young woman inside her, plotting escape. Barbara was about to meet a turning point in her life. In those days South African farm workers were paid little and partly in wine. Alcoholism, a scourge Barbara knew only too well, and malnutrition, were rife among farm hands and their families. One day in 1969 a young farm worker's wife came to Barbara with her baby son suffering from bronchial pneumonia. The baby died in Barbara's arms. Barbara went to work for *Kupugani* (Zulu for 'Uplift yourself') a scheme which bought up and processed some of South Africa's huge agricultural surplus and then sold it very cheaply to poor families. It also provided basic health education.

In 1970 the marriage to Turner broke down. He went to teach in Durban. She took their girls to Cape Town and became acting Regional Secretary at the Institute of Race Relations, then worked for *Kupugani* again, first as Regional Manager – Cape and Namibia (1971–74), then National Health Education Director (1975–78). On the rebound Barbara was briefly married to psychologist Gerald Stonestreet. In 1974 she married architect Les Broer and they had a son, Adam (1975). Barbara's ex-husband Richard, a critic of the apartheid regime, was 'banned' in 1973 and forbidden to travel. On 8 January (ANC Day) 1978 Jann and Kim, then 13 and 9, were staying with their father when he was assassinated in the early hours of the morning in their bedroom.

Three months later, Barbara, who was now running the Women's Movement for Peace was told that she too was about to be 'banned'. Barbara and family fled to England and lived in Farnham, Surrey. Barbara found work as Assistant Course Organiser and a lecturer on Africa for the Farnham-based Centre for International Briefing (1980–84) and joined the local Labour Party.

In 1983 Barbara was Labour's unsuccessful general election candidate in Woking. The difficulties she experienced then as a woman candidate convinced her that women should get additional help to fight elections. She also got to know local novelist Ken Follett. She married Ken in 1985 (and gained 2 stepchildren).

From 1984 to 1992 Barbara Follett was a freelance lecturer and consultant on cross-cultural management. She contested Epsom & Ewell for Labour in 1987. Again unsuccessful, and still unhappy with inequality in the system, she turned her mind to the problems of women candidates. She joined the Fawcett Society and the National Alliance of Women's Organisations. With three other women she founded the Labour Women's Network in 1987 and has served on its Steering Committee ever since. Later, she was inspired by women in the USA who, in 1985, founded EMILY's List, which raised funds for women Democrat candidates and was so-called because Early Money Is Like Yeast (it makes the dough rise!). Barbara imported the idea into Britain for the Labour Party. She became the Director of EMILY's List UK in 1993 and since then it has backed 52 women seeking selection.

During this period Barbara obtained a BSc(Econ) in Economic History at the LSE. She was selected as the candidate in Stevenage (1995) before her postgraduate course could get under way. She concentrated instead on work as Visiting Fellow at the Institute of Public Policy Research (1993–97).

Barbara's younger daughter, Kim, herself had a daughter, Alexandra, in 1993. It was then Barbara discovered that pre-eclampsia was a hereditary family condition which had killed a sibling Barbara never knew, nearly killed the young Barbara, and, later, Kim and Alexandra. It can be detected and managed with regular tests in pregnancy. It is typical of Barbara that, after Kim's scare, she became a patron of Action on Pre-Eclampsia (APEC), an organisation for raising awareness of the condition and the need for testing.

In Parliament, as ever deploying her interests and the trials of her life to best effect for the Party, Barbara went on the Select Committee on International Development (July 1997), as well as becoming Chair of the All Party Retail Industry Group; Chair of the Eastern group of Labour MPs; Vice-Chair of the Parliamentary Film Industries Group; a member of Labour's backbench Treasury Committee; Joint Secretary of the Population, Development and Reproductive Health Group; and Treasurer of the Sex Equality Group.

In May 1999 Barbara became a member of the Britain in Europe Council. She is also a member of the Fabian Society Research Committee, of the Socialist Environmental Research Association, Liberty and Charter 88. While many of her areas of concern have led to numerous official positions, Barbara has other interests, including Scrabble, photography and Star Trek. As a former art student, Barbara is fascinated by the work of Johannes Itten, the colour theorist who taught at the Bauhaus in Weimar Germany, from 1919 to 1923. Harnessing this interest to assist Labour, Barbara Follett pioneered presentation training in the Labour Party, teaching senior Labour figures the science of colour and some of the requirements of a TV- and fashion-conscious age. So closely associated was she with this smartening-up of Labour that it has been called 'Folletting'. With husband Ken, Barbara has helped raise substantial funds for the Labour Party. If somebody ever devises a way to make Scrabble or Star Trek work for the Labour Party, we can be sure Barbara Follett will be guiding the operation, while still finding as much time as possible for her and Ken to spend with their five children and two grandchildren.

Rex Osborn

Michael Foot   (1913–)

In his essay 'Mind and Motive', William Hazlitt wrote: 'Happy are they who live in the dream of their own existence, and see all things in the light of their own minds; who walk by faith and hope; to whom the guiding star of their youth still shines from afar; and into whom the spirit of the world has not entered! They have not been "hurt by the archers", nor has the iron entered their souls. The world has no hand on them.' There is surely no better description of the virtues of Michael Foot, Hazlitt's most famous modern disciple. To stand by the guiding star of your youth in an age of political opportunism and cynicism is not an easy task, yet Foot continues to do so with style, intelligence and wit. How many other 85-year-olds would produce a book as timely as *Dr Strangelove, I Presume*, his critique of nuclear proliferation in South East Asia. But then Michael Foot is no ordinary politician. Since his political debut as Labour candidate for Monmouth in the 1935 election he has dazzled us with the greatest range of skills and talents of any twentieth century politician. No one can match his brilliance as an essayist, political journalist, biographer, orator and parliamentarian. Although genius is a word whose value has cheapened in modern times, due to the cult of media personality, it can most definitely be applied to Michael Foot.

Michael Foot's significance to the history of the Labour Party is threefold: firstly he played a leading part in the battle for the soul of the party that was fought between the supporters of Aneurin Bevan and Hugh Gaitskell during the 1950s; secondly he acted as the left's conscience inside and outside parliament under the 1964–1970 Labour Government; and finally he led the party during a period when it was utterly unleadable. Throughout his leadership he was vilified in the most grotesque manner by the media and the Conservative Party, yet he still managed to maintain his decency, integrity and optimism. To its shame the Labour Party has never properly acknowledged the sacrifice that Michael Foot made between 1980 and 1983; there is no doubt that history will treat him more kindly.

Michael Foot was born on 23 July 1913 at 1 Lipson Terrace in Plymouth. His parents were both liberal dissenters, and from a young age he was encouraged to take an interest in political matters. Although afflicted with eczema and asthma, he excelled in History and English Literature at Leighton Park School, Reading. He also succeeded at sports, showing promise in rugby, cricket and soccer. In the summer of 1931 he successfully sat for a History exhibition to Oxford University and that autumn he took up his place at Wadham College where he studied Philosophy, Politics and Economics. During his time at Oxford he remained a Liberal and was President of the Liberal Club – but he was showing signs that he was ready to switch allegiance to the Labour Party.

After university Foot took a job in Liverpool working for Blue Funnel Line, a shipping company. He stayed in Liverpool for nine months but spent more time at work trying to write a biography of Charles James Fox than advancing his career. His spell in Liverpool was more significant for the fact that it was there that he switched from the Liberal Party to the Labour Party – pinpointing his conversion to reading the work of Hazlitt.

When Stanley Baldwin decided to call a general election in November 1935, Foot stood as candidate for Monmouth at the tender age of 22 in the full knowledge that he had no hope of winning the seat. His election speeches, however, had a rhetorical flourish which essayed the language of New Labour by fifty years: 'I want to see a government in this country which will serve the interests of the deserving many, and not those of the wealthy few.'

Following the election he embarked on his career as a journalist. A brief spell under Kingsley Martin at the *New Statesman* paved the way for a staff job on *Tribune* (then called *The Tribune*) when it was launched in January 1937. A year later he resigned in protest at the sacking of the magazine's editor, William Mellor. But it was in his next job that he made his journalistic reputation. On Aneurin Bevan's recommendation Lord Beaverbrook took Foot on as an *Evening Standard* feature writer. Though Beaverbrook was seen as a dangerous and reactionary figure by the left, Foot warmed to his personality and came to regard him as a second father. From writing features Foot moved on to leader writer and eventually became editor in 1942. It was during his five years at the *Standard* that he wrote (and co-wrote) four highly popular polemics: *Armistice 1918–1939, Guilty Men, The Trial of Mussolini* and *Brendan and Beverley*. All four contained hallmarks of Foot's later speaking and writing style: deadly invective, satirical wit and a wide reading of English literature.

In the 1945 general election Foot was elected member for Devonport. Whilst his great friend Aneurin Bevan began to build the National Health Service, Foot played a leading part in the Keep Left Group of Labour MPs and continued his journalistic career – mainly in the pages of *Tribune*. Bevan's resignation (with John Freeman and Harold Wilson) over charges for dental treatment and spectacles in the April 1951 Budget triggered the next most significant phase in Foot's Labour Party career. In *Tribune*, Foot denounced the measures in forthright terms: 'There is no case whatever for this proposal on the grounds of merit … a fundamental blow at the essential principle of the Health Service … Mr Gaitskell has delivered a frontal attack on the Health Service.' This style of attack continued throughout the 1950s as the Bevanites and Gaitskellites fought over the direction of the Labour Party. It was fundamentally a clash of political styles rather than policy programmes: in one corner the emotional intensity and verbal imagination of Bevan and in the other corner the empiricism and cool rationality of Gaitskell.

Foot lost his seat in the general election of May 1955 and turned to writing, producing his most significant work to date, *The Pen and the Sword*, an account of Jonathan Swift's battle against the Duke of Marlborough during 1710 and 1711. At the same time he was caught up in a battle of his own: the battle against the British H-bomb, which was first tested on Christmas Island during the summer of 1957. That autumn the Labour Party gathered for its annual conference in Brighton deeply divided over the bomb issue. Despite their closeness, Foot was in no way prepared for Bevan's devastating denunciation of the left's unilateralist stance. The 'naked into the conference chamber' speech caused a deep rupture between the two men that was only partially healed in the months before Bevan's death.

At the 1959 general election Foot was again defeated at Devonport and considered retiring from frontline politics to concentrate on journalism and writing. However, Aneurin Bevan's death in July 1960 gave him the opportunity to return to the Commons and he duly did so as member for Bevan's constituency, EbbwVale, which he would represent for the remainder of his parliamentary career.

During the 1960s Foot emerged from Bevan's shadow to become leader of the left, fighting a number of issues that made him unpopular with the Labour leadership and precluded his participation in HaroldWilson's 1964–1970 government. He was the left's most effective critic on nuclear disarmament, prices and incomes policy, theVietnam War, immigration policy and the trade union reforms contained in the 1969 white paper *In Place of Strife*. He found time too for the first volume of his biography of Aneurin Bevan, published in 1962 (the second volume being published in 1973).William Rees-Mogg described the first volume as 'One of the great political biographies of this century.'

In 1968 he formed an unlikely alliance with Enoch Powell to scupper Richard Crossman's bill to reform the House of Lords. Foot wanted outright abolition of the Lords, whilst Powell wanted to preserve the status quo, and together they used their considerable parliamentary wiles to block the legislation. Many parliamentary observers believe that Foot was at the peak of his oratorical powers during the debates on the Bill. He was certainly at his most scathing of the Conservatives:'Look at them, these unlikely novices for a new Trappist Order, these bashful tiptoeing ghosts, these pale effigies of what were once sentient palpable human specimens, these unlarynxed wraiths, these ectoplasmic apparitions, these sphinx-like sentinels at our debates – why are they here?'

It was to everyone's great surprise when Foot, having turned down the offer of office between 1964 and 1970, secured election to the shadow cabinet in July 1970, accepting a position on Labour's front bench as spokesman on Fuel and Power. Surely Foot could not control his radical instincts within the confines of collective shadow cabinet responsibility?Yet he did, becoming Shadow Leader of the House of Commons in January 1972 and securing re-election to the shadow cabinet every year until Labour's return to government in 1974 when, like Aneurin Bevan, he proved to be an excellent administrator as Employment Secretary. At the Department of Employment he successfully framed the legislation that established ACAS (the Advisory, Conciliation and Arbitration Service) and produced the Social Contract which played a major part in helping to control inflation until the breakdown of the Government's relationship with the unions in the autumn of 1978. He played a leading role in the 'Vote No' campaign during the 1975 EEC Referendum, again in partnership with Enoch Powell, and Labour ministers including Peter Shore, Barbara Castle andTony Benn.

Following Wilson's resignation in March 1976, Foot stood against Benn,Tony Crosland, Denis Healey, Roy Jenkins and Jim Callaghan for the Labour leadership. He lost in the third round to Callaghan by 39 votes, and in April 1976 became Lord President of the Council and Leader of the House of Commons. In October 1976, he defeated ShirleyWilliams in straight fight by 166 votes to 128 to become Labour's Deputy Leader, a post that had eluded him on three previous occasions. In July 1970 and November 1971 he had been beaten by Roy Jenkins, first by 133 votes to 67 (with Fred Peart limping in third with 48) and second by 140 to 126, afterTony Benn's 46 votes had transferred to Foot on the second ballot. In April 1972 he had been beaten by Ted Short, by 145 votes to 116,Tony Crosland's 61 votes splitting fairly evenly on second ballot. With Labour having lost its parliamentary majority by the spring of 1977, Foot had to use his full array of parliamentary skills to prevent government defeats whilst attempting to push through major bills such as the ones to establish devolution in Scotland and Wales. Eventually a pact was formed with the Liberals which kept Labour in power until the spring of 1979, when it faced a vote of no confidence in the aftermath of the unsuccessful Scottish and Welsh devolution referendums. During that debate Foot produced one of his most memorable turns and was at his most mocking for both Margaret Thatcher and David Steel whose Liberal Party was voting with the Conservatives against the government. Of Steel he famously said 'He has passed from rising hope to elder statesman without any intervening period whatsoever!'

Foot persuaded Jim Callaghan to remain leader of the Labour Party after the general election defeat of May 1979. But Callaghan was tired of the faction fighting which by then had gripped the party and resigned as leader shortly after the 1980 Blackpool conference. Initially Foot was reluctant to stand for the leadership and was intending to support Peter Shore. However, a number of Labour MPs and trade unionists (led by Clive Jenkins, the ASTMS leader) persuaded Foot to change his mind on the basis that only he could unite the party. He eventually defeated Denis Healey – in the last Labour leadership contest to be decided solely by the parliamentary party – by 139 votes to 129 in the second round of the ballot.

The period of his Labour leadership was not the happiest time for Foot. He had to contend with a sizable chunk of his party splitting off to form the Social Democratic Party in 1981; Tony Benn's challenge to Denis Healey for the Deputy Leadership of the party; the infiltration of the party's grassroots by the Trotskyist Militant Tendency; and constant attacks in the media on his age, appearance and speaking style.

Britain's victory in the Falklands War entrenched Margaret Thatcher as Prime Minister and the 1983 general election was always going to be a difficult one for Labour to win, irrespective of the policies on which the party would be fighting. The strength of the SDP-Liberal Alliance and the tabloid media's vitriol against the Labour Party were also decisive factors in the 1983 election. That the party collapsed to its worst performance since 1935 shocked everyone and Foot took full responsibility for the defeat with customary honesty and grace: 'I understand the scale of the defeat which we suffered at the general election ... I am deeply ashamed that we should have allowed the fortunes of our country and the fortunes of the people who look to us for protection most ... to sink to such a low ebb.'

Following his resignation as party leader Foot continued as member for Ebbw Vale (later renamed Blaenau Gwent) until the 1992 general election. In retirement he has concentrated on writing and, astonishingly for a man in his eighties, he has written major biographies of Byron and H.G. Wells. Michael Foot continues to live happily in the dream of his own existence. He married the filmmaker Jill Craigie in 1949; she died in 1999.

His publications include: *Armistice 1918–1939* (1940); *Guilty Men* (1940); *The Trial of Mussolini* (1943); *Brendan and Beverley* (1944); *The Pen and the Sword* (1957); *Guilty Men 1957* (1957); *Aneurin Bevan* (Volume One: 1962, Volume Two: 1973); *Harold Wilson* (1964); *Debts of Honour* (1980); *Another Heart and Other Pulses* (1984); *Loyalists and Loners* (1986); *The Politics of Paradise* (1988); *HG: The History of Mr Wells* (1995); and *Dr Strangelove I Presume* (1999). A biography, *Michael Foot*, by Mervyn Jones was published in 1994.

Jayant Chavda

Tom Fraser (1911–88)

Tom Fraser was the Transport Minister who introduced the 70 mph speed limit and the breathalyser to cut drink-driving, two of the most lasting achievements of the first Wilson government. His departure from office in December 1965, after little more than a year, meant however that it was his successor, Barbara Castle, who made his experimental 70 mph speed-limit permanent and made his bill introducing the breathalyser become law, albeit after she had removed Fraser's proposals for random breath tests.

As Transport Minister, his main task was to make a reality of Labour's commitment to an integrated transport policy. Appointed in the wake of the Beeching report to a department dominated by a road-building ethos, he had a fight on his hands to reverse, as there was substantial pressure from within the Labour Party to do, the programme of planned rail-closures. Fraser and Wilson initially sought to appoint Beeching to undertake the report on the co-ordination of all transport but leaking of the Cabinet revolt that ensued dissuaded Beeching from accepting the post.

The son of Tom and Mary Fraser of Blackwood, Lanarkshire, he was born on 18 February 1911 and attended Blackwood School and Lesmahagow Higher Grade School before going into the Lanarkshire coalmines at the age of 14. He worked underground until he was elected as MP for Hamilton in 1943 at the age of 32. From 1939 until 1943 he served as President of the Coalburn Miners Lodge and and as secretary of the Lanark CLP. Tom was an unassuming, modest, warm-hearted man. Popular amongst his Parliamentary colleagues he was close to Hector McNeil who became his senior on joining the Scottish Office as Secretary of State in 1950. By then, after some six months as PPS to the President of the Board of Trade in the wartime Coalition, Hugh Dalton, Tom had served five years as the Joint Parliamentary Under-Secretary of State for Scotland, but there was little or no animus between him and McNeil. Both were out of office after Labour's defeat in 1951 and went their different ways. Fraser became an opposition front-bench spokesman on Scotland, joining the shadow cabinet in February 1956. From November 1961 until 1964 he was principal Opposition Spokesman on Power but as the only Scottish MP in the shadow cabinet, he continued to spend much of his time on Scottish Office affairs.

Thirteen long years passed before he was plucked by Harold Wilson to be, not the Scottish Secretary as everyone, including Fraser himself, expected, but Minister of Transport. Thus Fraser joined the cabinet, as did his rival William Ross, who became Scottish Secretary to widespread surprise. These two were very different men, although both had supported Gaitskell over Wilson as Labour leader. Fraser was a particularly vocal opponent of unilateralism and the Bevanite rebellions of the 1950s. Gaitskell had died of a very painful illness called lupus erythematosis the year before, and Ross quickly became a Wilson ally. Fraser, on the other hand, had not a sycophantic bone in his body and, though not anti-Wilson, was more independent-minded. Within a year Fraser was sacked by Wilson. Wilson had decided he wanted to give Transport to his close ally Barbara Castle, and Fraser declined the Ministry of Aviation outside Cabinet. He never recovered from this setback.

In 1967 he was appointed (by Ross) as Chairman of the North of Scotland Hydro Electric Board, serving until 1973, and left Parliament. The consequent by-election produced the famous victory for Winnie Ewing of the SNP. He participated on various important committees, mainly about local government, but retired from public life in 1977. He died in 1988.

Rt. Hon. Dr. Dickson Mabon

John Freeman (1915–)

John Freeman spent only ten years as a Labour MP but during that time he made a sizeable impression on the Attlee Government as well as the Parliamentary Labour Party. Yet his subsequent media career considerably eclipsed the period spent as a politician.

Born on 19 February 1915, the son of Horace Freeman a Barrister-at-Law, Freeman was educated at Westminster School and Brasenose College, Oxford (where he was made an Honorary Fellow in 1968). He joined the Labour Party in 1933. He made his career in the immediate pre-war era as an advertising consultant (1937–40) and his political path followed one similar to that of his contemporaries. From 1940 to 1945, he saw active service in the Middle East, North Africa, Italy and North-West Europe and was commissioned in the Rifle Brigade in 1940. He was awarded the MBE in 1943. Rising to the rank of Major, he became Labour MP for Watford in 1945. He seconded the King's Speech following the war in his major's uniform. Roy Jenkins described Freeman as 'the very model of a modern Labour major'.

Freeman was a protégé of Hugh Dalton, who was one of the most respected members of the Labour Party leadership and Chancellor of the Exchequer under Attlee. Dalton's patronage of Freeman ensured that he was put on the fast track to a Cabinet position and much was expected of him. Appointed PPS to Secretary of State for War Jack Lawson in 1945, he became Financial Secretary (and Under-Secretary) at the War Office in October 1946. Yet it was as Parliamentary Secretary to the Ministry of Supply from October 1947 that Freeman had most impact – not for his work in the Ministry but for his resignation from the post on 22 April 1951.

When Bevan threatened to resign from his position as Minister of Labour over the plans of Hugh Gaitskell (then Chancellor of the Exchequer) to impose charges in the health system for dentures and spectacles, he was supported by Harold Wilson and John Freeman. Although both tried to dissuade Bevan from resignation, they failed and also felt obliged to resign. Freeman was more concerned with the issue of rearmament, which the charges were imposed to pay for, rather than the charges themselves. He was even offered promotion if he did not resign. The resignations rocked the Labour Government and it lost the election later that year. As far as the left was concerned, Freeman was a more important figure than Wilson, who was regarded with some suspicion. By the time that he decided to stand down from Parliament in 1955, he had distanced himself from Bevan by failing to support moves against an official Labour Party amendment to a Defence White Paper.

Freeman's decision to stand down disappointed his left-wing 'Bevanite' colleagues. Yet he had already begun to position himself as a serious political journalist, having contributed articles to *Tribune* and written pamphlets for the Fabian Society, and in June 1951 he became the assistant editor of the *New Statesman*. He had outmanoeuvred Richard Crossman, then an influential Bevanite MP, to gain the position. Freeman remained assistant editor until

1958 when he became deputy editor, and then, eventually, editor from 1961 to 1965. He had always lusted after the post, but the period of his editorship is not recalled as one of the greatest periods in the history of the *New Statesman*. Freeman failed to stamp his personality on the publication and, as under several of his successors (Paul Johnson and Crossman), the *New Statesman* became more conservative and closer to the opinions of the Labour Party leadership. He appeared happier adopting a backseat role than confronting the constant exposure of a frontline position in politics.

During the 1950s and '60s he also presented the television programme *Face to Face* – a hard-hitting, innovative and ground-breaking interview programme, which he chaired for ten years. The programme went on to become the standard by which all others were judged. During his time on the programme, Freeman undertook a series of classic interviews with the likes of Herbert Morrison and Adam Faith (a popular singer of the time), and even made the late Gilbert Harding (a combative media personality) cry openly. Freeman was often criticised for his 'aggressive' interviewing technique, also employed by him on other television programmes such as *Panorama,* but it came to be accepted practice.

Freeman had continued to enjoy a good relationship with Harold Wilson since their joint resignations in 1951, with Wilson having gone on to become Prime Minister in 1964. This association led Wilson to appoint Freeman to two diplomatic posts – British High Commissioner in India (1965–68) and British Ambassador in Washington (1969–71). His appointment to India appeared to be an indication of Wilson's desire to have a more active role in India and Pakistan, as well as a level of trust in Freeman which he did not have in the Commonwealth Office. The appointment to America took place in the expectation that Hubert Humphrey, a Democrat, would win the Presidential election. However, the election of Richard Nixon created some consternation as Freeman had openly criticised him as being 'a man of no principle' during his time at the *New Statesman*. Freeman initially offered to resign, but at the first dinner attended by Wilson, Freeman and Nixon, the newly-elected President used humour to 'clear the air'. Nixon claimed he understood that Freeman had criticised him in the past but now the tables had been turned and 'He has become the new diplomat while I have become the new statesman'!

Freeman continued his impressive career in the media when he was appointed Chairman of London Weekend Television in 1971. He saw the company through some challenging times until his retirement in 1984. He recognised the need to win peak-time audiences at the expense of local and minority coverage with the advent of cable and satellite television. Channel Four also started broadcasting and became a competing station (which initially led LWT to lose revenue, especially from advertising). He had originally planned to retire some three years earlier but the LWT board wished for rather more time to consider the future of the group and he agreed to stay on. He also held a number of posts which increased his overall contribution to the media, such as his presidency of ITN (1976–81), governorship of the British Film Institute (1976–82) and vice-presidency of the Royal Television Society (1975–85). He was even considered to be a candidate for the position of Secretary of the British Board of Film Censors when the position became available in 1985.

Following his retirement he commentated on bowls for Granada TV. A fan of the sport, he considered himself to be only 'a very ordinary bowler'. Despite protestations that he wished to 'drop out and do nothing on retirement', his final role was as Visiting Professor of International Relations at the University of California, Davies (1985–90). Freeman has had four marriages – to Elizabeth Allen Johnston (1938, dissolved 1948), Margaret Ista Mabel Kerr (1948, died 1957); Catherine Dove (1962, dissolved 1976) and Judith Mitchell (1976–).

Dr. Stuart Thomson

Hugh Gaitskell   (1906–63)

Hugh Todd Naylor Gaitskell was a middle-class, public-school-educated economist who came from a family steeped in the traditions of Empire and public service. His father Arthur was an official in the Indian Civil Service. He became the leading social democratic politician of his generation. He adopted socialism; it did not choose him. Born on 9 April 1906 in Kensington, he was known as a child as 'Sam' – a name which stuck with some people at least until the 1930s. He had a strong relationship with his mother and retained until the 1920s the probably rather endearing habit of blushing frequently while talking. He initially attended the Dragon School, Oxford before moving to Winchester. By the time he left Winchester – a school he had little affection for – he had learned to be self-reliant, to decide for himself on such things as friends, reading and holidays. Some writers have played down the impact of childhood and early life on Gaitskell, Roy Jenkins concluding in a 1973 portrait that Gaitskell's father had no impact and that this was 'to some extent true of all his family'. However he would have been a remarkable man indeed if the early death of his father, the frequent absences and then remarriage of his mother and the English public school system had had no effect on his personality.

There were two distinct sides to Gaitskell's personality: a warm, pleasant, emotional and giving side that was expressed in private and intimate relationships, and a cool, detached, pedantic and defensive side that came through in public and political situations. The public and private were kept separate, the emotional and the analytical divided. Gaitskell's growth as a politician, as a communicator and, perhaps, as a person, was about the way in which the cool, detached, pedantic man increasingly let, or could not prevent, the warm, passionate, emotional, intimate man into the public persona.

While it is straightforward to identify these sides to his character and the evidence for them is plentiful, connecting them to particular elements in his childhood and upbringing is perhaps more difficult. He had to develop at an early age considerable self-reliance; this was in turn enhanced by his experience at a public school he did not like and through the early death of his father. He idealised his brother Arthur, following him to school and college, competing with him and emulating him until developing his own personality and style. This world taught certain ways of behaviour and relating that, despite many later attempts to abandon, he never completely rid himself of. But most of all it reinforced an already highly developed work and public service ethic.

He was also Sam, the youngest son, with a deeply emotional mother who smothered him in love on her visits to England and indulged him as the youngest child. This was the side of his character that was to discover dancing and seek out fun with the same energy with which he could redraft a brief or a speech. That the two sides remained separate and that he kept, in the main, the people and the relationships that appealed to the two sides separate for much of his life, is not an accident; it is a consequence of his childhood.

From school he followed Arthur to New College and continued the dual aspects of his personality by living with the hard-working and serious Evan Durbin, while socialising with the utterly frivolous Maurice Bowra. He joined the Labour Party in 1926. After Oxford and a first in PPE, radicalised by the General Strike, he spent a year in the Nottinghamshire coal field lecturing for the WEA before moving to Bloomsbury. In April 1937 he married Dora Frost, née Creditor, with whom he had two daughters. He taught Economics at UCL until the outbreak of World War Two.

In the interwar period Gaitskell was one of a small group of economists who introduced the ideas of J M Keynes to Labour politicians like Hugh Dalton. He was Labour's unsuccessful Parliamentary candidate at Chatham in 1935. After wartime service on the home front, working closely with Dalton at the Ministry of Economic Warfare and the Board of Trade, he was awarded a CBE in 1945. He was elected MP for South Leeds in 1945 and served as Minister for Fuel and Power from October 1947 until May 1950, having been the Parliamentary Secretary at the department from May 1946. From February until October 1950 he was Minister for Economic Affairs before becoming the last Chancellor of the Attlee governments in October 1950. He delivered only one budget, which was dominated by the need for rearmament and which split the cabinet and contributed to the defeat of the government in 1951.

Power was the defining political experience of his life, more important than even the General Strike, because it determined him on the single unshakeable conviction which underpinned much of what was to come later: power was critical, power to put principles into practice. He learnt his politics in the age of power; he practised power in the most successful administration of the century. For the rest of his life he wanted it back; sometimes it prevented him from playing the political game as well as he might.

In opposition he was Shadow Chancellor, also serving as Party Treasurer 1954–56, and campaigned effectively for the leadership, which he won in December 1955 with 157 votes, defeating Bevan on 70 votes and the ageing Morrison on 40. He led the party with a zealous belief in the need for it to modernise. His leadership was characterised by a series of bruising internal conflicts. He initially went some way to reconciling the left and worked closely with Bevan on Suez in 1956, but his revisionist policies led to confrontations over nationalisation and Clause IV. He was also committed to the Atlantic alliance and collective security, which in turn led to more divisions over unilateralism. His belief in the Commonwealth led to a break with his own supporters over membership of the European Economic Community. These divisions resulted in the three great crises that summed up his period as leader.

Following a crushing defeat in the 1959 general election, Gaitskell proposed the updating of Clause IV of the party constitution to reflect modern concerns as revealed in the work of pioneering pollsters like Mark Abrams and in the political ideas of Gaitskell's close friend, Tony Crosland. Despite pinning his personal prestige to a new statement of party aims, he was defeated. This led to a concerted attack on his position as leader and the defeat of his defence policy by CND-inspired resolutions at the Scarborough conference of 1960. He responded to defeat with his famous 'Fight and fight and fight again' speech, which rallied supporters of NATO and saw CND defeated at the 1961 conference. At the 1962 conference he dismayed many of his supporters by opposing British membership of the EEC in an equally electrifying platform performance.

His attempt to change Clause IV and his two great conference speeches were typical of his style of leading from the front and his faith that the party could be persuaded to adopt his positions by the force of rational argument. This didacticism was matched by his faith in economic intervention as a means of improving society. He chose to be a socialist because he believed that it was right rather having been born into it, and he was impatient with those who did not share his faith. Though an inspirational leader for those who agreed with him, he inspired passionate dislike amongst his political opponents. In the final analysis his ability to hold the Labour Party together was questionable, though the substance of the policy differences between the two wings of the party in the 1950s appear much less profound in hindsight than they did at the time. For example, his revisionism was conducted within strict intellectual and emotional limits that rejected market economics in favour of Keynesian demand management and planning. Though he was convinced of the need to transcend nationalisation as the main means of achieving greater equality, he remained dedicated to the ends of social justice and retained a deep-seated faith in state action. Moreover, he did not believe that the historical Labour Party needed to be abandoned to achieve a modern and relevant approach, and was very much of the 1931 generation in his suspicion of pacts with other parties. He was wedded to the Labour Party and had a strong belief in its ability to change. His sudden death on 18 January 1963 in London robbed him of the opportunity of being Prime Minister and thus his career has an unfinished quality about it. Moreover, he made a major mistake in the 1959 campaign when he pledged that the Labour Party would not increase taxation. This focused the campaign on Labour as a tax-and-spend party. While his next campaign might have been more effective, he would not have been in as good a position to exploit Conservative problems over Profumo and other scandals, because of the nature of his own private life and his affair with the socialite Ann Fleming. He had undoubted qualities of leadership and revealed himself in the great struggles of his career as a man of the highest integrity and courage, but his single-mindedness, which could often appear as stubbornness, must leave a question mark over the claim frequently made for him as being the best Prime Minister Britain never had.

Hugh Gaitskell's legacy to the Labour Party was a style of confrontational leadership and a political approach of brutal frankness. He was intellectually and emotionally woven into the Labour Party and Labour movement in a way which his society love life could not obscure. His revisionism was a commitment to the future of the Labour Party as an independent political entity. He did not toy with coalition or merger with Liberals but advocated, in his attempt to replace Clause IV, the modernisation of the Labour Party so that it absorbed the radical centre. His brand of economic intervention and central belief in equality were entirely incompatible with liberalism. He did not believe that the destruction of the historical Labour Party was necessary for the formation of a revisionist Labour Party. His legacy is therefore of an alternative model of modernising leadership, one followed by Neil Kinnock and John Smith and espoused by the current Chancellor of the Exchequer and not the current Prime Minister. Tony Blair's modernising leadership contain flexibility on one issue, above all others, that Hugh Gaitskell contemptuously rejected after the 1959 election: the integrity of the Labour Party as an independent political force was not negotiable. The lessons of 1931 were burned into Labour leaders of his generation and he was not about to repeat the error. But that did not mean that the Labour Party should not change and that any debate on means was worth having. In this respect he has most in common with Gordon Brown, but he was also very much a man and a politician of his time and his central faith was in the power of economic theory to improve human life.

Hugh Gaitskell's publications include: *Chartism* (London 1929); *In Defence of Politics* (London, 1954); *The High Cost of Toryism* (London, 1956); *Recent Developments in British Socialist Thinking* (London, 1956); *The Challenge of Co-existence* (London, 1957); *Labour and the Common Market* (London, 1962); and, edited by Philip Williams, *The Diary of Hugh Gaitskell* (London, 1983). Works about Hugh Gaitskell include Bill Rodgers, (editor), *Hugh Gaitskell 1906–1963*, (London, 1964); E.J. Goodman, *Hugh Gaitskell and the Modernisation of the Labour Party*, (PhD, Nebraska, 1965 (University Microfilms International, Catalogue number 6601020); Stephen Haseler, *The Gaitskellites*, (London, 1969); Geoffrey McDermott, *Leader Lost*, (London, 1972); Philip Williams, *Hugh Gaitskell: A Political Biography*, (London, 1979); 'Hugh Gaitskell', in John Vaizey, *Breach of Promise* (London, 1983); 'Hugh Gaitskell' in Michael Foot, *Loyalists and Loners* (London, 1986); 'Hugh Gaitskell: The Social Democrat as Hero' in David Marquand, *The Progressive Dilemma*, (London, 1991); 'Hugh Gaitskell: 1955–1963' in Peter Shore, *Leading the Left* (London, 1993); 'Hugh Gaitskell' in Ben Pimlott, *Frustrate their Knavish Tricks* (London, 1994) and Brian Brivati, *Hugh Gaitskell*, (London, 1996).

Professor Brian Brivati

John Kenneth Galbraith   (1907–)

John Kenneth Galbraith is a Canadian-born economist and liberal Democrat whose ideas played a key role in preparing Labour for power in the early 1960s. Born in Ottawa on 15 October 1907, he emigrated to Berkeley, California, where he received a doctorate in Agricultural Economics in 1934. He worked briefly for the Agricultural Adjustment Administration (AAA) and the National Resources Planning Board during the New Deal, while teaching at Harvard. Galbraith worked for the Office of Price Administration, the most interventionist of the US wartime agencies, but was driven out by conservatives. In 1947, he became a founder member with Arthur Schlesinger Jnr and other anti-Communist liberals of the Americans for Democratic Action (ADA), the main liberal pressure group within the Democratic Party. Thereafter, he enjoyed a reputation for sparkling wit and intelligence in his studies of economics and society, and became a loyal radical within the Kennedy camp, serving briefly as Ambassador to India (1961–63).

Galbraith's importance for the Labour Party mainly derives from his book *The Affluent Society* (1958), in which his own admiration for the American radical Thorstein Veblen was expressed in sharp and satirical style. The book was an important modification of Galbraith's own earlier acceptance of corporate power in his *American Capitalism* (1952), in which he had seen corporate capital and labour as countervailing powers against monopoly in a modern economy.

Galbraith argued that unemployment and depression may have been conquered through the use of Keynesian economics, but the sheer abundance of marketable commodities and the obvious wealth of modern capitalist society had created new problems, so far unrecognised and unexamined, in their place. These problems of affluence were embedded in the quality of living rather than in the economic statistics of the increasing production of wealth. Material comfort may have been secured, but inflation and consumer debt were creating new anxieties, threatening both security and status. At the same time, there was a starvation of public services taking place side-by-side with these comforts. This disparity between domestic opulence and social austerity – 'private affluence and public squalor' – was the centrepiece of the book, as Galbraith pointed to the anomaly of air-conditioned cars travelling through badly-paved and litter-strewn cities, and to the irony of exquisitely packaged food eaten in picnics in parks which were a menace to public health and morals.

This fashionable best-seller, which ignored the real household poverty hidden in American society, was taken up as a means of healing the divisions in the Labour Party in 1960. In the aftermath of the disastrous 1959 election defeat, the revisionists called for the deletion of the commitment to a statified economy which they saw embodied in Clause 4 of the party constitution, while there was an increasing call on the left for a greater commitment to public ownership (even radical demands for industrial democracy) as an antidote to the immorality of private competition. As the party tore itself apart publicly over defence at the 1960 conference, there was a less-noticed rally around the ideas of Galbraith as a means of unifying the party's domestic policy. Its commitment to increased spending on public services appealed to the left, its implicit acceptance of corporatist planning appealed to Wilson, and its critique of an affluent society as ignoring the inadequacies of health and education appealed to the revisionists (see Crosland's *The Conservative Enemy*, 1962). For books, see Richard Pells, *The Liberal Mind in a Conservative Age* (1985)

Geoffrey Foote

Gerald Gardiner (Lord Gardiner)　　　　　　　　(1900–90)

Of all the Labour lawyers who have held political office, Gerald Gardiner was the most successful and important until the arrival of Derry Irvine. Gardiner was born on 30 May 1900 in London. His father was a businessman with interests in the theatre, and Gardiner initially considered a career on the stage. After Harrow he served briefly with the Guards in World War One and then went to Oxford. He was president of both the Union and the Oxford University Drama Society.

In fact three alternative worlds lay before him when he left Oxford. At the end of World War One he joined the Peace Pledge Union, which reflected what became a life-long commitment to peace and a growing interest in politics. In addition to politics he was also still interested in the stage. Finally, the law became an increasing focus of interest. He was sent down for two terms at Magdalen for campaigning for the rights of women in the university and publishing a pamphlet which attacked restrictions on their entry. This political bent did not, however, win out over the law. He was called to the Bar in 1925. He built a successful practice before the war and served with the Friends Ambulance Unit during the conflict.

In the post-war years he began to make a real reputation by combining his political interests – he joined the Labour Party in the 1930s in response to the rise of fascism – with his experience in the law. At the end of the war his advice lead to the creation of legal aid, and he continued campaigning for law reform, bringing his thoughts together in the 1963 book, *Law Reform Now*. In addition he took a number of high-profile cases, most famously the Lady Chatterley Trial, which pushed at the boundaries of censorship. His real chance to have a long-lasting impact on British law came in 1964. He had stood unsuccessfully for West Croydon in 1951, but had come to Harold Wilson's particular attention when he ran the National Campaign for the Abolition of the Death Penalty. Wilson nominated him for a life peerage in 1963 and he was made Lord Chancellor when Labour won the 1964 election.

Gardiner was one of the most progressive Lord Chancellors of the post-war era. During his tenure the whole set of reforms that ushered in the permissive society were passed, and law reform was a central part of this programme. Many of his ideas from *Law Reform Now* were implemented. In sum, capital punishment was abolished, abortion was legalised, homosexuality was decriminalised, the Law Commission was established, the first women judges were appointed and a system of compulsory training for JPs was introduced. Though he failed to make the most obvious reform, unifying the legal profession, he was the key figure in the modernisation of the English legal system, bringing it much more, if not completely, into line with contemporary society. He did not return to the Woolsack when Labour was re-elected in 1974 but served with distinction as Chancellor of the Open University – he enrolled and completed a degree in Social Science – and chaired many committees of enquiry. He was made a Companion of Honour in 1975.

Though a Labour politician, his calibre as legal expert was demonstrated when the Heath government asked three privy councillors to investigate the systematic abuse of interrogation procedures by members of the security forces in Northern Ireland. A majority report backed the security forces' use of techniques which contravened the Geneva and other human-rights conventions. Gardiner submitted a minority report that condemned what had been going on. Edward Heath accepted his report. Socially inept and cool, he did not have a politician's easy skill with people, but he lived a life of service to the causes he believed in. His first wife Doris Trounson died in 1966, while his second, Muriel Violette Box, the film producer and writer, survived him. He died at home in Mill Hill, London, on 7 January 1990.

Professor Brian Brivati

Anthony Giddens (1938–)

Anthony Giddens' reputation as the most widely read and cited social theorist of his generation has culminated in his rise to prominence as one of the intellectual architects of New Labour through his espousal of Third Way politics. Indeed, this position has led many to refer to him as Tony Blair's guru and favourite intellectual. His future eminence as one of the world's leading sociologists, which has seen him awarded fifteen honorary degrees from prestigious universities around the world and seen his appointment at, among others, Harvard University as a Memorial Lecturer and at the Sorbonnne as Descartes Lecturer, must all seem a long way from his childhood in Edmonton, North London, in which his first passion in life was his local team Tottenham Hotspur.

Anthony Giddens was born on 18 January 1938, the son of T G Giddens, and was educated at Minchenden School, Southgate. Although he confesses to being surprised at gaining a place at Hull University to read Sociology and Psychology, it was here that he became the first member of his family not just to go to university, but to graduate with first class honours in 1959 at the age of 21. This early success propelled him off to the LSE, where he secured a Distinction in MA Sociology in 1961, and then on to the University of Cambridge where he obtained his PhD in 1976.

During this period of academic success, Giddens married Jane Ellwood at the age of 25 in 1963; the couple have two daughters. As a family man, Giddens still finds time for other passions in his life – notably the theatre, cinema, playing tennis and supporting Spurs.

It is hard to deny Anthony Giddens at least a share in the credit for re-establishing sociology as an academic discipline after its years in the wilderness. The author of 35 books that have been translated into 29 languages, including *Capitalism and Modern Social Theory* (1971), *New Rules of Sociological Method* (1976), *Sociology* (1982) and *The Consequences of Modernity* (1990), Giddens is nothing if not prolific. In 1999 he delivered the prestigious BBC Reith Lectures. Choosing to speak on the theme of globalisation, Giddens presented his Runaway World lectures to an international audience from around the world, encompassing London, Hong Kong, Delhi and Washington DC.

Despite being rejected for promotion to a readership at Cambridge nine times in the 1970s and 1980s and encountering substantial criticism for his methods and approach to his discipline, he is still considered as the 'best-known British academic on the continent.' His contribution was formally recognised with his appointment as Professor of Sociology at Cambridge in 1986, and subsequently to the Directorship of the London School of Economics and Political Science in 1997, where he has promised to further the university's claim to be the 'guardian of social sciences'. Even as an entrepreneur, Giddens has remained faithful to the cause; in 1985 he co-founded Polity Press, of which he is still Chairman and Director, which has gone on to become one of the best-known social science publishers. In addition, he is the Director of Blackwell-Polity, a post he has also held since 1985.

Despite being a lifelong member of the Labour Party, and given the wave of attention he has attracted as the pioneer of Third Way politics, Giddens did not publish his first political work, *Beyond Left and Right,* until 1994 – the same year that Tony Blair became Labour leader. In it, Giddens contended that the conflicting ideologies of socialism and neo-liberalism, which had provided the framework for political debate in the post-war era, are now redundant as blueprints for political change. Set against a backdrop of intensive socio-economic and technological change, driven by the forces of globalisation and growing interdependence, Giddens argues that the traditional ideologies of both left and right have passed their sell-by date. In subsequent texts, spanning *The Third Way* (1998), *The Third Way and its Critics* (1999) and *The Global Third Way Debate* (2001), Giddens argues that they are to be substituted with a new politics emanating from a 'radical centre' which in turn constitutes a 'renewal of social democracy.'

Criticism has been widespread, with accusations flying in from both left and right that Third Way politics amounts to little more than Mrs Thatcher without the handbag. But whilst critics continue to try and derail the credibility of the Third Way, it is undoubtedly true that the ideas of Professor Giddens have found resonance at the heart of New Labour. In 1998 Tony Blair published a Fabian Society pamphlet entitled *The Third Way: New Politics for the New Century* which paralleled many of the ideas Giddens had been formulating. Indeed, Giddens is said to have the ear of the Prime Minister, a fact best illustrated in February 1998 when he accompanied Blair to a Third Way seminar in Washington hosted by the then President Bill Clinton. In the court of Number 10, Giddens' ideas are still said to wield influence. He is also a Trustee of the influential think-tank, the IPPR.

It remains to be seen whether a second Labour term will be a manifestation of the Third Way and the extent to which Giddens' influence will be felt on the policy making process. However it is hard to ignore Giddens' claim, that regardless of the criticism it has generated, 'Third way politics will be the point of view with which others will have to engage.'

Guy Lodge

John Golding (1931–99)

As a leader of the party's trades union right wing, John Golding, the former MP for Newcastle-under-Lyme and General Secretary of the National Communications Union, was one of the most powerful figures in the Labour movement at the height of the party's in-fighting in the late 1970s and early 1980s.

He was pivotal in recapturing the National Executive Committee from Tony Benn, Eric Heffer and Militant in 1982, paving the way for Neil Kinnock's leadership and reforms of the Party. Golding was instrumental, too, in thwarting Benn's leadership hopes by ensuring he was not selected, following boundary changes, for Chief Whip Michael Cocks' safer Bristol constituency. As a result, Benn lost his seat at the 1983 election and was unable to contest the succession to Michael Foot.

Until he retired in 1986, Golding was also one of the outstanding parliamentarians of the day. His record for the longest-ever Commons speech, an 11 hours and fifteen minutes filibuster to stall the privatisation of British Telecom until after the 1983 election, is unlikely ever to be beaten. With a mischievous sense of humour, Golding was thoroughly down-to-earth with no trace of pomposity. Indeed, he showed a childlike pride in his 1980s award by *The Guardian* as the Commons' worst-dressed MP.

He was born in Birmingham on 9 March 1931, but was brought up with his four sisters in Chester, as his father Peter – a chef, who died when Golding was in his teens – moved extensively looking for work. After Chester Grammar School, at 16 he joined the Ministry of National Insurance in London as an office boy, to help support the family.

After eventually studying at Keele University in Newcastle-under-Lyme, then at the London School of Economics, it was as a researcher with the Post Office Engineering Union that he was returned to parliament in a 1969 by-election in the constituency. It was then that he met his second wife Llin – a hospital radiographer and daughter of Ness Edwards, Postmaster General in Attlee's 1950 government, who drove him round during the election. Both were already married at the time, with separate families, but they tied the knot together in 1980.

Golding quickly joined the Wilson government, first as Parliamentary Private Secretary to

Minister of State for Technology Eric Varley from February to June 1970 then, after serving as an Opposition Whip 1970–74, as a Government Whip from February to October 1974. It was then, and during the 1970s miners' strike, that initial admiration turned to intense antipathy towards Benn. As Under-Secretary of State for Employment from 1976 to 1979, Golding was intensely proud of Labour's efforts to cushion the blows of unemployment and short-time working, despite the left's attempts to undermine the Callaghan government. He was chairman of the Commons Employment Select Committee 1979–82.

Tireless organisers, he and Llin made a formidable political team, instinctively loyalist 'Old Labour'. Llin succeeded him as MP in 1986, when Golding stepped down to become General Secretary of the new NCU and fight Militant in his own union. Golding had little time for the left-wing intellectuals, who to him defied common sense. Proud to be called a 'fixer', Golding was bloody-minded enough to use the left's tactics to the moderates' advantage and was much in demand in the Commons tearoom with threatened MPs untutored in the tactics of the pro-cedural rough house.

'I'm fed up of this fuckin' idiot. I'm going,' Heffer once screamed at a home policy meet-ing of the NEC after Golding stalled another fix with a two-hour-long insight into ordinary people's views on every subject under the sun. Alas, Heffer walked into a cupboard, then a broom cupboard, before slamming his papers down and shouting: 'Oh fuck it! I'm staying.' 'And these were people who thought they could run the country,' Golding remarked in the memoirs he was finishing before his sudden death from septicaemia on 20 January, 1999.

In more than 40 years of active politics, including 17 as an MP, Golding admitted he made more enemies than friends, and not only on the left. In Labour's darkest days, it often fell to Golding to step where others feared to tread. In 1983, during the leadership election, union tacticians calculated that Roy Hattersley could not beat Kinnock and would have to be satis-fied with the deputyship instead. Golding was deputed to deliver the black spot and later blamed Hattersley for being left out of the shadow cabinet.

A confidant of Kinnock, if he was bitter at the time, the scars never showed. In politics, his attitude was 'You win some, lose some'. 'I got Benn, then they got me,' he said after losing to the left the position he always kept as political officer in the POEU. That victory over Benn, the recapture of Labour's feuding NEC in 1982 after 'five years hard Labour', as he put it, was undoubtedly Golding's high point. Using a majority of just one, as Foot abstained, he ruthlessly removed Benn and his acolytes from all their positions of power.

To many, with Golding playing a key role in the 1983 manifesto, it remained a mystery why La-bour fought the election on 'the longest suicide note in history'. The answer was straightforward: Golding had already decided that, with all the feuding, Foot as leader and the Falklands, Labour had lost the election. He wanted, therefore, to allow the Bennites enough policy rope to hang them-selves so they could never again blame the right as they had after 1979.

Politics aside, Golding's great passions were fishing, horse-racing and Spanish. Just before his untimely death at 67, Golding took great delight in running rings round civil servants in his new appointment to a Ministry of Agriculture panel on the plight of British fresh-water fish-ing. Right to the end, fixing the fixers was a mischievous delight in itself.

Paul Farrelly MP

Victor Gollancz   (1893–1967)

'I don't suppose you have any conception of the impact you have made on the social life and history of this country', wrote the author John Gloag to Victor Gollancz on learning in June 1965 that the publisher had received a knighthood: 'The Left Book Club, a magnificent conception, was largely instrumental in swinging Labour into power after the Second World War, though the blind, ungrateful bastards ignored you then …'. The bastards had plenty to be ungrateful for, as Gollancz had performed signal service to the Labour Party by promulgating left-wing writing to a wide public, not only through Left Book Club literature itself but through the groups spawned by the club all over Britain, from which socialist ideas trickled down into the workplace and social gatherings.

Son of a wholesale jeweller, Victor Gollancz was born in Maida Vale, London, on 9 April 1893 and educated at St Paul's School and New College, Oxford. In 1914 he was commissioned in the Northumberland Fusiliers, only to spend most of the First World War seconded to the Officer Training Corps teaching Classics at Repton. In 1919 he married architect Ruth Lowy, and embarked on his publishing career in 1920 with Benn Brothers. Victor Gollancz Limited was started in 1928 – with the great typographer Stanley Morison a member of the board from its inception – and as its founder's socialist convictions deepened through the early 1930s the company became an ever more productive channel for his political drive.

Gollancz founded the Left Book Club in 1936, with John Strachey and Harold Laski joining him to form the selection panel. The Club proclaimed a simple aim: 'to help in the struggle *for* World Peace and a better social and economic order and *against* Fascism, by (*a*) increasing the knowledge of those who already see the importance of this struggle, and (*b*) adding to their number the very many who, being fundamentally well disposed, hold aloof from the fight by reason of ignorance or apathy.' Membership involved a commitment to buy one book a month at a cost of half a crown (12½ pence) from a choice of two titles, the first pair being *France Today and the People's Front* by Maurice Thorez (General Secretary of the French Communist Party) and *Out of the Night: a biologist's view of the future*, in which H. J. Muller made the case for genetic selection in a socialist society. Concerned to tackle general social issues such as unemployment and poverty, the club published George Orwell's *The Road to Wigan Pier* in March 1937 and *The Town that was Murdered*, Ellen Wilkinson's account of the Jarrow Hunger March, in September 1939.

Alongside the book publishing went the monthly magazine *Left Book News* and LBC rallies, the first of which at the Albert Hall in February 1937 attracted 7,000 people. Membership of the club peaked in 1939 at around 60,000, and during the early years of the Second World War titles proliferated despite paper rationing. But after the hostilities the prevailing mood was very different from before, and with Attlee's government in power and the threat of fascism pushed back, the Club's original aims were past their sell-by date. By the late 1940s membership was down to 7,000 and Gollancz was tired of the project: in October 1948 the Left Book Club slipped quietly away, having published 252 titles, including works by such authors as Richard Acland, Clement Attlee (*The Labour Party in Perspective*, 1937), G. D. H. Cole, Stafford Cripps, J. B. S. Haldane, Arthur Koestler, André Malraux, Philip Noel-Baker, Clifford Odets, Stephen Spender, Sidney and Beatrice Webb, Leonard Woolf and Michael Young – as well as Laski, Strachey, Orwell and Gollancz himself, who was a prolific author. Notable political figures published by Gollancz outside the confines of the LBC included Aneurin Bevan (*Why Not Trust the Tories?*, 1945) and Michael Foot, whose *Guilty Men* (written with Peter Howard and Frank Owen under the pseudonym 'Cato' in 1940) sold over 200,000 copies and was followed by *The Trial of Mussolini* (which sold 150,000 copies after publication in 1943), *Brendan and Beverley* (a broadside at Brendan Bracken and Beverley Baxter) in 1944, and *Guilty Men 1957*, an attack on the British government's handling of the Suez crisis co-written with Mervyn Jones. But Gollancz famously declined to publish George Orwell's *Animal Farm* in 1944:'I am highly critical of many aspects of internal and external Soviet policy: but I could not possibly publish … a general attack of this nature', he wrote to Orwell's agent. (Gollancz was not alone: Jonathan Cape and T. S. Eliot at Faber and Faber also declined *Animal Farm*, Cape withdrawing at a late stage after pressure from the government.)

It was not only in the political arena that Victor Gollancz Limited made its mark: the company was the original publisher of R. C. Sheriff's *Journey's End* in 1929 and Kingsley Amis's *Lucky Jim* in 1954, and other well known VG authors are Daphne du Maurier (including *Rebecca* in 1938), John Updike, Colin Wilson, A. J. Cronin, Elizabeth Bowen, Ford Madox Ford, Dorothy L. Sayers and Ivy Compton-Burnett.

During the Second World War much of Gollancz's energy was taken up with getting Jewish refugees out of Germany, and after it he continued to become closely involved with causes about which he felt passionately – Save Europe Now, Jewish Society for Human Service, Campaign for Nuclear Disarmament, the National Campaign for the Abolition of Capital Punishment and War On Want. Zealous, egotistical and passionate, Gollancz could be notoriously childish and difficult. Ernest Benn's experience that 'I spend alternate periods of three months each, hating him and loving him' was shared by many others who worked with him (though the periods tended to be a good deal shorter than three months), and he could be an exasperating employer: he declined to speak to one secretary for three weeks after she had mistakenly posted a letter to the USA by surface mail rather than air. Victor Gollancz died on 8 February 1967 at the age of seventy-three, and control of the publishing house passed to Livia, oldest of his five daughters.

The company remained independent until bought by the American publisher Houghton Mifflin in 1989, and was sold on to Cassell in 1993, changing hands yet again when the Cassell Group was taken over by Orion in 1998. The latter-day Victor Gollancz Limited showed occasional flashes of preserving the company's political traditions – Michael Foot's *Dr Strangelove, I Presume*, promoted as 'a wake-up call to the moribund peace movement', was published in 1999 – but such flickers of the flame were few and far between and Orion had little interest in maintaining the company's distinctive character. The death notice came in a story tucked away in the *Daily Telegraph* in September 2000: 'Victor Gollancz, the firm which in its heyday published George Orwell and Kingsley Amis and helped to form the political climate, is ceasing to publish general interest titles. The decision by Gollancz's owner, Orion, to restrict the imprint to science-fiction titles means the end of a maverick tradition.' Ironically, the very last non-fiction title to appear under the Victor Gollancz imprint was the *Left Book Club Anthology*, edited by Paul Laity and published in summer 2001.

The standard life is *Victor Gollancz: a biography* by Ruth Dudley Edwards (1987), while Gollancz's own most directly autobiographical works are in the form of book-length letters addressed to his grandson: *My Dear Timothy* (1952) and *More for Timothy* (1953).

Sean Magee

Arnold Goodman (Baron Goodman of Westminster)   (1913–95)

Lord Goodman was a lawyer who built up a network of influential connections that enabled him to act, both in public and behind the scenes, to broker legal and political deals, offer advice and defend high-profile Establishment figures. At the peak of his powers in the era of Harold Wilson, his ability to make a deal or argue a case was invaluable to the Party leader and Prime Minister as well as his many other clients.

He was born on 21 August 1913 in Hackney, London. His father, Joseph, a master draper and his mother, Bertha, gave him the name Aby, but his registered name was changed to Abraham a few months after his birth. It was not until after the Second World War that he became known as Arnold.

He was educated at the Grocers' School at Hackney Downs, and at University College London (UCL). After initially enrolling to study History of Art, he switched for a year to Economics and finally to Law. He graduated from UCL in 1933 and went on to gain a master's degree, LLM, with first class honours, and came second in the Law Society Finals. In 1936 Goodman continued his law studies at Downing College, Cambridge where he obtained two first-class degrees in Roman Law and Roman-Dutch Law.

He returned to London and joined a practice specialising in commercial conveyancing. At the outbreak of war he enlisted as an anti-aircraft gunner, but was soon moved to an administrative role. He was commissioned as second lieutenant in 1942 and rose to Major in the Ordnance Corps by the end of the war. On being demobbed he returned to his former practice, becoming a partner in 1947. He formed his own practice in a new partnership, Goodman Derrick, in 1954.

As well as specialising in work in the arts and media, a crucial link to the Labour Party was established through George Wigg whom he had met in the Army. Wigg was a close associate of Harold Wilson and although Goodman started to acquire clients from the left of British politics, his own politics, such as they were, were basically liberal.

Goodman made his first major impact in the 1957 *Spectator* libel trial. A report accused Aneurin Bevan, Morgan Phillips and Richard Crossman of heavy drinking and lack of attendance when visiting an Italian Socialist Party congress. The case made the front pages of the newspapers and eventually the jury awarded the plaintiffs damages for libel. Goodman's reputation as a libel lawyer was made. He began advising the Labour Party on legal matters when Gaitskell was leader in cases such as the Vassall spy inquiry in 1962, and after Wilson became leader advised him on Labour's stance in the Profumo scandal in 1963.

When Labour won power in 1964, Wilson's patronage became even more important. As with Marcia Williams (later Baroness Falkender), the fact that Goodman was not a rival to Wilson for a position in traditional party politics was probably an attractive attribute that enabled him to become a close and trusted confidant in frequent meetings. The range of his involvement with the Wilson administration was enormous. His experience in property development and property law was drawn upon as he linked up again with Richard Crossman, the new Minister of Housing. Crossman noted in his diary how Goodman was a 'resourceful man', 'full of ideas', an 'invaluable adviser' and that even if it meant offending senior civil servants he would 'be bound to use him' (R. Crossman, 1979, *The Crossman Diaries: Condensed Version*, Magnum Books, London, pp 35–36). The arts was the other area in which he became closely involved as chairman of the Arts Council from 1965. He was granted a life peerage in June 1965 as Baron Goodman of Westminster.

He also helped Jennie Lee clarify plans for introducing the Open University and conducted negotiations with the BBC to act as the University's broadcaster. He submitted a report to Wilson on the viability of the venture, but underestimated the cost considerably. He continued to support Lee in the project to find further funds and overcome scepticism. When the Open University was officially announced, Goodman was on the committee overseeing the launch. He acted in another capacity when he represented Wilson in negotiations over Rhodesia from 1966 to 1968, meeting Ian Smith in secret to arrange talks and discuss preliminaries. There were also many behind-the-scenes consultations on many of the difficult issues that arise in any government, issues on which Brian Brivati's excellent biography of Goodman goes into fuller details.

When the Conservatives won the 1970 election, Goodman continued to take a role in Rhodesian negotiations. Although he endorsed the final deal in public, he recognised its flaws and subsequently noted in his memoirs (p 226) 'I prefer a bad agreement to a prolonged disagreement'. He was appointed Chairman of the Newspaper Publishers' Association in 1970, reflecting his long involvement with the media in general and his position as chairman of the Board of Editorial Trustees of the *Observer* at that time. He acted as a link for Wilson to Rupert Murdoch in a manner not dissimilar to that adopted by Tony Blair over twenty years later. The *Sun* advised its readers to vote Labour in 1970 and 1974, just as it would in 1997.

When Wilson was returned to power in 1974, Goodman was still involved, but not as closely or over such a wide range as previously. There was, even, one issue on which he stood apart. He strongly, but unsuccessfully, opposed Labour's trade union legislation from 1974 to 1976 concerning the allowing of a closed shop. He was particularly concerned about the newspaper industry and argued that journalists and print unions could use their monopoly in a way detrimental to the freedom of the press.

Having acted for Labour and Conservative Party leaders, he now acquired the Liberal leader as a client. Goodman tried to keep knowledge of Thorpe's relationship with Norman Scott out of the public domain as long as possible, but once the story broke he worked to limit the damage. Thorpe resigned, but in August 1978 was arrested and charged with conspiracy and incitement to murder. Although Thorpe was eventually acquitted, Goodman's reputation had taken something of a pounding in the process.

Goodman became Master of University College, Oxford, in 1976. His legal practice continued, but his mobility was decreasing and the level of activity gradually declined. His final involvement with the Establishment was in advising Prince Charles, Princess Diana and Sarah Ferguson during their marriage break-ups. His memoirs were published following his eightieth birthday in 1993. He died on 12 May 1995. One newspaper described him as 'Britain's most distinguished citizen outside government'.

For an excellent biography see Brian Brivati's *Lord Goodman* (1999). His memoirs are published as *Tell Them I'm on My Way: Memoirs* (1993), and selected speeches and writings can be found in Lord Goodman, *Not for the Record* (1972).

Nick Cowell

Patrick Gordon Walker (Lord Gordon-Walker of Leyton) (1907–80)

Patrick Gordon Walker 'is certainly the leader of the Labour Party the Conservatives would regard as hardest to beat, and his solidity of character might well provide a solid platform for a Labour Government,' wrote William Rees-Mogg in the *Sunday Times* of 27 January 1963 on the death of Hugh Gaitskell. Indeed, the *Daily Express* had tipped him as Labour's next leader as early as 28 July 1958. For the *New Statesman* of 27 September 1963, 'the pipe-smoking exponent of moderating common-sense' was 'one of the most decent men in British politics.' Patrick enjoyed many friendships in the Parliamentary Labour Party but in reality had insufficient support to become leader. He stood aside to avoid splitting the Gaitskellite vote and nominated his friend George Brown, only for George to lose to Harold Wilson anyhow.

Wilson, not wanting to appoint Brown, made Patrick Shadow Foreign Secretary, a role he fitted like a glove. Patrick was no sycophant, however, and gave on the whole wise advice to Wilson whether he liked it or not, in good or bad times alike. Patrick was also very unlucky: he lost his seat despite Labour's 1964 General Election victory due to a campaign against Commonwealth immigration in his Smethwick constituency based on the slogan, 'If you want a nigger for your neighbour, vote Labour.' The winning Conservative candidate, Peter Griffiths, refused to condemn the use of this slogan. Griffiths was dubbed the 'Parliamentary leper' by Wilson but nevertheless later became the long-serving Conservative MP for Portsmouth North. Even more unfortunately, Patrick lost the Leyton by-election in January 1965 even though Wilson had appointed him Foreign Secretary, a post from which he now had to resign. The *Evening Standard* unkindly likened him to looking like a 'recently orphaned bloodhound.' Out of Parliament, Wilson sent him in spring 1965 on a fact-finding mission to the USA and South-East Asia to explore the potential role for Britain in progressing peace talks in Vietnam.

Finally winning Leyton at the 1966 general election, and now combining, according to the *Guardian,* 'a winning charm with a daunting toughness in debate,' he joined Wilson's Cabinet as Minister Without Portfolio in January 1967. This essentially involved negotiating the withdrawal of the British military presence from Malta and taking over the long-term review of social services from Douglas Houghton. He and the Chancellor, Jim Callaghan, eventually agreed to propose a means test for increased family allowances.

In August 1967 he was appointed Education Secretary and got to grips with plans to increase teacher training facilities and expand primary school provision. However, Patrick was again unlucky. Following the devaluation of November 1967, Cabinet was forced to agree a package of cuts. He agreed to end free school milk in secondary schools, but more was needed. The Cabinet meeting of 5 January 1968 was a fearful row. In order to save higher-education funding, with the backing of Wilson, Dick Crossman, Barbara Castle, Dick Marsh and Peter Shore, Patrick agreed to Roy Jenkins' demand to postpone raising the school leaving age from 15 to 16. Cabinet agreed only by eleven votes to ten. George Brown, who with Callaghan, Crosland and Michael Stewart had been in the minority, exploded: 'May God forgive you. You send your children to university and you would put the interests of the school kids below that of the universities.' Wilson replaced him in June and he became a backbencher and a Companion of Honour.

As Wilson's unpopularity grew, Patrick became a prime mover in the covert Wilson Must Go campaign amongst Labour MPs in the late 1960s. Working closely with Ivor Richard, Roy Hattersley, Dick Taverne and Chris Mayhew, he organised a group of over 100 backbenchers who at the right moment would seek to replace Wilson with Callaghan or preferably Jenkins. The right moment never came, however, and after Labour's defeat in 1970 Patrick tried in vain to bolster Wilson's position as a bulwark against the anti-EEC mood sweeping Labour. In 1974 he accepted a peerage as Lord Gordon-Walker of Leyton, and in 1974–75 he served as one of Britain's first MEPs. In the Lords he was an active supporter of the loyalist Manifesto Group and the Campaign for Labour Victory until his death in December 1980.

Patrick Gordon Walker was first elected in 1945 as MP for Smethwick and became PPS to Herbert Morrison in October 1946 before becoming Parliamentary Under-Secretary of State at the Commonwealth Relations Office in October 1947 and joining the Privy Council and the Cabinet as Secretary of State 1950–51. He played a key role in modernising the basis of Commonwealth membership so that newly independent India and Pakistan felt able to be members. Born in Worthing on 7 April 1907, he spent his early years in the Punjab where his father, Alan Lachlan Gordon Walker, was a judge in the Indian Civil Service. Donnish, he had been educated at Wellington and Christ Church, Oxford, where he taught history after graduation. Several visits to Germany in the early 1930s politicised him, and he began helping the Labour Party maintain contacts with persecuted social democrats in Germany. In 1934 he was Oxford University Labour Party Secretary and he was the Labour candidate for Oxford City at the 1935 general election. In 1938 it was Gordon-Walker who stepped down as Labour candidate in favour of the 'Popular Front' candidate, former Oxford Vice-Chancellor A D Lindsey, in the famous 'appeasement' by-election. He was well liked by his students but after the war broke out, being fluent in German and having been rejected by MI5, in 1940 he joined the BBC German Service until his 1945 entry into the House of Commons. He sponsored the post-war Koenigswinter annual gatherings to further Anglo-German relations and in 1946 became Treasurer of the British Council.

He blotted his copybook rather badly with his injudicious handling of the Seretse Khama affair while Commonwealth Secretary. Nevertheless he remained a key figure from 1951 to 1964 and from 1956 was an elected member of the shadow cabinet. He was an opposition spokesman on Commonwealth and then Treasury matters before becoming Shadow Home Secretary (1958–61) and Shadow Defence Secretary (1961–63). A close friend and ally of his patron, Herbert Morrison, he was a leading light amongst those in the early 1950s who urged Attlee first to take a stronger line against the Bevanites and then to retire to give Morrison his chance as leader. By 1955, however, Morrison's advancing age meant that he backed Gaitskell for leader. Patrick was soon functioning as Gaitskell's unofficial chief of staff, working particularly closely with the Campaign for Democratic Socialism in the fight against unilateralism and neutralism. Though not a great orator, his Commons attack in November 1958 on Prime Minister Harold Macmillan for using an advertising firm to promote himself like, 'Munchmallows, Payne's Poppets and Amplex' caused a great stir.

After the 1959 election defeat he was an early advocate of market research, or what would now be called 'focus groups', to find out why Labour had lost, and in a famous article in *Forward* pinned the blame on Labour's nationalisation plans and the poor performance of some Labour councils. Unlike Douglas Jay, who wrote a similar article for *Forward*, he did not advocate changing Labour's name, but he did privately agree with Jay on the need to rewrite Clause 4. Patrick had a very happy family life with Audrey his delightful wife, whom he married in 1934, his twin sons and three daughters. He published several books including *The Sixteenth and Seventeenth Centuries* (1935); *An Outline of Man's History* (1939); *The Lid Lifts* (1945); *Restatement of Liberty* (1951); *The Commonwealth* (1962), and *The Cabinet* (1970). His *Political Diaries 1932–1971*, edited with a lucid and informative introduction by Robert Pearce, were published in 1991.

Rt Hon. Dr Dickson Mabon

Joe Gormley (Lord Gormley of Ashton-in-Makerfield)   (1917–93)

Joeseph Gormley was the President of the NUM from 1971 to 1982. It was a period that saw the miners bring the country to a standstill with the first deployment of flying pickets in the strike of 1972, and with a second strike causing the three-day week and the 'Who runs Britain?' election of February 1974, which brought down the Heath government. Yet Gormley, who declared himself on his retirement to have been 'an anti-communist all my working life', was a self-confessed moderate whose message on bowing out of the Presidency in 1982 was to 'think before you strike'.

The context to this apparent dichotomy is probably to be found in his defeat in the pithead ballot of 1968 for the NUM General Secretaryship, which he blamed on his membership of Labour's NEC, where over the period 1963–73 he was a determined opponent of the Benn/Mikardo left. Despite Gormley being favourite to win, the unpopularity of the Labour government's incomes policy with rank and file miners meant they voted for his left rival, Lawrence Daly. As former Minister of Power and NUM MP Roy Mason recalled in his memoirs, Gormley was 'a much wilier bird than Scargill could ever hope to be', and when the chance came in 1971 to succeed Sir Sidney Ford as NUM President, Gormley pledged to make his members 'the highest-paid industrial workers in Britain'.

Though he defeated his communist rival, NUM Scottish Area President Mick McGahey, he was saddled with the decision of the 1971 NUM policy conference to reduce the majority for strike action required in a pithead ballot from 66 per cent to 55 per cent, making strike action a far readier weapon than before. Moreover, the NUM left was determined to use it, despite Gormley's counsels of caution. In 1974 Gormley sought compromise with the government via a negotiated settlement, but his communist Vice-President Mick McGahey sought 'not negotiation in Downing Street but it is agitation in the streets of this country to remove this government that is required'. Under the Labour government of 1974–79 Gormley backed the wage-restraint of the Social Contract and negotiated a 'Plan for Coal' which through investment and modernisation sought to improve productivity and competitiveness and thus secure a future for Britain's coal industry. He also secured the introduction of incentive bonus schemes, operated at a local level, linking productivity with earnings and reducing absenteeism. The overproduction of coal relative to a shrinking demand Gormley could not, however, solve, and by his retirement in 1982 there was clearly a need to close uneconomic pits. Gormley successfully sought to avoid national strike action and, through negotiation and subsidy, to secure as successful a future for British coal as possible. Tragically, his successor, Arthur Scargill, had a different agenda.

Born on 5 July 1917, he attended St Oswald's Roman Catholic School before joining his father down the mines at the age of 14. His father encouraged him to join the Miners' Federation of Lancashire and, having worked in eleven different collieries, he was in 1958 elected to the NUM National Executive and in 1961 elected over the left candidate as full-time Secretary of the North-West NUM. In his twenties he also served as a Councillor in Ashton-in-Makerfield. He was awarded an OBE in 1969.

In retirement he indulged his love of racing and became a director of United Racecourses. Created Lord Gormley of Ashton-in-Makerfield in 1982, he suffered two debilitating strokes the same year and in 1986 left his London home in Sunbury to retire to a bungalow near Wigan. He died on 27 May 1993, leaving his wife Nellie, whom he married in 1937, a son and a daughter. His autobiography, *Battered Cherub*, was published in 1982.

Lynn Williams

Bryan Gould   (1939–)

Bryan Gould, Labour's nearly man, was a moderniser too soon. A serious thinker and a first-class mind (which set him apart from the later, successful modernisers), he was Labour's rising star of the Eighties, a not-quite Leader by the Nineties, but ultimately he failed and withdrew to New Zealand in 1994. So he is referred to in the past tense here.

Born in New Zealand (11 February 1939) the son of a bank manager, he took Law at Auckland University and came to Oxford on a Rhodes Scholarship, reacting, as so many antipodeans do, against class accents and attitudes. He joined the Foreign Office and served in the Brussels Embassy, then became a Fellow of Worcester College from 1968 to 1974. He joined the Labour Party in the late 1960s and was selected for Southampton Test, narrowly winning it in the second 1974 election, with a majority of 374.

Bryan came in as a brilliant barrister with hands-on experience of Europe and Foreign Affairs, a man with prospects but in a party dominated by the men of the Sixties who disliked both his Euroscepticism and his expansionary economics. He was a voice crying in the wilderness as government struggled to shore up the post-war settlement, fighting inflation by incomes policy and low growth by high taxation. Gould, a self-taught economist, was contemptuous of the economic ignorance of backbenchers and critical of Denis Healey's 1976 cuts. This apprenticeship as a footsoldier in an army marching in the wrong direction was hardly enjoyable. He rose no higher than PPS to Peter Shore and was fired for voting against duties on New Zealand lamb.

In 1979 he lost his seat ,but the experience had strengthened two aspects of his politics which were of enduring importance – and the key to his ultimate failure. His Euroscepticism put him in a strong position when the old leadership went and Labour adopted withdrawal but was disastrous later. His expansionary economics, developed with his friends Shaun Stuart and John Mills in a series of Fabian pamphlets and a book, *Monetarism or Prosperity*, a critique of deflationary economics and monetarism, was coolly received in a pretty orthodox party.

Gould advocated expansion via a competitive exchange rate, low interest rates and a boost to the demand the orthodox were trying to cut. Those less subtle than Gould read this as perpetual devaluation, but it was really a recognition of the role of the exchange rate in translating

British costs into foreign prices, a return to Keynes's *Economic Consequences of Mr. Churchill* and a revival of the Croslandite emphasis on growth rather than deflationary cuts in living standards and public spending. Sadly, the left saw devaluation as an attack on wages, the right as an attack on the City and sterling, and both as the source of galloping inflation, even though the three authors showed convincingly that earlier devaluations had boosted the economy, not inflation. Radical economics put Gould on the outer track in a party which lacked confidence.

Out of Parliament Gould worked in television, where glittering prospects opened up, but his aim was always to get back into Parliament, which he did, after Southampton Test had rejected him, by selection for Dagenham. Safe seat, large majority, powerful industrial base, and one of the ablest minds in the party: he was well placed for success, a rising star, elected to the Shadow Cabinet in 1986 and writing the best of the several redefinitions of Socialism which came out as Labour tried to differentiate itself from both loony left and triumphant right.

However bright, Gould's star was a lonely one. Personable and friendly as an intellectual, he was viewed as too clever by half. He had no Labour background or union backing, kept apart from Solidarity and the Labour Co-ordinating Committee, and attached himself to the wrong candidate, his friend Peter Shore, in the 1983 leadership election. Kinnock and Hattersley won. Shore rewarded Bryan with a job in his Trade and Industry team, where he remained until 1986 when he became spokesman on the economy and party campaigns.

Gould became close to Kinnock, who liked and admired him but was always uneasy with him intellectually, as with anyone smarter than himself. Bryan also attracted the interest of Peter Mandelson, then beginning his courtier's progress in search of a court. Gould was a major influence on the 1987 campaign, successful in relaunching the party, less so in winning seats. After it the economic position he had wanted went to John Smith, the natural Shadow Chancellor, who disapproved of both his expansionary economics and his Euroscepticism.

Appointed Shadow Trade and Industry Secretary in 1987, Gould damaged his left-wing credentials at the 1987 Conference by advocating worker share ownership, but was more successful in the Policy Review by guiding it to devaluation and competitiveness and against Europe. This was to the annoyance of Gordon Brown and John Smith who had him moved to shadow Environment in 1989 while Smith and Brown took economic policy and steered it in a much more conventional direction and to the ERM.

Isolated on Europe and the economy, Gould was still a major figure, until everything fell apart after 1992. Kinnock, still his friend but a convert to Europe, stood down. Smith was the obvious, indeed inevitable successor, but instead of going for the Deputy Leadership, Gould unwisely challenged him for the top job. Kinnock advised him that Smith had it all sewn up, but 'won't last the course. It's important that you're there to pick up the pieces'. Bryan pressed on, unheeding the prophetic hint.

Supported by several of the best and brightest but not by the unions, Gould got only 10 per cent of the electoral college vote and came third to John Prescott as Deputy. Though proved right on the ERM, he now had no appetite for another long rearguard action against the Maastricht Treaty and was beginning to think 'that the task of rejuvenating British society, of freeing the British people from the weight of their own history would not be accomplished'. Gould ended up demoted to Shadow National Heritage Secretary. In this gloom he resigned his shadow cabinet position, always a basic mistake in Labour Party politics, and fought Maastricht as a backbencher.

Rescue came when he was head-hunted for the Vice Chancellorship of Waikato University in New Zealand. He decided to take the job rather than endure the loneliness of the long-distance dissenter, in a Euro-enthusiastic Labour Party where a younger generation of modernisers was taking over, and went ahead even though John Smith's subsequent death precipitated the leadership election which Blair won. His departure was criticised as sulking, a feeling encouraged by his disappointing autobiography *Goodbye to All That*, but was really eminently sensible. Why not take another rewarding career while still young enough to do so rather than sit around waiting for his bitch goddess, the Labour Party, to come to its senses? It hasn't yet.

Later, successful modernisers were less subtle and obsessed with presentation. Gould's focus was on ideas and policies. They were also more brutal. Gould had the same middle-class affection for the party as Tony Crosland, and the same anxiety to be thought well of by Labour. The younger modernisers viewed its tribalism, its trade union ties, its sectional appeal, its policies, with contempt. Each year in the long misery of opposition made Labour more amenable to their brutality.

Neither Gould nor anyone else of the generation which had come through the Seventies could have envisaged the total rejection of policies and past which ensued from Blair's leadership. Gould was as unlucky in his time as he was bad in his timing. Yet a successful politician perseveres in defeat and makes his own weather. Gould didn't. He liked to be liked, and lacked the guts for the fight, though his other failings cast a more favourable light on him than on the Party, for he lacked the killer instinct and was too nice and .too intellectually scrupulous to follow the herd.

To be an intellectual and a loner are badges of failure in a Party which prefers to be together rather than right, mistrusts intellectuals, and likes those who prate solidarity even as they plunge knives in other people's backs. Bryan couldn't do any of this. He wasn't born to achieve the high position he craved in our perverse, crude Party, and duly didn't get it. He was quite right to stop worshipping the brutal, fickle, goddess to whom he'd devoted twenty years of his life. Right, too, to do well for himself rather than a Party which didn't deserve him.

Austin Mitchell MP

Joyce Gould (Baroness Gould of Potternewton)   (1932–)

Amidst the celebrations in the Royal Festival Hall in the small hours of the morning of 2 May 1997, a young man approached a bespectacled, greying older woman and said 'We couldn't have done it without you, Joyce'. When the history of the Labour Party in the final quarter of the twentieth century is written, large sections of it will no doubt be devoted to the party's internal struggles and the role that the then Director of Organisation, Joyce Gould, played in saving the Labour Party.

Born in Leeds on 29 October 1932 to a Jewish family, Joyce Gould was educated at Roundhay High School for Girls and Bradford Technical College before moving onto Bradford

University. Although her father and one of her brothers were party members, Gould herself did not join the party until she was nineteen, largely as a result of the trade union activities of her then boyfriend, later husband, Kevin.

She grew up in a very different society from today, where politics were part of mainstream life. She remembers fondly running through the streets on polling day shouting 'Vote, Vote'. The 1945 election did not have a dramatic impact on the 13-year-old Gould, though she remembers recognising the big change brought by the creation of the National Health Service.

Her feminism, which she has maintained for the entirety of her career in the party, stems from a strong belief in what is right and in the drive toward equality between people. Despite her critics on the left, she describes herself as having been a Bevanite and holds that the mechanisms for delivery are what change and not the party's nor her own left-leaning ideology. She was active in CND in the 1950s and '60s along with Michael Foot and Fenner Brockway, and rose to become Secretary of CND Yorkshire.

Having joined the party, husband Kevin, unknown to her, nominated her to become branch secretary. This was the first of many party positions she held, culminating in her becoming the voluntary national women's representative for Yorkshire. During this time she stood for parliamentary selection on at least two or three occasions, but was always unsuccessful. However, she was a candidate in council elections in Leeds, but was never elected.

Thanks to supportive grandparents, Gould was able to work after the birth of her only child Jeannette in 1953. She eventually gave up work as a pharmaceutical dispenser in favour of an office-based job so that she would have Saturdays free to work for the party.

In 1969 it was suggested to her that she apply for the position of Assistant Regional Organiser and Women's Officer for Yorkshire, following in the footsteps of her good friend and now fellow Peer, Baroness Lockwood. In deciding to become a member of party staff, Gould effectively ended her parliamentary ambitions as at that time staff were prevented from being candidates.

In 1975 she became Assistant National Agent and Women's Officer, again following in the footsteps of Betty Lockwood. It was still rare to find women in positions of power in politics at this time, and Gould has always had respect for women like Barbara Castle more for what they achieved during this period than for who they were.

In 1985, the party was restructured and a new post of Director of Organisation was created, which Gould took up. That year saw Neil Kinnock's famous attack on the Militant Tendency at Party Conference. Militants had always been present in the party; however, there was evidence that entryism had grown significantly. Attention centred on Liverpool, and an enquiry by a committee of NEC members with Joyce Gould as the secretariat was begun. Their final report recommended expulsions; however, court action by Felicity Dowling temporarily stalled events. It was here that Gould first came into contact with the now Lord Chancellor Derry Irvine, who was acting as the Labour Party's QC.

Dowling's case centred on the issue of natural justice, accusing the NEC of being both judge and jury. The Party lost the case. In response the National Constitutional Committee was established, the rules of which were drafted jointly by Joyce Gould and Derry Irvine. Further enquiries followed and Gould was at the centre of preparing the detailed cases that would eventually go before the NCC. At one point she was spending upwards of three days a week in

Liverpool, alongside people like Peter Kilfoyle, gathering evidence. But at no time was she allowed out alone, such was the level of hostility she was experiencing.

Her work on behalf of the NCC earned her the title of 'witchfinder general' from Militant and praise from Kinnock who said, 'Nothing happens unless the Director of Organisation says so'. Enquiries in Bradford, Tower Hamlets and Brighton followed Liverpool, with Gould having to present the cases to the NCC on each occasion. During this time not one day went by when she did not speak to a solicitor.

As if the party was not already going through enough, Lambeth and other Labour councils kicked off a variety of madcap media-grabbing initiatives that also needed the Director's attention. The Party's Youth Section meanwhile had to be shut down due to Militant entryism and, under the guidance of Joyce Gould and other key officers such as Sally Morgan and Vicky Philips and the party's student wing, was rebuilt in the early 1990s as Young Labour.

The Militant episode finally culminated in 1987 with the expulsion of two Labour MPs. But it was not enough to save the party from defeat in the general election of that year. Indeed, Gould describes this defeat and that of 1992 as her two greatest disappointments. What sustained her during the whole period was, she says, her involvement with the women's section of the party. Gould retired in 1993 and was elevated to the House of Lords later that year, taking the title Baroness Gould of Potternewton, after an area in Leeds.

Now in the second half of her political career, Gould served as a Whip in opposition and in government, as PPS to the Leader of the House of Lords, Baroness Jay, and as a member of the Jenkins Commission looking at reform of the House of Commons. She retains a strong interest in international affairs having previously represented the party at the International Federation of Socialist Democratic Women. Also during her time at Party Headquarters she became involved in the American National Democratic Institute on the personal recommendation of Peter Mandelson, and travelled round Eastern Europe helping establish the new democracies. She was a member of the Council of Europe when she entered the Lords.

Having now been both part of the machine and a parliamentarian, Gould is clear that she wielded more influence in the three positions she held at HQ than she does as a parliamentarian. And it is an influence that we New Labourites should be thankful for, for without Joyce Gould, Neil Kinnock and others who stood firm in the mid-1980s, it is unlikely there would be a party for us to belong to.

Julie Minns

Philip Gould (1950–)

Philip Gould is Britain's leading professional political strategy and polling adviser. He played a key role in the modernisation of the Labour Party and the creation of 'New' Labour. He is a partner in the global political strategy firm of Gould, Greenberg, Carville Ltd (GGC), which he helped to create in 1997 and has been a director of the polling company NOP since 1997. He continues to advise Prime Minister Tony Blair.

Philip Gould was born in Beddington, Surrey, on 30 March 1950. He was educated at Knaphill Secondary Modern School, Woking (1961–66). Always inclined to anti-Establishment ideas and fascinated by politics, Philip joined the Labour Party in 1966 and has been an active member ever since. For a couple of years after 1966 the rebel in Philip took hold and he spent his time at rock concerts; on demonstrations; working for six months with recently discharged criminals in Camberwell, South London; working for six months with delinquent children in Pontefract, Yorkshire, on a Rowntree Trust programme; and working on building sites. But he saw that if he was ever to help create a better society he had to complete a formal education. He then went to East London College (1968–71), Sussex University, where he obtained a BA in Politics (1971–74), and the London School of Economics, where he obtained a masters degree in the History of Political Thought (1974–75).

After university Philip Gould embarked on a career in communications. For a decade, Philip worked in a succession of advertising agencies. He began as an Account Director with Wasey, Campbell-Ewald (1975–79). He became a Director of Tinker and Partners (1979–81). He was a founder partner of Brignull, LeBas, Gould (1981–83). He went on to be a Group Board Director of Doyle, Dane, Bernbach (1984–85). As a Sloane Fellow, he went to the London Business School (1984–85), where he passed with distinction. But after ten years Philip was looking for something more meaningful. The directorships, studies and extra qualifications were not enough for him. He felt a need to reconnect with fellow radicals. He felt he needed a change.

Big changes in all aspects of Philip Gould's life came in 1985. Philip met the new Director of Communications of the Labour Party, Peter Mandelson, and persuaded him that the ponderous Labour campaign machine could benefit from the advice of Labour supporters working in the advertising and communications industry. Philip set up his own company, Philip Gould Associates, to manage his various initiatives, including a burgeoning programme of advice and support to the Labour Party. Philip formed an invaluable partnership with another Labour supporter from the communications business, Deborah Mattinson, who worked with him on Labour party projects (for a time, between 1986 and 1989, the company was named Gould-Mattinson Associates). Also that year Philip married publisher Gail Rebuck. Philip and Gail now have two daughters.

The intervention of Philip Gould in Labour's internal discussions sparked a wholesale review of how Labour presented itself to voters. To support the review, Gould-Mattinson Associates created and managed a body called the Shadow Communications Agency (SCA). The purpose of the SCA was to marshal experienced communicators from the private sector who volunteered to advise and work with the Labour Party. Through this arrangement, and elsewhere, extensive public opinion research was done on Labour's behalf. Gould interpreted this research to develop a political strategy which demanded dramatic changes in how Labour conducted itself. Philip led the modernisation process in all Labour's communications and campaigning. This revamp covered language and style, colour and logo, advertising of all kinds, polling techniques, party television broadcasts (during and between elections), the themes used and the messages delivered. Philip also gave strategic advice to show how all these factors fit together in a campaign. He played a vital part in each of the '87, '92 and '97 elections.

His expertise and his reputation growing, Philip was called upon to advise Bill Clinton in the Presidential election of 1992, and again in 1996. He has also advised the governing, or left-of-centre, parties of Denmark, Greece, Jamaica, The Netherlands, Norway and Sweden on their national election campaigning. In the period 1993/4 he co-ordinated the European Parliament elections of the Party of the Group of European Socialists across the European Union. Since 1994 he has been one of Tony Blair's most valued political advisers. In a merger with similar talents across the Atlantic, Philip Gould combined with celebrated American political campaigners Stanley B. Greenberg and James Carville to form GGC in 1997.

After all that he has done to make Labour electable again, Philip Gould is aware that there is one more important truth which most Labour Party members have not yet grasped. In order to stay in touch with its supporters a political party must constantly re-assess and re-shape itself to suit its times. He has tried to drive this fact home by writing a book which documents how the party was renewed. It is called *The Unfinished Revolution – How the modernisers saved the Labour Party* (1998). The title alone makes Philip's point, that the process of renewal is not finished – nor can it ever be finished if the Labour Party wishes to continue as a relevant political force. We shall see if the party is paying attention.

Rex Osborn

Ted Graham (Lord Graham of Edmonton) (1925–)

Thomas Edward (Ted) Graham was born on Tyneside on 26 March 1925 and has been employed in one capacity or another by the Co-operative Movement all his life. Although passing what was called the Eleven Plus in 1935 he was deprived of that chance due to the economic circumstances of his family – his father was on the dole and he was the eldest of five children. When he left school at the age of 14 in 1939 he was top boy at his elementary school and his testimonial simply said 'This Boy is too good for a dead-end job'. He saw service in the Royal Marines during the war, and, in preparation for D-Day suffered severe injuries by what is now called 'friendly fire' – shot by his own men. He rose to the rank of Corporal.

He married Margaret in 1950 and they have two sons, Martin and Ian. He advanced up the ladder within the Co-operative Movement, being successively National Youth Organiser, Education Secretary, Co-operative Union Sectional Secretary and National Secretary of the Co-operative Party. He had began his taste for politics when he became the Prime Minister of the Tyneside Youth Parliament where, amongst others, his political opponents included Peter Cadogan, who went on to become the Secretary to the Committee of 100, and Lord Lambton. He had his first parliamentary contest in 1966 when he fought Iain MacLeod in Enfield West. He was a member and became Leader of the London Borough of Enfield Council 1960–68. He entered parliament as Member for Edmonton in 1974 until 1983. Having been PPS to the Minister of State for Prices and Consumer Protection 1974–76, Jim Callaghan put him in the Government Whip's Office in 1976, and when Labour lost office he continued in opposition until becoming deputy to Roy Hattersley and then Gerald Kaufman as Environment Spokesman. Having lost his seat in 1983, Michael Foot sent him to the Lords as Lord Graham of Edmonton, where he went straight into the Opposition Whips Office, also serving variously as an Opposition spokesman on the Environment, Northern Ireland, Defence and Tourism. He became Opposition Chief Whip in 1990 and served there until the General Election of 1997, completing almost 20 years in the Whips Office in both

Houses. Lord Richard, then Lords Opposition Leader, wrote a note (cited in Janet Jones' *Labour of Love*, 1999) to Tony Blair on 30 April 1997, the eve of the general election recommending that in the event of a Labour victory Graham be appointed Government Chief Whip: 'Ted Graham is the obvious and best candidate for the job ... Frankly, I think he is the only person who can be guaranteed to produce the attendance necessary from our somewhat elderly troops to make sure that we can keep a House.' Blair, however, chose to appoint a younger man.

Having missed out on early formal education, he became the first MP to gain a degree from the Open University, in 1976, and whilst other MPs have entered the House with an OU degree, or gained one after leaving he still remains the only MP to have gained the degree whilst in the Commons. He went on to be awarded an Honorary Master of the University, and served on the Council of the University for nine years.

In 1997 he became the Chairman of the United Kingdom Co-operative Council, the body which unifies the CWS, Co-operative Bank, Co-op Insurance and the newer forms of co-operation such as credit unions, housing, worker co-ops etc. He served as Chair of the Labour Peers Group from 1997 to 2000, and was made a member of the Privy Council in 1998. He remains the President of the Edmonton Labour Party, and a member of the Editorial Board of the *House Magazine*. He is the President of the Institute of Meat and a Freeman of the Worshipful Company of Butchers. Perhaps he will be remembered most for the more than forty obituaries of Labour colleagues he has written for the *House Magazine*, or for increasing awareness of deep-vein thrombosis.

Greg Rosen

Willie Graham (1887–1932)

The fall of the 1929–31 Labour government was a profound shock to the whole Labour movement. For some, it was said, the shock proved literally fatal. Willie Graham, President of the Board of Trade throughout 1929–31, had been one of its leading lights and had he lived would undoubtedly have been one of the heavy hitters of the Attlee government. Ironically, for it was Hugh Dalton himself who was in 1945 to fulfil this role, albeit later than he expected, Dalton's diary in April tipped Graham as being in his view the likely successor as Labour's Chancellor of the Exchequer to his friend and mentor Philip Snowden.

By the summer of 1931, Graham was increasingly taking Clynes' place in the government's so-called 'Big Five', alongside MacDonald, Henderson, Snowden and Thomas. It was these five who on 30 July 1931 were designated the Cabinet Economy Committee to consider the May Report. Although Graham was as passionately opposed to a revenue tariff as Snowden, unlike his mentor he was prepared to countenance it as an alternative to cutting the dole. 'There was,' as Roy Jenkins put it in *The Chancellors*, 'a bitter personal split as a result, which, such was the burning force of Snowden's personality to the few exposed to its direct rays, many people thought contributed to Graham's death at the age of forty-four five months later.'

His sudden illness and death at his Hendon home on 8 January 1932 came barely two months after he had lost his seat in the general election of 27 October 1931. With the fall of the government, he had on 26 August 1931 become joint Deputy Leader alongside Clynes, later presenting the shadow budget at the 1931 Labour conference. The 1931 election was the first in which broadcasting had played a full part and Graham gave one of three Labour broadcasts (Clynes and Henderson giving the other two).

He had been one of Labour's most able ministers. As President of the Board of Trade he had in February 1930 negotiated a 'tariff truce,' under which, in order to boost world trade, eleven countries including Britain had undertaken not to increase tariffs until April 1931. With Snowden's backing he secured Britain's ratification in the face of the growing protectionist instincts of MacDonald, Thomas and Hartshorn. He was extensively involved in the negotiations at The Hague and Geneva over German reparations payments and was responsible for the attempt to rationalise and reform the mining industry that comprised the coal mines bill. As Financial Secretary to the Treasury and Snowden's deputy throughout the 1924 Labour government, he had piloted two complex pensions bills through the Commons, and in late 1924 had been appointed a Privy Councillor.

In February 1922, *Manchester Guardian* editor C P Scott confided to his diary that Henderson was tipping Graham as a potential Labour Foreign Secretary. Graham himself, however, was interested primarily in becoming an economic minister and in avoiding the Scottish Office, which he regarded as a dead end. In opposition from 1924 to 1929 he served as both an elected member of the shadow cabinet and chair of the powerful Commons Public Accounts Committee.

In 1918 he had become Labour MP for Edinburgh Central, serving continuously until 1931. He was at first Edinburgh's only Labour MP, and his Parliamentary style was less confrontational and 'obstreperous', as he put it to his brother, than that of his Clydeside comrades. His manifest ability and expertise, particularly in economics, were swiftly recognised, and he was persuaded to serve on a veritable plethora of committees and enquiries including the 1919 Royal Commission on Income Tax; the 1920–21 Royal Commission on Oxbridge; the 1919–20 Speaker's Conference on Devolution; and the 1920 committee on railway agreements. Also in 1919 he married Ethel Dobson, the daughter of a Harrogate cashier, but they did not have children.

Born on 29 July 1887 at Peebles, he was the eldest of the seven children of George Graham, master-builder. Securing scholarships at Peebles Public School and George Heriot's, Edinburgh, he left school at 16 to spend two years as a clerk at the War Office, until in 1905 he went to work for a Selkirk newspaper. He joined the ILP in 1906. Spending the following years as an Edinburgh-based freelance journalist, by 1911 he had earned enough to begin an MA in Economics at Edinburgh University, graduating in 1915 and gaining a further LLB in 1917 and in 1927 an honorary LLD. At university he became a leading light in the Edinburgh University Fabian Society and expanding his political involvement further, was elected to Edinburgh Council in 1913. From 1915 to 1918 he was an economics lecturer for the WEA, 'but with rather more go than is usual in his type,' as Hugh Dalton rather condescendingly conceded to his diary of his non-Oxbridge rival. In 1921 he published *The Wages of Labour*. A biography, *Willie Graham*, by his brother T N Graham was published in 1948.

Greg Rosen

Bernie Grant   (1944–2000)

Bernie Grant wholeheartedly engaged with radical politics throughout his life. From the bauxite mines of Guyana to Britain's Parliament, Grant carved a political path few parliamentarians dared. As one of Britain's first black parliamentary figures, Grant was an outspoken populist. He often openly challenged the party line as an advocate for ethnic minorities, women, youths, the poor and the elderly. He also fought racism and intolerance in England as well in Europe as chairman of the Standing Conference on Race Equality in Europe (SCORE). As a result, Bernie Grant ended his life as a revered and respected politician, a dedicated constituency MP and a national and international anti-racism campaigner, who had gained the admiration of politicians across party lines for his tireless activism and commitment to issues of social importance.

Although Tony Blair counted him among his friends, describing him as a man of powerful convictions – a politician who did not hesitate to vote against his own government on behalf of his constituents – for most of his Parliamentary career Grant had to cope with press vilification. It began in 1985, when riots sparked in reaction to the death of Cynthia Jarrat erupted on the Tottenham Broadwater Farm estate. Jarrat, a resident of Broadwater Farm, died suddenly following an unnecessary police raid at her home. In the ensuing protests, a policeman, Keith Blakelock, was murdered. At the time uninformed of the policeman's death, Grant, then Labour Leader of Haringey Council, in an attempt to explain what had happened, commented that the youths on the estate felt that the police had received a 'bloody good hiding'. After he was told of the murder the next day, he issued a statement condemning the horrible assault, but the damage had been done; he was misquoted and condemned across the country. During the 1980s, he was branded with alarming regularity 'Barmy Bernie of the Loony Left' by tabloids, and along with other radical members of the party, he became anathema to a Labour leadership who considered his grassroots politics anachronistic to their increasingly centre-of-left policies. He was dubbed by Conservative Home Secretary Douglas Hurd a 'high priest of racial conflict'.

It was perhaps a label that Grant may have adopted proudly. For after all, he dedicated his life to illuminating the burning issues of race and class – issues that until black representatives began to question in respect to their urban constituencies were not considered serious variables in British political life.

Bernie Grant was born the second of five children on 17 February 1944 in Georgetown, British Guyana. His parents, Eric and Lilly, descendants of African slaves, were both schoolteachers. An ardent student, Grant won a government scholarship to St. Stanislaus College, a Jesuit-run secondary school.

In 1961, aged only 17, Grant left school to become a lab technician in the Guyana bauxite plants. Faced with the harsh realities of colonial inequality, Grant joined a radical youth wing and immersed himself in labour politics. These early years spent analysing economic, political and social injustice and, most significantly, racial oppression, helped mould the passion, vision and courage that would define his future politics.

In 1963 Grant moved to England with his mother Lilly and sister Rosamond, where they settled in the North London borough of Haringey. He attended Tottenham Technical College where he took his A levels. He continued his education at Edinburgh's Heriot Watt University, studying for a mining and engineering degree, but withdrew from the course in his second year in protest at whites' only work-experience scholarships to South Africa.

Back in London he became a railway clerk, a postal employee and international telephonist and in 1978 a NUPE Area Officer. He joined the Marxist Party briefly, but left it to join the Labour Party, which he saw as the only realistic force for delivering social justice to Britain's minorities and working class.

In 1978 he became a Haringey Borough councillor, where he met Sharon Lawrence, a fellow, white councillor whom he would eventually marry. Just one year later in 1979, Margaret Thatcher was elected Prime Minister, and race relations in Britain plummeted. Grant led a campaign against the rising white-supremacist National Front during this time and though many celebrated him for his efforts, the press ironically depicted him as a dangerous extremist. Grant continued to campaign hard within the Labour Party for a stronger voice for black people. In 1985 he was elected leader of Haringey Borough Council, becoming the first black leader of a local political body in Europe.

He became Tottenham's MP in 1987, replacing the veteran incumbent Norman Atkinson. He and fellow MPs Paul Boateng and Diane Abbott were the first black MPs to enter Parliament in half a century. Grant was the most senior, the one with the most radical grassroots background and certainly the most controversial parliamentarian. On his first day in Parliament, he cut a dashing figure dressed in African robes. It was a significant gesture not missed by his supporters. As representative of one of the most vibrant and diverse multi-ethnic areas in Europe, he had aligned himself with a transatlantic tradition of black freedom political figures firmly rooted in anti-colonial, anti-racist, radical democratic politics, who were nonetheless dedicated to working within existing political structures.

Bernie Grant worked tirelessly for his constituents. During periods of racial tension and stressful economic times, he was a champion for black youth and the black community. He was often the solitary voice in authority translating the frustrations and desires of his urban community to the rest of the country as well as to the party. He was also an effective bridge between a frustrated black community and the local police. When in 1993, Joy Garner died after an encounter with the police, Bernie Grant moved quickly to prevent another Broadwater Farm. This time round, entrusted with leadership by his community, he provided absolutely crucial political leadership and effectively defused rising tensions.

As controversial as he may have been perceived by wider society, Grant had enormous respect among black Britons. He attracted international friends and allies in South African Nelson Mandela and American Democrat Reverend Jesse Jackson. He campaigned for anti-apartheid and reparations for the descendants of slavery. He was a supporter of revolutionary governments, feminist causes, black studies and an inclusive school curriculum. But although he inhabited a politically left-of-centre terrain, he held several convictions to which natural allies took exception. He was, for instance, a monarchist, believing that the monarchy bound Britain to the Commonwealth. He supported Harriet Harman's decision to educate her children at an opt-out grammar school. While he sent his own children to local schools, he pointed out that middle-class parents could afford to take a principled stand over the future of their children's education. Their postcodes were a guaranteed passport to quality state schools where their children could be sure of getting over 5 GCSEs grade A to C and then three 'A' levels.

Increasing illness overshadowed the final years of Bernie Grant's political career. He continued to work as an MP in spite of heart trouble, kidney failure and failing eyesight. In October 1998, he had a triple bypass after a history of ill health caused by diabetes and phlebitis, a circulatory disease.

Grant continued to return to the House of Commons, even though he was clearly ill. He advised the Prime Minister and the Home Secretary Jack Straw on race relations and foreign affairs and was valued by central government as a serious politician and an authentic voice of his constituents. Indeed until his sudden death on 8 April 2000, Grant continued to campaign for an increase in black and Asian Labour Parliamentary candidates.

It was Grant's striving to understand the realities and needs of his constituents that forever ensure him the respect and unswerving affection that large segments of Tottenham still feel for him. It was his determined pursuit of justice for the underdog that made Bernie Grant a national and international leader for those who needed a voice, who needed someone to articulate wordless aspirations and misunderstood frustrations. It was Grant's alternative agenda – his hope rooted in a pragmatic, radical and economically just Britain – that his supporters continue to work towards today. He is succeeded by three children and his wife Sharon, who became not only his partner in life, but also his political ally in working toward a vision of an inclusive and truly representative politics.

David Lammy MP

Victor Grayson   (1881–1920?)

Victor Grayson is one of those rare people where the myth is far greater than the reality. He was only briefly in the public eye, yet he had great influence on generations of socialists and Labour activists in the first half of the twentieth century. Grayson was a charismatic figure and a powerful orator. He was only 25 when he was elected as an MP. He later married a beautiful actress, enlisted as a soldier in World War I and then disappeared in mysterious circumstances. It is easy to understand how the myth prevailed.

He was born in Taliesin Street in a working-class district of Liverpool on 5 September 1881. He received his early education locally at St Matthew's Church of England School. On leaving he was apprenticed as a turner at the nearby Bankhall Engine Works. As a teenager, religion caught his interest and the minister at Anfield Unitarian Church recognised Victor's potential, encouraging him to take Sunday School and even assist in services. Victor seemed to have found his vocation and in 1904, at the age of 23, he entered the Home Missionary College in Manchester. Socialist politics began to interest him. Towards the end of 1905 he increasingly was in demand to address meetings, which eventually led to him being selected in January 1907 as the Parliamentary candidate for Colne Valley.

His selection led to a dispute with the Independent Labour Party (ILP) nationally but this was overtaken by events when a by-election was called for 18 July 1907. Time and place conspired for an eventful by-election. Grayson captured the imagination in this traditional Liberal stronghold. Socialists throughout the north flocked to his assistance. Keir Hardie send a message of support and Philip Snowden came to help. The Pankhurst family and the suffragettes descended on the constituency. The candidate's religious background found a resonance and over forty clergymen joined him under the slogan, 'Socialism – God's Gospel for Today'. The effect was unstoppable and Grayson won a spectacular victory as the Socialist and Labour candidate. Once an MP he quickly became the hero of party activists throughout the country. His flamboyant speeches and his dismissive attitude to his own Party's Parliamentary leadership only further enhanced his popularity. But it became clear he was not a team player.

His unsympathetic views towards trade unions, which he regarded as more sectarian than socialist, only accentuated his problems, and eventually, many of the Parliamentary leaders began attacking him with stories of his sumptuous life-style. He began to be absent from the Commons, and in 1909 only voted in 5.5 per cent of divisions.

During this period he wrote three pamphlets: *The Destiny of the Mob* (1908), *God's Country* (1908) and *The Appeal for Socialism* (1909). In addition he co-authored *The Problem of Parliament* (1909).

At the general election of January 1910 Grayson faced a determined Liberal campaign and came bottom of the poll. His core supporters remained loyal but he had alienated some moderates. Grayson moved to London and contested Kennington as the Socialist candidate in December 1910, coming bottom of the poll with a mere 408 votes. In Spring 1911 he agreed to become the Parliamentary candidate for Colne Valley but never contested the seat again. He continued to be active in left-wing politics writing regularly for Blatchford's *Clarion* and addressing meetings. In August 1911 he left the ILP and was instrumental in forming the British Socialist Party, but by now his interest was waning.

On 7 November 1912 he married a 25-year-old actress, Ruth Nightingale, at Chelsea Registry Office. His financial affairs worsened and he only avoided bankruptcy when his father-in-law intervened. On 13 April 1914 he became a father to a daughter, Elaine. In early 1915 Ruth obtained work with a Shakespearean Company on a tour of Australasia. Grayson accompanied her and he addressed pro-war meetings, eventually enlisting in the New Zealand Army on 28 November 1916. As 45001 Private Grayson he disembarked in France in September 1917. On 12 October he was wounded at Passchendaele and although recovering from a hip wound he was eventually discharged from the army on 7 March 1918 with neurasthenia. This was a severe blow to Grayson, for he much enjoyed his period in the forces and especially the camaraderie. Immediately prior to his discharge, he suffered an even more grievous blow when his wife died in childbirth on 10 February.

He returned to the public platform, in both an official and non-official capacity to support the war effort. Following the war his political links with the left were completely severed and he moved into a luxurious suite in St James's, London. He enjoyed an expensive lifestyle of drinking, dining and the theatre in association with the likes of Horatio Bottomley and Maundy Gregory, the man who sold the honours for Lloyd George.

In September 1920 Victor Grayson walked out of his apartment accompanied by two men, got into a taxi and was never positively sighted again. Key biographies of Grayson are Reg Groves, *The Strange Case of Victor Grayson* (1975) and David Clark, *Victor Grayson, Labour's Lost Leader* (1985).

Rt Hon. Lord Clark

Arthur Greenwood   (1880–1954)

Arthur Greenwood was a leading figure in the Labour party for almost three decades. A popular figure, he had great ability, but a serious drink problem held him back and, by the time of his death in 1954, he was a largely marginal figure in the party. Nonetheless, he was one of the leading Labourites of his generation, and made a significant contribution to the party's development.

Greenwood was born in Hunslett, Leeds, on 8 February 1880, the son of a businessman. He was educated at Leeds Higher Grade School and Victoria (now Leeds) University. He then became a school teacher, before moving on to become a Lecturer in, and Head of the Department of, Economics at Huddersfield Technical College. He also lectured for the Workers' Educational Association. In 1904 he married Catherine Ainsworth Brown, who outlived him: they had a son and a daughter. In 1914, shortly before the outbreak of the First World War, he became general secretary of the Council for the Study of International Relations, and was appointed to Lloyd George's secretariat after the latter became Prime Minister in 1916. From 1917 he served as assistant secretary of the Ministry of Reconstruction under Christopher Addison.

By this time Greenwood was closely involved in Labour politics, and at the December 1918 general election he stood as the party's candidate at Southport, but was heavily defeated. In March 1920 he took over from G D H Cole as secretary to the Labour Party's advisory committees, and in 1922 became secretary of the party's research department. At the 1922 general election he won Nelson and Colne for Labour, holding the seat in 1923. In the first Labour government (1924), Greenwood was appointed as Parliamentary Secretary to the Ministry of Health, under John Wheatley, where he was partly responsible for one of the administration's few concrete achievements, the 1924 Housing Act. At the 1924 election which followed the government's fall, Greenwood held Nelson and Colne very narrowly in a straight fight with a Liberal. From then until 1929 Greenwood's main work was in the Labour party organisation, and he was not once elected to the shadow cabinet.

At the 1929 election Greenwood held his seat by a convincing margin, and Ramsay MacDonald, in forming his second cabinet, appointed him Minister of Health. In difficult economic circumstances, Greenwood was as successful as any other home front minister. He finally succumbed to growing pressure to allow local authorities to offer advice on contraception. He piloted through the 1930 Housing Act, which gave subsidies to local authorities to clear slums and build replacement housing. Widows' pensions were also improved. In the crisis which led to the collapse of the government in August 1931, Greenwood was one of the leaders of ministerial resistance to any cut in unemployment benefit. After the fall of the government he emerged as one of the party's leading figures, but at the October 1931 general election he was defeated, losing Nelson and Colne to a Conservative on a massive swing.

In the aftermath of defeat, Greenwood returned to full-time work at Labour party headquarters, but was soon re-elected (albeit with a majority of just 344) to parliament at a by-election in Wakefield in April 1932. However, the leftist temper of the PLP under Lansbury was not to his more moderate taste, and he did not really emerge as one of the party's leaders in parliament; in any case, the need for Labour to develop policy was so obvious that the research department took up much of his time. When Lansbury resigned shortly before the 1935 general election, there were attempts to manoeuvre Greenwood into the position, but in the event Attlee took over. At that election, for which Greenwood drafted the party's manifesto, he held Wakefield, but Labour was heavily defeated overall. Immediately afterwards, Greenwood stood against Morrison and Attlee for the leadership, but he took only 33 votes out of 135 cast and was eliminated after the first ballot. In the run-off, most of his supporters – who included many who were, like Greenwood, Freemasons – switched to Attlee, helping the latter to defeat Morrison. Morrison refused to serve as deputy leader, so Greenwood took the post, retaining it until succeeded by Morrison in 1945.

In the later 1930s, Greenwood was called upon to act as Labour's leader during Attlee's periodic illnesses: in September 1939 Attlee's prolonged absence meant that Greenwood led Labour at the time of the outbreak of war. Greenwood's forceful support for action against Nazi aggression was important in forcing Chamberlain to declare war. That November, he was nominated for the leadership of the party against Attlee, but, along with Dalton and Morrison, refused to go forward to an election; by now, in any case, he was in poor health, exacerbated by continued heavy drinking. In May 1940, on the formation of Churchill's Coalition, he was appointed, along with Attlee, as a Labour member of the five-strong war cabinet, and in January 1941 he was placed in charge of reconstruction planning. He was not, however, a success, and was dropped from the war cabinet in February 1942 (in the same year his twenty-year tenure as head of the party's research department came to an end). He then served for the rest of the war as titular leader of the opposition and chairman of the PLP, an important post in terms of proceeding parliamentary business, but a clear demotion all the same. Even so, it was a sign of his continuing popularity in the party that he was elected as its Treasurer in 1943.

At the 1945 election Greenwood once again held Wakefield, almost doubling his majority, and was appointed Lord Privy Seal in the Attlee government; however, he was not a success in his main role of co-ordinating national insurance policy. In April 1947 Lord Inman succeeded him as Lord Privy Seal; he held on as Minister without Portfolio until that September, but was then, in effect, sacked. He held Wakefield in 1950 and 1951, and remained Party Treasurer until his death, despite considerable misgivings among his senior colleagues. Greenwood died on 9 June 1954. His son, Anthony Greenwood, went on to serve as a minister in the Labour government of 1964 to 1970.

Arthur Greenwood was a man of considerable ability. An 'intellectual', he was nevertheless able to draw support widely within the party, not least among trade unionists. As a minister, however, his record was, at best, mixed. In addition, distrust of his masonic connections and, more significantly, his drink problem created serious obstacles to him. Both of his last two periods in office ended with him being effectively sacked. Overall, Greenwood's massive potential was to a large extent unfulfilled.

Greenwood never wrote his memoirs, but did publish a number of works, of which perhaps the most significant were *Juvenile Labour Exchanges* (1911), *Public Ownership of the Liquor Trade* (1920), *The Education of the Citizen* (1920), *The Labour Outlook* (1929), and *Why We Fight: Labour's Case* (1940). Somewhat surprisingly, there is no published biography of Greenwood.

Andrew Thorpe

Tony Greenwood (Lord Greenwood of Rossendale) (1911–82)

Arthur William James 'Tony' Greenwood was born in Leeds on 14 September 1911, the son of Arthur Greenwood. He was educated at Merchant Taylors' School and Balliol College, Oxford, becoming President of the Union in 1933. He married Gillian Crawshay Williams in 1940 and they had two daughters.

Tony Greenwood joined the Labour Party at the age of 14, and before the war had been selected as prospective candidate for Colchester, but did not in fact contest the seat in 1945. He was a borough councillor in Hampstead and led the minority Labour group from 1945 to 1949. In February 1946 he successfully defended the highly marginal seat of Heywood and Radcliffe, Lancashire, in a by-election. During the Attlee government he was regarded as a very promising young MP, serving as PPS to the Postmaster-General in 1949–50 and vice-chair of the Parliamentary Labour Party 1950–51.

The boundary revision of 1950 abolished Greenwood's seat of Heywood and Radcliffe and dispersed its parts to join constituencies which had elected Conservative MPs even in 1945 – Royton and Bury, respectively. Greenwood was selected for Rossendale instead in 1950 and represented the seat for twenty years, although it was never safe – his majorities oscillated between about 1,500 and a peak of 4,109 in 1966. His favourable national and local profile (he was apparently sometimes called 'the mill girls' pin-up') and the trend to Labour in East Lancashire in the 1950s and 1960s helped him maintain a hold on a very marginal seat. Labour lost Rossendale in 1970, even with the redoubtable Betty Boothroyd as candidate.

Greenwood's star rose in the 1950s. He was one of the most articulate and attractive exponents of left-wing arguments in the Labour Party and a good performer on television and the platform. In 1954 he was elected to the NEC in the constituency section after Bevan stepped down to contest the Party Treasurership; he had become increasingly closely identified with the Bevanites in the early 1950s. In the split of the Bevanites in 1957 Greenwood was a unilateralist, and the following year he marched with CND at Aldermaston. He was drawn to the left primarily because of his beliefs about international affairs, not his rather unfocused domestic socialism.

Greenwood held a succession of shadow Cabinet posts, including home affairs and education. On 13 October 1960 Greenwood resigned from the shadow cabinet over defence, and announced that he would stand for the leadership, but on 29 October Harold Wilson said that he would stand, and Greenwood stood down and backed Wilson; it was felt that a centre-left candidate stood a better chance than the more left-wing Greenwood. Greenwood's own challenge to Gaitskell in November 1961 took place after Gaitskell had prevailed at the 1961 conference and the party was in the mood for unity. He attracted 59 votes to 171 for Gaitskell, and was persuaded not to stand in the 1963 leadership election to unite the left-wing vote behind Wilson. He was chairman of the party in 1963–64.

After Labour won the 1964 election Greenwood joined the Cabinet as Colonial Secretary, with a brief from Harold Wilson to 'work himself out of a job'. Greenwood was a sponsor of the Movement for Colonial Freedom and took the job gladly. The Conservative government in 1959–64 had overseen independence for the bulk of Britain's remaining colonies, but Greenwood accelerated the timetable even further. Gambia and the Maldives became independent in 1965; Barbados, Lesotho, Botswana and Guyana were independent in 1966 on the basis of Greenwood's work. It was the last substantial part of the British Empire, and the job of

Colonial Secretary disappeared in 1966. Greenwood was moved in a reshuffle in December 1965, before the post vanished, to become the minister for Overseas Development, but he only remained there until August 1966.

Greenwood's next ministry, Housing and Local Government, was the occasion of the decline of his political career and reputation. Housing was a key issue for Labour. The March 1966 manifesto proclaimed that 'housing is our top priority' and set a target of 500,000 houses for the year 1969/70, which had the status of 'not a promise, a pledge', according to Wilson. One of his techniques of expanding housing was a boost to the New Towns, one of the successes of 1945–51. The most ambitious project was the new city of Milton Keynes in north Buckinghamshire, which Greenwood designated in 1967. In 1968 more cut-price New Towns were designated at the existing large towns of Northampton and Peterborough.

Housing, however, was the victim of cuts in 1966 and, more seriously, of the post-devaluation retrenchment of early 1968. Greenwood's reputation suffered for being too 'helpful' to the Chancellor, and his predecessor Crossman was continually questioning his competence as a minister. Greenwood's alignment with Wilson led him into a humiliating episode in July 1968 when he was a candidate for General Secretary of the Labour Party. Wilson supported him for the post, and all appeared to be going well as he was recommended unanimously by the selection committee of the NEC. However, at the second meeting George Brown turned up and proposed Harry Nicholas instead, so two names went to the full NEC. The NEC voted by 14–12 to reject Greenwood and approve Harry Nicholas as the new General Secretary. It was one of the most unpleasant and uncomradely occasions in Labour history; Barbara Castle had 'seldom felt so nauseated by a meeting of the NEC and that is putting it very high indeed.' Brown, who had overseen this plot, argued that Nicholas would be better at the job, which had hitherto been organisational rather than front-rank political, but there was no doubt that Greenwood suffered because he was perceived as Wilson's man.

Very little went right for Greenwood after the defeat for the General Secretary job, which he did not particularly want in the first place. Housing continued to be deeply problematic, with the cuts making the 500,000 target totally impossible and the Ronan Point disaster bringing an abrupt halt to high-rise construction, and by the end of Greenwood's term of office the emphasis was shifting from massive new construction into rehabilitation of older properties. A ministerial reorganisation in October 1969 cost Greenwood his Cabinet position. The Ministry of Housing and Local Government was put under a large Ministry of Local Government and Regional Planning headed by Tony Crosland who spoke for it in Cabinet. Wilson, characteristically, described Greenwood's job as being 'a minister of Cabinet rank outside the Cabinet.'

In May 1970 Greenwood suddenly vacated his NEC place and his constituency, having been offered a seat on the board of the Commonwealth Development Corporation by Wilson. It was understood that he would become the Corporation's Chairman later on in 1970, but Labour's surprise defeat in the June 1970 election destroyed the plan. The incoming Heath government refused to confirm his appointment to the Corporation and he was left without a career or a livelihood. Created Baron Greenwood of Rossendale in 1970, he took several business directorships and worked for charities during the 1970s, and died suddenly at home of a heart attack on 12 April 1982.

Greenwood's legacy to the Labour Party and to British politics is insubstantial. His main achievement was putting his sincere belief in colonial freedom into practice, although by the time he became Colonial Secretary there was little of the empire left. His record at Housing is under-rated: his New Towns have been successful and he started to bring the era of mass demolition and high rises to a close. His promise was never fulfilled, partly because of the flimsiness of Bevanism as a political programme, partly through his own lack of drive. But most of all Tony Greenwood's career stands as a cautionary tale of what happened to a man who put too much loyalty and trust in Harold Wilson.

Dr Lewis Baston

James Griffiths (1890–1975)

James (christened Jeremiah) Griffiths was an outstanding example of the links between the unions and the Labour Party in its classic phase. Unlike many trade unionists, he proved to be a major figure in the political as well as industrial wing of the Labour movement in the era spanning the premierships of Attlee and Wilson. He also played a notable part in the political affairs of his native Wales.

He was born in Betws, Ammanford, Carmarthenshire, on 19 September 1890, the son of a blacksmith. He attended Betws board school and at the age of 13 went down the local anthracite pit. The area was strongly Welsh-speaking and chapel-going; his brother was a famous eisteddfodic bard. The young Griffiths was deeply influenced by the religious revival of 1904–5 and by local advocates of the 'new theology' of social Christianity. In 1908 he became a founder-member of the local branch of the Independent Labour Party. He also played a lively role in left-wing workers' forums at the 'White House', a former vicarage in Ammanford. He campaigned vigorously against British involvement in the First World War, and against conscription. In 1919–21 he was a student at the left-wing Central Labour College in London, along with other young miners such as Aneurin Bevan and Morgan Phillips. However his own socialism was always ethical rather than Marxist and he rejected class-war ideas.

He became prominent in the South Wales Miners Federation and was elected miners' agent in the anthracite district in 1925. Inevitably, he took an active part during the General Strike of 1926. He rose to become vice-president of the SWMF and in 1934 its president alongside communists like Arthur Horner. Griffiths launched a campaign to build up union membership, to repel company unionism and to gain for the miners a wage rise, the first for ten years. He handled with calm statesmanship the 'stay-down' strikes at Nine Mile Point colliery, Monmouthshire, in 1935, after which the blackleg 'Spencer' union was totally destroyed in South Wales.

Jim Griffiths (as he had become known) always had a passion for politics, and had been agent for the Labour Party in Llanelli from 1922 to 1925. In 1936 he was elected MP for Llanelli in a by-election with a majority of over 16,000, and resigned his presidency of the Miners' Federation thereafter. It was a rock-solid mining stronghold, and Griffiths held it with massive majorities until he retired in 1970. He became prominent in campaigns against the scourge of tuberculosis and published a pamphlet, *The Price Wales Pays for Poverty* in 1939, along with a Welsh pamphlet *Glo* [Coal]. During the war years, he was a major spokesman on social security. He had been prominent in drawing up Labour's scheme for social insurance early in 1942, many months before the Beveridge Report was published. In February 1943 he moved a motion condemning the Churchill coalition government for failing to promote Beveridge's proposals; in a remarkable rebellion for wartime politics, 121 other MPs joined him in voting against the government, among them the aged David Lloyd George. He was also a leading figure in plans for post-war economic and social reconstruction. When the Attlee government took office in July 1945, Griffiths as predicted became Minister of National Insurance, outside the Cabinet.

Along with his fellow Welshman, Aneurin Bevan, the Minister of Health and Housing, with whom he always had a somewhat wary relationship, Griffiths became a pioneer of the welfare state. His National Insurance Act of 1946 was a major measure which created a comprehensive system of social security and became a cornerstone of welfare policy thereafter. His Industrial Injuries Act of 1948 drew upon his own experience as a working miner. He was active on the party National Executive, and served as chairman of the party in 1948–49. Here he worked with Bevan in trying to push on with the public ownership of industrial assurance companies. But Herbert Morrison feared this would alienate ordinary policy holders and in the end 'mutualisation', a watered down version of Griffiths's scheme, fell by the wayside.

After the general election of February 1950 Griffiths entered the Cabinet as Colonial Secretary in succession to Creech Jones. He was much involved in promoting new constitutions in emerging colonial territories like Nigeria and Kenya. Despite his former pacifism, he also had to fight a fierce war against left-wing insurgents in Malaya. More controversially, he endorsed the idea of a Central African Federation for the Rhodesias and Nyasaland, but withdrew support after meeting the full force of black African opposition at the Victoria Falls conference in September 1951. He was an effective minister, and when Bevin, a dying man, left the Foreign Office, Griffiths was seriously considered as a replacement by Attlee, who wanted additional trade unionists in his government. In fact, the new Foreign Secretary was Morrison, who proved to be an undistinguished appointment.

After Labour's electoral defeat in October 1951, Griffiths played a leading part in the party's affairs in Opposition, topping the poll in the Shadow Cabinet elections of 1951–55. He sought to be a conciliator: in 1952 he was the only non-Bevanite elected to the Labour NEC. When Hugh Gaitskell became party leader, Griffiths was elected as his deputy in 1956, defeating Bevan by 141 votes to 111, and he remained in this post until October 1959 when Bevan briefly replaced him. Griffiths was always a moderate figure, clearly on the party right. He did not support the Campaign for Nuclear Disarmament, and when Gaitskell died in 1963 Griffiths cast his vote for George Brown as his successor.

Throughout his career, Griffiths had always been closely identified with the politics and the ethical socialism of his native Wales. He had unsuccessfully pressed for Wales to be recognised as an administrative unit in the nationalisation measures of the Attlee government. The adoption of a pledge to create a Welsh Secretary of State in the 1959 party manifesto owed much to Griffiths's influence over Gaitskell, and when Labour returned to government under Wilson in October 1964 Griffiths was appointed to serve as the first Welsh Secretary, at the age of 74. He developed the new office with some success, although a proposal for a new town in mid-Wales failed to be adopted. After retiring from the Cabinet in 1966 he championed the cause of Biafra in the Nigerian civil war. He also published a volume of memoirs, *Pages from Memory*, in 1969. He retired from Parliament in 1970, when Labour in South Wales faced an unexpected challenge from Plaid Cymru. He continued to write on behalf of Welsh devolution and membership of the European Common Market until his death at Teddington on 1 August 1975.

In 1918 Jim Griffiths had married a young socialist woman from Hampshire, Winnie Rutley, starting his first letter to her 'Dear Comrade'. Their marriage was exceptionally happy and they had two sons and two daughters. Griffiths was the embodiment of the nonconformist ethos so powerful in the making of the Labour Party, and his outlook was shaped by the comradeship of the pit and Welsh village community life. He was sometimes criticised for sentimentality and an excess of Welsh guile, but in general he was an extremely popular, warm-hearted politician. He was also a very capable minister under both Attlee and Wilson, successful as a welfare reformer, colonial minister and charter Welsh secretary. He became close to a whole generation of younger colonial leaders in Africa, Asia and the Caribbean; his wider interests included Welsh literature and rugby football. His career symbolized the 'labour alliance' of unions and party, and the ethos of Labour as a moral crusade with strong Christian overtones. He is undoubtedly one of the most notable trade unionists to have made a mark in Labour politics.

Apart from his autobiography, *Pages from Memory* (1969), biographical material on Griffiths may be found in J. Beverley Smith, *James Griffiths and his Times* (1976) and the chapter on Griffiths in Kenneth O Morgan, *Labour People: Leaders and Lieutenants; Hardie to Kinnock* (1987, new edn. 1992).

Professor the Lord Morgan of Aberdyfi

Ray Gunter (1909–77)

Ray Gunter was a key Cabinet figure in the 1964 and 1966 Wilson Governments, who enjoyed his role as Minister of Labour with its involvement with both trade unions and employers – an area of activity in which he had first-hand practical experience and knowledge. In the eyes of many he was also the best known and most prominent President the Transport Salaried Staffs Association has had, and during his term of office he played a key role in the campaign against the Beeching cuts in the national railway network. His resignation from the Labour Party and obvious feelings of alienation should not be allowed to detract from his many achievements.

Raymond Jones Gunter was born in South Wales on 30 August 1909. He was educated at Abertillery and Newbridge Secondary Schools. In 1934 he married Elsie (née Elkins) who died in 1971. They had one son. When he left school Ray Gunter started work as a clerk on the railways joining the then Railway Clerks Association in 1926 as a member of the Ebbw Vale branch. He took an active interest in the union and was a branch officer from 1929 to 1941, and also became Chairman of the Association's South Wales and Monmouthshire Divisional Council. He joined the Royal Engineers in 1941, was commissioned in 1943 and was Staff Captain from 1944 to 1945.

From an early stage Ray Gunter was deeply involved in politics and the Labour Party. From 1935 to 1939 he was Secretary and Agent for Abertillery Labour Party and was elected to the Railway Clerks Association's Parliamentary Panel in 1940. He was first elected to Parliament in 1945 when he won South-East Essex with a majority of 3,591. For the first time there were more railway employees than railway directors in the House of Commons. At the 1950 general election he stood and won in Doncaster, but lost the seat in the general election the following year by 384 votes. He returned to work as a railway clerk becoming a member of the Association's Paddington branch.

He was elected National Treasurer of the by now Transport Salaried Staffs Association in 1953, and held this position until 1956 when he was elected President of the Association. He remained President until 1964 when he resigned on being appointed a Cabinet Minister. The President and Treasurer are the two most senior lay positions in the union.

In 1955 he stood again for Parliament in Doncaster but lost by 1,660 votes. That same year he was elected to the National Executive Committee of the Labour Party. He returned to Parliament at the 1959 general election winning, Southwark in London. He became Opposition spokesman on Power in 1960 and a year later Opposition spokesman on Labour and Employment matters. He was Vice-Chairman of the Labour Party in 1963–64 and Chairman of the Labour Party in 1964–65.

With the return of a Labour Government in the 1964 general election Ray Gunter became Minister of Labour in Prime Minister Harold Wilson's Cabinet, a post he described as his 'bed of nails'. He was the first TSSA member to hold Cabinet rank. In February 1965 Harold Wilson announced that a Royal Commission on Trade Unions would be established. Initiated by Gunter, it was chaired by Lord Donovan. Gunter said that the purpose of the Royal Commission was to take an objective look at the trade unions in a world that was totally different from the one in which they had been created.

He was Minister of Labour until April 1968 when he became Minister of Power, a post he held for less than three months. His move from the Ministry of Labour and resignation as Minister of Power on 29 June 1968 caused a flurry in political circles, although some trade unionists were more than pleased to see his departure. In his role as Minister of Labour, he had been heavily involved with the implementation of the Government's Prices and Incomes Policy and the associated wage restraint, and had sometimes taken a tough line with trade unions, particularly when he felt there were 'red plots' behind industrial unrest. He was certainly extremely disappointed at Harold Wilson's decision to remove him from his 'bed of nails' as he had intended to produce his own trade union legislation. An indication of his intentions was revealed when he said that the White Paper, *In Place of Strife*, drawn up following the Report of the Donovan Commission by his successor Barbara Castle, was feeble in many respects but should be supported as a start.

Ray Gunter was by now a disillusioned man. Not only had he seen Barbara Castle take over his project, but her Ministry and authority had been greatly expanded. Following his resignation he accused Harold Wilson of overloading the Cabinet with intellectuals 'who fail to understand how ordinary people think'. Other comments were deemed equally unhelpful and Michael Foot and a number of other MPs complained that he had breached Labour's Code of Conduct. He was exonerated from this accusation and his Constituency Labour Party gave him their backing by 33 votes to 1.

Ray Gunter was appointed a Director of Securicor Ltd in 1969 and a Director of Industrial

Communications Ltd in 1970. In 1971 Gunter defied the Party Whip, with nearly 70 other Labour MPs, and supported the Conservative Government's motion to approve joining the European Economic Community. The same year he also abstained in the final vote on the Tory Government's Industrial Relations Bill. On 16 February 1972 Gunter resigned from the Parliamentary Labour Party and sat as an Independent until he applied for the Chiltern Hundreds just over two weeks later on 3 March 1972. Ray Gunter died on 12 April 1977.

Richard Rosser

Peter Hain (1950–)

Peter Hain was born in Nairobi, Kenya, on 16 February 1950 to Walter and Adelaine Hain. The eldest of four children, he spent most of his early life in Pretoria at the heart of South Africa where he attended Hatfield Primary and then Pretoria Boys High School. From early childhood he campaigned alongside his parents, who were members of the non-racial, but largely white, Liberal Party that opposed apartheid, which greatly influenced Peter's later political development. Their involvement led to a spell in jail when he was 11, and in 1964 his parents became the first couple banned from speaking to more than one person at a time and even from entering public buildings. This led to Peter giving his first political speech in 1965 aged just 15, at the funeral of a family friend, John Harris, hanged for a bomb explosion at Johannesburg station in July 1964.

A year later, in 1966, the family were forced to flee the apartheid security police and they left for England. They settled in Putney, South-West London, and Peter attended Emanuel School in Wandsworth. He later studied at Queen Mary College, London University, at which he gained a first class honours BSc Economics and later an M Phil at Sussex University.

Hain became involved in domestic politics almost immediately on arriving in the UK and joined the Young Liberals in 1968. In 1969, while a student at Queen Mary College, London University, he formed the successful pressure group for which he is now infamous – 'Stop the Seventy Tour'. Hain's direct action was so effective that Harold Wilson believed that further protests would destabilise the Government and forced the cricket authorities to cancel the tour. It was a significant blow to the apartheid state and the beginning of the worldwide isolation of South Africa. Twice he has ended up on trial at the Old Bailey, once in 1972 on trumped-up conspiracy charges and the second time in 1976, framed by BOSS (the South African security organisation), on equally dubious but serious bank robbery charges when a look-alike raided a Barclays in Putney. Both times after legal struggles he was found not guilty. He remained involved in the Young Liberals, becoming Chairman in 1971 and President in 1975. He opposed any coalition with the Tories in 1974 and any attempt to help the Tories topple the Labour government in 1977.

In 1977 he joined the Labour Party and a year later helped found the Anti-Nazi League, which became one of the most successful direct-action campaigns in post war British history. He worked for the Anti-Nazi League until 1980 when he became Assistant Research Officer for the Communications Workers' Union, becoming their Head of Research in 1987. He has been a member of the GMB Union since 1973 and served on the Labour Co-ordinating Committee between 1979 and 1987, including as Vice-Chair from 1982 to 1987.

He stood as the Labour Party candidate for Putney in the 1983 and 1987 general elections, where he was beaten twice by David Mellor, despite energetic electoral campaigns. After the 1983 election defeat he campaigned actively for Neil Kinnock in the Labour leadership election. Hain became Vice Chair of 'Time to Go' in 1988, a group campaigning for a gradual withdrawal of troops from Northern Ireland leading to reunification.

In 1991 Peter Hain was selected for the Neath constituency near Swansea, which he won in a by-election on 4 April 1991 with a majority of 9,000. On entering Parliament, Hain joined the left-wing Tribune group of MPs, of which he became Secretary in 1992 and remained a part until 1993. He became chair of the *Tribune* newspaper board in 1992, a position he held until the 1997 election. He introduced two bills in the House of Commons during his time as a backbencher: the Second Chamber (Reform) Bill in the 1992–93 session and the Regulation of Privatised Utilities Bill the following year.

Hain was Secretary of Labour's Trade and Industry Group between 1993 and 1995, before serving as Labour Foreign Affairs Whip in the Opposition Whips Office from 1995 to 1996. He joined the front bench as the Party's Shadow Employment Minister in 1996 and served in this post until the 1997 election.

After Labour's successful 1997 campaign he increased his majority to 27,000 and was appointed as Parliamentary Under-Secretary of State in the Welsh Office where he co-ordinated the Government's campaign for a 'Yes' vote in the referendum on Welsh devolution a successful campaign that led to the creation of the Welsh Assembly. In 1998, following Welsh devolution, he was campaign manager for Alun Michael's successful bid to become Labour's Leader in Wales and First Minister in the Welsh Assembly.

In the summer of 1999 he became Minister of State in the Foreign and Commonwealth Office, with responsibilities including South Africa. He used his position to be a strong advocate of a new ethical foreign policy. In January 2001 he was appointed Minister for Energy and Competitiveness at the Department of Trade and Industry. Although holding this position for only a few months until the June 2001 election, he used his time to fight vigorously for compensation payments for ex-miners and for a greater commitment to renewable energy.

At the general election of 2001 he was re-elected in his Neath constituency with over 60 per cent of the vote, although with a reduced majority of 21,000. After the election he returned to the Foreign and Commonwealth Office as Minister for Europe, with responsibility for the European Union, Western, Southern and Central Europe, Russia, Eastern Europe, Central Asia and the Caucasus. He was appointed to the Privy Council in June 2001. He is the author of a number of books and pamphlets: *Don't Play with Apartheid* (1971), *Radical Regeneration* (1975), *Mistaken Identity* (1976), *Policing the Police* (1979), *The Debate of the Decade* (1980), *Reviving the Labour Party* (1980), *Neighbourhood Participation* (1980), *The Democratic Alternative* (1983), *Political Trials* (1984), *Political Strikes* (1986), *Proportional Misrepresentations* (1986), *A Putney Plot* (1987), *The Peking Connection* (1995), *Ayes to the Left* (1995), *Sing the Beloved Country* (1996) and *The End of Foreign Policy?* (2001). Hain married Patricia Western in 1975 and together they had two sons. They remained married for 24 years before separating.

Phil Taylor

Joe Haines   (1928–)

Joeseph Thomas William Haines left an indelible mark on the relationship between Downing Street and the press. Of all those who have become No 10's press secretary, he, more than any-one, was the proverbial poacher turned gamekeeper. Although he was a fascinated observer of power and its trappings, he never forgot his humble origins. He realised that his early struggles were similar to those of millions of ordinary families and believed that Labour's duty was to help those people.

Joe – or, as he called himself officially, J T W – Haines was born on 29 January 1928 in Rotherhithe, which was then one of the worst slums in London. His father was a stevedore who died when Haines was two, the youngest of three children. His mother was left to bring up the family on a weekly state income of 18 shillings, which she swelled by scrubbing floors in the local hospital.

At 14 Haines became a copy boy on the *Bulletin* in Glasgow, where he learned shorthand – a skill he proudly demonstrated throughout his working life. He became a reporter and trans-ferred to the parliamentary lobby at Westminster in 1950, moving to the *Scottish Daily Mail* and then to the (pre-Murdoch) *Sun*, the successor to the *Daily Herald*. It was there that he was spot-ted by Harold Wilson, already Prime Minister, who in 1969 took Haines into Downing Street, first as deputy and then as press secretary.

Typically, before he took the job, Haines insisted on telling Wilson all those government policies with which he did not agree. Yet he quickly became part of No 10's kitchen cabinet, despite his abrasive relationship with Marcia Williams (later Lady Falkender), whom he be-lieved tried to get him sacked in 1970. When Labour lost the general election that year, Joe Haines stayed with Wilson throughout the four years of opposition, returning to Downing Street with him – travelling in the official car from the palace with Harold and Mary – after the victory of February 1974.

The Prime Minister relied heavily on Haines, particularly his brilliance with words, which was invaluable for speech-writing. His contribution did not end there, though. He played a key role in making early contacts with Republicans in Northern Ireland in an attempt to restore peace to the province. This led to a lifelong interest in the problems of Ireland and the devel-opment of his policy while at the *Daily Mirror* of a phased withdrawal of British troops.

The act for which he is best remembered, though, was his abolition of lobby briefings for journalists in June 1975. Officially he said at the time: 'I believe this is in the best interests of journalists and government alike' but privately he scorned journalists who, he felt, wanted to be spoon-fed information and liked the daily ritual of association with 10 Downing Street.

When Harold Wilson resigned unexpectedly in April 1976, he offered Haines a peerage. Turning the offer down, he replied: 'I want to destroy the House of Lords, not strengthen it.' Instead he wrote his account of life at the heart of Government, *The Politics of Power*, a fascinat-ing insight into the operation around the Prime Minister, though it became best known for his revelations about Wilson's resignation honours list – the 'lavender list', as it was called, because Haines revealed it had originally been drafted by Marcia Williams on lavender notepaper.

Haines then went to work for the *Daily Mirror*, initially as chief leader writer, later be-coming political editor of the group. He played a key role during this period in sustaining Labour's most important supporters in the press during a critical time for the party. He was instrumental in the papers staying with Labour rather than backing the fledgling SDP, which he scorned, even though he sympathised with many of its policies. He was tribal in his support for Labour, just as he was for Millwall football club.

When Robert Maxwell took over the Mirror Group, he relied heavily on Haines, whom he admired for his political brain and writing abilities, and Haines wrote the authorised biography of the publisher. Those who worked with Joe Haines in politics and journalism would testify to his fierce temper, fiercely-held opinions and fierce loyalty.

David Seymour

Richard Burdon Haldane   (1856–1928)
(1st Viscount Haldane of Cloan)

The life of R B Haldane reveals a great deal about the politics of the late nineteenth and early twentieth century. Haldane was a philosopher who applied his ideas to practical politics, as a Liberal MP and member of the Liberal Government from 1906 to 1915. He was also a passionate campaigner for education, achieving real successes in the promotion and development of higher and adult education. But from a Labour perspective, Haldane also provides an interesting example of the transference of ideas and politicians from the Liberal Party to Labour during this period, as Haldane was to serve as the first Lord Chancellor in MacDonald's 1924 Labour Government.

Richard Burdon Haldane was born on 30 July 1856 in Edinburgh into a distinguished Scottish family, including in its ranks senior politicians and renowned legal advocates, one of whom was a former Lord Chancellor, Lord Eldon. Holding high office was so much in the traditions of the family that it was prophesied by his nanny at an early age that R B Haldane would follow his relative on to the Woolsack. He was brought up at the family estate at Cloan near to Gleneagles and in Edinburgh, where he went to the Edinburgh Academy. At 16 he went to Edinburgh University, where his studies took him from Latin and Greek to philosophy and religion, whilst discussion groups brought him into contact with philosophers such as Benjamin Jowett and writers like Matthew Arnold.

Just before his eighteenth birthday, Haldane was refused permission by his parents to attend Balliol College Oxford, the natural place for students with a growing interest in Hegelian philosophy, as he now had. Balliol also had a reputation for promoting dubious religious doctrines. Instead he was sent to Gottingen University, where he was taught by the idealist philosopher Lotze. Yet if his parents had intended their actions to ensure Haldane's religious beliefs endured, they were to be frustrated. Upon his return, Haldane agreed to be baptised but recanted during the ceremony. His spiritual life had turned away from religion and towards an interest in philosophy and idealism. He graduated with first class honours in Philosophy in 1876.

Only a year after he left university, Haldane's father died. Instead of pursuing a legal career in Edinburgh, Haldane moved to London where he read for the Bar, starting in the chambers of William Barber. His work at the Bar was demanding, but he was also able to cultivate a wide network of political friends, including a fellow barrister and future Prime Minisiter, H H Asquith. Haldane also maintained his interest in idealist philosophy in this period, editing a collection of essays in memory of T H Green. The success of the Liberal Party in the election in 1880 inspired him to form the Eighty Club, a discussion group made up of like-minded colleagues. This election also fired his own political ambitions. By 1885, Haldane had secured a seat in East Lothian and he was elected as a Liberal MP in that year.

Haldane's rise within the Liberal Party ranks was not without its difficulties, as he was an independent-minded MP who was not afraid of speaking in favour of an issue he felt strongly about, irrespective of the Party position. He also maintained an active interest in Hegelian philosophy, giving the Gifford Lectures from 1902 to 1904, which were later published under the title *The Pathway to Reality*. Haldane's academic pursuits were in many ways remarkable for someone also serving as a senior political figure, but they also provided an opportunity for some of his Parliamentary colleagues to mock him – he was nicknamed 'Schopenhauer' by one – and his connection with German philosophy and Germany was later to be used against him.

The formation of the Liberal Government in December 1905 opened a new phase in Haldane's political career, as he was offered the Cabinet position of Secretary of State for War by the new Prime Minister Campbell-Bannerman. As War Secretary, Haldane's most significant achievements were to create an expeditionary force, which would assist the rapid mobilisation of troops in Europe were they to become necessary, and the reorganisation of the army in the Territorial and Reserve Forces Bill of 1907. In an attempt to provide some additional strength in the Upper House following the constitutional crisis between the Lords and Commons in 1910, which had caused the Liberal Government much difficulty, Haldane was in early 1911 sent to the Lords as Viscount Haldane of Cloan. He was offered the India Office but predrerred to stay at War, believing, rightly, that the Lord Chancellorship would soon become vacant. In June 1912 he was appointed Lord Chancellor, a position he held with great pride and esteem.

The early months as Lord Chancellor were the most happy in office for Haldane. It was not to last. Soon afterwards, with the deepening crisis in Europe, his record at the War Office and his alleged pro-German sympathies were being attacked in the British press. The fact that he had undertaken secret negotiations with Germany on behalf of the Government was manipulated by the press, who claimed Haldane had been briefing the Germans on British plans and had been aware of their own preparations for conflict. Unfortunately Haldane did very little publicly to defend himself and only subsequently published the full account of his record at the War Office and of his dealings with Germany. But it was too late for his political career, and in the negotiations about the formation of a National Government in 1915, Asquith faced demands from the Conservatives that Haldane should be removed. On 26 May 1915 he resigned as the Lord Chancellor.

For most politicians, their political life would end here. For Haldane it was simply the closing of one chapter. His removal from office and the crisis within the Liberal Party during the First World War provided a catalyst for Haldane to begin formal relations with the Labour Party. Informally, the connections between the two went much further back. Haldane had worked with socialists like R H Tawney for many years and he was a close personal friend of the Webbs. Whilst never a Fabian Society member himself, Haldane shared much with the views of leading Fabian members. He had also established ties with Labour figures as the barrister on the Taff Vale case. Haldane's emerging support for Labour was also in tune with his long-standing principles. He wrote to Balfour in 1894 that he hated the name Liberal and preferred to call himself a progressive, and he had consistently argued prior to 1915 for a new political formation which united radical Liberals and sensible Labour members. His sacking from the Cabinet should therefore be seen as less the reason for his switching support to Labour, and more the opportunity for its further development.

Between 1915 and 1923 Haldane gradually distanced himself from the Liberal Party, attacking them in the Lords in 1918 as a party which had 'lacked vision considerably, and lacks vision now', and arguing that the new movement which Labour represented would progress inevitably. In public he did not yet commit himself to Labour, but in private he was already meeting with Labour members at receptions and serving on advisory committees to the Party. These gradual movements became more formal in 1922, when Haldane rejected an invitation from Asquith to attend a Liberal Party meeting on education. He campaigned openly for Labour candidates in 1922, and in December 1923 Haldane wrote a manifesto supporting Labour in the election. When MacDonald was asked by the King to form a Government in 1924, Haldane was offered the position of Lord Chancellor.

Unfortunately, Haldane was no better at being a party loyalist for Labour than he was for the Liberals, and as Lord Chancellor he retained his independence and desire to support causes that were out of step with the party. But his experience and political interests helped to establish the credibility of the first Labour Government, despite its short life. After the fall of the Government, Haldane became Leader of the Labour Opposition in the House of Lords and he continued to serve the Labour Party, which he believed was the best vehicle to further the goals he worked all his life to promote: equality of opportunity and education.

Haldane's political career is only one aspect of his extremely busy life. He was also a passionate campaigner for education and did much work to establish higher education in Britain. In the 1890s Haldane worked with Sidney Webb to draft the legislation and win political support for a University of London, and he played a key role in the establishment of other educational institutions, like Imperial College and Liverpool University. Haldane also helped to found and served as President of the British Institute of Adult Education. Other interests included the campaign for female suffrage, which Haldane believed was essential if true equality of opportunity for all was to be achieved. Haldane was the sponsor of four Bills to promote the Women's Franchise League's proposals between 1889 and 1892 and he spoke on many occasions in the House in favour of extending the vote to women. He was also keenly interested in the workings of government and the state. His evidence to the Sankey Commission on the nationalisation of the coal industry was seen as significant by many Labour figures including Tawney, who wrote an introduction for it when it was published. This interest was furthered in 1922 when Haldane became the first President of the Institute of Public Administration. Haldane also maintained his philosophical interests, publishing *The Reign of Relativity* and a number of collections of his philosophical essays and speeches.

Finally there is a private side to Haldane's life. He never married – he was once engaged to Valerie Munro Ferguson in 1890, but she called it off suddenly – and so most of his life was dedicated to his political work. Perhaps he was speaking of this sorrow when he told a recently bereaved colleague: 'There is only one solace for personal grief and that is work for the country'. He also wrote to his mother on a daily basis for a period of many years, and this correspondence helps to reveal the private, reflective person that was hidden behind Haldane's reputation for political conspiracies and intrigue.

Haldane's life touched so many different spheres – philosophy, education, politics, social reform. It is a measure of his impact that in each of these fields Haldane's contribution is regarded as significant. Haldane was also one of a number of leading Liberals who saw Labour as the right party to promote the causes they had until recently been delivering in the Liberal Government. His decision to support Labour in the early 1920s is therefore important, in the context of a young Labour Party's need to replace the Liberals as the main challenger to the Tories. As well as bringing to MacDonald's government his authority and experience, Haldane brought to Labour a credibility that it had lacked. All this meant that, although defeated after less than a year in government, by 1924 Labour had established itself as a major party of power.

Haldane died on 19 August 1928 and was buried on the family burial grounds at Gleneagles. His key writings include: *Education and Empire: Addresses on Certain Topics of the Day* (London, 1902); *The Pathway to Reality: The Gifford Lectures 1902–3* (London, 1903); *Army Reform and Other Addresses* (London, 1907); *The Problem of Nationalisation* (London, 1921); *The Philosophy of Humanism and other Subjects* (London, 1922); *The Reign of Relativity* (London); *An Autobiography* (London, 1929). There is a two-volume biography by F Maurice, *Haldane 1856–1915: The Life of Viscount Haldane of Cloan* (London, 1937) and *Haldane 1915–1928: The Life of Viscount Haldane of Cloan* (London, 1939) and a further biography by Stephen E Koss, *Lord Haldane: Scapegoat for Liberalism*, was published (London) in 1969.

Matt Carter

George Hall (Viscount Hall of Cynon Valley)   (1881–1965)

By the time of his retirement in 1951, George Henry Hall had served in three governments, including the coalition during the Second World War. He became identified as a moderate within the Labour Party, and was for many years seen as a safe pair of hands to run affairs in the Admiralty, Colonial Office, or Foreign Office.

He was born on 31 December 1881 in Penrhiwceiber, Glamorgan. His father, also George Hall, an ostler in a local colliery, died when George junior was only eight years old, leaving his mother, Ann, to bring up the family of eight children. Educated at Penrhiwceiber Elementary School, Hall started full-time working at the age of twelve in the Penrikyber colliery. He was seriously injured in a pit cage accident at the age of twenty-one and during a long convalescence he had frequent discussions with the local vicar, the Reverend J R Jones, not only on religious matters, but also on the radical political issues of the time. When recovered, Hall recommenced his colliery job, but also started to become active in Labour politics.

He supported Keir Hardie as the successful Independent Labour candidate for his Merthyr Tydfil constituency between 1906 and 1910. Hall was elected to the Mountain Ash Urban District Council in 1908 and was appointed as a checkweigher at the colliery in 1911 and became treasurer to the colliery lodge. He married Margaret Jones in 1910 and became chairman of the Merthyr Tydfil Labour Party in the same year. By 1916 he was chairman of the District Council and he went on to maintain a special interest in local education, serving on the education committee for eighteen years. He continued to work in the colliery and as local agent for the South Wales Miners' Federation throughout the First World War.

Hall won the parliamentary seat of the Aberdare division of Merthyr Tydfil in 1922 and represented the constituency for the next twenty-four years. He was on Labour's back benches during the first MacDonald administration in 1924. In 1925 he became a Justice of the Peace in Glamorgan. He gained his first major appointment as Civil Lord of the Admiralty in the second Labour government of 1929, a post that involved responsibility for the Admiralty's industrial workers. He resigned from the post in the party split of 1931, but unlike most of his colleagues, he managed to retain his seat in the subsequent general election. Throughout the 1930s he did what he could to encourage the development of new industries in the high unemployment areas of the Welsh valleys and was elected to the shadow cabinet in November 1939.

When the wartime coalition government was formed by Churchill, Hall served in a number of offices for the rest of the war. First, in May 1940, he was appointed Parliamentary Under-Secretary of State at the Colonial Office. One of his main interests in this post was in colonial development and welfare. He was moved back to the Admiralty as Financial Secretary in February 1942 and made a Privy Councillor. Finally in 1943 he became Under-Secretary of State for Foreign Affairs, deputy to Foreign Secretary Anthony Eden. When he received a testimonial £2000 from his constituents to mark his twenty-two years in Parliament, he showed his continuing commitment to local education, by using the funds to found language scholarships for grammar school students in the Aberdare valley. He had also acted as governor of Cardiff University College and as chairman of the Welsh Youth Committee.

Following Labour's 1945 election victory, Hall was promoted to the Cabinet when, drawing upon his wartime experience, he was appointed Secretary of State for the Colonies. With Labour short of peers in the House of Lords, however, an experienced spokesman was needed and in October 1946 the ageing Hall accepted the title of Viscount Hall of Cynon Valley. This gave him the distinction of becoming the first former coalminer to sit in the Lords. His earlier experience was again brought to bear with his simultaneous appointment as First Lord of the Admiralty (outside the Cabinet), where he remained from October 1946 until indifferent health led in May 1951 to his retirement from government aged sixty-nine. He was Deputy-Leader of the House of Lords from 1947 until his retirement in 1951.

His contribution was recognised in two honorary degrees from the Universities of Birmingham and Wales. After his retirement he maintained an interest in industrial development in the Welsh valleys as a consultant to companies involved in nuclear power and electricity. From 1954 to 1962 he was chairman of Gwent and West of England Enterprises.

His first wife, Margaret, had died in 1941, and one of his two sons, Bruce, had died in the war. In 1964 he married Alice Walker. His first son, William George, who succeeded to the peerage, went on to become the first chairman of the Post Office Corporation. George Hall died on 8 November 1965 in Leicester.

George Hall had never been allowed long in any one post at the national level of government. In the general area of Admiralty and foreign affairs, however, it was recognised that he could always be relied upon to provide a steady hand and this contributed to him being moved around, wherever this quality was most required at the time. In local affairs, though, he was able to direct his efforts in a more sustained way, with education and development of the local economy gaining most from his contribution over many years to the life of the Welsh valleys.

Nick Cowell

Glenvil Hall   (1887–1962)

William George Glenvil Hall was born at Almeley, Herefordshire, on 4 April 1887. His parents William George and Elizabeth Hall were Quakers and his father worked for the Home Mission of the Society of Friends. Glenvil was educated at the Friends' School, Saffron Walden, and aged fifteen went on to work as a bank clerk in London. He devoted his own time to social work at Hoxton and Toynbee Hall to help the poor of the East End. He even moved to Whitechapel for some years to be part of the community he was helping and joined the Independent Labour Party in 1905. He divided his spare time between social work and political activity until 1914.

He volunteered for the Army at the outbreak of war and was commissioned in 1916. He was wounded whilst serving in the Tank Corps and mentioned in despatches, leaving the army with the rank of Captain. After the war he joined the headquarters staff of the Labour Party, becoming its finance officer for the next twenty years. In 1921 he married Rachel Ida Sanderson. After unsuccessfully contesting the Isle of Ely at the elections of 1922, 1923 and 1924, he was elected as the first Labour MP for Portsmouth Central in 1929. He was PPS to Frederick Pethick-Lawrence, the Financial Secretary to the Treasury 1929–31. Being one of the many Labour candidates who lost their seats in 1931, Hall later returned to Parliament in a by-election at Colne Valley, Yorkshire, in 1939 and retained the seat for the next 23 years. He was called to the Bar in 1933, but did not start practising until 1939, the same year that he recommenced his parliamentary career.

In the Second World War he was an officer in the Palace of Westminster Home Guard. After the war he was appointed Financial Secretary to the Treasury. Hall was the main defender in Parliament of the necessarily austere measures of the early post-war budgets. In these years Hall was also a representative at many international meetings: the last Assembly of the League of Nations, the Paris Peace Conference and the United Nations. He was made a Privy Councillor in 1947.

After leaving his Treasury post in March 1950 he was elected chairman of the Parliamentary Labour Party, a post he held until the fall of the Labour government in October 1951 when Attlee assumed the role (until 1970 the Party leader acted as PLP chair in Opposition). During this time he attended the Consultative Assembly at Strasbourg and travelled on behalf of the Commonwealth Parliamentary Association. He also worked for the NSPCC and became a member of the advisory council of the BBC. With the fall of the Attlee government, Hall was elected to the shadow cabinet, being re-elected every year until he retired from the front bench in June 1955.

He continued as an active MP until his death on 13 October 1962. His wife had died in 1950 and he was survived by a son and a daughter.

Nick Cowell

Willie Hamilton   (1917–2000)

Willie Hamilton was for 37 years one of the most famous of backbench MPs, an outstanding constituency Member, a distinguished chairman of major parliamentary committees and a fervent advocate of women's rights. Yet for the mass public, he was known for only one thing – his persistent and outspoken criticisms of the Royal Family and what he regarded as their essentially parasitical role.

William Winter Hamilton was born in Durham on 26 June 1917, the son of a militantly left-wing miner. He attended Puddock Stile elementary school in Newbottle, and by the age of nine, at the time of the 1926 General Strike, his anti-royal sentiments had already evolved. 'We were told a member of the Royal Family would pass our school,' he wrote much later, 'and we were all taken out to wave. The car came past, we duly waved, and that was that ... but I resented the fine car because I knew that we weren't able to put a coal fire on'. Hamilton's own instincts were reinforced by the views of his parents who, he wrote, taught him that the monarchy was 'the very apex of something evil, of that pyramid of wealthy privilege and exploitation; at the bottom of which writhed coalminers, dockers, textile workers and toiling masses everywhere'.

Hamilton went on to study at Washington Grammar School and Sheffield University, where he qualified as a teacher. He taught at a school in Huddersfield, and at the outbreak of World War II registered as a conscientious objector, not on religious grounds but because he thought that the war was irrelevant to the working class. At his father's urging, however, he joined up after Hitler attacked Russia in 1941, and rose through the ranks to become a Captain by the end of the War.

Hamilton had joined the Labour Party in 1936, and in 1945 he fought the West Fife constituency for Labour, losing to the popular Communist MP, Willie Gallacher, who had won the seat in 1935. Hamilton turned the tables in 1950, and arrived at Westminster, a tall, lean, red-haired man of 32. He was disconcerted to find himself cold-shouldered by many left-wing Labour MPs, despite the fact that his had been one of very few Labour gains at that election, which saw the virtual wipe-out of the crushing Labour majority of 1945.

It may have been, in part, to establish his own left-wing credentials that Hamilton lost no time in launching his first anti-royal broadside, objecting to a proposal by the Labour government to pay an allowance to Princess Margaret, whom he described as 'an expensive kept woman, who is not worth the money'. He returned to the charge throughout his parliamentary career, most notably during the 1970–74 Parliament, when he succeeded in getting himself put on a select committee to examine the royal finances, until then buried in the deepest obscurity. He greatly discomforted various royal functionaries by the persistence of his questioning, but this did not prevent the Queen from submitting a request for a review of the Civil List, which Hamilton characterised as 'the most brazen pay claim made in the last 200 years'.

It was probably true that a majority of Labour MPs privately agreed with Hamilton's views, but most of them were embarrassed to raise the issue, and only about two dozen of us joined him in the division lobby when he divided the House against the proposed increases. Hamilton spelled out his case in great detail in two books, *The Queen and I* (1975) and *Blood on the Walls: Memoirs of an Anti-Royalist* (1992), but these had less impact than his often gratuitously insulting remarks, which were regularly reported in the press.

Hamilton, an essentially kindly man, was not driven by any personal animus against royal personages; his anger was fuelled by a fierce hatred of privilege wherever he found it, not excluding the Labour movement, where he objected to trade union sponsorship of MPs, which, he said, led to Parliament being 'saddled by dim MPs selected by Tammany Hall methods'. He was also scathing about the use of the honours system, notably by Harold Wilson at the time of his resignation in 1976.

For many years Hamilton was held up as a bogey man by the Tory press, which led to him being widely regarded as a left-wing extremist. Yet he was a consistent supporter of what were then regarded as right-wing causes within the Labour Party – anti-Soviet, pro-NATO, pro-Europe. When the West Fife constituency was redistributed in 1974 and he had to seek selection for the successor seat of Central Fife, he declared: 'I am a Roy Jenkins man'. In fact, the potential Labour leader whom he most admired was Tony Crosland, and he took a leading role in promoting Crosland's unsuccessful bid for the Labour deputy leadership in 1972.

Hamilton was a dedicated House of Commons man, and took a keen interest in helping newly elected young Labour MPs find their feet, taking enormous pains to guide them through the tricky shoals of procedure. He once shyly confessed to me that his highest ambition was to become Speaker, a post for which he was well qualified by virtue of his chairmanship of important committees such as the Estimates Committee and the Select Committee on Procedure.

It was never on – nor was he ever likely to have been offered ministerial office, despite his substantial abilities. His views on royalty – undoubtedly more acceptable at the beginning of the new century than they were at the time – effectively precluded him from preferment. It was a waste of an unusual talent. Hamilton retired from the Commons in 1987, at the age of nearly 70, and died in Lincolnshire, aged 82, on 23 January 2000. He was married in 1944 to Jean Cullow, a nurse, who died in 1968, and by whom he had a son and a daughter. His second marriage, in 1982, was to a childhood friend, Margaret Cogle, who survived him.

Dick Leonard

Eric Hammond (1929–)

Eric Hammond continued a late-twentieth-century trade union tradition that owed much to the experience of leaders of the electricians union, the EETPU. He was no clone of Les Cannon or Frank Chapple, but he faced the strongest battle for the soul of the Labour movement in modern times. His leadership of the EETPU, and his eventual merging of that union with the engineers union, the AEU, guaranteed that the trade unions would not use their industrial power to overthrow elected government.

Eric Albert Barrett Hammond was born in North Kent on 17 July 1929, the son of a middle-of-the-road Labour man who was a labourer at the Bowater's paper mill. Eric's father eventually rose to head timekeeper. Eric Hammond was evacuated to Canada during the war, growing up in West Newfoundland with the Nichols family. He returned to England at the end of the war and became an apprentice electrician at Bowater's. During the early 1950s, he worked in construction, particularly on the BP refinery at the Isle of Grain – known to construction workers for years as 'Treasure Island'. He was elected as shop steward in 1954, and was constantly supported by the left. Hammond has never been a communist, but as early as the

1955 election was influenced by Richard Acland's Common Wealth ideas, and developed his social life through the Co-op youth structures. He was elected as a Labour Councillor on Gravesend Council in 1957, refusing to wear ceremonial regalia. Within the union he attended closely supervised Youth conferences during the CP era, and was elected to the union's executive in 1963 as a left candidate, standing out against the anti-left, post ballot-rigging trial mood of the members nationwide. Very soon afterwards he was short-listed for the Labour seat of Deptford, but chose his union executive career in preference to left Labour politics.

After two years on the executive, he had understood Les Cannon and Frank Chapple's vision for a modern union, and fell out with his North Kent political support within the union. He took a leading role in the reform of contracting through the establishment of the Joint Industry Board for electrical contracting. This body, a joint union-employer council with an independent chair and local boards, survives today. The structure was robust enough to resist left opposition when it won earnings rises of a third in two years for electricians to become graded according to skill. The industry was de-casualised. In 1970, he brought this analytical skill to the electricity supply industry in providing productivity evidence to support the union's successful evidence to the Wilberforce inquiry after a work to rule turned the lights out. Later, he was to lead for the union in a pre-Scargill unity of the energy unions in pursuing a realistic balanced energy policy, and spoke frequently for the union on the vital subject of industrial democracy – was it better to develop the sophistication of collective bargaining or go for the placing of a few 'workers' on the boards of companies? Hammond was always well briefed and deployed immense intellectual power behind his participation at the NEDO committees concerning the electronics industry, his Monopolies and Merger Commission work and the development of skills training for mid-life workers as well as apprentices. As chairman of the union's political structure, which he designed, he was resolute in support of Labour, even when the SDP was both briefly influential and looking to peel reputable union opinion away from a Labour Party that was electorally in turmoil. He maintained the union's political fund with a mixture of central grants and support for EETPU members running for office, along with support for any local Party that sought to democratise itself with one person one vote methods of deciding local candidates. His unequivocal support for Labour was vindicated in 1985 when the members voted overwhelmingly in the biggest turnout in any ballot to explicitly keep its political fund exclusively in the service of the Labour Party.

He was elected General Secretary of the EETPU in December 1982, to run in tandem with Frank Chapple until 1984. His first election was a 33 per cent turnout in which he beat two other candidates combined by 73,571 to 59,468 votes. He achieved the highest election result in the union's history when he was re-elected in 1987 by 108,146 to 36,684 in a huge 40 per cent secret postal ballot. His personal popularity was based on modest charm and a spry sense of humour. He is a keen photographer and serious gardener, and supports his local rugby team and town grammar school to this day. He reads widely, is familiar with Machiavelli's *The Prince* and Burke's ideas on the importance of offering constituents your judgement ahead of your agreement with their views.

His public reputation was based on his frequent spats with other unions in defence of the EETPU's insistence on democratic participation by the union's members. In the Isle of Grain dispute in 1979–80, the debate about the movement's response to 'Tebbitt's Law' and the 1984–85 miners strike, Hammond kept the focus on the issue of members' rights to be consulted. The miners strike made him a household name as he stood almost alone against several aspects of Arthur Scargill's leadership of the miners. Hammond said they should have balloted for a national strike. He objected to the crude and violent picketing of coal-using industries, notably steel at Ravenscraig, where other livelihoods would have been destroyed if the furnaces had gone cold. He attacked the violence against the police, counselling that however much state power it took, no elected government could be intimidated by industrial action. He was fearful that union violence in the end would provoke state violence that would destroy indiscriminately all trade union influence in society. Most of all, he was angered by the TUC encouragement for a dispute its leadership privately opposed. His speech to the 1984 TUC and the following year's Labour conference produced howls of opposition from delegations who would in later years accept Hammond's analysis of how the miners – 'lions led by donkeys' – had been misled and betrayed by false expectations.

All of this was on the moral high ground, as was his conviction in 1985 that it would be reasonable for the EETPU to be ejected from the TUC in company with the engineers union, the AEU, for taking government support for running elections with expensive postal ballots. But the same year, the EETPU were embroiled in the Wapping dispute. Rupert Murdoch needed machinery installed in his new plant in East London. Traditional print unions were wary of running the new plant until 'jobs for life' were assured. When Murdoch provoked the printers into strike action, he sacked them for being on strike, using the Tory labour laws. EETPU members stayed at Wapping after the installation of the machinery and ran it. Again, Hammond was appalled by the level of violence and criminality associated with picketing and opposition to the union – threats of violence that reached into his own family life. The *Financial Times* labour editor, John Lloyd, called the episode 'the sharpest of sharp practices'. Other unions were determined to attack the EETPU and used the issue of single union recognition to discipline the EETPU out of the TUC. The union signed agreements with employers where other unions felt they had rights of traditional spheres of influence in recruitment. Hammond was clear. If workers wanted to join his union or leave it – that was their right. It was not up to the TUC to prescribe which union people should be in. There was only ever going to be one result, and the EETPU were expelled from the TUC in 1988.

Hammond summarised the philosophical differences that had lain behind the union's relationships with the elements within the rest of the movement when he said to that silent Congress:

> With secret postal balloting ... our members made decisions on who was to lead them, what rules were to apply and what policies we were to pursue ... You (the TUC) listened to and were part of the unrepresentative politicos. We were at one with our members. That difference has meant that the opposition of our members to unilateral nuclear disarmament finds no echo among Congress decisions ... Our members' attitudes to strike ballots, law in society and violence in disputes are disregarded. There is a pathological, racist anti-Americanism here which finds little echo amongst our members. Above all, our members reveal an enthusiasm for the market system and its values which infuriates the sherry-party revolutionaries with their model resolutions and conference hall rhetoric ... this Congress constantly rejects the known views of members. For this Congress, the members are now the problem. If you seek to please

the activists, it is necessary to outwit the members. If you continue to allow committee decisions to have precedence over the views of members, the structure becomes part of the conspiracy against the members.

Outside the TUC, Eric Hammond's fears that there would be a thousand hand-to-hand combats for members failed to materialise. The union membership remained remarkably stable. There are few mass migrations of trade union members, even when leaderships fall out on fundamentals. The EETPU held its own, and continued to make its normal contribution within the Labour Party. Eric Hammond's last contribution to the union was to lead it into a huge merger with the AEU just before he retired in 1992. He remains convinced that this triumph will ensure the voice of skill and responsibility will be always heard in Labour circles and never drowned out by the bigger general and public service unions. He married Brenda Edgeler in 1953, with whom he has two sons. His autobiography, *Maverick*, appeared in 1992. This author's *Light and Liberty* (1990) also covers much of his period of office in the EETPU.

Dr John Lloyd

Keir Hardie (1856–1915)

James Keir Hardie, more than any other man, was the founder of the Labour Party. He was the first independent labour MP, and was central to forming the Independent Labour Party and the Labour Representation Committee. In 1906 he was the Labour Party's first leader. As strategist, evangelist and legend, he is foremost of the founding fathers.

He was born on 15 August 1856 in Legbrannock, Lanarkshire, the illegitimate son of a farm servant, Mary Keir. In 1859 she married David Hardie, a ship's carpenter; the young boy was known thereafter as James Keir Hardie. He had virtually no schooling and began working in a series of menial jobs in Glasgow at the age of nine. In 1867 the family moved to Newarthill in the eastern Lanarkshire coalfield and Hardie went down the pit at the age of ten. Later he worked in a pit at Quarter, near Hamilton. He worked as a 'trapper' in helping to ventilate the mine; it was dangerous work and the young boy saw many accidents and even fatalities. However, he taught himself to read serious works by Carlyle, Ruskin and others, and also became for a time a fervent member of, and lecturer for, the 'Morisonians' or Evangelical Union, fiercely committed to temperance. He also became a pioneer trade unionist. He was active in a strike of the Lanarkshire pits in the summer of 1880 and in 1881 helped organize the struggling Ayrshire miners. At the age of 23 he gave up the life of a working miner.

Politically still a Liberal, he now became an increasingly forceful journalist in the local Ayrshire press. However in 1886 his political philosophy dramatically changed. A socialist tone appeared in his writings, and also in the programme of the newly-formed Ayrshire Miners' Union. In *The Miner* he campaigned hard for the Scottish miners to organize. At the 1887 TUG, he launched a fierce attack on Henry Broadhurst and other Lib-Lab union leaders. Though not overtly a socialist, he was clearly pushing labour politics into new, radical directions. A key episode came in April 1888 when he stood as Labour candidate, against the Liberal, at Mid-Lanark. It followed his being turned down by the local Liberal Association.

He polled only 617 votes, but it gave him a new stature as a working-class leader. He confirmed this in the founding of a new Scottish Labour Party that August, and in further onslaughts on the Lib-Labs at the 1889 TUC.

His activities were taking him far beyond Scotland, however. He attended the new Socialist International in Paris. Then he was nominated for the London constituency of West Ham South. The local Liberals failed to put up a candidate and in the 1892 general election Hardie had a straight contest with the sitting Conservative. He was elected by a comfortable margin and was given a rousing send-off to launch his career at Westminster. Legend marked him down as 'the man in the cloth cap' but in fact he wore a deerstalker, rather like Sherlock Holmes.

His three years as MP for West Ham South, 1892–95, were mixed ones. A lone figure in the Commons, he generally supported the Liberal government. His main activities were outside the House. In January 1893 he presided over the meeting at Bradford that saw the founding of the ILP, the first avowedly socialist political party, albeit of an ethical, non-revolutionary kind. The next year he founded a weekly newspaper, *The Labour Leader*. He owned it and wrote all the editorial comment, even at times the women's and the children's column (under the pseudonym 'Daddy Time'). In parliament he made his main mark as 'member for the unemployed', focusing attention on the social consequences of the depression in trade. But he also caused uproar by denouncing the monarchy when a royal birth (the future Edward VIII) coincided with a mining disaster in South Wales. In the 1895 general election, Hardie lost the votes of many Liberals who now saw him as an extremist, and he was unexpectedly defeated by a Conservative.

The conclusion he drew was that independent labour on its own had little prospect of making headway as a small socialist sect without wider support. After an abortive attempt to form a 'socialist unity' coalition of the ILP and the Marxist Social Democrats, Hardie campaigned indefatigably for a grand alliance of the socialist bodies with the trade unions, to create a party to promote the cause of labour in parliament. In fact, the employers' attacks on unions in the courts and in suppressing strikes strengthened his arguments. In 1899 he won the backing of the Scottish TUC, and then the British TUC voted by 546,000 to 434,000 to attend a conference to 'secure the better representation of labour in the House of Commons'. This was held at Memorial Hall, Farringdon Street, London, on 27–28 February 1900. Here the Labour Representation Committee came into being. It was dominated by the trade unions, but the key figures on the 12-man executive were socialists like Hardie and Ramsay MacDonald. Weak though it was, a new political party to represent labour was launched. Hardie became its founder chairman.

He was shortly back in parliament. In a dramatic contest in October 1900, held during the Boer War which Hardie strongly opposed on both pacifist and socialist grounds, he failed at Preston but then won one of the two seats in the Welsh constituency of Merthyr Tydfil. He benefited from the rivalry between the two sitting Liberals. For the next few years, he worked to build up the fledgling LRC. He gained from the Taff Vale verdict which enraged the unions by undermining the right to strike, and many large unions now affiliated to the new party. It was a difficult time, exemplified by personal quarrels when Hardie had to sell up *The Labour Leader* in 1904. He was also somewhat uncertain about the affiliation of mass trade unions since their outlook tended to be labourist rather than socialist. However, he reasserted his stature with a strong personal crusade against unemployment in 1905.

The key issue, however, was relations with the Liberals. Hardie was always an uncertain supporter of a 'progressive alliance' but he went along with MacDonald's negotiation of the electoral 'entente' with the Liberal Chief Whip in 1903. As a result, Labour had a clear run in 30 seats in the 1906 election and 29 LRC candidates were returned. They called themselves the Labour Party and, by a one-vote majority over the trade unionist David Shackleton, Hardie was elected chairman.

His time as leader in 1906–08 was not a success. Hardie did not enjoy the compromises of leadership and MacDonald made far more impact in parliament. Hardie's health also suffered and he retired as party leader with some relief at the start of 1908. However, his career had taken important new directions. Hardie powerfully backed the women's suffrage movement, reinforced by his close friendship with Sylvia Pankhurst, perhaps his mistress. He clashed with some of the party rank and file in the priority he gave to the women's cause, social as well as political. He also took up key aspects of colonial freedom. On a world tour in 1907 he called openly for Indian self-government when visiting the sub-continent, and in meetings in South Africa he scandalized opinion by upholding the rights of black Africans. He wrote a rare book on India (1909) when he returned and also criticised the Union of South Africa Bill for its failure to protect the black majority.

In Britain itself, he was passionate in the defence of democracy. He pressed for local devolution rather than a Prussian-style state bureaucracy, urging that Scotland and Wales should be granted home rule alongside Ireland. He was also a fierce critic of the tactics of the authorities, including the police and the army, in putting down strikers during the disturbances in mining and other areas from 1910 onwards. A pamphlet, *Killing No Murder,* condemned the loss of life at Tonypandy and Llanelli in troubles there. He upheld the right to strike alongside the right to vote. He could lend support to radical outsiders like Victor Grayson and like James Larkin in Ireland. On the other hand, he argued both in the Labour Party and in the Socialist International on behalf of constitutional parliamentary approaches towards the socialist commonwealth. His book *From Serfdom to Socialism* (1907) condemned doctrines of class war.

His final crusade, and greatest disappointment, was on behalf of international peace. At Socialist Internationals he strove to carry a motion endorsing an international strike by the workers to prevent war, and he worked closely with German socialist comrades. When war broke out in August 1914, Hardie condemned the militarist fever, but his was a minority voice even in the Labour movement. A meeting in Merthyr was broken up by a jingo mob headed by local miners' leaders. The war years broke his spirit, and his health deteriorated rapidly. He died, a very old man of 59, on 26 September 1915. His death caused an immense outpouring of grief in socialist and labour circles. Bernard Shaw declared that after Hardie's death, his soul would go marching on. But at the resultant by-election in Merthyr, the seat fell to a pro-war union leader, C B Stanton, far removed from the pacific ideals of the former member. His daughter, Nan, later married the left-wing pacifist Labour MP, Emrys Hughes.

Keir Hardie was a complicated, passionate, romantic man. He dabbled in spiritualism and there was always a mystical aspect to his outlook. He had extraordinary charisma as a mass crusader; yet he could be difficult in personal relations, not least in money matters. His marriage to Lillie Wilson in 1879 was not tranquil, and he found happiness in friendships with young women socialists, including Sylvia Pankhurst. His socialism was essentially ethical and fraternal; he had little interest in economics or the techniques of government. He never held elective office: he was a politician of protest, not a man for power. Yet, both as a strategist and a prophet, he was unique. He took up great causes – unemployment, social welfare, women's suffrage, colonial freedom. In all, his judgement was broadly vindicated after his death. He was also a supreme strategist, politicising the working class by finding a middle way between Lib-Labism and direct action. No-one came close to equalling his achievement in building up a grand alliance of the mass unions and the socialist societies. Of all Labour's pioneers, he was the one that was truly indispensable, in Sylvia Pankhurst's words, 'the greatest human being of our time'.

The fullest biographies of Hardie are Kenneth O Morgan, *Keir Hardie, Radical and Socialist* (1975); Fred Reid, *Keir Hardie: the Making of a Socialist* (1978); and Caroline Benn, *Keir Hardie* (1992).

Professor the Lord Morgan of Aberdyfi

Harriet Harman (1950–)

At one time, Harriet Harman seemed to epitomise New Labour. A fluent, telegenic moderniser, she was one of Labour's most prominent female politicians while the party prepared for power. No surprise, then, that she was given the high profile job of Social Security Secretary in Tony Blair's first cabinet. Yet, just a year later, she was summarily sacked, a casualty of the new government's first uncertain year in office. Her departure, clutching a huge bouquet of lilies and smiling bravely, was one of the memorable images of the time.

When Harman became Social Security Secretary after the 1997 election, she quickly found herself at odds with her deputy, Frank Field, brought in by Tony Blair to 'think the unthinkable' about reforming the welfare state. Field's strategy sounded excellent in principle – radical, fair and coherent – but when the Treasury realised how much it would cost, they binned it, leaving Harman's DSS floundering for a new way forward. The barely hidden warring between the two Social Security ministers had an inevitably destabilising effect.

Then, in trying to push through the government's plans for cuts in benefits for lone parents, Harman faced a substantial rebellion from the party's own backbenchers. The Chancellor and the Prime Minister decided to make the cuts a question of their authority, yet left Harman to push them through without offering much support. It was her authority that suffered and made her an easy victim in the reshuffle.

At the time, the Prime Minister said she was taking 'a break from office', with the implication that she might one day return. She decided to take him at his word. Rather than carping from the backbenches, or giving up politics altogether, Harman set a fine example of how to behave after being sacked. She went back to campaigning for women's rights, something she had long fought for, and was influential in winning better maternity pay and conditions for women, as well as higher-quality and more accessible childcare. She had been the Minister for Women and continued to campaign for more female MPs, while setting up a series of seminars on the future of feminism with leading female politicians, academics and journalists.

Harriet Harman was born on 30 July 1950, the daughter of Dr John Harman, a consultant physician, and Anna Harman, a barrister and a former Liberal candidate. She qualified as a solicitor and first joined the Labour Party in 1978 while Legal Officer for the National Council for Civil Liberties, working alongside Patricia Hewitt. Harman was selected as Labour's candidate for Peckham, a deprived South-East London constituency in 1981 and won the seat in a by-election in October 1982. She was appointed as a Health spokeswoman in 1987, a post she held till 1992, when she became Shadow Chief Secretary to the Treasury. From 1994 to 1995 she was Shadow Employment Secretary, moving back to become Shadow Health Secretary (1995–96) and then Shadow Social Security Secretary from 1996 until the 1997 election. She then took office as Secretary of State for Social Security and Minister for Women until the reshuffle in 1998. Harman was a member of Labour's National Executive Committee from 1983 to 1998.

She is married to the prominent trade unionist, Jack Dromey, currently National Secretary of the Transport and General Workers' Union. They have three children, all of whom have attended selective grammar schools, something some members of the Labour Party have never forgiven her for. Her eldest son Harry attends the same school as Tony Blair's two sons, the London Oratory, and friends suggest she mopped up much of the anger felt towards him for this.

Would she come back? The odds were in her favour. Harman retains links with both Tony Blair and Gordon Brown. She was fired at New Labour's early low point and went with dignity. She quietly set about rethinking her political style and returning to her political passions. Once the target of much venom in the party and in the press, that is no longer, on the whole, the case. Her reward came in the post-election reshuffle of June 2001 with her return to government as Solicitor-General.

Jackie Ashley

John Harris (Lord Harris of Greenwich) (1930–2001)

John Harris had a long political life. Never himself of public fame or the front rank, he nevertheless spent over 40 years as a Westminster insider consistently promoting, as he saw it, the cause of mainstream social democracy. He can lay legitimate claim to be Labour's first spin doctor, working as Hugh Gaitskell's political assistant and press officer in the 1959 campaign and then as Labour's Director of Communications in Harold Wilson's 1964 victory. But his skills as a manager of the press and a moderniser of campaigning technique underestimate him.

John Harris worked intimately with Gaitskell in all the battles over Clause Four and unilateralism. It fell to him to announce Gaitskell's premature death to a stunned press and public in 1963. Hugh was his idol. A picture of his former boss that conveyed his unique warmth and passion stayed close beside his favourite armchair maintaining a watchfully benevolent eye over his protégé right until his death on 11 April 2001.

Yet despite his fierce loyalty to Gaitskell, he did not take a factional view of the Gaitskellite succession. He was one of those figures on the Labour right who concluded that George Brown's personal failings meant that he was simply not up to the job as Labour Leader. Harris backed Wilson despite all the reservations he shared, and in the 1964 campaign became part of Harold's inner circle. The good relationship he then formed with Marcia Williams played no small part in keeping the Labour show on the road through all the Wilson-Jenkins-Callaghan tensions of the succeeding years, despite the fact that in the leader's circle it was often Harris who was blamed for destabilising press briefings against Wilson himself.

As one of the first Special Advisers, he became Roy Jenkins's closest confidant: so close that without any apparent self-consciousness he adopted the great man's mannerisms and voice, playing a central role in all Roy's political endeavours from 1965 until John's death. This remarkable political partnership began at the Home Office at the time of the liberal reforms of the 1960s: no flinching then in the face of the usual reactionary press, but rather a flinty determination to pursue a radical agenda that has probably done more to achieve racial justice, more equal opportunity and the possibility of individual self-fulfilment than any other set of legislative changes in the last half century.

In the 1970s it was in the cause of Britain in Europe that he made his decisive contribution. Not for him the seductive and self-serving argument that whatever one's personal inclinations as a pro-European, other issues were far more important to Labour voters. He played a central role in the tense and at times bitter intra-party manoeuvrings that led to the 1975 referendum campaign and then its planning and success.

In the 1980s he never doubted the rightness of leaving Labour to set up the SDP. He was not a central figure in the break. In part this was because he was chair of the Parole Board at the time. But also early SDP-ers kept their distance. John had acquired a negative and unfairly Machiavellian reputation for someone of such natural buoyancy, humour and fun.

Nevertheless the SDP might have flopped in its first electoral contest at Warrington. More than anyone John Harris ensured that it did not. Quite unfazed and undeterred by others' sniping, he was ever-present in that by-election: three paces behind his candidate Roy Jenkins, his constant guide and protector, effortlessly gliding down the paths of housing estates to halt some awkward constituency encounter, always available to steer a pushy journalist in a hopefully more favourable direction. And then at a late evening dinner, those episodes were lovingly recalled with graphic descriptions and a jolly laugh over a bottle of claret and the fine cigar with which John's days nearly always ended.

John Harris was a journalist by trade. Born on 5 April 1930, he was of a generation where many grammar school boys did not go to university. Leaving Pinner County Grammar School at 16, he trained as a journalist in Bournemouth and Leicester. His lucky break in politics was when George Thomson appointed him as Assistant Editor of the Scottish Labour weekly *Forward* when it was moving to London to take on *Tribune* and become the voice of Gaitskellism against Bevanism. That brought the young John Harris to the approving attention of Hugh Gaitskell.

But for all the deep knowledge of the press on which Harris's political indispensability was founded, John always recognised that politics was fundamentally about policies making a difference. He showed this amply when in 1974 Roy Jenkins persuaded Harold Wilson to elevate John to the Lords and make him Minister of State at the Home Office. In this role he was a great hit. He developed a deep understanding of the full range of Home Office issues. Civil servants respected him, and several became close personal friends for the rest of his life. His second, brilliantly successful marriage was with Angela Smith a one-time private secretary. He won the confidence of the police and later became closely involved in the work of the Police Foundation.

From the SDP and later the Liberal Democrat benches of the Lords he was a consistent voice for a balanced, tough-minded and humane approach to criminal justice issues, defending the police in the 1980s against the lunacies of the left and in the 1990s standing up for justice, fair play and common sense against the populist remedies of the right.

In 1994 he became Liberal Democrat Chief Whip in the Lords: a role to which he dedicated himself for the remainder of his life. He was skilful and effective. Forthright in his condemnation of the Blair Government where he believed proposals were retrograde, as for example on the Mode of Trial Bill, he nevertheless played a significant and largely unrecognised role in securing the success of the Government's legislative programme in the House of Lords during its first Parliamentary term. On several crucial occasions he delivered the votes which the Labour Whips simply could not muster. He died in harness, struck down by cancer, to the very end a model of dedicated political commitment, sheer guts and courage as well as jolly good fun. Gaitskell would have been very proud of him.

Roger Liddle

Judith Hart (Baroness Hart of South Lanark) (1924–91)

Judith Hart was only briefly a member of Wilson's 1966–1970 Cabinet (as Paymaster General), and is better known for her achievements as Minister for Overseas Development, a post she held three times over the course of her Parliamentary career. The 1975 Lomé Convention, which introduced EEC aid for developing countries, was a testament to her tenacity and drive. A passionate socialist from her early teens to her death in 1991, she was a member of the hard-left tendency on and off the NEC and often a thorn in the Labour leadership's side. Barbara Castle's *Guardian* obituary of her described her as 'dynamic, physically attractive, courageous and challenging', and Hart's impact on Labour politics of the sixties and seventies was greater than her limited Cabinet career implies.

The daughter of a Lancashire linotype operator, Judith Ridehalgh was born on 18 September 1924 in Burnley. Academically talented, she won a place at Clitheroe Royal Grammar School, where she became school captain and head prefect, and then a scholarship to the London School of Economics (LSE), leaving with a first in sociology. She joined the Labour Party at 18, and when the LSE relocated to Cambridge during the war, she became Secretary of the Cambridge University Labour Club and Chair of Cambridge Labour Party.

At 22 she married scientist and fellow socialist Anthony Hart – a happy marriage that produced two sons and provided her with staunch support throughout her sometimes-turbulent political career. While she worked as a lecturer and research worker in sociology, his job took them to Dorset, where she stood for Parliament for the first time in 1951 for unwinnable Bournemouth West. By 1955, they had moved to Scotland, where Hart ran an energetic, although ultimately unsuccessful, campaign for Aberdeen South, which nevertheless brought her to the attention of the leadership. She was also becoming involved in the nascent anti-nuclear movement and, at the 1957 Party Conference, delivered an impassioned speech on disarmament, which further raised her profile. She was soon selected for Lanark, a winnable seat.

Despite Labour's drubbing at the 1959 general election, Hart held Lanark by 540 votes.

Her constituency included a declining coalfield and unemployment and deprivation were rife. Throughout her career, she campaigned hard for local interests, fighting factory closures and battling for redundancy terms often in opposition to the leadership, putting constituency before career.

Despite some early conflicts with Gaitskell, Harold Wilson was initially an admirer of hers, and when he became Prime Minister he made her Joint Parliamentary Under-Secretary of State for Scotland (1964–66) under Willie Ross. Chosen because she was one of the few Scottish Labour MPs who had voted for Wilson over Brown, initially she was seen as his woman in the Scottish Office, but soon made her own mark, particularly through her championing of the rights of pupils with disabilities. After the general election, she was promoted to Minister of State at the Commonwealth Office (1966–67) where Wilson gave her responsibility for the Rhodesia Committee which was monitoring negotiations with Ian Smith.

The resignation of right-winger Margaret Herbison brought the opportunity of promotion. Herbison had refused to introduce the social security cuts Wilson was seeking, and he made Hart Minister for Social Security in her place (1967–68). Hart was rewarded with promotion to Cabinet as Paymaster General the following year (1968–69). However, now she found herself running into conflict with Wilson. She believed in active intervention in industry, and that the public sector should be the spearhead in creating jobs. (Later, before the first 1974 election, she would campaign for the nationalisation of 25 leading British companies). In the summer of 1969 she campaigned with Dick Crossman against *In Place of Strife,* the Wilson/Castle plans for trade union reform, and was dropped from the Cabinet, but not before she had been elected to the NEC (1969–83), consolidating a powerbase within the party.

Wilson demoted her to Minister of Overseas Development, and she shadowed the post in opposition (1970–74). This was a brief she cared passionately about – she was an early pioneer of analysing how the economic and fiscal policies of the West impacted on developing countries, and requiring aid policy to reflect the interests and needs of recipient countries. In 1973 she published *Aid and Liberation,* setting out her own vision on aid and development policy.

She developed a keen interest in African policy and was Chair of Labour's Southern Africa Solidarity Fund. She also became deeply and personally involved with Chilean politics, an interest that lasted a lifetime. (Later she was to be a vocal critic of the Labour government over supplying arms to Pinochet). She was a personal friend of the wife of the murdered Chilean leader, Salvador Allende, and was instrumental in cutting off aid to Chile. She was eventually awarded that country's Order of Merit in recognition for her support.

Her biggest achievement came after Labour returned to power in 1974. She was central to the development of the 1975 Lomé Convention, spending days in negotiations with the Commission and 46 developing countries on trade, aid and co-operation. She fought hard in Whitehall for extra funding and won important concessions allowing the transfer of loans to developing countries into grants. Her contribution was recognised in 1985 when she was made an Honorary Fellow of the Institute of Development Studies at Sussex University.

However, it was not long before she came into conflict with Wilson again. She vigorously opposed Britain's entry to the EEC alongside left-wing Cabinet members like Foot and Castle and, with them, argued for a referendum and for members of the cabinet to vote with their consciences. Then in 1975, with Joan Lestor and Tony Benn, she received a public rebuke for going too far in anti-South African activities. She was offered a switch to Transport but refused to take it, instead insisting on making a personal statement to the House about her sacking.

James Callaghan brought her back to the front bench in 1977, giving her back control of her old department. Unsympathetic to her politically, the move was probably in recognition of the support she had within the party, particularly on the NEC. After her ministerial career ended with the defeat of the Labour Government in 1979, she remained a member of the NEC (Vice Chair 1980–81 and Chair 1981–82), retaining authority within the Party and allowing her a platform for her strong left-wing views: opposing the expulsion of Militant Tendency leaders; speaking out against cuts in spending; arguing for more nationalisation and import controls and, ever the pacifist, campaigning vigorously against the Falklands War. However, she did attract criticism from old allies when she accepted the award of a Dame Commander of the British Empire in 1979.

After boundary changes in 1983 her constituency was renamed Clydesdale, and she held the seat until she retired at the 1987 general election. In 1988 she was elevated to the Lords as Baroness Hart of South Lanark, but growing ill-health meant she spent little time there. She died in London on 8 December 1991 at the age of 67.

Ann Rossiter

Vernon Hartshorn (1872–1931)

If Ramsay MacDonald's decision to form the National Government in 1931 came as a shock to many, his decison to abandon the supposedly sacred tenet of free trade for protection would have come as less of one to anybody who had read the memoranda of his Lord Privy Seal, Vernon Hartshorn. Before his unexpected death at his Maesteg home on 13 March 1931, Hartshorn had been for nine months responsible, as deputy to its chairman, MacDonald, for running the Cabinet committee charged with conquering unemployment. Unable to appoint him to government in 1929 due to his membership, along with Attlee, of the Simon Commission on India since November 1927, MacDonald had appointed him Lord Privy Seal on 5 June 1930 in succession to the floundering J H Thomas.

Within a few months it had become clear that Hartshorn had been persuaded of the view of his most senior civil servant, Sir John Anderson, that what MacDonald had pejoratively termed 'relief works' were neither justifiable on grounds of economic utility, nor on grounds of curing unemployment. Hartshorn wrote on 18 August 1930: 'I confess that, before I had an opportunity of investigating matters for myself, I thought that a great deal more could be done … After fully examining the position, I am satisfied that not much more is possible.' He concluded that the only way out of unemployment was via protectionism: 'If present fiscal conditions are unfavourable to the expansion of certain established industries or the expansion of new ones, ought we not to be prepared to consider a modification of our fiscal policy?'

Hartshorn, with, Thomas and MacDonald, remained in a minority on this question within the Labour Cabinet and it was not until the formation of the National Government that his view became generally accepted, a development which precipitated the resignation of

Snowden. Whether Hartshorn would have followed them into the National Government remains, of course, a moot point. Though Hartshorn's other role as Lord Privy Seal was to further practical co-operation between Ministers and the Liberals, he had in his earlier life been a leading opponent of the Lib-Labbery of the older generation of miners' leaders and was branded an extremist by local Liberals in the bitter electoral battles of 1910 at Mid-Glamorgan. Moreover the consultation between Liberals and relevant departmental ministers regarding telephone development and rural housing was continued, a process continued and expanded by his successor, Tom Johnston, as a practical attempt to sustain the government, not a precursor to alliance with the Conservatives.

Born in Pontywaun, near Pontypridd, on 16 March 1872 the son of Theophilus Hartshorn, a miner and his wife Ellen, the daughter of a farm labourer, no fewer than five of his contemporaries from that little hill village were to become Labour MPs and three Presidents of the South Wales Miners Federation. He was largely self-taught: he went down the mines in boyhood, working also in a Cardiff colliery office before becoming a checkweighman and in 1905 a full-time miners agent at Maesteg, Glamorgan. His marriage, to Mary Winsor in 1899, brought him two sons and a daughter. His involvement in challenging the old-guard of the South Wales Miners Federation (SWMF) led him to top the poll for the South Wales representatives to the Executive of the Miners Federation of Great Britain (MFGB) in 1911. His patriotic line during the Great War and acceptance of membership of the wartime Coal Controller's Advisory Committee and the Industrial Unrest Committee, not to mention the consequent award of an OBE, served to alienate him from his more militant erstwhile comrades. He was one of the MFGB leaders to give evidence to the Sankey Commission and, following his unopposed election to Ogmore at the 1918 election, became a leading parliamentary critic of the Lloyd George coalition's failure to tackle the problems of the mining industry. In November 1920, after tactical disagreements over the conduct of the October 1920 miners' strike, he resigned from both the executives of the SWMF and the MFGB. However, in 1921, following the death of the incumbent, he was elected president of the SWMF and thus back to the executive of the MFGB, a position he retained until his appointment as Postmaster-General in MacDonald's first government.

He was regarded as an able parliamentary speaker; he had for seven years been a local Methodist preacher, and his popularity with colleagues contributed to his election in 1923 as chair of the Welsh Labour MPs. The *Fortnightly Review* wrote of him in 1921: 'Hartshorn knows every phase of the coal industry: he is master of all its intricate statistics, and completely master of himself when addressing the House ... He has always been ready for a fair deal and is the miners' true leader.'

Greg Rosen

Roy Hattersley (Lord Hattersley of Sparkbrook)   (1932–)

Roy Hattersley belongs to Labour's lost generation of politicians whose bright ministerial career prospects were interrupted in 1979, and, as one Conservative election victory turned into four, were never given the chance to be fulfilled. Despite the lack of high office Hattersley would have undoubtedly attained, his contribution to his party is immense. Labour's success in 1997 owes much to Labour politicians like Roy Hattersley who steered the party through perilous, uncharted waters throughout the eighties and early nineties.

Born in Sheffield on 28 December 1932 the son of Frederick, a local government officer and ex-Catholic priest, and Enid, later a Labour Lord Mayor of Sheffield, Roy Sydney George Hattersley was educated at Sheffield City Grammar School and Hull University where, having joined the Labour Party in 1949, he became chair of the student Labour Club and in 1956 national chair of the National Association of Student Labour Organisations (NALSO). A WEA tutor-organiser 1957–59, he served as a Sheffield City Councillor from 1957 to 1965, with a spell as Chair of Housing, and was Labour's parliamentary candidate for Sutton Coldfield in 1959. From 1959 until his election to Parliament in 1964 as MP for Birmingham, Sparkbrook, he worked as a Health Service PR Officer. In 1956 he married Molly Loughran who in a career encompassing spells as the headteacher at London comprehensive schools and Assistant Education Officer at the ILEA shared her husband's passionate commitment to comprehensive education. As a young Labour Party activist and councillor, Hattersley was a Gaitskellite, and remained on the revisionist wing of the Labour Party throughout his career. He wore his Yorkshire background as a badge of pride throughout his career, despite representing the Birmingham Sparkbrook parliamentary constituency from 1964 to 1997, and recalled his early life in *A Yorkshire Boyhood* and *Goodbye to Yorkshire*.

Hattersley began his Government career as soon as he was elected, as PPS to Peggy Herbison, Minister of Pensions and National Insurance from 1964 to 1967. During this period Hattersley became both political and social friends with fellow revisionists Tony Crosland and Roy Jenkins; the former became his philosophical mentor, the latter his political patron. A passionate pro-European, he was also from 1966–67 the Director of the short-lived Campaign for a European Political Community.

In March 1967, Hattersley was appointed Under-Secretary of State at the Department of Employment and Productivity under Ray Gunter and then Barbara Castle. In 1969, as Secretary of State, Castle failed to secure support for the *In Place of Strife* proposals, thus creating turmoil in the Labour Government. She also failed to persuade her own Minister Hattersley, who believed governments should not interfere in industrial relations.

At Denis Healey's request, Hattersley was in August 1969 appointed Minister of State for Defence Administration at the MoD, serving until Labour's defeat in 1970. In Opposition, he became deputy foreign affairs spokesman 1970–72, and was one of sixty-nine Labour MPs, including John Smith, to break the whip and vote with the Conservative Government in October 1971 in support of Britain's membership of the EEC. Unlike some of his pro-EEC allies, he did not, however, follow Roy Jenkins in resignation from the front bench, and it was to fill the place of one, George Thomson, that in April 1972 he was promoted to principal spokesman on Defence. Later in 1972, he moved sideways to speak on Education, resuming in 1974 his ministerial career, unexpectedly outside the Cabinet, as Minister of State at the Foreign and Commonwealth Office, with responsibility for the 'renegotiation' of Britain's place within the EEC, culminating in the 1975 referendum and his appointment to the Privy Council.

After supporting James Callaghan's bid to replace Harold Wilson as Leader of the Party and therefore Prime Minister, he joined the Cabinet in September 1976 as Secretary of State for

Prices and Consumer Protection, an office in which he served until the Conservatives' victory in 1979. Elected to the Shadow Cabinet in 1979, Hattersley was Shadow Environment Secretary 1979–80, and Shadow Home Secretary 1980–83.

When the SDP split from Labour in 1981, Roy Hattersley watched the bulk of his political allies desert the party, but he chose to remain inside Labour's ranks in the fighting spirit he had admired in Gaitskell twenty years earlier. With Peter Shore he became co-chair of the Solidarity group of Labour right-wingers with the aim of keeping Labour moderates inside the party and preventing the wholesale takeover by the left. He was elected Deputy Leader of the Labour Party in 1983 as the other half of the Neil Kinnock 'dream ticket' designed to balance and reunite the left and right of the party. Throughout the eighties, this leadership team grappled with the dispiriting and divisive effects of the miners' strike, the expulsion of Militant, the loss of the 1987 general election and the Benn-Heffer leadership challenge in 1988. From 1983 to 1987 Hattersley was Shadow Chancellor, and from 1987 to 1992 he was Shadow Home Secretary.

Hattersley published *Choose Freedom* in 1987, an attempt to create for Labour a socialist ideology to combat Thatcherism without recourse to Bennite extremism. His work of political philosophy starts where Tony Crosland left off in *The Future of Socialism*, and weaves in contemporary political thinkers, notably John Rawls. It has at its heart the notion that liberty can only be realised though equality. The significance of *Choose Freedom* was to provide Labour with a workable intellectual alternative to the extremes of left and right, and to underpin Labour's new statement of *Aims and Values* (1988) and the Policy Review.

An observer might also wonder how Hattersley as Deputy Leader of the Labour Party found the time, at the height of the Kinnockite battles with foes to the left and right, to write a Victorian triology *The Makers Mark, In That Quiet Earth,* and *Skylark Song,* based on his own ancestors. Throughout his career, Hattersley has been a prolific author and journalist, penning the weekly Endpiece column in the *Guardian*, and books including a biography of Nelson and collections of essays, making him by the 1990s the MP with the highest earnings outside his MP's salary.

After Labour's defeat in April 1992, Roy Hattersley resigned immediately as Deputy Leader, along with Neil Kinnock, and became a backbencher for the first time since his election in 1964. He decided not to seek re-selection and stood down as an MP in 1997.

After his elevation to the House of Lords as Baron Hattersley of Sparkbrook, in 1997, Hattersley continues to write frequently and speak out when he feels it necessary. When defending his cherished principle of comprehensive secondary education, he found himself siding with the Labour left against Tony Blair's leadership, an irony which earned him the name 'Trottersley'.

His career may have been unfairly curtailed by his party's inability to win an election from 1979 to 1997, but by sticking to his guns over Europe, defence, the unacceptability of the presence of Trotskyists inside the Labour Party, and the need for moderation and common sense in policy formulation, Hattersley can rightly be cited as one of the founding fathers of New Labour. Without those like Roy Hattersley who stayed true when so many deserted to the SDP in 1981, Labour's 18-year exile might have proved permanent, and Britain would have never known a Prime Minister Blair. Like Marx, who disavowed the label 'Marxist', Hattersley rejects the 'New Labour' tag, but without him, New Labour's success in 1997 and its success in governing since, might have never happened.

Paul Richards

Derek Hatton   (1948–)

In its hundred-year history, Labour has provided many 'red bogeymen' for the media to terrify its Home Counties readers with. From Keir Hardie and his deerstalker at the end of the nineteenth century there has been a long tradition of Labour leaders being demonised by the press, and the 1980s had the largest cast of pantomime devils – Scargill, Benn, Livingstone and Liverpool's Derek Hatton.

Born in 1948 the only child of a Protestant working-class family (his father was a fireman), Hatton grew up in a council house in Childwall Valley Road bordering the affluent suburb of Woolton. He passed the eleven-plus exam and went to the prestigious Liverpool Institute. Not taking to academic life, he concentrated on his football and acting – his love of applause was to feature throughout his later political career.

At sixteen, he started an apprenticeship at Plessy's Electrical Engineering firm which lasted six months before he and the company parted ways. After a year as an office clerk at the Royal Liver Friendly Society, he followed his father into the Fire Service.

Remember, Derek Hatton was a child of Liverpool in the sixties, a teenager in the early sixties – he appeared to be an ordinary lad of the time, a sharp dresser, out clubbing as much as possible and supporting Everton. He was, however, looking for something else in life and for a while was actively involved in the church until becoming disillusioned.

In 1968 he met, and a year later married, Shirley Ward, three years younger than him. Shirley was from the 'posh' side of the tracks and they married just before Hatton moved to London to study on a community workers' course at Goldsmiths College. Here he became involved with radical action, working with squatters' groups, but it was when he moved back to Liverpool as a community worker that he became involved with the Labour Party; joining the Edge Hill Labour Party in 1974 and canvassing for the well-known radical – Sir Arthur Irvine MP.

After a brief spell in Sheffield he became a community worker in Knowsley in 1975 and was recruited to Militant by Tony Mulhearn. The Labour Party he joined in Liverpool was like no other in the country. The council was Liberal-controlled and the party was very much a moribund shell. In many ways Liverpool was the home of Trotskyism in Britain, with a tradition dating back to the 1930s, and the party was rife for a take-over by well-organised, energetic activists.

He fought Tuebrook Ward in 1978 and was elected to the Council in 1979 for Netherley at the same time that Margaret Thatcher was elected Prime Minister and launched her own counter-revolution. With a Tory Government and a Liberal Council, Liverpool was in a ferment, with rioting in Toxteth, Croxteth School being occupied and Militant and their friends rapidly taking over the Labour Party. In 1983, his finest hour, Labour took control of Liverpool and the stage was set for Liverpool's tragedy to unfold, with Hatton having plenty of room to exercise his frustrated thespian skills.

Within less than four years, Hatton was to become a national figure reviled by the leadership of the Labour Party, demonised in the Tory press, expelled from the Labour Party in 1986, sacked from his job with Knowsley Council and surcharged by the district auditors. During this period he led Liverpool Council into a kamikaze battle with Thatcher's Government, and Liverpool became synonymous with Militant policies. The defeat of Militant became crucial for Neil Kinnock to show that the Labour Party had moved out of its 'Red Guard' period – but this is not a history of Militant, it's about Derek Hatton.

Nowadays, he has left Militant and is a radio talkshow host. He still has a public affairs company, but in terms of Labour politics is a spent force. He's certainly no Keir Hardie – the parallels are more with Victor Grayson – but the question is, as always, Could he have done more? Whilst it is always a pity to see a working-class lad go wrong, his temperament suggests it was always going to end like this.

Peter Wheeler

Ron Hayward (1917–96)

At the autumn 1979 Labour Party conference, held in the wake of the defeat of the Callaghan government at the general election a few months before, the hard left were baying for blood. The British electorate had, so they claimed, voted in Thatcher because the Labour government had not been sufficiently left-wing and had therefore betrayed the socialist aspirations of the British people. Tom Litterick, defeated Labour MP for Selly Oak, famously tore up a copy of the manifesto and threw it from the rostrum, declaring, 'Jim will fix it. Ay, he fixed it. He fixed all of us. He fixed me in particular.' What gave the hard left the cloak of respectability was the apparent endorsement for its attacks on the Callaghan government from the General Secretary of the Labour Party himself, Ron Hayward. Hayward declared: 'You have got to ask yourself: why was there a winter of discontent? The reason was that, for good or ill, the Cabinet, supported by MPs, ignored the Congress and Conference decisions. It is as simple as that... I wish our ministers and our Prime Minister would sometimes act in our interests like a Tory Prime Minister acts in their interests.'

It was almost by accident that Ron Hayward became first National Agent (1969–72) and then General Secretary (1972–82) of the Labour Party. EETPU General Secretary Frank Chapple, a member of Labour's NEC when in 1969 it had to decide on the successor to the formidable retiring National Agent Dame Sara Barker, recalled his 'cardinal error' in voting for the 'disastrous' Hayward over Assistant National Agent Reg Underhill: 'It was a close-run thing and my vote was important, especially since I swayed at least one other NEC trade-unionist [Andy Cunningham of the GMB] to follow me... I worried at the time that I might have cocked it up and I have always regretted that vote.' Eric Hammond, Chapple's successor as EETPU General Secretary, gave a pointer in his own memoir to the provenance of Chapple's 'error': 'I knew and did not take to Hayward when he was Southern Region Organiser. At Gravesend we had the best agent in the business, John Beadle. Hayward did not take to him and ... effectively blocked him working in the region... The [NEC] was deadlocked, evenly divided between Ron Hayward and Reg Underhill. Frank discussed the problem with me and

I contemptuously responded that I wouldn't vote for Hayward to be my Ward Secretary! However, at the time I was not seeing eye to eye with Frank. His unspoken reaction was, "Well, if Hammond is against Hayward, he must be the right man."' On such grounds are great matters all too often decided.

It was Hayward's platform as National Agent that gave him the base to become the Benn-backed candidate to succeed retiring General Secretary Harry Nicholas in 1972. Voting was along left/right factional lines, with Harold Wilson supporting Hayward on the grounds that his main rival, Assistant General Secretary Gwyn Morgan, was a Gaitskellite pro-European with the firm backing of both Roy Jenkins and Jim Callaghan. The NEC tied 14–14 and Benn was able to use his casting vote to give Hayward the job. On becoming General Secretary, Hayward secured a license to advocate publicly Labour conference policy whether or not this was in direct conflict with a Labour Cabinet, making his role considerably more political than that of his predecessors.

The essential tragedy of Hayward was that, having secured the General Secretaryship through the backing of the Labour left, he proved signally incapable of rising above narrowly perceived factional interest on issues as crucial as the threat posed by Militant, until profound and lasting damage had been done to the Party he had been appointed to serve. Hayward did nothing to counter the hijack of Labour Party Young Socialists (LPYS) by Militant, which from November 1974 secured them control of the Youth position on Labour's NEC and through it access to private NEC documents. In 1976 he appointed a Militant supporter, Andy Bevan, as Labour Party National Youth Officer at Transport House. Hayward's old rival Reg Underhill, who had finally succeeded him as National Agent in 1972, was sufficiently alarmed at the Militant threat to submit a report on it to the NEC in November 1975 detailing the nature of their activities and calling for action. Hayward's attitude was more relaxed. The Labour Party, he ruminated, had 'as many caucuses as Heinz had soups.' The NEC voted 16–12 that Underhill's report not be published and no further action be taken. In 1977, Underhill prevailed upon the NEC to set up a sub-committee to re-examine his report. The subcommittee divided on right/left lines. Tom Bradley and John Chalmers wanted action, but were outvoted by Michael Foot, Eric Heffer and Ron Hayward, who opposed expulsions and reported in favour of nothing more than a enhanced political education programme and recruitment drive to counter Militant influence within LPYS. Eventually, in December 1981, nearly a year after Michael Foot's election as Labour leader and the SDP split, Foot asked Hayward and Underhill's successor as National Agent, David Hughes, to prepare a new report into Militant. However, by the time it was presented, in June 1982, Militant's roots had penetrated the Labour Party too deeply to be removed without considerable trauma over a period of years.

Son of an Oxfordshire smallholder, Ronald George Hayward was born on 17 June 1917. After Bloxham Church of England School and several RAF technical colleges, he was apprenticed to a cabinet-maker aged 16, serving 1940–45 as an RAF technical training instructor. He became Labour Party agent in Tory-held Banbury 1945–47 and then from 1947–50 for Arthur Bottomley in Rochester and Chatham. Appointed Assistant Regional Organiser for Labour's Southern Region in 1950, he became Regional Organiser in 1959. Created a CBE in 1970, he served the Labour Party right up until his sixty-fifth birthday heralded retirement to his garden in Kent. He died on 22 March 1996, being survived by his wife, Phyllis, whom he married in 1943, three daughters and 10 grandchildren.

Laura Higgs

Denis Healey (Lord Healey of Riddlesden) (1917–)

Denis Healey was once described by his Oxford contemporary and rival, Roy Jenkins, as carrying 'light ideological baggage on a heavy gun carriage'. Between his appointment as Secretary of State for Defence in 1964 and his retirement from the front bench in 1987, Healey was one of the Labour Party's three or four genuine political heavyweights. Although he never became leader of the Labour Party or Prime Minister, he was Secretary of State for Defence from 1964 to 1970, Chancellor of the Exchequer from 1974 to 1979, and Deputy Leader of the Labour Party from 1981 to 1983. He was, in every sense, a big man, with interests ranging far wider than politics.

Denis Winston (after Winston Churchill) Healey was born at Mottingham in Kent on 30 August 1917. His paternal grandfather was a Yorkshire tailor who had emigrated from Northern Ireland. His father, Will, was an engineer who had won an engineering scholarship to Leeds University through evening classes and, when Denis was born, he was working at the Woolwich Arsenal. When Denis was five, his father was appointed Principal of Keighley Technical College and the Healey family moved back to Yorkshire.

Encouraged by his mother, Winnie, who was the driving force in his early life, Denis won a scholarship to the illustrious Bradford Grammar School. He was an outstanding pupil, good at Latin and Greek but even better at English, in which he was always top of the class. As well as the delights of literature, he also acquired a taste for the arts, especially painting, music, film and the theatre. The nineteen-year-old Denis Healey who won an exhibition in classics at Balliol College, Oxford in 1936 was clearly very bright, with exceptionally wide interests and self-confidence for his age. But it seemed far more likely that he would end up as an English lecturer or art historian or even a civil servant than that he would become a politician.

It was Oxford and the war which politicised Healey. When Denis first arrived at Balliol as a scholarship boy from a northern grammar school, he admitted to being uncharacteristically nervous. But he soon discovered that his intellectual prowess and his interest in the arts and later in politics bridged all barriers. Healey got a double first in Mods and Greats and helped set up the New Oxford Art Society, which held exhibitions of the surrealists and Picasso's current work. He was able to travel extensively in Europe. Above all he became involved in politics. The Oxford generation on the eve of the Second World War has been described by Healey as 'perhaps the most political generation in Oxford's history'. It included Tony Crosland and Roy Jenkins, as well as Edward Heath. Influenced by the Spanish Civil War and the threat of Hitler, their politics was mostly of the Left. Healey joined the Communist Party(CP) and became the Communist-backed chairman of the Labour Club in 1939. He did not break with the CP until after the fall of France, but his decision, on hearing the news of the war, was to volunteer immediately for the artillery, which showed his basic patriotism.

Denis Healey had 'a good war'. He even admitted to enjoying his five years in the army. In 1942, he volunteered for combined operations, learning how to become a Military Landing Officer in a Beach group. He proved himself in the Italian campaign, supervising an allied landing under enemy fire at Porto di Santa Venere in Calabria and playing a vital role both in the planning and execution of the logistically brilliant landing at Anzio. Healey was promoted to Major and was mentioned in dispatches. From the army, he learned the importance both of planning and of improvisation when planning went awry. He also learned at first hand the suffering which war had caused and was determined to play his part politically in building a better world.

Denis contested Pudsey for Labour in 1945, being defeated by 1,651 votes. Supported by NEC members from different wings, including Hugh Dalton, Harold Laski and Nye Bevin, he was appointed International Secretary of the Labour Party in November 1945 and became more influential than all but a handful of Labour MPs. Healey derived his clout not only from his considerable personal qualities but also from his relationship with the powerful Foreign Secretary, Ernest Bevin, whom he admired greatly. After seeing at first hand the communist take-over of Eastern Europe, he played a 'bit' part as one of Bevin's trusted 'irregulars' in helping bring about the new direction in foreign policy which led to the Marshall Plan, the Western European Union and the North Atlantic Treaty Organisation. He also defended Bevin's policies both within the Socialist International and inside the Labour Party. After Labour's defeat in 1951, Healey was so sickened by Labour's infighting that he hesitated before deciding to stand for Parliament. In April 1952, he won the South East Leeds by-election with a majority of over seven thousand on a low turnout.

As a foreign affairs and defence expert, Healey rapidly became indispensable to the Labour leadership. He spoke from the front bench under Clement Attlee and when his fellow MP Hugh Gaitskell became leader in December 1955, Denis, though he was never a member of the 'Hampstead set', became Gaitskell's chief foreign affairs adviser, helping to shape his views especially over Suez, disengagement in Central Europe and the Common Market. He was elected to the shadow cabinet in 1959 and was appointed Shadow Commonwealth and Colonial Secretary in 1960. In 1960 and 1961, he gave Gaitskell strong backing against unilateral nuclear disarmament, writing the Conference document 'Policy for Peace' and speaking up for the Gaitskellite position both inside and outside parliament. If Gaitskell had lived, Healey might, in time, have become Labour's Foreign Secretary.

After Gaitskell's death, the new leader, Harold Wilson, made Denis Healey Shadow Defence Secretary and, when Labour won the October 1964 election, Healey's Cabinet appointment was one of the first six announced. In the Labour Party of that time, Defence was not considered a glamorous job but Denis brought to it the unrivalled knowledge and contacts on both sides of the Atlantic which he had built up since the 1950s, as well as having 'a very clear mind, a lot of charm, and an unwillingness to take no for an answer' (according to Neil Cameron, one of his chief advisers). Healey tried to make defence decision-making more rational and coherent against a background of expenditure cuts and an overstretch of manpower and commitments. Following devaluation in November 1967, he accepted the logic of an East of Suez withdrawal, though he was extremely reluctant to cancel the UK order for the American F111 plane. Healey, who was Secretary of State for Defence from 1964 to 1970, refused other posts, though he would, of course, have accepted the Foreign Office, for which he was eminently well qualified, if it had been on offer.

After Labour's defeat in 1970, Healey became Shadow Foreign Secretary and was elected to the National Executive Committee of the Labour Party. In April 1972, Roy Jenkins resigned as Shadow Chancellor and Deputy Leader in protest against Labour's policy of holding a referendum over European entry. Healey, traditionally a reluctant European, had switched position over whether to support the Conservative Government's attempt to take the UK into the Common Market, and, though he was sceptical about a referendum, felt no inhibitions about accepting Jenkins' shadow appointment.

Then Labour unexpectedly won the February 1974 election and Healey became Chancellor. He faced a difficult situation. He was the first Labour Chancellor to have to deal with a world of floating exchange rates. The economy was threatened by hyper-inflation, caused by world oil price hikes and accommodating labour market and fiscal policies in the UK. In addition, he had never held an economic job in government.

Edmund Dell wrote in his authoritative book, *The Chancellors*, that there were three Healeys. The first was the Healey of the period from February to the October election and its aftermath, when he was an inexperienced, 'political' Chancellor intent on winning the election and doing little to bring the economy under control. The second was the Healey who dominated the struggle for an incomes policy in 1975 and in 1976 for an acceptable agreement with the IMF, by the force of his intellect and personality. By early 1978, with the economy back under control, the third Healey produced an expansionary budget, designed to help Labour win an autumn election. However, the Prime Minister, Jim Callaghan, deferred the election and the Labour government was subsequently destroyed by public sector strikes in 1978–79, the so-called 'Winter of Discontent'.

In normal times, Denis Healey would have been the obvious successor to Jim Callaghan. But Labour's defeat in 1979 and the growing power of the left in the constituencies and at conference undermined Healey's prospects for the succession. When Callaghan resigned following the 1980 party conference, Healey was narrowly defeated by Michael Foot by 139 to 129 votes in a ballot of Labour MPs. His defeat had a disastrous impact. It was followed by the SDP breakaway of moderate Labour MPs (a handful of whom had voted for Foot rather Healey in order to hasten a split) and the outbreak of civil war inside the Labour Party. Instead of accepting an invitation to be nominated as Secretary General of NATO, Denis doggedly fought on, through the long summer of 1981, to defeat Tony Benn's challenge for the deputy leadership in the newly set-up Electoral College. He won by 50.42 percent against 49.57percent for Benn, a victory 'by a hair of my eyebrow' as Healey called it. Healey's victory probably saved the Labour Party from complete disintegration, but it did not prevent the Tories under Mrs Thatcher from winning a crushing second election victory at the 1983 election.

After Labour's defeat, Healey resigned from the deputy leadership but lent authority to Neil Kinnock's leadership by continuing to serve as Shadow Foreign Secretary. In 1987 he left the Labour front bench and in 1992 he retired from the House of Commons and entered the Lords as Baron Healey of Riddlesden. Despite his retirement as a front-rank politician, Denis Healey has remained a national celebrity, instantly recognisable by his eyebrows and his voice.

Denis has had a long and happy marriage to Edna Edmunds, whom he met at Oxford and married in December 1945, and they have three children. Healey has written a number of books which reflect his wide 'hinterland'. These include *Healey's Eye*, a charming record of his photographic career, *My Secret Planet*, a linked anthology of his favourite books and poems, *When Shrimps Learn to Whistle*, a collection of his writings and speeches, and his excellent autobiography, *The Time of My Life*. Edna Healey is also an author who has written a number of biographies, as well as a portrait of Buckingham Palace. Edward Pearce is writing a major biography of Healey, while the present author compares Healey, Crosland and Jenkins in his forthcoming *Friends and Rivals*.

Rt Hon. Lord Radice

Eric Heffer (1922–91)

Eric Heffer was born into a lower-middle-class home in Hertford on 12 January 1922. His father had a small shoe-repair and boot-making business, whilst his mother was a freelance cook (or 'caterer', in today's parlance). He was educated in local schools – Bengeo Church of England Primary, and Longmore Senior School. He had a happy childhood and youth, without the deprivation then commonplace in many parts of the country.

Leaving school at fourteen years of age, Eric had various jobs including apprentice electrician, leatherworker, and, finally, as an apprentice carpenter. Conversation at home often turned to politics, and when hunger marchers passed through Hertford in 1936, it had a profound effect on the young Heffer. His burgeoning political consciousness fitted well with his incipient trade unionism, and his religious convictions. This matrix was to be his lifelong anchor.

Having initially joined the Labour Party, Eric resigned at the age of 17 to join the Communist Party. As Eric wrote: 'To me, Stalin was the greatest of men'. He remained a member of the Amalgamated Society of Woodworkers until, in 1942, he was called up into the Royal Air Force. After various postings, he was sent to a maintenance unit in Fazakerley (in the Walton constituency) where he was to meet his future wife, Doris, and where he was to make his political future.

Before and during his conscription, his life was a frantic round of political and trade union meetings and activities. His marriage in 1945 to Doris led initially to a return to Hertford, to live with his parents; but it did not work out. He and Doris returned to Liverpool, but not before he unsuccessfully contested a Hertford council seat in 1946. Working as a carpenter, Eric threw himself into political and trade union activism, leading to his expulsion from the Communist Party after ten years' membership. He lost not only his political allies but his circle of friends. Within six months, he had rejoined the Labour Party in the Toxteth constituency.

Locally, he made his mark, sitting on the executive committee of the Liverpool Trades Council from 1950 to 1964, and chairing it twice – in 1959 and in 1964. He also became a member of the executive of the North West Regional Labour Party, giving him a wider audience. However, he once again resigned from the Labour Party, in 1954, to join the Socialist Workers Federation. This, in turn, collapsed in 1957, leaving Eric to join the Labour Party for the third time.

Within three years, he became a councillor for the Pirrie ward (1960–66), and chairman of

Liverpool City Council's Direct Works Department in 1962. Yet a bigger stage beckoned. In 1963, he came from behind to win the Labour Party nomination as candidate for Liverpool Walton. In October 1964, he defeated Tory incumbent, Sir Kenneth Thompson, by nearly 3,000 votes. Eric fitted the House of Commons like a glove, and was to enjoy no finer compliment than to be described as a parliamentarian.

Betwen 1964 and 1974, Eric Heffer was a backbench journeyman, learning his new Parliamentary trade. Harold Wilson appointed him Minister of State in the Department of Industry in 1974, but was to sack him twelve months later for speaking in the House against the government on the Common Market. Eric immediately became an icon of the left, and was voted onto the National Executive Committee of the Labour Party.

This ushered in Eric's era of national celebrity. On the NEC from 1975 until defeated in 1986, he was Labour Party Vice-Chairman 1982–83 and Chairman 1983–84. During this period he secured election to the shadow cabinet for three consecutive years from November 1981, serving as European Affairs spokesman until October 1983 and as Housing and Construction spokesman until he failed to secure re-election to the shadow cabinet in October 1984. He also stood unsuccessfully against Neil Kinnock in the contest to succeed Michael Foot as Party leader in 1983. A later attempt for high office – alongside Tony Benn in 1988, challenging Kinnock and Hattersley – was another miserable failure.

Eric never recovered from his ignominious walk-out from the platform during Neil Kinnock's 1985 Conference attack on Militant. Later attempts for both a Shadow Cabinet place and an NEC place, in 1988, convinced him that his time had passed; and in November 1989 he announced his retirement at the following general election. In fact, he died of cancer on 27 May 1991.

A convinced Christian and a unilateral nuclear disarmer, Eric Heffer had been a founding member of the Tribune Group of MPs. He wore his opinions on his sleeve and was famed for his protests. Indeed, one protest led him to storm out of an NEC meeting, but he chose the wrong door, ending up in a cupboard rather than a corridor – an appropriate metaphor for a complex career. His autobiography, *Never A Yes Man*, was published posthumously in 1991. He also published *The Class Struggle in Parliament* (1970) and *Labour's Future* (1986).

Peter Kilfoyle MP

Arthur Henderson (1863–1935)

Arthur Henderson's political journey reflected several key influences on the development of the Labour Party: trade unionism, Nonconformist Christianity and Lib-Labbery. Like the Labour Party he progressed from protest to power, holding high office as Home Secretary and Foreign Secretary. In the traumatic years of 1931–2, Henderson was a crucial figure, eventually replacing MacDonald as Leader of the Labour Party when the National Government was formed. Always a popular figure among activists, he was to play a crucial role in developing trade union influence on the party.

Born in Glasgow on 20 September 1863, Henderson grew up in Newcastle-upon-Tyne, where he held an apprenticeship in an iron foundry. He was an active trade unionist as a member of the Iron Founders' Union, for which he became a district delegate in 1892. In this role, he was a proponent of the idea of co-operation between employers and employees in joint committees in order to settle industrial disputes. Until the end of the First World War he remained a prominent trade unionist, part of the 1919 National Industrial Conference, and the earlier National Industrial Council of 1919. His past as a trade unionist was to remain a constant influence on his career, and he was a vital bridge between the Labour Party and the unions.

A further influence on Henderson was Christianity. As a Wesleyan Methodist, he was both a widely-known lay preacher in the 1890s, and a speaker in favour of temperance. His first experience of party politics was as a member of the Liberal Party, though his relationship with the party was far from straightforward. A member of the Liberal Party, he was elected onto Newcastle City Council in 1894 under the Labour banner. In 1895, he was the Liberal general election agent for the two-member Barnard Castle constituency (having sought the Liberal nomination himself) and, three years later, became a 'Lib-Lab' member of Darlington Council, where he was mayor in 1903.

In the meantime, Henderson had been selected as the Labour Representation Committee candidate for Barnard Castle, and was elected at a by-election in 1903 – in the face of Liberal opposition. He remained very much a Lib-Lab MP, not joining any kind of socialist organisation until he became involved in the Fabian Society in 1912. He held his Barnard Castle seat until 1918, when he stood unsuccessfully in East Ham (South). A chequered election record for the remainder of his career saw him win Widnes in an August 1919 by-election, only to lose it in 1922. A January 1923 by-election win in Newcastle-upon-Tyne (East) kept him in the House no further than a defeat in the general election later in the year. He was therefore forced to fight and win Burnley in a January 1924 by-election, managing to hold the seat in both the 1924 and 1929 general elections. Further defeat came in 1931, and his final seat was Derbyshire Clay Cross, won in September 1933, and held until his death. Such electoral vicissitudes do not indicate any particular hostility to Henderson from the voters. Rather, they reflect the roller-coaster ride that was the inter-war Labour Party. One of Henderson's achievements was to stay on the train – and it was a mark of his popularity in the party, where he became known as 'Uncle Arthur', that he was able to carpet-bag from one seat to another so often.

Even greater success was seen when he won high office in the Labour Party. Serving as Chairman of the Parliamentary Labour Party (1908–10), he became Secretary of the Labour Party in 1912, holding the post until 1934. On the outbreak of war in 1914, he was again Parliamentary Chairman, taking over from Ramsay MacDonald. Henderson then entered Asquith's coalition Cabinet in May 1915 as President of the Board of Education, having already negotiated the Treasury Agreement on behalf of the unions in March of that year. He remained closely involved with the government's Labour relations, becoming Paymaster General in August 1916. Later that year, when Lloyd George became Prime Minister, Henderson was made a member of the five-man War Cabinet.

He had to resign in the summer of 1917 (being replaced as party chairman by William Adamson), after the infamous 'doormat' incident, when he was made to wait outside the War Cabinet for an hour while his colleagues debated and condemned his liaisons with socialists from abroad. Henderson had advocated Labour participation in an international socialist conference in Stockholm, attended by representatives from all countries, including Britain's wartime enemies. Having liaised with Russian communists over the matter, he gained a reputation as a 'hob-nobber with Bolsheviks', even though he had been an enthusiastic supporter of the Provisional Government in Russia in 1917. His final resignation came a week after the doormat incident, when Lloyd George had suspended him from the Cabinet. Out of office, Henderson devoted his energies to party organisation, especially revising the party's constitution, and securing union acceptance of the political levy. His work ensured that the unions dominated key areas of the party's decision-making for years to come.

When Labour came to power in 1924, Henderson served as Home Secretary, though he also took part in the negotiation of the Geneva Protocol, the doomed attempt to strengthen the League of Nations' Covenant. During this period, he became a fervent supporter of the League of Nations, and a critic of what he called 'the system of Versailles'. He believed that the League, backed by the military might of its members, was a far better mechanism for keeping peace than the situation in the early 1920s, which maintained aspects of the pre-Great War system of 'secret diplomacy', so strongly opposed by many in the Labour Party.

Henderson was not able to put all of his views on the League into practice when he became Foreign Secretary in the Labour government of 1929–31. Henderson certainly played an important role in securing the withdrawal of allied troops from the Rhineland. However, MacDonald's personal interest in foreign affairs reduced Henderson's influence. The Prime Minister took the lead in several areas, notably Anglo-American relations. In others, such as relations with France and Germany, they were actually rivals, with the effect that attempts to agree a loan to Germany in July 1931 fell apart.

Difficult relations between MacDonald and Henderson reached a climax in the July-August 1931 financial crisis. Initially Henderson's views wavered, but his instinctive support for the TUC eventually meant that he supported its opposition to cuts in social benefits, thus ensuring that the ministers opposed to MacDonald had an alternative leader.

With MacDonald forming the National Government in August 1931, Henderson found himself as Party leader. As leader of the opposition to the National Government, the MacDonald-Henderson personal rivalry had been formalised, but Henderson's time as leader was short-lived. Having lost his Burnley seat in the election of October 1931, he was replaced as acting leader of the parliamentary party by George Lansbury, the only remaining Labour ex-cabinet minister both inside Parliament and outside the government. Henderson formally retained his post of party leader until 1932 when he resigned, but it was Lansbury who was really calling the shots.

Having left Parliament briefly (he was to return in 1933), Henderson's ministerial experience and belief in collective security through the League made him an obvious choice to be President of the Geneva Disarmament Conference in 1932. Though the conference ultimately achieved little, his work there earned him the Nobel Peace Prize in 1934. He died on 20 October 1935. Henderson had married Eleanor Watson in 1889. They had one daughter and three sons.

In addition to articles and pamphlets, Henderson wrote *Labour's Way to Peace* (1935). Modern biographies are F M Leventhal, *Arthur Henderson* (1989) and Chris Wrigley, *Arthur Henderson* (1990). Other important studies include: David Carlton, *MacDonald versus Henderson: The Foreign Policy of the Second Labour Government* (1970); Ross McKibbin, *The Evolution of the Labour Party, 1910–24* (1974); and J M Winter, *Socialism and the Challenge of War* (1974).

Dr Richard S. Grayson

Margaret 'Peggy' Herbison   (1907–96)

'The miner's little sister' was an improbable, but true, description of the tiny, church-going spinster, who rose to become one of Harold Wilson's ministers, and whose reputation lives on in the Lanarkshire mining villages she so dominated in the post-war years. Winning the seat that had been held by the glamorous Jennie Lee, wife of Aneurin Bevan, Peggy could not have been more different.

A gentle but determined rebel, she resigned from the Wilson Government, but not before she had successfully secured the merger of her Ministry of Pensions and National Insurance with the National Assistance Board, creating a new Ministry of Social Security. Many claim to know why she resigned, but she herself, as a determined loyalist, would not allow her name to be used to attack a Labour Government. In August 1966, Dick Crossman noted in his diary that she 'can't let herself be associated any more with an attitude of which she disapproves; but on the other hand she can't let herself oppose her colleagues because she does not want to be accused of disloyalty.' She stuck to that until her death in December 1996.

In the mid eighties, unaware that one day I would be her successor in Parliament, I asked if she would allow me to make a TV documentary about her. She was not averse to the idea, but I was told that under no circumstances would she talk about that resignation, or attack the Party in any way that could be used 30 years later to damage Labour's election campaign.

In 1994, following the death of her protégé John Smith, I was to inherit the seat she won in 1945. She spoke in my by-election to a packed audience, many there to hear 'Peggy', totally disinterested in me and a young man called Blair. Then 84, she spoke for almost an hour without notes, holding her audience spellbound, and leaving the rest of us to scrabble for something left to say. Some claim she was known to all as Peggy; not true. It was drilled into me, and most of my generation, by parents who idolised her, that to us it was 'Miss Herbison'.

Born on 12 March 1907 in Shotts, a fiercely independent mining community that was to be her home for the rest of her life, Margaret McCrorie Herbison attended the local Dykehead School and Bellshill Academy, going on to Glasgow University where she graduated with an MA, as well as chairing the university branch of the Labour Party. Her father, and two of her brothers, one of whom was an Olympic boxer, were miners.

She taught English and History in Allan Glen's School in Glasgow and worked as a tutor for the National Council of Labour colleges, travelling every day from her parents' home in Shotts. She told me that when the local miners came to ask her to stand, she sent them away to find a man, but they stood their ground and she was swept to victory.

First elected to the NEC Women's Section in 1948, she served for some twenty years until her retirement from politics, becoming Chair of the Party in 1956–57. Appointed Joint Parliamentary Under Secretary of State for Scotland under Hector McNeil in 1950, she was the first woman Scottish Office Minister and the only woman to make party political broadcasts in the 1950 and 1951 elections.

In Opposition she was runner-up in the shadow cabinet elections of November 1951 with 84 votes to the 91 of Tony Greenwood who came twelfth, beating Hector McNeil, Patrick Gordon Walker and George Brown, but Attlee did not promote her beyond her status as a shadow junior Scottish Office Minister.

Gaitskill moved Peggy to Education in February 1956; her passion for the subject gave her a searing contempt for Margaret Thatcher. She returned to the Scottish Front Bench in 1959, moving at her own request to become Shadow Pensions Minister in 1962, although she continued to speak on Scottish Affairs in the Commons. She became a Privy Counsellor in 1964.

Fearless as a Minister in her battles with the Treasury, her ability to get her own way was limited by her Cabinet overlord, Douglas Houghton, who represented both her Ministry and Kenneth Robinson's Ministry of Health in the Cabinet, although he ran neither.

Her ideas were far sighted: it could be said she was the visionary behind the Minimum Income Guarantee. She supported wage-related benefits and wanted to increase family allowances, paying for it by increasing taxes on the more affluent. The Chancellor of the time, Jim Callaghan, feared the consequences of such a clawback, and advocated means testing. In July 1967, Peggy Herbison walked away from her Ministerial career.

Looking to the long term and her retirement from Parliament, she took under her wing the brilliant young Advocate John Smith: she was to outlive him. Passionate to the end about children, she would sit in her neat, sheltered house in Shotts and wait for the schoolchildren coming to see her on their way home.

The only real recognition of Margaret Herbison as a ground-breaking politician of national standing came when she served as the first Lord High Commissioner of the General Assembly of the Church of Scotland in 1970–71. The post, functioning as the Queen's representative in Scotland, replete with Ladies in Waiting and the mandatory title 'Your Grace', is the ultimate gathering of the Scottish Establishment. Always dignified, behatted, a church member of real Christian dedication, Peggy would have none of the flummery. She turned the traditional garden party over to the young people of Scotland.

Behind the staid image was a politician of principle and passion, earning criticism when she visited the United States and could not bite her tongue about the evils of segregated schooling. She loved the States but despaired of some of their politics, although she encouraged her niece, Karen Whitefield, who now represents the Airdrie & Shotts constituency that grew out of North Lanarkshire in the Scottish Parliament, to work as an intern on Capitol Hill.

A chain smoker who discovered training shoes in her latter years, she was much more fun than the picture painted of her by her contemporaries would suggest. She did not live to see the Labour Government, dying on 29 December 1996, but she would have approved of 'Wducation, education, education'.

Rt Hon. Helen Liddell MP

Patricia Hewitt (1948–)

Patricia Hewitt MP is an energetic Labour Secretary of State. All her working life Patricia has had an interest in the way policy ideas can be translated into social change through effective policy implementation. She is also strongly motivated by a desire to get things done. Consequently, she has made an important contribution to the shaping of the 'New' Labour Government and its programme. Her central part in this process began in 1983 when she embarked upon an overhaul of Labour's vision of a future society. It was an acknowledgement of this contribution, and, indeed, a recognition that the renewal process never ends, when Tony Blair appointed Patricia to his government in 1998.

Patricia Hewitt was born on 2 December 1948 in Canberra, Australia. She is the daughter of Sir Lenox Hewitt, the former First Permanent Secretary to the Australian Prime Minister's Department and former chairman of the Australian airline, Qantas. Patricia was educated at Canberra Girls' Grammar School and spent one year at the Australian National University, Canberra (1966). She then sat Cambridge entrance exams and, moving to the UK, attended Newnham College, Cambridge (1967–70) where she obtained a BA in English. In 1970 Patricia married Julian Gibson-Watt, but the marriage did not 'take' and they separated in 1974.

Patricia Hewitt's employment after college reflected her desire to correct injustices by effecting genuine change. She was Public Relations Officer at Age Concern (1971–73); Women's Rights Officer, National Council for Civil Liberties (NCCL) (1973–74) and then NCCL's General Secretary (1974–83). In this period she wrote numerous pamphlets and reports on various subjects, including women's rights. Her publications include *Your Rights* (Age Concern) in 1973; *The Privacy Report* (NCCL) in 1977; *Your Rights at Work* (NCCL) in 1978 (with a second edition in 1981); and *The Abuse of Power* (NCCL) in 1981. It was also in this period that she married barrister, Bill Birtles (1981). Patricia and Bill have a son and a daughter. She contested Leicester East for Labour in 1983 and in the process became convinced of the need to reconnect Labour with voters. Ever since that experience Patricia has been in the forefront of Labour's modernisation process.

Determined to re-establish that link between Labour and its supporters, Patricia Hewitt became Press and Broadcasting Secretary (1983–88) to Labour Leader Neil Kinnock. By 1983 it was obvious that the antiquated policy framework of defeated Labour lacked sufficient appeal to voters. Labour policy was like an Augean Stable requiring a thorough clear-out, and Neil Kinnock gave this Herculean task to Patricia Hewitt. Moreover, once the professionalisation of Labour's press relations had been achieved in 1987, the need for party policy reform became an even greater priority, and Patricia became Kinnock's Policy Co-ordinator (1988–89). But political events continued to overtake party structures. There was a pressing need for more imaginative Labour policy formulation and for a counter to the numerous right-wing policy 'think tanks'. A left-of-centre 'think tank', the Institute for Public Policy Research (IPPR), was set up in 1989 and Patricia became its senior research fellow (1989) and then deputy director (1989–94). She coupled this role with the part she played as Deputy Chair of the Commission for Social Justice (1992–94). This commission was the brainchild of party leader, John Smith. Its final report argued that social justice and economic success are mutually supportive in a modern economy – anticipating a key theme of 'New' Labour. The Commission also put forward several policies subsequently adopted by the Labour government.

An integral part of the modernisation process, touching on both the need to realign Labour with its constituency and on policy-making, was the need to redress Labour's shortfall of votes among women, the 'gender gap'. Patricia had been on the Secretary of State's Advisory Committee on the Employment of Women (1977–84) and on the National Labour Women's Committee (1979–83). She had written *Rights for Women* (NCCL) in 1975, and went on to co-author with Deborah Mattinson the Fabian pamphlet, *Women's Votes – the Key to Winning* in 1989; and to write *Your Second Baby* in 1990 and *About Time, the Revolution in Work and Family*

Life in 1993. She combined a theoretical with a practical understanding of a woman's relationship with the Labour Party. Labour's closing of the gender gap in 1997 owes much to Patricia's determined assault on Labour's old-fashioned approach to gender issues and her championship of a women's perspective within Labour.

For over a decade Patricia Hewitt wrote, or influenced, three Labour Party general election manifestos and innumerable policy initiatives. Thanks in great part to Patricia, fitfully but decisively, Labour policy extended its appeal to an ever greater proportion of the electorate.

Having done her bit to drag Labour into the modern age, there was a short period in which Patricia Hewitt was not directly involved in the Labour Party. She went to Andersen Consulting as Head (later Director) of Research (1994–97). But she was still influential. Having studied US election technique, Patricia strove to get Labour to adopt a rapid rebuttal approach during general elections. She travelled to the USA with her own team of Labour Party members made up of novelist Ken Follett, his wife, Labour candidate Barbara Follett, and a Management and Computer Systems Consultant, John Carr. The result was the successful Rapid Rebuttal Unit at Labour HQ in the 1997 election and the Excalibur computer system that powered it.

In 1997 Patricia Hewitt was elected MP for Leicester West. She was soon made a member of the Select Committee on Social Security. Not long after, together with Charles Clarke (with whom she had served in Kinnock's office), she was among the first of the May 1997 intake to get government posts. She was appointed Economic Secretary to the Treasury (1998) and played a key role in drafting the Financial Services and Markets Act, which sets out the regulatory framework for the new Financial Services Authority. She then became a DTI Minister of State with responsibility for small business and e-commerce in 1999. In this post, Patricia was the UK's first e-Minister and had responsibility for co-ordinating work on information age issues across government. Re-elected in 2001, Patricia was promoted to Secretary of State for Trade and Industry, as well as Minister for Women.

Patricia's energy is reflected in the many organisations she has been involved in, including council membership of the Campaign for Freedom of Information (1983–89); the Board of the International League for Human Rights (1978–83); Co-chairman of the Human Rights Network (1979–81); Vice Chair of Healthcare 2000 (1995–96); a Vice Chair of the British Council (1997–98); member of the Council of the Institute of Fiscal Studies (1996–98); Fellow of the RSA (since 1992); Associate of Newnham College (1984–97): Visiting Fellow of Nuffield College, Oxford (since 1992); member of the Fabian Society, including a period on its executive (1988–93); member of the Labour Campaign for Social Justice (since 1995). She still finds time for a little gardening.

In her e-Minister role, Patricia was charged with making sure we are all equipped to make the most of the technological changes that will alter every aspect of all our lives. Having been promoted (she is now the e-commerce Minister's boss and retains responsibility for e-issues generally at cabinet level), Patricia's role is vital to the way in which forward-looking ideas are not just translated into real change for the better but are also marshalled so as to serve British industry and the British economy. Her practical interest in getting things done suits her well to this job and will also benefit Labour for some time to come.

Rex Osborn

David Hill (1948–)

Robert Harris once described David Hill as the 'Bill Haley of spin doctors'. The description is literally true in the sense that he was the first to engage in what we now term political public relations. However, it would be more accurate to describe Hill as the Bruce Springsteen of spin doctors, for he had many of the same qualities as 'The Boss': a direct, no-nonsense approach backed up with enormous energy and commitment for his cause.

A laser-like focus on communicating Labour's message meant Hill had little time to engage in the promotion of his own profile – unlike some of his peers, who seemed to gain as much coverage as the stories they were promoting or rebutting. His inclination to get on with the job at hand endeared him to the political journalists whom he was engaged with on a daily basis. They had complete trust in him delivering the Labour Party's line. Steve Richards spoke for many of his colleagues when he said that Hill 'spun with integrity.'

Three things stand out about David Hill's career. The first was his loyalty to the Labour Party over the course of a thirty-year political career that saw him serve under every leader from Harold Wilson onwards. Although he was a Labour man through and through, there must have been occasions during the eighties when his patience and commitment was severely tested.

Secondly, he had a remarkable capacity to adapt to the changing needs of the party leadership whilst carrying out his tasks in the clear and consistent style to which the media had been accustomed. So he operated effectively as Labour's Director of Communications under Neil Kinnock despite his long service for Roy Hattersley. Likewise he managed a seamless transition from working for John Smith to working for Tony Blair.

Finally, the secret of his success over such a long period of time was his ability to connect with people whatever their political persuasion or background. He was able to connect because of his wide and varied hinterland. Whether extolling the virtues of the actress Susan Sarandon, or discussing the Rolling Stones's greatest singles or describing the delights of the Catalan region in Spain, there were few subjects that he could not talk passionately about. In the world of politics – where the key players more often confine their interests to the machinations of Westminster and Whitehall – this quality stands out like a beacon.

David Hill was born in Birmingham on 1 February 1948. He was educated at King Edward VI School, Birmingham, and Brasenose College, Oxford University, where he read philosophy, politics and economics. Following Oxford he worked for a brief period on industrial relations matters for Unigate.

In 1973 he began working for Roy Hattersley who was then Shadow Education Secretary. He quickly formed an effective partnership with Hattersley and began to operate many of the news management techniques that were to later form the basis of the Labour Party's communications under Peter Mandelson and Alastair Campbell.

As special adviser to Hattersley at the Department of Prices and Consumer Protection from 1976, he ran into trouble with civil servants who deemed his activities too political. He was again ahead of his time, as similar complaints were later made about the Blair Government's special advisers. However, Hattersley stood by his aide and informed civil servants that he would be more concerned if Hill was not carrying out his job in a politically attuned fashion.

Following Labour's 1979 general election defeat, he continued to work for Hattersley and played a pivotal role in a number of the party's significant moments in its first ten years of opposition. These included the 1981 special conference, the leadership contests of 1983 and 1988, and the policy review process that followed the 1987 election.

When Peter Mandelson resigned as Labour's Director of Communications in 1990, Hill applied for the job but was turned down in favour of John Underwood. Within a year, though, Underwood himself departed, and this time around Hill was successful in his application for the vacancy. He began his new job in a pugnacious mood: 'My task now is to help the Labour Party to win the general election whenever the Prime Minister has the guts to call it.'

Unfortunately, the 1992 election campaign was not a happy experience for either Hill or the Labour Party. He had to overcome a number of organisational problems, including the bizarre situation of having the election campaign team based in three different buildings. But it was fundamentally the Kinnock factor and the party's inability to effectively counter the Tory 'tax bombshell' campaign that did for Labour in 1992. There was very little that Hill could have done differently to improve the campaign or the party's result.

A year after Smith had taken over from Kinnock as leader, Hill was appointed Labour's Chief Media Spokesperson. This new role saw him working as both the Leader of the Opposition's spokesman and head of the Walworth Road press office. He worked effectively with the new Labour leader despite Smith's aversion to publicity. Shortly before Smith's death Hill had convinced him of the need to engage more closely with the media, including the Murdoch press.

Hill continued as Chief Media Spokesperson under Tony Blair and played an important part in Labour's 1997 election campaign. One of the most memorable sights on the evening of 1 May 1997 was Hill dancing away to Labour's anthem 'Things Can Only Get Better' at the party's Royal Festival Hall celebrations. His exuberance that night showed how much the victory meant to him.

A year after the election he decided he needed a fresh challenge and so moved into the world of public relations consultancy. He joined Bell Pottinger Good Relations, part of the Chime Communications empire of Lord Bell, Mrs Thatcher's former PR man. He continued to advise Labour, but his presence was missed by the party and lobby journalists alike. Most political insiders would agree with Alastair Campbell's verdict that he has been a 'a very, very hard act to follow.'

Jayant Chavda

Rita Hinden (1909–71)

Dr. Rita Hinden never became a Member of Parliament, never held high office in the state, the Party, or a trade union, and had such a gentle, modest manner that she was rarely in the spotlight. She did, though, achieve a level of influence that was widely recognised in the Party. She brought a consistently compassionate and informed view to any debate on social democracy, opening up narrow views to wider perspectives. She made two great contributions; first towards the clarification of Labour's colonial policy after the Second World War, and then as an important conduit for the revisionist debate about how Labour policy should develop after the Attlee administration's programme of reform had been exhausted.

Born on 16 January 1909, she was registered under the name Rebecca but was always known as Rita. After the failure of the family's ostrich farm, the family moved to Cape Town. She was educated at the Seminary of Good Hope and at Cape Town University for one year before, following their Zionist beliefs, the family emigrated to Palestine in 1927. Rita was sent to continue her education, first in Liverpool for a year and then at the London School of Economics (LSE), where she graduated with a BSc in economics in 1931.

During her studies she had met Elchon Hinden, graduate in Medicine at Cambridge. After her own graduation, Rita returned to Palestine and Elchon joined her to be married on 14 February 1933. They returned for a while to London, joining the Independent Labour Party, but once again, their Zionism drew them to Palestine in 1935. Rita worked as a journalist and researcher, but as nationalism intensified in reaction to developments in Hitler's Germany, the Hindens were becoming disenchanted with Zionism. In 1938 they finally decided to make England their permanent home.

Rita joined the Fabian Society and the Labour Party and returned to research at the LSE, obtaining her doctorate in 1939. She had started to specialise in colonial matters and was instrumental in founding the Fabian Colonial Research Bureau (FCRB) in 1940, with Arthur Creech Jones as chairman and herself as secretary, a post she held until 1950. The FCRB produced a constant supply of pamphlets, briefings, speeches and debate including Hinden's own book, *Plan for Africa,* in 1941. Hinden helped to take the Labour Party out of its parochial concentration on domestic policy and to develop for the first time a credible colonial policy based on recognising the need to move to democratic self-government for the colonies with a long-term investment and development programme in partnership with Britain. Her expertise became so respected that from 1945 onwards not only the Labour Party but also Colonial Office officials took up many of the FCRB ideas with Creech Jones appointed Colonial Secretary in 1946. Because of her pioneering of colonial freedom, Denis Healey referred to her as 'Rudyard Hardie' (quoted in K O Morgan's *Labour People: Leaders and Lieutenants, Hardie to Kinnock,* Oxford University Press, Oxford (1989), p 241). Once colonial policy was established along the lines Hinden had been advocating she started to look for a new challenge, whilst never losing her interest in colonial matters.

When the programme of nationalisation, welfare reform, and other elements of the 1945 administration's plans had been largely implemented, the Labour government seemed to be lacking a clear idea about what should be done next. A debate started about whether there should be more of the same or whether in the newly established conditions the programme needed revision. The Socialist Union was founded to argue the revisionist cause from the centre and right of the Party and took control of the monthly journal *Socialist Commentary.* Hinden was appointed editor, a role she filled for the rest of her life.

Socialist Commentary established itself as the unofficial voice of the Gaitskellites, and later of the Campaign for Democratic Socialism. Indeed, Gaitskell served as the treasurer of the 'Friends of Socialist Commentary' from 1953 until he was elected Party leader in 1955. In 1956 when Crosland's *Future of Socialism* and Strachey's *Contemporary Capitalism* made major contributions to the revisionist debate, Hinden, together with Allan Flanders, produced the Socialist Union's contribution, *Twentieth-Century Socialism.* Between the three works the whole range of revisionism was apparent, with Hinden's in the middle offering a vision of fellowship, liberty and equality that was firmly entrenched in the ethical traditions of R H Tawney.

In the same way that she had helped define Labour's colonial policy, now she commissioned policy supplements that raised the level of debate and helped to clarify future policy. Supplements on education, incomes policy and social services were amongst those that made a significant contribution to the policy debates within the Party. In 1960 Hinden commissioned the groundbreaking survey by Mark Abrams, *Must Labour Lose?* The only time she seriously departed from Gaitskell's position was in 1962, when despite the leader's opposition to the European Common Market, *Socialist Commentary* took a pro-European line. It was typical of Hinden's broad view, which always extended beyond Britain, that she believed Labour could work for the benefit of social democracy in conjunction with fellow parties on the continent.

For almost twenty years Rita Hinden sustained the influence of *Socialist Commentary.* The strength with which she adhered to her Tawneyesque principles was such that after Tawney's death it was she who was the obvious choice of his executors to edit a posthumous volume of his essays, *The Radical Tradition.*

It is remarkable the extent to which her views were listened to in discussions or through her editorials. All accounts of her are unanimous in their recognition of her compassionate and gentle approach that did not suit the hurly-burly of party politics and parliamentary life. This gentleness, however, never prevented her instilling purpose and clarity into any task she entered upon. She brought integrity, expertise and intelligence that was respected by politicians and officials alike and made her a quiet, but important, influence over the political life of the Party for a period of twenty-five years. She died on 18 November 1971 at the early age of 61 leaving Elchon, her son Jonathan and her daughter Judith.

There is a short biography in K. Morgan's *Labour People. Leaders and Lieutenants: Hardie to Kinnock* (first published 1987). See also R Hinden's *Plan for Africa* (1941), and the Socialist Union's *Twentieth-Century Socialism,* eds A Flanders and R Hinden.

Nick Cowell

Eric Hobsbawm (1917–)

A Marxist historian, Hobsbawm played a key role in the Communist Party and thereby exercised a strong indirect influence on the Labour Party at a critical period in the late 20th century, preparing the ground intellectually for the rejection of the Bennite Left in the 1980s.

Eric John Ernest Hobsbawm, born on 9 June 1917, was educated at Vienna, Berlin, and Cambridge. His academic career began with a lecturing position at Birkbeck College, London, in 1947 and continued with a Fellowship at King's College, Cambridge, from 1949 to 1955, before his return to Birkbeck. Along with many intellectuals in the 1930s, he saw the Soviet Union as the main bulwark against fascism and Nazi Germany and joined the Communist Party. Unlike most other intellectuals of the time, he has remained faithful to the Party through all its vicissitudes. He has always testified to the strength of the idea of the Popular Front, which attracted him to the communists at that time and which in different forms has remained the keynote of his politics ever since. This is the notion that political differences between the parties of the left should be forgotten in the face of the common enemy on the right; it is a politics which has led both the communists and Hobsbawm to bitterly criticise left-wing radicals, particularly the Trotskyists (and later the Bennites), for their insistence on a radical strategy which could isolate socialists.

Strongly influenced by the communist historians A L Morton and Dona Torr, he helped to form the influential Communist Historians Group with Christopher Hill, E P Thompson and John Saville. Here, his concern to demonstrate that the Communists were not an alien party directed from Moscow led him to argue that they were the heir to a native radical tradition in Britain stretching back through the Chartists to the Levellers. Unlike New Left historians such as Thompson and Saville, he remained within the Communist Party after the Soviet suppression of the Hungarian Rising in 1956. Instead, with Christopher Hill, he proceeded to contribute to the rich field of Marxist historiography with such works as *Primitive Rebels* (1959), *Labouring Men* (1964), and his monumental history of Europe from *The Age of Revolution* (1962) to *The Age of Extremes* (1994).

In the 1970s, as the communists experienced a new intellectual influx of Euro-communists and feminists, Hobsbawm became a figure of influence within Labour circles with his writings on the need for Labour to respond differently to its problems. In *The Forward March of Labour Halted?*(1978 – the question mark was subsequently dropped), he called on socialists and progressives to recognise that the idea of an inexorable advance of Labour and socialism had to be replaced by the recognition that Labour was losing ground in the electorate as a result of its inability to address the problems of ordinary people. While changes in the capitalist economy were making the reality of an industrial working class redundant, the dominant Bennite Left was fixated on the old problems of class-war rhetoric and public ownership. Hobsbawm called on Labour to be more responsive to the 'lost voters' of the South, and to be more relevant to young people 'who remember the date of the Beatles' break-up, and not the date of the Saltley pickets'.

Hobsbawm was listened to with enthusiasm by Neil Kinnock and other leftists concerned with Labour's declining popularity in the face of Thatcher's electoral success in the 1980s. The later writings of Philip Gould, in which the forgotten suburbanites are commended above the elitist bohemians of the left, are a reflection of the views of this quiet and studious historian.

There is an interesting article by Bill Schwarz, '"The People" in History: The Communist Party Historians Group', in *Making Histories: Studies in History-Writing and Politics* (Centre for Contemporary Cultural Studies, 1982).

Geoffrey Foote

J A Hobson (1858–1940)

John A. Hobson was one of the principal proponents of the 'New Liberalism' at the beginning of the last century. For the New Liberals, the cause of liberty could not be understood solely in its negative sense as an absence of coercion by the state. Instead, in a break with Gladstonian orthodoxy, liberty must mean a positive liberty for all, and this goal required an active state. Only through the state enabling people to realise their full potential could all people truly enjoy liberty. Without the state playing this role, liberty for the majority of people would remain a worthless facade.

In his book, *Liberals and Social Democrats* (1978), Peter Clarke charts the lives of the four leading lights of New Liberalism – L T Hobhouse, J L Hammond, Graham Wallas and Hobson. Whilst all four became disillusioned with the Liberal Party as the vehicle for their brand of social liberalism, it was only Hobson of the four that made the journey to the Labour Party.

John Atkinson Hobson was born on 6 July 1858 in Derby. He enjoyed a comfortable middle-class upbringing and attended Derby Public School between 1868 and 1876. From there he went up to Lincoln College, Oxford, to study Classical Literature. He graduated in 1880, obtaining a disappointing lower second class honours degree. After university, Hobson worked on the newspaper his father owned and edited, the *Derbyshire and North Staffordshire Advertiser,* for a short time before leaving to teach classics in Faversham. From here, he quickly moved to teach in Exeter where Hobson met his wife, Florence Edgar, the daughter of an American businessman. Florence and John had two children, Harold and Mabel.

It was also in Exeter that Hobson began his long and prolific writing career with *The Physiology of Industry* (1889). The tract was co-authored with Exeter businessman, A F Mummery. The book's significance lay in its introduction of the concepts of 'over-saving' and 'underconsumption' which came to dominate Hobson's work. It attacked the assumption underpinning classical economics that savings were an inherent good. Rather, for Hobson, the culture of saving was to blame for underconsumption and diminishing demand and, therefore, the direct cause of unnecessary unemployment in periods of downturn. Since it was only natural for individuals to save, the state must step in to remedy the situation through fiscal measures to check savings and encourage demand. Hobson described *The Physiology of Industry* in his autobiography as the first step in 'my heretical career' and the book certainly marked Hobson out for attack by the academic establishment.

In *Problems of Poverty* (1891), *The Evolution of Modern Capitalism* (1894), and *The Social Problem* (1891), Hobson developed the concept of underconsumption and broadened it to a wider attack on classical *laissez-faire* economics. To increase consumption amongst the masses, a larger proportion of the national income must be redistributed through progressive taxation on income, particularly unearned income.

Anti-imperialism was the other great cause to dominate Hobson's life. In 1899, he became a special correspondent in South Africa for the *Manchester Guardian*. His account of his time there, *The War in South Africa* (1900), was strongly critical of the British authorities and the 'stupid jingoism of the British public'. The attack was followed up in *The Psychology of Jingoism* (1901), and in his renowned *Imperialism* (1902), a work later cited by Lenin as a strong influence, much to Hobson's embarrassment.

It was in the early years of the century that Hobson aligned himself with the group of Liberal intellectuals that came to be known as the New Liberals. The New Liberals rejected classical liberalism, instead perceiving strong state action and a degree of socialism as necessary prerequisites of true liberalism. The work of the New Liberals largely centred around the journal *The Nation* and the *Manchester Guardian*. Hobson himself began full time work for *The Nation* in 1907. The influence of the New Liberals reached its zenith in Asquith's premiership and, in particular, Lloyd George's 'People's Budget' of 1909. However, disillusion quickly set in with the House of Lords rejection of the 'People's Budget'.

Hobson, in particular, attacked the Liberal Party's failure to take on the forces ranged against it in *Crisis in Liberalism* (1909) and *Traffic in Treason* (1914).

This disenchantment culminated in Hobson's break with the Liberals in 1916. It was his opposition to the First World War and the Liberals' conduct of it that provoked the final break. For Hobson, who still regarded himself as a Cobdenite, the abandonment of free trade and descent into protectionism was too much to bear. His break was confirmed when, in 1918, he stood for Parliament against the Liberals as an independent in a joint university seat which he narrowly lost.

Hobson had been moving closer to the Labour Party through his involvement in the anti-war Union of Democratic Control, and in 1918 he became chairman of the Labour Party Advisory Committee on Trade Policy and Finance. However, he did not join the Labour Party until 1924, joining at the same time he advised Ramsay MacDonald to risk forming a minority government.

Paradoxically, given his Liberal background, Hobson's influence within the Labour family was strongest on the ILP. Although he never formally joined the ILP, Hobson's thinking became the dominant source of its economic approach, most notably in his influential report, *The Living Wage* (1926), which recommended that the Labour Party adopt the minimum wage as a central plank of its policy. In 1931, Hobson rejected a peerage from Ramsay MacDonald in protest at what he saw as MacDonald's and Snowden's slavish adherence to economic orthodoxy.

In the last decade of his life, Hobson became less politically active and died on 1 April 1940 at the age of 81. Hobson's work, perhaps underestimated at the time, greatly influenced leading Labour radicals such as G D H Cole and Harold Laski. Keynes never fully accepted Hobson's underconsumptionist analysis, but nevertheless hailed Hobson's work as an 'epoch in economic thought' in his *General Theory*.

Whilst Hobson was the most prominent of the New Liberals to join the Labour Party, he never felt truly comfortable in his new home. For him, the majority of the Labour Party did not recognise that its historic task lay in the building of a reformed and more socially just capitalism, not the wholesale substitution of capitalism for a full-blooded socialism. In his autobiography, he wrote, 'For neither section of this Labour Party avowedly accepts that middle course which seems to me essential to a progressive and constructive economic government in this country.' In his advocacy of this course, Hobson can be seen as a true forerunner of Gaitskell, Crosland and the revisionist tradition within Labour that has reached its apotheosis in New Labour. As David Marquand concludes, 'In the struggle for intellectual ascendancy between socialism and New Liberalism, socialism won the first battles. Posthumously, and without acknowledgement, the New Liberals won the war.' (*The Progressive Dilemma*, 1991).

Key works in the life and writings of Hobson are *New Liberalism: The Political Economy of J.A. Hobson* (John Allett, 1981), *J.A. Hobson: A Reader* (ed. Michael Freeden, 1988), *J.A. Hobson After Fifty Years* (ed. John Pheby, 1994), and *J.A. Hobson* (Michael Scheider, 1996). The classic text on the New Liberals remains Peter Clarke's *Liberals and Social Democrats* (1978). Hobson also published an autobiography, *Confessions of an Economic Heretic* (1938).

Patrick Loughran

Stuart Holland   (1940–)

The political economist Stuart Holland was the main influence behind the more radical policy agenda that emerged in the Labour Party after the disappointments of the 1964–70 Wilson government. As an academic advisor to the Labour Party he played a key role in developing the more interventionist economic approach that provided the basis of stated policy of the late 1970s (though the Party leadership effectively disowned it) and, notably, the 1983 general election manifesto. Despite becoming an MP and sitting on the Labour front bench for several years, Holland is best remembered and had his greatest influence on the Labour Party for his time as an advisor during the 1970s when he was outside parliament.

Holland was born on 25 March 1940. After Christ's Hospital School he went to Balliol College, Oxford, where he graduated with a first in Modern History. He stayed at Oxford to research for a doctorate in economics at St Anthony's College. After a spell as an Economic Assistant to the Cabinet Office under Lord Balogh and then to the Prime Minister, between 1966 and 1988 he moved to academia, taking up a lectureship at the University of Sussex. From his base at Sussex he began to develop a critique of the Keynesian economic approach that had framed most Labour Party thinking about the economy since the 1950s and which had been given its most famous exposition by Anthony Crosland in *The Future of Socialism* (Cape, 1956). Holland's doctoral thesis, which he finally completed in 1971, gives an early insight into some of the sorts of issues that he subsequently developed. It looked at regional development in Italy and, in particular, it examined the role of the IRI – the Italian state holding company – in promoting economic development.

Holland had joined the Labour Party in 1962 and maintained an active role in it even after resigning from the Prime Minister's office. And though he was to become the major intellectual of the Party left he was initially associated with its revisionist or social democratic right. It was through the journal *Socialist Commentary*, which for many years had been the organ of Labour's social democratic wing, that he met Bill Rodgers who appointed him as an advisor to the Commons Public Expenditure Committe which he chaired. An article in the journal brought him to the attention of Roy Jenkins who recruited him to help draft a speech on public ownership that was given to the NUM in 1972.

However this association with the Party right was short-lived, and he was soon to become one of its hate figures as the chief intellectual figure on the Bennite left of the Party. He established himself in the Party policy-making arena through his membership of the Public Sector Group of the Party's Industrial Policy Committee, in particular developing proposals for a state holding company – along similar lines to the Italian IRI that he studied for his doctorate – to play a central role in economic policy. Whilst the concept of a state holding company owning stakes in private firms was not confined to the Party left and had supporters on its right as well, Holland was proposing to use it as an instrument of economic planning and control to a far greater degree than the right were happy to countenance. Holland found support for his proposals on the left from figures like Judith Hart (who appointed him her adviser in 1974 when she was Minister for Overseas Development) and Tony Benn.

The fullest statement of Holland's approach to economic matters in this period can be found in his most famous book, *The Socialist Challenge* (Quartet, 1975). In it he put forward a critique of the social democratic, Keynesian approach associated with Crosland. Karl Marx had been correct, claimed Holland, when he noted the tendency of capital to concentrate in monopolies over time, and now the Keynesian policies favoured by Crosland and his followers had been undermined by the increasing number of large multi-national companies able to circumscribe the policies of national governments and too dominant to be subject to the normal constraints of market competition. This sector of multi-nationals constituted a new 'meso-economy' outside the traditional economic focus on the national macroeconomy or the microeconomic level of individual firms. As a consequence of the emergence of this meso-economy the government was no longer able to exercise the control and direction of the economy that Holland felt necessary.

The solution that he put forward in *The Socialist Case* revolved around re-establishing the economic sovereignty that he felt the meso-economic sector had undermined. Public ownership was a central part of this. It was necessary to take significant numbers of very large firms into state hands in their entirety in order to re-establish the government's capacity to manage the economy in the nation's interests. But alongside the extension of public ownership of entire firms Holland proposed a far greater degree of planning over the private sector. Drawing on the experience of economic planning in post-war France and the Italian IRI that he had researched for his doctorate, Holland proposed a National Planning Agency to sit at the centre of national economic policy. This agency would reach planning agreements with firms in the private sector and play a key role in regional policy. The broad approach was labelled the 'siege economy', because it sought to insulate the UK economy from the international system. As a consequence its proponents opposed continued membership of the European Economic Community, which tended to be dismissed by the left as a 'capitalist club'. And yet despite the socialist rhetoric the general aim of the approach that Holland was putting forward was not as different from Crosland as the hostility between the left and right of the Party might imply. Crosland's approach sought to manage the economy to maintain steady economic growth that would ensure full employment, rising incomes and a well funded public sector. This was an aim that Holland shared, although he argued that far more interventionist policies were required to achieve it.

Holland left academia to become MP for Vauxhall in London in 1979 and held the seat until he left parliament in 1989. Throughout the 1970s he had been active in Labour politics (he was an Labour Co-ordinating Committee member, serving on their Executive 1978–81). By 1983 he had been promoted to the front bench as shadow spokesperson on Overseas Development Co-operation and he developed his analysis of the global economy in the direction of Third World development issues. He remained at Overseas Development until 1987 when he became a Treasury spokesman. But his stay there was brief and in 1989 he left parliament to return to academia as a Professor at the European University Institute in Florence. Once in parliament and in the wake of the disappointing election result of 1983, Holland was not able to exert the same degree of influence over Labour policy at the highest level that he had done during the 1970s. After leaving parliament he wound down the involvement with the Labour Party committees that he had been involved with, including the NEC on which he had sat from 1972–89.

But despite returning to academia and a less prominent role within the Labour Party he continued to contribute to the public policy debate and became particularly involved in

European Union initiatives. In place of their earlier attempts to insulate the British economy, many on the left began to look to the EU to achieve some the goals that they no longer saw as feasible in the domestic economy alone. Holland has argued for an expanded and more deeply integrated EU (*The European Imperative*, 1993) and also collaborated with Ken Coates, an old ally from the Institute for Workers Control during the 1970s who became an MEP, in developing socialist policy proposals at the EU level. He married Jenny Lennard in 1976 and is now director of an economic research company. Holland has written a large number of books, pamphlets and articles on a variety of aspects of politics, economics and policy. The disputes over policy within the Party during the 1970s have been covered by a range of academics, while Michael Hatfield's *The House the Left Built* (Gollancz, 1978) provides a detailed, journalistic account.

Dr Philip Larkin

Geoff Hoon (1953–)

Geoff Hoon MP is one of New Labour's rising stars, described by the BBC as 'talented, intelligent and ambitious', whose loyalty and ability have been rewarded by rapid promotion through the ranks of Government.

Born the son of a railwayman in Derby on 6 December 1953, he was educated at Nottingham High School and won a scholarship to Jesus College, Cambridge, to study Law. He was called to the Bar by Gray's Inn in 1978. He lectured in Law at Leeds University from 1976 to 1982 and was Visiting Professor of Law at the University of Louisville, Kentucky, in 1979 and 1980. He practiced as a barrister between 1982 and 1984.

In 1977 he joined the Labour Party, and was elected as MEP for Derbyshire and Ashfield from 1984 until 1994, serving on the European Parliament's Legal Affairs Committee. In 1992 Geoff Hoon won the parliamentary seat of Ashfield, Nottinghamshire, following the retirement of Frank Haynes. In Opposition, Hoon won praise for his forensic debating skills during the passage of the Maastricht Bill. In 1993 he won a *Spectator* magazine award for 'ingenious use of a parliamentary procedure' which forced a parliamentary vote on the Maastricht treaty on the beleaguered Major Government; it became known as 'Hoon's Hurdle'. In 1994 Labour Leader Tony Blair promoted Hoon to the Whips Office, and in 1995 to the post of spokesman on Trade and Industry.

Hoon entered Government in 1997 as Parliamentary Secretary to the Lord Chancellor's Office and was promoted in 1998 as Minister of State in the same department. He won a reputation as a moderniser by supporting legal reforms, including support for an end to judges wearing ceremonial wigs.

When Leeds MP and FCO Minister Derek Fatchett died suddenly in 1999, Hoon was appointed to replace him as Minister of State at the Foreign and Commonwealth Office, and later was promoted to Minister for Europe. In October 1999, following the Secretary of State for Defence George Robertson's elevation to the Lords and appointment as Secretary General of NATO, Geoff Hoon was promoted to be Secretary of State for Defence. He was re-appointed following Labour's second landslide in 2001.

As Secretary of State for Defence, Hoon has proved a tough and skilful operator. He has secured a £1.25 billion increase in defence expenditure from Gordon Brown, and has handled situations such as the bombing of Kosovo, protection of the no-fly zones over Iraq, the row over the European rapid reaction force and the deployment of British troops to Sierra Leone. He oversaw the lifting of the ban on gays in the Armed Forces, and has signalled support for women being allowed to serve in combat roles. Observers agree that Geoff Hoon is a politician whose star will continue to shine brightly, and, some suggest, whose ability will take him to the very top of the political ladder. Geoff Hoon is married to Elaine and they have three children. He is an avid Derby County football club supporter.

Paul Richards

Douglas Houghton (Lord Houghton of Sowerby) (1898–1996)

Douglas Houghton reached no higher among Labours pinnacles of power than the General Council of the TUC and Chancellor of the Duchy of Lancaster in the Wilson Cabinet. Yet as a modest man who found the distortions and over-simplifications of political debate and the rough and tumble of power and promotion distasteful, he much preferred the major role he did have as wise adviser and respected tribal elder. Unusually, he combined this with advocacy of the kind of single-issue causes which have become so much more important in recent years. On abortion (where he gave crucial support to the passing of the 1967 Abortion Act), women's rights and animal welfare, he was a passionate crusader.

Born Arthur Leslie Noel Douglas Houghton into a Liberal-radical family on 11 August 1898 in Long Eaton, Derbyshire, Houghton's belief in the dignity and strength of the people was nurtured after leaving county secondary school by infantry service at Passchendaele in the First World War, where he served in the trenches alongside Henry Moore. It found its full expression in the inter-war years, when he built up the Inland Revenue Staff Federation, becoming General Secretary in 1922, a position he held until 1960. In office he pioneered white collar unionism and advancing education as the instrument for promoting civil service 'clerks' who found difficulty in rising through the Service's rigidly stratified hierarchy.

He came to wider public attention as an early media star and one of the first to make the transition from media fame into politics. He began the popular advice programme 'Can I Help You' in 1941. As an avuncular, common-sense presenter of straightforward advice on tax, employment and social issues, he built up a considerable following on the, then, dominant BBC Home Service; the programme carried on to 1964.

Popularity and personal probity made him the perfect candidate to fight the 1949 Sowerby by-election in the West Riding when the sitting Member, John Belcher, was forced to stand down by a corruption scandal, mild by today's standards, but enormously inflated by the *Daily Express*. Houghton was persuaded to stand by his friend Herbert Morrison (he was an LCC Alderman 1947–49) and successfully maintained the 1945–51 Labour government's unbroken record of by-election victories in a difficult seat where the Liberals were always a threat.

By the 1950s he was a power in the trade union movement as member of the General Council of the TUC and Chair of the staff side of the Whiteley Council, while as an MP he was an early moderniser, disliking nationalisation and high taxation and advocating widening the appeal of both Labour and the unions beyond manual workers. He took little part in Labour's internal civil war, preferring his active role on the Public Accounts Committee, becoming its Chair when Harold Wilson stepped down to become Party Leader in 1963. Appointed Opposition Pensions Spokesman in 1959, he continued in this role as an elected shadow cabinet member from November 1960 before Wilson moved him to strengthen the Shadow Treasury team where he operated as Shadow Chief Secretary alongside his old friend and Inland Revenue Staff Federation protégé, Shadow Chancellor Jim Callaghan. He was then appointed to influential roles in Wilson's Cabinet as the Party came to power, as a non-departmental 'overlord' to the non-Cabinet ministries of Health and Pensions, charged with co-ordinating the reform of the welfare state. He served as Chancellor of the Duchy of Lancaster from October 1964 until April 1966 and as Minister without Portfolio until January 1967, when he was dropped as too old at 69. That same year he was made a Companion of Honour.

This began Houghton's Indian Summer as senior statesman of the movement and Chairman of the PLP, a position he held from April 1967 until 1974. He was sometimes accused of sour grapes, as when he opposed Wilson on Lords' reform, and over *In Place of Strife,* the attempt by Wilson and Barbara Castle to reform trade union relations, but both campaigns sprang from deep feelings about the issues and his close connections with the union movement. On other issues he was equally principled but less successful, as in 1971 when as a convinced European he was one of the 69 Labour MPs who defied the Whips to allow the Heath government to win its crucial vote on entry to the Common Market.

In 1974 he stood down as MP, and by the law of opposites, which then operated, the Sowerby party chose a left-wing, anti-European successor in Max Madden. Douglas become Lord Houghton of Sowerby and played major roles in many of the Royal Commissions we used to formulate policy before focus groups took over. He had already been a member of the Kilbrandon Commission on the Constitution, which first endorsed regionalism, and then served on the Commission on Standards in Public Life, as well as chairing the enquiry into teachers' pay in 1974, and the Houghton Committee on Aid To Political Parties. This made sensible recommendations for the kind of aid paid in Germany, but the Labour government had neither the majority, nor the will, to implement it.

Labour's loss of office in 1979, his own increasing age and the Party's headlong rush to folly in the early Eighties restricted Houghton's influence, though he remained active in pursuit of his causes in the Lords, attending with great regularity and speaking powerfully on protection of animals, advance of women's rights, protection of children, and in defence of abortion. More curiously, he also opposed reform of the Lords, seeing it as a protection against the elective tyranny of an over-powerful party system. His last speech in the Lords was given on 27 March 1994, a frail figure speaking briefly in support of his own Dangerous Dogs Amendment. The Bill did not pass. Two years later, at the age of 97 the oldest Parliamentarian, on 2 May 1996, Douglas Houghton was dead. His publications included a notable lecture to the Institute of Economic Affairs on 'Paying For The Social Services' (1968), which suggested closer inter-action between income tax and social security and an equal retirement age for men and women.

Austin Mitchell MP

Denis Howell (Lord Howell)   (1923–1998)

In his autobiography, Denis Howell wrote that throughout his life he had never been certain whether he was engaged in the sport of politics or in the politics of sport. He is remembered for his work in sport and for his ability to influence the weather. He was an active church member, with a great love of poetry and music. When Roy Jenkins and Shirley Williams abandoned the Party, he saw the Labour Movement in Europe through difficult times to become popular with the mainstream of the Party.

Denis Herbert Howell was proud of his Birmingham roots. He was born in Lozells on 4 September 1923. His father lost his job in the General Strike and had to move to Exeter for a time. His parents were great readers and strong supporters of the Labour Party. He chose King Edwards Grammar School, Handsworth, because football was played there rather than rugby.

Aged 22, he was elected Councillor for St Paul's ward in November 1946, serving until 1956. From 1950–55 he served as Secretary of the Labour Group, and from the Health Committee he was appointed to the Management Committee of Dudley Road Hospital, which he later chaired, the commencement of a long association with the NHS. Denis married Brenda Willson in 1955. They had four children, one of whom is a councillor in Birmingham. Born into a political family, he married into a political family and founded a political family.

Howell was elected MP for All Saints constituency in 1955. He continued as a football referee. It gave him popularity, reaching beyond party lines. Howell greatly admired Hugh Gaitskell and founded the Campaign for Democratic Socialism to support him in the battle over unilateralism. A keen advocate of the rights of immigrants, he spent many a Sunday afternoon berating Home Office Ministers on behalf of people refused entry. All Saints remained a marginal constituency. In 1969 he lost the seat. However, he won a by-election in the neighbouring Small Heath constituency in 1961, representing it until his retirement from the Commons in 1992.

Following the 1964 victory, Harold Wilson appointed him Under-Secretary at Education with special responsibility for sport, a post he held until, retaining responsibility for sport, he was appointed Minister of State at the Ministry of Housing and Local Government in 1969. Howell will be remembered as the first Minister for Sport – the politician of whom one of his successors said, 'Half the nation thinks Denis Howell was the best Minister for Sport we ever had. The other half thinks that he is still doing the job.' He can take real credit for involving the Government in the promotion of sport, which had previously been left to private initiative. Although his great loves were cricket and football, he argued, in government and out, for assistance to every sporting activity, particularly in schools. Howell believed that sport mattered and argued for its importance in a way which made men and women, in previously neglected sports, feel recognised. In opposition during 1970–74, he served as Front-Bench spokesman on Local Government and Sport.

During his two periods in government, 1964–70 and then from 1974–79 as Minister of State at the Department of the Environment, his responsibilities were far wider than sport alone. He was made a Privy Counsellor in 1976. He was responsible for environmental protection before that subject became fashionable and pioneered rehabilitation of Britain's waterways. During his last year in office he became famous for his crisis management, first during the drought and then during the freezing Winter of Discontent. Howell, an honest friend who never shirked from pointing out possibilities for improvement, was always a ministerial team player. Having fiercely argued his case he would unswervingly accept the majority decision and argue for it with great conviction.

Being from 1971 to 1983 the President of APEX, the white-collar union, he became involved in the Grunwick dispute. Throughout that period he endeavoured to bring about a sensible and fair solution. Regrettably the strike had become a political football, which the Opposition were determined to exploit as a protest against the government's industrial relations legislation, so all proposals to the company to resolve it were ignored.

In 1980 Margaret Thatcher sought a boycott of the Olympic Games in Moscow in protest at the invasion of Afghanistan. Howell led the opposition, because top athletes would have wasted five years of their lives, while no one else would have faced any sacrifice. He organised fund-raising to ensure that the absence of government finance would not prevent athletes attending.

Howell fought against extremist proposals after the defeat in 1979. Then in the contest for Leadership in 1983 he supported Roy Hattersley, but following Neil Kinnock's election he soon established a good relationship. When Roy Jenkins and Shirley Williams left the Labour Party, the Labour Committee for Europe was left leaderless. Howell took over the Chair and under the new name of Labour Movement for Europe, he rebuilt it, putting it in the mainstream of the Party. When he stood down it had more members and influence than ever before.

Created Baron Howell in 1992, he continued in the Lords to support and advocate those causes that he had worked so hard for all his life, including Birmingham's bid for the Olympic Games. He had many successes, because he had the drive to pursue his aims and the ability to mix with the great and ordinary alike and persuade them to support his passions. He published *Soccer Refereeing* in 1968 and his autobiography, *Made in Birmingham*, in 1990. He died on 19 April 1998.

Roy Grantham

Cledwyn Hughes (Lord Cledwyn of Penrhos)   (1916–2001)

Cledwyn Hughes was an outstanding Welsh Labour politician of his generation with an unusual background. Born in Holyhead, Anglesey, 14 September 1916, he came from a leading Liberal family in Anglesey and could say with truth 'Lloyd George knew my father'. The Rev Henry David Hughes, Minister of one of Holyhead's principal Methodist Chapels, was an intimate friend of Lloyd George's. But the young Cledwyn, after Holyhead Grammar School and University College of Wales, Aberystwyth, broke with the family Liberal tradition and joined the Labour Party in 1938.

In the 1945 General Election, as an RAF Flying Officer, he stood against his father's wishes as the Labour opponent of Megan Lloyd George in the Anglesey constituency. He fought a vigorous, but largely one-man campaign, making 50 speeches, 45 of them in Welsh, and reduced the Lloyd George majority to 1,081. He set up as a solicitor in Holyhead and in 1951, at the third attempt, he defeated Megan by 595 votes. Later they were Labour colleagues together in the House of Commons, and a reflection of this change was that by 1955 his majority rose to 4,568. He held the seat comfortably until retiring from the Commons in 1979 to go to the Lords as Lord Cledwyn of Penrhos.

Cledwyn Hughes remained the most Welsh of politicians to the end of his life, although he combined this with a leading role in UK politics and a deep involvement in Commonwealth affairs. Unlike most of his South Wales colleagues, he was a fluent Welsh speaker, dedicated to preserving the language. He was a leading figure at the Eisteddfod and a Druid. In his Maiden Speech on 8 November 1951 he pleaded for a separate Welsh Office.

In 1955, with other Welsh-speaking MPs, he started a petition for a Welsh Parliament, and was reported for this rebellion against party policy to the National Executive by the South-Wales-dominated Welsh Council of Labour. It was, therefore, his proudest moment that when he finally joined the Cabinet in 1966, it was as Secretary of State at the new Welsh Office. He was almost immediately overtaken by the Aberfan disaster. The Prime Minister, Harold Wilson, declared: 'Cledwyn Hughes has military-type powers.' He flew from Anglesey, and never left Aberfan for a week. He was tutor to Prince Charles on Welsh affairs when the preparations were taking place for his investiture as Prince of Wales. Again, in 1980, when civil strife threatened over Welsh language broadcasting, he was a key figure in the small group which persuaded Willie Whitelaw, as Home Secretary, to establish the independent Welsh Fourth Channel. His services to Wales, for which he was made a Companion of Honour in 1977, were legion, He was Pro-Chancellor of the University of Wales 1985–94 and President, University of Wales Bangor, from 1995 until his death in 2001.

Cledwyn Hughes began his political career as a member of the Anglesey County Council (1946–52) and was the Clerk of Holyhead Urban District Council. During 13 years in Opposition (1951–64) he became a front-bench spokesman on housing and local government (1959–64) and became active in Commonwealth Affairs. In 1958 he became the first (and only) British political leader to visit St Helena, and he produced an important report which improved conditions there. In 1964, when Labour returned to office, he became Minister of State at the Commonwealth Office, where he established relations of good will with leaders of the newly independent countries in Africa which served him well in the abortive efforts to prevent Ian Smith's UDI in Southern Rhodesia. He became a Privy Counsellor in 1966. Cledwyn Hughes's final cabinet post after the Welsh Office (1966–68) was as Minister for Agriculture (1968–70). Though not elected to the shadow cabinet in 1970, he remained Shadow Agriculture Minister until dropped from Wilson's team in 1972. An active pro-European, he became one of the Vice Presidents of the Britain in Europe campaign during the EEC referendum of 1975.

It was, however, in two behind-the-scenes roles, as Chairman of the Parliamentary Labour Party (1975–79) and House of Lords Leader of the Opposition (1982–92), that he made his biggest impact on the Labour Party. In 1974, having been unfairly passed over by Harold Wilson for fresh ministerial office, he led the fight of the moderates against militants in the Parliamentary Labour Party by defeating the sitting Chairman, Ian Mikardo, by 163 votes to 131. After going to the Lords in 1979, he became in 1981 the Deputy Opposition Leader and showed the same courage in challenging the increasingly ineffective right-wing role of his own leader, Lord Peart. In the tradition-bound Lords, this was an unprecedented situation, but Cledwyn Hughes triumphed over Fred Peart by 60 votes to

37. He proved an outstanding Lords Leader. At both ends of the Parliamentary corridor, with shrewdness, firmness and good humour, he did as much as anyone to moderate Labour's lurch to the left and to pave the way for the restoration of the Labour Party's electability under Neil Kinnock, John Smith and Tony Blair. He stepped down as Lords leader in 1992, but remained an influential member of the Political Honours Scrutiny Committee until 1999. He died of cancer in his native Anglesey on 22 February 2001 at the age of 84, nursed by his devoted wife, Jean, with whom he shared the same surname, and whom he married in 1949. They had two children, a son and a daughter. His funeral service in Anglesey was attended by over 700 people from all walks of life in Wales.

Rt Hon. Lord Thomson of Monifieth

Will Hutton (1950–)

William Nicholas Hutton was born on 21 May 1950 in Woolwich Arsenal, son of William Thomas Hutton and Dorothy Anne (née Haynes). He was educated at Chislehurst and Sidcup Grammar School and studied Economics and Sociology at Bristol University. He married Jane Atkinson in 1978. They have three children – Sarah, Alice and Andrew.

He began his career as an investment analyst at stockbrokers Phillips & Drew in 1971, rising to become a senior account executive. After completing an MBA at INSEAD (1977–78) he embarked on a career in the media, fulfilling roles as Producer/Director of *The Money Programme*, Economics Editor of *Newsnight* and a reporter for *Panorama*. In 1990 he joined Guardian Newspapers as Economics Editor, and became Editor-in-Chief of the *Observer* in 1996. He has written five books including *The State We're In*, edited a number of others and presented several topical television and radio series.

In 2000 he became Chief Executive of the Industrial Society, in his own words more of a do-tank than a think-tank. Outside the media he has had a number of external appointments including Chairman, Commission on NHS Accountability (1999); Chairman, Employment Policy Institute (1995–); Governor, London School of Economics (1995–) and Visiting Professor, Manchester University Business School (1997–). He was Political Journalist of the Year (1993), Honorary Fellow, Mansfield College Oxford, and holds six honorary degrees.

Hutton came to prominence as an intellectual figure in the Labour Party in the early 1990s. He joined the Labour Party on 10 April 1992, the day after Labour's fourth consecutive defeat, having been close to leading Labour figures for much of the 1980s. He was already well known as Economics Editor of the *Guardian* when he wrote his landmark book *The State We're In* (1995) – a treatise which was both a deconstruction of free-market economics of the late Thatcher era and a passionate advocacy of stakeholding as the centre-left political philosophy of the mid 1990s.

His central propositions were that British society was fragmenting, investment was too low and British democracy had structural deficits. His philosophy advocated keeping the merits of private ownership while reshaping the way it works, through a new financial architecture in which private decisions produce a less degenerate capitalism. The triple requirement, he argued, was to broaden the area of stakeholding in companies and institutions to create a bias to long-term commitment from owners, to extend the supply of cheap, long-term debt and to decentralise decision making.

Hutton played a crucial role in creating the intellectual climate for the return of the Labour Party to Government, exploring and developing many of his ideas through his publications and his weekly *Guardian* column. His offering was a serious social-democratic philosophy that came at a time when the Party needed an 'ism' to add intellectual weight to its aspirations for Britain. His influence carried more widely, popularising his ideas to a whole new generation in the post-Thatcher era, from his position as a highly regarded national commentator.

Hutton was very much a man of his time. He helped provide a springboard for Labour, but even as early as 1996 the party seemed to move on from Hutton. In credit to him, the stakeholding rhetoric stayed and indeed was used in many of Blair's speeches to the business and other communities. But the Party was anxious to create a strong partnership with business, and they were sensitive to criticisms that legislating for change, particularly to company law and the composition of company boards, would be too interventionist. Indeed other stakeholder advocates argued that this was not the best way to protect the interests of different and diverse stakeholders, for whom different mechanisms may be appropriate. Moreover, it was unclear to the leadership how they could actually translate Hutton's ideas into practical policies that would enhance competitiveness and success in the economy. Peter Mandelson, writing in the *Observer Review* on 15 April 2001 epitomised this view: 'Even if we tried to legislate for stakeholding, it is difficult to imagine how governments could alter corporate behaviour without drastic and unwieldy intervention.'

Hutton's lack of success in persuading the Blair circle to take on his ideas more fully would have been a disappointment to him, as someone who offered a vision, and strived not for a socialist utopia but a just capitalism consistent with a social-democrat approach, creating a win-win situation for business and society.

Hutton, a liberal social democrat, cites his main influences as Keynes on the economy, Durkheim on social policy, Beveridge on the Welfare State, Tawney on equality and Habermas for his views on the public realm. The pillars which underpin Hutton's political philosophy are four-fold, firstly, stressing democracy, citizenship and the importance of the public realm. For Hutton, the public way of making a difference is as important as the private and the private sector can diminish the public realm. He contends that it is a privilege for corporations to trade in our communities, in return for which there are democratic obligations.

Secondly, Hutton stresses the responsibility and obligation of the rich in society. Thirdly, there are the principles of equality and liberty – marrying universalism (e.g. a universal education system) with liberty. Fourthly, there is internationalism. Hutton is passionately pro-European, believing that the UK's values are closer to a European value system than the neo-conservatism of America. He is interested in reform of international trading laws, and supports a rules-based international trading order.

Hutton never stood for political office, something he later came to regret, but in 1986 was approached by some senior Labour figures to consider becoming a candidate. Aside from some uneasiness as to how the Party would transform itself, he decided not to stand for two very different reasons – firstly a desire to keep the independence he had as a journalist, and secondly a concern that he lacked the ruthlessness which may have been needed in politics. However his family did not completely escape political office – his wife became a Labour Councillor in Haringey in 1998.

Hutton does not 'born' political, but became politicised whilst working in the City. Politically, his achievement has been that he helped shape a national political conversation in which conservatism, in a historically conservative nation, was at a disadvantage. He also played some part in furthering the argument for an independent Bank of England, which he advocated in his writings. His contribution to other areas of change outside economic stakeholding should not be overlooked. He has been consistent in his support and involvement with Anthony Barnett and others in Charter 88, the constitutional reform pressure group, and remains a strong advocate for constitutional change in political and economic structures.

Seema Malhotra

H M Hyndman (1842–1921)

Henry Mayers Hyndman was the leading pioneer of Marxism in Britain. He has nevertheless been widely criticised for his idiosyncrasies, and in particular for his failure to move with the times; and his career on the left came to an inglorious end when he was effectively forced out of the movement he had created due to his jingoistic attitude during the First World War. Nevertheless, he was an important figure in the development of the British left.

Hyndman was born in London on 7 March 1842 into a wealthy family with business interests in the West Indies. He was educated at Trinity College School in Cambridge, and took a degree from Trinity College in 1865. Hyndman read for the Bar but did not complete the course, and lived a leisured life, based on a comfortable private income (he played cricket for Sussex between 1863 and 1868). Politically, he was at this stage a Conservative. In 1866, he was in Italy at the time of that country's war with Austria, and was employed as a war correspondent by the *Pall Mall Gazette*. Towards the end of the decade he travelled to Australia and the USA, and became concerned that Britain should develop closer links with its Empire. In 1876 he married Matilda Ware, who died in 1913; in 1914, he was to marry Rosalind Travers.

Hyndman came close to standing for parliament as an independent at the 1880 general election. By this time, he was being influenced by the ideas of the German socialist, Ferdinand Lassalle. He then read Marx's *Capital* in a French translation while cruising the West Indies, and was finally converted to socialism. At first Hyndman hoped to convince Lord Beaconsfield, the Conservative party leader, of the value of such ideas, but met a discouraging response, and in 1881 Hyndman was a leading figure in the formation of the Democratic Federation. His first book, *England for All*, was published in the same year, but its virtual plagiarism of Marx earned the undying antipathy of both Marx and Engels. He became a prolific writer: perhaps his major works were *The Historical Basis of Socialism in England* (1883) and his two volumes of memoirs, *The Record of an Adventurous Life* (1911) and *Further Reminiscences* (1912).

In 1884 the DF was renamed the Social Democratic Federation, a recognition of the movement's shift towards Marxian socialism. But the SDF was soon riven with factionalism, and some leading members, like William Morris, soon left to form the Socialist League.

Hyndman's domineering personality was clearly a problem, but at the same time his prestige and wealth made him almost invulnerable to challenge. The SDF did make some progress in the years that followed, and organised a series of demonstrations in 1886 and 1887. SDF members, ignoring Hyndman's own contempt for trade unions, became involved in the 'new unionism' towards the end of the decade. But the 1890s proved a difficult period for the SDF. At the 1895 general election, Hyndman, standing in the SDF stronghold of Burnley, was only able to take 12.4 per cent of the poll. Hyndman himself continued to predict revolution, but the tide of labour politics now appeared to be moving against him, and the development of the ethical socialist Independent Labour Party (formed 1893) further handicapped the SDF. The eventual success of the ILP's leadership in pursuing an alliance with the trade unions, with the formation of the Labour Representation Committee in 1900, confirmed the extent to which the SDF was being bypassed. Once again, Hyndman's own personality was often used as an argument against those ILPers who sought the creation of a united ILP-SDF Marxist party. Although the SDF initially affiliated to the LRC, it left after a year when the non-revolutionary nature of the new organisation became clear. Yet the departure of the extreme left 'impossiblists' to form the Socialist Labour Party (SLP) in 1903 further entrenched Hyndman's control of the SDF, and he was still seen as one of its main assets. But it continued to struggle – Hyndman's further parliamentary candidatures in Burnley in 1906, 1908 and December 1910 all ended in defeat – and in 1911 it was agreed that it should unite with left-wing members of the ILP to form the British Socialist Party (BSP). But this failed to stem the decline of the movement, and in 1914 a BSP membership ballot voted to apply for affiliation to the Labour Party.

On the outbreak of war in 1914, Hyndman became a member of the wide-ranging War Emergency Workers' National Committee. Although he worked hard there, with other leading figures in the Labour movement, to defend working-class interests, his rapid adoption of a virulently anti-German and superpatriotic line created massive problems within the BSP. It became increasingly clear that he was opposed by a significant proportion of the party's membership, and the denouement came at the BSP's Easter 1916 conference, when the majority opposed his views. He and his supporters walked out and formed the National Socialist Party which, after the war, reverted to the old SDF title. However, the revived SDF was a political irrelevance. Its marginality was merely confirmed by the formation (largely from the BSP) of the Communist Party of Great Britain in 1920. Although Hyndman continued to write and speak at public meetings, he was by now a throwback to an earlier age, and died on 20 November 1921.

Hyndman is often remembered with a mixture of condescension and contempt. He was not helped, of course, by the fact that there was no body of acolytes to keep his memory alive: had he died in 1913, for example, the CPGB might well have claimed him as one of its progenitors, but that was never likely given his conduct thereafter. His own high-handed methods and his failure to see the potential of the 'labour alliance' that created the Labour Party must certainly be counted against him. So, too, must his personal idiosyncrasies: it was no mean achievement that he managed to alienate the English-domiciled Marx and Engels, and his anti-Semitism hardly helped a party which might in other circumstances have hoped to garner more Jewish support. Yet, at the same time, he was an important figure. He, more than any other individual, sparked off and kept alive Marxist politics in Britain for the three decades after the formation of the SDF, and he was a prolific – if rather pedestrian – writer and propagandist for the cause. Those who have dwelt only on his failings and eccentricities have done little service to the truth.

The main biography is C Tsuzuki, *H M Hyndman and British Socialism* (1961), although M Crick, *The History of the Social-Democratic Federation* (1994) is also valuable.

Andrew Thorpe

Derry Irvine (Lord Irvine of Lairg) (1940–)

The Rt Hon. Lord Irvine of Lairg QC is probably the most powerful Labour Lord Chancellor in history. He has masterminded many aspects of Blair's constitutional reform programme, started a fundamental review of the legal system, and chairs many important cabinet committees. One of the finest legal minds of his generation, he gave up a lucrative career at the Bar and his own Chambers to take up what is usually one of the lowest profile jobs in Government. It is a supreme irony, that for most people, he is remembered for an argument about wallpaper and the fact that he asks his staff at the Lord Chancellor's Department to peel oranges for him.

Alexander Andrew Mackay Irvine was born into a working-class family in Inverness on 23 June 1940. His mother, Margaret Christina, worked as a waitress, and his father Alexander started out as a roof tiler. His mother never liked the name Alexander – both her husband and father had the same name – and so she called her only child 'Derry' for short. The name stuck for the rest of his life.

Irvine was a bright and extremely hardworking boy, and after Inverness Royal Academy won a scholarship to the well-known private Hutchesons' Boys' Grammar School in Glasgow. He won another scholarship from there to study at Glasgow University. Contemporaries remember that Irvine had an ambition to become a barrister from a very early age and he was certainly driven by a desire to impress and to please his parents.

At Glasgow, Irvine was a contemporary of John Smith, Donald Dewar and Menzies Campbell, although he was not particularly interested in politics at the time. John Smith became a particularly close friend as they were both studying Law. Friends recall how they used to drink together late into the night, both with an apparent endless capacity for alcohol, and displaying no ill-effects afterwards.

After achieving a distinction at Glasgow, Irvine went on with another scholarship to Christ's College Cambridge where he took a further BA and LLB (Postgraduate) degree, studying with the famous Professor Glanville Williams. He won firsts in both degrees, and won a prize for one of his papers in Jurisprudence. He married Margaret Veitch, and they lived together in Cambridge, while he both studied and lectured part-time and she worked as a teacher.

Irvine has since said that he turned down the offer of a fellowship at Cambridge as his first love was to practice at the Bar, and so after graduating from Cambridge, Irvine taught at the London School of Economics to see him through his Bar exams and pupillage. While there Irvine took a stand against the appointment of Dr Walter Adams as Director because of his earlier support for Ian Smith's government in Rhodesia, and was rewarded for his efforts by being made an honorary vice-president of the LSE Student's Union for life. It was the first time he had become involved directly in politics.

Unusually, Irvine failed to be offered a tenancy after completing his pupillage but was taken on soon after by Morris Finer QC at 2 Crown Office Row, where he began the start of his brilliant legal career. He made an odd move in 1970 when he was persuaded to stand as the Labour Party candidate for Hendon North constituency by John Smith, and was given some help in the selection by Labour HQ. Despite the fact that the seat was regarded as a winnable marginal, his chances were hampered by the fact that the selection was delayed until a few weeks before the election, and he lost to the Tory candidate John Gorst, who increased the Tory majority. After this initial flirtation with the idea of Parliament, Irvine stuck to his ambition of becoming a top-rate barrister.

Meanwhile Irvine had fallen in love with Donald Dewar's wife, Alison, which ended in his divorcing Margaret in 1974, and resulted in a history of enmity between him and Donald Dewar. It has always been a legend that Dewar and Irvine did not speak to each other until they both met up as pallbearers at John Smith's funeral, but both men denied this. Friends have commented that Irvine dotes on his wife and is completely different when she is around. They have two sons.

While working as a senior member of Michael Sherrard's Chambers at 2 Crown Office Row, Irvine developed a formidable reputation for the steamroller-like quality of his court work. Within Chambers he recruited many talented young barristers, all of with Oxbridge firsts, with whom he developed strong bonds of reciprocal loyalty. In 1976 Irvine received an application for pupillage from Tony Blair. Although Blair did not obtain a first from Oxford, Irvine took him on, despite his policy of only accepting candidates with the highest educational standards possible. As a consequence an exceptionally clever candidate, Cherie Booth, was denied the place, even though she had been offered it by Irvine, and instead went to 5 Essex Court. They kept in touch, however, and it was through Irvine that Blair met Cherie.

In an interview in 1997 Blair remarked that it was over a lunch with Lord Irvine that they realised they were in love. Irvine also introduced Tony Blair to John Smith and suggested that he produce a paper for Smith on the legal aspects of the Tory Government's privatisation agenda. Smith was impressed with his work, and they too became close friends. Tony Blair's relationship with Lord Irvine was cemented when he persuaded Blair not to re-stand for Beaconsfield and wait instead for a more winnable seat, a gamble that paid off in the form of Sedgfield. Once an MP Blair kept in constant contact with Irvine, asking for his advice on a number of issues, and they have remained close friends ever since.

Having taken silk as the youngest QC in 1978, Irvine's reputation continued to rise with the creation of a new set of specialised chambers, 11 King's Bench Walk, and he was granted a peerage in 1987 by Neil Kinnock. He also became the Labour Party's Lords Spokesman on Legal and Home Affairs up until his appointment as Shadow Lord Chancellor in 1992 by John Smith. It was predictable that after helping with Tony Blair's leadership campaign, he would become Lord Chancellor in 1997.

Irvine had produced a series of weighty papers and speeches on legal policy as Shadow Lord Chancellor but few in the legal profession were prepared for the major changes he was to bring in. The enactment of the Human Rights Act, the reform of the legal aid system, reform of the system of jury trial, and reform of the House of Lords, plus an attack on the high earnings of barristers, were just a few of the measures Irvine drove through.

However, Lord Irvine's policy output was more than overshadowed by a series of gaffes starting shortly after the 1997 election. His staff at the Lord Chancellor's Department were said to find his style aggressive, even bullying. His habit of treating his senior Clerk at Chambers as if he were a butler or valet did not go down well with the civil servants. Irvine loves oranges, and needs a constant supply as he often skips meals when working long hours. However, he also has big hands and finds it difficult to peel fruit. For this reason, he always asked his senior Clerk at 11 King's Bench Walk to peel the oranges for him. This apparently reasonable request caused a tabloid frenzy when staff at the Lord Chancellor's Department were shocked to be asked to continue the practice.

It was the refurbishment of the Lord Chancellor's apartments at the Palace of Westminster which caused the most trouble, however. While the initial decision to refurbish the apartments came from a cross-party committee, Lord Irvine certainly encouraged the contractors to use the best possible materials. He maintains that he will be thanked by future generations for the very highoquality refurbishment of what is, after all, a public building. However, there were opposition calls for his resignation when the costs were revealed. In particular, Lord Irvine made an amazing gaffe when he compared the wallpaper – costing £60–70 a roll – in his apartments to the 'cheap' stuff you find in DIY stores which might last 'one or two years'. Predictably, the tabloids, the Conservatives and the DIY stores themselves were outraged.

The most recent gaffe was in the run-up to the 2001 election, when Irvine allowed himself to act as host for a Labour Party fundraising event, writing out to senior barristers to invite them to attend. The Conservatives and the media again attacked his judgement, asking whether it was appropriate for the man who still held the power to appoint QCs and judges to invite many potential candidates for those positions to donate money to the Labour Party. It became known as the 'cash for wigs' scandal.

Despite repeated rumours of a rift with Blair, particularly during some of his press outbursts when Irvine has angered Alistair Campbell, he remains one of the Prime Minister's closest advisers and survived the 'ruthless' reshuffle of June 2001, much to the surprise of many observers. He has a lot of legislation still to push through, with the second stage of the reform of the House of Lords, the reform of the Criminal Justice System, the creation of the Community Legal Service and the completion of the reforms to legal aid, plus many other policy issues on which his legal advice will be vital.

Irvine is, however, still not well-liked by his cabinet, parliamentary and Labour Party colleagues and his style has been described by colleagues as 'arrogant', 'pompous' and 'self-promoting'. Irvine may be viewed by history as one of the most hardworking Lord Chancellors, but he is unlikely to become the most popular.

There is just one biography of Lord Irvine: *Irvine – Politically Correct?*, written by legal business journalist Dominic Egan (Mainstream Publishing, Edinburgh, 1999). It gives a good flavour of the Lord Chancellor, and the author has spoken to many of Irvine's friends and colleagues. However, it could not be said to be an impartial biography, and concentrates very much on the negative aspects of Irvine's reputation rather than the positive.

Howard Dawber

George Isaacs (1883–1979)

George Isaacs successfully combined careers as a trade unionist and a Labour MP. He was general secretary of NATSOPA from 1909 to 1949, a Labour MP for 23 years and a cabinet minister in 1945–51.

Isaacs was born on 28 May 1883 in Finsbury, where his parents occupied one room over a small shop. His father was a printer's assistant, a trade also followed by his grandfather and great-grandfather. His mother had worked as a milk-maid. The eldest of nine children, George was educated at the Wesleyan Elementary School in Hoxton. He won a scholarship but instead began work as a reader's boy (reading aloud to a proof-reader) at the age of 12 in order to support the family. He then had a variety of jobs in the printing trade, studying during frequent periods of temporary unemployment.

In 1901 he joined the National Society of Operative Printers and Assistants (NATSOPA), the only union that catered for non-craft print workers. Six years later he followed his father as Father of the Chapel at *Lloyd's News*. In 1909, at the age of only 25, he became general secretary of the union. The 'schoolboy general secretary' held this position until 1949, and under his direction membership grew from an initial 4,000 to 29,000 members. He helped to secure pay rises and also better conditions of service, to stem the tuberculosis from which so many printers suffered, and better educational facilities. In 1919 he established an annual NATSOPA scholarship to Ruskin College. This was also the year in which he secured a national wages agreement for his members, a 48–hour working week and a week's paid summer holiday. Out of this wide experience came his only book, *The Story of the Newspaper Printing Press* (1931).

Isaacs served on the General Council of the TUC from 1932. He was also President of the British Printing and Kindred Trades Federation from 1939 to 1945. In 1945 he was Chairman of the TUC. He presided over the World Conference of Trade Unions that year, and was looking forward to presiding at the 1945 TUC Annual Conference; but – much to the surprise of this humble though successful man – Attlee made him Minister of Labour in Cabinet. He therefore resigned from the TUC.

Isaacs' first political mark had been made in 1914, when he had been active in the formation of the London Labour Party. He failed to secure election to the House of Commons first in 1918 at North Southwark and then in 1922 at Gravesend. He was, however, Southwark's first Labour mayor (1919–21), and in 1923 he narrowly won the Gravesend seat. Defeated at Gravesend in 1924, he unsuccessfully contested North Southwark again in a by-election in 1927 before winning the seat at the 1929 general election. Ernest Bevin spoke for him, and a firm friendship grew up between the two men. He lost by a landslide in 1931 and more narrowly in 1935; but in a by-election in 1939 he won handsomely, a victory repeated in 1945. In 1950–59 he represented Southwark. He was PPS to J H Thomas during the first two Labour governments, but refused to follow Thomas into the National Government in August 1931. In 1942–45 he was PPS to A V Alexander at the Admiralty.

Isaacs' appointment in 1945 surprised the press. But Attlee kept him in this post for five and a half years, and he handled with efficiency the enormous problems posed by the demobilisation of millions of men, modifying and speeding up Bevin's plans. He also widened facilities for industrial training. Where his touch was far less assured was in handling industrial relations. His union experience predisposed him to favour minimal government interference in collective bargaining, and he argued that 'the right to strike is as much our inalienable right as the right to breathe', though he played a part in the TUC's acceptance of pay restraint. It was Wilson at the Board of Trade and Cripps at the Exchequer who did far more to promote industrial harmony. As early as 1947 Cripps remarked privately that 'George Isaacs should go'. He himself asked Attlee to be relieved of his duties in January 1951, but the Prime Minister's regard for him was shown by his appointment as Minister of Pensions, outside the cabinet. There he remained until Labour's defeat later that year.

In a speech-day address, Isaacs told the pupils that 'There's plenty of room at the top', adding *sotto voce* 'That's why I'm there'. All who knew him testified to his humility. He was a reserved man with no taste for high society. Attlee wrote that he had the typical Cockney virtues ('courage, good temper, humour and kindliness') and 'a genius for friendship'. These qualities, and his achievements in trade unionism and politics, are well brought out in the only biography, *George Isaacs: Printer, Trade-Union Leader, Cabinet Minister* by G G Eastwood (1952). Isaacs died in a nursing home on 26 April 1979.

Robert Pearce

Ken Jackson (1937–)

Creating the Amalgamated Engineering and Electrical Union (AEEU) was not easy. The merger process between the old engineers and electricians unions that had created the AEEU was a painfully drawn-out process that had still not been completed by the time Sir Ken Jackson took over the helm of the AEEU in January 1996, some four years after merger had nominally taken place. Jackson was the driving force who built, rationalised and secured the foundations and finances of the new AEEU. By the dawn of the new Millennium he had clearly established the AEEU, at 730,000 members Britain's third largest union, as not only the most powerful independent force within the British industrial and political arena, but a key bulwark of New Labour. In doing so he has won the trust and admiration of the Prime Minister.

In recognition of this, the June 2001 AEEU Policy Conference, in an unprecedented move, voted to extend his term of office beyond the normal retirement age of 65. Robert Taylor, *Financial Times* Employment Editor and historian of the TUC, wrote: 'In his championing of UK manufacturing industry and partnership agreements with companies, Sir Ken is widely seen as the main moderniser in the trade union movement. At the height of his powers of presentation and analysis, his prolonged period in office will be welcomed by both sides of industry.' For Jackson, the tragic destruction of British manufacturing under the impact of the Thatcher and Major recessions was a searing lesson to both management and workers in the need to embrace change and flexibility. Now, he believes: 'Improving the productivity of manufacturing in Britain will be a crucial challenge. British manufacturing increasingly operates in a globally competitive environment. Only by boosting investment and productivity can we secure the bright future that manufacturing in Britain and the jobs that depend on it deserve.'

It is not just in industry that Jackson has championed partnership. He has done so equally in the political arena, where his commitment to the strengthening and maturing of a genuine partnership with the Labour Party in government has been part of the key to the success of the

Blair government in its relations with the unions. For Jackson, Labour's union link 'gives Labour a direct line to millions of hard-working people, and it helps those same working people find their political voice.' Indeed, he argues that it was the link with unions such as the old AEU and EETPU that made modernisation possible, by keying Labour in to the instincts and values of aspirational, skilled workers, values far closer to the mainstream of the British electorate than the Bennery of what former EETPU leader Frank Chapple branded the 'lunatic left.' 'We fought for the expulsion of Militant, one member one vote, an end to the twin absurdities of unilateralism and the old Clause Four,' Jackson has said. 'We were proud to play our part. I still am.' Roy Rogers, seasoned industrial commentator of the *Herald,* has written: 'As head of the most pro-New Labour of Britain's unions, Jackson has emerged as a considerable power broker ready to criticise ministers where necessary, yet, as in the case of the Blairite contender for the head of the Welsh Assembly, be the first to deliver much-needed support too.' It was Jackson who, with John Monks, brokered the deal with government over trade union recognition in *Fairness at Work.*

Under Jackson's leadership, the AEEU began to punch its weight in the political arena for the first time since the merger. From only four EETPU MPs in the 1970s, there are now some 30 AEEU members in the Commons and ten in the European Parliament. A staunch pro-European of long standing, Jackson was active in the original Britain in Europe campaign during the Common Market referendum of 1975 and, since its foundation in 1999, has been the only trade-unionist on the Board of the new Britain in Europe campaign. His pamphlet, *Out of Europe – the Threat to Working People,* was published by the Britain in Europe campaign in February 2000. He has enthusiastically embraced the government's agenda of 'making work pay' through the New Deal and welfare reform. For Jackson: 'My members are furious at being ripped of as taxpayers by scroungers and fiddlers.'

He has also sought to defend Labour from the proponents of the politics of dissent and their allies on the oppositionalist left. Thus he has become the most effective opponent of those like Arthur Scargill and the Democratic Left (formerly the Communist Party of Great Britain) and its multifarious 'networks', who advocate proportional representation as a means to break up Labour as a party of government. Having spent much of his political life working for a Labour government sufficiently stable to deliver for working people the reforms Britain needs, for Jackson it would be 'absurd' to want to throw all that away in the name of 'progressive' theory. He believes that it is a delusion to blame the electoral system for Labour's defeats in the 1980s, when the real problem was the drift of the Party away from the bread-and-butter concerns of working people and onto the wilder shores of Bennery. Always prepared to work in partnership with business and political allies on issues such as Europe, his experience of the Liverpool Liberals in the 1970s and '80s left him under no illusions about the real agenda of many Lib Dems, and he points to the difficulty of any party which seeks support in large parts of Britain as the 'opposition' to Labour being a reliable partner in securing a stable reforming government.

For Jackson, the big political issue for Blair's second term is undoubtedly the improvement of public services. His keynote speech to the June 2001 AEEU Policy Conference dwelt on this at length: 'Our members are consumers as well. They want the best schools for their kids, the best hospitals for their family. My fear is that if we don't deliver what our members voted for on Thursday then they will lose their faith in us. And I don't think they will understand why trade unions seem prepared to stand in the way of the reform they want. I understand why people might be anxious over private finance in the public sector. But to get the investment we need, we have to look to the private sector as well. Public and private can work well together. This is not about privatisation. Privatisation of public services is not an agenda this union will support. The Conservatives proposed it – and the British people rejected it. This is about a choice. We can either work with Government to ensure the public services on which we rely are the best in the world. Or we can stand in the way, oppose new initiatives, and watch as the public questions our motives... If we spend more money than ever before without delivering real improvements then we will not just have lost the battle to provide better public services, we will have lost the whole argument for public services themselves. That is why we welcome reform – because we want a stepchange in delivery. Our guiding principle must be that what matters is what works. The private sector can work. In some areas the private sector must be used.'

Born in 1937 in Wigan, Lancashire, he attended the local St. Joseph's School before joining the RAF in 1956 as an electrical technician. Seeing service both in Britain and abroad (including Cyprus), he left the RAF in 1961 to work at Plessey's, where he became a shop steward in the old Electrical Trade Union (it became the EETPU after merger with the plumbers in 1967). In 1966 he became one of a group of full-time Branch Secretaries appointed under the modernising post-communist leadership of Frank Chapple and his Wigan mentor, Les Cannon. Cannon was a pioneer advocate of industrial partnership who had argued that it was not enough to react to change, it was necessary to initiate it. Had Cannon not been struck down by cancer in 1970, aged only fifty, he might have had a stature to rival Jack Jones and the giants of the trade-union left. Jackson still has a portrait of Cannon in his office, incidentally, the same office as used by Cannon as EETPU President rather than the one across the corridor used by Frank Chapple as General Secretary.

During the 1970s Jackson honed his political skills in the tough world of northern EETPU politics, soon becoming a Lancashire regional official. Securing the enmity of the communists and fellow-travellers of the union's left-wing for his determined effectiveness and political resilience, by the late 1970s he had become the union's key political organiser in the north of England, forming a formidable team with his friends and colleagues Pat O'Hanlon in Scotland and John Spellar in the south. As Political Secretary in the north during the 1980s, based in the EETPU's north-west regional office in Southport, Jackson led the battle against Militant on Merseyside, forming a friendship with Peter Kilfoyle. This was the period when Derek Hatton's power was at its height and Jackson was fortunate in having the comradeship of several men of stature, including ex-Wigan rugby union player John Clarke, on whom he could rely for support at meetings – the so-called 'Jackson Five'. In 1987 he was elected full-time Executive Councillor for the North-West and in 1992 President of the EETPU. In what little spare time he has he remains a devoted supporter of rugby league multi-champions Wigan, occasionally managing to fit in watching a match when visiting his grandchildren in Lancashire with his wife Rene. He was knighted in 1999.

David-John Collins

Douglas Jay (Lord Jay of Battersea)   (1907–96)

You did not need to know Douglas Patrick Thomas Jay well to realise that his was an outstanding intellect; but you did to feel the warmth that underlay his close friendship. As a result you felt yourself somewhat special to have discovered this spring of emotion within the well-disciplined thinker. It is not surprising therefore that those who recognised his brilliance were many, while those close friends who admired him, somewhat fewer. The famous comment of 'Too clever by half' was certainly not made of him, but is worth bearing in mind as illustrating the average response to outstanding mental powers. You may recognise them, you will probably envy them, but only a few will say, 'Here is a great brain: let us see that it is put to the best possible use in the national interest.'

Fortunately that is what happened. In 1945, Prime Minister Clement Attlee appointed him his Personal Assistant on economic matters: the Labour leadership played a full part in making it possible for him to become an MP in 1946. Chancellor of the Exchequer Hugh Dalton made him his economic advisor, so too did President of the Board of Trade Stafford Cripps. It would be difficult to imagine a more impressive trio to establish one's credentials. Against this background of exceptional ability and confident support it is not surprising that ministerial responsibility came quickly: Economic Secretary to the Treasury in 1947, advancing to Financial Secretary to the Treasury in 1950 and, when Labour next came to power in 1964, President of the Board of Trade. He became a Privy Counsellor in 1951.

These and other achievements rested on a secure foundation. Born on 23 March 1907, from Winchester, where his very clever contemporary Dick Crossman recognised him as being cleverer than himself, he won a scholarship to New College, Oxford, where he got a first followed by a Fellowship of All Souls. In 1929 he was snapped up by Geoffrey Dawson to work on *The Times* for four years, followed by four years on the *Economist*, leading to the City Editorship of the *Daily Herald* from 1937 to 1940. With the advent of World War Two he switched to the civil service, where he worked at a high level for five years, in the Ministry of Supply (1940–43) and at the Board of Trade (1943–45).

Doubtless it was this deep experience of the civil service at the higher levels that he was drawing on when he gave birth to the famous saying, 'The gentleman in Whitehall is usually right' – a phrase quickly vulgarised into, 'The man in Whitehall knows best' and used by any politician who wanted to criticise a minister for relying on his civil servants. It was also in a large measure this experience, together with his own dynamism, that enabled him to get large departments to move with speed and to achieve his reputation of being able to get things done. A well-known example of this characteristic at work was his achievement at the Board of Trade in getting factories set up in what were defined as Development Areas: areas of below average economic activity and above-average unemployment.

His deep concern for the unemployed throughout his political career illustrated the fact that beneath the cool head and the calm exterior – he never raised his voice and never seemed to get excited – lay a warm heart. There were many other illustrations, such as his action, when a Treasury Minister, in ordering the diversion of a ship carrying much-needed food intended for Britain, to famine-stricken India. Another public example of this is to be found in his letter of (enforced) resignation in August 1967 to Prime Minister Wilson, where he wrote of his regret at leaving the Board of Trade first and foremost because 'a great deal remains to be done by this government in the promotion of social justice …'

It is worth looking at the circumstances of that resignation in some detail, for no-one has ever suggested that Jay was not a thoroughly competent minister. He was, however, the most able of those who opposed the idea of joining the EEC. He was opposed with the whole of his being, emotionally as well as intellectually and as with every other important issue on which, after careful thought, he had made up his mind, he was unbudgeable. But Cabinet had agreed, after de Gaulle's effective opposition to Britain's joining, that Harold Wilson and George Brown as Prime Minister and Foreign Secretary, should go knocking at the doors of the capitals of Europe seeking support for Britain's application for membership .This was probably the most important political issue of the time, and the Prime Minister could not contemplate having a senior minister in his Cabinet who was known to be so completely opposed to the idea and felt he had to ask him to offer his resignation. Another reason, for what it was worth, was that Douglas was now sixty and Wilson was anxious to present a young Cabinet to the public, so that was the reason given. He never rejoined the government and remained an outspoken and implacable opponent of the European idea until his dying day, serving from 1970 to 1977 as the Chairman of the Common Market Safeguards Committee.

He had a rich family life. His first wife, Peggy, whom he married when he was 26, was much liked as a delightful person and much admired for her work in the Inner London Education Authority. They had four very able children, two sons and two daughters, the eldest son Peter, a distinguished economist, reaching the giddy heights of being Britain's Ambassador to the USA. Unhappily, difficulties arose and after nearly forty years the marriage, very sadly, broke up and Douglas remarried. He enjoyed throughout a very happy relationship with his children, whom he would take on long walks in his beloved Cornwall. He habitually holidayed in Cornwall, and with Douglas Jay a habit was really a habit. He never felt the urge to travel abroad. You could regard that as yet another idiosyncrasy or yet another example of his kind of patriotism.

Certainly he was well-known for his idiosyncrasies and his eccentricities – and indeed his near-asceticism. Less well-known is the fact that he was a very 'clubbable' man who enjoyed the company and conversation of fellow diners. One such dining club, of which he was a member in his later years, drew its membership from distinguished Oxford dons. Another (the 'XYZ' so called) consisted of Labour MPs and others from the City, all of whom shared an interest in financial and economic issues and support for Labour. It included among its members Hugh Dalton, ex-Chancellor of the Exchequer, Nobel Prize-winner Professor James Meade, the very distinguished economist, and Hugh Gaitskell, Labour leader and close friend of Douglas Jay for many years. It was at one of these dinners in a small dining room in the Commons that, disagreeing profoundly with the views of a fellow economist and Labour MP, he calmly (he was never ruffled or excited) got out of his chair, walked round the table and, while continuing, very rationally, to explain the errors of his fellow-member's thinking, picked up a glass of water and poured the contents over his head. It is a great tribute to his sportsmanlike qualities and his high regard for Douglas that the errant fellow-member's sole reaction to the cold water trickling down his neck was to roar with laughter. Of course it would be quite wrong to suggest that this practical display of eccentricity was in any way typical: but it would be fair to add that none of the members present was wholly astonished.

He continued as MP for Battersea North until 1983 and was created Lord Jay at the age of 80 in 1987. He was a regular Lords attender and spoke frequently in his ever calm, well-ordered, well-argued and unemotional way. Probably his style was more suited to the written, rather than the spoken word: certainly he wrote easily and well. *The Socialist Case* appeared as early as 1937, followed *by Socialism and the New Society* in 1962. He published *Who is to Pay for the War and the Peace* in 1941, *After the Common Market* in 1968 and *Sterling* in 1986. In 1980 he produced what was regarded as one of the best post-war autobiographies in the field of politics, *Change and Fortune*. In his later years he suffered a good deal from ill-health: he battled his way through, but only to emerge as an even more gaunt and lank figure than before. He died on 4 March 1996, just a few weeks short of his 89th birthday, in the heart of his beloved English countryside, after enjoying a loving relationship with his second wife Mary for nearly a quarter of a century.

Rt Hon. Lord Diamond

Margaret Jay (Baroness Jay of Paddington) (1939–)

Baroness Jay of Paddington has claimed in the past, some may argue wistfully, that she is most likely to be remembered in Labour history for her affair with the Watergate journalist Carl Bernstein, just as Lord Irvine of Lairg, the Lord Chancellor, will always be known for his expensive choice in wallpapers. In fact, Baroness Jay, as Leader of the House of Lords from June 1998 until June 2001, will be associated with one of the most fundamental constitutional achievements during Tony Blair's first term in office, namely the abolition of hereditary peers in the upper chamber.

Ironically, she has often been described as New Labour's only true aristocrat. Her father James Callaghan was Prime Minister, and when Tony Blair, a personal friend, was first elected she advised him on the sleeping arrangements at No 10. As Minister for Women, she led the campaign for the introduction of more family-friendly policies at the workplace, although she has infuriated some women rights' campaigners by refusing to call herself a feminist.

When she announced he decision in 2001 to step down from her Cabinet post, Baroness Jay blamed the long hours in the House of Lords, saying thst at 61 she wanted to spend more time with her family, particularly her granddaughter. But friends of the 'Posh Spice' of New Labour privately admitted that her constant hounding by the press played a significant part in her decision to leave frontline politics.

Margaret Ann Jay, née Callaghan, was born on 18 November 1939 in Maidstone, Kent, and her childhood was steeped in Labour politics. She joined the party at the age of 16. Her education at the Blackheath High School, South London, became the subject of a bitter battle with the media in 2000 after she claimed that it had been a 'pretty standard grammar school'. Critics insisted that she had misled the public because the school, now completely private, was then a direct grant school, which was largely fee-paying. After her secondary-school education she went on to read Philosophy, Politics and Economics at Somerville College, Oxford. She met Peter Jay, the son of Labour politician Douglas Jay, and the couple married in 1961 soon after completing finals.

After university, she joined the BBC for a career in journalism and had three children, a son and two daughters. In 1969, the Jays first moved to Washington and then in 1977 faced accusations of cronyism when Peter was appointed British Ambassador, with Margaret describing herself as the co-ambassador. The couple's private life literally became the stuff of Hollywood movies when her passionate affair with Carl Bernstein, one of the two *Washington Post* reporters who broke the Watergate scandal, became public knowledge. Bernstein was married to the then pregnant Nora Ephron, whose subsequent book about the affair *Heartburn* was later made into a film starring Meryl Streep and Jack Nicholson. The marriage with Peter Jay was dissolved in 1986.

After her affair with Bernstein ended in 1981, Jay returned to Britain and worked as a reporter on BBC's *Panorama* programme and *This Week*. She also became a producer on Thames TV between 1986–88 and a non-executive Director of Carlton Television between 1996–97. During a series of programmes about Aids, she met and interviewed Professor Michael Adler, chairman of the National Aids Trust. This led to her becoming founding director of the Trust and also to her second marriage to Adler in 1994. She was made a life peer by Neil Kinnock in 1992.

Her commitment to healthcare led to her appointment as Opposition spokesman on Health between 1995–1997. She was a natural choice as Health Minister in the Lords after the 1997 general election. But Tony Blair had even bigger plans for her. In the 1998 summer reshuffle, Baroness Jay was appointed both Leader of the Lords, charged with the difficult task of piloting House of Lords reform through Parliament, and Minister for Women. She succeeded in both. Her work as Minister for Women culminated in December 2000 when a Green Paper on family-friendly policies was published, arguing for a wide-ranging extension of parental rights and benefits.

Yet with her uncompromising, sometimes steely manner, Baroness Jay, a towering figure at six foot, has made many enemies and there are few on the Labour benches in the House of Lords who will praise her. At times, she has played into her critics' hands. Apart from the controversy over her schooling, Baroness Jay was criticised for saying she understood the problems of rural people because she had a 'little cottage' in the country, when in fact she owns a £500,000 house in Ireland and a substantial property in the Chilterns. But her allies blame the continuing force of sexism in Westminster for her retreat from politics. As Baroness Jay once said herself: 'You can make a speech in the House of Lords and they say she was wearing a red dress. If they did this to the men – he was wearing a horrible tie or looks as though he needs a haircut – everyone would think it was ridiculous.'

Sarah Schaefer

Clive Jenkins (1926–99)

A trade unionist through choice rather than birth, Clive Jenkins was born on 2 May 1926 and raised in Port Talbot, South Wales. The death of his father meant that he was forced to leave school at 14; he then began work as a technician and later a foreman in the local metal industry. He joined the Association of Scientific Workers (AScW) on starting work, was branch secretary within a year, and a member of that Union's national committee by the time he was 19.

In 1947, aged 21 he was appointed an assistant divisional officer of ASSET, the embryonic foremen's union, which at the time had just 8,000 paying members. In 1961 he was elected General Secretary. In 1968 he brokered a merger with his old union, the AScW, creating ASTMS, with around 90,000 members. By 1978 ASTMS had 450,000 members. This exceptional growth can be partly attributed to an economic, political and legal environment ideal for trade union organising. However Jenkins seized the opportunities that this environment created and it is unlikely that ASTMS would have grown so spectacularly without his skills as an organiser, negotiator, manager and above all his genius for public relations.

Jenkins' commitment to trade unionism stemmed from a basic political commitment to socialism. His early political activity allowed an outlet for his exuberant personality at a time when his work as a junior union official required self-discipline and conformity. He joined the Labour Party at 14 and was briefly a member of the Communist Party before rejoining Labour, becoming a councillor in St Pancras 1954–60.

Despite being elected General Secretary of ASSET in 1961, manual union distrust of a white-collar union official, distrust of his political views, and personal disdain for his flamboyance and abrasive personality kept Jenkins from the higher councils of the trades union and labour movement until the mid 1970s. Throughout this exclusion Jenkins exerted considerable influence on public opinion through regular appearances on television and radio, and authorship of newspaper articles and books. He used these platforms to argue against UK entry into the Common Market, and against incomes policies and wage restraint. His books took a longer view, propounding novel ideas like redundancy payments and industrial tribunals that have since become part of the landscape.

The growth of ASTMS meant that Jenkins could no longer be ignored by his peers. He was elected to the TUC's General Council in 1974, where he was a powerful opponent of the TUC orthodoxy, criticising the incomes policy of the Labour Government. The leftwards shift in the trade union movement that culminated in the 1979 Winter of Discontent carried Jenkins into the mainstream of the labour movement. He was to use his new-found influence in the immediate aftermath of Labour's election defeat.

In alliance with the TGWU's Moss Evans, Jenkins was a prime mover in the campaign to get Michael Foot elected leader of the Labour Party in 1980. Foot would probably have won even without Jenkins support because, at this time, the electorate consisted solely of MPs. More important was the support Jenkins gave Foot once he was elected, arranging for ASTMS to provide finances and staff to run Foot's private office. (Callaghan's private office had been bankrolled by the right wing EEPTU, who promptly withdrew their support when Foot was elected.) He also helped fight off attacks on Foot's position from right-wing union leaders, who thought that Foot was an electoral liability.

In the Wembley special conference of 1981, Jenkins and ASTMS backed the proposal that gave unions 40 per cent of the vote in future leadership elections, with 30 per cent each for MPs and Constituency Labour Parties. When this position was eventually carried, to the despair of Labour moderates, Jenkins' Machiavellian reputation was such that he was credited by the press with brokering the final deal. In the bitter battle for the deputy leadership between Denis Healey and Tony Benn that followed this conference, Jenkins sought to dissuade Benn from standing by presenting him with a teapot inscribed with the slogan, 'Don't do it, Tony'.

However Jenkins was unable to persuade ASTMS activists to back his judgement, so the union cast its votes for Benn.

In the immediate aftermath of Labour's defeat in the 1983 general election, Evans and Jenkins again plotted over the future leadership. They immediately agreed to support Neil Kinnock if Michael Foot were to stand down as leader. The speed with which Jenkins acted, and the show of trade union support that he orchestrated, formed an important contribution to Kinnock's victory. Jenkins retired in 1989, unable to gain the political influence he craved, and increasingly out of touch with the views of his own union's activists. His final act was to negotiate a merger with the draughtsman's union, TASS, to form MSF. He was succeeded by the communist TASS General Secretary Ken Gill, causing internecine strife within the union, and loss of influence for MSF in the TUC and Labour Party.

Clive Jenkins was able to exploit the opportunities of the post-war consensus to build a large and powerful trade union. His tragedy was that at the height of his powers, history turned against him. After the hubris of his rise he met nemesis in the form of Margaret Thatcher. For this reason, his influence on the Labour Party and Labour Governments was significantly less than he would have liked. He died on 22 September, 1999. He published his autobiography, *All Against The Collar*, in 1990. Other major publications include: *The Leisure Shock* (with Barrie Sheerman, 1981); *White-collar Unionism: The Rebellious Salariat* (with Barrie Sheerman, 1979); *The Collapse of Work* (with Barrie Sheerman, 1979); *Collective Bargaining* (with Barrie Sheerman, 1977); *Computers and Unions* (with Barrie Sheerman, 1977); *The Kind of Laws Unions Ought to Want* (with J E Mortimer, 1968); and *Trade Unions Today* (with J E Mortimer, 1965).

Andy Charlwood

Roy Jenkins (Lord Jenkins of Hillhead)   (1920–)

Roy Jenkins was probably the most all-round talented figure in the top ranks of the Labour Party during the second half of the 20th Century. He was an outstanding reformist Home Secretary and a dominant Chancellor of the Exchequer, and he would most likely have succeeded Harold Wilson as Prime Minister if his strongly pro-European views had not fatally alienated significant sections of the Party. He went on to become the President of the European Commission, and was subsequently a founder and the first leader of the Social Democratic Party. A fine writer, he has produced over twenty books, including highly praised biographies of Sir Charles Dilke, Asquith, Baldwin and Gladstone.

Roy Harris Jenkins was born an only child on 11 November 1920 near Abersychan, Monmouthshire. His father, Arthur Jenkins, had worked underground as a miner for 24 years, but was then a miners' agent and much later, from 1935–46, Labour MP for Pontypool. He became PPS to Clement Attlee, and was a junior minister for some months in 1945 before he resigned due to ill health, dying in April 1946 after a kidney operation. Roy's mother, Hattie Harris, was the third daughter of the manager of a local steel works, but had been orphaned and left penniless at the age of 17 and was, her son later recalled, 'very much a fringe member of the middle class'.

When he was six his father went to prison, having been falsely accused of fomenting a riot in the aftermath of the 1926 General Strike, when he had actually been attempting to calm it down. He served three months of a nine-month sentence before being released on the intervention of the Home Secretary. Jenkins' mother concealed from him that his father was in gaol, pretending that he was absent on a trade union delegation to Germany, and he only learnt about it several years later.

Apart from this episode, Jenkins' childhood was uneventful. He attended Abersychan Grammar School, from whence he proceeded to Balliol College, Oxford, in 1938, in fulfilment of an ambition long harboured by his father. At Balliol, he was a contemporary of both Edward Heath and Denis Healey, but Jenkins' closest friend and associate at Oxford was Tony Crosland, two years his senior and with whom he organised a breakaway from the communist-dominated Labour Club to found the Democratic Socialist Club. His main focus of interest was the Union Society, and he was deeply disappointed not to be elected its President, despite – highly unusually – making two attempts. In July 1941 he graduated with first class honours in Politics, Economics and Philosophy.

Jenkins joined the army later that year and rose to the rank of captain. He saw no military action, being drafted into the Intelligence Corps and assigned to Bletchley Park, where he was part of the top-secret team decoding German radio signals. Although this work was intellectually demanding, it left him much free time, which he spent mostly reading bulky volumes of 19th and 20th Century political biography, a genre which he was later to practice with distinction, and at rather shorter length. He was also able to attend numerous Labour Party functions, and actively sought nominations for several parliamentary constituencies, eventually being selected as Labour candidate for Solihull, which he unsuccessfully contested in 1945. In January 1945 he married Jennifer Morris, daughter of the Town Clerk of Westminster, whom he had met at a Fabian summer school in August 1940.

Demobilised in January 1946, he worked for two years as an economist for a banking corporation, during which time he published – with the Prime Minister's co-operation – his first book, an 'interim biography' entitled *Mr Attlee*. In 1948 he was selected to fight a by-election for the safe inner London seat of Southwark Central, a constituency, however, which was due to disappear under redistribution in 1950. He was duly elected, but immediately started to search for another seat which would guarantee him a long-term parliamentary career. After several false starts, he was selected for Birmingham Stechford, where he was returned in 1950 and which he continued to represent until he left to become President of the European Commission in 1976.

Jenkins was an active backbencher, specialising initially in economic policy which brought him into close contact with Hugh Gaitskell, who was Chancellor of the Exchequer in 1950–51. He supported Gaitskell in his dispute with Aneurin Bevan over his 1951 budget, and was one of his strongest supporters before and after his election as Labour leader in December 1955.

Earlier that year he had been appointed as a delegate to the Consultative Assembly of the Council of Europe at Strasbourg for a two-year term. As a result of this experience, and the contacts he made with European politicians, he became a convinced supporter of the European Economic Community and a firm advocate of British membership. This conviction was to have a determinant influence on Jenkins' subsequent political career. Early in 1960 he was appointed as a junior front bench spokesman, but resigned seven months later – to Gaitskell's chagrin – when he was advised that this position would debar him from speaking from the back benches in a European debate.

This episode did not seriously mar his relations with Gaitskell, but it foreshadowed a more fundamental breach in October 1962 when the Labour leader dismayed nearly all his closest associates by coming down heavily against the British application to join the EEC in a bravura speech at the Labour Party conference at Brighton. The speech was enthusiastically received by the great bulk of the delegates and earned Gaitskell his first ever standing ovation at the conference. With the feeling of delegates very much against him, Jenkins took part in the subsequent debate and made a courageous and passionate five-minute speech rallying the pro-European minority. This led to a temporary estrangement with Gaitskell, though they were reconciled, personally if not politically, within a couple of months.

Jenkins, who entitled a chapter in his memoirs 'The Evolution of a Gaitskellite', was devastated by Gaitskell's unexpected death in January 1963. He strongly supported, though not without misgivings, George Brown's candidature as Gaitskell's successor, and had difficulty in reconciling himself to Harold Wilson's election. Perhaps in reaction to this, he cut back on his parliamentary activities and concentrated more on his work as an author, completing his biography of Asquith in 1963 and writing a series of major pieces of investigative journalism for the *Observer*. These led to an attractive offer to edit *The Economist*, which would however have meant giving up his parliamentary seat. Jenkins was tempted, but declined, after receiving an assurance from Wilson that he would be included, though not at cabinet level, in the government which he was hoping to form after the 1964 election.

In the event, he was appointed Minister of Aviation in October 1964, and made such an impressive start that within three months Wilson proposed to promote him to the cabinet as Education Secretary in a reshuffle caused by the defeat of Foreign Secretary Patrick Gordon Walker in the Leyton by-election in January 1965. Showing immense temerity and self-confidence, Jenkins turned down the offer, preferring to gamble on the possibility of obtaining the portfolio which he most preferred, that of the Home Office.

This highly sensitive post had been regarded as the graveyard of ambitious politicians, but Jenkins had long since devised a comprehensive reform programme to liberalise that stuffy department and the policies for which it was responsible, which he had set out in his 1959 paperback *The Labour Case*. Among the projected reforms he listed were the abolition of the death penalty, homosexual law reform, the abolition of theatre censorship, divorce reform and the decriminalisation of abortion. Jenkins's gamble paid off, and he duly replaced Sir Frank Soskice as Home Secretary in December 1965. The death penalty had already been removed under Soskice, but he then proceeded to implement all the other overdue reforms. They were the subject of Private Member's Bills, but Jenkins was instrumental in achieving government time for their passage, and was a powerful advocate for each of them.

He also took energetic steps to overhaul the department, and to open it to external influences and personnel. During this time too, he established his reputation as a formidable parliamentary debater, probably the most effective in the House, in routing a series of challenges unwisely mounted by the Opposition, most notably following the prison escape of the spy George Blake in October 1966.

Together with Crosland, Jenkins had long been uneasy about the refusal of the Prime Minister and Chancellor of the Exchequer to consider devaluing the pound during their first three years in office. In October 1967 the inevitable happened, and James Callaghan resigned as Chancellor. He strongly recommended appointing Crosland, who was then President of the Board of Trade, as his successor and assured him that the appointment was virtually in the bag. Wilson, however, offered it instead to Jenkins, perhaps influenced by the fact that this would make it easier to keep Callaghan in the government by proposing a straight swap of jobs between the two men. Crosland, who had long coveted the post, was deeply disappointed, and thereafter a certain wariness entered into his relations with Jenkins, although outwardly they remained friendly.

The challenge facing Jenkins was formidable, and many regarded it as a poisoned chalice. In the wake of devaluation, he was forced to introduce deep and painful budget cuts, involving the reversal of four major government policies. The British military presence East of Suez was abandoned, a large order for F-111 fighter planes was cancelled, prescription charges were reintroduced in the National Health Service and the raising of the school-leaving age to 16 was postponed for several years, a decision which provoked the resignation of Lord Longford as Leader of the House of Lords. Despite these radical measures, there was an exceptionally long and nerve-shattering wait until the gaping deficit in the balance of payments began to improve. In the meantime, the government became deeply unpopular and lost a long series of by-elections, many of them in normally ultra-safe seats. Yet respect for Jenkins continued to grow as he played a cool and steady hand and retained his parliamentary dominance over the Opposition. In this period, while Wilson himself lost ground particularly within the Parliamentary Labour Party, Jenkins was regarded as his only possible replacement.

Finally, in the summer of 1969 the balance of payments position dramatically improved, and by the following spring it was showing a substantial surplus, while Labour was rapidly closing the gap with the Tories in the opinion polls. Jenkins came under pressure to produce a pre-election give-away budget, but resisted the temptation and followed his judgement that an only mildly expansionist one was justified. This was well received by the public, and it is highly improbable that if he had let things rip (as Tory Chancellor Reginald Maudling had done in 1964) it would have improved Labour's electoral chances.

As it was, Wilson was stampeded into an early election by the good local election results in May 1970, and all the indications were that Labour would win a decent majority on 18 June. In the event, Edward Heath led the Tories to an unexpected victory, largely due to an aberrantly bad set of monthly trade figures published a few days before polling day.

Although it was not clear at the time, this effectively ended Jenkins' prospects of becoming Prime Minister. Had Labour won, Wilson's intention had been to bow out after two years, making way for Jenkins as his probable successor. Jenkins was elected deputy leader of the Labour Party in July 1970, but his position was undermined by party divisions in the following year over the renewed British application to join the European Community. While the majority of the party, including Wilson, swung sharply against accepting the terms which Heath negotiated, Jenkins led a determined group of 69 MPs who voted in favour, in defiance of a three-line whip unwisely and vindictively imposed by the party leadership, while

20 others abstained. Their action caused great ill feeling in the party, and Jenkins lost his position as heir presumptive to Wilson.

Earlier, during 1968, when his public reputation had soared while Wilson's had slumped, he had been urged by many MPs to make an open bid for the leadership, but had declined to do so. He subsequently came to believe that a successful challenge could have been mounted, though it would have caused great turmoil in the party, which he was not prepared to provoke. In his memoirs he compared his position to that of R A Butler in 1953, when both Churchill and Eden had been incapacitated by illness. Had Jenkins become leader it is conceivable that the party's evolution into something like New Labour would have occurred 25 years earlier than it did.

Jenkins' subsequent career in the Labour Party was something of an anti-climax. He resigned the deputy leadership in April 1972 in protest against the decision to back a referendum on EEC membership, but rejoined the shadow cabinet in October 1973 in advance of the February 1974 election, which unexpectedly led to the formation of the second Wilson government. Jenkins rather half-heartedly accepted the Home Secretaryship for the second time, but the highlight of his last period in office was undoubtedly his leadership of the 'yes' campaign in the June 1975 referendum. Despite his earlier misgivings, he plunged into the campaign with great enthusiasm, and particularly appreciated the close contact which this gave him with pro-Europeans in the other parties. This undoubtedly contributed to his growing disillusionment with the Labour Party as it then was.

When Wilson resigned as Prime Minister in April 1976, Jenkins duly ran as a candidate to succeed him, but came only third out of six candidates, behind both Michael Foot and Callaghan, and dropped out of the contest. He hoped that Callaghan would appoint him as Foreign Secretary, but when this position was denied to him accepted an invitation to become President of the Commission of the EC. He served in Brussels from January 1977 until early 1981, when he returned to Britain and, together with David Owen, Shirley Williams and William Rodgers, founded the Social Democratic Party, of which he became the first leader.

He fought by-elections at Warrington in July 1981 and at Glasgow Hillhead, where he was elected in March 1983, but was defeated in the 1987 general election. He then became a life peer, as Lord Jenkins of Hillhead, and was subsequently leader of the Liberal Democrat peers. As such, he encouraged co-operation between Liberal Democrats and Labour, and indeed for a time became a valued if unofficial adviser of Tony Blair. He was appointed chairman of the Independent Commission on the Voting System, which in 1998 reported in favour of a change to a hybrid system with a strong proportional element. He continues to be active as an author and as Chancellor of the University of Oxford, to which post he was elected in 1987.

Roy Jenkins' memoirs, *A Life at the Centre*, was published in 1991, and his *European Diary 1977–81* in 1989. John Campbell's *Roy Jenkins* appeared in 1983. The official biography is being written by Andrew Adonis, but will not be published in Lord Jenkins' lifetime.

Dick Leonard

Brynmor John   (1934–88)

Brynmor Thomas John earned a strangely mixed reputation. Forthright and blunt in his views, he never concealed his contempt for hypocrisy, nor for those who used the Labour Party in its good years, but were missing when times were harder. In government, he was not always popular with officials, who preferred their ministers more pliant. Yet he was a gregarious character, whose company was enjoyed by his friends, and in his constituency he was widely liked.

Born in Pontypridd on 18 April 1934, he received his education at the local Pontypridd Grammar School. His mother, an energetic figure in Labour politics, exerted a decisive influence and he joined the Labour Party in his early teens. He took a law degree at University College, London, where he was Secretary of the Labour Society. He was admitted as a solicitor in 1957, but practice was delayed by national service in the education branch of the RAF. He then became a partner in a prestigious firm of solicitors, and acquired a reputation in the industrial accident field. His wife Anne, whom he married in 1960, was from a local family, and they had one son.

He was selected to fight his local constituency of Pontypridd and in 1970 was elected to the seat, which he held for the remainder of his life. His socialism, though deeply held, was in the moderate stream. He was not a charismatic speaker, but he spiced a thoughtful style with the occasional gem, as when he accused Sir Geoffrey Howe, then Chancellor of the Exchequer, of having been caught robbing pensioners, like 'a cat burglar who has stepped on a squeaking floorboard'.

In the Labour Government of 1974, he was appointed Parliamentary Under-Secretary for Defence (RAF) and acquired a reputation as an effective, if sometimes stubborn, minister. In a tightly-knit defence team under Roy Mason, he robustly resisted calls for defence cuts. When James Callaghan succeeded Harold Wilson as Prime Minister in April 1976, John was promoted to be Minister of State at the Home Office.

After the defeat of May 1979, he became Chief Opposition Spokesman on Northern Ireland, followed by Shadow Defence Secretary in December 1980. It was no feather bed. In the Labour Movement, social expenditure has always been more popular as a target for resources than defence, but additionally the Party was split between the supporters of unilateral nuclear disarmament and those who sought multilateral agreement. John was firmly multilateralist, and uncompromising in his belief that Britain's future was within NATO. He opposed demands by the NEC for cuts in the defence budget. In 1981, in the debate at Party conference he was not called to speak, and his indignation exploded to the point where he walked out of the hall. Though in November 1981 he became an elected member of the shadow cabinet for the first time, it came as no surprise when Michael Foot moved him to be Shadow Social Security Secretary in December 1981, a post he retained until 1983.

In September 1983 he co-nominated Roy Hattersley in his unsuccessful bid to become Labour leader. A month later he missed re-election to the shadow cabinet on the Solidarity slate by one vote, and was moved by Neil Kinnock to shadow Agriculture. He was runner-up in the shadow cabinet election the following year, and thereafter his vote steadily declined: in July 1987 he lost his post as Agriculture spokesman. He was the Chairman of the Welsh Group of Labour MPs 1983–86. His way with militants and their sympathisers was short, yet his concern was to build bridges in the Party for any who would respond. He was virtually the founder of Labour First which, as its name implied, believed that the Party was more important than any of its contending factions. And when Solidarity was formed to re-store the movement to its natural balance, he became a member of the Executive. An inter-nationalist in outlook, he developed a strong interest in American history and politics. He initially opposed devolution as insular and backward-looking, but later came to believe that a robust local culture can be consistent with a global vision.

The first foreboding of health problems came with an attack of MS in the mid-1980s, and although he recovered, his old energy appeared to have deserted him. In December 1988 he suffered a fatal heart attack. It was ironic. He would have been more at home in the fraternal Party of the 1990s than in the fratricidal battles of the earlier decade. He did not see the reali-sation of the unity to which he devoted his later years.

Rt. Hon. Lord Archer of Sandwell QC

Tom Johnston   (1881–1965)

Known in his lifetime as 'the uncrowned King of Scotland', there was a significant period when Thomas Johnston appeared a possible future leader of the Labour Party, destined for the highest office.

Born at Kirkintilloch on 2 November 1881, the son of a licensed victualler, he was edu-cated at Lairdslaw Public School, Kirkintilloch, Lenzie Academy and Glasgow University. In 1903 he won election to the Kirkintilloch School Board on a platform which included higher pay for teachers, a higher school leaving age and evening classes in citizenship. Ten years later he was elected to Kirkintilloch Town Council, becoming founder and chairman of the Kirkintilloch Municipal Bank Ltd., which aimed to benefit ratepayers by removing capital from 'the orbit of the private speculator in finance'.

The first issue of his campaigning newspaper *Forward* appeared on 13 October 1906. Keir Hardie, Ramsay MacDonald, George Bernard Shaw, H G Wells and Bertrand Russell all wrote for the paper. Johnston's own savage polemics included *The Case for Women's Suffrage* (1907); *Our Noble Families* (1909); and *The History of the Working Classes in Scotland* (1920).

His opposition to World War One was absolute. His report of a speech by Lloyd George, then Minister of Munitions, at the St. Andrew's Hall, Glasgow, on 24 December 1916, enraged the future Prime Minister who responded with a raid on the offices of *Forward*, followed by a ban which lasted five weeks.

In the general election which followed the war Johnston unsuccessfully contested West Stirlingshire and Clackmannan on behalf of the ILP. Four years later he won in the same constituency, earning his place in the most famous group of parliamentary dissidents ever dispatched from Scotland to harangue Westminster, the legendary Clydesiders. Ramsay MacDonald hoped to win power by appealing to the middle class. This was anathema to Johnston, who also opposed Labour forming a minority government in 1924. However, when the party suffered heavy losses, including West Stirling, in the election which followed MacDonald's resignation after only nine months in Downing Street, he refused to support calls for a change in the leadership.

The death of E D Morel, one of two MPs representing Dundee, a few days after the election, provided the opportunity of an early return to the House of Commons. He soon found Dundee Trades and Labour Council was deeply divided, especially in its relations with the ILP. Ahead of the next election Johnston announced he would be abandoning his safe city seat and returning to West Stirling.

West Stirling was an important Labour gain in 1929. Johnston's loyalty to MacDonald was rewarded with a place in the second Labour government — as Parliamentary Under-Secretary in the Scottish Office. Two years later he was named Lord Privy Seal, with a seat in the Cabinet. Five months to the day following his appointment, Johnston was one of nine Cabinet ministers who refused to vote in favour of a large cut in unemployment benefit as a means of maintaining the gold standard and defending the pound.

The future leadership of the Labour Party was almost certainly affected by the result of the 1931 election and Tom Johnston's failure to win an early by-election in Dunbartonshire when Ramsay MacDonald openly supported the Tory candidate. Highly regarded by other MPs, Johnston was just one of a dozen candidates from the previous parliament who could have been expected to defeat George Lansbury and Clement Attlee for the leadership.

Awaiting the next election Johnston busied himself with *Forward* and becoming head of a life assurance company, the City of Glasgow Friendly Society. On his return to the House of Commons in 1935, he was asked by Attlee to shadow Scottish affairs, anticipating Winston Churchill's decision to make him Secretary of State for Scotland in the wartime coalition.

Johnston was a life-long supporter of devolution, with a Scottish Parliament sitting in Edinburgh his primary goal. On two occasions he seconded Home Rule Bills which never progressed beyond second reading. He was a prominent member of the Scottish Home Rule Association for many years, and shortly before the outbreak of the Second World War he helped establish the London Scots Self-Government Committee.

Johnston began the war as Regional Commissioner in charge of Civil Defence. By the time it ended, with Churchill's considerable support, he enjoyed a greater degree of power and authority as Secretary of State for Scotland than anyone before or since. Coalition government, and the role of benign dictator, suited Johnston's pragmatic managerial style, with its emphasis on all shades of political opinion coming together to solve whatever problem presented itself.

His decision to quit parliament when the war ended surprised and disappointed many people. In fact, his place at the forefront of Scottish life barely altered. The new Labour government believed forestry, tourism and hydro power should be at the heart of a plan to invigorate the Highlands. Tom Johnston was entrusted with running all three!

A noticeable absence of honours attended his retirement from public life, reflecting the same scrupulous streak which prevented him from accepting any payment for his wartime service as Regional Commissioner and Secretary of State. A peerage, a viscountcy and membership of the Order of the Thistle were all declined. Pressed by Churchill, he finally agreed to become a Companion of Honour in 1953, adding to the honorary degree bestowed on him by Glasgow University and the freedom scrolls he received from several towns. He was also Chancellor of Aberdeen University from 1951 until his death 14 years later.

Tom Johnston died on 5 September 1965. His wife, Margaret Freeland Cochrane, whom he married in 1914, outlived him. There were two daughters. Johnston's published works include *Memories* (1952). Key biographies are *Without Quarter: A Biography of Tom Johnston 'The*

Uncrowned King of Scotland' by Russell Galbraith (1995) and *Thomas Johnston: Lives of the Left* by Graham Walker (1988).

Russell Galbraith

Arthur Creech Jones   (1891–1964)

Although built on a traditional trade union background, Arthur Creech Jones' political career was dominated by, and is remembered for, his involvement in colonial affairs. Born in Bristol on 15 May 1891, he was educated at Whitehall Boys' School. After a short period in a solicitor's office he joined the civil service in 1907, serving in a number of departments including the War Office and the Crown Agents' Office.

At the age of twenty he became secretary of the Camberwell Independent Labour Party, a post he held until 1915. During the First World War he was active in the anti-war movement, and was imprisoned as a conscientious objector from 1916 until 1919. The following year he married Violet Tidman. The year of his release from prison he took on a full-time position in the trade union movement, as Secretary of the National Union of Docks, Wharves and Shipping Staff. Following its amalgamation with the Transport and General Workers' Union in 1922, he served as the National Secretary of that union's administrative, clerical and supervisory group until 1929. That year he first stood for Parliament, unsuccessfully contesting Heywood and Radcliffe. He was the joint author of the ILP's Living Wage programme in 1926.

He was the Organising Secretary of the Workers Travel Association from 1930 to 1940, during which time he expanded on his interest in colonial affairs and visited Palestine. In 1935 he was successfully elected for Labour to the Yorkshire seat of Shipley. Just before the outbreak of war he successfully piloted the Access to Mountains Act 1939. On the formation of the coalition government he was appointed as Parliamentary Private Secretary to Ernie Bevin, the Minister of Labour. From 1942 to 1943 he was able to build on his experience with Britain's overseas possessions when he served as Vice-chairman of the Commission on Higher Education for West Africa.

Following Labour's 1945 election victory he was appointed as Parliamentary Under-Secretary of State for the Colonies, and on the retirement of George Hall in October 1946 he stepped up to be Secretary of State. This post had responsibility for relations with Britain's imperial possessions outside of India and Burma. The main focus was therefore twofold; Africa, and the thorny problem of Palestine, and it was Jones who announced to the UN in 1947 that Britain intended to terminate its mandate there and hand over control to the UN. He presided over the first African conference at Lancaster House in 1948 and that year saw the independence of the first colony with a non-European population, Ceylon. He set up the Colonial (later Commonwealth) Development Corporation.

Jones narrowly lost his seat in the 1950 election, and Labour did not regain Shipley until its 1997 landslide victory. He unsuccessfully contested Romford in 1951 before being elected for Wakefield in a 1954 by-election. As soon as he was back in Parliament he was the obvious choice to serve as opposition spokesman on Commonwealth and Colonial Affairs, and he held this post until his retirement due to ill health in August 1964.

In modern terms, Jones would be regarded as something of a 'quango king'. He held many Labour Movement-based posts including spells with the Fabian Commonwealth Bureau, the Fabian Africa Bureau, the Workers' Travel Association, the Pit Ponies Protection Society and the Labour Party Imperial Advisory Committee. Outside he served on the boards of a wide variety of bodies, including the Anti-Slavery Society, the Royal Commonwealth Society, the Colonial Office Education Advisory Committee, the Metropolitan Water Board, the Southern Electricity Board, the Royal Institute of International Affairs, the British Council, the Travel Association of Great Britain and the National Film Council. He died in London on 23 October 1964, just a week after Labour's return to power.

Matthew Seward

Elwyn Jones (Lord Elwyn-Jones) (1909–89)

(Frederick) Elwyn Jones was MP for Plaistow, West Ham (later West Ham South & Newham) between 1945 and 1974. He then served in the Lords until his death from cancer on 4 December 1989, from 1983 to 1989 as spokesman on home and legal affairs. Serving as PPS to Attlee's Attorney General from 1946 to 1951, he was Attorney-General 1964–70 and Lord Chancellor 1974–79. Knighted in 1964, he joined the Privy Council the same year and was made a Companion of Honour in 1976. With his background as a young man, as an MP he always had his feet on the ground, never considering ditching the ship when the going was hard. He believed in parliamentary democracy and used it in the Commons and Lords to further his socialist beliefs.

The first Labour government with a majority did not come until 1945, so aspiring young MPs in the 1920s and '30s could not look forward to a parliamentary career with much certainty. Elwyn was not converted by a blinding flash of light en route from Cambridge via Liverpool Street. He was born on 24 October 1909 into a socialist family in Llanelli; his father was a tin-plate roller man, a pillar of the Tabernacle Congregational Chapel and the Sunday School, as was his mother.

These roots influenced the wider Jones family of a sister and two brothers. They all obtained first class honours degrees and subsequent educational success. After Llanelli Grammar School and University College Wales at Aberystwyth, Elwyn read history at Gonville and Caius College, Cambridge, where he became President of the Cambridge Union. Joining Gray's Inn, he was called to the Bar in 1935. His brother was captain of the Cambridge University Rugby Club and played for Wales before becoming Chief Scientist to the National Coal Board. His sister was headmistress of the Llanelli Girls School. Education, religion and politics were intertwined in West Wales; they showed through in the personal lives and indeed attributes of the Jones family, who were all home-taught to speak clearly and succinctly.

The future Lord Chancellor's socialism was home-grown, but early on it spread its wings. He was recruited by the Fabians in the mid-thirties, responding to the activities of the Dolfuss fascists in Austria whose private army proscribed the Social Democratic Party there. Allied with the Fabians were the Quakers and the trade unions, who enabled Elwyn to act in the continental courts to ameliorate the severity of their sentences. Others, led by Hugh Gaitskell, acted more clandestinely.

The whole traumatic episode in Austria, developing into the horror of the Nazis and the Jewish refugees in Germany, convinced Elwyn that Nazism had to be stopped. He worked within the Labour Party, not least with Aneurin Bevan, to influence party policy in this respect. He also wrote three books for the Left Book Club on the Nazi threat: *Hitler's Drive to the East* (1937); *The Battle for Peace* (1938) and *The Attack from Within* (1939). Elwyn joined the Territorial Army. The time for talking was coming to an end, and he eventually served as a Major in the wartime Royal Artillery in the UK and Italy, where as Deputy Judge Advocate General he ensured that the 'Salerno mutineers' did not face the death penalty.

When the war ended, Elwyn Jones became an important member of the Nuremberg War Crimes Tribunal and subsequently, whether in government or by pressure groups, he worked to create legal means to support human rights. He represented before the courts the oppressed in many parts of the world including Africa and Asia. In this respect he was a founder member and trustee of Amnesty International, active in Justice and Chair of the Society of Labour Lawyers 1957–60. In government he significantly developed the number of Law Centres. He saw the need for these from his constituency work. From his legal activities he realised the need for a Law Commission, established in 1965 under Lord Scarman. He was counsel for the tribunal in the Aberfan colliery disaster inquiry and prosecuted in the Moors murder case. He was with Harold Wilson in the *Fearless* and *Tiger* talks on Rhodesian independence with Ian Smith. Within the party he spoke at party conference in support of the right of dissent by Party members and urged the retention of a liberal approach to Commonwealth immigration.

Elwyn Jones' politics grew out of the 'New Labour' of the time, aided as it was by the secondary (intermediate) schools born earlier in Wales than in England. Emerging democratic socialism needed civilised values; he epitomised these, aided and abetted by his painter wife, Pearl Binder. They married in 1937 and were survived by a son and two daughters. His autobiography, *In My Time*, was published in 1983.

Rt Hon. Lord Merlyn-Rees

Jack Jones (1913–)

It was during the period of James Larkin 'Jack' Jones's leadership of the Transport and General Workers Union – he was General Secretary from 1969 until 1978 – that the TGWU reached a record membership of over two million, larger than any union in the history of the British Labour Movement, larger than any union in Europe and probably in the non-communist world. It was an astonishing achievement and to this day ranks as Jones's trade union monument. But there are many other aspects to his achievements during the nine years this former Liverpool docker held sway over the TGWU and indeed across the entire Labour Movement. It was not pure idle malice that persuaded Paul Johnson, then editor of the *New Statesman* to dub him 'Emperor Jones', in September 1976. Johnson meant it – though not as a friendly salute.

Indeed a Gallup Poll taken at the time when Jones was at the peak of his power and influence placed his public image as 'the most powerful man in Britain'. That was in the mid-seventies when he bestrode the trade union movement (and the Labour Party) like a military commander. Many people genuinely believed he had more power than Prime Ministers and perhaps there were moments when some of his trade union colleagues might also have be-lieved that. Yet the remarkable paradox within the man was that he always remained a man of modest attitudes in the private sense, never seeking personal grandeur or baubles of office, and forever remaining with his wife Evelyn in a tiny council flat in South London. Emperor Jones he may well have been – but always a working class Emperor and Crusader.

He was born on 29 March 1913 in York Street, Garston, at the south end of Liverpool which he describes in his autobiography (*Union Man;* Collins, 1986) as 'a long street of poor and mean terraced houses.' Most of the houses were rat-infested, two rooms up and two down, no bathroom, just an outside toilet, and the rent was five shillings a week. You can't get more working class than that. He had three brothers and one sister, all older than him. He went to the local elementary school where the classes were huge, often fifty or sixty, the teachers lim-ited and the horizons nil. He says that as a youngster he never knew anyone who went to uni-versity. His eldest brother, Sydney, became a scoutmaster and was active in the local socialist Sunday School – which was Jack's first introduction to the world of political beliefs. When he left school at 14 , shortly after the 1926 General Strike, he wanted to follow his father into the docks but there were no vacant jobs there at the time and unemployment was soaring on Mer-seyside. He was lucky to find a first job as an engineering apprentice (at five shillings a week or 25p in today's money), but as soon as he could he switched to the docks alongside his father. And that was when Jack Jones began to cut his political teeth.

His father took him to hear Ernest Bevin speak to the Liverpool dockers – it was an occa-sion that remained engraved in his mind. The young Jones started a correspondence course with Ruskin College, Oxford, and then took a course in Economics at the Liverpool Labour College – his 'Universities'. He became a shop steward in the docks and a member of the TGWU docks branch committee – where he had to fight the constant threat of victimisation for trade union work. In 1934 he joined a Merseyside-organised Hunger March to London which combined the support of Labour Party and Communist Party activists.

Then came his involvement against Mosley's fascist campaign in the North West, as else-where, and in the fight against Franco's fascism in Spain. He wanted to join the International Brigade from an early stage and finally did so in 1937. Some of his close friends had already been killed at the battle of Jarama. One of Jack's jobs before leaving for Spain was to contact relatives of his friends who had been killed in Spain. That was how he met his wife Evelyn, whose first husband, George Brown, was killed in the battle of Brunete. Jack took the news of his death to Evelyn Brown, whom he had met before. But that was the meeting which brought them together, and Jack married the widowed Evelyn Mary Taylor in 1938 when he returned, wounded, from Spain. Jack was fighting on the Ebro front, clambering up the fiercely contested Hill 481 when he was hit in the shoulder by machine gun fire. It was a se-vere wound which refused to heal in a Spanish hospital, so he was sent back to England for medical attention.

When he recovered he returned to work in the docks, though he still spent much of his time in activities on behalf of the Spanish Republican Movement and in support of the anti-fascists. He also resumed his elected job as a Labour City Councillor in Liverpool (1936–39) which at that time had a Conservative majority. With the outbreak of the Second World War Jack left Liv-erpool to take up his first full-time union post. He was appointed Coventry District Organiser of the TGWU, and rubber-stamped by Bevin himself – his first step on the ladder to the General Secretaryship.

It was in wartime Coventry that Jones established his real trade union base and his commitment to 'shop floor power' and industrial democracy – hallmarks of his philosophy that, later, were to become the dominant theme of his TGWU leadership. He established a system of shop stewards' committees in the war production plants in Coventry that brought him into conflict with many local employers – and even his own union hierarchy, then under the command of Arthur Deakin, who was acting General Secretary when Ernest Bevin became a member of Churchill's War Cabinet as Minister of Labour. Deakin and Jones had many clashes during that wartime period and it left a permanent shadow over their relationship. Indeed he remained in Coventry after the war, rising only as high as District Secretary, and would probably have moved little further up the promotional ladder but for Deakin's death and the remarkable change brought to the TGWU when Frank Cousins was elected General Secretary. Jones and Cousins were old friends and Cousins moved Jones to Regional Secretary of the TGWU in the Midlands, a major union post, and then brought him to London by creating the new post of Executive National Officer, number three in the hierarchy to Cousins and Harry Nicholas. That move effectively secured Jones as Cousins' choice for succession. There is little doubt that without the 'Cousins' Revolution' in the TGWU Jack Jones would probably have remained a Midlands official.

When Frank Cousins moved into Wilson's Cabinet in 1964, Harry Nicholas became Acting General Secretary and Jones Deputy General Secretary. He also joined the Labour Party's National Executive and remained on the party NEC until 1967. By that time Cousins had resigned from the Wilson Government and returned to the TGWU as General Secretary. The two men then prepared for Jones's eventual succession. The ballot was held in 1968 and Jones was an easy winner, taking over from Cousins the following July. Harry Nicholas then moved across to become General Secretary of the Labour Party.

The nine years of Jones's leadership of the TGWU covered a period of widespread industrial upheaval. Indeed it began with a fierce clash over the Wilson Government's plan to introduce Barbara Castle's plan to curb unofficial strike, *In Place of Strife,* which Jones along with Hugh Scanlon of the AEU together helped to overturn. Then came the election of the Heath Government in June 1970, after which the Industrial Relations Act was quickly introduced to curb the powers of the unions. That brought the TGWU to the forefront of a two-year battle to fight, and then defeat, the Act.

The crucial moments came in 1972 in the London docks, when five members of the TGWU were jailed for their defiance of the Act. The TGWU had also been fined £55,000 for defying a ruling by the National Industrial Relations Court. In the end, as a result of a new dock workers' deal between Lord Aldington (Port of London Chairman) and Jones, the dockers were released from jail, the Government capitulated and the Act was effectively dead. There then began a series of discussions between the TUC and the Heath Government over pay, price control and productivity in which Jack Jones along with Vic Feather played a leading role. Jones writes in his book that the TUC came close to an historic deal with the Heath Government. But for the Middle-East oil crisis in 1973 and then the miners' strike, such a deal might have emerged.

In the event the election of February 1974 brought Harold Wilson back to Downing Street. They were the days when the Social Contract was being discussed – a plan which almost certainly originated in Jack Jones's mind, even if later it was claimed by others. It was certainly Jones's idea to establish a fixed £6 a week pay rise for all workers in 1975 – the basis on which the Social Contract was built. When he retired in 1978 the Prime Minister, James Callaghan, offered him a peerage – which Jones flatly rejected. He later accepted a CH. But in a sense he never retired. Immediately he vacated the TGWU leadership he set to work building up the TGWU retired members organisation around which he then established a National Pensioners Movement and in 1992 the National Pensioners' Convention, of which he became Chairman. Evelyn Jones died in December 1998, after sixty years of marriage. They had two sons, Jack and Michael. Jack Jones published his autobiography, *Union Man*, in 1986.

Geoffrey Goodman

Bill Jordan (Lord Jordan of Bournville)   (1936–)

William (Bill) Brian Jordan was born in Winson Green, Birmingham, on 28 January 1936, the son of Walter and Alice. He was educated at the Dudley Road Junior School. He started work at 15 at Stevens and Bullivants, training as a machine-tool fitter. Called up for National Service he served in the Royal Air Force with the rank of corporal and served in Jordan and Iraq. After the RAF he started work at GKN Smethwick where he became a shop steward and convener.

He became a prominent lay activist, president of the Birmingham West District Committee and a delegate to the National Committee, the AEU's 52–member policy-making body and its Rules Revision Committee. In 1977 he stood for full-time office as West Midlands divisional organiser. AUEW membership peaked nationally in 1979, and the West Midlands division had more members [130,000] than many national unions today. The massive workload in Birmingham and the West Midlands eventually persuaded the union's Executive to split the division and create extra district secretaries in Birmingham.

In 1978 he unsuccessfully ran for the Executive Council when Terry Duffy vacated the post to become President. However, he remained close to Duffy and was his choice to succeed him. Under the AEU's rules members could not contest two elections at the same time. Duffy used this rule by announcing he would retire early, so forcing an election to run for his successor at the same time as prominent political opponents faced elections for their own jobs, thereby assisting Jordan's campaign. Unlike Bill Carron thirty years before, the opponents did not gamble with their own jobs.

Jordan also took clever advantage of the engineers' row with the TUC over taking public money for ballots. At one point this row was of such significance that it led the Nine o'clock News, and he was seen on television supporting the union's leadership and by implication its members who had voted by a large majority to take the money. After two ballots he won a comfortable victory, becoming the AEU's ninth President in 1986, moving straight into that position from a divisional organiser post, effectively getting the top national job as an outsider to the union's full-time executive. As President he had to chair that executive, a difficult transition not faced by Bill Carron, Hugh Scanlon or Terry Duffy.

He was a careful and measured exponent of the moderate case. He readily understood the power of the media, for whom he was a thoughtful contributor. Unlike many of his contemporaries and predecessors who were distrustful of the media Jordan was always available. He applied the same professionalism to his speech delivery. A widely-read man, he strove to find the phrase which could be turned into a soundbite, and could often be seen polishing and re-writing minutes before being called to the podium. He wrote most of his own speeches. He was temperamentally very different to the union's General Secretary, Gavin Laird; though never close, they were well respected as an effective team at the top of the union

He was a strong supporter of partnership in industry and won a number of single union deals, including Toyota, with calm logic against the odds. Internally he was an impatient advocate of internal change and a strong supporter of a merger with the union's fellow moderate rival, the EETPU. The relationship between the unions had ebbed and flowed, with many attempts made to merge. On one occasion in the 1920s the EETPU had voted in favour, but not with the necessary turnout required by law. Despite his support the AEU's National Committee narrowly rejected the merger in 1989, only to reconsider and agree it in 1991. He, therefore, became the first AEEU President in May 1992.

In its initial stages the AEEU merger became a power battle between the AEU and EETPU camps. Whilst he was from an engineering background, Jordan had great respect for the structures of the electricians union, seeing it as a more modern version of the engineers'. Whilst both unions were membership-led, moderate and governed by full-time executives, their structures were very different. However, just as the merger seemed poised to take off he left the union.

In December 1994 he was appointed acting General Secretary of the International Confederation of Free Trade Unions – the world's largest international trade union organisation, with a world-wide membership of 156 million members in 148 countries. As President, Jordan played a prominent role in the Confederation of Shipbuilding and Engineering Union's Engineering Committee and, together with Alex Ferry (CSEU General Secretary) and Gavin Laird, successfully employed targeted strikes to win the 37–hour week for manual workers in 1989.

He also served the TUC with distinction for nine years, making a powerful impact on international issues and as Chair of the European Strategy Committee. Among many other wider fields he was a BBC Governor for ten years, a Governor of the LSE and the Manchester Business School, a member of the Engineering Training Authority and a fellow of RSA. He became a CBE in 1992 and Lord Jordan of Bournville in 2000. His wife Jean was a nursing sister at Birmingham Accident Hospital Casualty Department. They have three daughters.

John Gibbins

Tessa Jowell   (1947–)

Tony Blair brought Tessa Jowell onto the Labour front bench in his first reshuffle as Labour leader in 1995, triggering an ascent through the ranks that has now reached the Cabinet six years later, in the wake of the 2001 general election.

The daughter of Dr Kenneth Palmer and Rosemary Palmer, a radiographer, Tessa Jowell was born on 17 September 1947 and educated at St Margaret's School in Aberdeen before taking further education at a trio of universities: Aberdeen, Edinburgh and London. A career in social work then started at Lambeth Council in 1969 and, after serving as Assistant Director of MIND 1974–86, saw her rise to become Director of a Joseph Rowntree Foundation research project into community care before she became MP for Dulwich in 1992. A Camden councillor 1971–86, she unsuccessfully fought Ilford North for Labour at the 1979 general election.

After serving as an Opposition Whip 1994–95 and handling junior Opposition roles on both women (1995–96) and then health (1996–97), she entered the government at the Minister of State level in 1997. As Minister for Public Health, though, she hit her first major controversy over the government's decision to back down on a ban on tobacco advertising. The concurrence of this decision with Labour's acceptance of a million-pound donation from Formula One chief Bernie Ecclestone was causing trouble enough, but this was compounded when it emerged that Jowell (who was responsible for implementing the ban) was married to a director of the Benetton Formula One team, David Mills, whom she had married in 1979 and with whom she has a son, a daughter and three step-children. Her first marriage, to Roger Jowell in 1970, was dissolved in 1975.

She survived the 'scandal' and became Employment Minister at the DfEE in 1999. There she was able to consolidate her reputation (Ecclestone aside) as a hardworking and purposeful minister. But she did not remain free of controversy, and attracted scorn when she invited fashion magazine editors to Whitehall for a 'fat summit' and suggested establishing an agency to count the numbers of 'fat' and 'thin' models in magazines. Critics point to the episode as an example of an unfortunate ability to undermine a legitimate and well-supported cause by proposing absurd policy solutions, and whispered unkindly of a 'sanctimonious' and 'nannying' approach.

Nevertheless she again survived, and her promotion to the Cabinet in 2001 was seen as largely inevitable by the time of the election. Initial observations that her role as Secretary of State for Culture, Media and Sport is more marginal than she might have hoped may be misjudged. She will have to deliberate quickly on whether (and how) to authorise the launch of a range of publicly-funded TV and Radio channels by the BBC, and then tackle the thorny regulations of cross-media ownership in a new Communications Bill. On both of these issues, the commercial sector of which Rupert Murdoch is just one of several powerful members will be lobbying hard and will protest loudly if she is unable to balance their demands.

DCMS is a difficult department. It rarely provides the sort of regular high profile that ambitious ministers crave, and it also presents plenty of pitfalls: the difficult media issues pile up alongside the Dome, the Lottery and the new national soccer stadium in her in-tray. There is little scope for good news – but if she manages to solve these problems and deliver 'no news' on these issues, her cabinet star will be set to rise further.

Peter Metcalfe

Frederick Jowett   (1864–1944)

Throughout the history of the labour movement, there are many figures who have not become widely known, but whose influence on individuals' lives has reached much farther. Fred Jowett was one of those. Born in Bradford on 31 January 1864, he worked in a local textile mill from the age of eight, rising to become a manufacturer's manager following classes he took at Bradford Technical College.

A strong Christian Socialist, he was introduced to the subject of politics by his father (who was also a textile worker), joined the Socialist League and subsequently the Bradford Labour Union, which was created to support the Manningham Mills strikers. At the age of 28 he became the first socialist to be elected to Bradford Town Council and founded an ILP branch in the city soon after. Serving on the council for fifteen years crossing the turn of the century, he played a role in pioneering measures that were a feature of local government at that time. Jowett and the council successfully campaigned for slum clearance and reform of the Poor Law, but perhaps the most far-reaching reform was the introduction of the first-ever council-provided free school meals, a move which was actually illegal and could have been overturned.

Jowett became an alderman in 1895 and five years later contested West Bradford for the Labour Party. Losing by less than fifty votes, his opposition to the ongoing Boer War is thought to have been a factor in the outcome.

He was successfully elected in 1906 and sat for West Bradford until 1918. During this time he supported Lloyd George's measures to construct the early welfare state, notably the introduction of old age pensions. He also argued for legislation to extend the free school meals initiative that he had started in Bradford. It was the subject of his maiden speech and led to the Provision of School Meals Act of 1906, which allowed councils to provide such nourishment to children.

Jowett was Chairman of the Independent Labour Party from 1909 to 1910 and 1914 to 1917. He lost his seat in 1918 alongside other anti-war members like MacDonald, Lansbury and Snowden, and out of Parliament he was Chairman of the Labour Party NEC 1921–22. He was back in the House representing East Bradford from November 1922 until 1924, and when the first Labour government was formed, Ramsey MacDonald appointed Jowett to the Cabinet as First Commissioner of Works. During this time he ensured that funding was achieved for the modernisation of 60,000 government-built homes.

He was defeated again in the 1924 election, but was re-elected for the East Bradford seat in 1929. Jowett opposed the creation of the National Government and lost his seat in the huge defeat of 1931. In 1932 he and the ILP disaffiliated from the Labour Party, and when he stood as an ILP candidate in 1935 he was defeated.

He died on 1 February 1944 during the war, Britain' involvement with which was opposed by the ILP. His publications included *Socialism in Our Time* (1926), which advocated a national minimum income.

At the outbreak of war less than half of councils were providing school meals, but the programme took off after the war. Later legislation restricted it to those on low incomes and abolished minimum nutritional standards – the Labour government has announced that such standards will be reintroduced from May 2002.

Matthew Seward

William Jowitt (1st Earl Jowitt)   (1885–1957)

Lord Jowitt remains Labour's most successful Lord Chancellor, despite starting his political career as a Liberal MP and staying on in Ramsay MacDonald's National Government in 1931 only to lose his seat in the subsequent election. William Allen Jowitt was born on 15 April 1885, the only son of Rev William Jowitt, Rector of Stevenage, and studied at Marlborough and New College Oxford, gaining a first in Jurisprudence before starting a successful career at the Bar in 1909. He married Lesley McIntyre in 1913, with whom he had one daughter.

In the same Inns of Court as Stafford Cripps and Lord Parmoor, he became a KC in 1922 and sat as MP for the Hartlepools from 1922 to 1924. He was re-elected to Parliament in 1929, this time for Preston, but when he was appointed Attorney-General by MacDonald he re-took the seat under the Labour banner and with a knighthood to his name. Jowitt was one of only four Labour ministers who stood by MacDonald in 1931, but standing as a National Labour candidate for the Combined English Universities seat he was defeated and had to resign in 1932. It was not until 1939 that he re-entered Parliament as the Labour MP for Ashton-under-Lyne, serving in the Coalition Government as Solicitor-General (1940–42), Paymaster-General in May 1942, Minister without Portfolio (1943–4) and Minister of Social Insurance (1944–45). When Labour came to power in 1945 Attlee made him a baron and Lord Chancellor (he was also created a viscount in 1947). He remained Lord Chancellor until Labour lost in 1951, whereupon he became an Earl and from 1952–55 Leader of the Opposition in the Lords. His spell as Lord Chancellor brought phenomenal challenges, steering controversial Labour legislation through a largely Tory house and it is a measure of his success that the Government lost so few bills.

In his retirement he wrote two books, *The Strange Case of Alger Hiss* (1953) and *Some Were Spies* (1954). He died at his Bury St, Edmunds home on 16 August 1957.

Chris Bryant MP

Nicholas Kaldor (Lord Kaldor)   (1908–86)

Nicky Kaldor's contribution to history was largely as an economist. He was a central figure in the development of Keynesian economics after Keynes' death, and is considered by many to have been the best economist never to win a Nobel Prize. However, like Keynes, he was enthusiastic about emerging from academia's cloisters to play an active role in public policy debates. This interest is reflected in his prominence within Labour Party circles, culminating in his high-profile role as Economic Advisor to three Labour chancellors (James Callaghan from 1964 to 1967, Roy Jenkins from 1967 to 1968 and Denis Healey from 1974 to 1976; from 1968 to 1970 he was Special Advisor at the Department of Health and Social Security). On becoming a Labour peer in 1974 he maintained a high profile as a vociferous opponent of the emergent Thatcherite agenda.

Kaldor was born to a comfortable Jewish family in Budapest on 12 May 1908. His father, Dr. Julius Kaldor, was a prominent lawyer and his mother came from a family of bankers. He was educated at the Minta Gymnasium, an elite school that came under the control of the University of Budapest rather than the Department of Education and which produced a number of noted Hungarian academics, including his fellow Labour Party economist Thomas

Balogh (Balogh and Kaldor were very much linked in the public imagination and were nick-named, amongst other less flattering things, 'Buda and Pest'). After school he enrolled to study Economics at the University of Berlin before moving to the London School of Economics, graduating with a first in 1930 despite initially showing a greater enthusiasm for freelance jour-nalism than his studies.

The economics department at LSE at the time was very much under the sway of free mar-ket enthusiasts Lionel Robbins and Friedrich Hayek, despite the presence of prominent La-bour figures such as Hugh Dalton, R H Tawney and Evan Durbin on the staff, and Kaldor was very much seen as a protégé of Robbins. He also began to translate Hayek's early work from German. However by the time he was appointed a lecturer in 1932, after two years as a research student, he seems to have rejected Robbins and Hayek for Keynesian economics. By the time Keynes' magnum opus *The General Theory of Employment Interest and Money* was published in 1936 Kaldor was, in the words of his biographer A.P. Thirlwall, 'a complete convert'.

During World War II he became a vocal advocate of William Beveridge's plans for the con-struction of a comprehensive welfare state. He argued in articles, pamphlets, letters to the press and a talk for the BBC that, contrary to much conservative opinion, the Beveridge plans were readily affordable and would in no way prove an intolerable burden on the British economy. In Beveridge's second report, on Full Employment in 1944, Kaldor contributed an analysis of the implications for the public purse of the government assuming responsibility for the mainte-nance of full employment. Kaldor also took on important roles abroad, as chief of planning to the US Strategic Bombing Survey, as advisor to the socialist government in Hungary, and as an advisor to Jean Monnet preparing a plan for post-war economic stabilisation. But his most sig-nificant role was in the Research and Planning division of the recently established Economic Commission for Europe (a division of the UN set up to administer Marshall Aid from the USA for post-war reconstruction), notably drafting the report on National and International Measures for Full Employment. In 1949 he returned to academia, taking up a fellowship at Kings College, Cambridge.

But his report to the UN had made an impression on Hugh Gaitskell, a former academic economist and by now the rising star in the Labour cabinet. When Gaitskell became Chancel-lor he appointed Kaldor to a Royal Commission on Taxation of Profits and Income. Kaldor disagreed with the majority report of the commission and drafted a dissenting report recom-mending the imposition of capital gains tax. Kaldor's minority report recommendations found strong support from Gaitskell and provided the basis for the imposition of capital gains tax, which became Labour Party policy in 1959 and was introduced by the Wilson government in 1964. Kaldor built on his involvement with the commission to become an expert on the eco-nomics of taxation and acted as an advisor on tax matters to a number of developing countries.

As a high-profile economist with well-established Labour Party associations and personal friendships with prominent Labour figures like James Callaghan and Anthony Crosland, it was no surprise that when Labour won the 1964 election Kaldor was appointed Special Advisor on Taxation to the Chancellor of the Exchequer. Kaldor seems to have been frustrated by the po-litical side of his role. He was highly critical of the decision not to devalue the pound in 1964, a decision he felt severely hindered the British economy. But it was, predictably, in tax matters that Kaldor had his greatest impact on government, developing the Selective Employment Tax

(SET). He was of the opinion that UK industry was under-resourced. SET aimed to address this by levying a tax for each person employed but giving variable rebate on this. Manufacturing was given a 130 per cent rebate so the tax was effectively a subsidy to the sector. SET was later amended at Kaldor's behest with the introduction of Regional Employment Premiums designed to stimulate less productive regions of the economy. But his relationship with Roy Jenkins, who replaced Callaghan following the forced devaluation in 1967, was less close and he moved to advise Dick Crossman at the Department of Health and Social Security.

When Labour returned to power in 1974 Kaldor was re-appointed as Special Advisor to the new Chancellor Denis Healey, with a broader remit than merely tax matters. Despite this, however, he was to have a less constructive role in his second period of government. He had been frustrated by the Labour government's deflationary response to the forced devaluation of 1967 and regarded policy under the next government as similarly flawed. His employer Denis Healey on the other hand, whilst conceding Kaldor's economic brilliance, found his political judgement 'bizarre', as he put it in his autobiography, *The Time of My Life*. Frustrated by his lack of influence, Kaldor resigned his role as advisor in 1976.

This was not, however, the end of political activity. He was created Lord Kaldor in 1974 and used the Lords as a forum to continue contributing to public policy debate. He was a vehement critic of the emergent Thatcherite agenda which he predicted would cause untold damage to British manufacturing and undo many of the social advances made by the working class since 1945. A number of his Lords speeches were collected in *The Economic Consequences of Mrs Thatcher* (Duckworth, 1983), the title deliberately mimicking his mentor Keynes' attack on Winston Churchill. He remained an active critic of the Conservative government until his death on 30 September 1986.

Throughout his career Kaldor remained committed to the active management of the economy by government in order to maintain both economic growth and social justice. This faith in national economic growth underpinned his early opposition to British entry into the European Economic Community and in particular to the notion of a common European currency. Whilst best remembered for his contribution as an academic economist, Kaldor remained active within the Labour Party and the Fabian Society. As such he made a major contribution to both economic theory as well as public policy on a scale rarely equalled in post-war Britain.

Most of Kaldor's academic work is scattered throughout economic journals. *Nicholas Kaldor* by A.P. Thirlwall (Wheatsheaf, 1987), whilst focussing on his contribution to economics, has useful information on his periods in government.

Dr Philip Larkin

Gerald Kaufman   (1930–)

Gerald Kaufman's loyalty is absolute, to his friends, to his party, to Britain and to Israel. That loyalty is not blind; he is quick to recognise – and point out – the follies and faults of all of them. His frankness, however, does not mitigate his allegiances and it emphasises the hostility he shows to those whom he opposes, either personally or politically. He could easily be categorised as pompous, ponderous and pedantic, except that he uses these supposed defects to his advantage. It is difficult to sustain a charge of pomposity against a man who has a frequent twinkle in the eye, of being ponderous when his speaking style includes originality and wit, or of being pedantic when he meticulously questions a civil servant or minister in pursuit of the truth.

His devotion to the Israeli cause is unquestionable. Harold Wilson, for whom he worked as a political press officer from 1965 until 1970, considered sacking Kaufman in 1969 after receiving a cheeky card from him posted from Israeli-occupied territories to which Wilson had expressly forbidden him to go. He relented: the crime was not worth the punishment, especially as Wilson shared some of Kaufman's pro-Israeli sympathies, even if the Foreign and Commonwealth Office did not. But it was in Kaufman's character to declare, following a visit to Jordan in January, 1988, that 'after 20 years of deprivation of civil rights under military rule, the patience of the Palestinians in the occupied territories has finally snapped.' As Labour's Shadow Foreign Secretary under Neil Kinnock's leadership from 1987 to 1992, he tried to dissuade the US State Department from supporting Israel's refusal to negotiate with Palestinian Arabs, and was able to assert, in January 1989, that the time had come 'to end the spilling of blood in the Holy Land.' He alienated some Jews in Britain by his fierce criticism of the right-wing Likud party which from time to time governed Israel, but, unlike many others who were on the left, his socialism did not stop or begin at Dover.

Though he could occasionally, in private, be scathing about Wilson or his entourage, he never was so publicly. After being reduced to tears after an encounter with Lady Falkender, Wilson's personal and private secretary – 'She is a wicked woman!' he exclaimed – he returned to her office the next morning and kissed her, and he defended her against all criticism. Though he gave full support to his party, it was his description of Labour's 1983 general election manifesto as 'the longest suicide note in history' which is one of the few warm memories of a campaign in which Labour reached a depth of unpopularity unimaginable in 1945 or 1997. His remark more than a decade later that he had 'given grovelling support to every change Tony Blair has made in the way the Labour Party is run' gives the flavour of his approach to loyalty and his own self-mockery.

Gerald (Bernard) Kaufman was born on 21 June 1930, one of eight children of Polish Jewish immigrants, and was educated, formally, at Cowper Street Council School, Leeds, Leeds Grammar School, Queen's College, Oxford, and less formally, in the cinema, which was his abiding passion outside politics. 'Going to the pictures' is listed in Who's Who, along with travel, as a hobby. One of the survivors of the Holocaust filmed at the end of *Schindler's List* was a cousin of his mother's, which must have made his cinematic viewing more harrowing. He joined the Labour Party in 1948, was chairman of the Oxford University Labour Club in 1952, fought the then safe Tory seats of Bromley (against Harold Macmillan) in 1955 and Gillingham in 1959 and became MP for Ardwick in 1970, after five years on Wilson's staff as a political liaison officer. The retiring MP for Ardwick, Leslie Lever, was promised a peerage by Wilson if Kaufman was adopted as candidate, but the loss of that general election meant Lever had to wait.

If Kaufman never achieved the position in the party for which his understanding of politics and his intellect fitted him, the fault lay as much in himself as in others. An uncomfortable sense of humour is not a qualification for the greasy pole of politics, and under Blair he had to be content with the chairmanship of the Select Committee on Culture, Media and Sport, in each field of which he left many wounded. If there was a degree of anti-Semitism in the criticisms levelled against him from time to time, that ability to antagonise also played its part. In the early 1960s he was a contributor (as I was) to the notorious BBC satire programme, *That Was the Week That Was*, which was widely detested among politicians, including Harold Wilson and Tony Benn, an early member of Wilson's Kitchen Cabinet.

He also wrote – after his experiences in government under Wilson and James Callaghan, first as an Under-Secretary for Environment 1974–75, then at the same rank in the Department for Industry from June 1975 and finally as Minister of State for Industry from December 1975 until May 1979 – a light-hearted but penetrating volume entitled *How To Be a Minister* (1980 and 1997), more admired by commentators than by other ministers and civil servants. He was created a Privy Counsellor in 1978 and was appointed Opposition Spokesman on the Environment (1979–80). First elected to the shadow cabinet in November 1980, he was re-elected every year until his retirement from the front-bench in 1992, serving as Shadow Environment Secretary (1980–83), Shadow Home Secretary (1983–87) and Shadow Foreign Secretary (1987–92).

In an age when unfavourable personal descriptions were routinely denounced as sexist, it was surprising how many critics felt compelled to allude to his baldness, his spectacles and his garish taste in ties. The *Evening Standard,* not a newspaper noted for being peopled by Errol Flynn clones, called him a 'Kermit the Frog lookalike'. He was, according to a list drawn up by Andrew Roth, founder of *Parliamentary Profiles,* 'bald and beaky' and 'charming in a feline way' (*Guardian*), 'waspish' with 'a ferocious wit', 'pedant and dandy' and 'smilingly sinister' (various writers in the *Daily Telegraph*), 'poisoned-tongued' (*Sunday Express*) and 'Kaufman could start a fight in an empty room' (Matthew Parris, re-working an old cliché in *The Times*).

Hs emergence as a middle-ranking politician surprised those who knew him in his early days on the political staff of the *Daily Mirror* (1955–64) and as assistant general secretary of the Fabian Society (1953–55). That he was not chosen by Tony Blair to be a significant member of his Government owed more to New Labour's anxiety to wipe out its past than to any failings on Kaufman's part. If it was galling to him to see colleagues substantially inferior to him in ability being promoted while the call did not come to him, he concealed it while leaving few in doubt that it was New Labour's loss.

Joe Haines

Peter Kilfoyle (1946–)

One of the overworked clichés of modern politics is that there are no 'characters' left. Our MPs are increasingly cast from the same mould. Leave aside the fact that 'character' was usually a euphemism for pompous boor!

Peter Kilfoyle stands as living refutation of this idea. Born in Dovecot, Liverpool, on 9 June 1946, he was educated at St. Margaret Mary's Primary School and St Edwards College – a Christian Brothers institute. The Christian Brothers are a religious teaching order, renowned for a discipline which on occasions lapsed into barbarity. It is difficult to believe their example did not have its effect on the young Peter. On leaving secondary school he went to Durham

University in 1964 but did not last long – leaving disillusioned, to become a labourer on a building site back home in Liverpool.

He married Bernie in 1968 – a marriage which was to result in five children – three girls and two boys. He was persuaded by his former teachers that he was wasting his talents on a building site and went back into education at Christ's College, Liverpool, to train to become a teacher.

His early experiences in the Labour Party were mixed, as he was sued for libel in 1974 when acting as the election agent in Toxteth Liverpool. The family moved to Queensland, Australia, for a year, which turned into eight and saw two further children being born. Peter acknowledges learning some useful lessons in the battleground, which was Australian Labor Party politics at the time. Missing home, the family moved back to Liverpool in 1982, to a political scene, which was radically different. Militant was on the ascendant and Peter was right at the heart of the battle.

Appearing as it were out of nowhere, he must have been a fright for Militant and, after the 1985 Labour Party enquiry into Merseyside politics when Peter was appointed Labour's Merseyside Organiser, the rumours about him being a member of the Australian SAS were rife.

In 1988 he was appointed Labour's North West Regional Organiser but his sights were set on Westminster. As well as overseeing the dismantling of Militant in Liverpool, he was selected to replace Eric Heffer as MP for Liverpool Walton. Militant went bonkers. Walton had been their first and largest lasting stronghold. This was the period when Militant's traditional leadership under Ted Grant was being ousted. The lunatics were taking over the asylum and they walked straight into the trap. They stood against the official Labour candidate, managed 2,613 votes and saw hundreds of their canvassers expelled from the Labour Party.

Peter saw his majority increase from around 7,000 at the by-election to over 28,000 at the General Election less than a year later. Peter played an important role in Tony Blair's election as leader, acting as a foil to some of the more metropolitan advisors, and when Labour swept to Government, Peter became Under Secretary of State for Public Services, (having been an opposition Whip 1992–94 and an opposition education spokesman 1994–97) before moving to become Under Secretary of State for Defence in 1999.

Always capable of surprises, Peter resigned his Government post in January 2000, claiming it was 'the appropriate thing to do'. He wanted to 'speak out for Labour's core voters and the regions of England'. Later that year he published his story of his fight against Militant in Liverpool, *Left Behind*. Peter's reputation is such that any move he makes prompts speculation as to what is going on behind the scenes. His declared aim is to promote the interests of traditional Labour supporters – if they feel Labour has failed them, then the party's long term prospects will be bleak.

Peter Wheeler

Neil Kinnock (1942–)

In his nine years as leader of the Labour Party, Neil Kinnock rescued it from the verge of destruction and dragged it, sometimes brutally but always with courage and determination, far down the road back to electability. However, he never received the prize for which he strove.

By the time the party returned to power, he had left British politics to become a European Commissioner. Tony Blair, in his speech to Labour's first party conference after the 1997 general election, said of Kinnock: 'The mantle of Prime Minister was never his. But I know that without him, it would never have been mine.' Unlike some acts of polite genuflection, those words spoke the truth.

Kinnock was born on 28 March 1942 in Tredegar, South Wales – the same birthplace as Aneurin Bevan. His father was Gordon Kinnock, who worked for 24 years as a miner in Markham colliery and subsequently at Ebbw Vale steel works. Neil's mother, Mary, was a nurse. As a boy, Neil was a beneficiary of the Attlee government's programme of postwar social reform. At the age of four he started attending a newly-opened local nursery school. This not only helped his education; it allowed Mary to return to work as Tredegar's full-time district nurse. Her influence as a socialist and a committed chapel-goer left a strong mark on Kinnock's views on politics and community.

Despite a streak of classroom indolence – he later claimed his best subject was 'fooling about' – his intelligence and voracious appetite for books enabled him to pass the 11–plus in 1953, and sufficiently well to go to the prestigious Lewis School for Boys in Pengham, Cardiff, more than 20km away. At 15, while still at school, he joined the Ebbw Vale Labour Party, but politics was only one of his extra-curricular passions. Others included rugby, cricket, snooker and singing (he had an unusual ability to sight-read a score).

In 1961 Kinnock embarked on a three-year BA course in Industrial Relations and History at University College, Cardiff. As at school, he plunged into extracurricular activities, sometimes at the expense of his studies. He became a forceful debater at the Students' Union, winning first place for Cardiff in the perorations section of a Welsh inter-university Eisteddfod competition. His political passions were socialism, nuclear disarmament and the destruction of apartheid. In the end he had to resit his final year in order to gain his degree.

In his second year at university, Kinnock met Glenys Parry, the daughter of a militant official of the National Union of Railworkers. They married on 25 March 1967 at Holyhead, Anglesey (Glenys's home town). She wore a silver wedding ring, in order to avoid the danger of wearing a ring made from South African gold. By this time Kinnock was a tutor with the Workers' Educational Association, a post that could easily be combined with active work for the Bedwellty Labour Party. In 1969, when the sitting MP announced his retirement, Kinnock sought the nomination, with the support of his union, the Transport and General. At a tense selection meeting he tied with his main rival, 75 votes each. The meeting asked both men to speak again. Kinnock's oratory swung one vote: this time he won 76–74. In June 1970, as Labour lost power nationally, Kinnock entered Parliament with a majority of 22,279. Following boundary changes, the seat's name changed to Islwyn in 1983; Kinnock was re-elected by large majorities at six successive general elections before leaving Parliament in 1994.

After he had been an MP for just 18 months his parents died within nine days of each other; they were only in their early sixties. A few days later, the Kinnock's second child, Rachel, was born; a sister for Stephen, who had been born in 1970. At Westminster, Kinnock began to make his mark within the Tribune Group, actively supporting the coal miners' strike in 1972, and joining the unsuccessful campaign to withdraw Britain from the Common Market. When

Labour returned to power in 1974, Kinnock agreed reluctantly to serve as Parliamentary Private Secretary to Michael Foot, the new Employment Secretary. He told Foot privately that he would do the job for only a year; and in February 1975 he duly resigned.

In 1976 Kinnock was a prominent member of Foot's campaign to succeed Harold Wilson as party leader. When Foot was defeated by James Callaghan, the new Prime Minister asked Kinnock to become a junior minister at the Department of Industry. Kinnock declined the offer, and remained on the back benches. He used his position to gain public attention, as a writer – he contributed regularly to the *Guardian* and *Tribune* – and broadcaster. His ready wit and easy manner made him a popular choice for radio and television producers. He was also a rebel, voting frequently against the Callaghan government's economic policies, especially the public spending cuts it imposed in 1977. In 1978 he won election to Labour's National Executive, as a member of the main left-wing slate. Kinnock was also a committed opponent of devolution, and helped to persuade Welsh voters to vote down plans for a Welsh Assembly by 4 to 1 in the 1979 referendum.

Back in opposition after Margaret Thatcher's victory in the 1979 election, Kinnock agreed to join Callaghan's shadow cabinet as education spokesman. A forceful speech on education to that October's party conference brought him his greatest media attention yet; he began to be talked of as a potential future party leader. In January 1980 he defied the whips by voting in the Commons against the modernisation of Britain's nuclear weapons system. Callaghan threatened that another act of rebellion would lead to Kinnock's dismissal from the shadow cabinet. Kinnock did not defy the party line again.

In October 1980 Callaghan announced his retirement as Labour leader. Kinnock, with Clive Jenkins, the trade union leader, persuaded the 67–year-old Foot to stand once again. Foot defeated Denis Healey, who then agreed to serve as Foot's deputy. Kinnock continued as Shadow Education Secretary. The following three years were arguably the most hellish in Labour's history. In 1981 more than two dozen Labour MPs defected to the new Social Democratic Party. In 1983 Labour slumped to its worst election defeat since 1935. Foot's leadership was marked by ferocious in-fighting, of which the most spectacular example was Tony Benn's challenge to Healey for the deputy leadership in 1981. Kinnock was the most prominent left-wing MP to break with Benn, urging fellow left-wing MPs to abstain rather than back Benn's challenge in the October 1981 vote. Thirty-six MPs heeded Kinnock's call – enough to deny Benn victory in a desperately close contest. As the infighting continued, Kinnock became an increasingly committed opponent of Labour's hard left.

Immediately after the June 1983 election, Foot announced his intention to resign. There was never any doubt that Kinnock would succeed him. On 2 October he was declared the winner, obtaining 71 per cent of the electoral college vote, and comfortably defeating Roy Hattersley, his main rival, in all three sections of the college. In his acceptance speech he declared his intention to act as brutally as necessary to drag Labour back to electability: 'Remember how you felt on that dreadful morning of 10th June. Just remember how you felt then, and think to yourselves: June 9th, 1983, never ever again will we experience that.'

Kinnock's first policy action as leader was to scrap Labour's plan to withdraw from the European Community. Thus began a sequence of policy changes in which Kinnock led from the front and carried the party with him. During his eight years as leader, he also persuaded Labour to abandon support for unilateral nuclear disarmament, embrace the market system instead of state socialism, and – under the cover of endorsing Europe's social chapter – call for an end to trade union 'closed shops.' These changes went beyond a series of specific policy moves. They amounted to a comprehensive assault on left-wing ideology. He was the first Labour leader to do this effectively. Hugh Gaitskell had tried after Labour's 1959 defeat, but failed. Harold Wilson and Callaghan preferred to outmanoeuvre the left rather than take it on in open combat. Kinnock, with a detailed, insider's knowledge of the party, and a toughness of character that was a revelation to many, stood his ground, fought the fight and won.

The decisive moment in Kinnock's leadership came at the 1985 party conference in Bournemouth. His strategy for modernising Labour and expanding its appeal seemed stalled. Militant infiltrators has taken over Liverpool's Labour Party and, as a result, secured control of its City Council. At the same time a coal miners' strike was taking place, led by the left-wing Miners' Union President, Arthur Scargill. On successive days, Kinnock denounced them both. His denunciation of Militant's behaviour in Liverpool became arguably the best-remembered thing Kinnock ever said from a public platform ('… the grotesque chaos of a Labour council – a *Labour* council – hiring taxis to scuttle round a city handing out redundancy notices to its own workers …'). However, his impromptu speech the following day on the miners' strike was even more courageous for, even under Scargill, the miners tapped deeper than Militant ever could into ordinary party members' reservoirs of sympathy. Kinnock attacked the miners' leadership and the party's habit of passing resolutions that sound good in 'the comfortable, warm circles of the Labour Party Conference' but which repel ordinary voters. He also attacked the principle of passing retrospective legislation to help the strikers, which was what Scargill had demanded from the 'next Labour Government.' When the vote was called, Scargill's card-vote supporters just outnumbered Kinnock's; but the miners had failed to secure the two-thirds majority they sought, so the result amounted to a political victory for the party leader.

Kinnock entered the 1987 general election with complete control over his party, but was still regarded with some suspicion by the wider public. Some opinion polls suggested that Labour might be pushed into third place, at least in terms of the popular vote, by the Liberal/SDP Alliance. On the advice of Labour's Director of Communications, Peter Mandelson (one of a group of modernisers that Kinnock recruited to energise a creaking party machine), the decision was taken to build the campaign on Kinnock the man. This led to one of the most effective party election broadcasts ever made; indeed, it proved so popular that, uniquely, it was repeated towards the end of the campaign. It was a 10-minute profile made by Hugh Hudson (director of *Chariots of Fire*) and unashamedly appealing to emotion. It included an extract from a speech made that spring to the Welsh Labour Party Conference, when Kinnock asked 'Why am I the first Kinnock in a thousand generations to be able to get to university?' and concluded with his answer: 'Because there was no platform on which they could stand.'

In the event, Labour gained only 20 seats; the Conservatives still enjoyed a majority of 100. But the Liberal/SDP Alliance was pushed firmly into third place. Kinnock was credited with beginning the process of Labour recovery, rather than blamed for leading only a small advance. Following the 1987 election, Kinnock established a series of policy reviews, which took further the process of transforming the party. He was aided, unwittingly, by Tony Benn, who challenged him for the party leadership in 1988 on a platform of reclaiming Labour for traditional socialism. Kinnock won by 8–1, a margin that he claimed as a clear mandate for his process of reform.

By 1990, there seemed every prospect of a Labour victory at the following election. The party enjoyed 20–point-plus leads in the opinion polls. The Conservatives had introduced possibly the most unpopular domestic policy of modern times, the poll tax. Margaret Thatcher's ideological fervour was alienating more and more voters. However, in November that year the Conservatives replaced Thatcher with John Major, who promptly scrapped the poll tax and promised a gentler, less ideological approach to running Britain. Many voters who 'wanted a change' felt that their demands had been met. Nevertheless, Labour retaining a narrow lead in most polls during the run-up to the 1992 election. There still seemed a real chance of a change of government, despite virulent, hurtful and highly personal attacks on Kinnock in some tabloid newspapers, most notably the *Sun*. The disappointment was the more intense when the Conservatives won their fourth successive victory. Subsequent analysis showed that the polls had contained a clear Labour bias. In truth, Labour was always behind the Tories from the moment Major became Prime Minister. Moreover, there was considerable evidence that Kinnock himself was disliked by many voters, who regarded him as a political lightweight, a 'Welsh windbag,' and/or a man who still secretly believed in left-wing extremism.

On the Monday after the election, Kinnock announced that he would step down as party leader as soon as a new leader was elected. On 18 July 1992 he was succeeded by John Smith. During the following two years, Kinnock kept a low profile. His main foray into public debate took the form of two programmes for BBC Television in which he set out his views on the future of socialism. These included a proposal to rewrite the party's commitment, in Clause IV of its constitution, to public ownership. His prospectus – effectively a completion of the modernising journey he had begun in 1983 – foreshadowed with startling precision the reforms that Blair undertook after he became party leader in 1994.

At the end of 1994 Kinnock resigned as an MP to embark on a new career, as a European Commissioner. The man who had campaigned 20 years earlier for Britain's withdrawal from the Common Market was now one of Europe's top officials. He was appointed Commissioner for Transport. In 1999 he survived unscathed when the European Parliament exercised its power to sack the commission, following criticisms of malpractice at the commission generally, and of EC President Jacques Santer in particular. The new President of the Commission, Romano Prodi, appointed Kinnock as one of his two deputies, with special responsibility for rooting out nepotism, cronyism, fraud and mismanagement.

Two books of Kinnock's speeches have been published: *Making Our Way* (Blackwell, 1986) and *Thorns and Roses* (Hutchinson, 1992). The two main biographies of him, both simply called *Kinnock*, are by Michael Leapman (Unwin Hyman, 1987) and George Drower (The Publishing Corporation, 1994). In an introduction to Drower's biography, Gerald Kaufman wrote: 'I voted against Neil Kinnock in the 1983 Labour leadership election … [This] was one of the most serious mistakes I have made in nearly a quarter of a century as an MP. Kinnock turned out to be the most decisive, the strongest, the toughest and, in my judgement, the greatest leader the Labour Party has ever had.'

Peter Kellner

Alex Kitson   (1921–97)

Alexander Harper Kitson was a major figure in post-war trade unionism and in the Labour Party. Born on 21 October 1921, he left Kirknewton School in the Midlothian coalfield at 14 to become a van boy for the Co-op in Edinburgh and rose to be General Secretary of Scottish Horse and Motorman's Union (1959–71) and then Assistant General Secretary of the Transport and General Workers' Union (1971–80) and Deputy General Secretary of the TGWU (1980–86). He was Chairman of the Scottish TUC (1966) and Treasurer (1974–81). He also served on Labour's NEC (1968–86), where during the early 1970s he played a key role in swinging Labour Party policy in favour of backing Scottish devolution and was Chairman of the Labour Party (1980–81).

Alex was greatly influenced by his grandfather David Greig, an ILP member and railway union official in the 1920s, who became a Justice of the Peace in Midlothian. At the age of 23, Alex became the youngest full-time official in his union's history. Moving from van boy to driver, it was while Alex was driving his own milk float that he first met his near neighbour, the young Sir Sean Connery, who was brought up in an Edinburgh tenement near Alex's flat and the Co-op depot in Fountainbridge. James Bond's first assignment was with Alex Kitson, his mission – a milk boy. Connery never forgot his first 'boss' and sent a warm and tearful message to the family when Alex died. Afterward Connery worked with the STUC to establish a memorial fund in Alex Kitson's name.

As a trade unionist in the mould of Michael McGahey and Jimmy Knapp, Alex was a plain-speaking Scot. His passions – apart from his family – were universal education, international co-operation and Heart of Midlothian football club. He worked hard to ensure funding for union education projects, weekend schools and scholarships, especially promoting women in the union at a time when the movement's officers were predominantly male.

He worked with Willi Brandt, and from the 1950s on he was an active participant in the Socialist International. He was a frequent visitor to Eastern Europe and strove to maintain civilised dialogues between East and West after the invasion of Czechoslovakia in 1968. With Spain under Franco and Portugal under Salazar, Kitson worked with the transport unions in the Iberian peninsula and forged a life-time friendship with Mario Soares and other socialists who took power after the collapse of the last of the pre-war dictatorships.

His tough negotiating powers were at the fore in 1971 when the T&G's Jack Jones wanted to amalgamate with Alex's union and there was heated debate over future voting rights, as well as the union's handsome properties.

A left-winger who gave a controversial pro-Moscow speech in Russia to mark the 60th anniversary of the October Revolution, he avoided being stereotyped and played a critical part in shoring up the Labour leadership's position on Ireland. When Tony Benn was campaigning hard to take the troops out of Northern Ireland, Alex ensured that the votes of the T&G delegation backed the status quo. He knew from the large T&G membership in Northern Ireland that the bipartisan approach was vital to preventing violence spiralling, with the threat of all-out civil war. By 1992, Alex was in retirement and strongly supporting John Smith as Party leader.

Apart from his life-time commitment to the trade union movement he was a passionate Heart of Midlothian supporter. He also loved jazz and played the piano. His interest in transport was continued in retirement when he became chairman of Lothian Regional Transport Board, one of the most successful bus companies in Europe. In one of his last interviews, Alex said he had been more powerful as a trade union official and member of the Labour Party's ruling executive than if he had been an MP. He died in Edinburgh on 2 August 1997, survived by his two daughters; his wife since 1942, Ann Brown McLeod, predeceased him by several weeks

Nigel Griffiths MP

Ted Knight   (1933–)

Ted Knight, labelled 'Red Ted' by the press, gained national prominence as leader of Lambeth Council during the rate-capping disputes of the early to mid 1980s. In 1985 Lambeth councillors with Ted Knight at the helm refused to set a legal rate and thus, along with Militant-dominated Liverpool, became the first English politicians since Clay Cross to be surcharged and therefore banned from office as well as personally financially penalised.

Edward Knight, known as Ted, was born in Lambeth, South London, and spent most of his childhood and all his adult life living in the borough. Born in Brixton on 13 June 1933, Ted was educated initially at Rosendale School in West Norwood but evacuated to Tyneside and Scotland during the war years. He subsequently attended Strand Grammar School in Tulse Hill. He has been an active trade unionist since he started his first job in 1952 as an insurance clerk and has been a serving member of the MSF London Executive for the last eight years, having previously been active in its predecessor union ASTMS.

Aged fifteen Ted Knight joined the Labour Party League of Youth but was expelled eight years later in 1956 due to his involvement with the Socialist Labour League, the Trotskyist forerunner of the Workers Revolutionary Party for whom he worked until 1961. He was re-admitted into the Labour Party in 1970 and remains a member.

In 1972 he became Chair of Norwood Labour Party and remained in that position until elected Leader of Lambeth in 1978. Norwood was his base within Lambeth, and his influence over the Constituency Labour Party remained almost total until the early to mid 1990s when challenged by a new generation of activists under the auspices of Lambeth Labour Co-ordinating Committee.

In 1974 Ted Knight and Ken Livingstone were elected to Lambeth Council, representing Knights Hill Ward in Norwood. They formed a formidable team. Ken was influenced ideologically by Ted, whilst Ted Knight acknowledges that he learned from Ken Livingstone's ability to win wider support and form loose alliances. Over the following four years Ted effectively thwarted the efforts of the leader David Stimpson, exposing the administration's weaknesses and organising for the Labour Group elections in 1978.

In 1977 Ted Knight became Chair of Construction Services, and following the 1978 local elections he was elected as Leader of Lambeth Council, winning by 23 votes to 19. Within the Labour Group the prevailing mood was not hard left, but there was a desire for change and a commitment to high expenditure. Over the next few years he managed to build upon his control of the Labour Group, the Council machinery and the local Labour Party. Officers and members knew that Ted's approval was critical. As Ken Livingstone recalled in his *If Voting*

Changed Anything They'd Abolish It, 'Few people could be as charming or supportive as Ted Knight, or quite so obstructive when he was not.'

Initially, Ted Knight responded to Conservative Government cuts by putting up the rates locally; since he viewed the burden of rates as falling upon profitable businesses, rates tripled in Lambeth in three years. At one stage he and the Labour Group even proposed cuts in expenditure, but were overturned by the local Labour Parties.

In 1979 he unsuccessfully stood as a parliamentary candidate in Hornsey. In 1981, he stood in Norwood for the Greater London Council, but he paid the electoral price when the Tories mounted a very effective local campaign against a proposed supplementary rate increase. The inability locally to deflect responsibility for cuts or rate increases on to the Conservative Government influenced his later decision to go for a more confrontational approach. In 1980 he became a member of the Greater London Labour Party Executive Committee and in 1981 set up and became a joint editor of the weekly paper *Labour Herald*, along with Ken Livingstone and Matthew Warburton, Ted's deputy leader in Lambeth.

By 1984 Ted Knight had become a leading figure in the national campaign against the Conservative Government's new Rates Act and its attempt to cap 18 authorities, including Lambeth. The rate-capped councils, and nine others which were in conflict with central government, met in July 1984. Encouraged by the Tory government's recent climbdown in Liverpool, using his great oratorical skills, Ted succeeded in getting the majority to support the tactic of not setting any rate until the Government backed down. Yet despite the rhetoric, many local government figures were not convinced that the tactic would prove effective in bringing down the Government or in protecting services, and on a personal level they feared surcharge was a step into the wilderness. By early March 1985 ILEA, the GLC and a few of the other capped authorities had set a legal rate; quickly the others, with the exception of Lambeth and Liverpool fell in line. Bitter recriminations followed.

The question therefore remains as to what motivated Ted Knight, an experienced, astute politician, to lead Lambeth into making such a belated, isolated political gesture. Following removal from elected office as a result of being surcharged, Ted Knight remained involved in the Labour Movement, but over time his influence locally and nationally waned.

Cathy Ashley

Gavin Laird (1933–)

Gavin Harry Laird was born on 14 March 1933 in Clydebank, the son of James and Frances Laird. He was educated at Clydebank High School. He joined the AEU in 1949 and, like many of his generation, had a spell in the Young Communists. Before settling in engineering he was a merchant seaman. On returning to Clydebank he worked at Singers, becoming shop steward in the mid 1950s and factory convener in 1966. During this time he helped build a majority trade union membership amongst the predominantly female workforce.

He was active at all levels in the AEU, a representative on the Junior Workers' Committee, a member of the Glasgow District Committee, National Committee and Rules Revision delegate and its Standing Orders Committee. He was also chairman of the local Clydebank Labour Party.

He first stood for full-time office as Regional Officer for Scotland in 1972. Describing himself as militant but not irresponsible, he achieved a notable victory over an opponent supported by the recent heroes of UCS, Jimmy Reid and Jimmy Airlie. Three years later he faced Airlie in a straight fight, winning again, stressing his commitment to union amalgamations and equality.

Six months later he stood for the full-time executive, his predecessor Sir John Boyd having become AUEW General Secretary following the death of Jim Conway in the Turkish DC10 crash in Paris. This time he faced a straight fight with Jimmy Reid. Once again he won, making clear his support for postal ballots for electing full-time officers, which he had voted for at the 1970 Rules Revision. As convener at Singers he was, of course, well aware of the difficulties facing women and shift workers if they had to vote at branch meetings.

In 1982 Sir John Boyd retired as General Secretary and Laird stood for the position against Ken Brett, then Assistant General Secretary, but a principal organiser in Hugh Scanlon's victory over John Boyd for President in 1968. Laird this time scraped through with a tiny victory after two ballots.

So after five straight victories in ten years Laird found himself as the chief administrator of Britain's second largest union. The union had its headquarters in Peckham, South London and in contrast with its nineteenth-century image as the model modern union Laird found a rather conservative, unbusinesslike and old-fashioned administrative set-up. He was determined to modernise.

Laird was unfortunate to find himself at the helm of the union at a time when membership and union finances were under severe pressure. This constrained his ambitions, but he succeeded in refurbishing Peckham, revamping the union's staid magazine under the guidance of professional journalists. He also invested in Hamlet Television, a unique but ultimately ill-founded video-facilities house venture designed to communicate with members and stewards by electronic means.

He also liked to remain involved with industrial issues. With his close friend Alex Ferry, CSEU General Secretary, he achieved the breakthrough to 37 hours in 1989 by the novel strategy of targeted industrial action. This campaign generated a multi-million pound fund still awaiting the appropriate moment to push for 35 hours. His greatest disappointment was probably the failure to achieve a single union agreement for a new Ford plant at Dundee because of the opposition of the TGWU.

Financial restrictions also forced Laird to review all sources of union income and to start a process of modernising the union's structures, in part to control expenditure. One potential new source of income was Government money for postal ballots. TUC policy on this was to boycott, yet this made no sense to Laird. Not only did he and the union believe passionately in members electing their own officials by postal ballot it was in itself an expensive business, costing the union in a national election at least one hundred thousand pounds a year. So why turn down money for doing something the union did anyway?

This straightforward logic almost split the TUC. Laird persuaded the AEU Executive to ballot the members to submit claims. This achieved a large majority in favour. As a result the Union was threatened with expulsion at the 1985 Congress. With Terry Duffy seriously ill, Laird walked the tightrope, but the TUC backed down.

Internally Laird used financial difficulties to review every facet of the Union's structure, largely unchanged since the 1920 AEU amalgamation. With the assistance of a working party of lay members, the union began to reform itself. This process was ultimately completed by the AEEU merger with the EETPU, leading to a lay executive, policy-making determined largely by shop stewards and the appointment of officials.

Despite its objective of one union for engineering workers, the AEU had lost many potential merger partners including the craft unions, the boilermakers, metal mechanics, pattern makers, sheet metal workers and the white collar clerical workers in APEX. This was in part because of the disastrous and failed AUEW merger with TASS. Laird extricated the engineers from this in 1984 and achieved the merger with the Foundry Workers and Construction Engineers in the same year.

Logically the next step was merger with the electricians, but their expulsion from the TUC in 1988 was a serious obstacle. By a handful of votes the AEU National Committee rejected the merger in 1989. Unlike Bill Jordan, Laird was cautious but eventually agreed the details with Eric Hammond, leading to a merger on 1 May 1992 and the eventual return of the EETPU to the TUC.

The union's gain was Laird's personal loss as this agreement only allowed him to serve two years as the AEEU's first General Secretary. The early death of John Smith was also a bitter blow, as they were close friends and political allies. He retired in 1995 to concentrate on his extensive business links. He was a director of the Bank of England for two terms from 1986–94, chairman of Manchester Buses 1994–97 and, inter alia, a non-executive Director of Scottish Media (formerly STV) and FS Assurance. He married Catherine in 1956 and has one daughter. He was awarded the CBE in 1988 and knighted in 1995.

John Gibbins

George Lansbury (1859–1940)

George Lansbury was a Labour pioneer, leading pacifist, Christian Socialist, tireless campaigner against poverty, and Leader of the Labour Party between 1932 and 1935. The historian A J P Taylor called him 'the most loveable figure in modern politics'. When Harold Wilson claimed Labour was a 'moral crusade', it was surely men like Lansbury that he had in mind. Lansbury's biographer said, 'His anger and pain at injustice or cruelty could affect him so violently as to make him momentarily ill.' He personified the socialist dilemma between principles and power, between ideals and practical politics, and in the end his principles meant he had to relinquish the party leadership.

Lansbury, the son of George Lansbury senior and Anne Ferris , was born in a tollhouse between Haleworth and Lowestoft, Suffolk, in 1859. He was one of nine children. When Lansbury was nine years old the family moved to East London. George started work in an office at the age of eleven but after a year he returned to school, where he stayed until he was fourteen. This was followed by a succession of jobs as a clerk, a wholesale grocer and working in a coffee bar. Both his parents were alcoholics, and Lansbury became a life-long teetotaller.

Lansbury then started up his own business, working as a contractor for the Great Eastern

Railway. In 1880 he married Elizabeth Brine at Whitechapel. In 1884, now with three children, the Lansburys decided to emigrate to Australia. After one year, they returned to England, embittered by the conditions suffered by émigrés, and Lansbury founded the Emigration Information Department to reveal the truth behind the propaganda about emigration.

In the 1886 general election Lansbury joined the local Liberal Party. Later that year he was elected General Secretary of the Bow and Bromley Liberal Association. He broke with the Liberals in 1892 over their unwillingness to support legislation for a shorter working week. Lansbury joined the Gasworkers and General Labourers Union and in 1889 joined a local strike committee during the London dockers' strike. Here he met H M Hyndman, the leader of the Marxist SDF. Lansbury joined the SDF and in 1892 established a branch of the SDF in Bow.

In the 1890s he was influenced by the Christian Socialism of Philip Snowden. Lansbury became a Christian Socialist and helped convert Keir Hardie to Christian Socialism in 1897. In 1892 Lansbury was elected to the Poplar Board of Guardians, which ran the Poplar Workhouse. The Guardians worked to improve conditions in their workhouse. They also established, with funding from an American businessman, a farm colony in Lainden, Essex, where they provided work for the unemployed.

In the 1895 general election Lansbury fought the Walworth seat as the SDF candidate. He only obtained 204 votes in that election but in 1900 he fought the seat again and won 2,558 against the Conservative Party candidate who won with 4,403 votes. In 1903 Lansbury left the SDF and joined the ILP. He was elected as Poplar borough councillor in 1903. He unsuccessfully fought the 1906 general election in Middlesborough. He served on the London County Council between 1909 and 1912.

Between 1905 and 1909 Lansbury was a member of the Royal Commission on the Poor Laws, and along with Beatrice Webb and other members, signed the Minority Report. In 1906 the government ordered an inquiry into the running of the Poplar Workhouse. The Board of Guardians was accused of wasting ratepayers' money by their generous treatment of paupers and the funding of the Laindon Farm Colony. Lansbury, who had been joined as a Guardian by John Burns, another leading Christian Socialist, argued the case for treating people in workhouses with dignity.

In the 1910 general election Lansbury was elected as Labour MP for Bow & Bromley with a majority of 863, and he and Hardie launched headlong into the campaign in Parliament for votes for women. In October 1912, Lansbury in a typical display of principle over practicalities, resigned his seat in the House of Commons in order to fight a by-election on a platform of votes for women. He was defeated by 731 votes. The following year he was imprisoned for making speeches in favour of suffragettes who were involved in illegal activities. While in Pentonville prison he went on hunger strike and was eventually released under the 'Cat and Mouse Act'.

For the next ten years Lansbury was out of the House of Commons and concentrated on journalism. In 1911 he helped start the *Daily Herald* and two years later became the editor. Lansbury and his newspaper, the *Daily Herald*, was opposed to the First World War. In the 1918 General Election, Lansbury, like other anti-war Labour Party candidates, was defeated. In 1920 he visited Russia, and met with Lenin, 'the best loved and best hated man in the world.'

In 1921, Lansbury became Mayor of Poplar. The council took the decision to increase the amount of money spent on poor relief, in defiance of the LCC precept. This brought the council into conflict with the Government, and in 1921 Lansbury and the majority of the local council were imprisoned for over four months. Their experiences were recounted in a pamphlet *Guilty and Proud of It*. 'Poplar-ism' provided the precedent for future refusals by Labour local government to set rates prescribed by central Government, notably Liverpool and Lambeth councils in the 1980s.

In the 1922 general election Lansbury was elected as the Labour MP for Bow & Bromley with a majority of 7,000, a seat he retained until his death. Elected to the Parliamentary Labour Party Executive (shadow cabinet) in 1923, and in every subsequent opposition year until he became Labour leader, he was given to expect Cabinet office on the formation of Labour's first government in 1924. Instead he was offered the post of Transport Minister outside Cabinet, which he declined. In 1925 he started *Lansbury's Labour Weekly*. The newspaper rapidly reached a circulation of 172,000 and provided an important source of news during the 1926 General Strike.

Lansbury was elected Party Chairman in 1928, and published his autobiography *My Life*. In 1929 he joined Ramsay MacDonald's Cabinet as First Commissioner of Works, combining responsibility for the royal parks and ancient monuments with public works projects for the relief of unemployment. It was Lansbury who created the mixed-bathing Serpentine Lido. Less successfully, he advocated retirement pensions at 60. With Oswald Mosley and Tom Johnston he served on J H Thomas's Cabinet Committee on unemployment and became increasingly frustrated with its failure to agree a programme for the relief of unemployment through public works. Unlike Mosley, he did not let his frustration on this issue push him to resignation, but he shared many of Mosley's views on the issue. In February 1931 he wrote to Lloyd George urging him to join the Labour Party and help conquer unemployment: 'Your help would be invaluable, as one of us.' It was to no avail. It was in Lansbury's Ministerial office that the cabal of Ministers opposing proposals to cut unemployment benefit gathered in the summer of 1931. In the 1931 election following the formation of MacDonald's National Government, Lansbury was the only former Labour Cabinet Minister to retain his seat. In 1932 he therefore succeeded Arthur Henderson, who had lost his, as Labour Leader and the Leader of the Opposition.

When Italy invaded Abyssinia he refused to support the view that the League of Nations should use military force against Mussolini's army. After being criticised by several leading members of the Labour Party, Lansbury was effectively deposed as leader of the party in October 1935 and was replaced by his deputy, Clement Attlee, though he remained an MP. Ernest Bevin accused Lansbury of hawking 'your conscience round from body to body, asking to be told what to do with it.' After Lansbury's resignation Bevin remarked, 'Lansbury has been going about dressed in saint's clothes for years waiting for martyrdom. I set fire to the faggots.'

Lansbury published a variety of books and pamphlets including *Unemployment: The Next Step* (1909), *Your Part in Poverty* (1918), *These Things Shall Be* (1919), *What I Saw In Russia* (1920), *Jesus and Labour* (1924), *The Miracle of Fleet Street* (1925) (the story of the *Daily Herald*), *My England* (1934), *Looking Backwards and Forwards* (1935), *Why Pacifists Should be Socialists* (1937) and *My Quest for Peace* (1938).

Lansbury spent the last few years of his life trying to prevent another world war. After having talks with Hitler, he believed it was possible to reach agreement with the Nazis and prevent war. He died of cancer at his home, 39 Bow Road, London, on 7 May 1940. Biographies include the *Life of George Lansbury* (1951) by his son-in-law Raymond Postgate and *George Lansbury* (1990) by Jonathan Schneer.

Paul Richards

Harold Laski   (1893–1950)

'No one can teach politics who does not know politics at first hand' was the sentiment expressed by Harold Laski in 1939; and he practised what he preached. Along with R H Tawney and G D H Cole, he was one of the leading British socialist intellectuals of his era. His fame, or notoriety, was sustained not only by his academic contributions to political science and his extensive range of Labour Party activity, but also by the high-profile court cases that meant controversy was never far away.

Harold Joseph Laski was born on 30 June 1893 into a wealthy cotton shipping merchant's family in Manchester, where his father Nathan was a leading figure in the Jewish community, a magistrate, and a staunch Liberal. His mother, Sarah, was chair of the Board of Guardians and a city councillor. The young Harold had early exposure to the highest levels of politics when his father played an important role in the 1906 and 1908 election campaigns of Winston Churchill. He was educated at Manchester Grammar School and went on obtain a first class degree in History at New College, Oxford, having switched from science. He had met Frida Kerry, a militant suffragette, in 1909, and in 1911 they eloped to be married at Gretna Green because of the anticipated opposition from his parents at his marrying a gentile. At the outbreak of war he was rejected by the armed forces because of his weak heart, but was soon appointed to his first academic post as lecturer at McGill University in Montreal.

He started to establish his academic reputation as he moved on to Harvard University from 1916 to 1919, but it was also there that the first of his entanglements in public controversy arose. His support of striking police in Boston ended with him being labelled by the conservative press, not for the last time, as a Bolshevik. He resigned, and on returning to Britain was offered a post as politics lecturer at the LSE. He was appointed Professor in 1926 and continued his association with the LSE for a total of thirty years.

His early inspiration had been found in the New Liberalism of J A Hobson and L T Hobhouse as well as the older liberalism of J S Mill, but as he increasingly moved to socialism he sought to establish intellectual links between liberty and equality. In his best-known book, *A Grammar of Politics* (1925), he fused Fabian socialism with his earlier pluralism in an attempt to balance the obligations of the state to its citizens with the duties owed by individuals to society as a whole.

Laski joined the Executive of the Fabian Society in 1922, and in 1924 the new Labour Prime Minister, Ramsay MacDonald, offered him a role as an unofficial assistant. His politics continued to drift slowly leftwards and he grew more sceptical of the Party's leadership, but he nevertheless continued to campaign vigorously for a Labour victory in 1929.

During the ensuing second Labour administration he acted as an unofficial adviser on Empire matters in East Africa and India. One of his former students, Krishna Menon, formed the India League seeking full independence, and Laski became one of the strongest advocates within the Labour Party for Indian independence. He also worked as a link between Henderson's committee dealing with Palestine and Zionist circles. In addition he served on the Donoughmore Committee on ministerial powers from 1929 to 1932 and published *Liberty and the Modern State* (1930) in which he examined the limits of political and economic power.

It was the failure of the Labour government's economic policy and MacDonald's 'betrayal' of 1931 that helped to push Laski further to the left. He became the major publicist for the left with his articles in the *Daily Herald,* and he helped establish the Socialist league that was to become the main focus of left-wing activity within the Labour Party. Another controversy blew up in his face over his series of lectures in Moscow in 1934, during which he had discussed the possibility of revolution in Britain. Despite Laski's conclusion that revolution was unlikely in the immediate future, a prolonged debate in the press concluded with the LSE being proclaimed by its own MP to be 'a hotbed of Communist teaching'.

Together with publisher Victor Gollancz and John Strachey he established the Left Book Club in 1936. His belief in a 'Popular Front' with the communists developed with the rise of Nazism and was strengthened by the outbreak of the Spanish Civil War. He attached his signature to the 'unity manifesto' and helped launch a new left-wing weekly, *Tribune.* He stood for election to the constituency party section of the Labour Party Executive in 1936, was elected, and continued to serve on the NEC for twelve years. In 1938 Laski became concerned that the Communist Party's policy under the direction of Moscow did not seem to be facing up to fascism. He changed sides and prepared the first draft of the pamphlet 'Labour and the Popular Front' which set out the leadership's argument against a popular front. His criticism of Stalinism saw him attacked this time from the left, when *Pravda* denounced him as 'a prop to bourgeois civilization'.

Throughout the war he came top of the constituency section polls every year in the Executive elections, but still continued to be a thorn in the side of the Labour leadership with his outspoken criticism of policy. He saw in the war a not-to-be-missed opportunity for socio-economic transformation. Some of the radical statements in *Reflections on the Revolution of Our Time* in 1943 caused something of a stir, even though in essence the book stressed the need to reconcile economic planning with the maintenance of personal self-expression for autonomous individuals. He called for the introduction of socialist ownership of the means of production and social reforms at a pace greater than that of the Party leadership, whom he saw as compromising within the government coalition.

He became deputy Chair in 1944 and was elected Chair in 1945, but became the centre of public controversy again when Churchill and the Conservatives portrayed him as a 'red bogey' in the 1945 election. He also created controversy within the Labour Party with a call on Attlee to resign and a dispute over the role of the NEC and the influence it should continue to have over Labour policy when the Party formed the government. The problem of this relationship was an argument that was to re-emerge in the Labour government of the 1970s.

Laski soon became embroiled in the most damaging of his public controversies. He was accused in a letter to the *Nottingham Guardian,* 18 June 1945, of inviting revolution, by violent means if necessary. Laski replied that he was actually advocating revolution by consent as preferable to a drift into violence and issued a writ claiming damages for libel against the author of the letter, Conservative county councillor H C C Carlton, and the two local newspapers that had published the letter. In the court hearing the judge directed the jury to not only consider whether or not Laski actually used words inciting violence, but to consider 'are these the sort of words which Mr Laski would be likely to use?' (quoted in M. Newman, (1993), *Harold Laski: A Political Biography,* Macmillan, London, p277). The jury found the newspaper reports to be fair and accurate and Laski's reputation never fully recovered. He continued on the NEC for two years after this case and also continued his academic work, but his influence seemed to be steadily declining. In his lecture tours in the USA in 1948 and 1949 vilification continued as he was branded a communist, with some venues being cancelled. He resigned from the Executive in 1950, but still wrote the introductory section of the Party programme and made many speeches in the general election campaign of that year. He died shortly afterwards on 24 March 1950.

His inspirational teaching over several decades had made him an influence in India, Europe and the USA as well as at all levels of the British Labour Party. Of the Labour MPs elected in the landslide of 1945, no less than 67 had once studied with him as university students, on Workers' Education courses, or in wartime officers' courses. He had been the major publicist for the left of the Party and a constant source of ideas as well as criticism of the leadership. He may be remembered for his left-wing views, but throughout he tried to reconcile his socialism with concern for individualist liberalism combined with a pluralist concern for devolution and diversity. Although his work seems to have fallen into relative obscurity compared to the continued interest in G D H Cole and R H Tawney, the advent of New Labour and its concern for some of those same factors that so interested Laski in his earlier years may have made his work worth revisiting.

Biographies include M Newman's *Harold Laski: A Political Biography* (1993), and I Kramnick's *Harold Laski: a Life on the Left* (1993). See also A Deane's *The Political Ideas of Harold J Laski* (1955).

Nick Cowell

Jack Lawson (Lord Lawson of Beamish)   (1881–1965)

John James 'Jack' Lawson was born on 16 October 1881 in the bustling port of Whitehaven, one of ten children of John Lawson, a seaman who at times also worked as a miner (a not unusual combination in that area), and his wife Elizabeth Savage, whom her son revered as an indomitable woman of 'lava-heated, ungovernable temper'. He was educated at National schools, the last at Boldon in Durham, where the family moved when Jack was nine years old. At the age of 12 he began work at Boldon Colliery, reading in his spare time to continue his education. He 'read like a glutton' for the rest of his life. Initially he worked as a trapper, earning 10d a day for a 10-hour shift; but over the next 11 years he gained wide experience and eventually became a face worker.

In 1901 he made a commitment to Wesleyan Methodism, beginning a 60-year stint as a lay preacher, and at the same time began to take an informed interest in politics. He joined the ILP in 1904 and also helped to organise adult education classes. Two years later he married Isabella Scott and, borrowing money and selling his possessions, was able to become a student at Ruskin College, Oxford. For two years his wife worked as a domestic servant to support him. Returning to the North East, he was an ILP speaker, acted as an election agent in 1910 and became checkweighman in West Pelton the following year. He was elected to Durham County Council in 1913, worked as a driver in the Royal Artillery during the First World War, and was elected MP for Chester-le-Street in 1919 in a by-election, having failed to enter parliament for Seaham in 1918. In 1922 he, along with Clement Attlee, became Parliamentary Private Secretary to Labour leader Ramsay MacDonald, and in the first Labour government of 1924 he was Financial Secretary at the War Office, whilst Attlee was Under-Secretary. In the second Labour government he was Parliamentary Secretary under Margaret Bondfield at the Ministry of Labour.

As one of the small number of Labour survivors of the debacle of the October 1931 election, Lawson now had a higher profile than before. Though not a gifted or natural parliamentarian, he spoke frequently on the plight of the unemployed and was an outspoken critic of the household means test. He was an automatic choice for Labour's Parliamentary Committee. A loyal ally of the leadership, he voted for Attlee in the 1935 leadership contest. He also found time to write, developing a vivid, effective style. In 1932 an early volume of autobiography appeared, *A Man's Life* (1932), followed by a novel, *Under the Wheels* (1934) (which the *Manchester Guardian* described as 'moving, beautiful and even heart-rending'), a biography of a Durham miners' leader, *Peter Lee* (1936), and a study of the president of the Miners' Federation Herbert Smith, *The Man in the Cap* (1941). In 1945 appeared his collected broadcasts and sketches, *Who Goes Home?*

During the war Lawson was Deputy Regional Commissioner for Civil Defence, Northern Region, helping to prepare air defences from his base in Durham, an activity Hugh Dalton believed kept him fully occupied. He also visited Greece and China as a member of parliamentary commissions, and he was appointed Vice-Chairman of the British Council in 1944. After the 1945 election victory, Attlee made Lawson Secretary of State for War, with a seat in the Cabinet. In some ways this was a surprising appointment; but Attlee knew Lawson's steady worth and wished to see the Durham miners represented. Lawson was also, according to J R Clynes, a man of prodigious energy: 'I never knew anyone who spared himself less than Jack Lawson'. Lawson's main role was to oversee demobilisation. He believed firmly in the principle 'first in, first out', a policy he explained personally during 60 mass meetings of troops in Egypt, Singapore, Hong Kong and India; and he threatened to resign in November 1945 when it was mooted that the release of doctors should be given priority. He did resign on 4 October 1946, after a serious illness and a major operation. He continued as an MP until 1949, when he became Lord Lieutenant of Durham, the first working-class man to hold this position. In 1950 he was created Baron Lawson of Beamish. He continued to live in his miner's cottage at Beamish and died on 3 August 1965. According to his obituary in *The Times*, Lawson 'brought to high office in the service of state and country those qualities of sturdy self-respect, natural dignity, and robust vigour which flourish in the hardy mining communities of Durham'. A biography has not yet been written.

Robert Pearce

Fred Lee (Lord Lee of Newton) (1906–84)

Fred Lee was a far more important member of the Labour government 1964–66 than he was ever given public recognition for. He had the ear of the Prime Minister. Lee was, after all, the one member of the shadow cabinet that Wilson had inherited from Gaitskell who had voted for Wilson in the leadership contest of the spring of 1963. Born on 3 August 1906, Frederick Lee was a Mancunian through and through. Educated at the Langworthy Road School, he left at 15 to go to his father's place of work, Metro-Vickers. A talented engineer-craftsman, he rose in the shop-steward movement to become Chairman of the Works Committee of Metro-Vickers. The greatest moment of his life (he told me), other than becoming a Cabinet Minister in 1964 was organising the platform and speaking at the rally of some 35,000 workers at Trafford Park in the run-up to the 1945 election, addressed by Attlee and Ernie Bevin. By that time he was also a member of Salford City Council and the National Committee of the Amalgamated Engineering Union (1944–45).

Elected to what was the Hulme division of Manchester in 1945, he was in 1948 chosen by Stafford Cripps, Chancellor of the Exchequer, as his PPS. Cripps wanted a trade-union, working-class, sensible left-winger, respected by both his Parliamentary colleagues and the trade union leaders. In 1950 he became MP for Newton, Merseyside. In the short-lived 1950–51 Labour government, Lee became Parliamentary Secretary at the Ministry of Labour and National Service. As a National Serviceman at the time, I retrospectively applaud what Fred Lee told me, when I became an MP in 1962, of his efforts to persuade the forces (on the whole, successfully), to give 18–20 year olds some technical training. It certainly worked for the Royal Armoured Corps!

The thirteen years in Opposition was a difficult period, faction set against faction. Lee was not a core Bevanite, but sympathetic to the Left: 'I was uncomfortable at pleasing nobody!' Actually, he resisted herd-instinct, and showed courageous independence, which appealed to trade-union Labour Members, who were his power-base in being elected to the shadow cabinet in 1959 and thereafter. From 1955–59 he shadowed the Ministry of Labour, becoming principal Opposition Spokesman on Power in 1959–60 and on Aviation 1960–64. On the retirement of Jim Griffiths as Labour's Deputy Leader in November 1960, Lee stood unsuccessfully against George Brown and Jim Callaghan in the contest to succeed him.

Wilson's reasons for appointing Lee in October 1964 to the then critically important job of Minister of Power were sound. He was not a miner, but the NUM could accept a Minister with an impeccable working-class trade-union background, and he was an engineer who championed nuclear power, steel nationalisation and the whole White Heat of the Technological Revolution.

Albeit a hesitant performer at the Commons Despatch Box, he was respected by civil servants and both sides, management and unions, in the coal industry. His undoing came in the last week of January 1966, when there were widespread industrial stoppages through gas and electricity breakdowns, mainly caused by mechanical failures and late deliveries of plant and components. Lee was not at home on nightly television, and the Prime Minister felt the Government case was going by default.

So, after the election, Wilson moved his loyal old friend to the less high-profile job of Secretary of State for the Colonies. After six months, in which he showed himself a thoughtful Minister in dealing with incoming delegates and visits to colonies, Parliamentary disaster struck on 31 October 1966. Unexpectedly, he had to answer a Private Notice Question, after

Parliamentary Questions, on Gibraltar. Not being himself involved in the negotiations of Wilson and George Brown, Lee appeared ill-briefed and prevaricating. Wilson, ever loyal to those who had been loyal to him, tactfully excluded him from the Cabinet, and in January 1967 gave him the fig-leaf of becoming Chancellor of the Duchy of Lancaster, the first Lancastrian with a Lancashire seat to hold the post since 1914. His main task was to help Michael Stewart at the Department of Economic Affairs. With the end of the DEA in autumn 1969, Lee returned to the backbenches without complaint at the age of 63, remaining there until he was created Lord Lee of Newton after the election of February 1974. He died on 4 February 1984. In 1938 he had married Amelia Shay, by whom he had one daughter.

Tam Dalyell MP

Jennie Lee (Baroness Lee of Asheridge)   (1904–88)

Jennie Lee became an MP aged 24, before she was old enough to vote. The youngest woman MP ever elected, men, but rarely women, were besotted by her dark smokey beauty and arrogant sexuality. Gifted, passionate and quite lovely, she sank her own parliamentary prospects to promote those of her husband, Nye Bevan. In the Bevan-Gaitskell battles of the 1950s, she was seen as Nye's 'dark angel', his Lady Macbeth, pulling him away from compromise and the centre and, true to her ILP roots, into confrontation, resignation and Opposition. Later, she became the first and possibly the finest Minister for the Arts and the minister entrusted by Harold Wilson to deliver a University for the Air (the Open University).

Born Janet Lee on 3 November 1904 in Lochgelly, Fifeshire, the third of four children, the older two of whom died in infancy, she was the only daughter but unusually was brought up as the son of the family, free of female domestic responsibility and free also to join her father James, a miner and friend of ILP leader James Maxton, in his ILP activism. Her early years spent at socialist Sunday school, collecting ILP subscriptions, joining great anti-war pacifist rallies, celebrating the 1917 Russian Revolution and organising politically-correct lorry deliveries during the General Strike, meant she was always destined for politics. After Cowdenbeath Secondary School she left Edinburgh University in 1926 with an MA and LLB, by which time, with her vivid gypsy good looks and passionate evangelical style, she had become known as one of the finest platform orators in Scottish Labour politics. Fighting and winning Tory-held North Lanark for the ILP at a by-election of February 1929, she held the seat until Labour's electoral debacle of 1931. In Parliament she was introduced by Maxton, befriended by Ellen Wilkinson and Nye Bevan, mentored by Education Minister Sir Charles Trevelyan and educated in Hobsonian economics by her lover, MP Frank Wise. Dismissive of feminism, which she regarded as a middle-class women's issue, she was preoccupied primarily with the failure of MacDonaldism to tackle unemployment.

When the ILP disaffiliated from Labour in July 1932, Jennie followed the party into the wilderness. She failed to retake North Lanark at the general election of 1935, this time against an official Labour candidate. Out of Parliament she helped Bevan, Stafford Cripps, William Mellor and the young Michael Foot launch *Tribune* and became involved in the anti-fascist Popular Front. The war finally weaned her from ILP pacifism, and having resigned from the ILP in 1942 she fought and nearly defeated the official Tory candidate in the February 1943

Bristol Central by-election on an independent pro-Beveridge ticket, backed by Sir Richard Acland's Common Wealth Party.

Rejoining official Labour in December 1944, she became MP for Cannock at the 1945 general election. By then the death of her married lover Frank Wise from a brain haemorrhage in November 1933 had led her to marry her friend Nye Bevan on the rebound on 24 October 1934. 'You know, Nye, we could be brother and sister,' she had once said. 'Mmmm – with a tendency to incest,' he had replied. They chose to have no children. After Nye's death from cancer on 6 July 1960, a desolate Jennie turned to drink and largely withdrew from the public gaze. Harold Wilson revived her as his Arts Minister, first as Parliamentary Secretary at the Ministry of Public Building and Works (1964–65) and then as Parliamentary Secretary and from 1967–70 Minister of State, at Education. She became a Privy Counsellor in 1966.

A Policy for the Arts, the First Steps, her White Paper of February 1965, stated that the traditionally elitist arts could become accessible – diffused to the regions, to young people, to the trades unions, to the unemployed – without diluting their excellence. Trebling the Arts Council grant, despite stringent government financial controls, she brought new money to arts outside London whilst continuing to support the traditional flagships within it.

In creating the Open University she tackled widespread opposition from the existing universities, who insisted that open access was incompatible with academic excellence; from the adult education movement, who argued that the priority ought to be remedial adult education; from the Labour left, who wanted a working-class rather than an open university (which might attract mere 'housewives'); and from those on Labour and Tory front benches who thought it an expensive white elephant. However, with the help of Lord Goodman she drove it through and faced down the Tory threat to abolish it. In January 1971, six months after Labour's defeat, it accepted its first students and by 1984 it was Britain's largest university.

By then she was in the Lords as Baroness Lee of Asheridge, having lost her seat in 1970 on over twice the national average swing, probably because she neglected Cannock and Cannock deeply distrusted her love of London and the arts. Initially active in the Lords, bad health, including cancer, set in after the publication of her autobiography, *My Life with Nye,* in 1980. Increasingly confined to her Chelsea home, she died of pneumonia on 16 November 1988.

Baroness Hollis of Heigham

H B 'Bertie' Lees-Smith (1876–1941)

Bertie Lees-Smith was a typical example of the kind of progressive Liberal who came over to Labour around the time of the First World War. Although only briefly a cabinet minister, he was a significant second-rank player in Labour party politics from the mid-1920s to the early 1940s, and played a leading role in the formation of policy on defence and, to a lesser extent, education in the 1930s.

Hastings Bertrand Lees-Smith was born at Murree, North West Provinces, India, on 26 January 1876, into an Army family. Educated at Aldenham Junior Military Academy and the Royal Military Academy at Woolwich, his initial hopes for a military career were dashed by chronic asthma. Instead, he went in 1895 to study History at Oxford, graduating in 1899.

Thereafter he worked as general secretary of the newly opened Ruskin College, Oxford. From 1906 he also taught Public Administration at the LSE, becoming a Reader in 1924 and teaching there, with breaks, down to his death.

Before the First World War Lees–Smith was a radical Liberal, and became MP for Northampton in January 1910. Retaining his seat at the fresh poll that December, he supported 'advanced' positions on issues such as railway nationalisation. On the outbreak of war in 1914 he emerged as a leading critic of 'secret diplomacy', and became closely involved with the Union of Democratic Control, where he worked with, among others, Labour figures like Ramsay MacDonald. Although serving in the army (in the ranks, where he attained the rank of corporal) from 1915, he made a number of speeches in parliament condemning the illiberal policies of the Asquith and Lloyd George Coalitions, such as conscription. At the 1918 election he fought and lost the Don Valley seat in Yorkshire as an independent radical.

Lees–Smith joined the Labour party in 1919, and in 1922 he was elected as Labour MP for Keighley. But his defeat there by a Liberal at the following year's election meant he was out of parliament during the tenure of the first Labour government, and so could not be considered for office. However, he regained the seat in 1924, and was elected to the shadow cabinet every year between then and 1929. However, his worsening relations with MacDonald meant that he had to make do with the non-cabinet post of Postmaster-General when Labour returned to office in 1929. When, however, C P Trevelyan resigned as President of the Board of Education in March 1931, he finally entered the cabinet as his replacement.

Lees–Smith's ministerial career was disappointingly brief. The party's plans to raise the school-leaving age to 15 had collapsed, and there was severe downward pressure on public expenditure. In any case, the government was soon in its death-throes. That August, in the face of severe financial crisis, he backed MacDonald's call for a cut in unemployment benefit; unlike some others, however, he was not tempted to follow the premier into the National government. Instead, he went into opposition, being elected to the Shadow Cabinet and serving on the party's economic policy committee. But at the October 1931 election he was heavily defeated. Following this, he returned to full-time work at the LSE, while continuing his work on Labour's economic policymaking through such bodies as the XYZ Club.

At the 1935 general election Lees–Smith narrowly regained Keighley, and was elected once again to the shadow cabinet in November 1935 and in every subsequent year until his death. Here, his interest in education policy was increasingly replaced by concern with military matters. Along with Dalton and Alexander, he was a leading figure in changing the PLP's line from voting against to abstaining on the Service Estimates in 1937, and on the outbreak of war in 1939 he was appointed to liaise with the Secretary of State for War. Lees–Smith was not appointed to the Churchill Coalition in 1940, but he did act as Chairman of the PLP and Leader of the Opposition so that parliamentary business could be transacted properly. He died in London on 18 December 1941.

Bertie Lees–Smith was an unglamorous politician, but he had a quiet competence and loyalty that made him a respected colleague and a useful front-bench figure in Labour oppositions for almost two decades. His ministerial career merits no more than a footnote, but overall he was by no means insignificant in the development of the Labour party during the inter-war period. There is no published biography. Among his own works, the most significant are *India and the Tariff Problem* (1909) and *Second Chambers in Theory and Practice* (1923); he also edited *The Encyclopaedia of the Labour Movement* (1928).

Andrew Thorpe

Joan Lestor (Baroness Lestor of Eccles) (1931–98)

Joan Lestor was born in Vancouver on 13 November 1931. The daughter of Charles and Ethie Lestor (the former described as a 'political organiser'), Joan was initially educated in Monmouth, South Wales, prior to a family move to London where she continued with her education at William Morris School, Wandsworth. She then completed a Diploma in Sociology (then very much an 'up and coming' discipline) at London University, and a teacher training certificate. Joan developed a growing interest in education, perhaps intrinsically connected with the latter qualification, throughout her political career. She joined the Labour Party in 1956, a year that saw the publication of Crosland's *The Future Of Socialism*. However, Lestor was not to see eye-to-eye politically with the Gaitskellite revisionists such as Crosland, Jay and Jenkins in her Parliamentary years.

Between 1959 and 1968 she ran her own kindergarten, unsuccessfully contesting the West Lewisham parliamentary by-election in 1964. She continued to work with infants before winning the seat of Eton and Slough in the 1966 General Election. She was an active backbencher before finally being given office as Under-Secretary of State at the Department for Education and Science (DES) under Ted Short in October 1969, serving until Labour's election defeat in 1970. Most of her colleagues, including Short, Gerry Fowler, Jennie Lee and Alice Bacon, also had an educational background.

Lestor became prominent as a left-winger after securing election to the Constituency Section of the NEC in 1968 (continuing until defeated in 1982 by hard-left Audrey Wise after her failure to back Tony Benn for Labour's Deputy Leadership, and subsequently as a member of the Women's Section 1987–96). She was Labour Party Chair during the year 1977–8.

She was a vocal critic of the *In Place Of Strife* trades union legislation, claiming that support for the Bill came almost exclusively from those who wished eradication of the unions altogether. Joan's liberal stance on race relations was clear in her opposition to the government's imposition of tight controls on immigration into Britain for passport-holding Kenyan Asians fleeing persecution. 'Race' and 'Foreign Affairs' would continue to take precedence in her politics for many years to come.

In Opposition, she became Chair of the NEC Sub-Committee on Education (in April 1971) and, at her first meeting, came close to becoming a victim of a letter-bomb attack. She was unharmed, but the experience was disturbing and distressing to both her and her colleagues who witnessed the event. On wider issues, she was a prominent critic of Britain's entry into the Common Market alongside Tony Benn, Peter Shore and Eric Heffer.

Back in government in 1974, Lestor was appointed an Under-Secretary of State at the Foreign Office until being transferred back to Education on 12 June 1975, again as an Under-Secretary of State, where she was a strong advocate of pre-school education. However, faced with proposed cutbacks in government education spending, she resigned her post in February 1976.

She was replaced by Margaret Jackson (now Margaret Beckett), then the new MP for Lincoln. This was to be Joan Lestor's last experience of government.

Following the successful defence of her Slough seat in the 1979 defeat for Labour, Lestor continued as the MP until 1983 when she was deposed at the seat she had represented for nearly seventeen years. After Labour's 1979 election defeat she became embroiled in the internal party strife that came to a head with the challenge of Tony Benn to Denis Healey for the Labour Deputy Leadership in 1981. Surprisingly, Lestor chose not to back her old friend Benn (after initially fancying him as a serious leadership prospect in 1980), opting instead to abstain. Later, she was to declare that if the 1983 election was lost, it was due to the 'Deputy Leadership fiasco', not to the rising Militant problem within Labour's ranks.

In 1983 she lost her seat, becoming in 1984–85 the Head of Lambeth Council Police Unit and Director of the Trade Unions Child Care Project 1986–87. Returning to the Commons as MP for Eccles, Neil Kinnock appointed her Opposition Spokesperson on Development Co-operation 1988–89. Having been elected to the shadow cabinet, she became spokesman on Children 1989–92, on Children and the Family 1993–94 and for Overseas Development 1994–96. By 1996 she was 65 and decided to relinquish her seat on the NEC and to retire from the Commons at the next election. She had served instinctively and professionally under five successive Labour leaders, converting her expertise and experience into action in both government and opposition. She was created Baroness Lestor of Eccles in 1997. She died in a London hospice on 27 March 1998.

Phil Miles

Harold Lever (Lord Lever of Manchester)   (1914–95)

Harold Lever – as he was universally known to all his friends and Parliamentary colleagues during his 34 years as a Manchester Labour MP – was a delightful, many-sided man: as warm-hearted personally as he was brilliant in his understanding of finance; as outgoing and chatty as he was able as a Treasury Minister; as much at ease with the poorest of his constituents as with his guests in his luxury flat in one of the pleasantest squares in London's West End, and as urbane and charming in his personal contacts as he was pointed and imaginative in his debating speeches in Parliament. A legendary bridge player, he claimed to have made most of his wealth through share dealing in his spare time. Not surprisingly with so rich and varied an endowment, he successfully rose from being a well-liked and highly-regarded backbencher to become one of the chairmen of Standing Committees and ultimately a Cabinet Minister.

When that Labour government ended in 1979 he was created a life peer as Lord Lever of Manchester and was able to devote his many talents to his various business and financial activities in addition to fulfilling a number of important offices in charitable, academic and political organisations. In spite of suffering a severe stroke in 1973 which rendered one arm quite useless, he carried on with undiminished energy and died following further strokes on 6 August 1995 at the age of 81, rich in honours and having made a major contribution to the welfare of his countrymen.

He left behind a devoted wife, Diane, whom he had married in 1962, and their three daughters, in whom he delighted. Diane could always be seen in the gallery of the House of Commons whenever her husband was about to make an important speech, listening intently. It was a very happy marriage and deservedly so, for his second wife Billie, with whom Harold was very much in love, was snatched from him in 1948 by leukaemia after only three years of marriage – but not before giving birth to a very clever daughter.

Norman Harold Lever was born in Manchester on 15 January 1914, the younger son of Lithuanian Jewish immigrants, and joined the Labour Party as a schoolboy in the 1920s in reaction to the poverty he witnessed in Manchester. He was educated at Manchester Grammar School and Manchester University and was called to the Bar in 1935. After serving in the RAF during World War II he fought and won the Manchester Exchange (later renamed Cheetham) seat in 1945 and held it with comfortable majorities until his retirement in 1979. His elder brother Leslie sat for Manchester Ardwick for 20 years and became Lord Mayor of the city. Appointed Joint Parliamentary Under-Secretary at the Department for Economic Affairs in January 1967 and promoted in August of that year, just before devaluation, to Financial Secretary to the Treasury, he joined the Privy Counsel and Cabinet as Paymaster General in October 1969, working at MinTech under Tony Benn. Chairman of the Public Accounts Committee from 1970–73, he was elected to the shadow cabinet in 1970, serving as Shadow Minister for Europe until October 1971 when Wilson moved him to Shadow Minister for Fuel and Power. In April 1972, with his pro-European colleagues Roy Jenkins and George Thomson, he resigned over Labour's support for a referendum on membership of the EEC. Re-elected to the shadow cabinet in November 1972 he served as deputy to Benn in the shadow Trade and Industry team. In February 1974, waiving the salary, he was appointed to a non-departmental Cabinet role as Chancellor of the Duchy of Lancaster, remaining there as a key economic and financial advisor to the Prime Minister until 1979. It was in this capacity that he played a key role in the rescue of Chrysler and putting together the IMF economic rescue package of 1976.

He subsequently fulfilled a variety of important posts, devoting his time to his financial and banking interests. He was Director of the *Guardian* and *Manchester Evening News* from 1979–90, Chairman of the Trustees of the Royal Academy 1981–87 (he had an impressive collection of French Impressionists, some of which decorated the walls of his office in the Treasury), and chairman and director of finance houses and public companies including the London Interstate Bank 1984–90, Authority Investments 1986–91 and Brittania Arrow Holdings 1983–92. In 1983 he served on Lord Franks's Committee of Inquiry into the Falklands War. He was Treasurer of Socialist International 1971–73 and a Governor of the LSE from 1971, of Manchester University from 1975 and of the ESU 1973–86. He received Honorary Doctorates in Law, Science, Literature and Technology and was joint author of *Debt and Danger*, published in 1985.

One event and one anecdote serve to put flesh on this statistical record. His Parliamentary colleagues always remember how, when the practical circumstances of the moment required it, the Honourable Member for Cheetham once rose to his feet and, without a note or the opportunity to prepare for the occasion, made a dilatory speech lasting over two hours. The content was interesting and the delivery good-humoured and very witty. Even more important, it was in order: it satisfied the very strict rules which bar irrelevancies and which are enforced by the hawk-eyed occupant of the chair. This back-bench MP managed, with great skill and relevance, to bring into his speech, for example, quite a lengthy dissertation on the coelacanth, a prehistoric fish long thought to be extinct but very recently discovered alive and well in the Indian Ocean. Clearly it takes a kind of brilliance over and above the skills of a clever politician and well-trained barrister to achieve that kind of result.

Finally the anecdote. At the time of his marriage to Diane, Harold Lever was by no means a poor man, but his fiancée, the daughter of well-established Lebanese bankers, was reputed to be worth a staggering three million pounds – and this was in the days when bankers and Treasury officials spoke in millions and never in billions. Inevitably his detractors alleged that he married her for her money. 'Not true,' retorted Harold: 'I would have married her if she'd only had one million.'

Rt Hon. Lord Diamond

Helen Liddell (1950–)

The first female General Secretary of the Scottish Labour Party and the first female Secretary of State for Scotland, Helen Liddell is regarded by friends and foes alike as tough and able, having made her reputation as Scotland's 'Nat-basher-in-chief'.

Helen Liddell was born Helen Lawrie Reilly in the Scottish Labour heartland of Lanarkshire on 6 December 1950, the only child of Hugh Reilly, a bus-driver and shop steward, and Bridget Lawrie. Educated at St. Patrick's High School, Coatbridge, and then at the University of Strathclyde where she gained a BA in Economics, she joined Airdrie Young Socialists in her teens, later marrying its Chair.

She worked for the Scottish Trades Union Congress (STUC) from 1971–76 as Head of the Economics Department and then Assistant Secretary, before joining BBC Scotland as their economics correspondent from 1976–77. In the General Election of 1974, she made her first attempt to become an MP, standing in the Fife East constituency.

After two years at the BBC she became, aged only 26, the first female General Secretary of the Scottish Labour Party, a position that she held for eleven years, until 1988. A long-standing supporter of a Scottish Parliament within the UK, she starred alongside Labour MPs John P Mackintosh and Jim Sillars and Edinburgh councillor George Foulkes – her deputy at the Scotland Office 27 years later – in the 1974 Party Election Broadcast which announced Labour's commitment to creating a Scottish Assembly to harness 'Powerhouse Scotland'. She steered the party through the abortive 1979 referendum on the Callaghan Government's devolution plans, keeping Labour's campaign for a 'Yes' vote separate from those of the other pro-devolutionists.

She went on to play a key role in keeping the Scottish Labour Party together during the difficult years of the early 1980s. So successful was she that while elsewhere Labour was losing scores of seats to the Tories, in Scotland it was actually gaining them. In 1985 she was the candidate of the Manifesto/Solidarity right to succeed Jim Mortimer as Labour Party General Secretary, but was in the event to be the runner-up to GMB official Larry Whitty, the candidate of the soft left.

In 1988 Robert Maxwell appointed her Public Affairs Director for the *Daily Record* and

Sunday Mail. After his death in 1991 she played a leading part in salvaging the Mirror Group pension scheme which he had pillaged.

Since entering the Commons in the bitter Monklands by-election following the death of the Labour leader John Smith, she has gained a reputation as a pugnacious performer. In 1994 she faced a ferocious challenge from the SNP and the Labour majority was cut to 1,640. In the 1997 general election the seat changed to Airdrie & Shotts and she increased her majority to 15,412, retaining the seat in the 2001 general election with a majority of 12,340. Swiftly promoted to the front bench, she was an Shadow Scottish Office Minister 1995–97.

In the Labour Government of 1997, she was made Economic Secretary to the Treasury, making an immediate impact by forcing pension providers to compensate members of the public who had been mis-sold private pensions. The following year she was promoted to Minister of State and Minister for Education at the Scottish Office, where as Donald Dewar's deputy she paved the way for devolution; she also headed Labour's campaign for the first Scottish Parliament elections in 1999.

Devolution accomplished, she was made Minister for Transport at the DETR, but was quickly moved to the DTI as Minister for Energy and Competitiveness in Europe. In this capacity she speeded up the payment of compensation to ex-miners, including many in her home constituency, who had contracted chest diseases in the pits.

In 2001 she was famously made the first female Secretary Of State for Scotland. That spring she headed Labour's general election campaign in Scotland, in which the party, against expectations, held all 56 seats it had captured in the landslide of 1997.

Helen is married to Alistair, and has a son, Paul, and a daughter, Claire. She is also the author of a political thriller *Elite* (1990), a novel about a female Scottish MP who becomes Deputy Prime Minister. Watch this space …

Lindsay McCoy

5th Earl of Listowel (William Francis 'Billy' Listowel)   (1906–97)

There can be few Cabinet Ministers whose crowning achievement can be said to be the abolition of their job and scarcely more who, on having been in Cabinet, would be content subsequently to play the role of junior minister. The shy and mild-mannered fifth Earl of Listowel, the last Secretary of State for India and Burma, did just that. Having served in the wartime coalition as Parliamentary Under-Secretary of State for India from November 1944 to May 1945 and, as the only Labour peer in the coalition government, as Deputy Leader of the House of Lords, William Francis 'Billy' Listowel became Attlee's Postmaster-General in August 1945.

He combined the restoration of pre-war postal deliveries and, after the nationalisation of Cable and Wireless, the expansion of the telephone network, with an innovative approach to linking inland night air-mails with the railways. He joined the Privy Council in 1946 and the Cabinet as Secretary of State for India and Burma in April 1947 to replace the ailing Pethick-Lawrence in seeing through the final independence negotiations. He played a key role alongside Mountbatten, the last Indian Viceroy, in securing the consent of the Indian Princely States to independence and partition. In Burma, his friendship with the soon-murdered Aung San, the father of the present democratic leader Aung San Suu Kyi, did much to smooth the process of independence. The India Office was abolished by August and the Burma Office by January 1948, whereupon he left Cabinet to serve as Minister of State at the Colonial Office until February 1950. He also had to apologise to the King for not returning his seals of office, which the India Office had actually managed to lose.

At the Colonial Office, responsibility for the British Empire then comprised three geographical areas, of which Listowel dealt with South-East Asia and the West Indies. An early journey was to Malaya to preside over the inaugural session of the Federal Legislative Council, the first step towards eventual independence. He also visited Australia and New Zealand to secure their agreement to India becoming a republic within the Commonwealth. Other expeditions led him to see a different side to Empire: in the jungle of British Guiana, Listowel discovered that Amerindian schoolchildren were taught English from textbooks helpfully beginning with the words, 'The Scottish nobleman strode out of his castle into the snow.' After the Colonial Office he served from November 1950–October 1951 as Parliamentary Secretary at the Ministry of Agriculture, an area of which he knew little and a further demotion from his status as a full Minister at the Colonial Office.

In opposition, colonial liberation remained his passion, and as the last Governor-General of Ghana from 1957 to 1960, Listowel helped to smooth the path for Ghana's emergence as the first African republic within the Commonwealth. He had always maintained friendly relations with Ghana's left-wing leader Kwame Nkrumah, on whose advice he was appointed Governor-General and GCMG by the Queen. Though some were surprised when Harold Wilson did not give him office in 1964, his appointment a year later as Chairman of Committees and Deputy Speaker of the House of Lords gave him a post for which his amiable and consensual approach made him eminently equipped and which he held until 1976.

Despite his meek manner, he had a determinedly rebellious streak. It was perhaps the strength of this that made him a socialist in his Eton schooldays, well in advance of his contemporary Lord Longford, and encouraged him in his later years to become president of the League Against Cruel Sports, having as a boy had to endure the enthusiasm of his High Tory family for blood sports. After Eton, his brief stint at Balliol College, Oxford, and membership of the Oxford Fabians was terminated by his father who, fearing that Balliol had exacerbated his son's socialist inclinations, removed him to Magdalene College, Cambridge, only for his son to join Cambridge University Labour Club and become a frequent advocate of socialist causes at the Cambridge Union.

After Cambridge and the Sorbonne, whilst studying for his PhD at the University of London (published in 1933 as *A Critical History of Modern Aesthetics*), he worked at Toynbee Hall in East London. There, living on £3 a week, he helped create 'Neighbours Ltd', an organisation to distribute the funds of the rich amongst the poor. As the eldest son of the 4th Earl of Listowel, the young Billy Hare (as he insisted on being addressed, refusing the courtesy title of Viscount Ennismore) had from his birth on 28 September 1906 been likely to become very rich indeed. However, after his father's death in 1931 (which ended his hopes of a Commons career), though he succeeded to both the Irish earldom of Listowel and the UK barony of Hare (which gave him a vote in the House of Lords), he found that his father had diverted most of his wealth to Billy's non-socialist younger brothers: John Hare, later as Lord Blakenham chairman of the Conservative Party, and Alan Hare, who became an MI6 officer and chairman of the *Financial Times*.

Making his maiden speech of 1932 on colonial liberation, Listowel joined a band of only a bare half-dozen Labour Peers. What he lacked in experience he made up for with enthusiasm, introducing bills to reform the jury system and the divorce laws. Appalled by Nazism and fascism he also travelled Europe to see its growth at first hand and, having visited Germany in 1934, was later that year, with Ellen Wilkinson, expelled from Spain for his pains. In 1936, he became vice-chair of the National Joint Committee for Spanish Relief following the outbreak of the Spanish Civil War. When Japan invaded China, he chaired the Friends of the Chinese People, becoming president of the China Campaign Committee. He also became president of the Euthanasia Society and Joint President of the Anti-Slavery Society and was very active in the Fabian Society Colonial Bureau.

Listowel volunteered for war service in 1939, but bad eyesight meant he initially ended up a private in the Royal Army Medical Corps before being recruited to join the Intelligence Corps as a second lieutenant. Based in London, he succeeded in remaining active in the Lords and on the death of Labour's Chief Whip in 1941, Listowel was invited to take over, being released from the army in consequence. From 1937–46 he also represented East Lewisham for Labour on London County Council.

He married Hungarian aristocrat's daughter Judith de Marffy-Mantuana in 1933, and they had a daughter. After their divorce in 1945, he married jazz singer Stephanie Wise in 1958. They too had a daughter before in 1963 he divorced again and then married Mrs Pamela Read, ex-wife of a middle-weight professional boxer and daughter of a Croydon bus driver, with whom he had two sons and a third daughter. He continued to attend the Lords until his death at home in London on 12 March 1997.

Greg Rosen

Ken Livingstone   (1945–)

After he managed, at the GLC, to transform his image from Red wrecker to cheeky Cockney champion of local democracy, those outside politics often ask why Ken never managed to rise in the Labour Party and was always marginal in the Parliamentary Party, and above all why the Party moved heaven and earth to stop him being Labour's candidate for Mayor of London though his popularity with many activists remains. To those who have worked closely with him, there is no mystery to Ken Livingston's politics. He is an old fashioned socialist, a conviction politician, still genuinely believing that politics means mobilising the state, at local, national and international level, to tackle society's problems. Ken's democratic socialism places public authority, not market forces, at the centre of civic society, and he sees a profound antagonism between democracy and the free market.

Born in South London on 17 June 1945, he attended Tulse Hill Comprehensive School with little academic success. He worked as a laboratory technician, growing ever more disturbed about the treatment of the research animals in his care. Eventually, as his interest in politics grew, he returned to study at Philippa Fawcett Teacher Training College, completing the course successfully but later deploring the lack of challenge presented to students by the lecturers there.

After joining a largely moribund Norwood Labour Party, he rapidly became a Lambeth councillor (1971–78), serving as chair of the housing committee in succession to John Major when Labour won back control of the council from the Tories. First elected to the Greater London Council in 1973, he represented several different constituencies until its demise in 1986. He was also a Camden Councillor between 1978 and 1982.

His career has been largely centred in London politics because his real views are not widely shared either in the Labour Party or the country as a whole. He would have liked to have been a Minister, even Prime Minister, but apart from five years as Leader of the old GLC, and his current term as Mayor of London, public office has been denied him because he has never managed to make the compromises necessary. There would be no point, for Ken, in doing this; it would contradict his whole reason for being in politics.

He is the great British political escapologist, able to switch alliances and abandon one struggle to move on to another. Like T S Eliot's Macavity, when the crime's discovered, Ken Livingstone's not there. He flirted with Labour's Trotskyist entrists in the 1970s and 1980s, but his aim was to use them. For all their centralist discipline, he ended up less damaged than they were by the series of temporary alliances.

The Law Lords, in December 1981, supported the case brought by Conservative-controlled Bromley Council and declared illegal the GLC's policy of subsiding London Transport to keep Tube and bus fares low. The GLC Labour Group split almost down the middle, some among Livingstone's leading moderate supporters opting for legality. There was a fractional majority for defiance. Had the GLC voted not to accept, British local government would have entered uncharted waters.

The GLC Conservatives, sensing that Labour and Livingstone would lose power, decided to abstain. The Labour moderates did not want to plunge over the abyss, but there were not enough of them. A handful of GLC Conservatives were also more concerned to preserve the principle of local government in London than to step into the unknown. Livingstone allowed GLC officers to design a package which raised fares a little. Livingstone and the left then voted against it, but were defeated by the other half of the Labour Group, three Conservatives and three Liberal-SDP Alliance members. The escape route opened up and Livingstone escaped the blame for the switch. Illtyd Harrington, veteran moderate-left Labour GLC member, commented: 'I think Ken was opportunistic because he knew that the law would have to be obeyed, but he knew that other people would see that it was done.'

Livingstone fought Hampstead in 1979. The left had tried to oust sitting MP Reg Freeson (an ex-minister, Barbara Castle's one-time PPS and a former editor of *Searchlight*) from the Brent East seat before the 1983 election to replace him with Ken, but party officials stepped in and suspended the local party for breaching the rules. They did not make the same mistake in 1987.

The Thatcher Government, after the 1983 election, determined to restrict local authority spending by capping the level of rates which they could levy. (They also went ahead with plans to abolish the GLC, but that, and the fight against it, is really a separate story.) In July

1984, Livingstone was prominent among those calling for defiance by refusal to set a rate or to make cuts.

In March 1985, the resisting authorities were to pass resolutions refusing to set a legal rate, facing the Government with the alternative of taking them over or caving in. But the GLC was in a different position from other councils. The law was clear: it had to set its rate precept. Illegality, disqualification and even personal bankruptcy stared GLC councilors in the face. Bankrupts cannot be MPs. The law was much less clear on the specific responsibilities of the other councils.

Livingstone then claimed to have discovered that the GLC, luckily, had a fall-back. It could set a legal precept yet avoid cuts. The GLC left was incensed. They continued to vote not to set a rate. Livingstone urged support for the fall-back position as an alternative to a Tory proposal for much greater cuts. The Labour right came up with a compromise which the Tories could support. A legal precept was set. Livingstone voted, with the left, against it. Once again, others saved him.

Once in Parliament in 1987, Livingstone was cold-shouldered. The moderate left rallied behind Neil Kinnock, and the activities of the GLC and left-wing councils were generally thought to have contributed to Labour's marginalisation. Livingstone lost his NEC seat in 1989, only two years after he had secured it. He expected that every defeat would cause the party to turn back to the left. While he occupied himself with international economic theory, Labour changed again and he began to look quite irrelevant.

Yet he retained the ability to charm the media and even business audiences, and was never quite forgotten among Labour's rank and file. Their heads saw that under Tony Blair Labour had a chance to govern and that in government, advances were possible, albeit small ones in comparison with Labour's aspirations; in opposition, nothing could be done. Yet their hearts responded to Ken's warning that without higher taxation Labour could never pay for radical social measures.

The opportunity offered by an elected Mayoralty for London was his last chance. But the gap between what Ken stands for and New Labour was unbridgeable. True to form, Ken swore to Labour activists that he would abide by the Party's decision on who should be its candidate. At that same time, he was telling private gatherings that, come what might, he would run.

Hearts would have won had London Party members been allowed a vote. Unedifying manoeuvring to deny him the Labour candidacy hurt Frank Dobson, a good man strong-armed into sacrificing himself for the Party he loved. Former casualties of the many broken alliances at the GLC were the leading critics of Ken's candidacy.

In opposing the Government's proposed public-private partnership (PPP) for London Underground, Livingstone has support from economists and transport planners. But as ever, he is playing to the hearts of Labour activists and public sector trade unionists, who are deeply suspicious of the whole of the private sector.

Those around Livingstone expect a Labour government to fail to deliver at some point, when activists and voters will turn back to the traditional left. The 2001 election gave no indication of this happening. The Government will push through PPP. Livingstone will take them to court, as he did successive Conservative governments. London and the Tube will not have changed much by the time he stands for re-election in 2004: but Ken will dodge any blame for that.

Phil Kelly

Earl Longford (Frank Pakenham)   (1905–2001)

Frank Longford brought character and variety to the Labour Party ever since he became a socialist in 1936, persuaded following a stormy Oxford meeting addressed by Oswald Mosley. He had been a Conservative and had worked in the Conservative Party Research Department from 1930–32. On joining the Labour Party he announced 'I am a socialist because I am a Christian', and his faith grew in influence on his work. He was soon adopted as Labour's prospective parliamentary candidate for West Birmingham, though he stood down on his adoption as candidate for Oxford City in 1938, which he eventually fought unsuccessfully at the 1945 general election. He was elected a Labour Oxford City councillor at a by-election in 1937 and re-elected in 1938. He joined the Catholic church in 1940.

Born Francis Aungier Pakenham on 5 December 1905, his father was killed leading his brigade at Gallipoli in 1915. He was educated at Eton and New College, Oxford, where he took a first class degree in Modern Greats in 1927 and became friends with Hugh Gaitskell and Evan Durbin. He was a Workers' Educational Association tutor in Stoke on Trent from 192 to 1931. Returning to Oxford after working at Conservative head office, he became a politics lecturer at Christ Church in 1932, the young Chris Mayhew, whom Longford saw as a future Labour leader, being amongst his students. In 1931 he married Elizabeth Harman, who was to stand as Labour candidate for Cheltenham at the 1935 election, precipitating her new husband's resignation from the Carlton Club. They had eight children: four sons and four daughters (one died in 1969). Had the growth of their family not persuaded her to resign as the Labour candidate, she would almost certainly have been elected MP for Kings Norton, Birmingham, in 1945.

During most of the Second World War (1941–44), he served as personal assistant to William Beveridge. He was created the first Baron Pakenham by Clement Attlee after the 1945 election and was appointed a Lord in Waiting (government whip) in October 1945, being promoted to ministerial office as Under-Secretary of State for War in October 1946. From April 1947 until May 1948, as Chancellor of the Duchy of Lancaster, Pakenham had responsibility for the British-controlled zones of Germany and Austria. Controversially, he publicly demonstrated compassion for Germans suffering the after-effects of war, but was later to be commended for doing so by Churchill. He became convinced that the separation of eastern Germany was inevitable and was opposed to the government's policy of dismantling Germany's industrial base, almost to the point of resignation. In May 1948 he became a Privy Counsellor and joined the Cabinet as Minister of Civil Aviation, where he presided over the restructuring of the various airlines into more financially sound businesses. From February 1950, the aviation ministry was reduced to non-cabinet status and in May 1951 Pakenham was moved to become First Lord of the Admiralty, remaining in post until the fall of the Attlee government.

During Labour's years in opposition, Pakenham served, from 1955 to 1963, as Chairman of the National Bank of Ireland. The death of his elder brother, the 6th Earl of Longford, in 1961 meant that the first Lord Pakenham became in 1961 the 7th Earl of Longford. Harold Wilson appointed him to the Cabinet as Lord Privy Seal and Leader of the House of Lords in 1964, combining this role between December 1965 and April 1966 with that of Colonial Secretary. Back in government, however, as previously, Longford never appeared at home with his Labour colleagues. He was an eccentric Bertie Wooster character who often did not consider the consequences of his actions. Furthermore, his stance on ethical issues was often at odds with those of colleagues. He resigned from the government in January 1968 while his position was under threat, unable to support a delay in raising the school leaving age, and was succeeded as Leader of the Lords by Lord Shackleton.

It was as a campaigner against pornography and for penal reform that Longford became best known. The anti-pornography reputation originated with his chairing of a committee in 1971–72 to examine the issue. It resulted in a farcical visit to Copenhagen, where he marched out, shocked, from a strip show, and produced a considered report recommending restrictions on pornography that went against the grain of liberal society.

Longford chaired various committees on crime and penal reform, but also applied his concerns practically in the foundation of The New Bridge, designed to advise ex-prisoners. This was in addition to his work with individual prisoners, somewhat clouded by publicity generated by contacts with high-profile criminals such as Myra Hindley. He also established a youth centre, New Horizon. It is not hard to conclude that he courted publicity deliberately, perhaps to highlight his work. Together with an eccentric and single-minded approach to issues, this sometimes had the effect of obscuring its serious nature or the motives behind it. Ultimately however, he is remembered for a clear and public Christian sense of right and wrong.

He was made a Knight of the Garter in 1971 and was the author of several books including a memoir, *Avowed Intent* (1994); *History of the House of Lords* (1988); *Diary of a Year* (1982) and *Peace by Ordeal* (1935). He died on 3 August 2001.

Stephen Beer

Dickson Mabon (1925–)

When Hugh Gaitskell pledged to 'fight, fight and fight again' to save the Party he loved, there were few more doughty fighters at his side than Jesse Dickson 'Dick' Mabon, who on the day of Attlee's resignation as Labour leader on 7 December 1955, as the 26-year-old Labour soon-to-be victor of the Greenock by-election, had declared publicly for Gaitskell as Attlee's successor. Born on 1 November 1925, the son of Jesse Dickson Mabon and Isabel Simpson Montgomery, he had attended Possilpark, Cumbrae and North Kelvinside Schools. From 1944–48 he had worked in coalmining before army service. Whilst completing a medical degree at Glasgow University he stood as Labour candidate for Bute and North Ayrshire and West Renfrew at respectively the general elections of 1951 and 1955. For the next quarter-century, Mabon was to be a lynchpin of Labour's social-democratic right, using the organising skills he had honed as Chair of the National Association of Labour Students (1949–50), which as the Chair of Glasgow University Labour Club (1948–50) he had helped create. Student politics had also taught him how to debate. A winner of the *Observer* Mace, a debating trophy that now bears the name of his great friend John Smith, he was elected President of that cradle of Scottish debating, Glasgow University Union, in 1950–51, and in 1954–55 of the Scottish Union of Students.

The election in 1974 of Ian Mikardo as Chairman of the PLP showed that, with

Gaitskell now thirteen years dead, the hard left was a rising tide even in Parliament. Mikardo had won chiefly because of the split vote between several moderate opponents. It was Mabon who organised the loyalist counterattack and on 17 December 1974 launched the Manifesto Group of Labour MPs as a rallying point for those Labour backbenchers who did not regard defending the government as a betrayal of socialism, becoming from 1974 until his return to government in 1976, its Chair. Manifesto's membership of over 80 MPs ranged from younger Turks such as Ian Wrigglesworth, Phillip Whitehead, Giles Radice and John P Mackintosh to veteran ex-Ministers such as Tom Urwin, Father of the House George Strauss and ex-Foreign Secretary Michael Stewart. Importantly, its membership was not dedicated either to the leadership aspirations of one man or to the pro-European cause: whilst some like David Marquand were the epitome of Jenkinsite pro-Europeanism, others like Jim Wellbeloved and Mike Thomas were Callaghan supporters or like George Cunningham, Ken Weetch, Brian Walden and John Horam, of a Eurosceptic persuasion. Michael Stewart recounted in his memoirs: 'We did not repeat the error [of the Keep Calm Group of 1952] of looking for conciliation where none was possible; our object was avowedly to resist the left and assert the wishes of what we believed to be the decisive majority of Labour MPs. That we were right in this belief was shown by our success in the elections for significant posts within the PLP: we organised for these elections as thoroughly as the Tribune Group had ever done.'

In 1975 the hard work of Mabon's team paid off and Mikardo was ousted as PLP chairman by the loyalist ex-Minister Cledwyn Hughes. With the resignation of Wilson as Labour leader in April 1976, Mabon was a key player in the leadership campaign teams first of Roy Jenkins and then, after Jenkins' withdrawal from the race, of the victor, Jim Callaghan. Callaghan valued his ministerial ability and in reconstructing his government decided that Energy Secretary Tony Benn could be less dangerous in Cabinet than on the backbenches so long as someone like Dick Mabon was actually running the department. Mabon therefore served as Minister of State for Energy from 1976 until 1979, joining the Privy Council in January 1977. As a Scot, Callaghan thought him particularly well-suited to handle North Sea oil.

Though Benn and Mabon got on well personally, Benn's flirtation with the militant Marxist left was for Mabon a cause for deep concern. As Benn's diary of 21 February 1977 records: 'Dick, whom I like personally very much, was talking about the "legitimate left", and I said, "Am I a member of the legitimate left?"' "Oh yes, but the legitimate left has got to be careful it doesn't pave the way for others to come in." So I said, "Well, if I am the legitimate left I regard you as the authentic right".'

From 1974 to 1976, Mabon combined his role as Manifesto Group Chair with the chairmanship of the Labour Committee for Europe. A longstanding pro-European, he would almost certainly have joined the Cabinet had he not resigned as deputy Shadow Scottish Secretary over Labour's policy U-turn over Europe in 1972. During the 1975 EEC referendum campaign Mabon chaired Scotland in Europe and was, with Lord Houghton and Bill Rodgers, one of the three most senior Labour figures on the Britain in Europe campaign Executive. He was Chairman of the European Movement 1975–76 and Deputy Chairman 1979–83. From 1970 to 1972 and 1974 to 1976 he was a member of the WEU Assembly and the Council of Europe.

Mabon was also the most senior figure amongst Scottish Labour Parliamentarians of the 1960s and 70s actually to believe in Scottish devolution. This put him at odds with Wilson's long-serving Scottish Secretary Willie Ross, under whom he worked as Under-Secretary of State (1964–67) and Minister of State (1967–70), serving enthusiastically on Dick Crossman's devolution committee. Unlike his friends Donald Dewar and John P Mackintosh, however, Mabon had far too great a base amongst Scottish MPs for Ross to be able to block his promotion, a point made all too apparent to Ross by Mabon's election as Chair of the Scottish PLP (1972–73 and 1975–76).

In Opposition from 1955 to 1964 he had been a political columnist for the *Daily Record* and from 1958 to 1964 was a Visiting Physician at London's Manor House hospital. In February 1963 Shadow Foreign Secretary Patrick Gordon Walker asked him to be his PPS. Opposition in 1979, however, brought bad tidings: he was now a senior ex-Minister without an apparent role. Most of the new intake were of the left, depleting the Manifesto Group, now led by Mabon's friends George Robertson and Giles Radice, relative to the Tribune Group. Mabon, now a backbencher, set to work organising for Denis Healey's leadership bid but, like his own candidacy for the Vice-Chair of the Scottish PLP, the new Parliamentary arithmetic meant it was doomed. With Labour's constitutional changes agreed in 1980 and the departure of many Manifesto stalwarts to the SDP in early 1981 appearing to enshrine the dominance of the hard left, Mabon feared that Labour was condemned to become an unelectable Marxist party. The narrowness of Healey's defence of the Deputy Leadership against Benn at the September 1981 conference and the votes for EEC withdrawal and unilateral disarmament appeared to confirm this, as did the impotence of the loyalist right to do anything about it. Having persuaded his old PPS, veteran Glasgow MP Jimmy White, to stay put, Mabon joined the SDP in October 1981, becoming spokesman on Scotland and Energy and a member of the National Committee (1984–88).

The local Liberals were deeply antagonistic, however, to their old adversary and insisted on opposing him at the next election despite all the pleas of David Steel. With the boundaries of his Greenock & Port Glasgow seat being redrawn, he therefore decided to contest Renfrew West & Inverclyde and became one of only a handful of former Labour MPs nearly to hold their seats for the SDP at the 1983 election. Most came third. Although he unsuccessfully contested Lothians at the 1984 European election and Renfrew West again in 1987, he concentrated primarily on business work with the North Sea oil industry.

With Kinnock's decision to initiate the policy review of the late 1980s, Mabon's old friends Smith, Dewar and Jack Cunningham persuaded him that Labour was re-embracing a social-democratic approach, and he rejoined in 1990. Blair's success in reforming Clause 4 and modernising the Party was, to Mabon, the realisation of what Gaitskell had tried and failed to do. Campaigning in both London and Scotland for the 1992 and 1997 elections, at the initiative of Jack Cunningham he also undertook a review of Labour's energy policy in the mid-1990s under the auspices of the Labour Finance and Industry Group. He married Elizabeth Zinn in 1970. They have one son.

Greg Rosen

Gus MacDonald (Lord MacDonald of Tradeston)   (1940–)

Gus MacDonald's is a classic rags-to-riches story. He is a former Glasgow shipyard worker who rose to the Board of the Bank of Scotland and became a peer of the realm, via media presentation and management. Angus John (Gus) MacDonald was born on 20 August 1940, the son of Colin and Jean MacDonald, and initially educated at Scotland Street School, Glasgow. Brains were evident early when Gus won a scholarship to the selective Alan Glen's School, but he left to work on the Clyde in 1955. Early experience in trade unionism proved a good grounding for future negotiating skills and gave him an appetite for campaigning, as well as a desire to move on to better things. In 1963 he married Alice McQuaid, with whom he has two daughters, and moved to London to work for Michael Foot. His task on *Tribune* was boosting the circulation of the newspaper in 1964 when Harold Wilson won his first term of office for the Labour Government. Gus was an early supporter of black rights in South Africa, creating *Anti-Apartheid News* which for three decades was the voice of the anti-apartheid movement. One of the first writers Gus recruited was the legendary James Cameron. From Cameron, he learned the importance of clear thought and concise, forceful expression, and joined the *Sunday Times's* 'Insight' team under Harold Evans. The following year Gus returned north to the *Scotsman* where he honed his journalistic skills as a feature writer, then business editor from 1965 to 1967.

It was his eight-year stint at *World in Action* that allowed him to make his mark as a hard-hitting investigative journalist. As presenter of *Right to Reply* he honed his skills as a no-nonsense interviewer and viewers' champion. In 1975 he became head of current affairs at Granada and a decade later moved back to Scotland. As director of programmes for STV, then managing director, he gained a reputation as an axeman, but even his critics tempered this by the recognition of his talents, and the talent he recognised in others, like Carol Smillie and Kirsty Young whose TV careers he helped launch and who went on to become multi-million-pound presenters with UK TV companies.

Gus Macdonald is a deal-maker extraordinaire. When Margaret Thatcher auctioned Scottish Television, he bought it for £2,000 – having first spent massively securing contracts with almost every independent producer in Scotland. He bought the *Glasgow Herald* newspaper and merged STV with Grampian to create Scotland's biggest media company, overcoming any opposition to such a concentration of media ownership. His company is worth £500 million. His peers voted him Corporate Leader of the Year in 1997 and he received the CBE in the same year. Self-taught, with an awesome appetite for books, he founded the Edinburgh Television Festival and is a double BAFTA winner – for investigative programmes and for a life-times achievement.

In 1998, the call came from Prime Minister Tony Blair offering him a job as Scottish Industry Minister and the peerage necessary to perform this role. As a multi-millionaire, he needed neither a ministerial salary nor a car, but he did have to divest himself of any financial involvement with his Scottish Media Group. For Labour in Scotland, this was a great appointment, giving the Government heavyweight credibility with a still sceptical and conservative business community. In 1999 Gus became Transport Minister with a non-voting place at the Cabinet table. Privatisation had brought chaos to the maintenance of the railways, and 2000 was the system's worst year in a generation. Such events have destroyed political careers, but Gus ensured that the Railtrack owners set about the job of renewing the lines and making the system safe. He set tough deadlines and accepted no excuses. By 2001 he was being talked about as Tony Blair's Lord Young – Margaret Thatcher's Cabinet Minister running trade and industry – and his post-election reshuffle appointment as Cabinet Office Minister should give him ample opportunity to display his ability.

Nigel Griffiths MP

Ramsay MacDonald (1866–1937)

A J P Taylor once wrote that 'MacDonald, was a pathetic, almost tragic figure. Yet it is difficult to feel sorry for him. He was the architect of his own downfall.' There is, indeed, some truth in this statement, although the economic circumstances of the early 1930s had more to do with his fate than Taylor admits. Nevertheless, no twentieth-century British political leader has been more reviled than Ramsay MacDonald. His decision to offer the resignation of the second Labour government and to accept the King's Commission to form a National Government during the financial crisis of August 1931 provoked much animus amongst his former supporters and sustained the view that he had planned to ditch the second Labour government all along. It was for a long time an axiom that his actions in 1931 marked him as a traitor, and William Lawther remarked that MacDonald was 'bereft of any public decency'. To many Labour activists, the man who helped form the Labour Party had helped to undermine it.

(James) Ramsay MacDonald was born in Lossiemouth in Scotland on 12 October 1866, the illegitimate son of Anne Ramsay and, possibly, John MacDonald, a ploughman. He was educated at a local school and expected to become a teacher but, in 1880, took up various clerical posts in Bristol and London. He acquired wide political experience in the late 1880s, joining the Social Democratic Federation whilst in Bristol, working for Thomas Lough, a Liberal Radical MP, and in socialist circles. He had ambitions of becoming a Liberal MP but his candidature for Southampton was thwarted in 1894 and he turned instead to the Independent Labour Party (ILP), the first major socialist party to be committed to electoral politics, in July 1894, becoming the ILP and Labour Electoral Association candidate in Southampton in 1894, on whose behalf he was thoroughly trounced in the 1895 General Election.

During the early 1890s MacDonald joined the Fabian Society, a body of largely middle-class socialists committed to gradual social change through parliamentary and municipal politics. He acted as a Fabian lecturer in 1892, touring South Wales, the Midlands and the North East. In 1896 and 1897 he was also a member of the Rainbow Circle, which first met in the Rainbow Tavern, Fleet Street, London, and brought together some collectivist Liberals, such as Herbert Samuel, who believed that the old Liberal Party was about to disintegrate. The group published papers and, briefly, the *Progressive Review,* in the hope of encouraging the formation of a new centre party in British politics. MacDonald's own hope was that a centre party with socialist ideas would emerge. This desire, as well as his interest in foreign policy, were two abiding passions which MacDonald pursued throughout his political career.

MacDonald married Margaret Gladstone in November 1896 and this provided him with the financial security he needed to develop his political career, since Margaret brought with her a settlement of up to £300 per year. The couple moved to 3 Lincoln's Inn Fields, London, which was later to be a base for the Labour Representation Committee, an alliance of socialists and trade unionists which was later renamed the Labour Party, in its formative years. Margaret, who died on 8 September 1911, bore MacDonald six children, one of whom, Malcolm (born in 1901), followed Ramsay into politics.

MacDonald's career began to blossom in the 1890s. He joined the Executive Committee of the Fabian Society in 1894 and sat on the National Administrative Council of the ILP in 1896. He remained a prominent member of the ILP until the First World War, often acting as chairman or secretary. Thereafter he drifted away from the ILP, although he did not formally resign until May 1930. His contribution to the ILP would fill most lifetimes, but his real claim to fame arose from the fact that he was largely responsible for the early development of the Labour Party.

The Labour Representation Committee was formed in February 1900 and formally changed its name to the Labour Party at the beginning of 1906. MacDonald was its secretary from 1900 to 1912, its treasurer in 1911 and 1912, and chairman of the Parliamentary Labour Party from 1911 to 1914. From the start he was committed to winning trade-union support for the embryonic organisation, and was helped in this respect by the attack upon trade union funds by the Taff Vale judgement of 1901. Yet such support only emerged slowly and, with only four MPs in 1903, MacDonald embarked upon a series of eight secret meetings with Jesse Herbert, confidential secretary to Herbert Gladstone, the Liberal Chief Whip, to arrange the infamous 'Lib-Lab' pact of 1903. This allowed the Labour Party candidates a straight run against the Conservatives in about thirty Parliamentary seats in return for a similar arrangement for the Liberals. In the 1906 general election only five of the twenty-nine successful LRC candidates faced Liberal opposition, and the arrangement had worked for Labour.

The general election result was a personal triumph for MacDonald who was able to run a party which now had its own Parliamentary Party, initially led by James Keir Hardie. MacDonald also helped to direct the Party in a gradualist, and eventually socialist, direction by creating a Socialist Library to which he contributed his own books, such as *Socialism and Society* (1905) and *Socialism and Government* (1909). The dominating theme of his work was that a form of social Darwinism ensured that private organisations would get bigger, the state would have to intervene, and that socialism would emerge from the success, not the failure, of capitalism. Because of the influence of MacDonald and the Webbs during the First World War, these essentially Fabian views became the defining influence in the socialism the Labour Party espoused after 1918.

From 1906 to 1918, MacDonald was MP for Leicester, sometimes secretary of the Labour Party and, for four years, chairman of the Parliamentary Party (PLP). However, he was strongly criticised for helping lead the Party and the PLP into alliance with the Liberal Party. Nonetheless, his reputation for radicalism was restored, briefly (though it allowed him to win the post of Labour Leader in 1922), by his opposition to Britain's involvement in the First World War. This resulted in venomous attacks upon him by the press. The most notable instance of this hostility was the occasion when Horatio Bottomley, editor of *John Bull,* published MacDonald's birth certificate and revealed that he was illegitimate, registered as James MacDonald Ramsay after his father. Bottomley further suggested that MacDonald was both an impostor and a traitor, and should be taken to the Tower of London and shot at dawn.

This and similar hostility to MacDonald's wartime position led to the loss of his Parliamentary seat at Leicester in the 1918 general election and to him losing a by-election in a Labour seat in 1921.

In the immediate post-war years, relieved of his Parliamentary duties, MacDonald concentrated his efforts upon building up the Labour Party. Nevertheless he was returned as Labour MP for Aberavon in 1922 and shortly afterwards became Leader of the Parliamentary Labour Party, largely as a result of the support of Independent Labour Party MPs who, influenced by the dominant group from Clydeside, voted almost to a man for MacDonald in the leadership contest. After Stanley Baldwin failed to win support for his protectionist measures in the 1923 general election, after some delay MacDonald was invited to form the first Labour Government at the beginning of 1924. This was a minority government and lasted little more than ten months. MacDonald was both Prime Minister and Foreign Secretary, becoming the first Prime Minister to assume that dual role since Robert Cecil, the third Marquess of Salisbury. The defeat of the first Labour government at the general election of 1924 occurred in the climate of the infamous 'Zinoviev Letter', or the 'Red Letter Scare', which suggested that the Soviet Union was intending to use the Labour Party in its revolutionary objectives. Whether this letter was real or a fake, it seems to have made only a small difference to a Party which seemed certain to be, and was, defeated.

During the next five years MacDonald led a Labour Party to which he was increasingly becoming a stranger. Yet in the May 1929 general election, MacDonald was returned for the parliamentary seat of Seaham, having left his less safe Aberavon seat, and, at the head of the largest party, formed his second, minority, Labour government. Unfortunately within six months of its return the Wall Street Crash had occurred and, as a result of the world recession, unemployment rose from about one million to three millions in less than two years. The Labour Government grossly overspent its budget and faced a financial crisis in August 1931. The Cabinet attempted to find the spending cuts demanded by the opposition parties but split over the decision to cut unemployment benefit by 10 per cent. MacDonald offered the resignation of his government to King George V but returned with a mandate to form a National Government, which was to include both the Conservative and the Liberal parties as well as any National Labour support he could muster.

These actions led L MacNeill Weir to produce his book *The Tragedy of Ramsay MacDonald* (1938), which suggested that MacDonald was never a socialist, but an opportunist who had schemed to ditch the Labour government, and was guilty of betrayal. However, David Marquand has suggested that such accusations are, at best, half-truths. Indeed, he argues that MacDonald was probably as good a socialist as any other leading figure in the Labour Party and that he was a principled opportunist (he gave up the Labour leadership to oppose the First World War), who did not scheme to replace the Labour government with a coalition but may nonetheless have been guilty of betraying his former Labour supporters.

MacDonald was Prime Minister of the National Government, which won a landslide victory at the 1931 general election, between 1931 and 1935. During this period his premiership depended upon the support of the Conservative Party, which encouraged moves towards protectionism. Apart from being Prime Minister, MacDonald indulged himself in foreign policy and was deeply involved in two conferences in 1932 – the Geneva Disarmament Conference and the Lausanne Conference, which was concerned with German reparations. Thereafter, his career declined and he found himself attacked by both his former colleagues, such as Philip Snowden, and his new political friends. He went into physical and mental decline and was forced to, resign as Prime Minister on 7 June 1935. Subsequently, he lost his seat at the 1935 general election to, Emmanuel Shinwell, who had put him forward as Parliamentary Labour Party leader in 1922. MacDonald was found a seat for the Scottish Universities but thereafter played a diminishing role in the activities of the National Government. MacDonald died of heart failure on 9 November 1937 while cruising in the Caribbean on the *Reina Pacifico*. His body was returned to Britain and cremated on 26 November 1937. His ashes were interred in the Spynie graveyard, near Lossiemouth, next to those of his wife.

A J P Taylor was, perhaps, rather harsh in his assessment of MacDonald's failures. MacDonald was certainly a tragic figure, but he was not entirely the architect of his own downfall for the economic conditions of 1929 to 1931 and the divisions within the Labour Party also helped to determine the events of 1931. It must also be remembered that whilst he is seen as a traitor within the Labour Party he did much to build up the Labour Party into the second party of government between 1900 and 1931. Not surprisingly Chris Wrigley concludes that MacDonald remains a mixture of saint and sinner in Labour history. The key biography on MacDonald is David Marquand, *Ramsay MacDonald* (1977). In addition Chris Wrigley has written an excellent short chapter, 'James Ramsay MacDonald, 1922–1931', in Kevin Jefferys (ed.), *Leading Labour: From Keir Hardie to Tony Blair* (1999).

Professor Keith Laybourn

John P. Mackintosh (1929–78)

The failure of social-democratic thinkers to produce a worthy sequel to Crosland's *Future of Socialism* owes much to the premature death of John Pitcairn Mackintosh, whose thinking in many respects foreshadowed much of 'New' Labour. As MP for Berwick and East Lothian from 1966 (with a brief break between temporary defeat in February 1974 and re-election in October of that year) until his death of a heart tumour on 30 July 1978, Mackintosh shone out as one of the brightest stars in the political firmament. Reputedly with Enoch Powell and Brian Walden one of the three most commanding backbench orators of his era, he was a perceptive analytical thinker and a compelling polemicist. His pro-European speeches at the great Labour EEC Special Conferences of 1971 and 1975 were 'unscrupulously brilliant' even by the standards of that great anti-Marketeer Barbara Castle. A leading light in the loyalist Manifesto Group of Labour backbenchers, whose call to arms, a 1977 pamphlet entitled *What We Must Do*, he co-wrote, he was much in demand as a platform speaker by its grassroots campaigning wing, the Campaign for Labour Victory.

A steadfast opponent of Labour's fundamentalist left, he also sought to modernise the Croslandite social democracy of the right. Although he was to die before he could produce a systematic synthesis of his ideas in book form, his critiques of revisionism were as incisive as they were wide-ranging. He had yet to formulate all the answers, but he nevertheless asked the questions. His article 'Has Social Democracy failed in Britain?', published in the *Political Quarterly* of July 1978, expounded a persistent theme in Mackintosh's thought: that Crosland's position was fundamentally flawed by the absence of any rationale for the existence of a thriving private sector within the mixed economy it professed to advocate. Writing in the *Scotsman* of 10 April 1978, he attacked the 'basic error' of Croslandism in talking 'endlessly about the distribution of wealth, its taxation and use for this and that but very little about the creation of wealth... the central task of justifying and producing a thriving mixed economy remains.' His pamphlet *Change Gear! Towards a Socialist Strategy*, published on the eve of the October 1967 Labour Conference and co-written with two other Young Turks of the 1966 intake, David Marquand and David Owen, called for some measures – such as the creation of the DHSS, wider legislative safeguards against racism and the establishment of Parliamentary select committees – that the Wilson governments were to implement or pilot. Thirty years on, devolution, a minimum wage, the establishment of 'educational priority areas', road pricing and welfare reform are key planks of the Blair/Brown agenda.

Mackintosh's causes and polemics ranged widely. He championed electoral and Parliamentary reform including the creation of the Select Committee system, the reform of Scotland's arcane Calvinist licensing laws, and the importance of improving standards in schools, which he believed to have been undermined by the abandonment of setting in classes according to ability. The crusade for which he is most remembered today is undoubtedly the cause of devolution and the restoration of a Scottish Parliament. His formulation of the intellectual case for devolution even now, some thirty years after the publication of his seminal Penguin Special *The Devolution of Power: Local Autonomy, Regionalism and Nationalism* in 1968, underpins Labour's creation of the Scottish Parliament and the Welsh Assembly. As Gordon Brown told the author, it was Mackintosh who kept the flame of Labour's commitment to devolution alive during the lean years of Willie Ross's dour stewardship of the Scottish Office. In his lifetime, Mackintosh, through his friend Dick Crossman, helped secure the creation of first a Cabinet Committee on devolution and then the Kilbrandon Commission which backed devolution in the early 1970s and helped secure Labour's reversion to the pro-devolution stance of the days of Keir Hardie and Tom Johnston. Furthermore, it was the people Mackintosh inspired, like Helen Liddell and George Foulkes, who post-1997 were to put the ideas he espoused into practice. Indeed, Liddell, Foulkes and Jim Sillars had co-starred with Mackintosh in a party election broadcast of October 1974 which, on the basis of Mackintosh's scripting, committed Labour to giving a Scottish Assembly economic development powers ('Powerhouse Scotland', as it was dubbed) far in excess of what his great enemy, Scottish Secretary Willie Ross, had anticipated.

The antipathy of Willie Ross and the distrust of Harold Wilson and the Whips Office goes a long way to explaining why such a talented and energetic MP as Mackintosh never secured office. Ross saw Mackintosh's kamikaze commitment to devolution as a personal challenge to his authority over the Scottish Labour Party and Mackintosh's acerbic wit, talent for mimicry and sense of mischief went down badly with a Whips Office suspicious of 'intellectuals' at the best of times. Mackintosh seemed un-whippable, and sometimes, such as his rebellion with Brian Walden over the Dock Work Labour Scheme of 1976, he was. Mackintosh's persistence in raising the 'great unmentionable' of the late 1960s, devaluation, and in plotting the overthrow of Harold Wilson did not endear him to Numbers 10 or 12

Downing Street. Despite the friendship of Roy Jenkins, whose leadership candidature he promoted more relentlessly than even the candidate did himself, Mackintosh was never part of the Oxford/Hampstead set or the 1963 Club or XYZ Club groupings of Gaitskellite intellectuals who largely lived in London. His base was in Scotland, where he was an assiduous and intensely popular constituency MP.

For Mackintosh, given that the civil service bureaucracy that ran Scotland had already been devolved to St Andrews House in Edinburgh, 'the case for devolution is the case for democratic control of the machine'. The infamous West Lothian question, posed by his friend Tam Dalyell, Mackintosh showed to be underpinned by a 'complete myth about Parliament'. Writing in the *Political Quarterly* of April 1978 he said: 'The House of Commons does not sit down and make or devise educational policy for Bedford or for Liverpool. Policy is made by the government and the point of having MPs is to determine which party forms the government. Once this happens 99% of the legislation is passed. The case that it is intolerable to have Scots MPs helping to decide which Party is to form the Government is a case against the continuation of the UK.' Such was his public stature, Tam Dalyell and many others remain convinced that, had Mackintosh lived, the 1979 devolution referendum would have led to the creation of a Scottish Assembly.

Mackintosh explained the rise of the SNP in the late 1960s and early 1970s in terms of a dual Scottish-British consciousness: 'With a dual identity, there is a simple alternative; if the pride in being British wanes, just be Scottish.' The argument continues to underpin the Scottish Labour Party's belief that the Scottish people want a parliament but not independence, regarding themselves as both Scottish and British, and indeed also European. Mackintosh believed that only a period of successful Westminster government, rebuilding pride in Britain, could reverse the march of the SNP, a prescription, as New Labour strategist and MP Douglas Alexander wrote in the *Scotsman* of 17 August 1998, 'that holds true today'.

Such was his seemingly boundless energy that in 1978 alone, despite suspect health, he combined his duties as MP with those of Professor of Politics and Head of Department at Edinburgh University, co-editor of the *Political Quarterly*, fortnightly columnist in the *Scotsman* and regular columnist in *The Times*. He was also serving on the steering committees of the Labour Committee for Europe and the Anglo-German Koenigswinter Conference. For his Professorship, which he began in the autumn of 1977, he took on teaching the whole first year, a task that involved writing and delivering a course of seventy-five lectures from scratch. He contributed a prodigious stream of articles to journals ranging from *Socialist Commentary* through *Encounter* to *The Listener,* and was a regular broadcaster. His books included the groundbreaking analysis of post-Bagehot 'prime-ministerial' government, *The British Cabinet* (1962); one of the most lucid textbooks on British politics of the postwar period, *The Government and Politics of Britain* (1970); *Nigerian Government and Politics* (1966); and a two-volume collection of essays, *The British Prime Ministers* (1977).

Born in Simla on 24 August 1929, the eldest son of Colin Mackintosh, a cotton piece goods sales rep, and Mary Victoria Pitcairn, a teacher-training college teacher, it was only with the outbreak of war that his family returned to Edinburgh. After Melville College he secured a First in History from Edinburgh University in 1950 before graduating additionally in PPE from Balliol, Oxford, in 1952. Active in Labour politics at Edinburgh (in 1948 as Secretary of the Labour Club he had helped found the National Association of Labour Students' Organisations), he found the disdain with which many of his Balliol colleagues treated his Scots academic qualifications a source of great frustration and was glad to return after postgraduate work at Princeton 1952–53. After a year as a junior history lecturer at Glasgow University and seven as a lecturer at Edinburgh, where in 1957 he married one of his students, Janette Robertson, he took up a professorial post at Ibadan University in Nigeria. This meant abandoning the opportunity to be Labour's candidate in the 1960 Paisley by-election, for which, after his performance as the unsuccessful Labour candidate at Edinburgh Pentlands in 1959, he had the backing of STUC General Secretary George Middleton. He returned to a Senior Lecturership in Politics at Glasgow University in 1963, also in that year leaving his wife, son and daughter for Catherine Margaret Una Maclean, a lecturer in social medicine, with whom after remarriage he had a further son and daughter. He unsuccessfully fought Berwick & East Lothian at the 1964 election. In 1965–66 he was the first Professor of Politics at the University of Strathclyde, being forced to give up his academic work on his election to Parliament at the 1966 general election. Two posthumous collections of his essays were published in 1982 under the general editorship of Bernard Crick: *John P. Mackintosh on Parliament and Social Democracy*, edited by David Marquand, *and John P. Mackintosh on Scotland*, edited by Henry Drucker. 'John P. Mackintosh: His Achievements and Legacy,' by Greg Rosen was published in the *Political Quarterly* of April-June 1999.

Greg Rosen

John Mann and Phil Woolas   (1963– and 1959–)

In June 2001, immediately after Labour's epic victory at the polls, the new MP for Bassetlaw made his way to the green benches of the House of Commons. He recognised his old friend, Phil Woolas, the MP for Oldham East and Saddleworth since 1997, and sat beside him. Recognising Greg Pope, Caroline Flint and others, John remarked: 'This place looks like the National Union of Students Conference of 1984!'. Woolas, glancing opposite to the threadbare Conservative benches, replied: 'That's Paul Goodman – he's the Tory we put on the NUS Executive!'

John Mann and Phil Woolas met in October 1978. They lived on the same corridor in a Hall of Residence at Manchester University. Mann was born and bred in the Leeds Labour Party, where his father was a major figure; his family had helped to establish it at the turn of the century. Born on 10 January 1963, Mann attended Bradford Grammar School. Woolas was born on 11 December 1959, 30 miles across the Pennines in Burnley, East Lancashire, attending Nelson Grammar School. Both had been members of the Labour Party since their mid-teens but it was something much more important that brought them together – John was organising a football team and Phil was anxious to add his silky skills to the squad! As an avid supporter of Leeds United, Mann was naturally hesitant in allowing Woolas, a Manchester United fan, into his team.

Within a few years, Mann and Woolas were the leading figures in the student movement and sitting down with Neil Kinnock to discuss how to wrestle control of the Labour Party youth organisations back from the Militant Tendency. Their contribution to Labour is not that they are now Labour MPs. It is because Mann and Woolas were the leaders of a new generation in the Labour Party in the 1980s. They played a critical role in the Kinnock modernisation of the Labour Party and in so doing helped Labour in its long march back to electability.

At Manchester University, their first task was to take control of the University Labour Club which, like the National Organisation of Labour Students (NOLS) at the time, was dominated by Militant. By 1980, teaming up with a future Labour Assistant General Secretary David Gardiner, they had recruited over 1,000 members – nearly one tenth of the University. Mann and Woolas then turned their attention to taking control of the Students' Union – then dominated by Conservatives – which was achieved when Woolas was elected President in 1981.

Woolas and Mann used their power base at Manchester to lead a growing army of NOLS moderates in the pro-Kinnock Clause IV group. By 1984, with the election of Woolas as National President, NOLS managed to take control of NUS from the Left Alliance (an amalgamation of Liberals and Communists). At the same time, Mann was elected NOLS Chair, beating a candidate from the Militant Tendency.

Mann and Woolas' number one objective was to defeat the factionalism that was ripping the Labour Party apart. As Woolas says today: 'I believe the path back from oblivion for the Labour Party started in the redbrick universities in the late seventies and early eighties. Many of the people who shaped what became New Labour had their political roots as the sons and daughters of working-class people who had been the first in their families to go to university. In fact, the phrase "Third way" was first used in university Labour clubs. Clause IV was the vehicle that was used to defeat Militant and the Bennites. Our enemy was factionalism, and to defeat it we organised the hardest, most ruthless faction of them all'.

Key to their contribution was that both knew that they must, in Mann's own words, 'kill dead' the SDP in the universities. In the NUS, the SDP refused to join the Left Alliance. After taking the NUS presidency from the Left Alliance, Woolas and Mann knew that they must keep the Left Alliance in existence and thereby split the Liberals from the SDP – much to the annoyance of David Steel, David Owen and the leader of the SDP students in Scotland, Charles Kennedy. Labour knew that the universities were potentially a very dangerous recruiting ground for the SDP. Kennedy emerged, but without the policy of crushing the SDP, there would have been many more like him.

In the wider Party, Kinnock encouraged Mann and Woolas to smash Militant. Together they wrote an influential pamphlet published by the Fabian Society on the way forward for the Party's youth structure. This led in turn to the so-called 'Sawyer Proposals', the starting point in taking out Militant in the Labour Party Young Socialists (LPYS). As Woolas states: 'We backed Kinnock when he was education spokesman. He had used the universities, and the Labour Students, as his base. Kinnock then backed us – very strongly'.

In 1983, after he had been elected Leader of the Party, Kinnock summoned Woolas and Mann to a meeting in his office with Charles Clarke. As well as backing them in the crusade to defeat Militant, he asked the two young student leaders if they wanted any help from the Leader's Office. They asked for help in exposing the Conservative Students as being right-wing extremists who had, amongst other things, called for heroin to be sold on the free market and for Nelson Mandela to be hanged as a terrorist. Kinnock suggested they organise parliamentary questions as part of their campaign and offered them the services of one Tony Blair. 'He's come in the new wave after the election,' said Kinnock. 'But he's very good!'

Mann argues that their approach worked because they believed in the Labour Party having the broadest possible appeal, attracting support from people who had never supported Labour before. Mann, a fierce champion of the politics of organisation, attributes Woolas as being key to the strategy of wide appeal. Apart from his natural northern charisma, Mann has said: 'Phil's great strength was in popular appeal. He had the ability to always know where that was'. Arguably what Mann contributed, apart from being the finest speaker of his generation, was to do what all great politicians must do; namely be prepared to be unpopular but right. In the end the partnership worked.

Both remained totally committed to the Labour Party and never considered joining any other party. 'We wanted to save ours', says Woolas. Key to this was the uniting of the soft left and the old right behind the leadership of Neil Kinnock. Mann wrote to the *Guardian* the day after Labour's massive election defeat in 1983 saying: 'The Left that listens is the Left that wins'. He called on the Party to build broad appeal, but to do this through the Party.

Mann and Woolas wanted Labour to become the natural party of government. But key to this was that they were not prepared to take short cuts with coalitions with other parties. They had the faith to know that everything could be achieved through the Party and that the Party could eventually win outright. There are obvious lessons in this for Labour's ultra-modernisers and those who believe that PR and Lib/Lab coalitions are the only salvation for a 'progressive century'.

After student politics, Mann and Woolas eventually went to work for the trade unions, and it has become a well-trodden path for working-class university graduates to go into the manual unions as full-time operators. Both believed passionately in the importance of Labour's link with the trade unions. They understood that the link not only serves to keep Labour relevant and in touch with working people, but that the unions had a key role in modernising the Labour Party and making it electable.

In 1985, Mann went to work for the AEU, the forerunner of the AEEU, and eventually became Head of Research. After a stint at the TUC – which saw him establish the European College – Mann was appointed as the National Trade Union Liaison Officer for the Labour Party in 1995, earning a reputation as the Party's fixer and bag man for the unions. His selection as Labour candidate for the safe Labour seat of Bassetlaw in 2000 came after a stint as a Labour candidate in the European elections in 1999.

After working as a researcher and producer for TVS, the BBC and ITN, Woolas served as Director of Communications for the GMB from 1991 to 1997, famously running the successful 'fat cats' campaign. Woolas was also the Labour candidate in the 1995 Littleborough and Saddleworth by-election and, following boundary changes, he eventually beat his Liberal Democrat opponent, Chris Davies, in the 1997 general election. He held the seat in the 2001 general election.

Today Phil Woolas and John Mann remain close friends and allies. Woolas, having served as PPS to Transport Minister Lord MacDonald from 1999 to 2001, was appointed a Government Whip. Mann is already making his mark as a new MP, frequently asking questions and making contributions on the floor of the House of Commons. Their contribution in the 1980s, in ridding the Labour Party youth and student organisations of the Militant Tendency, means that their place in Labour history is assured. It remains to be seen what part they will play as MPs or Ministers in Labour's future.

Michael Dugher

Tom Mann   (1856–1941)

The term pioneer is often used, but in Tom Mann's case the number of times the word 'first' appears in his biography is a measure of just how much he pioneered many aspects of the labour movement. He was acknowledged as one of the most talented organisers, agitators and speakers of the early British labour leaders. A founder of the Independent Labour Party that went on to be one of the original socialist societies involved in the formation of the Labour Party, he subsequently took up syndicalism and turned to the support of communism. Throughout his life he retained a talent for being in the centre of action in many of the controversies of his time.

Born on 15 April 1856 at Foleshill in the mining district of Warwickshire, Thomas Mann worked on a farm from the age of 9 to 11 and then in the local pit from 11 to 14. His father was a clerk in the colliery, but when the family moved to Birmingham Tom completed a seven-year engineering apprenticeship. At the age of fifteen he started attending evening classes at a mechanics' institute. He educated himself through the public library and became deeply interested in the Christian religion, although never taking a fully orthodox approach in any sect. When he reached the age of 21 he moved to London as a journeyman engineer, joined the Amalgamated Society of Engineers in 1881 and immediately became interested in trade unionism and socialism. In 1885 he joined the most radical of Britain's leading socialist societies, Hyndman's Social Democratic Federation (SDF). His first key campaign was for shorter working hours, which exposed the limited understanding of working-class conditions amongst politicians of the day and helped highlight the need for the workers to organise their own party.

He will always be associated with the London dock strike of 1889, along with Ben Tillett and John Burns. He controlled the distribution of the strike funds, and shared out relief money. He was in the thick of the action, creating discipline, inspiring solidarity and acting as a model for the New Unionism that spread to the unskilled labourers when previously unions had only been for skilled craftsmen. Following his help in the London dock strike he became the first president of the Dockers' Union (1889–1893). He founded the International Federation of Ship, Dock and River Workers in 1896, and was the moving force behind the founding of the Workers' Union in 1898.

In 1891 Mann produced the pamphlet *The Eight Hour Day: How to Get It by Trade and Local Option*. He proposed the first May Day demonstration to the London Trades Council and sat on the Royal Commission on Labour from 1891 to 1894. Here he repeated calls for an eight-hour day and was one of the signatories of the minority report. At the end of the commission's work he allied with Keir Hardie and became the first Secretary of the Independent Labour Party (ILP) for three years. Always one to take a broad view, Mann often pressed for the various socialist societies to link together. Eleanor Marx described Mann as Keir Hardie's 'henchman', and the staunch but not entirely orthodox Christian beliefs of both were one of the factors that bound them together. Mann was accused of softness by Engels, but it was perhaps a softness that emanated from a toleration of the wide interpretations of socialism that contrasted with the confrontational factionalism that existed between many socialists of the different varieties that co-existed in these formative years.

1902 to 1910 were spent in New Zealand and Australia, organizing labour in a turbulent period of industrial unrest and suffering a spell in gaol as a result of a campaign for free speech. On returning to Europe he went to France to study syndicalism, an approach he supported for the rest of his life. When back in Britain, he worked to spread syndicalism, preaching workers' control. He directed the Liverpool dock strike to such effect that the government even sent gunboats to the Mersey. Throughout his active political life he was an important pamphleteer, author and journalist. He edited the *Industrial Syndicalist* and when he issued a 'don't shoot' appeal to the troops he ended up in prison again for incitement to mutiny. He was the dominant voice of British syndicalism in the pre-war years.

Mann joined the British Socialist Party in 1916, and when the Communist Party was formed after the Russian Revolution, Mann was one of the first members. In 1919 he was appointed general secretary of the Amalgamated Society of Engineers and then from 1920 to 1921 became the first general secretary of the new Amalgamated Engineering Union (AEU). Three years later during one of a number of trips to Moscow, he helped launch the Red International of Labour Unions. As chairman of the British section he launched the Minority Movement in 1924 that aimed to unite unions into one syndicate for each industry and win workers' control. The following year he was pressing for more thorough organisation for the impending General Strike, but it was an appeal that was ignored by most of the more moderate trade union leaders, with catastrophic results for any possibility of success for the strike. Although the TUC moved to the right following the failure of the General Strike, Mann did not lose faith in his syndicalist approach.

He journeyed to China in 1927 to meet leading members of the Communist Party. He also travelled to Canada, but was deported. When there were riots in Belfast in 1932 over the plight of the unemployed, two people died in clashes with the police. At the age of 76, Mann spoke at the funeral and was arrested for sedition and imprisoned again for three months. He faced a further sedition trial in Swansea in 1934, but this time he was acquitted. He was a member of the presidium of the British Communist Party throughout the thirties, and at the age of 82 he was in Sweden campaigning for the Swedish Communist Party in the elections. He suffered a seizure in November 1939 and after a long illness died on 13 March 1941.

Tom Mann is not easy to categorise. His biographer described him as 'union leader and official, organiser and agitator, free-lance lecturer, labour journalist and editor, political party office-holder, leader and candidate for Parliament' (White, J., (1991), *Tom Mann*, Lives of the Left Series, Manchester University Press, Manchester, p xii). He noted that although in each area he had his equals or even superiors, it was the ensemble of his talents that was unique. It was as a founding figure in the British labour movement and as an advocate of a politics of socialism from below that Mann was a leading personality in the labour movement for almost fifty years.

For a biography see Joseph White's *Tom Mann* (1991) and there is also *Tom Mann's Memoirs* first published in 1923, with a new edition containing a preface by Ken Coates (1967). For examples of his work, see *Tom Mann: Social and Economic Writings,* (1988), ed John Laurent.

Nick Cowell

Dick Marsh (Lord Marsh of Mannington)   (1928–)

Dick – no one ever called him Richard in his Labour Party days from 1942 until the 1970s – was, when I arrived at the House of Commons in 1962, one of four identifiable future Labour Prime Ministers; the other three at the time were Roy Mason, Gerry Reynolds, who died tragically young, and John Stonehouse, who came to grief. This note concentrates on his Labour Party days, rather than his high-powered business career after 1971 when he went, to borrow the title of his autobiography of 1978, *Off the Rails.*

Richard William Marsh was born on 14 March 1928 in Swindon; exactly a week previously his grandfather had been killed while working as a labourer on the Great Western Railway. During his time as a prominent Parliamentary Under-Secretary at the Ministry of Labour (1964–65), working to Ray Gunter, he elevated 'industrial safety' brilliantly into one of the causes of the Labour government, with its wafer-thin majority of three. His father William, a foundry worker, he describes in his autobiography as, 'a caricature of a gawd-bleeding-blimey cockney kid from South-East London.' By 1930 he had turned into an active, militant trade-unionist. He suffered a nasty bicycle accident with a motor-car, which resulted in his being off work, sacked by the GWR ('God's Wonderful Railway', as Marsh had it) and family poverty.

'We were poor. Unfortunately, my parents never had the foresight to deprive me of shoes,' Marsh wrote in his autobiography. This was a biting, sarcastic reference to Harold Wilson's pretence that he came from a poor background. My personal view is that one – perhaps the most important – reason why this exceedingly able, decisive man left Party, Parliament, and political future, was that he was chronically unable to conceal his contempt for his Prime Minister. He exasperated even Dick Crossman, whose PPS I was, by being cheeky and gratuitously rude about and to Wilson's face. In October 1969, Wilson merged Transport into the Department of the Environment, asking Marsh to remain in post but as Minister of State outside Cabinet. Marsh declined and, as he recorded in his autobiography, 'gained the distinction of becoming the youngest sacked Cabinet Minister this century.' Though Wilson re-appointed him Shadow Housing Minister in 1970, it was less than a year before in April 1971 he resigned his seat to become Chairman of the British Railways Board. 'I had ceased to be seriously interested in Parliamentary politics. I was finding the familiar procedures frustrating and the phoney Party battles boring… I had my own business interests in the morning …'

Having left Jennings School in Swindon aged 14 and moved to London with his parents, Marsh had joined Abbey Wood Ward of Erith Labour Party aged 16, founding Erith and then Dartford Young Socialists, and contested the safe Conservative seat of Hertford in the 1951 election. The Chairman of the Erith Labour Party was Charlie Pannell, later cockney AUEW member for West Leeds. Very often in the 1960s I would join them for lunch at a table in the Members Dining Room, with George Strauss, Bob Mellish, Douglas Houghton and others. Marsh with his sardonic wit sparkled.

He would recount killingly amusing episodes from his time at Woolwich Polytechnic, Ruskin College Oxford, his time as Health Services Officer at NUPE 1951–59, his membership of the Whitley Council 1953–59, and his election for Greenwich at the October 1959 election. In 1961 he was lucky to come up in the ballot for Private Members Bills and promote a much-needed Offices Act.

His main task on coming to office in 1964 was to pilot the Industrial Training Bill through the House of Commons and to dash round the country setting up Industrial Training Boards. But as a highly successful Under-Secretary he was plucked out in October 1965 to rescue the Prime Minister. Wilson had put C P Snow, the novelist, and Frank Cousins of the TGWU in charge of the Ministry of Technology, which was not only brand new but a monster organisation. Neither of them had any experience at all of Parliament. Marsh was added because it became obvious that there had to be, after Cousins' 'clangers', a Parliamentarian in the Ministry. Wilson intended the new Ministry to give effect to his speech at the 1963 Labour conference in Scarborough about the White Heat of the Technological Revolution. It had a remit to 'guide and stimulate a major national effort to bring advanced technology and new processes into British industry.'

As Marsh observed, in Whitehall even the sickliest-looking acorns soon grow into massive oak trees, meticulously following the principles laid down by Professor Parkinson, the Ministry could before long boast a staff of 38,000! But in spite of initial misgivings about himself from the Gaitskellite Right working with the tribune of the left, Marsh came to recognise Cousins' considerable character and judged him to be very much under-rated by the public.

Promoted to Cabinet and the Privy Council after the 1966 election, Marsh handled the nationalisation of steel and the decimation of the coal industry as Minister of Power. He became a *bête-noire* of the NUM. I think the truth is that Marsh just thought that the price of mining coal was often the price of emphysema or silicosis and too often the price of life itself – and if nuclear power made it unnecessary for men to risk health, life and limb down a pit, so be it. Credit accrued to him by overruling the Ministry and his Inspectorate of Mines and insisting on going straight to the site of the 1967 Aberfan disaster.

Marsh recounts how he became Transport Minister: Wilson 'indicated that he wanted Barbara Castle to move from the Ministry of Transport to the Ministry of Labour, and that he wanted me to take her position at Transport. I was flabbergasted. I had spent two years at the Ministry of Power and had only just reached the stage where I had developed good working relationships with the many diverse personalities with whom we were dealing. I was deeply involved in a number of major initiatives which were coming to fruition and I could not see the slightest reason why I should be shifted into a Ministry about which I knew nothing and cared less. Harold was obviously taken aback by my attitude. I asked him why I was being moved. "Well, quite apart from the fact that I need Barbara at the Ministry of Labour," he said, "we are moving towards a General Election and I think we need somebody at Transport who operates reasonably well on television." I replied with increasing irritation that I did not regard myself as an entertainer… He said with growing surprise that this was a promotion and then added the classic Wilsonian phrase, "I think, Dick, the captain of the team is entitled to place the field."'

Marsh was an astonishingly quick learner and soon became deeply interested in transport to which he was to contribute fresh thinking on rail, both as Minister and subsequently

Chairman of the British Railways Board (1971–76). My considered opinion is that if Dick Marsh had stayed in Parliament, the PLP would have preferred him to either Denis Healey or Michael Foot as Jim Callaghan's successor in 1979. Had he been chosen he would have patronised Mrs Thatcher as Leader of the Opposition, refused to endorse the Falklands expedition and become Prime Minister in 1984. He would have been an effective and probably a great occupant of 10 Downing Street. Knighted in 1976, he was created Lord Marsh of Mannington in 1981, sitting as a cross-bencher. An opponent of Common Market entry throughout his political career, he launched the Business For Sterling group in June 1998. His first marriage of 1950 to Evelyn Andrews, with whom he had two sons, was dissolved in 1973. His marriage to Caroline Dutton in 1973 ended tragically with her death in a car accident in 1975. He married Felicity MacFadzean in 1979.

Tam Dalyell MP

Willie Marshall (1906–94)

Willie Marshall is one of the unsung heroes of the Labour movement. As Secretary of the Labour Party in Scotland from 1951 until September 1971, not only did he mastermind victorious by-elections at Glasgow Kelvingrove (March 1958), Glasgow Bridgeton (November 1961), West Lothian (May 1962), Glasgow Woodside (November 1962), he also coordinated brilliant Labour campaigns in East Fife in 1961, when John Smith, later Party leader, was a student candidate in his early twenties, and in Perth & Kinross (November 1963), where the Conservative candidate, Alec Douglas-Home, happened also to be Prime Minister. The picture of Willie Marshall handling the entourage of the Westminster lobby correspondents and the national and international press corps on a golden autumn morning in Dunkeld will remain a delicious memory. He gave them an insight of how it was coming about that in Scotland, where in 1951 the Tories had a majority of seats, they were on their way to political extinction – a reality that came about in 1997, when not a single Conservative Westminster MP was returned. More than any other individual, Willie Marshall was responsible for the Scottish Westminster results being against the national trend in the 1950s and 1960s. Without the Scottish example of loyalty to Labour, there would surely not have been the way paved for Wilson's wafer-thin majority of 1964. Marshall was the architect.

Marshall was born in Lochore, Fife in 1906 and went to school in juxtaposed Ballingry. Aged fourteen, he left school on a Friday and was down the pit first shift on a Monday morning. As a teenager, his intelligence brought him to the notice of Willie Adamson, guiding light of the Fife miners in their struggles to create a union. Adamson as Ramsay MacDonald's Scottish Secretary became famed for his frequent response to Parliamentary questions of, 'I'll give that matter my due consideration.' Exasperated Tories asked, 'Cannot the Rt Hon. gentleman give an answer other than that he will give us his due consideration?' Memorably, Adamson would reply, 'I'll give that my due consideration too!' To my first-hand knowledge, Marshall would respond, 'Yes I'll give it due consideration.' And he did. He was a thoughtful, straight person, who not instantly, but reasonably promptly, would give a response. Along with Cllr Willie Ewing, Provost of Cowdenbeath, and Joe Westwood, Scottish Secretary 1945–47, he was the leader of the active Labour element in the Fife miners, where communists in the form of Alec Moffat and the young Michael McGahey held sway.

He married in 1926. Elected Fife's youngest-ever county councillor for Ballingry Central on 6 December 1938, he was active and influential before resigning as a councillor on 4 December 1946 on being appointed Assistant Secretary of the Labour Party in Scotland.

A Labour official of wit, laughter and considerable charm, Marshall was shrewd and abhorred the cheap. It was typical of Marshall that as Willie Hamilton's election agent in 1945 he ordered Hamilton not to attack the communist Willie Gallagher's patriotism, two Gallagher sons having been killed in the war. Hamilton never forgave Marshall, as he thought (probably wrongly) that given free rein, he would have won. Hypersensitive to working-class opinion, Marshall knew that personal attacks on Gallagher would be counter-productive. Years later, in 1958, Marshall was insistent that there should be no rudeness to the Conservative candidate in Kelvingrove, Kay, Lady Elliot of Harwood. 'You attack policies, not people,' he taught us – and among Marshall's MP 'pupils' were Bruce Millan, Dick Mabon, Judith Hart, John Smith, Neil Carmichael, Donald Dewar, Alec Eadie, Harry Ewing and myself. We owe him a debt of gratitude.

His friend, Bob Brown, the distinguished Scottish correspondent of the *Economist*, wrote in the *Glasgow Herald* of 1 April 1971 on the occasion of Marshall's last Scottish conference: 'The job (then as now) was less a five-day week than a forty-hour weekend. It fed on dedication and only latterly paid a salary ... The break with Fife began in wartime when he was carried home from the Mary pit, near to death after a roof fall. He recovered, joined the technical civil service and then enlisted as a political agent. Twenty-five years on, Marshall retains his miner's residual style; but tough as a brick, he can also compromise and wheel and deal in politically narrow places as the roof crumbles away. Naturally he has critics who complain how his political sap ran dry from too much machine-minding and arid organising. Perhaps that is true; he might admit himself to developing into the man in the grey flannel suit, to delivering the election goods, spinning the web, soothing the party's tantrums in dingy back-street halls, to waiting on lonely rail platforms, and riding home by late-night bus. But MPs and local councillors often believe their divine right is to treat party officers like dirt. Not all want to see big men grow bigger. Marshall's role in Scotland would have proved even more decisive had he seized or been ceded authority to operate primarily as Labour's political secretary – instead of as organiser, agent, lawyer and constitutionalist.'

As a postscript, on Labour's reelection in 1974, I (and I was by no means the only one) asked the all-powerful Scottish Secretary, Willie Ross, to find some post like Chairmanship of the Herring Board for Marshall: 'Mind your own business!' I was told. For 25 years, Willie Marshall vanished from the life of the Party he did so much to serve. He died in Glasgow in 1994.

Tam Dalyell MP

Roy Mason (Lord Mason of Barnsley) (1924–)

Roy Mason served continuously on Labour's front bench for over twenty years under Gaitskell, Wilson, Callaghan and Foot and remained throughout one of the most combative members of Labour's Old Right. Marcia Falkender, Harold Wilson's former Political Secretary, contended in her memoir of 1983, *Downing Street in Perspective*, that Wilson saw Mason as a potential Labour Party leader.

Born in a Barnsley pit village on 18 April 1924, at 14 Mason left Carlton and Royston Schools and followed his father Joseph down the mines. His mother died of cancer in 1944 shortly after she had nursed his father back to health after he had almost died in a mining accident. Mason married his teenage sweetheart Marjorie Sowden in 1945, with whom he has two daughters. Becoming active in the NUM, he was selected as Labour's prospective Parliamentary candidate for Tory-held Bridlington in 1952. Then an unexpected by-election in March 1953 made him Barnsley's MP aged only 28: 'My horizons were bounded by muckstacks which smoked and smouldered and cast a pall of dust and sulphurous filth over the brightest day ... I was sworn in as Member of Parliament in my best suit. In fact it was my only suit ... Dad stayed at home ... he didn't have the money for the fare from Barnsley and I was in no position to help.' Attlee gave him two pieces of advice, to stay out of the bars and to specialise, which Mason did, in defence and nuclear issues. An advocate of German rearmament as a bulwark against Soviet expansionism even before he entered Parliament he was staunchly pro-NATO and anti-unilateralist. 'After the Berlin blockade of 1949 and the savage suppression of the Hungarian uprising of 1956,' Mason wrote in his memoirs, 'nobody but a blinkered fool could possibly doubt the militaristic nature of Soviet Communism.'

From 1959 to 1964 he was an Opposition spokesman on the Post Office. In 1963 he helped campaign for George Brown as Gaitskell's successor and in 1964 was appointed Minister of State at the Board of Trade by the victor of that campaign, Harold Wilson. One of Mason's responsibilities was for shipping and shipbuilding, which he found in a poor state, as he recorded in his memoirs: 'The sheer backwardness of our operations: old-fashioned welding, old-fashioned riveting, men in flat caps which they doffed whenever their bowler-hatted bosses walked past. I once went to a lunch where the owner of the yard stood at the table with a great tureen of soup before him. We guests, along with everybody else, had to pass our plates along for him to fill. I doubt if you could find more antiquated aloofness than that. I was tempted to do an Oliver Twist and ask for more.' The ship-owners he found disinclined to invest and the trade unions equally reluctant to accept modernisation that sacrificed their restrictive practices and traditional demarcation lines. Nevertheless, he secured government fiscal incentives to encourage the plethora of small and inefficient privately owned shipyards to amalgamate and modernise.

In January 1967 he was appointed Minister of Defence for Equipment, under Denis Healey, and in early 1968 he was made a Privy Counsellor before, in April of that year, he was appointed Postmaster-General, the office he had hoped for in 1964. His stint was brief – terminated by the sudden resignation of Minister of Power Ray Gunter and Wilson's decision to redeploy Mason to fill his Cabinet vacancy. Thus Mason's achievements as Postmaster-General were confined to marking Celtic's achievement in being the first British football team to win the European Cup with the issue of commemorative stamps and repainting the Post Office's green engineering van fleet in a yellow sufficiently bright to enrage the sensibilities of many of his fellow Parliamentarians.

In July 1968, Mason became Minister of Power and one of the youngest Cabinet members: 'I think Roy Mason is one of the most promising new [Cabinet] Members and one of the ablest, infinitely superior, for example, to Dick Marsh', Dick Crossman noted in his diary (9 March 1969). Mason went on to serve as President of the Board of Trade from October 1969 until Labour's defeat in June 1970, where perhaps his greatest concrete legacy is the decision he took to build the National Exhibition Centre in Birmingham rather than London. Despite failing to secure election to the shadow cabinet, he was Principal Opposition Board of Trade Spokesman 1970–74.

A trenchant pro-European, along with Roy Jenkins, John Smith and 66 other Labour MPs Mason famously defied a three-line whip to support EEC membership in 1971. That same year he wrote a pamphlet on why the NUM should embrace the EEC. During the EEC referendum of 1975 Mason battled in Barnsley, at times physically, with anti-Europeans from the NUM: 'Scargill and all the other Communists and fellow travellers in the Union took the opposite view … a strong, united and prosperous Europe might prove inconvenient to their beloved Soviet Union.'

In 1974, Mason returned to Cabinet as Defence Secretary, where he saved the Sea Harrier and the Chevaline modernisation of Britain's Polaris submarine-based nuclear deterrent. Bernard Donoughue, Head of the Downing Street Policy Unit 1974–79, wrote of Mason in his book, *Prime Minister*, as 'a solid, tough, patriotic, authoritarian Yorkshireman… well organised, well dressed and his contributions to Cabinet were blunt and to the point… he was more military than the military and appeared to carry their confidence.' In September 1976, after Jim Callaghan, with whom Mason had become close, had succeeded Wilson as Prime Minister, Mason became Northern Ireland Secretary. He served until Labour's defeat in 1979, a notoriously troubled period. With the collapse of the Sunningdale power-sharing executive Mason's tenure in the Northern Ireland Office was perhaps the last real attempt to find a 'security solution' to the conflict. Uncompromising support for the interdiction and arrest of the terrorists earned Mason the respect of RUC and Army. The relationship he built with the mainstream Unionists helped head off another Paisley-engineered Protestant workers strike. Unfortunately it also alienated Gerry Fitt and the SDLP from the government and was the main reason for Fitt's failure to support Labour in the Commons confidence vote that saw the government defeated by one vote, precipitating the 1979 general election. His involvement in Northern Ireland required him to live under constant armed police escort, an escort he retains to this day.

Elected to the shadow cabinet in 1979, he became Shadow Agriculture Minister, despite lacking enthusiasm or experience for the portfolio. He backed Healey in vain to succeed Callaghan as leader in 1980 and opposed the imposition of the electoral college for future leadership elections: 'arguably the most disastrous single decision ever taken by a Labour conference,' as he trenchantly put it. Retiring from the shadow cabinet in November 1981, he remained one of the most combative opponents of the Bennite left and became Arthur Scargill's *bête noire* in Barnsley. Despite sharing the policy views of the Gang of Four and having an admiration for his 'tough and very able' former deputy at Defence, Bill Rodgers, he did not join the SDP. His relations with Jenkins and Owen, whom he saw as arrogant and aloof, were poor, and he felt Shirley Williams to be overrated. Moreover, unlike ex-Oxford University MPs like Roy Jenkins and Michael Foot who lived primarily in London, Mason was one of the many MPs from a trade-union background who based their families and social lives in their constituencies and for whom the Labour Party was not just a party label but a community and a way of life. Thus, though Mason's relationship with Hugh Gaitskell during the early 1960s was 'so close that he was godfather to my second daughter,' he was never part of the ex-Oxbridge 'Hampstead Set', his only education post-14 being a TUC scholarship year at the LSE in 1951.

He was a Callaghan man and like Callaghan believed the right needed to stand fast. Mason writes poignantly in his memoirs of the relevance of those dark days for today: 'If anyone these days complains about Tony Blair's stage management, they should remember the venomous shambles of the 1979 Conference and those that followed. This was when decisions were taken that would keep Labour out of power for nearly a generation ... the left-wing malignancy which came so close to destroying Labour has been cut out and Tony Blair leads a Party which is not only in power but seemingly unbeatable. I think that those of us who spent a lifetime fighting our often unfashionable corner played some part in that transformation.'

After the 1983 election, now a backbencher, he backed Roy Hattersley over Neil Kinnock for the leadership, but was pleasantly surprised by Kinnock's preparedness to abandon his previous support for unilateralism and withdrawal from the EEC, and in hindsight acknowledges that Kinnock was the man for the job. Retiring from the Commons in 1987 he was created Lord Mason of Barnsley. He is a keen cravatologist (designer of ties) and President of the Lords and Commons Pipe and Cigar Club and of the Lords and Commons Fly Fishing Club. He published his autobiography, *Paying the Price*, in 1999, with an introduction written by former premier Jim Callaghan.

Joe McGowan

Deborah Mattinson (1956–)

Deborah Mattinson is a businesswoman and political researcher who has made a significant contribution to the renewal of Labour. Deborah brought to Labour the skills and the professional rigour of scientific opinion research. In so doing she gave Labour the insight into its electoral strengths and weaknesses which showed the way forward for the party.

Deborah Mattinson was born in Darlington, County Durham, on 17 September 1956. She was educated at Cheadle Hulme School in Manchester and obtained a Law degree from Bristol University (1975–78). After college she became a graduate trainee at McCann Erickson Advertising. In 1983 she won a Market Research Society diploma and that same year joined the Labour Party. In 1984 Deborah moved to Ayer Barker as an Account Director. The following year she formed the dynamic partnership with Phillip Gould through which Deborah advised Labour on how to conduct and interpret its public opinion research. This work led to the formation of a company called Gould-Mattinson Associates (1986), which advised a number of organisations as well as the Labour Party. Gould-Mattinson managed the Shadow Communications Agency, which in turn co-ordinated Labour supporters from the professional communications sector who assisted Labour on a voluntary basis. In this structure Deborah advised on opinion polls and focus groups while Gould translated this into Labour strategy, although the division of labour was not strictly applied. This partnership reformed all aspects of Labour's communications and campaigning, including logo design, party political broadcasts, advertising, the language used in speeches, and the inter-relationship of all these elements. Deborah had an overarching communications role during the 1987 election and, focusing more on polling, oversaw the private research during the 1992 election.

In 1989, out of the Gould–Mattinson business, Deborah Mattinson set up a new company, the GMA Monitor partnership. This is the company of her freelance political research work. Over some years GMA Monitor has worked for the TUC, Greenpeace, Liberty, the European Parliament and many local authorities. Also in 1989, Deborah married David Pelly, the Research Director at the Institution for Professionals, Managers and Specialists (IPMS). Deborah and David have a daughter and two sons.

Deborah Mattinson established Opinion Leader Research in 1992, an innovative company specialising in research among opinion formers. This company was sold in 1998, though Deborah remains a non-executive director. In 2000, in another groundbreaking move, Deborah became a founder Director of the SMART Company, advising big companies and organisations on corporate social responsibility.

Deborah has published widely on market research and political research. She has worked on some seminal Fabian pamphlets, in particular *Women's Votes – the Key to Winning,* with Patricia Hewitt in 1989, and the series *Southern Discomfort* (1992*), More Southern Discomfort* (1993) and *Any Southern Discomfort* (1994), with Giles Radice MP and Stephen Pollard, highlighting Labour's need to address voters in Britain's populous South East. Most recently she co-wrote the pamphlet *Winning for Women* (2000) with Harriet Harman MP. For BBC's *Newsnight* Deborah provides regular updates on focus group research among swing voters.

Since 1985 Deborah Mattinson has played a prominent part in all the studies that shaped 'New' Labour and has overseen many of the consequent changes in the party's approach. Using polls, focus groups and scientific method, Deborah Mattinson taught Labour the language of voters. She also taught that it was not enough to know whether voters were supporting Labour – it is also necessary to know why. Having now moved on, Deborah has left Labour contemplating an even harder lesson – that the renewal process never ends.

Rex Osborn

James Maxton (1885–1946)

When James Maxton died in 1946, he was mourned in every continent and on every side of the British political spectrum. A compelling public speaker with dramatic physical features, his place in Labour history would have been secured by his provoking oratorical skills alone. James Maxton was one of Britain's most charismatic socialist politicians of the inter-war years. However, he was also a leading architect of the most ambitious British socialist project of his time: a programme for socialism that offered a 'Third Way' between the views of Ramsay MacDonald and Vladimir Lenin.

James Maxton was born on 22 June 1885 in Glasgow to a family of teachers, in whose footsteps he too would initially follow. By the age of 19, he regarded himself as a socialist and joined the Independent Labour Party. It was the beginning of his dedication to an enduring cause.

Maxton trained to be a teacher at Martyrs Public School and Glasgow University. One of his earliest teaching posts was at St James School in Glasgow's Bridgeton, where many pupils suffered from poverty-related illnesses. There is little doubt that the squalor and overcrowding of Bridgeton advanced Maxton's socialism from the abstract to the practical. He saw the task of socialism not as the eventual production of a distant better world but as a remedy, immediate if at all possible, to the hideous problems he saw every day in children he taught.

Maxton became immersed in the political campaigns of the ILP, gaining prominence particularly through his oratory skills, and was selected as the Parliamentary candidate for Montrose Burghs in 1914. But his time for Westminster had not yet come. Instead came the bloodshed of the First World War, which split the Left in Britain. The ILP campaigned unequivocally against it and Maxton, himself a pacifist, moved to the forefront of the opposition to war. Following a demonstration in 1916 where he had called for munitions workers to strike, he was arrested, charged with sedition, and imprisoned for a year.

He was released on 2 February 1917. Having been expelled from the teaching profession, he found a job at the one shipyard on the Clyde not engaged in war work, and resumed his intense political activities. As Chairman of the Scottish Divisional Council of the ILP, a member of the Labour Party's Scottish Executive, and soon to be on the Labour Party's National Executive, Maxton was at the forefront of developments within the Party and set about working on an election programme.

With the end of the war in 1918, the focus once again was on elections. Though already selected as the candidate for Montrose Burghs, the Bridgeton Labour Party asked Maxton to stand as their candidate instead. Though Maxton polled Labour's biggest vote in Bridgeton, he failed to win the seat.

Maxton then worked as an organiser for the ILP, which gave him the means to marry his girlfriend, Sissy McCallum, and they wed on 24 July 1919. He also ran successfully for a seat on the new Glasgow Education Authority – his first public office. Sissy gave birth to their first child, James, on 16 May 1921, but the baby developed complications and required continuous attention. Sissy, in poor health already, fell seriously ill and died on 31 August 1922. The child, however, recovered fully and was raised by Maxton's mother.

In the general election of 1922, Maxton finally was elected MP for Bridgend. He made his mark in the Commons from the start. No respecter of Parliamentary conventions, he was corrected by the Speaker for his robust language in his maiden speech. The following year, in a speech on the effect of poverty on child health, he referred to Conservative members as 'murderers'. He refused to withdraw the comment and was expelled from the House. It was not to be last time that Maxton was rebuked and expelled from the Commons.

Maxton's greatest political legacy, however, is the programme he set out in the ILP's *Socialism in Our Time* during the 1920s. *Socialism in Our Time* offered a non-violent road to full employment, social equality and public control over the economy. Maxton knew that socialism could not be achieved by the palliative adjustments that characterised MacDonald's leadership, but he knew also that Labour had to stand against the ultra-left and its belief that change must inevitably be violent. He believed it was a third way between communism and gradualism. Maxton appreciated the necessity for a coherent, effective, yet still Parliamentary democratic socialism which took account of British conditions. Hence the vehemence with which he tried to promote *Socialism in Our Time* in the interwar period. It failed, however, to win mass appeal within the Labour Party or beyond.

Maxton was the most consistent critic of the Labour Party leadership of the 1920s and 30s. If Ramsay MacDonald represented Labour in government, Maxton represented Labour in Opposition, as the conscience of the left. Maxton never considered himself a potential party leader. He saw his role as that of propagandist, a crusading politician rather than a career politician.

In 1926 Maxton was elected Chairman of the ILP and was prominent in the General Strike that same year. Following the 1929 general election and the formation of the National Government, Maxton successfully persuaded the ILP to break away from the Labour Party.

By the 1930s Maxton's influence had waned as he became engulfed in the sectarian socialist controversies of the period. As a pacifist, he opposed rearmament in the 1930s and supported the appeasement policies of Neville Chamberlain. In March 1935, Maxton married Madeleine Glasier who had worked as his political assistant. Maxton remained an MP for Bridgend until his death on 23 July 1946 at Largs. His biography, *Maxton,* by Gordon Brown, was published in 1986.

Rt Hon. Gordon Brown MP

Chris Mayhew (Lord Mayhew of Wimbledon)   (1915–97)

Christopher Paget Mayhew – 'Chris' to his friends – joined the Labour Party in 1934 and left it for the Liberals 40 years later. He was a prominent and distinctive figure in the intervening years but never quite fulfilled his early promise. He was a natural candidate to become Commonwealth Secretary in 1964, but Harold Wilson only appointed him as a middle-rank Minister for the Navy (he had been Shadow War Secretary 1960–61 and an Opposition Foreign Affairs Spokesman 1961–64). This was alternatively attributed to his right-wing views - although he had accepted Wilson as the best available candidate to become leader on Gaitskell's death – or the strength of his pro-Arab views in an essentially Zionist Labour Party. Whatever the case, in February 1966 he resigned on a question of principle, defence cuts, although more generally he was out of sympathy with the drift of the Government. He showed no real bitterness but continued to pursue the causes in which he believed with the open, sometimes mischievous, enthusiasm and hint of muscular Christianity that were so much his style.

The son of Sir Basil Mayhew, KBE, Chris Mayhew was born on 12 June 1915 into a comfortable professional family. He was sent to Haileybury, a public school where C R Attlee had been a pupil many years before, and then to Christ Church, Oxford. He was active in Labour politics and became President of the Union. About this time be became a protégé of Hugh Dalton – a great talent spotter, especially from amongst good-looking and lively public school boys – who then picked him in wartime to join the Special Operations Executive, conducting dangerous assignments in occupied Europe. Major Mayhew was an impressive figure when he fought the Norfolk South constituency in 1945 and found himself on the crowded Labour benches in the House of Commons. It was no great surprise when he became Under-Secretary of State at the Foreign Office in October 1946, remaining in post until he lost his seat at the general election of 1950.

Ernest Bevin, the Foreign Secretary, made as deep an impression on the young Mayhew as he did on his devoted officials. In turn Mayhew served Bevin well through the critical early years of the Cold War and the creation of NATO. He was a clear and bold critic of the Soviet Union at a time when many Labour MPs still saw it, rather than the United States, as Labour Britain's natural friend. Apart from inheriting many of Bevin's views, he also inherited Bevin's Woolwich East seat after he had lost his own Norfolk seat and Bevin had died.

It was from Bevin and his dealings with Palestine in the bloody final days of Britain's mandate when the state of Israel was created that Mayhew apparently acquired his passion for the Arab cause. At all events, it became a dominant interest that made a number of his friends uncomfortable. But in the thirteen years of Opposition after 1951 he also made a name for himself in television, helping to present some of Labour's first election broadcasts as well as conducting successful television interviews and doing major current affairs programmes. During those dark and unrewarding years for the Labour party he was something of a media star – Woodrow Wyatt and John Freeman were others from amongst his contemporaries – although his unequivocal right-wing views, especially on nuclear disarmament, made him enemies. Another very different interest he pursued with his usual tenacity was mental health, and he became Chairman of MIND.

In the controversies over defence Chris Mayhew was a lucid opponent of unilateral disarmament and in 1961 organised his own, marathon non-stop talk-in at Central Hall, Westminster. He joined the Liberal Party in July 1974 and fought Bath twice as a Parliamentary candidate. He became a life peer in 1981 and was the Liberal, then Liberal Democrat, spokesman on defence in the House of Lords almost until his death in July 1997. He was married for almost 50 years to Cicely Ludham. *Party Games* (1969) dealt with his falling-out with Labour and *Time to Explain* (1987) was his autobiography.

Rt Hon. Lord Rodgers of Quarry Bank

Joan Maynard (1921–98)

Infamous as 'Stalin's Granny' and 'Sheffield's answer to Rosa Luxemburg', Joan Maynard was Labour MP for Sheffield Brightside from October 1974, following the deselection of Labour loyalist Eddie Grifiths by the hard left local party, until her retirement in 1987. She was the leading Parliamentary representative of the pro-Soviet left during the 1970s and 1980s. A regular conference and platform speaker for the hard left, she won a seat on Labour's NEC Women's Section in 1972, which she retained apart from her defeat in 1982–83 until her final defeat in 1987. Her defeat in 1987 was precipitated by her having been one of seven hard-left members who walked out of the NEC, causing the collapse of the disciplinary hearings into Militant in Liverpool. Had she not been defeated in 1982, she would, on the principle of 'Buggins turn', have become Chair of the Labour Party for the general election year, having been Labour's Vice-Chair in 1980–81.

She was nothing if not firmly consistent in her views. Active in communist front organisations like the British Peace Committee (of which she was chair) and the World Peace Council, she opposed Gorbachev's Glasnost and protested that the sale of Harrier jump-jets to China would be an affront to the Soviet Union. The President of the pro-Sinn Fein Labour Committee on Ireland, she demanded the withdrawal of British troops from Northern Ireland and to know whether the British army was setting up brothels in Belfast for espionage purposes. She was anti-NATO, anti-Common Market, anti-devolution, anti-electricity pylons, anti-factory farming and opposed Callaghan's Lib-Lab Pact. She advocated unilateral nuclear disarmament, the wholesale nationalisation of the banks and the land and was the first MP to sponsor Ken Livingstone's Socialist Campaign for a Labour Victory, which created the *Labour Herald, Socialist Organiser* and *London Labour Briefing*. She was a leading advocate of the mandatory selection of MPs and the election of Labour's leadership by an electoral college rather than One Member One Vote.

She backed Tony Benn's leadership ambitions in 1976 and on every subsequent occasion he stood, co-nominating Eric Heffer for Labour leader and Michael Meacher for deputy during Benn's enforced Parliamentary absence in October 1983. On Neil Kinnock's victory she warned him ominously: 'You walk with your shoes straight or else.' On the failure of the Tribune Group to back Benn's continuing leadership ambitions she co-founded the breakaway Campaign Group of Labour MPs, of which she remained Chair until her retirement from Parliament. Tam Dalyell once sought her reaction to her sobriquet 'Stalin's Granny': 'Matter-of-factly, she challenged the nickname on the surmise that Stalin's real grandmother was probably a pillar of the Russian Orthodox Church in Georgia, "which might be difficult for me."'

Noisy though she was in the pursuit of her causes, her legacy is rather more muted. Firstly, it might be said that the article she wrote in the communist *Morning Star* in 1971 urging the abolition of the list of Marxist organisations proscribed by Labour's NEC, presaged the NEC's decision to do so the year after she joined it, in 1973. This NEC move, of which she was a leading proponent, was to facilitate the infiltration of the Labour Party by Militant and other extremist groups over the next decade and a half, profoundly damaging the organisational fabric and electoral credibility of the Labour Party. Secondly, her determined campaigning undoubtedly stiffened the resolve of the Labour government in passing the Rent (Agriculture) Act of 1976 which, with the exemption of estate workers (a necessary concession to placate the landed interests of the Lords), effectively heralded the abolition of the tied-cottage system, giving agricultural workers security of tenure and the rights enshrined in the Rent Acts.

Her devotion to the interests of agricultural workers was genuine and longstanding. She was to serve on the Parliamentary Agriculture Select Committee without a break from 1975 to 1987. It was from her father, a seventeen-acre smallholder, that she inherited her passion for rural issues. Born on 5 July 1921 in Easingwold, North Yorkshire, Vera Joan Maynard was educated at Ampleforth village school, moving to to Thornton-le-Street in the late 1930s to help her parents run a post office and smallholding. Joining the Labour Party in 1946, she was soon branch secretary and was Labour Party agent in Thirsk from 1953–74. Elected to South Kilvington District Council in 1952, she became a North Riding County Councillor 1956–61 and also a local magistrate. From 1954 to 1978, she was Yorkshire County Secretary of the Agricultural Workers' Union, becoming national Vice-President of the Agricultural Workers' Union from 1966 to 1972, surviving several attempts to unseat her. In support of wage demands she urged (albeit largely unsuccessfully) farmworkers to strike, barricade creameries and blockade markets. She never married and died on 27 March 1998 after a long illness, at her home, a cottage in Sowerby, North Yorkshire, where she had lived since 1953.

Greg Rosen

Jack McConnell (1960–)

Scotland's Education Minister and former Scottish Labour General Secretary, Jack McConnell at the age of 41 has emerged as a key figure in post-devolution Scotland. Never far from controversy, he has consistently delivered change and progress as a councillor, general secretary and now as a Scottish Minister.

Born in Irvine on 30 June 1960, Jack grew up in Arran, where he attended Arran High School in Lamlash. His father was a tenant sheep farmer while his mother ran a local tearoom. Jack's non-political family still live in Arran where they have always served as an escape from political life. At Stirling University he twice served as Student Union President and became Depute President of NUS Scotland. Contemporaries in student politics included John Reid, Charles Kennedy and Phil Woolas.

After University Jack taught as a Maths teacher at Lornshill Academy in Alloa (1983–92). An active member of the Labour Party during this period, he sat on Labour's Scottish Executive and stood for Parliament in Perth & Kinross in 1987. Jack was elected to Stirling Council in 1984 and became leader in 1990. As council leader he introduced Scotland's first 'Customer Contract' and introduced quality systems to overhaul council management complaints procedures. He ensured Stirling took a national lead on equal opportunities and environmental issues and became more and more visible nationally. In 1992 he was appointed Scottish Labour's General Secretary.

The position of General Secretary can often be a poisoned chalice for those who aim to go on to elected office. Members have mixed memories of Jack McConnell's period in the post. While many choose to remember the stunning 1997 general election and referendum results, the youth movement that was started from scratch and the increase in membership during this period, others have a different view. As General Secretary, McConnell was often caught between leadership and activists, inevitably collecting enemies; some councillors, traditional MPs and trade unionists still seek revenge. A strong supporter of all-women shortlists, Jack met resistance from local organisations who did not share his enthusiasm.

However, the 1997 general election was his biggest success in the post. Working with George Robertson, then Shadow Secretary of State for Scotland, Jack delivered the best Scottish results Labour can remember. On 2 May not one Tory MP remained and a record number of women went to Westminster from Scotland.

From 1989 to 1998 Jack McConnell sat on the Scottish Constitutional Convention, which played a key role in designing the Scottish Parliament later established by the new Labour government. Membership of the Convention confirmed Jack's long-standing commitment to Scottish Devolution. This commitment can be traced back to the establishment of the Home

Rule pressure group Scottish Labour Action in 1988. Legend has it that the pressure group was started after a meeting of likeminded young guns was held in Jack's living room in Stirling.

Following the election in 1997 Jack stayed on as General Secretary to manage the referendum 'Yes, Yes' campaign. The result was decisive and the course was set to establish a Scottish Parliament.

Standing down as General Secretary, Jack sought selection to be the Member of the Scottish Parliament for Motherwell and Wishaw, a former steel and coal area in Lanarkshire where Jack had strong links with local activists and politicians. Despite his high profile he found himself engaged in a close contest with AEEU official Bill Tynan (now MP for Hamilton South). The vote was close, the winning margin only two votes. However election followed and Jack has since moved to Wishaw with wife Bridget, daughter Hannah and son Mark.

During the 1999 campaign Jack was Environmental Affairs spokesperson, and was then appointed Finance Minister in Donald Dewar's first cabinet (a position he was to remain in until Donald's untimely death). Jack prepared the first budget for the Parliament, and used the new position to radically overhaul the financial support for local government. While cautiously managing spending in the early days, he began work which was to lead to the modernisation of quango appointments and greater diversity in civil service management.

However, this first year was by no means a smooth ride for Jack McConnell. The *Observer* alleged that a former employer had influenced him and Jack was involved in the first standards investigation of the Scottish Parliament. The accusation did not stand up and Jack was cleared of all wrongdoing. The young Minister had an abrupt introduction to the realities of national office.

October 2000 saw Donald Dewar's tragic death, Jack McConnell contested the position of Labour Leader in the Scottish Parliament with Henry McLeish. An electoral college of MSPs and the Scottish Executive of the party decided the new leader, meeting in Stirling's council chamber. Jack had returned to his old stomping ground as leader of the council, but he was not to leave as the leader of Labour. By 44 votes to 36 Henry McLeish was elected leader of Labour in the Scottish Parliament. While the ballot was held in secret, the lion's share of votes cast by the MSPs were thought to go to Jack. This speculation was supported by the result of a ballot of MSPs for the Channel 4 Scottish Parliamentarian of the Year 2001, where Jack won support from across the chamber.

Since his failed leadership bid he has been appointed Minister for Education, Europe and External Affairs, a position in which he has already made his mark. In keeping with his record of 'getting things done', his short period in office has seen pay modernisation for teachers (during which time his experience as a former teacher was appreciated), action on school discipline and a drive to raise standards for children in care. His role developing Scotland's growing influence in Europe is no surprise to those who remember his commitment to anti-apartheid and other international causes in the eighties. Indeed he still quotes Nelson Mandela as the person he most admires.

While unsuccessful in his leadership bid, Jack has and will remain a senior figure in the Scottish Executive and the Scottish Labour Party. At the relatively young age of 41 the future is clearly still bright for Jack McConnell.

Peter Hastie

Margaret McDonagh   (1961–)

Maragaret McDonagh was Labour's first ever woman General Secretary, the youngest ever to hold the post, and the first to reach the job by rising up from being a grassroots activist.

McDonagh was born into a family of staunch Labour-supporting Irish Catholics in Mitcham, South London. She still lives in the area in Colliers Wood. Born on 26 June 1961, her parents Brigid and Cumin McDonagh were then a psychiatric nurse and a labourer working on building sites. She was educated at Holy Cross secondary school, New Malden, and then studied Government at Brunel University in Uxbridge. Later she was awarded a Master's Degree in Advanced Marketing at Kingston Business School.

As a student at Brunel, McDonagh was very much not part of the then dominant clique in the National Organisation of Labour Students, which espoused liberation politics and proportional representation, was highly focused on the NUS, and saw itself as simultaneously linked to the domestic soft left and Gramscian Euro-communism. McDonagh would have been disdainful of this middle-class posturing – her own politics have always been rooted in a more practical, organisational, tribal right-wing Labourism. She has never been terribly impressed by the products of the NUS/Labour Co-ordinating Committee machine ever since, and this has led to not very well disguised friction with some of its leading products.

McDonagh joined the Labour Party aged 17 in 1978, at a time when the party was about to descend into an orgy of internal infighting. The formative experiences of her early years in the party were attending the Party Annual Conference in 1981, the year of the brutal fight between Tony Benn and Denis Healey for the Deputy Leadership, and the parliamentary by-election in her home constituency, Mitcham & Morden, in 1982. Moderate local Labour MP Bruce Douglas-Mann was a late defector to the SDP. Unlike every other Labour MP who crossed the floor, Douglas-Mann was principled, or naïve, enough to resign and fight a by-election in a bid to get a fresh mandate from his constituents. Unfortunately, Mitcham & Morden is a gritty suburb at the far end of the Northern Line, with little time for the party of claret and Europhilia, and he lost the seat to Tory candidate Angela Rumbold, with Labour trailing in third.

McDonagh and her sister Siobhan vowed to work to win the seat back for Labour, and she found herself volunteer Agent for the constituency at the age of just 22 in the general election of 1983. Amidst the carnage of Labour's *annus horribilis,* Labour clawed its way back into second place in Mitcham. By the next time the seat was fought in 1987, the Labour candidate was none other than Siobhan McDonagh. On her third attempt, Siobhan was elected in 1997, and has gone on to build a reputation as an assiduous constituency member and stalwart government loyalist.

This tough electoral fight for a historically marginal area has given Margaret McDonagh the political analysis that other New Labour figures have reached through more academic methods. Her support for New Labour is based on the pragmatism of knowing that skilled working-class and lower-middle-class voters in seats like Mitcham & Morden only vote Labour when it is moderate and embraces their values on issues like crime and defence.

Meanwhile, Margaret built a career first as a Regional Organiser for the National Association of Licensed House Managers, then as a Research Officer for the EETPU. The EETPU link, through its successor union, the AEEU, has given McDonagh a powerful set of contacts and allies on the trade union old right of the Party.

McDonagh moved over to become a Labour Party staffer in 1987. Her first post was as Assistant Regional Officer of the Greater London Labour Party (GLLP). This was at a time when the 'loony left' in various London boroughs were damaging Labour's reputation nationally and losing it a string of marginal seats in the capital. McDonagh developed a reputation as a hammer of the far left during her time in London.

She has been at Labour Head Office since 1994, when she worked on the successful campaign to modernise the party's aims and values (Clause IV). Then, as the Key Seat Task Force Leader, she initiated and managed the implementation of Labour's key seat strategy, focusing resources, time and effort on the seats the party needed to win to form a government. As General Election Co-ordinator from October 1996 to May 1997, she was responsible for the delivery of Labour's general election campaign. She was appointed Deputy General Secretary in September 1997.

As Tom Sawyer approached the end of his time as General Secretary, his Deputy began to take on more and more of his functions and was emerging as the heir apparent. However, she had strong rivals, both with very different styles to her, in the persons of David Gardner and Matthew Taylor, the two Assistant General Secretaries. McDonagh won through, allegedly with the blessing of Tony Blair, and her rivals swiftly moved on to jobs outside the party after she was appointed by the NEC in July 1998.

McDonagh broke the mould of previous General Secretaries not just in her age and gender, but also in the fact that she was promoted from within the Party staff rather than brought in from a senior position in a trade union like her predecessors.

McDonagh's management style was controversial – she does not suffer fools gladly – and sometimes terrifying for junior staff who are expected to deliver superhuman results by the day before yesterday, but arguably has been effective in ridding the Party machine of the last vestiges of its old *mañana* style of operation. She was not afraid to make enemies but has a tenaciously loyal group of allies who have watched her back.

McDonagh has been unlucky to see her record as General Secretary marred by factors largely outside her control: a small decline in party membership after the growth of the early Blair years, and debacles in the selections and elections for the Welsh Assembly and London Mayor. However, in the plus column are the fact that Labour has survived the parliament unscathed in by-elections, that the internal changes of Partnership in Power have been successfully adopted, and that the Party won a record second general election landslide in a row. McDonagh announced her decision to retire within weeks of the general election of June 2001. What comes next for Labour's youngest ex-General Secretary will be very interesting.

Locally rooted, she remains a regular attender of Colliers Wood branch Labour Party and the Mitcham & Morden GC. She and Siobhan host BBQ and coffee mornings for local members and she enthusiastically canvasses (or, to use the New Labour phrase, carries out Voter ID) every Sunday – she is disdainful of the sort of MP or staffer who does not get stuck in to campaigning at a local level. McDonagh is a workaholic and extremely tough and driven. This can be intimidating for lesser mortals as she expects others to match her own workload and perfectionism. It does, however, deliver results.

Luke Akehurst

Henry McLeish   (1948–)

Henry McLeish was born on 15 June 1948 to a Fife mining family. Leaving school at the age of 15 he became a professional footballer briefly with Leeds United before returning home to play for East Fife and Scotland under 18s. McLeish returned to education to study planning at Herriot Watt University, a subject he went on to lecture on throughout the seventies and eighties. It was at University that McLeish became increasingly political, joining the Labour party in 1970.

His political career began on Fife Regional Council (1982–87) where he was notable for carrying out a radical agenda including such New Labour staples as nursery places for all four-year-olds and free television licences and bus passes for pensioners. A Tribunite and member of Unison, he contested Fife North East in 1979 before using his council power base to unseat the famously anti-monarchist Labour MP Willie Hamilton to win the Central Fife seat in 1987. He would hold the seat at Westminster until 2001.

In Westminster Henry quickly established himself as a conscientious and diligent parliamentarian. A keen statistician with a knack for working through paperwork, he acted as a serial deputy throughout the nineties (Scottish Affairs 1988–89; Employment 1989–92; Scottish Affairs 1992–94; Transport 1994–95; Health 1995–96; Social Security 1996–97). Such was McLeish's reputation that when Tony Blair worked with him in opposition and needed a particularly complicated matter dealt with, he would 'unleash the McLeish', passing the task to his junior colleague.

Henry's life was touched by tragedy when he lost his first wife to stomach cance,r leaving him to raise their two children. He remarried in 1998.

When Donald Dewar charged McLeish with delivering the biggest constitutional change in over 300 years, his eye for detail and diligent preparation for parliamentary debate was put to full use. If Dewar can be described as the father of devolution it was McLeish who played nanny to the Scotland Bill, driving it through Parliament to become the first Act passed by the Blair administration.

McLeish stood down as Scottish Office minister to win the Central Fife seat at the 1999 Scottish Parliamentary elections. When the LibDems claimed the role of Deputy First Minister of Scotland, the ever ambitious McLeish was said to be bitterly disappointed; however many still viewed him as Dewar's political deputy. Given the role of Minister for Enterprise and Lifelong learning, McLeish, true to form, 'got his head down' and avoided the predicted coalition crisis over the abolition of tuition fees. He also emerged undamaged from the exam results fiasco of summer 2000 when he was shielded from blame by Education Minster Sam Galbraith.

When Dewar died in late 2000, his long-faithful deputy was viewed by many as the automatic choice as replacement. In a short leadership contest Jack McConnell, then Finance Minister in the Scottish Executive, mounted an impressive challenge, pushing the favourite closer than many had expected. With ministerial and union backing McLeish was felt to be a safe pair of hands. On the day of the leadership ballot, the front page of Scotland's top selling paper, the *Daily Record*, screamed 'It has to be Henry', and so it was.

McLeish has been dogged by bad publicity since his election as first minister. His critics in the media have attacked his dramatic use of vocabulary and serious image, labelling his soundbites as 'McClichés'. However this concentration on the First Minister's style ignores what has already been a radical administration. McLeish has shown a greater willingness to use the Parliament's devolved powers. On issues such as long term care for the elderly and the use of private finance in public services his approach has seen markedly different policies from Labour at Westminster.

At the time of writing it is too early to access McLeish's performance in any meaningful way. However it is clear that Labour will face a challenge at the next Scottish Parliamentary elections with a mid-term Blair Government in London. McLeish must convince the Scottish electorate that the election is not a popularity poll for Tony Blair but a judgement on Labour's record in the Scottish Parliament and he must convince that it is a record of success.

Blair McDougall

Tom McNally (Lord McNally) (1943–)

Born on 20 February 1943 to John P and Elizabeth McNally on the outskirts of Blackpool, Tom McNally has had a career never too far away from where the major decisions were made. Joining the Labour Party at sixteen, he was educated at the College of St Joseph, Blackpool, and University College London, where he became President of the Students' Union in 1965–66. His political career kicked off where so many young Labour politicians earn their spurs within the National Union of Students. A Vice President in 1966–67, his career was over-taken by a radical Jack Straw who went on to be the NUS President.

Nevertheless, McNally remained one of the Labour Party's rising stars. Appointed Assistant General-Secretary of the Fabian Society in 1966, from 1967–69 he was a Labour Party Researcher before becoming one of its youngest senior officers with his appointment as International Secretary in 1969. In this capacity he helped draft the 1970 general election manifesto. From 1974–76 he was appointed special adviser to the new Foreign Secretary, Jim Callaghan.

His tour of duty included expulsion from the pre-reformed Portugal, being present at the Cyprus Peace talks and being barred from Rhodesia by Ian Smith – a wise decision by Smith as it was Labour's refusal to sell out on Rhodesia which in some part led to the collapse of the Smith regime. This was reinforced by his hard work in supporting Callaghan in his efforts to renegotiate a dialogue with black South Africa. McNally also worked to ensure that the Labour government had a tough line on Chile during this time.

Not a Eurofanatic, McNally worked to ensure the referendum on Europe backed staying in, whilst maintaining as much as possible Labour's unity. In all these areas McNally worked closely with Tom McCaffrey, one of the senior civil servants in the Foreign Office, and remembers him as being a major influence.

From 1976 to 1979, with the election of Callaghan as Leader, McNally served as Head of the Number 10 Political Office, where he backed Policy Unit Head Bernard Donoughue in urging council house sales and action on education. McCaffrey accompanied them on their move from the Foreign Office to Downing Street, becoming Callaghan's Press Secretary. In this role he did a lot of the background briefing of the Press and believes strongly that if Callaghan had gone to the electorate in 1978 then he would have won a second term. The reasons why Callaghan did not call the election in 1978 are complex and varied, but prominent among them is that Callaghan wanted a full three years for some of his initiatives to settle in.

McNally was perhaps proudest of Labour's success in addressing the extra-parliamentary challenges to the democratic authority of Parliament that had proliferated during the 1970s. Central to this was repairing the Party's bitter relationship with the press. How successful this was is still a matter of debate, but McNally sought to develop positive media relationships to influence political coverage, avoiding the more toe-to-toe approach of Wilson's Press Secretary, Joe Haines.

Though 1979 saw the fall of the Callaghan government, McNally, despite attempts by the hard left on Labour's NEC to block the selection of a Prime-Ministerial employee, was elected as Labour MP for Stockton South. However, a hard-left faction in his constituency never gave up trying to deselect him, and in the wake of the disastrous Labour conference of that year, in October 1981 he joined the SDP, seven months after its formation, serving as SDP spokesman on Education and Sport until he lost Stockton South at the 1983 election. In February 1982 he was one of five rebel SDP MPs who voted with Labour against Norman Tebbit's trade-union reform bill. He also served from 1979 to 1983 as a member of the Commons Trade and Industry Select Committee.

Created Lord McNally of Blackpool in 1995, he was a key link in creating the Lib-Lab Cabinet consultative committee in 1997. He is currently the Liberal Democrats' Home Affairs spokesman in the Upper House. Outside Parliament, McNally was public affairs adviser to GEC Marconi in 1983–84, and Director General of the British Retail Association (now Consortium) 1985–87. From 1987 to 1993 he was Head of Public Affairs at Hill & Knowlton, subsequently becoming Vice Chairman of Shandwick. He married his second wife Juliet in 1990, and they live in St Albans with their three children, John, James and Imogen.

Mark Glover

Hector McNeil (1910–55)

In the late 1940s at the United Nations General Assembly and Security Council, Hector McNeil shot to national and international prominence because of the McNeil/Vyshinsky debates. Heard and seen by millions on radio, newsreels and television in America and all over the world, these debates were riveting. Both men were in effect the deputy Foreign Ministers of their countries, McNeil to his boss Ernest Bevin and Andrei Vyshinsky to Molotov, and the Cold War among the world's Big Five was getting very cold, as witness the Berlin airlift of 1948.

Both men were excellent debaters, the much younger McNeil having an extensive record in student debates in Scotland, Oxford, and, in 1931–32, the USA, which sharpened his wits and encouraged spontaneity. Born on 10 March 1910, the second son in the seven-child family of a Glasgow shipwright, he had gone to Glasgow University by way of Woodside School in Glasgow. On leaving University he had combined journalism, originally free-lance but latterly on the *Scottish Daily Express*, with a six-year membership of Glasgow City Council. First elected at the age of 22, he was by 26 also a Glasgow magistrate. In the 1935 general election he fought the Conservative Agriculture Minister at Glasgow Kelvingrove, and a few months later he increased the Labour vote in a by-election at Ross & Cromarty. In 1941 McNeil was elected MP for Greenock at a by-election and was swiftly appointed PPS to Philip Noel Baker on Noel-Baker's appointment in 1942 as Parliamentary Secretary at the Ministry of War Transport in Churchil's Coalition Government. In 1945 Attlee appointed McNeil Under-Secretary of State at the Foreign Office, promoting him to Minister of State in 1946.

Vyshinsky, older than McNeil, a veteran of the 1930s Stalin show trials, was a skillful negotiator and propagandist for the Russians. Vyshinsky and McNeil were equally matched. To western audiences McNeil's pugilistic stance, enhanced by a very definite Glasgow accent, was endearing. He refused to be brow-beaten by his scowling, bad-tempered Soviet opponent. The Americans loved it and McNeil too. His fame was international.

After the 1950 General Election, McNeil returned to terra firma with only a slight bump. He was promoted to Attlee's last Cabinet as Secretary of State for Scotland. He did the job well but longed for the Foreign Office. This was not to be: though Attlee did consider him as Bevin's successor, he was felt to be too young. Labour was defeated in the 1951 general election and McNeil ceased to be part of Government. In addition to his Parliamentary duties, McNeil was invited to work part-time for the American-owned Encyclopedia Britannica. He accepted and his fame in America continued. He was a frequent visitor to the United States. Disaster struck while he was crossing the Atlantic aboard the Queen Mary liner. In September 1955 he suffered a severe cerebral shock. He never recovered consciousness and died in hospital in New York on 11 October.

A staunch Gaitskellite, in the 1950s he was very much in the front-line in the party battles with the Bevanite left. Later colleagues would speculate that had he lived, fully recovered, he would have been a strong candidate to succeed Attlee or Gaitskell as Labour leader. Instead he became one of Labour's many 'lost' leaders.

Rt. Hon Dr. Dickson Mabon

Michael Meacher (1939–)

Meacher ranks as one of Labour's greatest survivors. He has been an MP for over 30 years and is now virtually the only serving member of this Government to have held office in any pre-1997 Labour Government. Born on 4 November 1939, he was educated at a public school, Berkhamstead, on a scholarship and at New College Oxford. He became a university lecturer in Social Administration at York (1966–69) and the LSE (1970). He fought unwinnable Colchester in 1966 before being selected for the 1968 by-election in Oldham West, a Labour seat which the party lost at the height of the unpopularity of the Wilson Government. He won it back in 1970 and has represented the area ever since.

He served in the 1974–79 Government as Parliamentary Under Secretary of State at Industry from March 1974 until June 1975, at Health & Social Security until April 1976 and finally at Trade until the fall of the government in May 1979.

Identified in the early 80s with he party's far left, he stood for the deputy leadership of the Labour Party in October 1983 against Roy Hattersley, Denzil Davies and Gwyneth Dunwoody. Neil Kinnock (from the 'left') had promised his support to Hattersley (from the 'right') as part of the 'dream ticket' to reunify the party. Meacher came second, with just short of 28 per cent of the electoral college vote.

Tony Benn, who had led the upheaval in the Labour Party after the 1979 defeat, lost his seat at the 1983 election and was therefore ineligible to stand for top office. Meacher was widely described as 'Benn's vicar on earth'. Though he supported left-wing groups including The Institute for Workers' Control, he was not as one-dimensional as the term implies. He had sided with the left after 1979 to a great extent out of genuine concern that the Callaghan government had not taken any serious steps to tackle poverty, particularly among the elderly.

He was never on close terms with Kinnock and after 1983 was regarded with suspicion by the Labour modernisers, though the activists elected him to Labour's NEC for six years running (1983–89). He was among the earliest victims of Labour's culture of leaking against colleagues, particularly after 1987, when Peter Mandelson became Director of Communications for the party and embarked on the project which after 1992 surfaced as 'New Labour'.

Meacher is however an astute and capable politician and parliamentarian. Among fellow MPs, even those who do not share his political views, he earns a grudging respect. At the height of the unsourced disparagement which he was suffering, the Parliamentary Labour Party nevertheless elected him to the shadow cabinet in every year between 1983 and 1996. Every year, the press would be fed with speculation that Meacher was about to lose his seat because he was so far off message. Every year, by careful activity in the Commons tearoom and the astute trading of block votes, he was re-elected by his colleagues.

In opposition, party rules dictate that the leader must give each elected shadow cabinet member a portfolio. Meacher was shifted from job to job, serving as Principal Opposition Spokesman on Health & Social Security, 1983–87, Employment, 1987–89, Social Security, 1989–92, Overseas Development & Co-operation, 1992–93, Citizen's Charter & Science, 1993–94, Transport, 1994–95, Education & Employment, 1995–96 and Environmental Protection, 1996–97.

His principal political interest is and remains social security. In that shadow post from 1989–92, he was closely monitored by the then Shadow Treasury Chief Secretary Margaret Beckett, lest in the course of a speech or interview he gave a spending commitment which would dent Labour's carefully crafted image of fiscal responsibility.

As shadow Employment spokesman, he clashed with the party leadership over rights for trade unions when industrial relations policy was re-shaped as part of the Party's post-1987 Policy Review. He was regarded as too sympathetic to the restoration of trade union rights removed under the Conservatives, at a time when the focus group polling was telling the leadership that Labour's association in the voters' minds with trade unions and industrial militancy was costing it support. He was eventually replaced in the Employment brief by the up-and-coming Tony Blair.

He embarked in 1990 on an ill-advised libel action against the *Observer* newspaper, which had described him as 'middle class', and lost heavily. Both bringing the action and his defeat could well have damaged his reputation to greater measure than turned out to be the case. In fact, he continued to attract support from colleagues who had privately deplored his lack of judgement.

He is undoubtedly still of the left of the Labour Party. As late as 1992, he was writing of the need to 'revive socialism'. He is a comparative rarity among politicians. His approach is academic, as befits his training. He believes that policy should come from a rational analysis of the situation, evolving radical but workable solutions, which are then implemented on a consistent basis. He would be the last to provide the Prime Minister with 'eye-catching initiatives' to overcome temporary unpopularity.

He is not without warmth and humour, and can be charmingly indiscreet, even about colleagues. He is, however, at base a thinking and quite private man and not very clubbable. Some think him vain.

As a shadow cabinet member at the time of the 1997 election, he was pointedly excluded from the Cabinet itself by Blair. After shadowing the then non-existent 'Environmental Protection' portfolio in Opposition for a year, he got the job in Government, though not at Cabinet rank. As those close to him might have predicted, he took the task seriously, grasped the details and is regarded as having made a good job of it. He saw the Countryside Act on to the statute book. Predictions that he would perish in each of the reshuffles after the 1997 election again proved untrue. He has skillfully balanced the scientific/industrial and environmental lobbies on issues like GM foods, tackled unpopular no-win issues like waste disposal and displays a sure touch when under attack by the broadcasting rottweilers like John Humphrys.

He has certainly mastered his brief. He has proved to the Party leadership that he is an asset and not a liability. Reappointed to effectively the same responsibilities in the new Department for the Environment, Food and Rural Affairs after the 2001 election, he has a good few years in Government yet. But at some stage during this Parliament, a role as elder statesman and conscience of the Party surely beckons. His publications include *Socialism with a Human Face – the Political Economy of the 1980s* (1982) and *Diffusing Power – The Key to a Socialist Revival* (1992). He has two sons and two daughters by his first wife, Molly Reid, whom he married in 1962. After their divorce in 1987 he married Lucianne Sawyer.

Phil Kelly

Bob Mellish (Lord Mellish of Bermondsey)   (1913–98)

When Bob Mellish first stood for Parliament as the Labour candidate in the Rotherhithe by-election, he was handicapped by the fact that he had been imposed upon the constituency by the power of the Transport and General Workers Union at a time when a considerable segment of the local party preferred to nominate a local doctor. The T&G regarded Rotherhithe as one of its seats; Sir Ben Smith, whose resignation caused the by-election, had been a taxi-driver member before he entered Parliament. But the union was in bitter rivalry with the Stevedores' and Dockers' Union, whose membership was strong in Rotherhithe and whose General Secretary, Dickie Barrett, was a local man and a communist. Mellish's principal rival was a shady Liberal, Edward Martell. Apart from a victory in the exceptional circumstances of 1931, Conservative candidates for the seat customarily lost their deposit. For Mellish, to win the nomination was to win the seat.

At one of his early hustings meetings, Mellish, anxious to demonstrate he was working-class through and through, proclaimed, 'I am just like one of you. I am no different.' A burly docker stepped forward. 'I don't want someone like me representing me in Parliament', he said. 'I want someone better.' Mellish ignored the rebuke. Though he was never a docker, he revelled in the title of 'Dockers' MP.' An avid football fan he was later President of Milwall FC.

Robert Joseph Mellish was born on 3 March 1913 and attended St Joseph's School, Deptford. A devout Roman Catholic, he married his wife Anna in 1938, with whom he had five sons. He became a T&G official in 1938. During the Second World War he was in the army and emerged as a captain, rejoining the T&G as a paid employee until succeeding to the Rotherhithe seat. He was briefly a PPS at the fag-end of the Attlee government to, first, the Minister of Supply and then to the Minister of Pensions. When Labour returned to office in 1964, promotion was slow. Mellish was not a natural supporter of the new Prime Minister, Harold Wilson, though he grew to admire him and to declare, in the sentimental language which often belied his tough image, that he 'loved the man.' From 1964 to 1967 he was Joint Parliamentary Secretary at the Ministry of Housing, an unlikely lieutenant to Dick Crossman, particularly as Mellish never hid his contempt for 'intellectuals.' After a reshuffle in 1967, he became Minister of Public Building and Works and then, in 1969 until defeat in June 1970, Government Chief Whip. He returned to that post after the February 1974 general election, with the difficult task of imposing discipline on a minority Labour Party in government. It was his finest hour, an hour prolonged until Jim Callaghan dropped him from the Government he formed after Wilson's retirement in 1976.

Throughout Mellish's second term as Chief Whip, the party, government and nation were in crisis, but, apart from one brief moment in 1975 when, feeling slighted by Wilson, he resigned and then promptly withdrew his resignation, he never wavered. At an informal Cabinet meeting at Chequers in the spring of 1975, Wilson was faced with demands by several of his colleagues, including Roy Jenkins, Reg Prentice, Shirley Williams, Denis Healey and others, for the imposition of a compulsory incomes policy. I sat close to Mellish and could feel him boiling up. At the end of the discussion, Wilson turned to Mellish: 'What do you say, Chief Whip?' he asked. 'I don't care what you effing intellectuals round this table think,' exploded Mellish, (though he did not say 'effing'), 'but I'll tell you I'll never get the effing thing through Parliament.' 'I think that settles it,' said Wilson.

Appointed to serve as Deputy Chairman of the London Docklands Development Corporation 1979–85, Mellish nevertheless continued in the Commons until 1982, but increasingly at odds with the left-wing flow of the Party. In 1982 he resigned his Commons seat and caused a by-election, supporting a local party stalwart who stood against the official Labour candidate, Peter Tatchell, who was totally unsuited to the constituency. The split caused both to be ignominiously defeated by the Liberal, Simon Hughes. He became Lord Mellish of Bermondsey in 1985 and died on 9 May 1998.

Joe Haines

Alun Michael (1943–)

Born on 22 August 1943 in Anglesey, Michael was brought up in a religious family and his religion has been a driving force behind his politics. He is a first language Welsh speaker – and proudly so – and ensured that his own children were educated at a Welsh Language School and bought up speaking Welsh themselves.

Alun was educated at Colwyn Bay Grammar School and went on to Keele University where he studied for a BA Hons degree in Philosophy and English. Keele at the time was still a small university and Michael was not active in politics but was an active member of the Christian Union and contributed to the student newspaper. It was here that he met his wife, Mary Sophia.

After university Alun decided to pursue a career in journalism, and for the period from 1966 to 1972 worked on the *South Wales Echo*. However, it was clear that this was not going to be a career that satisfied him, as he was much more interested in the work of helping people – in particular young unemployed people. He has been involved in many voluntary organisations and community initiatives throughout his life, first in North Wales and then in South Wales, and felt that this was more suited to him than journalism. Alun switched careers in 1972 to become a youth worker, first for Cardiff County Council and then from 1974 until he entered Parliament in 1987 as a Youth and Community Worker for South Glamorgan CC.

It was his interest in helping those young people that led to him taking a more active interest in politics as a way of effecting change. In particular he was interested in the circumstances that keep young people away from crime. He had become a magistrate in 1972 – on the juvenile bench, which he went on to chair in 1986–1987. In 1973 he was elected to Cardiff City Council which he served on until 1989 – staying as a member for two years after being elected to Parliament. His main interest on the Council was economic development, including the redevelopment of central Cardiff and setting up the Enterprise Agency to aid business development. He became a strong advocate for the Cardiff Bay Development which was to create conflict with other members of the Labour Party that spilled over into Parliament. He was also a passionate advocate for devolution for Wales – again in conflict with many in his own party who would later switch to its cause when Labour finally came to power.

It was also whilst on the city council that he met John Reynolds, who was to be a great role model, as a politician and through his belief and support for the Co-operative movement. Alun became a member of the Co-operative Party and he still serves as a Labour and Co-operative MP. His belief in the co-operative ideals and their belief in the concepts of sharing and fairness are as fundamental to his political beliefs as are his Christianity and his experiences working with unemployed young people.

In the 1983 general election he had served as press officer to Jim Callaghan and was there on the night during the campaign when Jim Callaghan famously condemned the Labour Party's policy of unilateral disarmament – without prior warning and without Alun's knowledge. It was this period of Margaret Thatcher's rule, with cuts to the programs he was working on in Cardiff and an economic climate that would give little hope to the unemployed youths he was working with, that led him to the decision to stand for the Cardiff seat when it was vacated by Jim Callaghan in the 1987 General Election.

Almost immediately on his election he was made an Opposition Whip by Neil Kinnock. Barely a year later, in 1988, Kinnock summoned him to the office to tell him that he was to send him to the Welsh team. Alun was reluctant as he felt that he needed more time in the Whips office to get used to the world of Parliament but Kinnock was keen to give Alun his chance and so from 1988 until the general election in 1992 Alun was Shadow Minister for Welsh Affairs.

Immediately after the general election in 1992 Alun was promoted again – this time by

John Smith – to become Shadow Minister for Home Affairs, as deputy to Tony Blair, and the team began to make important headlines on law and order through Blair's use of the phrase 'Tough on crime, tough on the causes of crime'. Law and order was prime Conservative turf, but the Labour team slowly began to prise it away from them with this dual approach. Alun also retained his commitment to the voluntary sector, joining the board of Crime Concern from 1993–97.

In 1994 John Smith died, and Alun Michael put his support behind the head of his team, Blair, for the leadership, not only because they had worked closely together but because Michael felt that they shared the same values. Both were modernisers in the Labour Party. Like Blair, Michael was also active in the Christian Socialist movement. Blair was elected leader and for a short time Alun stood in as Shadow Home Secretary. This period also included the long debate on the Criminal Justice and Public Order Act, where there was a great deal of anger within the Labour Party at the severity of some of the measures within the Bill, but Labour showed not for the first time that it would not be tripped up by the Tories but would argue for sensible and effective measures.

Jack Straw was appointed to the position of Shadow Home Secretary by Blair after his election and Alun remained as number two in the Home Office team. Michael also asked that he be allowed to take responsibility for the voluntary sector – an issue that had passed to the National Heritage department from the Home Office but which represented an important area of policy for him personally. He was now dealing with the issues that had launched him into politics and he used the opportunity to instigate a review of the voluntary sector and to push forward his views on youth crime initiatives that were to lead to the decision by the Labour Party to have a commitment to halving the time from arrest to sentence for youths as one of the key pledges for the 1997 general election. In 1997 he also published *Building the Future Together,* which set out a blueprint for partnership between the new Labour Government and the voluntary sector, for which he took lead responsibility in Government after the 1997 election.

With the general election victory in 1997 Alun became Minster of State at the Home Office, responsible for Criminal Policy, the Police and the Voluntary Sector. Alun was also officially named 'Deputy Home Secretary' on the request of Jack Straw, the new Secretary of State. There he began to work on some of the reforms to the criminal justice system – through the Crime and Disorder Act which he steered through Parliament – that he had been working for thirty years inside and outside of politics to instigate. In opposition he had argued strongly for more action to get young people off dole and into work, and in Government he was a member of the Cabinet Committee which designed and launched the New Deal. He also dealt with other legislation such as the Bill to ban handguns.

However, in 1998 events led to the resignation of the then Secretary of State for Wales, Ron Davies, and Alun was suddenly promoted to the Cabinet in his place. Although he would be able to see the devolution of which he had long been a passionate supporter be implemented in Wales, it was not a situation either of his making or of his desire. In addition he would be asked, against his better judgement, to stand to be leader of the Welsh Labour Party – a move which would inevitably lead him to stand for the Welsh Assembly. This period of political manoeuvring was to be reflected on as a mistake as a reluctant Michael was hoisted on to the equally reluctant Welsh Labour Party, and the ensuing political fall-out probably led to the closer than expected result in the Welsh Assembly elections. A Labour Party that had always been strong in Wales found itself with no overall control, and the first Assembly for Wales was to face a turbulent period. Alun had been vilified in the Welsh press and his opponents in the Labour Party managed to convince the media in Wales and in England that the fervently pro-devolution first-language-speaking North Wales man was in fact a London-centred control freak.

The result was that as First Secretary of the Welsh Assembly Michael was in for a torrid time – including from his own party, who had felt cheated out of their popular choice by an electoral college system that was seen as a 'fix'. With a combination of a hung Assembly to try and work with and no deal being brokered, Alun's was doomed to be a minority administration.

As First Secretary of the Welsh Assembly he led the way in forming the Partnership Councils to create dialogue between Assembly members and the business, voluntary and local government sectors in Wales, continuing the work he had done in Westminster in encouraging a partnership approach to Government, using the best of local agencies and business to adapt solutions to local needs. He also promoted a new framework for the youth service in Wales, which is now being implemented by the Assembly. Michael had to work hard in the early period of establishing the National Assembly for Wales, in the face of the difficulties over the election result not creating a clear majority and the fact that many Welsh still needed to be convinced about the Assembly, as it had only been supported by a close vote in a knife-edge referendum of the Welsh people. His priorities within the limited scope of the Assembly's powers were economic development, re-structuring post-16 education and reforming the health service in Wales.

After a year of pressure from within and externally, Michael finally resigned. The question of his leadership came to a head ostensibly on the issue of whether the money was available for implementing Objective One. The minor parties in the Assembly challenged Michael with a vote of no confidence over the matter which acted as a hook on which to hang discontent. Although the allegation was untrue – and he was totally vindicated shortly afterwards – he felt he had to resign to protect the integrity of the Assembly. Michael also decided to resign from the Welsh Assembly and returned to Westminster, where he was still an MP, to sit on the backbenches. His constituency party overwhelmingly convinced him to stay on at the 2001 election, although he had earlier announced his intention to stand down to concentrate on the Assembly.

Still a politician bounding with energy despite the setback in Wales, Alun has spent his time working with the voluntary sector, and also took up the Presidency of Cardiff CAB and the Chair of the Wales Committee of NACRO. He also still serves as a member of the Co-operative Party NEC, is active in the Christian Socialists and is involved in work on volunteering and the New Deal. His patience, loyalty and hard work were rewarded in Tony Blair's June 2001 post-election reshuffle with his return to government as Minister of State for Rural Affairs in the new Department of the Environment, Food and Rural Affairs.

Ian Moss

Jim Middleton   (1878–1962)

Jim Middleton was the first Secretary of the Labour Party (as the post of General Secreary was then called) not to be a Parliamentary politician in his own right. He played a key, and to modern ears unsung, role in keeping the party organisation together during the splits of the MacDonald era and rebuilding its strength for the campaign in 1945.

Born in Retford in 1878, James Smith Middleton became in 1903 the part-time assistant to the secretary (and only paid official) of the Labour Representation Committee, Ramsay MacDonald. During the general election of 1906 Middleton, was one of a handful of officials working out of the back-bedroom of MacDonald's Lincoln's Inn Fields flat, this being the nearest there was to a party headquarters. His father, A E Middleton was an ex-London journalist and printer who had in 1888 bought and revitalised the ailing local journal the *Workington Star*. Leaving school at twelve, Jim Middleton had joined his father's paper as printer's devil, machinist, compositor, linotype operator, office boy and amateur reporter. An early recruit to the ILP, he was secretary of Workington Trades Council by the age of 22 and secretary of his local LRC shortly thereafter. Moving to London in 1902 for a job as a newspaper compositor, he had within a year taken up a post with Ramsay MacDonald. He had married fellow socialist Mary Muir in 1900 who became Secretary of the Woman's Labour League. She became great friends with MacDonald's wife Margaret, and after Mary's untimely death in 1911 Margaret MacDonald founded the first baby clinic in Britain as a memorial to her friend. Jim Middleton was very much the backroom boy and it was only after some thirty years as Labour Party Assistant Secretary that in 1935, following his appointment as Secretary, he was to make his first Labour Party Conference speech.

During the First World War he served as Secretary of the War Workers Emergency Committee – as Margaret Cole put it, 'a clumsy name describing what was in fact the first real national combination of all the working-class and socialist forces.' Arthur Henderson was its Chairman and Sidney Webb, in effect, its chief draughtsman.

In 1924, when his boss, Arthur Henderson, became Home Secretary, Middleton took over day-to-day running of Labour's headquarters. When the situation recurred on Henderson's return to Cabinet in 1929, rumours began to circulate that Henderson would soon retire. It was Herbert Morrison who was initially the favourite to succeed. Morrison certainly wanted the post, as did Arthur Greenwood, but Henderson and Ernest Bevin were both determined that the next General Secretary ought not also to be a leading parliamentarian. Bevin's view was 'one man one job', whilst Henderson was keen that Morrison concentrate on making a success of the LCC. Unhappy at the prospect of being succeeded by either Morrison or Greenwood, Henderson remained technically in situ, though his role in the Disarmament Conference meant he was increasingly abroad. Middleton was therefore increasingly filling Henderson's shoes. When in 1934 Labour's NEC finally forced Henderson to announce his resignation, he was well placed to succeed him. With Parliamentarians like Morrison and Greenwood kept out of the running, and with Henderson's backing and encouragement, Middleton was in November 1935 chosen by the NEC as the new Party Secretary. His success from a short list of six that included Arthur Woodburn and Arthur Creech-Jones, both later members of Attlee's Cabinet, was undoubtedly helped by his reputation for organisational diligence and his ostensible lack of enemies. Morrison was never entirely reconciled to his failure to secure the post of Party Secretary and in consequence, his biographers George Jones and Bernard Donoughue were to note, 'maintained an undercurrent of criticism against Middleton for inefficiency.'

In May 1930 he declined an honour from MacDonald. They remained in touch even after MacDonald gave up the premiership in 1935. In 1931, Middleton wrote to MacDonald of feeling 'almost the deepest sadness I have ever known,' at the latter's decision to break with his party and form the National Government. For Middleton Labour was his life, but his stalwart devotion and personal loyalty to friends was unbreaking. He died in 1962, survived by his third wife, Lucy Cox, whom he had married in 1936 and who was from 1945 to 1951 the Labour MP for Plymouth Sutton. His second wife, Alice Todd, whom he had married in 1913 and by whom he had a daughter, died in 1935.

Greg Rosen

Ian Mikardo (1908–1993)

Ian Mikardo was a key member of the left-wing Bevanite faction that battled with the Gaitskellites for the soul of the Labour Party during the 1950s. But unlike a number of his Bevanite colleagues such as Harold Wilson, Dick Crossman and Barbara Castle, Mikardo never gained a ministerial post. Nonetheless he maintained a high profile from the backbenches as a critic of governments of both Parties.

'Mik' was born on 9 July 1908 in Portsmouth into an impoverished family of Jewish migrants. His father Moshe (anglicised to Morris) was a tailor who had arrived in London from Poland with so little command of English that he allegedly thought that he was in New York. His mother Bluma had arrived in Britain from Ukraine. He did well at school and won a scholarship to Aria College to train as a rabbi though, like his classmates, did not complete his training. Much to his mother's disappointment he had already begun to show a greater enthusiasm for the work of R H Tawney than for his rabbinical studies.

He continued his political education in the discussion groups and socialist societies of the Jewish East End before joining the Labour Party and *Poale Zion*, a Jewish socialist movement affiliated to the Party, in 1930. He married Mary Rossette, also the daughter of Jewish migrants, in 1931 and moved in with her extended family in London. He was earning a living drifting between bookkeeping jobs before enrolling on a course in 'Scientific Management' which was to provide him with the basis for his later career as a management consultant. After being employed in small consultancies he was inspired to set up on his own, he claimed, after seeing three laundry vans from the same firm making simultaneous deliveries in the same street. He rang the laundry firm the following day offering his services.

After war broke out his management skills were put to use in the aircraft industry and it was a contract from a factory in Berkshire that brought him from the East End of London to Reading where he was to make his first serious in-roads in the Labour Party. He was a surprise selection as the candidate for the election that was to follow the war, ahead of Jim Callaghan amongst others. The seat seemed to offer little prospect of a Parliamentary career, a fact that seemed not to bother Mik overly, developing as he was a successful career in consultancy. But he was swept to Parliament in the Labour landslide of 1945 and was, with only a brief interlude, to remain there until he retired in 1987.

He had, however, made an impression on at least one senior Labour figure before he arrived in Parliament. At the 1944 Party conference he moved the 'Reading resolution' calling for significant extensions of state ownership of industry which was carried against the wishes of much of the Labour leadership. Following Mik's speech Herbert Morrison introduced himself with the words 'That was a good speech you made but you realise, don't you, that you've lost us the General Election?' This event provides early indication of Mik's faith in state ownership and of his capacity to irritate senior figures in his own party.

Once in Parliament he soon fell in with other young newcomers on the left of the Parliamentary Party such as Dick Crossman and Michael Foot. It was with these two that he published *Keep Left* in 1947, a pamphlet criticising the conduct of international affairs under the Attlee government and calling for Britain and Europe to set out a democratic socialist model distinct from American capitalism and Soviet communism. The *Keep Left* pamphlet acted as the manifesto for the Keep Left group of disillusioned backbenchers, though with most of its membership being relatively young and inexperienced the group had a relatively low profile. This was to change, however, in the wake of the resignations of three ministers, Nye Bevan, Harold Wilson and John Freeman, from the government in 1951. The Keep Left group became the focus of parliamentary dissent within Labour, and in particular it became a focus of support for Nye Bevan as a future Party leader. Following the resignations Keep Left was transformed into the Bevanites and grew in significance and was to provide powerful left opposition to the Labour leadership in the 1950s, especially after Gaitskell had beaten Bevan to the Party leadership in 1955. Mikardo played a central role in organising the group.

But unlike a number of the Bevanites such as Crossman, Castle and the economist Tommy Balogh, Mikardo was not included in his erstwhile Bevanite colleague Wilson's 'kitchen cabinet'. For Mik's part he claimed not to have trusted Wilson from the early 1950s and maintained that this distrust had been vindicated by Wilson's move to the right once in office. On the other hand, from Wilson's point of view, Mik's unstinting commitment to public ownership, Zionism and the right of the Party membership to hold the Parliamentary Party to account made him a potentially troublesome minister despite his managerial experience. On a more trivial note Mik's physical appearance also may have mitigated against a high-profile public post. Whilst always popular with grass roots activists his slightly scowling expression would not have been any more appealing to the easily intimidated floating voter than his views on public ownership. On seeing him for the first time, Churchill is alleged to have asked whether he was as nice as he looked whilst another commentator observed that he looked as if he was perpetually walking into a stiff breeze. More significantly though he was out of Parliament at a crucial time.

Reading was always a marginal constituency that Mikardo had unexpectedly won in 1945 and even more improbably held in the general elections of 1950, 1951 and 1955. This was due in no small part to the application of his organisational skills to constituency campaigning. He developed the 'Reading system', identifying and focussing campaigning efforts on potential Labour voters in the constituency rather than wasting time on committed Conservatives who were never likely to be won over. He was returned to Parliament in 1964 as MP for Poplar, a seat in his spiritual home of London's East End, and was to hold the seat through name changes and boundary changes until he retired. However he was absent from Parliament in the crucial years of Wilson's rise to the leadership.

During his time out of Parliament he continued to work as a management consultant, an activity that he had been pursuing during his time as an MP anyway. And he also continued his role as a middleman for firms trading with the communist countries of Eastern Europe which he had also begun to develop whilst still in Parliament. These had provided him with quite lucrative additions to his MP's salary as well as an income once he was ousted.

On returning to parliament he resumed his advocacy of his traditional causes – public ownership, greater Party democracy and Zionism – and was happy to attack the Labour government where it failed to meet his standards on these issues. Public ownership and the calls for MPs to be held to account to the Party membership gained in popularity after Labour lost the election in 1970 and again after a second disappointing Labour government in 1979. But he kept his distance from Tony Benn who had become the self-proclaimed champion of them. Mikardo remained loyal to his former *Keep Left* collaborator Michael Foot and played a key role in organising his successful campaign for the Party leadership in 1980. But after Labour's unsuccessful 1983 election campaign he played a lower-profile role in Parliament, perhaps disillusioned and with some of his early fieriness missing. He decided not to contest the 1987 election.

Despite never holding the ministerial post that his organisational flair might have warranted, Mikardo maintained a high public profile from the backbenches, briefly securing election as chair of the Parliamentary Labour Party in 1974–75. He contributed to Labour Party affairs as an assiduous long-term member of the NEC (1950–59 and 1960–78) and of Parliamentary select committees. He established himself as the Parliamentary bookmaker and rarely lost. He played a key role in building up the ASSET trade union. He also remained truer to his original values than perhaps any colleagues. After retiring he wrote his memoirs, appropriately titled *Backbencher* (Weidenfeld & Nicholson, 1988). He died on 6 May 1993.

Dr. Philip Larkin

Alan Milburn (1958–)

There are those who would regard Alan Milburn as being one of the 'Project's' nastier members, inasmuch as he has a reputation for never suffering fools gladly and has an almost tribal approach to political debate: 'either you are with us or you are not and, if you are not, you're toast'. This reputation, at the robust end of politically antagonistic, is unfair, but perhaps it is understandable how it has arisen.

Alan Milburn was born on 27 January 1958 in Birmingham, the son of a single mother, and raised in the mining village of Tow Law in County Durham. Educated at John Marley School in Newcastle upon Tyne and Stokesley Comprehensive, he went on to study at the University of Lancaster and the University of Newcastle. During his student days Milburn's interest in politics came to the fore while at Lancaster University, and later when returning to the North East to begin a PhD into the origins of the Labour movement in the region. His Damascene conversion from 'old Labour' to the 'Project' was therefore more thoroughly based in an academic analysis of Labour's past failures than the opportunism that thwarted Tories have so frequently previously claimed of Milburn and his ilk.

To this extent, Milburn is typical of much which characterises the genesis of New Labour's 'shock stormtroopers': politicians determined to effect deep-reaching social change and, therefore, unimpressed by the niceties of 'old school' politics which (many New Labour adherents would accuse) cheerfully sacrificed 'achievement' for the maintenance of cross-party relations. Milburn is discernibly part of New Labour's technocracy, determined to forge a new social contract between the people and Government.

After university, Milburn worked for the Trade Union Studies Information Unit, providing briefings and other services around labour issues to trade unions and local authorities. He became involved in a number of high-profile campaigns, most notably that to oppose the closure of the Sunderland Shipyards. He ran a highly visible campaign, which – while ultimately unsuccessful – did nonetheless successfully mobilise public opinion behind the cause of the shipyard workers. Passionately, he argued the case for the viability of shipbuilding in the North East. Milburn still speaks of his anger at the Government's 'wanton act of industrial vandalism' that resulted in over 2,500 job losses. Today, Milburn may no longer see the need to fight valiant but doomed battles to protect 'heavy' British industry in a global market: undeniably, however, he has never lost the sense of outrage and pain he then felt as he witnessed a Tory government sacrifice an entire region on the alter of Thatcherism. The Sunderland shipyard campaign made Milburn realise that the only real way to stem the decline in manufacturing in the North East was to act from within Parliament, rather than from outside, and it was at this point that he determined to become an MP.

Having been selected in 1990, Milburn fought off the Tory, Michael Fallon, to win the seat on a 5 per cent swing to Labour, securing a majority of 2,798. His victory was all the sweeter for having swept away the 'back-to-basics' dirty campaign that strove to make an electoral issue out of Milburn's complicated, but not unusual, private life. In his maiden speech, Milburn (who has never abandoned the roots of his empathy with the working men who drove British industry) praised Cleveland Structural Engineering (of Darlington) for their having secured the emblematic contract to build the Tsing Ma suspension bridge in Hong Kong.

Once established in Parliament, Milburn quickly gained a reputation for assiduously attacking the Government over issues such as the dearth of funding for the regional development corporations (compared to, as he saw it, Thatcher's favoured bastard child, the London Docklands Development Corporation, with its huge tax breaks and subsidies), which he described as 'the biggest white elephant in the history of UK property development.'

In October 1993, Milburn was elected Chairman of the Parliamentary Labour Party Treasury Committee: in many ways the first step upon his route to national prominence. He continued to attract attention – being seen as a rising star and, indeed, one who could be relied upon as being a thorn in the Government's side – over issues such as the internal market in the NHS. His legislative interests, however, must be seen as going more broadly than just the tribal skirmishes of Tory versus Labour. He proposed an amendment to the Criminal Justice Bill, finally to change the ancient Common Law rule of a 'year and a day' limit to bringing a charge of murder – one of his constituents had been comatose for more than a year before dying. Although he was successfully thwarted by Michael Howard, the then Home Secretary (whom some would argue was the most legally conservative and uniconoclastic of post-war holders of that office), he continued to fight for this legal reform.

In 1994, when sitting on the Public Accounts Committee, Milburn claimed that leaked documents from the Employment Service revealed that unemployed claimants were being deliberately offered low-paid, hard-to-fill vacancies in out-of-the-way parts of the country to 'con' them out of benefits. Milburn, no doubt driven by the ire he has always felt for the way in which Thatcher's administration condemned a generation of working men to premature obsolescence, relentlessly pursued the Government saying 'ex-miners, who have been made redundant through no fault of their own, risked losing their benefit entitlements if they turn down jobs as hairdressers and debt collectors.' He evangelised the cause of industrial workers in the North East at precisely the time when many London-centric journalists had lost interest in the Northern industrial classes.

A tough Parliamentary operator, Milburn was promoted in October 1995 to serve as Assistant Spokesman on Health, serving under Harriet Harman. On his front bench debut he accused the Tory government of wasting millions of pounds on NHS bureaucracy: it was to prove a tough, but invaluable, training ground for his later Government role.

Appointed Assistant Spokesman on the Treasury in 1996, a promotion that caught the eye of many political watchers, he continued to harry the Government over its economic record, regularly attacking the then Chancellor, Kenneth Clarke. Later in 1996 he finally succeeded in seeing the law for murder changed when his Law Reform (Year and a Day) Bill went through the Commons in just one minute and fifty seconds, thus ending a 700-year-old law which said that a person had to die in 366 days for the offence to be considered murder. He richly savoured his victory over Michael Howard, by then the *bête noire* of the left's caucus of lawyers and law reformers.

Like most of Labour's vanguard, Milburn's 1997 electoral victory was historic for its scale, seeing his majority rise to 16,025 on a 14.1% swing to Labour. Since entering the Government (as a Minister of State, in the Department of Health) Milburn has deepened his reputation as a safe – if occasionally bellicose – pair of hands that Downing Street can rely upon in even the most difficult of circumstances. His brief stint as Chief Secretary to the Treasury – a promotion he earned in 1998 – arose as part of the 'musical chairs' that was played after the (first) fall of Mandelson. As Chief Secretary, he was steadfast in maintaining the Downing Street axis between numbers 10 and 11 that there was to be no 'raiding' of the Government's war chest. Millburn's ascension to political prominence in a spending ministry came after the doomed shunting of Frank Dobson into Blair's London Mayoral adventure. Despite the heavy increase in spending that Gordon Brown has gifted to the NHS, Millburn has retained a reputation which combines political toughness, genuine empathy for the ordinary family but, however, a willingness to embrace the new, even at the risk of assaulting the vested interests of middle-class doctors.

Richard Elsen

David Miliband (1965–)

David Miliband's reluctance to develop a personal media profile means that he is rarely grouped together with the cadre of young special advisers who are alleged to dominate New

Labour from behind the scenes. Yet he headed Blair's unit of policy advisers from when the PM became Labour Leader in 1994 right up until he became MP for South Shields at the June 2001 election, and his influence on the actual substance of Labour policy has been more profound than that of any other adviser.

It is unsurprising that he has clung to his low profile, though: it has served him well. A year into Blair's leadership, the first rumblings of discontent from the Labour Party began to appear over the 'Kremlin' leadership style of Blair and his team. Miliband was initially fingered as being one of the 'politburo' of advisers creating all the trouble, but the higher profile of other targets (Powell, Campbell and Mandelson in particular) drew the fire away from him, and he subsequently got on with his job relatively quietly.

The son of Marxist historian Ralph Miliband, David grew up in Hampstead and attended the local Haverstock Comprehensive School. Obviously bright, he progressed to Oxford and gained a first class degree in Politics, Philosophy and Economics at Corpus Christi – a degree he has subsequently supplemented as a Kennedy Scholar at America's MIT.

Born on 15 July 1965, he became a research fellow at the Institute of Public Policy Research at the age of just 24. It proved a useful first job, for in 1992 the IPPR was named as the secretariat to the Commission on Social Justice established by Labour Leader John Smith, and Miliband became its secretary.

The Commission brought him into closer contact with some of the leading intellectuals of the left, such as Gordon Borrie, Patricia Hewitt and David Marquand. In the event Smith had died, and Miliband been appointed Blair's head of policy, before the final report of the Commission was issued. But although not all of the Commission's proposals have been adopted as policy, some, such as the minimum income guarantee for pensioners, have been, and its general theme of a shifting emphasis towards 'workfare' has become a New Labour staple.

By the time the Commission reported, Miliband had gained a reputation for intellectual brilliance, even though at university he was seen as a talented all-rounder rather than a blinding genius. Doubtless, it is the all-rounder in him that makes him so indispensable for politicians faced with policy questions from all angles.

Nevertheless it took him a year after the general election to be confirmed in the post of Head of Downing Street Policy Unit, since in the meantime Blair had set off on a fruitless attempt to find a high-profile businessman to take the job.

Amiable and diplomatic, Miliband shows none of the arrogance that might be expected in one who has become so intellectually powerful so young. It is this manner as much as anything that has won him the ability to work with Cabinet Ministers on their departmental policies without provoking them into jealous territorialism.

Peter Metcalfe

Bruce Millan (1927–)

Born on 5 October 1927, Bruce Millan was educated at Harris Academy, a private school in Dundee. He married Gwendoline May Fairey in 1953 and they had one son and one daughter. Millan trained, then worked, as a chartered accountant from 1950 until entering the House of Commons in 1959 as the MP for Glasgow Craigton, the seat where he had stood in the previous election in 1955 but in which he had been defeated at that time by the Conservative J N Browne. He was re-elected to the same seat in the subsequent elections of 1964, 1966, 1970, 1974 (both) and 1979, and then to the re-named and re-organised seat of Glasgow Govan in 1983 and 1987. Throughout his elected political life, his colleagues and his opponents regarded Millan as a thoughtful political moderate.

Following Labour's election success in the 1964 elections, Millan was appointed Parliamentary Under Secretary of State for Defence (RAF) until the general election of April 1966. Following the election of another Labour Government, Bruce was appointed Parliamentary Under Secretary of State for Scotland, a role in which he served until Labour's defeat in the general election of 1970, moving then to the Opposition front bench as a spokesman on trade and industry.

The return of another Labour Government in the first general election of 1974 saw Millan appointed as a Minister of State at the Scottish Office. Millan was not known amongst his colleagues as a devolution enthusiast yet found himself during this time ordered by Harold Wilson to sort out the Scottish party's policy on devolution following the SNP's rise in support in the elections of 1974.

Millan was appointed Privy Counsellor in 1975 and on the election of Jim Callaghan as Labour leader and therefore Prime Minister in April 1976, joined the Cabinet as Secretary of State for Scotland in 1976, serving until Labour's defeat in the 1979 general election. He was Shadow Scottish Secretary 1979–83, winning election to the shadow cabinet twice in November 1981 and November 1982.

After almost 30 years in the House of Commons, Bruce Millan resigned his Govan seat in 1988. The fears of some regarding the scope for an SNP advance in Govan were borne out by the election victory of Jim Sillars in the subsequent Govan by-election (later regained by Labour's Ian Davidson in the 1992 election) and to this day the Govan constituency (albeit reorganised again) remains a supposed key target for the SNP in Scotland.

Less than 12 months after his resignation as a Member of Parliament, Millan was appointed by Margaret Thatcher as a member of the Commission of the European Community (EC) where he served one term as a European Commissioner. Prime Minister Major replaced him as Commissioner with Neil Kinnock following the latter's defeat in 1992. Many felt that Millan was retired, at the age of 68, against his will to make way for a major UK player who had outgrown the UK stage.

Millan's time in semi-retirement saw him serve as Convenor of the Charity Children in Scotland and as a member of the Board of the Scottish Association for Mental Health. His experience in the latter role led to his appointment in 1999 by the then Scottish Office Minister for Health, Sam Galbraith MP, as Chair of a Committee established to conduct an assessment and review of Scotland's mental health legislation. Millan's remit in this regard covered everything from the definition of mental disorder to arrangements for the sentencing and treatment of serious violent and sexual offenders.

This committee (referred to by the political establishment as 'The Millan Committee') recommended numerous changes to legislation, practices and procedures and most notably proposed extending the definition of 'nearest relative' in the Scottish Parliament's flagship Adults with Incapacity (Scotland) Bill to include couples in same-sex relationships, thus allowing them to act as legal guardians of a partner who becomes mentally or physically incapacitated.

Millan therefore entered the twenty-first century as he had served in the twentieth, a capable consensus politician able to adapt with ease his well-honed political skills to new environments to constructive effect. A man who is perceived by some as a Labour patrician, Millan never entered the House of Lords as may have been expected and, at the time of writing, lives in Glasgow and maintains a relatively low profile in spite of his continuing good works.

Eric Joyce MP

Eddie Milne (1915–83)

The story of Eddie Milne does the Labour party no credit. The worst that could be said of him was that he was stubborn and obsessive, but he was a transparently honest man in a region and at a time when the party was infected with corruption. Yet he was made to suffer, while more questionable characters prospered.

A docker's grandson, he was born on 18 October 1915 in Aberdeen, while his father was away at war, from which he returned with his health shattered by a severe wound. He was educated at Kittybrewster Primary School, Sunnybank International School and Robert Gordon's College, Aberdeen. His first job was working in his father's small shop, while his interest in politics was stimulated by the General Strike and by a by-election in Aberdeen won for Labour by Wedgwood Benn. This led him into the ILP, and, after lecturing at the National Council of Labour Colleges (1942–49), into full-time work from 1951 to 1960 for the shopworkers' union, USDAW, in Central Scotland. He unsuccessfully contested Glasgow Rutherglen at the 1959 General Election. In 1960, with USDAW backing, he was selected to fight a by-election in Blyth, in Northumberland, after its MP, Alf Robens, had been appointed head of the Coal Board. He held the seat with a 16,057 majority.

From the start of his Commons career, Milne became interested in the business affairs of public figures, and the potential for corruption. Some of his public statements were well intentioned but unwise: the Tory minister, Ernest Marples, successfully sued him for libel before 1964.

Afterwards, he came increasingly into conflict with Labour MPs and councillors, especially those who were doing business with the corrupt architect, John Poulson. Milne later said that he was amazed by the deference which his fellow Labour MPs from the North East showed towards T Dan Smith, the charismatic and corrupt Leader of Newcastle City Council, who had business links with Poulson. The nearest he came to government was as PPS to Home Secretary Sir Frank Soskice (1964–65).

By early 1973, when the Poulson scandal had become public knowledge through his bankruptcy hearings, Milne had become wholly isolated from the Northern Labour group. He refused to campaign in a by-election in Chester-le-Street in February 1973 because the candidate, Giles Radice, was a nominee of the local boss of the GMB, Andy Cunningham, who would soon be jailed for corruption. Milne was blamed for Labour's poor showing in the by-election, because of comments of his reported in the local paper.

He also made enemies in the Blyth Labour Party, notably the local agent, Peter Mortakis.

In February 1974, with a general election looming, the Blyth party voted not to adopt him as their candidate, later choosing in his place Ivor Richard, who as Lord Richard was a member of Tony Blair's Cabinet in 1997–98.

Milne defiantly fought and held Blyth in February, for which he was automatically expelled from the party and abandoned by every important figure in the Labour Party, left or right. In October 1974 he was defeated by the new Labour candidate, John Ryman, whose parliamentary career began and ended scandalously. Mortakis, Ryman's agent, was convicted of falsifying his election expenses, and Ryman himself was under investigation when he quit the Commons in 1987, and was later jailed for fraud. Milne himself lived quietly in Blyth after his defeat and died on 23 March 1983. His autobiography, *No Shining Armour,* was published by John Calder in 1976.

Andy McSmith

Dick Mitchison (Lord Mitchison of Carradale)   (1890–1970)

Despite his late start in Parliamentary politics (he was already 55 when he became MP for Kettering in 1945), Major Gilbert Richard ('Dick') Mitchison CBE QC was elected to the Shadow Cabinet at his first try in June 1955, serving continuously until his retirement from the Commons in 1964. The reasons were twofold and were nothing to do with his political standing in the party or his likelihood of receiving senior Cabinet office: he was never a particularly heavyweight political player.

Firstly he was highly personable, counting amongst his friends both leading Gaitskellites and Bevanites at a time when such was the feuding that few could do likewise. In his memoirs, *High Tide and After,* Hugh Dalton recollects Mitchison's people skills in acting as, 'one of our best human water-softeners.' House-guests at what Barbara Castle called the substantial 'rustic Scottish retreat' that the Mitchisons bought in the 1930s in Argyll ranged from Castle via the young Jim Callaghan through to Gaitskell, whom he had helped to get selected for Parliament. Not many Labour MPs, it is also true, other than the Eton and Oxford educated Mitchison (he had a First in Greats from New College) actually had such a place. Other friends included Bevan, Jennie Lee and Dick Crossman, for whom even in March 1957 he was 'a dear old thing.'

Secondly, he was an assiduously hard Commons worker and a good team player always happy to put his legal advice (he became a QC in 1946) at the service of the lowliest backbench newcomer. Why it was that this donnish public-school lawyer so consistently outshone his more ambitious younger rivals in shadow cabinet elections was explained by a frustrated Crossman in his diary on 19 March 1959: 'The rank and file party Member spends a large part of his life upstairs in these Committee Rooms, listening to frontbenchers, hour after hour, arguing the detailed Amendments. Of course a number of backbenchers, including all the trade-unionists, were bound to resent the fact that we intellectuals, and particularly the journalists and lawyers, never turn up for this morning work because we are earning a very good living outside. I can see why Dick Mitchison gets such a big vote. It's because he is always there in the mornings, when the work of the Party is really done.'

Already in February and April 1955, Hugh Dalton's diary records conversations with both Attlee and Gaitskell in which Mitchison featured as the likely Solicitor-General in a Labour Government. After securing election to the shadow cabinet in June of that year Mitchison was Principal Opposition Spokesman on Housing and Local Government 1955–59. In November 1959 he became deputy spokesman on Treasury and Trade under Harold Wilson, combining this from November 1961 with shadowing Works and Science (which he particularly relished). In February 1963, to his great frustration, Labour's new leader Harold Wilson replaced his three shadow spokesmanships with the job of Shadow Pensions Minister, which he regarded as demotion.

In 1964 Wilson asked him to go to the Lords and under the unflamboyant former Shadow Education Minister Fred Willey (the only other shadow cabinet member to be given a Ministerial job by Wilson outside Cabinet), he enjoyed an eighteen-month Indian summer as Parliamentary Secretary at the Ministry of Land and Natural Resources (1964–66). Crossman considered Mitchison 'first rate' and unsuccessfully sought to retain him when the Ministry of Land and Natural Resources was merged into his Ministry of Housing in 1966, but Wilson insisted that Lord Mitchison of Carradale was far too old and must be retired. He died on 14 February 1970.

Mitchison's career was varied as well as long. Born on 23 March 1890, the son of Arthur Mitchison and Mary Russell, he joined the Queen's Bays in 1914–18, suffering a serious head-wound whilst serving in France. In 1915 he was GSO 2 at the British Mission to French forces in Italy, being awarded the Croix de Guerre. In 1916 he married Naomi, sister of his Etonian contemporary J B S Haldane and later a famous novelist and close friend of Hugh Gaitskell; the couple had three sons and two daughters. Called to the Bar at the Inner Temple in 1917 he found his legal work unfulfilling and, under the influence of his wife and G D H Cole, he became in 1931 Treasurer of the New Fabian Research Bureau (NFRB), remaining so until its amalgamation into the Fabian Society in 1939. In July 1932 he was, with his wife, Hugh Dalton, Pethick-Lawrence and others, part of the NFRB study trip to Soviet Russia, from which he returned impressed. The NFRB published the impressions of the study group as *Twelve Studies in Soviet Russia* (1933). He became a proponent of planning, including, by way of import quotas, tariffs and trade boards, in the field of foreign trade.

He was Labour's Parliamentary candidate at Kings Norton (in succession to Cole) in 1931 and 1935. Whilst serving on the Executive of the Socialist League he published *The First Workers Government* (1934), which argued for the prompt redistribution of wealth and large-scale nationalisation by an incoming Labour government by means of an enabling act and for the abolition of the Lords, and also envisaged the disappearance of City of London and private housing. In later years, it is clear, these views became more moderated.

Greg Rosen

John Monks (1945–)

As Trades Union Congress General Secretary from September 1993, John Monks presided over a restoration of the organisation's influence and authority. In his thoughtful, constructive and practical way, he was soon able to articulate a New Unionism for the modern age. Monks was a substantial moderniser, aware of union weaknesses and decline, and determined to set an agenda for the trade unions based on the principles of social partnership in a market economy. A passionate believer in Britain's future inside the European Union, he made the TUC the foremost body in the country that supported membership of the Single Currency. Labour's May 1997 landslide election victory certainly assisted Monks's new approach. But he was well aware there was going to be no return to the formal contracts and concordats between the TUC and Labour governments that had characterised previous periods. Monks accepted Prime Minister Tony Blair's promise that under him the trade unions could accept fairness but not favours.

Born on 5 August 1945 in Manchester, the son of Charles Edward Monks, a district parks supervisor, after Ducie Technical High School in Manchester Monks gained a degree from Nottingham University and then spent a short time as a management trainee with Plessey. But he soon grew frustrated at the prospect of a life as a manager and was appointed to a post with the TUC's organisation department in September 1969. He married Francine Schenk in 1970, with whom he has two sons and a daughter. At the TUC he quickly became a highly effective and industrious diplomat in helping devise TUC strategies in the face of government efforts to limit trade union power by law. Monks was a prudent, shrewd and calming proponent of a sensible pragmatism at a time when union leaders were divided bitterly on ideological lines. But he always sought agreement and consent, displaying an endless patience in seeking to reconcile differences without any abandonment of principle. It was no surprise when he was made TUC Deputy General Secretary under Norman Willis in September 1987.

Monks was determined to seize the initiative from the moment he took over at Congress House, keen to show trade unions were not part of Britain's problems but part of their solution. He stressed the need for unions to develop a more aggressive organising culture to appeal to young workers, women and the ethnic minorities. But Monks was also keen to articulate social partnership between unions and companies as well as the TUC and the state in line with best European Union practice. He pursued – with the support of his colleagues on the TUC General Council – what he described as a revived social democracy, which would embrace orderly change, a reduction in inequalities, protection for people at work and a strong welfare state. Monks made some headway in advocating workplace modernisation where competitiveness and social justice were to act in harmony. He even went so far as to accept that bad industrial relations and union inadequacies must take some of the blame for Britain's inadequate post-war economic record.

Monks was often irritated by Tony Blair's negative view of trade unionism. He believed the Labour Prime Minister was too ready to dismiss or overlook the changes which were taking place in most unions as they modernised their views and structures. On one occasion he upset the government by likening union leaders to embarassing elderly relatives at a family reunion. But Monks was a man that Mr Blair could neither ignore nor patronise. His reasonableness and sheer intellectual ability made him a formidable figure. Although it could often be a painfully bruising and troublesome process, the successful implementation of a wide-ranging employment relations agenda between 1997 and 2001 owed much to Monks's ability to negotiate and lobby not only with the Prime Minister but other sources of power in the Labour administration.

The real value of Monks was to bring the TUC back from the wilderness. Once again, it became an organisation whose views were sought out and listened to with respect. But his contribution was perhaps at its greatest in providing the TUC with a new sense of purpose. More than any other General Secretary since George Woodcock in the 1960s, Monks nurtured a vision of what the TUC ought to be for in the new world of private services, information technology and flexible labour markets. He accepted the TUC could not restore for itself the weak corporatist role it had enjoyed with governments in the first three decades after the Second World War. But he did believe the TUC could become a vital body in the creation of a social market economy in Britain with strong worker and union rights designed to increase security and self-esteem in the workplace.

Robert Taylor

Rhodri Morgan (1939–)

Rhodri Morgan would not like the comparison with Ken Livingstone, but it must be made. Rhodri has said 'I am not a Welsh Ken Livingstone', but both have fought and won battles against the massed ranks of New Labour, both are recognised in Labour circles just by the use of their first names, and both have the tendency to get themselves into trouble with their taste for off-the-cuff witticisms which can send any self-respecting press officer into paroxysms of despair.

But the main area where New Labour tried to draw the comparison between Ken and Rhodri does not stand up to scrutiny. Rhodri is less demonstrably a serial oppositionalist and his political agenda is less clearly out of touch with the New Labour leadership. In fact he has remained remarkably loyal considering the flack he took when he had the temerity to run against both Ron Davies (by no means a favoured son of Blairism himself) and Alun Michael for the leadership of the Wales Labour Party.

Since the Labour victory of 1997, he voted with the leadership on the issue of student funding, a brave decision considering the number of students in his Cardiff West constituency. He voted in favour of bombing Iraq, a move guaranteed to lose him any left-wing credibility he had built up in his battle against Millbank. And he made a remarkably loyalist speech to the 2000 Labour Party conference in his role as First Minister for the National Assembly of Wales.

Morgan was born on 29 September 1939 and achieved his goal of leadership of the Welsh Labour Party on 11 February 2000. Between these two dates he was a brilliant student at Whitchurch Grammar School in Cardiff, St John's College Oxford and Harvard, became the highest-paid civil servant in Wales as Head of the European Commission Office in Wales, was elected MP for Cardiff West in 1987 and Assembly Member for Cardiff West in 1999. A successful career in academia, civil service and politics is not bad going for a boy whose great-great-grandfather shot Colonel Napier during the Rebecca Riots and whose great-great-great-grandmother attacked a sergeant with a frying pan when the Yeomanry came to arrest him.

Rhodri Morgan is incredibly popular amongst Labour members and the public in Wales. They regard him, rightfully, as one of their own. He was born and brought up in Cardiff, grandson of a grocer and a miner and son of a teacher and a Welsh language lecturer. He is a long-time supporter of devolution and is a product of solid, centre-left Labour, but has never really sat comfortably with many of those who control the Labour Party machine in Wales, being described by one as being 'too clever by half'. During the debacle of the first Welsh Assembly elections in 1999, when Labour lost such South Wales heartlands as Islywn, Rhodri recorded the only pro-Labour swing in the country.

Despite his persona as 'a colourful gadfly' (Andrew Rawnsley) and 'a mad professor' (Andy McSmith), he is entrenched in the South Wales 'Taffia' that runs Labour in the country. In 1990 the selection for Cardiff Central, eventually won by Jon Owen Jones, was a battle between 'his wife, his researcher, his former researcher and his next-door neighbour, who also happened to be his secretary's husband'. His wife Julie (2 daughters and one adopted son), was eventually selected to fight Cardiff North, which she won in 1997. Despite this place at the heart of South Wales Labour politics, he lost both elections he fought to be Leader of the Welsh Labour Party after the unions backed his opponents Davies and Michael as a result of a Millbank-based desire to ensure that its people won these selections.

He has served the Labour Party in opposition as Assistant Spokesperson on Wales between 1992 and 1997 and as Energy Spokesperson between 1988 and 1992, but was not offered a job after Tony Blair's landslide victory of 1997, as he was said to be too old at 57. He argued, perhaps with cause, that it was actually because he was not part of the 'Taliban of New Labour', closely reminiscent of Ken Livingstone's attacks on the 'Millbank tendency'.

However, Rhodri seemed destined to lead the Wales Labour Party and become First Minister of the Assembly. He fought Ron Davies, lost and then saw the victor self-destruct after a 'moment of madness' on Clapham Common. Rhodri then fought Alun Michael, the anointed representative of Tony Blair in Wales, but failed to secure sufficient support amongst the trade unions. Rhodri was finally given his chance to lead when Michael resigned before facing a 'no confidence' vote in the Welsh Assembly. And it is in this role that the real battle for Morgan's legacy to Labour will be fought.

There is no doubt that Rhodri was a Labour star in the dark opposition days of the late '80s and early '90s. He was one of those laid-back, witty parliamentarians who can destroy a Minister with a joke that is just a little too close to reality for comfort – witness his description of Margaret Thatcher's commitment to cleaning up litter by paraphrasing John F. Kennedy, 'Ich bin ein binliner'. The real question about Rhodri is can he prove wrong the Millbank analysis that he can't govern with the skill that he showed in opposition?

He has made a good start, cutting a clear figure as spokesperson for the whole of Wales and standing up to Gordon Brown over funding for the principality. But the real test for Rhodri will be whether Labour can stop the march of Plaid Cymru into the once ultra-safe citadel of the South Wales valleys when the next Welsh Assembly elections are held in 2003.

Lee Whitehead

Sally Morgan (Baroness Morgan) (1959–)

Sally Morgan became a life peer and Minister of State at the Cabinet Office in June 2001, having been Political Secretary to Prime Minister Tony Blair 1997–2001. She is a tough-minded organiser with a common touch and has repeatedly ensured that the Labour machine achieved whatever was demanded of it.

Born in Liverpool on 28 June 1959, she went to Belvedere School in Liverpool then obtained a geography degree at Durham University (1977–80), followed by a Post Graduate Certificate of Education and MA (Educ.) from London University (1980–81). She later taught Geography in a London secondary school (1981–85). At Durham Sally joined the Labour Party and met fellow student John Lyons, whom she married in 1984. Sally and John have two sons.

Sally's progress towards a teaching career was continually interrupted by involvement in student and youth politics. This experience led to her appointment as Labour's Student Organiser in 1985 and she has been a servant of the Party ever since. Sally's overriding aim, slightly diverted by her four years on Wandsworth Borough Council (1986–90), has been to make Labour a modern, campaigning political party.

The most delicate of Labour's modernising tasks have frequently been allotted to Sally Morgan. If these tasks had not been completed then New Labour would not have been possible. As Student Organiser, she masterminded removal of the Militant Tendency and other entrists from Labour's student and youth wings. As Senior Targeting Officer (1987–90), she supervised Labour's first positive responses to modern feminism and Britain's ethnic minorities. As Key Seats Officer (1990–93), she organised the disproportionately successful Labour campaign in its 1992 general election target seats. As Campaigns Director (1993–95), she ran Labour's successful European Parliament election of 1994.

On election as party leader in 1995, Blair lifted Sally out of Party HQ and made her Head of Party Liaison in his private office. Following the 1997 general election victory, she became Political Secretary in Number 10. This job required many skills but Sally Morgan added to them an instinct for what constitutes a potential political problem and the courage to deal with such problems swiftly.

Rex Osborn

Bill Morris (1938–)

Bill Morris's life can perhaps best be understood as a series of journeys. The journey from Jamaica to Britain as a teenager; from the shopfloor of a Birmingham engineering firm to the Court of the Bank of England; through the hierarchy of Britain's second biggest union to its summit, the office of General Secretary; and perhaps most interestingly of all, the journey from left-wing candidate for high union office to the position of 'supportive yet critical friend' to a New Labour government.

Bill Morris was born William A Morris in Bombay, Jamaica, on 19 October 1938 and lived with his parents (his mother was a domestic science teacher, his father a part-time policeman) in a small rural village, Cheapside, Manchester. He was educated at nearby Mizpah School where his ambition was to play cricket for the West Indies.

His plans to attend a prestigious agricultural college had to be rethought in 1954, when he joined his recently widowed mother in Britain, living in the Handsworth district of Birmingham. The cultural differences were considerable – as was the weather – but he coped with the snow and the rain and started work at the Birmingham engineering company, Hardy Spicers, attending day-release courses in engineering skills at Handsworth Technical College. He later married and had two sons, Garry and Clyde, and now has two grandchildren, Una and Rohan. His wife, Minetta, died in 1990. He now lives in Hemel Hempstead with his partner Eileen.

Bill's trade union life began in 1958 when he joined the Transport and General Workers Union. While at Hardy Spicers, he and his fellow workers were unhappy at the lack of provision of protective gloves for their work. A deputation was organised to see the management, and in the absence of the shop steward Morris spoke up for the workers. Soon after he was elected shop steward at Hardy Spicers, and in 1964 he was involved in his first major industrial dispute, over the issue of trade union recognition.

He was appointed a full-time TGWU Officer in 1973, as Nottingham/Derby District Organiser, and later as Northampton District Secretary. In 1979 he was appointed National Secretary for the Passenger Services Trade Group, responsible for leading national negotiations in the bus and coach industries. In 1986, Morris applied for the position of Deputy General Secretary, then a post appointed by the TGWU Executive. Morris put in what was regarded to have been an impressive performance in front of the Finance and General Purposes Committee, yet the committee, which was controlled by representatives of the union's right wing, did not shortlist him. Incensed at the committee's failure to shortlist the person he felt was the outstanding candidate for the job, the then General Secretary Ron Todd insisted that Morris's name go forward to the 39–strong executive. He duly did so, and beat the union's executive officer Larry Smith by 20 votes to 17.

He became Deputy General Secretary in 1986 and, as a result of a change in the law, was confirmed in the position by postal ballot four years later. His industrial duties included executive responsibility for the union's four transport sectors, the car industry, energy and engineering and white collar workers. He was also responsible for the union's educational activities, equal opportunities and development of policies and services for women and young members.

In 1991, Bill Morris contested the election for General Secretary, lining up against the man who Ron Todd had defeated in 1986, the union's regional secretary for Wales George Wright. As contemporary accounts record, the campaign was notably lacking in fraternal spirit. Wright was backed by the union's right wing while Morris was backed by the broad left grouping, which had supported Ron Todd as General Secretary. During the campaign, Morris made much of the differences between the two candidates, saying that he believed in lay member democracy, while Wright did not. Both candidates' supporters accused the other camp of playing the race card, though in different ways.

He was set to become the first black general secretary of a trade union and arguably one of the most influential black people in Britain. But he made it clear he did not wish to be known or judged as a black General Secretary: as he said at the time of his election, 'I am not the black candidate, rather the candidate who is black.'. In the event, Morris won comfortably, polling 118,206 (48 per cent of those voting) to Wright's 83,059 (33.8 per cent).

Under John Smith's leadership, Bill Morris opposed One Member One Vote (OMOV), casting the TGWU vote against it in the crucial 1993 Labour conference ballot. It is often forgotten that on that day the conference also voted to back a TGWU motion, proposed by Bill Morris, which opposed the Smith plans outright. However, a vote on rule changes, which was also passed meant that the leader's plan was accepted.

In 1995, the TGWU's National Organiser, Jack Dromey challenged Bill Morris for the position of General Secretary. Dromey had originally backed Morris in the 1991 contest, but had failed to secure Morris's backing for the post of deputy general secretary which became vacant upon his own elevation. The contest between Morris and Dromey was ill tempered. During the campaign, Dromey accused Morris of being out of touch with members, and of only appearing on television in order to attack the Labour leadership. He was critical of Morris's failure to ballot the TGWU membership over the union's decision to oppose Tony Blair's new Clause 4 in the summer of 1995. For his part, Morris accused Dromey of lacking principles and loyalty. He said that if Dromey were elected, control of the TGWU would in effect pass to Mr Blair, whilst under his leadership, the union would continue to be 'a strong, independent industrial organisation'. He also suggested that Dromey's wife, the then Shadow Employment Secretary Harriet Harman, would find herself in an impossible position due to the conflicting loyalties of her husband on issues such as the minimum wage.

Morris emerged triumphant from another bitter contest, winning 158,909 votes to Dromey's 100,056. His record as general secretary suggests that there is much for him to be proud of. He has succeeded in driving through a reorganisation of the TGWU itself, creating trade groups more relevant to the new economy, turning a £7 million deficit into a healthy surplus, and overseeing the union's odyssey from the old Smith Square HQ, via a soulless office block in Victoria, to a new, purpose-built Transport House in Holborn. While TGWU membership fell during most of his period as general secretary, along with other major unions in Britain, an aggressive recruitment campaign had started to show results by 1999, with small overall increases in membership being reported.

Although Tony Blair (a TGWU member throughout) was careful not to make his own position known, many supporters of Labour's modernisation project openly supported and campaigned for Dromey, with the effect that Morris' victory, always likely, was seen as a rejection of the modernisation project itself. Some claim Morris' victory was a precursor of the difficulties faced by the Labour leadership in Wales and London, where candidates backed by the leadership were rejected by the rank-and-file. Yet the TGWU has rarely been an accurate barometer of the prevailing mood within the Labour party as a whole, and the truth is that, as a relatively new, popular and high-profile incumbent, Morris was always likely to win.

In the years after re-election, Morris established stronger links with the Labour leadership, taking the chair of the Party-Union Liaison Committee, though he was rumoured to have been unhappy with the minimal use the party made of him during the 1997 election campaign. Naturally a rather reserved and private man, by now his public appearances had become more confident, helped by his deep, lilting voice, with its Jamaican and Brummie tones.

For 18 years the TGWU had been locked out of the corridors of power, but now its General Secretary was swamped with opportunities to contribute to public life. Something of a workaholic, he took on several extra roles (some said too many) among them membership of the Royal Commission on the Reform of the House of Lords and the Court of the Bank of England. His desire to serve in a wider context was perhaps due in part to a desire to prove that the TGWU general secretary could play a constructive role in society at large. Morris was always aware of the dangers of being pigeonholed as an old-fashioned trade union baron, yet he remained sensitive to any accusation of 'selling out'.

His graduation, as some saw it, to the ranks of the 'Great and The Good' did not stop him criticising the Labour Government on a range of policy areas. He attacked both the level of the minimum wage, and the existence of separate youth and trainee rates, while also criticising what he saw as the timidity of the 'Fairness at Work' employment legislation – which he said must be 'a first step, not a final word'.

During Labour's first term, Morris was often described as being close to the Chancellor, Gordon Brown, and his interventions in the debate over the single currency were scrutinised for evidence of the Chancellor's influence. Traditionally wary of European integration, Morris insisted he was in favour of the single currency in principle, but did not want Britain to rush into entry, lest public spending cuts be required to meet the necessary convergence criteria.

Yet despite his friendly relationship with the Chancellor, Morris was not afraid to criticise policies with which Gordon Brown was associated, notably over pensions. At the 2000 Labour conference, he was instrumental in inflicting Blair's first major conference defeat since 1994, on the issue of restoring the link between pensions and earnings, despite last-minute arm-twisting and meetings between the Chancellor, the Prime Minister and the leaders of the main unions, Morris included.

For all his insistence that he is a general secretary who is black, and not a black general secretary, as one of the most high-profile black people in public life, and the most senior black figure in the Labour movement, his interventions in debates on race have carried a great deal of weight.

If he was criticised in December 2000 for comparing William Hague's comments on the MacPherson report to Enoch Powell's 'rivers of blood' speech, many felt he was right to use such a lurid comparison in order to address the issue of how politicians speak about race matters. He has also been critical of his own party on the issue, most tellingly in April 2000, when in an interview with *The Independent* he said that the Government's policy was 'giving life to racists' and 'playing a hostile tune for black Britons'. He accused Jack Straw and his Home Office Ministers of allowing a 'climate of fear and loathing to foster around asylum and immigration issues' and contrasted the Home Secretary's warm response to the MacPherson report with his actual response in policy terms.

He followed this attack up with other broadsides at the Government's asylum policies, notably the scheme that provided asylum seekers with vouchers to buy necessities. His attacks at the Labour conference of 2000 succeeded in winning a review of the voucher scheme and changes to the way the vouchers are paid. Further criticism of the Labour government's policies followed in 2000 and 2001, most notably on public sector reform, though his criticisms were often accompanied by a frustration that the Labour Government was not doing more to publicise some of the progressive measures they had put in place.

In 2000, following press reports that he was considering stepping down early, Morris confirmed that he will remain as General Secretary until 2003, when he will be 65. Then the TGWU may face a problem created by their good fortune in having such a recognisable and popular figure as their general secretary – namely the lack of any significant public profile among the possible successors. Bill Morris refuses to respond to suggestions that he will one day accept a seat in the Upper Legislature he helped to shape. Apart from devoting more time to his position as Chancellor of the University of Technology in Jamaica, he says that he intends to make use of a rocking chair that he was given many years ago: 'When I retire from the TGWU, I may get out my old pipe and sit in my rocking chair, reflecting on what a great life I've had and what a great privilege it has been to lead the TGWU'. He will certainly have earned the rest, after almost half a century of sterling service to his union, its members and the Labour movement.

David Mills

Estelle Morris (1952–)

Estelle Morris is that rarity at Westminster, a rising politician for whom nobody has a bad word. Her promotion to the Cabinet as Secretary of State for Education and Skills was highly popular among both colleagues and civil servants in the Department – if not entirely unexpected after she emerged as the highest-profile woman in Labour's campaign. Her progress has been swift, reaching the Cabinet Room at the age of 48, just nine years after entering Parliament. Any fears that, having served in only one Department, she would lack the political clout to be effective are likely to prove misplaced. As School Standards Minister, she made a strong impression in Downing Street, and improving education is of central importance to the success of Tony Blair's second term.

Estelle Morris comes from a political dynasty. Her father, Rt Hon Charles Morris, was Labour MP for Manchester Openshaw 1963–83, serving as PPS to Tony Benn when Postmaster-General, Deputy Chief Whip 1969–70, PPS to Harold Wilson as Leader of the Opposition 1970–74, and then Minister of State at successively the Department of the Environment and the Civil Service Department in the 1974–79 government. His younger brother, Alf Morris (Lord Morris of Wythenshawe), represented Manchester Wythenshawe for 33 years to 1997, and was the first Minister for the Disabled. Lord Morris has said that it was an 'accident of inevitability, not just probability', that his niece would enter politics.

Born on 17 June 1952, at Whalley Range High School in Manchester she famously failed her French and English A levels. She has explained since that she simply failed to do enough work, having never properly made the transition from primary school. Smoothing that process is one of her priorities. The experience of failure at school has shown her, she now believes, the importance of education. In fact, she is passionate on the subject.

Despite the early setbacks, she went to Coventry College of Education, where she received a teacher's certificate, and then a BEd from Warwick University. Eighteen years of teaching followed at Sidney Stringer School and Community College, a tough mixed comprehensive in Coventry where she took PE and Humanities, becoming Head of the Sixth Form. She was also elected as a councillor, serving for twelve years on Warwick District Council from 1979, eight of them as Labour Group Leader.

She was elected to Parliament for Birmingham Yardley in April 1992, by the margin of just 162 votes. She quickly became Vice-Chair of the Labour backbench Education Committee, and a Whip in 1994. In 1995, she was promoted to the front bench on Education and Employment, and was a natural appointment as Parliamentary Under Secretary (School Standards) in 1997 under Stephen Byers as Minister of State, being promoted into his post the following year. Her rise has been earned by being good at the job, with primary school standards – especially in English and Maths – showing significant improvement in Labour's first term.

On her promotion to the Cabinet, *The Times* called her 'one of the unexpected successes of the last Parliament'. The promise was there in Opposition, notably to those who saw her performance on the Conservative government's last Education bill in 1996–97. Fluent and fully on top of the subject, she puts her arguments with conviction and common sense, while always being absolutely reasonable in her approach. She is straightforward and can be tough without ever needing to be heavy-handed. Firmly in line with the Blairite approach, she is non-ideological and describes herself as a pragmatist. Her emphasis will be on 'whatever works best'.

Education, with Health and Transport, forms one of the key public services on which Tony Blair has staked the success of his second term. With the credibility of her teaching experience, Morris will hope to win back some of the support of teachers, which turned to frustration and anger after 1997 at continuing criticism of the profession and a still-rising tide of paperwork. Union opposition to increasing the role of the private sector could, however, be stiff.

The overriding priority is to drive up secondary standards – notably in English and Maths for 11–14 year olds, where many pupils fall back – mirroring the improvement at primary level. Labour's ambitions are massive: Morris has spoken of a 'transformation' in standards which will become 'entrenched'. Teachers may oppose a literacy hour for younger secondary pupils, especially if it involves retraining out of hours. At the same time, however, Morris will be expected to resolve objections by teachers to their workload. Raising standards will be coupled with strong encouragement to continue full-time education until 18.

Structural reforms, first outlined in the Queen's Speech 2001, are expected to lead to a doubling of specialist schools, with elite schools taking over failing comprehensives. The private sector will be encouraged to take over successful as well as unsuccessful schools, sponsor new City Academies and bid for local authority services. Heads of successful schools will also be enabled to buy in services from the private sector without LEA agreement. The hope is that private sector experiments in raising standards will lead by example. A large expansion of Church schools will also be encouraged. Answering LEAs', teachers' and parents' fears that these measures will create a two-tier secondary structure akin to grammar and secondary modern schools will be one of Estelle Morris's main challenges. Local education authorities are also likely be concerned at any reduction in their overall role in planning and provision.

As well as standards, the second main priority will be tackling teacher shortages, by increasing recruitment and retention and by attracting back teachers who have left. Morris moved early to signal greater opportunities for the 44,000 extra classroom assistants recruited since 1997 to qualify as teachers by taking their degrees while working. Other priorities will be to get more students into higher education towards the target of 50 per cent of under 30–year olds, and to reduce adult illiteracy and innumeracy.

One political uncertainty for Morris is the attention she will also need to pay to defending her Parliamentary seat. When she took Yardley it had been a classic Tory/Labour marginal, changing hands seven times since the Second World War and backing the Conservatives since 1979. In 1997, the Conservatives ceded second place to the Liberal Democrats, who then led the popular vote in the 1999 European elections and took 61 per cent in council elections in May 2000. By 2001, Yardley was the Liberal Democrats' tenth target seat against Labour with a longstanding candidate, businessman John Hemming, well known from the sale of Rover. A shiver went round Labour counting agents on election night at a rumour that Morris was in trouble. In the event, her majority was halved to 2,578 on a 2.74 per cent swing to the Liberal Democrats.

Estelle Morris is an interesting and engaging politician. Her performance as Education Secretary will contribute heavily to Labour's success or otherwise in delivering the improvements in public services on which its second term will be judged.

Damien Welfare

John Morris (Lord Morris) (1931–)

When he became Attorney General in May 1997, John Morris started the final chapter of an extraordinary political career. He was the only member of the Blair Government with Cabinet experience, and as Labour's longest continuously serving MP had seen eight Labour Party leaders. He had first been elected to Parliament when Tony Blair was just eight years old and he served a record-breaking 33 years on Labour's front bench.

Morris was born in Cardiganshire on 5 November 1931, the son of a respected sheep farmer whose family had farmed the same land for over a century. His brother David went on to become Principal of the Welsh Agricultural College. Morris was educated at Aberystwyth's Ardwyn Grammar School, the University College of Wales Aberystwyth and Gonville and Cauis, Cambridge, where he was awarded an LLM. He went on to the Academy of International Law in the Hague.

Although Morris' family leant towards the Liberals and Conservatives, he joined the Labour Party at 21, and after National Service, where he was commissioned in the Royal Welsh Fusiliers and Welsh Regiment, began his twin-track career in politics and at the Bar. He was called to the Bar at Gray's Inn in 1954, where he was a Holker Senior Exhibitioner. He became Deputy General Secretary and Legal Advisor to the Farmers' Union of Wales from 1956 and a comfortable life at the Bar might have been assured. In 1957, however, he was unexpectedly selected for the safe Labour seat of Averavon. He won the seat in 1959 at the age of 28.

Morris sat on the back benches for six years, although he was a member of the Council of Europe from 1963 to '64. He began his long front bench career when he was appointed Parliamentary Secretary at the Ministry of Power by Harold Wilson in October 1964. In this post he served as Chairman of the National Pneumoconiosis Joint Committee, looking at this illness which struck down many miners across the country. Morris was moved to Parliamentary Secretary at Transport under Barbara Castle in January 1966. At Transport, Morris shook off an early disaster when he sat down too early after a speech, allowing the Conservatives to 'talk out' a Money Bill, and as the main author of the Railway Policy White Paper in 1967 set out a radical shake-up of British Rail management. His talents won him promotion to Minister of State at Defence in April 1968 and he kept this job as Deputy Defence Spokesman into opposition after 1970, despite competition from the likes of David Owen and Brian Walden.

After the election defeat of 1970, Morris went back to his career at the Bar and he took silk (became QC) in 1973. His Chambers was headed by Lord Havers and later included MPs Sir Derek Spencer (former Solicitor General) and Francis Maude.

In opposition, Morris served as a Delegate to the North Atlantic Assembly from 1970 to 1974 and as Chairman of the PLP Defence Group (1971–74). He was Chairman of the Welsh PLP Group (1970–71), and then the re-named Welsh Parliamentary Party (1972–73).

When Labour returned to power in 1974, Wilson gave Morris the job of Secretary of State for Wales, with a remit for delivering devolution. Morris was widely regarded as a success in Wales, winning special development area status for North West Wales and developing Welsh-language road signs among other lasting monuments. Losing the devolution vote so comprehensively (four votes to one) left him philosophical: 'When you see an elephant on your doorstep, you recognise it' he said.

Morris went back into the law in 1979, becoming first a Deputy Circuit Judge and then a Recorder of the Crown Court from 1982. Remaining on the Front Bench, he was appointed Shadow Attorney General and Opposition Spokesman on Legal Affairs in 1979 but was dropped by Michael Foot in 1981. Morris threw himself into Labour's internal battle over nuclear disarmament, chairing the multilateralist Labour Defence and Disarmament Group which aimed to reverse the unilateralist change to Labour defence policy.

In 1983, he nominated Roy Hattersley for Leader and Deputy Leader. Reappointed to the Front Bench by Kinnock in 1983, he spent the 14 years of opposition making occasional but often telling attacks on the Conservatives from a legal perspective. His training was particularly effective during the Arms to Iraq affair and the sleaze scandals of the early 1990s, when he was appointed as the senior Labour member of the Standards and Privileges Committee.

In May 1997, Morris became Attorney General, Labour's only remaining senior Commons QC. His two years in the job were marked by controversy and some major reforms to the legal system. On the positive side, Morris set up the Glidewell review of the Crown Prosecution Service, which resulted in regional decentralisation of the CPS. He introduced the Law Officers Bill, which allowed the Solicitor General to act as his deputy. On the negative side, his appointment of Philip Sales from Lord Irvine's Chambers as Treasury Devil brought controversy as it appeared to be a political favour. He was back in the newspapers when Home Secretary Jack Straw's son was caught by the Daily Mirror selling cannabis. Morris appeared to be blocking publication of the story against Jack Straw's own wishes. During the Kosovo War, despite a show of unity, Morris was reported to have serious concerns about the legality of many of the NATO bombing targets. Finally he was criticised for making a decision not to prosecute 'spy granny' Melita Norwood in 1999.

Morris offered his post to Blair in the April 1999 reshuffle, officially on grounds of ailing health, and shortly afterwards he also announced that he would be standing down from his Aberavon seat at the 2001 general election. By retiring, he deprived himself of the chance to succeed Sir Edward Heath as Father of the House. He was created a life peer after the June 2001 election.

Morris was appointed to the Privy Council in 1970 and knighted in 1999 after his retirement. He holds Honorary Fellowships of University College Wales, Aberystwyth, Trinity College Camarthen and University College Swansea. He was awarded an Honorary Doctorate from the University of Wales in 1985. He remains Vice-Chairman of Aberavon Rugby Club. Morris was married to Margaret Lewis, a nursery school teacher, in 1959 and he has three daughters.

Howard Dawber

William Morris   (1834–96)

To the general population William Morris is the world's premier Arts and Crafts designer of wallpapers, furniture and stained glass. For British socialists he was one of the founding figures of the Social Democratic Federation and the Socialist League, and the author of the hugely influential utopian dream, *News from Nowhere*. In Morris' own mind there was no contradiction between the aesthete, the poet and the political philosopher. All three careers were expressions of the same imaginative desire to expose the ugliness of a society that organised itself in a way that prevented its workers from enjoying the beauty which life should afford.

Morris was born to wealthy parents in Walthamstow on 24 March 1834 and was educated at the new Victorian public school of Marlborough before starting at Exeter College Oxford. Here he met the two young painters Edward Burne-Jones and Dante Gabriel Rossetti, with whom he founded 'the brotherhood', the progenitor of the Pre-Raphaelite Movement of which they were to be the main exponents. On leaving university in 1856 Morris was articled to the eminent architect George Edmund Street but within a year the Brotherhood were painting frescos for the Oxford Union. The following year, with Burne-Jones, Rossetti, Philip Webb and Ford Madox Brown, he formed the design company Morris, Marshall, Faulkener & Co, committed to the aesthetic and political principles espoused by the art critic and Oxford Professor John Ruskin. In 1859 Morris married Jane ('Janey') Burden, the young daughter of a travelling Oxfordshire agricultural worker who had originally sat for Rossetti. There is no record of any member of Morris' family attending the ceremony and it seems clear that polite society regarded the match as unequal and improper.

Meanwhile, Morris' company was immensely successful in transforming Victorian aesthetic values and major commissions were completed at the Red House in Upton (1859), the Armoury and Tapestry Room in St. James's Palace (1866) and the Dining Room in the Victoria and Albert Museum (1867). The partnership was dissolved in 1874 and the following year Morris formed his own business, Morris & Company. In 1877 he founded the Society for the Protection of Ancient Buildings.

At the heart of Morris' work was a passionate and religious belief in a just society modelled on mediaeval principles, but it was not until the 1870s that he took a direct interest in national politics. At first a Liberal, Morris became disillusioned with Gladstone's 1880 Government. In 1883 he helped found the Social Democratic Foundation but he soon fell out with its leader, H M Hyndman. In December 1884 Morris took Eleanor Marx, Walter Crane and Edward Aveling with him as he seceded from the SDF to form the Socialist League. From 1884 until his death Morris wrote extensively about socialism and many of his works soon became essential reading in the socialist canon, including *Chants for Socialists* (1883), *The Pilgrims of Hope* (1885), *The Dream of John Ball* (1888), *Socialism, Its Growth and Outcome* (1893), *Manifesto of English Socialists* (1893), *The Wood Beyond the World* (1894) and *Well at the World's End* (1896). It was, however, *News from Nowhere,* the fantasy he wrote for the Socialist League journal, *Commonweal*, that was his most-loved contribution to socialism, with its dream of a communist England free from industrial squalor where all were free, healthy and equal. Morris was not just a philosophical socialist. He spoke regularly at trade union meetings around the country and in 1887 he was arrested at a demonstration in London and was involved in the Bloody Sunday riots.

Throughout his life Morris remained an active poet and designer and in 1890 he founded the Kelmscott Press from his house at Kelmscott in Oxfordshire, publishing his own works and reprints of classic English texts.

Morris' political views were passionate and idealistic. He wanted everyone to share in the beauty of great art. 'What business have we with art unless we can all share it?' he asked. He believed in the dignity of labour, especially manual labour. He disliked modern society, believing that 'God made the country, man made the town, and the Devil made the suburbs'. He hoped for a return to a simpler, more cohesive world order along the lines of the mediaeval world that featured so prominently in his poems and drawings. He believed in using natural colours and patterns in his designs and he saw capitalism as an ugly and violent political system. As he put it, 'It is not this or that tangible steel or brass machine which we want to get rid of, but the great intangible machine of commercial tyranny which oppresses the lives of us all'.

Despite ill-health, Morris supported both the socialist and the syndicalist wings of the growing 1890s Labour Movement and was a friend of both George Lansbury and Keir Hardie. He was never to see the formation of the Labour Party, however, as he died on 3 October 1896. His wife Jane died in 1914.

There are countless biographies of Morris, the first being J.W. Mackail's 1899 volume and the most recent Fiona MacCarthy's *William Morris: A Life for Our Time* (Faber, 1994).

Chris Bryant MP

Herbert Morrison (Lord Morrison of Lambeth)   (1888–1965)

Herbert Morrison remains one of Labour's greatest forgotten heroes. He was Labour's first and most prominent Leader of the London County Council; the Home Secretary who sustained London through the blitz; the dominant figure in masterminding Labour's 1945 victory; and the Deputy Prime Minister in the Attlee Cabinet who can claim probably more credit than anyone else for the 1945–51 government's domestic and legislative programme.

The best contemporary indicator of Morrison's prominence is perhaps his thirty-three years of service on the NEC – longer than any of his distinguished colleagues and rivals – stretching between 1920 and 1955. There were, however, two revealing one-year breaks, which give us hints as to why he never made it to the very top. The first was when, as a result of Ernie Bevin's intervention in denying him the Transport Workers' bloc vote, he was defeated by the near-alcoholic Arthur Greenwood for the party Treasurership in 1943. The second was when he was unceremoniously booted out of the constituency section along with Hugh Dalton in the great Bevanite surge at the 1952 Morecambe conference.

But first and foremost, Morrison was the quintessential political organiser – chiefly responsible for rebuilding Labour's electoral base after the disaster of the 1931 defeat. He was a consistent moderniser throughout his career in politics, and championed a 'one nation' conception of democratic socialism that sought to reach beyond the manual working class for its support. Morrison was particularly sensitive to the need for political parties to consistently renew their policies and present their ideas in a credible fashion.

Herbert Morrison was born on 3 January 1888 in Brixton, London, into a traditional working-class family. His father Henry was a policeman. Life was hard although most basic material needs were met, and the family were more fortunate than most of a similar environment and social class in early twentieth century Britain. He attended St Andrew's Church of England School, Lingham Street.

Morrison began his political life very differently to how he ended it. Employed as a shop assistant and grocery deliver from the age of 14 on five shillings a week, he was a committed revolutionary. But the self-taught Morrison soon progressed from Marx's set texts to the business of reading agendas and chairing meetings, skills for which he became known far and wide in Labour circles. He had struggled from nothing but the most basic education available to a boy of his background. He therefore understood well the need to extend to the many the life-chances that were enjoyed by only a privileged few in society.

Having originally joined the Brixton ILP in 1906, following a brief interlude in the Social-Democratic Federation, he had become by 1910 the secretary of the South-West London Federation of the ILP. His reputation was made when he became the second secretary of the London Labour Party on 27 April 1915, following the death of his predecessor after less than a month in office. He was so attached to this role that even as a minister he insisted on being seconded to government and not replaced as secretary. By 1920–21 he was Mayor of Hackney, and from 1922 he was a member of the London County Council, to become a Member of Parliament in 1923 for Hackney South.

His first post in government was as Minister of Transport in MacDonald's 1929 administration, where he authored the London Passenger Transport Act, the beginning of the capital's integrated transport system. But the 1931 defeat saw him out of Parliament. Had Attlee not clung on in Limehouse it is inconceivable that he rather than Morrison would have emerged as party leader, but when both were contesting the post in 1935 Attlee had the advantage of a parliamentary seat between 1931 and 1935.

From 1934 to 1940, Morrison further established himself as Labour's first leader of the London County Council. There are unnamed memorials to his leadership across London. The green belt and housing estates still stand as models of good public housing compared to the socially engineered monstrosities of the 1960s and 1970s. This was the high tide of municipal socialism, exemplified by the South Bank that emerged from the Festival of Britain, pioneered by Morrison in 1951.

The war was a turning point for Herbert's career in many ways, principally because he was able to turn himself from an essentially municipal to a fully national figure. He did this not just through an increasingly adept use of the media, but by using his substantial influence inside the political system to shape detailed policies for the post-war world. Back in the Commons for Hackney South since 1935 he was appointed Minister of Supply in May 1940, and then Home Secretary and Minister of Home Security from October 1940 until May 1945 in Churchill's coalition War Cabinet.

It was natural that Morrison should be put in charge of the preparations for the Labour Party's coming election campaign. On the NEC in the 1930s he had already done a great deal to help reconstruct the Labour Party as a credible alternative government after the disaster of 1931. His watchful eye (he had been blind in the other since birth) was trained on every aspect of policy and organisation. With Hugh Dalton he took over manifesto planning. Nobody rivalled his experience or challenged his authority: he relished the fight and was thoroughly at home driving the party machine. He also made the extraordinarily bold step of forsaking his own safe seat to take on and win Tory-held East Lewisham because he felt this was the sort of place where Labour had to prove it could win.

Following the 1945 victory, Morrison continued in government in much the same role as he had held in the wartime coalition. He became Lord President and Leader of the House of Commons, co-ordinating economic and domestic policy and driving Labour's substantial legislative programme through parliament. Having succeeded Arthur Greenwood as Labour's Deputy Leader (a post he retained until 1956) he was as deputy Prime Minster the government's anchorman.

In March 1951 he was appointed to relieve Ernie Bevin as Foreign Secretary. But it was not a happy berth for him. Distracted by the need to manage rebellious colleagues in the Cabinet, it did not receive his full attention. To Foreign Office officials he was not their beloved Ernie and if Morrison let himself down, the Foreign Office did not do much to break his fall. Within 15 years he was dead. In fact he died on 6 March 1965, two months after Winston Churchill. He was to die disappointed at never having been elected leader of the Labour Party.

It is possible to cite three significant personal and professional attributes of Herbert Morrison as a practising politician. First, he was keenly aware of the importance of social and economic ideas in improving the conditions of the people. In 1935, the Editor of the *New Statesman*, Kingsley Martin, supported him as Labour Party leader on the basis he was, 'dynamic, open to ideas, keen to argue, and above all keen that the Party should succeed and win'.

Second, Morrison was insistent that the party had to represent interests that extended far beyond the organised working class. He understood that trade unions were limited in their pursuit of sectional interests rather than the fulfilment of wider political objectives, and that there was always a wider community interest to be served. In this sense Morrison was extraordinarily modern in his outlook.

Finally, Morrison considerably enhanced his status as a minister by always taking the views of his civil servants seriously, and by surrounding himself with experts and intellectuals who would challenge and enhance him. He was always interested in the machinery of government and in 1955 published a work based on his visiting fellowship at Nuffield College, Oxford: *Government and Parliament: a View from the Inside*.

Morrison retired from politics in 1959 when, true to his principles, he declined a hereditary peerage and settled for a life one instead as Lord Morrison of Lambeth. He did little else in his remaining years apart from presiding over the British Board of Film Censors and fighting the replacement of the London County Council by the GLC, though from 1961 he spoke out in favour of Britain's joining the EEC.

What lessons does Herbert Morrison have for New Labour today? An electorally successful Labour Party requires a broad appeal across the social classes. While the party in government must continue to put forward policies that address the plight of the needy and vulnerable, this will simply never be sustainable if pursued in outright opposition to other groups in society. Populist attacks on 'class enemies' do not in the end help us to implement progressive policies. That is as powerful a truth as any for a politician of the centre-left to bestow on the movement he leaves behind.

The key biography on Herbert Morrison is *Herbert Morrison: Portrait of a Politician* by

B Donoughue and G W Jones. Morrison published his memoirs, *Herbert Morrison: An Autobiography*, in 1960, and the seminal work *Socialisation and Transport* in 1933.

Rt Hon. Peter Mandelson MP

Jim Mortimer (1921–)

Jim Mortimer was General Secretary of the Labour Party during one of the bleakest periods of the Party's history (1982–85). He supervised Labour's election-fighting machine during Labour's most serious electoral debacle, the general election defeat of 1983.

James Edward 'Jim' Mortimer was born on 12 January 1921. He was educated at the Junior Technical School, Portsmouth; Ruskin College, Oxford (1945–46); and the London School of Economics. As a young man Jim Mortimer worked for several years in a variety of engineering jobs. He was an apprentice ship fitter, a machinist and a planning engineer. But after his spell at college, Jim Mortimer began a long career working full time in the trade union movement. He worked in the TUC Economic Department (1946–48) and then for the Draughtsmen's and Allied Technicians' Association (DATA) for twenty years (1948–68). Jim Mortimer went on to become Director of the London Co-operative Society (1968–71); a member of the Board of the London Transport Executive (1971–74); then chairman of ACAS (1974–81).

In this period Jim Mortimer wrote several publications. These include *A History of the Association of Engineering and Shipbuilding Draughtsmen* (1960); then, with the late Clive Jenkins, *British Trade Unions Today* (1965); also with Clive Jenkins, *The Kind of Laws the Unions Ought to Want* (1968); then *Industrial Relations* (1968); *Trade Unions and Technological Change* (1971); *A History of the Boilermakers' Society, Volume I* (1973), followed by *Volume II* (1982), and finally *Volume III* (1993); and with Valerie Ellis, he wrote *A Professional Union: the Evolution of the Institution of Professional Civil Servants* (1980). He also wrote two key articles in 1981 editions of *Personnel Management* – namely 'ACAS in a changing climate: a force for good IR?' in issue 13(2) and 'ACAS and the development of collective bargaining', in issue 13(3).

Towards the end of this period he was also Visiting Fellow, the Administrative Staff College, Henley (1976–82); Senior Visiting Fellow, Bradford University (1977–82), with an Honorary DLitt from Bradford (1982); Visiting Professor, Imperial College of Science and Technology, London University (1981–83); Ward-Perkins Resident Fellow, Pembroke College, Oxford (1981).

If he had retired then, at the age of 60, Jim Mortimer would be remembered, if remembered at all, as a quiet, low-profile, but committed toiler for the Labour movement, who had devoted his life to the trade unions, lectured widely and written authoritatively on trade union affairs. Instead he was persuaded to take charge of Labour's HQ and so became one of the most controversial general secretaries in Labour's history.

The early 1980s proved to be a time of rapid technological change in the field of communications, and this was bound to affect the conduct of elections and national political debates. Jim Mortimer had been schooled in the trade union discussions and election techniques of a bygone age and failed to see what was required of a modern political party. Reacting to the use of communications professionals by other political parties, Jim Mortimer said: 'I can assure you that the Labour Party will never follow such a line of presentation in politics. The welfare of human beings, the care of people and the fact that we want to overcome unemployment – these are the tasks before us, not presenting people (politicians) as if they were breakfast food or baked beans.'

And thus in a couple of phrases, despite the fine sentiments, Jim Mortimer betrayed, with his own words, his misunderstanding of the nature of modern communications and his inability to see that voters had lost touch with the very Labour ideals which Jim Mortimer supported so passionately. Consequently Labour's 1983 election campaign was unprofessional, poorly informed and badly organised, unable to settle on a clear message, impenetrably wordy, gaffe-prone and ultimately knocked off course. The electorate was unable to imagine the Labour leader, Michael Foot, as Prime Minister. So the defining moment of the 1983 campaign occurred when, to a packed early morning press conference, Jim Mortimer himself announced, suddenly and inexplicably, that the Labour Party had 'full confidence' in its leader, Michael Foot. The film footage of this incident shows Jim Mortimer in the seconds after he made this announcement, bewildered by the journalists' reaction. He was clearly unaware that what he had said caused the entire country to question Foot's leadership and Labour's unity of purpose or that this incident symbolised the amateurishness of Labour's election-losing campaign.

Jim Mortimer soldiered on as General Secretary until 1985 when, having skilfully staved off a disaster in Labour's finances, he entered into a period of recalcitrant retirement. He became Chair of the Editorial Committee of *Socialist Campaign Group News* in 1987 and he became a member of the Executive Committee of the Institute of Employment Rights in 1989. He has continued to write, notably by producing his autobiography, *A Life on the Left* (1999). Jim Mortimer is also a long-standing Vice Chair of Labour Action for Peace. He has remained active in the trade union movement, notoriously being one of six Manufacturing Science Finance (MSF) members who made a legal challenge to Labour's disqualification of London MSF votes in the Mayoral candidate selection process of 2000. But the courts found in Labour's favour since London MSF had not paid its party dues for three years. The six were ordered to pay costs, making their entire effort an expensive fiasco. This is apt, because Jim Mortimer's name will forever be linked in the minds of Labour Party members with expensive fiascos.

Rex Osborn

Sir Oswald Mosley Bt (1896–1980)

There are not many politicians in the twentieth century whose lives have been sufficiently eventful and interesting to justify being immortalised in a film or television dramatisation. One thinks of productions such as *Young Winston* or *The Life and Times of David Lloyd George*. Yet in 1998 these rare examples were joined by a four-part drama about Oswald Mosley, entitled *Mosley*. Such a programme serves as testament to the enduring fascination of the tragic and still debated story of Mosley's life.

Oswald Ernest Mosley, the eldest of the three sons of the fifth baronet Sir Oswald Mosley, was born on 16 November 1896 at 47 Hill Street, Mayfair. Aged five, his parents separated and he went with his mother Katherine to live in Shropshire. After West Down private school and Winchester, he attended Sandhurst for the first six months of 1914, was rusticated in June but recalled there at the outbreak of the First World War in August and commissioned into the 16th Lancers in October. In December he transferred to the 6th Squadron, Royal Flying Corps, and from December 1914 until April 1915 was an observer. Trying to obtain his pilot's licence back in England, he managed to break his ankle, leaving him with a permanent limp. After a brief time in the trenches with the 16th Lancers his injury invalided him out of the army and he spent the rest of the war in Whitehall, at the Ministry of Munitions and the Foreign Office.

This proximity to the senior levels of government introduced him to a number of politicians through whom he was able to procure the Conservative candidacy for the Harrow constituency, winning it at the 1918 general election. He further cemented his place in the Establishment by marrying Lady Cynthia Blanche, daughter of Lord Curzon, on 11 May 1920.

Following the war, his self-perception was as part of the vanguard of a new generation of younger politicians seeking to break free of the normal boundaries of political parties and thinking. After making a number of critical speeches in late 1920 attacking excessive military expenditure and the operation of the 'Black and Tans' in Ireland, he became an independent, and was bolstered by backing from his local party. But by 1922 they were demanding assurances of party loyalty Mosley was not prepared to give and they selected a new candidate; Mosley was however re-elected in that year's general election with a large majority, defeating an official Conservative candidate.

In many ways Mosley personified the flux being experienced by the British party system in the early 1920s and which laid the foundations of the essentially 'two and half' party system which has endured since then. He retained Harrow in 1923 with a reduced majority, which signalled to him that he would need some sort of party base if he were to survive. After initial flirtation with the Liberals, he soon saw the way the wind was blowing and joined the Labour Party in March 1924, a couple of months after its first government was formed by Ramsay MacDonald, who described Mosley that year as 'one of the greatest and most hopeful figures' in politics. In the next general election in 1924 Mosley came within 77 votes of defeating Neville Chamberlain at Birmingham Ladywood, and returned to the Commons in the December 1926 Smethwick by-election.

Whilst out of the Commons he evolved his economic thinking along Keynesian lines. He gained support on the left during the General Strike and with his combination of self-confidence, arrogance and ambition was already being tipped as a future Labour leader.

In 1928 he succeeded to his father's baronetcy and the following year was returned for Smethwick, an election in which Cynthia was also elected as MP for Stoke-on-Trent. In the second Labour Government of 1929 he took ministerial office for the first time as Chancellor of the Duchy of Lancaster. Though outside Cabinet, Mosley had a senior post with a key place alongside J H Thomas, George Lansbury and Tom Johnston on the Cabinet unemployment committee. Within the government, there was growing tension between the not insubstantial egos of Mosley on the one hand and Thomas and the Chancellor, Philip Snowden, on the other. In 1930 Mosley took it upon himself to pen a memorandum recommending radical changes in policy to deal with the Depression, which included extensive state intervention and a public works programme. On 20 May, following the rejection of his memorandum by Cabinet, he resigned from the government. A further attempt to get these policies adopted by the Labour Party failed at the Annual Conference of October 1930.

Mosley by this point began to believe his own press: his experience of winning parliamentary seats as an independent, along with his self-belief in his broad political support, talked up by the media, led him to plan the creation of the New Party, which was launched on 1 March 1931. At first this was just a Parliamentary venture – Mosley, his wife and four other MPs – and a spectacularly unsuccessful one at that: two MPs remained members for only one day and a third, John Strachey, resigned in June. All 24 of its candidates were defeated in the 1931 election.

Early the following year Mosley visited Mussolini's Italy. He concluded that parliamentary politics had had its day and that the dictatorships springing up around Europe were the way forward. On his return therefore he started planning a fascist movement, British-style, which bore fruit in October 1932 as the British Union of Fascists (BUF). Initially influenced by Italian fascism, the BUF in its early couple of years was relatively successful and great efforts were expended to gain respectability amongst the traditional right, which was achieved amongst some Conservatives.

But this was all undermined by the violence that was clearly on show at the party's June 1934 rally at Olympia. The true face of ugly extremism and anti-Semitism was made plain for all to see, and from later that year anti-Semitism became a major policy theme of the BUF. These events lost the party any middle-class support it might have hoped to get (and quite a lot of its membership), and it took its arguments (and violence) to the streets.

The party ditched its economic policies inspired by Mosley's 1930 memorandum and committed to policies based on totalitarianism, now much more influenced by Nazism. The rapid marginalisation of the BUF was largely complete by 1935, by when it was of little significance and far from political influence and power.

Cynthia had died in May 1933, and in 1936 Mosley married one of the Mitford sisters, Diana Guinness, at a ceremony in Berlin in the presence of Hitler. Following the outbreak of war, Mosley was interned along with other BUF leaders and sundry suspicious characters on the right under the Defence of the Realm regulations. He was released in November 1943 on health grounds, but any political influence he might have had had now completely evaporated, and for many years after the war the BBC banned interviews with him.

He devoted himself to a series of self-justifying books such as *My Answer* (1946) and *My Life* (1968), along with others that sought to outline his views on various topics such as *Atrocities, Britain First, European Socialism,* and *Revolution by Reason and other essays*. Living mainly in France for the rest of his life, he became particularly interested in the cause of European unity, but of course based on racial lines, as Leader of the Union Movement 1948–66. He made disastrous forays into parliamentary politics in 1959 and 1966, losing his deposit at North Kensington and Shoreditch respectively.

He died in Orsay, France, on 3 December 1980. He left two sons and a daughter by Cynthia, and two sons by Diana. His eldest son is Nicholas Mosley, the 3rd Lord Ravensdale and baronet, a noted author. Another son is Max Mosley, President of the FIA, which oversees Formula One and came to political light in recent times during controversies on tobacco advertising in the early years of the Blair government.

The debate about Mosley's abilities is in many ways a continuing one. He clearly lacked judgement and was prone to endorsing simplistic theories and strategies. Although he argued that he was part of a new generation leaving behind the old Establishment ideas and politics, he was nevertheless steeped in its traditions with the advantages of birth and position, including great arrogance and total confidence in his own abilities and in his own views. Yet at almost every turn he seemed to take the wrong decision to advance himself or his ideas. A combination of ambition in excess of ability, unfulfilled promise in the 1920s and a fatal impatience make Mosley a character quite unparalleled in British politics.

The classic biography is *Oswald Mosley* by Robert (Lord) Skidelsky, first published in 1975 with an updated edition in 1990. Nicholas Mosley wrote a two-part biography of his father, *Rules of the Game: Sir Oswald and Lady Cynthia Mosley 1896–1933* (1982) and *Beyond the Pale: Sir Oswald Mosley 1933–80* (1983).

Matthew Seward

Mo Mowlam (1949–)

Unconventional, brave, erratic and enigmatic, Mo Mowlam proved to be one of the most popular politicians of her generation. More than for most, her style was her politics. She hugged, provoked, shocked and surprised, a one-woman refutation of the view that New Labour had to be bland and conventional. As a result, she was at one stage achieving higher popularity ratings than even the Prime Minister, Tony Blair.

His 1998 party conference speech was overshadowed by an emotional standing ovation at the mention of her name. Privately, she wondered whether this lèse-majesté marked the date when her problems began. Just two years later she was bidding the party conference farewell, having announced that she was to step down from politics at the next election.

Though she was among the lesser authors of the New Labour project, her greatest contribution to national life was undoubtedly her effort to kick-start the Northern Ireland peace process at a critical time in the province's history. As Secretary of State for Northern Ireland in Tony Blair's first administration, she oversaw the signing of the Good Friday agreement and the achievement of the first lasting ceasefire in Northern Ireland for many years. But she will most be remembered as the politician who lived and worked through a brain tumour, scarcely stopping for a moment as the illness took its toll.

She was born Marjorie Mowlam in Watford on 18 September 1949, into what she described as a 'dysfunctional' family with an alcoholic father. While her father worked for the Post Office she attended George Tomlinson Primary School in Southall in west London before moving to Coundon Court school in Coventry, one of the country's first comprehensives. It was during her final years at school that she became known as 'Mo', a name which has stuck despite attempts by Labour spin doctors to give her gravitas by calling her 'Dr Marjorie' when she joined the Cabinet. She took her degree at Durham University before going on to gain a doctorate at the University of Iowa in the United States.

Mowlam joined the Labour Party when she was just twenty years old – in 1969 – but began her working life as an academic, teaching politics at Newcastle University and the Northern College in Barnsley. During the nineteen eighties she decided she wanted a parliamentary seat and after several attempts was selected for the North-East constituency of Redcar, which she won in the 1987 election.

Mowlam quickly established herself as one of Labour's modernisers and ten months after being elected to Parliament was promoted to the Opposition front bench by Neil Kinnock, the then Labour leader, as a spokeswoman on Northern Ireland. A year later she moved to the Trade and Industry team under Gordon Brown as spokeswoman for the City and Corporate Affairs. There she was part of Labour's 'prawn cocktail' offensive, using a series of lunches with bankers and stockbrokers to reassure the City that Labour was not what it was – and was not to be feared.

In 1992 Mowlam was elected to the shadow cabinet for the first time, taking on responsibility for Women's Issues and for shadowing William Waldegrave at the Office of Public Service and Science. That job mutated to the post of Shadow Heritage Secretary in 1993 – a job she loved. But a year later she was moved back to the Northern Ireland Office, this time as the Shadow Northern Ireland Secretary. In 1995 she was elected to Labour's ruling National Executive Committee.

At the beginning of 1997 Mowlam was diagnosed with a brain tumour – a secret she managed to keep from all but her closest confidantes while she underwent treatment. She came clean about the illness after a journalist compared her to a 'Geordie trucker' because she had put on so much weight as a result of steroid treatment. Despite months of gruelling treatment she carried on in her job, and actively fought the 1997 election, winning plaudits from even her political enemies for her courage.

After Labour won the 1997 election, Mowlam became Northern Ireland Secretary and immediately cut a very different style from her predecessors there. Her 'touchy-feely' approach endeared her to the general public, but was not appreciated by some of the Ulster Unionists. Her language could be coarse, her style direct. A favourite trick was to fling off her wig (needed because she had lost most of her hair during her illness) whenever negotiations were reaching a tricky stage, declaring it was 'too hot'. Her gutsy style – and her controversial decision to talk to terrorists in the Maze prison – alienated the Unionists and by 1999 Prime Minister Tony Blair felt the need to become more directly involved in the peace negotiations himself, leaving Mowlam to complain to President Clinton that she was 'just the tea lady'. She resisted a move from the Northern Ireland Office in the July re-shuffle that year, but by October found herself shifted out to make way for Peter Mandelson.

Mowlam became Minister for the Cabinet Office, known at Westminster as 'minister for the *Today* programme', as part of her task was to present a united front for the government in the media. It was a job she never really took to, despite doing some useful work on drugs policy, which was also part of her portfolio. Even in this comparative backwater, she was never one to bite her tongue, causing a small furore when she admitted smoking cannabis in her youth, and a much bigger one when she suggested the Royal Family should move out of Buckingham Palace.

In 1995 she married the banker Jon Norton, who has two children by a previous marriage. The couple enjoyed life at Hillsborough, the official residence of the Northern Ireland Secretary, but after Mowlam's move from the job she seemed to lose her appetite for politics. By 2000, newspapers were briefed by anonymous sources that she was not fully engaged and her health was again questioned. She announced her decision to quit politics, insisting it was nothing to do with the mutterings against her, but because she wanted to do something else with her life. With most politicians, that would have been taken as a quitter's excuse. For 'Mo', a fully paid-up member of the human race, it was entirely credible.

Jackie Ashley

Geoff Mulgan (1961–)

Geoff Mulgan, born in 1961, came from a conventional middle-class family in Highgate; both his parents were professionals, one a music publisher, the other a teacher. So the question is, Where did his interest in societal change come from? Mulgan himself suggests that his social alchemy is the result of other influences in his early life; that the Liverpool docker, who cleaned for his parents, gave him an insight into what life is like from the bottom up. His social conscience was already apparent in his early teens when he first became an active canvasser and organiser for the Labour Party before the legal aid of admission, which was 15. At the young age of 14 he was also recruiting teenagers for NUPE and organising campaigns against the National Front via the AntiNazi League. At the age of seventeen, after finishing at Westminster School, he took a gap year to Sri Lanka during which time he met an elderly German man who lived in the jungle. It was with him that the conversations about how society should change for the better began.

Later, Geoff Mulgan graduated from Oxford University with a first class degree and subsequently completed a PhD at the University of Westminster. In 1984–86 he was an investment executive at the Greater London Enterprise Council, developing first cultural policy and then the cultural industries strategy that later became the template for many other urban administrations around the UK and globally. This formed the basis for his book *Saturday Night Sunday Morning* which set out a radically different cultural policy for the Labour Party, and also made the case for reviving the much stronger cultural strand that had shaped the labour movement earlier in its history.

In the latter part of 1986 he became a Harkness Fellow, which took him to study at the MIT. In 1987 he went to work for the Democrats in the United States, encountering the likes of Al Gore and Jesse Jackson. In 1988 he became a lecturer at the University of Westminster, a consultant to the European commission and a member of the Comedia consulting group. Mulgan also at this time became a regular contributor to *Marxism Today*, which during this period was a forum for radical thinking on the British left. He wrote keynote essays on the new-networked organizational forms that the left needed to embrace, on public sector reform and on the importance of the politics of responsibility.

Following this in 1990 he became a policy advisor to Gordon Brown MP, publishing numerous pamphlets on unemployment, quangos and taxation. Mulgan was particularly prominent in urging the Party to embrace a more communitarian policy stance, publishing his ideas in *Renewal* and *Tribune*.

In 1993 Geoff Mulgan really made his mark: he founded a political think tank called Demos, in London, and became chairman of its advisory council. Demos was described by the *Financial Times* as a 'courageous and ambitious creation' to reinvigorate thinking about public policy. It has helped shape the political agenda here and in other countries, on issues such as social exclusion, joined-up government, employment, welfare to work, social entrepreneurs, local government reform, and finally urban policy. Alongside launching Demos, Mulgan was also involved in the conception and launch of Redwedge, the University of Industry and most recently the Social Exclusion Unit. He left Demos in 1997 to become a policy advisor at No 10 Downing Street, although he remains the chairman of Demos' advisory council.

In 2000 Geoff Mulgan, the man once called the 'prince of wonks', moved from being a political appointee to being a civil servant, becoming Director of the new Performance and Innovation Unit (PIU). Created as an innovative Whitehall-based think-tank to think the unthinkable at the highest level of government policy, it reports regularly to Tony Blair. Mulgan's aim for the PIU is 'to branch out somewhat and put emphasis on creativity. I would like to ratchet up the innovation side of the creative agenda'.

Geoff Mulgan sees his role as about modernising government and encouraging Whitehall to abandon old and outdated procedures and practices. In his first month as director of the PIU, he had completed a large-scale work on the issues of privacy and data sharing and migration. Mulgan has been a regular contributor to print and broadcast media. As an author his most recent works are *Connexity* (1997) and *Life After Politics* (1997).

Samantha Cunningham

Fred Mulley (Lord Mulley of Manor Park)   (1918–95)

Now remembered most colourfully as the Defence Secretary who fell asleep during the Queen's Silver Jubilee flypast, Fred Mulley was one of the unsung workhorses of the Wilson and Callaghan governments, remaining on Labour's front bench throughout the period 1964–79, though never becoming an elected member of the shadow cabinet. A cautious, unflamboyant and hard-working government loyalist, he was the epitome of the so-called 'safe pair of hands'. A solid pillar of the pro-European, pro-NATO social-democratic right, he was a prime deselection target of the militant left in the aftermath of the 1979 election defeat. Mulley combined his parliamentary work with his role as APEX member of the trade union section of Labour's NEC 1958–1980, in which capacity he was in 1974–75 chair of the Labour Party and of the Special Conference called in April 1975 on the EEC. In 1971 he and USDAW President and fellow former minister Walter Padley joined Roy Jenkins, Jack Diamond, Shirley Williams and Tom Bradley in the defeated minority when the NEC voted to call for Labour MPs to oppose Heath's attempt to join the EEC. Of the six, only he and Padley, neither of whom were close to Jenkins socially, did not later join the SDP.

A keen pro-European, he nevertheless did not want to risk splitting the Party over the EEC and on 29 March 1972 he joined the NEC majority in backing a referendum. He was far closer to Callaghan than to middle-class socialist intellectuals either of the right like Crosland (whom he resented as an overlord at the Department of the Environment) or of the left like Barbara Castle and Dick Crossman, for whom he was 'a bore'. On 26 March 1969 he joined Callaghan on the NEC in voting down Barbara Castle's *In Place of Strife* and during the 1970s her diaries note with a certain relish Mulley 'bleating pathetically' over his relative failure to protect the education budget as compared to her DHSS budget.

Born 3 July 1918 in Leamington Spa, where his father, W J Mulley, was a local labourer he attended the Church of England School, Leamington, followed by Warwick School, joining Labour in 1936. Leaving school after the loss of his father's job, the evening classes he attended whilst working as a clerk secured him a scholarship to Ruskin College, Oxford, in 1939. Joining the Worcestershire Regiment at the outbreak of war, Mulley used his time as a POW in Germany 1940–45 to teach himself economics, gaining a BSc from London University. His essay, *The Economics of a Prison Camp*, describing the operation of a currency system based on cigarettes, won him an adult scholarship to Christ Church, Oxford, in 1945.

Unsuccessfully contesting Sutton Coldfield at the 1945 general election, he graduated with a First in PPE in 1947. After a year at Nuffield he took up an Economics fellowship at St Catherine's College, Cambridge, remaining there until elected MP for Sheffield Park in 1950, a constituency he continued to represent until his deselection by the hard left at the 1983 election. In his spare time he read Law, and in 1954 was called to the Bar at the Inner Temple.

As a backbencher, he had long shown interest in defence issues, publishing *The Politics of Western Defence* in 1962 and serving on the Council of the Institute for Strategic Studies 1961–64. A delegate to the Council of Europe and the WEU (1958–61), he was from 1979 until 1983 the WEU Assembly President. Shadow Air Minister 1960–64, on Labour's election victory in 1964 he joined the Privy Council and was appointed Minister for the Army and Deputy Defence Secretary. Reshuffled to the post of Aviation Minister in December 1965 he inherited the burden of Concorde, a project begun under the Conservatives which he would have liked to have cancelled had it not already been so far progressed.

Appointed Minister of State for Disarmament at the Foreign Office in January 1967 he was 'a skilled negotiator', according to the memoirs of his chief, Michael Stewart. His priorities, and in particular his attempts to secure a complete nuclear test ban, were 'unexpectedly progressive' even by Barbara Castle's unsympathetic standards, as she duly noted in her diary. In October 1969 he was appointed Transport Minister outside the Cabinet, a post he held until Labour's defeat in 1970 and continued to shadow in Opposition. Re-appointed Transport Minister in 1974, Wilson promoted him to Cabinet as Education Secretary in succession to Reg Prentice on 9 June 1975.

With the growing economic difficulties which were to culminate in the so-called IMF crisis in late 1976, Mulley spent most of his time battling to minimise cuts to the education budget. He tried in vain to secure from his civil servants a workable scheme to remove charitable status from private schools. It was at a meeting with Mulley on 21 May 1976 that Jim Callaghan spelt out his Prime Ministerial priorities for tackling education standards and poor teaching as later encapsulated in the Ruskin speech. 'Fred rather blanched' at this, according to Callaghan's biographer Kenneth Morgan and in consequence he was appointed Defence Secretary in the reshuffle of September 1976.

Together with Callaghan, Healey and Owen, Mulley was a member of the government's secret Nuclear Defence Policy Group which supervised the Chevaline upgrade of the Polaris nuclear deterrent and considered its replacement with Trident and the deployment of US cruise missiles from British bases. He was a firm advocate of a three per cent NATO-wide increase in defence spending, and of the, ultimately unsuccessful, British Nimrod airborne early warning system over its US rival.

Created Lord Mulley of Manor Park in Sheffield in 1984, he remained a loyal Labour backbencher until his death on 15 March 1995. He served from 1988 until 1991 as Deputy Chair of the Sheffield Development Corporation He married Joan Philips in 1948, with whom he had two daughters.

Greg Rosen

Chris Mullin   (1947–)

Not many choose genuinely to leave government in order to spend more time sitting on a Select Committee, but Chris Mullin's decision to do that after the 2001 general election is both typical of the man and a sign of the way in which Parliament is likely to develop. Chris was a stalwart of the left-wing push for control of the Labour Party after the collapse of old Labour ideas and authority which led to the debacle of the 1979 defeat. Later, others were to draw different conclusions from the impact of the 1979–83 period. For Mullin, old Labour had failed, letting down its supporters, partly because of its limited aspirations, but largely because it had not been able to manage the business of governing.

Born on 12 December 1947, his father was an electrical engineer working for Marconi, his mother a secretary with the same company. He attended a Catholic boarding school, St Joseph's, near Ipswich and read Law at Hull University, graduating in 1969. Even in the late 20th century, the combination of history and the Catholic Church's approach to education contrives to mark the products of Catholic grammar schools with a different approach to life and politics.

He was Labour candidate in two unwinnable seats in 1970 (Devon North) and February 1974 (Kingston upon Thames). With the BBC World Service and as a freelance he travelled and reported extensively in China, South East Asia and India. The material found its way into his two later novels, *Last Man out of Saigon* and *The Year of the Fire Monkey*, and he married a Vietnamese; they have two children.

The huge mistakes made by the United States in Vietnam and the inability of the Wilson Government to influence its ally had a major impact on him. The Campaign for Labour Party Democracy and the other groups which welcomed the leadership of Tony Benn were the new Labour modernisers of their day. Many ascribed the 1979 failure mainly to betrayal, but Mullin knew that it was more complex than that. While there were weak and incompetent individuals, the main reason was that Labour did not understand the state.

Widespread disillusion with those who had led the 1974–79 government brought dissatisfaction focussed on MPs identified with that old order. Mullin's 1981 pamphlet, *How to Select or Reselect Your MP*, was a useful focus for the media which neither understood the depth of despair among Labour's rank-and-file nor knew those village Hampdens who became the architects of attempts to replace, as it turned out, a mere handful of them. Widely mis-titled 'How to Deselect your MP', it was taken as a sign that quite alien forces were loose inside the Labour Party.

There were Trotskyist entrists about, but the mood went wider than that. Previous attempts to remove unpopular MPs had been thwarted because the Party's staff were adept at finding technical breaches in the Party's rules to invalidate selection procedures. The incumbent stayed. The pamphlet was a practical handbook intended to ensure that everyone knew what the rules were.

Those targeted were not quite so sanguine, and Mullin was extraordinarily unpopular with the right and centre of the party. Tony Benn narrowly missed being elected deputy leader of the Labour Party in a bitter campaign against Denis Healey in 1981. An older generation of the Labour left, with Labour leader Michael Foot, had backed John Silkin as a centre candidate. When Mullin, among Benn's leading backers, became editor of *Tribune* in 1982, Silkin led a move to wrest control of the paper from him. It failed. *Tribune* under his editorship was regarded with suspicion by the Kinnock leadership. The two were never close, but Mullin moved on before the broad front of the early 1980s fell apart as the soft left moved in behind Kinnock. Before long, the conventional wisdom was that the CLPD left and the right they had fought so bitterly were actually the same – 'old Labour'.

Mullin's 1982 novel, *A Very British Coup*, depicted a socialist Labour Government led by a Sheffield steelworker ousted by the Establishment using the security services. It was a clever extrapolation of the plots and schemes which undoubtedly were mounted against Harold Wilson's Government. It was no mere political tract, but a good tale well told. Adapted for television, it focused attention on the activities of people who would rather not have been noticed and changed perceptions of the limits of elected Government to bring about change.

Mullin was an indefatigable investigative journalist, a discipline which has informed his politics. The publication in 1986 of *Error of Judgement* followed several years of his investigation into the miscarriage of justice which wrongly convicted six Irish men of the 1974 Birmingham pub bombing. It led to their release. It also led to wider reforms – the creation of a review body for criminal cases, an important corrective to a system which until then had, as Mullin put it, been based on judicial incompetence corrected occasionally by journalism.

The keys to effective journalism are knowing which questions to ask, not accepting the first answer, and judgement based on experience about the value of material from various sources. These are skills which Chris Mullin was able to bring to bear as a member of the Commons Home Affairs Select Committee, which he joined in 1992 and chaired between 1997 and 1999. He was 'Parliamentary Questioner of Year' in 1999.

When he became MP for Sunderland South in 1987, he was probably closer to the hard left Campaign Group. Some around Neil Kinnock were not prepared to forgive him for his Bennite period. He regarded that as mainly a problem for them. Given his record and his views, he did not expect to be asked to become a Minister, but Tony Blair, who had not even been an MP in the poisonous times of 1979–83, was prepared to reward talent. Mullin was Parliamentary Under Secretary of State, Department of the Environment, Transport and the Regions 1999–2001 and Department for International Development from January 2001.

Mullin had no illusions that becoming a Parliamentary Under Secretary would place the levers of power in his hands; after all, *A Very British Coup* argued convincingly that many of these levers were not even in the hands of the Prime Minister. But it was an experience which he did not want to turn down. Office did not change his views about the limitations of Government.

He announced his return to the back benches with a stinging question to Tony Blair about Britain's role in the development of America's new 'star wars' missile defence strategy. It seems highly likely that in the new Parliament he will chair the Home Affairs Select Committee. Holding the executive to account is what he does best. Many trees have suffered in the interest of debating the growing impotence of Parliament against the executive. If there is to be a resurgence of Parliament, it will come from the detailed forensic scrutiny of departments through the select committees. Chris Mullin will be among a new wave of practical modernisers.

Phil Kelly

Paul Murphy (1948–)

If Paul Murphy pulled out of politics tomorrow he would have left two indelible marks on the 21st century British political landscape. In both Wales and Northern Ireland he has used his political nouse, tact, drive and intelligence to shape the new, devolved institutions.

Murphy's success in Wales has been to sculpt an important and relevant role for a Welsh Secretary in a post-devolution political landscape. Though Conservatives questioned the need for his post at all, partly as a result of his success in the role, they were forced to back away from this position in their 2001 Welsh manifesto. Murphy has proved that a cabinet position provides a lynchpin between Government in Westminster and the Assembly in Cardiff. He also provides a useful counterweight to the sometimes-nationalist colleagues in the Assembly. Like Kinnock, Murphy was a long-time devolution sceptic; he was treasurer of the Labour Campaign against a Welsh Assembly in 1978. In fact it is probably this innate scepticism of the need for the body at all – one that was shared at the time by the majority of the Welsh people – that has made him the right man for the job.

Whilst others have courted nationalist sentiments, Murphy is a traditional Welsh socialist – a mild-mannered Bevan who has instead poured his political energy into transforming the lives and opportunities of people in Wales. He has spoken in the Commons on issues of poverty and employment, and has consistently asked questions which grasp the nettles that politicians would rather shy away from. It was his question in 1990 that forced the then Conservative government minister Ian Grist to admit that a total of 20,800 dwellings in Wales lacked a WC inside the dwelling, a figure that might have been more expected at the beginning of the century than the end. Murphy insists the appeal of the Labour Party in Wales should be across cultural and language barriers, that Labour should be a party for the English and Welsh in Wales. He raised concerns when Welsh was made compulsory at GCSE level that Welsh students would lose out in modern foreign languages. His Welshness is a Welshness of the South Wales valleys; he has spoken of traditional Welsh democratic traditions and Welsh community values. Indeed, according to a friend, his grasp of the Welsh national anthem 'makes John Redwood look like a Welsh patriot'.

Murphy's rise to the Cabinet has been rapid. After entering the Commons in 1987 he was quickly promoted to be an Opposition Spokesman for Wales in 1988 before going on in the next Parliament to be shuffled along the opposition front bench from Northern Ireland and Foreign Affairs to Defence. He was made a Minister of State for Northern Ireland in 1997. He was appointed to the Privy Council in 1999.

An unsung hero, according to George Mitchell in his book about the peace process, Paul Murphy is widely acknowledged to have played a vital role in securing the lead-up to the Good Friday Agreement. Working under Mo Mowlam and responsible for political development,

Murphy developed a reputation as a man who could be trusted. Appointed partly because of his religion he became respected by all sides. Ulster Unionist leader, David Trimble was said to have admired him for his meticulous grasp of detail. His consistent optimism and realism won respect from all sides. His reward was a resounding Yes vote in the referendum and a cabinet post.

Born 25 November 1948 and brought up in the not very Welsh corner of Wales that is Usk, Murphy's parents – his father a miner and his mother a shopworker – were a formative influence on his life. Like his family a devout Catholic with a Catholic education, Murphy regularly attends Mass. His moral views on abortion were evident when he voted to lower the abortion time limit to 22 weeks in 1990.

After graduating in history from Oriel College, Oxford, in 1970, Murphy worked as a management trainee for the Co-operative Wholesale Society for a year before he took up a position lecturing in History and Politics at Ebbw Vale College, Gwent. He has maintained links with his former profession and since 1995 has been an adviser to the National Association of Teachers in Further and Higher Education. Lecturing had the added benefit of allowing Murphy to pursue his political career. He became a Borough Councillor in 1973 until he stepped down following his parliamentary selection. He chaired the Finance Committee for ten years from 1976 where he no doubt cut his negotiating teeth.

Following the retirement of Leo Abse, he won the Parliamentary selection to fight Labour's 11th safest seat in Wales, Torfaen. Dominated by the new town of Cwmbran with a population of 40,000, Torfaen is a constituency with a strong Welsh industrial heritage; the smaller towns of Blaenavon, Abersychan and Pontypool still conjure up images of iron, coal, terraced housing and male voice choirs. A Labour heartland, that it is industrial, trade-union dominated and male is perhaps best illustrated by the controversy which surrounded the selection of Torfaen's Welsh Assembly candidate, Lynne Neagle, following Labour's twinning arrangements for those selections. The seat also has more council housing than any other seat in Wales, again helping to explain Murphy's commitment to combating poverty.

Murphy's practical approach to politics coupled with his determination to see politics have a tangible impact upon people's lives, be it though education, employment or housing, means he sits squarely in the moderniser camp. He has little time for ideologues or nationalists. His socialism is about what can be achieved. After just fourteen years on the green benches he has already achieved a lot.

Mari Williams

Len Murray (Lord Murray of Epping Forest)   (1922–)

As TUC General Secretary between September 1973 and September 1984 Len Murray led the organisation at the height of its supposed greatest power and influence during the Social Contract period between the TUC and the Labour government in the 1970s, and he also presided over the start of its precipitous decline in the face of Margaret Thatcher's anti-union government. A shrewd, likeable but cautious and often self-effacing figure, Murray was perhaps over-sensitive in his early years in the office to the need to act effectively as custodian of the majority views of the TUC General Council. His keen intelligence as well as an ability to get to the guts of a complex issue and explain it to others in a cogent no-nonsense manner was usually appreciated by his trade union colleagues, but for the most part he tended to move only at the pace of the slowest, aware of the limitations on the ability of any TUC General Secretary to give an effective lead if this meant coming into conflict with others.

Born on 2 August 1922 in Shropshire, the son of a farm labourer, Murray attended Wellington Grammar School and briefly the University of London before he served in the army during the Second World War and was struck down in action in the Normandy landings. He married Heather Woolf in 1945, with whom he has two sons and two daughters. After a short stint in the Communist Party and work as a store-keeper in Wolverhampton, Murray went to New College, Oxford, where he graduated in Politics, Philosophy and Economics in 1947. From there he went to a job in the TUC economic department, where he became head in 1954. In April 1969 he was made Deputy General Secretary to Vic Feather.

Murray was very much a consensus man, who disliked vote-taking on the TUC General Council. He was never pompous nor vain, with a healthy disrespect for the baubles of public life, though he accepted an OBE in 1966, was made a Privy Counsellor in April 1976 and accepted a Labour life peerage on his retirement. Privately he feared the TUC was being asked to take on too many responsibilities by Labour governments in the 1970s. An effective, reasonable and articulate TUC voice to the outside world, Murray worked effectively to create and develop the Social Contract. While successful in negotiating wage restraint in 1975 and again in 1976 to help a Labour government facing an economic crisis, he was always aware that such agreements were inherently unstable and temporary, depending more on instincts of political loyalty than economic logic. Murray was unable to convince Labour ministers that a more restrictive approach to pay in 1978 and 1979 would be impossible in the face of trade union resistance. The resulting industrial conflicts in the so-called Winter of Discontent did enormous damage to the moral credibility of the trade union movement and threw the close TUC-Labour alliance into serious question.

Murray sought to act as a calming influence, seeking to find ways through the impasse. But he was never comfortable with the view that the TUC should become a more effective partner in the management of the democratic state. Instead he preferred to defend the autonomy of trade unions and their independence from government control. Later on he admitted he had been too complacent about the increasing hostility towards trade unionism manifest in public opinion during the 1970s. The divisions within the TUC over the Social Contract with Labour forced Murray into retreat. With the retirement of the giant union leaders Jack Jones and Hugh Scanlon in 1978, he found himself having to fill a power vacuum in the TUC, a task that was never going to be easy.

The election of Margaret Thatcher and the Conservatives to government in May 1979 was at first received complacently by the TUC. Murray admitted later on that he and other union leaders believed she would be compelled by the force of events to seek a deal with the TUC, especially as unemployment began to soar. When she refused to change direction despite worsening economic conditions and industrial conflict the TUC found it hard to respond. Legislation was passed in 1982 to expose trade union funds to fines and sequestration in the case of unlawful disputes. The TUC's defiance of such a measure was to prove short-lived.

After Labour's landslide defeat in the 1983 general election, Murray made a belated attempt to spell out the painful realities to the trade unions. An exponent of New Realism, he argued that the TUC could not regard itself as an alternative government like Brother Bonnie Prince Charlie waiting to be summoned to power from exile. Murray's new-found resolve reflected his alarm at the widening gap he saw opening up between union leaders and their own members. He feared unions were no longer representing rank and file opinion and were out of touch with social and economic trends. He risked his own position by refusing to accept that the TUC should underwrite the unlawful actions of the National Graphical Association, print union in its battle against the *Stockport Messenger* newspaper. Although successful on that occasion, Murray's moderating position was quickly undermined by Mrs Thatcher when she outlawed trade unions at the government's intelligence-gathering centre in Cheltenham. The TUC offered to negotiate a no-strike agreement for staff at the establishment but this was rejected by the Prime Minister. Murray's New Realism met with no positive response from the government.

The outbreak of the miners' strike over pit closures in March 1984 dealt a further blow to his efforts to make the TUC more reasonable. Although the TUC was kept out of the dispute in its early months at the request of the Mineworkers' Union, Murray grew more pessimistic about its consequences, worried by the outbreaks of violence and in despair at the rejections of compromise on all sides. He decided to take early retirement. Murray took a Labour life peerage in 1985 as Lord Murray of Epping Forest and turned into a grey but respected figure in the House of Lords, an eloquent champion of the more civilised forms of industrial relations.

Robert Taylor

Harry Nicholas (1905–97)

That there was a 1974–79 Labour government at all owes a lot to the sensible, balanced devotion to the Party of its often-derided 'caretaker' General Secretary Harry (no one called him Herbert Richard) Nicholas, who held Transport House together 1968–72. It was a dangerous moment for Labour. The Party had been allowed to shrivel somewhat by those in government, after the internecine battles with the unions over Barbara Castle's ill-conceived White Paper, *In Place of Strife*. Albeit unexpectedly, Heath won against the odds in 1970, with the help of an over-cautious budget from Chancellor Roy Jenkins. Nicholas told us all quietly and gently to pull ourselves together and rebuild the Party – and above all, restore fraternal relations with the trade union movement. He had the bearing of an army officer, moustachioed and immaculately smart – but managed to get some discipline as he was perceived, rightly, on all sides, as wanting nothing for himself.

Born on 13 March 1905 of a docker's family (Richard Henry and Rosina Nicholas), he left Avonmouth Elementary School aged 14, becoming for seventeen years a clerk in the Port of Bristol Authority. There he came to the notice of another Bristolian, Ernie Bevin, who plucked him out to be Gloucester District Officer of the TGWU 1936–38, where he and his wife Rosina (née Brown, they had married in 1932) were such a success that Bevin made him Regional Officer for Bristol 1938–40 and brought him to London in 1940 to fill the National Officership for the crucial London Commercial Road Transport Group. In 1942 he became responsible for the Chemical Section and in 1944 for the Metal and Engineering Group, a post he held for twelve years. He was awarded an OBE in 1949.

It was assumed that as Arthur Deakin's anointed successor he would succeed to the General Secretaryship. That it was not to be is perhaps encapsulated in the view of Jack Jones: 'Nicholas managed to avoid the wrath of many of Deakin's opponents (including myself) by his courteous and friendly nature. But there was no doubting his conformity with Deakin's ultra-right wing approach ... He also found it difficult nevertheless to apply Deakin's authoritarian stance in dealing with members in dispute and the shop stewards in the various industries. His smooth, polished nature helped to avoid too much trouble but he did not fit in easily with the rough and tough problems of the shop floor. In trade union circles generally, he was renowned for smart debonair appearance, invariably wearing an Anthony Eden hat and nice clothes. One newspaper reporter during the automation strike in the west Midlands during the 1950s mistook him for a Scotland Yard detective.'

Geoffrey Goodman's perceptive *Guardian* obituary of Nicholas highlights a further reason for his failure to succeed Deakin: 'When Deakin needed to appoint a new Assistant General Secretary in the late 1940s he favoured Harry Nicholas ... And Harry would have been appointed but for the discovery that his union card had accidentally fallen into arrears because his wife, Rose, had been in hospital for two months. Under union rules this meant that his candidature for the job was invalid.' It was thus Arthur 'Jock' Tiffin who became the Assistant General Secretary and Deakin's successor on his death in May 1955. The TGWU executive meanwhile backed Frank Cousins over Nicholas to succeed Tiffin as Assistant General Secretary by a single vote and it was Cousins who succeeded Tiffin on his unexpected death in December 1955, Nicholas serving as Assistant General Secretary 1956–68.

Nicholas stood in as acting TGWU General Secretary 1964–66, somewhat to the detriment of his health, when Frank Cousins became Minister of Technology in Wilson's Cabinet. He also rendered valuable service as Labour Party Treasurer 1960–64 and on Labour's NEC 1956–64 and 1967–68. His elevation to the Labour Party General Secretaryship is a fascinating part of Labour history. Wilson, Crossman and Benn have all given their accounts; but the most fascinating is that of George Brown's memoirs, *In My Way*: 'We [the NEC sub-committee] had various meetings but nobody of really the right stature emerged, and gradually it began to appear that the favoured candidate of the Prime Minister himself was Anthony Greenwood.' Brown and Callaghan, however, preferred Nicholas.

Crossman agreed, noting in his diary for 24 July 1968: 'On the whole I must say I thought Harry Nicholas a far better choice. To take a failed politician and shove him into Transport House is an insult both to the unions and to the party workers. Harry will be quite an efficient administrator though he can't be the second focus of power which we recommended in the advisory Commission's Report last year. The fact is that Tony would have been the PM's stooge and that's why he lost.'

Crossman's verdict in his diary entry of 21 January 1969 was that Nicholas was, 'very much better, firmer, more efficient, and more confident a General Secretary than Len Williams.' A substantial preoccupation was with fundraising, for which Nicholas conceived the 'fighting fivers' campaign to persuade Labour supporters to donate financially to improve Party organisation and constituency services. Wilson knighted him in his 1970 dissolution honours and he retired aged 67 in October 1972, his own anointed successor, Gwyn Morgan, being rejected by the NEC in favour of National Agent Ron Hayward on the casting vote of Tony Benn. He died on 15 April 1997.

Tam Dalyell MP

Philip Noel-Baker (Lord Noel-Baker)   (1889–1982)

Philip Noel-Baker was awarded the Nobel Peace Prize in 1959 for his work on arms control and the international regulation of conflict. A Quaker from a privileged background, he was son of the Canadian Joseph Allen Baker, who as a Liberal represented East Finsbury on the LCC and in the House of Commons before and during World War One. Baker was an immense influence and inspiration on his son and Noel-Baker's (he formally added his wife's name to his own) lifelong work on the prevention of war was a natural extension of his father's pacifism and their shared religious faith. Born Philip John Baker in London on 1 November 1889, he was educated at Bootham School in York, at Haverford College in Pennsylvania and at Kings College Cambridge.

Noel-Baker was decorated three times in World War One for bravery as he commanded his Quaker ambulance unit; he was an athlete of international standing and world statesman by the time he was in his thirties. He participated in the formation, the administration, and the legislative deliberations of the two great international political organisations of the twentieth century – the League of Nations and the United Nations. In 1918–1919, during the Peace Conference in Paris, he was principal assistant to Lord Robert Cecil on the committee which drafted the League of Nations Covenant; from 1920 to 1922 a member of the Secretariat of the League, being principal assistant to Sir Eric Drummond, first secretary-general of the League; from 1922 to 1924 the private secretary to the British representative on the League's Council and Assembly. Meanwhile, he also was acting as a valued adviser to Fridtjof Nansen in his prisoner-of-war and refugee work. From 1924 to 1929 he was Cassell Professor of International Relations at the University of London and from 1929 to 1931 he was a member of the British delegation to the Assembly of the League and then for a year an assistant to Arthur Henderson, the chairman of the Disarmament Conference.

He combined this international career with a domestic political one from 1929 onwards and also pursued an academic career in Law. He was MP for Coventry 1929–31; for Derby 1936–50; and for Derby South from 1950 to 1970. Elected to Labour's National Executive Committee from 1937 to 1948, in 1946 he succeeded Harold Laski as chairman of the party. He was vice-chairman of the foreign affairs group of the Parliamentary Labour Party in 1961 and its chairman in 1964. He saw distinguished home front service in the coalition government as Joint Parliamentary Secretary to the Minister of War Transport from February 1942 until May 1945.

Appointed Foreign Office Minister of State, Bevin's deputy, in August 1945, and a Privy Counsellor, he applied his experience to the creation of the United Nations. Bevin never rated him, preferring Hector McNeil, and prevailed upon Attlee to have him moved. He became Secretary of State for Air in October 1946, and was promoted to Cabinet as Secretary of State for Commonwealth Relations in October 1947. Attlee famously concluded of Noel-Baker's

Cabinet performance that 'he has not advanced his reputation. He was talkative but not illuminating ...' In February 1950 he was demoted to Minister of Fuel and Power outside the Cabinet, where he continued to serve until the defeat of the Attlee government in October 1951.

In the 1950s, Noel-Baker returned to his studies on disarmament, though remaining a front-bench spokesman on UN and disarmament issues. He had published a long book in 1936, *The Private Manufacture of Armaments*. In *The Arms Race: A Programme for World Disarmament*, published in 1958, he summarised the results of extensive research combined with personal experiences which began at the Peace Conference in Paris in 1919. This comprehensive, historical, and analytical study won the Albert Schweitzer Book Prize in 1961.

Noel-Baker's position within the Labour Party was as a technician of international affairs and disarmament rather than as an effective political force, though he was an elected Shadow Cabinet member from 1951 until defeated in 1959. Close to the Gaitskellites, he always remained rather aloof from party factionalism around the issue of disarmament and relied on his immense personal moral authority to support his positions. In the battles over unilateral nuclear disarmament of the late 1950s and early 1960s he sided with the multilateralists without losing the respect of the other side. He never rose to high office, in part because of age and in part because of a disinclination to make the necessary political calculations and alliances. Though naturally and vigorously competitive, his morality and Quakerism were perhaps impediments to a really successful political career. However, there are few people in the history of the Labour movement who did more practical work for peace. Created Lord Noel-Baker in June 1977, despite growing blindness he launched the World Disarmament Campaign with his friend Fenner Brockway in 1980 (though Brockway supported unilateral disarmament, Noel-Baker remained a multilateralist) and continued to be politically active until his death in London on 8 October 1982. His wife, Irene Noel, the daughter of a British landowner in Achmetaga, Greece, whom he had married in 1915, predeceased him in 1956. He did not remarry, despite the expectations of his mistress since the late 1930s, Lloyd George's daughter Megan, on whose decision to leave the Liberals and become a Labour MP he had had considerable influence. His son Francis Noel-Baker was Labour MP for Brentford and Chiswick 1945–50 and for Swindon from 1955 until his resignation in 1968, later joining the SDP and in 1984 the Conservative Party.

His publications include: *J. Allen Baker, Member of Parliament: A Memoir* (London, Swarthmore, 1927); *The Arms Race: A Programme for World Disarmament* (London, Stevens, 1958); *Disarmament* (London, Hogarth, 1926); *Disarmament and the Coolidge Conference* (London, Leonard and Virginia Woolf, 1927); *The Geneva Protocol for the Pacific Settlement of International Disputes* (London, King, 1925); *Hawkers of Death: The Private Manufacture and Trade in Arms* (London, Labour Party, 1934); *The League of Nations at Work* (London, Nisbet, 1926); 'A National Air Force No Defence', 'Peace and the Official Mind' and 'The International Air Police Force', in *Challenge to Death*, ed. by Storm Jameson (London, Constable, 1934); 'The Obligatory Jurisdiction of the Permanent Court of International Justice', in *The British Year Book of International Law* (1925), pp. 68–102; *The Present Juridical Status of the British Dominions in International Law* (London, Longmans, Green, 1929); *The Private Manufacture of Armaments* (London, Gollancz, 1936); 'UN, the Atom, the Veto', Speech at the Plenary Assembly of the United Nations: 25 October, 1946 (London, Labour Party, 1946); *The Way to World Disarmament-Now!* (London,

Union of Democratic Control, 1963). 'A Tribute to Philip Noel-Baker' by Bertrand Russell appeared in *International Relations*, 2 (1960) 1–2, and a biography by David Whittaker, *Fighter for Peace*, was published in 1989.

Professor Brian Brivati

Sydney Haldane Olivier (Lord Olivier)　　　　　　(1859–1943)

George Bernard Shaw described him as looking like 'a Spanish grandee in any sort of clothes, however unconventional.' As a young Fabian he was renowned for his fondness for a brown velvet smoking jacket which he persisted in wearing beyond the point of its disintegration. At the Colonial Office, Olivier had dipped the white ostrich feather plumes on his court hat in ink when the Lord Chamberlain insisted black ones must now be worn. When Ramsay MacDonald sounded him out about joining the first Labour Cabinet, he replied that he would prefer the Colonial Office but was happy with India. MacDonald created him 1st Lord Olivier in 1924 and appointed him Labour's first Secretary of State for India in his Cabinet of 1924.

When it came to the problems of India, however, Lord Olivier was nothing if not conventional. Although Ghandi was released, Olivier as he himself put it, 'came to the conclusion that the problem of India was at present insoluble'. In consequence he rejected the Swarajist demand for a new Round Table Conference to discuss changes in the three-year-old Montagu-Chelmsford reforms and defended Britain's presence in India on the basis that Britain had made India what it was.

Sydney Haldane Olivier was born in Colchester in April 1859 of Hugenot descent, the second of ten children, to a stern Anglican, the Rev. H A Olivier. He himself described his father as 'a somewhat bitter religious bigot'. Moving in early childhood to Lausanne where he began his education he returned to school in England, first at Kineton and then to Tonbridge. Reading Philosophy and Theology at Corpus Christi, Oxford, he had become much influenced by the philosopher August Comte. Indeed, according to Shaw he was the only Fabian so influenced. Before joining the Fabians in May 1885, joining the same day as his friend and fellow Colonial Office clerk Sidney Webb, he was briefly involved with the team writing the periodical *Christian Socialist,* joined the committee of the Land Reform Union and began teaching a Latin class at the Working Men's College.

In 1882, having headed the Civil Service open competition list, he had joined the Colonial Office. Whilst at the Colonial Office, which opened at 11 am, he spent the earlier part of his mornings inspecting slums for the Lisson Grove district Sanitary Aid Committee. One morning he had to report having found the tenants smoking haddocks in the lavatories using lighted newspaper. These activities, and his appointment as Secretary of the Fabian Society from 1886–1890, do not appear to have unduly ruffled ostrich feathers in the Colonial Office. One reason may be that the Fabians had considerably less public profile than now, and indeed were considerably smaller. It was said, indeed, that the entire records of the society were at the time stored in a Colonial Office desk drawer. Along with Ramsay MacDonald, he was also a member of the progressive Rainbow Circle 1894–99 and 1913–31.

Promotion, however, meant overseas postings, which in turn meant divesting himself of some of his Fabian responsibilities. In 1890–91 for example he was appointed Acting Colonial secretary of British Honduras and in 1895 Auditor-General of the Leeward Islands. In 1896 he was in Washington negotiating on behalf of the West Indies colonies and from 1899 to 1904 he served as Colonial Secretary of Jamaica. Returning to Whitehall he continued to cover West Africa and the West Indies before his appointment as Governor of Jamaica in 1907, a position he occupied until his return to England in 1913 when appointed Permanent Secretary at the Board of Agriculture and Fisheries, where he remained until 1917. From 1917 until his retirement in 1920, he served as Comptroller and Auditor of Exchequer.

In his long retirement first in the Cotswolds and then in Sussex, broken only by his service in the Labour Government of 1924, he devoted himself to writing. Though Margaret Cole called Olivier's contribution to *Fabian Essays,* an essay on the moral basis of socialism 'easily the dullest of the essays,' he authored one of the early, and best-selling, Fabian Tracts: No. 7, *Capital and Land.* Published in 1888 and frequently reprinted thereafter, this was a trenchant attack on the supposed panacea of the Single Tax. He also continued to give lectures to organisations ranging from the Marxist Social Democratic Federation, the progressive Rainbow Circle, and Cambridge University Fabians whose membership include the young Rupert Brooke and Hugh Dalton, in addition to his own daughters, on whom, in the light of the interest of HG Wells, he was forced to keep a wary eye.

'Socialism is nothing else but common sense,' he had declared in his contribution to *Fabian Essays.* In 1942 he wrote to H G Wells, 'It has taken eighty years for what appeared reasonable to us to appear reasonable to the nation.' His books include *The Anatomy of African Misery* (1927), *White Capital and Coloured Labour* (1929) and *The Myth of Governor Eyre and Jamaica* (1936), *Jamaica, The Blessed Island* (1936). *Sydney Olivier,* by Margaret Olivier, was published in 1948. He died at Bognor Regis on 15 February, 1943.

Greg Rosen

Stan Orme (Lord Orme) (1923–)

Sometimes a parliamentarian is acknowledged wholly in his or her own right, but sometimes their reputation rests in part on an association with another – or others. When Stanley Orme entered the Commons as the Member of Parliament for Salford West in 1964 he did so at the same time as Eric Heffer, who represented the Liverpool seat of Walton. For almost ten years they were invariable seen as a partnership both in campaigns and Parliamentary activities. Eric was always slightly to the left of Stan, but they happily combined their not inconsiderable talents on the left in Labour Party terms. They advanced up the ladder together, each in time becoming a Minister of State and each making a mark both in Parliamentary as well as Party terms. Stanley also made another partnership with his Parliamentary neighbour, Frank Allaun, who represented Salford East. Yet again, as by his membership and association with his trade union – the Amalgamated Engineers Union – he formed yet other partnerships, notably with Charlie Pannell, a legendary organiser and wit who represented a Leeds constituency. Another famous duo was that formed at the time by Jack Jones and Hughie Scanlon, trade union leaders par excellence. But Stanley was his own man and made a personal contribution to post-1964 politics.

Stanley Orme was born on 23 April 1923 in Sale, Cheshire, the son of Sherwood Orme, and was educated in elementary and technical schools. Like so many in the broad labour movement of his era, he was also educated through the Workers Education Association(WEA) and the National Council of Labour Colleges (NCLC). The range of subjects taught by both these institutions covered the broad economic and social field as well as a grounding in both writing and public speaking – all attributes which stood him in good stead when he entered trade union and public life. During the war he served in the Royal Air Force (Bomber Command) as a Warrant Officer Air Bomber Navigator.

He joined the Labour Party in 1944 and served as a member of the Sale Borough Council from 1958 to 1965, and had his first Parliamentary contest in 1959 when he contested Stockport South. As a skilled engineer he specialised in industrial matters in the period immediately after entering the Commons, but once in Opposition after 1970 he handled the Northern Ireland brief, and became the Minister of State at the Northern Ireland Office and a Privy Counsellor when Labour came to power in 1974. Early after the election defeat of 1970 Stan made a powerful speech in the PLP on the situation in Northern Ireland. Afterwards in the tea-room, Harold Wilson told Stan that he was impressed by it and invited him to join Merlyn Rees as Spokesman for the Opposition. When Jim Callaghan became Prime Minister in April 1976 he moved Stanley to become Minister of State at the Department of Health and Social Security. In September 1976 he promoted him to be Minister for Social Security with a place in the Cabinet, promoting both Roy Hattersley and Bill Rodgers to the Cabinet that same day.

After the defeat in 1979 Stan Orme continued to play a prominent part in the affairs of the Parliamentary Labour Party, being elected to the shadow cabinet every year up until the General Election of 1987. He served as Shadow Health and Social Security Secretary 1979–80, as Shadow Industry Secretary 1980–83 and as Shadow Energy Secretary 1983–87. His greatest service to the Party, however, came when he was elected as Chairman of the Parliamentary Labour Party in 1987, serving until 1992. He beat, amongst others, Merlyn Rees and Bruce Millan for the post. Chair of the PLP is a comparative recent innovation. Until Harold Wilson decided to change the situation, the chair was occupied by the Leader of the Party in Government and in Opposition. In 1964 he decided that as Prime Minister he wanted another to occupy the Chair of the PLP, and Manny Shinwell was the first elected Chair, to be followed over the years by Douglas Houghton, Ian Mikardo, Cledwyn Hughes, Fred Willey, Jack Dormand, then Stan Orme, Doug Hoyle and today it is Clive Soley. This gave him a place in the shadow cabinet and the important role of being the link between the backbench MPs and the Government, especially the Prime Minister and in his case the Leader of the Opposition. All his experience gained over the years was needed. As a member of the Manchester Area Committee of the AEU which had 29,000 members, Stan had had a long apprenticeship for the post and by common consent he was a most effective voice both for backbenchers and for the Government when needed.

His sagacity was recognised by becoming a member of the important Commons Committee of Privileges (1995) and then the Committee on Standards in Public Life (1996). Very much a 'man of the people', Stan was well-liked because of his diligence in the tasks he undertook. From his days with Eric Heffer as a critic of the Labour governments of the sixties he could always be relied upon to be well-prepared for any argument in the Chamber or upstairs in a

Committee Room. He was proud to succeed Charlie Pannell in 1976 as Chair of the Parliamentary AEU group, and subsequently of the AEEU group until 1996, and took his responsibilities seriously. His joint stewardship with Frank Allaun over the interests of the City of Salford was a model for two MPs who represented adjoining constituencies and where it was possible to tread on other's toes. They never did. He retired from the Commons and was created Lord Orme of Salford in 1997.

Stan has been a fan of Manchester United all his life. The greatest night of his life was to be in Barcelona when they beat Bayern Munich and added the European Cup to those of the English FA Cup and the Premier Division Championship, bringing off that unique treble. The best players of his day were those of the Busby Babes who were killed in the Munich air disaster of 1958, especially Duncan Edwards. He married Irene Mary, daughter of Vernon F Harris, in 1951.

Rt Hon. Lord Graham of Edmonton

George Orwell (1903–50)

A writer, novelist and essayist can sometimes have more influence on the mentality of political activists than the most reasonable of politicians or the most serious of purely political writers. Orwell once said that 'Above all I wanted to make political writing into an art'. That he did, and his provocations, however seeming perverse or extreme, were always deliberately intended to make his readers think twice, or at all.

His real name was Eric Blair and he was born in India in 1903, son of an official in the Opium Service, but was brought to England by his mother at the age of three. His family were of what he called ironically, the lower-upper middle class', that is the 'upper-middle class without money'. He was crammed for a scholarship to Eton, but did little work there, already being something the odd man out 'agin the system'. Most of his school friends went on to Cambridge, but he entered the Burma Police, a satisfyingly second-class part of the Imperial Civil Service. He stuck it for five years, but resigned in 1927, having come to hate the social pretentiousness of the British in Burma, especially their indifference to Burmese culture. All this poured out in his first published novel, *Burmese Days* (1935).

Burmese Days is often taken to be socialist because it is anti-imperialist and because we know from his *Down and Out in Paris and London* that he had lived among the poor and destitute, to see if we treated our poor as we did the Burmans. He thought on the whole that we did. But between 1927 and 1934 Orwell often called himself, when asked 'Where do you stand?', simply 'a Tory anarchist'. He was an individualist who resented one man or one culture imposing its values on another; and though familiar with socialist arguments about economic exploitation, he did not feel himself a socialist until 1935. In 1936, in *The Road to Wigan Pier*, a clinical but moving account of living among the unemployed, he added an eccentric but provocative section announcing both his conversion to socialism and his scorn for the indifference to freedom of so many socialist intellectuals bemused by 'the myth of Soviet power'.

He went to Spain to fight for the Republic, not to write, but *Homage to Catalonia* (1938) resulted. It sold badly at the time but is now seen both as a classically honest description of war and as one of the shrewdest polemics against the Stalinist attempt to dominate both the

Spanish Republic and the whole international left. For a brief period until 1939 he was militantly anti-war, close to pacifism, a member of the Independent Labour Party, often mistakenly called Trotskyite, being strongly left-wing, egalitarian and both anti-Labour Party and anti-communist. He scraped a thin living as a novelist and reviewer, but with the outbreak of war he left the ILP and, moved by hatred of fascism and Hitlerism, argued with fervid optimism in a great polemic, *The Lion and the Unicorn* (1941), that a social revolution was taking place in the ranks of the British army. He set out to rescue patriotism from nationalism, trying to show that the roots of English patriotism were radical as much as Conservative.

Being tubercular, he was not accepted for military service and wasted two years in the BBC's Far Eastern Service before becoming Literary Editor of *Tribune* until the end of the war, a wholly congenial post with Aneurin Bevan as the Editor. He was an 'English Socialist' of the kind of Michael Foot and Bevan: left-wing but libertarian, egalitarian but anti-communist, but quite untheoretical, almost anti-theoretical. Early in the war he conceived a grand design for a three-volume novel of social analysis and warning which would deal with the decay of the old order, the betrayal of the revolution and what a subsequent English totalitarianism would be like. This design never came to be, but the pre-war novels like *Keep the Aspidistra Flying* and *Coming Up For Air* have some such connection with his masterpiece *Animal Farm* (1945) and with his most famous work, *Nineteen Eighty-Four* (1949). *Animal Farm* is a story of how the revolution of the animals for liberty and equality is betrayed by power-hungry (Stalinist) pigs. It was not a parable of the impossibility of revolution; and *Nineteen Eighty-Four* was not a morbid prophecy of what will happen but a savage, Swiftian satiric warning of what *could* happen if power is pursued for its own sake. Many right-wing American critics read him in a contrary sense, some mistakenly, others deliberately. His values remained those of a left-wing socialist until his early death from tuberculosis in 1950, only that his hope of seeing 'the Republic' emerge from 1945 had vanished. In the British press he criticised the Attlee government for losing the chance to establish 'real socialism', but typically in American left-wing journals he explained realistically the difficulties of doing so in a virtually bankrupt post-war Britain. He argued for a democratic socialist United States of Europe.

There is so much more in Orwell than his books. Some critics plausibly see his genius as an essayist. 'A Hanging' and 'Shooting an Elephant' are both ambiguously short-story or personal recollections, but both contain didactic or moral writing of great stature. His *Tribune* 'As I Please' columns virtually invented mixed column journalism, polemical and discursive. Sardonic humour is found throughout his essays, as when he would mock the fierce urban readers of *Tribune* by describing the pleasure of watching toads mating and hares boxing or the glory of a sixpenny Woolworth rose, all of which would form part of the good life, especially in the classless society.

He wrote major essays on censorship, plain language, the social beliefs of boys' magazines, and against pornography and violence: he believed passionately in liberty, but also in condemning harshly the morally and aesthetically bad. He wrote, like Dickens, Morris and Wells before him, for those whose only university was the free public library or the extra-mural class. All in all he became the living embodiment of that old English socialism that was not anti-parliamentary but was always suspicious of what power or its pursuit can do to people — as he once put it 'the backstairs crawlers and the arse-lickers of the Parliamentary Labour Party.' But he voted Labour, of course, although it is doubtful that he ever joined the party. Had he done so, he would have said, as he did when a member of the ILP, 'no writer can be a loyal member of a political party'. Any party needs members like that.

Key biographies are George Woodcock, *The Crystal Spirit: A Study of George Orwell*; Bernard Crick, *Orwell: A Life* (1980); and Michael Shelden, *Orwell: the Authorised Biography* (1991). And see also John Newsinger's admirable *Orwell's Politics* (1999).

Professor Bernard Crick

David Owen (Lord Owen) (1938–)

Throughout his political career David Owen provoked strong reactions from both friend and foe. His self-assurance and determination were attributes which stimulated deep loyalty from some, and violent antagonism from others. He had a meteoric rise in the Labour Party and was seen as one its brightest hopes. But launching and then leading the breakaway SDP made him a deeply unpopular figure in Labour ranks.

David Anthony Llewellyn Owen's early background was not typically Labour. He was very conscious of his non-metropolitan Welsh and West Country ancestry. His parents and the comfortable professional middle-class families from which they came had a strong tradition of public service. Both were independent councillors. That tradition, along with Christianity and medicine, were the powerful formative influences which led him to the Labour Party. They also nurtured his antagonism towards Establishment and particularly metropolitan elites with their 'cultivated effortless superiority'.

He was born on 2 July 1938 in Plympton in Devon. His mother was a dentist and his father a local doctor. He attended Mount House Preparatory School before boarding at Bradfield College near Reading. He read medicine at Sidney Sussex College, Cambridge, and at St. Thomas's Hospital, London, becoming Neurological and Psychiatric Registrar from 1964 to 1966 and a Research Fellow in the Medical Unit from 1966 to 1968.

He joined the Labour Party in 1960 after arriving in London as a clinical student at St Thomas's Hospital. As he said subsequently: 'The poverty I found in Lambeth around St Thomas's Hospital shocked me, for I had lived so far a very sheltered, relatively prosperous southern life.' He became the Labour candidate for Torrington whilst at St Thomas's and cut his campaigning teeth during the 1964 general election.

At the 1966 general election he then took the seat of Plymouth Sutton in his home town by defeating the serving Conservative member by the unexpectedly large majority of 5,222. He arrived at the House of Commons surprisingly ignorant and innocent about the internal politics of the Labour Party. At a dinner of the Gaitskellite 1963 Dining Club attended by Tony Crosland, Roy Jenkins and other right-wing luminaries, he had to ask Jack Diamond what CDS (the Gaitskellite Campaign for Democratic Socialism run by Bill Rodgers) actually was.

He still retained his direct interest in medicine at St Thomas's for some time after being elected and medicine retained its attraction as an alternative to politics for some years to come. He was appointed PPS to Gerry Reynolds, the Minister for Defence Administration, shortly after entering the House. From seeing it at close quarters he became increasingly disillusioned by

Harold Wilson and his administration. However, with a Navy constituency, Wilson's offer of the Navy Minister's post at the Ministry of Defence in July 1968 was understandably irresistible.

It no doubt helped him to hold on to his seat at Plymouth Sutton by a mere 747 votes when Ted Heath won the 1970 general election. The following four years in Opposition proved a traumatic time as the Party changed its position on the Common Market. David Owen was one of the 69 Labour MPs who voted against a three-line whip on the UK's entry to the European Community. The revolt was led by Roy Jenkins, then Deputy Leader, and Owen was heavily involved in all the manoeuvrings and consequences, which included his resignation as a front-bench defence spokesman in 1972. These events had a significant influence on the eventual split in the Labour Party and the establishment of the SDP less than a decade later.

This period also saw Owen's first taste of commercial life as Chairman of Decision Technology International. It was an invaluable experience of the private sector which was later to have a significant influence upon his thinking on industrial and economic policy issues. It was also a precursor to his involvement in a number of businesses after 1992, particularly as Executive Chairman of Middlesex Holdings Plc.

In February 1974 he was re-elected by the even narrower margin of 437 votes in the constituency of Plymouth Devonport. He was immediately appointed Parliamentary Under-Secretary of State for Health and in July that year Minister of State for Health, spending two and a half effective and enjoyable years in the Department with Barbara Castle as Secretary of State. During that time he was re-elected at Plymouth Devonport in the October 1974 General Election and succeeded with great difficulty in carrying through the phasing out of pay beds from NHS hospitals.

In March 1976 Harold Wilson resigned as Prime Minister and was replaced by Jim Callaghan. That September he moved David Owen to the Foreign Office as Tony Crosland's Deputy. The following February Tony Crosland unexpectedly had a stroke and died. No one was more surprised than David Owen when Jim Callaghan asked him to be Crosland's successor as Foreign Secretary. So began an eventful two years as Foreign Secretary. During that time the Government's majority in the House of Commons vanished and the Lib-Lab Pact was established. The Government eventually fell in 1979 following the 'winter of discontent' and its difficulties in carrying through its devolution legislation.

He was impatient with the Foreign Office culture, which he tried to reform, ruffling a lot of feathers by doing so. But he had a successful period as Foreign Secretary. He paved the way for the Rhodesian settlement which was concluded by his successor, Lord Carrington. He and Jim Callaghan, with whom he worked well, were able to sustain good relations with the Carter Administration in the US, marred only by embarrassment over the appointment of Peter Jay, Callaghan's then son-in-law, as the UK's Ambassador in Washington. Inevitably there was some tension with Roy Jenkins in his role as President of the European Commission, but he was responsible for successfully resisting Argentinian designs on the Falklands and coping with developments in Namibia and other events such as the fall of the Shah in Iran.

He was returned at Plymouth Devonport at the 1979 general election with a majority of 1001. So began the turbulent and divisive period in opposition which was eventually to end with him leaving the Labour Party and the founding of the SDP in 1981.

The battle lines between right and left had already been drawn up while he was still Foreign Secretary, but inevitably his involvement had been somewhat restricted by the demands of office. The Campaign for Labour Victory had been established during 1977 in the Party in the country to complement the Manifesto Group of the Parliamentary Labour Party in its resistance to the left.

Returning to the new House of Commons, David Owen was elected to the shadow cabinet in June 1979 and became Shadow Energy Secretary. That November, Roy Jenkins gave the Dimbleby Lecture, stimulating much discussion about the formation of a new Party. David Owen was not close to Roy Jenkins at this time and had an uneasy and suspicious relationship which was to grow into serious conflict in the later years of the SDP. But it was not until June 1980 that the onward advance of the left and the anti-Common Market groups in the Party provoked the first joint statement from David Owen, Bill Rodgers and Shirley Williams – dubbed from then on the 'Gang of Three'.

The rifts and the sense of disillusionment grew. The 'Gang of Three' published a policy statement in the *Guardian* that August. The September Party Conference supported policies for full withdrawal from the EEC, unilateral nuclear disarmament, the establishment of an electoral college and mandatory reselection. Callaghan resigned in October and Michael Foot was elected Leader in November 1980.

The stage was set. David Owen had led a group of dissident MPs in the House of Commons throughout the autumn. He did not stand for re-election to the shadow cabinet. Then Roy Jenkins returned from Brussels in January. A Special Party Conference at Wembley, addressed by a defiant David Owen, adopted a proposal for an electoral college to elect the Party Leader. The following day, 25 January 1981, from David Owen's home in Limehouse, the 'Gang of Four', as it had become with the addition of Roy Jenkins, issued the Declaration establishing the Council for Social Democracy which turned into the SDP.

David Owen was Chairman of its Parliamentary Committee until 1982, when he became Deputy Leader to Roy Jenkins. He was Leader from 1983 until the 1987 general election. He then led the fight against merger with the Liberal Party and continued as Leader, until their demise in 1992, of those who did not join the Liberal Democrats. He became Baron Owen of the City of Plymouth in 1992 and sits on the cross-benches in the Lords as an Independent Social Democrat. His non-federalist view of Europe is reflected in his chairmanship of the campaigning organisation New Europe.

He married his American wife Debbie in 1968. She has been a successful literary agent, and a powerful influence upon him. They and their two sons and daughter form a very close family.

David Owen is a man of prodigious energy and determination. Whilst in the Commons he produced an endless stream of statements, speeches and publications. At no time was this more apparent than during his years as SDP Leader from 1983 to 1987 when he built a formidable reputation in the House of Commons and a very high profile in the media. At times he displayed considerable courage, bordering on bravado. As in his sailing, he enjoyed the danger of a spill. He relished a challenge and was prepared to fight like a tiger for his interests and his beliefs. As he himself acknowledged, he frequently came over as arrogant and aloof and did not always suffer fools gladly. This often masked a depth of emotion and commitment he did not find it easy to reveal. He showed considerable leadership qualities and left the Commons with many thinking that, given the circumstances, he could have achieved even more than he did.

His publications include: *A Unified Health Service*, 1968; *The Politics of Defence*, 1972; *In Sickness and in Health*, 1976; *Human Rights*, 1978; *Face the Future*, 1981; *A Future that Will Work*, 1984; *A United Kingdom*, 1986; *Personally Speaking (to Kenneth Harris)*, 1987; *Our NHS*, 1988; *Time to Declare* (Autobiography), 1991; *Seven Ages* (a poetry anthology) 1992; and *Balkan Odyssey*, 1995.

Sir Ian Wrigglesworth

Baron Parmoor of Frith (Charles Alfred Cripps)　　(1852–1941)

The invitation to former Tory MP Lord Parmoor to join the first Labour Cabinet probably owed more to his being Beatrice Webb's brother-in-law than to his involvement in party politics. Nevertheless, he was to remain on the Labour front bench until the formation of Ramsay MacDonald's National Government nearly eight years later.

Alfred Cripps was born near West Ilsley, Berkshire, on 3 October 1852, the sixth of eleven children. His father, William Henry, was a leading parliamentary and ecclesiastical lawyer, a QC by 1886, and author of the classic text on Ecclesiastical Law, *The Law relating to Church and Clergy*. Educated at Winchester and New College Oxford, Alfred followed in his father's legal footsteps and was soon so successful that he was able to buy Parmoor, his father's 200-acre Buckinghamshire estate, and take up farming as a recreation. In October 1881 he married Theresa, the daughter of Great Western Railway Chairman Richard Potter and sister of Beatrice, wife of Sidney, Webb. They had five children, the youngest of whom, Richard Stafford, was to become Chancellor of the Exchequer under Attlee. Always frail, Theresa died after a brief illness in May 1893.

Possessing a high-Anglican scepticism of Liberalism over Irish Home Rule and Church schools in particular, he was elected Unionist MP for Stroud in 1895; he lost it to the Liberals in 1900 and switched to win Stretford, Lancashire, in 1901. Losing again to the Liberals in 1906 he gained South Buckinghamshire for the Unionists in 1910. In 1910 Alfred declared that he 'stood for the union and co-operation of all classes, for the union of the Empire and Kingdom; and let them all be Patriots and Imperialists'. A firm free-trader, he also advocated proportional representation. In the Lords reform battle of 1910–11 he favoured concession and this probably played a role in Haldane's request to Asquith that Cripps be offered a peerage and a place on the Judicial Committee of the Privy Council. He became 1st Baron Parmoor of Frith in 1914.

His political involvement was closely paralleled by his involvement in the Anglican Church. Having represented Oxford in the House of Laymen since 1890, he became its Chairman in 1911 and in 1913 initiated the process which by 1919 inaugurated the National Assembly of the Church of England, the House of Laity of which he was elected the first Chairman. It was, moreover, his Christian pacifist opposition to the First World War that was to divide him from his erstwhile Tory colleagues. He co-founded the League of Nations Society and presided over the initial meeting of the League of Free Nations Association in May 1917. Subsequently, his involvement in an International Christian Conference and the linked organisation 'Fight the Famine' led him to meet and marry Marion, daughter of Quaker Liberal MP John Ellis in 1919. In 1921 he joined the Labour Party.

In 1924, as Lord President of the Council he took responsibility for League of Nations affairs in Cabinet and the generality of foreign policy in the Lords, securing a room, albeit a small one, in the Foreign Office. He worked closely with Arthur Henderson on the Geneva Protocol which provided for multilateral disarmament, automatic sanctions against aggressors and compulsory arbitration of international disputes. MacDonald and others in Cabinet were notably antipathetic to aspects of the Protocol, in particular the provisions for sanctions and collective security. It is therefore likely that only the resignation of the government in October 1924, just a week after the publication of the protocol, saved it from an embarrassing split on whether or not actually to sign.

In 1928 he succeeded Haldane as leader of the small band of Labour peers. Aged 77, he returned in 1929 to Cabinet as Lord President of the Council and Leader of the House of Lords, combining this role with responsibility for League affairs. His continuing free-trade commitment manifested itself in his role in the Cabinet revolt over tariffs, which led to the ratification of an international 'tariff truce' under the aegis of the League in spite of the reluctance of MacDonald, J H Thomas and Vernon Hartshorn. By 1931 he was increasingly feeling his age and in March indicated a desire to retire. Moreover, with the worsening financial crisis, his free-trade convictions were less representative of the mainstream cabinet view. By August 1931 he was in a minority in opposing a manufacturing tariff. Though he did not oppose MacDonald's proposal to cut unemployment benefit, he opposed the National Government and retired to the Labour backbenches. He died on 30 June 1941.

His publications include: *A Retrospect, Looking Back over a Life of More than 80 Years* (Heineman 1936); *A Proposal for Equal representation* (Gilbert and Rivington 1884); *The Foundation Oration, 'Do Well and Right and Let the World Sink'* (UCL 1915); and *A Treatise on the Principles of the Law of Compensation in reference to the Lands Clauses Consolidation Acts* (H Sweet, 1881).

Greg Rosen

Fred Peart (Lord Peart of Workington)   (1914–88)

When one thinks of the hereditary principle in politics it is not unusual these days after the recent fundamental change in the House of Lords to think of that applying to great families who, down the ages have been represented in Parliament and especially the House of Lords as a result of such honour being bestowed on an ancestor centuries ago. This place and title is thereafter passed 'down the line' until, in the year 1999, there were more than 700 members of the House of Lords who sat as a result of inheriting a title, many centuries old but others not. Neil Kinnock once famously said that he was the first Kinnock to go to university in a thousand years, and so Fred Peart was the first Lord Peart of Workington in history, but some would say that he came from as good stock as others who graced the red leather benches of the Lords.

Thomas Frederick Peart was born on 30 April 1914 into a socialist home in County Durham; his father, Emerson Featherstone Peart, was leader of the Durham County Council, and his mother equally prominent in working-class life. He was educated at Crook Council

School, Wolsingham Grammar School and Henry Smith's School in Hartlepool and at Bede College, Durham University, where took his BSc, was President of the Union, played football and boxed for the University. He studied for the Bar at the Inner Temple but decided to became a schoolmaster and lecturer in Economics. He was prospective parliamentary candidate for Scarborough and Whitby in 1938–39 and for Sunderland from 1939 to 1945. Having joined the Labour Party in 1930 he served on Easington Council from 1937 to 1940. His connections with Easington were at a time when that constituency boasted a recent Member of Parliament – Ramsay MacDonald – who went on to become the first Labour Prime Minister in history, and where at the time Manny Shinwell was the local MP, to be followed in 1970 by Jack Dormand who went on to become the Chairman of the Parliamentary Labour Party.

Fred Peart had a kind of charisma or charm which rapidly propelled him to the top in the Labour Party, especially the Parliamentary Labour Party, and when he won the seat of Workington in 1945 he immediately got a foot on the ladder of promotion when he became the PPS to the then Minister of Agriculture, the legendary Tom Williams, remaining in post for the entirety of the Attlee government. Whatever his inclinations, that first small step under such a great man undoubtedly helped Fred to learn the parliamentary and ministerial ropes to such an extent that he was eventually to join the Cabinet as the Minister for Agriculture himself in 1964 when Harold Wilson entered No.10 for the first time, serving until April 1968. For the next 20 years Fred was never out of the top echelons of Parliamentary life.

What Labour called 'the thirteen wasted years' from losing office in 1951 until regaining it in 1964 were years of frustration for Fred Peart. He was busy and in demand as a speaker in both Agricultural and increasingly on Common Market issues. From 1959 to 1964 he was Shadow Agriculture Minister, with a brief break at Gaitskell's request 1960–61 when he was Labour's spokesman on science. He was a delegate to the Council of Europe from 1952 to 1955 and a member of the Nature Conservation Council 1961 to 1964. Another agriculture-related interest was represented when he served as the Privy Council representative on the Council of the Royal College of Veterinary Surgeons (1953–64), when on joining the Cabinet he became a Privy Counsellor proper. Fred's style of rich bonhomie was deployed to good effect in both the Commons (where he had to deal with the 1967 outbreak of foot-and-mouth disease) and increasingly in Europe, although at that time Britain had not yet entered the EEC. During the war he had served in the Royal Artillery in North Africa and in Italy and he was never opposed to the concept of European co-operation, but his backing for the British farmer and the availability of cheap Commonwealth imports led to a hostility to the operation of the Common Agricultural Policy. When there was a threat to devalue the pound during the 1966–1970 administration the Labour Government executed a volte-face and applied for EEC membership, and Peart was one of four members of the Cabinet who resisted. However, he had another opportunity to influence affairs in 1974 when Labour again came to power and as Agriculture Minister 1974–76 he was by the side of James Callaghan when they renegotiated the terms of United Kingdom membership. He had found that the Commonwealth beef and sugar producers wanted to exploit rising world prices to the full and that their governments offered grudging concessions to help Britain obtain supplies at cut rates. On the other hand the EEC offered immediate practical help and he decided that political and commercial togetherness formed part of the same pattern.

He was Leader of the British delegation to the Council of Europe 1973–74 and the Western European Assembly 1973–74 and was Vice- President of the Council of Europe 1973–74. In the Shadow Cabinet 1970–74 he served as spokesman on Parliamentary Affairs 1970–71, Shadow Agriculture Minister 1971–72 and Shadow Defence Secretary 1972–74.

In 1976, James Callaghan created him Lord Peart of Workington and appointed him Lord Privy Seal and Leader of the House of Lords, thus completing a rare double, for he had been Leader of The House of Commons and Lord President of the Council from October 1968 until Labour's defeat in the 1970 election. His period in the Lords was not a happy one. In opposition from 1979, he failed to lead Labour peers effectively, and he was replaced in an election of Labour peers in 1982 by Cledwyn Hughes. After he relinquished his leadership he was for two years the Chairman of the Retail Consortium. Tragically, he and his wife were brutally attacked in their home in 1984 and although he put up a spirited defence he never really recovered and died in hospital in Tooting on 26 August 1988. He married Sarah Elizabeth Lewis in 1945, with whom he had a son.

Rt Hon. Lord Graham of Edmonton

Frederick Pethick-Lawrence (1871–1961)
(Baron Pethick-Lawrence of Peaslake)

Frederick Pethick-Lawrence first came to the public's attention as a radical campaigner for women's suffrage and later as a pacifist in the First World War. He went on to serve for 22 years as a Member of Parliament (with a gap of four years), before being created a peer and being an active member of the House of Lords for a further 16 years. He was Secretary of State for India and Burma during the critical independence negotiations after the Second World War.

Frederick William Lawrence was born on 28 December 1871 in London. It was only on marriage that he prefixed his wife's name to his own. His father, Alfred, was a prosperous building contractor, but died when Lawrence was only three years old. His mother, Mary Elizabeth, brought him up in the Unitarian faith. He was educated at Eton and then Trinity College, Cambridge, gaining a double first in Mathematics and Natural Sciences. In 1897 was elected to a fellowship, but decided against an academic career and left for a world tour.

On his return, he renewed acquaintance with a Cambridge colleague, Percy Alden, who was then warden of Mansfield House, a nonconformist settlement in Canning Town. He became treasurer and combined his social work with law studies, being eventually called to the Bar in 1899. On the death of his elder brother in 1900 he inherited property and had the independent means to consider a career in Parliament. He was selected as Liberal-Unionist candidate for North Lambeth in 1901.

When he married fellow social worker Emmeline Pethick in 1901, Frederick, now Pethick-Lawrence, abandoned his candidacy for the Liberal Party to work with Emmeline to try to improve conditions for the poor in the East End. He purchased an evening newspaper, the *Echo,* following Percy Alden as its editor. The paper campaigned for the ideas of the newly forming Labour Party, but ceased publication with financial problems in 1905.

That same year he was asked to defend three suffragettes accused of disorderly conduct and this started a long commitment of both Pathick-Lawrences to the cause of women's suffrage. They became joint editors of *Votes for Women,* close colleagues of Emmeline and Christabel Pankhurst, and acted as publicists for the Women's Social and Political Union. Emmeline Pethick-Lawrence was among those arrested for causing a disturbance in the House of Commons, receiving a prison sentence. She was imprisoned again in 1909 for suffragette activity. Frederick was funding the WSPU and he later calculated that he stood bail for over 1,000 women. The couple were both arrested together with Mrs Emmeline Pankhurst after a demonstration in the West End and charged with conspiracy to incite damage. Despite Pethick-Lawrence's excellent advocacy in their own defence they were convicted and sentenced to nine months' imprisonment. All three went on hunger strike and were force-fed, but were released after five weeks. Pethick-Lawrence and Mrs Pankhurst had been ordered to pay costs and when he refused he was declared bankrupt, although this was annulled a year later.

The Pethick-Lawrences now split from the Pankhursts after deciding that a more moderate route to women's suffrage would be the better way of achieving results. The outbreak of war in 1914 returned Pethick-Lawrence to one of his earlier concerns. He had been opposed to participation in the Boer War and was now equally opposed to Britain's involvement in the war in Europe. He declared himself a conscientious objector when he was called up for military service. He was a leading propagandist for the Union of Democratic Control and contested the by-election in South Aberdeen as a 'peace by negotiation' candidate. He lost this election.

In 1922 he was unsuccessful at South Islington, this time as a Labour candidate, but in 1923 won the seat of West Leicester, defeating Winston Churchill who was standing for the last time as a Liberal. He remained MP for this constituency until 1931 and was appointed Financial Secretary to the Treasury in the 1929 Labour government. He had opposed the return to the gold standard in 1926 and believed the financial crisis of 1931 could have been overcome without giving way to the pressure being exerted by the banks. He refused to join MacDonald in the National Government and, along with most of his Labour Party colleagues, was defeated in the 1931 general election.

After being re-elected to parliament in 1935 as member for East Edinburgh, he became a privy councillor in 1937. He had been a member of the India Round Table Conference in 1931 and contributed significantly to debates on Indian affairs throughout his second spell as an MP. When war was declared in 1939, this time he reluctantly supported it as necessary because dictators such as Hitler and Mussolini were not open to peaceful persuasion. Throughout the war he sat on the Labour front bench.

When his autobiography, *Fate Has Been Kind,* was published in 1942, it celebrated and acknowledged the importance of Emmeline as a partner in all his ventures. Not only was there a customary dedication, but the account opened with a touching poem written for his wife whilst she was away in South Africa in 1930. Emmeline had already written her own account in *My Part in a Changing World,* published in 1938.

After the Labour victory in 1945 he was created a peer and appointed Secretary of State for India and Burma for what was to be a crucial phase in Indian affairs. The Cabinet mission to India in 1946 was led by Pethick-Lawrence, but Sir Stafford Cripps was the driving force; he seemed to have greater access to the Prime Minister's ear on Indian policy than the less decisive Pethick-Lawrence. The mission had to return without obtaining any agreement, but did convince the Indian leaders that the offer of independence was genuine. In February 1947, it was announced that the transfer of power would occur by no later than June 1948. Lord Mountbatten was appointed Viceroy and in April Pethick-Lawrence, now aged 75, resigned as Secretary of State. The process was speeded up and independence was brought forward by ten months.

Emmeline died in 1954 and in 1957 he was married again to Helen Millar, a friend for forty years since their involvement in women's suffrage campaigns. Pethick-Lawrence continued as an active member of the House of Lords, where the last words of his last speech on 27 July 1961 returned to his early concern for economic inequality as he attacked tax reductions for the rich. He died on 10 September just six weeks later.

Frederick Pethick-Lawrence's quiet and considerate manner and concern to hear all sides may have often made him seem indecisive compared to some of the more dynamic figures around him. He had, nevertheless, always been committed to the cause of the underdog and had devoted much of his life and his financial resources to championing the causes he believed in. Had he lived a few months longer, a dinner in his honour had been planned by the Fawcett Society for his ninetieth birthday to recognise, in particular, his great contribution to the cause of women's suffrage.

For further reference see Vera Brittain's *Pethick-Lawrence: A Portrait* (1963), Frederick Pethick-Lawrence's autobiography, *Fate Has Been Kind* (1943), or Emmeline Pethick-Lawrence's *My Part in a Changing World* (1938).

Nick Cowell

Morgan Phillips (1902–63)

Morgan Phillips was the powerful secretary (later General Secretary) of the Labour Party in the crucial years of government and opposition after 1945, and perhaps the most important organiser that the party has ever known.

Morgan Walter Phillips was born at Aberdare on 18 June 1902, the eldest son of a miner. He attended Bargoed elementary school until he was 12 and then began work in the local Rhymney Valley pits. By the age of 22 he had risen to become agent of the Bargoed Steam Coal Lodge. He was much influenced by the socialist and syndicalist currents powerful in the Welsh coalfield during and after the war, and in 1926–28 was a student at the famous 'marxisant' Central Labour College in London, where Aneurin Bevan and Jim Griffiths had also been students earlier.

He decided to stay on in London to work within the Labour Party. He had been secretary of the Bargoed Labour Party in 1923–25, and in 1928–30 served as secretary and agent of the West Fulham Labour Party. In 1934 he moved on to become agent in Whitechapel. He also served on the Fulham Borough Council in 1934–37. His reputation for organisational skills grew rapidly, and in 1937 he joined Transport House as propaganda officer. After a brief spell as Eastern Counties organiser, he became Secretary of the Party Research Department in 1941. He had already much impressed Dalton and others, and in early 1944, after the retirement of the veteran Jim Middleton, was elected Labour's National Secretary, defeating better-known figures such as the National Agent, George Shepherd, and Morrison's close friend, Maurice Webb.

Phillips established his reputation as head of party organisation and the policy-making apparatus during the 1945 election, and Labour's landslide victory redounded to his credit. Along with Attlee, Dalton, Morrison and Greenwood, he was a member of the 1945 campaign committee. But his initial impact was as a key manager of the Party machine, who also embodied the close relationship between the Party and the trade unions. He proved himself a valuable lieutenant to Attlee: with Morrison his relations were always more wary. He was exceptionally skilful in managing party conference, including the key matter of determining the agenda, and was also a brisk instrument of discipline, notably in expelling fellow-travellers such as Platts-Mills and Zilliacus in 1948–49 and in chastising those who had signed the Nenni telegram. His list of 'proscribed organisations' became ever more lengthy, while he also kept close contacts with the press.

He became involved in policy areas as time went on. Transport House became more of a powerhouse of ideas, especially in international affairs. His earlier leftishness disappeared as he strongly backed Bevin's foreign policy and built up a strong cadre, including the youthful Denis Healey, in the International Department at Transport House. He also worked closely with the Socialist International. Labour's electoral defeat in 1951 had a powerful impact on Phillips and his role in the party. He frequently clashed with his fellow-Welshman, Aneurin Bevan, whose revolt against the leadership he deplored. He used his influence against key Bevanites and worked assiduously against *Tribune* after its attacks on union leaders. However, he argued against the expulsion of Bevan from the Parliamentary Party in 1955 and became a leading reconciler thereafter.

He backed the policy stances of Hugh Gaitskell on such issues as German rearmament and Britain's retaining nuclear weapons. He strove hard to keep the party organisation in centre-right hands, from the National Executive to the youth section which he had rebuilt. But he never had total confidence in Gaitskell's judgement as party leader, and the two often clashed. Phillips was even less enamoured of Harold Wilson. In the 1950s, his strong position in Transport House was gradually eroded by election defeats in 1955 and 1959. Harold Wilson criticised the Party organisation as 'a penny-farthing in the jet age', and the youth movement was disbanded after evidence of communist infiltration. Phillips's lifestyle was also attacked when he, Bevan and Crossman had to sue over an (accurate) account in the *Spectator* that they had been drunk during a socialist congress in Venice.

After the defeat in 1959, Phillips turned his mind to the possibilities of entering parliament and tried in vain to win a nomination for North-East Derbyshire, a mining seat. He did, however, make an impact in the debate over policy when he largely wrote *Labour and the Sixties* (1960), which urged that Labour should appeal to middle-class voters, especially white-coated workers, women and young people. Its talk of a 'scientific revolution' anticipated Harold Wilson's famous 'white-heat' speech three years later. The 1964 Nuffield survey compared Phillips's pamphlet with Butler's Industrial Charter of 1947 as an exercise in party re-thinking.

However Phillips suffered a serious stroke in 1960. The main organising work was now undertaken by Len Williams. Phillips died, relatively young, in London on 15 January 1963. Funeral addresses were given by Donald Soper and James Griffiths. His widow, Norah, whom he had married in 1930, became a life peer and his daughter Gwyneth Dunwoody, unlike her father, a long-term Labour MP.

Phillips ended his career a frustrated man, unable to find a parliamentary seat, failing to make sufficient impact as policy-maker and unappreciated by party leaders such as Gaitskell. His assaults on the Bevanites in the early fifties made him many enemies. But his contribution in making Labour an organised national striking-force was immense. It imposed a stamp of professionalism and central control upon a notoriously factional party. In its golden period in the wartime and post-war years, Morgan Walter Phillips was unquestionably one of Labour's unrecorded heroes.

Biographical material may be found in John Saville's excellent entry in the *Dictionary of National Biography* and Kenneth O Morgan's essay on Phillips in *Labour People: Leaders and Lieutenants. Hardie to Kinnock* (1987).

Professor the Lord Morgan of Aberdyfi

Frank Pickstock   (1910–85)

Frank Pickstock was one of those rare grassroots politicians who made a significant contribution to the direction of the Labour Party. In the autumn of 1960 he was a moving spirit in launching the Campaign for Democratic Socialism that helped Hugh Gaitskell 'save the Party which we love'. Pickstock was the organiser of an Oxford Group of local Labour activists that teamed up with a group of London-based Gaitskellites to start CDS. Pickstock drafted the CDS Manifesto with Tony Crosland. He was on the platform at the October press launch alongside Bill Rodgers and Denis Howell. And he played a key role in the organisation of the initial stages, using his extensive database of nationwide contacts in trade union adult education to build up CDS grassroots support.

Pickstock described himself at the launch of CDS as 'one of the NCOs and platoon commanders of the party'. This remark was typical of Pickstock's modesty. The truth is, had he taken the risk of seeking a Commons seat in the 1940s, he would quickly have risen to be part of Labour's officer class.

But Pickstock's self-description as an NCO is also revealing. Frank was a believer in leadership as an essential quality in politics: in his later life he saw only Hugh Gaitskell and Roy Jenkins as having that quintessential quality on the national scene. But within his own domain Frank saw a duty to lead himself. At General Committee meetings and Labour Groups, he would rise up time and again, 'frankly speaking' as he would say, to explain and argue for the truth as he saw it. Most working-class members of the party loved him for it. Elements of the middle-class left in the Oxford party often found it harder to take as Frank carefully dissected the latest emotional spasm.

It was with good reason that Pickstock saw himself as one of the Labour Movement's senior NCOs. The son of a miner, Frank was born in the Potteries in 1910. He did well enough at school to get a job as a railway clerk and join what was then the 'aristocracy of labour'. He immediately became a stalwart of the Railway Clerks Association (now the TSSA), which has probably a more consistent record of good sense in the cause of moderate social democracy than any other affiliated organisation.

At the age of 19 he was vice-chair of Stoke Divisional Labour Party when in 1929 the dazzling Cynthia Mosley, first wife of Oswald and daughter of Lord Curzon, descended on Stoke to be adopted as Labour's candidate. Frank recalled the awe they all felt.

It was the WEA that provided Frank with his ladder of opportunity. In 1934 he won a scholarship to Queens College, Oxford, to read PPE. Remarkably, after his degree he went back to the railways and the Potteries to be a stationmaster.

After the war Pickstock established himself in Oxford. A D Lindsay, the then Master of Balliol (and the non-party progressive who was the anti-appeasement candidate in the famous Oxford by-election) had had him appointed to what was then the Extramural Delegacy, later renamed the Department for External Studies.

Pickstock was a pioneer of trade union education, though he later recognised that, with the extension of educational opportunity, the era of the self-improving working classes attending night classes and weekend schools had long passed. In its place he tried with mixed success to develop workplace industrial relations classes for shop stewards, together with the wider availability of adult education in the liberal arts by local authorities.

Frank stayed put at the Department for External Studies until his retirement as Deputy Director in 1977. He was elected a Fellow of Linacre College in 1966 – a mark of recognition by the University, which greatly pleased him. In retirement Frank served as secretary of the Oxford Preservation Trust.

Before that Pickstock had given 25 years' unbroken local government service to the city as a Labour councillor, alderman and Lord Mayor. He was first elected to Oxford City Council for Headington (Dick Crossman's ward in the 1930s) in 1952. Frank was a remarkable councillor. Way before his time he was deeply interested in what we would now call questions of delivery. He spotted early on for a social democrat that 'Finance isn't the real constraint – it's the ability to make things happen'. And unusually in the local government of his day, he devoted himself to quality of life issues, with consistent and effective advocacy of better planning, recreation facilities, culture and conservation. He understood very clearly that old-fashioned class politics was becoming an electoral and ideological cul-de-sac for Labour.

He acted always in the spirit of the social democratic aspiration for a better life so well expressed in the closing section of Crosland's Future of Socialism. Crosland was a great personal inspiration to Frank, even though his later record, particularly on Europe, disappointed him. Frank believed in loyalty and felt Tony had not stuck with his CDS principles.

It was no surprise when in 1981, after 55 years of Labour party membership, he followed Roy Jenkins and Bill Rodgers into the SDP, believing at the time that the Labour Party had no future. He died in 1985, after a spirited battle with cancer, when it was still unclear whether it had. In the intervening period, as someone who was always 'a Fabian with a good filing system', he devoted his considerable organisational energies to the new party despite failing health.

Frank had a happy married life. His half-century partnership with Winifred was political as well as affectionate. Her father had been a prominent railway trade unionist and she herself, as a magistrate, made a big contribution to Oxford city life. They had one son. Apart from his family and peers, the fondest memories of Frank are held by those who passed their early years in Oxford and enjoyed being one of his protégés.

He was 'always on the look out for talented young people'. He took infinite trouble. He was a marvellous source of good stories, wise advice and strong encouragement. As a social democrat, he was almost the perfect model.

Roger Liddle

David Pitt (Lord Pitt of Hampstead) (1913–94)

David Thomas Pitt was the leading black politician of his generation and ought to have been Britain's first black MP. He had the ability, the determination and, having predictably failed to defeat the sitting MP for Hampstead and Tory Home Secretary, Henry Brooke at the 1959 General Election, was well-placed to secure nomination in a winnable Labour seat in later years. In 1961 he was elected London County Council (LCC) member for Hackney, serving continuously on the LCC and its successor, the Greater London Council (GLC), until 1977. He was Deputy Chair of the GLC 1969–70 and in 1974–75 became the first Black Chair of the GLC. He became London's first black magistrate, and during 1985–86 was the first general practitioner to hold the Presidency of the British Medical Association. He was appointed a member of the National Committee for Immigrants in 1965, chairman of the Community Relations Committee from 1968 to 1977 and was the founding and only Chair of the Campaign Against Racial Discrimination. From 1979 to 1990 he was chairman of Shelter and in 1988 was Deputy Lieutenant for Greater London.

Having vainly sought a parliamentary nomination through the 1960s he was finally adopted as Labour's candidate at Clapham (Wandsworth) for the general election of 1970. Defending a Labour majority of over 4,000 he suffered an anti-Labour swing double that of neighbouring seats and was defeated. There is no doubt that race was a major factor in his defeat. Despite all, however, he remained a passionate moderate on the issue of race relations throughout his life, declaring that, 'Some blacks regard me as being an Uncle Tom, while some whites regard me as a Black Power revolutionary. So I reckon I must be about right.' His patience and perseverance were finally rewarded with a peerage from Harold Wilson in 1975. As Lord Pitt of Hampstead, the town in Grenada of his birth as well as the place of his first British parliamentary contest, he distinguished himself in the Lords as a conscientious Party loyalist, Kinnock ally and determined opponent of Tony Benn's leadership ambitions. Pitt's Labour colleague Lord Graham of Edmonton remembered him as 'a natural orator with a sometimes disconcerting high range of invective. One always knew when David felt passionate and excited, because the speech which started in low key suddenly and electrically took off, reached a higher plane and stayed there until he decided to come down towards the end.'

Born in Hampstead, Grenada, on 13 October 1913, after St David's Roman Catholic elementary school and at the Boys' Secondary School, in 1932 he won the island's single scholarship to Edinburgh University, where he graduated in Medicine. His socialism and Labour Party membership was rooted in his experience of Edinburgh during the Depression years.

Whilst at Edinburgh too he had his first experience of representative politics, becoming the first Junior President of the Students' Representative Council. The university was a happy time for him, his fellow students apparently more worldly than the white boys he had encountered when, aged fifteen, he had represented Grenada at the 1929 World Scout Jamboree in England, who had wet their fingers to see if they could wipe the black off his face.

Returning to the West Indies he became District Medical Officer at St Vincent in 1938, and later physician at the San Fernando Hospital, Trinidad and a GP, meeting and marrying his wife Dorothy, with whom he had a son and two daughters. In his spare time he founded the West Indian National Party, of which he became President and became deputy mayor of San Fernando. Moving to London in 1947, originally as a temporary move whilst he lobbied the Attlee government for independeance for Trinidad, he joined St Pancras Labour Party and established a general practice in Gower Street which he ran for over thirty years. A passionate cricket enthusiast, a first-class fast bowler in his youth and a longstanding member of the MCC, he died of cancer in a Hampstead hospice on 18 December 1994.

Greg Rosen

Raymond Plant (Lord Plant of Highfield) (1945–)

Professor Raymond Plant, Lord Plant of Highfield, is a major thinker of international renown in the area of modern political and social philosophy whose ideas have had immense intellectual influence on the evolution of Labour thinking.

Born in Grimsby on 19 March 1945, the only son of Stanley Plant, a fireman, and his wife Marjorie, he was educated at Havelock School Grimsby and Kings College London. After obtaining his PhD from the University of Hull, where his dissertation was examined by Michael Oakeshott, the eminent Conservative philosopher, his academic career began in 1967 at the University of Manchester where he was Lecturer in Philosophy. He was then appointed Professor of Politics at the University of Southampton between 1979 and 1994 before he took up the post of Master of St. Catherine's College in Oxford from 1994 to 2000. Currently Professor at the University of Southampton, he will shortly be taking up the post of Professor of Jurisprudence and Moral Philosophy at King's College London, where he first received his BA in Philosophy in 1966.

A pre-eminent example of an academic actively engaged with issues and imperatives rooted in the world of the practical, Raymond Plant was asked by Neil Kinnock in 1990, then leader, to chair the Labour Party Commission on Electoral Systems. The Plant Commission opened up and advanced the debate on electoral reform within the Labour party, advocating a form of preferential voting, the Supplementary Vote. In 1992, he was made a Labour life peer and was Opposition Spokesperson on Home Affairs in the House of Lords, serving until 1996.

He has held numerous other offices including President of the National Council for Voluntary Organisations and Chair of the Fabian Society Commission on Taxation and Citizenship. He was also Chair of the Board of Trustees of Hope, a leading medical research charity, and chaired the Winchester Diocese Working Party on Faith in the City. Professor Plant was instrumental in the founding of the Academy of Learned Societies in the Social Sciences, of which he is President, whose purpose is to give recognition to the contribution of academic work to public policy.

Author of some ten books and countless academic articles, Professor Plant has also written widely for the broader press, regularly contributing to newspapers, magazines and thinktanks both here and abroad. He was also a regular columnist for *The Times* between 1988 and 1991. A world expert on the thought of the German philosopher Hegel, the influence of Hegel is discernible in his other work on social justice, citizenship, welfare and public policy.

As a member of the then extant Socialist Philosophy Group of the Fabian Society in the 1980s, Plant's contribution to Labour Party thinking through his wider political writings as well as through his academic work makes him without doubt a major figure in Labour's intellectual tradition, along with others such as Crosland and Marquand.

His detailed analysis and critique of the arguments of Hayek and the New Right provided a powerful antidote to the perceived intellectual force of Thatcherism. Rigorously taking the arguments on their own grounds by exposing their inconsistencies and deficiencies, Plant's work was an important intellectual counterblast to their attempts to deny the legitimacy of social justice in the name of individual liberty and protect an unconstrained market without regard for social and wider moral limits.

At the same time, Plant's own positive views of social justice and citizenship presented an important intellectual alternative to a dominant strand of left thinking hostile to liberalism and to the market, providing a valuable intellectual bridge in the modernisation that led to the emergence of New Labour. Accepting the importance of liberty and a market economy subject to certain moral constraints, Plant's view of social justice posited an alternative, more inclusive and more liberal conception of political community in the form of a conception of social citizenship that contrasted with a conception of socialist community rooted in narrow class-based interests and class solidarity. Social citizenship à la Plant posited a unifying conception of citizenship based on a universal entitlement to a set of rights that can serve common fundamental needs and secure the freedom to choose between different ways of life. For Plant socio-economic rights, including welfare rights, are a logical extension of liberal civil rights, differing from them in no significant way.

Selina Chen and Richard Crossick

Reg Prentice (Lord Prentice of Daventry)   (1923–2001)

It would be easy to dismiss the turbulent political life of Reg Prentice as marginal to the history of the Labour Party: the unhappy tale of a confused maverick who earned notoriety on the left as the first Cabinet Minister since Winston Churchill to cross the floor of the House and join the Conservatives. In fact, in several fundamental respects, Prentice's career prefigured the emergence of New Labour – albeit at many years' distance.

Prentice's sensational defection on the eve of the 1977 Tory conference was one of the first portents that Labour was about to lose all middle-class respectability – a loss it would take the party 20 years to correct. The manner of his deselection foreshadowed the vicious constituency battles with the militant left of the 1980s. And his calls for Labour moderates to 'stand up and be counted', frustrated at the time, were eventually answered: first by the splitting away of the SDP, and, second, many years later, by the victory within the party of the Blairite modernisers.

Reginald Ernest Prentice was born in Croydon, Surrey, on 16 July 1923, and was educated at Whitgift. Between 1942 and 1946 he served in the Royal Artillery, before proceeding to the London School of Economics where, like so many leftwingers of his generation, he was profoundly influenced by Harold Laski. Prentice's disenchantment with the union movement would eventually drive him from the party, but it was there, as an official with the Transport and General Workers' Union after 1950, that his political roots lay. He contested three seats unsuccessfully, before capturing East Ham North in May 1957 – a constituency he continued to represent until February 1974 when he became MP for the new seat of Newham NE.

In his long and varied career as a Labour minister, Prentice displayed an ideological complexity which is too readily obscured by his final act of apostasy. Appointed Minister of State for Education in October 1964, he was, for instance, an early and passionate advocate of comprehensivisation, and a powerful inspiration to Anthony Crosland's subsequent campaign to abolish the grammar schools. Prentice also believed in root-and-branch reform of the public schools. 'But Reginald,' CP Snow teased him once, `does that mean I can't send my children to Eton?' Asked on a visit to that venerable institution what he planned for its future, he replied: `We're going to make it into a special school for the deaf'.

In 1966, Prentice was given his own department, Public Building and Works, becoming Minister for Overseas Development in August 1967. His closely-connected belief in the importance of overseas aid and fierce opposition to racism were at the heart of his politics: he was a leader of the the the all-party Fair Cricket Campaign, which succeeded in its battle to have the 1970 South African tour of England cancelled.

Yet for Prentice there was an all-important difference between idealism and ideology. His politics were Gaitskellite: he often cited his fallen hero's 'fight, fight and fight again' speech to the 1962 Labour conference. As the party drifted to the Left, he became more and more uncomfortable. He did well in shadow cabinet elections from 1971, but found himself increasingly at odds with the militant caucuses within the party. In November 1973, as Shadow Employment Secretary, he fell into open conflict with Tony Benn over whether to support strikers who broke the law. As Secretary of State for Education and Science after March 1974, he began to speak out beyond the parameters of his ministerial brief in a way which enraged his colleagues.

Prentice claimed it was his duty to confront those 'prepared to sacrifice the working people of this country on the altar of their Marxist ideology'. Michael Foot, then Employment Secretary, denounced such outbursts, with Harold Wilson's backing. But Wilson knew that Roy Jenkins would resign if he sacked Prentice and so moved him back to Overseas Development.

Meanwhile, Prentice faced a vicious battle in his constituency, where militants – the 'little gang' as he called them – launched a campaign to unseat him. Newham in east London fast became a bloody microcosm of Labour's future traumas, as Trotskyites fought with Labour moderates – including the young Julian Lewis, later to become a right-wing Tory MP. In March 1975, the Newham NE executive passed a vote of no confidence in its candidate, and deselected him four months later.

At the 1976 Labour conference, Prentice bitterly denounced the NEC's endorsement of his local party's action as 'political cowardice as the price of political survival'. After abstaining in a key vote, he resigned from the Government in December 1976, before his defection the following October, a decision he took, he said, to help stop Britain 'lurching further down the Marxist road'. The party's Chief Whip, Bob Mellish, called Prentice 'a nauseating traitor', a view shared at the time by many of his fellow Labour moderates – including Shirley Williams – who were later to jump ship themselves.

The defector was found a Tory seat in Daventry in 1979, which he represented until 1987. As Margaret Thatcher's Social Security minister, the politician who had started his career as a union official ended it by removing unemployment benefit from strikers. By the end of 1980, however, the drugs he was taking for hypertension made it difficult for him to carry on as a minister and he withdrew to the back benches in 1981, this time for good. He was knighted in 1987 and ennobled in 1992. In his last years he was president of the local Conservative Association in Michael Ancram's Devizes constituency. He died on 18 January 2001, survived by his wife and daughter.

Matthew d'Ancona

John Prescott (1938–)

John Prescott will probably be remembered in history as the man who punched the voter. If so, that would be a pity. The man the media loves to bait has been at the heart of Labour politics for nearly 40 years and has shaped more of its policies than many of his detractors will admit.

Born in Prestatyn in North Wales on 31 May 1938, he was the son of Bert Prescott, a railwayman and lifelong union and Labour activist, and Phyllis Prescott. He was educated in Yorkshire and then Liverpool and left school at 15 to join the merchant navy. It was his experiences at sea which did most to shape his political approach.

He was appalled by the way seafarers were treated. The relationship between captain and crew was still governed by merchant navy legislation dating back to the 18th century. He quickly became involved in the union, the NUS, and gained a reputation as a troublemaker both within the union and the companies. He became a union radical, largely because he was appalled at the failure of the union's right-wing leadership to take a stand in favour of better wages and conditions for seamen.

This culminated in the infamous seamen's strike of 1966 whose leaders, including the young Prescott, were denounced by Harold Wilson as a 'tightly knit group of politically motivated men'. Although Prescott did cooperate with the communist and other left-wing union leaders, he was never really a Marxist. The lesson he learnt from the strike was that the lot of the seamen could only be improved by parliamentary action. Whatever syndicalist tendencies he may have had before the strike, he lost through the experience. It was a lesson he remembered during the 1980s miners' strike.

Elected in 1970 in the seaport constituency of Hull East, he identified himself with the left of the Parliamentary Labour Party. He was anti-Common Market and demanded tougher opposition to the Tory Industrial Relations Act. In 1972, when Imperial Typewriters closed its factory in his constituency, he supported the worker occupation and its attempts to create a workers' co-operative. But he also identified himself with unpopular causes in his constituency.

During the so-called cod wars of the early 1970s, Prescott supported the right of Iceland to declare a 50-, then a 200-mile fishing limit.

He was seen by much of the Party establishment as an outsider, a left-wing trade unionist out to cause trouble. But he did get a break by being appointed Parliamentary Private Secretary to the then Trade Secretary Peter Shore in 1974. His relations with Shore were never really warm and Prescott supported Tony Benn for the party leadership in 1976.

In 1976, he was also appointed to the then indirectly elected European Parliament and in November he was elected Leader of the Labour Group. This was a reflection of his political pragmatism. An anti-marketeer, he immersed himself in Brussels and Strasbourg politics and made a name for himself pioneering inquiries against multinational corporations and in fighting for a tougher stand against apartheid South Africa. He also successfully urged the Labour Party not to boycott the first direct elections to the European Parliament, held in 1979.

Following the election defeat, he was appointed to the Commons front bench as a transport spokesperson. Two events occurred of significance: he published a pamphlet and met Peter Mandelson.

The pamphlet was an otherwise unremarkable policy document. But its significance is in what it tells us about Prescott. In 1980, blood was being spilled in every corner of the Labour party. The left was obsessed with mandatory reselection procedures for MPs, withdrawal from the Common Market, and unilateral nuclear disarmament. No-one was interested in policy, except Prescott. Unusually for a Tribunite, he was never active in CND or the Campaign for Labour Party Democracy, the main left-wing vehicle of the time. He did not like factionalism, even though he identified himself as a left-winger.

Prescott worked with Mandelson who was researcher to Albert Booth, the then chief Transport spokesperson, to produce a policy statement. Some of the ideas remained with Prescott. He advocated a national transport authority, which is now called the Commission for Integrated Transport. He called for investment in rail and shipping, both of which he attended to 20 years later in government. And he became obsessed with finding ways of getting round what he called 'silly Treasury rules', namely that investment in the railways, even when the money was borrowed against assets, still counted against the public sector borrowing requirement. It was the seed from which public-private partnerships grew.

In 1982, Michael Foot appointed him shadow regional affairs spokesperson. A new post, the brief was to find a policy for the English regions which would allow devolution for Scotland and Wales to proceed. The devolution bill had wrecked the last Labour government and much of the opposition to it had come from North Eastern Labour MPs who felt that Scotland already enjoyed far more benefits politically and economically than the English regions.

Prescott's answer was regional development agencies followed by political devolution. He published his ideas in a pamphlet, *Alternative Regional Policy,* the main tenets of which were to be implemented 15 years later.

Following the catastrophic defeat of 1983, Prescott was elected to Kinnock's new shadow cabinet team and was appointed Shadow Transport Secretary. The main high-profile issue was opposition to privatisation of British Airways and the British Airports Authority (BAA). He challenged a union leader at the time, asking 'Why no strike, then?' The unions had threatened strike action if BA were privatised. 'Well John, they've promised no compulsory redundancies and it was a bit of a holiday camp before.' Prescott was appalled. He became sceptical of the reality of public sector companies and the attitudes of the unions. He also struck up a strong and lasting relationship with John, later Lord, King, appointed by Thatcher to be chairman of BA.

Prescott was a rising star and Kinnock wanted to reward him and in 1984, appointed him Shadow Employment Secretary. It was not an easy brief. The Tories were intent on implementing employment legislation to place further restrictions on unions and bring about compulsory balloting on strikes and for the election of union officials. Britain was also faced with mass unemployment and Labour was saddled with policies demanding huge state intervention.

On trade union law, Prescott shifted the ground. As a seafarer, he told the union movement that he had fought for ballots in the NUS precisely to guarantee union democracy. He shifted party policy but kept the unions on side. On employment, he built on his regional policy, demanding a decentralised approach to job creation and economic planning. His document published in 1985, *Planning for Full Employment*, advocated a regional approach to economic growth. But crucially, it was based on an acceptance of the market, something most on the left were unwilling to accept at that time.

But Prescott fell out with Kinnock. They were too alike: both from working-class backgrounds, both strident socialists, both with chips on their shoulders against the Oxbridge intellectual set in the Labour Party.

Following the 1987 election, Prescott was demoted to Shadow Energy Secretary and in 1988 returned to Transport. He didn't mind. He loved transport. But the party was in disarray and Prescott decided to mount a challenge to Deputy Leader Roy Hattersley in 1988. He did so on the platform of making the Deputy Leader lead the campaigning and trench-warfare aspects of the Labour Party.

Kinnock was incensed. He persuaded Prescott to withdraw at one point with the proviso that there would be a proper debate at conference on party organisation. However, Eric Heffer's decision to challenge Hattersley anyway gave Prescott the opening he needed and he fought a campaign which earned him plaudits and a place on the NEC – but he was way behind Hattersley.

Following the 1992 election defeat, Prescott again ran for Deputy Leader against Bryan Gould and Margaret Beckett. Again, he fought on the issue of party organisation and mass membership and again ran a respectable but unsuccessful campaign. New Leader John Smith re-appointed him to the Transport portfolio. Again, he argued the case for transport investment through borrowing and leasing not counting against the PSBR. Smith agreed that he could do further work on it, and was surprised when he produced a coherent policy in favour of public-private partnerships based on risk-sharing between government and the private sector.

But Prescott's real use to Smith was on the NEC. Smith had failed to manage the politics on the NEC in favour of one member, one vote (OMOV). At the conference, it looked as if Smith would be defeated. He asked Prescott to speak from the platform in favour of the Leadership position. In an impassioned speech, Prescott succeeded in turning the conference. He was rewarded with promotion back to Shadow Employment Spokesperson.

Smith's untimely death shattered Prescott. Smith was a Labour right-winger Prescott could do business with. He knew he would run for Deputy Leader again, but he also decided to run for Leader. He liked Blair from the start: he felt that he could have a good argument with Blair and resolve differences.

Blair and Prescott spoke at the beginning of the campaign and they established a rapport. When Brown announced on television that he was nominating Margaret Beckett for Deputy Leader, Blair made his anger known and authorised his campaign organiser Mo Mowlam to announce that she was nominating Prescott.

Blair likes and respects Prescott and values the role that he plays within the party. Despite misgivings, Prescott supported the change to Clause 4 of Labour's constitution. But he knew he had to carve out his own position in a future Labour government.

He insisted on the title Deputy Prime Minister and on the creation of a new department combining environment, transport and the regions. It brought together most of Prescott's policy interests. In government though, many criticised the unwieldy behemoth of the DETR.

Prescott had significant successes. His leadership of the UK and EU teams at Kyoto secured agreement. He also helped to ensure that the Jubilee Line extension finished on time and re-negotiated the contract for the Channel Tunnel rail link.

His time at DETR was overshadowed by two rail tragedies (Ladbroke Grove and Hatfield) and two major political difficulties, NATS and London Underground. The rail tragedies turned round what was becoming a good news story for the railways. Passenger numbers and rail freight were both improving. Pressed by the Treasury, the NATS PPP went through parliament but cost Prescott political support. Similarly, the London Underground PPP attracted considerable opposition from within the party and without.

Following the 2001 general election, Prescott became Minister for the Cabinet Office in addition to his role as Deputy Prime Minister. He sees the role as similar to the one performed by Michael Heseltine, chairing cabinet committees, banging heads together, and representing the Prime Minister abroad.

Though at times turbulent, Prescott's career has placed him at the centre of Labour movement politics for nearly 40 years. Contrary to the views of his detractors, he is ferociously intelligent, hard-working and a loyal person to work with. But like many other politicians, he is quick-tempered and can bear a grudge for a long time. Without doubt, he adds value to the Labour cabinet. He personifies the party, for all its strengths and weaknesses. He is first and foremost a politician and political operator in an administration where political skills are often undervalued.

Mike Craven

Giles Radice (Lord Radice) (1936–)

Giles Radice was one of the most influential post-war Labour politicians never to hold ministerial office. This was largely because his political maturity coincided with Labour's self-imposed exile from power from 1979 to 1997. However, he had every reason to expect a job from Tony Blair when that exile ended, perhaps as Minister for Europe in the Foreign Office. It may be that he was blocked by Robin Cook, the Foreign Secretary, ironically in view of Mr Cook's later conversion, on the grounds that he was too pro-European. Mr Blair tacitly admitted his claim when he made him a Privy çounsellor in 1999.

Giles Heneage Radice was born in London on 4 October 1936, the son of a businessman under the Raj. He was educated at Winchester, which today would seem an improbable background for a Labour politician but was then *alma mater* to a leader, Hugh Gaitskell, and a cabinet minister, Dick Crossman. After Magdalen College, Oxford, and a brief spell working for Francis Noel-Baker, a somewhat eccentric Labour MP, Radice became head of research at the General and Municipal Workers' Union, then a bulwark of loyalist right-wing proletarian virtues. Not that this affected Radice's choice of researchers, who included a future deputy governor of the Bank of England, and a number two at *The Times,* for he was more interested in ability than class.

The GMWU then controlled a number of parliamentary seats, particularly in the North East, and eventually Chester-le-Street became vacant in 1973. The by-election was a torrid one: Radice, who was typically letting out the basement of his Hampstead home at half the market rate to a deserving case, found himself pilloried since the sum involved, £20 a week, sounded astronomic in Chester-le-Street. He won though, with a shrunken majority, and never again had to fear for reelection there, or in the Durham North constituency which succeeded it.

As an active Fabian, Giles Radice had been friendly with Shirley Williams, the Society's darling, and was made her Parliamentary Private Secretary at the Department of Education in 1978. However, Labour's loss of the 1979 general election, and its abrupt shift to the far left, put a halt to his ministerial career prospects.

Mrs Williams, together with many of Radice's natural allies in the Labour Party, split off in 1981 to form the Social Democratic Party, and his arm was naturally twisted to follow suit. The courage of those who left was much remarked on at the time; but in retrospect, it took more courage to stay and fight what then seemed a hopeless corner. Yet Radice did: at the 1981 Anglo-German Königswinter conference, as Mrs Williams and David Steel, the Liberal leader climbed the Drachenfels to finalise their compact, Radice and George Robertson, later General Secretary of NATO, were themselves climbing it, cementing their decision to stay and fight. One result was their building-up of the Manifesto Group of loyal Labour MPs determined to stop the party's drift to the left, work that laid the foundations of the party's slow recovery of its sanity.

Radice combined this work with his responsibilities as an opposition spokesman: on foreign affairs, in 1981, on employment in 1982–83 and as chief spokesman on education and a member of the shadow cabinet, from 1983–87. However in the latter role he kowtowed insufficiently to the teachers' unions, and never again held official office. Instead, he became an early intellectual prophet for New Labour, with his revisionist books *Labour's Path to Power* in 1988 and *What Needs to Change,* a collection of essays with a foreword by Tony Blair, in 1996. He was also an untiring and unrepentant pro-European, writing books on Britain and Europe and on Germany as well as innumerable press articles. He became chairman of the cross-party European Movement in 1995.

Important consolation for his exclusion from ministerial office came with his appointment in 1997 to chair the Treasury Select Committee of MPs, perhaps the most influential of the

Commons' select committees. He showed his fibre by refusing to bow before a powerful chancellor in Gordon Brown, for example, pushing through nomination hearings for members of the Bank of England's Monetary Policy Committee and criticising those who flunked them. Off the back of his natural friendliness and a carefully modulated vague eccentricity, Radice was a man who had opponents, but no enemies. With his beloved wife, Lisanne, and their assorted children, he enjoyed an exceptionally happy private life. He retired from the Commons at the 2001 election and accepted a life peerage afterwards.

Lord Lipsey

Merlyn Rees (Lord Merlyn-Rees)   (1920–)

It is a mistake to overlook the element of continuity in the history of the Labour Movement. We are not fond of new beginnings, but it is possible to point to a few dates which qualify as watersheds. One such was 1945. Previously, Labour's leading spokespeople in Parliament were usually individuals whose early lives had been spent in other trades or professions, and who had entered full-time politics in middle age, predominantly through the trade union movement or local government. After 1945, recruitment was increasingly from those who had chosen a political career from the outset, and who had first earned notice within the machinery of the Party itself.

Merlyn Rees was part of the transition. He joined the Labour Party in 1938, and entered politics as a young man, but he had experienced a world outside. Moreover, he was old enough to remember the sufferings and the battles of the inter-war period, and while he has rarely indulged in histrionics, he never forgot his roots in working-class Labour. Born on 18 December 1920 in Cilfynydd, in South Wales, he still remembers how his father, denied work in the coalfields, walked to London to find employment. The family settled in East Harrow, then part of the emerging urban spread. But they missed the close communities of working-class Wales, and never lost their links with their former home. Intending a career as a schoolteacher, Rees enrolled for a teacher training course at Goldsmiths College, but quickly displayed a flair for political debate, and became Chair of the Labour Society and President of the Students Union.

His plans were interrupted by the War. He enrolled in the RAF, emerging as Operations Officer on the staff of a fighter wing, with the rank of Squadron Leader. He saw service in Italy, and later France. After the War he declined an offer of a permanent commission, and like many of his generation, availed himself of the Further Education and Training scheme. In 1946 he enrolled for a degree, and later a postgraduate course, at the LSE, and proceeded to teach economics and history at his former school, Harrow Weald Grammar School. In 1949 he married Colleen Cleveley, and there were three sons.

But by now his sights were set on a political career. He was selected for the unpromising seat of Harrow East, which he fought unsuccessfully in 1955 and 1959, and again at a by-election later in 1959. In 1960 the Party was planning the Festival of Labour, which materialised in 1962. It consisted of a series of events designed to project a much-needed sense of comradeship and fun into Labour politics. Morgan Phillips, then General Secretary, asked Rees to organise it, and he spent two years learning the internal workings of the Party, and meeting the leading figures in the Labour Movement. It proved to be an effective launching pad for an aspiring politician.

He had been noticed by Hugh Gaitskell, and on the impending retirement of Morgan Phillips his name was canvassed as a successor, with Gaitskell's support. But he was not attracted by smoke-filled rooms.

He let it be known that his ambitions were centred on the House of Commons, and when, in 1963, Gaitskell died unexpectedly, Rees succeeded to his seat in South Leeds. His arrival narrowly preceded the return of a Labour Government in 1964. He had met James Callaghan during his by-election, and their friendship ripened with the Festival of Labour. When in 1964, Callaghan was appointed Chancellor of the Exchequer, Rees became his PPS. They remained close personal friends. In his autobiography, *Time and Chance*, Callaghan referred to him as 'my closest friend'. Promotion came quickly. In December 1965 he was appointed Parliamentary Under-Secretary of State at the Ministry of Defence (Army), moving sideways within the MoD in April 1966 to take responsibility for the RAF. When in 1967 Callaghan was moved to the Home Office, Rees followed him shortly afterwards, becoming Under-Secretary of State there from November 1968 until June 1970.

In Opposition, in 1970, he became part of Callaghan's Shadow Home Affairs team. In 1972, with Northern Ireland in crisis, Stormont was prorogued, to be replaced by 'Direct Rule', and William Whitelaw became Secretary of State. Rees was appointed to shadow him, and shortly afterwards, in November 1972, was elected to the shadow cabinet. When Labour was returned to office in 1974, he became a Privy Counsellor and Secretary of State for Northern Ireland. The most immediate concern was to restore peace and security to the streets, and for the moment there was a bipartisan approach between Government and Opposition. The Sunningdale Agreement had been concluded while Whitelaw was in office, and there was a pressing need to secure consensus between representatives of the two traditions as to how administration could proceed on a power-sharing basis. Disappointingly, it proved impossible to reach agreement. There was no alternative to rule from Westminster by ministerial order. But Rees succeeded in dispelling some of the heat by announcing the ending of internment without trial, and by the end of 1975 the last internee had been released.

In 1976, the unexpected retirement of Harold Wilson led to an election for the leadership of the Party, and consequently for the Premiership. Rees was Callaghan's campaign manager, and contributed substantially, not only to the successful outcome, but to an agreement with Stan Orme, who led the campaign for Michael Foot, which limited the risk of a damaging schism within the Party. When, shortly afterwards, Roy Jenkins departed for the European Commission, Rees became Home Secretary.

The strong libertarian tradition within the Party ensures that no Labour Home Secretary enjoys a comfortable seat. It fell to Rees to decide the fate of Philip Agee and Mark Hosenball, two American journalists who were alleged to have maintained regular contacts with foreign intelligence officers and 'disseminated information harmful to the security of the United Kingdom'. Rees announced that he proposed to deport them. He found himself in the unfamiliar situation of attracting praise from Conservative sources and angry protests from within the Labour Movement. He maintained that he could not discuss publicly the nature of the evidence on which be had acted. They availed themselves of the right to make representations to the independent advisory panel, but again it was impossible to reveal what advice the panel had tendered. They were deported, but in a Parliamentary debate thirty-six Labour members voted against the government.

Rees remained in the shadow cabinet until 1983, until December 1980 as Shadow Home Secretary and then after a spell as Shadow Energy Secretary he became, from 1982–83, the Principal Opposition Front-bench Spokesman on Industry and Employment Co-ordination. In 1982 he was a member of the Franks Committee of Enquiry on the Falkland Islands. It was not until 1992 that he left the Commons and accepted a life peerage as Lord Merlyn-Rees. He remains active in public life, and has been Chancellor of the University of Glamorgan since 1993. His book *Northern Ireland, a Personal Perspective*, published in 1985, is essential reading for the period with which it deals.

Rt Hon. Lord Archer of Sandwell QC

John Reid (1947–)

Dr John Reid was born on 8 May 1947 in the Scottish Labour heartland of Lanarkshire. His father, Thomas, was a postman. His mother, Mary, in common with many of her contemporaries, had worked in a local factory during World War II.

Having passed the then Scottish version of the eleven-plus , Reid entered St Patrick's Senior Secondary (now St Patrick's High School), a selective state school for Roman Catholics. St Patrick's is also the *alma mater* of a number of serving MPs today, including Helen Liddell, who succeeded Reid as Secretary of State for Scotland (see below). Reid did not enter higher education from school, preferring instead to enter employment directly. At 22 he married Catherine McGowan. They had two sons together and in 1975 Reid entered Stirling University as a mature student. He left in 1981 with an honours degree in History and a doctorate in Economic History.

From 1979 to 1983, John was the Scottish Labour Party's Research Officer. During this period his talents were spotted by Neil Kinnock who, as new party leader in 1983, installed Reid in his office as a key political adviser. Here, alongside current cabinet luminaries such as Charles Clarke MP and Patricia Hewitt MP, Reid served with distinction in the intellectual and political vanguard of the Labour modernisation project. In 1985, he moved to become the Scottish organiser for the TUL (Trade Unionists for Labour).

In 1987, Reid was elected Member of Parliament for Motherwell North, a seat he went on to hold at the 1992 general election. He was given his first role as opposition spokesperson on children in 1989, a role which lasted only a brief period as his abilities as a sound performer within and outwith the House became widely recognised. In 1990 Neil Kinnock appointed Reid an opposition spokesperson on defence, a role which new leader Tony Blair enhanced in 1995 by appointing Reid Shadow Armed Forces Minister.

Reid's crucial place in the shadow defence team is perhaps best exemplified by the fact that he was chosen to speak against a premature amending of the rules regarding homosexuals in the armed services. That is to say, Reid comes from a traditional working-class culture which shares, ostensibly at least, some conservative social mores and instincts with those social classes that have traditionally provided the senior echelons of the armed forces with talent. George Robertson, who in this respect came from a similar mould, once noted accurately that he, as Defence Secretary, and Reid, as Armed Forces Minister, would never have gained entry to the Army's most prestigious regiments. Yet each served with great distinction at the Ministry of Defence, in part not in spite of but because of their social backgrounds.

Subsequent ministers at the MoD during the first Blair administration included Peter Kilfoyle and Doug Henderson, then, in the second, Adam Ingram. All of these appointments, working-class MPs of considerable ability, could be seen as testimony of the Blair administrations' intent, in respect of the Ministry of Defence, to accept slower movement on social issues within the military in return for high military effectiveness in pursuit of Labour's foreign policy objectives. This broad strategy has yielded one of the closest relationships between the government and the armed forces in the post-war era, and has contributed handsomely to the government's ability to actively factor security issues into an increasingly proactive international development programme.

In 1997, Reid was elected to the new political constituency of Hamilton North and Belshill and, as expected, appointed Minister for the Armed Forces, where he was regarded by politicians of all parties, and by defence chiefs, as an unquestionable success. Success in his political career at this time was counterbalanced in his private life by the sudden and tragic early death of his wife, Catherine.

Reid was subsequently moved to the then Department of Environment, Transport and the Regions as Transport Minister. This role saw him attend cabinet, on the verge of entering the top political echelon. Then, in May 1999 he took over the role of Scotland Secretary, following Scottish devolution. During his time as Scotland Secretary, George Robertson left the UK political stage to become NATO Secretary General, and many were surprised when Reid was not appointed his successor.

Instead, over the following months, Reid was deployed by the Prime Minister as a utility heavyweight politician, firefighting such issues as the 2000 fuel protests, rarely off the television. Then, following the resignation of Peter Mandleson MP as Northern Ireland Secretary in early 2001, Reid took on the role and became, finally, a heavyweight UK politician in his own right. At the time of writing, few would predict that his rise will stop at the Northern Ireland Office.

John Reid is a fast-rising politician who has had behind-the-scenes successes in four government departments yet is only now, at the beginning of the new century, entering the public consciousness as a senior politician at the very centre of the Labour modernisation project. His future progress, perhaps to the top few political offices, will owe less to his Glasgow boxer's physiognomy and natural assertiveness and more to his deserved, but sometimes overlooked, reputation as one of the cleverest politicians of his generation. We may never actually see Reid carrying a men's handbag, in the European fashion, but his future progress will be certainly marked by his great intellectual and social sophistication, and by his ability to weave his brief into a wider tapestry of social modernisation and progress begun by Neil Kinnock and his team back in 1983.

Eric Joyce MP

Ivor Richard (Lord Richard of Ammanford)   (1932–)

If 'New Labour' is about traditional values in a modern setting, then the appointment of Lord Richard as Lord Privy Seal and Leader of the Lords in Tony Blair's first Cabinet was its personification. Richard had been a Labour Party member since 1953 and having unsuccessfully contested South Kensington in the 1959 general election, had served as MP for Baron's Court, Fulham, from 1964 until 1974, when the Boundary Commissioners abolished his constituency. A card-carrying Gaitskellite and CDS supporter, at 27 he had been the youngest of fifteen former parliamentary candidates to sign an open letter to the press organised by Bill Rodgers and Dick Taverne endorsing Gaitskell's leadership and the need for Party reform in the wake of the 1959 election defeat. The eldest signatory, fellow Welshman Merlyn Rees, was to become one of his closest friends. Born 30 May 1932 the son of Seward Thomas Richard, he had attended St Michael's School, Bryn, Llanelly and Cheltenham College before becoming Wightwick Scholar at Pembroke College Oxford. Graduating in Jurisprudence in 1953 he was called to the Bar. Joining Inner Temple in 1955 he practised in London from 1955 to 1974, taking Silk in 1971.

In Parliament, his membership of the 1963 Club of Gaitskellites translated by the late 1960s into a core role in the covert 'Wilson Must Go' campaign to replace Wilson with Jenkins or Callaghan. In June 1968, Patrick Gordon Walker's diary records meetings of the plotters taking place in Richard's secluded barrister's room in Temple. He was, wrote Dick Crossman in his diary in May 1966, 'a very powerful right-wing London lawyer who carries a great deal of weight.' In October 1968, Crossman, indeed, favoured the 'extremely able' Richard as his junior minister at DHSS. Roy Jenkins also sought to get him into government, but it was not until October 1969 that Richard, having had a spell in 1966–67 as Denis Healey's PPS, secured office under Healey at Defence, becoming until Labour's 1970 election defeat the Under-Secretary of State for the Army.

An Opposition Spokesman 1970–1974, first on Broadcasting, Posts and Telecommunications and then, from 1971, as Deputy Shadow Foreign Secretary under Jim Callaghan, his staunch Atlanticism and his participation in the pro-European rebellion of 69 Labour MPs in favour of EEC entry on 28 October 1971 were undoubtedly responsible for his failure to secure a new seat in London in the light of the abolition of Baron's Court in 1974. Instead he went down to defeat at Blyth in Northumberland against the rebel ex-Labour MP Eddie Milne in a campaign dominated by the impact of the furore surrounding the Poulson corruption scandal on the local Labour establishment. Richard, an outsider, had been completely uninvolved, but his campaign was torpedoed nevertheless. On a happier note, his Atlanticism and pro-Europeanism probably helped secure his appointment as UK Permanent Rep to the UN (1974–79), a role in which he chaired a special conference on Rhodesia, and as Labour's member of the European Commissioner in Brussels (1981–84).

His postings abroad did not, however, insulate him from Labour politics. His time at the UN during Callaghan's period as Foreign Secretary deepened a growing admiration, whilst David Owen's appointment as Foreign Secretary exacerbated a personality clash apparent when the two were Defence Ministers which, according to Bill Rodgers, was to remove any political attractions Richard might otherwise have found in the SDP. Indeed, outgoing Commission President Roy Jenkins noted in his diary of a lunch with Richard on 7 November 1980: 'Intelligent and agreeable but somehow … misconceiving the job I think, seeing it as far too much a propaganda job to be done in England with the object of reconciling the Labour movement and the trade unions to Europe. This admittedly would be a wonderful objective, but not I think achievable, and certainly not by a Brussels based Commissioner.' Richard was, however, not to be deterred: Barbara Castle's memoirs record her fury that in the 1983 election, 'pro-marketeers enlisted Labour's member of the European Commission, Ivor Richard, to declare that Labour's plan to withdraw from the EC would cause unemployment to reach 5 million.'

In 1985 he became a Bencher and Chair of the World Trade Centre Wales. His peerage as Lord Richard of Ammanford in 1990 brought a return to frontline politics and he became Opposition Spokesman on Home Affairs until in 1992 he was elected Leader of the Labour Peers in succession to the veteran Cledwyn Hughes. From 1992 to 1993 he shadowed Treasury and Economic Affairs and from 1992 to 1997 Civil Service and European Affairs.

As Lord Privy Seal and thus a non-departmental Minister, he served on more Cabinet Committees than virtually any other member of Blair's Cabinet. He did not, however, seem to feel an integral part of Blair's Cabinet team and was frequently frustrated by what he saw as a lack of consultation over issues such as the creation of new peers. His replacement by Margaret Jay in July 1998 was nevertheless a shock to Richard and a surprise to many commentators, for whom Richard was one of the success stories of Blair's Cabinet. He was, perhaps, a casualty of Blair's desire to promote more women to his Cabinet. His determination to replace the Lords with an at least partly elected second chamber may also have played a part: Blair and other Ministers appear to give more weight to the concern that another elected Chamber could risk legislative gridlock, as is the case in the US Congress, and would fail to encourage legislators from a more diverse range of backgrounds than comprise the Commons. Moreover, his relationship with Blair's longstanding friend and legal mentor, the Lord Chancellor Derry Irvine, was at times testy, particularly in relation to the Pugin wallpaper.

He had two sons and a daughter before the dissolution of his marriage of 1 June 1962 to Alison Imrie. On 1 September 1989 he married Janet Jones, with whom he has one son. Janet Jones published the eminently readable *Labour of Love, The 'Partly –Political' Diary of a Cabinet Minister's Wife* in 1999 after her husband's enforced retirement from Cabinet. Ivor Richard was himself joint author of *Europe or the Open Sea* (1971) and *We, the British* (1983).

Greg Rosen

Jo Richardson (1923–94)

Josephine (Jo) Richardson was born on 28 August 1923 and educated at Southend-on-Sea High School for Girls. Jo was not inexperienced in Labour politics prior to becoming MP for Barking in 1974. She had been a Hornsey Borough Councillor for four years and Alderman for six, as well as sitting on Hammersmith Council for three years. She had also become the Secretary of the Keep Left Group in 1948 and remained so for thirty years as it metamorphosed via its Bevanite phase into the Tribune group.

It was during these thirty years that Jo repeatedly attempted to secure a Parliamentary seat. She fought unsuccessful campaigns in Monmouth (in 1951 and 1955), Hornchurch (1959) and Harrow East (1964), eventually succeeding in winning the moderately solid Labour seat of

Barking in the February 1974 poll. From this base, Richardson was to build considerable standing in the Parliamentary Labour Party. Beginning with her election as 'Chairman' of the Tribune Group in 1978, she secured election to the Constituency Section of Labour's NEC in 1979, retaining her seat until 1991. Throughout this time she championed the policy agenda of the Labour left, but focused her major efforts on advocating rights for women. Jo was to become synonymous with this cause, and was appointed by Neil Kinnock to become Opposition Front Bench Spokesperson on Women's Rights in 1983. While in this post, Jo spoke at the 1986 Blackpool Conference, against the NEC line, for a resolution that called for a Labour government to install a Minister for Women in a future Cabinet. The resolution was carried by a margin of 3.3 million votes to 2.9. Kinnock had feared that this post would expand a future Labour Cabinet to an unworkable size, but the shadow post was approved and would help further the cause of women's representation at a higher level in intra-party developments in the coming years. Elected to the shadow cabinet 1987–92, Jo served as the Shadow Minister for Women's Rights. She also sat variously on the Home Affairs, Nationalised Industries and Procedure and Expenditure Select Committees.

Within the Labour Party Jo also sat as Chair of the Women's Committee and the Black and Asian Advisory Group. The latter caused her problems in 1986 when demands for Black Sections of the Labour Party came from certain prominent members of the PLP. At a meeting to launch the body she was branded 'a racist' from the floor of the committee room of the House of Commons – a verbal lash that caused her to threaten to resign as Chair at the Party Conference in 1987. Nevertheless, she became Party Vice-Chair in 1988–89 and Chair in 1989–90. In addition to these important roles, her work also included serving on committees set up by Labour to look into the workings of the electoral system – an occupation that was to see no discernible outcome by the time that Jo was forced to effectively withdraw from politics through illness by late 1993.

Having backed Michael Foot in the leadership contest of 1980, she became a close colleague of Tony Benn, supporting his bid for the Deputy Leadership in 1981. However, by the time of her election to the shadow cabinet in 1987, she was dubbed a 'YAK' (Young, Able and Kinnockite)! It is doubtful that Richardson had discarded her affinity to the left as much as Kinnock was beginning to by this stage – but to call her 'young' at 64 was certainly a compliment!

A member of the post-1979 Election Commission of Inquiry (into party finances and internal reform), she contributed vociferously in favour of nuclear disarmament as part of the internal debate on the party's defence policy of the early 1980s (she was a Vice-Chair of CND). In addition she continued her ceaseless campaigning on women's issues and civil liberties throughout her career. A left-winger who had argued for the new electoral college for internal elections in 1980 and had been part of the infamous walk-out from the NEC meeting to expel Militants in March 1986, Jo had also contributed to party progress. Touted herself as a plausible candidate for the leadership elections in 1983, she had gone on to challenge the validity of Tony Benn's challenge in 1988 as well as playing a part in the important policy reviews of the late 1980s. Overall, her career was appreciated for her application and belief in the issues that she saw as imperative and, after her death from a long illness on 1 February 1994, she was considered to be a considerable loss to the reforming Labour movement.

Phil Miles

Alfred Robens (Lord Robens of Woldingham)   (1910–99)

Alf Robens was born in Manchester on 18 December 1910 to a working-class family, and attended elementary and the Ducie Avenue Secondary School in Manchester, leaving at the age of 15 to work in a shop selling umbrellas, before becoming a clerk in the Manchester and Salford Co-op. His involvement in Labour politics came through the co-operative movement and his activities, from the age of 17 onwards, in the shop workers' union USDAW. He became a full-time union official in 1935 and served on Manchester City Council from 1941 to 1945 while he was medically disqualified from active war service.

Robens was elected MP in July 1945 for the Wansbeck constituency in Northumberland, and after 1950 followed the Blyth portion of the seat into a newly named constituency. Wansbeck and Blyth were working-class mining areas, and Robens rapidly acquired an interest in the coal industry although he did not take a close interest in local constituency and council matters in Blyth. His successor after 1960, Eddie Milne, did not take such a retiring attitude and became increasingly concerned about the corruption that existed in the council and the Labour Party in Blyth, leading to his standing successfully as an Independent in February 1974.

Robens became PPS to Alfred Barnes, the Minister of Transport, in 1946, and Attlee gave Robens his first job in government on 7 October 1947, when he was made Parliamentary Secretary at the Ministry of Fuel and Power under Hugh Gaitskell and then Philip Noel-Baker, dealing with the newly nationalised coal industry. Robens became a passionate Gaitskell loyalist, describing him as having 'the rare combination in a political leader of courage and complete integrity.'

When Bevan resigned as Minister of Labour and National Insurance Robens was appointed to replace him on 24 April 1951, becoming a Privy Counsellor. Robens was only in the Cabinet for six months, as Labour lost the election of October 1951. The orthodoxy of the Ministry of Labour then was for productivity initiatives and close co-operation with trade unions, an orthodoxy which fitted well with Robens's instincts. In opposition in 1951–55 Robens was a competent, pugnacious spokesman in several portfolios. Robens had considerable charm and was a popular figure within the Parliamentary Labour Party, elected continuously to the Shadow Cabinet every year from November 1951 until November 1959, the final time he stood.

Gaitskell made an error by appointing Robens Shadow Foreign Secretary in 1955. Robens had little grasp of the subtleties of foreign policy or the currents of opinion within the Labour Party, and his speeches were poorly delivered. Gaitskell thought that that 'Alfred has not got the intellectual quality which is needed for this absolutely top level work.' Discontent with Robens's performance grew among his colleagues and he was attacked in the *Daily Mirror*, although he still came second in the 1956 Parliamentary Committee elections. It was a troubled period for Robens, with family problems as well as the decline of his career, and he told Gaitskell that he did not want the job any more. In November 1956 Bevan took his place and Robens returned to the more congenial world of shadowing the ministries of Labour and Power, where he remained until he left parliament.

The 1959 election was a great disappointment for the Labour Party, and Robens took it worse than most. He questioned whether Labour could ever win again and despaired at the prospect of a lifetime of futile opposition, until Harold Macmillan controversially offered him the Chairmanship of the National Coal Board in 1960. Robens resigned his seat in parliament, joined the Board in October 1960 and started what he called his 'Ten Year Stint' as Chairman on 1 February 1961, now styled Lord Robens of Woldingham. The NCB in the 1960s was a good place to be for someone as interested in power as Robens was. He was allowed a great deal of managerial freedom by governments of both parties, faced a pliant Board under him, and was effectively ruler of an industrial empire that was then at the heart of the nationalised sector and Labour movement consciousness. His self-importance – and also his belief in communication – was apparent with the number of speeches and pit visits he made as Chairman.

Robens drifted away from his Labour roots during the Wilson government in 1964–70, for ideological and personal reasons. Robens had been regarded as a potential Labour leader during the 1950s and had made a historic misjudgement about the party's prospects in 1960. Had he still been a Labour MP in good standing in 1963 he would have been likely to have stood for the leadership after Gaitskell died and polled better than George Brown had against Wilson; Wilson was enjoying – or at least experiencing – what could have belonged to Robens. Robens also had numerous battles with the government and the frequently reshuffled industry and power ministers over coal industry policy; the rate of pit closure was faster than he wanted.

Robens had been close to Cecil King since the 1950s. In 1954 King started to provide him with money to 'make it possible for [him] to stay in politics'. King joined the Coal Board in 1966, and Robens became a director of the Bank of England the same year; the two grandees shared a contempt for Wilson and increasingly considered the dream of a 'National Government'. This government would be nominally non-party and be composed of moderate, Establishment figures from both main parties and from business. Its programme would be the restructuring of Britain along business management lines. Two of the senior business figures in such a government would naturally have been Robens and King, with Robens a potential Prime Minister. The 'Cecil King coup' dissolved into farce in 1968 but Robens did not let go of the idea of a national government.

Robens was the Dr Beeching of the pits, although his surgery was performed with more finesse and more anaesthetic than Beeching's hacking away at the railway network. He inherited an industry employing 583,000 miners at 698 pits in 1960, and left it in 1971 with 283,000 men and 292 pits. The amount of coal produced fell less dramatically, from 194,000 tons in 1960 to 147,000 tons in 1971, reflecting greatly increased productivity – 6 per cent a year. Robens expressed his views about productivity, which he regarded as a social as well as a technical issue, in his 1970 book *Human Engineering*, and these views were central to his later political beliefs.

The 1960s rationalisation of the coal industry was a striking piece of industrial modernisation achieved at a surprisingly low social cost. Robens had the support of the NUM President, Will Paynter, who shared his belief that rapid modernisation was the future of the coal industry. Industrial relations in the coal industry were generally good, although militancy was building among Yorkshire miners as the 1960s drew to a close. Compared with the harsh run-down of the industry in the 1980s and 1990s there was little industrial bitterness, and ex-mining communities were treated with care and did not become pools of unemployment and poverty.

The greatest blot on Robens's reputation was the Aberfan disaster of 21 October 1966, in which a coal tip slid off a hillside onto the village and engulfed its school. 144 people were killed in the disaster, including 116 schoolchildren. Robens decided to continue that day with his investiture as Chancellor of the University of Surrey in Guildford, a public relations blunder even in an age that expected few demonstrations of emotion from its public figures. The Coal Board stalled throughout the public inquiry into Aberfan before admitting its responsibility at the very end of proceedings, while in Aberfan arguments over insurance and liability left the ruined buildings standing for a year. The cost of removing the tips that loomed over Aberfan was borne by the disaster relief charity which had been set up with public subscriptions, not the NCB which had built them up in the first place. Welsh Secretary Ron Davies returned the £150,000 it cost to the charity in May 1997. Robens feigned an offer of resignation after the Aberfan report was published, but simultaneously briefed that there was no reason for him to resign, and even dictated the wording of the minister's letter refusing his 'offer'.

Robens redeemed himself somewhat for Aberfan by his chairmanship of the committee to review Britain's health and safety at work legislation from May 1970 to June 1972. The report recommended abolishing the complex web of specific regulations which had grown up to govern occupational health and safety and replacing it with broad duties on employers to provide a safe working environment and assess risks in the workplace. Robens also argued for extending the scope of health and safety regulation beyond industrial workers, the traditional focus of concern, to workers in health and education.

The recommendations were enacted in the Health and Safety at Work Act 1974, which has remained basically in place ever since. The Health and Safety Commission is one of the few surviving tripartite institutions. Rates of fatal injury at work have dropped to a quarter of what they were in the early 1970s. Although this also reflects the decline of the most dangerous industries – mining, fishing, heavy industry, dock handling – much of the improvement is due to Robens. The Robens approach to health and safety has been emulated in other countries.

Robens left the National Coal Board in 1971 and moved into private industry. He accumulated the chairmanships of Vickers, Johnson Matthey and MLH Consultants in 1971 and served as a director of numerous other enterprises such as Trust House Forte and Times Newspapers. Politically, Robens continued to veer to the right. In a speech to a business audience in October 1976 he returned to the theme of 'Great Britain Limited', implicitly with himself as Chairman of the Board, commenting that 'What we need is not a political coalition. We really need for five years a Council of State, composed of all parties and of none, and of the trade union and business world. Such a government could identify very clearly what was required to be done to put the country back on its feet. They would require to forego their political theories and concentrate on a single aim. The country needs today good, efficient business management.'

This address summed up Robens's political creed, of which aspects had always been apparent, that there was a common-sense solution to Britain's problems and that a transformation could be wrought by a marshalling of the talents of the political centre and successful business and the construction of a more efficient, and more truly corporate, corporate state. In the 1940s and 1950s he believed that the Labour movement was the core of a more efficient means of governance, and that public ownership was a way of avoiding industrial conflict, but in the

1960s and 1970s he was an enthusiast for big business – in the public and private sectors – and felt that the best way of encouraging good industrial relations was to assist internal union democracy. Robens was never very interested in political theory and this left his political views rather rudderless and prone to change according to his own circumstances.

Robens endorsed the Conservatives in the 1979 general election, and claimed that the 1979 'Winter of Discontent' had been caused by communist infiltration of trade unions 'which had largely succeeded'. Although his business activities continued into the 1980s he did not speak in the House of Lords after 1982, suffering the first of two disabling strokes in 1993, becoming wheelchair-bound after the second in 1994. He died of pneumonia at the age of 88 on 27 June 1999, leaving his wife Eva Powell, whom he had married in 1936, and their adopted son. His effect on the Labour Party was small, but the Labour movement's effect on him was massive. It was the ladder of ascent from poverty-stricken childhood to captain of industry.

Lewis Baston

George Robertson (Lord Robertson) (1946–)

In his career George Robertson has had a great impact on politics in Scotland, Europe and now the world. He is known as a 'canny Scots moderate and a pillar of Labour orthodoxy' but perhaps his greatest legacy to Labour is that the party is now trusted by both the public and the generals on defence. But it is not all over yet – and it would be a foolish man who would bet on his posting in Brussels being the end of his career.

George Robertson was born on 12 April 1946 in Port Ellen on the Hebridean island of Islay, the son of Police Inspector George P Robertson. He was educated at Dunoon Grammar School (which also educated fellow Labour MPs John Smith and Brian Wilson) and secured an Economics MA from Dundee University in 1968. Having joined Labour aged 15, he was active within the University Labour Club and became co-chair (with the Edinburgh University-based Robin Cook) of the Scottish Association of Labour Student Organisations.

Appointed Scottish Research Officer for the then General and Municipal Workers Union (now the GMB) in 1969, from 1970 to 1978 he was the full-time G&MWU official responsible for the Scottish whisky industry. In the union, he was chief negotiator for manual workers for the main company and industry-wide agreements. From 1973 to 1979 Robertson served on the Scottish Executive of the Labour Party, being its chair 1977–78. He married Sandra Wallace in June 1970, with whom he has had two sons and a daughter.

In 1978 he was elected as MP for Hamilton (latterly Hamilton South) in a by-election, beating the SNP's star campaigner Margo MacDonald. This was the only Wednesday parliamentary by-election in British history. His ability won swift recognition and, albeit brief, promotion; he was appointed PPS to David Ennals, the Secretary of State for Social Services, for the dying months of the Callaghan government from February to May 1979.

After the general election defeat he was appointed an opposition spokesman on Scotland, being reshuffled to defence in 1980, and then to Foreign Affairs in 1981. As importantly, he became in 1979 Secretary of the loyalist Manifesto Group of Labour MPs, working closely with Giles Radice and Bill Rodgers' ex-PPS Ken Weetch to sustain the pro-NATO, anti-unilateralist, social-democratic tradition within the Party during the traumas of the early 1980s. On 22 September 1980 he was one of twelve Labour backbenchers, dubbed the 'Dirty Dozen,' who signed a letter to *The Times* calling for the introduction of 'one member, one vote' (OMOV) in the selection of candidates, constituency officials and the Party leader, and the reform of the NEC to represent ordinary members, local councillors and MPs. Robertson and his allies were ahead of their time – OMOV had to wait until John Smith's leadership and reform of the NEC to Tony Blair's, and by 1983 all eleven signatories apart from Robertson had either been forced to retire or joined the SDP. Robertson remained to a play a prominent role in the battle to oust the Militant Tendency in particular, whom he described as a 'cancer' which had to be cut off, and against the hard left in general. He stood constantly against the grain of the party, supporting some restrictions on abortion, rejecting calls for unilateral nuclear disarmament and supporting European integration.

From 1984 to 1993 he served as principal spokesman on European affairs and was consistently pro-European. He was the Chairman of the British/German Parliamentary Group and in 1991 the President of Germany awarded him the Grand Cross of the German Order of Merit. In 1986 he travelled to Moscow to become the first non-communist Briton to attend a Soviet Communist Party Congress. In 1993 he was named Joint Parliamentarian of the Year, along with his successor at the MOD Geoff Hoon, for his role in exposing Conservative divisions over the Maastricht Treaty.

Whilst being one of Labour's well-known pro-Europeans, Robertson has always been a solid supporter of the 'special relationship' with the USA. He was a member of the Council of the Atlantic Conference and occupied a post on the Council of the British Atlantic Committee from 1979 to 1990.

In 1993 Robertson was elected to the shadow cabinet, becoming Shadow Scottish Secretary of State for Scotland. In the summer of 1996 he had to front an embarrassing U-turn on Labour's policy towards a referendum for a Scottish Parliament. The Labour leadership became increasingly concerned that the legislation needed for the new parliament could clog up the legislative process, as had happened under Callaghan with the 1978 Devolution Bill. It was decided that a referendum on the issue would give the mandate necessary to spearhead the change through Westminster. However, up until then Robertson had declared that 'the general election will be the referendum,' and he was left with egg on his face when the policy changed. He took the criticism on the chin, and won support from the Party membership for the two-question referendum. It is now seen as being a major reason for the success of devolution.

After the 1997 general election Tony Blair appointed Robertson as Defence Secretary. He said the appointment was 'a huge privilege and an honour' and went on to pledge to 'ensure as strong and effective a defence of our country as any Government ever has.' He won over the military with his wit and straight talking. One anecdote he regaled concerned an abusive letter he received which said, 'You are the worst Defence Secretary ever, I don't like your face or your wig.' He replied 'Dear Madam, I respect your views about my capabilities and appearance – but if I had a wig, do you really think I would have bought one with a hole?' At the MoD, Robertson masterminded a strategic review of British forces, which called for reorientation of military structures, purchasing and military doctrine around the concept of rapid reaction forces. He also pioneered plans for the rationalisation and integration of the capability of European armed forces. In March 1999 he said, 'Without effective military capability to back up European foreign policy goals, we are wasting our time. We risk being an economic giant, but a strategic midget.' He also developed the 'special relationship' with the USA. *The Guardian* obtained private correspondence between Robertson and his American counterpart William Cohen and compared the contents to love notes. Robertson wrote to Cohen: 'On a personal level, I would like you to know that your constant readiness to give us everything we need and your wise advice makes a tremendous difference. It is extremely reassuring to know that we stand alongside a faithful friend and ally as we face the challenges of these difficult times.'

During the Kosovo conflict of 1999 Robertson came into his own. He became renowned for his vitriolic attacks on Slobodan Milosevic – describing him as a 'serial ethnic cleanser' encircled by 'sadistic henchmen' in charge of a 'brutal murder machine.' He earned the support of generals and soldiers alike with his interest in weaponry and its procurement, and won plaudits for initiatives to encourage servicemen to gain educational and civilian skills. After the war, Kosovar Albanians welcomed him to Pristina as 'George Robinson' – but despite the confusion over the name, the affection was genuine. Political pundits declared that Robertson had 'a good war' and he was tipped as a successor to Robin Cook.

However, in August 1999 Robertson was elevated to the House of Lords as Lord Robertson of Port Ellen and in October became the tenth Secretary General of NATO. Tony Blair said Robertson had 'exactly the right mix of defence expertise, along with the political and diplomatic skills necessary for the job,' whilst President Clinton praised his 'extraordinary leadership in the Kosovo conflict' and his 'tremendous contribution to the United Kingdom's effort to modernise its military forces.' Robertson himself said that 'straight talking, plain common sense and dogged determination' were perhaps the qualities that made him the ideal candidate for the job. The main challenges facing him now are to increase co-operation between European armies, to consider NATO enlargement, to improve NATO's troubled relations with Russia, and to build relations with the new Bush administration.

James Connal

Geoffrey Robinson (1938–)

Geoffrey Robinson's influence on the 1997–2001 Labour Government has been enormous – but hardly any of it has been exercised through the ministerial post he commanded from 1997 until his resignation in 1998 (Paymaster General).

It was his loan to Peter Mandelson that brought down not only the Minister but also the Chancellor's press secretary, Charlie Whelan. It was his book, *The Unconventional Minister,* that re-opened the wounds of that debacle and exposed the personal divisiveness of the government in 2000. And it is the recurring, if unproven, suggestions of financial murkiness that have threatened to send shockwaves against the recipients of his patronage – including the office of Gordon Brown in opposition.

Robinson's obvious (although denied) bitterness at finding himself now comprehensively outside the Labour leadership's loop is understandable. He has been Labour MP for Coventry

North West since a 1976 by-election, entering the House as one of Labour's brightest prospects after a business career successful in that it saw him become Chief Executive of Jaguar Cars in 1974–75 at the age of 35. Born on 25 May 1938, following three years as a Labour Party Research Assistant he became in 1968 a Senior Executive of Tony Benn's Industrial Reorganisation Corporation, from 1970–72 the Financial Controller of British Leyland and in 1972–73 the Managing Director of Leyland Innocenti. Not bad for the son of working-class parents (the late Robert and Dorothy Robinson) who secured his places at Clare College Cambridge and Yale on the back of a scholarship to Emmanuel School in South London.

Initially he was associated with the Bennite left of the party (his role as unpaid chief executive of the tragically doomed Meriden Triumph Motorcycles Co-operative from 1978 to 1980 made him a temporary hero of the proponents of an Alternative Economic Strategy). He soon fell out with them, however, and was briefly a junior front-bench spokesman under Foot and Kinnock (Science 1982–83, then Regional Affairs and Trade and Industry 1983–87). From 1982 to 1985 he was also a Director of the West Midlands Enterprise Board. After that, he concentrated on his business interests in the ten years prior to the 1997 election.

But his absence from the front bench in this period should not be taken as indicating a lack of involvement in the affairs of the Labour leadership. He funded the offices of Kinnock, Smith, Brown and Blair. He lent Blair his Tuscan home for his summer holidays. And in 1994 he bought the struggling *New Statesman*, bailing it out and inspiring hopes amongst the young Blairites that it would become a vehicle for promoting modernisation.

The fact that he got the blame for the Mandelson loan affair whilst Mandelson himself was so swiftly rehabilitated must obviously grate. But Robinson is not entirely a victim – his dealings have been the subject of four parliamentary investigations since 1997. Whatever the truth of the allegations surrounding him, this is accident-prone to say the least and more than enough to foreclose the prospect of a revived ministerial career.

Successful businessmen accustomed to taking decisions that turn into actions often view politics with contempt and consider it to be easy. When they try their hand at it, most of them find it is not as easy as they thought. Geoffrey Robinson's constant ability to undermine his own obvious talent by getting into unnecessary 'scrapes' about his finances probably earns him a place in precisely this category.

And for someone obviously sensitive enough to be hurt at the way he has been treated, the support he gets from his constituency must be welcome: 'We can't fault him, he's a great MP' says his agent. And when he contemplates what has happened, there is little doubt his very considerable wealth dulls the pain as well. Married since 1967 to Marie Giorgio, they have a son and a daughter.

Melissa Robinson

Kenneth Robinson (1911–96)

Kenneth Robinson was Harold Wilson's Minister of Health from 1964 until Wilson's decision to merge the Health Ministry into the new super-department of Health and Social Security under the overlordship of Dick Crossman in November 1968. A highly regarded minister, he negotiated the General Practitioners' Charter, which formed the basis of the successful development of primary care in Britain. But he never made Cabinet. Writing in the *Guardian* shortly after Robinson's death, Roy Jenkins recollected him as 'the least self-seeking and most quietly civilised man I ever encountered in parliamentary or ministerial politics... He was a highly competent but hardly swashbuckling minister, and I always wondered how much he enjoyed the high-wire acts of politics.' Shirley Williams agreed: 'He was, indeed, more public servant than politician, devoted to his department, incapable of pushing himself, not good at manipulation... He was wonderful to work for. From 1964 until January 1966, I was his Parliamentary Private Secretary, encouraged to attend departmental meetings and to offer my own comments and ideas.'

It broke Robinson's heart to leave the Ministry of Health, which he had shadowed in Opposition from 1959 to 1964 as deputy spokesman under Edith Summerskill. His performance as Minister of Land and Planning in the Ministry of Housing and Local Government under Tony Greenwood compared badly with his record at Health, partly because it was said he had made the unworkable pledge that he would solve the housing problem in three years, but largely because his heart was not in it. When in October 1969 his ministry was abolished, he returned to the back benches, retiring from Parliament at the 1970 election.

He then embarked upon another life as director of social policy at the British Steel Corporation 1970–72 and managing director (Personnel and Social Policy Division) 1972–74, serving briefly as acting chief executive in 1973. From 1974, until the Tory GLC victory in 1978, he served as Chairman of the London Transport Executive. In addition he was from 1972 to 1977 Chairman of the English National Opera and from 1977 to 1982, Chairman of the Arts Council of Great Britain. He was knighted in 1983 and between 1983 and 1988 was joint treasurer of the Royal Society of Arts.

Born in Warrington on 19 March 1911, the early death of his doctor father forced him to leave his public school, Oundle, aged only 15 and put paid to his own hopes of becoming a doctor. Instead, he became a clerk at Lloyd's insurance brokers, remaining until he joined the RNVR as an able seaman in 1939. By 1945 he had become a Lieutenant Commander on the battleship *King George V.* He married Elizabeth Edwards in 1941 whilst on leave, and they were to have one daughter.

Elected a Labour councillor in St Pancras in 1945, where he founded the St Pancras Arts and Civic Council, he worked back at Lloyds until elected Labour MP for St Pancras North at a by-election in March 1949. Appointed a Junior Whip in April 1950, he continued in the Oopposition Whips office after 1951 until relieved of his post in May 1954 over his support for Nye Bevan's rebellion against the Party line on nuclear weapons. It proved a liberation, freeing him up to campaign for liberal causes in which he believed. He made an important contribution to the Mental Health Act of 1959, which ended the status of suicide as a common law crime and, in the wake of the 1960 Wolfenden Report became a leading champion of the then unpopular cause of homosexual law reform. He also became a leading campaigner for reform of the laws on divorce and abortion. His biography of the novelist Wilkie Collins, a social outsider and friend of Charles Dickens who wrote sympathetically of the plight of one-parent families and opium addicts, was published in 1951. He died on 16 February 1996. His wife predeceased him in 1993.

Greg Rosen

Bill Rodgers (Lord Rodgers of Quarry Bank) (1928–)

Bill Rodgers served as a Minister in six different departments during the Labour administrations from 1964 to 1970 and from 1974 to 1979, the last three in the Cabinet as Secretary of State for Transport. During those eleven years only a handful of Labour Members of Parliament served as long and none served in as many departments. But despite his extensive Ministerial career Bill Rodgers is still perceived by many as the arch-organiser of Labour's right wing during the 1950s and 1960s, reinforced by his support in the 1970s for the Campaign for Labour Victory. That played a critical role in the run-up to the establishment in 1981 of the SDP, of which he was one of the founding 'Gang of Four'. However, the perception of arch-organiser and political in-fighter masks a politician who was an effective Minister and, in later years, became a successful Leader of the Liberal Democrats in the House of Lords. His political roots were deeply embedded in the Labour Party and his fundamental convictions have changed very little from those that drew him into Labour in Liverpool in the 1940s.

He was born in Wavertree on 28 October 1928. Son of a local government officer who for much of his career was clerk to Liverpool's Health Committee, he went to the local council school and then on to Quarry Bank High School. As his title in the House of Lords suggests, this school had a formative influence on the young Rodgers. So too did life during the war years in Liverpool with its Pier Head and docks followed by national service in Germany in the immediate aftermath of the war.

In January 1949 he entered Magdalen College, Oxford, on an Open Exhibition. It was a new world from which many of his future political and public service colleagues came and in which he soon became fully immersed in the activities of the Labour Club. Following graduation he rapidly continued down the political path with appointment in 1953 as Assistant Secretary and then General Secretary of the Fabian Society. In 1955 he married Silvia and started a partnership and a close family that were to provide him with support that would be of great significance in his subsequent career.

The Fabian Society was a springboard into national Labour politics and the intellectual cauldron of Labour in the '50s. It led to him working closely with many of the heavyweights of the earlier generation like Crosland, Jenkins, Healey and Wilson, as well as immediate contemporaries like Shirley Williams. But he also cut his political teeth on the door-step at the sharp end of campaigning as Parliamentary candidate in Bristol West in 1957 and as a councillor in St. Marylebone from 1958 to 1962.

As General Secretary of the Fabians he was inevitably in the thick of the revisionist debates of the period. These battles between left and right, focusing particularly on public ownership and unilateral nuclear disarmament, led, after Gaitskell's defeat on defence at the Scarborough Conference of 1960, to the establishment of the Campaign for Democratic Socialism. Rodgers was the obvious person to run it. His organisational skills, knowledge of the Party and, above all, its success in a very short period of time, led to the establishment of his reputation as the arch-fixer of the Right.

He left the Fabians in 1960 and was employed briefly at the Consumers' Association where he left as a memorial to his brief sojourn the very successful *Good Food Guide*. He also during this period spent a short but enjoyable time in publishing, to which he was to return later. But in 1962 he successfully fought the safe Labour seat of Stockton-on-Tees in the North East of England. It was to provide him with a safe political base right through to SDP days in 1983.

The early 1960s were the dying days of thirteen years of Tory rule, with sex and security scandals, the resignation of Harold Macmillan, and the selection of Alec Douglas-Home as his successor to fight the watershed 1964 General Election. The Labour victory, led by Harold Wilson, took place against a background of high hopes for the country's future, driven, in Wilson's phrase, by 'the white heat of the technological revolution' and great faith in the virtues of state economic planning. Rodgers was very much part of a new breed of young Labour politicians, and his ministerial career began immediately as Parliamentary Under-Secretary of State in the newly formed Department of Economic Affairs, which began work drawing up the new National Plan under the mercurial leadership of George Brown.

So began Rodgers' wide-ranging ministerial career. He moved over to the Foreign Office from 1967 to 1968, was Minister of State at the Board of Trade from 1968 to 1969 and at the Treasury from 1969 to the General Election in 1970. This gave him very considerable insight into the workings of government and the depressing internal mistrust and jockeying for position in the Wilson administration. This was not only between right and left. Rodgers suffered more than once from rivalry between leading figures on the right.

A number of vignettes from this period in government illustrate Rodgers' centre-left instincts. For instance, despite internal opposition, he stopped an official from the Royal Mint at Heathrow en route to signing a deal with the Greek military junta to make commemorative medals. To promote openness, he started moves to set up the first Foreign Affairs Select Committee, although this was unfortunately quashed by the then Foreign Secretary. Or again, when asked to entertain the visiting Richard Nixon, some time before he became President, he refused to have anything to do with him because of his McCarthyite record. He continued in this vane when he became Chairman of the Expenditure Committee on Trade and Industry during the years in opposition leading up to the 1974 election, during which time he was also Opposition Spokesman on Aviation.

The Committee's work caught attention. There were inquiries into the role of private money in the public sector, the effectiveness of regional development incentives and the wages and conditions of South African workers employed by UK firms in South Africa. The enquiry and recommendations of this last report made a considerable impact. Within a short period its code had been adopted not only in the UK but by the European Community for all EC companies operating in South Africa. It made a direct impact upon the lives and welfare of tens of thousands of people and Rodgers was rightly proud of it.

However, the most significant event during the years in opposition from 1970 to 1974 was the rebellion on a three-line whip by 69 Labour Members on the October 1971 vote on entry to the European Community. Much of the organisation and the collection of names of the Labour pro-Marketeers was undertaken by Rodgers. He was sacked from his shadow post by Wilson for his efforts. The rebels included Shirley Williams, David Owen and the then Deputy Leader of the Party, Roy Jenkins. Jenkins' later resignation marked the beginning of the end of his claim for the leadership of the Party. It would have been his for the taking in the aftermath of the 1970 election. But events within the Party dismayed and demoralised Jenkins and close supporters like Rodgers. These events were part of a shift in policy built on the disappointment of many Party activists with the 1964–70 Government. The changes eventually alienated not only Rodgers and the Jenkinsites but also the electorate.

The events of this period marked out people's positions and opened a fissure in the Labour Party that was to make an indelible imprint upon it over the subsequent decade and beyond. Rodgers' commitment to membership of the European Community was deep and long-standing. During the decade ahead he continued as a leading campaigner for continued EU membership right up to the breakaway to form the SDP in 1981.

That was particularly the case after the February 1974 election when Rodgers was Minister of State for Defence in the minority Labour Government. He played a leading role with the Labour Committee for Europe and in the all-party campaign on the referendum on Britain's EU membership.

Shortly after Callaghan replaced Wilson as Prime Minister in 1976 and Jenkins left Government for the Presidency of the European Commission, Rodgers, along with Hattersley, at last entered the Labour Cabinet as Secretary of State for Transport. As such he was at the centre of the ongoing economic turbulence which dominated that period of government. This started with the IMF loan crisis, followed by the vicissitudes of pay and prices policy, industrial disputes, the Lib-Lab Pact, ending with the 'Winter of Discontent' and the election of Margaret Thatcher in May 1979.

His period as Secretary of State for Transport was marked by a White Paper outlining a policy of strengthening public transport and limiting new roads to those that met economic and environmental objectives. He succeeded in battles over the introduction of tachographs, the first national scheme to provide pensioners with concessionary fares and the abolition of Vehicle Excise Duty. He sought with difficulty to introduce a European dimension to transport policy and introduced the first government Seat Belt Bill, which fell because of the general election but was successfully re-introduced by the new Government after it.

The period from 1974 to 1979 also saw an increase in the ferocity of the battles between the centre right and the left. The Manifesto Group was established in the PLP in 1974 to resist the advances of the left. Its offshoot, the Campaign for Labour Victory, was launched with Rodgers in the chair at a meeting in Central Hall, Westminster, in February 1977. Following Labour's defeat in 1979 the battles over defence, the Common Market, mandatory re-selection, and the formation of an Electoral College to elect Labour's Leader continued. Rodgers stood and was elected to the shadow cabinet in 1979 and 1980, being appointed Shadow Defence Secretary by Callaghan. But the election of Michael Foot as Leader and his unwillingness to offer Rodgers a serious shadow portfolio led to a further feeling of detachment from the Labour Party.

Rodgers, along with Shirley Williams and David Owen penned a substantial article on the state of the party in the *Guardian* in August 1980, leading to the birth of the sobriquet 'The Gang of Three'. Joined by Roy Jenkins on his return from Brussels in January 1981, they became the 'Gang of Four'. They published the Limehouse Declaration in that same month, on the day after the Special Labour Party Conference at which the electoral college proposal was adopted. They then went on in March to launch the SDP. Leaving the Labour Party was an enormous emotional wrench for Rodgers. He found it more difficult to reconcile himself to it than others within the SDP Leadership.

He played a leading role in the launch of the SDP and in its early years. He was a strong advocate of the merger with the Liberal Party in 1988, clashing strongly with his former colleague,

David Owen, who wished to retain the SDP's independence. He was unsuccessful when he stood in his old Labour seat in Stockton North as an SDP candidate in the 1983 election and again when he stood as an SDP/Alliance candidate in Milton Keynes in 1987. Between 1987 and 1994 he was Director General of the Royal Institute of British Architects and since 1995 has been Chairman of the Advertising Standards Authority. He entered the Lords as Baron Rodgers of Quarry Bank in 1992 and became Leader of the Liberal Democrats there in 1998.

His publications include: *Hugh Gaitskell 1906 – 1963* (ed.), 1964; *The People into Parliament*, (jointly with Bernard Donoghue), 1966; *The Politics of Change*, 1982; *Government and Industry*, (ed.); 1986, and his autobiography, *Fourth Among Equals*, 2000.

Sir Ian Wrigglesworth

Willie Ross (Lord Ross of Marnock)   (1911–88)

Throughout the Wilson years, 1964–70 and 1974–76, Willie Ross dominated politics in Scotland. Not since Charles II placed total confidence in Lord Lauderdale, or at least Pitt the Younger in Dundas, has there been anything quite like it. As far as the British Prime Minister was concerned, what his 'old basso profoundo' – his affectionate sobriquet for his Secretary of State – wanted for Scotland, got the Prime Ministerial imprimatur.

Whether Ross's monopoly of 10 Downing Street's ear was good for Scotland and for the Labour Party is another matter. Even Ross's admirers – and they were and are numerous – concede that he never was a man to heed other people's opinions. Yet, even this had a good side. Asked, hesitatingly, by civil servants as to whether he wanted the 'political advisor' to which he was entitled, he sent them away with a flea in their proverbial ear: 'I dinnae need any young man to teach me my politics!' But then he sent many of us away with a flea in our ear on occasions when we deserved proper consideration.

William Ross was born in Ayr on 7 April 1911, the son of a senior LMS railwayman and prominent Ayrshire County Council Labour Group member. Always a Lad o' Pairts, one of his favourite categorisations in later life, he got into Ayr Academy, well-known for its disciplined scholarship in the 1920s, and Glasgow University, from which he graduated in English in 1932. Becoming a schoolmaster, rather than a teacher, he taught philology to clever pupils at Glasgow schools. Pupils in later life remembered him with enormous gratitude and respect and were hardly astonished that their pre-war dominie became the post-war master of drafting the pedantic Parliamentary amendment. The 1939–45 War changed everything. Ross volunteered as a private soldier on the outbreak of hostilities, exuded officer qualities, and was soon commissioned into the Glasgow Regiment, the Highland Light Infantry. In 1943, he was posted to India and attached to the Royal Signals in the campaign against the Japanese. Soon, he was promoted a staff officer, but before the end of hostilities returned to Britain to participate as Labour candidate for Ayr in the 1945 election. It was his long-term good fortune that he just failed to beat the long-serving Tommy Moore, by 22,593 votes to Ross's 21,865. Had he won the seat, he would certainly have been defeated in 1950 or 1951. As it was, after campaigning for only a few days, he won golden opinions for reducing the Conservative majority from 12,619 to 728. If it was his father's influence in promoting the cause of his talented son, serving his country in Asia, it was this immensely creditable result which secured him the safe Labour Kilmarnock seat when Mrs C M Shaw resigned for health reasons in December 1946.

He married an extremely smart WREN officer, Elma Aitkenhead, who was to be an enormous asset to him throughout his political life. They had two daughters. Never was there a whiff of scandal for the simple reason that there was no scandal to report. And his Private Secretary, (Sir) William Kerr Fraser, later Scottish Office Permanent Secretary and Glasgow University Vice-Chancellor, recollects how fastidious he was about declining to accept gifts from hosts at any function to which he was invited as Secretary of State.

At first, partly because he had arrived 18 months after the Labour landslide intake, he was a somewhat mischievous back-bencher, making, almost to the point of disloyalty, the life of Joe Westwood and particularly that of his successor, Arthur Woodburn, something of a misery. His activity was as nothing compared to the way, night after night, he would keep Tory Ministers out of their beds during the 13 long Opposition years, challenging every Order of Legislation into the wee small hours of the morning, on Mondays, Tuesdays, Wednesdays and Thursdays until it was time to catch the night sleeper from Euston to Scotland.

Actually, this late-night filibustering by Ross, George Willis, Cyril Bence, Willie Hamilton and others, with the constant refrain that Scotland was being disadvantaged in relation to England, turned out to be a double-edged sword. People in Scotland began to believe that somehow they were being cheated. Their late-night sillinesses gave credit to the SNP case that it would not otherwise have had. If ever politicians made a rod for their own back …!

As front-bench spokesman on Scotland in the never-had-it-so-good early 1960s, his arguments were directed to planning the UK economy so as to share wealth around. In this he was pushing at an open door: Macmillan's Ministers were sympathetic to schemes for encouraging the Midlands car industry, for example, to move north, to Bathgate and Linwood.

As Scottish Secretary from 1974, Ross planned to carry this process on more dynamically and set to it with a will, at Westminster, in Scotland and behind the scenes. It was an idea that fitted into Labour's National Plan. Unfortunately, by this time, many economic bubbles were beginning to burst. The competitive power of the whole UK was in jeopardy, and the evidence accumulated that to tamper with natural market forces could be counter-productive. Successes included schemes run under the auspices of the Scottish Development Office and Highlands and Islands Development Board , but Ross felt increasingly frustrated and contemplated resignation as Scottish unemployment rose.

He was also, often, out of sympathy with the 1964–70 Cabinet mood: these were the Swinging Sixties and the ideals of the Permissive Society were not his. Nevertheless, he stayed the course and indeed came back to the Scottish Office during Wilson's next term in 1974–76. But he was becoming increasingly estranged from a new element in the party in Scotland, who saw him as sticking stubbornly to an outmoded style of socialism that was part of the UK scheme of things: Scottish devolution was now the vogue. Devolution was espoused by the Labour Government, but Ross was never enthusiastic. He was dropped from Cabinet when James Callaghan succeeded Wilson.

Before leaving the Commons, Ross was appointed the Queen's Representative, the Lord High Commissioner to the General Assembly of the Church of Scotland – a role that he and

Lady Ross fulfilled with real distinction. Created Lord Ross of Marnock in 1979, he remained an Opposition workhorse in the Lords until the last year of his life. But the abiding memory for Labour people is the spectacle of Willie Ross, on the last afternoon of Scottish conference, at Perth, Dunoon, Aberdeen, or Largs, making his rallying calls, laced with quotations from Burns, orated as only a man from Ayrshire can. He died on 10 June 1988.

Tam Dalyell MP

John Ruskin (1819–1900)

Ruskin was one of the most influential polymaths of his age. A distinguished artist and art historian, a formidable writer on social issues, a skilled author and teacher, he was considered one of the great if troubled minds of his era and influenced a vast array of British socialist thought. His socialism sprang from the same source as that of the ethical socialists like William Morris and the Christian Socialist F D Maurice, and although he spent his latter years fighting madness his ideas were at the heart of the early Labour movement.

Ruskin was born on 18 February 1819, the son and eventual heir of an extremely prosperous London sherry merchant. At Oxford University he won the Newdigate Prize for Poetry but failed to finish his degree thanks to the first of many bouts of mental illness. Yet by the age of 24 he was a successful art historian, publishing his robust and successful apologia for the painter John William Mallord Turner, *Modern Painters I*. In his subsequent volume *Modern Painters II* he championed the cause of the Pre-Raphaelites.

These books, together with *The Seven Lamps of Architecture* (1849), made him the most prominent of Victorian cultural critics, but they not only embraced aesthetic themes but incorporated views on social ethics, economics and politics. Extensive foreign travel helped frame Ruskin's aesthetic taste, but it was his close friendship with the Christian Socialists F D Maurice, Thomas Hughes and Charles Kinglsey, at whose Working Men's College he taught drawing from 1854 to 1858, that led him to his peculiar brand of socialism. His political message was simple, although it could often be couched in colourful language: as a political, personal or economic principle, greed was wrong. Society should be built on cooperation, not competition. From 1859 he devoted himself to political and economic thought and throughout the 1860s his ideas gained him a reputation as a fiery and uncompromising thinker. His books *Unto this Last* (1862) *Essays on Political Economy* (1862) and *Time and Tide* (1867) all reiterated his central beliefs in the dignity of labour, the need for a national education system, the importance of labour organisation to combat poverty and for a new social principle of cooperation. He also practiced what he preached, giving away a large proportion of his inherited wealth, building (with Oscar Wilde and others) a road from Oxford to Binsey and founding an agrarian communist group called the St George's Guild – which soon foundered.

Ruskin was far from happy in his personal life. In 1847 he unwisely married Euphemia Gray, but the marriage was doomed to fail and six years later it was acrimoniously annulled, as Effie went to live with Ruskin's friend, the painter John Everett Millais. His extravagant later love for the young Rose La Touche ended in similar distress.

In 1869 Ruskin was appointed the first Slade Professor of Art at Oxford and an Honorary

Fellow at Corpus Christi (despite his fourth-class degree). His lectures, with their mixture of art, polemic and rhetorical flourish, were immensely popular, but by 1872 his mental health was beginning to deteriorate. Severe collapse came in 1878 and although he was briefly reinstated as Slade Professor in 1883, the remaining years of his life were spent fighting extreme depression and mental illness – a battle he finally succumbed to in 1889, after which he never left a coma before dying on 20 January 1900.

Nevertheless between 1871 and 1884 he intermittently published *Fors Clavigera: Letters to the Workmen and Labourers of Great Britain*, and between 1885 and 1889 his complex autobiography *Praeterita*. Ruskin was never directly involved in the early labour or trade union movement, but the power of his arguments for socialism provided forceful inspiration for the early leaders of the movement and when he died he was both a national institution and an icon of socialist thought.

Chris Bryant MP

John Sankey (1st Viscount Sankey) (1866–1948)

A candidate for the post of Lord Chancellor need not demonstrate great political experience, so long as he has at least exhibited some competence in his practice of the law. John Sankey was certainly a very competent, if undistinguished, practitioner of law, but his practice of politics was rather more limited. This limitation was to prove both an advantage in his appointment as Lord Chancellor at the beginning of Macdonald's second tenure as Prime Minister and a supporting factor for his dismissal.

Sankey was content with his achievements as a lawyer and a judge. Politics held little interest until in late middle age chance dictated that they could no longer be avoided. Only then did he immerse himself in the study of politics, the result of which was a commitment to the Labour Party. It was a commitment that came at an unfortuitous time for the Party and like so many other figures, Sankey was to suffer from the split that arose from the formation of the National Government in 1931. This was to prevent Sankey from being the radical Lord Chancellor for which his earlier career had shown signs of potential.

John Sankey was born on 26 October 1866 in a small general shop owned by his father, Thomas, in Moreton-in-Marsh. When, in his early childhood, his father died, John's mother, Catalina, moved with her family to Cardiff. He was educated at the local Anglican school in Stacey Road before going to Lancing College, a small public school on the South Downs where his expenses were met by a local vicar. This ecclesiastical heritage was to remain with him for the rest of his life.

From Lancing, Sankey went on to Jesus College, Oxford, in 1885. There he achieved a second class degree in Modern History. The rest of his university record is noteworthy only for his interest in athletics.

He now had his mind set on a career at the Bar, joining the Middle Temple in 1889 and achieving a third class pass in the Bar exam two years later. He was called to the Bar in June 1892. His training was completed with a pupillage at the chambers of William Pickford, a commercial practice. Money was scarce, but Sankey was supported by a devoted family.

Sankey began to practice as a barrister on the South Wales circuit, an experience that eventually would inspire his political motivations. From 1897, he specialised in workers' compensation cases and thereby acquired a personal insight into the dangers of a miner's life. However, in 1907 Sankey moved back to London to further his career. He was duly made a KC in May 1909.

If he had any political leanings at this time they were probably those of an orthodox Conservative, a reflection that his ecclesiastical upbringing still had a stronger sway than his experience as a miners' lawyer. In 1910, he contested the LCC elections at Stepney for the 'Municipal Reform Party', a disguised term for London Conservatives. Sankey later referred to his election addresses as follies of youth. Sankey's legal career continued to flourish with his appointment as High Court judge in 1914. Nor was it hindered by the First World War, since he served as chairman of the Aliens Advisory Committee in 1915 and oversaw many of the cases resulting from the Easter Uprising in 1916. For this he received the CBE in 1917. Also in that year, Sankey produced a separate constitution for the Church of Wales that was to survive the Church's disestablishment in 1930.

It was through his appointment as chairman of the Commission to inquire into the coal industry in 1919 that Sankey unwittingly made his mark in politics. He often began meetings of the Commission with the words, *'Digon o waith a chalon I'w wnead'* (Plenty of work and a heart to do it). In his own report on the Commission's findings, he recommended nationalisation as the only viable remedy to the defects in the coal industry. The report was shelved by Lloyd George, who was dependent on the support of Conservative MPs, who in turn would now regard Sankey with suspicion.

Sankey now also had the more positive attention of the Labour leadership. MacDonald would probably have appointed Sankey as his Lord Chancellor in 1924 had Haldane not refused to join the Labour Cabinet except in that capacity. By the time Macdonald was called on again to form a government, Haldane was dead and Sankey was now a Lord Justice in the Court of Appeal, which made him an unsurprising choice as Lord Chancellor. He was given the Great Seal on 8 June 1929. His first speech in the Lords was one to introduce the Coal Mines Bill, in which he accepted minor reforms instead of his preference for nationalisation.

Perhaps his most lasting legacy was the setting up in 1934 of the Law Revision Committee to come up with proposals for legal reform on a regular basis. Consisting of judges, lawyers and academics, it later became the Law Commission. However, Sankey was also drawn into other, more controversial, issues outside the remit of his department, such as the chairmanship of the Round Table Conference on India. But the formation of the National Government in August 1931 was to have a debilitating impact on both himself and his office.

Sankey was a supporter of MacDonald and stayed in the Cabinet, but he was not to suffer the vilification that others in a similar position received. This was due to a combination both of his low profile within the Labour Party, and also of the respect for him within it. Beatrice Webb confided to her diary of 10 May 1930: 'Intrigue, manipulation and sophisty are altogether "out of bounds" for Sankey's pious soul … As a conversationalist he is slow, even a trifle ponderous; he has none of Haldane's wit and clever characterisation of men and women; he has no intellectual subtlety, no comprehension of metaphysics, no liking for abstruse science, technology or scholarship; neither does he claim to be a lover of music, or art, or poetry. He is just a plain man with goodness and sweet reasonableness writ large in his thoughts and feelings, in his words and acts.

Perhaps of all the members of the Cabinet he is the most trusted and the least feared by his colleagues; he may be ignored by some, he is not disliked by any.' But he was not highly regarded in the Cabinet that continued. Never confident at cabinet meetings, he would bring an atlas to discussions on foreign affairs so that he could look up countries that were referred to.

Nor did Sankey endear himself to the legal profession. He had to respond to a threatened rebellion by the judiciary in 1932, which objected to a 20 per cent cut in its pay resulting from the National Emergency Act 1931.

There were plenty of interested parties, therefore, when Sankey returned the Great Seal on 7 June 1935 as Baldwin became Prime Minister. This might have been expected on MacDonald's departure, but MacDonald himself made no defence of Sankey, preferring instead to sanction his dismissal in return for a cabinet post for his own son.

Sankey remained sympathetic to the Labour Party, in spite of the ordeals he suffered. However, he no longer played much of an active part in public life. His last speech was in February 1943, when he spoke in favour of the Beveridge Report. He died on 6 February 1948 and was buried in Moreton-in-Marsh only 200 yards from where he had been born.

John Sankey was a competent lawyer, judge and Lord Chancellor, but he had never had a strong inclination towards politics. His experience as a lawyer, however, taught him that he could not avoid political controversy if the injustices which he witnessed were to be put right. Coming to the Labour Party late in life insulated him to an extent from the hiatus of the 1930s, but he was also seen as expendable when events moved on. Yet throughout all this, Sankey was not bitter, being instead a man who was both mild and pious in the true meaning of the word.

Kevin Bonavia

Tom Sawyer (Lord Sawyer of Darlington) (1943–)

Next to the triumvirate of Kinnock, Blair and Brown, Tom Sawyer played probably the greatest individual part in the birth of New Labour. As Chairman of the NEC's Home Policy Committee and, subsequently, as the Party's General Secretary, Sawyer steered through changes to Labour's policies, organisation and constitution that made it the most successful political machine in Europe. His background as a left-wing trade union activist, combined with his quiet and unflashy personality, helped to give modernisation credibility with grassroots party members and trade union supporters.

Tom Sawyer was born on 12 May 1943 in Darlington, County Durham. Brought up in a terraced row behind the Cleveland Bridge Manufacturing Company, he attended Dodmire and Eastbourne schools, finishing at Darlington Technical. He left school at age 15 to become an engineering apprentice with Robert Stevenson and Hawthorne. 'Stivvies' were locomotive builders in a direct line of descent from Stevenson's *Rocket* doomed, like so much of British traditional industry, to disappear. When the firm closed down in 1963, Sawyer found himself, at age 20, unemployed and with a wife and baby to support.

He headed south and, through a friend, managed to find work as an Engineering Inspector with Lockhead Brakes in Leamington Spa. He was in the Midlands only two years, but it marked the start of his political and trade union activism. A communist AEU shop steward, 'with a beard like Karl Marx', took him under his wing, gave him books and pamphlets to read and made him a shop steward at the age of 22. Sawyer was impressed with his mentor's confident disputations with the management and nearly joined the Communist Party but was put off by the thought of having to 'go into a pub and talk to blokes about Marxist Leninism.'

With his wife homesick for the north, Sawyer moved back to Darlington where Chrysler had set up a new factory and found work as a Work Study Officer with Cummins Engines. Sawyer left the AEU because, as a traditional crafts union, they refused to organise the white-collar inspectors. Sawyer organised them instead into the white-collar section of the rival TGWU. There followed a long battle for recognition, and Sawyer was warned by his bosses that one day he would have to choose between his work and his trade unionism.

In the meantime, he rose to become Secretary of the local Trades Council and Ted Fletcher, local MP and an ex-engineer, told him he should join the Labour Party. Sawyer did so, though, he said later, 'not out of massive conviction'. Sawyer was restless, and when he saw a *Tribune* advert for a NUPE Officer, he took a pay cut of £500 a year (or a third of his salary) to get the job. According to colleagues, he soon started to wear the official NUPE uniform of black leather jacket and beard. (By the 1990s, the latter had been modernised to a designer stubble.) More importantly, Sawyer formed a partnership with the then Northern Regional Officer, Rodney Bickerstaff. Bickerstaff was the charismatic orator and leader; Sawyer's role was that of deputy and organiser. In 1975, Sawyer succeeded Bickerstaffe as Northern Regional Officer. As such, he played a front-line role during the 1979 'Winter of Discontent' but he rejected the more extreme tactics used elsewhere. 'I didn't have any of that,' he said later. 'We dug the graves and buried the dead in my region.'

From 1981 to 1994, Sawyer was Deputy General Secretary, first of NUPE, then of the new super-union, Unison. Again, acting as the organising chief executive under Bickerstaff and displaying the openness to new methods which were later to distinguish him, he took the leading players from NUPE, COHSE and NALGO to Cranfield Business School to learn how to manage the process of change in the new organisation. But he was still firmly identified with the Bennite left when he was elected to Labour's NEC in 1982.

His experience on the NEC was as important as Labour's continued electoral failure in persuading him of the virtues of modernisation. In 1984 a Benn/Heffer motion in the NEC for a general strike to support Scargill's striking miners struck Sawyer as the worst kind of gesture politics. With David Blunkett and other moderate trade union leaders, Sawyer helped to shape the emerging 'soft left' which both Brown and Blair were later to use as a springboard to power within the party. In 1985 Margaret Beckett and Tom Sawyer were sent to Liverpool to investigate the activities of the Militant Tendancy. Sawyer began by being sympathetic to the Militant-led council, but when he arrived he found ordinary workers, gardeners, refuse collectors, school caretakers complaining of a 'pyramid of lies and deceit ... threats and intimidation'. Sawyer moved the NEC resolution that led eventually to the expulsion of Militant.

After Labour's third successive election defeat, Tom Sawyer became Chair of the Home Policy Committee and immediately argued for a comprehensive and radical review of the policies which had lost the Party so much support. In an article in *The Times* he wrote that 'our task is to win at least three million new voters, most whom looked at what Labour offered and chose an alternative.' In internal memos, he identified unilateralism and Euroscepticism as policies which would have to go and argued that the party needed 'new approaches to enterprise and wealth creation'. His style as Chair of the committee was not to promote his own ideas, however, but to mould those of others into a consensus which he would then steer deftly through the party decision-making process.

When Tony Blair became leader of the Party in 1994, Tom Sawyer was his personal choice to become General Secretary. He was charged with ending the organisational 'shambles' in the Party and with building, according to Blair 'the best political fighting machine in this country.' Again, Sawyer looked to Cranfield Business School for advice, and this time took the NEC with him. He set out about dismantling the hierarchical party bureaucracy and replacing it instead with 'small groups of dedicated people assigned to specific tasks to do them well...that's how the best businesses work and that's how the Labour Party will have to work.' The new methods soon proved their worth during the review of parliamentary boundaries when a small team under David Gardner won a series of favourable judgements from the Parliamentary Boundaries Commission and helped swell Labour's majorities in 1997 and 2001.

Sawyer also played a key role in selling Blair's wider reforms to the party membership and to traditional 'Old Labour'. The campaign to change Clause 4 triggered the biggest ever consultation process inside the Party and delivered a striking victory for modernisation. Through it all, Sawyer projected an aura of calm common sense. He was clearly determined to drive through the modernising changes which would make Labour electable again but his reticence and discretion allowed him to do so with a minimum of bruised egos. His final act as General Secretary was to deliver 'Partnership in Power' a long-overdue transformation of the Party's policy-making. Instead of the gladiatorial clashes at the annual Party conference so familiar from the past, and so prone to generating into unseemly squabbles, Sawyer put in place a rolling review involving forums of party members reporting regularly to the Conference for approval.

In 1998, Sawyer stepped down as General Secretary and was appointed to the House of Lords as Lord Sawyer of Darlington. Previously a member of the Post Office Advisory Board, The Nurses and Midwives Whitley Council and Investors in People UK, he has kept busy serving as Chairman of Notting Hill Housing Association. He is a non-executive Director with the Britannia Building Society and with Reed Executives as well as a Visiting Professor at Cranfield Business School. An enthusiastic antiquarian book dealer and collector, he has one son from his first marriage and two sons from his second to Elizabeth, a former shop steward.

Calum MacDonald MP

Hugh Scanlon (Lord Scanlon) (1913–)

Hugh Scanlon was one of the most important and influential trade union leaders of the 1960s and 1970s, both in the country as a whole and in Labour Party politics. Scanlon as leader of the AUEW (Amalgamated Union of Engineering Workers), along with Jack Jones, leader of the TGWU, were said to run the country. Both were subject to unwarranted attention and vitriolic attack by the British media and were nicknamed the 'terrible twins'. Whilst subject to many taunts and the surveillance of the security services, Scanlon refused to be driven from his path.

Born in Australia on 26 October 1913, Hugh Parr Scanlon came to the UK at the age of two. Raised in a Labour family, his grandparents were members of both the Labour Party and the Co-op, and they involved him in weekend educational schools from the age of 16. His formal education took place at Stretford Elementary School (Manchester), and on leaving he took on an engineering apprenticeship. Serving his apprenticeship not only taught him to be an instrument-maker but also enabled him to become involved in sports activities such as swimming, boxing and football which, Scanlon believes, broadened his vision and helping him in later activities.

He soon became involved in trade union activities as a shop steward-convenor with the AEU (Amalgamated Engineering Union) in the giant Metro-Vickers factory. Rising through the AEU's ranks, using his experience and reputation as a shop steward, he went on to be the union's divisional organiser in Manchester (a full-time, elected position) from 1947 to 1963, when he was elected to the union's Executive Council (1963–1967). But it was on being elected President of the union in 1968 (with talk of communist connections) that he really came to the attention of the public.

Scanlon's election marked a leftward shift in the leadership of Britain's big trade unions. Scanlon had been a member of the Communist Party (1936–55) and even stood for the party in Stretford in 1945. In contrast to their predecessors, Scanlon and the new generation of union leaders were often openly critical and used their 'block vote' power at Party conferences to voice their dissent or even defeat the leadership. Scanlon had never been a Labour activist and was brought to power on a wave of shop-floor militancy. He continued to speak at conferences held by the Institute for Workers' Control well into the 1970s.

The first major confrontation with the leadership of the Labour Party came in 1968 with their announcement of the *In Place of Strife* proposals. Secretary of State for Employment and Productivity, Barbara Castle, suggested reform of the trade union laws which would impose such concepts as compulsory strike ballots. Scanlon, along with others, was fundamentally opposed to the reforms, and in a number of meetings with Wilson (then Prime Minister) and Castle made his position quite clear. Trade union opposition, along with a failure by Wilson and Castle to build support within the Labour Party, doomed the reforms to failure. Scanlon had taken on the Government and won. Wilson's comment, 'Get your tanks off my lawn, Hughie', was intended to be a threat to Scanlon not to interfere with Government, and it proved to be a hollow one.

This form of opposition continued in the 1970s with the fight against the Industrial Relations Act (1970), which the Conservative Heath Government introduced. The intricate proposals confused many, but the unions were particularly hostile to the financial damages which they would face in the event of involvement in unlawful disputes. Scanlon believes that the unions should have sought greater unity when opposing the Act. His AUEW led the opposition, whilst others paid lip service to opposition to the Act but in reality conformed to its requirements. The AUEW refused to pay £75,000 demanded of it by the National Industrial Relations Court and this non-compliance, along with the opposition of other unions, led to the Act's successful repeal.

Following these years of Government-union conflict, the Labour Party and the Trades Union Congress (TUC) sought to 'prove' that the unions would work for the benefit of the country and that the Labour Party was the only political party that could ensure this. The signing of the Social Contract was a landmark in trade union politics, and Scanlon was crucial to its design. Whilst initially opposed to a wages policy, Scanlon, and other trade union leaders, saw the threat which inflation and economic collapse would pose to their members. A Social Contract appeared the best way forward.

This was the height of the so-called 'beer and sandwiches' era of British politics, when trade union leaders were said to call around to No 10 Downing Street to discuss the running of the country. Whilst this was always some way short of the truth, the Social Contract was central to the Labour Government's policies. Whilst the unions restrained their pay demands, the Government delivered improvements in the 'social' wage such as increased maternity provisions and better protection from unfair dismissal. Scanlon and Jack Jones backed the wages policy and worked with the Government to periodically renegotiate the Contract so that it could react to pressures and continue to function effectively.

A member of the National Economic Development Council (the 'Neddy 6'), which brought union leaders and leading Government figures together from 1971, he served on the TUC General Council (1968–78) and its Economic Committee (1968–78). He was made Chairman of the Engineering Industry Training Board (1975–82), the first time that a union boss had been put in charge; Vice President of the International Metalworkers' Federation (1969–78); President of the European Metalworkers' Federation (1974–78); member of the Metrication Board (1973–78); member of the NEB (1977–79); and member of the Government Committee of Inquiry into the Teaching of Maths in Primary and Secondary Schools in England and Wales (1978–).

Scanlon (in 1978) and Jones retired from their respective positions around the same time and with new leaders in charge of the AUEW and the TGWU, the Social Contract collapsed into the Winter of Discontent and the fall of the government. The new leaders were less able to 'control' their membership. Scanlon became a peer in 1979. One of Scanlon's final acts as President of the AUEW was to upset many on the left and to bring into even further disrepute the block vote at conference. Against the wishes of his delegation, Scanlon 'forgot' to vote for the measure on the mandatory reselection of MPs (opposed by the Party leadership). This upset many – in his own union, the wider labour movement and the Party – appearing, as it did to those critics, to demonstrate an arrogance and misuse of power.

From being a leading left-winger, often in conflict with the Labour leadership, Scanlon, in the 1970s, became more supportive. Initially critical of the Attlee Government, he later recognised the good in its nationalisation programme (railways, mines, gas, electricity). The anti-trade-union legislation and privatisations in the 1980s made him even more pro-Labour. Ill-health has blighted Scanlon's time in the Lords, limiting his contributions. He retired, with his wife Nora, by whom he had two daughters, to live on the Kent coast.

Dr. Stuart Thomson

Arthur Scargill (1938–)

Arthur Scargill, the miners' leader, came to represent a generation of militant trade unionists whose actions in the 1980s were a direct challenge to the authority of Margaret Thatcher's hard-line government committed to curbing trade union power. The trial of strength was un-equal, and doomed to failure. Scargill's resilient ego was unbruised, but the labour movement was permanently weakened.

'King Arthur', as he was called by admirers and critics alike, first came to prominence in 1972 at what became known as the Battle of Saltley Gate. The miners were engaged in their first national strike since 1926, for bigger pay. Scargill was a young official of the National Union of Mineworkers at Woolley Colliery in South Yorkshire. He claimed credit for the shut-down, after three days of mass picketing, of the Saltley coke depot in Birmingham, vital for fuel supplies in the city.

This triumph over inadequate policing shook the civil authorities. It set in train a review of strategy that eventually outlawed secondary picketing and put the unions in a legal straitjacket from which they have yet to emerge. For Scargill, it was simply 'the greatest day of my fife.'

Arthur Scargill was, born on 11 January 1938 in a two-room miner's house in Worsborough Dale, a pit village outside Barnsley. His father Harold was a miner, and a devout communist. His mother Alice worked in a bobbin mill and was an equally devout Christian. He was an only child, very close to his mother, and her death when he was eighteen years old devastated the young miner, who had followed his father down the pit at the age of 15.

He also followed his father into the Communist Party, standing unsuccessfully as a CP candidate for the local council and visiting Russia, Hungary and Cuba. He also became active in the NUM, leading his first strike as a teenager. In 1961 he married Anne Harper, a miner's daughter, and soon after he quit the CP, offering various (and sometimes conflicting) reasons. His real motive was to climb the greasy pole of union politics at a right-wing Labour pit, and the sacrifice paid off in 1964 when he became Woolley's delegate to the powerful Yorkshire coalfield executive. He was also in charge of the colliery's home coal scheme, which took him off the coal face.

Scargill's big chance came shortly after Saltley, when he beat off opposition from left and right to become the Yorkshire area compensation agent, a key job servicing tens of thousands of miners and their families. His forensic skills and hard-driving application were much admired, and the wide-ranging nature of the post made him the best-known miner in the biggest area of the NUM, well-placed to succeed the ageing national president, Joe Gormley, an outstanding leader and negotiator. He was elected to the Yorkshire area presidency in 1973.

A second national strike in 1974, which precipitated the downfall of Edward Heath's Conservative government, consolidated his position, and when Gormley manipulated the rulebook to ensure that his communist deputy, Mick McGahey, leader of the Scottish miners, did not succeed, Scargill assumed the mantle of heir-apparent. He was confirmed in that role, with some reservations, by the union's influential left-wing machine, which brought together Labour and communist activists, By now, he was a Labour Party member, though restive and truculent.

On Gormley's retirement in 1981, Scargill won by a landslide, taking 70 per cent of the votes cast by more than 200,000 miners. The union had just won a confrontation with Margaret Thatcher over pit closures. Her relatively new, untried government was not ready for the all-out conflict with Scargill that she knew, and intended, would come. Scargill moved the NUM head office from London to Sheffield, losing many of the union's loyal staff in the process, and set in motion a personality cult that outlasted the collapse of the industry and the union.

Twice, he failed to take the union into a national strike via a pithead ballot, and in March 1984 he began a rolling stoppage in Yorkshire against colliery closures, which spread across the country through vigorous, and sometimes brutal, unlawful secondary picketing. He almost brought the industry to a standstill, but the National Coal Board's new chairman, the Scots-American capitalist Iain MacGregor, handpicked by Thatcher after a stint at British Steel, doggedly wore down the dispute by a mixture of bribes to strike-breaking pitmen and resort to the new industrial relations law. The NUM was eventually sequestrated, heavily fined and put into receivership. Scargill, having refused to ask for help from the TUC, now found only token support from other unions. Amid great hardship, the strike dragged on for a year before petering out in a welter of mutual recrimination. Many miners lost their mortgaged homes. Scargill bought Treelands, the second-largest house in his native village, under the name of his daughter's fiancé.

The so-called Great Strike destroyed the NUM. Nottinghamshire miners, most of whom worked through the dispute, split to form the Union of Democratic Mineworkers. Pit closures accelerated to terrifying proportions, which Scargill claimed showed that he had been right. Then, in 1990, the *Daily Mirror* accused Scargill of various financial irregularities during the strike, involving money from Libya and Russia. A union inquiry, chaired by Gavin Lightman QC, found 'a number of misapplications of funds and breaches of duty.' A prosecution by the government-appointed Certification Officer failed, but Scargill was compelled by the executive to repay to the NUM funds of more than £700,000 scattered in bank accounts around Europe. In 1992, the Inland Revenue agreed that the secret accounts set up to avoid sequestration and receivership were valid trusts and not the property of the union, and the waters closed over the scandal.

Scargill virtually disappeared from the public gaze until 1992, when the Tories announced a final round of pit closures prior to privatisation of the industry. Unaccountably, public opinion rose up in defiance of John Major's new government. The NUM leader was at the head of a 100,000-strong protest march through London. Industry Secretary Michael Heseltine backed down, offering huge subsidies to coal. The money was never spent. After the furore died down, the pits closed, only twenty surviving into privatisation.

Despite the consummate failure of his industrial and political strategy, Scargill had one trick left in his book. In 1994, when Labour ditched the nationalising Clause IV, he formed his own party, the Socialist Labour Party, fielding candidates in the general election in 1997. Scargill stood against a Conservative turncoat, Alan Howarth, in Newport, Mon, and saved his deposit with 1,951 votes. Subsequently, the SLP was riven by internal conflict as Scargill sought to impose his personal authority. He stood again in 2001, against Peter Mandelson in Hartlepool, taking only 912 votes and coming fourth. Throughout the campaign, he repeated his mantra: 'I was right'. His tragedy was that he believed it.

Paul Routledge

Ted Shackleton (Lord Shackleton) (1911–94)

Ted Shackleton was the youngest of the children of the famous explorer Sir Ernest Shackleton, who led the National Antarctic Expedition two years before Ted's birth on 15 July 1911. Ted

(Edward Arthur Alexander) Shackleton never really got to know his father well, as he continued on expedition during much of Ted's early life and died on board ship off South Georgia when Ted was 11.

As a result, he was largely raised by his mother and grandmother, attending Radley College, followed by Magdalen College, Oxford. Whilst he naturally gravitated towards exploration, determined not to follow exactly his father's path he became a surveyor on the Oxford University Expedition to Sarawak in 1932, which became well known due to the first known ascent of Mount Mulu. Spurred by this success, he organised and acted as surveyor on another Oxford expedition, to Ellesmere Island in the Arctic, in 1934–5. His book based on his experiences, *Arctic Journeys*, published in 1937, became a best-seller. In 1938 he married Betty Homan.

He worked as a Talks producer with the BBC until signing up with the RAF at the outbreak of war. Serving in intelligence, he worked on anti-U-boat planning and with naval and military intelligence in the Air Ministry. Before the war ended, Shackleton fought hopeless Epsom & Ewell for Labour at the general election, and the fame that came with his surname helped in his selection at short notice to fight the November 1945 Bournemouth by-election which saw the return to Parliament of Brendan Bracken.

He did sufficiently well in increasing Labour's vote to be selected to fight the Preston by-election the following year, when he defeated Harmar Nicholls by 6,471 votes. This proved to be a precarious seat – Shackleton won in 1950 by 149 votes, in 1951 by only 16, and lost by 474 in 1955. During the Labour government he served as PPS to George Strauss as Minister of Supply from 1949–50, and to Herbert Morrison from 1950–51 when he was Lord President of the Council and Foreign Secretary. It was during this time that he became close to and advanced the cause of the young Harold Wilson, which was to stand him in good stead in the future.

Once out of the Commons, he wrote books including a biography of Fridtjof Nansen, who was the League of Nations High Commissioner for Refugees, an explorer, oceanographer and Nobel Peace Prize winner. Shackleton took a job as a senior executive and Director of John Lewis. When it became clear that he was unlikely to win Preston again, he accepted the offer to become one of the first life peers in 1958.

Back in government following Labour's 1964 election victory, he served as Minister for Defence for the RAF from 1964 to 1967, Minister Without Portfolio 1967–68 and Paymaster-General 1968, during which time he was also head of the mission to southern Arabia which led to the withdrawal from Aden and Southern Arabian independence. Wilson appointed him to the Cabinet in 1968 and he became Leader of the House of Lords and Minister in charge of the Civil Service Department.

As Lords leader he had two big responsibilities – civil service reform following the recommendations of the Fulton committee and House of Lords reform. On the latter, he reached agreement with Lords Carrington and Jellicoe on the Tory side, but was defeated in the Commons by the cross-party alliance led by Michael Foot and Enoch Powell.

Shackleton's difficulties over Lords reform showed the problem with attempting to remove the hereditary peers at the same time as instituting further reform and were central to informing the two-stage approach later adopted by Tony Blair's government.

He continued as Opposition Leader in the Lords during the Heath government, whilst also returning to his first love as President of the Royal Geographical Society in 1971–4. He worked in various senior board roles with the RTZ Corporation between 1973 and 1983, but was also retained as one of the 'great and good' of the British Establishment, becoming a Knight of the Garter in 1974. He was Chairman of the British Standards Institution, Chairman of the Political Honours Scrutiny Committee from 1976 until 1992, and conducted the 1978 review of UK Anti-Terrorist legislation.

But one of his most famous roles was as a rather prophetic, if lone, voice as Chairman of the Economist Intelligence Unit Economic Survey of the Falkland Islands. Reporting in 1976, he concluded that the islands' population 'is firm in its desire to remain British' and recognised the opportunities offered by economic development opportunities and an extended airfield. These were, however, rejected by the government. Following his post-war second report in 1982, the government eagerly took up his recommendations. The Islands repaid his commitment to them when in 1988 he became the second person to receive the freedom of Port Stanley after Margaret Thatcher. He died on 22 September 1994 in Lymington, Hampshire.

Matthew Seward

George Bernard Shaw (1856–1950)

In standard histories of the Labour Party Shaw is all but forgotten, but from the late 1890s through to the end of the 1920s he was possibly the most nationally famous and influential of socialist propagandists, not merely a close friend of Beatrice and Sidney Webb but someone they regarded (somewhat bravely) as their mouthpiece. Shaw acknowledged Sidney Webb as his mentor and, with typical humour, said that 'all I could do for Webb was to beat the big drum in front of his booth'. There was some self-deception on both sides, but not too much. Shaw was both thinker and agitator. If intellectuals in the inter-war period typically were (or thought to be) socialist, Shaw was as much the cause as either Methodism or Marx.

He was born in Dublin in 1856 to a drunken father in a genteel-poor household filled by his aspiring, frustrated mother with poor musicians and writers (often poor in both senses). After a few years of clerical jobs, he followed her to London in 1876. There, overcoming a great shyness with greater braggadocio, he gradually established himself as a well-know music, theatre and even art critic. After a brief spell of Hyndman's pilfered Marxism (the time Shaw was seen in the British Museum Library with *Das Kapital and* Wagner's *Rheingold* open side by side on his desk), he polemicised against the labour theory of values and joined the Fabian Society in 1884, attracting the attention of the Webbs. By 1889 he was the editor of the famous *Fabian Essays in Socialism*; then followed two decades of astounding creative activity that produced his first plays and *The Quintessence of Ibsenism* of 1891. His advocacy of Ibsen is a clue to the character of his advocacies for socialism. The theatre should and could raise social problems (of poverty, financial dishonesty, infidelity, social disease and public health) that polite literature ignored. And this theatre could reach a middle-class and professional audience to arouse a social conscience. So far so close to Fabianism, but the technique he used in the plays he carried over into the famous Prefaces (polemical, provocative tracts) and into street-corner oratory and then – as he became more and more in demand – into public lectures widely and fully reported in the press. The technique in the early plays was, as with Ibsen, to have naturalistic characters in naturalistic settings, but who became involved in or raised issues normally re-pressed, and did so with a dramatic and provocative exaggeration to catch the imagination of a potentially radical middle class. To shock could also be to entertain, but never, unlike the satiric cynics of today, for its own sake.

This makes him difficult to pin down. The imagination and the badinage could allow of-fensive things to be said that most of the audience would not take fully seriously – clearly 'over the top', as we would say. But his point was to get them thinking at all. Could the poor really 'not afford morality' (as when Mr Doolittle sold his daughter for phonetic experiment); or if 'literal equality of incomes, and I mean just that' was impossible, were the present gross in-equalities justifiable? His vegetarianism was genuine and resolute but his adoption of hand-woven tweeds as a rational costume, half bohemian and half 'New Age', was probably more to keep his hard-won notoriety; certainly it left him open to H G Wells' gibe, when they quar-relled bitterly over the direction of the Fabian Society (Shaw then the gradualist and Wells the extremist), that 'for most people the simple life is prohibitively expensive'.

Sixty years later Shaw boasted to Kingsley Martin that he had helped the Webbs sweep the 'Perfect Lifers' and 'all the nonsense and bohemian anarchism' out of the Fabian Society, which was true enough; but he made an exception of himself. For obviously Fabianism was a some-what dull doctrine to catch the imagination of a potentially radical middle class. Shaw knew that 'infiltration and permeation' were effective for immediate reforms but hardly warmed the blood, although equally if the tactics of the trade union and working-class labour movements of the time were 'to organise and agitate', it was only the latter that interested him. He had lit-tle contact with the trade union movement and its leaders, though he was feted and tolerated in society.

Perhaps his practice of a cult of personality, albeit for egalitarian ends, coupled with the ad-mitted elitism of the Fabian Society, eventually betrayed him in the late 1920s into his own ver-sion of Carlyle's 'great man' theory of history, his Bergsonian twist to Darwinian evolutionary theory. The worst of this was his period of admiration for Mussolini, one rhetorician falling for another man's futuristic rhetoric. But even in *Man and Superman* it was clear that the force for the future lay not in the talkative intellectuals who hogged the scene, but in their chauffeur, Henry Striker, who went to 'the Poly' in the evenings. Interesting to recall, both Shaw and Wells saw 'the Poly' (the Regent Street Polytechnic as was) as the model for progress: a techni-cal education for potential working-class leaders and, even more important (as with Orwell), the lower middle class, whose allegiance and leadership would determine whether socialism or fascism would come to dominate. By the 1930s he was preaching the case for a kind of benevo-lent autocracy of a socialist elite. By his death in 1950 he was forgotten as a political influence even if famed as a man of the theatre, albeit also someone who saw the use of theatrical meth-ods in political persuasion. Even his elitism, the flirtation with eugenics and heroic leadership, may simply have been coat-trailing for the old 'inevitability' of gradualism, expressed in his Preface to the 1908 edition of *Fabian Essays*:

> In 1885 the Fabian Society, amid the jeers of the catastrophists, turned its back on the barricades and made up its mind to turn heroic defeat into prosaic success. We can set ourselves two definite tasks: first, to provide a parliamentary programme for a Prime

Minister converted to socialism as Peel was converted to Free Trade; and second, to make it as easy and matter-of-fact for the ordinary respectable Englishman to be a Socialist as to be a Liberal or a Conservative'.

The key biography on Shaw is Michael Holyroyd, *Bernard Shaw* (3 vols, 1988).

Professor Bernard Crick

Rt Hon Tom Shaw MP CBE (1872–1938)

As Minister of Labour in Ramsay MacDonald's Cabinet of 1924, Tom Shaw was in the front line in the battle with unemployment. There were some notable achievements: unemployment insurance benefits were raised for both men and women (though men still received a sixth more) and the children's allowance was doubled. In addition, the conditions of receiving un-covenanted benefit were liberalised, ending the three-week 'gap' after twelve weeks of uncov-enanted benefit, during which benefits were withheld to deter idleness, whilst the disqualifica-tion from benefit of those 'not genuinely seeking work' was introduced. Shaw also introduced a Bill to ratify the provisions of the 1919 International Labour Organisation's Hours of Labour Convention. The Convention incorporated statutory rights to an eight-hour day and forty-eight-hour working week in industry, and fittingly had been adopted by the ILO's 1919 Wash-ington conference at the recommendation of a committee chaired by Shaw himself. Had this Bill not been lost on the fall of the government, it would probably have joined measures such as the extension of unemployment benefit to 14–16 year-olds in being a casualty of the gov-ernment's minority status. However, the government's main objective was not just to tackle the symptoms of unemployment but to cure the cause – in modern parlance, to get people off welfare and into work – and in this Shaw failed.

Shaw initially chaired the unemployment sub-committee of the Cabinet committee on housing and unemployment under Sidney Webb. Though it convened frequently, it proposed little and concluded that the major unemployment in the shipbuilding, engineering and cot-ton textiles industries could not be cured apart from by a revival in world trade. When, on 30 July, proposals were announced by Snowden for arterial road-building, afforestation, a massive electrification programme (including the construction of a national grid) and a feasibility study for a Severn barrage, it was because the Cabinet had lost patience with Shaw's committee and reconstituted a new and more powerful unemployment committee under Snowden.

On 10 March, taunted mercilessly by his Commons critics, Shaw had been forced to admit his failure to bring forward schemes to reduce unemployment additional to those already ini-tiated by previous governments: 'Yes, they have been agreed to by the previous Government. Does anybody think that we can produce schemes like rabbits out of our hat?' So far as finding work for unemployed women was concerned, he declared himself 'baffled'. On 29 May, the Commons debated Tom Shaw's salary and such was the government's fear of defeat that MacDonald decided personally to wind up in the debate for the government.

Born in 1872 at Colne, Lancashire, his father was a local miner and he went to elementary schools in the town before starting half-time work in the cotton mills at the tender age of ten. He continued his education at night school and technical classes, developing an interest in languages which would stand him in good stead when in later life he would be involved in international affairs. By the age of 21 he had become an official, and subsequently secretary, of the Colne Workers Association. Soon afterwards he became secretary of the Northern Counties Textile Trades Federation and joined the Central Executive of the Amalgamated Weavers Association. In 1911 he became secretary of the International Textile Workers, and during the Great War he served as Director of National Services in the West Midlands Region. In 1921 he became, with Friedrich Adler, the joint secretary of the Second International.

Elected MP for Preston in 1918, he served as a Whip and as one of the Labour members of the Holman Gregory Committee on Workmen's compensation before being elected to Labour's shadow cabinet in eleventh place out of twelve (1923). After the fall of the first Labour government he was re-elected to the shadow cabinet, this time in seventh place, and returned briefly to his role as secretary of the Second International before in 1925 he resigned to return to his earlier post of secretary of the International Association of Textile Workers. In 1929, having rejoined the shadow cabinet in 1927, he was appointed Secretary of State for War in MacDonald's second government.

His experience in international affairs failed to translate well to the War Office and his apparent lack of interest in his departmental brief undermined his credibility both amongst the military and his departmental officials. In his memoirs, *Lead with the Left*, his then junior minister Manny Shinwell recollected Shaw as a 'somewhat portly gentleman' who 'was inclined to be somewhat indolent and, indeed, remarked to some of my colleagues that he "wore the feathers and Shinwell did the work"'.

Although in 1931 he supported MacDonald at the moment of crisis, he declined MacDonald's offer for him to continue in post in the National Government and within days announced his intention to retire from Parliament at the next election. He died in 1938.

Greg Rosen

Hartley Shawcross (Lord Shawcross)   (1902–)

Sir Hartley Shawcross is often remembered, thanks to a clever invention by Bernard Levin in the 1950s, as 'Sir Shortly Floorcross' because of his tenuous moorings in the Labour Party. He never actually physically crossed the floor of the House of Commons, but he became alienated from the Labour Party during the latter half of his long and productive life.

Hartley William Shawcross was born on 4 February 1902 in Giessen, Germany, where his father John Shawcross was in post as Professor of English Literature. Hartley was among the first individual members of the Labour Party. He canvassed in Wandsworth during the 1918 general election and served as ward secretary while at Dulwich College and as election agent for Lewis Silkin in 1922. He acted as interpreter for the British delegation to the first post-war meeting of the Socialist International in Geneva, and was persuaded by Herbert Morrison to start a legal career to facilitate his political ambitions. His first career was as a barrister; he trained at Gray's Inn and was called to the Bar in 1925, and appeared in celebrated cases such as the Gresford Colliery disaster inquiry in 1934 and several murder cases, taking Silk in 1939. He married Alberta Shyvers in 1924, although their life together was blighted by her ill health. She died in 1943. He married his second wife, Joan Mather, in 1944, and they had three children, including the journalist William Shawcross.

Hartley was Regional Commissioner for the North West in 1942–45, was knighted in 1945, and was approached by both Labour and the Conservatives to stand in the post-war election. He accepted the Labour nomination for the safe seat of St Helens, Lancashire – Labour in every election since 1918 except 1931 – which he duly won in July 1945 and represented until his resignation in 1958. His brother Christopher won Widnes

Shawcross's Labour career was a singular product of the hope and idealism that surrounded the victory of 1945; he was angered by the gap between wealth and poverty and impatient at the inefficiency and even corruption he encountered in private business, and had faith that Labour could do something about it. His legal expertise made him the obvious choice for Attorney General when the Attlee government was formed. Among his responsibilities was acting as the British prosecuting counsel at the Nuremberg War Crimes Tribunal, which was the most notable episode of his legal career. He has retained an interest in international and human rights law, which he played an important part in developing at Nuremberg.

As a front-bench speaker in the Commons, Shawcross spoke in the forceful style of the law courts, which occasionally got him into trouble. He is much quoted as having boasted in 1946 that 'We are the Masters Now', when introducing the bill repealing the 1927 Trade Union Act, but like many such oft-cited remarks it is recorded inaccurately: he actually said that 'We are the masters at the moment' in response to a challenge from Churchill.

Shawcross occasionally prosecuted criminal cases as Attorney General, including William 'Lord Haw-Haw' Joyce and Haigh, the acid bath murderer, but his role in the Lynskey Tribunal of 1948 into allegations of corruption at the Board of Trade was most notable. His questioning of the accused minister, John Belcher, was brutal, although he made little headway with the confidence trickster Sidney Stanley. Shawcross, with Attlee very much behind him, enforced the puritanical standards of conduct expected in the Labour government of 1945–51.

After the resignation of Nye Bevan Shawcross enjoyed a brief period in the Cabinet, as President of the Board of Trade from 24 April 1951. He had hoped to be appointed Foreign Secretary after Bevin, but Morrison took on the post instead to the detriment of his historical reputation. He started work on ending Resale Price Maintenance but left the Board of Trade before it could be accomplished.

Hartley Shawcross was one of the stars of Labour's very first Party Election Broadcast. He appeared with Christopher Mayhew (the future careers of Labour's early television figureheads are diverse – see also Woodrow Wyatt and Tony Benn). The broadcast presented two articulate, upper-middle-class Labour MPs talking about their commitment to Labour's values. Mayhew addressed the camera: 'You may, for instance, be wondering how somebody so obviously well-off, well-educated, well-dressed as Sir Hartley Shawcross comes to be in the Labour Party. What is your answer to that, Hartley?' Shawcross replied: 'My answer to Christopher Mayhew is "Why on earth not?" It may be surprising to have a working man amongst the Tories. But in the Labour movement there are tens of thousands like me.'

The broadcast was something of a triumph, but it did not bring the middle class flocking back to Labour despite the well-educated, well-dressed advocacy of Sir Hartley. In the party civil wars of the 1950s Shawcross was a partisan of the right wing, and was regarded by some commentators as a potential leader, but he was increasingly discontented with party politics and although a regular speaker at Labour weekend meetings he was an irregular attender in the House of Commons. On returning to opposition Shawcross resumed practising, prolifically, as a barrister, but in 1957–58 he stepped down both from the Bar and from parliament to concentrate on family life and a steadily expanding set of commercial interests. Among his many directorships were Shell, EMI, Morgan Guaranty, *The Observer* and Upjohn & Co; he also served on bodies such as the British Hotel and Restaurant Association and the Press Council. He was appointed Baron Shawcross of Friston in the second set of life peerages in 1959 and took up a position on the cross-benches in the House of Lords; he allowed his Labour Party membership to lapse.

Shawcross did not particularly approve of the social changes of the 1960s, condemning the prurience and sexual content of the press during the Profumo affair and the 'malaise' of society and popular culture: 'The new morality ... is too often the old immorality condoned.'

Never an admirer of Harold Wilson, Shawcross became highly critical of the record of the Labour government in 1964–70 and was reported as calling for Wilson's resignation in January 1968. When the parlour game of forming a potential 'national' or 'non-party' coalition was played in the late 1960s and early 1970s, Shawcross always seemed to be in play. He became close to Cecil King, the deposed head of the Mirror Group and an inveterate anti-Wilson plotter, and considered a joint statement during the 1970 election that a Labour victory would be an economic disaster. During the early 1970s he was a sought-after source for *Private Eye* and others about Wilson's career.

Shawcross suffered a cruel loss in January 1974, when his wife was killed in a riding accident. After 1974 he continued City and commercial activities on a modest level, including being Chairman of Thames Television and running the City panel which investigated takeovers. He intervened occasionally in the Lords, including helping to impede the passage of the War Crimes Act in 1991. In 1995 he published his memoirs, *Life Sentence* (London: Constable). Although an important minister in the Labour government of 1945–51, the political career of Sir Hartley Shawcross was rather an interlude between the Bar and business.

Lewis Baston

Malcolm Shepherd (Lord Shepherd of Spalding)   (1918–2001)

One of the few Labour hereditary peers and certainly one of the latest, Malcolm Shepherd was the recipient of a hereditary peerage when his father, created in 1946, died in 1954. During the Lords Reform Act of 1998, whilst Hereditary Peers lost the right to sit and vote in the Lords, living Hereditary Peers who had been Leaders of the Lords were given, in addition to their hereditary title, a Life Peerage. Thus Malcolm Sheperd became Lord Shepherd of Spalding. During his Ministerial life he had more than once moved in unconventional ways up or down the slippery pole of advancement and he has the enviable record of having been both the Government Chief Whip as well as the Leader of the House of Lords, amongst other distinguished offices of state.

Malcolm Newton Shepherd was born on 27 September 1918. His father had been the

National Agent of the Labour Party and had been created a peer by Clement Attlee in 1946. Earlier he had been the Labour Agent in Blackburn to the nationally famous Philip Snowden, and when Churchill sent for Attlee as the Leader of the Labour Party in 1940 with the request that Labour enter into a wartime coalition, it was with Malcolm Shepherd's father that he negotiated the terms. Entering the House of Lords, he quickly established his qualities as an organiser and disciplinarian and became the Government Chief Whip, and with it the style and title of the Captain of the Yeomen of the Guard and the Captain of the Honourable Corps of the Gentlemen at Arms – in other words, the King's Bodyguard. Malcolm was not to be outdone, and so in due time he also achieved the same status from 1964 until July 1967, having been an Opposition Whip from 1959 to 1964. He had been educated at Friends School, Saffron Walden and in 1941 he married Alison. They had two sons, Graeme George, born 1951, and Douglas Newton, born 1954.

Malcolm Shepherd served in the Royal Army Service Corps and saw service in North Africa, (El Alamein), Sicily and Italy, ending the war with the rank of Captain. The detail of his service is shrouded in mystery for he became a member of what was called 'Special Services' – real cloak and dagger stuff. The period from 1964 when Labour came to power under the leadership of Harold Wilson was a testing time. Hitherto when Labour was in power (1945 to 1951) the nature of the House of Lords was substantially different. The House had to adjust to the fact that it was no longer the Upper House to a Lower House invariably controlled by the Conservatives, and the small band of Labour peers had to fashion their own modus operandi, creating for instance the 'Salisbury-Addison Convention' , a convention agreed between Lord Salisbury, the Leader of the Conservatives, and his Labour opposite number Lord Addison, which recognised that measures which had been in the Labour Manifesto would not be automatically opposed at Second Reading when they came to the Lords.

When Malcolm Shepherd first entered the Lords in 1954 there were about 25 to 30 Labour peers. When in January 1964 he became Opposition Chief Whip on the death of Lord Lucan, there were not many more, but they all had great experience both in and out of politics. Wilson made him the Government Chief Whip in 1964, and he had already come to terms with the fact that it was the Tories who ran the Lords regardless of who was in Government. Thus he made a successful job of working with them on many issues, and by trimming legislation he was able to deliver most, if not all, of the Government's business. He became a Privy Counsellor in 1965 and Minister of State at the Commonwealth Affairs Office in July 1967 and, on the merger of his department with the Foreign Office, at the Foreign and Commonwealth Office from October 1968 until Labour's defeat in 1970. During this period he endeared himself to the citizens of Gibraltar by writing into their Constitution that Britain would never give up sovereignty over Gibraltar without the consent of the citizens – taking a positive stance in the uneasy situation that then existed with Spain. Thereafter whenever he visited Gibraltar he received a hero's welcome.

He played a reduced role on Labour's front bench after the election (though he was nominally Deputy Lords Opposition Leader) and returned to a successful business career he had started earlier. However, when Harold Wilson returned to No10 in 1974 he sent for him and made him Leader of the Lords. He had given commitments to return to his business interests on a particular time-scale, and so he left office in mid-1976 when he was succeeded by Fred Peart. His non-Parliamentary career included the chairmanships of Mitchell Cotts, Fielding Brown and Finch, Cheque Point International, the Sterling Group of Companies, and a Directorship of Sum Hung Kai Ltd. He was the chairman of the Civil Service Pay Research Unit Board 1978–81 and the National Bus Company 1979–84.

During the intervening years he grew into an elder statesman both within the Labour ranks but also within the House of Lords. He had established happy relationships over more that 30 years with leading Tories, like Lords Carrington, St Albyn, Whitelaw and Denham. He was always conscious of the fact that, when it came to numbers, Labour would not win any battle, but if he worked with the Tories and made their lives less difficult than they might have been, he could achieve much for the Labour Party. He made management of Lords business his speciality, and he set a pattern for future Labour Chief Whips which has been followed to this day.

Malcolm Shepherd always was proud of his roots – not only his father but also his mother, Ada. Whilst her husband rose to the top in the Labour Party, she spent much of her time in strengthening the role of women in society and used the trade unions to fulfil that end. His mother was a contemporary of Margaret Bondfield and Mary MacArthur, and in one dramatic fight for a living wage for women she was almost abandoned by trade union leaders, but stoutly supported by the Quaker families of Cadbury, Fry and Rowntree.

He was a realist and recognised the limits of power in the world before the change in the composition both of the House of Lords and within the Labour Party itself. He never fought a Parliamentary election and succeeded his father before he could do so, but he recognised how fortunate he had been to do just that and was always content with what he had achieved. There can be few within Labour ranks and especially within the House of Lords who carried a more impressive record and who were accorded so much respect for what they did in their time. He died on 5 April 2001.

Rt Hon. Lord Graham of Edmonton

Manny Shinwell (Lord Shinwell of Easington) (1884–1986)

Emanuel 'Manny' Shinwell made his reputation as a socialist orator, reared in the tough politics of Clydeside in the early twentieth century. He was a prominent figure in the Labour party for more than half a century, serving in the governments of the 1920s and 1940s and acting as chairman of the PLP in the 1960s.

Shinwell was born in Spitalfields in the East End of London on 18 October 1884, the eldest of 13 children of Samuel Shinwell, a clothing manufacturer. He left school at the age of eleven and was apprenticed to the tailoring trade, but for several years he drifted through a variety of poorly paid jobs.

As a young man he moved to Scotland, where he became actively engaged in politics, joining the Independent Labour Party in 1903. At the age of 22 he was elected to the Glasgow Trades Council, of which he was twice president, and he devoted much of his time to the development of trade unionism among the seamen of the Clyde ports. Employment in the shipping industry meant he was in a reserved occupation during the First World War, which he initially supported, though by 1917 he backed the campaign for a negotiated peace.

Shinwell first came to national prominence on 'Red Friday' in January 1919, when he was one of the organisers of a strike (aimed at securing the introduction of a 40–hour working week) that saw violent clashes with the police in Glasgow. He was arrested and imprisoned for five months – on the charge of inciting a riot – though accusations that he was a 'revolutionary' were at odds with his moderate demands throughout the dispute.

After seven years as a Glasgow councillor Shinwell was elected as MP for Linlithgow in 1922 – a seat he first contested, unsuccessfully, in 1918. He was soon known for his effective debating skills, honed by assiduous reading that gave him a command of language unusual among those with little formal education. He was an enthusiastic supporter of Ramsay MacDonald and served for a few months as Parliamentary Secretary to the Department of Mines in the first Labour government, but he lost his seat at the 1924 election, only to regain it at a by-election in 1928. He was Financial Secretary to the War Office in 1929–30, and then returned to the Mines Department until he lost his seat when Labour was heavily defeated at the 1931 general election.

Shinwell's volatile nature was evident in two episodes during the 1930s. Angry at what he regarded as the betrayal of the party's leaders in 1931, he launched a vitriolic campaign against Ramsay MacDonald at the 1935 election, winning the contest for the Seaham constituency in Durham (which he held until 1950) and driving his old chief out of politics at the same time. Three years later, provoked by the comments of his opponents, Shinwell crossed the floor of the House and hit the Conservative MP Commander Robert Bower, a former naval boxing champion, before storming out of the chamber.

After the formation of the wartime coalition in 1940, he turned down the offer of a junior ministerial post and became instead a vocal critic of Churchill's conduct of the war. He did little in these years to endear himself to colleagues. His alliance with the Tory war critic Lord Winterton earned the label 'Arsenic and Old Lace', and his attacks on Labour ministers for not pressing hard enough for socialist policies inside the coalition aroused resentment among many in the PLP.

He was nevertheless considered sufficiently worthy – or too much of a loose canon – to be offered a senior post when Labour came to power in 1945. Attlee appointed him as Minister of Fuel and Power, and he set about the task of implementing Labour's commitment to nationalise the mines. His bill was the first to come forward in the government's extensive nationalisation programme, but expectations that a change of ownership would boost production were dashed when the vesting date of 1 January 1947 found Britain facing a fuel crisis.

Shinwell gave several advance warnings of possible coal shortages, but he always denied that this would cause dislocation across industry or factory closures. He therefore faced a storm of criticism after announcing that much of industry would have to shut down temporarily. Amidst the snow and ice of a freezing winter, 'Shiver with Shinwell' became a potent slogan for the Tory opposition, and after a series of poor performances in the Commons he was fortunate to survive in office.

In October 1947 he was moved to become Secretary of State for War. Shinwell bitterly resented this demotion to a post outside Cabinet rank, but he proved to be more adept at dealing with military matters than he was at handling the problems of industry. By March 1950 he had returned to the Cabinet as Minister of Defence, a post in which he adopted a hawkish posture on the need for large-scale rearmament following the outbreak of the Korean War.

Shinwell's influence within the party waned when Labour lost office in 1951. He was MP for Easington in Durham after 1950 (through to 1970), but after nine years he lost his seat on the NEC and failed in his attempts to gain re-election in the early 1950s. In 1955 he left the shadow cabinet and published – apparently without any trace of irony – an autobiography entitled *Conflict Without Malice*. By this time he was assuming the mantle of a Labour veteran, speaking his mind by defending the principle of public ownership and arguing for Britain to contract out of the 'club' of nuclear powers.

When Labour returned to power in 1964, ministerial office was out of the question for Shinwell at the age of 80, but his continuing vigour and enthusiasm for politics was such that he was elected chairman of the PLP. For a while the one-time rebel proved successful at containing a new generation of critics, though murmurings against him increased as Wilson's government lost its sense of direction and popularity. Unable to enforce discipline as strictly as he wished, Shinwell resigned in 1967 and returned again to the back benches, where he spoke forcefully against the principle of British membership of the EEC.

He was made a life peer – Baron Shinwell of Easington – in 1970, and into his nineties he remained an outspoken member of the House of Lords, well-informed on the major issues of the day. He surprised many commentators when he resigned the Labour whip in March 1982, protesting against the left-wing drift in policy. He remained a party member, but thereafter sat with the Independent group in the Lords.

Shinwell was married three times. His first wife, Fay, died in 1954 after more than fifty years of marriage. In 1956 he married Dinah Meyer, from Denmark, who died in 1971. A year later he married Mrs Sarah Hurst, who also predeceased him, in 1977. He celebrated his hundredth birthday in 1984 in the Royal Gallery of the House of Lords. Much of the conversation was about the miners' strike of the day, and thoughts went back some sixty years to the time when Shinwell supported the miners during the 1926 General Strike.

By the time he died in London, aged 101, on 8 May 1986, Shinwell's firebrand years were a distant memory and he had become a figure of affection among political friends and enemies alike. In many ways he shared the virtues and shortcomings of the early generation of Labour leaders. He was a tough and instinctive champion of the underdog, a quick-witted and skilful platform speaker. But in office he lacked administrative expertise and the capacity to plan ahead. As one of his juniors commented, as a minister – as in life – he acted on impulse, in fits and starts.

Peter Slowe's biography *Manny Shinwell* was published in 1993. In addition to *Conflict Without Malice*, Shinwell wrote further volumes of recollections: *The Labour Story* (1963); *I've Lived Through It All* (1973); and *Lead with the Left: My First Ninety-Six Years* (1981).

Kevin Jefferys

Clare Short (1946–)

Clare Short has had a tempestuous political career which has seen her move from Bennite radical in the early eighties to scourge of Trotskyism in the 1990s and Cabinet Minister in the 2000s. She has consistently put principle before preferment, resigning twice from the front bench. She shows an almost reckless willingness to speak her mind irrespective of the consequences and has been a sometimes vocal critic of the style of New Labour. Her political survival owes much to a certain star quality, and to the fact that she represents an intellectual tradition within the Party which connects New Labour to its grassroots. In her own terms, she views socialism as 'an ethical and not an economic system' – her politics are not primarily about class, but about the diverse needs of the powerless and excluded, including ethnic minorities and women. This belief system has underpinned her political career, bringing her into conflict variously with the Bennite left, the popular press, Neil Kinnock and New Labour. She remains the chief exponent of this tradition within the Cabinet.

Clare Short was born in Birmingham on 15 February 1946, the second of seven children of an Irish Catholic teacher (Frank) and a bookkeeper (Joan). She excelled at school and won a place at St Paul's Grammar School and then at the Universities of Keele and Leeds, where she studied Political Science. She met and married her first husband while still an 18-year-old student. It emerged only later that she had had a child at this time, who she gave up for adoption. They were reunited in 1996.

Before she left university she had assumed that she would go into teaching, like her father. Instead she sat the civil service exams, and entered the Home Office in 1970, the same year she joined the Labour Party. She spent five years running the office of a Tory Minister, Mark Carlisle, and his Labour successor, Alex Lyon MP, whom she married in 1982.

Frustrated by the enforced neutrality of civil service life, she left to become Director of the charity All Faiths for One Race. She took on the Directorship of Youth Aid in 1979, and of the Unemployment Unit in 1981. Her experiences in the voluntary sector were formative, and her political career has been marked by a campaigning zeal for tackling poverty and discrimination. In particular, race has been an issue of abiding interest.

In 1978 she published *Talking Blues: A Study of Young West Indians' Views of Policing* and the *Handbook of Immigration Law*. Early in her parliamentary career she launched the All-Party Group on Race Relations, only to resign a year later declaring that the Conservative and SDP Vice Chairs were totally disinterested in the issue. Her affinity with the needs of the poor and excluded have been fostered by the close connection she has maintained to her native Birmingham – she has represented its Ladywood constituency since 1983.

She made her mark on Parliament, and her reputation for outspokenness, early in 1983 when she accused Alan Clark MP, then Under-Secretary of State for Employment, of being drunk at the Dispatch Box. Three years later, her Ten Minute Rule Bill to ban pictures of partially naked or naked women in mass circulation newspapers and the attendant campaign bought her to the attention of the press and its readers. The backlash from the newspapers involved, particularly the *Sun*, was highly charged and highly personal. She was labelled 'Crazy Clare' and suffered press intrusion into her private life. However, her response was robust and she widened her campaign to target magazines and the shops that stocked them, leading to a direct-action raid on W H Smith. Her feminism made her an easy target for Tory MPs, but she was influential in the debate within the Parliamentary party about increasing the number of women MPs in the House, publishing a Fabian pamphlet, 'Quotas Now', in 1990.

She was first appointed to the front bench in 1985 as an employment spokesperson, only to resign three years later when she found herself in opposition to the front-bench line on the

Prevention of Terrorism Act (PTA). She believed that the PTA drove young people into an involvement with terrorism, and could not bring herself to support it. A year later she returned to a then politically uncontentious position as a Shadow Minister for Social Security, under fellow Campaign Group member Michael Meacher MP, only to resign again in 1991 over the Party's stance on the Gulf War. Warned by Neil Kinnock to be silent on the issue or to be sacked, she chose to resign.

During her early years in the House, she voted and worked with fellow members of the Campaign Group. However, she broke with the group in March 1988 over the decision that Tony Benn should challenge the then leader Neil Kinnock for the leadership of the Party. She was elected to the NEC in 1989, backed by the TGWU, and served as Chair of the Women's Committee 1993–96 and as Chair of the International Committee in 1996. She voted against the Bennites on the Committee, and worked for the expulsion of Militants from the Party, including MPs Terry Fields and Dave Nellist. She also supported preventing Liz Davies from standing as a Labour candidate before the 1997 general election. She was Vice-Chair of the Party from 1997 to 1999.

In 1992, Neil Kinnock brought her back on to the front bench as a spokesperson on environmental protection. Under John Smith's leadership she was promoted, to her delight, to Shadow Minister for Women in 1993. Blair brought her into the Shadow Cabinet as Secretary of State for Transport in 1995, supplanting her former boss, Michael Meacher. However, she again ran into trouble when she refused to condemn London Underground staff's one-day strikes. This, combined with public statements in favour of a public debate on the legalisation of cannabis and higher tax rates for people like her, saw her moved to the less high-profile position of Shadow Minister for Overseas Development a year before the 1997 general election.

A very successful Secretary of State, she has won a commitment from the Chancellor to increase aid spending, and has published the first White Paper on Development in more than two decades. She has declared that she has 'undoubtedly the best job in government. A fabulous job. It is by definition noble.'

Ann Rossiter

Ted Short (Lord Glenamara) (1912–)

Edward Watson Short – always known as Ted – was born in Warcop, Westmorland, on 17 December 1912, the son of Charles and Mary Short, and educated at Bede College, Durham. After service in World War II as a Captain in the Durham Light Infantry, he became Headmaster of Princess Louise County Secondary School in Blyth, Northumberland. It was whilst there that he became a Newcastle City Councillor and became the Leader of the Council in 1948. He was elected as the Member of Parliament for Newcastle Central in 1951 and served there until 1976. He had a distinguished Parliamentary career, rising to become a member of the Cabinet in more than one Labour administration

His experience as Leader of the Newcastle Council soon gave him an entry into the Labour Whip's Office, which he took in 1955, going on to become Deputy Opposition Chief Whip in 1962 and finally making it as Chief Whip to Harold Wilson from October 1964 until

1966. As will be seen, this was a most turbulent time, especially in a Government Whips Office with barely a majority. It led to him writing an account of his time as *Whip to Wilson*, published in 1989, which broke new ground, for it is the unwritten code of the Whip's Office that the secrets garnered there remain what they are – secret. Whilst it is undoubtedly true that much was revealed, it will be true also to say that much, much more was concealed. In later years the anatomy of a Government Whip's Office was dissected with forensic skills by Michael Cockerell for both the Thatcher years and those of James Callaghan, to be shown to a wider audience via television; nevertheless, Ted Short's account of how to survive with a majority of four made fascinating reading.

Most who rise to become Chief Whip of their Party often look back on that period as the peak of their Parliamentary achievement. If that was how it is seen, there can be no better testimony than is contained in a letter written by Harold Wilson when Ted Short left the Whip's Office to become Postmaster General in July 1966. He wrote: 'I will say no more than this: between you, you have saved the Labour Government and what we will be able to do, in all the years we remain, will be due to your efforts at this testing time. On behalf of the Labour Movement and everyone here and overseas who may depend on us – thank you for what you have done.'

When he left the Whips Office to become Postmaster General, even he was uncertain that it was a promotion, but after the volatile and tempestuous times in the Whips Office he welcomed the opportunity of having a department of his own. It was, he said, one of the happiest periods of his Ministerial life, made so by the support he received from civil servants and colleagues alike. He was succeeded as Chief Whip by his deputy, John Silkin.

He was promoted to Cabinet as Secretary of State for Education and Science in April 1968, serving until the fall of the Labour Government in 1970 and continuing as Shadow Education Secretary until 1972. It was during this period that he presided over the establishment of one of the jewels in the crown of that Labour administration when the Open University was created. He took immense pride in this. His wife Jennie went on to became a graduate of the Open University and he himself gained an honourary Doctorate from the OU. It was Harold Wilson who said that if he was to be remembered for one act he would wish it to be the establishment of the Open University. Ted Short became the Chancellor of the University of Northumbria in 1984 and continues there today.

Undoubtedly a highlight in his Parliamentary career came in April 1972 when he defeated Michael Foot and Tony Crosland to be elected to the position of Deputy Leader of the Labour Party under Harold Wilson when Roy Jenkins resigned over the Party's attitude to the Common Market. When Labour came back into power in 1974, Wilson made him Lord President of the Council and Leader of the House of Commons. He retired from the government at the same time as Harold Wilson, in April 1976, and from Labour's Deputy Leadership and the House of Commons in October 1976 to take up the Chairmanship of Cable and Wireless, holding the post from 1976 to 1980. He became a Companion of Honour in 1976 and in 1977 he was created Lord Glenamara. In the Lords he played no major role, but was always to be relied on to be of assistance to the Labour front bench, especially on educational matters and in deploying his special interest and knowledge of Middle East Affairs, especially supporting the cause of Israel. He was also active in the field of helping the disabled, and became the President of Finchale Abbey Training College for the Disabled in 1985, serving there to this day.

Despite his many achievements and glittering prizes, he will be remembered most for instituting what became known as 'Short Money'. When Leader of the House of Commons he crafted an arrangement of immense benefit to all opposition parties. Whilst the government of the day had the support of the whole Whitehall machine, opposition parties had to fend for themselves. It was agreed on an all-party basis that after each election the party managers would agree a formula taking into account the party balance in the Commons which would provide in hard cash a sum to enable the opposition parties to fund proper policy advice and research support. Currently this amounts to more than £1 million to the main Opposition party. Similarly, in the Lords, a scheme has been created, called 'Cranborne Money', after Lord Cranborne when Leader of the House.

He had busied himself with writing for some time, and wrote *The Story of the Durham Light Infantry* (1944), *The Infantry Instructor* (1946), *Education in a Changing World* (1971), *Birth to Five* (1974), *I Knew my Place* (1983); and *Whip to Wilson* (1989). He married Jennie Sewell in 1941: they have a son and a daughter.

The forty years from 1950 to 1990 – from City Councillor to Lord President of the Council – is a remarkable journey. Whilst Leader of the Newcastle City Council he was responsible for initiating plans for the new laying out of the City which, forty years on, is seen to have been spectacular. The cry then was to house the people in better housing than early Victorian slums, which were the lot of thousands. He was followed into the leadership by T Dan Smith, who also left his mark more widely, both on the city and local government and who was to be instrumental in appointing the first 'City Manager' a position that has grown into the City Supremo we know today. Short really blossomed as a fierce debater when he carried out his role as Leader of the Commons, for on numerous occasions he wound up important debates and demolished the Opposition with his forensic debating skills.

Rt Hon. Lord Graham of Edmonton

John Silkin (1923–87)

Coming from a political family can have both benefits and drawbacks. John Ernest Silkin (the third youngest son, born on 18 March 1923) had to follow in the footsteps of his father, Lewis Silkin (later Baron Silkin of Dulwich). Lewis Silkin had been fundamental in Britain's post-war reconstruction, being responsible, when Minister of Town and Country Planning, for the 1947 Planning Act, which led to the construction of new towns. John Silkin's impact on the Labour Party and the wider political environment was much narrower and he never quite escaped the shadow of his father.

Raised in South-East London, Silkin was, from an early age, surrounded by the company of politicians, Ramsay MacDonald, Herbert Morrison and Jimmy Maxton all being regular visitors to the Silkin household. His entry into politics was only, therefore, a matter of timing, and he joined the Labour Party in 1939 whilst still at Dulwich College. After attending the University College of Wales for a short period, he was called up to serve in the Navy where, in the Intelligence Corps (as Lieutenant Commander), he saw active duty in the Far East. After being demobilised, Silkin went on to study at Trinity College, Cambridge, where he earned a

BA (1946) and an LLB (1948). He entered the family law firm and acted for, amongst others, future Labour Cabinet minister Tony Crosland. Silkin's brother, Sam, also studied Law and went to the Bar before becoming Attorney-General.

Silkin's first attempt to win a Parliamentary seat came at Marylebone (an unwinnable seat for Labour in London) in the February 1950 general election. It was during this campaign that he met his wife, Rosamund John, the beautiful actress who had starred in several British post-war films (they had one son, Rory Lewis). Silkin went on to fight West Woolwich (1951) and South Nottingham (1959) before finally fighting a seat successfully in a by-election in 1963 for the London constituency of Deptford – which he represented until his death. More or less as soon as he entered Parliament, Silkin began his rise through the ranks of the Parliamentary Labour Party.

In July 1966 he became Chief Whip, having been a Junior Whip (1964 – January 1966) and then Deputy Chief Whip, and worked closely with the Leader of the House, Richard Crossman, to establish a more liberal regime (Silkin was also Deputy Leader of the Commons, 1968–69). He drew up a new code of conduct for MPs and widened the concept of conscience in votes, preferring friendly relations with parliamentary colleagues and employing the power of persuasion. This proved highly popular with Labour Members of Parliament, but it came to an end when Harold Wilson and Barbara Castle's *In Place of Strife* trade union legislation could not be forced through the party. Silkin was replaced by the tougher Bob Mellish in 1969, but regardless of this setback he remained a close confidant of Marcia Williams, Wilson's influential Personal and Political Secretary. Leo Abse has described Silkin as 'the most gentle and probably the most successful Whip in Labour's history'.

His appointment as Chief Whip represented the height of his achievements, his ministerial appointments in the Governments of 1964–70 and 1974–79 being less exciting. He first gained his own ministry in 1969 with Public Buildings and Works, shadowing Environment 1970–74. Appointed Minister of Planning and Local Government outside Cabinet in March 1974, although he joined the Cabinet in October, his Ministry remained under Tony Crosland's Environment Department. Despite parallels with his father's political career, John Silkin's Community Land Act proved to be an expensive failure. He was much happier at the Ministry of Agriculture from September 1976 until May 1979, where he was able to utilise his anti-EEC convictions to great effect. He saved Britain's doorstep milk deliveries in spite of the opposition of other member states and refused to allow British fishing grounds to be taken over. He also helped to defuse a potentially damaging rumour of a food shortage. After the Winter of Discontent and the election defeat of 1979, he held the difficult position of Shadow Industry Secretary (1979–80).

This anti-EEC position helped create the Social Democratic Party. Silkin was active in the Common Market Safeguards Committee and his public backing for the next Labour Government to withdraw from Europe without a referendum was instrumental in bringing together David Owen, Shirley Williams and Bill Rodgers in the 'Gang of Three'. He supported the 'Alternative Economic Strategy' encompassing import controls, and opposed the cuts in public expenditure proposed by the International Monetary Fund (IMF) during the Labour Government of 1974–79.

Silkin saw himself as being capable of holding the highest office in the Labour Party and believed that he had the support of others. Yet this support did not come to fruition when he stood for the party leadership in 1980 and, backed by his union, the TGWU, the deputy leadership in 1981. In these contests, Silkin saw himself as the 'soft-left' compromise candidate between the right and the 'hard' left of the party. He greatly miscalculated his standing within the party, for whilst he considered himself a heavyweight, others did not. However, he remained in the shadow cabinet as Shadow Leader of the House (1980–83) and the pro-unilateralist Shadow Defence Secretary (1981–83). This period was the nadir of the party's organisation, leading to such infamous incidents as Silkin, Michael Foot and Denis Healey announcing three different version of Labour's defence policy on the same day.

Silkin was always identified as being from the left of the party, and in 1970 became a member of the Tribune group of MPs. Silkin put much effort into the running of the group's newspaper, *Tribune*, and fought hard to prevent its takeover by the 'hard' left. Its then editor, Chris Mullin (who became an MP himself in 1997 and was made a junior minister under Tony Blair), attacked the Tribune Group and this greatly angered Silkin. The disagreement led to a legal battle with the paper, after Silkin had organised a shareholders' coup (supported by Lord Bruce, Russell Kerr and Jennie Lee). Vocal opposition from his local party almost led to him being deselected as the candidate for the 1983 election. Mullin even embarked on a speaking tour of Silkin's constituency, calling for his deselection. Such struggles led him to announce his plans to step down at the following general election (1987), and it was widely assumed that he would be elevated to the House of Lords on standing down. His untimely death, prior to the election, prevented this.

Shortly before his passing, Silkin completed a book (*Changing Battlefields*, 1987) analysing the problems of the Labour Party and offering solutions. It was published shortly after his premature death on 26 April 1987 at the age of 64 from a heart attack.

Dr Stuart Thomson

Lewis Silkin (1ˢᵗ Baron Silkin of Dulwich)   (1889–1972)

Lewis Silkin was, as Minister for Town and Country Planning in the first Attlee government of 1945–50 the minister responsible for the historic New Towns Act of 1946, the Town and Country Planning Act of 1947 and the National Parks and Access to the Countryside Act of 1949. Michael Stewart, who was the Whip on the Town and Country Bill, wrote in his memoirs, *Life and Labour* (1980): ' It was the first measure on the subject with real teeth. It put a stop to ribbon development outside cities which was the curse of pre-war urban growth and it saved numerous beauty spots from the despoilers. It provided also that when land increases in value because the community needs it, the increase should go to into the public purse. The repeal of this provision by the Tories in the 1960s has robbed successive Chancellors of revenue they could have obtained without doing injustice to anyone: it has also made more difficult any kind of incomes policy – for how do you persuade people who work for their livings to exercise restraint in wage claims when they can see that the really large fortunes are made, not by work at all, but by the mere ownership of land?' The New Towns Bill created the modern Stevenage and Hemel Hempstead whilst the National Parks act has conserved the beauties of the English countryside for future generations.

Born on 14 November 1889, he was the eldest of seven children of Baltic immigrant parents. After junior school in Stoke Newington and the Central Foundation School, City Road, he won an open Mathematics schollarship to Worcester College, Oxford, but was precluded from taking it up by the poverty of his parents. After a year at London University he worked as a solicitors clerk before becoming a solicitor himself and founding the firm of Lewis Silkin and Partners. Unsuccessfully fighting Central Wandsworth at the general election of 1922, Hartley Shawcross, his under-age agent depicted him in his memoirs as 'a fairly young solicitor, very fat as I remember (I drove him around at reckless speeds on a motorcycle and side-car) and a man of character and ability ...' In 1925 he secured election to the LCC and, working closely with Herbert Morrison, he soon became a leading expert on the problems of public housing and health in London. Whilst Morrison was Transport Minister in the MacDonald government of 1929–31, Silkin led the Opposition LCC Labour group, and on Labour's victory in the LCC election of 1934 he became Chair of the Housing and Public Health Committee, serving until 1940. From 1940–45 he was Chairman of the LCC Town Planning Committee. Having visited and studied continental housing developments Silkin became an advocate of the advantages of flats over houses in solving London's housing inadequacies, but sought also to utilise the best of British architectural tradition.

Having been MP for Peckham since a by-election in 1936, his failure to secure a new seat following the demise of his existing perch under the boundary review put a stop to his ministerial career at the 1950 General Election. He had been created a Privy Counsellor in 1945. Leaving the Commons, where he had been a legendary chess player, if a poor speaker, he was created the hereditary Baron Silkin of Dulwich in 1950 and enjoyed an Indian summer as Deputy Leader of the Opposition under A V Alexander from November 1955 until 1964. He was thrice married: to Rosa Neft in 1915, with whom he had three sons and, a year after her death in 1947, to Mrs Frieda M Johnson, a widow who died in 1963, and finally in 1964 to Marguerite Schlageter. He died on 11 May 1972. His eldest son Arthur succeeded him to the peerage whilst his younger sons John and Sam both followed their father into the House of Commons and were to be senior members of the Wilson and Callaghan governments: John as Chief Whip and Agriculture Minister and Sam as Solicitor General, 1974–79.

Greg Rosen

Jim Sillars (1937–)

It is a matter of the deepest personal regret that in 1976 Jim Sillars severed his links with the Labour Party to continue a political journey with his independent Scottish Labour Party 1976–79 and subsequently as SNP MP for Glasgow Govan from the November 1988 by-election until the general election of 1992. The following year he left politics to become the valued assistant to the Secretary-General of the Arab-British Chamber of Commerce, one of the causes in which he had had a lifelong belief.

James 'Jim' Sillars was born in Ayr on 4 October 1937 into a railway family. His father, Matthew Sillars, was a respected regular attendee at conferences of the Scottish Labour Party. Educated at Newton Park School and Ayr Academy, he left to the disappointment of the teachers, who hoped he would go on to university, for a succession of labouring jobs ending up in the Fire Service. He became an official of the Fire Brigades Union, but in 1963 was appointed by the Ayrshire Federation of Labour Parties as a full-time agent in the marginal constituency of Ayr, where the candidate was Alex Eadie of the NUM, later MP for Midlothian 1966–1992 and Under-Secretary of State for Energy 1974–79 with responsibility for the mining industry. I spent a week (staying in the house of Willie Ross MP) and thought Sillars marvellous as a dynamic agent and attractive, forthcoming personality. He had been elected to Ayr Town Council in his mid-twenties and quickly became their representative on the Ayr County Council Education Committee. Suddenly he had become a tremendous leader. In 1968, he was a natural choice, in the view of Jimmy Jack, to become Head of the Organisation and Social Services Department of the Scottish TUC.

Just as he was beginning to make a mark at the STUC, Emrys Hughes, the veteran left-wing MP for South Ayrshire and Keir Hardie's son-in-law, died. At the adoption meeting, one of the best organised constituency Labour parties in Britain chose Sillars: not only did he prove himself an outstanding speaker – yes, orator – and a superb candidate, but with the super-efficient and loveably popular agent, Jim Tanner, and a committed local party behind him, he delivered an outstanding result. Alas, Harold Wilson did not fully comprehend that candidate, party and local tradition in South Ayrshire were almost unique. On the basis of Sillars' result, Wilson decided to call the election early in June 1970, with dire consequences. Had he waited until October 1970 and not been beguiled by South Ayrshire, political history might have been different.

One other event should be recalled. At a huge meeting in the Cumnock Town Hall, Willie Ross, political king of the Scots, Wilson's 'basso profoundo', announced, 'Here is the young man who will have my job'. This was not to endear him to most of his future colleagues in the House of Commons!

Sillars did not like Westminster, though it was quite untrue, as he was later reported as claiming, that English MPs laughed at his Scottish accent; no MP in my 39 years experience has been laughed at on account of a Scottish or regional accent. The pull of his family in Scotland also drew him away from Westminster. (In 1981 he was to remarry: the former SNP MP Margo MacDonald). Part of the trouble lay, in my personal opinion, elsewhere.

The Americans invited two young Labour MPs to undertake a speaking/debating tour of the States. The Chief Whip chose Sillars and a young, red-headed Welshman, elected for Bedwelty in the 1970 general election by the name of Neil Kinnock. Kinnock was a roaring success, Sillars less so. This was a partial cause of tensions in the Tribune Group, of which both were prominent members. Above all, having been the author of Labour Party pamphlets on Scottish Nationalism, Sillars changed his mind on devolution and from being the 'Hammer of the Nats,' began to espouse policies after 1974's two elections which were indistinguishable from those of the SNP.

My abiding memory of Jim Sillars will always be the 18 public debates we did against each other from Fort William in the West, Elgin in the North, to Cumnock, Glasgow and Edinburgh. They were the only political forums in the run-up to the 1979 referendum. He was sincere, passionate, a true orator and a charming travelling companion.

Tam Dalyell MP

Dennis Skinner (1932–)

Dennis Edward Skinner is one of the few advocates of the class struggle left in the Parliamentary Labour Party. His solidly left-wing outlook is one which has moved out of fashion in the party, yet he remains one of the most recognised names and faces in the Party, regardless of the fact that he has never held a front bench position. Skinner is one of only two Labour MPs to enter the House of Commons in or before 1970 who has failed to gain the title Rt Hon. (the other being Tom Cox). His razor-sharp wit and aggressive manner bring fear among both friends and foes alike.

Skinner has always tried to remain true to working-class roots among the Derbyshire coal pits and mining villages, constantly citing the lessons learnt in this environment. Born on 11 February 1932, he was raised of what *Who's Who* calls 'good working-class mining stock'. Most of his immediate family worked in the mines, and much the same was expected for the children of miners. His father, Edward, was a miner and his mother, Lucy (Dudley), took in washing. However, Skinner's ability to pass exams enabled him to enter a grammar school, Tupton Hall Grammar School, entering it at the age of 10 after leaving Clay Cross Infants. Yet, on leaving school, he went on to become a miner, firstly at Parkhouse Colliery and then, when this was closed (1962), at the larger Glapwell Colliery.

It was on entering the mines that Skinner became involved in Labour Party (joining in 1956) and trade union politics. The solidarity of the mines meant that there was a certain 'expectation' that trade union membership would be sought. He was asked to stand for Clay Cross Unitary Development Council (1960–70) by those who wished to ensure Labour's majority and Derbyshire County Council (1964–70). Clay Cross is still referred to as 'Red Clay Cross' or 'Skinnerville' to indicate its left-wing nature. During Skinner's time, the UDC campaigned on a platform of low rents and public spending and did not lose a seat – 'a little bit of socialism in raw capitalism', as Skinner himself described this period.

This party political activity was combined with his trade union activities. He was elected as an area delegate for the National Union of Mineworkers (NUM) to the Derbyshire council, with a particularly large number of votes, before going on to become Vice President and then President of the Derbyshire NUM in 1966. This was a lay position, not a full-time one, and involved him chairing meetings on a Saturday morning. Much of the work Skinner undertook in the NUM was on the medical appeal tribunals and as a member of the Scarsdale Valuation Panel, fighting to obtain compensation for miners such as those who had been disabled.

Due to his activity in the NUM, Skinner was offered a place at Ruskin College. The NUM in Derbyshire ran a course, funded jointly with the Coal Board, at Sheffield University which taught successful applicants such as Skinner political theory, economics etc. He successfully completed the course and won a scholarship to Ruskin College, but did not feel able to accept the offer because of the commitment of council meetings. He was eventually to attend Ruskin College in 1967 as part of a Parliamentary course to ensure that all Labour candidates were of a certain 'quality'.

Skinner's real political break came when the previous MP for Bolsover decided to stand down in the 1970 election. Skinner was the choice of the NUM as replacement. Their wish to have one of 'their people' had been all the more urgent since the likes of David Marquand had been elected in the neighbouring Ashfield constituency, and his credentials, as far as the NUM saw, were questionable. Skinner still considers his selection to be a 'fluke'. He often tells the story that on the Monday following his election he went down the pit because he thought that an MP had to be sworn in before any pay was received.

Ever since entering Parliament in 1970, he has attempted to abide by a set of rules. He always works a full day; never drinks in the Commons bar; has never been a member of an all-party group; does not indulge in trips paid for by others; does not eat alongside Parliamentary colleagues in the dining rooms; does not believe in the power of patronage, so has never held a position to which he has not been elected; refuses to leave the Commons during the Queen's Speech; and has never been 'paired' with a Conservative MP. This failure to mix with Parliamentary colleagues has always meant that he has remained an outsider.

Skinner demonstrated his popularity in the party by being elected 1978–92 and 1994–98 to the National Executive Committee, whereas his relations with the leadership of the party have rarely been favourable. The peak of his influence came with the rise of the left in the late 1970s and early 1980s, and his prominent support for Tony Benn. Skinner was also vice-chair of the party (1987–88). Yet where other former supporters have discovered 'modernisation', Skinner has stayed true to the same set of beliefs. Despite numerous defeats he continues to battle, and does see occasional successes such as the large increases in pensions following a defeat for the party leadership at the 2000 Party Conference. His constant opposition to most of the Labour leaderships' policies since around 1984 has led to a problem of credibility. His solid anti-Common Market views (Skinner is one of the few to refer to the European Union in this way) has been one of his mainstays. His case is built around a perceived threat to the British state by un-elected officials.

There is a wide admiration for Skinner's Parliamentary skills, and one of his proudest achievements during his time as an MP remains defeating Enoch Powell's Private Member's Bill to ban all embryonic research. Whilst his colleagues remained at a loss as to how to stop Powell, who had himself cleverly used Parliamentary procedure to increase his chances of success, it was Skinner who used the rules of Parliament to introduce the Brecon & Radnor by-election and then talk out, along with others, the time available to Powell.

His non-Parliamentary activities seem a world away from his class-warrior image and demonstrate that politics do not dominate – totally. A keen marathon runner from the 1950s, he has also played nearly every sport under the sun (football, cricket, table tennis, tennis), and enjoys cycling (he has even developed a route around his constituency which takes in all the parishes and enables him to contact his constituents) and road walking (heel and toe). His true love has remained athletics. Yet it is his passion for flora and fauna which surprises many. His intimate knowledge of all the London parks and their plants even led to a role in the Radio 4 programme *Breakaway* as an expert on the subject. Skinner married Mary (Parker) in 1960 and went on to have three children – Dennis (born 1963), Dawn (born 1962) and Mandy (born 1966). He separated from his wife in 1989 and since 1993 has lived with his American researcher, Lois Blasenheim.

Skinner retains a passionate belief in the Labour Party and what the party can achieve – any hint of criticism of the Blair Government brings a stinging rebuke mentioning the advances made, even though it is claimed by some that he berated the newly elected Blair (1983) for lacking socialist principles. He may have reservations about some of the party's policies but he has always remained a Labour person. The so-called 'Beast of Bolsover', or 'left-wing firebrand', retains the same ideas with which he entered Parliament in 1970 and his battle against cancer has done little to mellow his attitudes.

Dr Stuart Thomson

Robert Smillie   (1857–1940)

In his autobiography, *The Time of My Life,* Denis Healey declared: 'My faith in the moral values which socialism represents, and in those who try to put them into practice, however imperfectly, remains undiminished'. On those occasions when a Labour activist's faith momentarily slips from this zenith, he or she would be well advised to turn to the story of miners' leader and Labour MP Robert Smillie for the inspiration with which to strengthen her/his conviction. It is a personal and political life most movingly rendered in Smillie's autobiography, *My Life for Labour* (1924), the very title of which communicates the sheer extent of Smillie's commitment to the moral vocation of socialism.

Smillie was born of Scottish Protestant parents in Belfast on 17 March 1857. After a sporadic education Smillie, aged nine, entered the world of work as an errand boy. Two years later he began work in a local spinning mill before, at the age of fifteen, emigrating to Scotland to join his brother Jack who, two years his senior, was already living in Glasgow.

Smillie gained work in a brass foundry and at some point as a riveter at two Clyde shipyards before, aged sixteen, becoming a miner at Summerlee Colliery, Larkhall. He started work at Summerlee as a hand-pumper before becoming a coal tub drawer and eventually a face worker, the job renowned as the most physically arduous and perilous in the mining industry. 'The flame of Socialism' was kindled within Smillie's heart by his experience of the physical and emotional misery the industrial system inflicted upon the Lanarkshire miners. The image of 'the form of an old miner, his back bent, his joints twisted, his voice hoarse with many freezings' was indelibly imprinted upon Smillie's mind, spurring him on to fulfil his youthful vow 'to give my life to the betterment of the conditions under which, even then, the miner still dragged out a life which was no life for a man made in God's image'.

Smillie was instrumental in the unionisation of the Lanarkshire miners, being elected Secretary of the newly formed Larkhall branch of the Lanarkshire Miners' Association in 1885. The post brought Smillie into contact with Kier Hardie, then Secretary of the Ayrshire Miners' Union.

In 1894 he was elected President of the Scottish Miners' Federation, a position in which he served until 1918 and then from 1921 until 1940, whilst he was Chairman of the Scottish TUC (an organisation in whose formation he was a key player, from its inaugural conference in 1896 until 1899). One of Smillie's main contributions to the Labour movement was his major role in securing the affiliation of the Miners' Federation of Great Britain, led by supporters of the Liberal Party, to the Labour Party in 1909. In 1912 Smillie was elected President of the MFGB, a post he held until 1921. As President of the MFGB Smillie played a pivotal role in the formation in December 1915 of the Triple Alliance, of which he was Chairman, with the NUR and the TGWU. In 1917 Smillie became a member of the TUC's parliamentary committee and he was a member of the General Council of the TUC from

1920 to 1926. The skill and knowledge of Smillie, a long-standing advocate of a nationalised mining industry, was decisive in persuading the majority of the 1919 Sankey Commission to recommend coal nationalisation. However, Lloyd George's Government, despite a pledge to follow the Commission's recommendations, rejected the proposal of nationalisation. It was not until Attlee's Government that Smillie's vision was fulfilled.

Smillie stood in nine Parliamentary elections. He stood unsuccessfully in General Elections in 1895 (Glasgow Camlachie), 1906 (Paisley), January 1910 and December 1910 (Mid-Lanark) and in by-elections in 1894 (Mid-Lanark), 1901 (North-East Lanarkshire) and 1906 (Cockermouth). Having long since dispensed with his ambition of pursuing the Labour interest through the national legislature, Smillie was strongly encouraged to stand in the Morpeth by-election of June 1923 (caused by the death of Labour MP John Cairns) by, amongst others, William Straker, Secretary of the Northumberland Miners' Association. Smillie was persuaded and won the by-election with a handsome majority, which he increased at the general election in December of the same year. Though suffering from poor health (refusing an offer of a place in MacDonald's Government of 1924), Smillie was Chairman of the PLP in 1924 and was until 1927 a member of its executive committee. Due to ill health Smillie stood down from Parliament in 1929, retiring to Dumfries, where he died on 16 February 1940.

Smillie was renowned as a great orator: audiences could not fail to be struck by his overwhelming sincerity and his passion for the Labour movement. The American poet Claude McKay, who visited England in 1920, spoke for many when he recalled that Smillie's 'face and voice were so terribly full of conviction that in comparison the colleagues around him appeared theatrical' and that 'When he stood forth to speak the audience was shot with excitement, and subdued'. A key figure in the early organisation of the Labour movement and the formation of the Labour Party, and one of the miners' greatest ever leaders, Smillie lives on as an inspiration to all those who in the twenty-first century strive to achieve the Labour Party's goal of a truly just society.

Richard Burgon

Andrew Smith   (1951–)

Looking back over the first Labour Government in 18 years, two of the key strategic aims of the Government are now clear. Firstly, to rebuild the United Kingdom's public services, primarily in the areas of Education and Health. Secondly to ensure that all citizens of the UK have the opportunity to develop their skills, and share in the country's economic prosperity through Employment.

Andrew Smith, as much as any member of the Labour Party, has worked to achieve these fundamental aims and hence will be seen as a key player in determining the success of the 1997 Labour Government. Born in Wokingham, Berkshire, on 1 February 1951, he grew up in Burghfield, Berkshire, and was educated at Reading School and St John's College, Oxford, with a BA in PPE (Politics, Philosophy and Economics) and a BPhil in Sociology.

Before his election to Parliament in 1987, Andrew worked for the Oxford & Swindon Co-op as Member Relations Officer, and as a tutor at the Open University. Andrew served as a

Councillor on Oxford City Council from 1976 to 1987, representing the Blackbird Leys estate. As a councillor he chaired the Planning, Recreation and Race Relations Committees.

Selected as the candidate for the constituency of Oxford East in the 1983 general election; he fought but narrowly lost a tight battle against Steve Norris. He was, however, destined to win an equally tight battle four years later in 1987, being re-elected as Member of Parliament of Oxford East in 1992 and 1997.

In Opposition, Andrew was Shadow Higher Education Minister (1989–92), Shadow Treasury Minister (1992–94), Shadow Chief Secretary (1994–96) and Shadow Transport Secretary (1996–97).

On 6 May 1997, following the Labour Party's landslide May Day victory, Andrew joined the Government as a leading figure in DfEE, as Minister for Employment, Welfare to Work and Equal Opportunities. He took responsibility for the success of the New Deal programme, a core pillar of Labour's employment, economic and social security policy, aimed at breaking the cycle of long-term unemployment. At the end of the first Labour term (1997–2001) expansion of the New Deal programme was planned, and the words 'full employment' were being mentioned for the first time in generations.

Whilst at the DfEE, Andrew also had responsibility for Labour's strategy for a Disability Rights Commission and had a wider role as the Government's representative on the EC's Social Affairs Council,

On 11 October 1999 Andrew was promoted to the Cabinet as Chief Secretary to the Treasury, his main responsibility being that of overseeing the Government's annual spending programme of £370b, and ensuring the delivery of quality public services. During his period in office he has played a key role in the development of the Public-Private Partnerships programme and negotiating Public Service Agreements. During summer 2000, he also co-ordinated the Government's Second Spending Revie, which has set out public spending well into the next parliament.

As Chief Secretary to the Treasury he is widely considered to be destined for higher positions within the Government, following such previous holders of the post as Alistair Darling (1997–98), Stephen Byers (1998) and Alan Milburn (1998–99).

Andrew lives on the Blackbird Leys estate, in Oxford, which he represented as a councillor. He is married with one stepson, his wife Valerie having also represented Blackbird Leys estate as a councillor for 12 years. Outside his Ministerial duties Andrew is also currently President of Oxford Blackbirds Boys Football Club, President of Pathway Sheltered Workshop, a Patron of the Radcliffe Medical Foundation and Patron of the Oxford Reserve Forces and Cadets.

Andrew Smith

Chris Smith (1951–)

Do nice guys not fit well in politics? Can a Minister think too much? Chris Smith's removal from the job of Secretary of State for Culture, Media and Sport after the 2001 election might indicate so. DCMS was never a 'Ministry of Fun' for Labour, but there are many who feel that his abrupt departure had at least as much to do with the fact that he is not closely identified with either of Labour's 'big beasts', Tony Blair and Gordon Brown, as the undeniable difficulties which his Ministry encountered.

Christopher Robert Smith was born on 24 July 1951 in Watford, where he lived until the age of ten. He attended George Watson's College in Edinburgh, his family having moved after his father, a civil servant, was transferred to the Scottish Office there. He read English at Pembroke College, Cambridge, from 1969 to 1975. He was President of the Union and chairman of the Fabian Society. His doctoral thesis was on 18th-century poetry, with particular emphasis on Wordsworth and Coleridge. He spent a year at Harvard as a Kennedy Scholar, and worked in the unsuccessful primary campaign of Arizona Democratic Senator Mo Udall.

Perhaps it was the Islington connection which did for him. Contrary to the media myth, Tony Blair might have lived in Islington, but he was never part of the local political scene. Chris Smith was and is. There are at least two Islingtons. On the one hand is the place where the media live, with its smart restaurants and trendy bars along Upper Street. On the other is the deprived, inner city borough of council estates and long disappeared jobs – in crafts like jewellery and with the large public sector employers like the railways and the Post Office.

Smith worked for the Housing Corporation and two housing associations. A borough councillor between 1978 and 1983, an Islington MP since then and Culture Minister for four years, he has a foot in both Islingtons. The media stalwarts flock to his £100 a plate constituency dinners; having chaired the Council's Housing Committee 1981–83, he is very aware of the problems of a borough where homes are either on run-down estates or unavailable for less than a high six-figure sum.

He was selected as candidate for Islington South as part of the shift to the left in the Labour Party after 1979. The old guard in the local party defected in large numbers to the SDP (Islington briefly becoming in consequence the one SDP-controlled council in Britain). The then Labour MP, George Cunningham, havered and wavered but, without support in the local party, lost the contest. After that, he too swapped. Given Smith's Scottish background, it was poetic justice that a left-wing London Labour constituency chose him to replace the man who inserted into Labour's 1970s devolution legislation the 40 per cent participation hurdle which eventually scuppered the 1979 referendum on a Scottish Parliament.

Fighting Cunningham, Smith's 1983 majority was just 363. Until 2001, when a resurgent Liberal Democrat Party scored its best vote since then, it grew steadily. Environmental issues were among his first political concerns, but this was no rural green idealism. He was a member of the Commons Select Committee on Environment (1983–87), before becoming a junior Treasury spokesman (1987–92). He sponsored a Private Member's Bill, the Environment and Safety Information Act 1988. It is precisely in the cities that pollution worst affects the daily lives of those who cannot escape. He was the first senior Labour politician to bring environmental concerns in from the fringes to become a major consideration for economic and industrial policy, no mean feat in a party born out of the era of heavy manufacturing and before the Green Party's 1988 European election performance shocked even Mrs Thatcher into making Green gestures. He was elected to the shadow cabinet following the 1992 general election and appointed Shadow Secretary of State for Environmental Protection, 1992–94.

He came out as gay in 1984, the first MP to do so. Though it was no secret locally, contingency plans had been made during the 1983 election campaign to deal with the issue had it been raised by the notoriously homophobic old-Labour types who ran the local SDP. Coming out on his terms enabled him to gain the respect of the gay community, which he still has, while not being branded as a one-issue MP.

It seemed that Blair trusted Smith's political skills and intellectual ability. He was appointed Shadow National Heritage Secretary 1994–95 and the following year, as Shadow Secretary of State for Social Security (1995–96), to tackle the tough problem of sorting out a fiscally viable but humane policy on pensions and social security benefits. What emerged was not perhaps fiscally tough enough for the real modernisers. But influenced by schemes in the USA, Smith produced a policy document which enabled the leadership to start moving the Labour Party away from its traditional support for a benefits culture and towards one based on helping the socially marginalised into work. He laid the basis for Labour's current approach to social security. It may be that he was trusted to take this on because, like Blair, he takes his Christian beliefs seriously. He served as Shadow Health Secretary 1996–97.

He had a troubled four years at DCMS. He is still to the left of the real modernisers in the Blair project (he was Tribune Group Secretary 1984–88 and Chair 1988–89). Calling the directors of the National Lottery franchisee Camelot 'fat cats' showed a lack of certainty in his political touch. The later debacle over the renewal of the Lottery franchise, in which the Lottery Board, which he had appointed, found its decisions overturned by Camelot in the courts, did not go down too well with the leadership.

He found himself up against powerful lobbies in the traditional arts world. He is no philistine, but his view that the arts should be accessible and non-elitist was wilfully misinterpreted as 'dumbing down'. In suggesting that the large opera companies might look to run their businesses more effectively, he offended some well-heeled state pensioners who regarded subsidies as a right. Traditionalists resented his view that the arts were a major sector of the economy. But he was undoubtedly right to stress that the industry was a major employer and exporter, and that no Government could ignore this, having a responsibility instead to further the arts-based economy. Yet others derided his advocacy of a higher profile for the arts and design in public life as paternalist and overbearing. His reorganisation of the Arts Council was also not well received, portrayed as political interference. Nevertheless, he has many friends in the arts who appreciate his genuine understanding of the contribution they make to national life.

The Chairman of the BBC Governors, Sir Christopher Bland, dismissed him as 'just another licence payer' when he involved himself in the row over the timing of the BBC's television news. It is a supreme irony that he is a believer in public broadcasting. The private broadcasting organisations, including Rupert Murdoch's Sky, have always regarded him as less than enthusiastic about their role. Yet the private sector will have to make a major contribution if Labour is to achieve its stated policy goal of moving broadcasting over to digital standards. Smith never quite mastered this part of his brief. The fact that no major broadcasting legislation was ready for the new Parliament after the 2001 election was unfairly laid at his door.

He was never given the major role in organising the Millennium celebrations, handed first to Peter Mandelson and then to his fellow Islington resident Charles (Lord) Falconer. In view of the problems of the Dome he may well have been relieved to pass up one more poisoned chalice.

The problems of the creation of a new National Stadium as the centrepiece of a British bid for the 2006 football World Cup (and at one point a bid for the Olympics) may have been the final nail in his coffin. He was accused of forcing changes in the design of the stadium, deciding that it could not have facilities for athletics as well as football. Uncertainty was said to be a major reason for difficulties in securing sufficient private sector funding. A public disagreement shortly before the election with his Junior Minister, Kate Hoey, over the responsibility for the lack of progress on the new stadium may well have been the last straw. Afterwards, Blair sacked all of the DCMS Ministerial team.

As a backbencher he will have plenty to do locally, where the Liberal Democrats have taken control of his local council. He is an active member of Red Rope, the socialist mountaineers' organisation. He was often a companion of the late John Smith on expeditions to climb the Munroes – the Scottish mountains over 3,000 feet; he has climbed all 277. Many in the arts world would welcome him as a powerful and informed advocate. There are more mountains for him to climb.

Phil Kelly

John Smith (1938–94)

The paradox about John Smith, the fifteenth Labour Party leader, is that throughout his career he was regarded as being on the party's right wing, but posthumously he became an almost iconic favourite of the left. The view of Smith's admirers is that, if he had lived, he would have won the 1997 election and would have been a more radical Prime Minister and more emollient party leader than Tony Blair. The harsher view, taken by more partisan Blairites, is that he threw away the 1992 election and might have done the same again in 1997.

Smith remained doggedly consistent through his long career in his belief in social democracy as expounded by Hugh Gaitskell and Anthony Crosland. To the Bennite left, he was barely distinguishable from the founders of the SDP, but by the late 1990s his views on redistribution through taxation seemed 'old Labour'.

The son of the headmaster of a village school, born 13 September 1938, he grew up in the tiny town of Ardrishaig, in West Scotland. After Dunoon Grammar School, he read Law at Glasgow University, where he was the leading figure in a promising Labour Club (he was Chair in 1960), whose other stars included a future Scottish Secretary and First Minister, Donald Dewar, and a future Lord Chancellor, Lord Irvine. Having been talent-spotted by officials at the party's Scottish head office, Smith was a parliamentary candidate at the age of only 22, in a by-election in East Fife in 1961, a safe Tory seat in which he did well to come second. He unsuccessfully re-fought the seat at the 1964 general election. He then took a break from politics to establish himself as a lawyer and start a family. In 1967 he married a contemporary at Glasgow University, Elizabeth Bennett, and had three daughters, Sarah, Jane and Catherine. For the whole of Smith's political career, the family home was in Edinburgh, not London.

Smith returned to politics by winning North Lanarkshire with a majority of 5,019 in the 1970 election. He was considered to be a reliable and hard-working backbench MP with a fine grasp of detail, but no firebrand. His political tactic was – as his friend Roy Hattersley put it – to be 'on the right but not deeply involved in the right.' He avoided making enemies and generally did as directed by the whips, except on one significant occasion: in 1971, when he was among several dozen pro-marketeers, led by Roy Jenkins, who broke a three line whip and secured the UK's entry to the Common Market.

He was quickly forgiven for this, and for turning down the first government job offered him by Harold Wilson in 1974, as a Scottish law officer. After serving briefly as PPS to Scottish Secretary Willie Ross, in October 1974 he was appointed an Under-Secretary of State at Energy, with special responsibility for the new North Sea oilfields. Eight months later he found himself working alongside Tony Benn, who respected him enough to demand his promotion to Minister of State level in December 1975 (and to vote for him in the 1992 leadership election). Together they created the British National Oil Company. Smith vehemently protested when the company was later privatised by the Conservatives.

In April 1976, James Callaghan sent Smith to work as deputy to Michael Foot, Leader of the Commons, as Minister of State at the Privy Council Office. His job was supervising the extremely complex legislation to create devolved assemblies for Scotland and Wales. The number of parliamentary days the legislation required was a post-war record, but Smith finally saw it through. By the time devolution was killed off by referendums in the two countries, he had been promoted Secretary of State for Trade (as of 11 November 1978), making him the youngest member of the Cabinet, just after his fortieth birthday.

In opposition, Smith set a unique record as the only person to be re-elected to the shadow cabinet every year for three whole parliaments, until he became party leader. This was despite his threadbare record in the early years, when much of his time was spent reviving his law practice. As Shadow Secretary for Trade, Prices and Consumer Protection (1979–82), during 1981 he made only two brief speeches to the Commons. In 1982, he did not speak at all until after he had been promoted to the post of Shadow Energy Secretary in December. In 1983, he qualified as a QC.

He became a much more significant figure in the Labour Party after the 1983 general election and the subsequent resignation of Michael Foot. A boundary change in that election meant that he was returned as MP for Monklands East, with a majority of 9,799. He ran Roy Hattersley's campaign for the party leadership. Under pressure from unions like the GMB and AEUW, Neil Kinnock appointed him Employment spokesman in October 1983, then promoted him to be Trade and Industry spokesman a year later. His reputation as one of Labour's best parliamentary performers was established during the Westland crisis, an argument over the future of a Cornish-based helicopter firm, during which Smith played a large part in forcing the resignation of Leon Brittan, his opposite number in the Cabinet.

After the 1987 election, Smith was appointed Shadow Chancellor, which made him deputy leader of the party in all but name, and the most obvious putative successor to Neil Kinnock. He was privately approached by some MPs who wanted him to run against Kinnock, but turned them away. Perhaps understandably, his relations with the leader were cool, and deteriorated until their inability to get on became an impediment to Labour's election chances. The origin of the problem was that Kinnock wanted to hurry ahead with a radical policy review, whilst Smith was reluctant to commit himself early, and moved only when he felt that the time was right.

An example of how nimbly he could move, when he thought it necessary, was during the Cabinet crisis which led to the resignation of the Chancellor, Nigel Lawson, brought on by Margaret Thatcher's opposition to Europe's Exchange Rate Mechanism (ERM), the prelude to the euro. Labour had always opposed British membership of the ERM, but in the middle of a parliamentary speech in October 1989, Smith casually announced a new policy, which favoured joining if certain 'prudent' conditions were met. The switch, which had not been agreed by the shadow cabinet, was adroitly timed to maximise the advantage of the Lawson-Thatcher rift. Smith was notably vague about what the 'prudent' conditions for ERM membership might be.

His popularity in the party was undiminished by the political risk he took in January 1988, during a free vote on abortion. Smith and the Monklands West MP Tom Clarke, his Parliamentary neighbour, were the only members of the shadow cabinet to support a proposal to tighten the abortion law by reducing the upper time limit to 18 weeks.

Politically, he may have been assisted by the sympathy he attracted after he had suffered a heart attack at the age of 50, just after the 1988 annual party conference. It might have killed him but for the lucky chance that it hit him whilst he was in hospital, after being cajoled by Mrs Smith to go in for a check-up. It took him out of politics for the latter part of 1988 and the early part of 1989. Whilst he was convalescing, he came second in the shadow cabinet election, topping the poll the next year.

At the time, Smith appeared to be a cautious Shadow Chancellor, keen to make Labour acceptable to business, and anxious not to repeat the expensive manifesto commitments which had bedevilled Labour's 1987 election campaign. He imposed a rule that no shadow minister was allowed to enter into a new spending commitment. However, he did not demur from expensive promises to raise pensions and child benefit, and to pay for them he proposed what amounted to a 19p in the pound income tax increase for the highest paid. This threatened increase, freely misinterpreted by the Tories and their supporting newspapers so that even the relatively low-paid imagined that it applied to them, was possibly the single biggest cause of Labour's 1992 defeat.

Nevertheless, when Neil Kinnock retired, it was almost a foregone conclusion that Smith would be his successor, despite the mistrust he had aroused among modernisers like Tony Blair. He easily saw off his only challenger, Bryan Gould, an opponent of ERM, and was virtually able to choose his own deputy in Margaret Beckett.

His brief leadership was characterised by what one admirer called 'masterly inactivity'. It frustrated the modernisers, who wanted to push ahead with party reforms and with another drastic revision of party policy. Smith was not to be hurried. He displayed a fondness for setting up commissions and committees to mull over difficult issues. The most prominent was the Social Justice Commission chaired by Lord Borrie, which produced a long, erudite and widely read report on reforming the welfare state, with little obvious impact. There were other commissions or committees handling topics like economic policy, electoral reform, and the role of the trade unions within the Labour Party.

On this last issue, Smith again displayed his capacity for moving quickly and decisively when he chose. The committee was examining the time-honoured method of using union 'block votes' in the election of party leaders and selection of parliamentary candidates. With union full-time officials around the table, there was no sign that it would produce any radical reform until Smith made a sudden appearance at its meeting in July 1993 to pronounce that nothing less than a one-member, one-vote system would do.

At the time, Smith seemed to be heading towards certain defeat, because a rule change had to be agreed by the annual party conference, which was itself dominated by union block votes. Three of the four biggest unions were opposed to introducing OMOV. Yet Smith persisted, against the odds, cajoling and exhorting the leaders of the smaller unions and privately hinting that he would resign if he lost. In the end, the reform was agreed by a tiny majority at the party's annual conference in October 1993. It was possibly the single most important change to the Labour Party's rule book in its entire history, whose most obvious beneficiary was Tony Blair. John Smith, meanwhile, was hit by a second and fatal heart attack in his London flat early in the morning of 12 May 1994.

Key books include: Andy McSmith, *John Smith: A Life 1938–1994* (Mandarin, 1994); Gordon Brown & James Naughtie, *John Smith, Life and Soul of the Party* (Mainstream, Edinburgh, 1994); Christopher Bryant (ed), *John Smith, An Appreciation* (Hodder & Stoughton, 1994).

Andy McSmith

Philip Snowden (1ˢᵗ Viscount Snowden)   (1864–1937)

Philip Snowden was a profoundly controversial figure in the early years of the British Labour movement. His name is closely associated with that of Ramsay MacDonald in the 'betrayal' of 1931, which saw the collapse of the second Labour government, an event which many construed as having arisen from his policies as Labour's first Chancellor of the Exchequer. Nevertheless, Snowden is also associated with the development of both the Independent Labour Party and the Labour Party. A powerful ethical socialist, he was, with Ramsay MacDonald, Keir Hardie and J Bruce Glasier, one of the four dominant political figures in the Labour Party before the First World War.

Snowden was born on 18 July 1864 in the remote Pennine moorland parish of Cowling, near Keighley, in the West Riding of Yorkshire, the son of John and Martha Snowden, cotton and worsted weavers. He was raised in a small textile community where nonconformity, particularly Wesleyan Methodism, shaped the life of the community. He received a basic elementary education, worked as a clerk and eventually joined the civil service. A bone deformity, either from an accident or due to an illness, meant that he was forced to leave. While he was recuperating, in January 1895 he became involved in the activities of the Liberal Party, and then the Independent Labour Party, which was then active in the West Riding.

In local politics, and on Labour's behalf, Snowden was elected on to the Parish Council (1895), the Cowling School Board (1895), Keighley Town Council (1899) and Keighley School Board (1899). He was also the editor of the *Keighley Labour Journal*. Nonetheless, it is for his Parliamentary activity that he is most famous. After two unsuccessful Parliamentary contests, at Blackburn in 1900 and Wakefield in 1902, he was returned as MP for Blackburn in 1906 and twice again in 1910. However, his opposition to the First World War led to his defeat at Blackburn in the 1918 general election. Indeed, up to polling day he was attacked in the press by Joseph Burgess, who had once been a leading figure in the early days of the Independent Labour Party, who wrote that 'There are some politicians who are termagents. Mr. Snowden belongs to this type.'

Nevertheless, Snowden's political life was not terminated. Indeed, he was returned as MP for Colne Valley in the 1922 general election, being returned there at four general elections until he was raised to the House of Lords as Lord Snowden of Ickornshaw in November 1931. During his time in the Commons, Snowden was Chancellor of the Exchequer in the first two Labour governments in 1924 and between 1929 and 1931. As Viscount Snowden of Ickornshaw, which he became in November 1931, he was briefly a member of Ramsay MacDonald's National Government, acting as Lord Privy Seal until his resignation on 28 September 1932.

Throughout his life Snowden adhered to radical Liberal sentiments. He opposed the First World War, was a dedicated free trader and abhorred borrowing. Indeed, he was an old Gladstonian Liberal in his economic policies. His wife Ethel Annakin, whom he married in March 1905, also directed him towards the issue of women's suffrage. He was a staunch member of the Independent Labour Party and acted as Chairman and Treasurer at various times between 1900 and 1921. During the First World War he also mounted the ILP's Peace Campaign of 1917 based upon the three issues of allied terms, no annexations and the involvement of the people – all made the more relevant by the Russian revolutions of 1917 and the move towards a Russian withdrawal from the First World War. Inevitably, he was drawn to attend the Workmen's and Soldiers' Council Convention held at Leeds in June 1917, where a mixture of Marxists and socialists sought to force international peace in the wake of the first Russian Revolution of 1917. Attempts to develop such a movement throughout the British working class soon expired, but Snowden earned the undeserved reputation of being a revolutionary at this time in his career, the authorities often breaking up his meetings in Colne Valley according to the memory of at least one Labour supporter.

From 1922 onwards, having been returned as MP for Colne Valley, Snowden made the Labour Party his political home. He was frustrated at Ramsay MacDonald's return as Labour's Parliamentary leader in 1922 but served under him as Chancellor of the Exchequer and Shadow Chancellor. In the former role he gave full vent to his notion of balancing the budget, reducing the National Debt and, if necessary, deflating the economy. In 1924 he was alarmed at the rhetoric of his fellow Cabinet ministers which gave the impression of great increases in expenditure when, in fact, little extra was being spent.

The problem was that Snowden's economic philosophy was based upon Britain's commitment to returning to the Gold Standard and the implementation of free trade. That being the case, he felt that budgets had to be balanced and that socialist measures could only emerge from a surplus on government income. Thus he had no Keynesian vision of spending and deficit budgeting in order to stimulate the economy out of a slump. Indeed, to strengthen the pound he was committed to pursuing a course, as one critic put it, of 'deflation with almost ghoulish enthusiasm'. Therefore his 'Housewife's Budget' of 29 April 1924 differed little from those of his Conservative predecessor and offered only minor reductions in indirect taxation on sugar and tea and announced the removal of the McKenna duties on motor cars, motor-cycles and various other items. His main concern was to demonstrate his financial soundness and economic orthodoxy by stressing that a reduction in the National Debt was an essential precursor of industrial growth and real tax cuts. The limitations of his blinkered thinking were exposed five years later when Labour's second minority government was in office.

Although Snowden's tenacity brought him some personal success, and Britain some economic savings at The Hague conference on reparations in 1929, it is clear that his policies, were inappropriate to the economic climate of 1929–31. The Wall Street Crash of November 1929 reverberated around the world and led to a rise in unemployment in Britain which increased Government expenditure enormously. Faced with an enormous deficit of between £100 and £170 millions, representing between a quarter and a fifth of the national budget, there was downward pressure on the pound and a serious economic crisis.

Snowden, concerned about sound finance, advocated the twin policies of a 10 per cent cut in unemployment benefit and increased taxation upon the middle classes, which was referred to as 'equality of sacrifice'. The Labour Government was deeply divided on the cuts even though Snowden maintained that they were demanded by the international bankers in order to justify the loans to Britain to restore economic confidence in the pound. The indecisive vote on unemployment benefit cuts on 23 August 1931, the tax increases having been abandoned, led to the resignation of the second Labour government and the formation of the National Government on 24 August 1931. Snowden assumed the post of Lord Privy Seal in that Government and was somewhat alarmed when Britain was taken off the Gold Standard on 21 September 1931, although he assured himself that it was only a temporary situation and not the basis of a move to protectionism.

Controversially, during the general election of October 1931, Snowden attacked the Labour Party's policy, which had previously been his own, as 'Bolshevism run mad', and thus conformed his position as Labour's 'Traitor No. 2', behind Ramsay MacDonald. He became Lord Privy Seal in the National Government, but after less than a year resigned because he could not accept its abandonment of free trade. Subsequently, although a spent force in British politics, he engaged in making personal attacks on MacDonald in his *An Autobiography* (1934). He died of a heart attack, following a long illness, on 15 May 1937.

Philip Snowden remains an immensely fascinating and controversial figure. Rather like MacDonald he has been enveloped in a cloud of criticism and consigned to a 'traitor's grave' by the Labour Party and its historians. The epithets have flowed fast and furious. He has been described as visionless, venomous, narrow-minded, spiteful and bitter. Indeed, he probably deserves many of these epithets. Nevertheless, he was one of those early Labour leaders who ensured the rapid growth of the Labour party in the early twentieth century. His problem was that he was consistently committed to Gladstonian economic policies and was unwilling to change these when faced with the 1931 crisis, which required the abandonment of the Gold Standard and free-trade frugality and required deficit budgeting. Yet, in the end, it did not matter, for as the *Leeds Weekly Citizen* of 21 May 1937 noted in its obituary of Snowden: 'Philip Snowden was a man of rare and distinguished gifts and for one great service he will ever be remembered in the Socialist movement: he was in the forefront of those who created so powerful a movement that when he tried to destroy his work he failed in the attempt and went into oblivion.'

The key biographies are C. Cross, *Philip Snowden* (1966) and Keith Laybourn, *Philip Snowden: A Biography, 1864–1937* (1988).

Professor Keith Laybourn

Donald Soper (Lord Soper) (1903–98)

The Revd Dr Donald Soper was the first Methodist Minister to become a member of the House of Lords and in many regards embodied the old precept that 'the Labour Party owes more to Methodism than to Marx'. For nearly five decades his name was at the head of every campaign list. He opposed blood sports, smoking, vivisection, apartheid, gambling, horse racing, nuclear weapons, and war of every kind and he was an ardent teetotaller. Long associated with the Bevanite wing of the party, he preached at Nye Bevan's memorial service on the hills above Ebbw Vale and was a long-term friend of successive Labour leaders, most especially Michael Foot for whom he wrote for two decades a weekly column in *Tribune*.

Born in Streatham on 31 January 1903, the son of a marine claims adjuster and a schoolmistress, he studied at Haberdashers'Aske's School.As a young man Soper was an expert cricketer and even considered a professional sporting career, but when a batsman died as a result of a blow above the heart from one of Soper's fast balls, he turned to religion.

Studying first History and then Theology at St Catherine's College Cambridge, Soper was heavily influenced by the Student Christian Movement and two great Christian Socialists, William Temple, who was later to be Archbishop of Canterbury, and Maude Royden. By the time he left Cambridge with a First he was already committed to seeking ordination as a Methodist minister, although he also found time for a doctorate at the LSE, where he was tutored by Harold Laski.

Accompanied by his wife Marie, whom he married in 1929, Soper's lifetime's work was to be spent in London, first at the London Mission, then in Highbury and then from 1936 to 1978 at the West London Mission at Kingsway Hall. Such a permanent position – unusual for Methodist ministers – gave him both a secure base from which to build a loyal congregation and a home for a wide array of his special interests, including providing homes for the homeless and for unmarried mothers. In 1953 he was President of Methodist Conference and he was a Labour (appointed) member of the London County Council until its abolition in 1963.

For decades he was one of the most entertaining and effective speakers at Speakers' Corner and at Tower Hill, and his dry sense of humour leant humanity to his often absolutist stances on the political issues of the day. He it was who on arriving in the House of Lords in 1965 as one of Harold Wilson's Labour Peers announced that the institution was 'proof of the reality of life after death'.

The strongest suit in Soper's politics was his pacifism and although a committed anti-fascist he joined the Peace Pledge Union with Bertrand Russell,Vera Brittain, Siegfried Sassoon and George Lansbury in 1937 and spoke out in loyal opposition to the Second World War. His arguments were considered so persuasive that he was banned form broadcasting on the BBC throughout the War.With Tom Driberg and R H Tawney, Soper also formed the Christian Socialist Movement in January 1960 and was its founding Chairman.

After many years of crippling arthritis – which rarely prevented him from preaching at Speakers' Corner – Soper died on 22 December 1998. Often referred to as 'the Labour Party's National Chaplain', Soper's controversial reputation as a leading Christian radical, alongside figures like BishopsTrevor Huddleston and Mervyn Stockwood and Archbishop William Temple, helped give a moral edge to Labour's politics which could be both disturbing and inconvenient for the professional politicians. HaroldWilson commented that ideals of Soper's order rarely survive the rough and tumble of political life. Nevertheless Soper was not as austere as his reputation might suggest. He loved cinema and was a fine jazz pianist.

Soper was a great wordsmith and produced countless pamphlets and books, most notably *Christianity and Its Critics* (1937) and his 'autobiographical enquiry', *Calling for Action* (1984). There is a fine if hagiographic biography by Brian Frost, *Goodwill on Fire* (1999).

Chris Bryant MP

Frank Soskice (Lord Stow Hill)   (1902–79)

Frank Soskice was born in Geneva on 23 July 1902, the son of a Russian revolutionary who in 1917 was a member of Kerensky's secretariat. Soskice senior escaped from Kiev pogroms in 1881 and had to flee Russia in 1893 to escape arrest. He arrived in London the same year and became a journalist. He was foreign correspondent for the *Guardian* and later Petrograd correspondent for *Tribune*. Soskice junior grew up in a culturally and politically rich émigré world in Geneva and London and was educated at St Paul's and Balliol College Oxford, becoming naturalised in 1924. Inheriting a liking for politics from his father but lacking the same brand of revolutionary zeal, Soskice was called to the Bar in 1926 and became an internationally respected barrister before the Second World War. During the war he served with some distinction in the Oxfordshire and Buckinghamshire Light Infantry and in the Political Warfare Executive and Dalton's SOE.

Soskice was elected Labour MP for East Birkenhead in 1945 but was thereafter blighted by boundary changes: his constituency was abolished and he had to switch to Neepsend, Sheffield, from 1950 to 1955, which was also then abolished. He finally settled in Newport, the seat that he held until 1966. His ability to get selected for new seats was based on much more than his status within the party and reflected his popularity. This aspect of his character is also clearly reflected in the fact that he was many MP's first choice as Speaker in 1959. He preferred to remain in active politics. Attlee had appointed him as Solicitor-General in 1945, his natural job in government, and he also both took silk that year and accepted a knighthood. His period as Solicitor-General was followed by a short stint as Attorney General from April to October 1951. He followed this with being UK delegate to the United Nations General Assembly in 1950. His cosmopolitan background and language skills, coupled with his natural tact and diplomacy, made him a great success.

Elected to Labour's shadow cabinet every year from November 1952 until Labour's return to office in 1964, with the exception of June 1955–November 1956, he served as a Shadow Law Officer throughout the period. His decision not be become Speaker in 1959 was perhaps the central mistake of his political career, compounded by Wilson's decision to make him Home Secretary in October 1964. His reactionary views on immigration (he also doubted the value of race relations legislation despite presenting the 1965 Race Relations Bill) and his inability to make decisions, which infuriated his civil servants, made him a disappointing appointment. In December 1965 he was made Lord Privy Seal, a position he held for less than four months, being replaced as Home Secretary by Roy Jenkins.

In the difficult transition period after the 1964 election he did little to help prepare the ground for the 1966 election. He acknowledged this and decided not to stand again, retiring from Cabinet and Commons in April 1966. Though ill health contributed to his decision, it was also recognition that his combination of skills and character were not suitable for the major offices of state. Created Lord Stow Hill in 1966, he had a quiet retirement in the Lords and died on 1 January 1979 at his home in Hampstead, which he shared with his wife Susan who he had married in 1940 and with whom he enjoyed a singularly happy and successful private life. Perhaps if he had returned to his old job as one of the government law officers his contribution to the Wilson government might have been greater; as it was, his distinguished career ended with a whimper.

Professor Brian Brivati

John Spellar (1947–)

'Part sophisticated Oxford graduate; part unreconstructed South Londoner' was how the *Guardian* described John F Spellar during the 1982 Birmingham Northfield by-election. Philip Bassett, then Labour Editor of the *Financial Times*, called Spellar: 'bearded, conspiratorial and engaging'.

In many ways John is a man of apparent contradictions. He is straight-talking, even rough, yet intellectual and philosophical. He is at home with the horny-handed sons of toil, yet his education – state scholarship at Dulwich College and Oxford University – is not exactly 'shopfloor'. He is a busy Minister who attends Cabinet, yet he makes time to hack with delegates at the regional Labour conferences – and he openly criticises those MPs who feel such tasks are beneath them. He is an ideologue of the traditional Labour centre-right, but at the same time a thoroughly old-fashioned pragmatist, cautious and gradualist.

Born on 5 August 1947, Spellar's time in the sun as a high-profile Labour Minister was earned surely, like many of his generation. Elected to Parliament in the by-election in Birmingham Northfield in 1982, he went on to lose the seat at the general election in 1983, remarking that 'it was all going rather well until the national party poked its nose in'. He was one of the many victims of Labour's lurch to the left. But it would be wrong to say that this was the event that fuelled his hatred of Labour's hard left in the 1980s. He had always hated them, and the feeling was mutual.

On hearing that Spellar had been elected at the 1982 by-election, the editorial in the *Herald* said: 'It is with a heavy heart that we welcome to the Parliamentary Labour Party John Spellar – Frank Chapple's leading henchman'. He took it as a compliment from the people he often referred to as 'the mad, bad and dangerous to know'. And he knew that Machiavelli was right – it is better to be feared than loved.

His contribution to Labour in opposition was vast. In common with others on the Labour right in the early 1980s, Spellar was convinced that the hard left, clamouring around Tony Benn, had launched a coup against the Labour Party. More than most, Spellar knew that the left was unrepresentative of either rank-and-file Labour members or, more critically, of British voters. Long before commentators talked of 'projects', Spellar was prominent in the project to reclaim the party for its members and prepare it for government. Politically he believed that

Labour had lost its way in its opposition to Europe, pandering to CND on defence and refusing to accept the realities of the market economy. At a TUC Congress in the mid-1980s, John Lloyd, now a National Officer with the AEEU, remembers how someone said to Spellar: 'Don't you electricians get bored with being moderate all the time?' To which Spellar replied: 'We're not moderate, mate, we're right-wing!'

Others remember how, during his time as the EETPU's political officer and head of research, Spellar had stand-up rows with any member of staff who expressed sympathies for the breakaway SDP, which he vociferously opposed. Having established the successful 'Liberal Watch' network, he remains a militant opponent of the Liberal Democrats and, similarly, of the folly of proportional representation. One research officer, who had been employed by the EETPU to work on the electricity supply industry, remembers casting some doubt as to the legitimacy of the state of Israel in a casual conversation during the coffee break. Without any hesitation or humour, Spellar quickly informed the young researcher that if he'd known his views prior to interviewing him, he would not have got the job. With Spellar, there *is* such a thing as black and white. Like the AEEU today, the EETPU in the 1980s was an intensely political place, with Spellar's cheerful aggression and Stakhanovite work ethic dominating the building.

But Spellar's contribution, in the 1980s as now, is not primarily as a right-wing Labour ideologue; he is first and foremost an organiser. He saw that by the late 1970s, Labour had allowed key parts of its organisation to be dominated by the unrepresentative left. Quickly gaining the nickname 'John Exspeller' for his efforts in defeating Militant, he led coalitions with other Labour moderates, in local government and the unions, to win back the National Executive Committee and thereby control the key appointments within the Party machine and restore confidence to the parliamentary party. Labour First, the grassroots network of Labour moderates, is still dominated by Spellar and to a large extent owes its heritage to Solidarity, the Campaign for Labour Victory, the Social Democratic Alliance and to Mainstream.

Spellar knew that the left's arguments needed challenging in the party at every level. On One-Member-One-Vote, something that Spellar had always championed, he knew that open public debate would rightly expose the Bennites as elitist. Accordingly he knew that there would have to be a confrontation if the left's arguments were to be defeated. He saw it as the role of the EETPU, as well as in providing invaluable resources and the organisational framework, to create that confrontation.

After he failed to take the Northfield constituency in 1987, reflecting the disappointment of that year's general election, Spellar was selected for the safer Black Country seat of Warley for the 1992 campaign. After the election, he was quickly appointed as a Whip by the late Labour Leader John Smith. From 1995, under Tony Blair, Spellar was appointed first as spokesman for Northern Ireland and then for Defence. After years of battling against the left it is fitting that the Prime Minister Tony Blair – perhaps judging that all governments need a few Spellars in their camp – rewarded Spellar's loyalty in opposition by appointing him Under-Secretary of State at the Ministry of Defence in 1997. After his successful role in implementing the Strategic Defence Review (particularly on equipment issues), and then steering the Government through the Kosovo crisis, he was promoted to Minister of State for the Armed Forces in 1999.

Spellar's promotion to the Cabinet as Minister for Transport was little reported in the media after the General Election of 2001, but it came as little surprise to those who know that he is one of the few Ministers who can 'get things done'. The *New Statesman* said that colleagues describe Spellar as 'a real thug' – his close friend Sir Ken Jackson, General Secretary of the AEEU, remarked: 'John will take it as a compliment!' Certainly friends argue that Spellar's tough, unpretentious attitude – together with a fierce intellect, an attention to detail and shrewd political antennae – is exactly what is needed in an age when the public demand 'delivery' and not just spin.

A contemporary of John Spellar's in the Oxford University Labour Club, Roger Liddle, once said that he found Spellar's consistency quite remarkable in that his basic political outlook was almost identical in 1998 as it was when he first knew him thirty years before. Whereas Liddle jumped ship for the SDP, only to return shortly before the 1997 election, Spellar always stayed loyal to the Labour Party to fight the good fight. Roger Liddle must also have reflected on whether or not he might have been a Labour Minister and not a perpetual advisor if he had shown the same fortitude, vision and conviction that John Spellar had shown in the dark days of the early 1980s.

Michael Dugher

Nigel Stanley (1955–)

Nigel Stanley is Head of Campaigns and Communications at the Trades Union Congress. He has a methodical approach, a vision and an arid sense of humour. His political analysis and advice have been decisive in paving the way for what has come to be called New Labour.

Nigel Stanley was born in Hayes, Middlesex, on 7 April 1955. He was educated at Westminster City School and Southampton University where he obtained a degree in Electronics (1973–76) and a Post Graduate Certificate in Education (1976–77). He joined the Labour Party while a student (1974) and was heavily involved in student politics. He came to national prominence in the Labour Party as Chair of the National Organisation of Labour Students (1977–78).

Nigel Stanley became the Labour Co-ordinating Committee (LCC) Organising Secretary (1978–83). The LCC had been set up towards the end of the 1974–79 Labour government by ministers and advisers close to Tony Benn MP, initially as a focus for work on policy formulation. But after the 1979 defeat the LCC was drawn into the Labour Party's bitter internal debate as a high-profile ginger group and part of a loose arrangement called the Rank and File Mobilising Committee. This body brought together mainstream and ultra-left groups that wanted to increase party democracy and promote a Bennite view of Labour's role.

Many mainstream activists, particularly those with experience of ultra-leftism and Trotskyists in the student movement, were wary of such alliances, and were unhappy at the credibility given to them by some LCC leaders. The influence of such alien groups distorted Labour's image and language, and damaged its electability. Nigel decided to transform the LCC from what could have become merely an ultra-left embarrassment into a cutting edge, mainstream left organisation. Many played a part in this transformation but it was Nigel, as Organising Secretary, whose role was pivotal. Nigel had the courage and the sophistication to confront the ultra-left. Under Nigel's tutelage, the LCC led the only effective opposition, through argument instead of mere name-calling, to infiltration of Labour. This was crucial to the development of the so-called soft left in the early 1980s who, while unhappy with the record of the previous government, rejected hard-left nostrums.

Nigel Stanley's most important achievement at the LCC was to turn the organisation into a force for modernisation in the Labour Party. In the process the LCC became the only ginger group within Labour to take an interest in campaign technique, policy and the nature of Labour's support among voters. A climax came when, in the wake of Labour's 1983 electoral disaster, the LCC organised a series of discussions examining the debacle and Nigel wrote *After the Landslide,* an analysis of what had occurred. It sparked a debate that was long overdue.

Robin Cook MP, then a modernising Labour frontbencher, employed Nigel Stanley as his Research Assistant in 1983. It was a key role at a key time. For much of the period Cook was Labour's Campaigns Co-ordinator and Nigel helped to guide Labour's first faltering steps as a modern campaigning political party. From 1986 to 1992 Nigel was Political Adviser to Bryan Gould MP, another moderniser who also spent some time as Campaigns Co-ordinator and deployed Nigel in key campaigning and policy tasks. Nigel drafted important Policy Review documents on economic policy, and an early green approach to the environment.

Following Gould's failure in the Labour leadership elections and his resignation from Parliament, Nigel took some time out to recuperate from many years at the centre of Labour politics. Until 1994 he was a freelance journalist and consultant. But Nigel Stanley could not stand being away from Labour movement work for too long. Nigel went to work for the Trades Union Congress, first as Parliamentary Officer (1994–97) then as Head of Campaigns and Communications (since 1997).

Nigel Stanley's work at the LCC and his years working for Labour front-benchers involved him in the early years of the great reassessment which culminated in the political approach that underpins New Labour. The TUC's current renaissance has much to do with the leadership of its modernising General Secretary, John Monks, but it is possible to see an important contribution from Nigel's campaigning expertise and political good sense in the background – which is where Nigel always seems happiest.

Rex Osborn

Michael Stewart (Lord Stewart of Fulham) (1906–90)

Michael Stewart was the safest safe pair of hands that the Labour government of 1964–70 possessed. Despite having made his name in opposition as a remarkable spokesman on housing (1959–64), when the government came in he was made Secretary of State for Education and a Privy Counsellor. Three months later, Patrick Gordon Walker, the then Foreign Secretary, failed to win a by-election in Leyton and left the government. In January 1965 Michael Stewart therefore moved to the Foreign Office.

In August 1966, following George Brown's dramatic resignation, he became First Secretary of State and Minister for Economic Affairs. In this role he was effectively Deputy Prime Minister, and would, if anything had happened to Harold Wilson, probably have been called upon by the Queen to serve as interim Premier. He was charged with responsibility for introducing the Labour government's controversial Prices and Incomes policy. His attitude to that is best summed up by a remark of his in July 1967, when he said: 'I look forward to a time when you can work the Prices and Incomes policy, not in a harsh, unfriendly atmosphere, but as a permanent feature of our national life'.

In March 1968 he was back in the Foreign Office again after the departure, this time permanently, of George Brown. He was made a Companion of Honour in 1969. He remained as Foreign Secretary until the government fell in 1970. Thereafter, he held no ministerial office.

Born in Bromley on 6 November 1906, Michael Stewart was the son of Robert Stewart, a London schoolmaster who died when he was four years old, leaving the family in reduced circumstances. The young Michael was sent to a council school in Catford, but won an LCC scholarship to Christ's Hospital. From there he gained a classical scholarship to St John's College, Oxford, where he obtained first class honours in Classical Moderations, and a First in PPE; chaired the University Labour Club and succeeded Quentin Hogg as President of the Union.

After a short spell in Geneva, he took a job as Assistant Master at Merchant Taylor's School, but had to resign when he fought West Lewisham for Labour in the 1931 general election. He failed to win the seat and returned to teaching at another London school, The Coopers. In 1942 he joined the Intelligence Corps and was later transferred to the Army Education Corps. In 1945 he was returned as the Member for Fulham East, a seat that he held until he went to the Lords in 1979. Appointed a Government Whip under Attlee in August 1945, he was promoted within the Whips Office to become Comptroller of HM Household in April 1946 and Vice-Chamberlain in December 1946. Ministerial office followed with his appointment as Under-Secretary and Financial Secretary at the War Office from October 1947 until May 1951, when he became for some six months the Parliamentary Secretary at the Ministry of Supply under George Strauss. In Opposition he served as a spokesman on Education 1955–59 and on Housing and Local Government 1959–64. He was an elected member of the shadow cabinet 1960–64.

Michael Stewart was an intellectual politician, but of the quiet sort. He was never flamboyant, and there was nothing pretentious nor overbearing about his thinking, not having the ebullient thought processes of a Crossman nor the academic attractiveness of a Crosland. He was essentially a quiet, thoughtful man who liked to make his mind up in his own time and his own way but who, having decided on a course of action, rarely, if ever, allowed himself to be diverted. His politics were essentially practical. He was not a great lover of theoreticians' political abstractions. His overriding interest was for the policy to have a practical and beneficial aspect.

His achievements as Foreign Secretary were mixed. Admired for his constancy in furthering British interests, he attracted criticism within the Party for his unwavering support of the US in their intervention in Vietnam, and of the Federal Nigerian government in the Biafran civil war. His attitude on these issues, coupled with his strong denial of the practicability of using force against Smith in Rhodesia, meant that while he earned considerable respect, particularly in the House itself, his position in the party deteriorated to such an extent that when the government lost the 1970 general election, Michael Stewart failed to be elected to the shadow cabinet. On Europe he was a strong pro-European, and one of the 69

Labour MPs who voted with the Conservative government on entry into the Common Market. After 1970 he was appointed leader of the British Labour MPs at the Council of Europe, and from July 1975 until November 1976 was the first elected leader of the British MPs who until direct elections served as Members of the European Parliament.

His personal style was quiet and restrained. Diffident to the point of embarrassment in private conversation, he sparkled when faced with an audience, and the bigger and more difficult the audience, the more he sparkled. Then his power of advocacy was considerable, but it was always advocacy – rarely oratory.

He was devoted to his wife, Mary, a strong Fabian and former chairman of Charing Cross Hospital, who preceded him to the Lords in 1975 (he himself became Lord Stewart of Fulham in 1979). They were married for 42 years, and were a happy and devoted couple. After his wife's death in 1985, he carried on as before and was quoted as agreeing with Tawney that 'to have useful and interesting work to do, and enough money and leisure to do it properly, is as much happiness as is good for the sons of Adam'. His autobiography, *Life and Labour*, was published in 1980 and other publications included *The British Approach to Politics* and *Modern Forms of Government*. He died on 10 March 1990 at the age of 83.

Rt Hon. Lord Richard QC

Richard Rapier Stokes (1897–1957)

Richard Rapier 'Dick' Stokes, born on 27 January 1897, was one of the that band of patrician public school socialists, who included Hugh Dalton and Clement Attlee, who fought in the First World War and came out of it filled with battle honours and a burning determination that never again should anyone have to earn them. He held important ministerial jobs in 1950–51 but died comparatively young without achieving the high office for which he had seemed destined. He was a tall, patrician figure, wealthy, and personally kind and generous, administratively skilled, and politically honourable if not always astute.

Born in South London, his father was a barrister and his mother – whose maiden name, Rapier, he was given as his middle name – came from a wealthy family of Ipswich industrialists. A devout Roman Catholic all his life, he was educated by the Benedictines at Downside in the West Country, one of Britain's four top Catholic public schools, and Trinity College Cambridge, and at both of these institutions he played cricket, football and rugby with distinction, even once playing for England at Twickenham against New Zealand. Between the two he served as an officer in the First World War, retiring as a major in 1919 with an MC, bar and Croix de Guerre.

An engineering graduate, he went into the family business and became managing director at the age of 30. His business took him regularly to the Middle East – a connection which was to have important consequences for his political career.

He contested Glasgow Central for Labour in 1935 and lost, but won a remarkable by-election victory in his home town of Ipswich in 1938, turning a 7,250 Conservative majority into a 3,161 Labour majority. He was convinced that the only way to head off war was to stand up to the dictators, but when war did break out, he became one of the leading critics of government policy, lining himself up with Aneurin Bevan and often going further than even Bevan was willing to do.

He brought to the arguments a certain technical mastery which Bevan and his other colleagues lacked, especially when the two men were receiving leaked evidence about failure in the quality and quantity of British tank production.

He vigorously opposed the bombing of German cities, talking of 'the indiscriminate bombing of civilian centres' which was 'both morally wrong and strategic lunacy'. Attlee acidly but unconvincingly advised him to turn his attention to 'those who began it'. He campaigned tirelessly for the release of those – fascists and others – who had been imprisoned without trial under wartime Regulation 18B. He called the body set up to search for the non-existent fifth column 'this rather odd secret Gestapo' and according to Robert Benewick (*The Fascist Movement in Britain*) he seems to have accepted, wrongly, that Mosley's fascists had never been funded by Mussolini.

These activities, in the overheated atmosphere of wartime politics, brought stupid accusations that he was helping Hitler, and made him unpopular in his own Party, for Churchill would have released all the internees by 1943 had Labour not insisted on keeping them locked up. Combined with the fact that he was an Arabist with many friends and business connections in Arab countries – he had received the Order of the Nile from King Fuad of Egypt for his work on irrigation – it even led some people to suggest that he was anti-Semitic. He was not, though many Arabists were – like St John Philby, the father of the spy Kim Philby, who became an Arabist in much the same way as Stokes, and stood as an anti-war parliamentary candidate. Even today, the little group of diehards who uphold the sacred memory of Sir Oswald Mosley regard Stokes as an icon, which would horrify Stokes. Perhaps this reputation played some part in his heavy defeat when he stood for election to the Administrative Committee of the Parliamentary Labour Party in 1942.

Behind the scenes he helped the war effort, travelling with Bevan to Dublin in an unsuccessful effort to persuade Prime Minister Eamonn de Valera to allow American and British shipping to use Irish ports. It was almost certainly Stokes's wartime politics which led Attlee to deny him office in 1945. Stokes seems to have crossed a line which Bevan just stayed the right side of. But after the 1950 election he got the Ministry of Works, and was responsible for the completion of the Festival of Britain exhibition on London's South Bank.

In April 1951 he joined the Cabinet as Lord Privy Seal after the death of Ernest Bevin, who had been given the job just a month previously to ease his departure on health grounds from the Foreign Office. Attlee seems belatedly to have recognised his administrative qualities, and in August we find Stokes writing to the Prime Minister: 'Thanks for your kind words of confidence in my efforts at the Cabinet yesterday.' In the autumn of that year Attlee sent him as his emissary to try to persuade the new Iranian Prime Minister, Dr Mohammed Mossadeq, not to nationalise the Anglo-Iranian Oil Company (now better known as BP). The British press was in a terrible lather about it, though Mossadeq was a benevolent enough figure, had a good case to argue, and was supported by pretty well everyone in the Arab world. Mossadeq conducted his interviews with Stokes from his old iron bed.

Labour lost office in October 1951 and in opposition Stokes got the defence portfolio, being elected to the shadow cabinet 1951–52 and 1955–56. When Attlee stood down as leader

Stokes noisily and energetically supported Herbert Morrison, showing perhaps the fallible political judgement which had denied him high office. A skilled politician would have seen that Morrison's day had come and gone and the real battle was between Bevan and Hugh Gaitskell. It was also surprising, for Morrison had been the wartime Home Secretary who enthusiastically locked up Mosley and Mosley's supporters and earned angry condemnation from Stokes for doing so. More recently, Morrison had been the Foreign Secretary whose fumbling and inept bellicosity over the Iranian problem had led Attlee to take control himself and send Stokes in. Morrison would have used troops; Stokes and Attlee were determined not to, and they prevailed. In July 1957 he had a serious car accident. Complications set in and he died on 3 August, aged 60.

Francis Beckett

John Stonehouse (1925–88)

Infamous as remains the story of the disappearance of Lord Lucan in the early 1970s, the consequences of his apparent discovery by Australian police in December 1974 proved to have far more profound consequences. The Victoria State police, it turned out, had initially made a mistake. Joseph Arthur Markham and Clive Mildoon, the one man with two false passports they arrested in Melbourne on Christmas Eve, was not Lord Lucan but the Rt Hon. John Thomson Stonehouse, Labour MP for Walsall North since 1974 (and for Wednesbury since a by-election of 1957), who had been missing, presumed dead, since his disappearance off a Miami beach on 21 November 1974.

Stonehouse, the then chair of the ASTMS group of MPs, was a not insignificant political figure and had been regarded in the 1960s as a rising protégé of Harold Wilson, who had even once lent Stonehouse and his family the Wilson holiday bungalow on the Scilly Isles. After his arrest and extradition, an Old Bailey trial revealed his involvement in financial irregularities at the British-Bangladesh Trust bank which had underpinned his £1 million debts and £100,000 horde in a Swiss bank account. His conviction on eighteen charges of theft and false pretences and imprisonment in Wandsworth prison was a profound embarrassment to the then Labour government. In the consequent by-election of 4 November 1976 the seat was lost to the Conservatives on a 22 per cent swing, even though Stonehouse himself had already resigned the Labour whip and renounced the party in April of that year, depriving the Callaghan government of a Commons majority on its first day in office.

Born in Southampton on 28 January 1925, the youngest of four children, his family were enthusiastically involved in local Labour politics. His father, William Mitchell Stonehouse, a Post Office engineer, was secretary of his local trade union branch, and his mother Rosina was a Southampton councillor and alderman (1936–70), President of the local Co-op society and Mayor of Southampton in 1959. His elder sister recruited him into the Woodcraft Folk, where he was nick-name 'Falcon'. He grew up in a Southampton council house and attended Tauntons School, where he was taught English by Horace King, later Labour MP for Southampton Test and Speaker of the House of Commons 1965–70. At 16, King told him he had little ability and ought to become an apprentice butcher; instead, in 1941 he joined the Southampton Probation

Department as a clerk and typist. Leaving for the RAF in 1944 he trained as a pilot in the USA before going to the LSE in 1947, where he was Labour Club Chair, graduating with a BSc (Econ) in 1951. At the LSE Harold Laski encouraged him to put his name forward for Parliament. Stonehouse, still in his mid-twenties, was Labour's unsuccessful candidate at Twickenham in the general election of 1950 and for Burton in the election of 1951. In 1948 he married Barbara Smith, with whom he had a son and two daughters.

Before his election to Parliament in the Wednesbury by-election of February 1957 (caused by the deselection of the sitting Labour MP, former minister Stanley Evans, over his support for Suez), where he defeated Tory candidate Peter Tapsell, having already beaten the favourite, Ray Gunter, in the selection, Stonehouse worked at home and abroad in the Co-op movement. From 1952 to 1954 he lived with his wife and young family in Uganda, building the African Co-op movement and establishing the credentials which would make him Vice-Chair of the Movement for Colonial Freedom under Chairman Fenner Brockway. On a visit to Rhodesia in 1959, his speech calling for black Africans to 'lift your heads high and behave as though the country belongs to you' led to his arrest and forcible deportation by the minority White Rhodesian government, experiences he chronicled in *Prohibited Immigrant* (1960).

Closer to home he became Director of the London Co-operative Society 1956–62 and its President 1962–64, narrowly beating a communist candidate in the election.

Wilson appointed him Under-Secretary of State at the Ministry of Aviation in 1964, under Roy Jenkins, where he set about vainly promoting the virtues of the British Super VC Ten versus the rival Boeing 707. In April 1966 he was moved sideways to the Colonial Office, where he furthered the process of granting independence to Mauritius and Botswana. In January 1967 he became Minister of Aviation in his own right, taking on responsibility for Concorde and Airbus, Anglo-French projects that persuaded him to drop his previous opposition to Britain joining the EEC. With the merging of the Aviation Ministry into the Ministry of Technology in February 1967, six weeks into his appointment, Stonehouse became Minister of State at MinTech under Tony Benn, retaining responsibility for aviation. Created a Privy Counsellor in June 1968, in July he succeeded Roy Mason as Postmaster-General (redesignated Minister of Posts and Telecommunications from October 1969) where he unsuccessfully tried to ditch what he regarded as the technological white elephants of his ministerial predecessors: namely postcodes and Girobanking.

It was then, however, that his career peaked: though he finally got to run his own ministry, he never made Cabinet, and after Labour's defeat at the 1970 election he was dropped from the front bench. Perhaps it was the Czech spy scandal that finally raised doubts in Wilson's mind about Stonehouse's reliability (in 1968 Stonehouse was named by a defector – though cleared – of being an informer for the Czech Secret Service). As Stonehouse himself wrote in his memoir, it was deeply ironic that as Minister for Posts and Telecommunications, unbeknown to him, his telephone was bugged on the orders of the Home Secretary. Nevertheless, the doubts of senior Labour figures like Barbara Castle and Roy Jenkins seem to have had no appreciable impact in retarding Stonehouse's prior career progression (Jenkins had resisted Stonehouse as his deputy at Aviation in 1964, preferring Tom Bradley, but Wilson had insisted on Stonehouse). Dick Crossman's views were typical of those like Castle and Jenkins whose doubts were ignored. He noted in his diary of 23 January 1969:

A tall, dark rather sleek young man ... [Stonehouse] has this rather insolent, handsome face, and when he is nervous an incipient stutter. I have always had the profoundest suspicion of his moral reliability. I met him first in Kampala in 1954 when I was reporting on the Mau Mau. He was Secretary of the Uganda Producers' Co-operative, which closed down in a great stink and he had to fly the land ... He certainly used pretty rough tactics in 1962 when he got himself made President of the London Co-operative ... When Harold gave me the job of investigating that great scandal at the Ministry of Technology, I found that there was no doubt that John Stonehouse had behaved in the most extraordinary way ... I have watched him in every job – for some reason he gets advancement – and I think he is a kind of dangerous crook, overwhelmingly ambitious but above all untrustworthy.

He was released from prison in 1979, having served three and a half years, half his sentence, during which time he underwent heart surgery after suffering several heart attacks. Having divorced his first wife in 1978, in 1981 he married his mistress and former Commons Secretary Sheila Buckley, with whom he had planned to start his new life in Australia. They had one son. His memoir, *Death of an Idealist,* had appeared in 1975 and three novels were published from 1982 to 1987: *Ralph* (1982), *The Baring Fault* (1986) and *Oil on the Rift* (1987). In 1985 he founded a company manufacturing electronic safes. He collapsed at his home in Totton near Southampton on 15 April 1988 and was dead on arrival in hospital.

Greg Rosen

John Strachey (1901–63)

John Strachey is one of that relatively rare breed known both as prominent Labour politicians as well as political theorists of considerable note. But his contribution as both politician and theorist was also notable for its extreme fluctuations. As a theorist he moved from being Britain's leading exponent of communism to Keynesian social democrat and avowed anti-communist. As a politician he moved from the Independent Labour Party (ILP) via the New Party (from which the British Union of Fascists emerged) to the fringes of the Communist Party and back to the Labour Party, where he ultimately became associated, albeit slightly peripherally, with the revisionist social democrats clustered around Hugh Gaitskell.

That Strachey joined the Labour Party at all gives an early indication of his later political volatility. Evelyn John St Loe Strachey was born on 21 October 1901 into the upper class. His father was John St Loe Strachey, the owner and editor of *The Spectator,* and a prominent figure in the British Establishment. John went to Eton and then to read history at Oxford in 1920 before joining *The Spectator* where he seemed destined to take over its editorship and ownership from his father. However within two years of leaving Oxford he had declared himself a socialist, joined the ILP, and beca,e its prospective parliamentary candidate for the potentially winnable seat of Aston in Birmingham, eventually winning it in the general election of May 1929 that brought to office the ill-fated MacDonald government.

Strachey's involvement in Left politics in Birmingham brought him into contact and then close friendship and collaboration with Oswald Mosley. Mosley was already regarded as a political maverick having joined the Labour Party in 1924 after being elected a Conservative MP in 1918. Mosley and Strachey were united in a rejection of the economic approach of Labour in the 1920s. In *Revolution by Reason* (Leonard Parsons, 1925) Strachey developed the expansionist economic proposals he and Mosley had been working on. In place of Labour's commitment to balanced budgets and a continuing faith in the Gold Standard to end the recession and return the British economy to its pre-1914 economic status, Strachey proposed the nationalisation of the Bank of England and a policy centred on the maintenance of effective demand – more active state management of the economy was imperative if economic crisis and the resulting class conflict was to be avoided. Despite the limited impact of *Revolution by Reason* within the Labour movement, it earned him a sufficient profile to win the editorship of the ILP journal *Socialist Review* in 1925, a position from which he was able to air his, and indeed the whole ILP's, frustrations with the economic approach of Ramsay MacDonald and his Shadow Chancellor Philip Snowden.

As the 1920s progressed his political views were increasingly influenced by Marxism. He became convinced that a Labour government could only rule within parameters set by the capitalist class. As such, only moderate moves could be made until the working class was prepared to unite and take full control of the state. This interest in Marxism, though by no means unique within the Labour Party at the time, does point to the more radical transformation in his political thought that was to come. This Marxist influence did not, however, prevent him from marrying the American heiress, Esther Murphy in 1929. It also did not prevent him from immediately becoming PPS to Mosley, who was now Chancellor of the Duchy of Lancaster

But despite his position he was soon publicly critical of Chancellor Snowden's orthodox economic policies. After a protracted internecine struggle between supporters of Mosley's expansionist proposals and those loyal to the policies of Snowden and MacDonald, Strachey resigned from the Labour Party to join Mosley's New Party. However this was a relatively short and ill-fated association. Strachey had hoped that the New Party could be a distinctively socialist party, but within months the rightwards trajectory of Mosley that would culminate with fascism was clear. However, as the MacDonald government collapsed in 1931, he was convinced of the futility of rejoining the Labour Party and by 1932 he was effectively a representative of the Communist Party. He also left Esther, marrying in 1933 Celia Simpson, a vicar's daughter whom he had known since Oxford and with whom he had been having an affair for some time.

Despite having his Communist Party membership application rejected, he became closely involved with the Party as its propagandist, seeking to attract disillusioned ILP members and to broaden its appeal as a mass anti-fascist movement. In 1932 he published *The Coming Struggle for Power* (Gollancz) in which he argued that capitalism would lead to violence and misery and communism remained the only route to a peaceful, civilised society. The book, along with later work such as *The Nature of the Capitalist Crisis* (Gollancz, 1935), was a significant influence on a generation of idealist young people seemingly faced with the alternative of fascism as a way out of the impasse that capitalism appeared to have reached in the 1930s. His work received a particularly high level of attention through his association with the Left Book Club, which he established with publisher Victor Gollancz and the academic Harold Laski.

Despite establishing himself as the foremost communist author in Britain, by the end of the 1930s he was once again shifting his ideological position. He had turned to communism as a means to save civilisation in despair at the failure of the Labour government. However by 1938 he was no longer convinced that capitalism's failures would inevitably lead to communism, fearing that they were more likely to result in fascism. As a result it was vital for a progressive government to develop the means to manage capitalism to fend off such a crisis. In *A Programme for Progress* (Gollancz, 1940) he argued that, in the medium term at least, capitalism might be managed in an expansionist, redistributionary way toward this end. *Programme for Progress* brought together Keynesian economics and socialist ideals, and in doing so paved the way for the post-war, revisionist Strachey. It was largely dismissed as liberal reformism within the Communist Party which, coupled with its soft line on Germany, precipitated his move back to Labour.

In the Labour landslide victory in 1945, Strachey returned to parliament as Labour MP for Dundee and was made Under-Secretary of State for Air. In May 1946 he was promoted to be Minister of Food before being moved to be Secretary of State for War in February 1950, following his introduction of bread rationing and a very publicly unsuccessful attempt to convert large parts of Africa to groundnut production; he remained there until the fall of the government in 1951. His time as Minister of War was also difficult; his enthusiasm for higher defence spending to contain Soviet expansion was one of the factors behind the imposition of charges on dentures and spectacles – a move which led to the resignation of his erstwhile ally and former Mosley acolyte Aneurin Bevan, as well as John Freeman and Harold Wilson.

After the fall of the Attlee government in 1951, Strachey was a fairly peripheral figure in the factional struggles between followers of Gaitskell and Bevan and reverted to his role as thinker and writer, publishing perhaps his best-known book *Contemporary Capitalism* (Gollancz, 1956). In it he continued the fundamental refutation of his communist past that had begun with *Programme for Progress*. Despite being right about much, Marx, he claimed, had underestimated the ability of progressive forces to use the state for their own ends, particularly through Keynesianism and public ownership.

Despite a good reception *Contemporary Capitalism* (and the judgement that it was 'built to last' [B. Crick 'Socialist Literature in the Fifties' *Political Quarterly* Vol.31 (1960), p.368]) was rather overshadowed by the furore surrounding Anthony Crosland's *The Future of Socialism* in the same year. Despite being lumped together as examples of Gaitskellite social democracy there remained differences between the two books, with Strachey putting far greater emphasis on state economic controls and public ownership as the *sine qua non* of the Labour Party. Rita Hinden, reviewing the book, considered it an inconclusive debate between the post-war reformist Strachey and his inter-war Marxist self ['Old Etonian versus Marx' *Socialist Commentary* (Sept 1956) p.28–9].

In opposition during the 1950s, Strachey shadowed the Air and War ministries before becoming Shadow Aviation Minister in 1960 and finally Shadow Commonwealth Secretary from 1961 until his death in 1963. His links with the Gaitskellites strengthened over the period and he sided with the leadership in the votes on revising Clause IV of the Labour Party constitution committing it to 'common ownership of the means of production' and the rejection of unilateralism. He also became increasingly committed to closer European integration, a testament of faith to many Gaitskellites (though not Gaitskell himself). He also concerned himself with issues of development, arguing for redistribution towards the developing world as a means to prevent the spread of communism.

By the time of his sudden death on 15 July 1963, Strachey was one of the most experienced politicians on the Labour benches, having been involved in the 1929 government and having held a ministerial post throughout the Attlee administration. He also had an established reputation as a Party intellectual. But he perhaps did not achieve the prominence or influence that he might have. Had he lived he could have expected a good job in the Wilson government though not one of the best ones, never actually securing election to the shadow cabinet. As a theorist he was most influential in his communist phase. As a social democrat in the 1950s he was, as Hinden notes, playing catch-up with many of those he had converted to communism in the first place and he never made the impact that Crosland did. His Parliamentary career was overshadowed by his communist past and prevented him from rising to the senior posts in the Party. His political volatility then prevented him from achieving greatness either as a Labour thinker or as a reforming politician. Strachey's work, though largely out of print, remains a substantial oeuvre. There are substantial biographies by Hugh Thomas, *John Strachey* (1973), and Noel Thompson, *John Strachey: An Intellectual Biography* (1993), and the much shorter *John Strachey* (1989) by Michael Newman.

Dr Philip Larkin

Gavin Strang (1943–)

Gavin Strang is one of Labour's most experienced MPs, joining Parliament in 1970 at the age of 27. Born on 10 July 1943, the son of James Steel Strang, a Perthshire tenant farmer, his upbringing and PhD in Animal Genetics made him highly qualified as a Labour spokesman on agriculture. After Morrison's Academy he studied at Edinburgh University – like his MP colleagues Robin Cook and Gordon Brown – and briefly at Cambridge and was active in the Labour Party there. Elected Labour MP for Edinburgh East in 1970, his diligence and abilities were recognised early by the former Prime Minister and then Opposition leader Harold Wilson, who appointed him as opposition spokesman on the Highlands within three years of Gavin's entry into Parliament.

When Wilson won his third term of office in February 1974, Wilson appointed him Under-Secretary of State for Energy, which Gavin had shadowed since 1973. This was the pioneering era of North Sea oil exploration and development. Oil companies were demanding tax concessions and a liberal licence regime. Gavin wanted a revenue stream and the most advantageous terms for the government. This was not a job where friends were made of these powerful multi-national companies. After the next election in October 1974, the Prime Minister moved Gavin to the hot seat of Agriculture, as Parliamentary Secretary, where Gavin continued to fight for the rights of tenant farmers and their families, ending oppressive tied cottage laws and gaining inheritance rights for widows and sons. This was a debt of honour to his boyhood friends. Likewise, his excellent reputation as a constituency MP was reinforced by championing AIDS victims. This came from his experience of constituents in Edinburgh where soaring unemployment during the Thatcher years blighted whole communities like Craigmillar, leaving people in the depths of despair unknown since the Depression years. Nor was Gavin's campaign a one-off. When blood supplies were contaminated by HIV in the 1980s and '90s, he campaigned for compensation for the victims.

An early champion of animal welfare, he opposed the transport of live animals over long distances and secured international advances in fish conservation. His years in opposition after 1979 were marked by shadow posts in Agriculture (1979–82), Employment (1987–89), and Food, Agriculture and Rural Affairs (1992–97).

A strong supporter of CND and a member of the Campaign Group of Labour MPs, he backed Tony Benn's socialist campaigns in the 1980s. In 1990 he voted against the UK's involvement in the Gulf War. With a terrific work-rate throughout the 1990s, he eventually was elected by his peers to the shadow cabinet in 1994, serving as the chief spokesman for Agriculture and Rural Affairs. But the spinning against him followed swiftly after this, with a newspaper report before the 1997 election that, as Prime Minister, Blair would drop him from the Cabinet. Such reports continued after his appointment as John Prescott's deputy in charge of Transport, with a seat in Cabinet, and in July 1998 the axe fell. This was not the first time that Tony Blair had moved Gavin Strang. Nearly ten years earlier, Gavin was dropped from Labour's Employment team when Tony Blair gained his first major promotion. After he ceased to be a minister in 1998, he became an outspoken critic of the Government's plans for air traffic control. He married Bettina Morrison in 1973, with whom he has one son.

Nigel Griffiths MP

Jack Straw   (1946–)

Jack Straw is one of the most underrated politicians of his generation. A ministerial career as Home and then Foreign Secretary ought, on its own, to confirm him as one of the 'big beasts'. In opposition, too, Straw displayed a rare mixture of courage, insight and determination, arguing against the prevailing Labour tide and being ready to re-examine Labour shibboleths at great risk to his own status, well before such behaviour was commonplace. His career displays all the marks of a man of stature and principle.

And yet Straw has never received the recognition that ought to be his due. His somewhat plodding image, a quiet manner, a lack of histrionics and a refusal to play the Westminster game of briefing and counter-briefing have all played their part in keeping the lid on his reputation. His Commons performances are competent, if never especially dominant, in part because of his tinnitus. As Shadow Home Secretary he failed to score in front of an open goal when the then Home Secretary, Michael Howard, sacked the Director of the Prison Service. Indeed, he suffered the humiliation of Tony Blair intervening in his speech to tackle Mr Howard himself.

Jack (or John Whitaker, the names he was given at birth) Straw was born on 3 August 1946 in Buckhurst Hill, Essex. One of the reasons Straw was so successful as Shadow Home Secretary in selling the first part of Labour's 'tough on crime, tough on the causes of crime' approach was that he was brought up on a council estate in Loughton, an upbringing which gave him an instinctive grasp of the sort of law and order policies a party supposedly upholding the interests of the poor ought to be espousing.

Left politics was in his blood: his father, an insurance clerk and conscientious objector, met his mother, a teacher, in the Peace Pledge Union. His parents divorced when he was ten and he was brought up by his mother. Straw was political almost as soon as he was born; he went on an Aldermaston march when he was just 12 and he joined the Labour Party at 15. He was a precocious child, winning a boarding scholarship to Brentwood School, where he passed ten O-levels at 14. At Leeds University, he became President of the Students' Union in 1967; two years later he entered national politics as President of the National Union of Students, after which he joined Islington Council in May 1971 (on which he remained for seven years). A clue to his later 'bread and butter' brand of socialism was given in his time at the NUS; Straw spent his time in office concerned primarily with issues such as the student grant and housing, rather than the more broad-brush campaigns that were the norm. Famously, he is often said to be the only 1960s student who took no drugs.

Straw was called to the Bar in 1972 and practiced until, after the February 1974 election, he became Special Adviser to Barbara Castle and then, on her sacking in 1976, to Peter Shore. It was at this time that he met his second wife, Alice Perkins, now a senior civil servant.

His appointment as Foreign Secretary in June 2001 brought his long track record of Euroscepticism to public attention. In Castle and Shore, he had two of the most passionate opponents of British membership of the then Common Market and he was instrumental in the setting up with Shore of the Labour Common Market Safeguards Committee.

One of the continuing threads of Straw's career has been loyalty. Just as Straw has been one of Tony Blair's most trusted and loyal colleagues since his election as Labour leader in 1994, so Straw has always stayed loyal to his former employers. When Barbara Castle left the Commons in 1979 to enter the European Assembly, Straw took over her Blackburn seat and, as a rising star of the PLP, he played a key role in Shore's two leadership campaigns; in 1980, when it looked as if Shore might win, and again in 1983, even though at this second attempt there was never a hope of victory. Unlike some, he chose not to nail his colours to the mast of the obvious victor, Neil Kinnock, but to remain loyal.

In his early parliamentary career he was thought to be on the left (or, in the language of the time, 'soft left') of the party but, above all, his loyalty is to Labour. Thus he urged Tony Benn against forcing his destructive deputy leadership contest in 1981, but was equally condemnatory of the so-called 'Gang of Four' for leaving the Labour Party as he was of the Militant Tendency and hard left whose dominance provoked them to go.

In 1987 he entered the shadow cabinet as Shadow Education Secretary. Although in today's terms Straw remained a relatively unreconstructed supporter of the 'bog standard' comprehensive, he forced some genuine changes on Labour, for which he took much flak, arguing that it was sensible to have 'schools managing more of their own affairs', proposing testing at 7, 11, 14 and 16, distancing Labour from the teaching unions, and arguing that Labour was the party of 'standards, of quality control and consumer choice'.

This ability to be ahead of his time was repeated in many other aspects of his career, not least when in 1993, to the fury of John Smith, he published a pamphlet arguing for the abolition of Clause IV. At the time there was little for him to gain, and much to lose: Smith looked set fair to remain leader – and then probably Prime Minister – for years and by raising the spectre of Clause IV Straw was very much out on a limb. Tony Blair, for instance, had made no such case (and had indeed argued that Clause IV was an irrelevance). Straw was not to know that his words would be heeded only a year later by the new leader, Tony Blair.

In 1994 Straw took over the Home Affairs brief from Blair, and stayed in that post until June 2001. To some, his tenure as Home Secretary was characterised by authoritarianism, attacks on civil rights and an undue deference to the *Daily Mail's* worldview. In fact, he was far more subtle. Whatever its rights or wrongs, for instance, his proposal to restrict the right to jury trial for some petty criminals was a reaction to the widely recognised problem of criminals 'playing the system'. On some definitions it was illiberal; to the view of those for whom Labour of all parties should be ridding estates of petty criminals, it was a sensible reform. In other areas, Straw was able to use tough rhetoric to mask liberal interventions.

Home Secretaries have been blown into oblivion by far less critical events than those dealt with by Straw. His political skill was never more clearly demonstrated than by the furore over the arrest of the former Chilean dictator, General Pinochet. Despite months of political, diplomatic and judicial chaos, Straw managed to extricate himself from an impossible situation and packed him off to Chile with no detriment to his reputation.

After four years as Home Secretary, and then becoming Foreign Secretary, it would be foolish to ignore Jack Straw as a possible contender for the leadership of the Labour Party once Tony Blair departs.

Stephen Pollard

Edith Summerskill (1901–80)

Dr Edith Clara Summerskill was both imposingly tall and the leading Labour woman Parliamentarian from the death of Ellen Wilkinson in 1947 until her own retirement from Labour's front bench in 1964. Though never actually in Cabinet, after Wilkinson's death she was the most senior woman minister of the Attlee government. The 1949 milk pasteurisation legislation, secured whilst she was Parliamentary Secretary to the Ministry of Food 1945–50, was one of her proudest achievements. From February 1950 until the fall of the government in October 1951 she ran her own department as Minister of National Insurance. She was the only woman elected to the shadow cabinet during the period 1951–64 (from 1951–57 and after her defeat in November 1957, re-elected in November 1958–59), and she served as Shadow Health Minister throughout the 1950s up until her elevation to the Lords as Baroness Summerskill in 1961. A member of Labour's NEC from 1944 until 1958, she was Chair of the Labour Party 1954–55.

Born in London on 19 April 1901 the youngest daughter of the progressively-minded Dr William Summerskill and his wife Edith, she was educated at Eltham Hill Grammar School, Kings College and Charing Cross Hospital, where she met fellow student Dr Jeffrey Samuel. They married in 1924. They had two children, Michael and Shirley, both of whom became active in the Labour Party (though Michael later joined the SDP) and were office-bearers of Oxford University Labour Club. Self-consciously feminist, Edith was one of the few women of her generation involved in politics who kept her maiden name after marriage. Her children also took her name and retained it through marriage: Shirley Summerskill followed in her mother's footsteps to the extent of becoming a doctor, an MP (Halifax 1964–83), a minister

(Under-Secretary of State at the Home Office 1974–79) and a Solidarity/Manifesto Group backed member of Labour's NEC 1981–83.

In the late 1920s Edith became active in the Socialist Medical Association and in Wood Green Labour Party, where she practised as a doctor. In 1934 she won a by-election for Labour on Middlesex County Council. She was less successful as Labour's candidate in a Parliamentary by-election at Putney the same year and as Labour's candidate for Bury at the 1935 general election, where she was colourfully denounced for her support for the rights of women to family planning. So bad was the abuse that, when writing to the Leeds South Constituency Labour Party to recommend her for consideration as a candidate in 1936, New Fabian Research Bureau Secretary John Parker MP added a considerable caveat: 'A good speaker and a live and active woman. If there are many Catholics in the division I would not recommend her as she is a strong advocate of birth control.' In a by-election of 1938, however, she was victorious in the Conservative-held seat of West Fulham, which she held until its abolition under boundary review led to a move to Warrington in 1955, a seat she held until her elevation to the Lords.

In 1936 she had joined Ellen Wilkinson and Nye Bevan in supporting the hunger marches of the unemployed. During the 1930s Summerskill was a great admirer of Bevan, and he would often come round to her house and play with the children. By the 1950s their differences on policy and party loyalty had produced a split, though she pinned more blame on Ian Mikardo for the excesses of the Bevanites than Nye himself. Dick Crossman recorded in his diary her outburst of 19 May 1954, quoting her as saying: 'Nye, Barbara [Castle] and Dick [Crossman] – I've got nothing against them. They are the victims of their temperament. The real danger here, the real organiser of subversion, is that man Mikardo!' She backed Gaitskell and Morrison against Bevan over the introduction of dental and eye charges in 1951 and advocated withdrawing the whip from Bevan over his nuclear rebellion in 1955. Her own views on 'the bomb' were idiosyncratic: pro-NATO and collective security, she combined a virulent anti-communism with a fear of the radiation risks associated with strontium-90 and therefore appears to have developed an aversion to Britain's retention of nuclear weapons on grounds of health risk. Gaitskell found her occasional unreliability irritating. Over Suez, Gaitskell believed she was 'pro-Nasser because she once met him or once went to Egypt.' 'She is extremely emotional, she does not listen very carefully,' Gaitskell recorded in his diary in August 1956, ' she is not really intelligent … is a woman whose political views are almost entirely dependent on personal contacts.'

In the Lords she proved a redoubtable campaigner on issues ranging from equal pay and the rights of women to matrimonial property, via opposition to Leo Abse's attempts to liberalise divorce law to her attempts to ban boxing. She died at her London home off Pond Square, Highgate, on 4 February 1980. Her books included *Babies without Tears* (1941); *The Ignoble Art* (1956); *Letters to My Daughter* (1957); and the autobiographical *A Woman's World* (1967).

Eleanor Jupp

Dick Taverne (Lord Taverne of Pimlico) (1928–)

Dick Taverne was Labour Member of Parliament for Lincoln from March 1962 until October 1972. Then, following a by-election, he sat for the same seat as Democratic Labour for some eighteen months, from March 1973 until September 1974. He was an Under-Secretary of State at the Home Office 1966–68 and successively Minister of State and Financial Secretary at the Treasury 1968–1970. He became a Liberal Democrat peer as Lord Taverne of Pimlico, in 1996.

Dick Taverne was born on 18 October 1928 of a Dutch father and English mother. He remains a Dutch speaker. He was educated in England at Charterhouse and Balliol College, Oxford, where he was an outstanding classical scholar. In 1954 he was called to the Bar and became a QC in 1965. He has been married to Janice (Hennessy) since 1955.

At Oxford, Dick Taverne held senior office in the Union and was Chairman of the Labour Club. Later, he became active in local Labour politics and as a member of the Fabian Society. He helped to organise protests against the Suez War in 1956 and became Labour candidate for Putney in the 1959 general election, reducing the Tory majority against the trend. After the Election, he became one of the leaders of the Campaign for Democratic Socialism in support of Labour's leader Hugh Gaitskell. When he won the Lincoln by-election in March 1962 he was Labour's second youngest MP.

He admired Harold Wilson's 'white heat of the scientific revolution' speech at the Labour Conference of 1963, although he became disillusioned with Wilson's performance as Prime Minister. He was one of the best of the young Ministers in the 1964–1970 Government both in the House of Commons and his departments.

With Labour now in Opposition, he was amongst the 69 Labour MPs who, in 1971, voted to take Britain into the Common Market against a three-line whip. But his vote for Europe brought to a head a simmering row with a powerful left-wing faction in his constituency. They had strongly objected to the short-list from which Taverne had been selected, all of whom had been on the right of the party. They had also been critical of the Government in which Taverne had served. By temperament, Taverne liked an argument and he could be uncompromising in debate. A Granada *World in Action* television programme exposed the bitter conflict and although it brought him sympathy and support from constituents and from well-wishers nationwide, it removed any chance of reconciliation. When a vote calling for his retirement was carried by a margin of 3:2, and his appeal to the National Executive Committee was turned down, he decided in October 1972 to resign his seat, leave the Labour party and fight a by-election.

His courage was widely applauded in the country, especially by those who had become alarmed by Labour's drift to the left. But there was embarrassment amongst many of his friends who were not ready to turn their backs on Labour or felt he had mishandled his constituency affairs. Taverne won the by-election in March 1973 and held the seat in the first General Election of 1974. But in the second Election of that year, he lost to Margaret Jackson (who later married his leading opponent in Lincoln to become Margaret Beckett).

A difficult period of political isolation followed. But his legal and financial talents, and his quick and innovative mind, opened up business opportunities. He served on the boards of several public companies and created the Institute of Fiscal Studies, which became an important think-tank. He also became Chairman of Prima Europe, a business and public affairs consultancy.

When the SDP was launched in 1981, he was united with his old political allies. Many social democrats looked back to his Lincoln experience as presaging the crisis in the Labour party that had now arrived. He played an active part in policy making and contested the Peckham by-election of 1982 and Dulwich in the 1983 general election.

Dick Taverne was generous in acknowledging Labour's recovery in the 1990s and in supporting policies consistent with his own steadily held beliefs. He contributes with authority to debates in the House of Lords, supports charities and good causes of various kinds and finds time for sailing his much-loved sea-going yacht. *The Future of the Left* (1974) was Dick Taverne's account of his break from the Labour Party over events in Lincoln.

Rt Hon. Lord Rodgers of Quarry Bank

Richard Henry Tawney   (1880–1962)

In reviewing one of R H Tawney's collections of essays in 1953, Tony Crosland compared Tawney's legacy to that of other leading socialists. They simply influenced one element of policy or organisation, he argued: Tawney gave Labour a coherent and comprehensive philisophy. Crosland was certainly right in that Tawney represents one of the most significant socialist theorists of the twentieth century, and his ideas permeated deep into the political consciousness of the Labour Party. However Tawney also made a significant contribution to the formation of Labour Party and Government policy, particulary on education, and though he never served in Parliament, his life is of great interest to political historians of the last century.

Richard Henry Tawney was born on 30 November 1880 in Calcutta where his father, C H Tawney, was the Principal of Presidency College. Tawney spent most of his childhood in Weybridge and was educated at Rugby, where he struck up a lifelong friendship with the future Archbishop of Canterbury, William Temple. Yet Tawney's formative years came at Balliol College, Oxford, which he entered in 1899. Even sixteen years after the death of its leading exponent, T H Green, Balliol was still under the sway of the philosophical school of idealism. Through his relationship with his tutor, Edward Caird, Tawney was drawn into the idealist tradition, and, though he never regarded himself as a philosopher, his political and economic writings clearly display their concepts. While at Oxford he joined the Christian Social Union, whose founders Henry Scott Holland and Charles Gore also shared many aspects of idealist thought. Gore was another of Tawney's tutors and through this network of philosophers and philanthropists at Oxford, Tawney developed an ethical tradition which had idealist foundations and which reached up towards the Christian Socialist heavens.

To the great disappointment of his father, Tawney only gained a second in Greats. Together with his Balliol colleague, William Beveridge, Tawney left Oxford to take up Caird's challenge to 'discover why with so much wealth, there was also so much poverty in London'. Tawney went first to the East End settlement, Toynbee Hall, named after another Oxford idealist and economic historian, Arnold Toynbee. From there, he moved on to work for the Children's Country Holiday Fund, where he met his future wife and sister of William, Jeannette Beveridge. They married in 1908.

The central part of Tawney's adult life was divided between his career in teaching and academic education, and his political role as an educational and moral campaigner. His first job came in 1906, when he was appointed by Professor William Smart to teach Economics at the University of Glasgow. In 1908, Tawney became the first tutor for a series of university extension courses aimed at workers in Rochdale, under the wings of the newly founded Workers'

Educational Association. His academic prowess was recognised by the London School of Economics and Political Science in 1913 when he was appointed the Director of the Ratan Tata Foundation, working alongside the leading New Liberal theorist L T Hobhouse.

Following the Great War, in which Tawney served with distinction as a sergeant and was seriously wounded on the Somme, he returned to the LSE to take up a Readership. In 1931 he was made Professor of Economic History at the University of London, a position he held until his retirement in 1949.

His writings during the interwar years were the most significant of his life. An essay for the Fabian Society in 1919 was turned into *The Acquisitive Society* (1921), an attack on the growth of a valueless society that placed acquisition above ethics and the common good. Modern life created an unreal dualism, with morality squeezed out of economics and the public realm. Individuals were given 'natural' rights that bore no relation to any social function. Instead Tawney argued that all social institutions should be made to work to social ends and rights were to be derived from this common good.

The impact of this ethical view of human conduct was further developed in his Henry Scott Holland Memorial Lectures, later published as *Religion and the Rise of Capitalism* (1926). The view of society as an organism, a perspective which religion had helped to sustain in the sixteenth century, was abandoned with the development of capitalism. Ethical relationships were replaced by selfish individualism and a cash nexus. The comradeship and citizenship that Tawney believed lay at the heart of humankind were undermined by a social philosophy that created huge social inequalities. The sickness of modern society, he argued, was caused by the lack of a proper moral ideal.

Central to all his writings was the concept of equality, and his most famous work *Equality* was published in 1931. Tawney used equality in two different ways: firstly to argue that everyone possesses equal moral value; but also to justify differences in material equality provided they were justified by the common good of society. In *Equality* Tawney argued every individual should be recognised as a moral personality and therefore be treated as an end in themselves, not simply a means to an end. Individuals were to him essentially divine, and to act in a way that ignored the moral worth of a person was to sin against God. Therefore one of his main attacks against nineteenth-century capitalism was that many individuals were used as 'tools', 'instruments of acquisition', perpetuating a society divided into masters and servants. However this fundamental weakness in capitalism did not justify total material equality. Complete moral equality was for Tawney consistent with material differences: indeed the latter were desirable in order to enable individuals to act freely and to fulfil their potential. His target was unjustified and unwarranted material inequality. Based on his notion of common good, Tawney argued that inequalities in wealth and power were justified when they served the social purpose. Society was justified in awarding exceptional rewards as incentives to individuals to perform difficult jobs, or ordering itself in a hierarchy of power, or paying unequal incomes, all provided such measures were justified and related to the function being performed. His complaint about the world of the 1930s was that most inequalities were not supporting the social purpose at all, but were founded on privilege, tradition and cultural differences. Therefore Tawny proposed an expansion of the role of the state to deliver for all individuals the means of civilisation – that which everyone needed to make the best of themselves. This was to be achieved principally through improved education, health and social services.

Tawney's life would be remarkable for his writings alone. However there remained another side to his life, that of the politician, the educational and ethical campaigner within the Labour movement. Tawney joined the Fabians in 1906 and the Independent Labour Party in 1909. However his ethical idealism meant Tawney rejected the gradualist approach of his Fabian socialist colleagues. Change was not inevitable, he argued, nor would improvement be brought about simply through increased state action. Instead Tawney's goal was to bring about measures to enable self-development and the improvement of character. Despite serving on the Fabian Executive from 1921, he fundamentally disagreed with his close friends and leading Fabians, Sidney and Beatrice Webb. 'They tidy the room', he wrote in his Commonplace Book, 'but they open no windows in the soul'.

Education was Tawney's life-mission, no doubt because it represented a key means of self-improvement. Tawney was a key member of the Workers' Educational Association, elected to its Executive in 1905 and as its President from 1928 to 1944. As well as the WEA, he was also influential on education policy through his role on numerous education committees and working groups, like the Consultative Committee of the Board of Education which reported in 1926. As one of his biographers, Tony Wright, put it: 'From the Fisher Act of 1918 to the Butler Act of 1944 Tawney's influence is writ large over the history of educational thought and policy in Britain.'

His interests were not restricted to education alone. For example he served on the Coal Industry Commission in 1919, led by Lord Sankey, where his contribution was seen as significant by senior Labour figures. Tawney was also active in Christian Socialist circles. Through his close friendship with Charles Gore, he served on many discussion groups investigating the cause of social problems, such as the Committee of Inquiry into *Christianity and Industrial Problems*, which reported in 1917. He also took a leading role in the Christian Politics, Economics and Citizenship conference in 1924.

Tawney's great interest in social and political matters also found expression in his influential role within the Labour Party. Tawney was never an MP – he stood for Parliament unsuccessfully three times, in Rochdale (1918), Tottenham (1922) and Swindon (1924). He was offered a safe seat in 1935 but by then his interest in elected office had waned. Tawney also refused Ramsay MacDonald's offer of a peerage in 1933, characteristically replying 'What harm have I ever done to the Labour Party?' Yet despite never sitting on the benches in Westminster, Tawney was extremely important in the development of Labour Party thinking and policy in the interwar years, and his ideas and thoughts can be seen clearly in Labour's election manifestos. He was also involved in key debates in the Labour Party, most notably in 1931 after MacDonald's resignation and the formation of the National Government, and in the early 1950s debate about nationalisation and unilateralism.

At the outbreak of the Second World War, Tawney went to Washington as a Labour attaché to the British embassy. Following the conflict, he returned to his political and historical writings and published *The Attack* (1953), a collection of political essays, and *Business and Politics under James I* (1958), which focused on his main academic interest, seventeenth-century economic history. While in this period Tawney worked on many different areas, his publications were infrequent. As A J P Taylor put it, 'The unwritten works of Tawney are among the lost masterpieces of the twentieth century.' He celebrated his eightieth birthday in 1960 with a party in the House of Commons. He died two years later, in January 1962.

Tawney's life can truly be said to be one of the most significant in terms of the development of British socialist thought in the twentieth century. He was able to draw the key elements from the idealist Liberal tradition of thought and marry them with a Christian faith and an understanding of economic history. The ideological mixture that emerged was an ethical socialism rooted in a fundamental belief in individual moral worth, equality of opportunity and social responsibility. Tawney's ideas were widely influential in the Labour Party, not only on a policy level, but also in terms of the way British socialism saw itself. It is no co-incidence that Tawney has been referred to by successive Labour leaders, from Gaitskell through to Tony Blair, as the pre-eminent socialist thinker. With the growth of moral relativism, multiculturalism, and a declining Christian faith, it is true that Tawney's ideas face a new challenge in the modern world. Yet a fresh look at Tawney's moral approach to politics and life might provide new directions for the left in the next century, just as it provided the inspiration for socialists in much of the last. His key writings include: *The Acquisitive Society* (London, 1921); *Religion and the Rise of Capitalism* (London, 1926); *Equality* (London, 1931); *The Attack and other Papers* (London, 1953); *The Radical Tradition: Twelve Essays on Politics, Education and Literature* (London, 1964) and *R.H. Tawney's Commonplace Book* (ed. J M Winter and D M Joslin; Cambridge 1972). Key writings on Tawney include: Tony Wright, *R.H. Tawney* (Manchester, 1987); R Terrill, *R H Tawney and His Times: Socialism as Fellowship* (London, 1974); N Dennis and A H Halsey, *English Ethical Socialism: Thomas More to R H Tawney* (Oxford, 1988).

Matt Carter

Ann Taylor (1947–)

Ann Taylor became the first woman to serve as Chief Whip when she was appointed to the post in 1998, and was also the first Chief Whip to serve as a full member of the Cabinet. Always more suited to the role of organiser rather than policy-maker, the appointment fulfilled a long-standing personal ambition. A member of Old Labour's old rightwing, and something of a traditionalist, she was one of 'the forces of conservatism' within the shadow cabinet Tony Blair inherited when he took over as leader rather than a politician in his own mould, and was one of only a handful of those in Blair's Government who had served in the previous Labour administration. With David Blunkett, she privately opposed the repeal of Section 28 and once abstained on, and once voted against, a lowering of the age of consent. It is suggested that her 'Old Labour' views on the public services and her scepticism about the single currency were behind her being dropped by the Prime Minister after the 2001 election. She was also criticised by some in the Labour ranks for her machismo as Chief Whip – her 'one of the boys' style disappointed those hoping for a more gentle approach from the Whips Office.

She was born Ann Walker in Motherwell in Scotland on 2 July 1947, but the family moved to Bolton when she was four. Her grandfather and father, John, a Post Office engineer, were both Labour Party activists and she inherited their strong political beliefs. She joined the Labour Party very young, at 14, and was actively involved from an early age. She met her husband, David, a civil engineer, at a Young Socialist meeting, marrying him in 1966 before she went to Bradford University (BSc Hons). She went on to Sheffield University where she gained an MA in Economic

History, and started studying for a PhD on the Conservative-supporting textile trade unions of 19th Century Lancashire, while working part-time as an Open University lecturer and serving as a Member of Holmfirth Urban District Council (1972–74).

But her political life took precedence, and she was elected as an MP for Bolton West at the October 1974 election before she had a chance to complete her studies. She was something of a curiosity then as a young, attractive woman in the House of Commons, but she enjoyed the Parliamentary life and flourished. After the boundaries of the seat were redrawn, she lost the Bolton North East seat at the 1983 election, shortly after the birth of her son. She retains an affection for the town, and is a still a Bolton Wanderers supporter.

Her first stint as an MP was marked by a quick start up the Parliamentary ladder. She served as a PPS 1975–1977 before being made a Government Whip (the youngest ever woman) in the dying days of the last Labour Government. Contemporaries noted her strong political instincts, and a forthrightness and genuineness that endeared her to colleagues. After Labour lost the election, she was made an Opposition Spokesperson on Education (1979–81), Neil Kinnock's deputy, before becoming Opposition Spokesperson on Housing (1981–83).

She spent her four years out of the Commons raising her son, Andrew, and daughter, Isabel, and working as a Monitoring Officer for the Housing Corporation (1985–87). In 1987 she was back in the House as the MP for Dewsbury, winning the Tory-held seat by 445 votes. She was immediately brought back onto the front bench as Roy Hattersley's deputy on Home Affairs. She again impressed Kinnock with strong Commons performances and, in 1988, was made Opposition Spokesperson on the Environment, responsible for fighting the Conservatives' plans to privatise the water industry. She was popular with the Parliamentary Party and, in 1990, won election to the shadow cabinet and, with it, promotion to Spokesman on Environmental Protection. As part of the environment team, she wrote part of Labour's green policy statement, as well as a thoughtful book on environment policy: *Choosing our Future – Practical Politics of the Environment* (1992).

After John Smith was elected leader, he made her Shadow Secretary of State for Education (1992–94). She was not an unequivocal success in the post, and was reluctant to engage with the then-shifting Labour agenda on education, with its focus on testing and standards, doubting the wisdom of a head-on collision with teaching unions. After John Smith's death, Blair made her Shadow Leader of the House (1994–97) and Opposition Spokesperson on the Citizen's Charter (1994–95). This was a role in which she could shine, and her baiting of the Tories over growing accusations of sleaze, while retaining, for Labour, the moral high ground, won her much admiration. She served as a member of the Standards in Public Life Select Committee in 1995 and of the Standards and Privileges Committee from 1995–97, where she was merciless in interrogating witnesses during the investigation into the Neil Hamilton affair.

When Labour took power in 1997, she became Leader of the House (1997–98), as well as chairing Cabinet Committees on the legislative programme and anti-drugs policy. In Opposition she had been vocal about the need to reform the Commons, and her appointment was greeted with some enthusiasm by Parliamentary modernisers, who expected radical reform. She instigated and took the Chair of the Modernisation Committee, which passed to Margaret Beckett when she took over from Ann Taylor as Leader of the House in 1998. But those wanting to see major change were critical of its (lack of) impact on the Commons' long-hours and family-unfriendly culture, and saw Beckett and Taylor as representative of an older generation of women MPs who had grown up in a heavily male-dominated Commons, and accepted the status quo to too great an extent. But some reform did result. Debates for backbenchers in Westminster Hall were brought in, the order paper was made clearer, Prime Minister's Questions were consolidated into 30 minutes on a Wednesday, early departures on Thursdays, and breaks coinciding with half-terms were introduced. These moderate, but not insignificant reforms, are likely to be the things for which Ann Taylor is best remembered.

Ann Rossiter

Matthew Taylor   (1960–)

It is difficult to properly assess Matthew Taylor's contribution to the Labour Party as he only recently turned forty years old and, therefore, has many years ahead in which to add to his distinguished achievements. However, three things are clear regarding his period as a senior Millbank apparatchik. Firstly, he provided boundless energy, enthusiasm and ideas to all the tasks that he was asked to perform. Secondly, he brought a commitment to project management and quality in the delivery of services that had often been lacking at Labour Party headquarters. And finally he played a significant role as a member of the party's senior management team in the run-up to the 1997 general election.

Matthew Taylor was born in London on 5 December 1960. He was educated at Emanuel Grammar School (now a private school but then direct grant), the University of Southampton and the University of Warwick. Prior to joining Labour Party headquarters he was a Research Fellow at Warwick's Local Government School. During this period he served as a Warwickshire county councillor and also stood as the Labour candidate for Leamington & Spa in the 1992 general election.

Matthew Taylor arrived at Labour's headquarters at Walworth Road in January 1994 to take up the post of Campaigns Researcher in the party's Campaigns and Election Directorate. He began shortly after the then leader of the Party, John Smith, had instituted a shake-up of Walworth Road's structures in preparation for the following general election campaign. The inability to rapidly rebut Tory attacks had been identified as a key weakness in Labour's operation during the 1992 campaign. So one of Taylor's key tasks was to set up a robust rebuttal system which would ensure that next time Labour were fully equipped to counter the Conservatives.

He worked with senior Labour officials to raise the funds necessary to purchase the Excalibur database, which had been used as a key rebuttal tool in Bill Clinton's 1992 campaign team. The role of Excalibur has acquired near-mythic status in the history of New Labour but in reality it was basically a very large electronic library that stored public information such as newspaper cuttings, press releases, speeches, think tank pamphlets and Hansard. The strength of the system was that it enabled users to retrieve information speedily and accurately – essential requirements for those working in the feverish climate of a general election campaign.

Shortly after setting up the Rebuttal Unit, Taylor applied for the post of Director of Policy after the resignation of Roland Wales, the former Bank of England economist who had been appointed by John Smith in 1993. At this time –late 1995 – the Labour Party had been reorganised into a taskforce structure and the role of policy director had changed accordingly. The role was now less about overseeing the development of policy and more about distilling and disseminating the contents and themes of the party's key policies. It was therefore perfectly suited to Taylor's ability to see the 'big picture', and his ingenuity in constructing innovative ways to deliver the party's core messages.

Nevertheless, Taylor had to work hard to secure his appointment which was in the hands of the party's National Executive Committee. He had the backing of the new leader, Tony Blair, but was up against a very strong candidate in Joe Irvin, later John Prescott's special adviser, who appealed to the more traditional members of the NEC. In the end Taylor was appointed by just one vote – perhaps the closest Tony Blair ever came before 1997 to being defeated by the NEC.

His appointment coincided with Labour's move to new headquarters at Millbank Tower in Pimlico and the arrival of Peter Mandelson as Head of Election Planning. Taylor quickly struck up an excellent working relationship with Mandelson, whom he impressed through his surefooted management of the policy team. He strengthened his reputation with the party's leadership by managing the delivery of high-quality campaign materials such as Labour's Policy Guide and the Daily Brief, the latter being a one-page summary of the party's key daily initiatives and messages which was distributed to all MPs, candidates and regional offices.

The development of his team was something that Taylor took seriously, and he tried to be as systematic as possible in managing their activities. Although he was often a demanding manager, he was also generous in praising the efforts of his team. Taylor was particularly proud when a significant number of those who worked under him went on to become special advisers in the Labour Government.

Taylor played an important role in two other major areas during his spell as Director of Policy. He worked very closely with David Miliband, Tony Blair's policy head, during the party's 'Road to the Manifesto' process in 1996 which brought together the key themes and policies which would eventually make up Labour's 1997 general election manifesto.

In addition, following the May 1997 election victory he wrote the *Partnership in Power* document which set out a new framework for the relationship between the party and the leadership when Labour was in government.

He eventually left the party in November 1998 to take up the post of Director of the Institute for Public Policy Research, and has managed to successfully raise the profile of the organisation whilst remaining a 'critical friend' of the Labour Government.

Jayant Chavda

Vincent Tewson (1898–1981)

General Secretary of the Trades Union Congress from September 1946 until September 1960, Vincent Tewson was a modest and self-effacing figure who made little positive impact on the organisation's development. This turned out to be a tragedy both for himself and the British trade union movement. The years immediately after the end of the Second World War provided the TUC with genuine opportunities to advance its role as a key institution in the making of a new Britain based on social justice and economic prosperity, but this was not to happen.

Tewson was overshadowed by the leaders of the large unions on the TUC general council and he was unable to make his mark. After the imaginative and effective growth of the TUC during the Second World War, when it became almost an Estate of the Realm, the organisation was a loyal but defensive ally of the 1945–1951 Labour governments, supporting wage restraint for two years and seeking to improve productivity.

Tewson helped to ensure the TUC maintained a friendly relationship in the 1950s with Conservative governments, keen to avoid any confrontation with the trade unions and determined to maintain full employment. But he was criticised for not developing new ideas and responding positively to the growing popular criticisms levelled at the trade unions for being allegedly obstructive and increasingly prepared to take strike action in pursuit of higher wages. Tewson was hostile to the rising power of the shop stewards and concerned to see unions maintain a strong discipline. In 1946 the TUC was said to have entered a new era of responsibility. By the time of Tewson's departure in 1960 the organisation was seen as a slow and unadventurous body in need of urgent reform.

Born on 4 February 1898 in Bradford, he was the youngest in the family of three sons and two daughters of Edward Tewson, a nursery gardener. Leaving elementary school at 14, apart from four years service in the West Yorkshire Regiment from 1916 (he won an MC in 1917 on the Western front in France and was promoted to be a lieutenant), Tewson spent his whole working life in the service of the trade union movement, starting as an official with the Amalgamated Society of Dyers. He joined the ILP and at the age of 25 became the youngest member of Bradford City Council. At the age of 27 he was appointed to the newly formed TUC organisation department, where he was responsible for encouraging friendly inter-union relations. In 1931 Tewson became Assistant General Secretary to Walter Citrine, a post he held for 15 years before his election as TUC General Secretary.

His years in office were not entirely barren. It was under Tewson that the TUC was to establish – for the first time – its own separate head office in the Bloomsbury district of London. Congress House was opened officially in 1958, and it soon became a landmark and a listed building. Tewson was also a strong force in the running of the Brussels-based International Confederation of Free Trade Unions, established in 1949 as a result of the onset of the Cold War. A determined anti-communist, Tewson became a powerful ally of the American labour movement in resistance to Soviet designs among trade unions in Africa and Asia. He was also a keen enthusiast for the training and education of aspiring union leaders in parts of the British Empire which were to achieve their independence in the 1950s and early 1960s. He died on 1 May 1981 in Letchworth, Hertfordshire, leaving his wife Florence Moss, a fellow former TUC employee whom he had married in 1929, and two adopted sons. He had received a CBE in 1942 and a knighthood in 1950.

Robert Taylor

George Thomas (1ˢᵗ Viscount Tonypandy)   (1909–97)

George Thomas remained throughout his life a major party and political figure in Wales; but until his election as Speaker of the Commons, he never commanded a similar status within British politics or within the British Labour Party. This can, perhaps, be explained by the ambivalent role and stance he took within the Labour party at key stages in its post-war development. George Thomas' background was an immaculate one in terms of a Labour movement upbringing. Although born Thomas George Thomas in Port Talbot on 29 January 1909, his childhood and politically formative years were spent in what is considered the cradle of early socialism, the Rhondda Valley. His mother, Emma Jane, was an archetypal woman of the early movement, an activist in local ward politics and the women's co-operative guild. 'Mam' remained a huge personal and political influence upon her son. His father, Zacharia Thomas, was a drunkard who deserted his mother, leaving her to bring up five children in considerable poverty.

These childhood experiences, his Christian socialist upbringing which brought him the Vice-Presidency of the Methodist church, and his trade union activities within the NUT (after Tonypandy Secondary School and University College Southampton, he was a schoolmaster from 1931) informed his political thinking throughout his life. From such a background came a natural, instinctive passion for justice and fairness, especially for the 'small man' threatened by or trodden upon by authority. He retained a remarkable rapport with his own Cardiff Central (1945–1950) and Cardiff West (1950–1983) electorate, and, indeed, could achieve an instant rapport with any audience or in any gathering. He had an elephantine memory for people. 'People', a word distinctively pronounced in almost every speech, remained his passion throughout his political life. It was encapsulated in his twenty-five-year-old and ultimately successful campaign to reform the leasehold system, which had allowed, in his view, the great ground landlords to exploit the small, poorer homeowner.

But George Thomas' natural socialist instincts were progressively tempered by a compelling wish to climb the greasy pole of parliamentary and party politics. His ministerial ambitions were also partly spiced by a keen sense of rivalry with his parliamentary lifelong Cardiff colleague, Jim Callaghan. There remained between them a strong competitive element which was carried from local Cardiff politics to the national stage, but which ultimately brought one the highest political and the other the other the highest parliamentary office.

In his memoirs George frankly admitted that his early foray into the wider and international scene, a controversial meeting with the Communist leader, General Mareas in 1947 during the Greek civil war, had revealed naivety. He became increasingly careful not to repeat such a mistake. More revealing was his ambivalent attitude towards one of the great issues of postwar politics, nuclear disarmament. His strong pacifist instincts attracted him to the campaign. He attended the founding meetings of what became CND (Campaign for Nuclear Disarmament) and, in one instance, rather shamefacedly paraded around Westminster bearing a billboard highlighting the dangers of nuclear war. But he never joined the Campaign, never took part in the famous Aldermaston marches, or spoke prominently at any of the great rallies which could have propelled him onto the British political stage.

Similarly, within the Parliamentary Labour Party he instinctively identified himself with Aneurin Bevan. He personally and politically disliked Hugh Gaitskell and supported Bevan for the leadership. However, George Thomas never became a 'Bevanite' and never consistently sustained or supported the left within the PLP during the divisive debates of the 1950s. As a consequence he never emerged as a major figure within the British Labour Party. From the early 60s until his effective retirement from party politics in 1974, George attached himself both publicly and personally to Harold Wilson. He surprised his Cardiff colleague Jim Callaghan by actively supporting Wilson's bid for the leadership after Gaitskell's death, and remained a devoted loyalist until Wilson's retirement in 1976.

George was rewarded by ministerial office between 1964 and 1970 (during the Attlee years the nearest he came to office was as PPS to the Minister of Civil Aviation from July to November 1951). He served as Parliamentary Under-Secretary of State at the Home Office from 1964 to 1966, and for a year as Minister of State, Commonwealth Office 1967–68, in both cases competently but uninspiringly. His two terms at the Welsh Office, first as Minister of State from April 1966 until January 1967 and between April 1968 and June 1970 as Secretary of State for Wales within the Cabinet, followed by his period as Shadow Secretary 1970–1974, absorbed his final party political energies. As Minister of State George had to cope with the devastating Aberfan disaster and the contentious, hugely emotional question of clearing the tips and the Government's proposal that a part of the disaster fund be spent on their clearance. While frequently having to act as a go-between for the local community and the Cabinet, George's skills, in personal people relationships and his obvious empathy with the Valley carried him and possibly the government through the crisis.

However, as Secretary of State, George had to address the rising tide of Welsh nationalism, partly fuelled by the escalating pit closure programme, and by the resurgence of Cymdeithas yr laith Cymraeg (the Welsh Language Society). Whereas most commentators have concentrated upon the controversies surrounding the investiture of the Prince of Wales, and George's apparent sycophantic approach to royalty, of greater party and political significance was his approach toward the nationalist threat. His robust and vivid denunciations of nationalism were not for the faint-hearted within the Labour Party, and exposed underlying longstanding fissures within the Party in Wales, in part personified by him and Cledwyn Hughes, whom he had replaced as Secretary of State.

George bitterly opposed the devolution/home rule wing of the Welsh Labour Party. He shared with the majority of South Wales miners' members, Ness Edwards (Caerphilly), Will John and Elfed Davies (Rhondda) and Arthur Pearson (Pontypridd), a bitter hostility to any concession to nationalist opinion. He did little to temper the rebellion within the Welsh Parliamentary Labour Party which scuppered Cledwyn Hughes' proposal to incorporate an elected Welsh Council as part of his local government reorganisation plan. His stance on nationalism was both highly personal and also coldly politically calculated. He found it a total personal affront that he and the vast majority of Welsh people should be considered second-class citizens because they were not Welsh-speaking.

George also believed that nationalism had to be challenged as vigorously and as verbally violently as it was promoted. The loss of Carmarthen in 1966 and the bitterly contested Rhondda and Caerphilly by-elections revealed the real threat Plaid Cymru presented to Labour's hegemony in South Wales. The majority had to be awoken to the nationalist hidden agenda which would discriminate in favour of a minority of Welsh speakers in jobs, education and broadcasting. He went as far as to warn that Wales could be the next Ulster! George claimed success for his strategy. At the 1970 election, Carmarthenshire was regained and Plaid Cymru failed to break through in the Valleys.

However, such success was at a price. The carefully constructed post-war Labour Party appeal to North and South, urban and rural, had been fractured. Party divisions over the response to the nationalist challenge remained. George Thomas' critics were to claim that his tactics cost the Party the Caernarvon, Merionydd and Ynys Mon seats. George paid a personal political price when Harold Wilson heeded his critics within the Welsh Labour Party and preferred John Morris as Secretary of State for Wales in February 1974. As George admitted later, he felt resentful and hurt at not being re-appointed Secretary of State and, instead, being offered the chairmanship of Ways and Means (Deputy Speaker) with the prospect of succeeding Selwyn Lloyd as Speaker. George Thomas' election and service as Speaker from February 1976 to June 1983 completed a remarkable Commons career, a fitting conclusion for someone who remained a passionate believer in the British parliamentary system.

These strongly held convictions had always been a factor in his agnostic views upon the Common Market and the European Union. He expressed them most trenchantly in his sparse contributions in the Lords, in which he sat as 1st Viscount Tonypandy from 1983. He argued that the transfer of sovereignty undermined British parliamentary democracy and threatened the peculiar qualities of the British way of life. To the anguish of many within the Labour Party, he went so far as to endorse Sir James Goldsmith's Referendum Party before the 1997 election.

George was never far from controversy. Even as Speaker of the House he was at the centre of a number of contentious rulings which discomforted the minority Labour Government between 1976 and 1979. As he controversially revealed in his later memoirs he bitterly resented pressures that he claimed ministers including Michael Foot, Leader of the House, sought to bear upon his rulings, and especially upon the issue of the hybridity of the Aircraft and Shipbuilding Industries bill. That led to the 'infamous' seizure of the mace by Michael Heseltine. Speaker Thomas' skilful defusing of a parliamentary row, in serious danger of getting out of hand, helped to establish his reputation in the Chair.

His memoirs, *George Thomas Mr Speaker*, published in 1985, appeared to many to have been written to pay off some old personal scores. They in fact reflect the struggle George had always felt throughout his political life to be acknowledged and recognised as a political and public figure of equal status to his contemporaries such as Jim Callaghan and Michael Foot. Attempts, as he saw it, by ministers to impinge upon his hard-won higher authority as Speaker, were, therefore, taken personally. These reactions and resentments were strangely felt by those with whom he had to work most closely, the clerks of the House, a number of whom complained, in private, rather bitterly of his haughty manner in dealing with them.

This, however, contrasted sharply with his public image and persona as Speaker Thomas, whose distinctive calls to 'Order' and whose natural love of his role transmitted itself to a wide general public. The revelations by Mr Leo Abse of George's homosexuality appear to have done nothing to diminish the enormous affection and the particular place in Welsh political and British public life that George Thomas commanded. He died in Cardiff on 22 September 1997.

Ted Rowlands MP

J H Thomas (1874–1949)

Jimmy Thomas meant to make a mark on his times. He did, but not quite the one he intended. Coming from the humblest circumstances to be the boon companion of the King of England, a leading trade unionist and a cabinet minister in three administrations was no mean achievement. But these accomplishments were all consistent with what his enemies claimed: that deep down he was an apologist for the Establishment, provided it opened its doors to his class.

This 'painful but disarming personality' as the shrewd German observer Egon Wertheimer called him, James Henry Thomas was always known by his initials or his diminutive. As time went on he called his eldest son after himself, and found a PPS and even a racehorse to bet on with the same name.

He was born on 3 October 1874, a few weeks before Winston Churchill, but in very different circumstances. He was the son, as he thought, of a seaman's widow, Ann Thomas, who had struggled to raise six children while working as a washerwoman in Newport, Mon. Jim was the youngest. Only many years later did he discover that his real mother was the older 'sister' who had gone into service after he was born. Although she remained in Newport she refused to meet him, and his desperate desire to be liked must have some roots in his early life.

The future creator of the National Union of Railwaymen left Angus Board School and became an engine-cleaner on the Great Western at 15, then worked on the footplate with coaling trains. This early life gave him a plenitude of anecdotes about frying his breakfast as he drove, which demonstrated to the railwaymen he aspired to lead that he was one of their own. In truth, Driver Thomas was always a tank engine man; he never graduated to the main line because he was already absorbed by union politics. He was president of Newport Trades Council at 23, and a Labour councillor in Swindon at 26. Initially he had joined ASLEF, then as now the train drivers' union, but soon transferred to the larger Amalgamated Society of Railway Servants (ASRS), which had never been able to mobilise or focus the collective strength of its disparate membership. Thomas, a formidable speaker and organiser, changed all that. Under the blows of the Taff Vale judgement and aggressive attitudes by the railway company owners, the ASRS was ready for a spark. Its General Secretary, Richard Bell, had already been elected as one of the first Labour MPs in Derby in 1900, but he was out of sorts with the membership for much of the time. The young Jimmy Thomas rose swiftly in the union, becoming president of the ASRS in 1905. By then he already had a wife, Agnes Hill from Newport (another fatherless child), and a young family of his own. All were to support him loyally through the vagaries of his career. He was soon appointed a full-time organiser and, when the disaffected Bell resigned, acclaimed by the railwaymen of Derby as their parliamentary candidate.

In the elections of 1910 Thomas proved to be as effective a politician as he was an organiser, targeting the House of Lords for its obstructions with 'end not mend' rhetoric directed at the source of the anti-union Osborne judgement on the political levy. From then on until 1931 Thomas pursued two careers, in the union and in the foremost ranks of the infant Labour Party. To both he brought a brash self-confidence and ribald humour which sometimes screened his effectiveness as an organiser and negotiator. He carried the main credit for welding 300,000 railwaymen from disparate unions together in the National Union of Railwaymen in 1913. ASLEF stood aloof, but the new union could stand shoulder to shoulder with the transport workers and the miners in a combination that could unnerve any government. Jimmy Thomas became its General Secretary in a ballot at the end of 1916.

By then Britain had been two years at war – a war which Thomas supported, though not conscription. He was at odds with his old parliamentary leader, J. Ramsay MacDonald, and it took both courage and generosity publicly to defend MacDonald's civil liberties. At one NCCL meeting in Cardiff both MacDonald and Thomas were in danger of serious injury from a patriotic rabble. Lloyd George would have found a place in his all-party coalition government for Thomas, but the only available war cabinet position was reserved for Labour's current parliamentary leader, Henderson. Thomas took care to tell his annual conference that he refused office, 'solely by my love of my society and my love for my class' when it was pressed on him again.

He knew, and his parliamentary colleagues acknowledged, that his great strength was as a persuasive negotiator. Those across the table from him always knew that if there was a genuine deal on offer he would take it and that he would only use the strike weapon with a heavy heart. In 1919 he was able to outmanoeuvre Lloyd George and the Geddes brothers by just this insistence, winning the battle for public opinion when the NUR and ASLEF took defensive strike action to protect their working conditions. When the miners attempted to fight cuts in their own wages in 1921 by calling for a triple alliance, Thomas was always the principal doubter. The militant miners could not carry their allies, and it was Thomas who came out of Unity House on 'Black Friday' to tell the press, 'It's over, boys'. Right across British industry the fall in wages continued.

Thomas was unrepentant. When greeted with chants of 'Jimmy's sold you', he would say, 'I've tried my very best, but I couldn't find a bloody buyer.' The private man echoed the public bravado. King George V, who regarded Thomas as his ideal patriotic socialist, asked for his opinion of his fellow railway leader, John Bromley of ASLEF. 'Speaking as man to man,' Jimmy replied, ''e's a bloody 'ound'. Encounters with the monarch multiplied after the 1922 election, in which the Labour Party became the second largest, with 142 seats. Thomas, Henderson, Clynes, Snowden and eventually MacDonald made their acquaintance with court dress, and soon afterwards with government. Baldwin's snap election in December 1923 further increased Labour's parliamentary strength to 191, including a Labour running mate for Thomas in Derby, Will Raynes. In the MacDonald minority government Thomas became Colonial Secretary. The post gave him a delight in the bracing effects of foreign travel, and in the Empire which provided it. The press verdict was that his time in office, one long unabated loyal toast, proved that Labour was 'fit to govern'.

Others saw the fall of the first Labour government and its moderate members differently. In 1926 industrial militancy again led by the miners' leaders, re-opened the unfinished business of Black Friday. Stanley Baldwin had first bowed to the miners' demand for a subsidy for the coal industry, on what became known as Red Friday. Then, confronted with coal owners and cabinet hawks who wanted a strike as much as the militant miners' leaders did, he prepared for a showdown. Thomas thought it all disastrous. 'Stanley Baldwin talks to me like a pal,' he told Citrine of the TUC. 'Who is this strike against? It is not against the coal owners, it must be against the state.' Thomas and his TUC fellow negotiators held out for a compromise solution, which could pull the miners back from the brink. Baldwin might have accepted it, but when the *Daily Mail* compositors refused to set a rabid leader by the editor, this 'gross interference with the freedom of the press' gave the game to the Cabinet hardliners.

The TUC, left to run a General Strike for which it had no stomach on constitutional grounds, effectively sued for peace after nine days. On the constitutional issue, plausibly put by Baldwin, with the support of *The Times* and the infant BBC, Thomas was never in doubt. He feared syndicalism and workers' councils more than the victory of the coal owners. It was no surprise that the only trade unionist allowed to broadcast after the strike was over was J H Thomas. If he had expected Baldwin to be as magnanimous in his deeds as in his broadcasts he was disappointed. The miners went down to a bitter defeat and a new Trade Disputes Act struck once more at the basis of the political levy.

In 1926 Thomas was at the height of his powers, quick-witted, irreverent, conciliatory. If his own side did not always trust him, the other one did, and that gave him a peculiar strength in negotiation. He was to win three more elections in Derby, where his hold was never broken over 25 years. He was one of the most popular speakers in the land. But high-living began to sap him in his fifties. The cartoonist Low dubbed him 'Right Hon. Dress Suit' and indeed after nightfall he never seemed out of it. Society opened its doors, and he went through. In full court dress he looked more like some visiting shogun than a Labour politician. In 1929, when a second minority Labour government took office, it was not only Thomas's clothes which did not fit. He had wanted the Foreign Office. What he accepted was the title of Lord Privy Seal and the responsibility for tackling unemployment, the scourge of the hour. The historian Robert Skidelsky summed up with cruel accuracy what the appointment meant. 'Totally devoid of constructive ideas, intimate with the City and big business…his appointment gladdened the conservatives and dismayed the radicals.'

One such radical was the newly-socialist baronet Sir Oswald Mosley, only 32, a reader of Keynes and a merciless critic of the old Gold Standard orthodoxies. Mosley was also appointed to the advisory unemployment committee. There would be no more trenchant critic of Thomas's timid proposals for employment creation, which depended heavily on limited public works at home and in the colonies and on the willingness of the Dominions to buy more from Britain. As the slump worsened and unemployment rose, Thomas floundered, unable or unwilling to challenge Treasury orthodoxies. Mosley and his sympathisers did this with relish, in a memorandum which called for all the powers of the state to be used for a rationalisation of productive industry, public works and job creation.

The memorandum went to MacDonald. It was rejected by the cabinet, for whom an aggrieved Thomas replied. Mosley thereupon resigned, and put his criticisms to a vote in the PLP. He lost and began his own long descent into the authoritarian abyss, but he had fatally wounded Thomas. A few days later over 60 Labour MPs signed a motion calling for Thomas to be dismissed. Instead on 5 June 1930, he was allowed to slump gratefully into the Dominions Office. Even there he had no respite. The Commonwealth prime ministers, arrived for an Imperial Conference on tariff preferences, found themselves denounced for ''umbug' in the Commons. The great negotiator was losing his touch. So was the government itself.

Faced with a clamour for more economies, including cuts in the dole and in public sector salaries, the government fell apart. Most ministers felt that the whole administration should resign, others that the run on the currency called for an all-party government. MacDonald left for the palace and returned – still Prime Minister – to announce that he had been asked to form a National Government. His accurate instinct was that Thomas (whom he asked to wait after stunned colleagues filed out) would join him. So did Snowden and Sankey, but it was Thomas who counted. He had a following in the country, and in the TUC. He was still, in political terms, a man with a future, at 56. He was the Palace's favourite socialist too, but he entertained hopes that his own class would support him. Its leadership did not. He was expelled from the Derby Labour Party, after a bitter meeting at which Raynes disowned him. The NUR instructed him to resign from the National Government. Instead he resigned from the NUR, and walked out of Unity House for the last time. It was literally ending in tears all round. The working-class response generally was less severe. Thomas was returned at the head of the poll in Derby, when the National Government called an election. His vote went up by 10,000, whereas Raynes crashed to defeat. His biographer calculates that two out of five Labour voters stayed with him: 'The message has gone forth that Derby is true to Jimmy,' he said at the declaration. 'What an answer to my own union.' The NUR answer was to refuse him a pension, despite 27 years as a high official. His twilight income would have to be elsewhere.

For the moment he was secure on a cabinet minister's salary (now combining the Dominions Office with the Colonial Office). He revelled in travel, not always abroad. Few race meetings had to bear his absence. In 1935, when the National Government was re-elected, he was little more than the creature of the Conservative machine. It duly re-elected him, nervous and not entirely sober, in Derby. But for the first time in seven elections he was second to his (Tory) running mate. 'Reid's top,' he kept repeating, as he denounced his new allies. The papers suppressed the report of his maudlin behaviour and Jimmy went on, after 22 November 1935 in the reduced circumstances of the Colonial Office. There, one final embarrassment awaited him. He was accused of leaking budget secrets to one Alfred Cosher Bates. It was never absolutely proved that he had, but the tribunal that examined the matter gathered such evidence of his financial dependence on his drinking companion Bates – a powerful figure in journalism, betting and insurance – that he was obliged to resign, first as Colonial Secretary in May 1936 and then as MP for Derby. His were not the only tears to flow as he made his resignation speech under the kindly but merciless eye of Stanley Baldwin. The grim ritual over, he was allowed to fade away, plaintively enquiring to old comrades he met from Derby and elsewhere, 'Do you think the party would have me back?' He was out, but not entirely broken. His autobiography, *My Story*, appeared in 1937. His wife and family remained devoted to the end. And when that end came there was a last reminder that he had been a great man in the union, and the land. When they took his ashes to Swindon for burial, on a cold 21 January in 1949, 300 railwaymen stood silently by to shake the hand of the widow of their former leader.

Phillip Whitehead MEP

C B Thomson (Lord Thomson of Cardington)   (1875–1930)

At 2am on 5 October 1930, Britain's R101 airship crashed during fierce winds into a field at Beauvais, Northern France. The pride of British aviation, she had been Britain's attempt to lead the world in lighter-than-air craft and her flaws were now cruelly exposed. Her crash, only hours into her maiden voyage to India, had fatal consequences not just for the development of British airships but also tragically for the man who, as Secretary of State for Air in Ramsay MacDonald's 1924 Cabinet had been largely responsible for initiating Britain's airship programme: Lord Thomson. Thomson, back in post as Secretary of State for Air since Labour's return to power in 1929, was one of the R101's passengers. He was not one of the handful of survivors.

Thomson's death, at the hands of his own prestige project, the day before Labour Party Conference in Llandudno, came as a particularly bitter blow to MacDonald. Thomson had been his golfing partner in Lossiemouth and probably his closest friend in politics, partly due, according to Beatrice Webb, to his hinterland being outside it. He was also one of the more able of MacDonald's peers and, unlike some, actually had a connection with Labour. He had left the army in 1919 with the rank of honorary brigadier-general to stand unsuccessfully as a Labour candidate at a by-election in Bristol. He re-stood at Bristol in the 1922 general election and contested St Albans in 1923, also unsuccessfully. He took part in several Labour Party fact-finding deputations to contemporary trouble spots: Ireland in 1920 and the Ruhr in 1923. In 1921 he served on an International Red Cross committee on the condition of refugees in Russia and the Near East. He was created Lord Thomson of Cardington and joined the Privy Council on accepting office in MacDonald's 1924 government.

During the opposition years 1924–29 he had been one of the most active of the tiny band of Labour peers. He maintained his links with aviation, becoming chairman of the Royal Aero Club, and in 1928 represented Britain at an international aviation conference in New York. In his spare time he was also a keen huntsman.

In Cabinet, he was a firm advocate of the expansion and enhancement of the RAF as Britain's main defensive force. He believed, as Beatrice Webb recorded in her diary, in deterring war via airpower: 'Make them convinced that their own capital will be destroyed half an hour after they have bombed yours.' This envisaged 'a relatively small fleet of aeroplanes and ships, but a perfectly up-to-date one in machines and men: excel in quality but not in quantity.' It meant also that he advocated redistribution of expenditure, from the Navy in particular, to the RAF. He also backed the use of air power as a tool of peacekeeping, authorising the use of air strikes in Iraq against marauding tribesmen during 1924. An effective speaker, due to the scarcity of Labour peers he was also frequently deployed in defence of the government in the Lords on issues outside his brief, particularly on foreign affairs.

Born Christopher Birdwood Thomson into an army family at Nasik in India on 13 April 1875, his father David was a Royal Engineer major general and his maternal grandfather was General Christopher Birdwood. After Cheltenham College and the Royal Military Academy, Woolwich, he joined the Royal Engineers in 1894. He served with distinction in Mashonaland, Mauritius and from 1899 to 1902 in the South African War. Subsequently serving as an instructor at the Engineering School, Chatham, in Sierra Leone, and from 1909 to 1911 at the Staff College, Camberley, he became a Captain in 1904. After serving briefly at the War Office he became military attaché to the Serbian Army in 1912, returning to the War Office in 1913. With the outbreak of war, Thomson served as a liaison officer with the Belgian army and then with the British I Corps. In February 1915 he began a two-year stint as military attaché to Bucharest, after which, via the Inter-Allied Conference at Petrograd, he joined the 60th division in Palestine. He commanded a brigade at the capture of Jericho and received the DSO before becoming in 1918 a brigadier-general on the staff of the Supreme War Council at Versailles, serving on the British delegation to the Paris Peace Conference. He received a CBE in 1919. An accomplished linguist and writer, he was the author of *Old Europe's Suicide* (1919); *Victors and Vanquished* (1924); *Smaranda* (1926); and *Air Facts and Problems* (1927). He was unmarried.

Greg Rosen

George Thomson (Lord Thomson of Monifieth) (1921–)

The highpoint of George Thomson's contribution to Labour politics was the Common Market struggle of the early 1970s, leading into his service as Labour's first-ever European Commissioner. Little apart from his immediate ministerial experience prior to 1970, marked him out for the major role he was then destined to play. And after his return from Brussels, while he successfully put together a long and distinguished second career of varied public service, he never regained the same heights of public prominence. But when the spotlight of history shone on him, he played a quality part.

George Morgan Thomson was born in Stirling on 16 January 1921. His father was a self-educated Socialist and Fabian who was a commercial traveller for the biscuit manufacturers, Carr's of Carlisle. When George was two, the family moved to the village of Monifieth, then as now a haven of lower-middle-class respectability on the outskirts of proletarian Dundee. It was Dundee East that George was to represent in the Commons from July 1952 to 1972 and Monifieth from which George took his title when he was elevated to the Lords in 1977 on his return from Brussels.

George was a high-flying pupil at Dundee's Grove Academy, but he left full-time education after passing his Highers to train as a journalist with Dundee's media barons, DC Thomson (no relation). His family would have preferred him to be articled to solicitor but a streak of creative independence in his prudent Scottish nature asserted itself, not for the last time. When the onset of war removed his older journalistic colleagues into National Service, George became editor of the *Dandy*, the children's comic, which was far more widely read than any of his later journalistic and political ventures. In due course George himself became an RAF conscript and had a relatively uneventful war working on radar at various locations in Britain. He wrote pieces for the *Guardian* on the experience of being a national serviceman, read voraciously and toured the country attending Labour meetings.

It was in the period after 1945 that a series of events pushed him into a life of full-time politics. First, his original intention had been to return to DC Thomson as a journalist, but the politically maturing George refused the offer of a post because the management would not allow him join a trade union. Instead he started work on the Scottish Labour weekly, *Forward*, of which he shortly became editor. This meant a move to Glasgow and that brought what turned out to be his second lucky break, his marriage to Grace Jenkins, a vivacious Fabian activist and railwayman's daughter brought up amidst the unemployment and poverty of the Glasgow tenements of the 1930s, who then devoted every aspect of her life and talents to his political success. His third lucky break was a by-election in his hometown of Dundee in 1952. The sitting MP Tom Cook was a young man thought to have a long political life ahead of him, but he was killed in a car crash. George was the lucky beneficiary of this tragedy, having fought a vigorous campaign in the then safe Conservative constituency of Glasgow Hillhead in 1950. The by-election was also a high point for Labour in the 1951–55 Parliament, with George winning an 8,000 majority in what was then thought to be a Scottish marginal – a success widely attributed to public hostility to the Conservative decision to lift a lot of remaining post-war price controls.

George was an unusual Scottish Labour MP – both then and now. While maintaining his parents' home as a base in the constituency, he moved his family to the London region, where they lived first in Harlow New Town (where they became good friends with the Shores, a personal affection that survived their later disagreements over Europe) and then Herne Hill in South London. George's interests were from the start internationalist. (His ambition was most definitely not to become Secretary of State for Scotland). It was through his involvement in the cause of the Commonwealth and colonial freedom, serving as he did as an Opposition Colonial Affairs spokesman 1959–64, that he came to Jim Callaghan's notice. He supported Callaghan, not George Brown, in the 1963 leadership contest, though later as Minister of State at the Foreign Office he rescued George, the Foreign Secretary, from many a late-night drunken resignation in the growing belief that he had far more integrity than Harold Wilson. (He served there as Minister of State 1964–66 and after a spell as Chancellor of the Duchy of Lancaster outside Cabinet, returned to the Foreign Office as Minister of State January-August 1967, joining the Privy Council in 1966).

In the Labour politics of the 1950s George was firmly on the centre right. He was one of those slightly innocent figures who arrived in the House of Commons believing that all the talk of Labour factionalism was got up by a hostile press – only to discover that the reality was far, far, worse, with Aneurin Bevan the clear culprit in his eyes. George was a social world apart from the Hampstead intellectuals who surrounded Hugh Gaitskell, though he gained some entrée into the more sophisticated world of upper-middle-class socialists through the senior member for Dundee, John Strachey. Rather, George rose steadily through the ranks of the PLP and was widely judged to be one of the ministerial successes of the 1964 Government. He won a place in the Cabinet as Commonwealth Secretary in the summer of 1967, securing election to the shadow cabinet in 1970 and 1971, becoming Shadow Defence Secretary 1970–72, and was even talked of as a future Labour Leader. But by then the die had been cast which little though he knew it at the time, was to lead his career out of Labour politics.

In the autumn of 1969 Harold Wilson appointed him Chancellor of the Duchy of Lancaster with responsibility for leading the negotiations for our entry to the Common Market. Apart from George's proven negotiating skills in the international arena, the political attraction of giving George this job was that he was not known to be *parti pris* on the already divisive subject of Europe. But ideal for Harold Wilson as was the choice of George for this task in government, it proved extremely damaging for him after the 1970 defeat. George refused to tread the Wilson path of rejecting 'Tory terms' that he knew in all conscience he would have recommended to the Cabinet. What's more, it caused an enormous sensation when he decided to say so in a very public way. From that moment on, the die was cast for George. The anti-Marketeers were outraged. He became identified as one of the leading Jenkinsite traitors in defying the Labour Whip on the Common Market entry vote, though up to then he had never been one of the *collaborateurs,* resigning fatefully from the shadow cabinet in 1972.

The whole Common Market episode greatly disillusioned George with the general direction of the Labour Party. When Edward Heath offered to nominate him as one of our first European Commissioners, he did not pause long for reflection, even though it meant giving up his seat in the Commons. In Brussels he continued to be active in promoting the European cause in the Labour Party, and the referendum victory in 1975 was a sweet triumph, only marred by the knowledge that the centre right's position in Labour politics had in the course of the struggle been fatally eroded. George was also a successful European Commissioner, responsible for the development of the Community's regional policy, which ironically was in the following decade to play a key role in winning round hearts and minds at Labour's grass roots to the European cause.

But for George his time in Brussels was the beginning of a graceful exit from the political front line. There were to be many more curtain calls and handsome bouquets in a wide variety of public service he then undertook, most notably as chairman of the Independent Broadcasting Authority 1981–88, a member of the Nolan Committee on Standards in Public Life in the 1990s and Chancellor of Heriot Watt University 1977–91. He was chair of the Labour Committee for Europe 1972–73, of the European Movement 1977–80, and was Liberal Democrat spokesman on Foreign Affairs and Broadcasting 1990–98, having joined the Liberal Democrats in 1989. What he, along with the other pro-Europeans, may have lost in Labour's internal power struggles, they won in public respect for their integrity and courage.

Roger Liddle

Will Thorne (1857–1946)

The founder of the National Union of General and Municipal Workers and one of the great pioneers of mass trade unionism in Britain, William James Thorne was also a Labour MP for 39 years.

Thorne was born in Birmingham on 8 October 1857. Both his parents worked as brickmakers, as had their parents; but when his father died after a fight with a horse-dealer in 1864, the family suffered from acute poverty, receiving aid from the Birmingham guardians. Thorne had no schooling and started work at the age of six, turning a wheel for a rope-maker for over 10 hours a day. On Saturdays, when he would finish at one o'clock, he earned an extra shilling by helping his uncle, who was a barber, by lathering the faces of his customers. But when the rope-maker sought to reduce his wages, Thorne took a job in a brickyard and thereafter had a variety of arduous manual jobs – dangerous jobs too, as his hands were badly burned with acid in a munitions factory.

He left home age at the age of 18, when his mother married a man who was an ever heavier drinker than his own father had been, and far more violent. He worked as a navvy on the Birmingham-Derby railway and then took a job (12 hours a day, seven days a week) at the corporation gas works at Saltley. Widely regarded as a militant agitator, he led a successful campaign for an end to Sunday work. Several times he walked to London for seasonal employment, and in November 1881 he settled in London with his wife, whom he had married in 1879, and their three children. He now joined the Social Democratic Federation and met most of the prominent socialists of the day. Eleanor Marx helped him to improve his reading and writing skills. In 1889, aided by Ben Tillett, he helped to form the National Union of Gas Workers and General Labourers (from 1924 the National Union of General and Municipal Workers), the first of the New Unions, with membership fees set at only 2d a week. He was its first general secretary. Success was rapid: employers accepted, without a strike, that three eight-hour shifts should replace the existing two shifts of 12 hours. This was a great victory, and it helped inspire the famous London dock strike of 1889, to which Thorne lent his full support, and then the formation of the dockers' union with Tillett as General Secretary.

Thorne remained General Secretary of his union for 45 years. Soon membership grew to around 40,000 men, and in 1921 it peaked at 490,000. The more diverse the union, he reasoned, the more strikers could be supported by the subscriptions of those from other trades who were still at work. His union affiliated to the TUC in 1890 and Thorne sat on its parliamentary committee (later General Council) from 1894 to 1933. He was chairman of the parliamentary committee in 1897 and 1911–12, and president at the annual Congress in 1912. He threw himself into his work without reserve. It was, he later wrote, 'a religion, a holy mission. I gloried in it.' He was also a real internationalist, attending more international socialist conferences than any other British trade union leader before 1914. With good reason do the Radices describe him as 'amongst the two or three leading trade unionists of his generation', a man of remarkable aggressiveness and perseverance.

Thorne became a town councillor for West Ham in 1891, becoming deputy mayor in 1899 and mayor in 1917–18. By this time he was also an MP, winning West Ham in 1906 and holding the seat for Labour until 1918, when he became MP for the Plaistow division of West Ham, giving up the seat at the age of 88 in 1945.

Thorne was not at his best in the House of Commons. His oratory was far more suited to open-air meetings than the debating chamber. Nor did he harbour any political ambitions; and though continuing to use the language of the class war, he moved gradually to the right. By the 1920s much of his old vigour had gone. No one would have predicted that this man, described as a 'full-blooded socialist' in his earlier years, would in the 1930s have cemented a political friendship with Lord Winterton. The turning point perhaps came in the Great War. Thorne became colonel of a volunteer regiment, inspiring intense criticism from the pacifist wing of the Labour Party, especially Philip Snowden, who also mocked his inability to pronounce certain words correctly. He was awarded a CBE in 1930 and became a Privy Counsellor in June 1945.

By his long career Thorne had earned the respect of the whole Labour movements. J R Clynes wrote that his life story was 'an inseparable part of the history of the Labour and Socialist Movement' and that he 'inspired fondness in every class and distrust in none'. He died of a heart attack on 2 January 1946, aged 89, having seen the formation of the first majority Labour government.

His autobiography, *My Life's Battles* (n.d. but 1925), covering the period up to 1918, is a very useful source for his early years. There is a good short biography, *Will Thorne: Constructive Militant* by Giles and Lisanne Radice (1977).

Robert Pearce

Glenys Thornton (1952–)

Baroness Thornton of Manningham is an active Labour peer with responsibility for departmental liaison between the Lords and the Department of the Environment, Transport and Regions. She has a gritty political style typical of the new breed that will one day form a Lords majority as the chamber moves irreversibly away from its aristocratic remoteness towards parliamentary democracy. She has given most of her adult life to the Labour Party.

Baroness Thornton was born Glenys Thornton in Mirfield, Yorkshire, on 16 October 1952. As a child she had a socialist upbringing and was taken on numerous demonstrations by her radical parents. By the age of eight she was attending Bradford Socialist Sunday School and had been expelled from her local branch of the Brownies for refusing to believe in God. She joined the Young Communist League in 1968. Glenys was educated at Thornton Comprehensive School in Bradford, where she risked expulsion by setting up a Schools Council in 1970, and the London School of Economics (LSE) (1973–76), where she was active in student politics and became chair of the London Students Organisation (1975–76). She also obtained a BSc (Econ) in Government. In 1974 Glenys joined the Labour Party and in 1976 the Co-operative Party. At LSE she met John Carr, whom she married in 1977. Glenys and John have one son and one daughter.

Baroness Thornton's career is a catalogue of organisations for which she has acted as a political guide and mentor. After the LSE she was National Co-ordinator of Gingerbread, the one-parent family organisation (1976–78). She was then North London Area Officer of the Greater London Citizens' Advice Bureaux (1978–79) and, soon after that, Project Director of the Institute of Community Studies (1979–81). Glenys then worked for over a decade with the Co-operative Movement, first as Political Secretary of the Royal Arsenal Co-operative Society (1981–85) then as Public and Political Affairs Adviser to the Co-operative Wholesale Society and Co-op Bank (1985–92). Since 1992 she has continued this kind of work on a freelance basis for a number of organisations including Macmillan Cancer Care, NCH Action for Children and the National Asthma Campaign.

Glenys Thornton chaired the Greater London Labour Party (GLLP), from 1986 to 1991, in a period when it required a tough individual to steer it through GLC and ILEA abolition. In all she spent ten gruelling years standing for 'Kinnockite' good sense in the London Labour Party, starting with a spell as its Vice Chair (1981–86) and including time as chair of its Women's Committee (1983–86). In 1991 she wrote *The Future of London's Government,* which went on to become New Labour's blueprint for the Greater London Authority.

As an active feminist, Glenys's wise counsel contributed greatly to the Labour Women's Network (founder member 1987) and Emily's List UK (founder member 1992). As an active Fabian, Glenys revived Fabian Society fortunes from 1993 to 1996, when, as Development Director and, before that, Acting General Secretary of the Fabians, she committed the organisation to the modernisation process and turned it into a New Labour think tank. Breaking with the tradition of taking only funds from trade unions or charities, Glenys arranged the first business sponsorship the Fabian Society ever received for its activities.

Glenys Thornton has made one other extraordinary contribution to the Labour Party. Her husband, John Carr, is a management consultant specialising in advice on computer systems. When the Labour Party moved its HQ from Walworth Road to the Millbank Tower, Carr volunteered to set up the new, computerised telephone and address system. Carr had to choose Labour's new postcode address because the new address had none. He came up with (SW1) 4GT, so Glenys Thornton contributed even her initials to the Labour Party.

Glenys has argued and debated – and sometimes kicked and punched – her way from the Manningham red-light district in which she was raised, by way of Aldermaston marches and Grosvenor Square street fights, to the red benches of the House of Lords. She represents a new type of peer.

Rex Osborn

Ben Tillett (1860–1943)

Ben Tillett belonged to a generation of socialists and trade unionists, to which we might add Hardie, Lansbury, John Burns, Tom Mann, and Ramsay MacDonald, who had few advantages save their convictions, and innate talents for persuasion, organisation, oratory and leadership. Tillett, born into extreme poverty and abuse, became the founder and leader of a major trade union, led and won the Great Dock Strike of 1889, was a founder of both the Independent Labour Party in 1893 and the Labour Representation Committee in 1900, served as MP for Salford North twice, and was President of the Trades Union Congress.

He lived in a state of persistent quarrel with the other great figures of the Labour Movement, notably Keir Hardie (who called him as 'a dirty little hypocrite'), and later Ernest Bevin, but retained the loyalty and affection of those he led. His role as midwife to the birth of a new political party is uncontested, and his achievement in trade unions organisation is unsurpassed.

Ben Tillett was born in Bristol on 11 September 1860, the son of a stevedore in Bristol Docks, an occupation with which he would have a lifelong association. He endured great cruelty at the hands of a succession of stepmothers, and ran away to the circus to become an acrobat. In 1873 he joined the Royal Navy, and then the Merchant Marine, and travelled widely before being invalided out of the service. He married and settled in Bethnal Green, in East London. Like many Labour pioneers, Tillett was wholly self-educated, devouring the works of Lamb, Hazlitt, Spencer, Carlyle, Ruskin and Darwin.

His first involvement in trade unionism was in 1887 as a member of the Boot and Shoe Operatives Union, and as a founder of the Tea Operatives' and General Labourers' Association within the wharf where he worked shifting sacks of tea. He founded the Dock, Wharf, Riverside and General Labourers' Union in 1889, and served as General Secretary until 1922 when the Transport and General Workers Union was founded from smaller unions. He was involved in every strike or industrial action by dockers during this period.

In 1889, he overcame his lifelong stammer to become a great mob-orator, and led tens of thousands of men and women in the Great Dock Strike in London, which was successful in securing the 'docker's tanner' and an end to casualisation in the London docks. Indeed some have argued that the very word 'docker' to describe the various types of dock worker was coined by Tillett himself as a way of unifying disparate groups of workers. Philip Snowden MP wrote that Tillett had the gift 'to move vast bodies of men by his eloquence and sincerity. Workers thronged to his meetings in their thousands, and came away having seen the vision of the new Earth.' The 1889 Dock Strike succeeded because of the strikers' iron discipline, brilliant organisation and prevention of blackleg labour, because of widespread public support, and because of financial donations from supporters all over the world, notably Australia. Tillett was in large part responsible for all of these factors.

As a proponent of 'New Unionism' Tillett played a central role in unionising unskilled and disorganised groups of workers which the traditional trade unions and craft associations had excluded, and by creating common cause between skilled and unskilled workers helped create a Labour Movement which was capable of creating a unified Labour Party twenty years later. He served as President of the Trades Union Congress in 1929, but was blocked from becoming President of the newly-created Transport and General Workers Union in 1921 by Ernest Bevin.

Tillett's political views shifted over the period of his life, ranging from extolling the virtues of direct action to extreme jingoism and nationalism during the First World War. He was a founder of the Independent Labour Party in 1893, and of the Labour Party in 1900. He was a member of the Fabian Society. However, Tillett's career as a politician was not a great success. In 1906 he published a pamphlet *Is the Parliamentary Labour Party a Failure?* (which concluded it was.) After four unsuccessful attempts as a parliamentary candidate, he was elected as 'independent Labour' in a by-election in Salford North in 1917. He served as Labour MP for Salford North until 1924, and from 1929 to 1931, but rarely spoke in the House of Commons and claimed 'I am the rottenest politician in the world. I don't believe I was made for it.'

In his later years he retreated into a religious sect, the Moral Rearmament League, and was known for heavy drinking. The communist leader Harry Pollitt recalled Tillett and his old pal Tom Mann wending their way down the Strand arm in arm via the pubs giving 'a few coppers to every flower girl and match seller'. James Callaghan, the future Labour Prime Minister, remembered Tillett towards the end of his life as a frequent attendee of the now-defunct Trades Union Club off Trafalgar Square, including a memorable occasion when Tillett was 'ensconced on a sofa and engaged in a salty conversation' with the economist J M Keynes.

Ben Tillett, despite illness throughout his life, lived to the age of eighty-three. He died on 27 January 1943. At his memorial service at St. Martins-in-the-Fields, London, the Leader of the Labour Party, Clement Attlee, said 'His memory will live not so much in the minds of the wealthy few as in the hearts of the toiling masses. Ben Tillet is dead but his voice and ideals live on.'

Paul Richards

Richard M Titmuss (1907–73)

Richard Morris Titmuss is an example of a certain type of socialist intellectual who, without having much direct influence on policy, exercises a profound influence on the climate of opinion in which policy is formed. From the 1950s onwards his writings were widely discussed. As a result, assumptions about the nature of the postwar Welfare State changed, and new perceptions of poverty and social need informed Labour thinking on health and welfare until at least the end of the 1970s. The research and social analysis of Titmuss (and others associated with him, such as Brian Abel-Smith, Peter Townsend and Tony Lynes) at times influenced aspects of policy, and occasionally too provided a basis for criticising the tardiness and inadequacy of government measures.

Titmuss was born in 1907 in Bedfordshire, the son of a small farmer. Due to his family's straightened circumstances he left school at fifteen to work as a clerk in an insurance office. In his spare time, before and after his marriage in 1937, he began to write. His first publications in the late 1930s and early '40s on demography, population problems and vital statistics drew upon his expertise in insurance and also his interest in eugenics. In 1937 he joined the Eugenics Society, and quickly becoming prominent in it, for a time during the War editing its *Review*. Although the controversy which had always clung around eugenics was increasing because of Nazi racist theory, many intellectuals in Britain remained committed to it, not least on the left, where its appeal was linked to a belief in social engineering; and Titmuss and others significantly shifted its focus, to the relationship between environment and genetic inheritance, in a way that distanced it from crude racism. They even managed to give eugenics a radical edge by arguing that at the lowest social levels many people were denied the opportunity to use their natural ability.

Titmuss's role in the Society gave him important contacts. He was exempt from military service on health grounds, and in 1942 Keith Hancock invited him to join the newly formed Historical Section of the Cabinet Office, to work on the civil history of the war. It was the publication in 1949 of the volume he wrote for this series, *Problems of Social Policy*, which made his reputation and enabled him to apply successfully in 1950 for the chair of Social Administration at the London School of Economics. He held this until his death.

It may be ironic that, having made his reputation with an account of social progress during the War, Titmuss consolidated it with two books, *Essays on 'the Welfare State'* (1958) and *Income Distribution and Social Change* (1961), which demolished the belief that in postwar Britain full employment and rising living standards had reduced poverty and inequalities of wealth and income to virtual insignificance. Titmuss, however, was the defender much more than the critic of the Welfare State, in particular defending the National Health Service and its underlying principles against various kinds of attack.

In the 1950s Labour thinking on retirement pensions reflected and were influenced by his views. The basic state pension Titmuss saw as inadequate in two senses – failing both to provide an acceptable minimum income in old age for those without other resources, and to prevent a huge decline in living standards on retirement. He also argued that official demographic projections and calculations about the future burden of ageing were mistaken, and that the cost of improving state pensions was bearable, particularly if contributions were graduated according to ability to pay (or graduated more steeply after the Conservatives had introduced a small graduated element in 1959). This analysis underpinned Labour's policy statement, *New Frontiers for Social Security*, in 1962, and led eventually to the introduction of state earnings-related pensions in 1975. In the 1960s his most direct involvement in policy was with the reorganisation of local government services. He was one of the academic experts who advised the Scottish Office on the implementation of the Kilbrandon Report; and the social work departments, which resulted from their advice, were the forerunners of unified social service departments in England and Wales.

By the time of his death he had an international reputation, particularly as an expert on health care. The memorandum which he and Abel-Smith wrote for the 1956 Guillebaud Report stilled alarm over the NHS's initial cost and opened the way for spending to improve the service. In the 1950s he advised the Mauritius and Tanganyika governments on health policy. *The Gift Relationship*, which he published in 1970, was a study of blood donorship in Britain and the USA which demonstrated the superiority the voluntary British system over the American commercial one. It was probably his most influential book. The American edition in 1971 attracted considerable attention, and he was consulted by the Nixon administration before it introduced tighter supervision of donorship and commercial firms.

Titmuss died in London 6 April 1973. There is no full biography. Ann Oakley, *Man and Wife, Richard and Kay Titmuss: my Parents' Early Years* (1996) is valuable for the first part of his life.

Dr John Brown

Ron Todd   (1927–)

The subject of bitter attacks from the Conservative press in the Eighties, Ron Todd took over the leadership of the T&G in the middle of the Thatcher years, when the political fortunes of the Labour Party and the trade unions were at their lowest ebb. Stockily-built, with an East London accent, Ron Todd is a left-winger who stuck to his views in a period when revisionism was in vogue, and was not afraid to challenge the party leadership over issues which he held dear, notably unilateralism. Yet despite the vehemence with which he argued his case, his integrity, generosity and personal warmth ensured that he is held in great affection by the Labour movement.

Ron Todd was born in Walthamstow on 11 March 1927. He attended St Patrick's School, Walthamstow, and went on to perform his National Service from 1945 to 1947 in the Far East in 42 Royal Marine Commando. He was posted to Hong Kong, where he was involved in the liberation of Allied troops held in Japanese war camps, and was detailed to guard Japanese prisoners of war. His experience of the social inequalities in Hong Kong had a profound effect on him, causing him to question and ultimately lose his Catholic faith and become a socialist.

On his return to Britain in 1947, he joined the Labour Party, canvassing for his local MP, Clement Attlee. He found work as a gas fitter in Walthamstow but in 1954, with a young family to support, he went to work as an engineer at the new Ford plant at Walthamstow. Here he joined the T&G, rapidly becoming a shop steward, then deputy convenor. In 1962, he became a full-time T&G officer, based at the Edmonton office, working for the metal, engineering and chemicals group.

In 1969, T&G General Secretary Jack Jones moved him to the Stratford office, so he could use his experience of working at Ford to look after the interests of Ford workers at Dagenham. Having built up a strong reputation as an effective negotiator, in 1975, Ron was appointed Regional Secretary for London and the South East, a region with over 500,000 members. When his close friend Moss Evans became General Secretary in 1978, Todd replaced him as national organiser, the fourth most senior position in the union and one of the most central.

It was as national organiser that Todd first rose to national attention as the officer in charge of the Ford pay negotiations in Autumn 1978. Todd secured a pay rise of 17 per cent, breaching the government's pay norm of 5 per cent and forcing a Commons vote of confidence in the Government's pay policy. However, like his General Secretary, Todd was convinced that he was right to put the interests of his members before the pleas of the Labour Government. Todd still has no regrets, maintaining that trade unions exist to negotiate on behalf of their members, and that it was the Labour government that destroyed the Labour government, not the trade unions.

Ron expected to serve his time as national organiser and retire at the same time as Moss Evans. However, following Evans's decision to retire due to ill health he decided to contest the election for General Secretary in 1984. Todd won the election comfortably, beating his nearest rival, the Regional Secretary for Wales, George Wright However, following allegations that ballot boxes had been stuffed with votes for him by supporters, he refused to take office unless another ballot were held, despite the fact that an inquiry had found no evidence of malpractice and that, at any rate, even if the votes in areas where allegations were made were disregarded, he would still have won a clear majority.

In the second ballot, Todd almost doubled his majority over Wright, winning 325,586 votes to Wright's 248,746 in a 40 per cent turnout. Todd's refusal to take office unless another ballot was held was hailed at the time as a tactical masterstroke. However, the real motivation behind the move was twofold – to prevent the Conservative press from exploiting the allegations to besmirch the T&G's name and to prevent his own executive from using the allegations against him in years to come: as he puts it, 'to be my own man'.

As T&G General Secretary, Todd was not afraid to challenge the Party leadership when he felt they were pursuing policies at odds with his union's own interests. The most celebrated example was his speech to the 1988 *Tribune* conference, when he urged both 'nostalgics' and 'modernisers' to recognise that they did not have all of the answer to Labour's electoral difficulties. The Conservative-supporting press savaged him, spotting a stick with which to beat Neil Kinnock. Even Labour-supporting newspapers attacked him, with Robert Maxwell's *Mirror* leading the pack. He was accused him of being a 'dinosaur', and dubbed the 'Tyrannosaurus', while Fleet Street's finest trawled his private life (unsuccessfully) for ammunition they could use against him. (Ironically, Todd is a keen fossil collector).

The party leadership was horrified, and several leading figures criticised him in intemperate terms. However, over the next decade and a half, Todd's warning, that 'without principles, you do not have power, you have office' was echoed by many who grew to have doubts about the modernisation of the Labour Party.

One of Ron Todd's most lasting achievements as General Secretary was his leading role in the development of the body linking the trade unions with the party, Trade Unionists for Labour (TUFL). When he took over as Chairman of TUFL in 1985, he brought the EETPU and the AUEW on board, assuaging their fears that the body would use its role to dictate policy by promising to resign as chairman if such demands were made. Under Todd's chairmanship, TUFL played a vital role in securing Labour's finances not least by enabling the party to plan future campaigns on the basis of knowing how much money they would have. He also provided TUFL with a secretariat at Transport House, enabling them to wage their successful fight to ensure victories in the ballots over the trade unions' political levy.

The policy area which Todd took the most interest in, and in which he had the greatest impact, was unilateral nuclear disarmament. A lifelong supporter of unilateralism, he was on the first CND march to Aldermaston in 1958, and from the days of Jack Jones he always moved the T&G resolution on unilateral nuclear disarmament at TUC and Labour conferences. Todd was bitterly disappointed that the policy was dropped by Neil Kinnock, arguing that Labour's internal polling in the 1983 and 1987 elections showed that the policy was not a vote-loser. Todd always maintained that it made no sense to drop a policy of nuclear disarmament when *glasnost* and *perestroika* were in the air. As a member of the Labour Party's Policy Group on Defence, he joined Peter Mandelson and Gerald Kaufman on trips to Washington and Moscow in the mid-Eighties to discuss Labour's future defence policy. Although Kaufman had promised him that the Moscow meeting was going ahead with no preconceptions, Todd felt that the Labour team's questions were phrased in such a way as to lead Gorbachev into supporting a change in Labour's unilateralist stance, and upon his return to Britain he produced a minority report, reiterating his support for unilateralism.

Todd's most recent foray into Labour politics came in April 2000, when he announced in a

Tribune article that he was going to vote for Ken Livingstone in the London Mayoral election. His article spoke of his sadness over the government's direction, particularly its treatment of pensioners, and his anger at Millbank's 'alleged rigging' to stop the ex-GLC leader winning the party's nomination. Though rumours of disciplinary action were heard, no action was taken.

In a decade when many in the Labour Party were content to look inward, Todd made an important contribution to broadening the outlook of the Labour party and the trade union movement. As chairman of the TUC's International Committee, Ron Todd was quick to spot the potential for trade unionists and socialists in Europe. He welcomed the seminal speech to the 1988 TUC Conference by European Commission President Jacques Delors, saying 'the only card game in town at the moment is in a town called Brussels and it is a game of poker where we have got to learn the rules and learn them fast'. Todd was also unafraid to challenge anti-Europeans in his own union to recognise that the European dimension, both political and industrial, was one which trade unionists should learn to exploit.

He also played a major role in supporting the struggle against apartheid in South Africa. He regularly met with representatives of the ANC and COSATU in Zimbabwe, Botswana and Zambia, as well as in South Africa itself. On one TUC-led trip in 1988, a visit to Bishop Desmond Tutu prompted an unscheduled trip to Alexandra township to see at first hand the conditions in which black families were living. While talking to a South African family living in a tiny Alexandra hovel, Todd and TUC General Secretary Norman Willis were surrounded by police armoured vehicles. After being held for an hour, they were escorted out of the township at gunpoint.

Todd retired as General Secretary in 1992, handing over to the man who had served as his deputy, Bill Morris. In retirement, Todd stays in close touch with the T&G and former colleagues from the Labour movement, regularly attending Labour Party, TUC and T&G conferences. In the late Nineties, he underwent surgery to replace both arthritic knees, refusing to use private medicine despite his family's entreaties.

When he is not tending the garden of his terraced house in Dagenham, Todd may be found composing verse. He has produced three anthologies of his work – *On His Todd, Still On His Todd* and *Odd Thoughts In Retirement* – the proceeds of which were donated to charity. In addition to his fossils, he collects Victorian sheet music (his mother was a semi-professional piano player, providing music for silent films at the cinema) and political autographs, having built up a collection of original Prime Ministerial signatures dating back to Sir Robert Walpole. His wife Josephine died in 1996, after 51 years of marriage. He is close to his son and three daughters, and his five granddaughters. He is an Honorary Vice-President of the Campaign for Nuclear Disarmament, and is a Vice-President of the Institute for Employment Rights.

David Mills

George Tomlinson (1890–1952)

Whilst much of the energy of the Wilson years was put into fulfilling the public-school educated Tony Crosland's pledge to 'destroy every fucking grammar school in England, and Wales, and Northern Ireland,' the Attlee government spent its energy in implementing the

1944 Education Act to create them. To do it Attlee appointed the flame-haired firebrand 'Red Ellen' Wilkinson, having decided that he needed its co-author, Chuter Ede, as his Home Secretary. Her early death in February 1947, however, meant that for the remainder, and therefore for most, of the Attlee government, the Education Minister was George Tomlinson, a football-loving Lancashire Methodist lay-preacher.

As Martin Francis illuminates in his masterly *Ideas and Policies under Labour 1945–51*, 'For the majority of the Labour Party, Ellen Wilkinson and George Tomlinson had fulfilled the essential criteria of a socialist education policy.' This was because 'only the grammar school offered the working class high acheivers the opportunity to compete on equal terms with the products of the independent schools for the prizes of university places and the top jobs in the professions and government service.' This was the approach endorsed by the only Fabian pamphlet on education policy of the period, Joan Thompson's *Next Steps in Education* (1947), and of the Workers' Educational Association proposals for educational reconstruction. Tragically, though the grammar schools, as Manny Shinwell recalled, 'were for many working class boys the stepping-stone to universities and a useful career,' the failure to invest properly in the secondary modern and technical schools under the post-1951 Conservative government, combined with the inflexibility of the eleven-plus, meant that the majority of Britain's children still received an inadequate education.

Nevertheless, Tomlinson saw through successfully the raising of the school leaving age to 15 in April 1947 and built a record number of schools each year to facilitate it in the context of a massively enhanced birthrate. As Minister of Works from August 1945 until February 1947 he had delivered the mass production of prefabricated classrooms under the Hut Operations for Raising the School Leaving Age Scheme (HORSA), which had helped deal with the issue in the short term and at the Education Ministry he established a new architects and buildings branch to provide a more permanent solution.

Tomlinson 'epitomised the common sense and humour of the Lancashire worker, which he joined to a deep religious faith,' recalled Attlee in his memoir *As it Happened*. 'Bevin, who was a very shrewd man, picked him out in 1941 as the right man to help him at the Ministry of Labour [Tomlinson was Joint Parliamentary Under-Secretary at the Ministry of Labour and National Service February 1941–May 1945]. During the war he did very good work there, particularly in the work of changing over the textile workers to munitions and in organising the rehabilitation centres which enabled so many disabled workers to work again. But perhaps his best work was done as Minister of Education. The first former half-timer to occupy the position, he brought to the work great experience gained in local administration, while his humour and sympathy endeared him to all.'

He also had a wider role in Cabinet, as Attlee recalled in *A Prime Minister Remembers*: 'You've got to have a certain number of very solid people whom no one would think particularly brilliant, but who between conflicting opinions can act as middle-men, give you the ordinary man's point of view. I'll tell you who was an ordinary man and a very useful man ... George Tomlinson ... I can remember a thing coming up which looked like a good scheme, all worked out by the Civil Service. But I wasn't quite sure how it would go down with ordinary people, so I said: "Minister of Education, what do you think of this?" "Well," says George, "it sounds all right but I've been trying to persuade my wife of it for the last three weeks and I can't persuade her." A common-sense point of view like that's extremely valuable.' In the notorious Bevan/Gaitskell row over the restoration of dental and eye charges, it was Tomlinson who tried and failed to secure a commonsense compromise whereby Gaitskell's money was raised some other way and Bevan's resignation avoided.

Born on 21 March 1890 at Rishton, Lancashire, after leaving Rishton Wesleyan Day School at the age of twelve he began work as a half-timer at the cotton mill alongside his father, two brothers and two sisters. His early ambition was to be a Wesleyan minister, and initially he studied for this in the morning before his shift. A year later, however, he was working at the mill full-time. His father, John Wesley Tomlinson, had started working there when eight and the mill had also employed his mother, Alice Varley, and his wife-to-be, Ethel Pursell, by whom after marriage in 1914 he had a daughter. Apart from three years' agricultural work away from home after his registration as a conscientious objector in 1916, he continued to live and work in the area, running a small shop in Farnworth in the 1920s. His election to Parliament at the 1938 Farnworth by-election, an area covering Rishton, came after extensive involvement in the Rishton and Distict Weavers Association (of which he was President aged 22 and Secretary from 1935) and local government. He served on the urban district council (UDC) intermittently from 1914 and on Lancashire County Council from 1931. It was in local government that he developed his interest in education, becoming chair of the education committee of the UDC for seven consecutive years from 1928 and President of the Association of Education Committees 1939 and 1940. He remained MP for Farnworth until his death following an operation on 22 September 1952, though the illness that set in after Labour's defeat in 1951 had curtailed his activities.

Greg Rosen

C P Trevelyan   (1870–1958)

C P Trevelyan is probably the only British politician of the twentieth century to have resigned from governments of two different political parties, each time on a matter of principle. This fact gives a clue to his nature, which was idealistic, unbending and outspoken often to the point of tactlessness. These characteristics inevitably limited his achievements in ministerial office, but he is notable as one of the Liberal politicians who, departing his erstwhile party as it began to fall apart in the 1920s, helped to give the rising Labour Party an ideological backbone it would otherwise have lacked.

Charles Philips Trevelyan was born in London on 28 October 1870, the descendant of an old West Country Liberal family. His father, George Otto Trevelyan, served in Gladstone's and Rosebery's cabinets as Chief Secretary for Ireland (1882–84), Chancellor of the Duchy of Lancaster (1884–85), and Secretary for Scotland (1885–86 and 1892–95); in 1869 he married Caroline Philips, daughter of another Liberal MP, and they had three children. Charles' two brothers were each to enjoy a distinguished career, Robert as a poet and scholar and George as a historian, and unsurprisingly for such a brilliant family, Charles carried, and felt he carried, a particular burden of expectation as the eldest son. He did not enjoy his father's and brothers' academic excellence, either at Harrow or at Trinity College, Cambridge, where he read history, and regarded his second-class degree as a failure. It was this highly developed sense of self-criticism, combined with an upper-middle-class background that stressed a responsibility and duty to serve those less fortunate than himself, that nurtured Trevelyan's idealism, endless capacity for hard work and tendency to intolerance.

Trevelyan had identified himself as a Liberal from his schooldays, and became secretary to the University Liberal Club. After Cambridge, and a brief period as private secretary to Lord Houghton, Lord Lieutenant of Ireland, he set about trying to enter Parliament. In the 1895 election he fought and lost North Lambeth, and in 1896–97 served on the London School Board. In 1899 he held the Elland division in the West Riding of Yorkshire in a by-election after the sitting MP retired. He soon became an accomplished speaker, and held Elland comfortably at the four succeeding general elections. He was firmly on the Radical wing of the Liberal Party, a vigorous supporter of issues such as education reform, taxation of land values, and graduation of income tax. He was friends with the Webbs, and joined the Fabian Society and the Rainbow Circle (a Liberal-Socialist discussion group), but along with other Fabian-inclined Liberals remained suspicious of socialism, which he saw as essentially destructive. He also regarded himself as an Imperialist, though in the sense of a strong Empire being the best foundation for a stronger society and progressive social reform, rather than any support for an aggressive foreign policy.

Although Trevelyan's abilities were widely recognised, his principled refusal to promote himself, combined with his tendency to outspokenness, denied him any ministerial position after the Liberal landslide victory of 1906. After two and a half years as Third Charity Commissioner, however, in October 1908 he was appointed Under-Secretary at the Board of Education, where he tried to extend secular and nondenominational teaching. He stayed in this position until 3 August 1914, when he resigned over the Government's ultimatum to Germany over the invasion of Belgium. He was not a pacifist, but he despised Foreign Secretary Sir Edward Grey's construction of alliances and secret treaties, and suspected that Britain's covert alliance with France had goaded Germany into aggression. He soon became a leader of the small Liberal anti-war group, and in September, along with E D Morel and Ramsay MacDonald, helped to form the Union of Democratic Control to campaign against the war and the balance-of-power diplomacy and expansion of armaments which had caused it. In practice the UDC achieved very little and Trevelyan's attachment to it cost him friends and political supporters. The result was to push him, along with other Liberal opponents of the war, towards the Labour Party, particularly after Labour left the wartime coalition in August 1917.

In November 1918 Trevelyan followed his younger brother Robert into the Independent Labour Party, though he was too late to fight Elland as a Labour candidate and campaigned as an independent, polling only 5 per cent of the vote in a four-cornered fight. In September 1919 he was selected as candidate for Newcastle Central, and won the seat easily in the 1922 election, holding it for the following nine years. He served as Labour's spokesman on Education in the 1922–23 Parliament, and, when Ramsay MacDonald formed Labour's first government in January 1924, Trevelyan entered the Cabinet as President of the Board of Education. 'I no longer have only six children,' he said to his wife. 'I have six million.' Already experienced in central government, he was one of Labour's undoubted successes, removing spending restrictions on local education authorities, expanding state grants, scholarships and maintenance allowances, and increasing free secondary school places.

In the 1924–29 Parliament Trevelyan kept his position as spokesman for education, and helped to commit Labour to raising the school leaving age to fifteen, arguing that it would help to reduce unemployment by cutting the number of entrants to the labour market. In 1929 he was reappointed as President of the Board of Education, but his second period in the post was far less successful than his first. The new Cabinet was even less progressive than its cautious predecessor, and Trevelyan frequently found himself frustrated by MacDonald's timidity and vacillation. In trying to raise the school leaving age to fifteen, which of course required an expansion in school classes, he found himself unable to reconcile the bitter Catholic and Nonconformist arguments over the issue of state support for denominational schools. After two abortive starts, in October 1930 he introduced a bill to raise the school leaving age and provide limited grants for low-income households. The Catholic group of Labour MPs, with Conservative support, amended it to introduce state support for denominational schools, and what was left of the bill was rejected by the Lords on 18 February 1931 in the light of the growing economic crisis. The next day Trevelyan resigned from a ministerial post for the second time, blaming MacDonald for his lack of support for socialist measures.

Along with most of his colleagues, Trevelyan was heavily defeated in the election of October 1931. Although he remained popular on the left wing of the Labour Party (in 1932 he joined the Socialist League, along with Cripps, Laski and Tawney), he increasingly became disillusioned with parliamentary politics, and in 1934 turned down the offer of the safe seat of Morpeth. But he led an active life at home. As Lord Lieutenant of Northumberland he reorganised the magistracy of the county, making it more representative of all sections of society. He was a prime mover in the founding of the People's Theatre in Newcastle. Together with his wife, Mary Katherine Bell, whom he had married in 1904, he restored the family house and estate of Wallington, providing all employees with a week's paid holiday a year and paying child allowances to every family on the estate (almost twenty years before Attlee's Government introduced family allowances). They made most of the estate's grouse moors over to the Forestry Commission and in 1941 gave the whole estate to the National Trust, continuing to reside there as tenants. He loved showing visitors round his house and the estate, and Wallington became a meeting point for young people interested in politics.

He died at Wallington on 24 January 1958, at the age of eighty-eight. With his wife Molly, he had four daughters and three sons, the eldest of which, George Lowthian (born 1906), succeeded to the baronetcy. His papers are kept at Newcastle University Library, and there is one biography, which draws extensively on his correspondence but misses much of the political context: *C P Trevelyan 1870–1958: Portrait of a Radical*, by A J A Morris.

C P Trevelyan played an important role in the growth of the Labour Party. He was one of the key group of Liberals, including Haldane, Wedgwood, Buxton, Ponsonby, Addison, Jowett and Wedgwood Benn, who felt themselves driven out of the Liberal Party by its disastrous split in 1916, its subsequent division into two warring factions and its loss of radical zeal. In general they did not regard their move as involving any significant adjustment of their political beliefs; rather, they came to see the Labour Party simply as the more vibrant and reformist wing of the old pre-war Progressive Alliance. They helped mould Labour policy, adding a strong idealistic element, particularly over foreign policy issues, including free trade and control of armaments, civil liberties and land value taxation, to its existing labourist, trade union-focused beliefs. They helped give Labour the image of respectability and competence in government that Ramsay MacDonald so coveted, because of their backgrounds and their administrative competence.

And Trevelyan, in particular, was important to many others. As a friend wrote to him on his eightieth birthday: 'Anyone who knows you appreciates that you made your policy from your own reasoning and whatever the inconvenience and unpopularity you act unflinchingly and conscientiously to work out your own policy. You know what you think you should do, and you do it.' This was his strength, and his weakness. It prevented him achieving what other, more flexible, politicians might have managed; but it also established him as a real inspiration for thousands of others.

Duncan Brack

Reg Underhill (Lord Underhill) (1914–93)

Reg, later Lord, Underhill was the last of the breed of organisers who grew up in Labour's machine and built it up as a professional backbone for the mass Party. He gave nearly half a century of his life to keeping the organisation efficient and relevant, rather than using it as the springboard to self-advancement today's apparatchiks and chaps might prefer. A canny machine minder, he subordinated self to Party, sustaining Labour in power locally and nationally.

Born on 8 May 1914, Henry Reginald Underhill grew up and was educated in Leyton, East London, leaving Norlington Road Elementary School and Tom Hood Central School in Leyton at 15 to work for Lloyds Underwriters. He joined the Labour Party in 1930, going to Transport House at 19 in 1933 to serve the Party there until 1979, apart from four years with the National Fire Service in the war and a stint from 1948 to 1960 as Regional Organiser in the West Midlands. In 1960 he returned to Transport House as Assistant National Agent but was pipped at the post as National Agent by Ron Hayward, succeeding to that job only in 1972, when he was too old to have any prospect of the top job of General Secretary.

The National Agent is in charge of the machine. Never as centralised or as well financed, Labour's was a penny farthing compared to the Tory Rolls Royce, but by combining the efforts of unions, big city machines and constituencies through the personal networks and contacts which held it all together, Underhill kept it on the road, and winning. He also became the hammer of all disruptive, infiltrating separatist groups in both the early Sixties when he was successful, and the Seventies, when he was less so against Militant because a left-dominated NEC refused to back him, effectively suppressing the Underhill Report on infiltration, forcing him to publish it later at his own expense. His achievement was to expose Militant rather than break it, though his exposures paved the way for its elimination in the Eighties.

Reg Underhill retired in 1979, and to the surprise of snobs and elitists Jim Callaghan sent his mechanic to the Lords. There he assiduously learned the ropes, the Standing Orders, the procedures and techniques, and turned himself into a master of procedure and an effective speaker, becoming Labour's Deputy Leader in 1982, a post he held until ill health forced him out in 1989.

In the Lords he earned the respect of the Labour minority, fighting its rearguard action against Thatcherism, and of the whole House. Right up to his death in 1993 he remained an effective defender of the unions, public transport, electoral reform (he was on Labour's Plant Committee) and of the EEC, spending his last years in a happy and productive Indian summer in the clublike atmosphere of the Lords, working with old mates from both party and unions, and dying in harness on 12 March 1993. He married Flora Philbrick in 1937, with whom he had two sons and a daughter.

Austin Mitchell MP

Eric Varley (Lord Varley) (1932–)

Eric Varley was a first-rate Labour MP who in a different age might have made it to the front rank of British politics. He got close. But in the end history was against him. There is no question that if Healey had won the leadership in 1980, Varley would have been a serious contender for the succession. Yet in the 1970s and early 1980s a cultural revolution was sweeping the Labour Party that made it impossible. By 1983 Varley sensed that the right wing of the labour movement was an increasingly busted flush. Realising that the Labour Party looked finished in British politics, but unprepared to contemplate the unbearable act of leaving it, Varley departed from politics altogether. It was a considerable loss.

Eric Graham Varley was born on 11 August 1932 at Poolsbrook, Derbyshire, into a mining family. His father, Frank, was a branch secretary of the National Union of Mineworkers in the days when the union was an important moderating influence within the British labour movement. Eric left school at 16 to take up an apprenticeship as a mining electrician, as well as fulfilling his talents as a young footballer with Chesterfield Town.

He married Marjorie Turner in 1955, with whom he had one son. In the same year he joined the Labour Party and was elected to the Derbyshire Executive of the NUM in 1956. He quickly became a protégé of Bert Wynn, General Secretary of the Derbyshire Miners. In 1960 Varley made his first speech at the NUM Annual Conference, arguing in favour of reducing the voting age to 18.

In June 1963 he narrowly won the selection to become the Labour Party candidate for Chesterfield, succeeding the veteran Labour MP George Benson. In his selection literature Varley described himself as, 'a left of centre unilateralist'. He was elected at the general election in October 1964.

In Varley's first term as an MP he reinforced his reputation as a figure from the Party's centre-left. In February 1965 he complained that the Home Secretary Sir Frank Soskice had wrongly refused to delay the deportation of the American peace activist Bert Benson, who had been arrested on a CND demonstration; and in May 1967 he was one of 36 MPs who rebelled against joining the European Economic Community.

Despite this act of mild rebellion, in July 1967 he achieved his first significant promotion when he was appointed as Assistant Whip in the first Wilson Government. However, his increasingly close links with Harold Wilson and his entry into the Wilsonite inner circle meant that in November 1968 Varley became the Prime Minister's Parliamentary Private Secretary.

Varley's affiliation with Harold Wilson stemmed not just from personal rapport, but the feeling that both men drew their support and friendship from the left in the Labour Party, yet were actually on the social democratic right in their outlook. They did not believe that there was any alternative to the market economy, favoured partnership rather than confrontation with industry, and sought vigorously to defend private enterprise. It was the paradox of Wilson, and in many ways also of Varley, that they were perceived as men of the Bevanite left.

Varley's entry into the Wilson camp was also a product of his close association with Gerald Kaufman. Ironically, Varley began his career as a protégé of Kaufman, yet by the mid-1970s he was the more senior figure as a member of the Cabinet. Kaufman remained a close personal friend and influence throughout Varley's political career.

In November 1969 Varley achieved further promotion and was appointed as Minister of State for Technology under Tony Benn, after Reg Prentice had resigned four days after having been reshuffled from his beloved Ministry of Overseas Development. In Opposition from 1970 to 1974 he served in the Trade and Industry team shadowing the regions 1970–72 and fuel and power 1972–74. From 1971–74 he was also the Chair of the Trade Union Group of Labour MPs.

The major breakthrough in his career came with his appointment as Secretary of State for Energy, following Wilson's unexpected election victory in February 1974. Varley was the youngest member of the 1974–76 Labour Cabinet. In his first period as a Minister, he stuck to the prevailing interventionist ethos of the mid-1970s, awarding a £600 million subsidy to the National Coal Board, and 'picking winners' by choosing a British Nuclear Power generator over its American rival.

In June 1975, Varley achieved his second promotion to become Secretary of State for Industry, as Wilson demoted Benn to the Department of Energy in a straight swap. Varley seized the opportunity to make his mark, and over the following months enjoyed a dizzy rise in reputation as a leading Minister in the Labour Government. He was even talked of as a future leader of the Party.

Varley had by now adopted a centrist position in the Labour Government, and from his position at the Department of Industry he sought to moderate Tony Benn's influence on Labour's industrial policy. Benn had begun to spark serious confrontations between the Labour Government and private companies, believing that centralisation and state planning were the only route to economic modernisation. But neither Wilson nor Varley were prepared to accept the Bennite left's 'alternative economic strategy' (AES). In essence the AES had two consequences for industrial policy. First, that Governments through the National Enterprise Board should purchase stakes in private sector companies to safeguard the long-term future of British industry. Second, that the Secretary of State for Industry should have the power to set planning agreements with large corporations on productivity and efficiency in order to add dynamism to the national economic effort.

These policies were strongly opposed by Wilson and Varley who were determined to protect the private sector from excessive government interference. As an NUM-sponsored MP and former mining electrician, Varley thus emerged as a leading pro-business Minister in the Wilson-Callaghan Government. His term of office at Industry led to much improved relations between the Labour Government and business. Two years earlier, few would have predicted his rise as the darling of the British corporate establishment.

In this sense Varley was a rare figure in the Labour Party of the 1970s. Few other Ministers, with the exception of Edmund Dell, were prepared not just to tolerate the private sector, but to argue actively for the left to embrace the market economy.

Yet it was Varley's almost unique commitment within the Government to protecting private enterprise which meant that in November 1976 his career suffered a serious setback. He was bruisingly and publicly defeated over the Government's decision to award a subsidy to the ailing Chrysler factory in Scotland.

Up to 25,000 jobs were at stake. Varley had followed the advice of his officials and recommended that the unprofitable factory should be closed down. Benn called for Chrysler to be re-nationalised and for car import controls to be imposed. It should have been a defining moment in the battle between left and right for the soul of the Labour Government. But Callaghan, terrified of the political impact of heavy job losses in the face of a rising tide of support for nationalism in Scotland, relented and ordered a Government subsidy to keep the factory open. Labour's reputation as a competent manager suffered immeasurable long-term damage.

Other politicians would have turned such humiliation to their advantage by striking out at the Government in protest, building an alternative power base within the Party to challenge the leadership. Indeed, Varley could have emerged as the leading social democrat of his generation. Jenkins had departed for Brussels; Crosland was engrossed in the Foreign Office; neither Rodgers nor Hattersley were experienced enough to seize the reins. There was a real opportunity to manoeuvre against Callaghan were the Government to have been fatally damaged by the ensuing economic crisis.

But this course of action would never have been acceptable to Varley. He was a committed Party loyalist, dedicated to the cause of competent, credible Labour Governments. He refused to rock the boat and remained Industry Secretary until the 1979 General Election.

Elected to the shadow cabinet following Labour's defeat, Varley became Shadow Employment Secretary and worked with those who sought to moderate the Party's leftward drift. He supported One Member, One Vote reform in March 1980, and helped lead Denis Healey's campaign for the Party leadership in October. He became Party Treasurer in September 1981 after ousting the hard left incumbent Norman Atkinson with AUEW support, and from his position on the NEC opposed the endorsement of the Militant Tendency's Peter Tatchell and Pat Wall as Labour Party candidates.

In November 1982 Varley successfully resisted Michael Foot's attempt to oust him in favour of Neil Kinnock as Labour's Employment Spokesman, with the backing of 40 trade union-sponsored MPs. But after Kinnock's overwhelming victory as Labour Party leader in 1983 Varley announced he would not contest the next round of shadow cabinet elections.

In March 1984 Varley stepped down as Labour MP for Chesterfield to be replaced, ironically, by Tony Benn who had been defeated at Bristol South. He was increasingly uncomfortable with the leftward drift of the Party as it became marginalised from mainstream public opinion. Describing his own politics, he once quipped, 'I've always been an extreme centrist'. The NUM was also coming under the control of Arthur Scargill and the militant Yorkshire miners.

In 1982 Varley publicly opposed the inclusion of unilateral nuclear disarmament in the Party's general election manifesto. But he was an increasingly lone voice. He did not believe that Neil Kinnock, who chose to stay outside the 1974–1979 Labour Government to argue against its policies from the left, offered the route to salvation for his Party.

By now completely disillusioned with the moderates' cause, but too deeply rooted in the ethos and traditions of the labour movement to defect to the Social Democratic Party (in addition to being unsypathetic to their enthusiasm for the EEC), he was essentially finished in British politics. From the mid-1980s he played no further part in Labour's slow return to sanity.

Varley was subsequently appointed as Chairman and Chief Executive of Coalite, where he served until 1989. He also held a number of non-executive directorships. In 1990 he was created Lord Varley of Chesterfield. He was a man of great talent and foresight who never achieved his potential to more radically shape post-war British politics.

Patrick Diamond

Stephen Walsh   (1859–1929)

Stephen Walsh, or 'Little Stee' as he was known to his mining comrades, 'was five foot high and looked as unlike a uniformed soldier as, say, a timid village curate would look like a local tavern keeper,' recollected J R Clynes of his Cabinet colleague. In the climate of uncertainty that surrounded Labour's attitude to defence and security, including as it did several pacifists and former opponents of the Great War amongst its leaders, MacDonald had to be careful in his choice of the first Labour Secretary of State for War. The appointment of Walsh, with his clear patriotic commitment to the welfare of the armed services, was shrewd.

Born in 1859 in Liverpool of Irish parents, he was orphaned at an early age, spending his time until the age of 14 at the Kirkdale Industrial School. Moving to Makerfield, he spent the next eighteen years as a miner in the Wigan coalfield, at first underground and latterly as a checkweighman, marrying Anne Adamson, a miner's daughter, in 1885. His intelligence and literacy led to his often being called upon by fellow miners for advice and assistance in disputes and he soon became embroiled in the creation of both a district Miners Union and then the Lancashire and Cheshire Miners Federation. In 1901 he was appointed full-time agent for the Wigan district of the Lancashire and Cheshire Miners Federation and was soon Vice-President of the Miners Federation of Great Britain, President of Wigan District Trades Council and, from 1914–1920, Vice-President of the English Miners Conciliation Board. He was also an active member of the Co-operative Movement and the Society of Oddfellows.

Following eight years on Ashton-in-Makerfield UDC, he became in 1906, following the decision of the Miners Federation to contest the seat, MP for the Ince Division of Lancashire South-West, beating handsomely the Tory colliery proprietor incumbent. An able speaker and avid reader, particularly of Shakespeare, his home in Wigan was reputed to resemble a library and as Clynes recollected, 'Walsh flavoured many of his speeches with classical allusions and fitting quotations from the poets or from drama. But the substance of his speeches was the condition of the people and the urgent necessity for improvement.'

Though an opponent of conscription before the First World War, he became a vocal advocate when the course of the war convinced him of its necessity. He had no truck with the pacifist left and firmly backed Labour's support for the wartime coalition. Appointed Parliamentary Secretary to the Ministry for National Service in March 1917 and subsequently to the Local Government Board from June 1917 until January 1919, it was only with great reluctance that he was persuaded to abandon the Lloyd George coalition and join the rest of the Labour Party in opposition. In 1921 he became with J H Thomas joint Vice-Chairmen of the Parliamentary Labour Party (PLP) and in 1922 joint PLP Deputy Leader with Josiah Wedgewood.

Joining MacDonald's first Cabinet as Secretary of State for War in 1924 one of his first acts, and one whose impact perhaps had the most far-reaching consequences, was to secure the young Clement Attlee as his Under-Secretary of State. By all accounts, Walsh's popularity in the Labour Party was replicated in his popularity with the services. He took a hard line on the communist left, for example favouring prosecution over the 'Campbell case', when the acting editor of the communist *Workers' Weekly*, John Campbell, wrote an editorial urging British workers not to fire on fellow workers in 'the class war nor in a military war.'

With the fall of MacDonald's Government Walsh sought to remain active in opposition and secured eighth place in the 1925 shadow cabinet elections. However, ill-health soon began to restrict his activities and at the end of 1927 he had to turn down MacDonald's offer to make him, with Attlee, one of Labour's representatives on the Statutory Commission on India under Sir John Simon. He died at his home in Wigan on 16 March 1929.

Greg Rosen

Sam Watson   (1898–1967)

Sam Watson, secretary of the Durham miners for 37 years, was a key figure in the Labour Party in the immediate post-Second World War period. He was above all a shrewd and influential figure who provided the necessary loyal support for the Labour leadership during difficult times as a member of the party's National Executive Committee from 1941 to 1963. As a young miner he was on the left, but like others he moved to the centre-right in later life and became a close friend of Hugh Gaitskell. At one time he was even considered by Labour Prime Minister Clem Attlee as Ernest Bevin's successor as Foreign Secretary, but it was said he would never move from his beloved Durham and it was hard to see how he could conduct the country's foreign policy from the North East of England.

Watson was a kind of Metternich of the Labour Movement – immensely shrewd, far-sighted and despite his confirmed right-wing stance, surprisingly fair and sensitive to the left, as the left-wing Michael Foot observed in his biography of Aneurin Bevan. A perceptive view of Watson can be found in Denis Healey's autobiography, where he is portrayed as a Durham miner of unusual intelligence and total integrity. A small, sturdy figure with balding head and twinkling eyes, he was typical of the working-class intellectuals whom society had denied a university education.

Although on the right, he was never closely identified with the trade union junta that dominated the Labour Party from 1945 until the mid-1950s. Watson was an admirer of Aneurin Bevan and was instrumental in urging him to speak out in defence of the British nuclear deterrent at the 1957 party conference. But he backed Gaitskell and not Bevan when the Mineworkers' Union threw its support behind the old Wykehamist rather than the miner from Tredegar for the Labour treasurership in 1954, a victory that was correctly seen as a clear sign of who would be Attlee's successor as party leader. Gaitskell secured the overwhelming support of the Mineworkers' Union-sponsored MP›s in the leadership election just over a year later and this owed much to Watson's influence.

Watson was born in Boldon, County Durham, on 11 March 1898, He was educated at Boldon elementary school and then went down the local pit. Watson worked underground until he was 38 years old and was elected secretary of the area miners' association. A self-educated man, a lay preacher and socialist Sunday-school master, Watson was well read in history and literature. *Who Was Who* relates that his pastimes were reading, walking and unravelling knots. In his Durham bailiwick he became a solid and proud pillar of the Labour community – a county councillor, a National Health Service grandee, a member of Durham University's governing body. Later in life he worked for the National Coal Board and the nationalised electricity industry. Watson was one of those unsung figures in the Labour movement in its prime who served the Party without fuss but with distinction.

But it was in his work on the arty National Executive Committee that Watson exercised power and influence. As chairman of the Party's International Committee he ensured that Labour remained solidly behind Britain's membership of NATO and opposed unilateral nuclear disarmament. At the 1960 Scarborough conference he led off on the defence debate in which the narrowly defeated Hugh Gaitskell made his famous 'fight again' speech. Watson warned on that occasion that 'the final arbiters of the future of this party do not sit in this conference but are the British electorate and the British people'.

Although a member of his union's executive, Watson was not a prominent figure in its post-war history. His talents lay in strengthening trade union links with the party rather than in the industrial arena. Watson never doubted that the union-party connection should remain dominant, even as some Labour right-wingers began to question whether it should continue when seen by many as an increasing electoral liability. Although an admirer of Gaitskell's, he was opposed to his leader's intention to drop Clause 4 on public ownership from the party's constitution in 1960. Watson may have approved of Labour's modernisation, but not to the extent of abandoning its core values.

A close friend of the United States and that country's influential labour attaché Sam Berger, Watson was also an important connection between American administrations and the Labour leadership. His daughter was to marry one of the sons of Joe Godson, a colleague of Berger's at the US Embassy in London. Watson died on 7 May 1967.

Robert Taylor

Sidney and Beatrice Webb (1859–1947 and 1858–1943)
(1ˢᵗ Baron and Lady Passfield)

The Webbs were, in Beatrice's words, a partnership. This was how they saw themselves, and also how others saw them, quite rightly, for in assessing their achievement it is impossible to separate what each contributed. Sidney Webb had a parliamentary career and served in the first two Labour cabinets. However, he never saw himself as an important politician and nor did anyone else. The Webbs were influential through their writings, and through other shared activities, which brought the Fabian Society into prominence, established the *New Statesman*, helped to create the London School of Economics, and laid down much of the basis for modern Labour history. They exercised a potent influence on the character of the Labour P`arty, its self-image and the nature of its commitment to socialism. Fabianism, of which they were the main architects, can be described and judged in various ways. But in giving priority to the practical and immediate, and in believing both that profound improvements can be achieved piecemeal, and that ruling elites can be won over to this kind of social transformation, they provided intellectual ballast for the moderate reformism of Labour governments.

During their courtship, when Sidney was pressing a reluctant Beatrice to marry him, he once remarked that at least they came from the same class. This was true only if the term 'middle class' can be stretched to cover a vast social gulf. Sidney was born on 13 July 1859 in London into a family whose mainstay was his mother and her hairdressing business. His father, described variously as an accountant or a hairdresser, seems to have provided neither a steady income nor emotional stability. Sidney and his brother were partly educated abroad, in Switzerland and Germany, to some extent because of tensions between their parents. As a result he came to know French and German without losing his lower-middle-class London accent and manners. In contrast Beatrice was born into a very wealthy family, at Standish House near Gloucester, on 22 January 1858, the second youngest of the nine daughters of Richard Potter, a railway entrepreneur and businessman. After a largely conventional upper-class upbringing, educated at home, on her mother's death in 1882 she acted as her father's hostess until his death. Only gradually, even hesitantly, did she detach herself from the upper-class milieu into which she had been born.

Sidney rose socially through passing exams. After a brief spell as a clerk in a commercial firm, he joined the civil service through competitive exam entry and moved departments to gain promotion in the same way. He also passed the Bar exams and took a third class London LLB. In 1885 he joined the Fabian Society, rapidly becoming one of its most active members, and contributing to *Fabian Essays on Socialism* (1889). He and his close friends in the Society, George Bernard Shaw, Edward Pease and Graham Wallas, purged it of any remnants of utopianism and anarchism and steered it away from Marxist error towards the truth of the new economics of Jevons and Marshall, which corrected and filled gaps in classical theory. Socialism for them had more or less the same meaning as it had in ordinary speech at the time. As they used it, the word stood as shorthand for municipal ownership, government regulation and the provision of public services; and what socialists needed to do, therefore, was to further a change in the character of the state that had already begun. The essential task was to establish what Sidney Webb called 'a national minimum,' through regulation and intervention. This described a standard of living below which no-one would fall, not initially to be set at a specific level, for once it had been established it could subsequently be raised.

Beatrice's early life had an unusual aspect despite its upper-class conventionality. One of her father's closest friends was the political philosopher Herbert Spencer, whose extreme individualism he shared. Spencer encouraged Beatrice's intellectual side (ironically, since in the extremism and huge scope of his theory he is the nearest thinker to a Marx that the far right has ever had). She followed her sister Kate into charitable work, as a rent collector and housing manager of model buildings, but found it dissatisfying. (Later she was to become a critic of the voluntary sector's value in meeting social needs.) A far more formative influence was her work for Charles Booth's survey of London life and labour. Booth's methodology, his systematic accumulation of detailed information and rigid distinction between findings and policy recommendations influenced the Webbs' subsequent research; and her investigations for Booth (who was her cousin) into the sweated tailoring workshops and the Jewish community of the East End brought her for the first time into some public prominence. She resisted suggestions that she go on to investigate women's employment in favour of studying consumers' co-operation, partly because she refused to be typecast as a woman interested in women's rights. When she became a socialist, Booth and Marshall and others who had encouraged her were disturbed, as were her relatives. Her conversion was also more complex than she later allowed in her autobiography, *My Apprenticeship* (1926), though this drew heavily on the diaries she kept at the time. It came about, it seems, through a combination of knowledge of working-class conditions, a feeling of upper-class guilt, and a growing interest in social organisation, which had been aroused by the trade unionists she met as well as by Co-operative activists. The last was probably the most important influence.

Beatrice's book *The Co-operative Movement in Great Britain* was published in 1891. The year before, she and Sidney had met for the first time. He resigned his post as First Division Clerk in the Colonial Office on their engagement. In 1892 they married and started life together in London, supported by her inherited wealth.

The Webbs' partnership was a mixture of research and writing and involvement in practical affairs. Their *History of Trade Unionism* was published in 1893, and three years later their two-volume study, *Industrial Democracy*, a description of the animating spirit of trade unionism. As an LCC councillor Sidney immersed himself in the development of London schools and technical education. He was a member of the Royal Commission on trade union law in the wake of the Taff Vale decision and signed its Report, though it failed to give the unions what they wanted. (As a basis for legislation the Report was set aside in 1906 by the new Liberal government.) Much more significant was Beatrice's appointment in 1905 to the Royal Commission on the Poor Laws and Relief of Distress. Together she and Sidney wrote its long and complex Minority Report, which she, George Lansbury and two other members signed in 1909. The others on the Commission signed an equally weighty and complex Majority Report. In fact the Majority and Minority recommendations had a great deal in common and were later reconciled by the Maclean Committee in 1917 during wartime reconstruction planning.

The Webbs miscalculated both their influence with Liberal ministers and the extent to which both Reports had been pre-empted by the Liberal government's commitment to national insurance. Nevertheless, they launched in 1911–12 a great public campaign for what was called first 'the Break-Up of the Poor Law,' and then 'the Prevention of Destitution,' aimed at forcing the government to accept the Minority proposals. Its inevitable failure meant that for the first time they began to see the Labour Party as the political vehicle for their ideas.

During the First World War the Webbs involved themselves far more closely than before in party affairs. Sidney worked closely with Arthur Henderson in drafting the new Constitution of 1918 and the policy statement for the election of that year, in which he stood unsuccessfully as Labour candidate for the London University seat. In the 1922 election he was elected MP for the Seaham constituency, and served as President of the Board of Trade in the 1924 government.

Afterwards he told his constituency association he did not intend to stand again. He and

Beatrice felt it was time to accept semi-retirement at least, and moved from London to a house in the country, Passfield Corner, near Liphook in Hampshire. They wrote and published the final parts of their history of English local government, which included a volume on the last hundred years of the Poor Law, in which they had been historical actors. In 1929, however, Sidney was persuaded to accept the title Baron Passfield and to serve as Colonies and Dominions Secretary (he ceded the Dominions Office to J H Thomas in June 1930) in the second Labour Cabinet. As a minister his hesitancy and lack of positive ideas only underlined the absence of any distinctive Labour colonial policy.

In 1932 the Webbs visited the Soviet Union for the first time, having turned down earlier chances to go there, and Sidney returned in 1934 alone, to check earlier impressions and gather more facts. The result was their *Soviet Communism, A New Civilization?*, published in two volumes in 1934. It was an enthusiastic account of Stalinist Russia; the question mark was famously dropped from the title of the second edition. The book can be seen as a betrayal of their commitment to social democracy. In the 1920s Beatrice, for example, had said that fascist Italy and the Soviet Union were different instances of the same type of government. But if they were deluded, so were many others. Fellow travellers were numerous in the 'thirties, and the Soviet Union with its Five Year Plans was widely taken as offering an example of successful and rational social planning to a Western Europe mired in an economic depression and mass unemployment.

Beatrice Webb died at Passfield Corner on 30 April 1943. Sidney died there on 13 October 1947. There is a joint biography by Margaret Hamilton, *Beatrice and Sidney Webb* (1933). As well as *My Apprenticeship* (see above), Beatrice prepared a second volume of autobiography based on her diary which was published posthumously, *Our Partnership* (1948). Subsequently two further volumes of the diaries were published, edited by Margaret Cole, covering 1911–1932. These earlier versions of the diary are superseded by the edition of Noman and Jeanne Mackenzie, published in various volumes since 1982. Royden J. Harrison, *The Life and Times of Sidney and Beatrice Webb, 1858–1905* (2000) is the first volume of a joint biography which will be definitive when completed.

Dr John Brown

Josiah Wedgwood (1st Baron Wedgwood of Barlaston) (1872–1943)

Josiah Wedgwood was not untypical of the radical Liberals who came over to Labour around the time of the First World War, and who went on to achieve some prominence in their new party. Like Arthur Ponsonby and Charles Trevelyan, though, he was to find that early preferment was followed by increasing disillusionment with aspects of the trade union-based ethos of much of the Labour Party's activity, and, like them, he was by the 1930s increasingly out of sympathy with the party on a range of issues.

Josiah Wedgwood was born at Barlaston, north Staffordshire, on 16 March 1872. His background was prosperously upper middle class, and he was educated at Clifton College. He worked as a naval architect before serving in the Army during the Boer War. Due to the ill-health of his wife, Ethel Kate Bowen (whom he had married in 1894), he returned to Britain in 1904, and became involved in Liberal politics as a strong supporter of Henry George's land taxation proposals. At the general election of 1906 he was elected as Liberal MP for Newcastle-under-Lyme, which he then represented without a break until he was elevated to the peerage in 1942. During the First World War, Wedgwood served in the forces, being awarded a D.S.O. for his role at Gallipoli in 1915. However, he was badly wounded in May of that year, and was invalided out, first to work in the Ministry of Munitions, and then serving on the Royal Commission on Mesopotamia. By now he was moving away from the Liberals, not least because of their increasingly rightward drift under the pressure of war. At the 1918 general election he was returned unopposed at Newcastle as an Independent Liberal, but in 1919 he joined the Labour Party. In 1919 he was divorced; he then married Florence Ethel Willett.

At the general elections of the 1920s, Wedgwood easily held Newcastle as a Labour candidate. He made rapid strides in his new party, serving on the parliamentary executive (shadow cabinet) from 1921 until January 1924, when Labour formed its first government. Wedgwood was appointed to the cabinet as Chancellor of the Duchy of Lancaster, but he was not a particular success as a cabinet minister, and emerged after the fall of the government as a strong critic of MacDonald. These factors were sufficient to guarantee that he would not be found a place in the 1929 Labour government. In any case, he was increasingly out of sympathy with the direction in which the party was moving: land taxation was not a priority, and he was irked by the increasing centralisation and discipline of his adopted party. Although elected to the parliamentary committee in December 1924, he lost his place the following November, never to regain it. In the late 1920s he played a leading role in ensuring that Newcastle remained independent of nearby Stoke-on-Trent, and served two terms (1930–2) as mayor of the town. At the 1931 election he was refused endorsement by the Labour party, on the grounds that he had refused to sign the new, stricter, PLP standing orders; but it made no difference, and his popularity in the town was such that he was returned unopposed. He did not face opposition in 1935, either, by which time he had returned to the official Labour fold. He was now very far from the leading circles of the party, and most of the last period of his life was taken up with advocacy of the Jewish cause in Palestine and the promotion of the *History of Parliament* project. He was elevated to the Lords in 1942 as 1st Baron Wedgwood of Barlaston, but heart trouble dogged him, and on 26 July 1943 he died in London.

Wedgwood was a man of ability and drive, but he lacked the finesse and ability to compromise that are features of the successful politician. Passionate about various causes to the point of obsession, he could be seen as a great man of principle, but it is hard to avoid taking a more critical view of him as something of a bore, and there can be little doubt that he owed his presence in cabinet in 1924 to the paucity of the other material in the Labour Party at that time. But he was important, nonetheless, as a symbol of the way in which Labour had taken over at least some of the highminded radicalism of the late nineteenth century, and his contribution to Newcastle-under-Lyme should not be underestimated.

Wedgwood published two volumes of autobiography: *Essays and Adventures of a Labour MP* (1924) and *Memoirs of a Fighting Life* (1940). The chief biography remains C V Wedgwood, *The Last of the Radicals: Josiah Wedgwood, MP* (1951).

Andrew Thorpe

Sid Weighell   (1922–)

Sid Weighell was a figure of true Yorkshire grit, small, neat, terrierlike, and from the last authentically working-class generation of trade union leaders. He held his own in the generation of Jones and Scanlon, when such leaders believed they had a giant's strength and did not shrink from using it. Weighell always knew it should be exercised for the public good, but from birth onwards was fated not always to get his point across.

Sidney Weighell was born on 31 March 1922, in the North Riding town of Northallerton. His mother meant his first name to be Sydney, in celebration of the great industrial contract that had just come to the region (Dorman Long was to build the Sydney Harbour Bridge) but the Registrar would have none of it. From his father Tom, a signalman who had taken part in the 1911 strike for recognition by what was still the Amalgamated Society of Railway Servants, he got his lifetime commitment to the railways. After a basic but thorough education at the local Church of England school, he went to work at the LNER Motive Power at Thirsk, followed by long hours on the footplate through the war years. This could have taken him into the élite train drivers' union ASLEF, but he remained in the NUR, where his father was branch secretary, and later on the national executive.

Weighell briefly felt the tug of other interests. As a footballer he did two years with Sunderland reserves, supplementing his fireman's wages, but his destiny was the union, closely linked with the Labour Party. He was the Labour agent for Richmond through three elections, until his rapid rise in the union forced him to concentrate his energies – to such effect that he was on the NUR national executive himself at the age of 31, and a divisional officer at Unity House in 1954. Like most northerners who moved south to London, he frequently went home to the north. Tragedy struck in 1956, in a head-on crash at Newark railway bridge, which killed his young wife Margaret and his four-year-old daughter. Weighell himself survived, as did his son Anthony, but wrote in his autobiography that it took him five years to make a physical and mental recovery. Eventually he was married again, to Joan Willets in 1959, and rebuilt his union too. In 1965 he was elected Assistant General Secretary of the NUR, and soon became the Union's effective voice, as the lugubrious General Secretary, Sidney Greene, diligently kept himself out of the spotlight while the railway system was being decimated.

Weighell, with his gift for the vivid phrase and his innate hostility to what he saw as the greed and indifference of the biggest unions, was happy to move centre stage. His final apprenticeship was three years as the NUR representative on the Labour Party National Executive, where the left, under the leadership of Tony Benn, its chairman in 1971–72, were bent on preparing a shopping list of 25 major companies for nationalisation. Weighell opposed this, and threw himself into a public campaign to save the railways through an integrated transport policy. The phrase survived as an aspiration through long years of attrition for the railways. Transport 2000, established in 1972, owed much to Weighell as its first secretary.

Thus, when Greene retired as General Secretary, the succession of the second Sidney was assured. Weighell gained an absolute majority of votes on the first ballot, and it says much for this combative character that all his three rivals, Frank Cannon, Russell Tuck and Charlie Turnock, continued to work closely with him thereafter. A natural supporter of the in-coming Labour government's Social Contract, he found himself caught in a game of leapfrogging wage claims. At its height his NUR executive actually rejected a tribunal award of 27.5 per cent in favour of an illusory 'going rate' of 30 per cent. The final rise was 29.8 per cent. Weighell pronounced himself 'a happy man tonight', but privately became (and remained) a firm believer in the policy of wage restraint combined with social justice advocated by the Labour government which lasted for three years. It was in line with his kind of socialism, to 'benefit workers, maintain an orderly control of the allocation of resources to labour costs, and keep industrial relations at a level which resembled rational behaviour'. By 1978, however, many of his colleagues on the TUC had had enough – or believed their members had. The minority government's appeal for further wage restraint was rejected, but in the unspoken belief that there would soon be a general election. Instead Jim Callaghan chose to soldier on, and Weighell was one of his loyal allies who went down fighting at Labour's Annual Conference.

Weighell's speech at Conference derided some of the wage claims which challenged the Government's imposed 5 per cent limit. 'My union helped to create this party …I am not going to stand here and destroy it. But if you want the call to go out to this conference that the new policy in the Labour Party you believe in is the philosophy of the pig trough – those with the biggest snouts get the biggest share – then I reject it.' 'Snouts in the trough' was a phrase that travelled badly, and Weighell's bluntness made him enemies who would be merciless when their turn came. The TUC General Council tried to shuffle back into a position of neutrality on wage policy, but on the crucial vote Weighell was absent – broadcasting in support of it – and a 14–14 tie left it uncarried. The 'Winter of Discontent' might have followed anyway, but the TUC was needlessly naked to face its moral rigours.

Weighell fought hard throughout the Seventies to save and to expand the railway network. Ministers came and went. The ablest, Anthony Crosland, was the least sympathetic to an extension of public support. The NUR made its own case (helped by a good working relationship between Weighell and British Rail's chairman Sir Peter Parker), though it was handicapped by the constant and bitter rivalry with ASLEF, the drivers' union. The two were at odds over the issue of flexible rostering and the joint 1982 rail strike, for which Weighell never hid his distaste.

Internally Sid Weighell was a moderniser. He tried to make the NUR National Executive more representative, purchased Frant Place in Kent as a union training centre for his members, and rebuilt Unity House. The hallowed headquarters of the old Amalgamated Society of Railway Servants, to which his father had come as an executive member before him, was demolished. In the Labour Party itself the NUR General Secretary meant to be a force. A political officer, Keith Hill, was recruited. The Parliamentary panel was much expanded. Rank-and-file union members were prepared for the rigours of Westminster and council selections at Frant.

In normal times this would have ensured the NUR a constructive role in a resurgent Labour Party. But these were not normal times. The Labour defectors to the SDP discredited the right of the party (although every NUR-sponsored MP remained steadfastly loyal). And Labour's malign antibody, the Militant Tendency, was emboldened to produce its own tract for the railways, *A Fighting Programme for the NUR*. Sometimes fighting was literal. Weighell and his mild-mannered union president, Tommy Hamm, were physically attacked at one meeting at Unity House. In 1982, with Labour hideously split, the tactics of the rail strike hotly debated, and a majority of his National Executive often against him, Weighell was buoyed up by the support of his delegate conference. There, at least, the hard left could not prevail. He now fatally overreached himself.

The 1982 Labour Conference marked the first ebbing of the Bennite tide. The standard bearer of the left was narrowly defeated by Denis Healey. Four additional moderates had been elected to the Labour NEC. Then it became clear, from a fortuitous recount of votes in the trade union section, that Weighell had switched the NUR block vote away from the NUM candidate, despite being mandated by his own delegate conference to vote for the full agreed 'slate'. He had given his enemies a sword, and they used it. On the long drive back from Blackpool he decided to resign before he was dismissed, thus allowing a final appeal to the NUR's own conference, which had been recalled to ratify a recent pay award. The delegates voted, by 41–36, that his resignation should be accepted. Then they took the fallen General Secretary's advice in his last speech, and accepted the award.

That was the end. Weighell was treated vindictively by his executive, and struck out of its history. When the new Unity House, his real monument, was opened in May 1983, he was not invited. The officers of the union and its president never joined the ostracism. Nor did the NUR MPs. Identification with Weighell counted heavily against his favoured candidate, Charlie Turnock, in the election of his successor, the much underestimated Jimmy Knapp.

Sidney Weighell went home to North Yorkshire, and remains there still. One moment of folly cost him his job, a place at the heart of Labour's eventual revival, and all the normal perquisites of retired General Secretaries. But he had the courage to fight his corner, a class act among class posturers, in a cause that might have foundered without him.

Phillip Whitehead MEP

Joseph Westwood (1884–1948)

Joe Westwood was born at Wollescote in Stourbridge on 11 February 1884, the son of Solomon Westwood, coalminer, and Harriet Sideway. He worked as a draper's assistant after leaving school at 13: he had, however, received a sound traditional Scottish education at Buckhaven Higher Grade School, Fife. Pit closures in Worcestershire had forced his family to move north in 1887. He began work down the pit in 1898: in 1916, the Fife miners appointed him as their industrial organiser.

In days when MPs had virtually no salary, he remained Political Organiser of the Scottish Miners 1918–1929, albeit he was elected for Peebles and South Midlothian, a mining seat, 1922–1931. At the fag end of the Labour Government he became Under-Secretary of State for Scotland, working for his friend, Willie Adamson, whose PPS he had been since 1929.

Swamped in the deluge of 1931, he came back for Stirling and Falkirk Burghs in 1935. In Churchill's Coalition he was from 1940–45 Under-Secretary of State, ministerially responsible for the clean-up of Clydebank and other blitzed areas. He displayed frenetic energy and effectiveness.

Having been Convenor of the Housing Committee of Kirkcaldy Town Council and having served for many years as a prominent member of Fife Education Comittee, arguably the most progressive in Scotland at the time, it was natural that Westwood should play a crucial role in the run-up to the Scottish Education Act of 1945, which did for Scotland what the Butler-Ede act of 1944 did for England. He was made a Privy Councillor in 1943 for his work which, in fact, shouldered an important burden, above that of Under-Secretary.

On the formation of the Labour Government, Attlee appointed Westwood as his Secretary of State for Scotland with cabinet status. He championed the poor with all the enthusiasm of the active Salvation Army Officer that he was. At the age of 63, Attlee asked him to make way for a younger man, which he accepted with grace and lack of resentment.

In 1906 he married Frances, daughter of James Scarlett and Frances Harvey, who gave him three sons and five daughters. Tragically, Joe and Frances were killed in a car accident at Strathmiglo, Fife, on 17 July 1948.

He was a much-loved cock-sparrow of a politician. The funeral service would have been held at the local Salvation Army Hall, but there were too many mourners and the large Sinclairtown Parish Church was used. The service was appropriately conducted by the General Secretary of the Salvation Army in Scotland, Colonel Edwin Calvert. At the London Memorial Meeting at the Crown Court Church, the Scottish Church in Russell Street, Bloomsbury, Clem Attlee, Ernie Bevin, Stafford Cripps, Hugh Dalton, Herbert Morrison and Emmanuel Shinwell were among the mourners.

Tam Dalyell MP

John Wheatley (1869–1930)

For many, Wheatley was the archetypal early Labour Member of Parliament. A miner from a working-class Irish family, he rose through the ranks of Scottish local government and attained a brief and successful period in Cabinet as Minister of Health, but much of his life was spent campaigning with zeal and passion against the injustices of the capitalist world and making a nuisance of himself on the back benches as the leading 'Red Clydesider'. Unusually for many prominent Labour leaders Wheatley was also an active Catholic and businessman.

John Wheatley was born one of ten children (two died young) on 19 May 1869 in Bonmahon, County Waterford, but the family moved to Braehead in Lanarkshire when he was seven. Although he joined his father down the mine when he was 14, between 1893 and 1901 Wheatley ran his own business, first as a publican and then running a grocery shop with his brother.

Thanks to the support of his parish priest and regular hikes into Glasgow for evening classes at the Athenaeum, Wheatley was an able writer by 1901, when the business collapsed, and on landing a job (as advertising canvasser and then reporter) on the *Glasgow Observer* he read widely in Catholic social teaching and soon became an expert self-taught polemicist. It was Irish politics that brought him into socialism however, becoming first the chair of the local Shettleston branch of the United Irish League and then in 1906 election agent for the Labour Representation Committee. That same year he formed the Catholic Socialist Society and in 1907 he joined the Independent Labour Party.

In 1912 Wheatley was elected for Shettleston to the Lanarkshire County Council, and when it was amalgamated with Glasgow he became a Glasgow City Councillor, rapidly establishing a name for himself by showing up the inadequacy of the Liberal Corporation's housing plans. In 1913 he argued for replacing Glasgow's tenements ('the slaughter-houses of the poor') and in 1915, whilst also opposing conscription in the War, he successfully led the Glasgow Rent Strikes.

Although Wheatley stood for Parliament in 1918 it was not until 1922 that he was elected for Shettleston (where he and his wife Mary lived) as one of Glasgow's ten Labour MPs. Less than two years later Ramsay MacDonald made him Labour's first Minister of Health. Few would disagree that Wheatley's Housing Act was one of the major achievements of the first minority Labour government, with its 15–year plan to build 2.5 million affordable council homes. The Liberal MP Charles Masterman commented, 'He has been the conspicuous success in the new parliament. A short, squat, middle-aged man with a chubby face beaming behind large spectacles, he trots around like a benign Pickwick'.

Wheatley's period in office was brief, however. When Labour lost the 1924 election he commented that Labour had been 'freed from a difficult position' and he soon became as virulent a critic of MacDonald's realpolitik and Labour's tacking to the centre as he was of the Tory Government – an attitude he continued from the backbenches when Labour again won power in 1929. By the time he was fighting Margaret Bondfield's National Insurance Act, though, he was an ill man, and he died from a cerebral haemorrhage on 12 May 1930.

Some have seen Wheatley as a hero of the uncompromising left, with his savage and often vituperative attacks on MacDonald. Others have pointed to his failures – most notably his inability or refusal to address the issues of birth control and health provision as Minister for Health. The truth is, however, that his greatest success lay in establishing (despite often virulent clerical opposition) a coherent argument for Catholics to espouse socialism and thereby helping win large reaches of the country for Labour at a time when Labour support for Irish Home Rule was waning. Wheatley wrote and published many pamphlets on socialism and Catholicism, and Ian Wood wrote the only full biography, *John Wheatley,* for Manchester University Press in 1990.

Chris Bryant MP

William Whiteley (1882–1955)

William Whiteley was one of the least known of Labour MPs outside the House of Commons, but as Chief Whip during Attlee's 1945–51 government he exercised a powerful influence behind the scenes at Westminster. Whiteley's early life and career confirmed the adage that the Labour Party owed more to Methodism than to Marx. It also owed much to the coal industry. He was born in the mining village of Littleburn, near Durham, on 3 October 1882, the fourth son of Samuel and Ellen Whiteley. His father was a miner and checkweighman at the local colliery, as well as being a Methodist lay preacher.

The influence of this home background was long-lasting. William attended Brandon Colliery School near his home until the age of 12, after which he began work in the local pit. At fifteen he became a clerk in the offices of the Durham Miners' Association, supplementing the family income by teaching subjects such as book-keeping and shorthand at local night schools.

In 1901 Whiteley married Elizabeth Swordy Jackson, daughter of James Urwin Jackson, a blacksmith at Littleburn colliery; they were to have one son and one daughter. Whitely grew into a tall, powerfully-built young man who excelled at sport, particularly soccer. There was some possibility that he might become a professional footballer, but his father – a strict teetotaller – discovered that his team changed in public houses, and proceeded to burn his son's boots and football kit.

Whiteley devoted much energy to the local Methodist church, but he became increasingly interested in political activity. He joined the nascent Labour Party in 1906; helped to found the Durham City Labour group; became a miners' agent in 1912; and from 1915 to 1922 was on the executive of the Miners' Federation of Great Britain.

In 1918 he fought his first parliamentary election for the Blaydon division of Durham, but he was defeated. He was successful second time around in 1922 and held the seat until Labour's crushing defeat at the 1931 general election. During this period he spoke infrequently – usually on mining issues – in the House of Commons. But he was recognised as a figure of integrity and authority, and in 1926 he became a party Whip. When Ramsay MacDonald became Prime Minister for the second time in 1929, Whiteley was appointed as Lord Commissioner of the Treasury, a post he held until the débâcle of 1931.

Whiteley was one of many Labour MPs who were defeated in 1931, and to earn a living he resumed his teaching of evening classes, as well as working in the public assistance department of Durham County Council. In 1935 he won back the Blaydon constituency – which he was to hold until his death – and continued to build his reputation through steady committee work rather than notable speech-making.

After the formation of Churchill's wartime coalition in 1940, Whiteley's career prospered. He was first appointed Comptroller of His Majesty's Household, and then in March 1942 he became Joint Parliamentary Secretary to the Treasury and Chief Labour Whip. For the next three years he worked successfully alongside his Conservative counterparts in maintaining support for the coalition. This was no easy task, as MPs on both sides hankered after an early return to traditional two-party politics. There were rebuffs along the way, notably when Labour back-benchers defied the whips to vote for the immediate introduction of the Beveridge Report, but Whiteley's firm yet conciliatory approach meant he came through the war with his reputation enhanced.

The pinnacle of his career came after Labour's landslide victory at the 1945 election. The new Prime Minister, Attlee, had no hesitation in appointing him as government Chief Whip, a position he held until Labour lost office in 1951. Attlee's massive majority meant there was little prospect of defeat in the lobbies, but this did not mean the Chief Whip was given an easy ride. There were numerous episodes where he had to contain unrest by small groups of Labour MPs (usually on foreign policy issues), which he did with a combination of tact and admonition. Whiteley was an imposing figure in these years – tall and always immaculately dressed – and his qualities helped to ensure that there were few parliamentary impediments to the introduction of Labour's programme of nationalisation and welfare reform.

His task was more challenging after Labour's majority was reduced to single figures at the general election in February 1950. With great energy and attention to detail, Whiteley marshalled his troops (ferrying in the sick through the lobbies when necessary) to ensure that Labour lost only five of 234 divisions in the 1950–51 parliament, none on the major issues of the day. The strain took its toll when, having been in good health throughout his life, he suffered an attack of shingles which kept him away from his duties for a lengthy period.

He continued to act as Labour Chief Whip after the party returned to opposition, but this was a less happy period. The emergence of the 'Bevanite' group posed more difficulties for party management than he had experienced while Labour remained in power, and it was with relief that Whiteley retired from the fray in 1955.

He always maintained close links with his native Durham, becoming a Deputy Lieutenant of the county. He had a keen interest in education – serving as a member of the county education committee and as a governor of several schools – and for many years he was president of the Durham Mineworkers' Home Association and of the Durham Miners' Approved Society. It was at hospital in Durham that he died at the age of 73 on 3 November 1955. As Attlee reflected, he was by common consent 'one of the greatest of all chief whips'.

Kevin Jefferys

Larry Whitty (Lord Whitty) (1943–)

If life had taken a different turn, Larry Whitty could have been treading the boards rather than playing a prominent role on the political stage. An enthusiastic actor at Cambridge University, the theatre's loss was to be the labour movement's gain and Larry was quite simply one of the best, if not the best, General Secretary the Labour Party has had.

He took over the post from Jim Mortimer in 1985 when a bitterly divided Party was still reeling from a devastating election defeat and the SDP posed a threat to the centre-left. When he left a decade later, the party's fortunes had been transformed, with Tony Blair and New Labour poised to be the beneficiaries of the tough times Larry Whitty had to face managing a National Executive Committee at times resistant to change.

The machine he bequeathed to Tom Sawyer was incomparably better than the ramshackle organisation he inherited. The Labour Party, for instance, knew for the first time who its members were and for once its finances were well into the black!

Once elected, he saw his role as working for the whole of the Party during a period when factions dominated the NEC. He became a trusted link to all sections of the party. For instance he played a key role in 1992 and 1993 in rescuing the relationship between the Party and the unions at a point when it was in danger of floundering. He was also the man who was responsible for modernising the financial organisation of the Labour Party, initiating the new policy making processes and the reorganisation of the responsibilities of Labour headquarters.

Larry believed in the power of persuasion, though the expulsion of Derek Hatton and his entryist Militants displayed his tougher side as he fought and defeated a group that quite simply refused to play by the rules. Larry did much of the spade work under Neil Kinnock and John Smith while enjoying little of the credit, The roar of approval that greeted his valedictory speech left many in the party believing Blair should have kept him on. He was very loyal to his friends in the machine, even when they were not always delivering. Alas, they were not always loyal to him. In truth, Larry had wanted to move on before Blair took over, John Smith persuading him to stay on in 1992 when he had thought of quitting to write a book on politics that to this day is still unwritten.

Blair later made him the Party's European co-ordinator, and was quickly impressed by his ability to spot the devil in the detail as well as the significance of ideas and major events. A peerage was accepted in 1996 despite misgivings, and Baron Whitty of Camberwell in the London Borough of Southwark was to serve 12 months as a Whip after Labour's election victory before becoming a minister in John Prescott's Department of the Environment, Transport and the Regions. The talent for organisation that served him so well in the party HQ once more came to the fore and he piloted the Countryside Bill into law without losing a single vote to the Tory landowners who dominated the second chamber.

The son of Frederick and Kathleen Whitty, he was born on 15 June 1943 and attended Latymer Upper School in London. Before St John's College Cambridge, where he received a BA in Economics, and thespianism, Larry was by his own admission a pretty poor draughtsman at Hawker Siddeley Aviation (1960–62), his inability to draw in that pre-computer-graphics era proving something of a handicap. In 1965, after Cambridge, he joined the Ministry of Aviation Technology, working with Tony Benn, before spending three years at the TUC from 1970, then around a dozen at the GMB before moving to Walworth Road.

At the GMB he built up a research department that was the envy of employers as well as other unions, sending officials into negotiations armed with killer facts as well as campaigning on issues such as health and safety. Cool, he never got flustered or threw a wobbly while Labour's General Secretary and would never ask anyone to say or do anything he was not prepared to say or do.

In preparation for party conferences he was a hands-on party manager. He wasn't one to hide away in the General Secretary's suite, instead visiting union receptions and meeting delegates, receiving brickbats as well as bouquets which were less forthcoming in the early years. And, unusually for a senior figure in any political party, Larry wrote his own reports of up to 100 pages, and the quality of his work and his analysis was remarkable. After the 1987 and 1992 election defeats, I did not read a better assessment of Labour's strengths and weaknesses.

His grey mane and neat 'tash have sometimes left him confused with Des Lynam, the TV sports presenter. After trying to explain who he really was to an enthusiastic and, it must be admitted, disappointed autograph hunter, Larry confessed he was relieved he had not been taken for the much older Dickie Davies, before wondering aloud whether Des Lynam was ever pestered by people thinking he was Larry Whitty.

I had dinner with Larry at his home in October 1994, the night before the NEC voted for a new General Secretary. I put it to him that he must be bitter and angry, at the very least feeling cheated that he had made the Party ready to win an election only to find that he would not be at its head when we won at the polls. Not even in a moment of such privacy did he criticise or condemn those who had failed to support him, displaying a loyalty lacking in some of his colleagues. Larry Whitty is a remarkable man and politician. He deserves the recognition and praise he never, ever courted. His first marriage, to Tanya Margaret, with whom he has two sons, lasted from 1969 until they divorced in 1986. He married Angela Forrester in 1993.

Fraser Kemp MP

George Wigg (Lord Wigg)   (1900–83)

George Edward Cecil Wigg was born on 28 November 1900 in Ealing, the first child of Edward William Wigg and Cecilia Comber. His father, the youngest of 13 children, ran a dairy business. The family drifted apart and he was brought up by his mother, described in his autobiography as 'of immense vitality and drive,' in Basingstoke, where he was educated at Fairfield's County School and, as a scholarship boy, at Queen Mary's Grammar School, 'a twentieth-century version of Charles Dickens's Dotheboys Hall,' he recalled in his memoirs. The social and educational system of the time thwarted the development of his considerable intellectual gifts. This accounted for his sometimes belligerent attitude towards those he dubbed the 'intellectuals in the Labour leadership.'

Wigg joined the army at seventeen, joining the Tank Corps in 1919, and spent eighteen happy years in the ranks. He served in Turkey at the time of the Chanak incident, in Mesopotamia, where he was befriended by the indomitable Arabist Gertrude Bell, and in Egypt. 'My years in Iraq and Egypt were lonely,' he recalled in his autobiography. Though he wrote of his enjoyment of 'racing and riding and swimming ... the friendship and life of the sergeants mess,' he also valued 'beyond price the privacy of my own bunk, where I could be alone with my books and my thoughts.' He read extensively about the history of the Great War and about the organisation of the armed forces, becoming a great admirer of R B Haldane's 'genius' as Secretary of State for War pre-1914. 'Organisation, administration, quartering and supply were my basic interests in military affairs and the core of many of my speeches in the House of Commons. Neglect of these problems brought us near to defeat in both World Wars. In my view the cause of neglect was the ossified class structure of British society.'

Class obsessed Wigg. It was as a soldier that he learned to stand up for himself and to use King's Regulations – as he later used Erskine May, with an ingenuity that I suspect was never shown before and to my certain knowledge never shown since – to confound bullies and cheats.

Stationed in Canterbury in the 1930s, he became involved with the Workers Educational Association (WEA). In 1937 he left the army for a full-time WEA post, working directly for one of his heroes, Sandy Lindsay, Master of Balliol, founder of Keele University in north Staffordshire. On the outbreak of war he was commissioned in the Royal Army Education Corps. He became MP for Dudley in July 1945, serving for 22 years. Substituting for his friend, Dick Crossman, at 24 hours notice, I went to Dudley Constituency Labour Party (CLP) in 1963. Since George terrified us all, Harold Wilson not excluded, it was quite simply the most daunting CLP meeting I have ever experienced. Wigg seemed to have imbued in his CLP members the same inquisitorial skills that he possessed so formidably. Obviously, his constituents thought the world of him – and rightly, since no MP ever raised such hell in Whitehall if he thought there was injustice.

He served as PPS to Emmanuel Shinwell, 1945–51, first at the Ministry of Fuel and Power (which was the origin of his distaste for Gaitskell) and subsequently at War and Defence. In October 1964, I was phoned at home – the inevitable call-sign, 'Wigg here' – and asked to propose the nomination of my predecessor but four as MP for West Lothian, Shinwell, as Chair of the Parliamentary Labour Party.

After 1951, from his front-bench seat below the gangway – flanked often by Sidney Silverman – he played a leading part in the Reform of the Army Act. He fought the implications of the defence White Paper of 1957, the Blue Streak project, achieving a mastery of parliamentary tactics – 'Wiggery-Pokery', as Tory Ministers wryly soubriquetised it.

Wigg's autobiography, *George Wigg* (Michael Joseph, 1972), gives an account of the Portland and Vassal trials of fascinating insight. As a new MP, I sat in the Chamber, uncomfortable at the *ad hominem* onslaught on Profumo, yet spellbound. This was not the silly name-calling and sound-bites of the year 2000 – it was devastating, intensely felt Parliamentary investigation into wrong-doing. Norman Shrapnel wrote: 'Above all one remembers him through the Macmillan years in endless running battles with what seems in retrospect like whole battalions of defence and serv-ice ministers ... his scorn for the stock uninformative reply was peppered with rich serviceman's comment ... "half-baked nonsense!" he would shout at Mr Soames, sometime Secretary of State for War ... He would make speeches about the army at enormous length – longer, people were already beginning to think, than it would take to fight a contemporary all-out war ... He re-sented an army in which, as he appeared to think, the well-being of soldiers was so often disre-garded that all too often they would desert and go off to fight by-elections.'

In 1963, on the death of Gaitskell – 'while there is death there is hope', boomed George – he became a manager for Wilson's leadership campaign, being appointed Paymaster General and a Privy Counsellor by Wilson in 1964. What he did was a mystery to most of his colleagues. All I know, staying with R H S Crossman in 9 Vincent Square Mondays to Fridays, was that Wigg phoned about 8am most mornings. He was interminable. Quite often Crossman would come down to an overcooked breakfast I had prepared and sigh, 'That was George – he's been on to Harold, haranguing him for forty minutes this morning.' Wigg had a unique relationship with Wilson 1964–67 – albeit as a devourer of Prime Ministerial time.

Mercifully, in 1967 Wigg accepted with alacrity the chairmanship of the Horserace Betting Levy Board, on which he had served 1958–64, and resigned his seat to accept a peerage. No si-necure! Betting and horses had been a passionate interest. From the unlikely quarter of my constituent, the Sixth Earl of Rosebery, KT PC DSO MC, owner of Derby winners, whose colours were famous at Newmarket and elsewhere for thirty years, came a glowing judgement: 'George knows what he is talking about!' From a dour aristocrat and wartime Cabinet Minis-ter, that was an accolade. He served until 1972.

My last memories of George are of going regularly to see him in his basement flat at 83 The Green, Clapham Common, for advice on opposition to Mrs Thatcher's Falkland's war – a reckless adventure that lost serviceman's lives for no long-term purpose. George never mel-lowed to his dying day: 11 August 1983. He was survived by his wife and three daughters.

Tam Dalyell MP

Ellen Wilkinson (1891–1947)

Ellen Cicely Wilkinson, dubbed 'Red Ellen' by the press, was a feminist, left-wing socialist, trade unionist and Fabian, and the first woman Education Minister. As a campaigner against unemployment she led the Jarrow Crusade, and as a pacifist and anti-fascist she led the cam-paign against Franco and Hitler in the 1930s. She was a founder of *Tribune*, and remained on the left wing of the Labour Party throughout her life.

Ellen Wilkinson was born in Manchester on 8 October 1891, daughter of a textile worker. Her parents, Richard Wilkinson and Ellen Wood, were both Methodists, and her father voted

Conservative. She was educated at Ardwick Higher Elementary School. In 1906 she won a teaching bursary to enter the Manchester Day Training College for half the week, and for the rest of the week taught at Oswald Road Elementary School.

Her first direct political involvement came with being encouraged to stand as the socialist candidate in her school mock election (probably in 1905), which led her to read Robert Blatchford's *Merrie England* and *Britain for the British*. At the age of 16 she joined the Independent Labour Party and at her first branch meeting was particularly impressed with the speech by the Fabian pioneer Kathleen Glasier at the Manchester Free Trade Hall.

In 1910 she won a scholarship to Manchester University, where she studied History under George Unwin. At Manchester University she became in 1912 joint secretary of the University Fabian Society. From there she became active in the Fabian Women's Group, a volunteer in the Fabian Reserarch Department and was co-opted to the Executive of the University Socialist Federation, serving as Vice-Chair to GDH Cole in 1915. She remained an active and enthusiastic Fabian throughout her life, serving on the Executive 1940–47.

She campaigned with the suffragettes, and was election organiser for the National Union of Women's Suffrage Societies from 1913 to 1915. In 1915 she became organiser for the Amalgamated Union of Co-operative Employees, a forerunner of USDAW, the shopworkers' union. During the First World War, Wilkinson was a supporter of the Non-Conscription Fellowship, and opposed to the war.

In 1920 Wilkinson was a member of the Labour committee investigating the activities of the Black and Tans during the conflict in Ireland. In July 1920 she became a founder member of the Communist Party of Great Britain, attending the Moscow Conference of Red International Labour Unions in 1921, though by 1924 she had resigned. At this time communists were yet to be banned from the Labour Party, and at the 1923 general election she was the Labour candidate at Ashton-under-Lyne. She served as a Labour Manchester City Councillor between 1923 and 1926.

Wilkinson was elected as Labour Member of Parliament for Middlesborough East in 1924, and became known as 'Red Ellen' for her politics and her vivid red hair. The *Daily Telegraph* said that she had 'hair of a stunning hue.'

In 1925 she was President of the Conference of Labour Women, and she served as Parliamentary Private Secretary to Arthur Greenwood MP, Minister of Health in the 1929 Labour Government. Wilkinson was defeated in 1931 as part of the National Government Landslide.

Out of parliament, Wilkinson wrote three books – *Peeps at Politicians* (1931), *The Terror in Germany* (1933) and a political novel, *The Division Bell Mystery* (1932). She also penned two pamphlets – *Why War?* (1934) and *Why Fascism?* (1934).

In 1935 she was elected as Labour member for Jarrow, where she served as MP until her death in 1947. In the year of her first election at Jarrow, nearly 80 per cent of the workforce were unemployed. Of 8,000 skilled manual workers, only 100 were in work.

In 1936 she organised and took part in one of the defining moments in Labour history—the Jarrow March against unemployment. Perhaps one of the most enduring images of the 1930s is the photograph of Jarrow marchers with Ellen Wilkinson at the their head. Writing in *Tribune* she called for action: 'Any government really alive to the appalling plight of masses of people – suffering from unemployment over long periods, from enforced malnutrition, from abominable housing conditions, from neglect, from despair – would move heaven and earth to bring immediate amelioration.' Her polemic against slump and unemployment and its effects on her constituents was published as *The Town That Was Murdered* (1939). In 1936 she published an account of her early life, *Myself When Young*.

In 1936, Wilkinson joined Victor Gollancz, Stafford Cripps, Aneurin Bevan and George Strauss to launch the weekly newspaper *Tribune*. She also became active in calls for a Popular Front, joining with communists and others to oppose fascism. In December 1936, she visited Spain with Clement Attlee to see the effects of the Spanish Civil War and the bombing of Valencia and Madrid. Wilkinson's Private Members Bill on hire purchase reform became successful in 1938, protected millions of people against repossession of their goods and unfair terms and conditions. In 1937 she was elected onto the Labour NEC, in the women's section. In 1944/45 she was to be chair of the Labour Party.

In 1940 Labour joined the wartime coalition, and on 17 May Wilkinson became Parliamentary Secretary at the Ministry of Pensions. On 8 October she was appointed Parliamentary Secretary for Home Security, serving until Labour left the coalition in May 1945 under her friend Herbert Morrison at the Home Office. There, she was in charge of introducing air raid shelters to the civilian population. The 1945 New Year's Honours list announced her appointment to the Privy Council.

Ellen Wilkinson became on 3 August 1945, following Labour's 1945 landslide, the first woman to be Minister for Education, and the only woman to serve in Attlee's Cabinet. She introduced the School Milk Act in 1946, guaranteeing free school milk to the nation's school children, which lasted until Margaret Thatcher scrapped it in 1973. Her determination and drive, moreover, were critical in bringing to fruition her first pledge as Minister, the raising of the school leaving age from 14 to 15 by 1 April 1947, in the teeth of profound anxieties amongst many in Cabinet, led by Stafford Cripps, regarding the administrative and economic practicalities of the short timescale she had set. To train sufficient extra new teachers, she secured resources to create the fast-track Emergency Training Scheme for ex-services personnel, which by 1951 had trained over 35,000 extra teachers. She was not, however, able to fulfil her medium-term goal of raising the school leaving age to 16.

Dispirited by the lack of pace of change, Ellen Wilkinson took an overdose of barbiturates and died, aged 56, on 6 February 1947. Jennie Lee writing in *Tribune* spoke of 'her gift of courage, of laughter, and generosity of spirit.' Her obituary in the *Times Educational Supplement* said 'Had Ellen Wilkinson lived longer, there is little doubt that the children of England and Wales would have had reason to bless her name.' A biography, *Ellen Wilkinson*, was published by Betty D Vernon in 1982.

Paul Richards

Francis Williams (Lord Francis-Williams)   (1903–70)

Francis Williams was the first real press secretary to a Labour Government, yet he is remembered for much more than that. He was a chronicler of the Labour movement, editor of the *Daily Herald*, prolific writer and a pioneer of debate shows on television.

Francis Williams was born at St Martins in Shropshire on March 10, 1903. He went to Queen Elizabeth grammar school at Middleton and then worked for a number of small local newspapers before joining the *Herald's* city desk. There he was spotted as a bright, though young, prospect. In 1936 he became editor of the *Herald* at a critical time for the country and Labour movement. He did not find it easy dealing with the paper's dual ownership by the TUC and Odhams. After four years in the editor's chair he left, and early in the war became Controller of News and Censorship at the Ministry of Information. For this work he received the CBE and US Medal of Freedom.

When Labour won the 1945 election, Clement Attlee made him his press secretary at No 10. With his background of journalism and propaganda, he seemed perfect for the post, particularly as the Labour Government began its great reforming programme. Yet by the time the NHS was formed, Williams had gone. He never stayed long in any job, even one as exciting as that.

He was a BBC governor for a couple of years in the early 1950s and then editor of the socialist weekly *Forward* for four years. He became a regular on television as that medium developed its political and current affairs coverage. His relaxed manner in all roles, whether he was chairman, interrogator or debater, soon made his face familiar to millions of viewers. Later he was one of those who set up Television Reporters International, which produced documentaries and current-affairs prorammes.

In 1962 he was made a Labour life peer as Lord Francis-Williams, and at his introduction he affirmed instead of taking the oath – 20 years earlier he had declared that he had 'no formal religion and no belief in the supernatural assumptions of the Christian religion'.

Throughout his life Williams was a prolific writer. He produced *Democracy's Last Battle* (1941), *Tomorrow's Politics* (1942), *Press, Parliament and People* (1946), *The Triple Challenge, The Future of Socialist Britain* (1946) and *A Pattern of Rulers*, a study of three prime ministers. He wrote an acclaimed life of Ernest Bevin, histories of the Labour Party and trade unionism, and in 1961 produced a book of conversations, *Attlee – A Prime Minister Remembers.* In his classic, *Dangerous Estate,* he told the story of newspapers from their origins 300 years earlier. Few knew more about their history. Later he wrote *The Right To Know: The Rise of the World Press* (1969). Shortly before his death on June 5, 1970, at the age of 67, Francis Williams published his autobiography, *Nothing So Strange.* It had indeed been a strangely varied and full life.

David Seymour

Gareth Williams (Lord Williams of Mostyn)   (1941–)

Gareth Wyn Williams, the Lord Williams of Mostyn, entered the Cabinet as Leader of the House of Lords in 2001 after a string of successful junior ministerial appointments, and just nine years after entering the House.

Born on 5 February 1941, the son of Albert and Selina Williams, Williams is a product of Rhyl Grammar School and Queen's College Cambridge, where he studied History and then for an LLB. In 1962 he married Pauline Clark, with whom he had a son and two daughters, remarrying in 1994, following his divorce, V M Russell, with whom he has a daughter. He was called to the Bar at Grays Inn at the age of 25 and set about creating a fearsome reputation as a libel lawyer. As well as being a successful lawyer he also had ambitions within the institutions of the legal profession, becoming Vice Chairman of the Bar Council in 1991 and then Chairman the year after. His elevation to the Lords in 1992 was as part of Neil Kinnock's dissolution honours, and there was speculation that Kinnock would have made him Lord Chancellor had he won. That of course did not happen, and the election of John Smith as leader saw Lord Irvine of Lairg become the prime candidate – a position that became a reality under Blair.

Nevertheless Williams went straight onto the Labour front bench as Legal Affairs spokesman in 1992, a position he held right up until the election of the Labour government, serving in addition, from 1993, as a spokesman on Northern Ireland and during 1995–96, on Wales. After the election, Blair made him a Parliamentary Secretary at the Home Office (in charge of constitutional affairs through the Scottish and Welsh devolution efforts) and then promoted him a year later to Minister of State at the same department.

At the same time as his promotion within the Home Office, Williams also became Baroness Jay's Deputy as Leader of the House of Lords. A year later, when he returned to his legal roots with a promotion to Attorney General (1999), he held onto his Deputy Leader role. Such was his success, that in 2000 he was named *The Spectator's* Peer of the Year.

Lord Williams' relatively low profile throughout this rapid ascent to the Cabinet should not be taken as indicative of a lack of forthright views. Indeed, his appointment as Attorney General was greeted with some trepidation by members of the legal profession who recalled his suggestion when Chairman of the Bar that judges should have to retire at 65, that all judicial posts be advertised, and that a Judicial Appointments Commission be set up.

He was recently given cause to wish this latter suggestion had been taken up. In early 2001 he was caught in the mini-furore over a Labour fundraising dinner at the Atlantic Bar and Grill hosted by Lord Irvine, at which the invitees were barristers and solicitors likely to be vying for judicial appointment. The criticism stuck mainly to Irvine, but Williams was there too and his participation will have been duly logged by journalists and Opposition alike for later use.

As Leader of the House of Lords he will have to ensure the success of the government's legislation, and with the Commons once again heavily stacked in the government's favour it is most likely to be peers who offer effective opposition. Given the large number of ex-trade union General Secretaries who are now clad in ermine, Williams will have to be skilful if the Upper House is not to become the apex of trade union opposition to the Blairite public service reform agenda.

Peter Metcalfe

Len Williams (1904–72)

(Arthur) Leonard Williams' lifelong career in and devotion to the trade union and Labour movement was inevitable and predestined. His was not just a commitment due to birth and circumstance, however, since at every stage of his life his constantly questioning mind threw up new elements and fresh attempts to sharpen and deepen his political convictions.

Len Williams was born on Merseyside on 22 January 1904 and educated at Holy Trinity Church of England Elementary School, Birkenhead, and the Labour College, London. At the age of sixteen he was already active in the National Union of Railwaymen, serving on the Liverpool and North Wales District Council (1920–21), and in 1923–24 he was made Secretary of the Birkenhead and District Joint Committee.

Williams' gigantic appetite for reading and research, wedded to a natural proselytising urge, formed the basis for his progression to the post of Staff Tutor, Liverpool Labour College (1924–26) and of Tutor-Organiser, National Council of Labour Colleges (1926–36). These years were, by Williams' own admission, among the happiest and most fulfilling of his life. He had the opportunity to immerse himself in Labour history and the development of international socialism. He travelled widely and met Labour students eager to learn in diverse circumstances and widely differing social conditions.

Williams was never starstruck by a possible Parliamentary career, although he did present himself as Labour candidate in Southport (1929) and Winchester (1935). He was unsuccessful on both occasions.

He became Secretary of Leeds Labour Party (1936–42) and joined Labour Party Head Office Staff in 1942. After a stint as Regional Organiser in the East and West Ridings of Yorkshire (1942–46) he moved on to the top echelons of the Party. He was Assistant National Agent and Deputy General Secretary (1959–62) before becoming General Secretary of the Party from 1962 to 1968.

During this period Williams contributed uniquely to maximising the impact and efficiency of Labour's largely voluntary army of workers and to professionalising Labour's small team of full-time agents.

Pragmatic and principled as he was, Len Williams saw his major obligation as preserving the health of the Labour Party as such. He was too discreet to declare it in public, but among his intimates he made no secret of his dislike for the 'capricious antics' of some of his Parliamentary or even Ministerial colleagues who, in his view, placed personal ambition well before any concern not to damage the Party.

Williams was forthright and courageous in expressing his concerns to the Prime Minister and Cabinet Ministers, as he was when the same ladies and gentlemen were leaders of the opposition. This he did in the privacy of the Party and not by public utterance.

Although Williams did not seek to emulate the more publicly political role of his predecessor as General Secretary, Morgan Phillips, he was nevertheless an astute reader of the political dialogue within the Party and a vigilant custodian of Party policy. He presided attentively and protectively over such Party prerogatives as the 'Friday Ritual.' By Friday midday, all weekend speeches by Labour Ministers intended for official distribution by the Party had to be presented to Transport House. The speeches were scrutinised for adherence to Party policy, and where necessary the author was asked to accept necessary amendments. In the case of refusal the speech was not issued officially by the Party. Many were the loud complaints of the more egocentric Ministers, but Williams held out, and certainly up to his retirement as General Secretary, no Prime Minister or Party leader succeeded in changing this situation.

Williams was a voracious reader of the press, but the more he read the more critical he became. He was never at ease with the media, and would have found his job much more unpleasant if he were General Secretary in the present climate of exaggeration and conflict-searching. Perhaps he enjoyed his writing interludes as Editor of the *Leeds Weekly Citizen* (1937–44) and of *Labour Organiser* (1952–62) just because they were publications which fell within his own acceptable parameters.

Len Williams was a traditionalist in the sense that he had a great respect for the trade union base of the Party. He was more naturally at ease with the trade union leaders on Labour's NEC, and they in turn showed him great respect, not least because he possessed an intellect that would not wither before the honed products of Wycliffe or the older universities.

At the end of his period as General Secretary, Williams was pre-occupied by the already discernible trend for Number 10 to pre-empt functions that, in his view, belonged to the Party. This view in no way affected his loyalty to the Government, but it certainly weighed more and more on his mind.

Williams' affair with Mauritius was more firmly based than was generally known, or else some of the more derogatory remarks and negative attitudes of people like Dick Crossman, Barbara Castle, George Brown or Harold Wilson at the time of his appointment as Governor General of Mauritius might have been moderated. In 1966, in the run-up to Mauritian independence, the British Labour government appointed an Electoral Boundary Commission to draw up the constituencies in Mauritius. The somewhat academic results of the Boundary Commission would have favoured the Parti Mauritien (backed by the French government and financed by the French sugar plantation owners) who were actually opposed to independence within the British Commonwealth – all this to the detriment of the Mauritius Labour Party led by Sir Seewoosagur Ramgoolam.

'Ram,' as he was affectionately known, sent a Mauritius Labour Party deputation to Transport House to plead the Party's case against the findings of the Boundary Commission. Williams was convinced and presented the case to the Prime Minister via the Colonial Office. John Stonehouse, Minister at the Colonial Office, was dispatched to Mauritius to examine the situation. Upon his return his recommendation that the findings of the electoral Commission should be revised was accepted and acted upon by the Government. The Mauritius Labour Party won the election and the rest is history.

It was also Len Williams who instructed his international staff to help the Mauritius Labour Party to become members of the Socialist International and who personally supervised the procedure.

It was the unanimous wish of the Mauritius Cabinet that Len Williams should become Governor General. Ironically, given the later hesitation of Harold Wilson over endorsing Len Williams' appointment, the deal was actually struck in a conversation between the first Prime Minister of Mauritius, Sir Seewoosagur Ramgoolam, and the General Secretary of the Labour Party, Len Williams, in front of a blazing fire at Chequers during a meeting of Socialist International leaders hosted by Wilson in 1967.

On 3 September 1968, Sir Arthur Leonard Williams GCMG, GCVO assumed his post as Governor General of Mauritius. Lady Williams (née Margaret Wiggins – they married in 1930) and Sir Len were to serve in Government House, Le Reduit, Mauritius, with great dignity and service, engendering a real affection among the people of Mauritius. Sir Len died on 27 December 1972 and is buried in the cemetery of St John, near Le Reduit where he served the second great cause of his life.

Gwyn Morgan

Marcia Williams (Baroness Falkender) (1932–)

For 27 years, from 1956 to 1983, Baroness Falkender, best known under her married name of Marcia Williams, was personal and political secretary to Harold Wilson, leader of the Labour Party 1963–76 and Prime Minister 1964–70 and 1974–76. Without question, she was the single biggest influence, at times beneficial, at others malign, on his political career and much of his personal life.

Marcia Matilda Field was born on 10 March 1932, the younger daughter of Harry Field, a Northamptonshire builder, and sister to Anthony (Tony). Both Tony and the older sister, Peggy, were to work for Wilson, too, in the latter stages of his political career. Marcia liked to surround Wilson with people whom she believed she could control. She was educated at Northampton High School, where she reputedly organised a rebellion against the headmistress whom she accused of bullying a classmate – a practice she herself frequently displayed in Wilson's office and towards Wilson – and Queen Mary's College, University of London, where she gained an Honours degree in History. She married an engineer, George Edmund Charles Williams, in 1955, but the marriage was not a success and following some years of separation they were divorced in 1961. Subsequently, in 1968 and 1969, she had two sons by the political journalist Walter Terry, with whom she had her longest affair. Neither her husband nor her children were referred to in her *Who's Who* entry, and the existence of the children was successfully kept from public knowledge for several years. Though I worked with her from January 1969, I did not become aware of the children until June 1970, when Wilson told me of them and asked me, by surreptitious means, to let Roy Jenkins, his closest rival for the Party's leadership, know of the fact, without disclosing to Marcia that I had done so. It was a typical incident in a relationship whose bizarre nature accelerated over the years.

Lady Falkender first joined the staff at Labour's headquarters in the mid-1950s. She was, briefly, secretary to the then Labour General Secretary, Morgan Phillips, and to Jim Callaghan. As a secretary with excellent shorthand, she was present at the notorious Labour dinner for the Soviet leader, Nikita Khruschev, on 23 April 1956, which degenerated into a shouting match between George Brown and Khruschev. It was there that Wilson and she met, though each was later to give different versions of their first acquaintance.

She had a brilliant political mind – probably better than any other woman of her generation – and she undoubtedly helped to change Wilson from the dull, dry, statistical politician that he was – he claimed to me that Aneurin Bevan's celebrated description of Hugh Gaitskell as a 'desiccated calculating machine' was actually meant to apply to him – into the witty orator whose success against the Tory Government in the Commons led to his unexpected victory in the leadership contest after Gaitskell's sudden death in 1963.

She was fiercely protective of Wilson. Though she herself often in private treated him with scorn and even contempt (it was she who named him 'Walter Mitty') she demanded absolute loyalty from all those around him. Any colleague not for him was regarded by her as an opponent, an attitude which led to the promotion of a number of politicians whose merits did not warrant it and the exclusion of others who, on merit, should have been appointed or appointed earlier than they eventually were. After the general election successes of 1964 and 1966, for which some credit was due to her, her influence grew. She soon made an enemy of George Wigg, the Paymaster-General, commonly nicknamed the Spymaster-General because of his supervision of security matters. When he once refused to discuss security matters 'in front of a secretary' and asked that she leave the room, his membership of the government was doomed. Civil servants, including the secretaries known as The Garden Room girls, to whom she took a dislike, were transferred from 10 Downing Street. Her private life increasingly obtruded on Wilson's time, especially her affair with Walter Terry, with jealous fellow-journalists attributing, usually unfairly, his reporting successes to his relationship with her.

Her considerable political skills began to wane as the 1970 election approached and with two infants to care for. Her gift for cutting through cant and muddled thinking and her ability to construct the order of a Wilson speech so that it made the maximum impact, which had made her even more invaluable to him, were lost amid the distractions of motherhood and the secrecy with which she surrounded it. Nevertheless, Wilson owed much to her, if not so much as she eventually came to believe. She was awarded a CBE in 1970.

During the first general election campaign in 1974, newspapers discovered that she and Peggy and Tony Field were partners in the ownership of former slag heaps at Ince-in-Makerfield in Lancashire. Though nothing was published before polling day, the fear that it was about to burst upon us dominated the later stages of the campaign. Tony was negotiating to sell the land at a considerable profit to a man, Ronald Milhench, who did not have the means to purchase it and who was to be exposed as a forger of Wilson's signature on notepaper which he had stolen from Wilson's office. This so-called scandal at the heart of a Government which had condemned the exploitation of land values also occupied much of the time of the Prime Minister and his other staff during the run-up to the second election of that year. It was overblown, part of the feverish atmosphere of the time, but Wilson's attempt to justify it as 'reclamation, not exploitation' was jeered in the Commons. He responded, typically, by agreeing to her demand that she be made a peeress. His action shocked his other senior staff who tried desperately to prevent it but to no avail. It was greeted with derision by the press and much of the Party.

Though she regularly attended the House of Lords, she never made a speech there. Initially, she claimed, reasonably, that as the Prime Minister's secretary she could not become publicly involved in matters of Government policy, but she had a horror of speaking in public and continued her silence after Wilson retired in 1976. She found the theatre and film worlds fascinating, and Wilson appointed her to his Film Industry Working Party in 1975. She was also a member of the Interim Committee on the Film Industry, 1977–82, and was appointed to the British Screen Advisory Council in 1985. Sir James Goldsmith, before his knighthood, promised Wilson he would make her a director of his Cavenham Foods empire, but nothing came of it. She did, however, pick up several other small directorships, including the Peckham Building Society, the South London Investment and Mortgage Corporation and the Milford Dock Co. She had a spell as a (ghosted) columnist on the *Mail on Sunday* and was the author of two books – *Inside No. 10* (1972) and *Downing Street in Perspective* (1983). After 1970, she lived in a stylish home in London W1, employing several servants and sending both her sons to public school. It was a style of living far removed from her roots in Northamptonshire and considerably more expensive than any that Wilson was later to afford. Her latter years have been dogged with serious ill-health and after several months in hospital she returned to Northamptonshire, where she lives with her sister.

Joe Haines

Shirley Williams (Baroness Williams of Crosby) (1930–)

In 1935 the five-year-old Shirley Williams sent her first letter to her parents in Sunderland, where her father Gordon Catlin was campaigning as the Labour candidate. They gratefully read it out at meetings, and her mother Vera Brittain recorded in her diary that it 'always went down well.' The letter read 'Dear Mummie and Daddy, I hope you will get into Parliament'. They didn't, then or ever, whereas Shirley was to contest 12 consecutive parliamentary elections between 1954 and 1987. Win or lose, Labour or SDP/Alliance, she always went down well. Few if any of her contemporaries matched her appeal, although many outstripped her in ruthlessness, organisation and guile. She never made the political weather, but she seemed to get the best of the sunlight in the garden.

Shirley Vivien Teresa Brittain-Catlin was born on 27 July 1930, the second child of Professor G E G (later Sir George) Catlin and the writer and pacifist Vera Brittain. Through the family house in Glebe Place, Chelsea, passed much of British intellectual and literary life. It included a number of self-confident and articulate women writers – the doomed Winifred Holtby, Phyllis Bentley, Margaret Storm Jamieson, Naomi Mitchison and Rebecca West. Catlin's own teaching post at Cornell University and his constant travels across the Atlantic added another dimension to his children's lives. Under the shadow of war Shirley and her brother John were evacuated for safekeeping to the USA, where in a variety of schools she began that easy acceptance of American life and mores that always co-existed with her strong Europeanism. It was a fortunate childhood. On her return from the USA Shirley eventually went to St Paul's Girls School, from where she secured a scholarship at Somerville, and followed in her mother's footsteps to Oxford.

She joined what was the first truly post-war generation. The ex-servicemen had gone. The 1940s were almost over. Shirley Catlin found worlds to conquer. One of her contemporaries, who was to become a political ally over fifty years, noted in her diary that she was 'a rare character, a unique combination of mental ability, physical energy, friendliness and ambition, plus a vague element of sometimes straying from the whole truth which she would probably justify as a desire not to hurt anyone'. Bill Rodgers, who followed her as chairman of the Labour Club, was this early chronicler of her discreet charm. 'With a husky, persuasive voice, a brilliant listener who engaged the speaker with her full attention, head slightly cocked to one side like a sparrow approaching a crumb, she was an instant success, and an *Isis* "idol" when these profiles mattered.'

To her mother's friends and contacts she added her own. At the Labour Club she was launched among the political generation who, for the next thirty years, rotated easily among the Fabians, the Königswinter conferences and frequent visits to what was Shirley's second home, the USA. She toured there triumphantly with the OUDS, Cordelia to Peter Parker's Lear, and always remained one of the few politicians who was a fine, rather than a ham actor. She married the eminent philosopher Bernard Williams in 1955. Both knew that her absorption in politics would continue, and that with her lack of skill in organising her time that might be a problem later on. She had already become the first of her generation to run for parliament, at a by-election in 1954 and again in 1955 at Harwich, Essex.

She contested Southampton Test in 1959, but in that year of heavy defeat it was not for winning. For the moment, and long after, Bernard and Shirley Williams were added value for each other, quizzical, friendly, endlessly well-connected. They had a daughter, Rebecca Clare, in May 1961.

It was a time of political reappraisal. Already a leading Fabian, Shirley Williams applied to succeed Bill Rodgers as the Society's General Secretary in 1960. The job, as it always does, had a high political salience. Her conference speeches, in 1960 opposing the dominance of nationalisation in Labour thinking and in 1961 supporting the principle of entry into the infant Common Market, attracted attention. She came to be one of the prominent younger candidates associated with the Campaign for Democratic Socialism, in opposition to the attacks on Gaitskell's leadership. She became the candidate for Hitchin and was duly elected in the swing to Labour in October 1964. For this seat, with its changing population, technological links and new-town ethos she had a real affinity. She was to hold it, in its new form as Hertford and Stevenage, for fifteen years. Gaitskell had died in 1963, and his old rival Harold Wilson was the new Labour prime minister. He bore no malice to the Gaitskellite loyalists, and Shirley was swiftly assimilated, as PPS to the Minister of Health 1964–66 and then a junior minister at departments she would revisit throughout her career, Labour (1966–67), Education and Science (January 1967–October 1969), and Home Office Minister of State (1969–70). She thus had early experience with three of the big figures on the Labour right, George Brown, Tony Crosland and Jim Callaghan. The trade union leaders also got to know her better. She was popular with many of them, and in their branches. Her mellow tones brought more warmth to the word 'Comrades' than it had had for years. Her natural egalitarianism spoke for itself. For the brothers and sisters of the class war she soon became the forces' sweetheart. The reward was a place on the women's section of the National Executive from 1970 until she left the Labour Party itself. These eleven years marked the growing dominance of the left, and were increasingly painful for passionate moderates like Shirley Williams.

She held her seat in 1970, and was elected to the shadow cabinet in Opposition, serving as Shadow Social Services Secretary (1970–71), Shadow Home Secretary (1971–73) and Shadow Prices and Consumer Protection Secretary (1973–74). The troubles of the Heath government, on the economy and industrial relations, should have revitalised the Labour opposition. But Heath had taken up the British application to join the EEC, which had led to a rebuff for Wilson and Brown in 1967. At that time (in Crossman's estimate) the Cabinet had divided into ten pro, six anti and six maybe. Now, however, what was on offer, after a successful negotiation, was dismissed by a majority as 'Tory terms'. The pro-Europeans were dismayed by this Wilsonian formula. It would not hold the party together, and it could lose the last and best opportunity to enter the EEC. Roy Jenkins, who had become Deputy Leader after George Brown lost his seat in 1970, was the natural leader of the pro-Europeans. In a shadow cabinet utterly divided on the issue, Shirley Williams was his most effective ally. On 28 October 1971, 69 Labour MPs, including Jenkins, Williams, George Thomson and Harold Lever, voted against a three-line whip on the principle of entry. A further twenty abstained. The fallout lasted for a decade. Roy Jenkins was re-elected as Deputy Leader, but in the following year, he, Thomson and Lever resigned from the shadow cabinet rather than be committed to a referendum on EEC membership. Shirley Williams did not resign with her colleagues, and their victory in the subsequent referendum after a hollow 're-negotiation' of the terms of entry by the incoming Wilson government in 1975 showed that her instincts were correct. The wounds, however, continued to seep. Her Oxford contemporary Dick Taverne, challenged in his Lincoln constituency, won a by-election on the European issue. Others MPs were in difficulties. The antagonisms made life more difficult for the pro-Europeans in the party, and some drew more than comfort from the all-party coalition which fought and won the 1975 referendum.

For the moment, however, the Labour government elected in 1974 after Heath's 'Who governs?' campaign produced its muffled answer, stumbled on. Shirley Williams became first Secretary of State for Prices and Consumer Protection, and then in April 1976, when Callaghan succeeded Wilson as Prime Minister, also Paymaster General and, from September 1976, Education Secretary. Never the most organised of ministers, it was a difficult time for her, reconciling government, party and personal concerns. (Her marriage was by now effectively over). To this was added the chaos of the times. No one can be a truly effective minister in a minority government, always under the cosh. And education was one of its most divisive areas.

Callaghan had chosen to launch a great debate about education. A comprehensive system which would produce equality of outcome was Labour's aim. The Secretary of State found the right equally eager to make it an issue. There were legal challenges to the introduction of comprehensive education, the defection of many direct-grant schools from the state system after the tough line of her predecessor Reg Prentice, and a venomous campaign in the *Daily Express* and *Daily Mail* on 'the scandal of the dunces'. Shirley Williams, always the most popular of Labour politicians, was now the target of vituperation. Sometimes, as with Auberon Waugh, it long outlasted the great debate. She countered the press onslaught with some facts: 'The *Mail* tended to give a great run to the argument that standards were declining. It actually wasn't true. Most of the inspectors' reports indicated the opposite. In 1978 they suggested the standards of reading were the highest they'd been for a decade. But with the upsurge of numbers some of the teachers who came in at that time were not very motivated towards the profession.'

The activities of the radical left in education had produced a backlash, and some defectors. The Black Papers began to make the case for a counter-revolution in education. Patrick Hutber, who once upon a time had been Shirley's successor as chairman of the Oxford Labour Club, wrote in *The Decline and Fall of the Middle Class* that 'it had to make the Labour Party aware of its irreducible demands ...' The National Association for Freedom (NAFF) attacked 'the state of proto-communism' in the trade unions. In this mood of hysteria, Shirley Williams drew heavy fire when she, together with other moderate Labour ministers who were members of APEX, made a supportive visit to the Grunwick picket line in 1977. An anti-union employer had locked out workers at his photo-processing plant who tried to join the union APEX. The plant was blacked, NAFF took legal action to lift the postal ban, and the defiant Grunwick management stalled attempts to ballot the workforce. Mass picketing and scenes of violence followed a few weeks after the ministers' uncontroversial visit.

Shirley Williams was unfairly pilloried for her Grunwick appearance, and discomforted after another public outing when her predecessor Reg Prentice came under savage attack in his London constituency. Both Roy Jenkins and Shirley made supportive visits, harassed by the bed-sit entryists who were some (but not all) of Prentices's critics. Badly rattled, he repaid them by defecting to the Conservatives. She was taken totally by surprise, having thought him a comparative radical in education (he had taken blunt action on the direct-grant schools, leaving her with the legal actions which followed).

She was becoming more sensitive to the slippage of power to the Bennite left in the constituencies and the trade unions. With Edmund Dell as her principal ally, she acted to reduce the thrust of the Bullock proposals on industrial democracy when they were discussed in cabinet. On the NEC she saw the left in the driving seat, with the party's General Secretary, Ron Hayward, unwilling to take action against the Trotskyite infiltrators now evident in many constituency parties. The NEC majority, including some who later became hammers of the Militant, would not even publish the report on entryism prepared for it by Reg Underhill, the National Agent. Williams was the first Labour cabinet minister openly to challenge the democratic credentials of the Militant Tendency and similar Marxist groups.

In the autumn of 1978 Jim Callaghan astonished his cabinet by telling them that his minority government would soldier on, sans incomes policy and soon sans allies into the New Year. Under fierce press attack the competence of the Government and its alleged subservience to the unions became the issue. Shirley Williams, who was (and remains) a staunch defender of comprehensive education, had underestimated the backlash against it in some of the English shires (in Scotland it was uncontroversial), and sometimes became ensnared in the details of the fight. On the eve of the 1979 election forced on Callaghan by a vote of no confidence, she was subjected to a character assassination by Labour's newest foe, the *Sun*. She sued, and the *Sun* withdrew and settled out of court – two days after the poll! She was one of the fifty-plus casualties, characteristically writing to congratulate those who had survived before she took stock of her own fate. She was still on the NEC, but in depressing company. The leader and deputy leader were depressed, even shell-shocked. None of the many MPs on the NEC could win election to the shadow cabinet. The leadership of the party in parliament was fatally diverging from that in the country, and the PLP was further marginalized by conference votes that October in favour of mandatory reselection and NEC control of the manifesto. Denis Healey, the heir apparent, seemed more full of bluster than fight.

These were the circumstances before the fatal conference of October 1980. In the wings Roy Jenkins, now returned from his stint as President of the European Commission, had for the past year trailed the idea of a new party, 'breaking the mould' of British politics. Shirley Williams' rejection of the notion of a centre party had been brusque. It would have, she said, 'no roots, no principles, no philosophy and no values'. But in their different ways, she, Bill Rodgers and the impetuous ex-Foreign Secretary David Owen were nudging themselves towards the idea of a radically changed Labour Party. The pace quickened. There was a weak compromise, to which Callaghan and Healey were party, over the electoral college. There was the 1980 Conference at Blackpool, Tony Benn's most clamant hour, where the PLP was corralled on the conference floor under attack by a General Secretary who seemed determined to incite the party against them. In a speech on the fringe, intended to both frighten and rally the MPs, Williams spoke of 'red fascism'. Later, in her Blackpool hotel room, she told some of them that Britain would have an East European-style Marxist Party, in which social democrats would be silenced, within ten years. Some of her listeners thought this ludicrous. Others did not.

Some had plans of their own for counter-revolutionary defeatism. When the PLP came to its own leadership vote, in the second round between Denis Healey and Michael Foot, enough right-wingers cast a silent vote for Foot to see him elected. Shirley Williams,

Rodgers, Owen and their old mentor Roy Jenkins now, at varying paces, moved towards the setting up of a Council of Social Democracy. For Rodgers and Williams at least it was a traumatic break with a lifetime of Labour. Shirley Williams had taken the trouble to be reselected in Hertford and Stevenage. She was chairman of the Fabian Society. Even the most bigoted activist wanted her to stay. After the 'Gang of Four', as the press now dubbed them, had issued their Limehouse Declaration, 28 Labour MPs initially rallied to their cause. More followed later, as deselection loomed.

The new SDP found its painful place in the spectrum. At the Königswinter conference that year it seemed that two rival groups of democratic socialists were vying for the favours of Helmut Schmidt. Once the Fabians had voted narrowly to stay with Labour, a rival Tawney Society was set up. But the new party would rely on close relations with David Steel's Liberals. Steel had also been at Königswinter. In a long walk up the Drachenfels, Williams, Rodgers and Steel were able to map out a coherent collaboration. The Liberals would support an SDP candidate at the first available by-election. The new party hoped that the candidate would be Williams. When the chance came at Warrington, with its substantial Catholic vote to which she, as Labour's most prominent Catholic, would appeal, she demurred. Roy Jenkins seized his chance to carry the standard, and his performance propelled him forward to the leadership of the SDP. Shirley then further stumbled by bidding for the next contest, at Croydon, only to be baulked by the chosen Liberal, an unmemorable figure with a memorable name, William Pitt. Her chance finally came at Crosby, where she won on a huge swing from the Tories on a 69% poll. Opinion polls recorded 51 per cent support for the SDP-Liberal Alliance. Shirley Williams returned to Westminster, thirty months after she left it, in a blaze of glory. Yet, as the authoritative history of the party, co-authored by Shirley's old friend Anthony King, put it, 'the SDP's golden age was already over'. Ahead lay the Falklands War, and cold reality.

Once Roy Jenkins had returned in his turn to Westminster after winning the by-election in Glasgow Hillhead, he was always likely to become the SDP parliamentary leader and Shirley Williams the new party's president. The Liberals baulked at a collective leadership in the 1983 election; it is possible that in electoral terms Williams would have added to, where Jenkins appeared to detract from, the Alliance's overall appeal. It would not have affected the result for her personally. There were further boundary changes in Crosby. She was out, once more. So was Bill Rodgers. Neither ever returned to the Commons, though playing a distinguished role in the Lords from 1993, and a dextrous one in the destruction of David Owen's attempt to maintain a separate SDP, led by him. The cost of it all – 18 years of Thatcherism – was mentioned less often.

In the party which then became the Liberal Democrats, Shirley Williams remained a respected figure, Deputy Leader in the House of Lords since 1999. She had found personal happiness in her second marriage to Professor Richard Neustadt in 1987, bringing up the orphaned children of her brother John, and her stepdaughter, as diligently as her own. She became as familiar a figure in Harvard Yard as she was at Westminster and Oxbridge, generous with her time and sympathy, sometimes spread too wide. (What was she doing on the 'Council of Advisors to the Ukrainian Praesidium ...' some asked, as they tried to make sense of her timetable). The SLD, which she helped to found, became a Mark 2 Liberal Party, more effective than its predecessor, and now led by the youngest of the candidates the SDP had drawn into politics in 1983. And the Labour Party, shaken by the great defection, had reformed itself and in some ways became another version of the SDP, which this lifelong egalitarian could now criticise from the further shore.

Williams' publications include: *Politics is for People* (1981); *Jobs for the 1980s: Youth Without Work* (1981); *Unemployment and Growth in the Western Economies* (1984); *A Job to Live* (1985); and *Snakes and Ladders, a Diary of Political Life* (1996).

Phillip Whitehead MEP

Tom Williams (Baron Williams of Barnburgh)   (1888–1967)

Thomas 'Tom' Williams was a Labour MP for 37 years, from 1922 to 1959. He was one of those solid, loyal supporters of the party who often go unsung. Yet his speciality in agricultural affairs gave him a unique position in the party's history. In 1965 Attlee called him 'the greatest British Minister of Agriculture of all time'.

Tom Williams was born on 18 March 1888 at Blackwell in Derbyshire, one of fourteen children. His father, a miner, moved to Yorkshire to find work; and Tom, who left school at the age of eleven, followed the employment of his father and elder brothers. First he performed odd jobs underground, then for three years he was in charge of pit ponies, and eventually, when his strength developed, he became a face-worker. When his father was blinded by an accident, and a brother and brother-in-law both sustained serious spinal injuries, Williams was attracted to union and Labour politics.

In 1912 he was sacked for complaining about conditions and was unemployed for six weeks, until he became steward – and his wife, whom he had married 18 months earlier, stewardess – at a working men's club. This was an important period in his life, which he later referred to as his equivalent of university. Not only did he gain a greater understanding of human nature, but he studied in his spare time. Yet in 1914 he was drawn back to the pits, and the following year he was elected checkweighman at Barnburgh main colliery. Now he was independent of management and could uphold the interests of the workers. Already secretary of the Wath-upon-Dearne Labour Party, in 1918 he was elected to the Doncaster Board of Guardians, where he first came in contact with the rural poor. The following year he was elected to the local district council, and in 1922 he became Labour MP for the Don Valley.

His constituency was a mixed mining and farming area, but it was his appointment as Parliamentary Private Secretary to Noel Buxton, the Minister of Agriculture and Fisheries during the first Labour government in 1924, which led to his specialisation in agriculture. In 1929 he became PPS to Margaret Bondfield, the Minister of Labour, and was disappointed not to achieve a junior ministerial position; but he admired the work of Christopher Addison at Agriculture. Williams' real chance came after the debacle at the October 1931 general election. One of the few Labour survivors, he now took an important role in the Opposition. In 1932 he filled 274 columns of Hansard and asked 607 oral questions and 67 written ones. According to the *Daily Express*, he 'speaks on every topic every day'. His profile was raised by his leadership of a rescue party at Bentley main colliery, where five miners were buried. He was consistently re-elected to the shadow cabinet every year from 1931 to 1939.

The pressures eased after 1935, when Labour gained another hundred MPs. In this period he was instrumental in gaining for MPs a pay rise and a contributory pension scheme. He was reluctant, however, to support rearmament, Dalton commenting tartly that he should 'stick to his spuds'.

When war did come he was a critic of the Chamberlain government's lack of impetus; and when Churchill took over he was an obvious choice as a junior minister at Agriculture. Indeed the Minister, the Conservative R S Hudson, asked for him specifically. He formed a bond with the other Joint Secretary, the Duke of Norfolk, and also with the farmers. He was Chairman of the Dig for Victory Campaign, and of numerous other committees and sub-committees. The overall policy, of which Williams fully approved, was one of fixing farm prices and of guaranteeing a minimum wage for agricultural workers. As a result, Britons were reasonably well fed during the war, while the acreage under tillage rose by 68 per cent during the first four years of the conflict.

In 1945 Williams was the obvious choice as Minister of Agriculture. It was a difficult time to be in office. The food situation in 1946 was worse than in 1941, and became worse still after the severe winter of February 1947. Williams' answer was to maintain wartime controls, guaranteeing prices and markets. The Agriculture Act of 1947 put these arrangements on a permanent basis. Domestic agriculture was boosted, the consumer was benefited and valuable foreign currency was saved. Williams was convinced that a Conservative government would have allowed a disastrous return to market economics in agriculture. 'If any group has good reason to be grateful for the policies of the Labour Government,' remarked *The Economist* in February 1950, 'it is those farmers, as well as labourers, who make their living on the land.' Williams used to remark, wryly, 'that the farmers could never afford to pay their entrance fee to the Conservative Club until they had Labour agricultural policy'.

Williams' success is the more remarkable because, from June 1940 onwards, he suffered badly from rheumatoid arthritis. Despite severe pain he remained MP for Don Valley and a Front-Bench spokesman on Agriculture until 1959; and he was made a life peer in 1961. He died at home in his semi-detached house in Doncaster on 29 March 1967. His achievements have seldom been vaunted, and several books on the 1945–51 governments ignore the unfashionable but nonetheless vital topic of agriculture. Perhaps this is why no biography has ever been written. His autobiography, *Digging for Britain*, was published in 1965.

Robert Pearce

Norman Willis   (1933–)

As Trades Union Congress General Secretary from September 1984 until September 1993, Norman Willis saw the organisation he led sink into inexorable decline as it was pushed to the margins of political life in the aftermath of the miners' strike. To many observers Willis was a surprisingly comic and inarticulate figure, who seemed to lack seriousness. Inarticulate and jolly, he seemed to have a rich repetoire of jokes for every occasion. His years as TUC General Secretary were often characterised as its age of stagnation. Willis found himself having to organise a rearguard action as Margaret Thatcher's government launched an increasingly self-confident and aggressive strategy to weaken the political and industrial power of the trade unions. Often un-fairly he was made the scapegoat for TUC decline. But it is hard to believe anybody else would have done any better in his job at that time.

Willis was elected TUC General Secretary after seven years as deputy to Len Murray (1977–84). Unlike his predecessors he had not spent his entire working life at Congress House. Born on 21 January 1933, the son of Victor and Kate Willis, he was a graduate of Ruskin and Oriel Colleges, Oxford, having also attended Ashford County Grammar School. He spent many years in the research department of the Transport and General Workers Union, working closely with that union's General Secretaries, Frank Cousins and then Jack Jones. He always in-sisted that he did not move to the TUC as a result of any urging by Jones, but the support of the TGWU was of enormous assistance in his becoming Murray's heir apparent. He married Maureen Kenning in 1963, with whom he has a son and a daughter.

Willis had a number of important assets, despite his apparent outward frivolity. He ac-quired a formidable range of personal contacts, lacked any sense of malice and was well versed in the minutiae of industrial politics. In his early months as TUC General Secretary, he showed courage and goodwill as he sought to bring an end to the miners crisis. An at-tempt by striking miners at Aberavon in south Wales to intimidate him by lowering a noose in front of him at a public meeting brought him considerable sympathy. But he was unable to convince Mineworkers' Union President Arthur Scargill to make a compromise peace. Nor could he prevent the temporary departure of the EETPU electricians union from the TUC in 1988 despite strenuous efforts to avoid such a rupture, although he was able to en-sure this did not lead to further defections.

Although much of his time was spent in damage limitation as the trade unions went through a period of self-destructive introspective conflicts, Willis attempted to coax them to face realities. In close alliance with Labour Party Leader Neil Kinnock, he developed a new agenda for the unions under which they accepted most of the employment laws passed by the Conservatives during the 1980s and in return secured the promise of more individual worker rights. It was under his direction that the TUC also dropped its opposition to British member-ship of the European Union after inviting the charismatic EU president Jacques Delors to speak to the 1988 Congress in glowing language about the future of social Europe that brought delegates to their feet.

Much of Willis's legacy derived from his activities overseas. He became a personal friend of Lane Kirkland, president of the American AFL/CIO trade union federation and did much to restore a close relationship between the British and US labour movements. A strong supporter of the Polish Solidarity movement, Willis aroused some criticism in Moscow with his public denunciation of repressive behaviour towards dissident Russian workers.

But at home he found it difficult to make much headway. The TUC lost much of its direct access to government with the abolition of the National Economic Development Council and the Manpower Services Commission. Union leaders were unable to exercise the kind of influ-ence they were used to doing between 1945 and 1979. Government ministers did not regard Willis as a man they could do business with.

Efforts to reverse the sharp decline in union membership made little impact either. The TUC launched a recruitment offensive under Willis during the early 1990s in London's East

End and the Trafford Park industrial estate in Manchester, but this failed to win over workers in any significant numbers to the attractions of trade union membership.

Perhaps there was little he could have done to restore the TUC's authority and credibility. But under Willis it was possible to detect the first seeds of recovery in areas like employment law and Europe. There was more continuity with the New Unionism of his successor John Monks than was often recognised. Moreover, the object of cruel jokes and personal abuse, Willis kept his dignity and tolerance. But it is true he did little to modernise the TUC's administration and embrace information technology. To many he became a symbol of trade union irrelevance, a rambling and confused figure presiding over a movement in what looked like terminal decline.

However, in unprecedented times for the TUC, Willis kept the organisation more or less united, preparing for better days. This may not have looked like a notable achievement in the early 1990s but it was to be appreciated later on. Despite his innumerable weaknesses and follies, Willis deserves to be remembered for holding the TUC together and pointing the way out of its impasse, caused mainly by events outside his immediate control.

Robert Taylor

Harold Wilson (Lord Wilson of Rievaulx) (1916–95)

Harold Wilson's particular approach to politics and government is best understood first through his upbringing. His Northern non-conformist background continued to shine throughout his long career and was clearly reflected in his personal style of life, which remained authentically and commendably provincial and was never seduced by the glitter of the metropolitan Establishment into which moved but of which he never saw himself as a paid-up member. I shall below begin by describing Wilson's upbringing, then his remarkable career as Labour Leader and Prime Minister, and conclude with an attempt to sum up his personality. I hope to catch some of the many aspects of his complex character, including the light as well as the shade, on which most London newspaper commentators concentrated in the last twenty years of his working life.

James Harold Wilson (like his longstanding Labour colleague, Leonard James Callaghan, he dropped his first name quite early on) always saw himself as a Yorkshireman. Born in Huddersfield on 11 March 1916, his family traced back in the county to the fourteenth century and were, until his grandfather moved close to Manchester, based on Helmsley in the North Riding, close to the Abbey of Rievaulx, from which he later took his peerage title.

His father was an industrial chemist working in the dyestuffs industry. His mother was from a more clearly working-class background with strong trade union ties. From when he was one year old, his family owned their own homes in respectable middle-class districts, and they also bought a car when he was seven, so they could be placed as reasonably comfortable lower middle class, with aspirations to upward mobility, though this progress was halted by his father's periodic unemployment in the post-war slump. The Wilsons were a close family. Harold was the favourite child, always performing to please his parents and to show off his cleverness – as he was still doing to his kitchen cabinet family half a century later. He loved his mother best and was in some ways a typical 'mother's boy'.

Central to his family background was a strong non-conformism stretching back generations to the Cromwellian civil war. His parents were active Congregationalists and Harold
regularly attended church and Sunday school. Even at Oxford, unlike most of his more sophisticated contemporaries, he still went to college chapel, and he married the daughter of a
Congregationalist minister. He was himself not really strongly religious in the spiritual sense,
but he absorbed and reflected the nonconformist values which shaped him. The chapel tradition of Christian good works inspired his early politics. Linked to non-conformism was his
devotion to the Boy Scout movement, in which his father was a District Commissioner.
Harold joined as a Wolf Cub aged 8 and rose to be a King's Scout, of which he was always
proud. The movement was a strong formative influence on him, giving him solid standards and
a belief in self-improvement and clean living. He remained attached to the Scouts even in the
1950s, by when he was already Leader of the Labour Party. Observing him much later, I felt
that in a way the party manifesto was his adult version of the Boy Scouts Code, to be learned
by heart and obeyed.

His education was properly meritocratic. He attended a council elementary school, a Huddersfield secondary school, and then the excellent Wirral Grammar School, where he thrived
and became Head Boy. He was bright and studious but not considered to be intellectually exceptional. The same was true at Oxford, where he won an exhibition – not an open scholarship – to Jesus, one of the less distinguished colleges, and worked very hard to achieve a good
first. He never mixed in any of the glittering Oxford social sets – which included some contemporaries who were later to be Labour colleagues in Parliament and in Government. His
eyes were firmly on climbing the career ladder.

Throughout this career rise he remained authentically provincial, nonconformist, lower
middle class, always retaining his Yorkshire accent. These characteristics stayed with him
through life and when I first worked for him – when he was 58 and towards the end of a distinguished career in high office – he struck me as basically unchanged, with the limitations
and more often the virtues of that background. He was brought up and conditioned in the
non-conformist work ethic, striving for self-improvement, discipline, orderliness, thrift, respectability and the accompanying respect for educational and professional qualification. In
that background there was little sexual liberation, arty culture or social climbing. It was very
Gilbert and Sullivan and not Benjamin Britten or Bach. He stuck to those roots and values
and it was very much to his credit that he was not seduced by metropolitan glitz.

Politics of various kinds was always in his family background. His grandfather was an active
National Liberal, his great uncle was Liberal Lord Mayor of Manchester, his uncle was Keir
Hardie's agent in the ILP, and his father became a strong Labour supporter. He grew up in the
Colne Valley outside Huddersfield, with its radical tradition of nonconformist socialism. Colne
Valley had the oldest Constituency Labour Party in Britain and had been won in 1907 by the
flamboyant independent socialist Victor Grayson. When Harold was a youth it was held by Philip
Snowden, the first Labour Chancellor, and when Ramsay MacDonald formed the first Labour
Government his father took him for the famous photograph before the front door of Number
Ten. Aged 15, Harold wrote a school essay about introducing his first budget as Chancellor (a
prime ambition he never achieved) and was also even then talking of becoming Prime Minister.
But he did not commit himself to politics until his academic career was firmly established. At

Oxford he occasionally attended the Liberal, and less often the Labour Club, but he preferred study to juvenile politicking.

His first big step towards public life was when he had the luck to be offered a research post studying unemployment and the trade cycle by Sir William Beveridge, later the author of the epoch-making 'Full Employment in a Free Society' and usually perceived as the father of the Welfare State. Wilson had little affinity with the egotistical old tyrant, but the research confirmed his inclinations towards factual-based central planning and, most importantly, put him visibly on the appropriate public career ladder. He quickly moved into Whitehall with the Economic Section of the Cabinet Office and then again with Beveridge, dealing with coal production. His contacts there with the coal industry and the National Union of Miners helped him to get nomination for the safe Labour seat of Ormskirk. In July 1945, aged 29, he was elected and launched onto a remarkable 30-year career in politics and government.

His rise within two years to be the youngest Cabinet Minister since 1806 as President of the Board of Trade was meteoric, though almost without political trace. He happened to be, as is so often important in politics, in the right place at the right time, and he rode on the back of his then hero, Stafford Cripps, though in the party and the country few people knew of him.

Over the next sixteen years, twelve of them in opposition, he built a strong base in the party, negotiating a series of political hurdles which revealed his dexterity and flexibility but also created the widespread impression that he was slippery and unprincipled. His resignation with Bevan from the 1951 Cabinet was seen as deserting the sinking Labour ship – although he did actually agree with Bevan on giving welfare a higher priority than defence. Wilson quickly played an active part in the left-wing Tribunite media circus of the early 1950s, further alienating the Labour right. But when Bevan resigned from the shadow cabinet over German rearmament, Wilson, while agreeing with Bevan on the issue, took the opportunity to take Bevan's place at the top table. He had now offended both the left and the right.

After Labour's terrible defeat in 1959, he opposed the Gaitskellite revisionism, especially concerning the abolition of the Clause 4 commitment to wholesale further nationalisation (changes which this author actively supported). Wilson was inherently less radical than Gaitskell and the Young Turks, Crosland and Jenkins, then surrounding the Labour leader. Also, as a pragmatist, he saw no reason to split the party over a non-issue, since Clause 4 was to him just an aspiration with no hope or risk of being implemented. He was emphatically defeated when standing against Gaitskell in the 1960 leadership election. But he was by then established as the clear alternative leader. He had trodden on many sensitive fingers on the way up, but he was by then at the top of the ladder and was comfortably elected Leader after Gaitskell tragically died in 1963.

His standing in the party then was not ideal. He was loathed and mistrusted by the old Gaitskellite right, who never forgave him for stealing their hero's crown. He was mistrusted, though tinged with admiration by his natural constituency in the centre. And on the left he was mistrusted for having abandoned them, but they grudgingly supported him because he was the best hope they had. But most had come to respect his political skills. Over the next four years until 1967 Wilson put on a dazzling display of leadership and won over all but the intransigent right to admire him. Wilson quickly improved his previously pedantic public speaking and launched a blitzkrieg against the crumbling Tory Government, cruelly and wittily exposing Macmillan's faded Edwardianism and Home's economic illiteracy. He was surely the most effective opposition leader in post-war Britain. He also conciliated his old Gaitskellite enemies by giving them key positions in the shadow cabinet and by finally coming out firmly against his old accomplices in the unilateralist movement.

He was able to sidestep the perennially destructive left-right divisions – which he always derided privately as 'theology' – by basing his policy campaigns on his own genuine non-sectarian beliefs in achieving economic progress through planning and the use of science and technology. He launched his impressive 'white heat of technology' speech at the 1963 Scarborough conference and followed it up with more statements on the theme of a New Britain based on improved technology. These exposed the Tories as amateur and out of date whereas his 'newish' Labour Party was by contrast modern and professional (recent echoes there !). It is easy today to forget the excitement which Wilson then created across the media and the electorate. He was never of course really a radical thinker. His planning approach was rooted in the wartime conditions which he had experienced in Whitehall. His 'socialism' often seemed to me to be a mixture of nonconformism, natural dirigisme, and anti-establishment 'chip-on-the-shoulder'. But in its modern technological dressing, it offered then a kind of 'third way' between the antique Marxist left and the divisively revisionist Gaitskellite right. It was what Wilson genuinely believed in (it was not true as many critics asserted that he did not believe in anything). It also provided him with a reasonably coherent intellectual and political framework on which he could base his Government when he just scraped home in the 1964 election and roared to a landslide victory in 1966.

These years from 1963 to 1967 were Wilson's time of peak triumph. As Prime Minister, he towered above his Government colleagues, few of whom had Cabinet experience, and he often took the lead in their departments' policy areas. He imposed his views on modernising Britain, inspiring the 1965 National Economic Plan which reflected his commitment to improve Britain's dismal economic performance by central planning and coordinating technological resources. He strove to reform the antiquated Whitehall machine, with new departments and the Fulton Enquiry into the civil service. He created new ministers of Economic Planning and of Technology and appointed a distinguished scientist as Education Minister. He initiated a dramatic expansion of higher education, created his beloved Open University, and launched the new DHSS. Overseas he began Britain's long overdue withdrawal from East of Suez and also first prepared the way for entry into the European Economic Community.

Perhaps of most lasting significance, he oversaw a remarkable period of social reform which adjusted British laws to the more libertarian values of the 1960s. Between 1965 and 1969, capital punishment, theatre censorship and corporal punishment in prisons were abolished. Britain's primitive laws relating to homosexuality, divorce and abortion (despite his Catholic constituency) were liberalized, so individuals were no longer persecuted for their personal behaviour. He strongly supported the first law against racial discrimination. The initial impetus for these changes often lay elsewhere, especially with Roy Jenkins, a great reforming Home Secretary. But it is to Wilson's credit that, against all his non-conformist conditioning, he quickly promoted Jenkins to the Cabinet and then supported his liberal proposals. His Government in 1964–70 both reflected and shaped the changes of moral and social values in post-war Britain and put these more civilized values into a lasting legal context.

Wilson also showed advanced thinking in his support for Barbara Castle's 'In Place of Strife' proposals to reform Britain's neolithic trade unions. But by then in 1969 the gloss had gone from him, and he was defeated by the powerful forces of conservatism within the Labour movement and parliamentary party. A series of policy setbacks – the cuts to public services in 1966, the abandonment of the National Plan, the humiliating devaluation of 1967 (from which his credibility never fully recovered), the failure to bring the Rhodesian rebels under control – all these and more served to disappoint the high hopes raised in 1964. The press, which had at first praised him to the skies, now relentlessly vilified him without reference to facts or fairness. His personal poll ratings slumped from 57 per cent in early 1967 to 27 per cent a year later. Labour suffered a string of by-election disasters. In Cabinet and the party, right-wing and centrist malcontents began moves to replace him with either Callaghan or Jenkins, neither of whom did much to discourage the plots. Wilson retreated into his Number 10 bunker, supported by Marcia Williams and the kitchen cabinet. No modern Prime Minister (except perhaps for Major in 1995–97) has ever been so beleaguered and seemed so forlorn.

Although the economy picked up a little towards the end of his Government, and the polls with it, his electoral defeat in 1970 was rooted in disenchantment: that the great ambitions of 1964 had not been fulfilled. Certainly his key approach to the economy of central planning and interventionism had not worked; in fact it already began to look out of date as the supporters of a free economy gained ground.

On kitchen cabinet advice, he personalized the 1970 election into a 'presidential' campaign and so the defeat firmly attached to him. It was the worst setback of Wilson's political career and it devastated his self-confidence. The gloomy days of opposition in 1970–74 continued the bleak days for him. The press always referred to him as yesterday's man, devious and unprincipled, seeking only personal or party advantage. He clung on to the leadership, mainly because the supporters of Callaghan and Jenkins each reluctantly preferred to stay with the apparently doomed incumbent rather than to risk precipitating the accession of the other.

But slowly among wider Labour supporters a grudging respect arose for his durability as one of life's survivors and for his party management skills. This was confirmed in the 1972 crisis over entry to the Common Market. With the party deeply divided, he trimmed back from his earlier position of seeking entry to one of neutrality, belatedly grasping the referendum device to delay the European crunch and leave the decision to the electorate. He lost his deputy leader Jenkins and the hard core of the right. It also confirmed the impression that he would sail with any wind to keep the bulk of the party united and behind him as leader. But it did ensure that he could fight the 1974 election on a reasonably united platform, each side willing to wait for the referendum.

Like most commentators, Wilson thought he would lose the 1974 election. Had he indeed lost, he would have immediately resigned the party leadership and left the political stage at a low point and to very few cheers. In fact he ran a shrewd campaign and squeezed home with less votes but a few more seats than Ted Heath. His pleasure at erasing the bitter memory of defeat in 1970 was visible to those of us campaigning with him. A second modest victory in October appealed to his weakness of boasting about his genuinely remarkable record of winning four elections out of five as party leader.

His final premiership was conducted quite differently from the triumphal days of 1964–66.

He kept a distinctly low profile, with none of the earlier circus performance in the spotlight on the high wire. There was a touch of autumnal mellowness about him and – privately committed to retire in 1976 – some of the earlier demons of paranoid suspicions seemed to have left him (at least for colleagues, though not for the security services). He exuded some of Stanley Baldwin's 'quiet life'.

His relations with key colleagues, especially with Callaghan, were more relaxed, and he came to be seen by the public and the party as an old familiar, who had been around Westminster as long as most people could remember, with some characteristic tricks still up his sleeve, but with his faults well known. Above all he seemed essential to holding his fissiparous party together. That objective became his single over-riding political objective: and it was not a dishonorable one. In this unifying role he negotiated the Government into an incomes policy and to remaining in the Common Market without losing the trade unions or the left. The referendum, to Wilson's constant amusement, had secured Britain's membership of the EEC for Jenkins and his pro-marketeers, although Roy had passionately opposed the device, and defeated Benn's anti-marketeers, although Benn had actually invented it.

Wilson resigned in March 1976 at the age of 60, as he had long planned. Ironically he departed at virtually the only time in his leadership when there were no plots among colleagues to remove him, and when there was almost universal, if often passive and unenthusiastic support for his leadership of the party. He had finally convinced the right wing that he was not really a left-winger; the centre that, if anything, he was one of them; and the left that, although not really one of them, at least he understood their tribalism.

However, his resignation was clouded by the atmosphere of scandal surrounding his bizarre final honours list, which contained people whose contributions to public life – as opposed to contributions to his political office – were not easy to detect. Some of them were hardly known to Wilson, though close to Lady Falkender. He was puzzled by the public reaction, since he had personally never taken honours seriously, viewing them as just useful tools of patronage, rewards for loyalty or even silencers on the disloyal. But the resulting clamour damaged him, especially as it seemed to confirm longstanding suspicions about the nature of some of the odd businessmen who had fringed Marcia's entourage. It meant, sadly, that the final public and media view of Harold Wilson in action was besmirched and did not give credit to the remarkable achievements of his political career.

The furore also reflected the important role in his life, for good or ill, of his personal and political secretary, Marcia Williams\Falkender. She joined him in 1956, shortly before his mother's death, and became in a way his 'political wife', having huge influence, even an eerie control over him.

The ultimate source of this unusual control was never clear, though to some who worked close to him he seemed in fear of revenge, even of blackmail. Their intimacy was almost psychic, a shared obsession with politics and political power, which was the very air they breathed. Observers of their early years together noted the positive contributions Marcia certainly made. Wilson had a 'soft' personality, containing what one colleague perceptively described as 'a streak of unwillingness to wound'. That capacity to strike and hurt is essential in a political leader. She provided it. She was the jagged edge compensating for his natural plump complacency. She pierced through the flabby verbiage of most arguments and stabbed the central